CASEBOOKS ON THE COMMON LAW OF EUROPE

CASEBOOKS ON THE COMMON LAW OF EUROPE

Contract Law

General Editors

Professor Hugh Beale　　　　*Professor Arthur Hartkamp*
Professor Hein Kötz　　　　*Professor Denis Tallon*

Contributing Editors

1. **Introduction**　　　　　　　　　*Professor Denis Tallon*

2. **Formation**
   Section 1: Offer and Acceptance　　　*Hester Wattendorf*
   Section 2: Pre-contractual Good Faith　*Professor Martijn Hesselink*

3. **Invalidity**
   Section 1: Immoral and Illegal Contracts　*Professor Hein Kötz*
   Section 2: Fraud, mistake and　　　　*Professor Hugh Beale*
   　misrepresentation　　　　　　　*John Harrington*
   Section 3: Threats and abuse of　　　*Hugo van Kooten*
   　circumstances
   Section 4: Unfair Terms　　　　　*Remiert Tjittes*

4. **Interpretation and Contents**　　　*Professor Hein Kötz*

5. **Supervening events**　　　　　　*Professor Denis Tallon*

6. **Remedies**　　　　　　　　　　*Professor Hugh Beale*
   　　　　　　　　　　　　　　John Harrington

7. **Third party consequences**　　　　*Professor Hein Kötz*

Managing Editors

Professor Hugh Beale　　　　　*Professor Denis Tallon*
Dr. Ludovic Bernardeau　　　　*Robert Williams*

·H A R T·
PUBLISHING

OXFORD AND PORTLAND, OREGON

Hart Publishing
Oxford and Portland, Oregon

Published in North America (US and Canada) by
Hart Publishing
c/o International Specialized Book Services
5804 NE Hassalo Street
Portland, Oregon
97213-3644
USA

Distributed in the Netherlands, Belgium and Luxembourg by
Intersentia, Churchillaan 108
B2900 Schoten
Antwerpen
Belgium

Reprinted 2002

Hart Publishing is a specialist legal publisher based in Oxford, England.
To order further copies of this book or to request a list of other
publications please write to:

Hart Publishing, Salter's Boatyard, Folly Bridge,
Abingdon Road, Oxford OX1 4LB
Telephone: +44 (0)1865 245533 Fax: +44 (0)1865 794882
e-mail: mail@hartpub.co.uk
WEBSITE: http//:www.hartpub.co.uk

British Library Cataloguing in Publication Data
Data Available
ISBN 1-84113-237-3 (paperback)

Typeset by Hope Services (Abingdon) Ltd.
Printed and bound in Great Britain by
Biddles Ltd, www.biddles.co.uk

Preface

This book is the second of the series of *Casebooks on the Common Law of Europe* under the General Editorship of Professor Walter van Gerven, who was also the principal author of the first in the series, the casebook on *Tort Law*. Like that book, the present volume aims to explore the extent to which, despite differences in approach, concepts and terminology, common principles underlie the laws of contract of the EU Member States. It has been prepared by an international team, each of whom is primarily responsible for particular chapters or sections, as shown on the title page, subject to the guidance of the principal authors.

The authors share the hope of the authors of the *Casebook on Tort Law* that

> " . . . the book will be used as teaching material in universities and other institutions throughout Europe and elsewhere in order to familiarize future generations of lawyers with each others' legal systems and to assess and facilitate the impact of European supranational legal systems on the development of national laws and vice-versa."

We believe that looking at primary sources, both legislation and cases, to see how concrete situations are resolved in the various systems is of considerable value to students not only in helping them to see how other systems work but also in understanding their own laws. Comparing the results of cases with similar facts, and the solutions provided in concrete examples, is at the heart of the "functional" approach which is one of the keystones of comparative law.

In many ways, however, the present volume is no more than a beginning. First, for the most part, the Casebook on Contract covers only three laws of contract—those of England, France and Germany. Other systems are mentioned only in relation when they have particularly striking solutions to problems—as, for example, does Italian law on questions of good faith. The problem has not been lack of offers of help from other countries. It is simply that size and price impose severe limitations on what can be included. We have thought it better to cover a few systems in depth rather than many more superficially, and felt unable to take up the very kind offers we received. The Dutch authors felt they had even to give up any systematic treatment of their law, to the regret of us all. Perhaps these are matters which can be reviewed in a future edition.

The book does consider both the Unidroit Principles of International Commercial Contracts and, more particularly, the Principles of European Contract Law. The latter are used in two particular ways. First, because the Principles attempt to state the rules that are more-or-less common to the major legal systems in a way that does not depend too heavily on uniquely national concepts and terminology, the articles that are most relevant to the topic to be discussed are usually set out at the start of each section, to give in indication of the subject matter to follow and to "set the scene", as it were. Second, the Principles are frequently re-examined at the end of the treatment as a point of comparison to the national laws which have been considered. The question is then posed: do the Principles genuinely reflect rules which are common to the different systems?

Secondly, the book concentrates on how particular fact situations are handled in the various systems. There is always a danger that such a "case-oriented" approach will leave students without any clear idea of the overall shape each system studied and how its components—for instance, its laws of contract, tort and unjust enrichment—fit together. Partly for this reason the first Chapter compares particular features of each of the three systems and looks at tort and unjust enrichment as well as contract. Further, each chapter mixes primary materials with a considerable amount of commentary and explanation. But teachers using the book will need to be aware of the need to direct their students' attention to broader issues, and the interrelation of the law of contract with other parts of the law, within each legal system.

Thirdly, the book concentrates on cases, legislation and "black-letter" rules of law. We are very aware that such an approach has serious limitations; that there may be deeper differences of philosophy, of *"mentalité"*, which may be masked by a superficially similar result. A good comparatist should explore these, which requires a much more rounded study of the traditions and institutions of each legal system than is offered here. However, we think that a comparison of black-letter rules is a good place to start and therefore offer this collection to that end.

At this juncture, Professor van Gerven's Foreword to *Tort Law* bears further quotation:

> "It is not the intention of this book, or of the series as a whole, to unify the existing laws of tort or of the other areas of law that are to be covered. That would not be possible, nor would it be desirable. For indeed, the diversity of European legal systems reflects not only a variety of legal cultures – which are bound to converge in step with European integration – but also and perhaps mostly a variety of value judgments or policy choices which find their expression in the legal systems. In their effort to uncover common roots, the authors do not wish to express any preference for the solutions embodied in one or the other legal system, where that would imply endorsing the underlying value judgment over alternative judgments. In the absence of a common European legislature (outside the limited areas for which national competences have been transferred to the European Union), there is indeed no authoritative source, other than national legislation or case law, from which a common understanding as to the fundamental value judgments underlying national law can be derived. Although that should not prevent legal writers from expressing their own personal preferences, we would prefer not to do that, or to do it only exceptionally, in a book like the present one which is intended to inquire into the common core of principles in the national and supranational legal orders existing within the European Union."

This casebook is a only beginning in a fourth sense. We have not yet much experience of teaching students from differing legal traditions from materials covering a variety of legal systems. Authors of different chapters in the book have had different ideas as to how this is best done; and as we simply do not yet know which approach works best (or indeed whether different areas of contract law may not require different approaches), we took the deliberate decision not to try to harmonize the chapters completely. Instead we decided to have just a few common features, for example, to introduce sections by setting out the relevant articles from the Principles of European Contract Law just as a way of indicating what the section is principally about. We hope that colleagues who use the book will let us know which chapters they find "work best" and that we can then adopt the "best" models in a future edition.

We are also very conscious of the immense difficulties of translating legal texts. We are enormously grateful to our translators, in particular James Benn and Norton Sims, who have done the vast bulk of the work. We firmly believe that they have served us well. But in an ideal world we would like to have the original texts available to the enquiring reader. Originally we had hoped to make them available on a website but both lack of time and lack of resources have so far prevented this.

Time has been a constant enemy in the production of this book. There have been severe delays caused by authors' other commitments, promotion and in one case illness. Some of the chapters—in particular those of Precontractual Good Faith and Threats and Abuse of Circumstances—were completed as long ago as 1996 and it has been possible to do only limited updating since. Again in an ideal world we might have waited until that could be done but so many colleagues have asked us to publish what we have that we have decided not to delay any further and to offer this collection of material after a final editing which was carried out largely by Dr. Ludovic Bernardeau, with valuable assistance from Professor Denis Tallon and Mr. Robert Williams. Additional help was given by Nadia Motraghi and Oliver Radley-Gardner. I am most grateful to them all. Errors of course remain the authors' responsibility. Sincere thanks are also due to Richard Hart and Hannah Young of Hart Publishing, without whose help and patience the project would not have been completed. Your authors hope and believe that the book will be of value.

Hugh Beale
London, October 2001

For further information about the Ius Commune Casebooks on the Common Law of Europe project, please refer to the following websites:

http://www.rechten.unimaas.nl/casebook
http://www.law.kuleuven.ac.be/casebook

Table of Contents

CONTENTS

CONTENTS

CONTENTS

CONTENTS

CONTENTS

CONTENTS

CONTENTS

CONTENTS

CHAPTER FOUR
INTERPRETATION AND CONTENTS

CHAPTER FIVE
SUPERVENING EVENTS IN THE LIFE OF CONTRACT

CHAPTER SIX
REMEDIES FOR NON-PERFORMANCE

CONTENTS

CONTENTS

CHAPTER SEVEN
THIRD PARTY CONSEQUENCES

Table of Frequently Cited Works

The works mentioned below are referred to frequently in this book and have accordingly been abbreviated as follows:

BBF3	H. Beale, W. Bishop and M. Furmston, *Contract Cases and Materials* (3rd edn., London, Butterworths, 1995)
Carbonnier	J. Carbonnier, *Droit civil—Les obligations*, 21st edn. (Paris: PUF, 1998)
Cheshire & Fifoot	M. Furmston, (gen. ed.), *Law of Contract*, 13th edn. (London: Butterworths, 1996)
Chitty	H. Beale, (gen. ed), *Chitty on Contracts*, 28th edn. (London: Sweet & Maxwell, 1999)
Flume, *Rechtsgeschäft*	W. Flume, *Allgemeiner Teil des Bürgerlichen Rechts*, Vol. 2: *Das Rechtsgeschäft*, 4th edn. (Berlin: Springer, 1992)
Gerven, van, *Tort Law*	Cases, Materials and Texts on National Supranational and International Tort Law (Oxford, Hart, 2000).
Ghestin	J. Ghestin, *Traité de droit civil—La formation du contrat*, 3rd edn. (Paris: LGDJ, 1993)
Ghestin and Desché	J. Ghestin and B. Desché, *Traité des contrats—La vente*, (Paris: LGDJ, 1990)
Ghestin, Jamin and Billiau	J. Ghestin, C. Jamin and M. Billiau, *Traité de droit civil—Les effets du contrat*, 2nd edn. (Paris: LGDJ, 1994)
Kötz, *European Contract Law*	H. Kötz and A. Flessner, *European Contract Law*, Vol. I, transl. by T. Weir (Oxford: Clarendon, 1998)
Kötz, *Europäisches Vertragsrecht*	H. Kötz and A. Flessner, *Europäisches Vertragsrecht*, Vol. I (Tübingen: Mohr Siebeck, 1996)
Lando and Beale	O. Lando and H. Beale, *Principles of European Contract Law, Parts I and II* (The Hague/London/Boston: Kluwer, 2000)
Larenz, *AT*	K. Larenz and M. Wolf, *Allgemeiner Teil des bürgerlichen Rechts*, 8th edn. (München: Beck, 1997)

Larenz, *SAT*	K. Larenz, *Schuldrecht—Allgemeiner Teil*, 14th edn. (München: Beck, 1987)
Larenz, *SBT–I*	K. Larenz, *Lehrbuch des Schuldrechts*, Vol. II, part I: *Besonderer Teil*, 13th edn. (München: Beck, 1986)
McKendrick, *Contract*	E. McKendrick, *Contract Law*, 4th edn. (Basingstoke: Macmillan, 2000)
Malaurie and Aynès	Ph. Malaurie and L. Aynès, *Cours de droit civil—Les obligations*, 10th edn. (Paris: Cujas, 1999)
Medicus, *SAT*	D. Medicus, *Schuldrecht—Allgemeiner Teil*, 12th edn. (München: Beck, 2000)
Münchener Kommentar	K. Rebmann and F. Säcker, (eds), *Münchener Kommentar zum bürgerlichen Gesetzbuch*, 4th edn. (München: Beck, 2000)
Nicholas	B. Nicholas, *The French Law of Contract*, 2nd edn. (Oxford: Clarendon, 1992)
Palandt	P. Bassenge et al., *Bürgerliches Gesetzbuch*, 58th edn. (München: Beck, 1999)
Schlechtriem, *SAT*	P. Schlechtriem, *Schuldrecht—Allgemeiner Teil*, 4th edn. (Tübingen: Mohr, 2000)
Terré, Simler and Lequette	F. Terré, Ph. Simler and Y. Lequette, *Droit civil—Les obligations*, 7th edn. (Paris: Dalloz, 1999)
Towards a European Civil Code	A. Hartkamp, M. Heselink, E. Hondius, C. Joustra and E. du Peron, (eds.), *Towards a European Civil Code*, 2nd edn. (Nijmegen/The Hague/London/Boston: Ars Aequi Libri, 1998)
Treitel, *Contract*	G. Treitel, *The Law of Contract*, 10th edn. (London: Sweet & Maxwell, 1999)
Treitel, *Remedies*	G. Treitel, *Remedies for Breach of Contract* (Oxford: Clarendon, 1988)
Treitel, *Frustration*	G. Treitel, *Frustration and Force Majeure* (London: Sweet & Maxwell, 1994)
Viney, *Introduction*	G. Viney, *Traité de droit civil—La responsabilité: introduction*, 2nd edn. (Paris: LGDJ, 1995)
Viney, *Effets*	G. Viney, *Traité de droit civil—La responsabilité: effets* (Paris: LGDJ, 1988)
Viney and Jourdain	G. Viney and P. Jourdain, *Traité de droit civil—La responsabilité: conditions*, 2nd edn. (Paris: LGDJ, 1998)
Zweigert and Kötz	K. Zweigert and H. Kötz, *Introduction to Comparative Law*, 3rd edn., transl. by T. Weir (Oxford: Clarendon, 1998)

Table of Cases

Cases in bold are excerpted at the page number indicated in bold.

European Jurisdictions

European Community (in alphabetical order)

Others

Australia

Table of Legislative Instruments

European Legislation

European Community (in chronological order)

International

CHAPTER ONE
INTRODUCTION

It is no easy task to embark on a comparative study of the law of contract. Despite its apparent uniformity the law of contract varies from one country to another, and even within the same system. Those difficulties are compounded in dealing with systems based on Roman law and those based on the Common Law.[1] Plainly, much of this may be accounted for by history. On the Continent, there has been the major influence of Roman law disseminated above all by the universities, even in those countries which scarcely used Roman law as positive law. This influence was carried on by the canon lawyers and then by the school of natural law leading to voluntarism, the leading lights of which were Domat and Pothier and which carried all before it under the French Civil Code during the whole of the nineteenth century. Conversely, in England, though not in Scotland, Roman law has not had the same influence. It took longer for the notion of contract to be worked out and voluntarism went into an almost immediate decline.[2] The decline was hastened by the analyses of American writers, particularly following the famous article by Fuller and Perdue;[3] these went as far as proclaiming the death of the contract.[4] Yet contract is alive, and it continues to constitute the basic legal instrument used to regulate the economic relations between natural and legal persons. It is, however, a concept which has undergone a certain evolution and which, from a comparative point of view, does not take the form of a uniform model. A contract under common law is not exactly the same as under the German or French legal systems. For that reason, it is necessary to begin **(1.1)** with a study of the basic notion of a contract as it exists in the main legal systems with which we are concerned, in order to work out what it is that the various concepts found in those systems have in common. Once that has been done, it will be possible to determine **(1.2)** the relationship between the notion of a contract, as thus defined, and the other sources of law giving rise to obligations, such as torts and quasi-contract/restitution. After that, it will then be necessary to move onto a higher plane, by considering **(1.3)** what it is that gives binding force to a contract.

1.1. THE NOTION OF CONTRACT[5]

What does one understand by the terms "*contrat*", "contract" or "*Vertrag*"? It is doubtful whether this term is identical in the different systems of European law. Failing precise concordance, it may even be that the term is misleading. It is appropriate to start (1.1.1) with a comparative study of the definitions given by the various different legal systems,

---

[1] See Kötz, *European Contract Law*.
[2] P. Atiyah, *The Rise and Fall of Freedom of Contract*, (Oxford: Clarendon, 1990).
[3] "The Reliance Interest in Contract Damages " 46 Yale LJ 52 (1936).
[4] G. Gilmore, *The Death of Contract* (Columbus, Ohio: Ohio State University Press, 1974).
[5] See Kötz, *European Contract Law* at 1 ff.

and then (1.1.2) to consider where the law of contract is to be found (particularly in codified systems of law) and the sources from which it emanates (legislation, case-law, academic legal writings, etc.). The various classifications applicable to contracts may also (1.1.3) shed an interesting light on the very concept of a contract. In addition, it will be necessary (1.1.4) to clarify the specific elements of contracts inherent in each legal system.

1.1.1. DEFINITIONS

In searching for definitions, we need to look at the legislation, if any, in which they are to be found, and also, where appropriate, at the relevant case-law and/or academic legal literature. It is apparent from such an analysis that the various definitions differ according to the particular legal system in which they appear. In addition, there are two specific points on which the various national legal systems differ from one another, the first being concerned with the question whether gifts *inter vivos* constitute contracts, and the second relating to the question whether any obligation arises from a unilateral intention to contract involving a promise of reward (unilateral promise).

1.1.1.A. DEFINITION OF CONTRACT UNDER CERTAIN SYSTEMS OF LAW

If one has regard to definitions contained in the code, certain differences are to be found.

Code civil (French Civil Code)   **1.F.1.**

Article 1.101: A contract is an agreement (convention) by which one or more persons obligate themselves to one or more other persons to give, or to do or not to do, something.[6]

Codice civile (Italian Civil Code)   **1.I.2.**

Article 1321: Definition: A contract is an agreement between two or more parties for the purpose of creating, providing for or extinguishing amongst themselves a legal patrimonial relation.

Burgerlijk Wetboek (Dutch Civil Code)   **1.NL.3.**

Article 6:213: A contract in the sense of this title is a multi-lateral juridical act whereby one or more parties assume an obligation towards one or more other parties.

BGB   **1.G.4.**

§ 305: For the creation of an obligation by a juristic act, and for any alteration of the substance of an obligation, a contract between the parties is necessary, unless otherwise provided by law.

---

[6] According to G. Cornu, *Vocabulaire Juridique Henri Capitant*, 8th edn. (Paris: PUF, 2000): Agreement (Convention): Any agreement intended to produce legal effects.

Proceeding from the point of departure, which is the basic criterion of an agreement to create obligations, one may discern different approaches. Only under French law is the contract a species of agreement. Under German law it is the notion of the legal act to which reference must be made. As to the obligation to "give" (*dare*) mentioned in Article 1108 of the French Civil Code, this will be considered with the category of agreements for the transfer of property.

In English law there is no legal definition of contract. The American Restatement Second gives one.

Second Restatement on Contracts

§ 1: A contract is a promise or a set of promises for the breach of which the law gives a remedy or the performance of which the law in some way recognises as a duty.[7]

The definitions given by academic legal authors are not always the same. They tend to emphasize different elements. Certain definitions stress, for example, the need for the existence of a "bargain", that is to say, an exchange of promised benefits—which may appear to exclude all but synallagmatic contracts. In other definitions, the emphasis is placed on the existence of a "promise". According to those definitions, a contract appears to involve the superimposition of two "promises", rather than any single, all-embracing transaction. Then again, one finds yet further definitions, such as that contained in the American Restatement (see above), which stress the need for the availability of a remedy, and according to which the contractual right emerges principally when one party fails to perform, taking the form of the options available to the wronged party. It should also be noted that that definition—which is, in fact, a statement rather than a definition as such—attaches greater weight to the role played by law than to any intention to contract. Certainly, voluntarism has never been unreservedly accepted and the role played by the notion of "reliance" will be examined under Section 1.3.[8] A comparison of the various definitions of a contract shows the mixture in varying degrees of two components, namely the subjective element: the irreplaceable role of intention, and the objective element manifested by the role of the law. It is around these two axes that the contemporary law of contract in Europe is articulated.

1.1.1.B. CONTRACT AND GIFT

Is a gift a contract? Divergent views have been expressed regarding that question. If it is a contract, the concept of a gift presupposes mutual consent, that is to say, acceptance by the beneficiary and an agreement that the transaction is to be subject to the normal rules governing the validity of a contract. It is true to say that, in general, a contract of gift must—by way of derogation from the principle of consensualism—be a solemn form contract, that is to say, a contract which, if it is not to be null and void, must comply with certain formal requirements. Thus, in French law, a promise of a gift is void unless it is made in the form of an officially or notarially recorded instrument.

---

[7] Restatement of the Law Second, Contracts 2d (1981) vol 1.

[8] See also D. Harris and D. Tallon (eds.), *Contract Law Today: Anglo-French Comparisons* (Oxford: Clarendon, 1989), at 380–2.

3

The formal criteria applying in French law have been relaxed to some extent, but not in such a way as to call in question the classification of such a transaction as a contract. Thus, French law recognizes the validity of a gift from hand to hand (*don manuel*)—i.e. traditionally, the giving of a corporeal chattel by means of its being handed over—, an indirect gift—i.e. an act of giving carried out by means of a "neutral" transaction such as the remission of a debt—, a waiver, and even a disguised gift—i.e. one concealed within a transaction purporting to be for valuable consideration, such as a sale in which it is understood that payment of the purchase price will not be demanded.

gifts inter vivos: *Code civil*   **1.F.5.**

Article 931: All instruments for *inter vivos* gifts are to be entered into before a notary in the usual form of a contract. They shall be recorded failing which they shall be null and void.

Article 932: A gift *inter vivos* shall be binding on the donor and shall have effect only as from the date on which it shall have been expressly accepted.

Acceptance may be in the lifetime of the donor by subsequent notarial act of which there shall be a record, but in that case the gift shall have effect as regards the donor only from the date on which the act recording such acceptance shall have been notified to him.

Article 938: The gift duly accepted shall be completed by mere agreement of the parties and property in the items subject to the gift shall be transferred to the donee without there being any need for any other handover.

Cass., 15 July 1889[9]   **1.F.6.**

• incapacity can be claimed by successors in title not re gifts.

Unaccepted gift

A gift which has not been accepted is invalid; provisions applying to contracts by a minor do not apply.
Judgment: THE COURT:—Whereas on the first plea alleging misapplication of Article 935 of the Civil Code, an infringement of Article 1125 and the rules relating to nullity, a gift which is not duly accepted fails to fulfil one of the conditions necessary for its completion and for it to produce mandatory effect.
—Whereas although Articles 1125 and 225 provide that nullity based on the incapacity of a minor and a woman may only be invoked by them or by their successors in title, those provisions do not apply to gifts.—Whereas therefore, the judgment appealed against did not infringe the abovementioned provisions of law by declining to uphold a gift not accepted under French law;
—Whereas the appeal is therefore dismissed.

This is the case of a contract for the transfer of property; see Article 938 of the French Civil Code.

Under German law the contractual nature flows by implication but necessarily from § 516 BGB, with § 518 imposing the formal requirement of an officially or notarially recorded instrument. Note the procedure designed to prompt the beneficiary to accept the gift (§ 516, second paragraph) and the possibility of affirming a contract which would

[9] DP. 1890.1.100.

BGB: contract revolves around formalities

otherwise have been void for failure to comply with the formal requirements relating to execution (§ 518).

BGB 1.G.7.

§ 516: (1) A disposition whereby a person confers a benefit on another out of his own property is a _gift_ if both parties agree that the disposition is made gratuitously.
(2) If the disposition is made without the consent of the other party, the person making it may demand that the other party declare whether he will accept it within a fixed reasonable period. After the expiration of the period, the gift is deemed to have been accepted, unless the other party has declined it within the period. If the gift is declined, the return of what has been given may be demanded under the provisions relating to the return of unjustified benefits.
§ 518: (1) For the validity of a contract whereby an act of performance is promised gratuitously, notarial authentification of the promise is necessary. If a promise of debt or an acknowledgment of debt of the kind specified in §§ 780, 781, is made gratuitously, the same rule applies to the promise or the declaration of acknowledgment.
(2) Any defect of form is cured by the performance of the promise. *← way of making good the promise*

As in the case of a sale an agreement to make a gift does not entail transfer of property in the thing given.
On the other hand, under common law, a gift cannot be a contract because the promise made by the donor is by definition not supported by consideration, a gratuitous or non-bargain promise becomes binding only if it is contained in a deed, that is to say if it is made in a particular form or (but only in American law, not English law) if the recipient has acted on the basis of that promise, the so-called theory of promissory estoppel reproduced in section 90 of the Second Restatement on Contracts.

a gift is not a promise

but there is remedy:

Second Restatement on Contracts *promissory estoppel*

Section 90: Promise reasonably inducing action or forbearance.
(1) A promise which the promisor should reasonably expect to induce action or forbearance on the part of the promisee or a third person and which does induce such action or forbearance is binding if injustice can be avoided only by enforcement of the promise. The remedy granted or breached may be limited as justice requires.
(2) A charitable subscription or a marriage settlement is binding under sub-section 1 without proof that the promise induced action or forbearance.[10]

1.1.1.C. CONTRACT AND UNDERTAKING BY UNILATERAL PROMISE

Can the intention of one person alone be binding on that person without acceptance by the beneficiary, the other party? In other words can he be precluded from going back on his undertaking? The question whether a unilateral promise may give rise to a promise, in the absence of any specific legislative provision, is very controversial. It should be added that the unilateral promise is also used in order to account for rules contained in some

unilateral promise — binding?

[10] _Infra_ at 126–27.

systems of substantive law, thus, the value of the offer accompanied by a fixed period for acceptance. The classic example of a unilateral promise is the promise of a reward, but also the transformation of a natural obligation into a civil obligation. A recent example from French case-law—to be contrasted with the German lottery judgment[11]—may serve to illustrate this point.

Cass. civ. 1re, 16 October 1995[12]   **1.F.8.**

The different bet which won

An unenforceable ("natural") obligation may be changed into a binding one by a subsequent promise to pay.

Facts: A punter promised to pay to a colleague on whose behalf he usually placed bets a share in the winnings on a bet different from the one agreed between them and made instead of it.

Held: The Cour d'appel held that the agreement was binding. The Cour de cassation upheld the decision.

Judgment: THE COURT: *On the various branches of the single appeal ground*:—Whereas according to the confirmatory judgment appealed against (Metz Court of Appeal, 7 October 1993), Mr Frata won the sum of FF 1,495,777 by playing the correct combination of the "Quinte Plus"[13] at a horse race which took place on 8 January 1991 at Cagnes sur Mer. Mr D'Onofiro maintained that, together with work colleagues, Mr Frata was in the habit of entrusting him with validating the Quinte tickets with PMU which he was able to do owing to his particular working hours; as it was agreed that he would receive 10 per cent of any winnings; as since he was unable for this race to validate the ticket which Mr Frata had given him in the machine for validating the gaming coupons, Mr D'Onofrio obtained a new ticket but reversed the numbers chosen by Mr Frata and this initiative enabled Mr Frata to win the Quinte in the correct order; as after the race Mr Frata informed Mr D'Onofrio that he would receive his share but in the end he refused to honour his commitments; consequently, Mr d'Onofrio brought proceedings against Mr Frata for payment of the sum of FF 149,577.70, together with interest. His claim was upheld in the lower court.
—Whereas the appeal is brought against the judgment for confirming the lower court's decision, although, it is pleaded, novation presupposes the existence of a debt to be extinguished and the creation of a new debt. Since, it is claimed, the appeal court based its finding of liability against one of the parties on the novation of a natural obligation, thus upholding novation where there was no pre-existing civil law obligation, it infringed Article 1271 of the Civil Code; as the intention for there to be novation must be clear from the act;
—Whereas in upholding the existence of a novation the cour d'appel is said to have based itself on an interpretation of the record of a personal appearance by the parties and witnesses, thus infringing Article 1273 of the Civil Code; as moreover, by finding there to be liability on the basis of a natural obligation mentioned in the notes of the hearing made by the plaintiff, it is said to have infringed Article 913 of the new Code of Civil Procedure; as finally the court, by placing reliance on those notes, infringed Article 16 of the new Code of Civil Procedure;
—Whereas however, in the first place, since Mr Frata argued in his pleadings that his commitment had no civil law consequences the plea cannot avail the appellant as to its first two branches; as the transformation incorrectly referred to as a novation of a natural obligation into a civil-law obligation based on a unilateral promise to perform the natural obligation does not require the

---

[11] *Infra* **1.G.66**, *infra* at 92.
[12] D. 1995.155, annotated by G. Pignarre; see also P. Molfessis, D. 1997, Chron. 85.
[13] A wager on the first five horses in a race.

natural law obligation + civil law obligation

pre-existence of a civil obligation; as finally, the cour d'appel after finding that Mr Frata had tacitly waived the application of Article 1341 of the Civil Code in respect of which it correctly states that its provisions are not a matter of public policy, it is for that court to assess the scope of the evidence submitted to it;

—Whereas cour d'appel held therefore on proper grounds that Mr Frata had intended to transform his natural obligations into a civil law obligation from which it follows that the plea which is partly inoperative is also unfounded;

On those grounds the appeal is dismissed.

substitution of an old contract for a new one

Note

This judgment raises several interesting questions: the creation of a natural obligation by a commitment binding in honour, the transformation of the natural obligation into a civil-law obligation by means of a unilateral promise—and not by novation. German law has specific provisions dealing with promises of reward (§§ 657 *et seq.*) but under § 305[14] seems not generally to have recognised a unilateral promise. The reverse could be inferred from Article 1324 of the Italian Civil Code.[15]

BGB   **1.G.9.**

§ 657: A person who by public notice announces a reward for the performance of an act in particular for the production of a result, is bound to pay the reward to any person who has performed the act, even if he did not act with a view to the reward.

§ 658: (1) The reward may be revoked before the performance of the act. The revocation is effective only if is made known in the same manner as the reward, or by special notice.
(2) The revocability may be waived in the notice of the reward; in case of doubt a waiver is presumed from the fact that a period of time has been fixed for the performance of the act.

The position under English law is more surprising. At first sight the question does not arise because there can be no unilateral promise in the absence of consideration. However, according to a celebrated judgment, the promise of reward gives rise to a unilateral contract, that is to say in the English sense of the term, a contract which is accepted by the performance of an act, *Carlill* v. *Carbolic Smoke Ball Company*.[16] This should be contrasted with the German rules. However the rule of English law does not apply where the recipient did not know of the promise of reward at the outset.

Thus the legal uncertainties in this matter may be noted. The Dutch Civil Code (NBW) does not seem to deal with this question directly.

1.1.2. PLACE AND SOURCES OF CONTRACT LAW   *Sources.*

Where is contract law to be found? In the case of each of the laws studied the reply throws light on the foundations of those laws.

---

[14] **1.G.4**, *supra* at 2; this requires a contract to create obligations.
[15] **1.I.10A**, *infra* at 8; this states that the rules of contract are in principle applicable to unilateral promises.
[16] [1893] 1 QB 256, **1.E.103**, *infra* at 142.

7

1.1.2.A. FRENCH LAW

The general theory of contract is essentially contained in the Civil Code, as elucidated and complemented by case-law, to which should be added the rules on consumer contracts contained in the consumer code.[17] They must be looked for in all those places because none of the three books of the Civil Code is devoted to contract or even to obligations. It is true that the French Civil Code is not reputed for its rigorous design.

Code civil   **1.F.10.**

Preliminary title: Of the publication, effects, and application of laws in general	Arts. 1-6
Book I—Of Persons	Arts. 7–515
Book II—Of Property and of the Various Kinds of Property Rights	Arts. 516–710
Book III—Of the Different Ways in which Property Rights Can Be Acquired	Arts.711–2283

    General provisions
    Title I—Of succession
    Title II—Of inter-vivos donations and of testaments
    Title III—Of contracts and of obligations based on convention in general
    Title IV—Of obligations not based on contract
    Title V—Of the marriage contract and of the respective rights of the spouses
    Title VI to Title XIII—9 specific contracts
    Title XIV—Of suretyship
    Title XV—Of compromises
    Title XVI—Of arbitration
    Title XVII—Of pledges
    Title XVIII—Of liens and of mortages
    Title XIX—Of forced sale and of the ranking of creditors
    Title XX—Of prescription

It should be observed that:

(a) the contract is placed amongst the different ways in which property may be acquired, which says much about the spirit of the Civil Code which is sometimes described as the owners' code. The model contract, that of a sale, is an agreement for the transfer of property;[18]

(b) title III is entitled "of contracts and of contractual obligations in general", from which it may be inferred that the general rules on obligations are set out in regard to contract. This demonstrates the primacy of obligations freely entered into above all others. And the courts apply by analogy to all legal acts the rules laid down in relation to contracts.

This is made explicit in Article 1234 of the Italian Civil Code.

Italian Civil Code   **1.I.10A.**

Article 1324: Rules applicable to unilateral acts: Unless otherwise provided for by the law, the rules relating to contracts must be observed, as long as they are compatible, in the case of unilateral acts, *inter vivos*.

[17] **1.F.22,** *Infra* at 24.
[18] **1.F.16,** *Infra* at 20.

These provisions of the French code have been relatively little altered and there is no question of them being reformed at the present time. Since their terms are generally flexible the courts have been able to mould them to changing circumstances, see for example the third party contract and the interpretation by the courts of Article 1121.

1.1.2.B. GERMAN LAW

It is also mainly in the BGB that the general theory of contract is to be found. It is set out more scientifically than the French Civil Code but, on the other hand, is more complicated for the user since the rules are to be found in different parts of the code.

BGB	**1.G.11.**

Book I—General Principles	
Section I—Persons	§§ 1—89
Title 1—Natural Persons	
Title 2—Juristic Persons	
Section II—Things	§§ 90—103
Section III—Juristic Acts	§§ 104—185
Title 1—Disposing Capacity	
Title 2—Declaration of Intention	
Title 3—Contract	
Title 4—Condition, Limitation of Time	
Title 5—Agency, Power of Agency	
Title 6—Approval, Ratification	
(Section IV—Periods of time, Dates)	(§§ 186—193)
(Section V—Prescription)	(§§ 194—225)
(Section VI—Exercise of Rights, Self-Defense, Self-Help)	(§§ 226—231)
(Section VII—Giving of Security)	(§§ 232—240)
Book II—Law of Obligations	
Section I—Scope of Obligations	§§ 241—304
Title 1—Obligation of Performance	
Title 2—Default of the Creditor	
Section II—Obligations ex Contractu	§§ 305—361
Title 1—Creation of an Obligation, Scope of a Contract	
Title 2—Bilateral Contracts	
Title 3—Promise of Performances in Favor of a Third Party	
Title 4—Earnest, Penalty Clauses	
Title 5—Rescission	
Section III—Extinction of Obligations	§§ 362—397
Title 1—Fulfilment	
Title 2—Deposit	
Title 3—Setoff	
Title 4—Release	
Section IV—Assignment of Claims	§§ 398—413
Section V—Assumption of Debt	§§ 414—419
Section VI—Plurality of Debtors and Creditors	§§ 420—432
Section VII—Various Types of Obligations	§§ 433—853

The basic concept is that of a legal act—juristic act and not a legal transaction, as stated in certain translations. The basic rules of the contract *qua* juristic act are to be found in the third title of the general part and, more specifically, in Chapter 3. Another series of rules is to be found in Title 2 of Book 2, "Obligations arising out of the contract". That part also concerns obligations in general. These provisions also have been little altered, save in so far as general terms and conditions are concerned (AGBG 1976[19]). A recent draft amendment resulted only in certain *ad hoc* reforms.

The German courts have done major work in adapting the BGB to evolving circumstances and to fill gaps. In doing so, they have had recourse to general concepts (*Generalklausen*) contained in the code although, at that time, its authors did not attach great importance to them. These are, for example, moral standards (§ 138) or good faith (§ 242). § 242 has been used to work out rules relating to unforeseeability (disappearance of the transactional basis). See also below,[20] the judicial theory of positive breach of contract (*positive Vertragsverletzung*) developed in order to fill a troublesome gap left in the BGB.

Thus, in order to find the rules on contract, it is necessary to consult the general part, then the second part of the BGB and, possibly, the law on general terms and conditions (AGBG).

1.1.2.C. ENGLISH LAW

Under English law the general theory of the contract is not chiefly based on written law but on the common law, frequently supplemented or attenuated by the rules of equity. Worthy of note, however, are the codifying pieces of legislation (in actual fact consolidated legislation), such as the Sale of Goods Act 1893 (now the Sale of Goods Act 1979), certain specific enactments, such as the Law Reform (Contributory Negligence) Act 1945 and also consumer protection legislation—such as the Unfair Contract Terms Act 1977[21]—or the Contracts (Rights of Third Parties) Act 1999.[22] Owing to the fact that it is judge-made law, the English law of contract is less structured than codified laws. This is all the more so since the general theory of the contract emerged progressively and only belatedly. It should also be noted that contract law is generally studied separately and not in the context of the law of obligations, the latter being a concept that has only recently emerged in the writings of English academics.

Furthermore, contract law was not influenced directly by Roman law and by its commentators, and the so-called voluntarist theories which became widespread in the seventeenth century did not penetrate English law as profoundly as they did on the continent. It is through the intermediary of foreign authors that the principle of autonomy of intent has penetrated English law, albeit modestly.

Pothier, an author who inspired many provisions of the Civil Code and was translated into English at the end of the eighteenth century, was frequently cited by English judges in the nineteenth century.[23]

[19] See 3.4.3., *infra* at 513.
[20] *Infra* at 662.
[21] **3.E.139**, *infra* at 515.
[22] **7.E.9**, *infra* at 893.
[23] Simpson, "Innovation in Nineteenth Century Contract Law" (1975) 91 LQR 247.

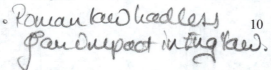

10

It is on the basis of the notion of a "promise"—which does not correspond to the French word "*promesse*"—that the law of contract was worked out, the contract not being considered in its overall context but rather as the juxtaposition of two promises.

House of Lords   **1.E.12.**

Moschi v. Lep Air Services Ltd [24]

[*The facts are not given in any detail as they are not relevant. The case concerned the enforceability of a contract of guarantee after the creditor had terminated the principal contract for non-performance by the debtor. The House of Lords held that this did not release the guarantor.*]

Judgment: LORD DIPLOCK: The law of contract is part of the law of obligations. The English law of obligations is about their sources and the remedies which the court can grant to the obligee for a failure by the obligor to perform his obligation voluntarily. Obligations which are performed voluntarily require no intervention by a court of law. They do not give rise to any cause of action.

English law is thus concerned with contracts as a source of obligations. The basic principle which the law of contract seeks to enforce is that a person who makes a promise to another ought to keep this promise. This basic principle is subject to an historical exception that the English law does not give the promisee a remedy for the failure by a promisor to perform his promise unless either the promise was made in a particular form, eg, under seal, or the promisee in return promises to do something for the promisor which he would not otherwise be obliged to do, ie, gives consideration for the promise . . .

Each promise that a promisor makes to a promisee by entering into a contract with him creates an obligation to perform it owed by the promisor as obligor to the promisee as obligee. If he does not do so voluntarily there are two kinds of remedies which the court can grant to the promisee. It can compel the obligor to pay to the obligee a sum of money to compensate him for the loss that he has sustained as a result of the obligee's failure to perform his obligation. This is the remedy at common law in damages for breach of contract. But there are some kinds of obligation which the court is able to compel the obligor actually to perform. In some cases . . . a remedy to compel performance by a decree of specific performance or by injunction is also available. It was formerly obtainable only in a court of equity . . . But, since a court of common law could make and enforce orders for payment of a sum of money, where the obligation was itself an obligation to pay a sum of money, even a court of common law could compel the obligor to perform it . . .

Note

Lord Diplock's reasoning raises questions on:

—the importance of remedies because it is on the basis of the means afforded to the disappointed creditor that the law of contract has been developed;
—the respective role of legal and equitable remedies;[25]
—the hierarchy of remedies;

To be noted also is the reference to the notion of obligation.

---

[24] [1973] AC 331.

[25] The distinction between legal and equitable remedies in English law goes back to the Middle Ages, when a party who complained that the rigidity of a rule at common law might appeal to the Chancellor (representing the King) for relief on the basis of "equity". In particular if the common law did not provide an adequate remedy, the Chancellor (sitting later in the Court of Equity) might grant one. Thus equity was a supplementary jurisdiction which would in effect supersede the common law rule. It became settled that the equitable rule would prevail, but until the nineteenth century the plaintiff would have to bring a separate action in the courts of equity; the common law courts would then defer. Since the nineteenth century Judicature Acts the same courts administer both sets of rules, always giving the final say to the rule of equity, but the two sets of rules remain largely distinct. See further, J.H. Baker, *Introduction to English Legal History* (3rd edn., London: Butterworths, 1990).

(margin note: contract law developed from promisor not keeping their promises)

[handwritten annotation: contract law - seperate / French/German law - comes under the law of obligations.]

The concept of the contract under English law is in certain respects a vague one and is not precisely the same as in Germany or France, as will be seen below. Moreover, contract law is studied separately in England, whereas in the two other countries it forms part of the study of the law of obligations. This is borne out by a comparison between the titles of the current textbooks.[26] It even happens that in the United States[27] reference is made to contracts in the plural as if there were no single uniform concept. It is also apparent when one compares the textbooks that there seems little willingness to construct a logical and coherent theory: see the 21 chapters of Treitel which are not grouped together in any way.

One final observation: a major influence on some academic writers has been exerted by American law, see, in particular, the publications of P.S. Atiyah.

In conclusion, there appears to be a fairly considerable gulf between the systems of law based on Roman law and the common law. Care should be exercised not to be taken in by superficial similarities. Many of these may be misleading, starting with the term "contract", as will be seen below.

1.1.3. CATEGORIES OF CONTRACT

In order to introduce order into the burgeoning array of contracts, legislation, case-law and academic writings have sought to establish a classification. This makes it possible for the applicable rules to be determined because each category has its own system of rules. We have already noted the distinction between contract and agreement ("*contrat/convention*") under French law to which the Germans prefer the distinction juristic act/contract ("*acte juridique/contrat*"), which has, moreover, also been accepted by French academic writers. I will mention here only those that appear to me to be the most important or those which raise difficulties from a comparative point of view. For certain distinctions which are important in one system of law are all but ignored in another or, something which poses more of a hazard for comparative students, distinctions which appear to be similar may in actual fact be considerably different.

I shall therefore swiftly review the distinction between commutative and aleatory contracts drawn in Article 1104 of the French Civil Code,[28] which is of use in particular in connection with the rules on damage, except in relation to corresponding provisions in other systems of law. The Civil Code also distinguishes between contracts with a special name and others (Article 1107), a distinction which is obviously to be found in other systems of law.

Code civil

1.F.13.

Article 1102: A contract is synallagmatic or bilateral when the contracting parties assume obligations reciprocally, each to the other.

---

[26] See Larenz, *SAT*; Malaurie and Aynès; Treitel, *Contract*.
[27] See Second Restatement and E.A. Farnsworth, *Contracts*, 2nd edn. (New York: Aspen Law & Business, 1998).
[28] *Infra* at 13.

Article 1103: It is unilateral when one or more persons are obligated to one or more other persons, and no obligation rests on the latter.

Article 1104: It is commutative when each party binds himself to give or to do something that is considered the equivalent of what the other party gives him or does for him.
　　　　　　　When the equivalent for each of the parties consists in a chance of gain or loss dependent upon an uncertain event, the contract is aleatory.

Article 1105: A contract of benevolence is one in which one party procures a purely gratuitous advantage for the other.

Article 1106: An onerous contract obliges each party to give or to do something.

Article 1107: All contracts, regardless of whether they have a special name, are subject to the general rules set out in this title.
　　　　　　　The special rules governing particular contracts are to be found under the titles dealing with each of them, the special rules governing commercial contracts are set out in the laws relating to commerce.

It should be noted that in the Common Law the rules were drawn up first for specific contracts before a general theory of contracts, whether specific or unspecific, came to be established.

There is also in every case a distinction to be found between once-and-for-all contracts and successive contracts or contracts providing for performance in successive parts. This is not provided for in the French Civil Code which nevertheless established a great number of distinctions. However, it is of importance, particularly as regards the annulment or termination of the contract. A contract providing for performance in successive parts is not at all the same thing as a long-term contract.[29] Nor is it a relational contract, a concept which is more sociological than legal.

There are three other distinctions which demand our attention: the synallagmatic or bilateral contract and the unilateral contract; the contract for valuable consideration and the contract without consideration; the contract giving rise to obligations and the contract for the transfer of property. In addition, there is the new category of consumer contracts.

1.1.3.A. THE SYNALLAGMATIC OR BILATERAL CONTRACT AND THE UNILATERAL CONTRACT

The definitions given by the French Civil Code correspond to those in Netherlands' Burgerlijk Wetboek.

BW   **1.NL.13A.**

6:261: (1) A contract is synallagmatic if each of the parties assumes an obligation to obtain the prestation to which the other party, in exchange, obligates himself toward him.
　　　　(2) The provisions respecting synallagmatic contracts apply *mutadis mutandis* to other juridical relationships intended for the reciprocal performance of prestations, to the extent that this is not incompatible with the nature of those juridical relationships.

---

[29] See Harris and Tallon (eds.), op. cit., at 195–242.

In §§ 320–326 the BGB provides rules governing the synallagmatic contract, and this distinction is well known to be significant in relation to cause, where mention is made of it, and above all in the event of non-performance, whether or not attributable to the debtor (theory of risk in French law). On the other hand, the concept of the unilateral contract is less clear, particularly owing to English law which is quite close but sufficiently different also to give rise to confusion, as is demonstrated by Diplock LJ's reasoning in the extract from the following case of the Court of Appeal.

Court of Appeal   **1.E.14.**
United Dominions Trust Ltd. v. *Eagle Aircraft Services Ltd*[30]

Recourse agreement

Where a contract is what is termed by English Law[31] a unilateral contract (that is, where one party promises to pay or do some other act if the other perform, but the latter party does not undertake that it will perform), the act stated must be performed precisely; there is no room for the doctrine found in synallagmatic contracts that whether the first party must perform despite an incomplete or late performance by the second depends on the seriousness of the non-performance.

Facts: An aircraft supplier had supplied an aircraft to a finance company so that the latter could lease the aircraft to an airline. It was a term of the agreement that if the airline defaulted and the finance company repossessed the aircraft, the supplier, if notified within a certain period of time, would repurchase the aircraft. The finance company failed to give notice within the time stated and the supplier refused to repurchase.

Held: The trial judge applied the doctrine of the *Hong Kong Fir* case (see *infra* at 765) and held that the supplier must repurchase unless the delay deprived it of the substance of what it had contracted for. The Court of Appeal disagreed with this approach.

Judgment: DIPLOCK LJ: . . . The present appeal does turn on the difference in legal character between contracts which are synallagmatic (a term which I prefer to bilateral, for there may be more than two parties), and contracts which are not synallagmatic but only unilateral, an expression which, like synallagmatic, I have borrowed from French law (Code civil, art. 1102 and art. 1103). Under contracts of the former kind, each party undertakes to the other party to do or to refrain from doing something, and, in the event of his failure to perform his undertaking, the law provides the other party with a remedy. The remedy of the other party may be limited to recovering monetary compensation for any loss which he has sustained as a result of the failure, without relieving him from his own obligation to do that which he himself has undertaken to do and has not yet done, or to continue to refrain from doing that which he himself has undertaken to refrain from doing. It may, in addition, entitle him, if he so elects, to be released from any further obligation to do or to refrain from doing anything . . . The mutual obligations of parties to a synallagmatic contract may be subject to conditions precedent, that is to say, they may not arise until a described event has occurred; but the event must not be one which one party can prevent from occurring, for if it is, it leaves that party free to decide whether or not he will enter into any obligations to the other party at all. The obligations under the contract lack that mutuality which is an essential characteristic of a synallagmatic contract . . .

. . . Under contracts which are only unilateral—which I have elsewhere described as "if" contracts—one party, whom I will call "the promisor", undertakes to do or to refrain from doing

---

[30] [1968] 1WLR 74.
[31] Note that this is quite different from the meaning of unilateral contract in French law: see note following the case.

THE NOTION OF CONTRACT

something on his part if another party, "the promisee", does or refrains from doing something, but the promisee does not himself undertake to do or to refrain from doing that thing. The commonest contracts of this kind in English law are options for good consideration to buy or to sell or to grant or take a lease, competitions for prizes, and such contracts as that discussed in *Carlill* v. *Carbolic Smoke Ball Co* [1893] 1 QB 256. A unilateral contract does not give rise to any immediate obligation on the part of either party to do or to refrain from doing anything except possibly an obligation on the part of the promisor to refrain from putting it out of his power to perform his undertaking in the future. This apart, a unilateral contract may never give rise to any obligation on the part of the promisor; it will only do so on the occurrence of the event specified in the contract, *viz*, the doing (or refraining from doing) by the promisee of a particular thing. It never gives rise, however, to any obligation on the promisee to bring about the event by doing or refraining from doing that particular thing. Indeed, a unilateral contract of itself never gives rise to any obligation on the promisee to do or to refrain from doing anything. In its simplest form (eg, "If you pay the entrance fee and win the race, I will pay you £ 100"), no obligations on the part of the promisee result from it at all. But in its more complex and more usual form, as in an option, the promisor's undertaking may be to enter into a synallagmatic contract with the promisee on the occurrence of the event specified in the unilateral contract, and in that case the event so specified must be, or at least include, the communication by the promisee to the promisor of the promisee's acceptance of his obligation under the synallagmatic contract. By entering into the subsequent synallagmatic contract on the occurence of the specified event, the promisor discharges his obligation under the unilateral contract and accepts new obligations under ther synallagmatic contract. Any obligations of the promisee arise, not out of the unilateral contract, but out of the subsequent synallagmatic contract into which he was not obliged to enter but has chosen to do so.

Two consequences follow from this. The first is that there is no room for any inquiry whether any act done by the promisee in purported performance of a unilateral contract amounts to a breach of warranty or a breach of condition[32] on his part, for he is under no obligation to do or to refrain form doing any act at all. The second is that, as respects the promisor, the initial inquiry is whether the event, which under the unilateral contract gives rise to obligations on the part of the promisor, has occurred. To that inquiry the answer can only be a simple "Yes" or "No" . . .

Note

It is to be noted that the definition of the synallagmatic contract corresponds to the French definition to which, moreover, reference is made, even if the remedies for non-performance are not exactly the same, particularly as regards performance in kind or termination of the contract (cf. Article 1184 of the French Civil Code). It is quite otherwise in the case of the unilateral contract, so much so that the terms are not interchangeable. The "if" contract or a contract on executed consideration is not necessarily a contract binding on only one of the parties. It is a contract under English law—but not necessarily under French or German law—which is accepted by the debtor acting in some way or refraining from acting. But, at the outset, he is in no way bound by it. The classic example in English law is provided by the celebrated judgment in *Carlill* v. *Carbolic Smoke Ball Co. Ltd.*[33] We come across this question in relation to the binding nature of a unilateral expression of intent. On the other hand, unilateral contracts under French law would not in general be deemed to be valid contracts at English law owing to the fact that they are

---

[32] This also is a test used by English law to determine whether the breach is or is not serious. See *infra* at 736.
[33] *Infra* at 142.

not supported by consideration. That highlights well the divergence between the Romanist system and the Common Law in regard to the very notion of contract.

1.1.3.B. CONTRACT FOR VALUABLE CONSIDERATION (*A TITRE ONÉREUX*) AND CONTRACT WITHOUT VALUABLE CONSIDERATION (*A TITRE GRATUIT*) OR CHARITABLE CONTRACT

The starting-point is provided by the definitions in the Civil Code (Articles 1105 and 1106[34]) and § 516 of the BGB.[35] The distinction is clear, even though the criterion, the gratuitous nature of the contract, is not simple and difficulties may arise in regard to charitable acts: see below on the intention to enter into contractual relations. It should also be noted that all synallagmatic contracts are contracts for valuable consideration whereas unilateral contracts, normally unsupported by consideration, may sometimes be for valuable consideration, for example the interest-bearing loan.

The distinction is an important one as regards the rules applicable to each category, for example in actions for recovery or declarations of nullity in the event of fraud, in assesssing the obligations of the parties, not to mention the rules applicable to gifts where the latter may be analysed as constituting contracts.[36]

Conversely, English law does not recognize transactions unsupported by consideration as a category of contracts. Gratuitous promises are without value, owing to the absence of consideration, unless they are incorporated in a deed, that is to say are embodied in a particular form. Moreover, the English courts have elaborated the theory of estoppel which may be used as a partial substitute for consideration. It is an equitable doctrine which here plays its corrective role. It is defined in section 90 of the Restatement and is elucidated by Lord Denning in the case of *Crabb* v. *Arun District Council*, below.[37]

The doctrine of consideration[38] requires that, for a promise to be binding in English law, the promise must form part of a bargain—that is to say, the promise must have been given in exchange for something else, either an act—or forbearance or a return promise. The exchange need not be for something of equivalent value—indeed English law routinely enforces promises which are given for purely nominal consideration, as when a lease is granted for a rent of a peppercorn or land is sold for £1. But if there is no exchange the promise will not be binding. Thus a promise to give money to a charity is not enforceable unless the need for consideration is avoided by the promise being made in a deed.[39]

It does not matter that there may be a very good reason for making the promise—e.g. that the promisee has just saved the promisor's life, even if he was gravely injured in the process; the act of saving the promisor was done before the promise and thus cannot have been in exchange for it—a rule summarized in the rather confusing phrase, "past consideration is no consideration".[40]

---

[34] *Supra* at 12.
[35] **1.G.7**, *supra* at 5.
[36] *Supra* at 3.
[37] **1.E.15**, *infra* at 18.
[38] *Supra* at 14–15.
[39] *Supra* at 5.
[40] See *Re McArdle* [1951] Ch 669; in the US, the courts have sometimes departed from this rule in deserving rescue cases, e.g. *Webb* v. *McGowin* 27 Ala App 82, 168 So 196 (1935). See also the *"donation rémunératoire"* in French Law.

THE NOTION OF CONTRACT

Equally in principle it makes no difference that the promisee has assumed that the promise will be performed and has acted in such a way that, if the promise is not performed after all, he will be left worse off than before—so-called detrimental reliance. Unless the promisor had asked the promisee to act as he did, the promisee's action was not done in exchange for the promise. The classic test is, did the promisor expressly or impliedly request the promisee to act as he did.[41] But in practice, when the promisee's actions have seemed reasonable and his case for compensation strong, English judges have sometimes striven to find a remedy. One approach is to "discover" a contract in which something done by the promisee is treated as consideration for the promise.[42] Another approach which has been widely (though not universally) adopted in the US has been to use a doctrine known as "estoppel".

In its traditional sense, estoppel is a principle known to many systems; it prevents a party from going back on what he has said or done (*venire contra proprium factum*). The traditional common law version of this was that if a party made a statement of fact which the other party relied on to his detriment—so that if the fact were not true he would be worse off than before—, then the first party could not deny the fact—so that if, had the fact stated been true, the relying party would have had some right or remedy, he will have that remedy anyway. Thus if the bank tells you that you have £1,000 in your account, and believing this to be true you spend that much money, the bank will have to pay the amount it said it owed you. But during the nineteenth century courts in the US started to use estoppel where a person had given a promise and the promisee had acted to his or her detriment on the promise.[43] It was said that, even though there was no consideration, once the promisee had acted to her detriment on the promise, the promisor was estopped from going back on the promise.[44]

This is inconsistent with the traditional English position, which is that estoppel does not apply to a promise, only to a statement of existing fact.[45] Also, English law would give a remedy only if there would be one had the fact stated been true. Even if the defendant had made a promise, the promisee would not have a remedy unless she had given consideration.[46] The American courts sometimes evaded this by saying that the promisor "was estopped from denying that there was consideration".[47] In an infamous case in 1947[48] Denning J attempted to introduce a rather similar doctrine into English law, in the context of a gratuitous promise to reduce the payment due under a contract. This caused a considerable debate, since it flew in the face of established authority that such a promise was not binding for want of consideration.[49] Ultimately the doctrine of promissory

---

[41] See *Shadwell* v. *Shadwell*, (1860) CB(NS) 159; (BBF3 119) and *Combe* v. *Combe*, [1951] 2 KB 215 (BBF3 at 148).

[42] See e.g. *de la Bere* v. *Pearson* [1908] 1 KB 280.

[43] See e.g. *Ricketts* v. *Scothorn* 77 NW 365 (1898) (BBF3 at 142), where a grandfather promised to pay money to his granddaughter, who gave up her job on the strength of the promise.

[44] See now Restatement, s.90, *supra* at 5.

[45] See *Jorden* v. *Money* (1854) 5 HL Cas 185 (BBF3 at 145).

[46] Which in *Ricketts v Scothorn* the court held she had not. See further *infra*, note 52.

[47] Which at least in *Ricketts* v. *Scothorn* was a complete fiction since the grandfather, doubtless being quite innocent of the niceties of contract law, had not said anything about consideration (all he had said was, "I have fixed something that you have not got to work any more. None of my grandchildren work and you don't have to.")

[48] *Central London Property Trust Ltd* v. *High Trees House Ltd* [1947] KB 130 (BBF3 at 146).

[49] See *Foakes* v. *Beer*, (1884) 9 App Cas 605 (BBF3 at 731).

estoppel, as it has come to be called, has been accepted by the Court of Appeal in England but only in the context of a promise not to enforce an existing contractual right.[50] In a case in 1951[51] even Denning—by then Denning LJ—had to admit that the doctrine could not be used as a substitute for consideration, to create a contractual obligation where none existed otherwise. Thus in English law the facts that a promise has been made and the promisee has acted on the promise to his or her detriment does not make the promise binding.[52]

However, in one particular context the strict English rule has been relaxed and a gratuitous promise which has been acted on will be enforced. This is where the promise is to confer some interest in land. In the nineteenth century case of *Dillwyn* v. *Llewellyn*,[53] a father said that he had given a piece of land to his son and encouraged the son to build on the land—but in fact the father never transferred ownership of the land to the son. After the father's death, his estate tried to reclaim the land, complete with the mansion the son had built on it. Rather than allow this injustice, the courts of equity compelled the father's personal representatives to complete the gift. The rule was gradually extended, first to cases in which the father said he would give the land and the son again built without the transfer having taken place,[54] and then, as the next case shows, to cases in which the promisee has not built on the land but had acted in some other way in reliance on the promise. The doctrine has come to be known as "proprietary estoppel".

Court of Appeal   **1.E.15.**
Crabb v. *Arun District Council*[55]

A land-locked property

A party who indicates that he will grant another a right in property and who encourages the other to act on that assumption in such a way that the other will lose if the right is not granted will be compelled to do justice.

Facts: This was an action for a declaration that the plaintiff had a right of access over the defendants' land in order to reach one of his plots which no longer had an access owing to the sale of part of his land. The plaintiff claimed that he would not have gone ahead with the sale of part of his property if the council representative had not given the clear impression in discussions that the plaintiff would be granted access from the Council's land at point B. The council at first left a gap at point B, but later fenced it off, denying the plaintiff access unless he paid £ 3,000 for such a right.

Held: The Court of Appeal granted the declaration.

Judgment: LORD DENNING MR: . . . When counsel for Mr Crabb said that he put his case on an estoppel, it shook me a little, because it is commonly supposed that estoppel is not itself a cause of action. But that is because there are estoppels and estoppels. Some do give rise to a cause of action.

---

[50] See *Alan* v. *El Nasr*, *WJ Alan & Co Ltd* v. *El Nasr Export and Import Co* [1972] 2 QB 189 (BBF3 at 746); the House of Lords has yet to pronounce on the doctrine.

[51] *Combe* v. *Combe*, *supra*, note 41.

[52] Thus in England, on the facts of *Ricketts v Scothorn*, the granddaughter would be without a remedy—unless the court were to decide—contrary to what the American court held—that the grandfather was asking the granddaughter to give up work in exchange for the promise of money, so that there would be consideration (in which case he would not have to pay if she went on working).

[53] (1862) 4 DeG, F & J 517.

[54] See *Inwards v. Baker*, [1965] 2 QB 29.

[55] (1976) Ch. 179.

Some do not. In the species of estoppel called proprietary estoppel, it does give rise to a cause of action. We had occasion to consider it a month ago in *Moorgate Mercantile Co Ltd* v. *Twitchings* where I said that the effect of estoppel on the true owner may be that :

> "his own title to the property, be it land or goods, has been held to be limited or extinguished, and new rights and interests have been created therein. And this operates by reason of his conduct—what he has led the other to believe—even though he never intended it."

The new rights and interests, so created by estoppel in or over land, will be protected by the courts and in this way give rise to a cause of action . . .

The basis of this proprietary estoppel—as indeed of promissory estoppel—is the interposition of equity. Equity comes in, true to form, to mitigate the rigours of strict law. The early cases did not speak of it as "estoppel". They spoke of it as "raising an equity" . . .

What then are the dealings which will preclude him from insisting on his strict legal rights ? If he makes a binding contract that he will not insist on the strict legal position, a court of equity will hold him to his contract. Short of a binding contract, if he makes a promise that he will not insist upon his strict legal rights—even though that promise may be unenforceable in point of law for want of consideration or want of writing—and if he makes the promise knowing or intending that the other will act upon it, and he does act upon it, then again a court of equity will not allow him to go back on that promise: see *Central London Property Trust Ltd* v. *High Trees House Ltd* and *Charles Rickards Ltd* v. *Oppenheim*. Short of an actual promise, if he, by his words or conduct, so behaves as to lead another to believe that he will not insist on this strict legal rights—knowing or intending that the other will act on that belief—and he does so act, that again will raise an equity in favour of the other, and it is for a court of equity to say in what way the equity may be satisfied. The cases show that this equity does not depend on agreement but on words or conduct. In *Ramsden* v. *Dyson* Lord Kingsdown spoke of a verbal agreement "or what amounts to the same thing, an expectation, created or encouraged". In *Birmingham and District Land Co* v. *London and North Western Railway Co*, Cotton LJ said that ". . . what passed did not make a new agreement, but what took place . . . raised an equity against him" . . .

The question then is: were the circumstances here such as to raise an equity in favour of Mr Crabb ? True the council on the deeds had the title to their land, free of any access at point B. But they led Mr Crabb to believe that he had or would be granted a right of access at point B . . .

The council actually put up the gates at point B at considerable expense. That certainly led Mr Crabb to believe that they agreed that he should have the right of access through point B without more ado . . .

The council knew that Mr Crabb intended to sell the two portions separately and that he would need an access at point B as well as point A. Seeing that they knew of his intention—and they did nothing to disabuse him, but rather confirmed it by erecting gates at point B—it was their conduct which led him to act as he did; and this raises an equity in favour against them . . .

Lord Denning's view is not universally accepted in full; see the somewhat more traditional view of Lord Scarman in the same case.[56] But all three judges in the Court of Appeal held that the plaintiff should have a remedy.

The theory of estoppel is relatively recent and doubtless has not yet reached its full maturity and, like any equitable remedy, leaves a wide margin of discretion to the courts. Here again, the divergent views of the doctrine are clearly apparent when one contrasts the Common Law with the systems based on Roman law.

---

[56] See also s. 90 of the 2nd Restatement on Contracts, *supra*, at 5.

1.1.3.C. CONTRACTS GIVING RISE TO OBLIGATIONS AND CONTRACTS TRANSFERRING OR CREATING PROPERTY RIGHTS

This time it is German law which differs from the others, even though in the other systems the distinction none the less exists without however entailing special rules. That is immediately apparent from Article 1101 of the French Civil Code which places on the same footing obligations to perform an act or to refrain from doing so and the obligation to give (*dare*, that is to say transfer property). However uncertain the current meaning of the obligation to give (some commentators take the view that it is of no practical significance owing to the transfer solely by way of agreement (*solo consensu*), it is established that under French law as under Italian law (and many others) and under English law, the sale is both a contract giving rise to obligations and an instrument under which property is transferred.

Code civil **1.F.16.**

Article 1582: Sale is an agreement through which one party is obligated to deliver an object and the other to pay for it.
It can be made by an authenticated instrument or by an instrument under private signature.

Article 1583: The sale is complete between the parties, and property passes by operation of law to the buyer, as against the seller, as soon as there is agreement on the object and the price, even though delivery has not yet been made or the price paid.

Sale of Goods Act 1979 **1.E.17.**

Section 1
(1) A contract of sale of goods is a contract by which the seller transfers or agrees to transfer the property in goods to the buyer for a money consideration, called the price.
(2) There may be a contract of sale between one part owner and another.
(3) A contract of sale may be absolute or conditional.
(4) Where under a contract of sale the property in the goods is transferred from the seller to the buyer the contract is called a sale.
(5) Where under a contract of sale the transfer of the property in the goods is to take place at a future time or subject to some condition later to be fulfilled the contract is called an agreement to sell.
(6) An agreement to sell becomes a sale when the time elapses or the conditions are fulfilled subject to which the property in the goods is to be transferred.

The position is the same for gifts[57] and contracts creating rights *in rem*. The rather complicated definition contained in the Sale of Goods Act is based on the same idea. Conversely, under German law and the systems which follow that model, the contract merely creates the obligation. Property is transferred or rights *in rem* created by means of another act, separate from the contract, pursuant to the principle of separability

---

[57] *Supra*, at 3.

(*Abstraktionsprinzip*). Under that principle the former may be null and void without affecting the validity of the latter instrument. This particular feature of German law will be examined below at 1.1.3.D.

It should be noted that French law does recognize a category of separable or "abstract" acts which may be detached from the underlying transaction. Such acts are valid irrespective of whether there is a valid underlying transaction. But this is an exceptional category in contrast to the system under German law (see below under cause—e.g. exchange transactions or first-call guarantees. Under German law the distinction is drawn and separability affirmed in §§ 433 and 929 BGB.

BGB	**1.G.18.**

§ 433: (1) By the contract of sale the seller of a thing is bound to deliver the thing to the purchaser and to transfer ownership of the thing. The seller of a right is bound to transfer the right to the purchaser, and if the right entitles one to the possession of a thing, to deliver the thing. (2) The purchaser is bound to pay to the seller the purchase price agreed upon and to take delivery of the thing purchased.

§ 929: For the transfer of ownership of a movable thing, it is necessary that the owner of the thing deliver it to the acquirer and that both agree that the ownership be transferred. If the acquirer is in possession of the thing, the agreement on the transfer of ownership is sufficient.

All acts of disposition are therefore abstract, whereas agreements creating obligations are nearly always based on reciprocity. There are however some acts which are abstract in the French sense: see for example the binding promise mentioned in § 780 BGB (*Schuldversprechen*) or exchange transactions. The principle of separability leads to injustices which are corrected by the application of the doctrine of unjust enrichment. An example is to be found in the judgment of the Supreme Court (*Reichsgericht*) of 25 June 1925 in a case concerning a gift to a concubine.[58]

1.1.3.D. CONSUMER CONTRACTS

The category of consumer contracts has emerged only recently, though the idea of protecting the weaker party is not new. Suffice it to recall the discussion concerning standard form contracts at the end of the nineteenth century, the case-law of the German courts on § 138 BGB (undue advantage) and § 242 (good faith), and the judgments of French courts[59] which, as from 1909, have held the commercial vendor to be irrebuttably presumed to have knowledge of the defect in the item sold (Article 1645 of the Civil Code), with all the consequences which that entails, not to mention the case-law on exemption clauses.[60] However, in the last 30 years specific legislation has been enacted to protect the consumer or private individual by making consumer contracts subject to special rules. This accounts for the emergence of the concept of the consumer contract enshrined in Council Directive 93/13/EEC of 5 April 1993 on unfair terms in contracts entered into

[58] See **1.G.27**, *infra* at 29.
[59] Cass. 10 May 1909, DP. 1912. 1.16.
[60] *Infra*, at 509 ff.

with consumers, which has sought to reconcile existing national laws. The Directive has given a boost to new legislation and the question now arises: what is now the notion of a consumer contract?

Council Directive 93/13/EEC of 5 April 1993 on unfair terms in **1.EC.19.**
contracts entered into with consumers

Article 1
1. The purpose of this Directive is to approximate the laws, regulations and administrative provisions of the Member States relating to unfair terms in contracts concluded between a seller or supplier and a consumer.
2. The contractual terms which reflect mandatory statutory or regulatory provisions and the provisions of or principles of international conventions to which the Member States or the Community are party, particularly in the transport area, shall not be subject to the provisions of this Directive.

Article 2
For the purposes of this Directive:
(a) "unfair terms" means the contractual terms defined in Article 3;
(b) "consumer" means any natural person who, in contracts covered by this Directive, is acting for purposes which are outside his trade, business or profession;
(c) "seller or supplier" means any natural or legal person who, in contracts covered by this Directive, is acting for purposes relating to his trade, business or profession, whether publicly owned or privately owned.

Article 3
1. A contractual term which has not been individually negotiated shall be regarded as unfair if, contrary to the requirement of good faith, it causes a significant imbalance in the parties' rights and obligations arising under the contract, to the detriment of the consumer.
2. A term shall always be regarded as not having been individually negotiated where it has been drafted in advance and the consumer has therefore not been able to influence the substance of the term.
The fact that certain aspects of a term or one specific term have been individually negotiated shall not exclude the application of this Article to the rest of the contract if an overall assessment of the contract indicates that it is nevertheless a pre-formulated standard contract.
Where any seller or supplier claims that a standard term has been individually negotiated, the burden of proof in this respect shall be incumbent on him.
3. The Annex shall contain an indicative and non-exhaustive list of the terms which may be regarded as unfair.[61]

German Law
Germany led the way with the 1976 law on General Terms and Conditions in Business (AGBG) which, notwithstanding its title, is indeed a law protecting the consumer by way of rules governing general terms and conditions in contracts. The legislation applies to general conditions to the exclusion of contract terms negotiated in detail by the parties, that is to say individual agreements. The rules differ depending on whether the contract is entered into with a trader or a private individual; it is the latter case which is of relevance for present purposes.

---

[61] The full text of the Directive will be found in Chapter 3 section 4, *infra* at 521.

AGBG 1976 **1.G.20.**

§ 1
(1) The general terms and conditions of business are all the standard contract terms used repeatedly in contracts which are imposed by one of the contracting parties on the other at the time when the contract is entered into. It is of little importance whether the provisions are contained in a document external to the contract or are incorporated in the contractual document itself; nor are the extent of the standard terms, the manner in which the contract is reduced to writing, or its form, of significance.

(2) The conditions negotiated in detail by the parties do not constitute general terms and conditions of business.

§ 9(1)
General contractual conditions shall be null and void if, contrary to the requirements of good faith, they place the person contracting with the party proferring the conditions at an undue disadvantage.[62]

In addition to the exclusion of individual agreements, it should be noted that contracts drawn up in advance for unique or limited use are also precluded. The law also establishes two categories of clauses: those which are prohibited and those whose validity is made to depend on the courts' appraisal; this is a technique which is mentioned only as an option in the Directive (and by French legislation).

In order to comply with the Directive, Germany chose to make a small amendment to the AGBG by the insertion into it of § 24(a) by the law of 19 January 1996.

AGBG, § 24(a), Law of 19 January 1996 **1.G.21.**

In the case of contracts entered into by a person carrying on an industrial, trading or occupational activity (entrepreneur) with a natural person, where the object of the contract is neither an industrial nor a trading activity nor an independent business activity (consumer), the provisions of this law shall be applied regard being had to the following terms:

1. The general terms and conditions of business are deemed to have been drawn up by the entrepreneur unless they were inserted into the contract by the consumer.

2. Sections 5, 6 & 8–12 must also be applied to standard terms and conditions drawn up in advance with a view to being used on one occasion, where the consumer has been unable to influence their contents owing to the fact that they were drawn up in advance.

3. All the circumstances surrounding the conclusion of the contract must be taken into consideration in the assessment of undue disadvantage under section 9.

Thus, it may be seen that some provisions also apply to standard contracts drawn up in advance to be used on a single occasion. However, the German legislation has sought to preserve as far as possible the AGBG by taking, according to some commentators, certain liberties with the Directive.

---

[62] The full text of the AGBG will be found in Chapter 3, Section 4, *infra* at 513, 527 and 538.

French Law

The legislation goes back to Law No. 78–23 of 10 January 1978, now Article L132–1 *et seq.* of the Consumer Code, and to Article 2 of Decree 24 of March 1978, and has been considerably widened by the case-law of the Cour de cassation. Article L 132–1 was amended by the law of 1 February 1995. It retains its initial point of departure, namely that of declining to take cognizance of the use of general conditions and of having recourse, if only in an optional manner, to the scheme of categories, which does not accord well with the spirit of French law.

Article L.132–1 of the Consumer Code   **1.F.22.**
Law No. 95–96 of 1 February 1995

Art. L. 132–1: Any clause contained in a contract concluded between a seller or supplier and a person who is not acting in the course of his trade, business or profession or a consumer shall be regarded as unfair if its object or effect is to create, to the detriment of that person or consumer, a significant imbalance in the rights and obligations of the parties to the contract.

Types of clauses which are to be regarded as unfair within the meaning of the first paragraph may be specified by decree(s) enacted by the *Conseil d'Etat* [Council of State] following delivery of an opinion issued by the committee established by Article L. 132–2.

There shall be annexed to this Code an indicative and non-exhaustive list of clauses which, if they fulfil the conditions laid down in the first paragraph, are to be regarded as unfair. In any proceedings concerning a contract containing such a clause, the onus of proving the unfairness of the clause in question shall lie with the plaintiff.

These provisions shall be applicable irrespective of the form of the contract or the medium in which it appears. The foregoing shall apply *inter alia* to any purchase order, invoice, guarantee, delivery note or delivery order, ticket or coupon containing stipulations, whether or not the same have been freely negotiated, or references to general conditions drawn up in advance.

Without prejudice to the rules of construction laid down in Articles 1156 to 1161, 1163 and 1164 of the Civil Code, the unfairness of a clause shall be assessed by reference, at the time of conclusion of the contract, to all the circumstances attending the conclusion of the contract and to all the other terms of the contract. It shall also be assessed in the light of the clauses contained in another contract where the conclusion or performance of each of those two contracts is legally dependent on the conclusion or performance of the other.

Unfair clauses shall be deemed not to exist (*reputées non écrites*).

Assessment of the unfair nature of any clause within the meaning of the first paragraph shall relate neither to the definition of the main subject-matter of the contract nor to the adequacy of the price or remuneration as against the goods sold or the service offered.

The contract shall continue in full force and effect as regards all provisions thereof apart from those held to be unfair, provided that it is capable of continuing in existence without the said unfair clauses.

The provisions of this Article are a matter of public policy.

The law therefore applies to consumer contracts, whatever form they may take. A consumer contract is a contract entered into by a business with a consumer. The legislator leaves it to the courts to give a definition of a consumer. After a period of hesitation the Cour de cassation has settled on a negative and narrow definition.

Cass. civ. 1re, 30 January 1996[63]   **1.F.23.**
SA Credit de l'Est c. Sté Andre Bernis Latitude 5 & Others

Minimum payment clause in business hire-purchase contract

Article L132–1 of the Consumer Code, striking down for abuse of bargaining power clauses in contracts entered into between businesses and consumers, does not apply to contracts for the supply of goods or services having a direct relationship to the business carried on by the other contracting party.

Facts: A clause held to be abusive had been inserted into a hire purchase agreement for the purchase of a computerized system for managing the buyer's customers' lists.

Judgment: THE COURT: *On the purely legal ground raised ex officio under the conditions provided for in Article 1015 of the new Code of Civil Procedure*:—Whereas Article L132–1 of the Consumer Code, striking down for abuse of bargaining power clauses in contracts entered into between businesses and consumers, does not apply to contracts for the supply of goods or services having a direct relationship to the business carried on by the other contracting party;
—Whereas the company Andre Bernis entered into with the company La Cogest, whose successor in title is Credit de l'Est, a hire purchase agreement for the acquisition of a computer system supplied by the companies Cresus & CMS which have since gone into judicial liquidation.
—Whereas pleading non-performance of their obligations by those two companies, Andre Bernis obtained a court order terminating the contracts and resulting in the termination of the hire purchase agreement; as Credit de l'Est sought application of a clause in the latter contract which provided that, in the event of termination of the sale, the hirer was to pay to the owner a sum exclusive of tax equal to one third of the purchase price of the equipment by way of lump-sum compensation for losses caused by that infringement;
—Whereas the judgment appealed against (Court of Appeal, Toulouse, Second Chamber, 29 June 1993) rejected the claim by Credit de l'Est on the ground that the owner was exploiting its financial power in order to impose on the other party a clause which gave it an undue advantage and which, therefore, had to be declared abusive;
—Whereas by so deciding, although the contracts at issue relating in particular to the acquisition of customer management software pursued the objective of managing the customer lists held by Andre Bernis and thus had a direct relationship with the business carried on by that company, the Court of Appeal misapplied and therefore infringed the above provision;
On those grounds the judgment is set aside and referred back to the Bordeaux cour d'appel.

Note
See also the judgment of the First Civil Chamber of 24 January 1995[64] concerning a contract for the supply of electricity to a factory: the Consumer Code did not apply since the customer was not a consumer.

[63] D. 1996, 228, annotated by G. Paisant.
[64] **3.F.149**, *infra* at 529.

The criterion of the direct relationship with the business is flexible, though uncertain. It would be a proper use of the power of the Cour de cassation to review the qualification of the criterion in order to make it more specific.

English Law

The Unfair Contract Terms Act 1977 is a complicated text which has recourse to several criteria.

Unfair Contract Terms Act 1977   **1.E.24.**

Section 3

(1) This section applies as between contracting parties where one of them deals as consumer or on the other's written standard terms of business.

(2) As against the party, the other cannot by reference to any contract term :

  a) when himself in breach of contract, exclude or restrict any liability of his in respect of the breach; or

  b) claim to be entitled :

    i) to render a contractual performance substantially different from that which was reasonably expected of him, or

    ii) in respect of the whole or any part of his contractual obligation, to render no performance at all,

except in so far as (in any of the cases mentioned above in this subsection) the contract term satisfies the requirement of reasonableness.

Section 12

(1) A party to a contract 'deals as consumer' in relation to another party if :

  a) he neither makes the contract in the course of a business nor holds himself out as doing so; and

  b) the other party does make the contract in the course of a business; and

  c) in the case of a contract governed by the law of sale of goods or hire-purchase, or by section 7 of this Act, the goods passing under or in pursuance of the contract are of a type ordinarily supplied for private use or consumption.

(2) But on a sale by auction or by competitive tender the buyer is not in any circumstances to be regarded as dealing as consumer.

(3) Subject to this, it is for those claiming that a party does not deal as consumer to show that he does not.[65]

The general criterion is contained in section 12 which is reminiscent of the current French criterion, but section 3 for its part adopts the criterion of general terms and conditions for different types of clause. Subsequently, and in order to comply with the directive, the United Kingdom enacted the Unfair Terms in Consumer Contracts Regulations 1994, later replaced by Unfair Terms in Consumer Contracts Regulations 1999. These follow the Directive fairly closely and define a consumer contract as a contract which has not been individually negotiated and a consumer as a person who does not make the contract in the course of his business.

---

[65] The full text of the Act will be found at **3.E.139**, *infra* at 515.

26

Unfair Terms in Consumer Contracts Regulations 1999   **1.E.25.**
Statutory Instrument 1999 No. 2083

Citation and commencement

1. These Regulations may be cited as the Unfair Terms in Consumer Contracts Regulations 1999 and shall come into force on 1st October 1999

[. . .]

Interpretation

3.—(1) In these Regulations—

[. . .]

"consumer" means any natural person who, in contracts covered by these Regulations, is acting for purposes which are outside his trade, business or profession;

[. . .]

Terms to which these Regulations apply

4.—(1) These Regulations apply in relation to unfair terms in contracts concluded between a seller or a supplier and a consumer.

(2) These Regulations do not apply to contractual terms which reflect-

(a) mandatory statutory or regulatory provisions (including such provisions under the law of any Member State or in Community legislation having effect in the United Kingdom without further enactment);

(b) the provisions or principles of international conventions to which the Member States or the Community are party.

Unfair Terms

5.—(1) A contractual term which has not been individually negotiated shall be regarded as unfair if, contrary to the requirement of good faith, it causes a significant imbalance in the parties' rights and obligations arising under the contract, to the detriment of the consumer.

(2) A term shall always be regarded as not having been individually negotiated where it has been drafted in advance and the consumer has therefore not been able to influence the substance of the term.

(3) Notwithstanding that a specific term or certain aspects of it in a contract has been individually negotiated, these Regulations shall apply to the rest of a contract if an overall assessment of it indicates that it is a pre-formulated standard contract.

(4) It shall be for any seller or supplier who claims that a term was individually negotiated to show that it was.

(5) Schedule 2 to these Regulations contains an indicative and non-exhaustive list of the terms which may be regarded as unfair.

Assessment of unfair terms

6.—(1) Without prejudice to regulation 12, the unfairness of a contractual term shall be assessed, taking into account the nature of the goods or services for which the contract was concluded and by referring, at the time of conclusion of the contract, to all the circumstances attending the conclusion of the contract and to all the other terms of the contract or of another contract on which it is dependent.

(2) In so far as it is in plain intelligible language, the assessment of fairness of a term shall not relate—

(a) to the definition of the main subject matter of the contract, or

(b) to the adequacy of the price or remuneration, as against the goods or services supplied in exchange.

The question will arise in English law as to the manner in which those rules are to be combined with those contained in the Unfair Contract Terms Act. That is no easy task since the two instruments largely overlap. As far as the definition of a consumer contract is concerned it is noteworthy that both the techniques laid down for French law and those applicable in German law are used.

Concluding Remarks
Although the notion of a consumer contract—or, according to the directive, of a contract entered into with a consumer—seems nowadays to be widely acknowledged, its definition continues to be shrouded in uncertainty. Sensitive points remain unsettled, for example the case of a businessman who makes a contract for the purposes of his business but outside the area in which he specializes, for instance the case of a lawyer who buys an alarm system for his offices.

This study also constitutes a valid exercise in comparative Community law: how have the different Member States reacted and are the provisions which they have enacted in conformity with the Directive?

Finally, consideration is needed on the difficult issue of harmonising domestic provisions, even in a system as structured as the Community system.

1.1.4. SPECIFIC PECULIARITIES

There are in each of the three principal systems studied categories or concepts which do not exist in the others. I have chosen three examples amongst those which occasion most surprise to foreign lawyers. I would recommend that the manner in which the functions of those foreign concepts are performed in the other legal systems be investigated.

1.1.4.A. GERMAN LAW: THE PRINCIPLE OF SEPARABILITY (*ABSTRAKTIONSPRINZIP*)

This is an extension of the distinction between contracts transferring property and contracts creating obligations which has been examined above. The Principle of Separability proclaimed by German law, and by certain other systems of law, asserts that the transfer of property is effected by two completely separate transactions and not by a single one, as in French or English law: see above. Under German law, any act of disposition is separable. This is how Zweigert and Kötz expound this principle:

Zweigert and Kötz[66] **1.G.26.**

Now if a legal system not only makes this distinction between the contract of sale and the real contract in this sense, but also makes the validity of each independent of the validity of the other, it accepts the doctrine of the "abstract real contract". By virtue of this doctrine, once a purchaser has made a "real" contract with his vendor and has received delivery of the purchased property from him, in principle he obtains ownership in the thing even if the contract of sale was void from the beginning, or is subsequently rescinded or is invalid in any other way: the real agreement is thus

[66] K. Zweigert and H. Kötz, *Introduction to Comparative Law* (2nd ed, Oxford: Clarendon, 1987) at 178–9.

"abstract" because, given delivery or constructive delivery, it transfers the property even if no valid contract of sale was concluded or if the contract of sale was originally valid but has subsequently lapsed. Of course in such a case the purchaser is not entitled to retain the property; he has become owner, but has done so in the absence of a valid contract of sale, that is, "without legal cause", and is therefore bound to retransfer the property to the vendor as an "unjustified enrichment" pursuant to § 812 BGB.

These rules apply in German law not only when property is sold but also when it is donated or given in exchange, or when it is transferred to a creditor as security for a loan or to a trustee for purposes of administration: in all these cases a distinction is drawn between the "basic transaction" or "causal transaction" (namely the contract of sale, or the declaration of gift, security or trust) and the "completion transaction" or "performance transaction", namely the transfer of property; the "abstract" completion agreement may be valid notwithstanding the invalidity of the basic transaction and thus the purchaser, the donee, the creditor or the trustee will have become owner. This is true not only in the case of things, moveable or immoveable, but also in the case on the transfer of a *claim*; here too the assignee may become owner of the claim which has been assigned, even if the "basic transaction"—namely the contract of sale, agency or security—was invalid in some way. Furthermore the same is true when a limited real right, such as a right of hypothec, is to be transferred; here too the law treats as independent the contractual agreement to give security and the "real contract" which creates the hypothec.

An illustration of the application of this principle is afforded by the judgment of the Supreme Court (*Reichsgericht*) of 25 June 1925 in relation to a gift to a concubine by a married man, a situation which is sufficiently frequent to allow a comparison with techniques in other countries.

RG, 25 June 1925[67]   **1.G.27.**

Transfer of property to mistress

A transfer of property made for immoral purposes is not invalid but the property may be recovered in an action for restitution.

Facts: The plaintiff was the sole heir of her husband who died on 29 August 1919. By means of a gratuitous act deposited with the Land Registry office, the deceased husband had transferred immoveable property belonging to him to a married woman with whom he had been having sexual relations. The wife sought restitution *de facto* and *de jure* of the property in question.

Held: At first instance her claim was upheld under § 187 BGB. An appeal on a point of law was dismissed by the Supreme Court.

Judgment:
Discussion:
It is a condition *sine qua non* for allowing an action based on unjust enrichment that the unjust enrichment must be established. Recognition of this situation was based on appeal on the following findings:—the gift was a consequence of the adulterous relationship in which the husband had lived with the defendant, a married woman;

The purpose of the gift was to dispossess the wife of the donor of an immoveable property in order to transfer it to the husband's mistress (adulterous woman).

---

[67] RGZE 111.152.

A gift of that kind constitutes an offence against good morals. Thus the transfer of property is null and void. In the lower courts it was agreed that there was no causal act in contravention of good morals the nullity of which would give rise to a right of restitution under § 812. Conversely, § 817 affords to the plaintiff a right of restitution, since, by accepting the gift of the immoveable property, the defendant contravened good moral standards.

However, according to the Supreme Court, inherent in that analysis of the situation was a contradiction, inasmuch as the gift of the property is allowed whilst the causal act relating to the transfer of property is rejected. A transfer presupposes an underlying cause which is not to be found in the contract creating the obligation. Under § 516 BGB a gift presupposes:
—agreement of the parties as to the gratuitous nature of the gift;
—a contract creating the obligation by which the agreement establishes the legal cause justifying the enrichment by way of the gift.

Such an agreement may be tacit, in particular where one of the parties discloses to the other his intention and where, in order to give effect to the gift, the two parties present themselves at the Land Registry Office without mentioning any performance in exchange. This was the position in the case under examination.

If the contract thus entered into constitutes an offence against good morals then it is null and void under § 138 and that nullity deprives of any legal cause the abstract act preceding the transfer. It is for that reason that it should be emphasised that the lower courts erroneously held § 812 not to be applicable. But that has no effect on the decision. Under settled case-law, § 812 is a general rule on which actions *in rem verso* may be founded.

According to the appeal the courts were wrong to hold that there had been an offence against good morals. Although it is to be emphasized that the defendant may be heard to say that there is no evidence that the gift was intended to make the defendant decide to continue the adulterous relationship, conversely it cannot validly be asserted that the gift was not shown to be motivated by the adulterous relationship and that the relationship was not wanted. It has not been demonstrated that the gift was motivated by the adulterous relationship and that that relationship was not wanted. Thus the defendant received a reward for the adulterous relationship with the donor. The gift constitutes *per se* by the nature of its content, motive and objective an offence against principles of justice and is therefore null and void under § 138 as an act against good morals. Nor can it be maintained that the transfer of the property in question could have been effected by other means without any contravention of good moral standards.

In the present case the gift benefits the adulterous woman but also places the lawful spouse in a disadvantageous position. Thus the preconditions of unjust enrichment are satisfied. Moreover, under § 826, if harm is found to have occurred there is a right to restitution. If the courts trying the case on its substance did not apply that provision, the Supreme Court is entitled to apply it where the plaintiff has suffered harm.

Note

This case is a good illustration of the principle of separability and its corrective, unjust enrichment. The contract is null and void by application of § 138 (good morals). The position would be the same under French law, owing to its immoral cause, where the gift is decisively motivated by the "formation, maintenance or resumption of immoral relations".[68] But under French law annulment of the contract automatically entails annulment of the transfer and gives rise to liability in restitution. Under German law the deed of transfer remains valid in accordance with the principle of separability and recourse must be had to

---

[68] Cass. civ. 1re, 4 Nov. 1987, Bull. civ. I.319; the solution has been reversed by Cass. civ. 1ère, 3 Feb. 1999, J.C.P. 1999. II.10083, annotated by Billiau.

the doctrine of unjust enrichment in order to secure restitution. The mistress unjustifiably enriched herself at the expense of the lawful wife. The principle of separability is controversial, even in Germany. It falls to be assessed in relation to the causal concept—absence of cause, unjust enrichment—the notion of property contract and of abstract acts.[69]

1.1.4.B. FRENCH LAW: THE ADMINISTRATIVE CONTRACT

Contracts entered into with individuals are subject in France to special rules—as in the Netherlands—,[70] whereas in Germany and in England they are governed by the ordinary law both as regards the rules applicable to them and the courts having jurisdiction to hear disputes arising out of it. Thus, in Germany, contracts entered into by the public authorities are governed by the BGB and by the ABGB (because frequently standard form contracts are involved) and, in the event of any dispute, are to be referred not to the administrative courts but to the ordinary courts of law. The same position prevails in Italy. Conversely, in France the category of administrative contracts is of great importance because these contracts are not governed by ordinary contract law but are subject to supervision by the administrative courts and thus, at last instance, to the Council of State which in its case-law has elaborated special rules for them to take account of the fact that the public interest is at stake. Accordingly, there are a number of exceptional rules— apart from the jurisdiction question—, in particular the right of the public authority unilaterally to withdraw from the contract or to amend it, subject to compensating the other party, recognition of the doctrine of unforeseeability—amendment of the contract in the case of an unforeseen event[71]—, power to enforce remedies without prior judicial authorization—subsequent judicial review of remedies. It is therefore important to be aware of the manner in which an administrative contract is defined. The Council of State has progressively elaborated two alternative criteria.

The first is taken from a celebrated judgment of the Conseil d'Etat of 31 July 1912 in the case of *Granits Porphyroides des Vosges* concerning exorbitant clauses. A contract is governed by the civil law where it is entered into in accordance with the rules and conditions applicable to contracts between individuals, that is to say without any exorbitant clauses in favour of the public authority.

Conseil d'Etat, 31 July 1912   **1.F.28.**
Société des Granits Porphyroides des Vosges[72]

Paving stones

A contract for supply of goods is not a public works contract subject to the Administrative Court.

Facts: This was a contract for the supply of paving stones to the town of Lille in the context of which the refusal of the town to reimburse a contractual penalty is challenged. The brief answer by the Council of State is that it

---

[69] See also see A. Rieg, *Le rôle de la volonté dans l'acte juridique en droit civl français et allemand* (Paris: LGDJ, 1961) paras. 278–282.
[70] See A. Hartkamp and M.M. Tillema, *Contract Law in the Netherlands* (The Hague/Boston: Kluwer, 1995) para. 319 ff.
[71] See chapter 5, *infra* at 629 ff.
[72] Rec. 909, 1916.3.35, Opinion by Blum.

is a private law contract because it was entered into in accordance with the conditions applicable under the ordinary law. The reference to works to be carried out may be accounted for by the fact that public works contracts are governed by special rules.

Judgment:—Whereas the claim by the Société des Granits Porphyroides des Vosges is for payment of the sum of 3,436.20 francs retained by way of penalty by the municipality of Lille from the price payable for a supply of paving stones, owing to delayed delivery.
—Whereas the contract entered into between the municipality and the company did not include any works to be carried out by the company and solely concerned supplies to be made in accordance with the terms and conditions of contracts between individuals;
—Whereas accordingly, the claim raises an issue which it is not for the administrative court to determine;
—Whereas consequently, the company's claim is inadmissible and must be dismissed.

Note

The second criterion which is of more recent date concerns contracts entrusting to private persons the performance of a public service even if there is no clause excluding the contract from application of the ordinary law. This is known as the "*Epoux Bertin*" doctrine of 1956.

Conseil d'Etat, 20 April 1956   **1.F.29.**
Epoux Bertin[73]

Contract to feed refugees

A contract to provide meals for refugees until repatriation is a public service contract.
Judgment: On jurisdiction:—Whereas the judicial investigation shows that by an oral contract entered into with the public authorities on 24 November 1944 the Bertin couple undertook in consideration of the payment of a lump sum of Ff 30 per man and per day, to feed the Soviet nationals sheltered at the Meaux repatriation centre pending their return to Russia; as that contract was intended to entrust the Bertin couple with the task of performing a public service which was to ensure the repatriation of foreign refugees then on French soil
—Whereas that fact is in itself sufficient to enable the contract in question to be classified as an administrative contract
—Whereas it follows that, without there being any need to investigate whether the contract included clauses exempting it from the ordinary law, the litigation turning on an additional undertaking to that contract whereby the authorities granted to the Bertin couple an additional bonus of Ff 7.50 per man and per day in consideration of the inclusion of new foodstuffs in the rations served comes within the jurisdiction of the administrative courts;
On the merits:—Whereas the Bertin couple has not adduced evidence of the existence of the above-mentioned additional undertaking;
—Whereas under those conditions it is not possible to uphold their claim for the setting aside of the decision of 1 June 1949 whereby the Minister for Veterans and Victims of War refused to pay to them the additional bonuses alleged to have been provided for in that undertaking;
  Application dismissed with costs.

---

[73] Req. 167, D.1956.433, annotated by Laubadère.

Note

The jurisdiction of the administrative courts was upheld because under the contract for looking after the Soviet nationals the Bertin couple became involved in the public service of ensuring the repatriation of the foreign refugees.

However, it should not be imagined that there is any great originality in the French law on this point. In this connection it is sufficient to read the conclusions of the Anglo-French group.

Contract Law Today[74]   **1.E.30.**

(ii) Contracts governed by public law compared with those governed by private law

French law adopts a dualistic approach in contrast to the unitary approach of English law, which has not developed an independent body of law for administrative contracts. In principle, English law takes the view that the rules of contract law apply to all contracts whether the parties are private individuals or public bodies.[75] In practice, however, the position is very different, because the public interest is recognized in England and special rules have been developed in the practice of public authorities. Thus, administrative contracts contain clauses which are completely unknown in commercial contracts and which lead to the result that the ordinary legal principles are subdivided or even abrogated.

In England, some general considerations have led to some special legal rules for contracts with public authorities. It has been decided that such bodies cannot bind themselves for the future by undertaking contractual obligations which are contrary to the purposes for which the bodies were granted their powers. This rule permits them, in spite of general contractual theory, unilaterally to release themselves from their obligations. The same position applies to administrative contracts in France. In many contracts in England, such as those by which the Government buys goods and services, the fact that one party is a public body leads to the adoption of standard terms in specifying the details of the agreement. All these contracts include virtually the same clauses, which are imposed by the public body, and which obviously favour it. Sometimes, the standard clauses even permit the public body to pursue a different public interest from that directly pursued by the contract in question. In this way, a kind of customary law on purchasing by public authorities has been created through the almost automatic practice of including standard clauses. The regular use of these clauses is different from the application of general principles laid down in a body of administrative law, but they are used so regularly that we can say that they should be properly analysed as rules of general application. The practical result is the same as if there were special legal rules for administrative contracts, although it is achieved by a different route.

English law permits the court neither to grant certains remedies against the Crown, nor to take certain enforcement measures against the Crown. For instance, an injunction cannot be granted against the Crown, nor can an order for specific performance be granted. If an award of damages is made against the Crown, there is no possibility of enforcing payment nor of any other form of

---

[74] Haris and Tallon (eds.), op. cit., at 382–3.

[75] In both France and England, certain matters fall outside the scope of contract. The reasons for this are completely different in each country and cannot be reconciled. French law has decided that in certain areas public authorities should unilaterally determine the content of some legal relationships, which are therefore not subjet to negotiation by the parties. Moreover, the public authorities cannot be prevented by the existence of acquired contractual rights from modifying or abrogating contractual obligations. So the following topics fall outside the scope of contract: arrangements for public services, for taxation, and for financial and administrative regulation. In England, the delivery of mail is not a matter of contract: there is no particular reason for this rule, which is simply a matter of traditional law. It was laid down that the Post Office does not enter into a contract when it carries mail.

execution. So the judge cannot issue orders to the Crown. In France, the problem is rather different because the Administration has its own judge. Nevertheless, many similar results are found. The administrative judge cannot grant an injunction against a public authority: only an award of damages may be given against it (although the remedy of *astreinte* is now available against it).

So the legal approach of the two systems is different because English law does not recognize a separate body of administrative law administered by special courts; but despite the fact that the two systems use legally distinct machinery, in both countries the scope and the contents of administrative contracts are often similar.[76]

1.1.4.C. ENGLISH LAW: BAILMENT

In English law there is an original doctrine on the margins of contract law known as bailment. This is the lawful holding of an item by a person who is not the owner thereof with the owner's consent—for example, depositary contract—or without the owner's consent—for example, the finder of lost property. Bailment gives rise to a legal duty to conserve and give up the item. The rules on bailment may overlap with those of contract where the bailment is with the owner's consent.

The legal rules on bailment sometimes differ considerably from the rules applicable to contract. For example, there is no requirement of consideration and the privity rules do not apply. An illustration of the doctrine may be afforded by the case of the stolen mink stole.

Court of Appeal   **1.E.31.**
Morris v. *C. W. Martin & Sons Ltd.*[77]

The stolen mink stole

A party who hands goods to a second party who entrusts them to a third may bring an action against the third party for loss of or damage to the goods on the basis of bailment even though there is no contract between them.

Facts: This was an action by the owner of a mink stole for its value brought against a firm of cleaners. The owner had sent her mink stole to one Beder, a furrier, for cleaning and Beder, with the owner's consent, gave it to the defendants to clean. The defendants' employee who was supposed to clean it stole it instead.

Held: The trial judge held the defendants not liable; an appeal to the Court of Appeal was allowed.

Judgment: DIPLOCK LJ: . . . Duties at common law are owed by one person to another only if there exists a relationship between them which the common law recognises as giving rise to such duty. One of such recognised relationships is created by the voluntary taking into custody of goods which are the property of another. By voluntarily accepting from Beder the custody of a fur which they knew to be the property of a customer of his, they brought into existence between the plaintiff and themselves the relationship of bailor and bailee by sub-bailment. The legal relationship of bailor and bailee of a chattel can exist independently of any contract, for the legal concept of bailment as creating a relationship which gives rise to duties owed by a bailee to a bailor is derived from Roman law and is older in our common law than the legal concept of parol contract is

---

[76] For more information on this reference should be made to: Nicholas at 25 ff.; A. de Laubadère, J.-C. Venezia and Y. Gaudemet, *Traité de droit administratif*, Vol. I, 15th edn. (Paris: LGDJ, 1999), at 279 ff.; and also to the Code on public contracts (*Code ° des Marchés publics*) which governs contracts entered into with public authorities.

[77] [1966] 1 QB 716.

giving rise to legal duties owed by one party to the other party thereto. The nature of those legal duties, in particular as to the degree of care which the bailee is bound to exercice in the custody of the goods and as to his duty to redeliver them, varies according to the circumstances in which and purposes for which the goods are delivered to the bailee. But we are concerned here with conversion. This is a breach of a particular duty common to all classes of bailment. While most cases of bailment today are accompanied by a contractual relationship between bailee and bailor which may modify or extend the common law duties of the parties that would otherwise arise from the mere fact of bailment, this is not necessarily so—as witness gratuitous bailment or bailment by finding . . .

One of the common law duties owed by a bailee of goods to his bailor is not to convert them, ie not to do intentionally in relation to the goods an act inconsistent with the bailor's right of property therein. (See *Caxton Publishing Co Ltd* v. *Sutherland Publishing Co*, per Lord Porter). This duty, which is common to all bailments as well as to other relationships which do not amount to bailment, is independent of and additional to the other common law duty of a bailee for reward to take reasonable care of his bailor's goods. Stealing goods is the simplest example of conversion; but, perhaps because in his classic judgment in *Coogs* v. *Bernard* Sir John Holt CJ discusses the circumstances in which bailees are liable to their bailors for the loss of goods stolen not by the servant of the bailee but by a stranger, some confusion has, I think, arisen in later cases through failure to recognise the co-existence of the two duties of a bailee for reward: to take reasonable care of his bailor's goods and not to convert them—even by stealing.

[The court went on to hold that the owner of the fur was bound by the terms of the sub-bailment agreed between Beder and the defendants; but that these terms were not adequate to protect the defendants from liability for theft by their employee.]

Appeal allowed.

Note

It may be seen that bailment corresponds to what in other sytems of law might be regarded as a sub-contract. To a certain extent bailment resembles what French law terms a real contract (*contrat réel*), that is to say a contract formed by the handing over of an item of property. But the doctrine is not universally acknowledged. For its part German law has made provision for property-related transactions (*sachenrechtliche Geschäfte*) which fall under the law relating to property.

CONCLUDING REMARKS ON SECTION 1

The notion of a contract clearly contains a solid central core which is common to the legal systems prevailing within the European Union. However, that core is limited to what is termed, in systems based on civil law, a synallagmatic or bilateral contract for valuable consideration, since it involves a state of affairs which is universally regarded as amounting to a contract. In cases extending beyond that central core, it is necessary to verify, in each legal system, whether or not a given legal transaction constitutes a contract.

It is principally by reference to that "common core" that an attempt will now be made to establish the relationship between contracts and the other sources of law giving rise to obligations.

1.2. THE SCOPE OF CONTRACT

From a theoretical point of view, since Roman law—Gaius—contract has been viewed as a source of obligations, alongside torts and quasi-torts which found the obligation to compensate another for damage caused, and quasi-contract, more complex and more controversial, based on unjust enrichment to another's detriment and giving rise to an obligation to make restitution. Finally, the law may also be the direct source of obligations. Indeed, it is always under the law that the other categories of obligations are recognized but there are also obligations which derive purely from the legislation such as maintenance obligations as between parents. That is however a particular category which need not detain us further here.

Conversely, it is necessary to delimit the scope of contract in relation to tortious liability (1.2.1) and quasi-contract (1.2.2) (which in certain countries is described as restitution).

1.2.1. CONTRACT AND TORT

These are two notions which stand side by side and sometimes overlap. Non-performance of a contract, like a tort, may cause damage to another person. Their respective domains must therefore be established, which first entails seeking their respective spheres before going on to elucidate the concerns which may prompt a need to distinguish them.

1.2.1.A. THE RESPECTIVE DOMAINS

The demarcation line must be drawn in terms of time and then in terms of persons—parties to the contract as against third parties.

Demarcation by time
It is important to determine precisely when the contract begins and ends because before and afterwards only liability in tort is possible, whereas during the currency of the contract both contractual and tortious liability may apply or exclusively contractual liability where the system of exclusive liability (*non cumul*) applies.[78] The issue is then one of pre-contractual or post-contractual liability.

Pre-contractual liability, which is dealt with below in relation to formation of the contract, is treated differently in English and French law on the one hand, and German law and the other legal systems following German law on this point—notion of *culpa in contrahendo*—, on the other. Under German law pre-contractual liability does not come under tortious liability but constitutes a specific category of liability developed by the courts under § 242 BGB.[79]

In French and English law matters occurring before the future parties are definitively agreed are matters for the law of torts. The same is true after the end of the currency of the contract. A good example of this in French law is afforded by the contract for the

---

[78] See 1.2.1.B, *infra* at 67.
[79] This imposes a general duty of good faith (*treu und glauben*).

transport of persons which, in contrast to English law, is subject to a contractual regime imposing an *obligation de sécurité*). The French courts were hesitant. After a period in which they distinguished between three phases, namely before the transport proper, during and after—platform accidents: a traveller who falls at the exit—, it limited the domain of contract to the actual carriage, where there is a duty to ensure a safe outcome (the *obligation de sécurité*).

Cass. civ. 1re, 7 May 1989[80]   **1.F.32.**

TRANSPORT ENDS WHEN PASSENGER LEAVES TRAIN

Icy platform

The obligation of security applies only from the moment a passenger boards the train to the moment he leaves it; but if the station premises are dangerous the railway may be liable in delict.

Facts: On 17 January 1982 Mr Valverde was found on the track alongside a platform of Pierrefitte station. His legs had been cut off by the wheels of a train. Mr Valverde brought proceedings against SNCF for a declaration and damages, alleging that, after alighting from a carriage, he had slipped on the icy platform; in this connection he claimed breach of contract by the transport undertaking which had neglected to clear an icy patch.

Held: The cour d'appel dismissed the claim. The Cour de cassation upheld this decision on the contractual claim but allowed the plaintiff's delictual claim.

Judgment:THE COURT: . . . *On the first appeal ground*:—Whereas Mr Valverde submits that the cour d'appel wrongly dismissed his claim on the grounds that it was common ground that the accident occurred after the traveller had finished alighting from the train and that therefore the transport undertaking was no longer bound by the duty to secure a safe outcome;
—Whereas, it was argued, the contract of carriage by train and the duty of care attached thereto commences when the traveller having validated his ticket gains access to the platform of the station of departure and terminates at the exit of the station of destination when it is no longer possible to exercise supervision by means of checks;
—Whereas thus by determining that the duty of care ancillary to the contract of carriage ceased to subsist after the passenger alighted from the train, when Mr Valverde was still walking on the platform of the station at which he had arrived, the judgment appealed against infringed Article 1147 of the Civil Code;
—Whereas contrary to what was claimed on appeal, the duty of care in conducting the traveller safely to his destination imposed by Article 1147 of the Civil Code is borne by the transport undertaking only during the implementation of the contract of carriage, that is to say from the time when the traveller begins to embark on the carriage until he has completely alighted from it;
—Whereas the appeal ground is therefore unfounded.

On the second appeal ground on a pure point of law:—Under Article 1384(1) of the Civil Code, outside the performance of the contract, the transport undertaking's liability to the traveller is governed by the rules on torious liability;
—Whereas in dismissing the claim, the judgment appealed against (Paris, 17th Chamber A, 4 November 1986) also states "that is for Mr Valverde to show that the SNCF by committing an error in this case by omitting to remove the icy patches from the platform has failed to fulfil its obligation to provide adequate means"; as and that in the present case Mr Valverde has not adduced proof that he fell on the platform after slipping on an icy patch allegedly left by the transport undertaking on the platform;

[80] D. 1991.1, annotated by Ph. Malaurie.

37

—Whereas it is therefore not established that SNCF committed any fault in connection with the accident;

—Whereas in so holding, although the accident occurred when the train from which the traveller had alighted, and which was under the control of SNCF, started, the court of appeal infringed the abovementioned provision.

On those grounds and without there being any need to give a decision on the third plea, the Cour de cassation refers the case to the cour d'appel Versailles.

Note

The contractual situation is well described in the judgment; it covers the time from the moment when the traveller begins to climb into the carriage until the moment when he has completely alighted from it. Outside that period of time, liability is only in tort and it is for misapplying the rules on tortious liability that the appeal judgment was set aside. It will be noted that although the court considers that the transport undertaking had charge of the train or the platform full liability is incurred under Article 1384(1) of the Civil Code which will have the same outcome as in the application of contract to ensure a safe outcome.

The case of a customer in a shop illustrates the way in which the regimes interract. In this case German law extends the period of contractual liability through the notion of *culpa in contrahendo*.

RGH, 7 December 1911[81]   **1.G.33**

RELATIONSHIP "SIMILAR TO CONTRACT" WITH PROSPECTIVE BUYER

Falling rolls of lino

When a customer enters a shop intending to make a purchase, the shop is under a duty "similar to contract" to take care towards her.

Facts: A shop's customer was injured by the fall of a linoleum roll incorrectly moved by the sales assistant who was showing the merchandise.

Held: The Court of Appeal held that the trader was liable in tort (§ 278 BGB). The Supreme Court upheld liability but also founded its judgment on liability in contract.

Judgment: According to the findings of the Court of Appeal the plaintiff, after making several purchases in the defendant company's department store, went to the linoleum department to buy linoleum floor-cover. She mentioned this to W, the sales assistant who served there, and looked through the patterns which he displayed for her to make a choice. W, in order to pull out the roll she pointed to, put two others aside. They fell, hit the plaintiff and her child, and struck both of them to the floor. The purchase of the linoleum was not completed because, in the plaintiff's words, she became seriously disturbed by the fall.

The Court of Appeal rightly attributed the plaintiff's accident to W's fault, on the ground that he had put the rolls, which were not stable enough because of their relatively small bulk, insecurely on one side, instead of furnishing them with lateral protection on leaning them against the wall, and this even though he could have foreseen that the plaintiff, as usually happens with the buying

---

[81] RGZ 78.239.

public, would approach the place where the goods she had asked to be displayed were stored. The Court of Appeal's view is comprised in the simple conclusion that the rolls would not have fallen if W had placed them carefully and regularly on one side.

The Court of Appeal's opinion that the defendant company is liable for W's fault under § 278 BGB cannot, in spite of the appellant's contention, be rightly objected to; and it conforms to the case-law of this Senate. W was acting for the defendant company (§ 164 BGB, § 54 HGB) when he entered into negotiation with the plaintiff. The plaintiff had asked for a piece of linoleum to be laid out for inspection and purchase. W had acceded to her request in order to make a sale. The proposal and its acceptance had for their purpose the conclusion of a sale, and therefore the production of a legal transaction. That was no mere factual proceeding, a mere act of courtesy, but a legal relationship came into existence between the parties in preparation for a purchase; it bore a character similar to a contract and produced legal obligations in so far as both seller and prospective buyer came under a duty to observe the necessary care for the health and property of the other party in displaying and inspecting the goods.

The judgments of this Senate have already proceeded on similar grounds, and it has been recognized in several decision of the Reichsgericht that duties of care for the life and property of the other party can arise from bilateral or unilateral obligations, which have nothing to do with the legal nature of the relation in a narrower sense, but nevertheless follow from its factual character.

The defendant company made use of W's services for the fulfilment of the aforesaid obligation to the prospective purchaser, and is therefore answerable for his fault. This is in line with the thought expressed in § 278 BGB, that whoever himself owes a performance that he must carry out with the required amount of care must, when he makes use of an employee, answer for his careful performance, and that accordingly the other person to whom the performance is due must not be put in a worse position because he does not do it himself but commits it to an employee. It would be contrary to the general feeling of justice if in cases where the person in charge of the business of displaying or laying out goods for exhibition, sampling, trial, or the like carelessly injures a prospective purchaser, the proprietor of the business—with whom the prospector wished to make a purchase—should be answerable only under § 831 BGB and not unconditionnaly, so that the injured person should, if the proprietor succeeds in exonerating himself, be referred to the usually impecunious employee.

There is no need to go here into the legally questionable view of the Court of Appeal that the mere entry into a department store of a prospective purchaser or even a visitor without any intention of buying creates a contractual relation between him and the proprietor, including the widely discussed duties of care . . .

Note

This represents an extension of the preliminary contract. Under German case-law there exists a contractual relationship between the customer and the vendor in order to prepare the sale. It is to be noted that there is an exception in regard to persons entering the shop with no intention of making a purchase. It enables the court to impose on the shop vicarious responsibility for the act of its employee, which in German law would not exist if the liability were purely delictual.

The situation of a customer in a shop prior to any purchase is dealt with differently in French and English law on the basis of tortious liability alone.

Cass. civ. 1re, 7 November 1961[82]   **I.F.34.**

<small>NO CONTRACTUAL LIABILITY FOR INJURY NOT RESULTING FROM BREACH OF CONTRACT</small>

A fatal fall

A customer who suffers an unexplained injury which is not the result of any non-performance of the contract he was contemplating has no contractual claim.

Facts: A prospective customer falls in a trader's storage area; the reason is not known.

Held: The cour d'appel declined to hold the trader liable and the Cour de cassation dismissed the appeal.

Judgment: THE COURT: *On the first appeal ground*:—Whereas Garibal went to the Balard Establishments in order to purchase some galvanized sheets and was taken into a shop installed on the unloading platform of the factory's own railway track; as at a certain moment for a reason which has remained unclear he fell on to the track situated 3.50 metres below and was killed;
—Whereas the judgment appealed against (Montpellier, 13 November 1959) is criticised for declining to render contractually liable a trader who had authorised a customer to gain access to a storage area although, irrespective of any contract of sale, the fact of inviting, with a view to profit, customers on to premises for which one is responsible in itself constitutes a contract which may give rise to a duty of care;
—Whereas however the cour d'appel was right to hold that in order for contractual liability to be incurred it is not sufficient for damage to have been caused in connection with a contract but the damage must arise from non-performance of one of the obligations imposed by the contract;
—Whereas the sales contract does not give rise to any duty of care towards the purchaser;
—Whereas it is pleaded in the appeal but to no avail that, independently of any sale, the trader assumes a duty of care in regard to any person gaining access to the commercial premises and who may be a potential purchaser. In such a case it is only the rules on tortious liability which play a role.
The plea is therefore unfounded.

Note

The Cour de cassation clearly reaffirms that the fall has no direct connection with the sales contract—not yet entered into—and that moreover the sales contract gives rise to no duty of care towards the purchaser. On the other hand there is no preliminary contract, unlike under German law, with the result that liability can only be tortious. In the present case no recourse may be had to full liability for events emanating from another person's property— in this case the premises—since in the present case they played only a passive role.
The route taken in English law is also that of tort.

Court of Appeal   **1.E.35.**
Ward v. Tesco Stores Ltd[83]

<small>DUTY OF CARE TO CUSTOMERS</small>

Spilt yoghurt

A shop is under a duty to take reasonable care to ensure that customers are not injured by dangerously slippery substances spilt on the floor of the shop.

[82] D.1962.146, annotated by P. Esmein
[83] [1976] 1 WLR 810.

Facts: The plaintiff went round the store, carrying a wire basket, as shoppers are expected to do in supermarkets. She was doing her shopping at the back of the store when she felt herself slipping. She appreciated that she was slipping on something which was sticky. She fell to the ground, and sustained minor injuries. She had not seen what had caused her to slip. It was not suggested that she had in any way been negligent in failing to notice what was on the floor as she walked along doing her shopping. When she was picking herself up she appreciated that she had slipped on some pink substance which looked to her like yoghourt. It was yoghourt. Later, somebody on the defendants' staff found a carton of yoghourt in the vicinity which was two-thirds empty . . .

Held: The trial judge held that in the absence of any other explanation he was entitled to infer that the defendants had failed to take reasonable care to clear up the spillage. The Court of Appeal (by a majority) upheld this decision.

Judgment: LAWTON LJ: This is an appeal by the defendants from a judgment of his Honour Judge Nance given in the Liverpool Country Court . . . whereby he adjudged that the plaintiff should recover against the defendants £178.50 damages and her costs . . . for personal injuries said to have been caused by the negligence of the defendants in the maintenance of the floor in their supermarket at Smithdown Road, Liverpool. [He stated the facts and continued:]

That is all the plaintiff was able to prove, save for one additional fact. About three weeks later when she was shopping in the same store she noticed that some orange squash had been spilt on the floor. She kept an eye on the spillage for about a quarter of an hour. During that time nobody came to clear it up.

The trial judge was of the opinion that the facts which I have related constituted a *prima facie* case against the defendants. I infer that this case, which involves only a small amount of damages, has been brought to this court because the defendants are disturbed that any judge should find that a *prima facie* case is established merely by a shopper proving that she had slipped on a supermarket floor.

At the trial the defendants called some evidence . . . The defendants did not call any evidence as to when the store floor had last been brushed before the plaintiff's accident. It follows that there was no evidence before the court as to whether the floor had been brushed a few moments before the accident, or an hour, or possibly an hour and a half. The court was left with out any information on what may have been an important matter . . .

In this case the floor of this supermarket was under the management of the defendants and their servants. The accident was such as in the ordinary course of things does not happen if floors are kept clean and spillages are dealt with as soon as they occur. If an accident does happen because the floors are covered with spillage, then in my judgment some explanation should be forthcoming from the defendants to show that the accident did not arise from any want of care on their part; and in the absence of any explanation the judge may give judgment for the plaintiff. Such burden of proof as there is on the defendants in such circumstances is evidential, not probative. The trial judge thought that *prima facie* this accident would not have happened had the defendants taken reasonable care. In my judgment he was justified in taking that view because the probabilites where that the spillage had been on the floor long enough for it to have been cleaned up by a member of the staff . . .

[Megaw LJ agreed with Lawton LJ. Ormerod LJ dissented on the ground that, as it had not been proven that the yoghurt had been on the floor for a significant length of time, an essential element of negligence had not been proven.]

Note
In the present case discussion turned essentially on the issue of proof of negligence on the part of the trader. It is not even alleged that there could have been a contract. It is to be noted that the accident occurred in a self-service shop, which raises the problem of the moment in time when the sales contract was concluded: see for example the judgment of the French Cour de cassation in Cass. civ. 2e, 5 June 1991.[84]

[84] D.1992.409.

As far as the facts are concerned, this judgment may be compared with the judgment of the German BGH of 28 January 1976[85] which applies the doctrine of *culpa in contrahendo* and so enables circumvention of prescription in the case of an action in tort.

In all cases the problem of the fault of the victim may arise, or that of the act of the creditor—duty of care—, as mentioned in certain of the decisions.[86]

Delimitation in terms of person

In principle only the parties to a contract may rely on its terms—see Article 1220 of the Civil Code. It is necessary to make a connection between the relative effect of the contract and the problem of the rights of third parties.[87] It is sufficient at this juncture to recall the distinction between the enforcement of the obligations under a contract and whether the contract may be relied on as against a person who is not a party to it. A particular issue is that of the third party involved in non-performance of the contract. In such a case the liability of the third party is only in tort. English law even recognizes a special tort of "inducing a breach of contract". At this point we encounter the rules on the overlapping of liabilities under different heads and also, under certain laws, on the extent of the right to compensation—the question of "economic loss", which does not arise in French law.[88]

To simplify, we will take three situations only: involvement of the third party in the contractual relationship under the technique of third party stipulations; chain contracts and the relationship between the contracting parties at the two ends of the chain; and finally the connected question of subcontracting, in French, English and German law.

a) French law

The courts have been inclined to extend the sphere of contract in favour of third parties. The first technique was to find in the contract a stipulation, more or less notional, in favour of a third party. A typical example of this is the contract of carriage.

Cass. civ., 6 December 1932[89]   **1.F.36.**

OBLIGATION TO PASSENGER IS STIPULATION IN FAVOUR OF DEPENDANTS

Fatal fall from train (I)

The obligation de sécurité owed to a passenger is an implicit stipulation in favour of his wife and children.

Facts: Noblet, an infantry captain, had taken a seat in a carriage headed for Angers. He fell on to the track and his death was instantaneous. The victim's widow, acting on her own behalf and that of her minor children, sought compensation for the loss caused to them as a result of the accident. No fault on the part of the company was shown.

Held: The court of first instance held that the widow could recover without proving fault on the part of the railway, and an appeal was dismissed.

---

[85] BGHZ 66.51.
[86] See also for French law: Cass. civ. 2e, 22 May 1978, Bull. civ. II.139.
[87] *Infra*, Chapter 7.1.
[88] *Infra*, at 49 ff.
[89] D.P.1933.1.137, annotated by L. Josserand.

Judgment: THE COURT: *On the first appeal ground*:—Whereas a certain Noblet, an infantry captain, had taken a seat in a carriage headed for Angers and he fell on to the track and his death was instantaneous; as the victim's widow, acting on her own behalf and that of her minor children, sought compensation for the loss caused to them as a result of the accident;

—Whereas since no fault on the part of the company was shown, the court of appeal declined to apply Article 1382; it none the less upheld the claim for damages pursuant to the rules on contractual liability and Article 1147 of the Civil Code; as according to the appeal ground, widow Noblet and her minor children were unable to recover the damages awarded to them under Article 1147 alone; as standing in the shoes of the victim, they were entitled under that article only to damages for the physical injury suffered by the deceased as a result of the accident, prior to his demise; since death was instantaneous, there was no injury of a kind to satisfy that provision; as thus, being unable to establish default on the part of the company, widow Noblet and her minor children were not entitled to damages.

—Whereas however, under the contract of carriage, the railway company assumes as regards the person to be conveyed an obligation to carry him safely to his destination, as in the event of a fatal accident occurring during the course of performance of the contract, there was a right to obtain compensation under Article 1147 of the Civil Code in favour of the victim's spouse and children for whose benefit also, and to the extent of their interest, the victim struck the bargain, without there being any need to do so expressly.

On those grounds the appeal is dismissed.

Note

The Court of cassation held that, on taking his ticket, the traveller is also contracting on behalf of his successors in title (it remains to determine who these are: see at I.39(3) below). This allows those persons who are the beneficiaries of a "*stipulation pour autrui*" the benefit of a direct action under the contract against the carrier, based on the obligation to provide safe carriage, which is very favourable to heirs, particularly in the event of sudden death. It is an implied provision. The same technique has been used in analogous situations. The sale to a client of contaminated blood has been held to entail an implied third-party provision in favour of persons receiving a transfusion: Cass. civ. 1re, 12 April 1995.[90]

However, it became necessary to determine who may benefit from the provision in order to limit the number of claims for damages. This the Cour de cassation did in the following year.

Cass. civ., 24 May 1933[91]   **1.F.37.**

"DEPENDANTS" ARE THOSE TO WHOM LEGAL OBLIGATION OF SUPPORT

Fatal fall from train (II): the sister

The railway's obligation de securité is presumed to be a stipulation only in favour of those to whom the passenger owed a legal duty of support.

Facts: A railway passenger fell to his death in unexplained circumstances. His sister, whom he had supported financially, brought a claim.

---

[90] JCP 1995.II.22467, annotated by P. Jourdain.
[91] DP.1933.1.137, annotated by Josserand.

Held: The lower court dimissed the claim and this decision was upheld on appeal.

Judgment: THE COURT: *On the sole appeal ground*:—Whereas the appeal alleges that the contested judgment (Paris, 11 July 1928) wrongly declined to award Miss Falduti damages for the injury occasioned to her as a result of the accidental death of her brother who provided for all her needs and who died following a fall from a moving train on the company's network from Paris to Lyon and the Mediterranean;

—Whereas however, the judgment shows that the causes of the fatal fall remained unknown and that the plaintiff neither proved nor offered evidence to prove that it was owing to the carrier's fault; as although a traveller who is the victim of a fatal accident must be presumed to have contracted in favour of the persons to whom he was legally bound by a duty of assistance, such a presumption may not be extended to a case in which, as in the present case, a plaintiff is unable to set up in support of her action any such legal duty;

—Whereas it follows that on the facts as found in the judgment and notwithstanding the incorrect reasoning challenged in the appeal, there is sufficient warrant in law for the operative provision of the judgment.

On those grounds the appeal is dismissed.

Note

The Cour de cassation ties the benefit of the third-party provision to the existence of a duty of assistance by the victim to the successor in title who must be a very close relative (spouse, parents and children). Thus, one legal fiction is supplemented by another in order to limit the effect of the first fiction.

Finally, in order to extend the fiction, the Cour de cassation allows waiver of the third-party provision.

Cass. civ. 2e, 23 January 1959[92]   **1.F.38.**

DEPENDANT MAY RENOUNCE STIPULATION AND SUE IN TORT

Drowning caused by negligence

The heirs of a deceased passenger may renounce the stipulation in their favour and sue in delict, thereby avoiding the effect of a contractual limitation of liability.

Facts: A passenger travelling under a contract which limited the defendant shipowners' liability was drowned through the negligence of the defendants' employees. His sons brought an action based on delict.

Held: The lower court allowed their claim in full and on appeal this decision was confirmed.

Judgment: THE COURT: *On the first two branches of the first appeal ground*:—Whereas it appears from the confirmatory judgment appealed against that Viaud-Grandmarais who had taken a passage on board the packet-boat Champollion met his death in attempting to swim ashore after the vessel had foundered off the Lebanese coast. Bernard and Hervé Le Roterf, his heirs, brought proceedings under Articles 1382 and 1384 of the Civil Code against Commander Bourde, the ship's captain and against Compagnie des Messageries Maritimes, the ship-owner, for damages for the loss suffered by them.

—Whereas the court below found that Commander Bourde had committed no fault and held that the death of Viaud-Grandmarais was attributable to a fault in the vessel for which the Compagnie des Messageries Maritimes was liable as the vessel's keeper;

[92] D.1959.281, annotated by R. Rodière.

—Whereas it is argued on appeal that the court below declined to have regard to a clause limiting liability included in the ticket, although the general obligation entered into by the passenger to limit his complaint to the amount stipulated, which was binding not only on him but also devolved with his estate on his successors in title, precluded those persons from bringing "an action contrary to that obligation";

—Whereas however, as Viaud-Grandmarais perished in the accident he was unable to transmit to the respondents the action in contract which would have been available to him if he had survived; and as the court below also found as a fact that the deceased's successors in title had waived the alleged third-party provision included in the contract in their favour, there was nothing to prevent them from bringing an action in quasi-tort for compensation for the loss occasioned to them as a result of the death of their father, which would be a different action from that to which non-performance of the contract at issue could have given rise;

—Whereas in so deciding the court of appeal violated none of the legislative provisions mentioned in the appeal. On those grounds the appeal in cassation is dismissed.

Note

The contractual route may be blocked by exemption clauses. According to this judgment, the victim is then entitled to waive the benefit of the third-party provision and his successors in title may claim in tort in regard to their own injury and not that suffered by the person transported. That represents an indirect breach of the rule against the overlapping of remedies.[93]

It should be stated that on questions of transport more recent enactments, which have generally been passed as a result of international conventions, have improved the position of carriers. But the technique of the third-party provision remains in use, though to a lesser extent, in other situations.

The question of chain contracts has also encountered a variable response in the French courts. Can the contracting party at the end of the chain act directly against the initial contracting party? A distinction is made between homogenous chains of contracts, for example chain sales, and chains made up of contracts of varying kinds (sale/service contract/sale, for example) as in the case which gave rise to the judgment discussed below.

Cass. ass. plén., 7 February 1988[94] **1.F.39.**

DIRECT ACTION FOR NON-CONFOMITY

Insulation not fit for purpose

Under a building contract, if material supplied by a manufacturer is not in conformity with the contract, the employer has a direct action against the manufacturer.

Facts: Insulating material supplied to a building contractor by MPI was not in accordance with the contract and caused water pipes to corrode. The employer brought a direct action against the manufacturer after the short time period in which it would have been necessary to make a claim for a latent defect.

Held: The lower court allowed the claim on the basis of delict. The Plenary Court upheld the decision on the basis of a direct contractual action.

[93] *Infra*, at 67.
[94] JCP 1986.II.20616, annotated by Malinvaud, D.1986.232, annotated by Benabent.

Judgment: THE COURT: *On the first appeal ground*:—Whereas according to the findings of the judgment appealed against (Paris, 19th Chamber B, 14 June 1984) the Residence Brigitte, insured by Union des Assurances de Paris (UAP) in 1969 entrusted the construction of a building to the architects Marty & Ginsberg (to whose rights the Ginsberg couple had succeeded), assisted by the consultants OTH and BEPET; as the company Petit which was responsible for the main structural work subcontracted to the company Samy the digging of trenches for the laying of services to be carried out by the company Laurent Bourillet; as Samy applied a product called Protexculate to those surfaces which was intended to ensure thermal insulation; as the product was sold to it by the Soc. commerciale de Matériaux pour la protection et insulation (MPI); as upon the occurrence of leaks of water the experts appointed at the interlocutory stage concluded in 1977 that there had been corrosion of the pipes caused by the Protexculate product which was aggravated by failings in the trench cutting;
—Whereas UAP brought proceedings against MPI, Petit, Samy, Laurent Bourillet and Messrs Marty & Ginsberg and the consultants for reimbursement of the compensation paid to the co-owners under an invoice givings rights of subrogation dated 30 October 1980;
—Whereas MPI argues that the court below was wrong to uphold that claim together with interest at the legal rate with effect from 30 October 1980 on the basis of liability in tort; as according to the appeal ground the employer (*maître de l'ouvrage*) has a right of action against the manufacturer of materials laid by an undertaking only as regards the guarantee against a latent defect affecting the item sold at the time of its manufacture; and that action, which is of necessity contractual, must be brought within a short period after the defect is discovered.
—Whereas thus, in the present case, by upholding the action brought on 28 January 1980 by UAP succeeding to the rights of the main contractor seeking a guarantee of a defect discovered by the court-appointed expert on 4 February 1977, and in respect of which compensation was paid by UAP on 30 October 1980, the cour d'appel which declined to examine whether the action ought to have been brought within a shorter time-frame misapplied and therefore infringed Article 1382 of the Civil Code and, by failing to apply it, Article 1648 of that Code;
—Whereas as however the employer (*maître de l'ouvrage*), in the same way as the sub-owner, enjoys all the rights and rights of action attaching to the item which belonged to the manufacturer;
—Whereas the owner therefore has a contractual right of action against the manufacturer based on the non-compliance of the product supplied;
—Whereas therefore, in finding that MPI had manufactured and sold under the name "Protexculate" a product which was not fit for the use for which it was intended and which was the cause of the injury suffered by Residence Brigitte, the employer (*maître de l'ouvrage*), the court d'appel found there to have been a breach of contract in respect of which UAP (succeeding to the rights of Residence Brigitte) was entitled to rely upon in order to make a direct claim for compensation within the time limits applicable under the ordinary law;
—Whereas on those grounds the cour d'appel underpinned its decision with proper legal reasons; . . .
  On those grounds the appeal is dismissed.

Note
This judgment is the culmination of a long line of court decisions. The conflicting opinions even as between chambers of the Cour de cassation have now been settled by the Plenary Court in a classic situation. A product is sold to the builder of a building which is sold. Does the purchaser have a right of redress under contract law against the manufacturer? Or is there a right of action in contract only as between the purchaser and the builder, there being another right of action as between the builder and the manufacturer? The reply is this time unambiguous: there is a direct right of action against the manufacturer, which avoids a multiplicity of suits involved in passing liability back up through

each link in the chain. In fact, there is a direct right of action based on non-conformity—or for a latent defect—because that right of action attaches to the product and is transmitted with it. Therefore, the Cour de cassation is giving priority to an analysis based on the ancillary nature of the action in relation to the product over other analyses proposed—implied third-party provision, implied assignment of chose in action. It is in fact an obligation *propter rem*, that is to say an obligation which runs with the product sold. This decision continues to apply after the *Besse* judgment.[95]

Finally, it should be noted that the manufacturer will normally be able to plead against the final contracting party the exceptions and defences which he would have been entitled to plead as against the intermediate contracting party such as, for example, a clause exempting the manufacturer from liability to give a guarantee, prescription periods, etc.

The next judgment concerns subcontracting and relations between the main contracting party and the subcontractor who are the contracting parties at either end of the scale in a chain of contracts.

Cass. ass. plén., 12 July 1991[96]   **1.F.40.**

NO CONTRACTUAL CLAIM AGAINST SUB-CONTRACTOR

Bad plumbing

An employer does not have a direct contractual claim against a sub-contractor for defective work.

Facts: Mr Besse asked Mr Alhalda, a builder, to construct a dwelling house. The builder subcontracted the plumbing work to Mr Protois. Since that work proved to be defective, Mr Besse brought an action based on delict against the subcontractor more than ten years after the handover of the works.

Held: The Nancy Court of Appeal declared the action inadmissible on the basis that, where a party liable to perform a contractual obligation has entrusted performance of that obligation to another person, the other party to the bargain merely has a right of action in contract against that person to the same extent as regards rights and obligations as the substituted party primarily liable. (It thus applied the case law of the first civil chamber and more particularly the principles laid down in the judgment of 8 March 1988 whose reasoning it adopted.) An appeal was allowed.

Judgment: THE COURT: *On the sole appeal ground*:—Under Article 1165 of the Civil Code agreements have effect only as between the parties to them;
—Whereas according to the contested judgment, more than ten years after the hand over of the dwelling house which Mr Besse had asked Mr Alhalda, the main contractor, to build, and in which a subcontractor, Mr Protois had carried out various items of plumbing work which turned out to be defective, Mr Besse brought proceedings against both of them for damages for losses sustained;
—Whereas in declaring inadmissible the claims against the subcontractor, the judgment notes that where a party liable to perform a contractual obligation has entrusted performance of that obligation to another person, the other party to the bargain merely has a right of action in contract against that person to the same extent as regards rights and obligations as the substituted party primarily liable; as it deduces therefrom that Mr Protois may set up against Mr Besse all the rights of defence based on the building agreement entered into by Mr Besse with the main contractor, as well as the legal provisions governing it, in particular the ten-year time-bar;

---

[95] Discussed *infra*, **1.F.40.**
[96] D.1991.549, annotated by J. Ghestin; JCP 1991.II.21743, annotated by G. Viney.

47

—Whereas in so deciding, where the subcontractor is not contractually bound to the owner who asked for the works to be carried out, the appeal court infringed the abovementioned provision;

On those grounds the Court quashes the judgment of 16 January 1990 by the Nancy cour d'appel, but only to the extent to which it declared inadmissible the claim against Mr Protois . . .

Note

This judgment calls a halt in a marked trend towards an extension of the sphere of contract. In a judgment which aroused considerable comment, the first Civil Chamber established in the *Soderep* case of 21 June 1988,[97] the principle that in a group of contracts liability in contract "*necessarily* applies to claims for damages by all persons suffering injury simply by virtue of the fact that they had some link with the initial contract. Therefore, since the party liable to perform under the contract must have foreseen the consequences of a failure by him to perform in accordance with the applicable contractual rules, a right of action in contract against him lies at the behest of the victim, even if there is no contract between them." The rule was very far-reaching and not very clearly circumscribed—how should the link with the initial contract be determined? It was widely criticized by academic writers. On a question of time-limits and concerning subcontracting, the *Besse* judgment succinctly retorts that the subcontractor is not contractually bound to the owner who asked for the works to be carried out, whereas the appeal relied on the principle formulated in the *Soderep* judgment. The action by the initial creditor against the subcontractor can therefore only be in tort and therefore, obviously, the clauses in the contract cannot be opposed to it. Henceforth the solution will be the same in all chains of contracts, except in the cases mentioned in the judgment of the full court of 1986 reported above, that is to say where property has passed.

In its judgment of 17 June 1992,[98] the Court of Justice of the European Communities, ruling at the request of the French Cour de cassation on the interpretation of Article 5 of the Brussels Convention of 27 September 1968, held that an action on a warranty by a subsequent purchaser against the manufacturer is not based on contract. The French courts have subsequently deemed that solution to concern only jurisdiction within the European Union and not to alter the substantive solution; but a recent judgment (Cass. civ.1re, 5 January 1999,[99] below) has just decided, in the case of a chain of contracts where the original sale was governed by CISG (Convention on the International Sale of Goods), that this Convention can apply as between the original seller and the sub-buyer only if there is a contract of sale between the supplier and the sub-buyer. This ignores the existence of the sub-buyer's *action directe*. Can this be right? One may wonder while we await confirmation of the new jurisprudence by the Plenary Cour de cassation.

What the court (Cass. civ.1re, 5 January 1999) said was this:

—Whereas according to those provisions, the Convention is applicable to international contracts for the sale of goods, and exclusively governs the rights and obligations to which such a contract gives rise between a vendor and a purchaser;

[97] D.1989.5, annotated by C. Larroumet; JCP 1989.II.2115, annotated by P. Jourdain.
[98] Rev. Crit. DIP 1992.726, annotated by H. Gaudemet-Tallon.
[99] D.1999.383, annotated by Cl. Witz.

—Whereas for the purposes of applying that Convention to the contractual relations defined by it in respect of the American company Thermo King, in its capacity as the manufacturer of a refrigeration system installed in a lorry belonging to the French company Transports Norbert Dentressangle, which had acquired it from the French company Frappa, the latter having itself been supplied with it by the company Sorhofroid, which acts as Thermo King's agent in France, the Grenoble cour d'appel held in its judgment of 15 May 1996 that, by issuing a guarantee to the user of the system, Thermo King had agreed to be bound by a contractual relationship with that user, who therefore had a right of action against the manufacturer in respect of defects in the system sold. In so ruling, without establishing the existence, as between Thermo King and Dentressangle, of a contract of sale governed by the Convention, the cour d'appel infringed the provisions referred to above; . . .

On those grounds, [the Court] quashes the judgment of the court below and refers the case to the Lyon cour d'appel.

b) English Law

The concept of a contract is more rigid. From the outset, the narrow concept of "privity" militate against any widening of the sphere of contract law until the recent reforms of the doctrine of privity. As we can see, English law is still less inclined than French or German law to include within the scope of a contract persons who are not parties thereto in the strict sense of the term, and is less disposed to conclude that contracts of a more or less notional kind exist in order to enable the rules of contract law to be applied instead of the rules of tort, particularly with a view to avoiding the limits imposed on damages in tort, which do not cover the purely economic loss for which contract law alone affords a right to compensation. It is not appropriate here to enter into a discussion of that vexed and uncertain question; the present analysis must be restricted to a consideration of the impact which it has on the notion of a contract. This is because the English courts tend on occasion to water down the principles involved, and do not hesitate to resort to certain stratagems in order to arrive at the desired result. This tends, in the situations under consideration, to give rise to a certain lack of clarity and even, sometimes, to decisions which are difficult to reconcile with one another.

Thus, in matters concerning contracts in the form of a chain, the judgment in *Simaan*, the facts of which are similar to those of the German judgment referred to,[100] provides an illustration of the strict approach.

Court of Appeal   **1.E.41.**
Simaan General Contracting Co v. *Pilkington Glass Ltd (No 2)*[101]

NOMINATED SUPPLIER NOT LIABLE IN TORT TO CONTRACTOR

Red glass

Facts: A contractor (Simaan) entrusted a subcontractor (Feal) with the installation of glass panes in a building under construction. The employer, a sheikh, required the glass to be obtained from the manufacturer, Pilkington

---

[100] See **1.G.48**, *infra* at 62.
[101] [1988] 1 All ER 791.

49

Glass. The glass was defective in that it was not green (in the country where the building was being constructed, the colour of peace) but tinged with red. The contractor sought compensation from the manufacturer for the loss incurred by him as a result of the owner's refusal to pay based on the defects in the glass. At first instance Pilkington's defence was unsuccessful. An appeal against the judgment was allowed.

Judgment: LORD BINGHAM: I can, I think, state my conclusions fairly shortly.

(1) I accept without reservation that a claim may lie in negligence for recovery of economic loss alone. Were that not so the *Hedley Byrne* case [1964] A.C. 465 could not have been decided as it was.

(2) I am quite sure that the defendants owed the plaintiffs a conventional *Donoghue* v. *Stevenson* [1932] A.C. 562 duty of care to avoid physical injury or damage to person or property. Suppose (however improbably) that the defendants manufactured the units so carelessly that they were liable to explode on exposure to strong sunlight and that one of the units did so explode, blinding an employee of the plaintiffs working in the building. I cannot conceive that such employee would fail in a personal injury action against the defendants for failure to prove a duty of care.

(3) There is no meaningful sense in which the plaintiffs can be said to have relied on the defendants. No doubt the plaintiffs hoped and expected that the defendants would supply good quality goods conforming with the contract specification. But the plaintiffs required Feal to buy these units from the defendants for one reason only, namely, that they were contractually obliged to do so and had no choice in the matter. There was no technical discussion of the product between the plaintiffs and the defendants.

(4) Where a specialist sub-contractor is vetted, selected and nominated by a building owner it may be possible to conclude (as in the *Junior Books* case [1983] 1 A.C. 520) that the nominated sub-contractor has assumed a direct responsibility to the building owner. On that reasoning it might be said that the defendants owed a duty to the Sheikh in tort as well as to Feal in contract. I do not, however, see any basis on which the defendants could be said to have assumed a direct responsibility for the quality of the goods to the plaintiffs: such a responsibility is, I think, inconsistent with the structure of the contract the parties have chosen to make.

(5) The *Junior Books* case has been interpreted as a case arising from physical damage. I doubt if that interpretation accords with Lord Roskill's intention, but it is binding upon us. There is in my view no physical damage in this case. The units are as good as ever they were and will not deteriorate. I bridle somewhat at the assumption of defects which we are asked to make because what we have here are not, in my view, defects but failures to comply with Sale of Goods Act conditions of correspondence with description or sample, merchantability or (perhaps) fitness for purpose. It would, I think, be an abuse of language to describe these units as damaged. The contrast with the floor in the *Junior Books* case is obvious.

(6) I do not accept that the *Hedley Byrne* case [1964] A.C. 465, and such authorities as *Ross* v. *Caunters* [1980] Ch. 297, establish a general rule that claims in negligence may succeed on proof of foreseeable economic loss caused by the defendant even where no damage to property and no proprietary or possessory interest are shown. If there were such a general rule, the plaintiffs in the *Candlewood* case [1986] A.C. 1 and *Leigh and Sillavan Ltd.* v. *Aliakmon Shipping Co. Ltd.* [1986] A.C. 785 would not have failed on the ground they did and the causes of action in the *Pirelli* case [1983] 2 A.C. 1 and *London Congregational Union Inc.* v. *Harriss & Harriss* [1988] 1 All E.R. 15 would have been complete at an earlier date. However attractive it may theoretically be to postulate a single principle capable of embracing every kind of case, that is not how the law has developed. It would of course be unsatisfactory if (say) doctors and dentists owed their patients a different duty of care. I do not, however, think it unsatisfactory or surprising if, as I think, a banker's duty towards the recipient of a credit reference and an industrial glass manufacturer's duty towards a main contractor, in the absence of any contract between them, differ. Here, the plaintiffs' real (and understandable) complaint is that the defendants' failure to supply goods in conformity with

the specification has rendered their main contract less profitable. This is a type of claim against which, if laid in tort, the law has consistently set its face.

(7) If, contrary to my view, these units can be regarded as damaged at all, the damage (or the defects) occurred at the time of manufacture when they were the defendants' property. I therefore think that the plaintiffs fail to show any interest in the goods at the time when damage occurred. I very much doubt if there was any time on site, whether in course of erection or after rejection, when the plaintiffs had a proprietary or possessory interest in the units, but I do not think it useful to pursue this, since neither was the time at which, if at all, physical damage occurred.

(8) I do not think it just and reasonable to impose on the defendants a duty of care towards the plaintiffs of the scope contended for. (a) Just as equity remedied the inadequacies of the common law, so has the law of torts filled gaps left by other causes of action where the interests of justice so required. I see no such gap here, because there is no reason why claims beginning with the Sheikh should not be pursued down the contractual chain, subject to any short-cut which may be agreed upon, ending up with a contractual claim against the defendants. That is the usual procedure. It must be what the parties contemplated when they made their contracts. I see no reason for departing from it. (b) Although the defendants did not sell subject to exempting conditions, I fully share the difficulty which others have envisaged where there were such conditions. Even as it is, the defendants' sale may well have been subject to terms and conditions imported by the Sale of Goods Act 1979. Some of those are beneficial to the seller. If such terms are to circumscribe a duty which would be otherwise owed to a party not a party to the contract and unaware of its terms, then that could be unfair to him. But if the duty is unaffected by the conditions on which the seller supplied the goods, it is in my view unfair to him and makes a mockery of contractual negotiation.

I would accordingly allow the appeal and answer the question posed by the preliminary issue in the negative.

Note

The loss at issue is regarded as economic loss and therefore not in principle recoverable in tort. The plaintiff had an action in contract against the subcontractor. For unknown reasons—insolvency?—the plaintiff preferred to bring an action against the manufacturer with whom he had no contractual link. The Court of Appeal pointed out that the situation is different from that which gave rise to the judgment in *Junior Books Ltd* v. *Veitchi Co Ltd*, discussed below at **1.E.42** and mentioned repeatedly in this judgment. Since the action is in tort, it was held in the judgment that, even if there was negligence, that does not allow recovery of damages for economic loss stemming from non-payment of the undertaking. For that it would have been necessary to retrace the chain of contracts link by link.

However in the *Junior Books* case a way was found to avoid this difficulty.

House of Lords   **1.E.42.**
Junior Books Ltd v. *Veitchi Co Ltd*[102]

LIABILITY IN TORT FOR DEFECTIVE GOODS WHERE SPECIAL RELATIONSHIP

Defective floor laid by sub-contractor

When an employer has nominated a particular firm to be employed by the main contractor to carry out a particular part of the work, there is sufficient relationship between the employer and the nominated

---

[102] [1983] 1 AC 520.

sub-contractor to make the latter liable in tort if it does its work without proper care, even if the defective floor is not dangerous and has caused no physical injury.

Facts: An owner asked an undertaking to build a factory. A subcontractor appointed by the owner was to build a special concrete floor. There was no contract between the owner and the subcontractor but only between the main contractor and the subcontractor. Cracks appeared in the floor after only two years. The owner sued the subcontractor and asked for the floor to be replaced and for restitution of the economic loss resulting from closure of the factory for the duration of the works. The Scottish courts declared the action admissible and their decision was confirmed by the House of Lords.

Judgment: LORD ROSKILL: . . . [I]n *Anns* v. *Merton London Borough Council* [1978] A.C. 728, 751, Lord Wilberforce, approving the earlier decisions of the Court of Appeal in *Dutton* v. *Bognor Regis Urban District Council* [1972] 1 Q.B. 373 and *Sparham-Souter* v. *Town and Country Developments (Essex) Ltd.* [1976] Q.B. 858, said of the trilogy of cases, *Donoghue* v. *Stevenson*, *Hedley Byrne*, and *Dorset Yacht*:

> "the position has now been reached that in order to establish that a duty of care arises in a particular situation, it is not necessary to bring the facts of that situation within those of previous situations in which a duty of care has been held to exist. Rather the question has to be approached in two stages. First one has to ask whether, as between the alleged wrongdoer and the person who has suffered damage there is a sufficient relationship of proximity or neighbourhood such that, in the reasonable contemplation of the former, carelessness on his part may be likely to cause damage to the latter—in which case a prima facie duty of care arises. Secondly, if the first question is answered affirmatively, it is necessary to consider whether there are any considerations which ought to negative, or to reduce or limit the scope of the duty or the class of person to whom it is owed or the damages to which a breach of it may give rise: . . ."

Applying those statements of general principle as your Lordships have been enjoined to do both by Lord Reid and by Lord Wilberforce rather than to ask whether the particular situation which has arisen does or does not resemble some earlier and different situation where a duty of care has been held or has not been held to exist, I look for the reasons why, it being conceded that the appellants owed a duty of care to others not to construct the flooring so that those others were in peril of suffering loss or damage to their persons or their property, that duty of care should not be equally owed to the respondents. The appellants, though not in direct contractual relationship with the respondents, were as nominated subcontractors in almost as close a commercial relationship with the respondents as it is possible to envisage short of privity of contract. Why then should the appellants not be under a duty to the respondents not to expose the respondents to a possible liability to financial loss for repairing the flooring should it prove that that flooring had been negligently constructed? It is conceded that if the flooring had been so badly constructed that to avoid imminent danger the respondents had expended money upon renewing it the respondents could have recovered the cost of so doing. It seems curious that, if the appellants' work had been so bad that to avoid imminent danger expenditure had been incurred, the respondents could recover that expenditure, but that if the work was less badly done so that remedial work could be postponed they cannot do so. Yet this is seemingly the result of the appellants' contentions . . .

Turning back to the present appeal I therefore ask first whether there was the requisite degree of proximity so as to give rise to the relevant duty of care relied on by the respondents. I regard the following facts as of crucial importance in requiring an affirmative answer to that question. (1) The appellants were nominated sub-contractors. (2) The appellants were specialists in flooring. (3) The appellants knew what products were required by the respondents and their main contractors and specialised in the production of those products. (4) The appellants alone were responsible for the composition and construction of the flooring. (5) The respondents relied upon the appellants' skill and experience. (6) The appellants as nominated sub-contractors must have known that the respondents relied upon their skill and experience. (7) The relationship between the parties was as close as it could be short of actual privity of contract. (8) The appellants must be taken to have known that if they did the work negligently (as it must be assumed that they did) the resulting defects would at some time require remedying by the respondents expending money upon the remedial measures as a consequence of which the respondents would suffer financial or economic loss.

My Lords, reverting to Lord Devlin's speech in *Hedley Byrne & Co. Ltd.* v. *Heller & Partners Ltd.* [1964] A.C. 465, it seems to me that all the conditions existed which give rise to the relevant duty of care owed by the appellants to the respondents.

I then turn to Lord Wilberforce's second proposition. On the facts I have just stated, I see nothing whatsoever to restrict the duty of care arising from the proximity of which I have spoken. During the argument it was asked what the position would be in a case where there was a relevant exclusion clause in the main contract. My Lords, that question does not arise for decision in the instant appeal, but in principle I would venture the view that such a clause according to the manner in which it was worded might in some circumstances limit the duty of care just as in the *Hedley Byrne* case the plaintiffs were ultimately defeated by the defendants' disclaimer of responsibility. But in the present case the only suggested reason for limiting the damage (ex hypothesi economic or financial only) recoverable for the breach of the duty of care just enunciated is that hitherto the law has not allowed such recovery and therefore ought not in the future to do so. My Lords, with all respect to those who find this a sufficient answer, I do not. I think this is the next logical step forward in the development of this branch of the law. I see no reason why what was called during the argument "damage to the pocket" simpliciter should be disallowed when "damage to the pocket" coupled with physical damage has hitherto always been allowed. I do not think that this development, if development it be, will lead to untoward consequences. The concept of proximity must always involve, at least in most cases, some degree of reliance—I have already mentioned the words "skill" and "judgment" in the speech of Lord Morris of Borth-y-Gest in *Hedley Byrne* [1964] AC 465 at 503. These words seem to me to be an echo, be it conscious or unconscious, of the language of section 14 (1) of the Sale of Goods Act 1893. My Lords, though the analogy is not exact, I do not find it unhelpful for I think the concept of proximity of which I have spoken and the reasoning of Lord Delvlin in the Hedley Byrne case involve factual considerations not unlike those involved in a claim under section 14 (1); and as between an ultimate purchaser and a manufacturer would not easily be found to exist in the ordinary everyday transaction of purchasing chattels when it is obvious that in truth the real reliance was upon the immediate vendor and not upon the manufacturer . . .

[Lords Fraser and Russel agreed, Lord Keith delivered a separate concurring judgment and Lord Brandon dissented].

Appeal dismissed.

Note
Most noteworthy in the judgment of the House of Lords is the statement by Lord Roskill: "the relationship between the parties was as close as it could be short of actual privity of contract". Without embarking upon the controversial question of how well founded it was for economic loss to be excluded in tort, the realism of the English judges is to be noted who here again seek to give effect to the reasonable intentions of the parties in their commercial relationships.

Thus, a quasi-contractual relationship may exist between the two ends the chain, based on "proximity" (but giving rise to liability in tort, not contract).

The same contrast exists between the following two judgments, which concern relatively similar facts.

House of Lords **1.E.43.**
Murphy v. *Brentwood District Council*[103]

NO LIABILITY IN TORT FOR MERELY DEFECTIVE HOUSE WHERE NO SPECIAL RELATIONSHIP

Inadequate foundations

A local council which had the power to inspect building work but which negligently failed to stop a house being built with inadequate foundations is not liable in tort to a person who subsequently purchases the property not knowing of the defect; nor is the negligent builder if there is no contract between it and the house-owner.

Facts: Mr Murphy purchased from a building company a house within a group of buildings constructed on a concrete slab. The plans and calculations for the construction of the slab in question were approved by the local council pursuant to the regulations in force. Cracks appeared, giving rise to a serious and dangerous situation which resulted, beyond any doubt, from negligence on the part of the experts engaged by the council. The owner, who did not have the means to pay for the repairs needed, sold his house at a substantial loss and claimed compensation from the council. He was successful in the proceedings at first instance and on appeal, but the House of Lords held that no contract existed between the council and the owner.

Held: Having considered what is known as the "complex structure theory", reminiscent of the French theory relating to sets of interrelated contracts, the House of Lords rejected that theory.

Judgment: The relative positions of the builder and the local authority . . .

. . . I have so far been considering the potential liability of a builder for negligent defects in the structure of a building to persons to whom he owes no contractual duty. Since the relevant statutory function of the local authority is directed to no other purpose than securing compliance with building byelaws or regulations by the builder, I agree with the view expressed in *Anns* [1978] A.C. 728 and by the majority of the Court of Appeal in *Dutton* [1972] 1 Q.B. 373 that a negligent performance of that function can attract no greater liability than attaches to the negligence of the builder whose fault was the primary tort giving rise to any relevant damage. I am content for present purposes to assume, though I am by no means satisfied that the assumption is correct, that where the local authority, as in this case or in *Dutton*, have in fact approved the defective plans or inspected the defective foundations and negligently failed to discover the defect, their potential liability in tort is coextensive with that of the builder.

Only Stamp LJ in *Dutton* was prepared to hold that the law imposed on the local authority a duty of care going beyond that imposed on the builder and extending to protection of the building owner from purely economic loss. I must return later to consider the question of liability for economic loss more generally, but here I need only say that I cannot find in *Hedley Byrne & Co. Ltd.* v. *Heller & Partners Ltd.* [1964] A.C. 465 or *Dorset Yacht Co. Ltd.* v. *Home Office* [1970] A.C. 1004 any principle applicable to the circumstances of Dutton or the present case that provides support for the conclusion which Stamp L.J. sought to derive from those authorities.

Note

In contrast to the previous case, the court felt unable to discern the existence of any such "quasi-contractual" relationship (note that in *Murphy* the *Junior Books* case was not overruled but was said to depend on a special relationship on the facts of the latter case). It is instructive to note the flexibility and relativity of the rules applied in the matter.

There was held to be no relationship of proximity between the owner and the council; nor, *a fortiori*, was there any contractual relationship between them. The poor owner was not entitled to any compensation for the loss in the value of his property.

---

[103] [1990] 2 All ER 908, HL.

The position was found to be different in the following judgment.

King's Bench Division   **1.E.44.**
Shanklin Pier Ltd v. Detel Products Ltd[104]

WARRANTY BY MANUFACTURER TO EMPLOYER

Paint for a pier

Where an employer contacts a manufacturer who gives an undertaking that its product will perform in a certain way, and consequently the employer instructs its main contractor to piurchase the product, the manufacturer will be held to have given a contractual "warranty" that its product will perform as stated. The consideration will be being nominated as the supplier.

Facts: The owner of a pier asked a paint manufacturer whether a particular paint produced by it was suitable for use in painting the pier. The latter replied that it would last for at least seven years. The owner therefore instructed the painting company to use it. The paint started to peel after three months. The owner claimed compensation from the manufacturer.

Judgment: MCNAIR J.: This case raises an interesting and comparatively novel question whether or not an enforceable warranty can arise as between parties other than parties to the main contract for the sale of the article in respect of which the warranty is alleged to have been given. [His Lordship stated the facts set out above and continued:]

The defence, stated broadly, is that no warranty such as is alleged in the statement of claim was ever given and that, if given, it would give rise to no cause of action between these parties. Accordingly, the first question which I have to determine is whether any such warranty was ever given. [His Lordship reviewed the evidence about the negotiations which led to the acceptance by the plaintiffs of two coats of D.M.U. in substitution for the paint originally specified, and continued:]

In the result, I am satisfied that, if a direct contract of purchase and sale of the D.M.U. had then been made between the plaintiffs and the defendants, the correct conclusion on the facts would have been that the defendants gave to the plaintiffs the warranties substantially in the form alleged in the statement of claim. In reaching this conclusion, I adopt the principles stated by Holt, CJ, in *Crosse* v. *Gardner* (1) and *Medina* v. *Stoughton* (2) that an affirmation at the time of sale is a warranty, provided it appear on evidence to have been so intended.

Counsel for the defendants submitted that in law a warranty could give rise to no enforceable cause of action except between the same parties as the parties to the main contract in relation to which the warranty was given. In principle this submission seems to me to be unsound. If, as is elementary, the consideration for the warranty in the usual case is the entering into of the main contract in relation to which the warranty is given, I see no reason why there may not be an enforceable warranty between A and B supported by the consideration that B should cause C to enter into a contract with A or that B should do some other act for the benefit of A.

Note
The decision was based on a contractual guarantee given by the manufacturer to the owner. This case provides an example of the manipulation of the notion of a contract in order to arrive at the desired result. The facts required to give rise to such a warranty seem very similar to those which would give rise to a "special relationship" as in the *Junior Books* case.

---

[104] [1951] 2 All ER 471.

Indeed, in some cases, it is only the dictates of practical necessity and/or imperative commercial requirements which justify the extension to third parties of an exemption clause agreed between the parties.

Privy Council (on appeal from New Zealand)[105]   **1.E.45.**
New Zealand Shipping Co Ltd v. *AM Satterthwaite & Co Ltd*[106]

PROTECTION ARRANGED ON BEHALF OF THIRD PERSON

Himalaya clause

A third person who is not directly a party to the contract may be protected from liability in tort by clauses arranged on his behalf by one of the contracting parties.

Facts: A bill of lading contained a clause[107] exempting the carrier from liability. The clause extended to protect independent contractors acting on behalf of the carrier. The carrier was said to make this arrangement as agent on their behalf and they were deemed to be parties to the contract. The defendants, independent stevedores, relied on the clause. The Privy Council, to which the case was referred by the New Zealand courts, upheld their claim.

Judgment: LORD WILBERFORCE, delivering the judgment of the majority, quoted the part of Lord Reid's speech in the *Midland Silicones* case in which Lord Reid stated the prerequisites for success of the "agency" argument:

"... [I]f (first) the bill of lading makes it clear that the stevedore is intended to be protected by the provisions in it which limit the liability, (secondly) the bill of lading makes it clear that the carrier, in addition to contracting for these provisions on his own behalf, is also contracting as agent for the stevedores that these provisions should apply to the stevedore, (thirdly) the carrier has authority from the stevedore to do that, or perhaps later ratification by the stevedore would suffice, and (fourthly) that any difficulties about consideration moving from the stevedore were overcome."

Lord Wiberforce continued :

The question in this appeal is whether the contract satisfies these propositions.

Clause 1 of the bill of lading, whatever the defects in its drafting, is clear in its relevant terms. The carrier, on his own account, stipulates for certain exemptions and immunities: among these is that conferred by article III, rule 6, of the Hague Rules which discharges the carrier from all liability for loss or damage unless suit is brought within one year after delivery. In addition to these stipulations on his own account, the carrier as agent for, inter alios, independent contractors stipulates for the same exemptions.

Much was made of the fact that the carrier also contracts as agent for numerous other persons; the relevance of this argument is not apparent. It cannot be disputed that among such independent contractors, for whom, as agent, the carrier contracted, is the appellant company which habitually acts as stevedore in New Zealand by arrangement with the carrier and which is, moreover, the parent company of the carrier. The carrier was, indisputably, authorised by the appellant to contract as its agent for the purposes of clause 1. All of this is quite straightforward and was accepted by all the judges in New Zealand. The only question was, and is, the fourth question presented by Lord Reid, namely that of consideration.

It was on this point that the Court of Appeal differed from Beattie J., holding that it had not been shown that any consideration for the shipper's promise as to exemption moved from the promisee, i.e., the appellant company.

[105] Until comparatively recently the Privy Council in London was the final court of appeal for several Commonwealth countries.
[106] [1974] 1 All ER 1015, PC.
[107] Often called a Himalaya clause after the name of the ship involved in one of the early cases raising this problem, *Adler* v. *Dickson* [1955] 1 KB 158.

   If the choice, and the antithesis, is between a gratuitous promise, and a promise for consideration, as it must be in the absence of a tertium quid, there can be little doubt which, in commercial
reality, this is. The whole contract is of a commercial character, involving service on one side, rates
of payment on the other, and qualifying stipulations as to both. The relations of all parties to each
other are commercial relations entered into for business reasons of ultimate profit. To describe one
set of promises, in this context, as gratuitous, or nudum pactum, seems paradoxical and is prima
facie implausible. It is only the precise analysis of this complex of relations into the classical offer
and acceptance, with identifiable consideration, that seems to present difficulty, but this same difficulty exists in many situations of daily life, e.g., sales at auction; supermarket purchases; boarding
an omnibus; purchasing a train ticket; tenders for the supply of goods; offers of rewards; acceptance by post; warranties of authority by agents; manufacturers' guarantees; gratuitous bailments;
bankers' commercial credits. These are all examples which show that English law, having committed itself to a rather technical and schematic doctrine of contract, in application takes a practical
approach, often at the cost of forcing the facts to fit uneasily into the marked slots of offer, acceptance and consideration.
   In their Lordships' opinion the present contract presents much less difficulty than many of
those above referred to. It is one of carriage from Liverpool to Wellington. The carrier assumes
an obligation to transport the goods and to discharge at the port of arrival. The goods are to be carried and discharged, so the transaction is inherently contractual. It is contemplated that a part of
this contract, viz. discharge, may be performed by independent contractors—viz. the appellant. By
clause 1 of the bill of lading the shipper agrees to exempt from liability the carrier, his servants
and independent contractors in respect of the performance of this contract of carriage. Thus, if
the carriage, including the discharge, is wholly carried out by the carrier, he is exempt. If part is carried out by him, and part by his servants, he and they are exempt. If part is carried out by him and
part by an independent contractor, he and the independent contractor are exempt. The exemption is
designed to cover the whole carriage from loading to discharge, by whomsoever it is performed:
the performance attracts the exemption or immunity in favour of whoever the performer turns out
to be. There is possibly more than one way of analysing this business transaction into the necessary components; that which their Lordships would accept is to say that the bill of lading brought
into existence a bargain initially unilateral but capable of becoming mutual, between the shipper and
the appellant, made through the carrier as agent. This became a full contract when the appellant performed services by discharging the goods. The performance of these services for the benefit of the
shipper was the consideration for the agreement by the shipper that the appellant should have the
benefit of the exemptions and limitations contained in the bill of lading. The conception of a "unilateral" contract of this kind was recognised in *Great Northern Railway Co.* v. *Witham* (1873) L.R. 9
C.P. 16 and is well established. This way of regarding the matter is very close to if not identical to
that accepted by Beattie J in the Supreme Court: he analysed the transaction as one of an offer open
to acceptance by action such as was found in *Carlill* v. *Carbolic Smoke Ball Co.* [1893] 1 Q.B. 256.
But whether one describes the shipper's promise to exempt as an offer to be accepted by performance
or as a promise in exchange for an act seems in the present context to be a matter of semantics. The
words of Bowen LJ in *Carlill* v. *Carbolic Smoke Ball Co.* [1893] 1 Q.B. 256, 268: "why should not an
offer be made to all the world which is to ripen into a contract with anybody who comes forward and
performs the condition?" seem to bridge both conceptions: he certainly seems to draw no distinction
between an offer which matures into a contract when accepted and a promise which matures into a
contract after performance, and, though in some special contexts (such as in connection with the
right to withdraw) some further refinement may be needed, either analysis may be equally valid. On
the main point in the appeal, their Lordships are in substantial agreement with Beattie J.
   The following points require mention. 1. In their Lordships' opinion, consideration may
quite well be provided by the appellant, as suggested, even though (or if) it was already under an

57

obligation to discharge to the carrier. (There is no direct evidence of the existence or nature of this obligation, but their Lordships are prepared to assume it.) An agreement to do an act which the promisor is under an existing obligation to a third party to do, may quite well amount to valid consideration and does so in the present case: the promisee obtains the benefit of a direct obligation which he can enforce. This proposition is illustrated and supported by *Scotson* v. *Pegg* (1861) 6 H. & N. 295 which their Lordships consider to be good law.

2. The consignee is entitled to the benefit of, and is bound by, the stipulations in the bill of lading by his acceptance of it and request for delivery of the goods thereunder. This is shown by *Brandt* v. *Liverpool, Brazil and River Plate Steam Navigation Co. Ltd.* [1924] 1 K.B. 575 and a line of earlier cases. The Bills of Lading Act 1855, section 1 (in New Zealand the Mercantile Law Act 1908, section 13) gives partial statutory recognition to this rule, but, where the statute does not apply, as it may well not do in this case, the previously established law remains effective.

3. The appellant submitted, in the alternative, an argument that, quite apart from contract, exemptions from, or limitation of, liability in tort may be conferred by mere consent on the part of the party who may be injured. As their Lordships consider that the appellant ought to succeed in contract, they prefer to express no opinion upon this argument: to evaluate it requires elaborate discussion.

4. A clause very similar to the present was given effect by a United States District Court in *Carle & Montanari Inc.* v. *American Export Isbrandtsen Lines Inc.* [1968] 1 Lloyd's Rep. 260. The carrier in that case contracted, in an exemption clause, as agent, for, inter alios, all stevedores and other independent contractors, and although it is no doubt true that the law in the United States is more liberal than ours as regards third party contracts, their Lordships see no reason why the law of the Commonwealth should be more restrictive and technical as regards agency contracts. Commercial considerations should have the same force on both sides of the Pacific.

In the opinion of their Lordships, to give the appellant the benefit of the exemptions and limitations contained in the bill of lading is to give effect to the clear intentions of a commercial document, and can be given within existing principles. They see no reason to strain the law or the facts in order to defeat these intentions. It should not be overlooked that the effect of denying validity to the clause would be to encourage actions against servants, agents and independent contractors in order to get round exemptions (which are almost invariable and often compulsory) accepted by shippers against carriers, the existence, and presumed efficacy, of which is reflected in the rates of freight. They see no attraction in this consequence.

Their Lordships will humbly advise Her Majesty that the appeal be allowed and the judgment of Beattie J. restored. The respondent must pay the costs of the appeal and in the Court of Appeal.

Note

The solution arrived at would appear not to observe the principle of the relative effect of the contract because the exemption clause may validly be relied on by a person who was not a party to the contract. The justification given by Lord Wilberforce is entirely pragmatic: to allow the stevedore the benefit of the clause is "to give effect to the clear intentions of a commercial document and can be given within existing principles", which is doubtless questionable. None the less, it is the case that a kind of "Ersatz" third-party provision is thereby recognized. (Now the same result could be reached directly under Contracts (Rights of Third Parties) Act 1999; see *infra* at 908). The pragmatism of the Common Law may also be noted.

Concluding Remarks on English Law

English law appears at first sight somewhat reluctant to permit any extension of the scope of a contract. It differs in that respect from the position which prevailed under French law prior to delivery of the judgment of 5 January 1999, which shrouded the issue in uncertainty. However, its decisions are marked by a certain pragmatism, reflected either by the discernment of a collateral contract or by the idea of an "almost" contractual relationship.

c) German law

In German law the same uncertainties are encountered.

Rather than imagining in a rather arbitrary manner fictitious third-party provisions, the German courts have created an autonomous category, namely contracts with protective effect in favour of third parties (*Vertrag mit Schutzwirkung für Dritte*). These do not create positive rights in favour of a third party but extend the protective effect of the contract to persons close to one of the contracting parties.

BGH, 17 January 1985[108]   **1.G.46.**

PASSENGER HAS RIGHTS AGAINST AIRLINE

Non-payment by charterer

A passenger who books a seat on a charter flight has an enforceable right against the airline to be given a seat.

Facts:The defendant, an airline company, agreed with T a return charter flight from Frankfurt to Santa Lucia and back from 9 to 16 December 1980. A number of seats were assigned by T to O, a travel agency. On 15 December 1980, T suspended payments. On 16 December 1980 the defendant airline company refused Mrs H who had booked a journey to Santa Lucia a place on a return flight to Frankfurt. That refusal was based on the fact that T had not paid for that flight. Mrs H and the other travellers took a flight with another airline. The courts trying the case on the substantive issues ordered O to reimburse the sum of $1,783.60 together with interest. The plaintiff, an insurance company, repaid to O the sums incurred by it in legal proceedings and the sum which it was found liable to pay in the proceedings. The total amount was then claimed from the defendant by the plaintiff.

Held: The courts trying the case on the substantive issues upheld its claim in part and ordered the defendant to pay the sum of DM 4,579.69. The appeal on a point of law was dismissed.

Judgment:The charter agreement entered into between T and the defendant is a genuine contract in favour of a third party within the meaning of § 328 BGB. Consequently, Mrs H had acquired as against the defendant a genuine right of transport.

By refusing to carry Mrs H the defendant incurred liability under § 325(1). By way of derogation from § 334 it was not entitled to set up as against Mrs H the right which it enjoyed against T in the event of a failure to pay, that is to say non-performance. In fact, as between the charter company and the travellers there can be no implied term as regards failure to pay since it is reasonable for travellers to consider that they have acquired rights not subject to any exception against the airline company.

O having compensated Mrs H the right to recover that sum passed to it under § 426(2). The defendant must alone provide restitution of the loss because, owing to its refusal, it was the cause of the loss. O had against the defendant a claim in the amount of the sum paid to Mrs H. This right passed to the plaintiff.

The contract entered into between the defendant and T must be analysed as a contract in favour of Mrs H. Under a charter contract the charter company undertakes to provide seats on planes.

[108] BGHZ 93.271.

Contrary to the appeals submission, § 651 does not preclude acceptance of a contract in favour of a third party. Certainly under § 651(a) the contractual partner of a traveller who has entered into a travel contract is the travel agent. The travel agent may cite the person liable to provide performance as a person charged with assisting in the execution of the contract. As determined by academic writers, a contract between a travel agent and the person promising performance must be analysed as a contract for the benefit of a third party which secures for the traveller a direct right of action against the person promising performance. The traveller's interest in a trouble-free journey thus affords him a right of action not only against the travel agent but also against the airline.

The defendant entered into the charter contract with T (travel agency) which assigned seats on a plane to O (also a travel agency). It had to make the seats available. It also agreed to have plane seats issued by T. The risk of payment was to be borne by it.

A charter entered into between an airline company and a travel agency may give rise as a contract in favour of a third party (in this case the travellers) to a right to transport. The airline company is not entitled to rely on failure to pay the charter by the travel agency in order to refuse the traveller's right to transport.

Note

This case clearly involved a contract genuinely conferring a right on a third party, that is to say, creating a real contractual right in favour of a person not directly a party to the contract—in the present case, the traveller. The latter had a direct right of action in relation to the performance of the contract and, in addition, a right to claim damages.

In the case of chains of contracts, in a case very similar on its facts to the *Simaan* judgment (*supra*), German law also employs the concept of a contract for the benefit of a third party.

BGH, 26 November 1986[109]   **1.G.47.**

SELLER'S APPRAISER LIABLE TO BUYER'S BANK

Tax consultant's "rosy view"

A tax consultant employed by the owner of a company to prepare a balance sheet for use in selling the company may, if the balance sheet is inaccurate, be liable not only to the purchaser but also to the bank financing the purchase.

Facts: A was the sole shareholder of a company which he wanted to sell. He requested the defendants, his tax consultants, to draw up a balance sheet. They were negligent in painting the company's financial position in too rosy a light. A copy of the balance sheet was passed on by A to B as a potential purchaser of the company, and B in turn passed it on to his bank, the plaintiff, in support of an application for credit to finance the purchase price. The bank was duly impressed and lent B DM 500,000, taking a pledge on the company's shares as security. The bank lost all its money when shortly thereafter both B and his newly acquired company became insolvent and went into liquidation, but it did not lose its action against the tax consultants.

Held: The Court awarded the plaintiff damages for a breach by the tax consultants of their contractual duty to use proper care in drawing up the balance sheet. This duty was primarily owed by them to A with whom they had a contract. The Court held, however, that they owed this duty also to third parties of whom they knew or ought to have known that they might rely on the accuracy of the balance sheet. This included not only B (and other potential purchasers of the company who might be shown the balance sheet), but also the bank to whom the balance sheet had been submitted in support of an application for a loan to finance the acquisition.

[109] NJW 1987.1758.

Judgment: . . . The present case affords grounds for supposing that the contracting parties intended to include third parties within the scope of protection provided by the contract. As stated above, it cannot be assumed that [the balance sheet] was intended solely for the edification of the defendant's client; on the contrary, it was meant to serve as the basis on which a third party—either the purchaser or a lender—might reach a decision. In such a case, it is clear that the third party is to be included within the scope of protection afforded by the contract. It cannot be argued, in opposition to the claim in the present case, that the interests of the purchaser or lender, on the one hand, and of the tax adviser's client, on the other, ran counter to each other. Where a person instructs another person recognised by the State as possessing expert knowledge in a particular field (e.g. a publicly appointed expert, chartered or certified accountant, publicly appointed surveying engineer or tax adviser) to produce an expert's report or to give an expert opinion (e.g. an accountant's or tax adviser's attestation) to be used in dealings with a third party, the client generally has an interest in ensuring that the results of the work carried out have the requisite probative value. This can only be guaranteed, however, if the author of the report or opinion produces it on an objective basis and does so to the best of his knowledge and belief, and if he is also able to vouch for it *vis-à-vis* the third party.

The inclusion of the plaintiff within the scope of protection afforded by the contract does not depend on whether the defendant was aware of the fact that [the balance sheet] was to be submitted to the plaintiff; it will suffice in that regard if the defendant realised, or ought to have realised, that the results of his work were intended either for a purchaser or for a lender (bank). The Bundesgerichtshof has previously held on numerous occasions that a duty of protection exists, in cases in which the person owing that duty was aware neither of the number nor of the names of the persons entitled to such protection [citations omitted]. This does not mean, however, that the group of persons to whom the duty of protection is owed may be extended *ad infinitum*; on the contrary, that duty must be restricted to a discernible, clearly circumscribed group of persons. Accordingly, it does not appear unacceptable to include within the scope of protection afforded by the contract the person for whom [the balance sheet] was clearly intended to serve as the basis for a decision, since in this case the scope of such protection would extend to cover only the purchaser and whoever might lend money to the purchaser.

Note

It is apparent from the facts of this case that the contracting parties intended to include third parties within the sphere of protection afforded by the contract. As stated above, it cannot be assumed that the interim balance sheet was to be used only for the purposes of providing information to the defendant's principal; instead, the balance sheet was intended to serve as the basis for a decision to be made by a third party—either the purchaser or a credit provider. It is not possible, in the case under consideration, to contest that conclusion by arguing that the interests of the purchaser or of a credit provider were in opposition to those of the agent for the tax adviser. Where a person commissions an expert's opinion— e.g. a certificate to be provided by a financial or tax adviser—from another person possessing, in the field in question, special knowledge and skills which are recognized by the State—e.g. a publicly appointed expert, a certificated financial adviser, a publicly appointed land surveyor or a certificated tax adviser—, with a view to using that opinion in dealings with a third person, the person commissioning the opinion will generally wish it to provide the probative force which he desires it to possess. However, that force cannot be guaranteed unless the author of the opinion has conscientiously drafted it from an objective standpoint and also accepts responsibility for its contents *vis-à-vis* the third person.

The inclusion of the plaintiff within the ambit of the protection afforded by the contract did not depend on whether or not the defendant knew that the interim balance sheet was to be submitted to the plaintiff; instead, the fact that the defendant could or should have realized that the balance sheet was intended to be relied on by a purchaser or a credit provider—a bank—was enough in itself. The BGH had previously held on a number of occasions that a duty of protection existed in favour of third parties where the person on whom that duty was incumbent was unaware of the number or names of the persons to whom the protection was owed. This does not mean, however, that the class of persons enjoying the benefit of the protection obligation can be extended *ad infinitum*. On the contrary, it is necessary to limit that protection obligation by restricting the persons to whom it is owed to a finite, clearly ascertainable class of persons. From that point of view, it does not therefore appear unreasonable for the class of persons included within the protection afforded by the contract to include the person whose decision was clearly based on the contents of the interim balance sheet, since, in such circumstances, the scope of protection could extend only to cover the purchaser and any bank granting credit to the purchaser.

The credit was granted by the bank to a customer on the strength of accounting documents provided, at the customer's request, by an expert. The latter's expert opinion was also intended to protect a third party, namely the bank. It was open to the bank to rely on it for the purposes of obtaining compensation for the loss resulting from the errors made by the expert. In contrast to the position prevailing in the case a contract genuinely conferring a right on a third party, the third party did not have any direct right of action with regard to the performance of the contract. This new class of contract enabled the court to avoid having improper recourse to the concept of a stipulation for the benefit of a third party; it is instructive in that regard to compare the situation under French law. Moreover, it is clear from the German case-law that this category of contract should likewise be invoked with moderation. The class of persons covered cannot be enlarged *ad infinitum*.

BGH, 28 June 1979[110]   **1.G.48.**

Isolar glass

A guarantee given by a manufacturer of glass for houses is a contract for the benefit of the house-owner.

Facts: In 1969 the plaintiff gave an order to the G firm to carry out the glazing of his house. Thereupon the firm inserted "I-Glass" units which had been manufactured under licence by the defendant. The delivery took place on 9 October 1969 by way of the F Company, which had ordered the material from the defendant and taken delivery on 7 October 1969. In September 1974 the plaintiff detected condensation on a part of the inserted plate. At the end of October 1974 the defendant was notified of claims by the plaintiff. The defendant, in a letter of November 1974, asserted that the limitation period applicable to the warranty had already elapsed. When that letter reached the plaintiff by way of the G firm on 14 November 1974, he learnt for the first time that the defendant included in its publicity a declaration under the heading "warranty", which read, inter alia, as follows:

[110] BGHZ 75.75.

"The manufacturers of 'I-Glass' warrant—for five years from the date of the first delivery—that under normal conditions the transparency of 'I-Glass' will be vitiated neither by the formation of film nor by the deposit of dust in the space between the plates . . . This warranty creates an obligation only to replace the defective 'I-Glass' units . . . The group of European 'I' manufacturers . . . have established a warranty fund to insure quality and warranty. This fund serves to provide extraordinary insurance of the 'I' warranty and makes ultimately independent of local conditions and circumstances. The warranty fund therefore supports the warranty issued by each 'I-Glass' licensee . . ."

The plaintiff in his action begun in January sued the defendant on this producer's warranty. He at first demanded twelve substitute glass units. In May 1977, he had the plates he objected to changed and claimed compensation for the cost of the materials.

Held: The lower courts rejected the claim. On the plaintiff's application for review the Bundesgerichtshof set aside the appellate judgment and sent the case back for reconsideration for these.

Judgment: 1. The Court of Appeal is of opinion that no direct contractual relation came into being between the defendant manufacturer and the plaintiff as ultimate acquirer of the glass plates. Whether that is correct may be left undecided; for the judgment under review cannot be upheld because by virtue of a contract between the defendant and the F Company a warranty came into existence for the benefit of the plaintiff as ultimate acquirer (contract for the benefit of their parties).

(a) . . .

(b) . . . The defendant's warranty . . . attached on the date of the first delivery, namely that of the glass of the F Company. Thus it is obvious that the contractual intention of the defendant also relates back to that moment. That answers to the interest of the middleman, who acquires advantages for himself as well as from the creation of the warranty in favour of the ultimate acquirer. If, that is to say, one of the defects covered by the warranty occurs, he will be free from his own liability to the other party in so far as the manufacturer is responsible for the defect by virtue of his duty to perform the warranty. Accordingly everything speaks in favour of the F Company's intending to establish the warranty as early as possible, in order to assure itself of the indirect exemption from liability connected therewith and its independence of later contingencies (e.g. the question whether the ultimate acquirer had notice as a third party of the warranty). The fact that the warranty fund set up intended the liability assumed by the defendant to be "independent of local conditions and circumstances" does not stand in the way. That turn of phrase emphasizes the material security of the warranty, but says nothing about the person to whom the defendant intented to direct his offer to make good the warranty. The custom sought by the warranty is not put in doubt on the ground that it initially operated on the middlemen in their relations with the manufacturer, for the last middleman will as a rule indicate to the ultimate acquirer the advantages implied in the warranty, in order to obtain a customer.

(c) As the interests of all concerned speak in favour of creating the warranty at once by means of a contract for the benefit of third parties (§ 328 BGB), it must follow that the defendant and the F Company intended to enter into a contract of that kind. . .

That the person of that third party was not ascertained when they made the contract does not affect the result. For the contracting parties the identity of the future ultimate acquirer played (to start which) no role. The agreement that whoever should happen to be the ultimate acquirer should be the third party beneficiary was enough. That made him sufficiently ascertainable.

2. The plaintiff claimed in good time under the warranty offered by the contract for his benefit. It is true that the defendant learnt of the occurrence to which the warranty applied only after the limitation period had run out. Since the F Company had taken delivery of the glass plates from the defendant on 7 October 1969, the five-year limitation period had already run out when the defendant obtained on 28 October 1978 knowledge of the complaint. That, however, is of no significance since according to the clear wording of the warranty, the period referred to is the period within which the material damage envisaged must occur and not the period within which the claim must be made.

The only decisive factor therefore is that the defect appeared in September 1974—and so within the warranty period. That at that moment the plaintiff's claim against the G firm was already time-barred, because it was based on VOB/B standard contract is irrelevant (because it was valid "independent of local conditions and circumstances"), and therefore irrespective of the contractual arrangements of the ultimate acquirer with the glazier.

3. If the glass plates manufactured by the defendant turn out to have the defect alleged by the plaintiff (which must be taken for granted for present purposes), it should make no difference to the plaintiff's action that he no longer demands their replacement but compensation.

The defendant's warranty is intended to give greater effect to the claims for defects that the ultimate acquirer has against the person (the glazier) employed by him to do the work. The contract of warranty is, therefore, ancillary to a warranty arising from a contract for work and labour. In the present case the plaintiff's contract with the G firm was one of sale and work concerning non-fungible goods; for the glass plates had been prepared to fit the special dimensions of the windows-frames in the plaintiff's house. That the defendant's contract with the F Company is one of sale is irrelevant. The decisive factor is the economic function the warranty has to perform for the ultimate acquirer as third-party beneficiary.

The plaintiff was at liberty to remedy the defects himself—assumed to exist for the purposes of the present appeal—and to demand money compensation from the defendant.

4. The plaintiff's claim under the warranty is not statute-barred. As has already been explained, the warranty was intended to give greater effect to the ultimate acquirer's claim for defective delivery based on the contract of work against the builder carrying out his order. In accordance with that purpose the claim under the warranty becomes statute-barred at the same moment as the corresponding claim of the ultimate acquirer. Here the glazing of all the windows in a house amounts to a building contract. The limitation period for a contract of work is five years. Accordingly, claims under the warranty also are subject to a five-year limitation. That the plaintiff agreed with the G firm that standard conditions of VOB/B should apply makes no difference. The warranty here for the ultimate acquirer was to be "independent of the circumstances of the particular case". It was to give greater effect to his claims of the final acquirer under the warranty arising from the contract of work and therefore according to its sense and purpose should in no way be subject to the agreed curtailment of the limitation period applicable to a contract of work.

The defendant by his warranty agreed to be responsible for all defects appearing within the limitation period. Accordingly that period for claims under the warranty cannot be taken to run from the delivery, fixing or acceptance of the glass. The better view is that the sense and purpose of the warranty require it to begin only with the discovery of the defect (cf. also BGH, NJW 1979, 645). Otherwhise defects which were first detected towards the end of the warranty limitation period could in many cases not be successfully invoked before the limitation operated. That is precisely shown in the present case.

The plaintiff here detected the defect in September 1974—within five years from the delivery of the plates—the subject of the action started in January 1977. Thereby the limitation was interrupted in good time.

Note

The guarantee given by the manufacturer must benefit not only the builder but also the purchaser. The latter was entitled to demand not only replacement but also compensation. It is also instructive to note the way in which the BGH managed to circumvent the rules on limitation. This case clearly involved a contract conferring a right on a third party. German case-law has conjured up another means of enlarging the circle of contracting parties, by establishing, through judge-made law, a new class of contract, the contract offering protection to third parties (*Vertrag mit Schutzwirkung für Dritte*): this does not create any direct right in favour of a third party, but it allows persons in a very close relationship to one of the contracting parties to plead non-performance of the contract for the purposes of obtaining compensation.

As regards subcontracting, German law is similar to the other systems of law studied.

BGH, 13 December 1973[111]   **1.G.49.**

SUB-CONTRACTOR HAS NO CLAIM FOR PAYMENT BY EMPLOYER

Direct invoices

The fact that a contractor which has been directed to delegate certain work to a sub-contractor arranges that, in order to save VAT, the sub-contractor will invoice the employer directly, does not give the sub-contractor a right to be paid by the employer.

Facts: From 1956 to 1958 the plaintiff carried out infrastructure works for the construction of a motorway bridge. The defendant, BRD, entered into a contract for the building of this bridge with K subject to the proviso that K would forward the plans for the infrastructure works to the plaintiff for the account and on behalf of the defendant.

The defendant's order form to K dated 21 May 1956 fixed the total remuneration relating to the bridge construction at DM 5,691,661.30 which excluded the plaintiff's offer relating to infrastructure amounting to DM 2,728,621.50. On 24 August 1956 the plaintiff and K entered into an agreement for performance and settlement of the order for the bridge (internal contract). During the construction of the bridge the services which the plaintiff was liable to perform were altered in relation to those which were originally agreed, which were moreover contested from the point of view of their extent and the payment therefor. In addition, the construction period was exceeded.

The defendant paid the plaintiff's invoice in the amount of DM 3,689,077.25 but the parties were in dispute concerning the plaintiff's additional claim amounting to DM 300,000. The plaintiff brought proceedings for the payment of DM 300,000 together with interest. The defendant invoked the penal clauses and price clauses concluded by it and K. The plaintiff claimed not to be bound by those clauses.

Held: The Regional Court (LG) upheld the claim. On appeal the question also arose as to whether there were direct contractual relations as between the parties, as alleged by the plaintiff and denied by the defendant. The Higher Regional Court (OLG) dismissed the claim on the ground that there was no right of action against the owner. The appeal on a point of law was dismissed.

Judgment: The court of appeal considered that there was no contractual relationship between the parties to the proceedings. The defendant did not instruct the plaintiff in respect of the infrastructure works. Consequently, the plaintiff had no right of action to recover from the defendant. It intervened in the carrying out of the infrastructure works on the instructions of K and could recover from K. According to the appeal it was argued that the plaintiff was not a subcontractor but a secondary undertaking to K, the main undertaking, and that therefore there was a contractual relationship between the plaintiff and the defendant.

1—Transmission of the order by the defendant

It is for the plaintiff to prove that by the order of 7 May 1956 the defendant confirmed that the plaintiff was a secondary undertaking and not a subcontractor. Under the additional contract of 16 May 1956 the defendant gave instructions to K as the sole contractual partner, admittedly subject to the proviso that K would transmit the order to the plaintiff in order to carry out the infrastructure works. The account given of the facts highlights the fact that there is no contractual relationship between the parties to the proceedings.

[111] WM 1974.197.

K's request to the defendant to place the order for infrastructure works directly with the plaintiff in order to save VAT did not form part of the contract negotiations with the defendant. Moreover, in the contractual document of 21 May 1956, reference is made only to K, the contracting undertaking.

(a) The Higher Regional Court is not disregarding the difference between a secondary undertaking who acts on the direct orders of the owner to carry out a portion of the works, and the subcontractor who assists in the performance of the contract by the principal undertaking without there being any contractual relationship between him (the subcontractor) and the owner.

(b) In the appeal it is argued that the term main contractor used both by the defendant and by K means nothing else than the general contractor (as opposed to secondary) and thus covers not only a subcontracting relationship but also that of a secondary undertaking.

(c) K entrusted the works to the plaintiff on behalf of the defendant in order to avoid double liability to VAT. At the outset the defendant wished to contract and deal only with K as the contractor for the whole of the works.

2—Transmission of the order to the plaintiff

The court of appeal also considers that no contractual link was created subsequently between the parties. If K was in fact obliged to transmit instructions to the plaintiff on behalf of the defendant, no evidence has been adduced of a delegation of authority to that effect or of a subsequent ratification. Moreover, the 1959 negotiations with regard to possible set off do not enable the view to be taken that a contract was created.

The court of appeal could not infer the existence of a delegated authority solely on the basis of an act indicative of an intention to enter into contractual relations.

The saving in terms of VAT benefits K, the main contractor. That benefit derives from an internal contract entered into between the plaintiff and K. Thus, the plaintiff made out its invoices directly to the defendant which paid the plaintiff direct. Those methods of deduction and payment do not alter the contractual relationships and give rise to no direct contractual relationship.

The changes in the services to be performed under the contract stem from the fact that K delegated the infrastructure works to the plaintiff. The payments by the defendant to the plaintiff should not lead one to think that there is a contract between them but rather may be analysed as mere payments in favour of a third party on the instructions of the person with a right of action for payment.

3—Unjust enrichment

The Higher Regional Court dismissed the claim under that head. The plaintiff maintains that it carried out major and additional infrastructure works not provided for in the initial order. If those additional works were carried out in the absence of any contract with the defendant, then the defendant would have unjustly enriched itself. Those claims were to no avail.

If the plaintiff carried out additional work the beneficiary thereof is K and not the defendant. It provided services under the contract with K and therefore did not do so for no consideration. Payment for those services is a matter for its contractual partner K and not for the defendant.

The plaintiff mistook its defendant. On that ground its claims were dismissed.

Note

This was indeed a case of subcontracting and not of a secondary undertaking. The Court confirms that there is no contractual relationship between the owner and the subcontractor even if the former became directly involved in the contractual process. Also worthy of note is the fact that there was no recourse to the doctrine of unjust enrichment, consideration for the enrichment of the owner being the contract entered into with a third party, in this case the main contractor:

d) Comparative conclusion

A certain consensus may be discerned between the systems of law studied in favour of an extension of the contractual sphere to certain third parties involved in the contractual process either by the acceptance of more or less fictitious third-party provisions or by the creation of related concepts (contracts protecting third parties), or on pragmatic grounds. On the other hand, the problems arising from groups of contracts, which have been the subject of more recent studies, have given rise to rather hesitant or contradictory decisions, except as regards subcontracting. The boundary between contract and tort is a difficult one to draw, particularly as the interest in distinguishing between them may differ from one system of law to another.[112]

1.2.1.B. THE INTERESTS TO BE WEIGHED ON DECIDING WHETHER TO BRING AN ACTION IN CONTRACT OR IN TORT

Before we enumerate those interests—which it is not intended to study in depth at this stage—, the question arises whether one may choose between rights of action where the preconditions of both categories of remedy are met.

Concurrent liability (cumul or non-cumul)
Is there a possible option between the two rights of action when the preconditions of a right of action in tort and in contract are both met? French law speaks ambiguously of "*cumul*" or "*non-cumul*". There is no need to specify that there can be no right to double compensation. But each right of action may have its own advantages.

Without legislative backing but on the basis of settled case-law, French law—and, to a lesser extent, Belgian law—upholds the principle of non-overlapping. In the most recent decisions the principle is stated peremptorily.

Cass. civ. 1re, 11 January 1989 [113]   **1.F.50.**

NON-CUMUL

Dishonest insurance agent

The creditor of a contractual obligation cannot rely, as against the debtor of that obligation, on the rules of tortious liability, even where there is an interest in doing so.

Facts: An insured person brought an action against the insurance company and the local agent for payment for compensation which he alleged was payable to him under the law on insurances, but the court trying the case on its merits found the company liable on the basis of the principal's responsibility for the acts of its agent (who had mispropriated the funds), a tortious action based on Article 1384(5) of the Civil Code.

---

[112] On groups of contracts, a particular area of study in France, see Malaurie and Aynès, paras. 691 and 874.
[113] JCP 1989.II.21326 annotated by C. Larroumet.

Judgment: *On the second branch of the first appeal ground*: —Under Articles 1134 of the Civil Code and L. 114–1 of the law on insurance, the creditor of a contractual obligation cannot rely, as against the debtor of that obligation, on the rules of tortious liability, even where there is an interest in doing so; —Whereas Mr Bejottes was unable to obtain the compensation following two accidents causing physical injury to which he was entitled under the life and invalidity insurance policies which he had taken out with the insurance company La Protectrice; as Mr Bejottes therefore brought proceedings against the insurer and also against its local agent Mr Loustau who was criticised for not repaying to the insured the sums which he had received for that purpose from the company; —Whereas in ordering La Protectrice to pay the amounts claimed by Mr Bejottes whilst at the same time declaring the action for payment brought by him against the company on the basis of the insurance company under the insurance contracts to be time-barred under Article L114–1 of the insurance law, the judgment appealed against notes that the line of argument against the overlapping of contractual and tortious liability is inadequate since the claim against the insurer is also based on the tort commited by Mr Loustau, deemed to be an agent of the company, who is therefore liable under Article 1384(5) of the Civil Code; —Whereas in so deciding, whereas the fault imputed to Mr Loustau did not enable Mr Bejottes to bring an action against La Protectrice in conditions other than those afforded to him by the insurance contract, the cour d'appel infringed the above mentioned laws.

On those grounds the judgment given on 18 June 1986 between the parties by the Pau cour d'appel is set aside in that it ordered La Protectrice jointly and severally with Mr Loustau to pay to Mr Bejottes the principal sum of 50,160 Francs and 5,000 Francs under Article 700 of the new Code of Civil Procedure and the matter is referred to the Bordeaux cour d'appel for a fresh judgment.

Note

The principle is succinctly upheld: "the creditor of a contractual obligation cannot rely, as against the debtor of that obligation, on the rules of tortious liability even where there is an interest in doing so". Contract law therefore predominates. The rule is frequently criticized by French academic writers who accuse contractual law of imperialism. See, however, the conclusion.

A noteworthy development is however the creation of a third right of action, that is to say special liabilities which are neither contractual nor tortious. This applies to traffic accidents and also to product liability.[114]

Article 1 of the law of 5 July 1985 to improve the situation of victims of road traffic accidents and to accelerate compensation procedures provides.

Article 1
The provisions of this chapter shall apply, even where they are transported under a contract, to the victims of a road traffic accident involving a terrestrial motor vehicle together with trailers or semi-trailers, to the exclusion of railways and tramways circulating on their own tracks.

The fact that there is a transport contract does not alter the rules on compensation laid down by the law. The same phenomenon is observable for product liability, as provided for in the Council Directive of 25 July 1985. However, under Article 13 of the Directive "any rights which an injured person may have according to the rules of the law on contractual or non-contractual liability or a special liability system . . ."

[114] See Art. 1386–1 of the French Civil Code inserted by the law of 19 May 1988 adopted in pursuance of the EEC Directive of 25 July 1985.

German law and English law allow overlapping, that is to say the creditor may choose between an action in contract and an action in tort. German law provides an illustration of the general theory of competing claims (*Anspruchshaufung*), The two actions are said to be competing.

BGH, 9 May 1957[115]   **1.G.51.**

THEORY OF COMPETING CLAIMS

Stolen suitcase

Facts: On 19 April 1946 the applicant handed over a suitcase at the main station in W to the defendant for onward transmission to X. In addition to clothing the suitcase contained a collection of stamps and a ring. On registration the case was stolen by an employee known as P. The theft was one of a series of such thefts recorded at the station of W between February and September 1946, when P was employed..

A part of the value of the stolen stamps was reimbursed and a part in poor condition was returned. Under the railway regulations, the defendant merely paid the sum of 2,868 Reichsmarks (that is to say Rm 200/kg).

Judgment: . . . The applicant sought full and complete restitution of his loss, relying on the provisions on tortious liability (§§ 823 and 831). In his view the company had been careless in its choice of employee and had not adequately supervised him.

The defendant company considered that the provisions of the Commercial Code and of the Railway regulations precluded the application of the provisions of the Civil Code on its liability in tort. Moreover, it chose carefully and duly supervised the employee. Finally, the applicant's right to restitution must be precluded owing to the applicant's own fault.

The applicant demands payment of the sum of DM 2,100. By a decision of the Düsseldorf Higher Regional Court of 2 July 1953, the company was ordered to pay to the applicant the sum of DM 2,100 under § 831 BGB (vicarious liability in tort for the acts of an agent). An action brought by the applicant before the Regional Court was dismissed. His appeal to the Higher Regional Court was successful in part, to the extent of the amounts of RM 2,868 and DM 2,100.

Discussion

1—Rights of action which for the same facts have several legal bases duly coexist on an independent basis alongside one another. Where a particular set of facts is governed by a special provision, that rule prevails over the general rule contained in the Civil Code where what is at issue is a provision on liability having the same legal basis. Book 7 of the Commercial Code (HGB) and the Railway Regulations govern liability in regard to contracts for the carriage of goods. Thus, they exclude the provisions of civil law relating to contracts for services. However, where there is a gap in those provisions, the rules of the Civil Code on tortious liability are not excluded. Consequently, the applicant was entitled to full restitution in respect of his losses under §§ 823 and 831.

2—This is a case of genuine competition between contractual and tortious claims where a contractual breach and an unlawful act coexist side by side. Whereas the law of torts covers breaches of the law and creates general legal obligations backed up by an obligation to pay damages, contract law concerns the specific obligations of two parties who, on the basis of their consensus ad idem, entered into a contract and with it obligations, and in respect of which a breach of contract will be visited by the legal consequences thus provided for.

According to the law of torts, a breach of the law entails an obligation (namely the obligation to afford compensation) only when it occurs whereas in contractual matters a pre-existing obligation

[115] BGHZ 24.189.

69

is transformed, in the event of its breach, into an obligation to afford restitution. When an act or an act or omission of negligence infringes both a general legal obligation and a contractual obligation, the provisions concerning tortious and contractual liability must both be considered in determining the legal consequences. Both give rise to claims for damages, but the conditions of their implementation, their content and realisation are distinct and subject to distinct sets of legal rules.

Note

The court confirms, though this point was not argued, that the two rights of action co-exist. In the present case it was more worthwhile to bring an action in tort given the limitation on damages which an action in contract would come up against.

And now another example, this time concerning the time-limit for bringing an action.

BGH, 24 May 1976[116]   **1.G.52.**

COMPETING PRESCRIPTION PERIODS

Wrong kind of anti-freeze

Where there were competing claims, one of which is now barred, the plaintiff may still claim on the other.

Facts: The applicant owns a transport company. Amongst his vehicles he possesses type SV lorries for which the manufacturer recommends the use of anti-freeze products. Thus, on 24 September 1969, the applicant orders through the intermediary of X 200 litres of anti-freeze. He maintains that X assured him that the product was suitable for lorries. However, the product supplied caused damage to the engines of four of the lorries, entailing expenditure of DM 12,990.45

Judgment: Following negotiations, the defendant on 27 July 1972 refused to afford restitution in respect of the damage. Accordingly, the applicant brought proceedings against the defendant for payment of the sum of DM 12,990.45, together with interest.

The defendant contends that the product was vitiated ab initio, that X made a mistake and finally that the obligation to give notice of the defect is not only time-barred but was also not observed. The lower courts dismissed the application, taking the view that it was time-barred. An appeal against that dismissal was upheld.

It is common ground between the parties that the claim for compensation is time-barred to the extent to which it is founded on the contract of sale. Such claim is subject to the short prescription period contained in § 477(I).

The question to be resolved is whether the short prescription period contained in § 477(I) in the case of actions for compensation based on a contract of sale impinges on the right to compensation at tort, thus supplanting § 852, where on the facts there is a cause of action in tort and in contract.

The appeal court chose to extend the shortened prescription period to actions in tort. The Federal Supreme Court rejects this solution and follows the majority view which is that claims for damages and interest based on a breach of contract and on tort are genuinely two competing rights of action. Where an event constitutes both a breach of contract and a tort, there is a right of action in both contract and tort. Each right of action must observe its own implementing conditions and is subject to its own rules on prescription.

---

[116] BGHZ 66.315.

Note

Here again, the action in tort is more beneficial owing to the short period for bringing an action based on the contract. It is to be noted that the rule allows the disappointed creditor to choose between the two causes of action. Each action has its own rules. However, German law gives pre-eminence to the contractual right of action by refusing to allow the action in tort to be availed of in order openly to circumvent the contract, for example where contractual liability has been formally excluded—for example in the case of a serious fault. But that does not affect exemptions which are not typically contractual.[117]

Where the buyer may claim damages and interest for defects in the item sold on the basis of a positive breach of contract (*positive Vertragsverletzung*) and on the basis of tort, the action in tort is time-barred after three years, irrespective of the rules applicable to actions in based on § 477 BGB—six-month prescription period for an action on a warranty.

In English law there might appear to be a certain amount of vagueness, certainly if one compares the dicta of Lord Scarman in *Tai Hing Cotton Mill Ltd* v. *Liu Chong Hing Bank Ltd*[118] with the peremptory assertion of Oliver J in *Midland Bank & Trust Co Ltd* v. *Hett, Stubb & Kemp (a firm)*.[119] Lord Scarman said:[120]

. . . Their Lordships do not believe that there is anything to the advantage of the law development in searching for a liability in tort where the parties are in a contractual relationship. This is particularly so in a commercial relationship. Though it is possible as a matter of legal semantics to conduct an analysis of the rights and duties inherent in some contractual relationships including that of banker and customer either as a matter contract law when the question will be what, if any, terms are to be implied, or as a matter of tort law when the task will be to identify a duty arising from the proximity and character of the relationship between the parties, their Lordships believe it to be correct in principle and necessary for the avoidance of confusion in the law to adhere to the contractual analysis on principle because it is a relationship in which the parties have, subject to a few exceptions, the right to determine their obligations to each other, and for the avoidance of confusion because different consequences do follow according to whether liability arises from contract or tort, eg in the limitation of action.

In contrast, Oliver J said:

There is not and never has been any rule of law that a person having alternative claim must frame his action in one or the other. If I have a contract with my dentist to extract tooth, I am not thereby precluded from suing him in tort if he negligently shatters my jaw.[121]

However in the important case of *Henderson* v. *Merrett Syndicates Ltd*[122] the House of Lords distinguished the *Tai Hing* case as dealing not with concurrent liability but with the separate question whether, as between contracting parties, "a tortious duty of care could be established which was more extensive than that which was provided for in the relevant contract".[123] The House held that where the duty in contract and the alleged duty of care

---

[117] See BGH, 20 November 1984, BGHZ 92.23.
[118] [1985] 2 All ER 947.
[119] [1978] 3 All ER 571.
[120] *Ibid.*, at 957.
[121] *Edwards* v. *Mallan* [1908] 1 KB 1002.
[122] [1994] 3 All ER 506.
[123] Per Lord Goff, *ibid.*, at 526.

in tort to avoid causing economic loss were the same, there would be concurrent liability. After an extensive discussion of the cases, Lord Goff—with whom all other members of the House agreed—said:[124]

My own belief is that, in the present context, the common law is not antipathetic to concurrent liability, and that there is no sound basis for a rule which automatically restricts the claimant to either a tortious or a contractual remedy. The result may be untidy; but, given that the tortious remedy is imposed by the general law, and the contractual duty is attributable to the will of the parties, I do not find it objectionable that the claimant may be entitled to take advantage of the remedy which is most advantageous to him, subject only to ascertaining whether the tortious duty is so inconsistent with the applicable contract that, in accordance with ordinary principle, the parties must be taken to have agreed that the tortious remedy is to be limited or excluded.

Note
The result was that investors were permitted to sue their managing agents in tort when actions against the managers for breach of contract would have been barred by limitation. In an analogous case French law would allow full recovery but would limit it to foreseeable damage (Article 1150 of the Civil Code) if the action is in contract. And there would be no choice.

The interests at issue
These are rather variable since the rules on tort differ considerably from the the rules on contract. That is frequently the case as regards prescription, whether that is a period laid down by law or contractually agreed. Also worthy of note is the contrast in French law between the short period allowed for a contractual action on a warranty for latent defects (Article 1648 of the Civil Code) and the prescription period of ten years for actions in tort (Article 2270(1) of the Civil Code).[125]

Also to be considered is the application of exemption clauses. An issue may be the question of the validity of these clauses in matters of tort: that is true of French law which declares such clauses to be null and void (but not of Belgian law).

Cass. civ. 2e, 17 February 1955[126]   **1.F.53.**

VALIDITY OF EXEMPTION CLAUSES

Fire spreads to warehouse

Clause cannot exclude liability which, were action brought in tort, could not be excluded.

Facts: By a contract dated 1 July 1945 SNCF let to Lafond a warehouse at Lyon station. It was stipulated that the lessee undertook to assume all the risks to which any items or goods stored in the warehouse might be exposed and also to guarantee SNCF against any judgments against it. On 6 August 1948 a container wagon of fuel caught fire close to the warehouse. The fire spread to the warehouse and to the goods stored there.

Judgement: THE COURT:—Whereas it is pleaded on appeal that the contested judgment was wrong to uphold the claim by the insurance company against SNCF for repayment of the amounts paid

---

[124] *Ibid.*, at 532–3.
[125] For the position in German law see cases *supra* at 69–70.
[126] **D.1596.17**, annotated by P. Esmein.

by SNCF to Lafond, and to have declared null and void the abovementioned clauses, even though an exemption clause is valid, even in the event of tortious liability, provided that it is not a serious fault equivalent to fraud, which is not so in this case.

—Whereas the warranty clause is distinct from that of an exemption clause, nullity of the latter clause could not, where the law was silent, entail nullity of the former;

—Whereas clauses exempting or restricting liability in matters of tort are null and void. Articles 1382 and 11383 of the Civil Code are a matter of public policy and their application cannot be neutralised in advance by way of agreement;

—Whereas the court properly considered that the two clauses inserted in the same article of the lease agreement "could not arbitrarily be separated."

—Whereas the terms employed "clearly showed assimilation as between abandonment of any action and liability on the warranty, the latter appearing to emphasise the former and the nullity affecting abandonment in regard to the current dispute also entails nullity of the warranty";

—Whereas it follows that the pleas on appeal are unfounded.

On those grounds the appeal is dismissed.

Note

The justification given, namely the mandatory nature of Articles 1382 and 1383, is frequently criticized, especially as the courts sometimes uphold clauses limited to the application of Articles 1384 *et seq.* dealing with liability for products and the acts of other persons. In order to justify different treatment of contractual and tortious clauses it has been observed that the commission of a tort is of general application whereas non-performance of a contract is dependent on the scope of the undertaking voluntarily entered into. The doctrinal discussion continues; the courts, however, remain consistent.

In English law a clause may exclude liability in contract and in tort (subject of course to the various statutory restrictions).[127] A question of interpretation arises: does the clause relate to both rights of action or to one of them only and, if so, to which one?

Subject to the statutory restrictions mentioned, it is possible to exclude liability for tort, for example liability in negligence, as well as liability for breach of contract. However, to exclude liability for negligence clear words must be used. For example in *White* v. *John Warwick & Co Ltd*,[128] a contract for the hire of a bicycle provided that "Nothing in this agreement shall render the owners liable for any personal injuries . . .". The plaintiff was thrown from the bicycle and injured when the saddle tilted as he was riding it. This was due to negligent maintenance of the bicycle by the defendants. The Court of Appeal held that the defendants were liable for negligence; the clause quoted excluded any liability for injuries caused by a breach of contract, but they were also under a duty in tort to take reasonable care and the clause did not cover that.

White v. *John Warwick* was a case in which, but for the clause, there would have been both liability in tort for negligence and strict liability for breach of contract. Some thought that this meant that if there was only a duty to take care—whether in tort or contract—, a similar clause must exclude all liability as otherwise it would be of no effect. However in *Hollier* v. *Rambler Motors (AMC) Ltd*[129] a garage which took the plaintiff's

---

[127] See *infra*, at 515.
[128] [1953] 2 All ER 1021.
[129] [1972] 1 All ER 399.

car for servicing negligently allowed it to be destroyed by fire. A clause in its standard conditions provided that "The company is not liable for damage caused to customers' cars on the premises". It argued that as its only duty was to take reasonable care of the car, this clause must be effective to exclude that duty, otherwise it would have no effect. The Court of Appeal disagreed: a reasonable customer might interpret the clause as a warning that the company would not be liable for fires which started by accident. To exclude liability it thus may be necessary either to refer to negligence expressly or to use some synonym such as "damage howsoever caused".

It has also been pointed out that duplication of rights of action or non-duplication is significant in English law for the purposes of calculating damages.[130]

In conclusion, pretty clear divergences may be discerned as regards the way the relationship between rights of action in contract and rights of action in tort is to be handled, whether the one excludes the other or whether they may be combined. The uncertainty of the dividing line is essentially due to uncertainty as to the very concept of contract.

The original views of B. Rudden may assist in guiding the discussion.

Rudden, in Contract Law Today[131]   **1.E.54.**

6. As a working hypothesis, we are treating contract as something which (a) changes legal relations and (b) creates one or more legal (and usually enforceable) obligations. Thus UCC, section 1–201, says "contract means the total obligation in law which results from the parties' agreement . . .". The Code civil, article 1101, appears to take a similar view: "contract is an agreement by which one or more persons bind themselves (s'obligent) to one or more others . . .". The Common Law, however, applies the requirement of both agreement and obligation quite strictly, and excludes the instant gift from the domain of contract since, although technically it requires acceptance to be complete, and alters legal relations, it creates no obligations. By contrast a long French tradition treats the don manuel as contract, focusing on the requirement of agreement (since the donee must accept) and ignoring the absence of obligation. This is not to say that the Common Law is hostile to gifts: once they are made it simply leaves them alone and, indeed, is much less likely than the Civil Law to revoke them on the grounds of the donee's ingratitude or in order to protect the donor's heirs (his creditors are an different matter). Furthermore, the system has a large section—the law of trusts—dealing with non-instantaneous gifts.

Because of this lack of obligation—or, looking typically from a remedial point of view, because there are no promises for the law to enforce—some recent US doctrine would not classify the cash sale within the domain of contract, although it is suggested that the author's explanation for the persistence of obligations as to title and quality as being "of a promissory character" is less than satisfactory.

7. Torts also change legal relations and create an obligation. The latter may well overlap with an obligation whose source is contract (or statute) and indeed there are those like Atiyah and Gilmore who aver that the law of tort is taking over the domain of contract. It is submitted, none the less, that there are certain obvious features by which the heartland of contract may still usefully be marked off.

---

[130] See *supra*, at 49 ff. the uncertainties in regard to restitution for economic loss and, in France, as regards the limitation of damages to foreseeable damage, see D. Harris and D. Tallon (eds.), *Contract Law Today: Anglo-French Comparisons* (Oxford: Clarendon, 1989), at 275 ff., paras. 23–25, for a comparison between English law and French law.

[131] D. Harris and D. Tallon (eds.), *Contract Law Today: Anglo-French Comparisons* (Oxford: Clarendon, 1989), at 83–84.

8. The first is so simple that it would be embarrassing to mention were is not for the fact that much of our law is simply a deduction from it: torts are bad things, contracts are good. The second is that contracts almost never come singly. The conclusion of any given contract is made possible only by the scores, or even hundreds, of contracts which lie behind it (hereafter called "upstream contracts"). Any two people can make a contract of sale of a pencil; no two people can make a pencil. Atiyah maintains that "the wholly executory contract is a legal peculiarity" and that "wholly executory contracts are rarer, more ephemeral in practice, and somewhat less binding than the classical model of Contract would suggest". But surely the main point of the division of labour is to allow some to concentrate on the production of goods for the future while others supply for current consumption. Adam Smith uses bows and arrows as an example of the first, and version for the second, and says:

> "As it is by treaty, by barter, and by purchase, that we obtain from one another the greater part of those mutual good offices which we stand in need of, so it is this same trucking disposition which originally gives occasion to the division of labour."

The more advanced an economy, the more of its assets consist of "work in progress"—capital equipment being constructed, raw material being worked up, and so on. Economists estimate that only about 20 per cent of total sales in Western countries are to the final consumer. Much of the investment capital needed for this upstream activity is raised on the stock market by countless contracts of sale, loan, and guarantee, many of which are never "performed" at all.

9. The third feature is that people have the choice whether or not to assume a particular contractual obligation. It will be objected that life may force us to contract; but even the pauper whose last pence go on bread is choosing not to buy cheese. On the supply side, since there is not enough of anything to satisfy every competing wish, we must choose which wish matters most. The science of economics studies choice, the law of contract embodies and enforces it. In the absence of initial ordering (by central Plan) of the relative importance of wishes, the market provides the mechanism by which no wish comes true at the cost of withdrawing more means (which could fulfil other wishes) than are needed to satisfy it.

10. The fourth feature is that, above all in upstream contracts, there is the possibility of pre-contractual negotiation in which each party may, however reluctantly, yield one thing in order to gain something which he value more: there is scope for trade-offs. The fifth is that (within limits) not merely the source but the content of the obligation is the wills (or, as the common law puts it, the promises) of the parties. The sixth is that, whereas tort law typically compensates losses caused by actions, contract law shelters expectations against inaction. If A sues B for painting A's door, his action could lie in trespass; but if A sues B for not painting his door, it is contract or nothing. If he wins in the first example he will be put—as far as money can do it—in the position he would have been if his door had not been painted; if he wins in the second example he will be put, financially, in the position he would have been in if it had. Tort law is retrospective and restorative, contract law prospective and productive. Expectations are realized, not just for their own sake, but because of all the downstream deals which depend on the sanctity of the upstream contracts as signalled by their prices. Certainly there is, at the boundaries, a blurring of categories: if a loss has been sustained the overlap may be with tort; if a benefit conferred, restitution. If, however, the only claim is that, because of inaction, an expectation has not been fulfilled, it is contract which creates the protection.

11. Furthermore, the protection supplied by the law of contract then becomes property. This may be seen in two ways.

(a) Firstly, where a forward sale is made, the seller's obligation in the hands of the buyer may immediately be traded on the commodity markets; similarly, the buyer's obligation may be discounted on the money market. The parties' expectations are not protected because they have sold them ("reliance"); if this were the case, the result would be that a party who had done so (a merchant) would be safe (but, since his buyer would be selling him protection, the price would reflect this), whereas one who had not sold, but had merely relied in this heart on performance of the obligation in order to satisfy his needs in specie, would be worse off. So the entitlements traded in the commodity and money markets are merchantable because they are safe,—the other way round. A striking example of dealings in wholly unperformed obligations is the rapidly growing market in "traded options".

(b) Secondly, the expectation enshrined in a contract for future performance is an entitlement which (via the law of tort) is immediately protected against (or "opposable to") those stangers who matter—rivals. In contracts for personal services, for instance, theatrical production are planned months or years ahead. As soon as an artist is engaged, however, rival managers either may be enjoined from enticing him or her away or be liable for damages. Once the contract is concluded, the creditor's entitlement, together with (often, but not necessarily) his investment in there project, is treated like a piece of property marked with the sign "No Trespassing". It is this which goes some way to explain how the law overcomes, almost unconsciously, the causation problem, holding that, although the immediate cause of the creditor's loss is the deliberate, willed act of the artist, yet a third person—the "trespassing" rival—may be ordered to compensate.

12. From the above, it seems that we may deduce one function peculiar to the law of contract: it handles the creation of wealth. The laws of gift and trust deal with its mere transfer; the rest of the law of property protects entitlements and confers upon their owner certain powers, but then leaves him alone. The law of tort does not (or did not) create wealth either: its aim is to restore the status quo ante. But when a contract is freely made, each party is—in his own opinion—better off. As the Austrian economist Ludwig van Mises put it:

> "An inveterate fallacy asserts that things and services exchanged are of equal value. Now we must realise that valuing means to prefer a to b. The basis of modern economics is the cognition that it is precisely the disparity in the value attached to the objects exchanged that results in their being exchanged. People buy and sell only because they appraise the thing they give up less than those received."

These remarks are not shared by all authors in an area which is evolving. Nevertheless they provoke interesting comparative thinking. It is worth noting the analysis of the gift, the inclusion of the theory of contract in the wider one of obligation—a rare analysis in common law, the idea that tort liability is retroactive and compensating, contract being prospective and "productive". The contact is indeed an asset producer, which is another theory deserving of discussion, as well as the relations between contract and property.

1.2.2. CONTRACT AND RESTITUTION (QUASI-CONTRACT)

It is now time to delimit the sphere of contract from that of a third source of obligations, that is to say quasi-contract—according to the terminology inherited from the Romanists—or restitution, as it is frequently referred to in English terminology, since quasi-contracts generally give rise to liability to afford restitution of an item unjustly obtained.

Nevertheless, these two expressions are somewhat ambiguous when examined from the standpoint of a comparative lawyer. They may occasionally pose in the guise of false friends: quasi-contracts are not always akin to contracts. And a contract may give rise to liability in restitution, such as contracts involving the restitution of property (*contrat réel*); the same applies in the case of bailment.[132] It will be helpful therefore to form an overall view of the notion of quasi-contract or restitution prior to contrasting it with that of contract.

The notion of quasi-contract and restitution

Here again, Roman law is in certain respects in opposition with the Common law.

a) Roman-law countries

The quasi-contract is regarded as a source of obligations, namely the obligation to afford restitution of an item of value unduly obtained. It is in that light that the French Civil Code presents the matter, albeit incompletely.

Code civil	**I.F.55.**

Article 1371: Quasi-contracts are the purely voluntary acts of a person resulting in liability of some kind towards a third party, and sometimes in reciprocal liability on the part of both parties.

This provision opens the first chapter concerning quasi-contracts, together with torts and quasi-torts, in Title IV of Book III: Commitments arising outside contract. This is followed by rules governing *gestion d'affaires* (Articles 1372–1375) and repayment of sums unduly paid (Articles 1376–1381). Based on these provisions, the courts have elaborated a third more general quasi-contractual doctrine, namely unjust enrichment, first enunciated in the landmark *Patureau* judgment[133] and underpinned by "an equitable principle which prohibits a person from enriching himself to another's detriment". Subsequent decisions have refined the conditions under which a right of action *in rem verso* might arise.

The trilogy of *gestion d'affaires*, recovery of sums wrongly paid and unjustified enrichment is to be found in the most up-to-date codes, but with a different presentation and localisation. Thus, the German code devotes Title 24 of Book II (§§ 812–822) to unjust enrichment, which includes recovery of sums wrongly paid, and deals with *gestion d'affaires* (§ 679 et seq.). The major role played by unjust enrichment is also known, owing to the principle of separability.

See in particular **1.G.26** and **1.G.27**, section I above.

German BGB	**1.G.56.**

§ 812: (1) A person who, through an act performed by another, or in any other manner, acquires something at the expense of the latter without any legal ground, is bound to return it to him. This obligation subsists even if the legal ground subsequently disappears or the result intended to be produced by an act to be performed pursuant to the legal transaction is not produced.
(2) Recognition of the existence or non-existence of a debt, if made under a contract, is also deemed to be an act of performance.

---

[132] See *supra*, at 34.
[133] *Cass. 15 June 1892, S.1893.1.281, annotated by Labbé.*

Just like the BGB, neither the Italian Civil Code nor the Netherlands Civil Code (BW) uses the concept of quasi-contract. The former devotes a title to each of the three quasi-contracts, the latter in Title 4 to Book 6: "Obligations arising from sources other than unlawful act or contract" governs them in three sections (Articles 198–212).

BW **1.NL.57.**

Article 6: 212: 1. A person who has been unjustifiably enriched at the expense of another must, to the extent this is reasonable, make reparation for the damage suffered by that other person up to the amount of his enrichment.
2. A decrease in the enrichment is not taken into consideration to the extent that it results from a cause which cannot be imputed to the enriched person.
3. A decrease in the enrichment during the period in which the enriched person did not reasonably have to foresee the existence of an obligation to make reparation for damage, is not imputed to him. In determining this decrease, the expenses which would not have been made had there been no enrichment, are also taken into account.

It appears that unjust enrichment constitutes the essential feature, not to say the sole justification, of quasi-contracts. It is therefore instructive to compare the definitions given in the codes and the case-law.[134]

b) English law

English law is vaguer and more ambiguous in its terminology; It speaks both of quasi-contract and of restitution, but does not always accord the same meaning to those terms.
 At the outset it may be noted that English law is unfamiliar with the trilogy known to Romanists: *gestion d'affaires* does not exist as a distinct concept, for fear of untimely intervention by third parties in the business of other persons.[135]
 Moreover it is difficult to determine with accuracy the relationship between restitution and quasi-contract. Thus, Beale, Bishop and Furmston speak of "restitutionary—or quasi-contractual—liability" as if they were one and the same thing,[136] whereas Treitel deals with unjust enrichment in relation to non-performance,[137] with recovery of money paid in connection with termination of contract for non-performance, and *quantum meruit* actions in the case of services unjustly obtained. Also, unjust enrichment is encountered as including repayment of sums wrongly paid in a chapter on restitution. For his part, G. Samuel[138] devotes one section to quasi-contracts and another to unjust enrichment. In *Orakpo* v. *Manson Investments Ltd* [1978] AC 95 Lord Diplock said:

. . . My Lords, there is no general doctrine of unjust enrichment recognised in English law. What it does is to provide specific remedies in particular cases of what might be classified as unjust

---

[134] See, for French law, *infra*, at 79–81.
[135] See S. L. Stoljar, *International Encyclopedia of Comparative Law*, Vol. X, Chap. 17: *Negotiorum Gestio*, 1987.
[136] BBF3, at 39.
[137] Treitel, *Contract*, at 714.
[138] G. Samuel, *Law of Obligations and Legal Remedies* (London: Cavendish, 1995), at 103 and 410.

enrichment in a legal system that is based on the civil law. There are some circumstances in which the remedy takes the form of "subrogation", but this expression embraces more than a single concept in English law. It is a convenient way of describing a transfer of rights from one person to another, without assignment or assent of the person from whom the rights are transferred and which takes place by operation of law in a whole variety of widely different circumstances. Some rights by subrogation are contractual in their origin, as in the case of contracts of insurance. Others, such as the right of an innocent lender to recover form a company moneys borrowed *ultra vires* to the extent that these have been expended on discharging the company's lawful debts, are in no way based on contract and appear to defeat classification except as an empirical remedy to prevent a particular kind of unjust enrichment.

This opinion is not exactly on all fours with doctrinal views. The link he makes between subrogation and unjust enrichment should be noted. These pointers would appear necessary for the purpose of discerning the relationship between contract and quasi-contract or restitution.

However, it has been claimed that the later decision of the House of Lords in *Lipkin Gorman* v. *Karpnale Ltd*[139] shows that a principle against unjust enrichment has been recognised by English law: "not only did their Lordships use the language of unjust enrichment but, more specifically, the defence of change of position was accepted for the first time and that defence can only be rationalised through unjust enrichment reasoning".[140]

Contract and quasi-contracts or restitution

Apart from terminological and conceptual difficulties, there is one point in common: quasi-contract exists where there is no contract or there is no longer any contract. *Gestion d'affaires* presupposes that there is no valid agency relationship between principal and putative agent; in the case of recovery of sums wrongly paid the payment must of course have been in error, that is to say that there was no contract to justify the alleged wrong payment. As regards unjust enrichment the contract may be the cause of one party enriching himself and the other party impoverishing himself.

French law speaks on the one hand of an absence of cause and on the other of subsidiarity.

Cass. civ., 28 February 1939[141]   **1.F.58.**

ABSENCE OF CAUSE

Lingerie not paid for

There is no unjust enrichment when the defendant has received no more than it was entitled to under a contract with another party even if the amount received has been increased by the other party's use of the plaintiff's property for which the latter was never paid.

---

[139] [1991] 2 AC 548.

[140] A. Burrows and E. McKendrick, *Cases and Materials on the Law of Resitution* (Oxford: Clarendon, 1997), at 39. These authors provide extracts and an extensive discussion on the competing views on the question to which English recognizes a general principle of restitution.

[141] DP.1940.1.5, annotated by G. Ripert.

Judgment: THE COURT: *On the first branch of the sole appeal ground*:—Under Article 1235 of the Civil Code, there is no unjust enrichment where the enrichment is derived from a legal act which legitimates it;

—Whereas it is clear from the grounds of the contested judgment that the undertaking, Lutetia, which is the owner of two trading businesses, entrusted the unimpeded running of them to the Noël couple; as under the terms of the agreements entered into by the parties, the equipment used in the businesses was to form part of the businesses and, at the end of the period of management, was to be returned complete and in good condition to Lutetia; as also, a certain Dambrin had supplied goods (lingerie) to the couple which had not been paid for and sought payment from Lutetia;

—Whereas the lower court upheld Dambrin's claim on the ground that the lingerie supplied by him had enabled the couple not only to build up the clientele and to ensure the operation and continuation of the businesses, but at the same time to supplement and enhance the equipment used in the respective businesses which, pursuant to the abovementioned agreements, was to be returned to Lutetia.

—Whereas that undertaking thus obtained without just cause from Dambrin an item of value which became part of its assets and was ordered to make restitution to Dambrin in the amount by which it had enriched itself.

—Whereas however in upholding Dambrin's personal and direct right of action against Lutetia, the court below merely stated that the defendant became richer without lawful cause', without giving an explanation, as it ought to have done, concerning the factual or legal grounds on which it declined to regard the provisions of the management agreement as affording justification in law capable of being set up as against third parties and legitimising the enrichment which in its view Lutetia had obtained;

—Whereas by so holding, the judgment appealed against failed to give proper legal grounds for its decision.

On those grounds, the Cour de cassation sets aside the judgment of the court below.

Note

Justification for enrichment is to be found in a contract entered into with a third party, in this case the clause in the letting agreement in respect of the business stating that the merchandise is to revert to the owner at the end of the contract. No matter that the supplier has gone unpaid, the enrichment of the owner is not unlawful. It has a legal justification which is for these purposes deemed to be the source of the enrichment. It is to be noted that this condition was not required in the first judgments recognizing unjustified enrichment, in particular in the *Patureau* judgment.

It is obvious that, in the case of a contract entered into between the person enriched and the person impoverished, the latter, unless there is serious injury or excessive advantage accruing, cannot plead unjust enrichment in order to go back on the contract and demand an additional price.

Cass. civ., 2 March 1915[142]   **1.F.59.**

ACTION IN REM VERSO ONLY WHERE NO LEGITMATE CAUSE

Work on baths

An action in rem verso can be allowed only where a person's assets have been increased without legitimate cause to the detriment of another person's assets.

Facts: The town of Bagnères had granted to a certain Mr Bréchoire the right to operate its thermal establishments and casino. It then authorized him at his own risk to carry out conversion and repair work for the payment of which it voted a lump sum of 160,000 francs. The works were carried out by various undertakings including by a certain Mr Brianhaut. The estimates were exceeded and Mr Bréchoire was deprived of his concession and Mr Brianhaut, to whom he owed money, claimed from the town the price of the additional work. On 24 February 1910 the Court of Pau upheld his claim under the principle that a person may not enrich himself at another's expense and appointed experts to determine the amount by which the town had benefited from the works in question. The town of Bagnères appealed.

Judgment: THE COURT: . . .—Whereas the town of Bagnères under the contract between it and Mr Bréchoire limited to a lump sum figure the liabilities which it was to assume in respect of the works to be carried out in the buildings belonging to it; as by dealing direct and in his own name with the undertakings, Mr Bréchoire was unable to impose higher charges on it. In order to recover his debt, Mr Brianhaut could take action not only against Mr Bréchoire with whom he had dealt but also against the town by exercising the latter's [Bréchoire's] rights under Article 1166 of the Civil Code. —Whereas an action *in rem verso* can be allowed only where a person's assets have been increased without legitimate cause to the detriment of another person's assets, and no action lies in favour of that other person under a contract, a quasi-contract, a tort or quasi-tort, in order to allow recovery of what is owed to that person.—Whereas such an action cannot be used in order to circumvent the rules under which the law has expressly defined the effects of a given contract, nor therefore by an undertaking in order to disguise a claim for an additional price which is prohibited by Article 1793 of the Civil Code in the case of a lump-sum bargain; —Whereas in deciding the case contrary to this provision, the judgment appealed against infringed that article by declining to apply it.

On those grounds the Cour de cassation sets aside the judgment of the lower court.

Note

This judgment sets out what may be termed the ancillary nature of the action *in rem verso* which may be availed of only where the impoverished person has no other right of action in contract or in tort. This right of action must be prevented from superseding other rules of law and taking over the whole area. The subsidiarity rule means that the action *in rem verso* is precluded where the person impoverished has available to him as against the person enriched or against a third party other means, even where the means afforded are ineffective owing to prescription, loss of rights or other bar or legal obstacle. Where there is a factual impediment, on the other hand, such as insolvency of the third party through whose intermediary the enrichment occurred, the action lies if the insolvency can be proven.

In German law as well, the contract may constitute the legal justification of the enrichment and thus debar the action. In that case, the contract in fact constitutes the legal ground justifying the enrichment (§ 812, 1, BGB).

[142] DP.1920.1.102.

OLG Hamm, 9 January 1974[143]   **1.G.60.**

<small>CONTRACT CONSTITUTES LEGAL GROUND JUSTIFIYING ENRICHMENT</small>

Car repairs ordered by husband of owner

A car owner is not unjustly enriched by repairs to her car which she did not order but which were ordered by her now-bankrupt husband.

Judgment: The applicant was the owner of a car repair workshop. The defendant was the owner of a Ford vehicle. The applicant claimed payment of the balance due for repairs carried out on the defendant's car.

On 1 August 1970, following an accident, the defendant's husband towed the vehicle to the applicant's garage and continued his journey to Denmark. From Denmark he sent a letter dated 3 August 1970 to confirm the request for repairs to be carried out. He also informed the applicant that he would pay by a cheque drawn on the savings bank of the town X. He asked the applicant to contact that bank and said he would come back for his car on 8 August 1970.

The applicant therefore went ahead and ordered spare parts and, on starting the repairs, he found that the damage to the vehicle was greater than at first thought.

On 3 September 1970 the defendant and her husband collected the vehicle which had been repaired. No invoice had been prepared as the applicant's computerised system had gone down. Nevertheless, the vehicle was handed over against payment of DM 2,000 (DM 500 in cash and DM 1,500 by cheque).

On 4 September 1970 the applicant sent the defendant an invoice for DM 4,765.15. The defendant asked for time to study the invoice. Following an exchange of correspondence the defendant alleged that she had not given her consent to the repairs. As she was refusing to pay, the applicant proceeded against the defendant's husband for payment of the amount remaining outstanding, namely DM 2,765.15.

Since the letter before action elicited no positive outcome, the applicant sued the husband in the Hamburg Regional Court. By a default judgment dated 29 March 1971 he was ordered to pay the sum of DM 2,765.15.

However, execution proved fruitless since the husband had neither liquid assets nor mortgageable property. Accordingly, the applicant once again demanded payment from the defendant of the sum remaining outstanding and brought proceedings on the debt.

The Regional Court ordered the defendant to pay the sum of DM 500 and dismissed the remainder of the applicant's claim. Both parties appealed against the decision. The applicant's appeal was dismissed whereas the defendant's appeal was allowed.

Discussion
I—The applicant has no right of action on the debt against the defendant.

(1) Absence of contractual relationship between the parties
Since the defendant's husband did not act as his wife's representative, there could be no ratification of the contract entered into between him and the applicant. The mere indication of the name of a third party on a registration document is not sufficient in order to establish agency.

The defendant did not acknowledge the debt.

(2) No action based on management of business
Certainly the intention to manage another's business may be presumed even where that other person performs an act of their own. In the present case an inference of this kind may be drawn from

[143] NJW 1974.951.

the statement of the defendant's name and the sending to her of an invoice. But it is important to ask the question whether the repairs were objectively in the defendant's interests. However, according to a witness statement, it appears that the defendant no longer wished to have major repairs carried out. Consequently, it may be inferred therefrom that an investment of that kind would no longer have seemed appropriate to her. In addition, the management of business was not ratified within the meaning of § 684 II.

(3) No action for enrichment under § 684 I

In the case of unauthorized management of business there is a right to recovery of the unjust enrichment. But § 684 I applies only in bilateral relations. In the present case such an action cannot be applied. In fact, the applicant performed a service on the basis of a genuine contract, that is to say on the basis of a legal ground. Thus, he cannot at the same time plead unjust enrichment under § 812.I,1,1.on the basis of a contractual right against the defendant's husband.

Note

The Court points out successively that there is no contract because there was no agency of one spouse on behalf of the other, no management of another's business because it was not established that the repair was beneficial, and no unjust enrichment because there was a legal ground justifying it, namely the contract entered into with the husband which became ineffective, it is true, as a result of the husband's insolvency.

The solution under French law would have been different because proven insolvency is regarded as depriving the enrichment of its justification, notwithstanding the existence of a contract: Cass. Civ. 1, 1 February 1973.[144]

The question whether there is a contract underlying the enrichment has also arisen in English law.

Queen's Bench Division **1.E.61.**

British Steel Corporation v. *Cleveland Bridge and Engineering Co Ltd* [145]

RESTITUTION CLAIM WHERE GOODS SUPPLIED WITHOUT CONTRACT HAVING BEEN CONCLUDED

Steel nodes

Where one party asks another to supply goods and the other does so although there is no contract between them because the terms of the proposed contract are still under active discussion, the recipient is liable in restitution for the value of the goods actually received.

Facts: The plaintiff (BSC) was in negotiations with the defendant (CBE) for the supply of nodes, for a construction project. During the negotiations a letter of intent was issued by CBE asking BSC to start the work and, with negotiations still under way. nearly all the nodes were delivered. Delivery of the final item was delayed by a strike and the nodes were not paid for. BSC claimed payment for the nodes on the basis of their reasonable value, in the absence of a contract. CBE counter-claimed for damages greater than that value for late delivery. BSC's claim was upheld.

Judgment: ROBERT GOFF J . . . I now turn to the first issue in the case, which is concerned with the legal basis for BSC's claim for payment, and in particular whether there was any binding contract between BSC and CBE and, if so, what were its terms. As I have already indicated, it is the

---

[144] *Supra*, at 81; for a Franco-German comparison, see A. Rieg, *Le rôle de la volonté dans l'acte juridique en droit civl français et allemand* (Paris: LGDJ, 1961).
[145] [1984] 1 All ER 504.

contention of CBE that there was such a contract; whereas BSC contends that they are entitled to payment in quasi contract . . .

Now the question whether in a case such as the present any contract has come into existence must depend on a true construction of the relevant communications which have passed between the parties and the effect (if any) of their action pursuant to those communications. There can be no hard and fast answer to the question whether a letter of intent will give rise to a binding agreement: everything must depend on the circumstances of the particular case. In most cases, where work is done pursuant to a resquest contained in a letter of intent, it will not matter whether a contract did or did not come into existence, because, if the party who has acted on the request is simply claiming payment, his claim will usually be based on a quantum meruit, and it will make no difference whether that claim is contractual or quasi-contractual. Of course, a quantum meruit claim (like the old action for money had and received and for money paid) straddles the boundaries of what we now call contract and restitution, so the mere framing of a claim as a quantum meruit claim, or a claim for a reasonable sum, does not assist in classifying the claim as contractual or quasi contractual. But where, as here, one party is seeking to claim damages for breach of contract, the question whether any contract came into existence if of crucial importance.

As a matter of analysis the contract (if any) which may come into existence following a letter of intent may take one of two forms: either there may be an ordinary executory contract, under wich each party assumes reciprocal obligations to the other; or there may be what is sometimes called an "if" contract, ie a contract under which A requests B to carry out a certain performance and promises B that, if he does so, he will receive a certain performance in return, usually remuneration for his performance. The latter transaction is really no more than a standing offer which, if acted on before it lapses or is lawfully withdrawn, will result in a binding contract.

The former type of contract was held to exist by Mr Edgar Fay QC, the official Referree, in *Turriff Construction Ltd* v. *Regalia Knitting Mills Ltd*, and it is the type of contract for which counsel for CBE contended in the present case. Of course, as I have already said, everything must depend on the facts of the particular case; but certainly, on the facts of the present case (and, as I imagine, on the facts of most cases), this must be a very difficult submission to maintain. It is only necessary to look at the terms of CBE's letter of intent in the present case to appreciate the difficulties. In that letter, the request to BSC to proceed immediately with the work was stated to be "pending the preparation and issuing to you of the official form of sub-contract", being a sub-contract which was plainly in a state of negotiation, not least on the issue of price, delivery dates, and the applicable terms and conditions. In these circumstances, it is very difficult to see how BSC, by starting work, bound themselves to any contractual performance. No doubt it was envisaged by CBE at the time they sent the letter that negotiation had reached an advanced stage, and that a formal contract would soon be signed; but, since the parties were still in a stage of negotiation, it is impossible to say with any degree of certainty what the material terms of that contract would be. I find myself quite unable to conclude that, by starting work in these circumstances, BSC bound themselves to complete the work. In the course of argument, I put to counsel for CBE the question whether BSC were free at any time, after starting work, to cease work. His submission was that they were not free to do so, even if negotiations on the terms of the formal contract broke down completely. I find this submission to be so repugnant to common sense and the commercial realities that I an unable to accept it. It is pershaps revealing that, on 4 April 1979, BSC did indeed state that they were not prepared to proceed with the contract until they had an agreed specification, a reaction which, in my judgment, reflected not only the commercial, but also the legal, realities of the situation.

I therefore, reject CBE's submission that a binding executory contract came into existence in this case. There remains the question whether, by reason of BSC carrying out work pursuant to the request contained in CBE's letter of intent, there came into existence a contract by virtue of which BSC were entitled to claim reasonable remuneration; ie whether there was an "if" contract of the kind I have described. In the course of argument, I was attracted by this alternative (really on the basis that, not only was it analytically possible, but also that it could provide a vehicle for certain contractual obligations of BSC concerning their performance, eg implied terms as to the quality of goods supplied by them). But the more I have considered the case, the less attractive I have found this alternative. The real difficulty is to be found in the factual matrix of the transaction, and in particular the fact that the work was being done pending a formal sub-contract the terms of which were still in a state of negotiation. It is, of course, a notorious fact that, when a contract is made for the supply of goods on a scale and in circumstances such as the present, it will in all probability be subject the standard terms, usually the standard terms of the supplier. Such standard terms will frequently legislate, not only for the liability of the seller for defects, but also for the damages (if any) for which the seller will be liable in the event not only of defects in the goods but also of later delivery. It is a commonplace that a seller of goods may exclude liability for consequential loss, and may agree liquidated damages for delay. In the present case, an unresolved dispute broke out between the parties on the question whether CBS's or BSC's standard terms were to apply, the former providing no limit to the seller's liability for delay and the latter excluding such liability altogether. Accordingly, when, in a case such as the present, the parties are still in a state of negotiation, it is impossible to predicate what liability (if any) will be assumed by the seller for, eg defective goods or late delivery, if a formal contract should be entered into. In these circumstances, if the buyer asks the seller to commence work "pending" the parties entering into a formal contract, it is difficult to infer from the buyer acting on that request that he is assuming any responsibility for his performance, except such responsibility as will rest on him under the terms of the contract which both parties confidently anticipate they will shortly enter into. It would be an extraordinary result if, by acting on such a request in such circumstances, the buyer were to assume an unlimited liability for his contractual performance, when he would never assume such liability under any contract which he entered into.

For these reasons, I reject the solution of the "if" contract. In my judgment, the true analysis of the situation is simply this. Both parties confidently expected a formal contract to eventuate. In these circumstances, to expedite performance under that anticipated contract, one requested the other to commence the contract work, and the other complied with that request. If thereafter, as anticipated, a contract was entered into, the work done as requested will be treated as having been performed under that contract; if, contrary to their expectation, no contract was entered into, then the performance of the work is not referable to any contract the terms of which can be ascertained, and the law simply imposes an obligation on the party who made the request, such an obligation sounding in quasi contract or, as we now say, in restitution. Consistently with that solution, the party making the request may find himself liable to pay for work which he would not have had to pay for as such if the anticipated contract had come into existence, eg preparatory work which will, if the contract is made, be allowed for in the price of the finished word (cf. *William Lacey (Hounslow) Ltd* v. *Davis*). The solution moreover accords with authority: see the decision in *Lacey* v. *David*, the decision of the Court of Appeal in *Sander & Forster Ltd* v. *A Monk & Co Ltd*, though that decision rested in part on a concession, and the crisp dictum of Parker J in *OTM Ltd* v. *Hydranautics*, when he said of a letter of intent that "its only effect would be to enable the defendants to recover on quantum meruit for work done pursuant to the direction" contained in the letter. I only wish to add to this part of my judgment the footnote that, even if I had concluded that in the circumstances of the present case there was a contract between the parties and that that contract was of the kind I have described as an "if" contract, then I would still have concluded that there was no obligation under that contract on the part of BSC to continue with or complete the contract work, and therefore no obligation on their part to complete the work within a reasonable time. However, my conclusion in the present case is that the parties never entered into any contract at all.

Judgment for the plaintiffs. The counter-claim was dismissed.

Note

The court found there was no contract. The letter of intent did not constitute a "binding contract" and there was also no conditional or "if" contract. Accordingly, there was a quasi-contract or, "as we now say", restitution.

English law has also concerned itself with restitution consequent on a void contract: Restitution lies unless such restitution would result in effect being given to a void contract.

Court of Appeal   **1.E.62.**
Westdeutsche Landesbank Girozentrale v. *Islington London Borough Council*[146]

RESTITUTION AFTER ILLEGAL CONTRACT

Swaps contracts

Party who has received money under an illegal contract may be required to make restitution.

Facts: A municipality entered into a swap agreement with a local authority. The agreement was set aside as being ultra vires. The bank was entitled to recover sums paid under it.

Judgment: The parties believed that they were making an interest swaps contract. They were not, because such a contract was ultra vires the local authority. So they made no contract at all. Islington say that they should receive a windfall because the purpose of the doctrine of ultra vires is to protect council taxpayers whereas restitution would disrupt Islington's finances. They also contend that it would countenance "unconsidered dealings with local authorities". If that is the best that can be said for refusing restitution, the sooner it is enforced the better. Protection of council taxpayers from loss is to be distinguished from securing a windfall for them. The disruption of Islington's finances is the result of ill-considered financial dispositions by Islington and its officers. It is not the policy of the law to require others to deal at their peril with local authorities, nor to require others to undertake their own inquiries about whether a local authority has power to make particular contracts or types of contract. Any system of law, and indeed any system of fair dealing, must be expected to ensure that Islington do not profit by the fortuity that when it became known that the contract was ineffective the balance stood in their favour. In other words, in circumstances such as these they should be unjustly enriched.

It is common ground that the interest swaps and Islington's payments were ultra vires the local authority, and that the contract was therefore void *ab initio*; that there was no illegalilty involved; and that the legal property in the money which was paid by the parties to each other under the swap contract passed to the recipient.

Where A has in his possession the money fo B under a void transaction, B should be entitled to reimbursement unless some principle of law precludes it. If the transaction was a contract, initially valid, the question will arise whether it has been partially performed. If so, the failure of consideration will not be total. But if the transaction as entered into by both parties in the belief, which proves unfounded, that it was an enforceable contract, in principle the parties ought to be restored to the respective positions from which they started. To achieve that, where there have been mutual payments the recipient of the larger payment has only to repay the net excess over the payment he has himself made.

---

[146] [1994] 4 All ER 890.

Hobhouse J said (at the first instance, [1994] 4 All ER at p. 929):

"In my judgment the correct analysis is that any payments made under a contract which is void ab initio, in the way that an ultra vires contract is void, are not contractual payments at all. They are payments in which the legal property in the money passes to the recipient but in equity the property in the money remains with the payer. The recipient holds the money as a fiduciary for the payer and is bound to recognise his equity and repay the money to him. This relationship and the consequent obligation have been recognised both by courts applying the common law and by Chancery courts. The principle is the same in both cases: it is unconscionable that the recipient should retain the money. Neither mistake nor the contractual principle of total failure of consideration are the basis for the right of recovery."

In my judgment that formulation is wholly accurate, provided that the contract in question is not a borrowing contract. If it were a borrowing contract, it would fall foul (as the judge recognised) of the principle in *Sinclair* v. *Brougham* [1914] AC 398 that restitution will not be ordered where to do so would have the effect to enforcing a void contract. That is not the case here. In relation to a contract other than a borrowing contract the effect of restitution is to put the payer into the position in which he would have been if the transaction had never been entered into.

. . . In *Rover International Ltd* v. *Cannon Film Sales Ltd (nº 3)* Kerr LJ expressed the test as being "whether or not the party claiming total failure of consideration has in fact received any part of the benefit bargained for under the contract or purported contract". That seems to me to be the test to apply here.

As Westdeutsche submitted, the fact that the payer had received a benefit did not mean that there had been no total failure of consideration, if the payer did not get the benefit for which he bargained. What in this case Westdeutsche bargained for were payments which would discharge a contractual obligation and which Westdeutsche were entitled lawfully to receive. What they obtained were payments made under a void agreement, which in equity remained the property of Islington and which even at law they were always entitled to recover back.

Islington criticised this formulation as artificial, contending that if the formulation of counsel for Westdeutsche in the court below, which appears to have been indorsed by Hobhouse J, is that Islington must also show absence of consideration, then the argument is circular. The payments by Westdeutsche were tainted by "absence of consideration" because they received payments from Islington which were recoverable because Islington received payments from Westdeutsche, which are recoverable by Westdeutsche, and so on. Islington argued that Westdeutsche here did not bargain for the right to receive repayment of their payment to Islington. No doubt it hoped to do so. It bargained for participation in a series of risks on specified days in the future on each of which the prevailing London Inter-Bank Offered Rate would be compared with 7.5 per cent and, if the risk favoured Westdeutsche, a payment would be made by Islington, and vice versa. It bargained for the risk-taking twice a year for ten years. It got two years. There was no total failure of consideration, only partial. It was so held by Hobhouse J.

There can have been no consideration under a contract void ab initio. So it is fallacious to speak of the failure of consideration having been partial. What is meant is that the parties did, in the belief that the contract was enforceable, part of what they would have been required to do if it had been. As it was, they were not performing the contract even in part: they were making payments that had no legal justification, instead of affording each other mutual consideration for an enforceable contract. In my judgment, the payments made are in those circumstances recoverable by Westdeustsche, in so far as they exceed the payments made by Islington, as money had and received to the use of Westdeutsche by which Islington have been unjustly enriched.

[The decision of the Court of Appeal was reversed on other grounds: [1996] A.C. 669. Lord Browne-Wilkinson said that the Court of Appeal was correct to hold that the money had been paid on a consideration that had wholly failed. He also said that in so far as *Sinclair* v. *Brougham* was based on the concept that the claim for the return of money rested on an implied contract, it should be overruled.]

Note

One is here confronted with what in other legal systems would be called repayment of sums paid in error. The concern shown by Hobhouse J not to give effect to an unlawful contract is partly covered, in French law, for example by the adage "*nemo auditur propriam turpitudinem allegans*", limited in French law, it is true, to contracts for an immoral purpose.[147]

Concluding Remarks on Section 2

Unlike what was found to be the case as regards the contract–tort relationship, and in spite of the differences in the classification of types of quasi-contract, there do not appear to have been major difficulties in drawing the demarcation line between the sphere of contract and that of quasi-contract.

1.3. BINDING NATURE OF CONTRACTUAL OBLIGATIONS

Why do certain undertakings have binding force or, more specifically, why do they give rise to obligations which the law will uphold? This is a classic question and the answers to it are many and varied. Two major themes may be discerned, and these are mingled together in varying degrees. The first is based on the moral imperative of *pacta sunt servanda*: a person's word, once given, must be his bond, on moral grounds. This is the great contribution of the Canon lawyers of the Middle Ages, carried forward by the Natural Law school and which is predominant in the Civilian conception of the contract. On the other hand, at Common Law, it is the economic idea of the bargain which is dominant: the contract is the most effective means of carrying out exchanges of value.

Stock has been taken of these two themes by an Anglo-French research group which highlighted a quotation from Oliver Wendell Holmes throwing into sharp, and no doubt exaggerated, relief the economic foundation of contract.

Contract Law Today[148]   **I.E.63.**

(a) The relative weight given to moral and economic arguments.

Several times in our study it was shown that the two systems take different views about moral arguments. French law gives greater weight to evaluating the behaviour of the parties, whereas English law, being more utilitarian than Kantian, is primarily interested in the exchange of economic value achieved by the contract. However, this contrast needs to be qualified and explained in more detail. Beginning with Domat and Pothier, French academic writing abandoned the concept of contract as an economic exchange in favour of the concept of contract as an exchange of consents; this took place at the expense of seeking equality in the value of the exchange of undertakings. It is the economists who have reintroduced the analysis of contract as exchange: they have influenced certain lawyers, particularly Maury in his thesis on *cause* as the equivalent willed by the obligated party. Today we can see in French academic writing an evolution towards this more utilitarian concept of contract; but it is marked with a concern, in the name of morality and justice, to take account of the inequality of the parties in making the exchange.

---

[147] For restitution due following termination of the contract, see *infra*, at 795.
[148] Harris and Tallon (eds.), op. cit., at 385–6.

But the orthodox views is still influential in France, where the canonists had a considerable influence on the development of contract law. In England, however, it was commercial practice which influenced contract law. Although French contract law has a general and abstract character and applies to any kind of agreement, English contract law is modelled on commercial transactions, which are treated by the judges as the paradigm of contract. For various reasons, English courts have not regularly handled non-commercial transactions, where an ethical view of contract would be more relevant to the litigation. Since commercial litigation has predominated in England, the ethical view has a less important role. We should add that American academic writing, which was the first to use economic analysis to study contract law (as, for example, with the theory of the efficient breach), has strongly affected much English academic work.

The contrast between the two approaches can be put in two statements: *pacta sunt servanda* for French law, which accordingly insists on exact performance of a contractual undertaking; and for the common law, Holmes's celebrated statement, which, although contemporary writers may treat it as exaggerated, none the less reflects a general attitude of mind. According to Holmes, in Anglo-American law the contractual promisor has a choice between performing his promise and paying damages: in a way, it is a kind of alternative obligation. It follows that French law resorts to issues of morality, such as fraud, serious fault, or good faith,[149] more readily than does English law. Even the English principles of Equity are based more on normal standards of commercial probity than on abstract moral values. The different weight given to moral arguments also explains why English law has not adopted institutions like the *astreinte* or accepted penalty clauses, which are designed to punish a party who fails to perform: and why English law gives much more weight to economic consequences, as discussed below. In the same way, English law is more willing to allow each party to protect his own interests, but is less willing to take into account inequalities between the parties, especially in regard to disclosing information and technical knowledge. (The exception is found in consumer protection, as with the example of the Unfair Contract Terms Act 1977). French contract law is both more "moral" and more dogmatic; English contract law is both more "economic" and more pragmatic.

Holmes[150]

The duty to keep a contract at Common Law means a prediction that you must pay damages if you don't keep it and nothing else.

These themes are well illustrated by the provision for remedies, with the emphasis being placed on mandatory performance or the payment of damages.

The theory of American origin known as the "efficient breach"[151] well illustrates the divergent viewpoints.[152]

The starting point on which there can be no doubt, in a liberal system, is the intention to give a binding commitment in accordance with the law. As a matter of principle there can be no imposed contract (unlike what happens under socialist systems of law). For that reason, it is necessary as a first step (A) to determine the components of intention. The question may then be raised (B) whether intention is sufficient and whether regard should

---

[149] E.g see the law on exemption clauses—which were not directly within our study—or on the foreseability of damage (Article 1150 of the Civil Code), etc.

[150] O.W. Holmes, *Collected Legal Papers* (1920), at 175.

[151] See Ogus, in Harris and Tallon, op. cit., at 259 ff.

[152] For a critique of this theory from the French point of view, see Ghestin, para. 219 ff.

be had to the reliance placed on another person's word. (C) Is something more necessary to make the contract effective, cause or consideration or (D) a requirement as to form?

1.3.1. INTENTION TO CREATE LEGAL RELATIONS

In a liberal society intention is necessary: no person may be contractually bound against his will. And that is without prejudice to the explanation given of this proposition.[153]

It is first necessary to examine what it is that one is committing oneself to. That is why it is important to bear in mind the existence of preparatory agreements (*avant-contrat*, *Vorvertrag*) and options, that is to say genuine contracts but ones which are provisional and whose purpose is to pave the way for the creation of the definitive contract.[154]

Conversely, there are very many situations, often closely analogous one to the other, where it may be wondered whether there is a contract or not. First, there are cases in which it is doubtful whether there was an intention to enter into a genuine agreement (**1.1.3.A**). Closely akin to those cases are situations where the parties wished to enter into binding arrangements, whilst waiving *ab initio* any recourse to legal remedies, that is to say gentlemen's agreements (**1.1.3.B**). Then, there are, under various headings—letter of intent, of patronage, or comfort, which are not infrequently equivocal, to do something for another (**1.1.3.C**). Finally, there are the agreements in principle, which are incomplete agreements (**1.1.3.D**). What value is to be attached to these different types of agreement? That varies according to the circumstances and very often it is a question of interpreting the intentions of the parties.

1.3.1.A. INTENTION TO ENTER INTO A CONTRACT

There may be arrangements in regard to which it is legitimate to ask whether they can give rise to legal obligations, so much so that it can be difficult to discern whether the parties intended to bind themselves at law. To this category belong acts of courtesy, social commitments, informal offers of help.

Such situations may be distinguished from unilateral obligations or unilateral contracts, though the line between them is sometimes difficult to draw.

Thus, in *Carlill* v. *Carbolic Smoke Ball Co* (1893),[155] it was legitimate to ask whether the "contract" was not too vague to have legal consequences. In some cases this may be in doubt.

Cass. civ. 1re, 6 April 1994[156] **1.F.64.**

INFORMAL AGREEMENT MAY NOT AMOUNT TO CONTRACT

Shared business trip

An agreement to share the costs of a business trip is not sufficient to establish a contract.
Judgment: THE COURT: *On the sole appeal ground*:—Whereas Mr De Stephano claims that the lower court (Besançon, judgment of 17 September 1991) ought not to have declared the Hague

---

[153] See below, Foundations of the binding force of contract, *infra*, at 115 ff.
[154] See *infra*, at 178 ff.
[155] See **1.E.103**, *infra* at 142.
[156] Bull. civ. I.136; RTD civ. 1994.866, annotated by P. Jourdain.

Convention of 4 May 1971 (on the law applicable to non-contractual liability resulting from a road traffic accident) applicable to the accident in Italy in which he was the passenger of a vehicle driven by Mr Spinelli and sustained injuries; as the appeal court, it is submitted, ought not to have applied the Italian law of the place of the accident and ought to have attributed to the facts at issue their proper classification by seeking to determine whether the agreement entered into between Mr De Stephano and Mr Spinelli to share the costs of using the latter's vehicle for a business trip, constituted, if not a contract of carriage, then at least an agreement excluding the application of the abovementioned Convention;

—Whereas however, the appeal court was correct to hold that the existence of an agreement to share the costs of the trip was not sufficient to establish between the parties a link such as to give rise to liability in contract founded on he duty of the driver to ensure the safety of his passenger;

—Whereas thus, in holding that there was no contract of carriage, the appeal court's decision was soundly based in law, Mr Spinelli's liability being only non-contractual and thus coming within the sphere of the Hague Convention of 4 May 1971;

—Whereas the appeal ground is therefore unfounded;

    On those grounds the appeal must be dismissed.

Note

In a case concerning the application of the Hague Convention on the law applicable to non-contractual liability in respect of a road traffic accident, the question arose whether an agreement between two persons to use the car of one of them for a trip, and to share the costs, constituted an agreement excluding the application of the Convention. The Cour de cassation considered that the agreement related only to the cost-sharing arrangement but that there was no agreement giving rise to any liability to ensure the safety of the other party. The parties did not intend to enter into a genuine contract of carriage.

House of Lords   **1.E.65.**
Albert v. Motor Insurers Bureau[157]

INFORMAL AGREEMENT NOT CONTRACT

Shared lifts in car

Facts: A stevedore drove some other stevedores to the place where they worked and it was agreed that they would pay him 5 to 10 shillings per week. Sometimes, he was also satisfied with cigarettes or beers; it sometimes happened that he did not ask for anything when the person carried had run out of money.

Held: The majority held that a vehicle was used to carry passengers for hire or reward if the driver was, on a systematic basis, going beyond acts of social kindness, even if there was no contract between the owner and the passengers: Quirk's vehicle had been so used.

Judgment: LORD CROSS [differing from the majority, held it was necessary to determine whether there was a contract, and continued]: I think that the judge was wrong in holding that the facts which he found warranted the inference that there were no legally binding agreements between Quirk and any of his passengers. It is not necessary in order that a legally binding contract should arise that the parties should direct their minds to the question and decide in favour of the creation of a legally binding relationship. If I get into a taxi and ask the driver to drive me to Victoria Station it is extremely unlikely that either of us directs his mind to the question whether we are entering into

---

[157] [1971] 2 All ER 1345.

a contract. We enter into a contract not because we form any intention to enter into one but because if our minds were directed to the point we should as reasonable people both agree that we were in fact entering into one. When one passes from the field of transactions of an obviously business character between strangers to arrangements between friends or acquaintances for the payment by the passenger of a contribution towards expenses the fact that the arrangement is not made purely as a matter of business and that if the anticipated payment is not made it would probably never enter into the head of the driver to sue for it disposes one to say that there is no contract, but in fact the answer to the question "contract" or "no contract" does not depend on the likelihood of an action being brought to enforce it in case of default.

Suppose that when one of Quirk's fellow workers got into touch with him and asked him whether he could travel in his car to Tilbury and back next day an "officious bystander" had asked: "Will you be paying anything for your transport?" the prospective passenger would have answered at once: "Of course I will pay." If the "officious bystander" had gone on to ask Quirk whether, if he was not paid, he would sue the man in the county court, Quirk might well have answered in the words used by the driver in *Connell's* case [1969] 2 Q.B. 494: "Not bloody likely." But the fact that if default was made Quirk would not have started legal proceedings but would have resorted to extra-judicial remedies does not mean that an action could not in theory have been brought to recover payment for the carriage. If one imagines such proceedings being brought a plea on the part of the passenger that he never meant to enter into a contract would have received short shrift and so, too, would a plea that the contract was void for uncertainty because no precise sum was mentioned. If the evidence did not establish a regular charge for the Tilbury trip the judge would have fixed the appropriate sum.

Note

According to Lord Cross, it is not necessary that the parties had wanted to create legal relationship for a contract to be. Or should one admit that there can be a legal relationship without any contract? The House of Lords does not rule on this.

A further, borderline situation may arise in connection with joint gaming or betting, where several persons take part and the prize is won. How is it to be shared out, given that there may, at best, have been merely a formal agreement? The French courts may apply the concept of an obligation existing by virtue of a unilateral intention.[157a] The German and English examples referred to below involved, in particular, the question whether there was a contract.

BGH, 16 May 1974[158]   **1.G.66.**

AGREEMENT TO PLACE BETS NOT ENFORCEABLE

Betting syndicate

An agreement to place a bet each week does not create a legal obligation so that the person who had agreed to place it will be liable if the bet would have won.
Judgment: The plaintiffs and the defendant formed an association for the purpose of placing wagers. Each week they wagered the sum of DM 50, that is to say DM 10 per person. The wagers were paid by the defendant who filled out and handed in the lottery ticket in his own name. For the

---

[157a] See **1.F.8**, *supra* at 6.
[158] NJW 1974.1705.

draw on 23 October 1971 the defendant neglected to hand in the ticket with the figures agreed. Yet at this draw those were the winning figures giving entitlement to a prize of DM 20,550.

Accordingly, the plaintiffs demanded the sum of DM 2,110 per head, together with interest and damages.

It was contended on the defendant's behalf that he was under no legal obligation as to his conduct. He claimed that for work reasons he was unable to hand in the ticket as agreed. Quite unexpectedly, he had been unable to leave his place of work before a quarter to six and, on his arrival at the betting office, he discovered that the last bet had been taken an hour before. Therefore, instead of filling out the agreed ticket, he placed other bets totalling DM 450.

The lower courts trying the case on its merits dismissed the claim for damages and interest. The Fed. Sup. Ct. dismissed the appeal on a point of law.

Discussion

I—The Higher Regional Court (OLG) dismissed the claim under § 762 BGB. Under that provision gambling debts and wagers cannot form the subject-matter of legal proceedings. However, that provision was held not to apply in this case. Taking responsibility to place a wager on behalf of a gaming association is not in itself a wager but an ancillary act enabling the wager to proceed. Moreover, according to settled case-law, § 762 applies only where a person invites another to participate in gaming which is not authorised by the public authorities.

II—The second question is whether the task entrusted to the plaintiff by the defendants constituted an act legally binding on the plaintiff and giving rise to an obligation on his part.

1—It must be determined whether the gaming association established by the parties constitutes a partnership and whether the agent is to be equated with a manager within the meaning of § 710 BGB. It is common ground that where the agent places a wager within the remit of his agency, he is required to share any resulting winnings.

2—Consequently, a legal link is established. But the question arises whether and to what extent an unsupported mandate gives rise to a legally enforceable obligation. It may be hard to resolve that question by reference to the express or implied intentions of the participants; thus, it is also necessary to have regard to the interests of each of the parties in light of the requirements of good faith and custom.

In the present case, upon weighing the interests at stake, it had to be decided that a mandate to complete and hand in a lottery ticket gives rise to no legal obligation. To find in favour of the existence of any such obligation would be too onerous to the agent. A simple error in selecting the numbers would rarely entail a risk of major loss. But where that loss is incurred, it can be particularly serious. The ensuing obligation on the agent to afford restitution could result in his total ruination.

Note

The facts are somewhat out of the ordinary, but so is the analysis of the legal aspects. This was not a case involving the exception relating to gaming which exists in various countries (e.g. Article 1965 of the French Civil Code and § 762 BGB), since there was no gaming within the meaning of those provisions. But was there a contract? The BGH clearly considered that a legal relationship had been formed, but declined to reach a conclusion based on any express or tacit intention shared by the participants, which would of necessity be a fiction. It preferred to approach the matter from the standpoint of the balance of interests. To impose a legal obligation on the person delegated to act as the participants' agent would be inequitable, since this could result in that person facing ruin if, for example, he made a mistake in filling out the lottery slip and, but for that mistake, the winnings would have been sizeable. The only commitment given to the principals was the obligation to share the winnings if the ticket was correctly filled out in accordance with the numbers jointly agreed on by the participants. Thus an objective approach was adopted by the court, similar to the approach found in the English case-law, which, on account of its specific characteristics, in particular the doctrine of consideration, provides rather different illustrations.

Queen's Bench Division   **1.E.67.**
Simpkins v. *Pays*[159]

AGREEMENT TO SHARE WINNINGS ENFORCEABLE

Competition in Sunday paper

An agreement between a house-owner, her granddaughter and a lodger to enter competitions and share any winnings may be intended to be legally binding.

Facts: Since 1950 the plaintiff had been living as a lodger in the house of the defendant, an elderly woman, in circumstances which had some element of a family circle. Each of the parties used to compete separately in newspaper competitions. From about the beginning of May, 1954, for a period of seven or eight weeks, the plaintiff, the defendant and the defendant's grand-daughter each sent in, each week, a separate entry on one coupon to the fashion competition of a Sunday newspaper. Each of the three contributed one forecast, and the coupon was filled in by the plaintiff but was made out in the defendant's name. The costs of postage and entry were informally shared, being sometimes paid by one and sometimes by another. When the question of sharing winnings first came to be considered between the plaintiff and defendant, the latter said that they would go shares. The grand-daughter was not present on that occasion but the plaintiff and the defendant both knew that she would join in the arrangement. The coupon sent in for 27 June 1954, was successful, the correct forecast being that of the defendant's grand-daughter, and a prize of £750 was paid to the defendant. The defendant refused to pay a third of the prize money to the plaintiff, claiming, among other things, that the arrangement to share the winnings was arrived at in a family association and was not intended to give rise to legal consequences, and that, accordingly, there was no contract.

Held: There was an enforceable contract, because there was a mutuality in the arrangement between the parties, and, therefore, the plaintiff was entitled to payment of a third share of the prize money.

Judgment: SELLERS J: . . . On each of the occasions when the plaintiff made out the coupon . . . she put down the forecasts in the way which I have indicated, and entered in the appropriate place on the coupon "Mrs Pays, 11, Trevor Street, Wrexham", that is to say, the defendant's name and address, as if the coupon had been the defendant's. There were, in fact, three forecasts on each coupon, and I accept the plaintiff's evidence that, when the matter first came to be considered, what was said, when they were going to do it in that way, was: "We will go shares", or words to that effect. Whether that was said by the plaintiff or by the defendant does not really matter. "Shares" was the word used, and I do not think anything very much more specific was said. I think that that was the basis of the arrangement; and it may well be that the plaintiff was right when she said in her evidence, that the defendant said: "You're lucky, May, and if we win we will go shares".

. . .

On the finding of fact that the plaintiff's evidence is right as to what was said about the shares, learned counsel for the defendant not unnaturally said: "Even if that is so, the court cannot enforce this contract unless the arrangement made at the time was one which was intended to give rise to legal consequences". It may well be there are many family associations where some sort of

[159] [1955] 3 All ER 10.

94

rough and ready statement is made which would not, in a proper estimate of the circumstances, establish a contract which was contemplated to have legal consequences, but I do not so find here. I think that in the present case there was a mutuality in the arrangement between the parties. It was not very formal, but certainly it was, in effect, agreed that every week the forecast should go in in the name of the defendant, and that if there was success, no matter who won, all should share equally. It seems to be the implication from, or the interpretation of, what was said that this was in the nature of a very informal syndicate so that they should all get the benefit of success. It would, also, be wrong, I think, to say from what was arranged that, because the grand-daughter's forecast was the one which was successful of those submitted by the defendant, the plaintiff and the defendant should receive nothing. Although the grand-daughter was not a party before the court and I have not had the benefit of her evidence, on this arrangement she would, in my opinion, be as entitled to a third share as the others, because, although she was not, apparently, present when this bargain was made, both the others knew, at any rate soon after the outset, that she was coming in. It is possible, of course, although the plaintiff is not concerned in this, that the grand-daughter's effort was only to assist the defendant. The grand-daughter may accept that, but it makes no difference to the fact that the plaintiff and the defendant entered into an agreement to share, and, accordingly the plaintiff was entitled to one-third. I so find and give judgment for the amount of £250.

Note

This case clearly raises a problem of interpretation: what was it that the parties had agreed? And there is a further problem, concerning characterization: in what way did the agreement fall to be analysed? The court considered that there had been something cautiously characterized by it as an "arrangement" which the parties had intended to have legal consequences. It even accepted that an "informal syndicate" was involved. The upshot was the same: the plaintiff was entitled to one third of the prize. The decision appears to have been given on the basis of equity—in the general sense of the term—rather than by reference to law.

It is apparent from a comparison of the three judgments that, in cases of this kind involving similar circumstances, the courts have been at something of a loss to find any legal basis for the conclusion reached by them. They have taken the view that it is difficult to determine what the parties really intended in such cases where joint gaming has gone wrong, and have had problems in deciding whether, on the one hand, to order payment of a proportion of the winnings or whether, on the other, to dismiss the claim for payment. The French judgment speaks of the transformation of a moral obligation into an obligation in law, non-performance of which entails a legal sanction, whilst the English and German courts refer to the interests in issue. This is without doubt an area lying at the very fringes of contract law.

We now turn, finally, to a judgment showing the special nature of English law in relation to family arrangements, the effectiveness of which in other European legal systems is open to debate.

NO INTENTION TO CREATE LEGAL RELATIONS

Allowance to wife

An agreement between a husband and wife that he will pay her an allowance, made while they were still on amicable terms, does not create a legal obligation.

Facts: A couple returned to England from Ceylon. When his leave was over, the husband went back alone, his wife remaining in England for health reasons. She maintained that before his departure her husband had promised to pay her the monthly sum of £30. Subsequently, the couple separated and the wife brought an action for the maintenance payments to be continued to be paid to her. She was successful at first instance. But the husband was successful on appeal.

Judgment: AKTIN LJ: The defence to this action on the alleged contract is that the defendant, the husband, entered into no contract with his wife, and for the determination of that it is necessary to remember that there are agreements between parties which do not result in contracts within the meaning of that term in our law. The ordinary example is where two parties agree to take a walk together, or where there is an offer and an acceptance of hospitality. Nobody would suggest in ordinary circumstances that those agreements result in what we know as a contract, and one of the most usual forms of agreement which does not constitute a contract appears to me to be the arrangements which are made between husband and wife. It is quite common, and it is the natural and inevitable result of the relationship of husband and wife, that the two spouses should make arrangements between themselves—agreements such as are in dispute in this action—agreements for allowances, by which the husband agrees that he will pay to his wife a certain sum of money, per week, or per month, or per year, to cover either her own expenses or the necessary expenses of the household and of the children of the marriage, and in which the wife promises either expressly or impliedly to apply the allowance for the purpose for which it is given. To my mind those agreements, or many of them, do not result in contracts at all, and they do not result in contracts even though there may be what as between other parties would constitute consideration for the agreement. The consideration, as we know, may consist either in some right, interest, profit or benefit accruing to one party, or some forbearance, detriment, loss or responsibility given, suffered or undertaken by the other. That is a well-known definition, and it constantly happens, I think, that such arrangements made between husband and wife are arrangements in which there are mutual promises, or in which there is consideration in form within the definition that I have mentioned. Nevertheless they are not contracts, and they are not contracts because the parties did not intend that they should be attended by legal consequences. To my mind it would be of the worst possible example to hold that agreements such as this resulted in legal obligations which could be enforced in the Courts. It would mean this, that when the husband makes his wife a promise to give her an allowance of 30s. or 2l. a week, whatever he can afford to give her, for the maintenance of the household and children, and she promises so to apply it, not only could she sue him for his failure in any week to supply the allowance, but he could sue her for non-performance of the obligation, express or implied, which she had undertaken upon her part. All I can say is that the small Courts of this country would have to be multiplied one hundredfold if these arrangements were held to result in legal obligations. They are not sued upon, not because the parties are reluctant to enforce their legal rights when the agreement is broken, but because the parties, in the inception of the arrangement, never

---

[160] [1918–1919] All ER 860

intended that they should be sued upon. Agreements such as these are outside the realm of contracts altogether. The common law does not regulate the form of agreements between spouses.
Their promises are not sealed with seals and sealing wax. The consideration that really obtains for
them is that natural love and affection which counts for so little in these cold Courts. The terms may
be repudiated, varied or renewed as performance proceeds or as disagreements develop, and
the principles of the common law as to exoneration and discharge and accord and satisfaction are
such as find no place in the domestic code. The parties themselves are advocates, judges,
Courts, sheriff's officer and reporter. In respect of these promises each house is a domain into which
the King's writ does not seek to run, and to which his officers do not seek to be admitted. The
only question in this case is whether or not this promise was of such a class or not. For the reasons
given by my brethren it appears to me to be plainly established that the promise here was not
intended by either party to be attended by legal consequences. I think the onus was upon the plaintiff, and the plaintiff has not established any contract. The parties were living together, the
wife intending to return. The suggestion is that the husband bound himself to pay 30l. a month
under all circumstances, and she bound herself to be satisfied with that sum under all circumstances, and, although she was in ill-health and alone in this country, that out of that sum she
undertook to defray the whole of the medical expenses that might fall upon her, whatever might be
the development of her illness, and in whatever expenses it might involve her. To my mind neither
party contemplated such a result. I think that the parol evidence upon which the case turns does not
establish a contract. I think that the letters do not evidence such a contract, or amplify the oral evidence which was given by the wife, which is not in dispute. For these reasons I think the judgment
of the Court below was wrong and that this appeal should be allowed.

[Warrington and Duke LJJ delivered judgments to same effect].

Appeal allowed.

Note
The first question is as to the existence of consideration. Lord Atkin is of the view that
there is indeed consideration, but that there was no intention to enter into a legally
enforceable contract. The underlying idea is that this kind of family arrangement falls
outside the purview of the law. It is not certain that the solution would have been the same
in other countries.

In short, in order to specify that there is intention to be bound a lot depends on judicial interpretation of the will of the parties.

It is not always easy to determine whether the parties, or the persons claiming to be parties, intended to establish legal relations and, what is more, contractual relations.
Borderline situations exist affording the courts a relatively wide discretion. Three trends
may be discerned. First, in contrast to the situation prevailing in certain legal systems and
at certain times in the past, the courts are somewhat reluctant to engage in artificial
enquiries into questions of intention, preferring to steer clear of a subjective approach.
Instead, as will be noted, they tend to have recourse to the concept of the balance of
interests, as favoured by Ihering. Finally, this cannot conceal a very distinct propensity
towards delivering rulings based on equity.

1.3.1.B. AGREEMENT IN HONOUR, "GENTLEMEN'S" AGREEMENT

This situation is closely related to the previous one, but with one slight difference: the parties deliberately include a clause ousting the courts' jurisdiction, in reliance on each

other's good faith. Is it possible for the courts to acquiesce in this ouster of their jurisdiction?

Court of Appeal and House of Lords   **1.E.69.**
Rose & Frank Co v. J.R. Crompton Bros[161]

GENTLEMAN'S AGREEMENT NOT BINDING

"Binding in honour only"

Although commercial agreements are usually assumed to be legally binding, the parties may agree that the arrangement shall not be legally binding.

Facts: The parties agreed to extend a supply contract for a predetermined period at prices to be fixed every six months. The agreement contained the following clause: "This arrangement is not entered into nor is this memorandum written, as a formal or legal agreement, and shall not be subject to legal jurisdiction in the law courts either of the United States or England, but is only a definite expression and record of the purpose and intention of the three parties concerned, to which they each honourably pledge themselves in the fullest confidence—based on past business with each other—that it will be carried through by each of the three parties with mutual loyalty and friendly co-operation."

None the less, one of the parties sought to repudiate the arrangement. The other brought an action for breach of contract and non-delivery of the goods before the repudiation. The Court of Appeal took the view that this arrangement was not a binding contract, and (by a majority) that nor was the acceptance of an order placed by the plaintiffs. The House of Lords agreed with the view that the arrangement described above was not a binding contract, but agrred with the dissenting judge in the Court of Appeal that the acceptance of the sepcific order did create a contract (this part of the judgments is omitted).

Judgment: SCRUTTON LJ: In 1913 the parties concurred in signing a document which gives rise to the present dispute. I agree that if the clause beginning "This arrangement" were omitted, the Courts would treat the rest of the agreement as giving rise to legal relations, though again of great vagueness. An agreement that Messrs. Brittain & Crompton "will subject to unforeseen circumstances and contingencies do their best, as in the past, to respond efficiently and satisfactorily to the calls of Messrs. Rose & Frank Co. for deliveries both in quantity and quality," is not very helpful or precise. But the clause in question beginning "This arrangement" is not omitted and reads as follows: "This arrangement is not entered into, nor is this memorandum written, as a formal or legal agreement, and shall not be subject to legal jurisdiction in the Law Courts either of the United States or England, but it is only a definite expression and record of the purpose and intention of the three parties concerned to which they each honourably pledge themselves with the fullest confidence, based upon past business with each other, that it will be carried through by each of the three parties with mutual loyalty and friendly co-operation." The judge below thinks that by itself this clause "plain as it is" means that the parties shall not be under any legal obligation to each other at all. But coming to the conclusion that without this clause the agreement would create legal obligations, he takes the view that the clause must be rejected as repugnant to the rest of the agreement. He also holds that if the clause merely means to exclude recourse to the Law Courts as a means of settling disputes, it is contrary to public policy as ousting the jurisdiction of the King's Courts.

In my view the learned judge adopts a wrong canon of construction. He should not seek the intention of the parties as shown by the language they use in part of that language only, but in the whole of that language. It is true that in deeds and wills where it is impossible from the whole of the contradictory language used to ascertain the true intention of the framers, resort may be had, but only as a last expedient, to what Jessel MR called "the rule of thumb" in *In re Bywater* of reject-

---

[161] [1923] 2 KB 261 and [1925] AC 445.

98

ing clauses as repugnant according to their place in the document, the later clause being rejected in deeds and the earlier in wills. But before this heroic method is adopted of finding out what the parties meant by assuming that they did not mean part of what they have said, it must be clearly impossible to harmonize the whole of the language they have used. Now it is quite possible for parties to come to an agreement by accepting a proposal with the result that the agreement concluded does not give rise to legal relations. The reason of this is that the parties do not intend that their agreement shall give rise to legal relations. This intention may be implied from the subject matter of the agreement, but it may also be expressed by the parties. In social and family relations such an intention is readily implied, while in business matters the opposite result would ordinarily follow. But I can see no reason why, even in business matters, the parties should not intend to rely on each other's good faith and honour, and to exclude all idea of settling disputes by any outside intervention, with the accompanying necessity of expressing themselves so precisely that outsiders may have no difficulty in understanding what they mean. If they clearly express such an intention I can see no reason in public policy why effect should not be given to their intention . . .
[The House of Lords agreed with this reasoning.]

Note
The House of Lords considered that it was not contrary to public policy to agree in advance that the jurisdiction of the courts should be ousted and that such a stipulation was to be observed by the parties. This is in contrast to the strict position in regard to penalty clauses where the courts may refuse to give effect to the intention of the parties.

In German Law, the use of the term "gentleman's" agreement does not necessarily imply that the parties have no intention to be legally bound, even if it was so construed in the following case.

BGH, 22 January 1964[162]   **1.G.70.**

OBLIGATION ARISING FROM GENTLEMAN'S AGREEMENT

Priority treatment

A gentleman's agreement for priority treatment may not be of no effect as good faith may be involved.
Judgment: The plaintiff was a manufacturer and distributor of pumps. It concluded with the defendant, a shipbuilding company, an agreement by which the defendant stated that the plaintiff would be given "priority treatment" for the purposes of the acceptance of tenders for the supply of pumps for the defendant's vessels. The plaintiff formed the view that the defendant had ceased to afford it the agreed treatment when ordering consignments of pumps. It demanded to be supplied with information in relation to all the pumps ordered by the defendant, as well as details concerning the defendant's other suppliers and the prices charged by its competitors.

The *Landgericht* and the *Oberlandesgericht* ordered the defendant to supply the information, apart from the names of the suppliers. On appeal by the defendant, the plaintiff's action was dismissed.

Discussion:
I The parties described their agreement as a "gentlemen's agreement". That term was not recognised by the court. According to the works of academic legal authors, a gentlemen's agreement is a

---

[162] DB. 1964 No 14.475.

statement made without any intention of giving rise to any consequences in law, since the result which it seeks to achieve must be based on trust in the word of the other contracting party, or "respect for morality" (meaning, in this context, the practices followed by business persons). Such an agreement may be discerned not only in the case of an agreement which is contrary to mandatory laws but also, and above all, in matters in which the parties merely enter into a simple agreement the detailed implementation of which is left to the sense of "morality" of the business persons concerned, without this conferring on the parties any legally enforceable rights. The Hamburg *Oberlandesgericht* accepted that this type of agreement is frequently entered into by business persons; and it based its approach on that fact when describing a gentlemen's agreement as a unilateral or bilateral guarantee governed by the goodwill and sense of morality of business persons, stating that—subject to the parties' intentions—such an agreement did not confer any legally enforceable rights, and observing that that interpretation, which was recognised by the courts, was in conformity with the view taken by the great majority of business persons. Since the use by the parties of the somewhat unusual term "gentlemen's agreement" must have been intended to have a particular meaning, it was necessary to conclude that all that could be expected of the defendant in the present case was that it should act in a gentlemanly way, without being legally bound to do so.

However, it is not possible to lay down any general rule to the effect that, whenever the parties call their agreement a "gentlemen's agreement", this necessarily means that they have no intention to be legally bound by it and, consequently, that they may rely only on their goodwill and sense of morality as business persons. Irrespective of the term applied to the agreement, it is necessary instead to examine, in accordance with the general rules of interpretation, whether the parties meant to bind themselves in law by creating legally enforceable rights, and if so, to what extent. The name given to the agreement may, within those parameters, form a starting-point for an analysis of the intention of the parties.

II The existence of such an extensive obligation to provide information was not apparent, either as a principal obligation or as an ancillary obligation, from the contents of the contract. Nor could it be generally inferred from the principle of good faith. The existence of such a contractual obligation to provide information has been upheld by case-law where, in the light of all the circumstances, the person concerned was not in a position to determine on his own the existence and scope of the right vested in him and that right could therefore be enforced, in accordance with the principle of good faith, against the other party, who was in a position to provide him with the information in question. In the present case, the facts were not such as to admit of any such presumption. Instead, the conclusion of what was termed a "gentlemen's agreement" showed that the parties merely intended to arrange for a system of amicable cooperation between them, enabling them to waive the need to carry out regular checks on all the information relating to the defendant.

In the present case, however, it was necessary for the court to examine whether, even in the absence of a proven breach of contract by the defendant, a request for information could be justified by the fact that the defendant had aroused the distrust of the plaintiff by virtue of the way in which the contractual clause providing for priority treatment had hitherto been implemented. . . . In such circumstances, it may be inferred from the principle of good faith (§ 242 BGB), which governs the whole of the law of obligations, that, in order for a plaintiff to invoke a right to be supplied with information, he simply needs to claim that he has reason to believe that the defendant has ceased to fulfil the criteria of amicable cooperation and mutual trust on the basis of which the contract was originally concluded.

Note

The definition by the BGH of a "gentlemen's agreement" is noteworthy as not being entirely free from confusion with an "agreement in principle". In actual fact, a gentlemen's agreement may be quite detailed. What is most interesting is the affirmation of the existence of an ancillary obligation of good faith which must be observed and upheld, to an extent, by the law. In order to be entitled to demand the information, the plaintiff in the present case had to show that it had grounds for doubting the defendant's good faith.

Cass. civ. 2e, 2 November 1985[163]   **1.F.71.**

PROMISE TO WAIVE RIGHTS TO SEEK CHANGE IN ALIMONY MAY BE BINDING

Alimony agreement

A promise by a divorcing person that she will not seek variation of an alimony order is not necessarily not binding.
Judgment: THE COURT: *On the second branch of the second appeal ground*:—Under Article 282 of the Civil Code;
—Whereas the judgment appealed against reduced, upon application by Mr A, the amount of alimony which he had been ordered to pay to Mrs de R de F, his ex-wife, by the decision declaring the parties divorced on the ground of a break-down of their marriage;
—Whereas in doing so, that judgment disregarded the commitment in honour entered into by the promisor on the occasion of the divorce, to waive the right to seek a subsequent alteration in the amount of the alimony, merely stating that such waiver was not legally enforceable as against the person making it;
—Whereas in so deciding, without stating the grounds of fact or of law on which it based its decision, the court of appeal deprived its decision of any basis in law;
On those grounds and without giving a decision on the other appeal grounds, the Cour de cassation sets aside and annuls the *inter partes* judgment given on 23 January 1984 by the Paris cour d'appel and consequently restores the cause and the parties to the state in which they found themselves before that judgment and, for a determination in accordance with the law, refers the case to the Amiens cour d'appel.

Note
The waiver of the right to seek an alteration in the amount of alimony is indeed described by the parties as a commitment in honour. The judgment of the Court of Appeal was quashed for not stating the grounds of "fact or of law" on which the appeal court held the waiver to be unenforceable. Thus, in principle a waiver of that kind may be lawful, which was not obvious before. This judgment may be contrasted with the judgment in *Balfour* v. *Balfour,*[164] where there was no commitment binding in honour or gentlemen's agreement.

1.3.1.C. LETTERS OF INTENT, OF PATRONAGE OR OF COMFORT

These are often ambiguous assurances, under various different guises and designations, whereby a person, generally a parent company, gives an assurance to a third party, for example a bank, that it will lend financial support to another, often its subsidiary. Depending on the case, that might be a genuine legal commitment, for example a guarantee, or a simple declaration of intent without any specific legal consequence. All turns on the interpretation to be given of the intention of the author of the letter.

---
[163] Bull. civ. II.178.
[164] *Supra*, at 98.

Court of Appeal **1.E.72.**

Kleinwort Benson Ltd v. *Malaysia Mining Corp. Bhd*[165]

STATEMENT OF INTENTION MAY NOT HAVE LEGAL EFFECT

Comfort letter

A statement to a lender by a parent company that it intends that its subsidiary, which is the borrower, should be able to meet its debts may not amount to a guarantee.

Facts: A broker in the tin market, M, obtained a bank loan, and a company sent that bank letters of assurance in which it stated: "it is our policy to ensure that the business of M is at all times in a position to meet its liabilities to you under the loan facility arrangements". And those letters added that the defendants would not reduce their current financial interest with M until those loans were repaid. Following a collapse in the tin market, M was placed in liquidation without repaying the loans. The bank sought repayment from the signatory of the letters and obtained it at first instance. The decision was reversed on appeal.

Judgment: RALPH GIBSON LJ. The central question in this case, in my judgment, is that considered in *Esso Petroleum Co Ltd* v. *Mardon* [1976] QB 801 on which counsel for the plaintiffs relied in this court but which was not cited to Hirst J. That question is whether the words of para 3, considered in their context, are to be treated as a warranty or contractual promise. Paragraph 3 contains no express words of promise. Paragraph 3 is in its terms a statement of present fact and not a promise as to future conduct. I agree whith the submision of counsel for the defendants that, in this regard, the words of para 3 are in sharp contrast with the words of para 2 of the letter: "We confirm that we will not" etc. The force of this point is not limited, as Hirst J stated it, to the absence from para 3 of the words "We confirm". The real contrast is between the words of promise, namely "We will not" in para 2, and the words of statement of fact, "It is our policy" in para 3. Hirst J. held that, by the words of para 3, the defendants gave an undertaking that now and at all times in the future, so long as Metals should be under any liability to the plaintiffs under the facility arrangements, it is and will be the defendants' policy to ensure that Metals is in a position to meet their liabilities. To derive that meaning from the word it is necessary to add the words emphasised, namely "and will be", which do not appear in para 3. In short, the words of promise as to the future conduct of the defendants were held by Hirst J to be part of the necessary meaning of the words used in para 3. The question is whether that view of the words can be upheld.

The absence of express words of warranty as to present facts or the absence of express words of promise as to future conduct does not conclusively exclude a statement from the status of warranty or promise.

The evidence does not show that the words used in para 3 were intended to be a promise as to the future conduct of the defendants but, in my judgment, it shows the contrary.

The concept of a comfort letter was, as counsel for the defendants acknowledged, not shown to have acquired any particular meaning at the time of the negotiations in this case with reference to the limits of any legal liability to be assumed under its terms by a parent company. A letter, which the parties might have referred to at some stage as a letter of comfort, might, after negotiation, have emerged containing in para 3 in express terms the words used by Hirst J to state the meaning which he gave to para 3. The court would not, merely because the parties had referred to the documents as a comfort letter, refuse to give effect to the meaning of the words used. But in this case it is clear, in my judgment, that the concept of a comfort letter, to which the parties had resort when the defendants refused to assume joint and several liability or to give a guarantee, was known by both sides at least to extend to or to include a document under which the defendants would give comfort to

---

[165] [1989] 1 All ER 785, CA.

102

the plaintiffs by assuming, not a legal liability to ensure repayment of the liabilities of its subsidiary, but a moral responsibility only. Thus, when the defendants by Mr John Green in June 1984 told the plaintiffs that Mr Green would recommend that credit lines for Metals be covered by a letter of comfort rather than by guarantee, the response of Mr Irwin, before any draft of a comfort letter had been prepared, was ". . . that a letter of comfort would not be a problem, but that (he) would probably have to charge a higher rate". The comfort letter was drafted in terms which in para 3 do not express any contractual promise and which are consistent with being no more than a representation of fact. If they are treated as no more than a representation of fact, they are in that meaning consistent with the comfort letter containing no more than the assumption of moral responsibility by the defendants in respect of the debts of Metal. There is nothing in the evidence to show that, as a matter of commercial probability or common sense, the parties must have intended para 3 to be a contractual promise, which is not expressly stated, rather than a mere representation of fact which is so stated.

Next, the first draft of the comfort letter was produced by the plaintiffs. Paragrah 1 contained confirmation that the defendants knew of and approved of the granting of the facilities in question by the plaintiffs to Metals, and para 2 contained the express confirmation that the defendants would not reduce their current financial interests in Metals until (in effect) facilities had been paid or the plaintiffs consented. Both are relevant to the present and future moral responsibility of the defendants. If the word of para 3 are to treated as intended to express a contractual promise by the defendants as to their future policy, which Hirst J held the words to contain, then the recitation of the plaintiffs' approval and the promise not to reduce their current financial interest in Metals, would be of no significance. If the defendants have promised that at all times in the future it will be the defendants' policy to ensure that Metals is in a position to meet its liabilities of the plaintiffs under the facility, it would not matter whether they had approved or disapproved, or whether they had disposed of their shares in Metals. Contracts may, of course, contain statements or promises which are caused to be of no separate commercial importance by the width of a later promise in the same document. Where, however, the court is examining a statement which is by its express words no more than a representation of fact, in order to consider whether it is shown to have been intended to be of the nature of a contractual promise or warranty, it seems to me to be a fact suggesting at least the absence of such intention if, as in this case, to read the statement as a contractual promise is to reduce to no significance two paragraphs included in the plaintiffs' draft, both of which have significance if the statement is read as a representation of fact only.

That point can be made more plainly thus: if par 3 in its original or in its final form was intended to contain a binding legal promise by the defendants to ensure the ability of Metals to pay the sums due under the facility, there was no apparent need or purpose for the plaintiffs, as bankers, to waste ink on paras 1 and 2.

As I have said, the absence of express words of promise does not by itself prevent a statement from being treated as a contractual promise. The example given in argument by counsel for the plaintiffs, namely of the shop stating by a notice that it is its policy to accept, within 14 days of purchase, the return in good condition of any goods bought and to refund the price without question, seems to me to be a case in which a court would be likely to hold that the notice imported a promise that the policy would continue over the 14-day period. It would be difficult on those facts to find any sensible commercial explanation for the notice other than a contractual promise not to change the policy over the 14-day period. It would not be satisfactory or convincing to regard the notice as no more than the assumption of a moral responsibility by the shop giving such a notice to its customers. In such a case, and in the absence of any relevant factual context indicating otherwise, it seems to me that the court would probably hold that the statement was shown to have been intended to be a contractual promise.

In this case, however, the opposite seems to me to be clear . . .

If my view of this case is correct, the plaintiffs have suffered grave financial loss as a result of the collapse of the tin market and the following decision by the defendant company not to honour a moral responsibility which is assumed in order to gain for its subsidiary the finance necessary for the trading operations which the defendants wished that subsidiary to pursue. The defendants have demonstrated, in my judgment, that they made no relevant contractual promise to the plaintiffs which could support the judgment in favour of the plaintiffs. The consequences of the decision of the defendants to repudiate their moral responsibility are not matters for this court.

I would allow this appeal.

[Nicholls and Fox LJJ agreed].

Appeal allowed.

Note

The letters of intent do not contain any formula limiting the scope of the commitment in the way one finds them in a gentlemen's agreement. But on the basis of their deliberately vague wording it may be asked whether there is indeed a legal commitment. In the present case the Court of Appeal considers there to be only a moral responsibility and no legal liability. It will be recalled that in *British Steel* v. *Cleveland Bridge and Engineering Co Ltd*[166] mention is made of letters of intent, but this seems to be a very extended use of the term. Goff J.—as he then was—provides a definition which covers preliminary agreements, the "if" contracts. An example of a comfort letter is to be found in *Walford* v. *Miles*.[167]

In other circumstances, the courts may regard this kind of document as a genuine obligation, or even as a guarantee.

BGH, 30 November 1992[168]   **1.G.73.**

LETTER AMOUNTING TO GUARANTEE

Letter of patronage

A Patronatserklärung may amount to a guarantee.
Judgment: The plaintiff, a Viennese bank, maintained business relations with the company, S GmbH, a wholly-owned subsidiary of P GmbH whose share capital is wholly-owned by the defendant company.

The plaintiff granted S Co. a loan of 25 million Austrian schillings. A "letter of patronage" from the defendant was to be provided by way of guarantee for the capital increases. In August 1986 the defendant company sent such a letter to the plaintiff, in which it agreed to guarantee a loan exceeding, by 10 million schillings, the sum of 30 million schillings, with a view to "constraining" the affiliated company "to fulfil its obligations".

. . .

Following negotiations between S Co. and the plaintiff, the defendant on 10 November 1986 sent a second letter of patronage to the bank, the contents of which were as follows:

---

[166] *Supra*, at 83.
[167] **2.E.64**, *infra* at 241.
[168] NJW 1992.2093.

"It has come to our notice that S Co., which is affiliated to P, has entered into a business relationship with you, and we are agreeable to this. P Co. is affiliated to our company as to 100%, and holds 100% of the capital of S Co. For as long as the above-mentioned business relationship continues to exist, or any debts are due to you from our affiliated company, we will maintain our participation at the same level. In the event that we intend to alter this state of affairs in any way, we will contact you in good time beforehand with a view to resolving the situation on an amicable basis. In addition, we irrevocably accept the obligation to exert our influence on our affiliated company throughout the period during which it has not yet repaid the loan in full, and to procure for it the requisite finance enabling it at all times to fulfil the obligations, present or future, which it owes to you. This declaration is governed by Austrian law."

On 28 December 1987 proceedings for court-supervised recovery were initiated against S GmbH. The plaintiff bank called in the loan and established the balance due at AS 18,545,418.99. Those proceedings were terminated by a compulsory settlement under which the bank was to have its claim satisfied as to 25 per cent. On 30 December 1997 like proceedings were brought against the defendant company. Under a settlement dated 6 October 1989 these proceedings were brought to an end. The compulsory settlement provided for the payment, in three tranches, of a 35 per cent proportion.

On the basis of the letter of patronage of 10 November 1986 the bank registered its claim in the amount of AS 3,110,453.03 which was disputed by the official receiver. In addition, under the settlement of 6 October 1989, the bank demanded payment of 35 per cent of its claim in three tranches.

The action for payment brought by the Bank was upheld by the courts trying the case on its merits which ordered the defendant to pay AS 6,490,896. The appeal on a point of law was dismissed by the Fed. Sup. Ct.

Discussion [extracts]:

1 The existence of a letter of patronage

. . . As the *Oberlandesgericht* acknowledged, the defendant is liable to pay damages pursuant to § 902 ABGB (the Austrian Civil Code) for failure to comply with its obligations as described in the (second) letter of patronage which it agreed to give and which it send to the bank. According to the terms of that letter, the defendant undertook to provide S Co. (the principal debtor) with finance enabling it to honour its debt to the plaintiff. That offer was accepted by the plaintiff in accordance with § 863 ABGB. According to that provision, acceptance may also be signified by "such conduct as, having regard to all the circumstances, affords no valid reason for doubting an intention to accept". In the proceedings at first instance, the plaintiff relied on the argument that its conduct had been conclusive, as was borne out by the fact that it had continued to abide by its commitment to provide credit to S Co. In the proceedings at second instance, it argued that, according to the defendant's letter of patronage, the latter had not expected any express acceptance of the terms of that letter. Silence in response to a contractual document corresponding to the matters agreed in oral negotiations was sufficient to constitute acceptance. . . . In the present case, the *Oberlandesgericht* held that the (second) letter of patronage enured to the benefit of the plaintiff alone. Unlike the first letter, dated 4 August 1986, it was not limited as to the amount of the guarantee. Moreover, it was formulated in more precise terms than the first letter and more clearly imposed an obligation on the party issuing it . . . Neither in Austrian law nor in German law could one expect to find a letter of patronage having greater force than that issued in November 1986 (. . .). In the present case, all those matters give rise to a very strong presumption that the second letter of patronage was firmly accepted. . . .

2 The effects of the letter of patronage

. . . A letter of patronage such as that in the present case is generally comparable to a form of security such as a bond or declaration of guarantee. In the event of the insolvency of the creditor, those two instruments acquire, in principle, the binding force of a guarantee having equal rank. In the case of a bond, this results from subparagraph 3 in the first paragraph of § 773 ABGB, and, in the case of an ordinary guarantee (not governed by the Code), from the general legal principles of entitlement to damages, to which it is subject. According to the general rules, the obligation to pay damages means not only that damages are payable in the event of default by the debtor but also that compensation is payable for the entire loss suffered, where appropriate on a joint and several basis with other persons owing an obligation. If, in the present case, the defendant parent company had properly fulfilled its obligations arising from the letter of patronage, the loan would have been repaid by the due date. However, in the event of wrongful failure to perform, a party undertaking to guarantee the performance of the contractual obligation of another is in principle fully liable to pay the debt due from the principal debtor, jointly and severally with the latter. . . .

Solution

In the present case the letter of patronage, as widened, must be regarded as a genuine guarantee under § 773(I)(3) BGB or a guarantee governed by the general principles of liability. Accordingly, full restitution of the loss suffered by the Bank must be afforded. The defendant, the promisor under the letter of patronage, is jointly liable for non-performance of the contractual obligations which the principal debtor was bound to perform.

Note

This is a declaration known as a *Patronatserklärung*, or letter of patronage. Again a problem of interpretation arises. The Court considers there to have been a legally binding commitment, notwithstanding the absence of express acceptance since silence here amounts to acceptance. The Court considers there to have been a genuine guarantee.

Cass. com., 21 December 1987[169] **1.F.74.**

CONTRACT OF SURETYSHIP MUST BE EXPRESS

French letter of comfort

A contract of suretyship requires express words.

Facts: A company signed a letter in the following terms to a lender of funds to its subsidiary: "As the majority shareholder of TV, we confirm our intention to follow and support our subsidiary in its financial needs and, should it be necessary, to substitute ourselves for it in regard to all commitments which it might enter into with yourselves, our concern being to ensure that it remains totally solvent. We confirm our intention, in the event of need, of immediately taking the necessary steps with our authorities in order to obtain authorisation to transfer the funds."

Held: TV was placed under judicial liquidation and the lender sought reimbursement from the parent company. The claim succeeded at first instance and on appeal but the judgments of the lower courts were set aside on cassation.

Judgment: THE COURT:—Whereas according to the findings of the judgment appealed against (Montpellier, 2nd Chamber, 10 January 1985), the company, Textiles du Vallespir (TV), a subsidiary of the company incorporated under Spanish law, Viuda de José Tolra (Tolra), obtained, by way of notarially attested deeds, drawn up in November 1973 and June and September 1974, respectively, three loans from the Société de développement régional du Languedoc-Roussillon (Solder) for the

---

[169] D.1989.112 annotated by Brill; JCP 1988.II.21113, concl. Montanier.

building of a factory; as in addition to the guarantee which it gave in respect of the repayment of the first of those loans, Tolra signed on 29 May 1974 a letter addressed to Solder in which it stated its intention to "support our subsidiary in its financial needs and, should it be necessary, to substitute ourselves for it in regard to all commitments which it might enter into with Solder", whilst expressing concern to ensure that it remained totally solvent, and confirming an intention, in the event of need, of immediately taking the necessary steps with the Spanish authorities in order to obtain authorisation to transfer the funds; as that letter was mentioned in the notarial deed dated 12 and 17 September 1974 relating to the third loan but referred also to the second loan; as following the order for court-supervised composition in regard to TV and the subsequent conversion of that order into a liquidation of assets, Solder brought proceedings against Tolra, on the basis of the letter of intent, for payment of the principal sum of the second and third loans, together with interest;

On the first two branches of the first appeal ground:—Whereas Tolra alleges that the appeal court took the view that the letter of intent was binding on it in contract, and found that it was under an obligation as to the result to be achieved, whereas, in the terms of the appeal submission, a unilateral declaration of intention gives rise to no obligation at civil law, save in exceptional circumstances;

—Whereas it follows from the facts as found by the court below that Tolra merely made a unilateral declaration of intention without any contract being created, there being no agreement between the parties;

—Whereas by taking the view that the letter of intention drawn up by Tolra could have given rise to an obligation upon it at civil law, the appeal court infringed Article 1101 of the Civil Code; as secondly, since the obligation as to the result to be achieved, namely taking the place of a debtor in order to honour undertakings given to a creditor is an obligation arising out of suretyship;

—Whereas such liability can arise only under a contract of suretyship which must be express and must have a specific or specifiable object;

—Whereas by taking the view that the letter of intent contained an obligation as to the result to be achieved distinct from a guarantee, the appeal court infringed Article 2011 of the Civil Code;

—Whereas however, notwithstanding its unilateral nature, a letter of intent may, according to the terms in which it is couched, and where it has been accepted by its addressee, and regard being had to the common intention of the parties, impose contractual liability on the party subscribing to it to act or not to act, which may go so far as to impose an obligation to ensure a certain result is achieved, even if it does not constitute a contract of suretyship;

—Whereas it is for the courts to give or restore a precise designation to such a document without dwelling on the terms attributed to its description by the parties; as the appeal court also found that Tolra, in its letter of 29 May 1974, gave to understand that it agreed that it would substitute itself, if need be, for its subsidiary to honour undertakings given to Solder; as that letter, the appeal court added, certainly referred to the second and third loans;

—Whereas although suretyship cannot be inferred and must be in express terms, a person who by means of an unequivocal and informed declaration of intent, declares that he will undertake to meet the obligation of the debtor towards the creditor, if the debtor does not do so himself, sets himself up as guarantor of that obligation;

—Whereas solely on this point of law, in place of those which were criticised, the appeal court's decision may be justified, inasmuch as it found that Tolra had undertaken to pay to Solder, in the event of TV'S failure to do so, the balance outstanding under the loans granted. It follows that none of the limbs of the plea can be upheld;

On the first branch of the second appeal ground:—Under Article 3 of the Civil Code and Article 3 of the law of 24 July 1966, in dismissing the claim by Tolra that, even if the letter of intent did constitute an obligation to pay, it was in any event null and void as it was not concluded in accordance with Spanish company law, the appeal court merely declared that it was seised "of a dispute arising out of facts and matters occurring in France to which French legislation must apply".

—Whereas in so deciding, despite finding that Tolra was a joint-stock company incorporated under Spanish law and in light of the fact that an appraisal of the powers of the directors of a company is a matter for the national law governing that company, the appeal court misapplied and therefore infringed the abovementioned provisions;

On those grounds the judgment is set aside.

Note

This judgment, based on carefully drafted reasoning, touches on most of the questions arising in connection with comfort letters and the different forms they take. They may be mere declarations without legal commitment, in the absence of a sufficiently well defined subject-matter and the agreement of the other party: an example of this is the promise to "do everything possible". This may be an obligation to provide the means, or may amount to a genuine obligation to secure a result, namely to take the place of the defaulting debtor, which constitutes a guarantee. In this case, the decision to provide a guarantee must be in accordance with the provisions of the applicable system of company law. In this case the judgment was set aside because it applied French law to a Spanish company. Under French law the authorization of the board of directors is required.[170]

In the final analysis, here again, it is all a question of interpretation which is all the more difficult to resolve since frequently the parties involved are careful not to be too specific in regard to the commitments which they are undertaking. The ambiguity is often intentional.

1.3.1.D. AGREEMENT IN PRINCIPLE (*ACCORD DE PRINCIPE*)

This is another of those intermediate situations. The parties are in agreement on the most important part of the contract, so much so that it may legitimately be asked whether the contract has been created or not. We already encountered a situation of this kind in *British Steel Corp.* v. *Cleveland Bridge and Engineering Co Ltd (1984)*[171] where it was found that, contrary to expectations, a definitive contract had not been created. This kind of situation may arise where negotiations are protracted and complicated and the contract comes into being in successive stages.

In a declaration of principle there is more then mere negotiations but less than a definitive contract. It has to be filled out. Does that mean to say that it is of no effect?

---

[170] See Article 98(4)of the law of 24 July 1966 and Cass. com., 8 November 1994, Bull. civ. IV.330.
[171] *Supra*, at 83.

AGREEMENT IN PRINCIPLE

Maize driers

A short agreement may be binding if it contains the necessary elements of a contract. Whether it does so is a matter for the appreciation of the court.

Facts: The company, S, in a letter dated 9 August 1977, stated to Mr B: "We confirm the agreements reached during your visit and grant you sole rights for the whole of France for our maize driers." The appeal court took the view that this was merely a declaration of principle and not a genuine contract.

Judgment: THE COURT: *On the first appeal ground taken in its three branches*:—Whereas it appears from the findings contained in the judgment appealed against (Bordeaux, 2nd Chamber, 9 May 1984) that Mr Betat bought from Mr Berger a business trading under the name of Italfrance (later Euromat) and that possession was to be given on completion before a notary, and that a deposit on account of the purchase price had been paid; as subsequently, Mr Betat sought to rescind the purchase, to recover the payment on account together with damages on the ground that he had been the victim of fraud, since the contract mentioning an exclusive distributorship agreement in respect of Pedrotti goods in France was, in Mr Betat's submission, entirely imaginary;

—Whereas the Berger couple criticise the judgment appealed against for upholding that claim since, as stated in the appeal, under Article 1101 of the Civil Code a contract is an agreement under which one or more persons enter into obligations towards one or more other persons to give, to do or not to do something;

—Under Article 1108 of the Civil Code such a contract is valid once the subject-matter is determined with certainty, the cause is lawful and the party assuming obligations has legal capacity to enter into contractual relationships and has given his unvitiated consent;

—Whereas in the present case, the letter from the Pedrotti company of 9 August 1977 expressly stated to Mr Berger: "We confirm the agreements reached during your visit and grant you sole rights for the whole of France for our maize driers"; as that letter in which Pedrotti, whose capacity and consent were not in issue, undertook to give Mr Berger exclusive sales rights in France in respect of its maize driers, did constitute a firm, precise and definitive contract granting exclusive rights.

—Whereas by holding that it was merely an "agreement in principle" and not a contract, the appeal court infringed Articles 1101 and 1108 of the Civil Code by misapplying them and by holding that the exchange of correspondence between the parties, in which Pedrotti stated clearly and unequivocally: "We confirm the agreements reached during your visit and grant you sole rights for the whole of France for our maize driers", was too vague to constitute a genuine contract but merely amounted to an agreement in principle, the appeal court distorted the plain evidence of that letter and consequently was in breach of Article 1134 of the Civil Code, since it was in the end not disputed by any of the parties to the proceedings that since 1977 Pedrotti had in fact been granting exclusive rights to Mr Berger to sell its maize driers; as by holding, however, that "the 1977 agreement was not followed up", the appeal court placed reliance on a matter of fact extraneous to the proceedings, thereby infringing Article 7 of the Code of Civil Procedure;

—Whereas however, in the exercise of its sovereign power to appraise the evidence, the appeal court held that no contract conferring exclusive rights had been entered into between Pedrotti and Mr Berger;

—Whereas none of the branches of the appeal ground therefore well founded . . .

[172] Annexed to I. Najjar, "L'accord de principe", D.1991, Chron.67.

Note

The Cour de cassation hides behind the appeal court's sovereign power to appraise the evidence in order to dismiss the appeal. The appeal court had found that the agreement did not constitute a "precise, firm and definitive contract". Doubtless too many important matters—duration, remuneration etc.—had been left unsettled. In the final analysis, its subject-matter was not sufficiently well circumscribed—Article 1108 Civil Code.

The notion of the agreement in principle was also used in slightly different circumstances in the following judgment.

Cass. soc., 24 March 1958[173]   **1.F.76.**

No AGREEMENT IF PARTY DOES NOT COMMIT ITSELF

Agreement to consider re-employment

A letter stating that an employer will consider re-employing an ex-employee if buiness improves imposes no commitment.
Judgment: THE COURT . . .: *On the sole appeal ground*:—Under Article 1134 of the Civil Code;
—Whereas under this provision, contracts created in accordance with the law have the force of law as regards those who have entered into them;
—Whereas although it is indeed for the courts to interpret agreements, this is on condition that they do not distort the plain meaning of their clear and unambiguous provisions;
—Whereas the judgment appealed against finds that Marchal had been employed until 19 December 1940 by Renault; as after the liberation he asked to be reinstated by registered letter dated 4 December 1944; as on 19 January 1945 he was sent the following letter in reply: "Although we would wish to accede to your request, our reply to your request in which you mention the status which you acquired in the Resistance is that the current operational activity of our works and the organisation of our departments which are already very busy whilst production remains slack, prevent us from giving you for the moment a favourable reply"; as on 24 March 1945 a reply along the same lines was sent to a third party who had intervened in Marchal's favour: "Following a fresh examination of the question I can inform you that our intentions as regards Mr Marchal have not changed and that, as soon as the resumption of car manufacturing permits, we will once again study the possibility of reinstating him in the Company";
—Whereas the lower courts inferred from those letters that Renault had given an undertaking to reinstate Marchal as soon as the post corresponding to his former duties had been recreated as a result of a recovery in the economic situation; as it was for the Company itself to advise Mr Marchal as soon as a suitable post became vacant, and it mattered little that Mr Marchal delayed until 18 May 1951 before reiterating his request;
—Whereas by holding that the abovementioned letters contained a firm undertaking on the part of Renault to reinstate Marchal, as soon as the first post fell vacant, the judgment appealed against distorted the meaning and scope of the clear and unambiguous terms in which those letters were couched; as under those terms Renault, desirous of acceding to Marchal's request, would, depending on the state of prosperity and development of the undertaking, study the possibility of reinstating him, which amounted only to an agreement in principle;
—Whereas it followed that the judgment appealed against had no legal basis;
On those grounds, the Cour de cassation set aside the judgment delivered on 23 March 1956 by the Tribunal Civil de la Seine and referred the case to the Tribunal Civil de Versailles.

[173] JCP. 1958.II.10868, annotated by J. Carbonnier.

110

Note

The interpretation of this judgment is finely balanced. The Cour de cassation took the view that the lower court, in holding there to be a firm commitment on the part of Renault to reinstate Marchal as soon as a post fell vacant, distorted the meaning and scope of the clear and unambiguous terms in which the letters to Marchal were couched, which sets the limit to the untrammelled power of appraisal. In fact the lower courts appear to have stretched the meaning of those letters. Does that mean that the agreement in principle found by the Cour de cassation is a formula having no legal scope? One cannot make such an assertion since the Cour de cassation used it knowingly. Accordingly, it may reasonably be supposed that Renault is required to re-examine Marchal's situation when the situation of the undertaking so permits.

The solution adopted by the German BGH. on 8 June 1962 also results in effect of a kind being given to an agreement in principle, but in a slightly different way.

BGH, 8 June 1962[174]   **1.G.77.**

PRELIMINARY CONTRACT

Consulting his lawyer

A preliminary contract may not be binding yet may create some obligations to complete arrangements.
Judgment: On 3 September 1958 the parties had a discussion and agreed to settle their differences concerning a licensing agreement entered into on 4 October 1950. A written settlement was drawn up on 30 September 1958 under which the parties signed a preliminary contract with a view to concluding a definitive agreement. However, the defendant wished to show the preliminary contract to his legal adviser in order to amend certain formal clauses and to ascertain the financial implications of what he was letting himself in for. However, there was no provision to this effect in the preliminary contract. The plaintiff sought conclusion of the definitive contract, whilst the defendant resisted this.
The plaintiff therefore brought an action for specific performance against the defendant whose defence to this claim was that he had never sought to commit himself contractually since he wished to consult his legal adviser. The lower courts granted the remedy sought and the appeal on a point of law was dismissed.

Discussion:
The *Oberlandesgericht* took the view that it had been established that the parties had agreed, in the course of the discussion which took place on 3 September 1958 between the plaintiff and W.B., the co-tenant and manager of the defendant, that the differences between them concerning the licence of 4 December 1950 were to be settled in the form agreed, as set out in the memorandum of the meeting held on 3 September 1958. It regarded that agreement as a preliminary contract drawn up with a view to achieving a written settlement on the same terms as those set out in the memorandum. According to the *Oberlandesgericht*, such a contract may be concluded orally, even though it is agreed between the parties that the definitive contract is to be in writing. It is true to say that W.B., in stating that he wished first of all to show the contract to a lawyer, gained for the defendant the opportunity of altering the forms of wording chosen, the scope of which he was unable to appreciate without the advice of a lawyer, whilst at the same time preserving the essential scheme of the

---

[174] NJW 1962.1812

111

contract. However, the draft contract did not contain such wording. . . . As an experienced busi-nessman, W.B. was aware of the general scope of that agreement, and was in a position to evaluate it without consulting a lawyer. In response to the plaintiff's statement that there was an agreement and that they should not part without agreeing the wording, he replied: "Of course we've got an agreement"; consequently, that reply cannot have meant, as the defendant asserts, that it was an agreement without legal force. Instead, it was an agreement which was intended to impose obliga-tions on the two parties, since they had not wished to part without reaching an agreement and had intended to be bound. Moreover, the agreement thus reached by both sides had been cemented by a handshake. . . .

The appeal on a point of law criticized the judgments of the lower courts for analysing the agree-ment as a genuine preliminary agreement. In that connection, the *Bundesgerichtshof* points out that academic writers and judicial precedents are at one in considering that a preliminary agreement gives rise to a genuine contractual relationship under which the parties are bound to enter into a subsequent principal contract.

The *Bundesgerichtshof* observes that the conditions governing the validity of a preliminary agree-ment are the same as those applicable to contracts in general, and also that the contents of the prin-cipal contract must be adequately adumbrated, although it stresses that the general principle is the immediate conclusion of the principal contract and that the conclusion of a preliminary contract is the exception to that rule. In cases involving preliminary contracts, it is necessary to examine very carefully whether the parties really intended to conclude such a preliminary contract, and whether it is itself intended from the outset to create principal obligations. Thus, a preliminary contract is in essence concluded where there are *de facto* or *de jure* obstacles preventing the execution of the definitive contract but the parties nevertheless wish to be bound from the outset. . . . Since those conditions were fulfilled in the present case, the *Oberlandesgericht*'s categorisation of the agreement as a preliminary contract cannot be contested on legal grounds.

However, the order of the *Oberlandesgericht* requiring the defendant to execute the contract can-not be upheld. The *Bundesgerichtshof* finds that the preliminary contract pleaded by the plaintiff was not the definitive contract; it merely obliged the parties to conclude a contract having the same general scope. Moreover, the contract to be concluded on the basis of the preliminary contract takes effect only from the time at which the decision ordering the defendant to enter into it acquires the force of *res judicata* (§ 894 ZPO). Consequently, when the contents of the contract were deter-mined, account should also have been taken of the changes which had taken place since the con-clusion of the preliminary contract. On that ground, the *Bundesgerichtshof* sets aside that aspect of the judgment, and refers the case back to the *Oberlandesgericht* with a view to the conclusion of a settlement under the supervision of that court.

Note

The question was to determine whether there was merely a pre-contract or an actual con-tract, which was the view of the OLG. The Federal Supreme Court adopted a balanced solution: there was an agreement but it was incomplete, and there were points on which the parties were not *ad idem*. The agreement had to be completed before the court to which the case was referred back.

Court of Appeal   **1.E.78.**
Eccles v. *Bryant*[175]

No binding contract before both sign

"Subject to contract"

When parties agree to the sale and purchase of a house "subject to contract", neither party is bound until each has signed his part of the contract and they have "exchanged contracts".

Facts: A house was sold by correspondence "subject to contract". The purchaser's solicitor sent the contract for signature to the vendor's solicitor. But the vendor had in the meantime had a change of mind and refused to sign. At first instance a decree of specific performance was granted. This was set aside on appeal.

Judgment: LORD GREENE MR . . . The parties were minded to enter into a contract for the sale and purchase of a house. The matter was put into the hands of their respective solicitors in the ordinary way. The basis on which the negotiations were being conducted was that the terms set out in the preliminary correspondence were stated to be subject to contract and survey. We are not troubled with the survey. The important words are "subject to contract". This is one of those cases where quite clearly and admittedly no contract came into existence in the earlier correspondence. It is common ground that the parties contemplated a definitive binding contract which was to come into existence in the future. One thing is quite clear on the facts of this case to my mind, that both firms of solicitors, one of whom—that is the vendors' solicitors—practised in East Grinstead and the other of whom, the purchaser's solicitors, practised in London, when they were instructed to carry this matter through by their respective clients, contemplated and intended from beginning to end to do so in the customary way which is familiar to every firm of solicitors in the country, namely, by preparing the engrossment of the draft contract when agreed in duplicate, the intention being to do what I have no doubt at this very moment is happening in dozens of solicitors' offices all over the country, namely, to exchange the two parts when signed by their respective clients. That, indeed is what anyone would have understood, I think, from the language of the earlier correspondence and the words "subject to contract"—that the contract would be brought about in the way I have mentioned, by an exchange of the two parts signed by the respective parties.

Vaisey J. pointed out that what he called the ceremonial form of exchange, namely, the meeting of solicitors in the office of one of them—the vendors' solicitors' office as a rule—and the passing of the two signed engrossments over the table may be taken to have fallen—and indeed, no doubt it has—into disuse to a certain extent, particularly when there are firms of solicitors in different parts of the country. He recognized that an exchange by post would, in many cases, take the place of the old more ceremonial exchange, but that an exchange was contemplated by both firms of solicitors from beginning to end appears to me to be clear from what took place and from the correspondence. I am prepared to assume—and I think I should probably be right in assuming—that their intention was that the exchange should take place by post. When an exchange takes place by post and a contract comes into existence through the act of exchange, the earliest date at which such a contract can come into existence, it appears to me, would be the date when the later of the two documents to be put in the post is actually put in the post. Another view might be that the exchange takes place and the contract thereby comes into existence when, and not before, the respective parties or their solicitors receive from their "opposite numbers" their parts of the contract. It is not necessary here to choose between those two views. I mention them particularly because Mr. Hopkins, for the purchaser, here tried to suggest an intermediate stage, that where the parties

---

[175] [1948] Ch 43.

contemplate an exchange by post the contract is completed not when an exchange takes place, but when one of the parties puts his part into the post. I am afraid I cannot accept that. It seems to me to be a contradiction in terms to speak of that as an exchange . . .

It is said that a contract took place when, in response to an alleged invitation on behalf of the vendors, the purchaser signed his part of the contract and communicated the fact to the vendors. It was argued that there is no necessity in this class of case for an exchange of documents at all, and that the references which have taken place in very many judgments in this court and other courts to an exchange are either inaccurate or wrong; a contract in this class of case, it is said, does not require exchange. The answer to that seems to me to be a simple one. When parties are proposing to enter into a contract, the manner in which the contract is to be created so as to bind them must be gathered from the intentions of the parties express or implied. In such a contract as this, there is a well-known, common and customary method of dealing; namely, by exchange, and anyone who contemplates that method of dealing cannot contemplate the coming into existence of a binding contract before the exchange takes place.

It was argued that exchange is a mere matter of machinery, having in itself no particular importance and no particular significance. So far as significance is concerned, it appears to me that not only is it not right to say of exchange that it has no significance, but it is the crucial and vital fact which brings the contract into existence. As for importance, it is of the greatest importance, and that is why in past ages this procedure came to be recognised by everybody to be the proper procedure and was adopted. When you are dealing with contracts for the sale of land, it is of the greatest importance to the vendor that he should have a document signed by the purchaser, and to the purchaser that he should have a document signed by the vendor. It is of the greatest importance that there should be no dispute whether a contract had or had not been made and that there should be no dispute as to the terms of it. This particular procedure of exchange ensures that none of those difficulties will arise. Each party has got what is a document of title, because directly a contract in writing relating to land is entered into, it is a document of title. That can be illustrated, of course, by remembering the simple case where a purchaser makes a sub-sale. The contract is a vital document for the purpose of the sub-sale. If he had not got the vendor's part, signed by the vendor, to show to the sub-purchaser, he would not be able to make a good title.

[Cohen and Asquith LJJ delivered judgment to the same effect].

Appeal allowed.

Note

The Court considered that the form agreed, namely the exchange of signatures by means of an exchange of correspondence between the parties' solicitors, is an essential element of the agreement and that, if that exchange does not take place, no contract has come into existence. The agreement in principle on the remainder of the agreement is without effect.

The solution would be different under French law, where, for some types of contract, once the intention of the parties has been established, the contract must be notarized.[176] But everything turns on the intention of the parties. For German law, see § 154 BGB under which there is a presumption, in case of doubt, that a contract has not come into existence as long as it has not been notarized.

All the cases considered above under the heading "Intention to create legal relations" raise the question whether a given undertaking—within the broad sense of the term— gives rise to a legal relationship and constitutes a contract. Such situations must be

---

[176] Cass. civ. 3e, 20 December 1994, JCP 1995.II.22491, annotated by C. Larroumet.

distinguished from those giving rise to *avant-contrats* (pre-contracts), *Vorverträge* (pre-contracts), unilateral promises to enter into a contract and options, which certainly constitute contracts in most legal systems but are in fact preliminary contracts intended to serve as preparatory steps towards a definitive contract. Such preliminary contracts will be considered in the section devoted to the formation of contracts.

The intention to enter into a binding undertaking is a necessary precondition to a contract, but not always easy to discern. There are intermediate situations which are not free from doubt. But is that precondition sufficient?

1.3.2. FOUNDATIONS OF THE BINDING FORCE OF CONTRACT

1.3.2.A. GENERAL

It may be wondered why a discussion on the foundations of the binding force of the contract finds its way into a casebook which concentrates on practical matters. The reason is that a discussion of that kind has an influence on the practical solutions arrived at by contract law, as will be seen from the numerous references which are made in this section.

Freedom of contract entails that a person is free to decide whether or not to bind himself by contract and to determine the content of his commitment. The corollary of that principle, namely *consensus ad idem*, means that intention will suffice, without there being any requirement as to form. These two principles, which still underpin the European systems of law, are generally speaking accounted for as being a manifestation of the philosophical principle of free will, that is to say the creative force of the will. It is true that those fundamental principles have been under assault for the past 100 years. Disputes have proliferated. There are those who take the view that intention plays only an ancillary role, or perhaps none at all, in the law of contract. In more general terms, in addition to intention, the role of objective matters is highlighted, which has repercussions as far as the substantive law is concerned.

The two following texts each offer a slightly different, though complementary, approach.

Kötz, *European Contract Law*[177]   **1.G.79.**

Why are contracts binding? Why do they give rise to enforceable claims for performance or damages for non-performance? Many explanations have been put forward. According to some of these theories, rooted in the classical contract law of the nineteenth century, the rules and structures derive from the basic tenet of liberalism that an individual has the right to determine his future conduct by decisions freely arrived at, and that his autonomy in this regard must be respected by the courts of the state. Savigny held that contractual obligations must be recognised and enforced because they were the product of the will of the promisor. Many of the outworks of this "will-theory" have now been abandoned; in particular we recognise today that while recognition must be accorded to the manifestation of a person's will—his "declaration"—what is binding is not what was willed but what was expressed, that he is bound not in the sense he intended but in the sense in which what he said would reasonably be understood by the addressee in the context in which he said it. This objection to the basic idea of the will-theory is not, however, crucial: autonomy does not

---

[177] H. Kötz, *European Contract Law*, at 7–9.

necessarly mean that one may disregard the interests of others or disclaim the import properly to be accorded to what one says.

Some modern writers, such as Werner Flume in Germany[178] and Charles Fried in the United States,[179] propound cognate theories. Fried derives the binding nature of contract from the "promise principle": "An individual is morally bound to keep his promises because he has intentionally invoked a convention whose function is to give grounds—moral grounds—for another to expect the promised performance". Fried accepts that he cannot derive all the actual rules of contract law from the "promise principle". He has to make considerable concessions. For example, he admits that the "promise principle" cannot explain why a promise is not binding if the promisor was fundamentally mistaken in making it, nor why a promise may cease to bind if performance turns out to be impossible or futile: "gaps" like these have to be filled by reference to *other* principles, such as the requirements of fairness, the protection of reliance or the proper allocation of risks.

This already suggests that it may not be possible to trace back to any single "principle" the complex web of rules which make up the law of contract.[180] This is confirmed by a glance at recent scholarship which, especially in the United States but also in England and Germany, has busied itself with questions of contract theory. Quite different proposals have been made.

Thus against Fried it is said that the dominant principle in the Common Law is that of *bargain*. It is true that in the common law a promise is not regarded as binding just because the promisor seriously intended to bind himself: he has to ask the promisee to render or·promise something in return, something regarded by the parties as the "price" for the promise. This is the doctrine of consideration. Fried's reply is that the courts no longer pay much attention to the consideration doctrine or the "bargain principle" based on it: they are on the way out. There is indeed some evidence for this. In certain circumstances, especially in the United States, a promise is regarded as binding even if no counter-performance is present. This is so in particular if the promisor must have realised that the other party would regard his promise as binding and make disadvantageous arrangements in consequence. If the other party was entitled to rely and did actually rely on the promise, the promisor here is prevented—"estopped"—from asserting that his promise is invalid for want of consideration.[181] Atiyah is in the forefront of those who talk of the *reliance principle*, and emphasise that where justifiable reliance has been betrayed the Common Law increasingly grants claims for damages, admittedly directed not to the "performance interest" but to the "reliance interest".[182]

[178] See Flume, *Rechtsgeschäft*, at 7: "The concept of contract is that what has been contractually agreed has validity because the parties in their free self-determination, have agreed that that should establish their rights and duties".

[179] C. Fried, *Contract as Promise, A Theory of Contractual Obligations* (Cambridge, Mass.: Harvard UP, 1981), reviewed by Kronman, 91 Yale LJ 404 (1981) and by P. Atiyah, 95 Harv. LR 509 (1981). See also P. Atiyah, *Essays on Contract* (Oxford: Clarendon, 1990) at 121 ff.

[180] See, for well-justified scepticism, T. Weir "Contracts in Rome and England", 66 Tul. LR 1615, 1647 (1992): "But many of the total theories do seem to be dotty in their assumption that social phenomena resulting from the manifold contributions by thousands of differently motivated persons . . . are susceptible of simple explanation, and that 'contract' must have an essence, be it will or consent or promise or reliance or whatever monosyllabic spell is thought most apt to unlock its complex treasures and lay them bare in easily assimilable order".

[181] The term used is "promissory estoppel". In cases involving a right in land English lawyers also use the phrase "proprietary estoppel".

[182] See P. S. Atiyah, "Contracts, Promises and the Law of Obligations" 94 LQR 193 (1978); also in *Essays on Contract*, op. cit., at 10 ff. Atiyah's views result from a comprehensive analysis of the history of contract law in the Common Law: see P. S. Atiyah, *The Rise and Fall of Freedom of Contract* (Oxford: Clarendon, 1979). Atiyah distinguishes three bases for contractual liability, namely (1) that the promise was not kept, (2) that justified reliance was falsified, and (3) that performance was rendered as agreed, but the recipient must return it because the contract has failed. Whether this third case is actually an instance of *contractual* liabilitiy may well be questioned. In Germany and France and even in England one would think that liability was based on the fact that

Thus the courts have occasionally held that even before the contract come into existence a party is bound to pay some heed to the interests of the other party, and may be liable in damages for breach of this duty.[183] Indeed in a very readable little book Grant Gilmore maintains that the "reliance principle", with damages claims covering the reliance interest much as in tort, is making such headway that it is already sounding the death knell of contract.[184]

Note

This extract illustrates the different theories: from voluntarism as renewed by C. Fried, through the theory of the bargain, and the reliance principle rediscovered in the United States and advocated in Europe by P. Atiyah, to the death of the contract announced by the American writer, Gilmore.[185]

Carbonnier[186]   1.F.80.

By what means does intention provide itself in the contract with its own rules? Many, viewing the matter from the promisor's vantage point, attribute the obligation to a power or creative immanent will (cf. Demogue, I, No 15): I want, therefore I make a promise to do something. The voluntarist psychology of Maine de Biran and de Jouffroy was able in the last century to predispose minds in such a way they received this account favourably. Neverthless, it is difficult to grasp how an obligation, which is perceived as coming from outside, could result from a purely internal phenomenon. Thus, philosophers have sought to shift the focus of the creative action of the will to its expression, namely speech. That is the meaning underlying the theory of acts of speech which is not unrelated to the modern vogue for linguistics (John R. Searle, *Speech Acts*, 1960): if I say, "I promise to pay you 500 francs", I am *ipso facto* under an obligation to do so. The words are the vehicle by which the promise is delivered. But is that not because there is a witness who heard the promise, that is to say society, as the custodian of the law?

Gorla (in *Il contratto: problemi fondamentali trattati con il metodo comparativo e casuistico*, 1955, I, 6) has provided a compelling critique of this idea that the will, by its own creative energy, imposes its own obligations on itself. In his account of the matter the focus shifts from promisor to promisee: what gives to the contract its binding force is the reliance of the promisee not the undertaking by the promisor.

Moreover, when the law restricts freedom of contract, is it to prevent promisors from making promises? It is rather to debar promisees from enforcing the promise. Emmanuel Levy (*Vision socialiste du droit*, 1926, and *Les fondements du droit*, 1933) has already highlighted the role played by legitimate expectations in the machinery of obligations. Even more so, the Natural Law School, in spite of the share of responsibility which it is tempting to attribute to it for exalting the creative will, conceived the matter rather pragmatically. Thus, Puffendorf in *Devoirs de l'homme et du citoyen*,

the recipient has been unjustifiably enriched, since if the contract goes off, the justification for the retention of the benefit ceases to exist, and the fact that the contract is invalid or never came about does not turn the duty to disgorge into a contractual obligation. On this see K. Zweigert and H. Kötz, *Einführung in die Rechtsvergleichung*, 3rd edn. (Tübingen: Mohr, 1996), at 557 ff. This dispute may be purely verbal.

[183] The leading case in the US is *Hoffman* v. *Red Owl Stores* 26 Wis. 2d 683, 133 NW 2d 267 (1965), and in England *Rox* v. *Midland Bank* (1979) 2 Lloyd's Rep. 391.

[184] G. Gilmore, *The Death of Contract* (Columbus, Ohio: Ohio State University Press, 1974) at 88: "We may take the fact that damages in contract have become indistinguishable from damages in tort as obscurely reflecting an instinctive, almost unconscious realization that the two fields, which had been artificially set apart, are gradually merging and becoming one".

[185] *Ibid.*

[186] Carbonnier, para. 24.

117

Book I, Ch. IX, expressly bases the binding force of the contract on the need to ensure security for promisees, and finishes on a note which is far-reaching indeed: "Apart from the fact it is always hard to accept that one has been fooled by a person because one took that person to be honest."

Nevertheless, if you are viewing the situation from the promisee's vantage point, the account you give will be valueless where there is in fact no promisee, namely in the case of a unilateral promise. Even if there is no other, there is one purely unilateral act, the last will and testament which seems to illustrate the creative force of the human will (unless it is deemed to be the will of religion or of death). Does the presence of the other person nullify that will? "Keep to others the promise you made to yourself; that is your contract." Those are the words of a poet (René Char, *Feuillets d'Hypnos*).

Note

J. Carbonnier places the emphasis on the arguments current in Continental Europe, and recalls the theory of E. Levy on legitimate expectations, which are close to those of "reliance". Also worthy of note is the discussion on the emphasis attached by some commentators to the position of the promisor, rather than that of the promisee, as launched by G. Gorla.

1.3.2.B. HISTORICAL BACKGROUND

As J. Carbonnier points out, the Natural Law School took a pragmatic view of things. Certainly, it acknowledged the role of the will but without exalting it. The importance of the will went without saying. Its philosophical basis was to be found in human freedom: as a matter of principle only a person who so wishes may bind himself; as a rule an obligation must be freely entered into. Its economic basis was in the *laissez-faire* advocated by Adam Smith and its moral basis, inherited from the Canon lawyers, the keeping of one's word once given.

That was the situation, as described by Pothier and Portalis, at the time when the French Civil Code was drawn up. But voluntarism must not be elevated to the status of dogma, which accounts for two basic provisions of the Civil Code.

Code civil   **1.F.81.**

Article 6:   No particular agreement can deviate from the rules concerning public policy and good morals.

Article 1134: Agreements legally formed are like a statute for those who have made them. (. . .)

These two provisions read in conjunction show that for the framers of the Civil Code the will has value only within the ambit of the law and that it is the law which gives effect to the will and, also, that the will is not omnipotent: it must observe public order and good moral standards. This is a combination of the subjective element, the will, and the objective element, namely the law. The binding force of the contract rests on a combination of those two elements.

Terré, Simmler and Lequette[187]   **1.F.82.**

If one takes the theory of the autonomy of the will to its most extreme conclusion, the contract would be self-sufficient. It would not require to be buttressed by any rule of law in order to be binding on

---

[187] Terré, Simler and Lequette, para. 27.

the parties. The will derives its binding force from within itself. Yet even a cursory reading of Article 1134 of the Civil Code is enough to show that its framers did not intend to adopt this view of things. Though they affirm the binding force of contract by means of a very high-flown comparison, viz: "contracts . . . are like a statute for those who have made them", they go on to state that that is the case only if the contracts are created "in accordance with the law". That means that the contract draws its binding force , not from itself, but from a rule of law which is external to it. The power conferred on the individual will is not primary *but secondary*.

Yet how could it be otherwise?

Under the doctrine of the autonomous will, the basis of liability is the will or more precisely the power of the will to bind itself. The promisor is bound because he wanted to be. But what, then, is to account for the fact that he continues to be bound even if his will changes? Is it not the "current, living will" which must take precedence over the "past dead will"[188]? If the will is really omnipotent what is to prevent it from undoing what it has done? The answer to that is that the wills of the contracting parties have come together. But that is simply to evade the issue. Why should acceptance crystallise into an obligation wills which are fundamentally free and untrammelled? However concordant they may be, the common intentions of the parties cannot be self-sufficient. They merely put forward a programme which would not be binding on the parties if it were not fixed and sanctioned on the date of the contract by some authority external to the parties. Otherwise, there would in fact be nothing to prevent either of the contracting parties from obeying a fleeting interest of the moment and following whatever fluctuating course his will might take. Therefore, the binding force of the contract does not come from the promise but from the value attached to the promise by the law. That value stems from an external rule which alone is able to secure the means necessary for enforcing the promise. The contract is therefore genuinely binding only when supported by a legal system which will lend to the promisee, if necessary, a portion of that force over which it has a monopoly. It may be seen, therefore, that the binding force of the contract is not a reality existing and imposing itself independently of any legal system. Without the assistance of the legal system, the contract remains a purely moral commitment, which is not nothing, but is not necessarily sufficient to constrain a recalcitrant promisor.

If one follows the theory of the autonomous will without, however, supporting its most extreme postulates, the theory of the enabling rule could be encapsulated in a single rule stating that the legal system strictly enforces agreements freely entered into. But it appears difficult to accept that a legal system should be prepared to uphold any agreement of the parties of whatever kind. The legal system cannot in fact lend its assistance to the enforcement of obligations where it disapproves of the manner in which they were created or the content thereof. More specifically, as far as contracts are concerned, all the legal systems concern themselves with the conditions under which they were entered into and make them subject to a whole series of requirements whose objective is to ensure a minimum level of protection both for the parties themselves and for third parties and for that part of the public whose interests could be affected by the transaction. The Civil Code is not an exception to this rule. To enter into a contract is not merely to want a thing; it is also to use an *instrument forged by the law*.[189]

This balanced conclusion concerning the roles played by the will and the law respectively seems to coincide with general opinion in France and Europe.

But that has not always been the case. For in the second half of the nineteenth century, the autonomy of the will was elevated to the rank of dogma under the influence of the

---

[188] G. Rouhette, *Contribution à l'étude critique de la notion du contrat*, Ph.D. diss., Paris, 1965, para. 113, at 407; V. Heuzé, *La réglementation française des contrats internationaux*, th. Paris I, 1990, para. 131, at 71.

[189] B. Ancel and Y. Lequette, *Grands arrêts de la jurisprudence française de droit international privé*, 2nd edn. (Paris: Dalloz, 1993), at 185 ff.

internationalists who sought to underpin autonomy by legal means in order to resolve conflicts of laws in contractual matters. Savigny was a precursor in this field. He was succeeded by French academic writers (Weiss, Foelix), and then by the Civilian Writers.

The formulation by Fouillée is still cited: He who says that it is contractually agreed says that it is fair ("*Qui dit contractuel dit juste*").[190]

This may be contrasted with the remark by Lord Devlin: "The common lawyers hardly recognise the principle of fair dealing as one that needed independant support. For them free dealing was fair dealing".[191]

The acme of the autonomy of the will, based on the idea of contracts being negotiated by persons of equal bargaining power, did not last long. Criticism mounted, led in France by the arguments of E. Gounod, who was to be killed shortly afterwards in the First World War, in his thesis, *Le principe de l'autonomie de la volonté en droit privé. Contribution à l'étude critique de l'individualisme juridique* (Dijon, 1912), which is critical rather than constructive. It has been noted that, in order to facilitate their criticisms, the authors caricatured the voluntarist theory. Anti-voluntarist thinking was carried forward in Italy by G. Gorla[192], and by G. Rouhette.[193, 194]

In England, P. S. Atiyah traced analogous developments in *The Rise and Fall of Freedom of Contract*.[195] For him, citing Pollock and Anson, the period 1770–1870 is the age of freedom of contract, the period 1870–1970 he describes as that of the decline and fall marked by the collapse of the classic system and the resurgence of liability founded on reliance. Plainly the year 1970 did not mark the end of that trend and it remains to be examined whether recent changes, such as the disappearance of most of the socialist systems of law and the advent of economic neo-liberalism, have ushered in a new era in which the pendulum has swung back.

1.3.2.C. THE THEORY OF RELIANCE

The notion that regard should be had to the trust placed by the promisee in the word of the promisor has always existed. The reliance interest may be traced back to Ihering's theory of interests which was availed of to a considerable extent by Fuller and Purdue in their article on "The reliance interest in contract damages",[196] which is regarded as the origin of the modern concept of reliance. What should be noted in this connection is the ferment of ideas in American academic writings and the great controversies, such as those between Fried and Atiyah, who is the apologist in England of American thinking.

It is therefore to American writings that we must turn for an account of the notion of reliance.

---

[190] A. Fouillée, *Science Sociale*, 2nd edn. (1884), at 410.
[191] Lord Devlin, *The Enforcement of Morals* (Oxford: OUP, 1965) at 47.
[192] G. Gorla, *Il contratto* (Milan: Giuffrè, 1954).
[193] Rouhette, op. cit., summarised in Ghestin, para. 191 ff.
[194] On the historical background in France, see V. Ranouil, *L'autonomie de la volonté. Naissance et évolution d'un concept* (Paris: Univ. Paris II, 1980).
[195] *Supra* note 182.
[196] 46 Yale LJ 52 (1936), 373.

Cohen, *The Basis of Contract*[197]   **1.G.83.**

The injurious-reliance theory
   Though this seems the favorite theory today, it has not as yet been adequately formulated, and many of those who subscribe to it fall back on the will theory when they come to discuss special topics in the law of contract. The essence of the theory, however, is clear enough. Contractual liability arise (or should arise) only where (1) someone makes a promise explicitly in words or implicitly by some act, (2) someone else relies on it, and (3) suffers some loss thereby.
   This theory appeals to the general moral feeling that not only ought promises to be kept, but that anyone innocently injured by relying on them is entitled to have the loss "made good" by the one who thus caused it. If, as Schopenhauer has maintained, the sense of wrong is the ultimate human source of the law, then to base the obligation of the promise on the injury of the one who has relied on it, is to appeal to something really fundamental.
   This theory also appeals to modern legal theorists because it seems to be entirely objective and social. It does not ask the court to examine the intention of the promisor. Instead, the court is asked to consider whether what the defendant has said or done is such that reasonable people generally do rely on it under the circumstances. The resulting loss can be directly proved and, to some extent, even measured. In emphasizing the element of injury resulting from the breach, the whole question of contract is integrated in the larger realm of obligations, and this tends to put our issues in the right perspective and to correct the misleading artificial distinctions between breach of contract and other civil wrongs or torts.

This article, which appeared not long before Fuller and Purdue's, discusses "injurious reliance", thus highlighting the link with liability in tort, and bringing out clearly the objective and social nature of the theory.
   Atiyah was to go on to elaborate these features, falling only a little short of nullifying contractual intent.

P. Atiyah, *"Promises, Obligations and the Law of Contract"*[198]   **1.E.84.**

And so far I have said nothing about one of the most obvious bodies of legal doctrine which is not easy to reconcile with the theory that contractual and promissory obligations rest on voluntary obligation. I refer, of course, to the so-called "objective-test" theory of contractual liability. Every law student is taught from his earliest days that contractual intent is not really what it seem; actual subjective intent is normally irrelevant. It is the appearance, the manifestation of intent that matters. Whenever a person is held bound by a promise or a contract contrary to his actual intent or understanding, it is plain that the liability is based not on some notion of a voluntary assumption of obligation, but on something else. And most frequently it will be found that that something else is the element of reasonable reliance. One party relies on a reasonable construction of an offer, or he accepts an offer, reasonably thinking it is still open when the offeror has revoked it but failed to communicate his revocation. All this is standard stuff but I suggest that cases of this type have for too long been regarded as of marginal importance only, as not affecting the fundamental basis and theory of liability. In a simple world of simple promises and contracts this might have been an acceptable perspective. But the arrival of written contracts and above all the standard printed form has surely rendered this approach much less defensible. A party who signs an elaborate printed document is almost invariably held bound by it not because of anything he intended; he is bound in the teeth of his intention and understandings except in some very exceptional cases of fraud or the like.

---

[197] 46 Harv. LR 553 (1933).
[198] In *Essays in Contract* (Oxford: Clarendon, 1986), at 33.

The truth is he is bound not so much because of what he intends but because of what he does. Like the man who is bound to pay his fare because he boards a bus, the man who sign a written contract is liable because of what he does rather than what he intends. And he is liable because of what he does for the good reason that other parties are likely to rely upon what he does in ways which are reasonable and even necessary by the standards of our society.

What I suggest then, is that whatever benefits are obtained, wherever acts of reasonable reliance take place, obligations may arise, both morally and in law . . . Now I want next to suggest that these cases of benefits received or of action in reliance, are more common than is suggested by our conventional image of the legal world. In conventional contract theory, the paradigm of contract is the executory arrangement. Executory contract theory has totally subsumed liabilities and obligations which arise from the receipt of benefits or from acts of reasonable reliance. But in practice, the wholly executory transaction is nothing like such a paradigm as it appears in the books. I have already said something of the difficulties involved in the very concept of a paradigm in this context, but he most cursory look at the world and at the law will reveal that many types of transactions do not fit the model of the wholly executory arrangement at all. Vast numbers of transactions are not in any real sense binding prior to something being done by one or both of the parties. This may partly reflect the fact that lawyers have traditionally implied promises very easily from transactions, and that in consequence today there are many situations in which the lawyer would assert that an executory arrangement involves implied mutual promises while the parties themselves might very well deny that they promised anything at all. The language of consumer transactions, in particular, is not couched in terms of promises. People "book" holidays, or air reservations, they "order" goods, they "accept" estimates, and so on. Even in business circles this sort of terminology is more common than the express language of promises and undertakings. Whether language of this kind is treated as creating an obligation is traditionally thought of as depending upon whether the language is tantamount to being promissory. But it is at least arguable that in many case of this nature the reality is otherwise. Frequently, both in law and in moral discourse we appear to determine whether there should be an obligation first, and then decide how the language should be constructed afterwards. And it follows that the existence or non-existence of the obligation is then being decided independently of the existence of any promise . . .

Now I must repeat that I an not arguing that consent, promise, intention, voluntary conduct, are irrelevant to the creation of obligations even where an element of reciprocal benefit is present, or some act of reasonable reliance has taken place. In the first place, where liability arises out of conduct rather than from the voluntary assumption of an obligation, the conduct itself is usually of a voluntary character. Even if liability on a part-executed arrangement can properly be said to the benefit-based rather than promise-based, a man is normally entitled to choose what benefits he will accept—normally, though by no means invariably. Similarly, with reliance-based liability; it is normally open to a person to warn others that they are not to rely upon him, but must trust to their own judgment. Obviously this raises difficulty when a person wants to have his cake and eat it, where he wants to influence others to behave in a certain manner but wants also to disclaim responsibility for their doing so. There is little doubt that in such circumstances the trend is towards insisting on the imposition of responsibility. The striking down of exemption clauses and disclaimers of liability are evidence of the unacceptability of these attempts to have things both ways. This trend may reflect the increased emphasis on reliance and the declining stress on free choice.

Notes

(1) This very detailed passage calls for a number of comments. The critique of the role of intention is to be noted and the role played in its stead by "the receipt of benefits or from acts of reasonable reliance". We encounter here a discussion of the role played by intent in the case of standard form contracts and in contracts highly regulated by the law,

such as consumer contracts. Does the negotiated contract still have any part to play? Also worthy of note is the distinction made between "executory contracts", that is contracts to which effect has yet to be given, and "executed contracts", a distinction already noted by Rouhette. Finally, according to its advocates, the theory of reliance breaks down the distinctions between tortious liability—where damages are calculated on the basis of reliance—, contractual liability and unjust enrichment—restitution interest. For Atiyah all these matters should be merged into a single law of obligations. For Gilmore that would signal the "death of the contract". It may be seen that this doctrine opens up vast perspectives which may or may not accord with reality.

(2) It must not be overlooked that there is a very close link with the theory and notion of the contract at common law. The doctrine of reliance comes under the heading of "consideration" and is discussed in connection with that doctrine. It is the rationale of estoppel, also a notion proper to the common law. Yet the majority of English commentators acknowledge the influence of reliance only in special situations, not (yet) as a general principle. In that respect applications of the doctrine may be found in other systems of law.

(3) Most authors would not yet accept reliance as a subsitute for consideration except in special circumstances.[199] They would accept that the court is more likely to find a contract where there has been reliance—e.g. if the contract contains some point to be agreed, but acts of reliance take place. They would also accept that it is relatively rare in practice that contracts which have not been relied on are litigated. However, they would insist that as a matter of principle a contract is enforceable even though it is purely executory and there has been no reliance.

1.3.2.D. APPLICATIONS

A prime example is afforded by the new Netherlands Civil Code.

BW   **1.NL.85.**

3.33: A juridical act requires an intention to produce juridical effects, which intention has manifested itself by a declaration.

3.35: The absence of intention in a declaration cannot be invoked against a person who has interpreted another's declaration or conduct, in conformity with the sense which he could reasonably attribute to it in the circumstances, as a declaration of a particular tenor made to him by that other person.

Note
Article 3.33 upholds the voluntarist principle; Article 3.35 acknowledges something akin to estoppel: the promisor is bound to an extent greater than desired.

The difference in approach is highlighted by the contrast between an English judgment which refers to reliance and a French judgment given in analogous circumstances, namely tacit termination of an agreement not applied for a long time where one party is claimed to have relied on the negative attitude of the other.

[199] See *supra*, at 18.

OBJECTIVE MEANING OF WORDS AND ACTIONS

Abandonment of arbitration agreement

The intention of a party should be judged by how it reasonably appeared to the other party.

Facts: A contract for the sale of a vessel contained an arbitration clause under which proceedings were started and pursued sporadically. In 1980 the buyer proposed that a date be fixed for the hearing. The seller sought a declaration that the arbitration agreement no longer subsisted. The House of Lords declined to grant the declaration sought on the basis of repudiation or frustration. It then wondered whether the contract had been abandoned and held that it had not.

Judgment: LORD DIPLOCK: . . . Abandonment of a contract ("the former contract") which is still executory, i.e., one in which at least one primary obligation of one or other of the parties remains unperformed, is effected by the parties entering into a new contract ("the contract of abandonment") . . .

To the formation of the contract of abandonment, the ordinary principles of the English law of contract apply. To create a contract by exchange of promises between two parties where the promise of each party constitutes the consideration for the promise of the other, what is necessary is that the intention of each *as it has been communicated to and understood by the other* (even though that which has been communicated does not represent the actual state of mind of the communicator) should coincide. That is what English lawyers mean when they resort to the Latin phrase consensus ad idem and the words that I have italicised are essential to the concept of consensus ad idem, the lack of which prevents the formation of a binding contract in English law.

Thus if A (the offeror) makes a communication to B (the offeree) whether in writing, orally or by conduct, which, in the circumstances at the time the communication was received, (1) B, if he were a reasonable man, would understand as stating A's intention to act or refrain from acting in some specified manner if B will promise on his part to act or refrain from acting in some manner also specified in the offer, and (2) B does in fact understand A's communication to mean this, and in his turn makes to A a communication conveying his willingness so to act or to refrain from acting which mutatis mutandis satisfies the same two conditions as respects A, the consensus ad idem essential to the formation of a contract in English law is complete.

The rule that neither party can rely upon his own failure to communicate accurately to the other party his own real intention by what he wrote or said or did, as negativing the consensus ad idem, is an example of a general principle of English law that injurious reliance on what another person did may be a source of legal rights against him. I use the broader expression "injurious reliance" in preference to "estoppel" so as to embrace all circumstances in which A can say to B: "You led me reasonably to believe that you were assuming particular legally enforceable obligations to me," of which promissory or *High Trees* estoppel [*Central London Property Trust Ltd.* v. *High Trees House Ltd.* [1947] K.B. 130] affords another example; whereas "estoppel," in the strict sense of the term, is an exclusionary rule of evidence, though it may operate so as to affect substantive legal rights inter partes.

LORD BRIGHTMAN: The basis of "tacit abandonment by both parties," to use the phraseology of the sellers' case, is that the primary facts are such that it ought to be inferred that the contract to

---

[200] [1983] All ER 34, HL.

arbitrate the particular dispute was rescinded by the mutual agreement of the parties. To entitle the sellers to rely on abandonment, they must show that the buyers so conducted themselves as to entitle the sellers to assume, and that the sellers did assume, that the contract was agreed to be abandoned sub silentio. The evidence which is relevant to that inquiry will consist of or include: (1) What the buyers did or omitted to do to the knowledge of the sellers. Excluded from consideration will be the acts of the buyers of which the sellers were ignorant, because those acts will have signalled nothing to the sellers and cannot have founded or fortified any assumption on the part of the sellers; (2) what the sellers did or omitted to do, whether or not to the knowledge of the buyers. These facts evidence the state of mind of the sellers, and therefore the validity of the assertion by the sellers that they assumed that the contract was agreed to be abandoned. The state of mind of the buyers is irrelevant to a consideration of what the sellers were entitled to assume. The state of mind of the sellers is vital to a consideration of what the sellers in fact assumed.

[Lords Brandon, Roskill and Keith concurred].

Appeal allowed. Cross-appeal dismissed.

Cass. civ. 3e, 8 April 1987[201]   **1.F.87.**

IMPRESSIONS CREATED AND GOOD FAITH

Rent not claimed

A party who creates an impression that she has gievn up a claim may not go back on that impression in a way that is contrary to good faith.

Facts: A house was sold in 1970. The purchase price was made up of a cash payment and an annuity. The contract for sale included a termination clause in the event of the non-payment of the annuity. On account of the affectionate relationship between the parties, the annuity was not claimed for more than 10 years. Dissension arose between them. The vendor claimed payment of the annuity. Upon the purchaser's refusal to comply with this request, the vendor sought termination of the sale under this clause. His claim was unsuccessful.

Judgment: THE COURT: *On the first three appeal grounds taken together*:—Whereas according to the judgment appealed against (Aix-en-Provence 20 June 1985), Mr Thomas sold a house in 1970 to Mr and Mrs André-Renouvier with an easement in favour of his wife and himself for a cash amount together with an annuity; as after the death of Mr Thomas, his wife invoking the termination clause in the contract for sale, gave formal notice to the debtors to pay the annuity which had never been claimed, and, upon Mr André and Mrs Renouvier refusing to pay, brought proceedings against them for repudiation of the sale;
—Whereas Mrs Thomas criticizes the judgment for dismissing her claim whereas, in the terms of her first appeal ground, the termination clause in the deed of sale of 17 December 1970 was entirely lawful and binding on the parties and the courts; as furthermore, in her submission, once the courts found that effect had not been given to the claims in the summons, they had no power other then to hold that the contract had been terminated;
—Whereas by excusing non-payment of arrears on alleged grounds of equity, the judgment appealed against infringed Articles 1134, 1184 and 1656 of the Civil Code;
—Whereas under the second appeal ground it is submitted that, although the court may examine points of law of its own motion, it must first invite the parties to submit their observations
—Whereas in holding there to have been an abuse of her rights by Mrs Thomas to the detriment of her adversaries the judgment appealed against infringed Articles 12 and 16 of the new Code of Civil Procedure.

[201] Bull. civ. III.88.

—Whereas finally, under the third ground it is submitted that the exercise of a right cannot degenerate into an abuse unless it is exercised with the intention of harming another person or constitutes a serious fault equivalent to deception to be established by the court; as that is argued not to be the case here since Mrs Thomas merely availed herself of a right which accrued to her only on the death of her husband some months earlier, and whose exercise could have been foreseen by the debtors;

—Whereas the judgment appealed against is therefore said to be without legal basis under Articles 1382 et seq. of the Civil Code.

—Whereas however, the court below found that, by omitting for more than 10 years to claim the annuity payment from the debtors, the creditor then, after his death, his wife had led the debtors to believe that the annuity would never be claimed, the spouses having a particularly affectionate relationship with Mrs Renouvier, who was the foster sister of the creditor, and that the sudden change in the creditor's attitude which was solely due to dissension in Mrs Renouvier's daughter's family constituted a situation which was unforeseeable as far as the debtors were concerned, and prevented them from bringing themselves into conformity within the period allowed;

—Whereas the judgment is lawful on those grounds alone from which the court of appeal was entitled to infer, without infringing the principle of *audi alteram partem*, that the termination clause had not been relied on in good faith.

On those grounds: The appeal is dismissed.

Notes

In a situation close to that in *The Hannah Blumenthal*, French law invokes good faith in line with case-law which is reluctant to admit that termination clauses should have automatic effect.[202] Where a promisee refrains for many years from requiring a contract to be performed and then suddenly insists on performance, he is acting contrary to the principle of good faith. It may also be pleaded against such a person that he has abused his right to demand performance. It is nevertheless true to say that the concepts of the abuse of a right and breach of good faith are very closely linked and are frequently interchangeable. One can also see in this, however, a glimmer of the idea of "reliance": the attitude of the promisee had instilled in the promisor "the firm belief that payment of the annuity would never be claimed". It must be pointed out that there is no exact equivalent in French for the term "reliance"; the closest phrase is perhaps "*confiance légitime*" (legitimate expectation).

Under English law abandonment of the clause may be by implied agreement—which presupposes consideration, not easily identifiable in this case but presumably the alleged implicit undertaking that each party would abandon its claims—or as a result of a reasonable belief on the part of one of the parties based on the conduct of the other. In the House of Lords' view, the facts of the case did not enable either explanation to be adopted. The account given by Lord Diplock well illustrates the role which "reliance" could have played—he even speaks of "injurious reliance"; others use the expression "detrimental reliance". Estoppel is not mentioned as it operates as a bar to admissibility, whereas, in his opinion, reliance may create rights.

The notion of reliance is also used in English law to explain or justify a certain number of solutions which will appear further on in this work.

---

[202] See Malaurie and Aynès, para. 752.

Thus, we shall encounter it:

—in the study of consideration and estoppel;
—in the study of the relationship between contract, tort and restitution;
—in the debate between inner intent and stated intent;
—in connection with the interpretation of the contract;
—in connection with the calculation of damages: expectation and reliance interest, positive interest and negative interest, as opposed to the principle of full compensation
—and again in connection with various rules of offer and acceptance.

Conclusion

The question of the basis of the binding force of the contract remains controversial and various theories, including that of reliance, have been put forward. If one leaves aside certain more or less Utopian points of view, such as the death of the contract, it is difficult to do other than conclude that it is neither possible nor desirable completely to remove the role played by intent in the formation of the contract. In any event that is not the current situation under the European systems of law. The notion of the imposed contract is regarded as dangerous. It stems from the Marxist theory of the contract[203] which in any event was not successful in completely excluding consent from planned contracts.

Another aspect must be considered: the return in force of economic liberalism. Is this neo-liberalism not giving rise to a resurgence of freedom of contract and, perhaps, to a stepping back by the legislator from interference with the contract? Is it not the case that excessive protection of the weaker party reduces him to a state of incapacity?

Now that the voluntarist dogma has been abandoned, if it was ever all-powerful, the binding force of the contract appears to result from a combination of subjective and objective elements; that combination varies from legal system to legal system and from one era to another.

1.3.3. CAUSE (OTHER THAN UNLAWFUL CAUSE) AND CONSIDERATION

Is anything else apart from intent needed for the valid formation of a contract? Once the adage *ex nudo pactu nulla obligatio oritur* was abandoned under the influence of the Canon lawyers of the Middle Ages, the question was whether a bare promise was self-sufficient or whether something was needed in order to ensure the seriousness and lawfulness of the engagement. There may thus be a requirement as to form.[204] But the seriousness of the engagement may also be ensured by the doctrine of the cause, as a reply to the question *cur debetur*. Thus inspiration was sought from the rather uncertain Roman law doctrine of the "*causa*", and it is this revived doctrine which is to be found in a certain number of Roman-law countries. English law took a different path with its doctrine of consideration. As for German law, it knows no doctrine of cause or consideration.

---

[203] See R. David and C. Jauffret-Spinosi, *Grands systèmes de droit contemporains*, 10th edn. (Paris: Dalloz, 1992) para. 254 ff.
[204] See 1.3.4 , *infra* at 154.

These theories raise major doctrinal controversies which this is not the place to embark upon. In the absence of matters in common, it is intended to proceed by juxtaposition rather than comparison:[205] French law: the cause; English law: consideration and German law: neither cause nor consideration.

1.3.3.A. FRENCH LAW: THE DOCTRINE OF CAUSE

This is a complex theory, much argued over in academic circles but still very significant as far as decisions of the courts are concerned. Following a general discussion, we shall successively examine its traditional applications and recent trends.

(a) General[206]
The requirement that there be a cause is written into French, Italian and Quebec laws.

<table>
<tr><td></td><td align="center">*Code civil*</td><td align="right">**1.F.88.**</td></tr>
</table>

Article 1108: Four conditions are essential to the validity of an agreement :
            the consent of the party who binds himself :
            his capacity of contract ;
            a definite object which forms the subject matter of the agreement ;
            a licit cause for the obligation.

<table>
<tr><td></td><td align="center">*Codice civil*</td><td align="right">**1.I.89.**</td></tr>
</table>

Article 1325: Conditions
            The conditions to be satisfied for there to be a contract are:
            (1) the agreement of the parties;
            (2) cause;
            (3) form, where prescribed by law, on pain of nullity.

<table>
<tr><td></td><td align="center">*Quebec Civil Code*</td><td align="right">**1.CAN.90.**</td></tr>
</table>

Article 1485: A contract is formed by the sole exchange of consents between persons having capacity to contract, unless, in addition, the law requires a particular form to be respected as a necessary condition of its formation, or unless the parties require the contract to take the form of a solemn agreement.
            It is also of the essence of a contract that it have a cause and an object.

Cause is also a term used in French law, this time by the courts in regard to unjust enrichment or enrichment without cause, that is to say without there being a ground justifying the enrichment or impoverishment, thus in a slightly different sense.[207]

---

[205] For a Franco-German comparison, see A. Rieg, *Le rôle de la volonté dans l'acte juridique en droit civil français et allemand* (Paris: LGDJ, 1961) at 250. For comparative studies, see Zweigert and Kötz, chapter 29; Kötz, *European Contract Law* chapter 4.

[206] See Malaurie and Aynès, para. 692 ff.; Terré, Simler and Lequette, para. 312 ff.

[207] See Malaurie and Aynès, paras. 953–954.

The history of cause is complicated because it draws on both the Roman tradition and the Canonist tradition which accounts for the two tendencies which are discernible in the notion of cause: the objective aspect linked, albeit uncertainly, to Roman law and expounded by Domat in the seventeenth century, which is sometimes referred to as the cause of the obligation; and the subjective aspect which is derived from the moralising, Canonist tradition. It should be stated, by way of simplification, that the objective *"cause"* is always the same for the same class of contract. In synallagmatic contracts, it is the consideration (counter-part) or, to be more precise, the prospect of the consideration to be given by the other party. In the case of gratuitous contracts, it is the unfettered, abstract intention to supply or provide something without demanding anything in return. In the case of a *"contrat réel"* (i.e. a contract which requires for its formation the effective delivery of the thing to which it refers in addition to the agreement of the parties, e.g. a deposit or loan for use), it is the delivery of the thing in question. The subjective *"cause"* is the individual motive which prompted the party concerned to commit himself: it is different for each contract. The Civil Code would appear to be inspired by both traditions.

Code civil   **1.F.91.**

Article 1131: An obligation without cause or one based on a false or an illicit cause cannot have any effect.

Article 1132: An agreement is valid although its cause has not been expressed.

Article 1133: A cause is illicit when it is prohibited by law or when it is contrary to good morals or to the *ordre public*.

The doctrine of cause was vehemently criticised by Planiol at the end of the nineteenth century but Planiol's arguments were easily refuted by the neo-causalists, such as H. Capitant and J. Maury, to the point where there may be said to be no more anti-causalists in France. The doctrinal controversies relate primarily to the importance to be attached to each of the two aspects respectively. For some they are two distinct concepts. J. Carbonnier may be permitted to close the debate.

Carbonnier[208]   **1.F.92.**

The twofold presentation of the doctrine (abstract cause and cause as motive) appears to have become a *locus classicus* (e.g. Flour-Aubert, No 267; Larroumet, Nos 44 et seq.; Malaurie and Aynès, No 336). It is convenient but its scope must not be exaggerated. It may be that academic writers have attached too much significance to the illegal or immoral cause (in this connection, see M. Defossez, Réflexion sur l'emploi des motifs comme cause des obligations, R.T., 85, 231: an overly psychological approach is not possible). A concept such as that of interest, which might have been a more appropriate translation of *causa*, clearly brings out the unity of purpose underlying Article 1131; interest must exist, must be serious and must also be legitimate (that is what is professed where the law expounds the doctrine of interest, namely under the law of procedure, in regard to the maxim "no interest, no action"). That may also serve to elucidate the relationship between the object and the cause: the latter is the interest of the promisor; the object (useful and lawful) is

---

[208] Carbonnier, para. 64.

the interest of the promisee. The assumption made by the law is that any step taken by a reasonably prudent person is dictated by a financial interest (contracts for valuable consideration) or a moral interest (gratuitious acts).

It is to be noted that these academic controversies do little to disturb the serenity of the courts. As regards the distinction between cause and object, denied by the anti-causalists, it is today easy to establish. The object must exist, be determined or determinable and lawful—Articles 1126 to 1130 of the Civil Code. In a synallagmatic contract the link is obvious: an obligation without a predetermined object or having an unlawful object renders the contract null and void in its entirety because the counterpart obligation is unsupported by an underlying cause and therefore null and void. The two concepts are therefore complementary. A contract may be unlawful as a result of its object or its cause. The analysis is more finely balanced than if it is based directly on illegality—e.g. § 138 BGB.[209] The loan of a sum of money will always have a lawful object: the payment of a sum of money. On the other hand, it will have an unlawful cause if, for example, it is intended to facilitate the commission of a crime.

Cass. civ. 1re, 12 July 1989[210] **1.F.93.**

ILLEGAL CAUSE

Hocus pocus

Facts: A professional soothsayer sold to his successor his occult paraphernalia, then contested the validity of the sale.

Judgment: THE COURT . . . —Whereas the cause underlying the buyer's obligations is indeed the transfer of property and delivery up of the items sold, the cause underlying the sales contract is to be found in the essential motive, that is to say the motive which, had it not been present, the buyer would not have committed himself;
—Whereas once they had established that the impelling and determining cause of a contract for the sale of various works on the occult and associated paraphernalia was to enable the buyer to engage in the occupation of soothsayer and fortune teller, which is an offence under Article R.34 of the Criminal Code, the lower courts correctly inferred that a cause of that kind, originating in a criminal offence, is unlawful . . .

Note
The items sold are not in themselves unlawful because what was at the time a criminal offence is the carrying on of the occupation of soothsayer. Yet the cause underlying the contract is the carrying on of the outlawed occupation and the seller knew that the purchaser was intending to carry on that occupation. It is to be noted that the Cour de cassation here distinguishes between the cause supporting the buyer's obligation—transfer and delivery of the items—and the cause underlying the contract—the essential motive.
  The articles of the Italian Civil Code (Articles 1343, 1344, and 1345) seem to refer only to the subjective cause. Yet academic writers and the courts both acknowledge the dual

---

[209] See however Zweigert and Kötz, at 381–2.
[210] JCP 1990. II.21546, annotated by Dagorne-Labbé.

nature of the cause.[211] The objective cause, which is sometimes described as the financial cause, ensures that it is possible to ascertain the reason justifying the transfer of value under the contract.

As for the Quebec Civil Code of 1993, the first draft abolished the cause, at least under that name. It reappeared in the definitive text, alongside the object. It would appear that its reappearance resulted from the realization that certain functions fulfilled by the "*cause*" could no longer be fulfilled. The definition of cause given in Article 1410—the "reason leading each of the parties to enter into the contract"—is consistent with the dual analysis of the cause.

(b) The Classic Applications of the Cause[212]

There must be an objective cause and a contract without a cause or based on an illegal or immoral cause is null and void. In the case of donations it is the intention to make a gift, in synallagmatic contracts it is the performance by the other party of his obligations. In the case of unilateral contracts—in the French sense of the term—the cause varies according to the category of the contract. In a contract for bailment the cause is constituted by deposit of the item which forms the subject-matter of the contract. It will be recalled that French law is also familiar with abstract acts, that is to say acts detached from their cause, though to a lesser degree than German law.[213]

The application of the cause in modern transactions is illustrated by the so-called dates of valuation case.

Cass. com., 6 April 1993[214]   **1.F.94.**

ABSENCE OF CAUSE

Delay in crediting accounts

Facts: Under a well-established banking practice, customer remittances are entered only after a certain period whereas payments by the bank are entered in the accounts with a date preceding the date of the transaction. This practice affects the calculation of interest.

Judgment: THE COURT:—Whereas according to the judgment appealed against (Aix-en-Provence, 2nd Civil Chamber, 3 October 1990), the companies Major, Jean Major, Suren and Ambre (the companies) which held current accounts with the Banco Exterior France (the Bank) sued the Bank for recovery of fees charged; as the Bank cross-claimed for an order that the companies should pay to it the amounts debited to their accounts;

—Whereas the companies allege that the lower court erred in holding that the Bank was not wrong to carry out a quarterly capitalisation of interest accrued due in regard to the current accounts opened by the companies, whereas, according to the terms of the appeal, if a current account agreement is a special agreement under Article 1154 of the Civil Code that provision stipulates that the capitalisation of interest can only be in respect of interest accrued due for a whole year; whereas by failing so to hold, the appeal court infringed Article 1154 of the Civil Code.

---

[211] See G. Alpa and M. Bessone, *Contratti*, Vol. III (Turin: UTET, 1991) at 461 ff.

[212] Excluding the illegal cause, subject to what was said *supra* at 129–30.

[213] See Malaurie and Aynès, para. 493 ff. and *supra* at 128.

[214] JCP 1993.II.22062, annotated by Stoufflet; D. 1993.310, annotated by C. Gavalda.

131

—Whereas however, the judgment appealed against found that Article 1154 aforesaid does not apply to the capitalisation of interest in the context of a current account. In fact periodic debit entries in respect of interest due are equivalent to payment of such interest which loses its autonomy by becoming merged in the balance due. Thus, the appeal court provided legal justification for its decision and the plea is unfounded;

On the first branch of the first plea:—Under Article 1131 of the Civil Code;
—Whereas the companies claimed that their obligation to pay interest was in part unsupported by any cause, inasmuch as the amounts on which interest was calculated were increased, without justification, by the application of "dates of valuation" to remittances in the form of cheques and cash and to withdrawals;
—Whereas in rejecting that claim, the lower court found that the practice of the Bank, which was condemned by the companies, was justified by the fact that "a remittance for the credit of an account, like a withdrawal debited to an account, takes time to collect or pay out", and that "the value of a cheque can be credited to an account only after collection which cannot be instantaneous";
—Whereas by so holding, although the transactions at issue, other than remittances of cheques for collection, did not involve, even for the purpose of calculating interest, the postponement or bringing forward of the dates on which such amounts were to be credited or debited, the cour d'appel infringed the abovementioned provision.
  On those grounds the judgment is set aside and the case referred to the cour d'appel, Lyon.

Note
As is borne out by the reference to Article 1131 of the Civil Code, the Cour de cassation is availing itself of the doctrine of cause in order to hold that amounts of interest received or paid are in part unsupported by any cause. Thus, in the case of the remittance of cheques for collection, postponement of the date from which interest becomes payable is justified by the delay involved in collection. Conversely, there is no such justification in the other cases—cash remittances, telegraphic transfers etc.; in such cases the interest charged is unsupported by any cause.
  The Bundesgerichtshof, in its decision of 17 January 1989,[215] provides a similar solution by ordering the deletion of a clause fixing the value date of a current account transaction at 24 hours after the transaction where it involves the remitting of funds or a bank transfer, since, in such circumstances, the deferment of the value debt cannot be regarded as a reimbursement of costs. In order to arrive at that conclusion, the BGH could not have recourse to the concept of a ground inherent in the facts—though not relied on by the parties—, which is not recognized in German law; consequently, it referred to the general conditions contained in the ABGB,[216] even though the clause in question appeared only on a leaflet. It considered that the customers were not given sufficient information and that there was a lack of transparency. It further stated that the fact that the clause was of a customary nature could not operate to save it. The reasons given for the court's decision were therefore of a technical nature and based on a particular form of wording, even though there was also a reference to "*Treu und Glauben*" (the principle of good faith and fair dealing) and, in addition, to the absence of any consideration. This prompts the

---

[215] NJW 1989.582.
[216] As to which see *supra*, at 23.

question whether it may be possible, in French law, also to invoke, in a similar situation, the rules laid down in the *Code de la Consommation* (Consumer Code) with regard to the unfairness of the clause.

Another example is provided by aleatory contracts, while non-occurence of the risk entails failure of the *cause*.

Cass. civ. 1re, 18 April 1953[217]   **1.F.95.**

No real benefit

The genealogist

An agreement to do research to discover facts which are already known and readily available is without cause.

Judgment: The Court:—Whereas the facts and reasoning of the decision under review, Aix, 17 July 1950, a decision which affirmed the decision of the lower court, indicate that, Doctor M having died on September 8, 1944, B., a genealogist, was asked by the family notary on the day of M's death to perform research in order to discover the heirs of the deceased; as on November 26, 1944, B. entered into a contract with Mrs P., the niece and sole heir of Doctor M., by virtue of which he promised to reveal an inheritance which was to come to her in exchange for a substantial share of that inheritance; as after the contract was signed, he informed her of the inheritance of Doctor M. and of her status as heiress.

—Whereas the appeal objects that the court of appeal declared the contract invalid for absence of cause at the request of Mr and Mrs. P. even though Mrs. P. had been running the risk of ignorance of the existence of the inheritance and of her status as heiress and that without the intervention of the genealogist it would have been impossible to discover the name and address of the said heiress;

—Whereas however the decision, in its own conclusions and those adopted from the lower court decision, and having seen the documents of the case and the results of an inquest, found that the address of Mrs. P. was known to the friends of Doctor M. and of the notary; as the notary had asked B. to do research pointlessly, with too much haste, and without consulting the documents he had at hand and in his files, and as he had given B. enough information to permit B. to find Mrs. P. with nothing left to chance; as B. had not rendered Mrs. P. any service and as he had not run any risk himself; as the existence of the inheritance would have come to the knowlegde of the heiress in the normal course without the intervention of the genealogist; as on these facts the cour d'appel could infer that no secret had been revealed and that the contract of November 26, 1944 was without cause . . . ;

For these reasons, the pourvoi is rejected.

Note

The contract is risky because the genealogist is not certain to find an heir. However, in the present case, the risk did not occur because the notary was in possession of the heir's address. The service rendered was non-existent and the contract was therefore unsupported by any cause. Certainly, the genealogist in that case has an action in tort against the negligent notary.

The case of the unilateral promise to sell subject to a "cancellation charge" affords an illustration of the role played by cause in this type of contract.

[217] D. 1953.403.

Cass. com., 23 June 1958[218]   **1.F.96.**

Cancellation charge on option

The cause of an undertaking by a purchaser who has reserved the right to buy a property to pay a cancellation charge is the advantage conferred on him by the promisor's undertaking not to assign the business to another person for a specified period.

Judgment: THE COURT: *On the sole appeal ground*:—Under Article 1131 of the Civil Code;

—Whereas according to the judgment appealed against (Orléans, 2 December 1953), Fisch, by a writing under hand dated 11 March 1952, promised to sell to Bellanger who reserved the right to acquire his bakery and confectionery business at the price of 3,500,000F, that promise to remain valid until 1 May 1952, the date fixed for the taking of possession; as it was stipulated that, should Bellanger not acquire the business within the period provided for, he would be obliged to pay to the vendor, by way of a fixed lump-sum cancellation charge, the sum of 400,000F; as on 20 March 1952 Bellanger informed Fisch that, for personal reasons, he would not be acquiring the business; as Fisch sought payment by Bellanger of the fixed cancellation charge and the judgment appealed against dismissed that action;

—Whereas the judgment appealed against was based on the fact that "Bellanger, the promisee could not be ordered to pay any sum to the promisor Fisch since, not having himself promised to acquire the business but having merely reserved an option to do so, he remained free to decide;

—Whereas consequently, the insertion into a unilateral promise to sell of a clause providing for payment of a given sum by way of cancellation charge must be deemed not to have occurred because it is without cause;

—Whereas the cause of the undertaking by the likely purchaser to pay a cancellation charge was constituted by the advantage conferred on him by the promisor's undertaking not to assign the business to another person for a specified period;

—Whereas by holding this not to be the case, the cour d'appel misapplied and consequently infringed the provision referred to above;

On those grounds the Cour de cassation set aside the judgment of the cour d'appel.

Note

The problem is to determine how to justify the payment of the "cancellation charge", in other words to identify the cause in return for which the undertaking is offered. The Cour de cassation regards it as being constituted by the tying up of the property which the promisee can no longer dispose of owing to his promise. The "cancellation charge" is the price of the service rendered to the promisee. A promise may also be made *ab initio* for valuable consideration where a promise is made to make an immediate payment of a sum to be imputed to the price if the sale is completed, or else retained.

Article 1131 deals also with the false cause, where one party is mistaken as to the existence of the cause: either it does not exist or is different. It is sometimes referred to as error as to the cause. In actual fact, error as to the cause is to be distinguished from the false cause in that the latter is sanctioned irrespective of the error, which merely serves to

---

[218] D. 1958.581, annotated by P. Malaurie.

explain it. It does not call for any study of psychological motives. Moreover, mistake as to the cause is visited by relative nullity whereas the absence or falsity of the cause is attended by absolute nullity.

Cass. civ. 1re, 10 May 1995[219]   **1.F.97.**

LACK OF CAUSE BECAUSE OF MISTAKE

Worthless services

A mistake as to the existence of the cause, albeit it inexcusable, warrants annulment of an undertaking given for that cause.

Judgment:—Whereas according to the findings of the lower court, Sominos was set up in 1961 in order, in particular, to build and operate on land granted by the Loiret Department warehouses and office or shop buildings and to carry on the management of all the buildings that the Department might consider appropriate for purposes of economic development. As from 1962 Sominos had as directors general persons proposed by one of its shareholders, SCET; as on 28 June 1972 Sominos signed with SCET an agreement under which SCET undertook, in return for a lump-sum remuneration, to provide it with assistance in legal, fiscal, administrative, technical and financial matters, and in regard to financial management; as article 11 of the agreement provided that Sominos could call upon SCET to provide it with "a qualified executive competent in the management of a mixed-economy company and capable of substituting in the absence or indisposition of the director"; as as from 1 June 1980 Mr Pellerin was delegated by SCET to Sominos in order to perform the duties of the director. After Sominos got into financial difficulties, La Fiduciaire de France was commissioned in December 1986 to carry out an audit of the company; it reported in 1987; as following the premature dissolution of Sominos in January 1988, SCET sought from Sominos payment of the sum of 212 881, 74 francs representing the redemption of retirement points in favour of Mr Pellerin pursuant to an undertaking which it had entered into by letter dated 14 November 1986; as Sominos claimed that SCET had failed to fulfil its obligations by providing it with an incompetent executive who was guilty of serious managerial errors; as it therefore sued for damages;

—Whereas the judgment appealed against (Orléans) dismissed the claim by Sominos and ordered it to pay to SCET the sum claimed. . . .

On the second appeal ground:—Under Article 1131 of the Civil Code;

—Whereas in ordering Sominos to pay to SCET the cost of redeeming retirement points in favour of Mr Pellerin, the court below was content merely to find that Sominos could not claim that the undertaking given in its letter of 14 November 1986 was vitiated by error, in light of the services rendered by Mr Pellerin, inasmuch as it was in ignorance at that time of the serious managerial mistakes of which Mr Pellerin was guilty; as it was for Sominos as principal to use its powers of supervision and authority over its chief executive;

—Whereas by so holding, although the mistake as to the existence of the cause, albeit it was inexcusable, warrants annulment of the undertaking for lack of cause, the court of appeal failed to give its decision any legal basis;

On those grounds, the Cour de cassation sets aside the appeal court's judgment (Orléans) of 20 November 1991 to the extent to which it orders Sominos to pay to SCET the sum of 212,881.74 francs; accordingly, restores the case and the parties to the *status quo ante*, and refers them to the Angers cour d'appel for a fresh determination.

[219] Bull. civ. I.194.

135

Note
The cause of the undertaking to pay was constituted by the services rendered by the beneficiary. Yet, after the event, it is noticed that those services were negated by serious managerial mistakes. It might perhaps have been possible to discern some failure by Sominos to perform the contract. However, the Cour de cassation expressly confined itself to considering the matter in terms of the *"cause"*. It clearly stated that there had been an error in that regard. Belief in the existence of the services rendered entails nullity of the undertaking, even though the error was inexcusable, a solution opposite to that which would have been reached in the case of consent vitiated by error.[219a]

(c) New trends
Certain recent judgments show the new uses to which the doctrine of the cause has been put in order to provide contracts with a greater ethical content. The *Chronopost* judgment is an interesting use of the cause to revive the case-law on exemption clauses.

Cass. com., 22 October 1996[220]   **1.F.98.**

LACK OF CAUSE BECAUSE OF FAILURE TO PERFORM

Chronopost

Payment for transport service is without cause if the transporter did not perform the fundamental duty under the contract.
Judgment: THE COURT: *On the first appeal ground*:—Under Article 1131 of the Civil Code;
—Whereas according to the judgment appealed against (Court of Appeal, Rennes, 1st Chamber B, 30 June 1993), the company Banchereau on two occasions handed to Chronopost, subrogated to the rights of SFMI, an envelope containing a bid in a tendering procedure; as those envelopes were not delivered before midday on the day following their despatch, as Chronopost had undertaken to do. Accordingly, Banchereau brought an action for damages against Chronopost in respect of the loss sustained by it; as Chronopost relied on the clause in the contract limiting compensation for delay to the cost incurred by it in transporting the packet;
—Whereas in dismissing Bandereau's claim, the court below found that, although Chronopost did not comply with its obligation to deliver the envelopes before noon on the day after despatch, its fault was not so serious as to preclude its reliance on the contractual clause limiting its liability;
—Whereas in so holding, the court of appeal infringed the abovementioned provision; as Chronopost, a specialist in swift transport guaranteeing the reliability and speed of its service, undertook to deliver the envelopes entrusted to it by Banchereau within a specified period; as owing to its failure to perform that fundamental duty, the contractual clause limiting liability, which contradicted the scope of the obligation entered into, was to be deemed not to have been incorporated in the contract.

Note
The courts will uphold the validity of exemption clauses and clauses limiting liability in contractual matters where non-performance is not due to a serious fault or fraud of the

---

[219a] For further discussion of error see 3.2.3.D, *infra* at 367 ff., esp. at 379.
[220] D.1997.121, annotated by A. Sériaux.

debtor—which is paralleled by the English doctrine of fundamental breach.[221] The *Chronopost* judgment lays down a new limitation: the contract limited the undertaking's liability to reimbursement of the cost of transport, a derisory indemnity in relation to the loss actually suffered by the sender, namely the loss of the chance of obtaining major contracts. Non-performance was not due to the serious fault or fraud of Chronopost: it was caused by unknown factors. Yet, the Cour de cassation held that there had been a failure to perform a fundamental duty under the contract, which was not merely to convey the packet, but to do so within the period stated. By referring to Article 1131 the Cour de cassation founded its reasoning on the doctrine of cause which is made to apply at two distinct stages: the payment of the transport service is without cause because the transporter did not perform the fundamental duty under the contract. And, again, the cause is applied in the definition of the fundamental duty under the contract: it is that duty which was the cause of the promisee's entering into the contract. The innovation as regards the penalty should also be noted: the clause is deemed not to have been incorporated in the contract whereas the normal sanction would have been the absolute nullity of the contract.

There is also a discernible trend in having recourse to the doctrine of cause to ensure that obligations and benefits are evenly distributed between the parties. Traditionally, the cause did not require a balanced performance as between the parties, since under French law cognizance was not generally taken of loss arising out of an imbalance in the parties' obligations under a synallagmatic contract.

Cass. civ. 1re, 3 July 1996[222]   **1.F.99.**

MISTAKEN PURPOSE AND CAUSE

The video club

A contract made for a purpose which cannot possibly succeed is without cause.

Facts: With a view to setting up a video club at V., Mr and Mrs Pillet hired from DPM, a newly incorporated company, 200 video cassettes for a period of eight months subject to payment of the sum of 40 000 F excluding taxes. DPM brought an action for payment before the cour d'appel which set aside the hire agreement on the ground that it was vitiated by a mistake.

The appeal court preferred the absence of cause to mistake as the basis of the contract's nullity. In the words of the appeal court "the cause, that is the determining motive for Mrs Pillet to enter into the contract, was the guaranteed distribution amongst her clientele of cassettes hired from DPM, which could not be achieved in V, a municipality numbering only 1,315 inhabitants". On the basis of these findings the appeal court held the hire agreement to be null and void for lack of cause (Court of Appeal, Grenoble, 17 March 1994).

The appeal by DPM alleged that the appeal court had confused cause and motives without making any finding as to whether they had entered the ambit of the contract.

Judgment: THE COURT: *On the two branches of the sole appeal ground*:—Whereas DPM alleges that the court below (Court of Appeal, Grenoble, 17 March 1994) set aside for lack of any cause the contract for the setting up of a "video club" and the hire of video cassettes entered into with Mr and Mrs Pillet; as it did this, it is submitted by finding the cause, namely the determining motive for the couple to enter into the contract, to be the guaranteed distribution of cassettes amongst their

---

[221] *Infra*, at 506.
[222] D. 1997.499, annotated by P. Reigne.

137

clientele, and further finding that the operation was doomed to failure in a community of just 1,315 inhabitants; as however, it was pleaded on appeal that in a synallagmatic contract the cause of one party's obligation is the obligation entered into by the other party; as applied to this case, the appellants submit, the cause of the Pillet couple's obligation was to be found in the making available to them of video cassettes, and determining motives cannot constitute the cause of the contract unless they have entered the ambit of the contract, which was not found to be the case by the appeal court;
—Whereas however, as the appeal court found, the contract was for the hire of video cassettes in order to operate a business; as performance of the contract according to the overall plan intended by the parties was impossible;
—Whereas therefore, the appeal court correctly inferred that the contract was unsupported by any cause once there was found to be no real consideration passing for the obligation to pay the price for the hire of the cassettes entered into by Mr and Mrs Pillet under an agreement for the setting up of a "video club";
—Whereas the judgment was therefore sound in law;
On those grounds the Cour de cassation dismissed the appeal.

Note
This is an innovative judgment, inasmuch as it imports a new idea into the doctrine of cause, at the same time quite deliberately declining to be swayed by the arguments drawn from traditional doctrine which were put forward on appeal. The cause of the contract is not merely the supply of the cassettes in consideration of the payment of the hire charge. The hirer knew the use to which the hire of the cassettes was to be put, namely the opening of a video centre in its turn hiring out the cassettes. The cause was to be inferred from the overall structure of the contract, including the actual motives of the parties. However, it proved impossible to achieve the objective pursued owing to the small size of the community and the inadequate number of foreseeable hirings out. The equilibrium sought by the parties was not achievable.

This case was therefore based on the idea of a contractual whole: the hire of the cassettes to the video centre and the hiring out of the cassettes by the centre to customers. The phenomenon of complex contractual networks has for some time now exercised academic writers. It has repercussions on the whole legal status of the contract and, in particular, of the cause. The complex web of contracts has a functional unity. It may be wondered whether it possesses a cause of its own. The question arises where one of the contracts in a series is set aside. Does the setting aside of one such contract entail the setting aside of the other contracts?

Cass. com., 4 April 1995[223]   **1.F.100.**

CAUSE AS BETWEEN RELATED CONTRACTS

Indivisible contracts

If one of two contracts cannot exist without the other, failure of one may lead to failure of both.
Judgment: THE COURT:—Whereas according to the judgment appealed against (Court of Appeal, Douai, 2nd Chamber, 30 June 1993), Mr Kessler entered into a contract with V, a company

---

[223] D. 1996.141, annotated by S. Piquet.

advising on applications, giving him access, by means of special equipment and software, to the telematic network of SEDRI, an industrial research and development company, in order to enable him to broadcast information and publicity pictures in his shop; as in order to finance the equipment and software Mr Kessler, on the suggestion of V's representative, signed a draft rental agreement with the Compagnie Générale de Location (CGL) which subsequently accepted the proposal subject to insurance cover to be paid for by SEDRI in the event of damage to the equipment or interruption in the payment of rental by the lessee; as it was proposed to Mr Kessler that SEDRI should take over responsibility for the rental payments in consideration of the assignment of rights over certain publicity pictures concerning him; as in August and September 1990 SEDRI, V and the insurance company acting as guarantor of CGL were put into liquidation under a court order, whereupon the broadcasting of pictures on the network was interrupted and termination of the contracts for the provision of services was notified to the traders by the court-appointed representative of the companies in liquidation. CGL claimed payment of rentals from Mr Kessler;

On both branches of the first and second appeal grounds taken together:—Whereas CGL criticises the appeal court for deciding that the cessation of the services provided by SEDRI entailed termination of the rental agreement for the equipment and hardware whereas, in the terms of the appeal, the trader was on the one hand pleading that the rental agreement for the telematic equipment between the trader and CGL, on the one hand, and the subscription agreement between the trader and the server SEDRI were objectively indivisible; as conversely, CGL claimed that there was no such link between those contracts; whereas the court of appeal found there to be no subjective indivisibility between those contracts, and held on the other hand that they were linked in such a way that termination of one entailed termination of the other;
—Whereas in so deciding, without determining in what way those two contracts were linked as to subject-matter or of necessity by a situation of legal dependence, the court of appeal deprived its decision of any legal basis under the terms of Articles 1134(1) and 1184 of the Civil Code, at the same time as it deprived its decision of a legal basis under Article 1165 of the Civil Code;
—Whereas moreover, the duty to ensure maintenance is a matter not for the lessor but for the lessee;
—Whereas in deciding to the contrary, the court of appeal infringed Article 1134 of the Civil Code;
—Whereas in the final analysis the maintenance obligation relates to the equipment hired and not to the supply of images by the server; in deciding to the contrary, the court of appeal infringed Article 1143 of the Civil Code;
—Whereas however the court below in its judgment pointed out that the equipment and software could not, without substantial alterations, have any use other than communication via the SEDRI network; as the lessor was aware of that specific feature and had indeed participated in drawing up the complex arrangements for the installation and financing of the communication system;
—Whereas by inferring from these findings that the contracts entered into by Mr Kessler both with V and SEDRI and with CGL, the court of appeal based its decision on proper legal grounds, irrespective of the reasoning criticised in the second plea which are superfluous;
—Whereas none of the appeal ground can be upheld.
On those grounds the Cour de cassation dismisses the appeal.

Note
The judgment does not expressly refer to the cause. It prefers to base itself on the unspecific ground of indivisibility. But it may be thought that fundamentally indivisibility presupposes that one of the contracts cannot exist without the other, that each is the cause of the other. That marks the emergence in embryonic form of the cause in groups of contracts.

In conclusion it is worth noting that the doctrine of cause in French law remains as vital as ever. It is a doctrine which is still much debated in academic circles, not to repudiate it but to search for its foundations, owing to its twofold aspect. It would appear that recent developments in case-law demonstrate that the doctrine of cause continues to find new applications in regard to which it may be wondered whether they represent a response to the considerations of Carbonnier[224] on the profound unity of the doctrine. Anyway, it is difficult to agree with some writers[225] that the cause is an ineffectual doctrine. On the contrary, a study of the cases shows that the French courts have found ways to use it in order to inject an ethical content into the contract, even in the case of the so-called objective cause.

1.3.3.B. ENGLISH LAW: CONSIDERATION

Consideration, which may be compared with the doctrine of cause inasmuch as it is a requirement additional to intention, is a strange notion for a lawyer brought up under the Roman system of law. As is often the case in the Common Law system, it is a product of history, a history, moreover, which is still somewhat obscure. It can be compared only obliquely with French law and German law. It is not possible in the confines of this work to dissect the doctrine in detail.[226]

This doctrine, peculiar to the Common Law, is still relatively ill-defined and controversial. Currently there is no consensus on its true scope or on the expediency of maintaining it in force.[227]

In General

The early history of consideration as an essential component of a simple contract binding in law is obscure. It seems to have become a requirement in the sixteenth century for bringing an action of assumpsit, the principal action for non-performance of a contract. Roughly speaking, it consists in the requirement of a counterpart in exchange for a promise doubtless laid down as a counterweight to contractual formalism—this link between form and consideration will be encountered again and is a characteristic of English law. The contract is upheld when the interests of business so demand, that is to say when there is a "bargain".[228] The attempts made in the seventeenth century to replace "consideration" with the "sovereignty" of the will, or at least to mitigate the effects of consideration (Lord Mansfield) all failed. Similarly, in 1937 the proposal by the Law Reform Committee to abolish the requirement of consideration, or at least its worst effects, also came to grief. Only in the United States has it been possible in part to achieve this result, in particular in the Uniform Commercial Code concerning sales, and in the 2nd Restatement on Contracts.[229] It should also be noted that the doctrine of consideration does not exist in Scottish law.

---

[224] *Supra*, at 129.

[225] Kötz, *European Contract Law* at 54.–55.

[226] In this connection reference is made to the standard works: Treitel, *Contract*, at 63 ff.; McKendrick, *Contract*, at 79 ff.

[227] For a comparative viewpoint, see: R. David, "Cause et Consideration", *Mélanges J. Maury* (1960); A.G. Chloros, "The Doctrine of Consideration and the Reform of the Law of Contract", 17 ICLQ, 137 (1968); Kötz, *European Contract Law* at 75–7.

[228] *Supra*, at 16.

[229] *Supra*, at 5.

There is no precise definition of consideration. Each definition, whether by academic writers or by the courts, places the emphasis on one aspect of the doctrine.

(a) Definitions of consideration[230]

1.E.101.

A valuable consideration, in the sense of the law, may consist either in some right, interest, profit or benefit accruing to one party or some forbearance, detriment, loss or responsability, given, suffered or undertaken by the other.
(*Currie* v. *Misa* (1975) LR 10 Exch 153, 162)

Consideration means something with is of some value in the eye of the law, moving from the plaintiff; it may be some detriment to the plaintiff or some benefit to the defendant, but at all events it must be moving from the plaintiff.
(Patteson J in *Thomas* v. *Thomas* (1842))

An act of forbearance of the one party, or the promise thereof, is the price for which the promise of the other is bought, and the promise thus given for value is enforceable.
(F. Pollock, *Principles of Contract*, 13th edn. (London, 1936) at 133, approved by Lord Dunedin in *Dunlop* v. *Selfridge* (1915))

Restatement 2nd Contracts, s. 71. **1.US.102.**

(1) To constitute consideration, a performance or a return promise must be bargained for.
(2) A performance or return promise is bargained for if it is sought by the promisor in exchange for his promise and is given by the promisee in exchange for that promise.
(3) The consideration may consist of
  (a) an act other than a promise, or
  (b) a forbearance, or
  (c) the creation, modification or destruction of a legal relation.

What is noteworthy about the Restatement is, *inter alia*, the relaxation of the rule in connection with amendments to the contract;[231] and also that alongside section 71 there is section 90, which creates liability when a promise made without consideration has reasonably been relied on by the promisee.[232]

However, the central point continues to be the notion of "bargain", as the counterweight to a promise; it may be a benefit conferred or some act of forbearance. It is consideration, rather than a consensus of intentions, which brings two promises together in a relationship of dependency. These definitions also show that "consideration" is an essentially objective concept; it does not include psychological aspects, as does the doctrine of cause under French law. This is particularly so in English law, where the courts may point to the fact that the parties have in fact made an exchange of some kind and hold that they have therefore made an agreement supported by consideration, even if the

[230] See BBF3 at 93.
[231] *Infra*, at 150 ff.
[232] *Supra*, at 5.

parties were perhaps not conscious of so doing—e.g. *de la Bere* v. *Pearson*.[233] The American Restatement, section 71, is more subjective, as it requires that each party sought for the other's counter-promise or performance; however, as just noted, section 71 is supplemented by s.90 which would cover cases such as *de la Bere* v. *Pearson*.

Finally, it is important to note that consideration applies only to certain contracts, that is to say simple contracts. Consideration is not necessary in the case of contracts by deed. In other words, the form replaces the requirement of consideration. Likewise, the requirement of consideration means that English law disregards gratuitous contracts which are by definition unsupported by consideration. It is more difficult to discover consideration in what are known in English law as "unilateral contracts", that is to say contracts which come into existence by virtue of the performance of an act.[234] The question was discussed and resolved positively in the landmark judgment in *Carlill* v. *Carbolic Smoke Ball Co.*

Court of Appeal   **1.E.103.**
Carlill v. *Carbolic Smoke Ball Co*[235]

TROUBLE TO PROMISEE MAY BE CONSIDERATION

The Smoke Ball

There will be consideration for a promise if the promisee incurs inconvenience in exchange for it.

Facts: The Carbolic Smoke Ball Company advertised that it would pay £100 to any person who used the Smoke Ball for two weeks and nonetheless caught influenza. Mrs. Carlill purchased a Smoke Ball from a third party and used it. She caught 'flu but the company refused to pay.

Held: The Company's promise was intended to create legal relations and was for good consideration.

Judgment: BOWEN LJ: A further argument for the defendants was that this was a nudum pactum—that there was no consideration for the promise—that taking the influenza was only a condition, and that the using of the smoke ball was only a condition, and that there was no consideration at all; in fact, that there was no request, express or implied, to use the smoke ball. Now, I will not enter into an elaborate discussion upon the law as to requests in this kind of contracts. I will simply refer to *Victors* v. *Davies* (12 M. & W. 758) and Sergeant Manning's note to *Fisher* v. *Pyne* (1 M. & G. 265), which everybody ought to read who wishes to embark in this controversy. The short answer, to abstain from academical discussion, is, it seems to me, that there is here a request to use involved in the offer. Then as to the alleged want of consideration. The definition of "consideration" given in Selwyn's *Nisi Prius*, 8th ed., p. 47, which is cited and adopted by Tindal CJ in the case of *Laythoarp* v. *Bryant* (3 Scott 238), 250), is this: "Any act of the plaintiff from which the defendant received a benefit or advantage, or any labour, detriment , or inconvenience sustained by the plaintiff, provided such act is performed or such inconvenience suffered by the plaintiff, with the consent, either express or implied, of the defendant". Can it be said here that if the person who reads this advertisement applies thrice daily, for such time as many seem to him tolerable, the carbolic smoke ball to his nostrils for a whole fortnight, he is doing nothing at all—that it is a mere act which is not to count towards consideration to support a promise (for the law does not require us to measure the adequacy of the consideration). Inconvenience sustained by one party at the request of the other is enough to create a consideration. I think therefore, that it is consideration enough that the plaintiff took the

---

[233] [1908] 1 KB 280.
[234] *Supra*, at 14 ff.
[235] [1893]1 QB 257, AC; see also **2.E.9**, *infra* at 187.

trouble of using the smoke ball. But I think also that the defendants received a benefit from this user, for the use of the smoke ball was contemplated by the defendants as being indirectly a benefit to them, because the use of the smoke ball would promote their sale . . . if you once make up your mind that there was a promise made to this lady who is the plaintiff, as one of the public—a promise made to her that if she used the smoke ball three times daily for a fortnight and got the influenza, she should have £100, it seems to me that her using the smoke ball was sufficient consideration. I cannot picture to myself the view of the law on which the contrary could be held when you have once found who are the contracting parties. If I say to a person, "If you use such and such a medicine for a week I will give you £5", and he uses it, there is ample consideration for the promise.

LINDLEY and A. L. SMITH L.JJ. delivered concurring judgments.

Note
It may be wondered whether there is not a certain artificiality in the discovery of consideration in this case. This landmark case is also controversial on other points.

Finally, the notion of consideration assumes a specific meaning in connection with "failure of consideration". This is very close to absence of cause in French law. An action lies for failure of consideration, to recover money paid.[236]

(b) Consequences of the doctrine of consideration

It is clearly impossible here to provide an in-depth analysis of all the extremely complex aspects of the concept of consideration.[237] Suffice it here to refer to major handbooks.

I will confine my remarks to the main consequences and to those which are of most interest from a comparative point of view.

First of all, an offer may be freely revoked, even if it is a firm offer expressed to be open for a specified period, because the offer was unsupported by consideration. This solution has been criticized and American law has disavowed it to an extent in the Uniform Commercial Code.

§2–205: An offer by a merchant to buy or sell goods in a signed writing which by its terms gives assurance that it will be held open is not recovable, for lack of consideration, during the time stated or if no time is stated for a reasonable time, but in no event may such period of irrevocability exceed three months; but any such term of assurance on a form supplied by the offeree must be separately signed by the offeror.

The requirement that there be consideration is attenuated to a limited degree; it must be an offer by a "merchant", the offer must be contained in a signed document with a preclusive time-limit of three months. To create a binding offer in English law it would be necessary either that the offeror make the promise to keep the offer open by deed or for the offeree to pay for the offer to be kept open—since the doctrine of consideration does not require that the exchange be of things of equivalent value, a nominal sum such as £1 would suffice.

The doctrine of consideration precludes the amendment of a contract or the waiving of a debt.

---

[236] See *Fibrosa Spolka Akcyjna* v. *Fairbairn Lawson Comber Barbour Ltd* [1943] AC 32. See also McKendrick, *Contract*, at 313.
[237] Hence the rule that consideration, whilst not needing to be adequate, must have some economic value. "Moral" consideration has no value.

1.E.104.

House of Lords
Foakes v. *Beer*[238]

PART PAYMENT OF DEBT NO CONSIDERATION

Debt paid without interest due

A debtor who pays part of the sum he owes does not thereby provide consideration for the creditor's promise to release the debtor from the rest of the debt.

Facts: Judgment was entered against F for the payment to B of a certain sum of money. B and F then entered into an agreement under which F on signing was to pay to B a certain amount, the remainder to be paid in quarterly instalments, in consideration of which B promised not to seek execution of the judgment debt. F paid all the instalments so that the principal sum was paid off. However, B sought payment of interest with effect from the date of the judgment. The House of Lords was divided on whether the agreement entered into included an undertaking not to claim interest but held that in any event such an undertaking would be of no value.

Judgment: THE EARL OF SELBORNE LC . . . But the question remains, whether the agreement is capable of being legally enforced. Not being under seal, it cannot be legally enforced against the respondent, unless she received consideration for it from the appellant, or unless, though without consideration, it operates by way of accord and satisfaction, so as to extinguish the claim for interest. What is the consideration? On the face of the agreement none is expressed, except a present payment of £500, on account and in part of the larger debt then due and payable by law under the judgment. The appellant did not contract to pay the future instalments of £150 each, at the times therein mentioned; much less did he give any new security, in the shape of negotiable paper, or in any other form. The promise de futuro was only that of the respondent, that if the half-yearly payments of £150 each were regularly paid, she would "take no proceedings whatever on the judgment." No doubt if the appellant had been under no antecedent obligation to pay the whole debt, his fulfilment of the condition might have imported some consideration on his part for that promise. But he was under that antecedent obligation; and payment at those deferred dates, by the forbearance and indulgence of the creditor, of the residue of the principal debt and costs, could not (in my opinion) be a consideration for the relinquishment of interest and discharge of the judgment, unless the payment of the £500, at the time of signing the agreement, was such a consideration. As to accord and satisfaction, in point of fact there could be no complete satisfaction, so long as any future instalment remained payable; and I do not see how any mere payments on account could operate in law as a satisfaction ad interim, conditionally upon other payments being afterwards duly made, unless there was a consideration sufficient to support the agreement while still unexecuted. Nor was anything, in fact, done by the respondent in this case, on the receipt of the last payment, which could be tantamount to an acquittance, if the agreement did not previously bind her.

The question, therefore, is nakedly raised by this appeal, whether your Lordships are now prepared, not only to overrule, as contrary to law, the doctrine stated by Sir Edward Coke to have been laid down by all the judges of the Common Pleas in *Pinnel's* Case (5 Rep. 117 a) in 1602, and repeated in his note to Littleton, sect. 344 (Co. Litt. 212 b), but to treat a prospective agreement, not under seal, for satisfaction of a debt, by a series of payments on account to a total amount less than the whole debt, as binding in law, provided those payments are regularly made; the case not being one of a composition with a common debtor, agreed to, inter se, by several cred-

---

[238] [1881–5] All ER 106, HL.

itors. I prefer so to state the question instead of treating it (as it was put at the Bar) as depending on the authority of the case of *Cumber* v. *Wane* (1 Sm. L. C. 8th ed. 357), decided in 1718. It may well be that distinctions, which in later cases have been held sufficient to exclude the application of that doctrine, existed and were improperly disregarded in *Cumber* v. *Wane*; and yet that the doctrine itself may be law, rightly recognised in *Cumber* v. *Wane*, and not really contradicted by any later authorities. And this appears to me to be the true state of the case. The doctrine itself, as laid down by Sir Edward Coke, may have been criticised, as questionable in principle, by some persons whose opinions are entitled to respect, but it has never been judicially overruled; on the contrary I think it has always, since the sixteenth century, been accepted as law. If so, I cannot think that your Lordships would do right, if you were now to reverse, as erroneous, a judgment of the Court of Appeal, proceeding upon a doctrine which has been accepted as part of the law of England for 280 years.

The doctrine, as stated in *Pinnel's* Case, is "that payment of a lesser sum on the day" (it would of course be the same after the day), "in satisfaction of a greater, cannot be any satisfaction for the whole, because it appears to the Judges, that by no possibility a lesser sum can be a satisfaction to the plaintiff for a greater sum." As stated in Coke Littleton, 212 (b), it is, "where the condition is for payment of £20, the obligor or feoffor cannot at the time appointed pay a lesser sum in satisfaction of the whole, because it is apparent that a lesser sum of money cannot be a satisfaction of a greater;" adding (what is beyond controversy), that an acquittance under seal, in full satisfaction of the whole, would (under like circumstances) be valid and binding.

The distinction between the effect of a deed under seal, and that of an agreement by parol, or by writing not under seal, may seem arbitrary, but it is established in our law; nor is it really unreasonable or practically inconvenient that the law should require particular solemnities to give to a gratuitous contract the force of a binding obligation. If the question be (as, in the actual state of the law, I think it is), whether consideration is, or is not, given in a case of this kind, by the debtor who pays down part of the debt presently due from him, for a promise by the creditor to relinquish, after certain further payments on account, the residue of the debt, I cannot say that I think consideration is given, in the sense in which I have always understood that word as used in our law. It might be (and indeed I think it would be) an improvement in our law, if a release or acquittance of the whole debt, on payment of any sum which the creditor might be content to receive by way of accord and satisfaction (though less than the whole), were held to be, generally, binding, though not under seal; nor should I be unwilling to see equal force given to a prospective agreement, like the present, in writing though not under seal; but I think it impossible, without refinements which practically alter the sense of the word, to treat such a release or acquittance as supported by any new consideration proceeding from the debtor. All the authorities subsequent to *Cumber* v. *Wane* (1 Sm. L. C. 8th ed. 366), which were relied upon by the appellant at your Lordships' Bar (such as *Sibree* v. *Tripp* (15 M. & W. 23), *Curlewis* v. *Clark* (3 Ex. 375), and *Goddard* v. *O'Brien* (9 Q.B.D. 37)) have proceeded upon the distinction, that, by giving negotiable paper or otherwise, there had been some new consideration for a new agreement, distinct from mere money payments in or towards discharge of the original liability. I think it unnecessary to go through those cases, or to examine the particular grounds on which each of them was decided. There are no such facts in the case now before your Lordships. What is called "any benefit, or even any legal possibility of benefit," in Mr. Smith's notes to *Cumber* v. *Wane*, is not (as I conceive) that sort of benefit which a creditor may derive from getting payment of part of the money due to him from a debtor who might otherwise keep him at arm's length, or possibly become insolvent, but is some independent benefit, actual or contingent, of a kind which might in law be a good and valuable consideration far any other sort of agreement not under seal.

My conclusion is, that the order appealed from should be affirmed, and the appeal dismissed, with costs, and I so move your Lordships.

LORD BLACKBURN:—I think, therefore, that it is necessary to consider the ground on which the Court of Appeal did base their judgment, and to say whether the agreement can be enforced. I construe it as accepting and taking £500 in satisfaction of the whole £2090 19s., subject to the condition that unless the balance of the principal debt was paid by the instalments, the whole might be enforced with interest. If, instead of £500 in money, it had been a horse valued at £500, or a promissory note for £500, the authorities are that it would have been a good satisfaction, but it is said to be otherwise as it was money.

This is a question, I think, of difficulty.

In Coke, Littleton 212 b, Lord Coke says: "where the condition is for payment of £20, the obligor or feoffor cannot at the time appointed pay a lesser sum in satisfaction of the whole, because it is apparent that a lesser sum of money cannot be a satisfaction of a greater. . . . If the obligor or feoffor pay a lesser sum either before the day or at another place than is limited by the condition, and the obligee or feoffee receiveth it, this is a good satisfaction." For this he cites *Pinnel's* Case (5 Rep. 117 a). That was an action on a bond for £16, conditioned for the payment of £8 10s. on 11 November 1600. Plea that defendant, at plaintiff's request, before the said day, to wit, on the 1st of October, paid to the plaintiff £5 2s. 2d., which the plaintiff accepted in full satisfaction of the £8 10s. The plaintiff had judgment for the insufficient pleading. But though this was so, Lord Coke reports that it was resolved by the whole Court of Common Pleas "that payment of a lesser sum on the day in satisfaction of a greater cannot be any satisfaction for the whole, because it appears to the judges that by no possibility a lesser sum can be a satisfaction to the plaintiff for a greater sum: but the gift of a horse, hawk, or robe, &c., in satisfaction is good, for it shall be intended that a horse, hawk, or robe, &c., might be more beneficial to the plaintiff than the money, in respect of some circumstance, or otherwise the plaintiff would not have accepted of it in satisfaction. But when the whole sum is due, by no intendment the acceptance of parcel can be a satisfaction to the plaintiff; but in the case at bar it was resolved that the payment and acceptance of parcel before the day in satisfaction of the whole would be a good satisfaction in regard of circumstance of time; for peradventure parcel of it before the day would be more beneficial to him than the whole at the day, and the value of the satisfaction is not material; so if I am bound in £20 to pay you £10 at Westminster, and you request me to pay you £5 at the day at York, and you will accept it in full satisfaction for the whole £10, it is a good satisfaction for the whole, for the expenses to pay it at York is sufficient satisfaction."

There are two things here resolved. First, that where a matter paid and accepted in satisfaction of a debt certain might by any possibility be more beneficial to the creditor than his debt, the Court will not inquire into the adequacy of the consideration. If the creditor, without any fraud, accepted it in satisfaction when it was not a sufficient satisfaction it was his own fault. And that payment before the day might be more beneficial, and consequently that the plea was in substance good, and this must have been decided in the case.

There is a second point stated to have been resolved, viz.: "That payment of a lesser sum on the day cannot be any satisfaction of the whole, because it appears to the judges that by no possibility a lesser sum can be a satisfaction to the plaintiff for a greater sum." This was certainly not necessary for the decision of the case; but though the resolution of the Court of Common Pleas was only a dictum, it seems to me clear that Lord Coke deliberately adopted the dictum, and the great weight of his authority makes it necessary to be cautious before saying that what he deliberately adopted as law was a mistake, and though I cannot find that in any subsequent case this dictum has been made the ground of the decision, except in *Fitch* v. *Sutton* (5 East, 230), as to which I shall make some remarks later, and in *Down* v. *Hatcher* (10 A. & E. 121), as to which Parke, B. in *Cooper* v. *Parker* (15 C. B. 828), said, "Whenever the question may arise as to whether *Down* v. *Hatcher* is good law, I should have a great deal to say against it," yet there certainly are cases in which great judges have treated the dictum in *Pinnel's* Case as good law.

For instance, in *Sibree* v. *Tripp* (15 M. & W. 33, 37), Parke, B. says, "It is clear if the claim be a liquidated and ascertained sum, payment of part cannot be satisfaction of the whole, although it may, under certain circumstances, be evidence of a gift of the remainder." And Alderson, B. in the same case says, "It is undoubtedly true that payment of a portion of a liquidated demand, in the same manner as the whole liquidated demand which ought to be paid, is payment only in part, because it is not one bargain, but two; viz. payment of part, and an agreement without consideration to give up the residue. The Courts might very well have held the contrary, and have left the matter to the agreement of the parties, but undoubtedly the law is so settled." After such strong expressions of opinion, I doubt much whether any judge sitting in a Court of the first instance would be justified in treating the question as open. But as this has very seldom, if at all, been the ground of the decision even in a Court of the first instance, and certainly never been the ground of a decision in the Court of Exchequer Chamber, still less in this House, I did think it open in your Lordships' House to reconsider this question. And, notwithstanding the very high authority of Lord Coke, I think it is not the fact that to accept prompt payment of a part only of a liquidated demand, can never be more beneficial than to insist on payment of the whole. And if it be not the fact, it cannot be apparent to the judges . . .

What principally weighs with me in thinking that Lord Coke made a mistake of fact is my conviction that all men of business, whether merchants or tradesmen, do every day recognise and act on the ground that prompt payment of a part of their demand may be more beneficial to them than it would be to insist on their rights and enforce payment of the whole. Even where the debtor is perfectly solvent, and sure to pay at last, this often is so. Where the credit of the debtor is doubtful it must be more so. I had persuaded myself that there was no such long-continued action on this dictum as to render it improper in this House to reconsider the question. I had written my reasons for so thinking; but as they were not satisfactory to the other noble and learned Lords who heard the case, I do not now repeat them nor persist in them.

I assent to the judgment proposed, though it is not that which I had originally thought proper.

[Lords Watson and Fitzgerald delivered concurring judgments].

Appeal dismissed.

Note

It seems to have been with a heavy heart that the House of Lords declined to give effect to agreements which appear reasonable from a business point of view, The reservations expressed by Lord Blackburn are particularly to be noted. One could get round the difficulty by deeming the amending contract to be a new contract and by acknowledging more readily the existence of consideration.[239] Section 2–209 of the Uniform Commercial Code, on the other hand, states that "An agreement modifying a contract within this article needs no consideration to be binding".[240]

Any modification and indeed any transaction may also be invalid for being based on past consideration, that is to say consideration passing in respect of a promise already executed.

[239] See *William* v. *Roffrey Bros & Nichols (Contractors) Ltd* [1990] 1 All ER 512, CA; BBF3, at 107.
[240] See also 2nd Restatement on Contract, § 74.

PAST CONSIDERATION

The share deal

The fact that the alleged consideration was an act which took place before the promise to pay for it was made does not render the promise without consideration if it was always understood that the act was to be paid for.

Facts: Pao assigned his shares in SO to SO of which Lau was the principal shareholder, in exchange for FC shares. Pao undertook not to resell his FC shares until at least twelve months after acquiring them. In an ancillary agreement Pao secured an agreement that 60% of his shares would be redeemed before the end of the year at \$2.5 per share. That agreement was modified by a new agreement on 4 May 1973 providing for compensation if the 60% of shares retained fell below the value of \$2.5 each. This eventuality occurred whereupon Lau refused to pay. At first instance he was unsuccessful, but the judgment was reversed on appeal. On appeal to the Privy Council the judgment at first instance was reinstated. The Privy Council found that the agreement was not contrary to public policy, was not signed under duress and above all was supported by consideration.

Judgment: The opinion of the Privy Council was delivered by LORD SCARMAN:
. . . The first question is whether upon its true construction the written guarantee of May 4, 1973, states a consideration sufficient in law to support the defendants' promise of indemnity against a fall in value of the Fu Chip shares.

Mr Neill, counsel for the plaintiffs before their Lordships' Board but not below, contends that the consideration stated in the agreement is not in reality a past one. It is to be noted that the consideration was not on May 4, 1973, a matter of history only. The instrument by its reference to the main agreement with Fu Chip incorporates as part of the stated consideration the plaintiffs' three promises to Fu Chip: to complete the sale of Shing On, to accept shares as the price for the sale, and not to sell 60 per cent. of the shares so accepted before April 30, 1974. Thus, on May 4, 1973, the performance of the main agreement still lay in the future. Performance of these promises was of great importance to the defendants, and it is undeniable that, as the instrument declares, the promises were made to Fu Chip at the request of the defendants. It is equally clear that the instrument also includes a promise by the plaintiffs to the defendants to fulfil their earlier promises given to Fu Chip.

The Board agrees with Mr Neill's submission that the consideration expressly stated in the written guarantee is sufficient in law to support the defendants' promise of indemnity. An act done before the giving of a promise to make a payment or to confer some other benefit can sometimes be consideration for the promise. The act must have been done at the promisors' request: the parties must have understood that the act was to be remunerated either by a payment or the conferment of some other benefit: and payment, or the conferment of a benefit, must have been legally enforceable had it been promised in advance. All three features are present in this case. The promise given to Fu Chip under the main agreement not to sell the shares for a year was at the first defendant's request. The parties understood at the time of the main agreement that the restriction on selling must be compensated for by the benefit of a guarantee against a drop in price: and such a guarantee would be legally enforceable. The agreed cancellation of the subsidiary agreement left, as the parties knew, the plaintiffs unprotected in a respect in which at the time of the main agreement all were agreed they should be protected.

Mr Neill's submission is based on *Lampleigh* v. *Brathwait* (1615) Hobart 105. In that case the judges said, at p. 106:

---

[241] [1980] AC 614.

"First . . . a mere voluntary courtesie will not have a consideration to uphold an assumpsit. But if that courtesie were moved by a suit or request of the party that gives the assumpsit, it will bind, for the promise, though it follows, yet it is not naked, but couples it self with the suit before, and the merits of the party procured by that suit. which is the difference."

The modern statement of the law is in the judgment of Bowen LJ in *In re Casey's Patents* [1892] 1 Ch. 104, 115–116; Bowen LJ said:

"Even if it were true, as some scientific students of law believe, that a past service cannot support a future promise, you must look at the document and see if the promise cannot receive a proper effect in some other way. Now, the fact of a past service raises an implication that at the time it was rendered it was to be paid for, and, if it was a service which was to be paid for, when you get in the subsequent document a promise to pay, that promise may be treated either as an admission which evidences or as a positive bargain which fixes the amount of that reasonable remuneration on the faith of which the service was originally rendered. So that here for past services there is ample justification for the promise to give the third share."

Conferring a benefit is, of course, an equivalent to payment: see *Chitty on Contracts*, 24th ed. (1977), vol. 1, para. 154.

Mr. Leggatt, for the defendants, does not dispute the existence of the rule but challenges its application to the facts of this case. He submits that it is not a necessary inference or implication from the terms of the written guarantee that any benefit or protection was to be given to the plaintiffs for their acceptance of the restriction on selling their shares. Their Lordships agree that the mere existence or recital of a prior request is not sufficient in itself to convert what is prima facie past consideration into sufficient consideration in law to support a promise: as they have indicated, it is only the first of three necessary preconditions. As for the second of those preconditions, whether the act done at the request of the promisor raises an implication of promised remuneration or other return is simply one of the construction of the words of the contract in the circumstances of its making. Once it is recognised, as the Board considers it inevitably must be, that the expressed consideration includes a reference to the plaintiffs' promise not to sell the shares before April 30, 1974—a promise to be performed in the future, though given in the past—it is not possible to treat the defendants' promise of indemnity as independent of the plaintiffs' antecedent promise, given at the first defendant's request, not to sell. The promise of indemnity was given because at the time of the main agreement the parties intended that the first defendant should confer upon the plaintiffs the benefit of his protection against a fall in price. When the subsidiary agreement was cancelled, all were well aware that the plaintiffs were still to have the benefit of his protection as consideration for the restriction on selling. It matters not whether the indemnity thus given be regarded as the best evidence of the benefit intended to be conferred in return for the promise not to sell, or as the positive bargain which fixes the benefit on the faith of which the promise was given—though where, as here, the subject is a written contract, the better analysis is probably that of the "positive bargain." Their Lordships, therefore, accept the submission that the contract itself states a valid consideration for the promise of indemnity.

This being their Lordships' conclusion, it is necessary to consider Mr. Neill's further submission (also raised for the first time before the Board) that the option given the defendants, if called upon to fulfil their indemnity, to buy back the shares at $2.50 a share was itself a sufficient consideration for the promise of indemnity. But their Lordships see great force in the contention. The defendants promised to indemnify he plaintiffs if the market price of Fu Chip shares fell below $2.50. However, in the event of the defendants being called on to implement this promise they were given an option to take up the shares themselves at $2.50. This on the face of it imposes on the plaintiffs in the circumstances envisaged an obligation to transfer the shares to the defendants at the price of $2.50 if called on to do so. The concomitant benefit to the defendants could be a real one—for example, if they thought that the market, after a temporary set-back, would recover to a price above $2.50. The fact that the option is stated in the form of a proviso does not preclude it being a contractual term or one under which consideration moves.

[His Lordship went on to hold that there was good consideration for the promise of indemnity despite the fact that the primary consideration was the promise given by the plaintiff to the Laus to perform their contract with FC: a promise to perform, or the performance of, a pre-existing contractual obligation to a third party can be valid consideration.]

Note

The efforts made by the Privy Council to circumvent the "past consideration" rule should be noted. It is certainly the case that the requirement that there be executory or executed consideration may cause arrangements which are otherwise perfectly reasonable to founder. The three conditions of "implied assumpsit" are not in fact always easy to satisfy.[242]

There is another obstacle stemming from another traditional rule: "the consideration must move from the promisee". This is the rule which, until the reforms recently introduced by the Contracts (Rights of Third Parties) Act 1999, precluded contracts in favour of a third party, as will be seen *infra*. It is sufficient to refer to the judgment in *Dunlop Pneumatic Tyre Co Ltd* v. *Selfridge & Co Ltd*.[243]

It is to be noted that the prohibition of such agreements arises out of the combination of two rules: the rule on the origin of consideration and the rule of privity of contract, and the result is the same in both cases.[244]

It seems unlikely that a general reform will be undertaken by legislative action. Yet attention should be drawn to a means which has been found of giving effect to some undertakings unsupported by consideration, which is known as promissory estoppel. We came across this earlier when considering gratuitous contracts.[245]

As is well known, estoppel was developed by equity as a corrective to the rigours of the common law.[246] The subject is attended by some degree of uncertainty and this is not the place to enter into a detailed discussion of it. But it is worth examining the manner in which promissory estoppel intervenes to mitigate the rigours of consideration, by studying the landmark judgment in the *High Trees House* case.

Queen's Bench Division   **1.E.106.**
Central London Property Trust Ltd v. *High Trees House Ltd*[247]

PROMISSORY ESTOPPEL

The High Trees case

A landlord's promise to reduce a tenant's rent will be binding without consideration if the tenant has acted on the promise in such a way that it would be inequitable for the landlord to go back on the promise.

Facts: The plaintiff, Central London Property Trust, granted to High Trees House Ltd a ninety-nine year lease on a block of flats at a ground rent of £2,500 a year. The war supervened and the lessor granted a reduction in

---

[242] See McKendrick, *Contract*, at 103, who states the other exceptions, this time legislative ones.
[243] [1915] AC 847, HL, **7.E.4**, *infra* at 882.
[244] See McKendrick, *Contract*, at 137 ff.
[245] *Supra*, at 17–18.
[246] On the different types of estoppel reference is made to McKendrick, *Contract*, at 108.
[247] [1947] KB 130.

rent of one-half to take account of circumstances. The reduced rent was paid regularly. By 1945 all the flats were again let and the lessor sought to recover ground rent at the full rate from the beginning of the term. It then reduced its claim to the difference with effect from the third quarter of 1945. Denning J (as he then was) allowed this claim.

Judgment: DENNING J. stated the facts and continued: If I were to consider this matter without regard to recent developments in the law, there is no doubt that had the plaintiffs claimed it, they would have been entitled to recover ground rent at the rate of £2,500. a year from the beginning of the term, since the lease under which it was payable was a lease under seal which, according to the old common law, could not be varied by an agreement by parol (whether in writing or not), but only by deed. Equity, however stepped in, and said that if there has been a variation of a deed by a simple contract (which in the case of a lease required to be in writing would have to be evidenced by writing), the courts may give effect to it as is shown in *Berry* v. *Berry* [1929] 2 K. B. 316. That equitable doctrine, however, could hardly apply in the present case because the variation here might be said to have been made without consideration. With regard to estoppel, the representation made in relation to reducing the rent, was not a representation of an existing fact. It was a representation, in effect, as to the future, namely, that payment of the rent would not be enforced at the full rate but only at the reduced rate. Such a representation would not give rise to an estoppel, because, as was said in *Jorden* v. *Money* (1854) 5 H. L. C. 185, a representation as to the future must be embodied as a contract or be nothing.

But what is the position in view of developments in the law in recent years? The law has not been standing still since *Jorden* v. *Money*. There has been a series of decisions over the last fifty years which, although they are said to be cases of estoppel are not really such. They are cases in which a promise was made which was intended to create legal relations and which, to the knowledge of the person making the promise, was going to be acted on by the person to whom it was made and which was in fact so acted on. In such cases the courts have said that the promise must be honoured. The cases to which I particularly desire to refer are: *Fenner* v. *Blake* [1900] 1 Q. B. 426, *In re Wickham* (1917) 34 T. L. R. 158, *Re William Porter & Co., Ltd.* [1937] 2 All E. R. 361 and *Buttery* v. *Pickard* [1946] W. N. 25. As I have said they are not cases of estoppel in the strict sense. They are really promises—promises intended to be binding, intended to be acted on, and in fact acted on. *Jorden* v. *Money* can be distinguished, because there the promisor made it clear that she did not intend to be legally bound, whereas in the cases to which I refer the proper inference was that the promisor did intend to be bound. In each case the court held the promise to be binding on the party making it, even though under the old common law it might be difficult to find any consideration for it. The courts have not gone so far as to give a cause of action in damages for the breach of such a promise, but they have refused to allow the party making it to act inconsistently with it. It is in that sense, and that sense only, that such a promise gives rise to an estoppel. The decisions are a natural result of the fusion of law and equity: for the cases of *Hughes* v. *Metropolitan Ry. Co.* (1877) 2 App. Cas. 439, 448, *Birmingham and District Land Co.* v. *London & North Western Ry. Co.* (1888) 40 Ch. D. 268, 286 and *Salisbury (Marquess)* v. *Gilmore* [1942] 2 K. B. 38, 51, afford a sufficient basis for saying that a party would not be allowed in equity to go back on such a promise. In my opinion, the time has now come for the validity of such a promise to be recognised. The logical consequence, no doubt is that a promise to accept a smaller sum in discharge of a larger sum, if acted upon, is binding notwithstanding the absence of consideration: and if the fusion of law and equity leads to this result, so much the better. That aspect was not considered in *Foakes* v. *Beer* (1884) 9 App. Cas. 605. At this time of day however, when law and equity have been joined together for over seventy years, principles must be reconsidered in the light of their combined effect. It is to be noticed that in the Sixth Interim Report of the Law Revision Committee, pars. 35, 40, it is recommended that such a promise as that to which I have referred, should be enforceable in law even though no consideration for it has been given by the promisee. It seems to me that, to the extent I have mentioned that result has now been achieved by the decisions of the courts.

I am satisfied that a promise such as that to which I have referred is binding and the only question remaining for my consideration is the scope of the promise in the present case. I am satisfied on all the evidence that the promise here was that the ground rent should be reduced to £1,250. a year as a temporary expedient while the block of flats was not fully, or substantially fully let, owing to the conditions prevailing. That means that the reduction in the rent applied throughout the years down to the end of 1944, but early in 1945 it is plain that the flats were fully let, and, indeed the rents received from them (many of them not being affected by the Rent Restrictions Acts), were increased beyond the figure at which it was originally contemplated that they would be let. At all events the rent from them must have been very considerable. I find that the conditions prevailing at the time when the reduction in rent was made, had completely passed away by the early months of 1945. I am satisfied that the promise was understood by all parties only to apply under the conditions prevailing at the time when it was made, namely, when the flats were only partially let, and that it did not extend any further than that. When the flats became fully let, early in 1945, the reduction ceased to apply.

In those circumstances, under the law as I hold it, it seems to me that rent is payable at the full rate for the quarters ending September 29 and December 25, 1945.

If the case had been one of estoppel, it might be said that in any event the estoppel would cease when the conditions to which the representation applied came to an end, or it also might be said that it would only come to an end on notice. In either case it is only a way of ascertaining what is the scope of the representation. I prefer to apply the principle that a promise intended to be binding, intended to be acted on and in fact acted on, is binding so far as its terms properly apply. Here it was binding as covering the period down to the early part of 1945, and as from that time full rent is payable.

I therefore give judgment for the plaintiff company for the amount claimed.

Judgment for plaintiffs.

Note

On this judgment, which upheld the reduction of rent under a lease during the war, the equitable doctrine of promissory estoppel was founded. Under that doctrine promises intended to create legal relationships and to be acted upon by the parties must be regarded as valid even if they are unsupported by consideration. We speak here of "reliance on non-bargain promise". The doctrine is used as a shield rather than a sword in the sense that it is applied to a promise to give up an existing contractual right, rather than to the creation of a new right. It will be noted that Denning J was careful to say that "The courts have not gone so far as to give a cause of action for breach of such a promise, but they have refused to allow the party making it to act inconsistently with it". That promissory estoppel cannot be used to make binding a promise to create a new right was confirmed by the Court of Appeal—including Denning LJ, as he had become by then— in *Combe* v. *Combe*.[248] This limit on promissory estoppel seems to be derived from the notion that estoppel does not confer a cause of action, it only helps to complete some other cause of action which would otherwise be incomplete. This restriction on promissory estoppel is not applied in the U.S. under Restatement section 90, nor now in Australia;[249] and it is not impossible that on this point matters might evolve.[250]

---

[248] [1951] 2 KB 215; BBF3 at 148.
[249] See *Walton Stores (Interstate) Ltd* v. *Maher* (1988) 164 CLR 387, High Court; BBF3 at 153.
[250] See McKendrick, *Contract*, at 118 ff.

Whatever the future may bring, it may be concluded that the doctrine of consideration is an additional feature which is rather burdensome to the validity of contracts; whenever possible the courts endeavour to mitigate its worst effects, in the absence of legislative reform, as has happened in the United States with the UCC.

1.3.3.C. GERMAN LAW: NEITHER CAUSE NOR CONSIDERATION

It is of course unsurprising that consideration, being a product of the Common Law alone, does not exist in German law. What is surprising is that the doctrine of cause, which originated in Roman law, plays no part in German law and the systems of law which have been strongly influenced by German law, such as Swiss law. Netherlands law in which the French doctrine of cause was incorporated in the 1838 Civil Code has abandoned it in the new code.

In German law the notion is not encountered in the BGB.[251]

The first important point to be noted is that German law attaches great importance to the act abstracted from its underlying cause, which includes all acts transferring property, in addition to the abstract acts known under the other systems. It is the doctrine of unjust enrichment (even here German law does not use the term "cause") which is applied in order to restore equilibrium.

In the case of other acts, intention does not need to be supported by a cause. How has it come to this?

The starting point is the same as in French law: the twofold influence of Roman law and Canon law. In the nineteenth century, in his theory on intention, the celebrated Pandectist, Windscheid, gave priority to the subjective argument by affirming that the cause is subsumed within the motive. As a reaction, under the influence of Lenel, the objective cause becomes prevalent: the cause as economic objective of the contract. The objective desired is revealed by the content of the contract. It in its turn becomes subsumed within intention. The cause does not limit intention but is subject to it. This is affirmed by § 812 BGB in regard to unjust enrichment.

BGB   **1.G.107.**

§ 812: A person who, through an act performed by another person or in any other manner acquires something at the expense of the latter without legal justification is bound to return it to him. This liability in restitution is also incurred where the legal justification subsequently disappears or the objective pursued by means of the legal transaction does not materialise.

The objective pursued is determined by the contents of the transaction. Motives not forming part thereof are left out of account. Thus, the doctrine of unjust enrichment deals in German law with matters which would be classified in French law as a failure of cause or a false cause. That may be perceived as an implied application of the objective theory of cause, as expounded by Domat. But the question is hardly touched on by academic writers. As regards the immoral or unlawful cause, German law does not go by the

---

[251] For comparative bibliography see Rieg, op. cit at 388, and Zweigert and Kötz, (*supra*, note 67).

object or the cause but directly reviews the unlawful aspects of a transaction without seeking to analyse the etiology of the unlawfulness.[252]

A fruitful area of research would be to determine how German law would resolve issues where French law has recourse to the doctrine of cause.[253]

In the Netherlands the new Civil Code no longer mentions the cause as a condition of the validity of the legal transaction: Article 3.33 requires merely that there be an intention to produce legal effects evidenced by a declaration.

There is, however, an underlying notion of the cause: in Article 3.40 under which "a legal transaction which by its content or scope is contrary to public policy or good morals shall be null and void". That seems to echo the unlawful object—content—and cause—scope. Likewise the notion of objective cause seems to emerge between the lines of Article 6.229: "A contract entered into in order to give effect to a legal relationship already existing between the parties may be annulled if that relationship fails to materialise". Is that not an application of the failure of cause?

It seems that this disguised continuance in force of the doctrine of cause may also be detected in Swiss law which, according to A. Simonius cited by R. David, is "causalist in principle but anticausalist in technique".[254]

In conclusion, it may be stated that, as demonstrated by German law, additional verification of the intent of the parties is not necessary. The verification carried out in French law by application of the doctrine of cause is however useful. Conversely, the doctrine of consideration under English law, which is peculiar to the Common Law, is more controversial and, in any event, would be hard to transpose to other systems of law.

1.3.4. FORMAL REQUIREMENTS[255]

The doctrinal discussion is ancient: is a bare promise (*nudum pactum*) sufficient to create a contract or must the parties' agreement be embodied in a special form?

For the consensualists, concurring intentions are sufficient. That is a consequence of the autonomy of the will in reaction to the requirements of Roman law which refused to accord any value to a bare promise. Formalism occurs where intent is not sufficient and the concurring intentions are required to take a specific form. Formalism may be intended to give effect to an act which, according to the general rules, would have no legal value: this is the function of a deed in English law, and of certain solemn acts in other legal systems; alternatively, it may involve an additional formality required in certain specific circumstances in order to give effect to an act which would be valid in other circumstances. This is the position in the case of certain consumer contracts, which would be valid under the ordinary law but which, being consumer contracts,[256] need in addition to comply with formal requirements. Formalism may intervene at several stages. It may apply to the validity of the contract: *ad validitatem*. That is direct formalism. It may apply only to proof of

---

[252] See Chapter 3, *infra.*
[253] See the cases *supra*, at 130.
[254] R. David, in *Etudes Capitant* (1939), at 759.
[255] See Kötz, *European Contract Law* at 78–96.
[256] *Supra*, at 23 ff.

the contract *(ad probationem)*: the contract can be proved only in accordance with certain formal requirements—as opposed to a system in which there is freedom of proof. The contract is valid but failing observance of the rules it cannot be proved, save in exceptional circumstances. There are also enabling formal requirements: to be effective the contract must receive the authorization *(homologation)* of an administrative or judicial authority. Finally, there are the formalities concerning publication and notification of the contract to third parties. Failure to observe those formalities in general means that the contract cannot be enforced as against third parties. In the case of "real" contracts *(contrats réels)* the handing over of the item may also be regarded as a necessary formality for the validity of the contract. But this category is known to be controversial.[257]

I shall confine myself to the formalities, properly so-called, which are required *ad validitatem*, but account must also be taken of the rules of evidence which are frequently difficult to distinguish from formal requirements in systems of law which have rules on proof laid down by law.

In the countries studied the prevailing principle is that of consensualism but formalism, even if it appears only exceptionally, occupies an important place, particularly in consumer law. The respective scope of consensualism and formalism may also vary according to the area of law in question. Thus, formal requirements *ad validitatem* or concerning public registration are normally laid down for complex or risky transactions, such as gifts or real estate transactions. The reciprocal advantages of both systems are much discussed. Formalism as a general rule precludes consent being given lightly and acts as a curb on disputes as to the existence and content of the contract. It also enables proof to be established in advance. Yet it is cumbersome, costly and may favour a party in bad faith who may seek to withdraw from a contract on the pretext that there has been a mere error of form.

It would be useful to organize a discussion around the two opposing viewpoints set out below, both canvassed by the same prestigious author.

Jhering[258] **1.G.108.**

50. Consensualism prevents "an honest man who is ignorant of affairs from being at the mercy of a wily and unscrupulous adversary, for the person who knows how to exploit formal requirements can make a noose out of them for the inexperienced person."

. . .

A sworn enemy of arbitrariness, formality is the twin sister of freedom. In fact, it serves as a counterweight to the tendency of liberty to degenerate into licence. It leads freedom on to a sure path where it can neither become dispersed nor go astray. It fortifies it within and protects it without. The fixed forms are discipline and order, consequently, freedom itself is a bulwark against external attacks. They yield but do not bend. Any people who has truly practised the cult of liberty has instinctively felt the value of formalism and known that in its formalities it possessed not something purely external but the bulwark of its liberty.

---

[257] *Supra*, at 35.
[258] R. von Jhering, *Geist des römischen Rechts* (Leipzig: 1852–1865), para. 50.

This is not the place for a detailed study of the rules as to form and proof. Apart from a general presentation, attention will be paid to practical aspects and some examples will be given, taken particularly from consumer law where formalism is sometimes taken very far: not only is writing required but the provisions often lay down its content and even the appearance of certain clauses. Thus, I will dwell, in the three systems of law studied, on the rules relating to the form which a contract of guarantee must take.

1.3.4.A. GERMAN LAW: MODERATE FORMALISM, FREEDOM AS TO PROOF

(a) General rules

German law is the least stringent of the three systems of law studied. § 125 BGB provides that legal acts which fail to comply with the formal requirements laid down by law are null and void. However, those formal requirements are rarely encountered. The principle is that of *"Formfreiheit"*. Also there are no rules governing the form which evidence must take for purposes of proof. Evidence is assessed freely by the judge (*freie Beweiswürdigung*) under § 286 ZPO. The formal requirement may be for a signed document: for example, the contract of guarantee: § 766 BGB, discussed below, or consumer credit transactions (§ 4(1) *Verbraucherkreditgesetz*). Certain contracts require notarization (*notarielle Beurkundung*): transfer of assets, acquisition or transfers of real estate, marriage contracts, certain leases on real estate and gifts. The role of the notary, the effectiveness of the act, and requirements as to form are governed by § 415 ZPO (Code of Civil Procedure) and by the *"Beurkundungsgesetz"* law on authentification of 28 August 1969, in a manner which differs considerably from the French régime governing authenticated deeds. Finally, there is a public legalisation requirement (*öffentliche Beglaubigung*) in § 129 BGB which provides for the notarial authentification of a person's signature. It is necessary where a declaration has to be entered in a public register—land registry, marriages, companies and business names registry.

The penalty attendant upon non-compliance with formal requirements is the nullity of the deed which may be pronounced by the courts even *ex proprio motu*.

(b) Applications

It will be noted first and foremost that the courts tend to apply the legal requirements flexibly.

BGH, 7 May 1971[259] **1.G.109.**

CONTRACT VOIDABLE FOR FORMAL ERRORS

Notary left to complete contract

Judgment: The parties appeared before a notary in order to enter into a sales contract relating to two pieces of real estate. The notarial deed dated 23 February 1966 was duly authenticated. The sales price amounted to DM 152,000. Payment was to be made partly by the constitution of three mortgages on the properties and partly in cash.

---

[259] BGHZ 56.159

Since the parties were unaware of the amount of the liability secured under the mortgages, they authorised the notary to determine the amount with the creditors, and to complete the authenticated deed accordingly. After deductions, the balance to be paid, as inserted by the notary, amounted to DM 30,483.67. That additional clause was not read out to the parties.

The plaintiff contested that estimate and sought payment of DM 36,350. The defendants contended that the balance to be paid was DM 7,483.67. They further consider that they are not bound to pay that sum since there was no agreement on the price.

Even if there had been agreement, the contract would be null and void for error or fraud.

The plaintiff (vendor) was unsuccessful before the lower courts and before the Fed. Sup. Ct.

The Regional Court (LG) held that the contract was voidable for error.

The Higher Regional Court (OLG) held that the contract was voidable on the ground that it was vitiated by formal errors (§§ 313, 725 BGB).

The Fed. Sup. Ct. was to adopt the latter solution.

Reasoning

The sales contract required as a matter of form the authentication provided for in § 313 relating to real estate. The contract was not effectively authenticated on several grounds.

The contract was not read out aloud, although that requirement also applied to the stipulations concerning the amount of the mortgage liability and the cash sum payable.

Whilst the notary was able to assess the amount of the mortgage liability and inform the parties thereof, he could not complete the contract without again complying with the requirements as to form.

However, it is correct that the additions made by the notary altered neither the vendor's obligation to give possession nor the purchasers' obligation to pay the purchase price. But the view to be taken must be that the question as to the method of financing is significant.

That is why the plaintiff cannot plead that the additions made by the notary did not have to comply with the formal requirements under § 313 on the ground that they did not give rise to new legal obligations.

Solution

The view to be taken is that formal requirements are intended to afford evidence of the contractual obligations assumed. The contract entered into on 23 February 1966 before the notary does not perform this function, as is borne out by the dispute which has arisen over the determination of the sales price.

Note

The court considers that the additions to the contract made by the notary may not be subject to the requirement of form since they do not create new obligations. However, the additions were necessary for determining the price, that is to say for providing proof of the content of the contract. The judicial technique for saving the contract could not operate in this case.

But there are other ways, notably through reference to good faith.

FORMAL REQUIREMENTS AND GOOD FAITH

Contract never put in writing

It may be contrary to good faith to rely on a formal defence, but this depends on the party's conduct.

Facts: The plaintiff was the daughter of the defendants. Together with her husband she sought to enforce an oral contract entered into in 1968 under which she acquired title with her husband to a dwelling house and her three sons jointly acquired title to another lodging in the defendants' house for a total sum of about DM 150 000. She also sought damages.

Following delivery by the *Landgericht* of a judgment in part finding partly in the plaintiff's favour, the *Oberlandesgericht* made an order against the defendant, based on the plaintiff's final ancillary claims and the defendant's consent to pay the sum of DM 121,520 plus interest, together with one half of the increase in the value of the two apartments between 1968 and 1972 (. . .). However, it dismissed the main claims, which sought an order (1) for the partition of the property (. . .), the preparation of a plan for the dividing up of the house (. . .), the issue of a declaration of partition (. . .) and guaranteed access to the land (. . .), and (2) acceptance of the purchase offers made by the plaintiff and her three sons, together with a declaration that the defendant was obliged to transfer ownership of the two apartments in exchange for a payment of DM 2 900 (the latter claim being dismissed as inadmissible), alternatively for payment of the sum of DM 216,720, half of which was to be held by the plaintiff "in her own hands" and one sixth by each of her three sons. The plaintiffs' appeal on a point of law was dismissed.

Judgment: The appeal court dismissed the claim as ill founded because the formal requirements (authentication) laid down in the case of real estate transactions had not been met. The appeal on a point of law cannot be upheld. The agreement in question was required to be in notarised form (§ 4, III NEG, § 313, 1 BGB). It was not . This defect was not cured by the transfer of property and by registration at the land registry (§ 313(2) BGB). Consequently, the agreement was null and void (§ 125 BGB).

However, the question is whether nullity on the ground of a formal defect (§ 125) contravenes the requirements of good faith (§ 242 BGB). As the Higher Regional Court (OLG) held, the reply must be in the negative.

It is settled case-law that an agreement for the sale of realty which is vitiated by a formal defect must be deemed to be valid in certain very specific cases, in particular where the consequences of nullity are incompatible with the requirements of good faith.

For such exceptions to be admitted strict conditions must be imposed in the interests of legal certainty. The mere fact that nullity harshly affects one of the parties does not suffice.

In the present case the Higher Regional Court (OLG) held that the financial consequences were harsh but not intolerable. From the point of view of good faith the present conduct of the defendants did not conflict with their past conduct. It was not established that the defendants left the plaintiffs under a misapprehension and that before 1971 they were not prepared to comply with their obligations and that, finally, they provoked the dispute in 1971 in order to cause the contract to disappear.

In order to constitute a breach of the requirements of good faith it is not sufficient either that the defendants were from the start keen on the plaintiffs' investing in the property.

The interpretation by the lower courts is free of any error in law, contrary to what was asserted in the appeal. The court made an overall assessment (§ 286 ZPO) and did not have regard only to

[260] WM 1974.1224.

the financial consequences but also envisaged the problem of the unlawful exercise of rights (abuse of rights) and, in particular, the contradiction between the defendants' past and current conduct.

As regards the need for the contract to be authenticated, both parties were in error and therefore there was nothing significant which could be secured by the plaintiff.

The claim for damages

The claim was dismissed by the Higher Regional Court (OLG) because in such circumstances there must be a fault committed by the defendant. However, that condition is not satisfied in the present case. There cannot be an indemnity based on the principle of a breach of trust which presupposes a fault on the part of one of the parties during the negotiations which frustrates the expectations of the other party to the contract by failure to conclude a contract whose coming into being was expected and where, in reliance thereon, that party incurred expenditure.

The case-law may be applied to the negotiation of contracts governed by the provisions as to form contained in § 313 BGB.

The breaking off of contractual negotiations by one of the parties to the contract without there being any such initial fault may found liability where the party responsible for breaking off the negotiations knew that the other party, in contemplation of the creation of the contract, had incurred considerable expenditure.

In its decision of 6 February 1969 the Second Civil Chamber of the BGH took the view that, by analogy with the case of rescission for mistake provided for in § 122, it was possible to obtain damages for refusal to enter into a projected contract, even where there was no initial fault, where there was a consensus between the parties as to the content of the future contract and the party refusing to proceed rejected the conclusion of the contract for no valid reason, although he had previously conducted himself in such a way as to lead the other party legitimately to expect that the contract would come into being, and thus to incur financial burdens.

What must be borne in mind is the concept of liability for present or future repercussions.

However, according to the case-law of the Fed. Sup. Ct., there can be no such liability if there is no initial liability founded solely on a refusal at the outset to enter into the contract, where the law lays down a requirement as to the form to be taken by the contract, such as the requirement of authentication under § 313 BGB, and that formal requirement is not met. In such a situation the precedents on rescission for mistake cannot be applied by analogy.

In fact, the purpose of the protection provided for by the rules as to formal requirements is to prevent any obligation from arising between the parties in connection with the actual subject-matter of the contract, where the rules as to the formal requirements have not been observed. In the present case, as was held at first instance, no liability on the part of the defendants has been established.

Note

Here again is an illustration of good faith stepping in to mitigate the rigours of formalism. In the present case neither good faith nor reliance can avail because the German courts do not wish to compromise the security of transactions governed by rules as to formal requirements. The contract is null and void owing to the lack of formal authentication and the nullity is not cured under § 313 BGB. The courts will allow nullity to stand against good faith only in certain specified cases: excessive financial hardship; not mere difficulties, and the past and current conduct of the party relying on nullity. It is to be noted that the concept of abuse of law (*abus de droit*) is considered in Germany more as a feature of bad faith than, as in France, a self-standing plea.

As regards the claim for damages, it is based on the detrimental reliance placed by the purchaser on the vendor's conduct. But, as far as the courts are concerned, the plea can succeed only if there was an initial fault by the vendor, which was not the case here. In other situations the courts have allowed good faith to intervene.

BGH, 22 April 1972[261]   **1.G.111.**

GOOD FAITH REQUIRES COMPLIANCE WITH INFORMAL CONTRACT

Defective house

It is contrary to good faith to rely on a formal defence if this would cause extreme hardship to the other party.

Facts: On 21 October 1963 the plaintiff (who was seeking to acquire a private residence) entered into negotiations with a co-operative society with a view to concluding a written sale/purchase contract with an option. The contract concerned the construction of a semi-detached house and the acquisition of two shares in the defendant co-operative society. The plaintiff paid the purchase price for the two shares (DM 1,000) and, in relation to the price of the house, which was provisionally estimated to amount to DM 78,500, the sum of DM 77,000 together with contributions in kind which he considered to be worth DM 2,000 and which the defendant considered to be worth DM 885.50. The plaintiff refused to pay the further sum of DM 7,047.58 which—in the light of the final construction cost of DM 83,900—was demanded by the defendant, pending the repair of certain defects found in the house. The plaintiff occupied the house from August 1965 onwards.

The *Landgericht* and the *Oberlandesgericht* ordered the defendant to take the requisite formal steps to transfer ownership. The defendant appealed on a point of law.

Judgment: . . . Whilst the contract must be regarded, in accordance with § 3132 BGB, as needing to be in a notarial form, and whilst, in the absence of compliance with that formal requirement, it must in principle be regarded as null and void (§ 125 BGB), nevertheless, such a result would be intolerably harsh as regards the plaintiff. Consequently, in the present case, the plea of nullity must, exceptionally, be rejected in favour of the need for the exercise of good faith ("*Treu und Glauben*", § 242 BGB). It is, however, settled case-law that such an exception may be made only in extraordinary cases and that the prospective purchaser of a private residence who, despite the absence of a contract executed before a notary, has nevertheless paid the purchase price and has lived in the house for a very long time is in principle entitled to claim only damages. . . . Be that as it may, such an exception, based as it is on the unacceptable nature of the situation, has previously been recognised in decided cases, since it involves criteria relating to the very existence of the party to the contract. . . .

In the present case, the plaintiff, aged 63, was a small-scale craftsman (whereas the defendant was a lawyer). If he had not been totally sure of becoming the owner of the property, he would never have invested so much money in that house. The plaintiff bought that house with a view to spending the rest of his days in it. He used all his savings (approximately DM 80 000) in order to acquire that property and paid a very large proportion of the purchase price in cash, the balance being disputed in view of the defects in the house. The plaintiff trusted in the validity of the contract, which contained a clause by which the parties declared their wish to dispense with the need for it to be in notarial form.

If the formal requirements laid down in § 313 BGB were applied to the present case, the plaintiff would be obliged to vacate the building and to look for a new home. This would seriously prejudice his material circumstances. It follows that, in the light of the duty to act in good faith laid down by § 242 BGB, such obligations are intolerably harsh.

[261] NJW 1972.1189.

Note

There are two aspects here: the situation of the applicant buyer, which is particularly worthy of note and "reliance". But, in contrast to earlier decisions, there is a lack of surefootedness in the choice and application of rules. Also worthy of note is the declared invalidity of the clause waiving the right to notarization.

However, it is important to highlight the efforts made by the German courts to find a happy medium between the dictates of good faith and observance of the purpose of the rules as to formal requirements.

It remains to examine the case of the contractual form, that is the form voluntarily chosen by the parties.

BGH, 2 June 1976[262]   **1.G.112.**

CONTRACTUAL REQUIREMENT OF WRITTEN NOTICE

Oral termination

A clause requiring that notice of termination be given in writing precludes a party relying on an unwritten notice.

Facts: The plaintiffs had let to the defendants property for the purpose of operating a supermarket. In the lease of 25 January 1972 it was agreed, *inter alia*, as follows:

> "S. 10—Any amendment or addition to the contract or any agreement to terminate it requires to be reduced to writing in order to be valid. For any waiver of that formal requirement, a written declaration is required."

On 24 March 1972 the plaintiff's representatives and the directors of the defendant met in order to decide who was to bear the costs of a fire installation (DM 350,000) without reaching an agreement. The defendants certified that the plaintiffs' representative orally proposed that the contract be terminated. By letter dated 27 March 1972, the defendant referred to the meeting of 24 March 1972: "After an examination of the difficulties which have arisen and since certain questions still remain open, we have decided to avail ourselves of your offer and no longer to proceed with the opening of a shop on your land".

The plaintiffs replied by telex dated 30 March 1972 and by letter dated 5 April 1972: "We refer to your letter of 27 March 1972and to our telex of 30 March 1972 and inform you that the signatory of the letter made no proposal at the meeting about shelving the opening of a supermarket by your company. In that connection we refer to Clause 10(2) of the lease of 25 May 1972 which unambiguously stipulates that amendments and additions to, and termination of the contract are required to be in writing in order to be valid."

The defendants persisted in their point of view. Since 1 March 1973 the hall has been hired out to other interests. The plaintiffs claimed payment of rent for the period from March to May 1972, together with VAT at 11%.

The Regional Court dismissed the claim. That judgment was set aside by the Higher Regional Court. The appeal on a point of law was dismissed.

Judgment: . . . The evidence given . . . has not shown that the parties agreed that the contract was to be terminated. The statements made by the plaintiff's representative are not such as to warrant the conclusion that he put forward in that connection any proposal which was contractually binding on them. In view of the requirement of written form, for which provision was made even in the event of termination of the contract, it would be contrary to the natural interests of the plaintiffs to find that they were bound by an oral statement of intent whilst affording the defendant the protection offered by the clause in question . . .

1 It is settled case-law . . . that, even where a contract stipulates that an agreement must be in written form if it is to be effective, the parties may none the less be bound by an oral agreement,

---

[262] BGHZ 66.378.

whether such agreement is intended to create contractual obligations, to supplement them or to limit them. Such informal agreements—which are not necessarily required to be spelt out in express terms—will be held to be valid if both parties intended that their agreement was to be definitive . . . Thus, the validity of an oral agreement will be upheld where the parties are deemed to have agreed to be bound by the requirement of writing only up until such time as their conduct indicated a contrary intention no longer to be bound by the contractual clause requiring the written form.

2 However, the contract in the present case, dated 25 January 1972, possesses an unusual feature, in that it provides that the parties may "waive the formal requirement only by means of a written declaration" (clause 10(2) of the contract). That clause is clearly designed to make it impossible to circumvent the stipulation as to written form by means of an oral undertaking by the contracting party, by oral declarations or by conclusive conduct . . . The principle of contractual freedom enables (traders) to bind themselves, in their legal relations, to observe certain formal requirements. In the present case, any waiver of the written form had itself to be in writing, since the parties intended by that means, *inter alia*, to cement their legal relationship. . . . For that reason, the defendants may not validly rely on the termination of the lease in March 1972. . . .

Note
Two contractual requirements are laid down: the first that to be valid an amendment to a contract must be in writing, and the second that any agreement to dispense with that requirement must itself be in writing. The principle of freedom of contract validates those two clauses. But oral termination is ineffective if the waiver of written form was not itself reduced to writing.

It will be noted that the solution under French law is different: see below.

(c) Formal Requirements Governing Suretyship
In the three systems of law studied suretyship (or guarantee) is regarded as a risky transaction and formal requirements are laid down in order to protect persons against obligations entered into without due premeditation. But, in each system of law, the measures laid down and the sanctions are different, which makes it difficult to compare them, even if such measures all pursue the same objectives. The question is merely as to their respective effectiveness.

In German law § 766 BGB provides that:

In order to be valid the contract of suretyship requires that the declaration of the surety be in writing. If the surety fulfils his obligations all defects of form are cured.

The above formalities are not required in commercial transactions (§ 350 HGB).

BGH, 29 January 1993[263]   **1.G.113.**

FORM IN COMMERCIAL AGREEMENTS

Jeans

Facts: The plaintiff, a company incorporated according to English law whose registered office is situated in Gibraltar, entered into an agreement signed under hand with R, a textile company in Bavaria, for the supply of 3 000 pairs of jeans. The contract stipulated in particular that:

[263] NJW 1993.1926.

(11) R was obliged to pay DM 84,000 for the supply of the jeans, such sum to be payable within 60 days of the invoice date.

(13) The defendant acted as surety.

On 28 July 1989 the notary, Dr H., of B., authenticated the declaration made by the defendant, as director and sole manager of the company, by which the latter agreed to stand surety for the debt of DM 84 000. Subsequently, on 31 July 1989, he sent that declaration, with the defendant's consent, by fax to his client's address in Malaga. On 1 August 1989 the plaintiff's representatives wrote to R Co. on the plaintiff's headed writing paper, accepting the order and the suretyship. . . . Thereafter, 2 813 pairs of jeans were sent by the defendant; the invoices sent, totalling DM 78 764, were not paid by R Co.

The plaintiff relied on the authenticated declaration of 28 July 1989 and brought an action for payment against the surety in the sum of DM 79 551 (the amount of the invoice plus 1% interest).

The claim was upheld by the lower courts. On appeal, the decision of those courts was set aside and the case was referred back for further determination.

Judgment:

1—German law was applicable.

2—Under German law, there was no valid contract of suretyship between the parties.

Under § 766(1) BGB, a suretyship must be accepted in writing. In the present case, the criteria laid down by § 350 HGB, according to which a contract of suretyship may be created in the absence of compliance with the formal requirements of § 766(1) BGB where it constitutes a commercial act on the part of the guarantor, were not fulfilled, despite the fact that the defendant was the sole manager of the company. The conditions prescribed by § 766(1) BGB were not met. The defendant had indeed had his declaration of suretyship authenticated by the notary, and had signed it himself; the declaration therefore fulfilled the formal requirements laid down by § 126(1) and (3) BGB. However, no formal delivery of the declaration had taken place. A declaration of suretyship is not formally delivered merely by reason of the deed having been signed. In order for it to be formally delivered, the deed had to be physically handed over to the creditor in such a way as to be held by the latter, even if only temporarily. That was not the position in this case.

(a) The transmission of the contents of the deed by fax could not be regarded as constituting formal delivery, in writing, of the declaration of suretyship.

According to § 126(1) BGB, the requirement of written form provided for by law is complied with only where the deed has been signed in his own hand by the person issuing it or initialled by him, such initialling being authenticated by the notary. A fax does not contain a holograph signature. Only the original bears such a signature, and that remains in the hands of the sender. Nor does it correspond to the objective of § 766(1) BGB whereby the fax transmission of a declaration of suretyship is regarded as constituting formal delivery in writing. The rationale for the formal requirement is to be found in the need to protect the guarantor, who must act with the greatest prudence and who must be protected against the consequences of any declaration made without sufficient forethought . . . That objective precludes the application of a line of case-law which has developed with a view to making it possible to meet the time-limits for the commencement of proceedings by using modern telecommunications. . . .

(b) The *Oberlandesgericht* took the view that case-law and academic authors had accepted that the transmission of a copy with the guarantor's knowledge and consent could be enough to constitute valid delivery of the contract of suretyship. It considered that, since the transmission of the wording of the deed by fax is equivalent to a copy, and since the notary had faxed the deed to the plaintiff with the defendant's consent, the latter had validly handed over his declaration. That argument cannot be accepted . . . He (the defendant) had simply requested the notary to send the plaintiff a fax of the deed; he had not authorised him to send the plaintiff an official copy of the deed or to act in any other way on his behalf. In those circumstances, the requirements of § 766(1) BGB were not met.

Note

The BGH is showing itself to be demanding here: it is refusing to accept substitute forms: a facsimile is not the same as a written document and authentication by a notary cannot cure the lack of signature by the surety.

This rigour may be contrasted with the solutions adopted by French and English law.[264]

(d) Conclusion

German law remains attached to consensualism. It is true that it lays down certain obligations as to form which always go to validity, owing to the rule of unrestricted production of evidence. Particularly worthy of note are the efforts by the courts, aided by the concepts of good faith and reliance, to limit the unjust consequences of a strict application of the rule of nullity on the ground of a formal defect.

1.3.4.B. ENGLISH LAW: LIMITED FORMALISM; RULE OF ALMOST UNRESTRICTED PRODUCTION OF EVIDENCE

Formal requirements play a somewhat different role in English law. They do not appear as an exception to the principle—unwritten—of consensualism but are primarily considered in relation to the doctrine of consideration.

According to McKendrick[265] consideration and formal requirements are rules identifying types of agreement which must be treated as enforceable contracts. Form and substance are confounded. Proof of that fact is that the form, namely the deed, replaces the requirement of consideration. Thus, one may effect by deed transactions which would otherwise be invalid owing to a lack of consideration: e.g. gifts, unilateral undertakings, options etc.

The formalities are quite complex and date back to the Statute of Frauds 1677, which has been many times amended and no longer governs more than a few residual contracts. In order to mitigate the rigour of this formalism, the courts have, as in the case of consideration, had recourse to the doctrine of estoppel.

Nowadays it is an enactment of 1989 which regulates deeds.

Law of Property (Miscellaneous Provisions) Act 1989 **1.E.114.**

Section 1: Deeds and their exception
  (1) Any rule of law which
      (a) restricts the substances on which a deed may be written ;
      (b) requires a seal for the valid execution of an instrument as a deed by an individual; or
      (c) requires authority by one person to another to deliver an instrument as a deed on his behalf to be given by deed,
  is abolished.
  (2) an instrument shall not be a deed unless
      (a) it makes it clear on its face that it is intended to be a deed by the person making it or, as the case may be, by the parties to it (whether by describing itself as a deed or expressing itself to be executed or signed as a deed or otherwise); and

---

[264] *Infra*, at 165 and 170 ff.
[265] McKendrick, *Contract*, at 74.

   (b) it is validly executed as a deed by that person or, as the case may be, one or more of those
      parties.
(3) An instrument is validly executed as a deed by an individual if, and only if
   (a) it is signed
     (i) by him in the presence of a withness who attests the signature; or
     (ii) at his direction and in his presence and the presence of two witnesses who each attest
       the signature; and
   (b) it is delivered as a deed by him or a person authorised to do so on this behalf.
(4) In subsection (2) and (3) above "sign", in relation to an instrument, includles making one's
mark on the instruments and "signature" is to be construed accordlingly.
. . .
(11) Nothing in this section applies in relation to instruments delivered as deeds before this
section comes into force.

Previously, a deed under seal was necessary. The requirement of a seal is now generally replaced by the attestation of the signature by a witness.

In addition to the deed, English law sometimes requires the contract to be reduced to writing: those are cases of real estate transactions,[266] certain consumer credit transactions—Consumer Credit Act 1974, sections 60 and 61—and negotiable instruments.

Moreover, written form may be required for purposes of proof, which was the rationale of the Statute of Frauds 1677 .

Statute of Frauds 1677 **1.E.115.**

S. 4: No action shall be brought whereby to charge any executor or administrator upon any special promise to answer damages out of his own estate; or whereby to charge the defendant upon any special promise to answer for the debt, default or miscarriage of another person; or to charge any person upon any agreement made upon consideration of marriage; or upon any contract or sale of lands, tenements or hereditaments, or any interest in or concerning them; or upon any agreement that is not to be performed within the space of one year from the making thereof; unless the agreement upon which such action shall be brought, or some memorandum or note thereof, shall be in writing and signed by the party to be charged therewith or some other person thereunto by him lawfully authorised.

All of section 4 has been repealed, save for the suretyship provision. The requirements concerning sales of goods of £10 and upwards have of course also been abolished.

Until 1989 contracts for the sale or disposition of land, under Law of Property Act 1925, section 40—a direct descendant of the Statute of Frauds—had to be evidenced in a writing signed by the party against whom the contract was to be enforced. The Law Reform (Miscellaneous Provisions) Act 1989, section 2, now requires such contracts to be in writing signed by both parties.

Needless to say there were many cases in which the parties had not satisfied the requirements of section 40 but nonetheless had acted as if there were a binding contract, for example by the purchaser paying the price and being given possession of the land. A doctrine known as the doctrine of part-performance was been used by the courts to mitigate

---

[266] *Infra.*

165

the effects of the statute: see *Wakeham* v. *Mackenzie*.[267] The principle was that where one party has done acts in part performance of his own obligations under a contract which should have been evidenced in writing, then, even though there be no memorandum of the contract, equity will admit a decree of specific performance of the oral contract if the acts of part performance be such as to justify the admission of oral evidence of the agreement. This doctrine no longer applies; it is expected that the courts will deal with cases where the requirements of the 1989 Act seem to cause hardship and which would have fallen under the doctrine of part performance by using promissory estoppel[268]—though whether this will cover all the cases remains to be seen.

One effect of the changes is that all the terms of the contract must be in the writing. If a party wishes to enforce some undertaking by the other which was not included in the writing, he may find himself in a dilemma. It would seem that either he cannot say that the undertaking was part of the contract, so he cannot enforce it; or, if he proves that it was part of the contract, then the contract is no longer wholly in the writing as required by the statute and thus the contract is wholly unenforceable! In fact the courts have mitigated this harsh result in two ways. First, they are sometimes prepared to accept that there was a second agreement between the parties, the contract for the sale of land and a so-called collateral contract containing the other undertaking—e.g. *De Lassalle* v. *Guildford*;[269] or, in cases in which the term was omitted from the writing by mistake, by ordering that the document be rectified[270] to bring it into line with what the parties intended. Whether giving rectification is really consistent with the purpose of the statute in requiring all the terms to be in writing might seem questionable, were it not that the statute specifically allows for it (section 2(4)).[271]

At one time, the rule that all the terms must be in the writing seemed to be applied not only to contracts which were required to be in writing but to any contract in which the parties had in fact put their agreement into writing. This was the effect of the so-called Parol Evidence Rule: "parol evidence cannot be admitted to add to, vary or contradict a deed or other written instrument". Parol is often taken to mean "oral". It is an old word meaning, originally, a statement not in a deed (the rule applied originally primarily to deeds); in this context "parol" is best understood as meaning "extrinsic", thus covering both oral agreements and agreements contained in a separate document (e.g. a letter) which is not referred to in the written contract. (This rule would appear to be akin to the second rule laid down in Article 1341 of the French Civil Code.)

The Parol Evidence Rule has been likened to the Holy Roman Empire (which it will be recollected was neither Holy, nor Roman, nor an empire), in that none of the three stated elements was correct. As just explained, it does not apply solely to oral agreements. Secondly, it was not a rule of evidence—if the rule applied, it did not matter in the slightest that there was ample other evidence of the additional term; the written document would still be treated as conclusive of what had been agreed as the contract; and it was not a rule. This last point refers to that fact that, if the court were convinced that the

---

[267] [1968] 1 WLR 1273.
[268] *Supra*, at 18.
[269] [1901] 2 KB 215.
[270] See *infra* at 348.
[271] See the discussion in *Chitty*, § 4-059.

oral or other extrinsic promise was in fact made, the court would simply evade the "rule" by saying that, as the contract did not contain the omitted term, the contract was not in writing within the meaning of the rule but only a partly written contract to which the rule does not apply. This makes complete nonsense of any notion that there is a "rule"—at the most, there is a presumption that the writing contains all the terms of the contract. The English Law Commission investigated the so-called rule with a view to abolishing it and concluded that there was in fact no rule to abolish.[272] So as far as English law in concerned—the parol evidence rule still seems to survive in some of the United States and in the Antipodes—, discussion of the Parol Evidence Rule may be consigned to the dustbin of history. This is to be contrasted with French law.[273]

Conclusion
Except as regards consideration, formalism is limited in English law. The Common Law is made by traders who do not need to be protected by formalities, and those which exist have been progressively reduced.

1.3.4.C. FRENCH LAW: A CERTAIN FORMALISM, MEANS OF PROOF LEGALLY CIRCUMSCRIBED

(a) General Survey
There is no doubt that the principle is consensualism: that is clear from Article 1108[274] which does not mention the form alongside the four conditions governing the validity of contracts—consent, capacity, object and cause. That also follows from the general acceptance of free will and the untrammelled formation of intent. Formalism can be only the exception. But the principal feature of the French system of law is the marked effect of the rules on evidence whereby the respective value of each method of proof is laid down by the law, the written form being the preferred method. There is thus a certain evidentiary formalism which takes its place alongside formalism properly so-called.

At the beginning of the nineteenth century there were only four solemn contracts— contract of marriage, gift, mortgage on realty, subrogation agreed by the debtor—which had to be entered into before a notary—by authentic act which confers on the deed a particular significance. These four solemn contracts continue to exist although the courts have freely accepted other forms of gift—disguised gifts, indirect gifts, gifts by transfer; for the latter the formal requirement is the handing over of the item. But since then a number of provisions have laid down formal requirements governing validity, mostly by contract under hand signed by the parties. Examples of this are the contract of insurance, the contract of apprenticeship, consumer contracts, etc. The penalty for non-compliance is not always nullity of the contract and the contract is often required to contain particulars by way of information. The courts have frequently[275] relaxed the legal requirements, in particular by construing them as mere requirements as to evidence.

Those requirements are laid down in particular in Article 1341 and Article 1347 which mitigates its effects.

---

[272] See Report No. 154, *Law of Contract: The Parol Evidence Rule* (Cmnd 9700, 1986).
[273] *Infra.*
[274] *Supra*, at 128.
[275] See further on suretyship, *infra*, at 171.

Article 1341: (Law No 80–525 of 12 July 1980): In respect of any item exceeding such sum or value as may be laid down from time to time by decree, including even the voluntary deposit of items, a document must be drawn up by a notary or signed by the persons concerned; no witness evidence shall be admissible to vary or contradict the content of such documents, or as to what may be alleged to have been said before, on the occasion of or since the coming into being of such document, even if a smaller sum or value is involved.

    The preceding clause shall be without prejudice to the rules concerning trade.

Article 1347: Exceptions to the abovementioned rules shall be admitted where there is *prima facie* written evidence ("*commencement de preuve par écrit*")

    This shall cover any written document emanating from the party against whom the claim is made, or his representative, and which would appear to bear out the veracity of the fact alleged.

    (Law No 75–596 of 9 July 1975). The courts may deem statements made by a party on his personal appearance, a refusal to reply or default of appearance, to be the equivalent of *prima facie* written evidence.

In 1980 the limit above which reduction to writing is required was set at FF 5,000. It is a traditional requirement dating back to the Moulins Decree of 1556. The guiding principle is that it is of the first importance that there be pre-existing proof in order to avoid disputes. That rule is complemented by another, which is akin to the parol evidence rule. Under that rule oral evidence is not admissible to vary or contradict a document, even where the amount at stake is less than 5,000 FF. As in England the courts have limited the scope of that rule, in particular by interpreting the contract.[276]

The requirement of writing as proof is subject to significant exceptions. First and foremost, according to the second paragraph of Article 1341 there are no limits on the evidence which may be adduced as between traders and as against a trader. Then, under Article 1347, evidence by writing may be replaced by witness evidence or by presumptions, where there is *prima facie* written evidence, as provided for in Article 1347, that is to say a written document which does not in itself constitute proof but which appears to bear out the veracity of the fact alleged. Such written evidence may also be replaced by statements to the court on a personal appearance or even by default of appearance. The use to which the courts have put this provision may be seen in connection with proof of suretyship.

Another possibility of providing proof in the absence of written evidence is afforded by Article 1348 which provides that proof may be by any method where "it has been substantively or physically impossible to obtain written evidence"; this is an exception of which the courts have made much.

There is also the "formality of the duplicate" which provides that in the case of synallagmatic contracts there must be as many copies as there are parties (Article 1325 of the Civil Code). A further formal requirement is laid down in Article 1326, a handwritten statement of the amount of money due under a unilateral undertaking. That will be encountered again in connection with suretyship.

---

[276] See Terré, Simler and Lequette, para. 146.

(b) Applications

The first question in connection with a requirement as to form laid down in a provision is of a practical nature: is it a formal requirement going to validity (*ad validatem*), that is to say where non-compliance will be visited by nullity, or is it a requirement as to proof (*ad probationem*), where a failure to comply will make it impossible or more difficult to prove the existence or terms of the document? Where the provision is not specific on this point, which is not infrequently the case, the courts tend to go for the second solution because of the greater flexibility which it offers.[277]

The second question, where formalism goes to the substance, is to determine the scope of the nullity: relative where the applicable rule seeks to protect the parties; absolute if the public interest is at stake, according to the theory of nullity.[278]

As regards contractual formalism, French law is less rigorous than German law. The form laid down by law is not a requirement non-compliance with which will result in nullity, where there is no doubt about the intentions of the parties. Tacit waivers are also possible.

Cass. civ. 1re, 6 July 1964[279] **1.F.117.**

FORM NOT REQUIRED WHEN PAYMENT RECEIVED AND POSSESSION GIVEN

The Desprez's house

Judgment: THE COURT: *On the two branches of the sole appeal ground*:—Whereas it is clear from the judgment appealed against, which upheld the decision of the lower court, that under a document under hand signed on 13 April 1956, Mr and Mrs Desprez promised to sell to the Société Parisienne de Diffusion Immobilière (SPDI), at a price of 250 old francs per square metre, land extending to 15 1/2 hectares situate at Verrières-le-Buisson; as it was stipulated that SPDI could by registered letter call for that promise to be executed until 15 April 1958; as thereafter the promise was to be considered null and void; as also, by a letter dated 29 March 1956 SPDI informed Mr and Mrs Desprez, further to the promise to sell made by them, that it agreed to pay the purchase price in three instalments, the first of 4 million (old) francs in cash, the second of 4 million within one year and the balance on completion by authenticated deed. Subsequently, Mr and Mrs Desprez refused to complete the sale;

—Whereas the Cour de cassation noted that the appeal court is criticised for reaching the determination that the promise to sell made by Mr and Mrs Desprez had been accepted by SPDI, thus constituting a sale, although the letter of 29 March 1956 laying down the dates for payment of instalments and the balance did not in itself constitute acceptance of the offer to sell and there was no acceptance in the form as provided for by the parties by means of a registered letter and the period laid down in the agreement was not observed;

—Whereas however, as the appeal court found, the agreement of 29 March 1956 was plainly concomitant with the promise to sell and their manifest intention to consider the offer accepted and the sale completed was to be inferred from the acceptance by Mr and Mrs Desprez on 13 April 1956, the date of the promise, of the payment on account stipulated in that agreement, their subsequent claim for compensation for late payment of the second instalment and the payment thereof, and

---

[277] **1.F.120**, *infra* at 172.
[278] Terré, Simler and Lequette no. 139.
[279] Bull. civ. I.369.

169

finally the actual occupation of the land as from April 1956 with the full knowledge of the couple;
—Whereas the judgement appealed against further points out that, by receiving those payments as payments on account and not as a deposit, and by executing the agreement of 29 March after acceptance of the promise by SPDI, the Desprez couple have rendered nugatory their allegation as to non-observance of the formal requirements laid down for effect to be given to the promise to sell;
—Whereas those being the findings of the courts, the cour d'appel was entitled to hold that the promise to sell had been, to the vendors' knowledge, accepted by the purchasers and constituted a sale and that the sending of a registered letter was pointless;
—Whereas the plea is without foundation in both its branches and the judgment, underpinned by reasoning, is sound in law;

On those grounds, the appeal against the judgment of the Paris cour d'appel of 25 January 1962 is dismissed.

Note

The pointlessness of the registered letter flows from the tacit waiver of that requirement which follows from acceptance of part payment of the price, and the taking possession of the land with the vendors' knowledge. The registered letter is thus rendered pointless. That is a fresh illustration of the courts' tendency to relax formalism, even of the contractual kind, where the party claiming non-observance appears to be in bad faith.

(c) Formalism of Suretyship

As in England and Germany, French law lays down rules as to the formal requirements governing suretyship. Those rules are the product of the uneasy association of two provisions.

Code civil **1.F.118.**

Article 1326: (Law 80–525 of 12 July 1980)—The legal act whereby one party undertakes to another to pay him a sum of money or to deliver generic goods must be recorded in a document bearing the signature of the person assuming that undertaking together with a statement, written in his hand, of the sum or quantity in letters as well as figures. If there is a discrepancy, the agreement under hand shall apply to the amount written in letters.

Article 2015: Suretyship may in no event be inferred: it must be express and cannot be extended beyond the limits within which it was entered into.

The first of these provisions applies to all unilateral undertakings to pay a sum of money, including under a contract of suretyship. The second is peculiar to suretyship. Under the commonly accepted interpretation, it does not elevate suretyship to the status of a solemn contract but simply gives interpretative guidance on the existence and scope of the suretyship: it cannot be inferred from the silence or conduct of the surety. In practice, a contract of suretyship must be in writing, if only to satisfy the requirement of the handwritten statement referred to.

The application of those two provisions gave rise to a spectacular instance of the Cour de cassation overruling itself. After some hesitation, the Cour de cassation decided that the requirements as to the handwritten statement referred to were not mere rules on proof but pursue the objective of protecting the surety, thus entailing the penalty of nullity—relative because it is for the protection of the parties.[280] The Court subsequently went on to hold that they were rules on proof.

Cass. civ. 1re, 15 November 1989[281]   **1.F.119.**

SEFCO

Judgment: THE COURT: *On the first branch of the sole appeal ground*:—Under Articles 1326 and 2015 of the Civil Code;

—Whereas the undertaking assumed by the surety must bear his signature together with a statement, written in his hand, of the sum or quantity in letters, as well as figures, of any obligation ascertainable on the date on which the undertaking was given;

—Whereas the rules on proof are intended to protect the surety;

—Whereas under a contract signed on 26 February and 2 March 1981 the company, Euro Computer Systems (ECS) hired computer equipment, at a monthly rent of 16,654 francs net of tax, for a period of fifty months, to the company Sefco Grand Delta, represented by Mr Delous, who on 25 February 1981 sent a letter to ECS in the following terms: "Further to the agreements between your company and Sefco Grand Delta, I have taken note of the fact that the rent on the IBM 370/125 equipment now being installed at 11 Avenue du Général Brosset, in Marseilles will be payable only from 1 September 1981. I, for my part, will personally stand surety for the rental payments commencing on that date under the current contract, namely 16,654 francs per month. However, the suretyship shall cease and determine if the equipment in question is transferred to a branch of the Sligos Group or if the capital of Sefco Grand Delta is taken over by a new group known to be solvent";

—Whereas Sefco Grand Delta did not pay the contractually agreed rental to ECS which, maintaining that Mr Delous had stood surety for that obligation, brought proceedings against him for payment of the rental;

—Whereas that claim was upheld in the judgment appealed against; as Mr Delous had argued that the abovementioned letter could not be deemed to constitute a contract of suretyship satisfying the requirements of Articles 1326 and 2015 of the Civil Code

—Whereas at second instance this defence plea was rejected on the ground that the letter in question included not only the signature of the person concerned but also the amount, written in his hand, of the debts for which he wished to stand surety.

—Whereas however, it was clear from the findings in the judgment appealed against (Toulouse, 21 July 1987) that that amount, whilst appearing in figures in the document at issue, is not written in letters as well;

—Whereas that is a mandatory requirement of the abovementioned provisions;

—Whereas failure to comply with it invalidates the contract of suretyship;

—Whereas accordingly, in reaching the determination which it did the cour d'appel infringed those provisions;

   On those grounds, and without there being any need to give a decision on the two other branches of the appeal ground, the Cour de cassation sets aside the judgment of the court below.

---

[280] See Cass. civ. 1re, 30 June 1987, Bull. civ. I.210.
[281] D.1990.177, annotated by C. Mouly.

Note

The Cour de cassation, whilst maintaining that the rules are for the protection of the surety, confirms that they are rules concerning proof. In the present case they were not satisfied, the amount not being mentioned in words. The document does not therefore constitute a valid contract of suretyship.

There is, then, a discernible tendency on the part of the courts to relax the rules as to formal requirements which appears to be confirmed in the following judgment—it should be noted that the "hard" solution for consumers has been enshrined by a legislative amendment: Article 311–1 of the Consumer Code.

Cass. civ. 1re, 15 October 1991[282]   **1.F.120.**

INSUFFICIENT WRITING MAY BE SUPPLEMENTED BY OTHER EVIDENCE

The surety

Judgment: THE COURT: *On the two branches of the single appeal ground*:—Whereas according to the findings of the lower courts, the Del Giudice couple purchased from the Arbomonts a property by notarised deed dated 30 August 1982 which stipulated that the price of 1,400,000F was to be paid as to 750,000F in cash and, as to the remainder, by way of a loan for 650,000F; as by a document under hand signed on the same day, the purchasers acknowledged that they owed to the vendors the sum of 700,000 F "being the balance of the purchase price for the property", and undertook to "return and reimburse" that amount within a one-year period; as a certain Mr Suma joined in the deed to act as surety for the liabilities of the Del Giudice couple; as the Arbomonts brought proceedings against the Del Giudices and Mr Suma, as well as the officiating notary, for payment of the sum of 700,000 F remaining outstanding, according to them, on the purchase price, notwithstanding the receipt given in the deed;

—Whereas the confirmatory judgment appealed against (Aix-en-Provence, 3 October 1989) considered that proof of the debt in favour of the Arbomonts was established and ordered the Del Giudice couple and Mr Suma jointly and severally to pay the sum claimed; as Mr Suma maintains in his appeal on a point of law that the court below ought not to have found against him when, in the terms of the plea on appeal, he asked for the judgment to be set aside on the ground that the contract of suretyship was null and void since it did not satisfy the requirements of Article 1326 of the Civil Code;

—Whereas accordingly, the cour d'appel, in his submission, was not able to reach the determination which it did without infringing Article 4 of the new Code of Civil Procedure and Articles 1326 and 2015 of the Civil Code; as in his further submission, if the contract of suretyship did not satisfy the requirements of Article 1326 of the Civil Code it was not possible to infer from that document that the surety's undertaking was genuine;

—Whereas in deciding as it did, the cour d'appel failed to found its decision on a proper legal basis;

—Whereas however, the cour d'appel was correct in stating that, even though the absence of the handwritten particulars required under Article 1326 of the Civil Code in the contract of suretyship entered into by Mr Suma constituted an irregularity, that document was none the less *prima facie* written evidence which could be supplemented by other matters; as thus, the court below rejected rather than disregarded the submissions going to the nullity of the suretyship;

---

[282] JCP. 1992.II.21923, annotated by P. Simler.

172

—Whereas, secondly, having taken note of the evidence adduced in addition to the document constituting *prima facie* written evidence of the contract of suretyship, the court below, acting within its jurisdiction, took the view that that additional evidence demonstrated that Mr Suma was aware of the nature and scope of his undertaking;

—Whereas the judgment of the cour d'appel was therefore sound in law, and none of the appeal grounds are well founded.

On those grounds, the appeal is dismissed.

Note

This judgment reaffirms that the requirement that there be handwritten particulars is indeed a rule on proof but it also affirms that a document which, whilst containing an irregularity, is not null and void may constitute *prima facie* written evidence which may be supplemented by other matters. That will often be the case. Thus, a way is found of preventing favourable treatment from being accorded to the party acting in bad faith.

French law is indeed marked by a certain formalism in legislation which is offset by a relaxation in formalism by the courts. That trend toward a relaxation in formal requirements may also be observed in regard to evidentiary formalism: the French system of legally recognized methods of proof does not operate unduly harshly owing to the attitude of the courts.

1.3.4.D. CONCLUSION

This conclusion must be a guarded one. The principle of consensualism appears to be alive and kicking. It is indeed reflected in the *Principles of European Contract Law*.

> *Principles of European Contract Law*   **1.PECL.121.**

Article 2:101: *Conditions for the Conclusion of a Contract*
   (1) A contract is concluded if:
      (a) the parties intend to be legally bound, and
      (b) they reach a sufficient agreement
      without any further requirement.
   (2) A contract need not be concluded or evidenced in writing nor is it subject to any other requirement as to form. The contract may be proved by any means, including witnesses.

And yet there is much talk of a re-emergence of formalism. The reason is perhaps that formal requirements, including those to do with proof, are a means of protecting the weaker or more naïve party. It is for the courts to ensure that formal requirements are not misused to the advantage of the contracting party acting in bad faith.

Concluding Remarks on Section 3

It has long been clear (see Article 1341–1 of the French Civil Code) that, in order for an agreement—that is to say, an understanding between the parties—to be effective, it must be "legally concluded". Moreover, it can no longer be disputed that it is the law which underlies the binding force of contracts. Purely voluntary acts are no longer accepted as being capable of forming the basis of a contract. The very role played by free will has been whittled down by certain concepts, in particular that of "reliance", according to which it is not the interests of promisors which need to be protected—voluntary acts being fatal to the existence of a contract—but rather those of a promisee who has placed his faith in the promisor. Nevertheless, in the law as it actually exists, the idea of willingness remains the basic element. It is sometimes difficult, however, to discern whether a willingness to enter into a commitment really exists, for example in the case of a letter of intent or a gentlemen's agreement. Areas of uncertainty, frequently raising difficult questions of interpretation, continue to exist.

The contrast between the opposing positions is more marked when one considers the role played by the immediate reason, or consideration, for agreeing to enter into a contract, which, in the common law system, for all the criticisms levelled at it, constitutes—in the case of consideration at least—an additional *sine qua non* over and above the requirement of consent. As far as the notion of the immediate reason for entering into a contract is concerned, this is a concept which is still very much alive in France, but is regarded as pointless and unnecessary in other legal systems, such as German law.

The position in relation to formal requirements is marked by more subtle differentiations. On the one hand, the principle of consensualism, that is to say, the idea that no specific formalities of any kind are necessary, continues to prevail, and the requirement that a contract must comply with certain formalities if it is not to be null and void remains the exception. But there can be no doubt that we are currently seeing something of a revival in the need for compliance with formal requirements, especially in the field of consumer protection. Consequently, formal requirements indirectly appear to represent a means of strengthening the role played by contractual free will, rather than a substitute for it.

Concluding Remarks on Chapter 1
Many jurists still believe that the law of contract is the same everywhere—and thus similar in all other countries to their own national law. They also think that it is immutable. It is a comforting idea to think that, in order to be an expert in contract law, all one needs to do is to learn one's own law and that, having learned it, that is the end of the story. This first chapter, which is intended to pave the way for an in-depth study of the comparative law of contract within the European Union, is designed to dispel that illusion and to show that there are, on the contrary, numerous aspects of contract law on which the various national laws differ from each other.

It will be seen from the outset, upon considering the various legislative provisions, judgments and passages from works by academic lawyers put forward for discussion, that whilst the very notion of a contract contains a solid core, and although the concept of the perfect reciprocal contract is found in more or less all jurisdictions, situations arise on the periphery of that solid core which may or may not be regarded as contractual, depending on which legal system is applied to them. The dividing line between contractual and tortious matters is often a grey area, particularly as regards the persons concerned. New concepts blossom forth (for example, in the field of groups of contracts). The different categories of contracts are far from immutable. Divergences exist, which are rendered all the more perilous by virtue of their being frequently hidden by terminological similarities (e.g. the difference between a *"contrat unilatéral"* and a "unilateral contract").

Developments also take place, as is shown by the distinction which has grown up in the field of consumer contracts between contracts concluded between, on the one hand, business persons and, on the other, persons not acting in the course of a business.

The same uncertainty reigns when one looks into the question of what it is that gives the "force of law" to an agreement between two or more parties. A crucial, indeed indispensable, factor is of course the existence of an intention to enter into contractual relations; but this no longer constitutes, as was formerly the case, the supreme, decisive element. Other concepts in addition to an intention to contract, such as the notion of reliance on what has been said or the existence of an immediate reason for entering into a contract, are dismissed or criticised—not to mention that curious principle of consideration which has evolved in English law but is, or at least appears to be, unknown to other legal systems.

It must be recognized, therefore, that the theory of what constitutes a contract within the European Union is elusive and, at times, not fully developed.

Thus, it remains to consider the potential effects which these various characteristic elements may have on the outcome of the specific cases analysed in the following chapters.

CHAPTER TWO
FORMATION

2.1. OFFER AND ACCEPTANCE

2.1.1. INTRODUCTORY NOTE

The *consensus ad idem* required to form a contract is traditionally analysed as an offer made by one party (the offeror) followed by an acceptance thereof by the other party (the offeree).[1] The meeting of the offer and the acceptance ("meeting of minds"[2]) constitutes the consensus. This analysis is essentially common to the different jurisdictions studied in this book. Indeed, this may be one area in which the common law borrowed directly from the civil law, and in which the writings of Ulpian, Pufendorf and Pothier were influential in shaping English law.[3]

This schematic representation of the formation of a contract has proved to be very useful for creating rules covering the formation phase. This chapter considers a number of important issues which arise in relation to the formation of contracts: how to distinguish offers from dealings which are merely preliminary to the conclusion of a contract (**2.1.2.A.**), what are the requirements as to the content of a declaration in order to qualify it as an offer (**2.1.2.B.**), whether an offer may be revoked before it is accepted (**2.1.2.C.**), how an offer may come to lapse (**2.1.2.D.**), the form which an acceptance may take (**2.1.3.A.**), whether an acceptance must be communicated to the offeror in order to take effect (**2.1.3.B.**) and what are the consequences where the acceptance deviates from the offer (**2.1.3.C.**). Indeed, in this final section, we will see that in some cases a contract may be concluded where it is difficult to identify a clear offer-and-acceptance between the parties, suggesting that the offer-acceptance diagram may be too simple to account for the entire law of contract.

This section of the chapter does not deal with one issue which is of key importance during the formation phase: the distinction between "subjective" and "objective" approaches to contract law; in other words, the way in which discrepancies between declaration and intention are dealt with when determining the legal relationship between the parties. The subjective and objective approaches reflect fundamentally different conceptions of "contract", and the distinction has therefore been discussed in Chapter 1; the practical effect of the distinction is discussed further in Chapter 3.2 in the section on Mistake. However, in practice, the distinction between the subjective and objective approaches may dictate whether a contract is formed at all, for example, where the offeree is subjectively,

---

[1] See Malaurie and Aynès, para. 342, Terré, Simler and Lequette, para. 98, Treitel, *Contract*, at 8; McKendrick, *Contract*, at 31; Larenz, *AT* at 516; Zweigert and Kötz, at 356–7; A. T. von Mehren, "The Formation of Contract", in *International Encyclopedia of Comparative Law* (1992), Volume VII, *Contracts in General*, chapter 9, at 63.

[2] Whincup, *Contract Law and Practice. The English System and Continental Comparisons* (Deventer, Boston: Kluwer, 1990) at 31.

[3] See Simpson, "Innovation in Nineteenth Century Contract Law" (1975) 91 LQR 247, 259.

but unreasonably, mistaken as to the terms of the offer. For this reason, the impact of the subjective and objective approaches, as explained in other parts of this book, should be borne in mind when considering the doctrine of offer-and acceptance.

2.1.2. OFFER

2.1.2.A. DISTINCTION BETWEEN PRELIMINARY DEALINGS AND OFFERS TO ENTER CONTRACT

Principles of European Contract Law   **2.PECL.1.**

Article 2:201: **Offer**
    (1) A proposal amounts to an offer if:
        (a) it is intended to result in a contract if the other party accepts it, and
        (b) it contains sufficiently definite terms to form a contract.
    (2) An offer may be made to one or more specific persons or to the public.
    (3) A proposal to supply goods or services at stated prices made by a professional supplier in a public advertisement or a catalogue, or by a display of goods, is presumed to be an offer to sell or supply at that price until the stock of goods, or the supplier's capacity to supply the service, is exhausted.

Article 2:103: **Sufficient Agreement**
    (1) There is sufficient agreement if the terms:
        (a) have been sufficiently defined by the parties so that the contract can be enforced, or
        (b) can be determined under these Principles.
    (2) However, if one of the parties refuses to conclude a contract unless the parties have agreed on some specific matter, there is no contract unless agreement on that matter has been reached.

Unidroit Principles   **2.INT.2.**

Article 2.2   (*Definition of offer*)
    A proposal for concluding a contract constitutes an offer if it is sufficiently definite and indicates the intention of the offeror to be bound in case of acceptance.

Article 2.13: (*Conclusion of contract dependent on specific matters or in a specific form*)
    Where in the course of negotiations one of the parties insists that the contract is not concluded until there is agreement on specific matters or in a specific form, no contract is concluded before agreement is reached on those matters or in that form.

CISG   **2.INT.3.**

Article 14: 1. A proposal for concluding a contract addressed to one or more specific persons constitutes an offer if it is sufficiently definite and indicates the intention of the offeror to be bound in case of acceptance. A proposal is sufficiently definite if it indicates the goods and expressly or implicitly fixes or makes provision for determining the quantity and the price.
    2. A proposal other than one addressed to one or more specific persons is to be considered merely as an invitation to make offers, unless the contrary is clearly indicated by the person making the proposal

Clifton v. *Palumbo*[4]

INTERPRETATION OF PRE-CONTRACTUAL DEALINGS

Clifton's Estate

The use of the word "offer" will not necessarily render a communication an offer. When construing a communication which may or not constitute an offer, it is legitimate to bear in mind the probability that the parties intended to enter into a contract of the given description under the given circumstances.

Facts: Palumbo was negotiating to purchase Clifton's estate, which was very large and subject to a number of leases. On 7 June 1943, without legal assistance, Clifton wrote to Palumbo as follows: "I . . . am prepared to offer you . . . my . . . estate for £600,000 . . . I also agree that a reasonable and sufficient time shall be granted to you for the examination and consideration of all the data and details necessary for the preparation of the Schedule of Completion." It was contended on behalf of Palumbo that the letter of June 7 constituted an offer to sell for £ 600,000 on the terms of an open contract which had been accepted by Palumbo. Clifton sought a declaration that there was no contract.

Held: No contract was concluded by the acceptance of the proposal in the letter of 7 June 1943, for that letter had not contained an offer.

Judgment: LORD GREENE: . . . At the threshold of the case lies a question which, if decided against the defendant's contention, is, as counsel for the defendant very fairly admitted, conclusive. It is a question of the construction of a short document. . . . The document in question is the letter of June 7, 1943. . . .

The negotiations, such as they were, between the parties down to June 7, had been conducted with some haste and with no real assistance, so far as the formulation of the terms of a bargain was concerned, from legal advisers. This document is a layman's document, and it was signed by laymen, neither of them having had any expert assistance in drafting it. The subject matter of the alleged contract was a very large estate spread over a very large area and comprising properties of various types which were subject to various sorts of lease, the whole being subject also to a jointure. There were mortgages outstanding in large sums. The transaction was one which any layman (and I suppose more particularly a layman in the position of the defendant, who was not inexperienced in dealing with real estate) would regard as one of great magnitude, and probably of considerable complication . . .

Therefore words like "agree", "offer", "accept", when used in relation to price are not to be read necessarily as indicating an intention to make, then and there, a contract or an offer as the case may be. Whether they do or do not must depend entirely on the construction of the particular document . . .

There is nothing in the world to prevent an owner of an estate of this kind contracting to sell it to a purchaser, who is prepared to spend so large a sum of money, on terms, written out on a half sheet of notepaper, of the most informal description, and even, if he likes, on unfavourable conditions; but I think it is legitimate, in approaching the construction of a document of this kind, containing phrases and expressions of doubtful significance, to bear in mind that the probability of parties entering into so large a transaction, and finally binding themselves to a contract of this description couched in such terms is remote. If they have done it, they have done it, however unwise or however unbusiness like it may be. The question is: have they done it? . . .

The document which is being referred to by the phrase "the Schedule of Completion" can only be the purchase contract which the parties, if one is entitled to regard them as reasonable persons,

---

[4] [1944] 2 All ER 497.

would have contemplated, and which, in the ordinary course, no one in their senses would dispense with in a transaction of this magnitude.

Court of Appeal 2.E.5.
Bigg v. *Boyd-Gibbins Ltd*[5]

OFFER DESCRIBED AS ACCEPTANCE

A quick sale

The question whether a letter constitutes an offer depends on the objectively ascertained intention of the purported offeree. The use of the language of acceptance will not therefore prevent a communication from constituting an offer.

Facts: Mr and Mrs Bigg and Gibbins were negotiating for the sale of certain freehold property belonging to the Biggs. The Biggs wrote to Gibbins stating: "As you are aware that I paid £25,000 for this property, your offer of £20,000 would appear to be at least a little optimistic. For a quick sale I would accept £26,000 . . ." In reply Gibbins wrote: ". . . I accept your offer . . ." and asked Mr and Mrs Bigg to contact Gibbins' solicitors. In their final letter Mr. Bigg said: "I am putting the matter in the hands of my solicitors . . . My wife and I are both pleased that you are purchasing the property." Mr and Mrs Bigg alleged that this exchange of letters constituted an agreement for the sale of the property and brought an action for specific performance.

Held: The Biggs' claim succeeded.

Judgment: RUSSELL LJ: . . . the defendants were correct in treating the first letter of 22 December 1969, as an offer to sell the property at £26,000 when they wrote "I accept your offer". Further than that, it seems to me that the last letter of 13 January is a recognition, an affirmation indeed, that the parties have come to agreement on the sale of the property . . .

I cannot escape the view, having read the letters, that the parties would regard themselves at the end of the correspondence, and would regard themselves quite correctly, as having struck a bargain for the sale and purchase of this property. We were warned at an early stage in the argument, quite rightly, that agreement on price does not necessarily mean agreement for sale and purchase, and we were referred to the warning phrases used by Lord Greene MR in *Clifton* v. *Palumbo*, where it was stated that "offer" does not always mean offer in the sense of an offer for actual sale, but might be related to a negotiation continuing, but with agreement on one term or one element of the contract which would or might subsequently be concluded. But bearing in mind those warnings, I am bound to say for myself the impression conveyed to my mind by these letters, and indeed the plain impression, is that the language used was intended to and did achieve the formation of an open contract.

Notes

(1) In English law the question whether a certain statement constitutes an offer depends on the objectively ascertained intention of the party making the statement.[6] Was that party prepared to be bound by an acceptance of his offer, or did he merely make an invitation to treat? The cases discussed above[7] indicate that the context in which the words are used will be taken into account when determining the intentions of the parties. However, the objective nature of the test is even clearer where the words used are conclusive: see

---

[5] [1971] 2 All ER 183.
[6] See Treitel, *Contract*, at 8; McKendrick, *Contract*, at 25–6.
[7] *Supra*, at 179–180.

Gibson v. *Manchester CC*,[8] in which the council had stated in a letter that it "may be prepared" to sell a council-owned property to the occupant. When the council changed its policy and decided not to offer the property for sale, the tenant claimed that council was already bound to sell it to him. It was held that the council's letter could not be interpreted as an offer capable of acceptance by the tenant.

(2) *Clifton* and *Bigg* also illustrate that the statement of a price by the seller is not decisive in determining whether he made an offer. Neither is the wording of a certain statement conclusive: although it contains the word "offer", it does not necessarily have to be one (the letter in *Clifton* v. *Palumbo*) and, conversely, if it does not contain the word offer but purports to be an acceptance, it can still be an offer—the letter in *Bigg* v. *Boyd Gibbins Ltd*.

(3) The party alleged to have made an offer may have intended simply to answer a question from the other party, as was the case in *Harvey* v. *Facey*,[9] where the plaintiffs telegraphed to the defendants "Will you sell us Bumper Hall Pen? Telegraph lowest cash price". The defendants telegraphed in reply, "Lowest price for Bumper Hall Pen, £900". It was held by the Privy Council that the price statement was not an offer, but only an answer to the second question in the first telegram.

The distinction between an offer and a mere invitation to make an offer or to negotiate is also made in German law[10] and in French law.[11] As in English law, the conclusive criterion is the—objectively ascertainable—intention with which a statement is made. The question to be asked is whether a statement has the purport to enable its addressee to conclude a contract by accepting it, or merely shows the intention of the person making the statement to be put in the position to conclude a contract.[12]

Cass. com., 6 March 1990[13]   **2.F.6.**

OFFER SUBJECT TO CONFIRMATION

Hugin Sweda

A company selling goods but which indicates that its proposal is not definitive and must subsequently be approved or accepted by itself will not be held to have made an offer.

Facts: Mr Borde ordered certain equipment from Messrs Hugin Sweda for the purposes of his business; that company had stated, in the general conditions of sale featuring in its order forms, that its offers did not become definitive, and did not constitute a binding commitment, until they were approved by it, and, moreover, that an order would not be regarded as definite until it had been accepted by the company. Before his order was accepted by Hugin Sweda, Mr Borde changed his mind and withdrew it.

Held: M. Borde had not accepted an offer, but had himself made an offer which had been withdrawn before it was accepted.

Judgment:—Under articles 1134 and 1583 of the Civil Code;—Whereas between traders, a proposal to enter into a contract constitutes an offer only if it states an intention on the part of the person making it to be bound by it in the event of its acceptance; . . .

[8] [1979] 1 WLR 294.
[9] [1893] AC 552.
[10] Medicus, *SAT* at 135; Flume, *Rechtsgeschäft* at 636.
[11] Ghestin at 261.
[12] Flume, *Rechtsgeschäft* at 637.
[13] Bull. civ. IV.74; JCP 1990.II.21583 annotated by B. Gross.

—Whereas in dismissing Mr Borde's claim for repayment of the sum paid by him on account, the cour d'appel held that the order form constituted "a firm purchase on the terms proposed by Hugin Sweda", and that the clause appearing in that form constituted a condition having suspensory effect which was intended solely for the benefit of the vendor and which did not entitle the purchaser to withdraw from a sale which had been definitively concluded by agreement between the parties as to the subject-matter and the price;

—Whereas in so ruling, despite the fact that, by complying with the proposal contained in the order form, Mr Borde had merely made an offer to purchase which he remained at liberty to withdraw until such time as the sale became definitive by acceptance on the part of the vendor, the cour d'appel infringed the legislation referred to above; . . .

Notes

(1) An offer subject to confirmation is not in reality an offer but only an invitation to make an offer, because it does not show the necessary intention to be bound by mere acceptance. Thus, when a buyer signs a seller's order form containing a condition that makes the seller's offer subject to confirmation of the latter, then the signing of the order form, and not the order form itself, constitutes the first offer. The decision reached in the present case would therefore have been the same if it had been given by a German or an English court; the English case of *Robophone Facilities* v. *Blank*[14] is precisely on point—although with regard to the revocability of the buyer's offer a different outcome from that in the present case would have been reached under German law.[15]

(2) The *Cour de cassation* uses wording identical to that of Article 14 paragraph 1 CISG and of Article 2.2 of the Unidroit principles.[16] Although the CISG is applicable to commercial contracts only, it is remarkable that the court limits the applicability of the rule to contracts between merchants: the given definition of an offer seems to be valid for every offer.[17]

(3) To prevent a prospective buyer from withdrawing between his signing of the order form and the confirmation of the seller, order forms sometimes contain a provision stipulating that the buyer will be bound definitively. Conditions of this nature are valid, but in France, the *Commission des clauses abusives* (Commission for Unfair Terms) has recommended that these clauses—and similar conditions—should be eliminated from contracts between consumers and professionals.

(4) The *Cour de cassation* seems to state as a general rule that an offer is revocable. As will be seen in 2.1.2.C., this rule is subject to major restrictions in French law. That no restriction was placed on the revocability of the buyer's offer in the present case may be explained by the fact that it was the seller who had taken the first initiative to enter into a contract.[18]

[14] [1966] 1 WLR 1428.
[15] See under 2.1.2.C. *infra* at 197.
[16] *Supra*, at 178.
[17] See annotation by B. Gross, JCP 1990.II.21583 and by J. Mestre, RTD civ. 19990.464.
[18] See D. 1991.317.

BGH, 8 March 1984[19]

2.G.7.

OFFER WITHOUT ENGAGEMENT

The Aeroplane Charter

The use of the words "without engagement" will not necessarily prevent a communication from constituting an effective offer.

Facts: The plaintiff, a tour company wishing to charter an aircraft for a flight planned for the 1979 summer season, sent a telex on 2 August 1978 to Messrs L, in which it requested that firm to submit an offer. It stated that it would prefer the departure day to be "if possible a Friday, Saturday or Sunday, but that is not an absolute condition". Since Messrs L did not have an aircraft available for the period requested, it passed the telex on to the defendant. The plaintiff, on being informed of this, sent a telex to the defendant on 4 August 1978, in which it referred to the telex sent to Messrs L and requested the defendant "if possible, to make that offer . . . by return". The defendant replied in writing on 4 August 1978, referring to the plaintiff's telex to Messrs L and stating that it was willing, "without engagement, and subject to availability", to offer a Caravelle SE 210 for one-day flights at a price of DM 18,016 per flight, inclusive of all ancillary costs but without commission. The plaintiff replied in writing on 11 August 1978, stating that it was interested in the offer and requesting the reservation of a Caravelle SE 210. The defendant sent a further telex to the plaintiff on 1 September 1978, in which it informed the latter of the flight operations permit issued to it; thereafter, by telex of 10 October 1978, it stated that, having completed its planning for the summer 1979 season, it had "no availability". The plaintiff was then obliged to charter another aircraft having greater passenger capacity. It claimed from the defendant compensation for the damage suffered by it, in the sum of DM 120,000.

Held: The plaintiff's claim succeeded.

Judgment:

1. The appellate court correctly found that the defendant's communication to the plaintiff of 4 August 1978 constituted an effective offer. It was not rendered ineffective by the proviso "without engagement and subject to availability" contained therein. Moreover, the content of the offer—in conjunction with the telex from the plaintiff to Messrs L of 2 August 1978, to which reference was made—was adequately specified.

(a) The legal meaning of the phrase "without engagement", when used in an offer, is disputed. The *Reichsgericht* (Supreme Court of the German Reich) has taken the view that an "offer without engagement" does not constitute an offer within the meaning of § 145 BGB, but rather a request made to the other party, asking it to submit a contractual offer. However, it held, in accordance with the principle of good faith, that a party making a request in such terms is obliged forthwith to comment on the application for an "offer without engagement" contained in the answer. If a party making an "offer without engagement" fails to fulfil that obligation to provide an answer, his silence will be regarded as constituting acceptance of the offer (see RGZ 102, 227 [229 et seq.]; 103, 312 [313]; 105, 8 [12]; RG, JW 1921, 393; 1926, 2674 [2675]). . . .

The case-law of the *Reichsgericht* has been partially accepted by academic legal authors, who have likewise regarded an "offer without engagement" as constituting merely a request for the submission of an offer, which is in turn deemed to be accepted in the event of silence on the part of the party making the request. . . . However, such an offer may also amount to a proposal within the meaning of § 145 BGB which, by reason of the revocation proviso expressly stated in the clause in question, may be revoked at any time *up* to acceptance by the other party. . . . By contrast, a different view has been expressed, to the effect that an "offer without engagement" constitutes not merely a request for the submission of an offer but, invariably, a proposal the binding effect of which is excluded and which can still be revoked forthwith even *after* notice of its acceptance has been received. . . .

[19] NJW 1984, 1885.

(b) The *Bundesgerichtshof* (Federal Court of Justice) has not yet expressed any definitive view concerning the legal meaning of the qualification "without engagement". In its judgment published at BGH, NJW 1958, 1628, it merely stated (*obiter*) that the use of such a qualification indicated a desire on the part of the seller not to be bound in any way. However, it did not rule on the question whether a statement subject to such a qualification constitutes merely a request for the submission of an offer or whether it amounts to an offer in its own right. It is not necessary in the present case to determine whether an "offer without engagement" must *invariably* be regarded merely as a request for the submission of an offer, since, in the circumstances of this case, the defendant's statement that it was willing to offer an aircraft "without engagement, *and subject to availability*" constituted in any event an effective *offer* within the meaning of § 145 BGB.

(aa) Both in its telex of 2 August 1978, addressed to Messrs L but forwarded to the defendant, and in its telex sent direct to the defendant on 4 August 1978, the plaintiff asked the defendant to submit an *offer*. In so doing—as the appellate court correctly points out—it did not merely make an enquiry of the defendant for the purposes of obtaining information; instead, it expressly requested the submission of an offer. Consequently, even though the response to that request, contained in the defendant's written answer of 4 August 1978, was qualified by the words "without engagement", it cannot be regarded as constituting, in turn, a request for the submission of an offer. On the contrary, that response amounted to "more than a mere request for an offer" (see Flume, § 35 I 3c, with comments in support), since the plaintiff was entitled to expect the defendant to make a specific offer in response to its enquiry. The defendant likewise had necessarily to assume that its reply, in which it expressly "offered" to provide a specific service, would be understood as constituting an offer. On the basis of those facts—as the appellate court correctly found—the use by the defendant of the qualifying words ". . ." could only be understood as amounting to the reservation of a right of revocation, by which the defendant declined, in a permissible manner, to be bound by the application made to it (see § 145 BGB). In those circumstances, there are no grounds for treating its response as an acceptance of a mere request for the submission of an offer. The appellate court was unable to discern the existence of any contrary trade practice.

2. By its written communication of 11 August 1978, the plaintiff accepted the defendant's offer.
. . .

3. There is no need to determine whether—as the appellate court found—the reservation of the right of revocation contained in the phrase "without engagement and subject to availability" ceased to have effect upon the coming into existence of the contract, or whether—in accordance with the view expressed by academic legal authors, as mentioned in 1(a) above—the defendant could still have revocation its offer even after receiving the confirmation of its acceptance. This is because the defendant did not decline the plaintiff's acceptance of its offer immediately after receiving that acceptance on 11 August 1978. On the contrary, it was not until it sent its telex of 10 October 1978 that it informed the plaintiff that it had "no availability". By that time, revocation by the defendant had ceased to be possible under any circumstances.

4. Consequently—as the appellate court rightly held—an effective contract came into existence between the parties.

Notes

(1) This case illustrates that, in German law, the words used by the parties must be interpreted by reference to the intentions of the parties. The fact that the telex was sent in response to a request for an offer indicated that the intended purpose of the communication was to make an offer rather than an invitation to treat or the mere provision of information. On that basis, the disputed words could be interpreted only as reserving a right of revocation, and that right had not been exercised on the facts of the case.

(2) The legal meaning of the word *freibleibend* (free of engagement) in an offer has generated some controversy in German law. Three possible views are mentioned by the *Bundesgerichtshof* with regard to. The first view is that such an offer is not a real offer but only an invitation to make an offer—this view had been adopted by the *Reichsgericht*, for example in the *Alcohol For Sale* case;[20] the second view is that it is a real offer, but one that can be revoked until its acceptance—the main rule in German law is that an offer cannot be revoked;[21] and the third view is that it is a real offer, but revocable even immediately after its acceptance. The *Bundesgerichtshof* in the present case avoids choosing between the three views, because the statement of the firm was not made without any commitment (*freibleibend*) in general, but without any commitment according to our availability and, moreover, it was not revoked immediately after it had been accepted. Anyway, the practical meaning of the difference between the first and the third view is small, especially when it is assumed that an offer that has been made on invitation of the offeree, may be accepted by silence.[22] In both views the person who used the term *freibleibend* is bound to a contract if he does not revoke his proposal immediately after the addressee has agreed to it.

Cass. civ. 3e, 28 November 1968[23]   *2.F.8.*

OFFER TO PUBLIC AT LARGE

Land for sale

An offer to the public at large is not merely an invitation to treat and is capable of being accepted so as to give rise to a contract.

Facts: Maltzkorn, having become aware of an advertisement published in the newspaper *L'Ardennais* on 23 May 1961, offering for sale a certain plot of land at a price of 25,000 francs, informed the owner, Mr Braquet, that he accepted his offer; however, Braquet claimed that he was not bound by Maltzkorn's offer to buy.

Held: Maltzkorn's claim failed, but this decision was overturned by the *Cour de cassation*.

Judgment:—Under article 1589 of the Civil Code;—Whereas an offer made to the public at large binds the offeror *vis-à-vis* the first person who accepts it, in the same way as an offer made to a specific person;
—Whereas the grounds for dismissal of Maltzkorn's claim for an order requiring the sale to be completed, as set out in the contested judgment, state that "an offer made in a newspaper for the sale of an asset which can only be purchased by one person cannot be equated with an offer made to a specific person; it constitutes merely an invitation to treat addressed to potential purchasers, and cannot therefore bind the person by whom it is made *vis-à-vis* a person who accepts it";
—Whereas in making that general ruling, despite its finding that Braquet, upon receiving notice of the acceptance, had stated that "the farm has not yet been sold", and without mentioning any factor which could have prompted it to infer that the advertisement constituted merely an invitation to enter into negotiations or that Braquet's offer was subject to any qualification, the cour d'appel failed to establish any legal basis for its decision; . . .

---

[20] Cit. in 2.1.3.A., *infra* at 216.
[21] See 2.1.2.C. at 197.
[22] See for acceptance by silence under 2.1.3.A., *infra*, at 213 ff.
[23] Bull. civ. III.507; Gaz. Pal. 1969.1.95; JCP 1969.II.15797.

185

Note

(1) This case illustrates that, in French law, an offer to the public is no less a valid offer than an offer to a particular person. A statement that is made to the public at large by means of an advertisement in a newspaper is therefore a "real" offer that is susceptible of being accepted.

(2) The French court speaks generally of "offers to the public". Later in this section, we discuss another case which would be treated in this way by the French courts: the display of priced goods in a shop.[24]

(3) According to French authors and case-law of the lower courts, if the offer relates to the conclusion of a contract for which the person of the other party is of particular interest to the offeror (*intuitus personae*), an exception is allowed to the rule laid down by the Cour de cassation concerning offers to the public.[25] The examples mentioned by these authors are employment contracts, credit agreements,[26] the rent of a flat and certain types of partnerships. In such cases, the offeror can be said to have made a reservation with regard to the person of the other party.

(4) Malaurie and Aynès are critical of the *Land for Sale* case,[27] and are of the opinion that the sale of real estate is an act too serious to be concluded in this way and that the advertisement should have been characterized as an invitation to enter into negotiations. On this basis, the prospective buyer would make the relevant offer by giving the vendor notice of his willingness to buy. The approach of the French courts certainly contrasts with that of the English courts in *Clifton* v. *Palumbo*,[28] in which the courts took into account the seriousness of a sale of land when construing a letter as merely preliminary to a binding contract.

(5) According to some French authors the distinction between an offer to the public and an offer to a particular person is relevant to the question of the revocability of an offer.[29]

(6) The approach taken in German and English law reflects the proposal of Malaurie and Aynès in their criticism of the French approach: the advertisement is a mere invitation to treat.[30] In support of this analysis, some German authors[31] have argued that a statement addressed to an indefinite number of persons can never be meant as an offer, because the person making the statement cannot perform the proposed contract an infinite number of times. However, German law does not entirely reject the notion of an offer to the public. The holding out of a slot machine is generally regarded in German law as an offer that can be accepted by putting in money.[32]

In the English case of *Partridge* v. *Crittenden*,[33] a notice in a periodical "Bramblefinch cocks and hens, 25s each" was held not to be an offer. Lord Parker stated the general rule in English law:

[24] See the English case of *Pharmaceutical Society* v. *Boots* , *infra*, at 189.
[25] Malaurie and Aynès, para. 383; Terré, Simler and Lequette, para. 108.
[26] Compare Cass. com., 31 janv. 1966, Bull. civ. III.64; D., 66.537, annotated by Cabrillac et Rives-Lange.
[27] Malaurie and Aynès, para 387, note 29.
[28] *Supra*, at 179.
[29] Malaurie and Aynès, para 211; Against this view, see Ghestin at 278. On the revocability of an offer, see 2.1.2.C. *infra*, 195.
[30] Treitel, *Contract*, at 13–14, McKendrick, *Contract*, at 36.
[31] E.g. Medicus, *SAT* at 135.
[32] Larenz, *AT* at 518; Flume, *Rechtsgeschäft* at 636.
[33] [1968] 2 All ER 421.

I think that when one is dealing with advertisements and circulars, unless they indeed come from manufacturers, there is business sense in their being construed as invitations to treat and not offers for sale.

The argument given for the rule is the problem of "limited stock", as in German law. However, the argument is not convincing: the offer to the public can be seen as implicitly including a clause which limits the validity of the offer to the exhaustion of the offeror's stock. The offer therefore lapses when the offeror's stock is finished. The better reason to deny an advertisement the character of an offer seems to be that the person placing the advertisement wishes to reserve to himself the final decision whether to conclude a contract, and therefore the proposal does not show the intention to be bound in case of acceptance. This will generally be the case for proposals *intuitus personae* ("with an eye to the person"); other considerations may also lead to the assumption that, unless otherwise indicated, a proposal to the public at large is only an invitation to make an offer. This is the view promoted by some French authors and French lower case-law.[34] The Dutch Supreme Court has used the *intuitus personae* argument, holding that an advertisement in which a specific thing, such as a house (as opposed to a generic thing), is offered for a certain price, has to be taken by prospective buyers, in principle, as an invitation to enter into negotiations, in which not only the price and other conditions of the sale but also the person of the prospective buyer can be of interest.[35]

Court of Appeal   **2.E.9.**
Carlill v. *Carbolic Smoke Ball Co*[36]

UNILATERAL CONTRACT

The smoke ball (again)

An advertisement setting up a unilateral contract constitutes an offer rather than an invitation to treat.

Facts: The Carbolic Smoke Ball Company, proprietor of a medical preparation called "The Carbolic Smoke Ball", inserted in some newspapers the following advertisement: "100*l*. reward will be paid by the Carbolic Smoke Ball Company to any person who contracts the increasing epidemic influenza, colds, or any disease caused by taking cold, after having used the smoke ball three times daily for two weeks according to the printed directions supplied with each ball. 100*l*. is deposited with the Alliance Bank, Regent Street, shewing our sincerity in the matter." Mrs. Carlill on the faith of the advertisement bought one of the balls, and used it in the manner and for the period specified, but nevertheless contracted influenza and claimed the 100*l*.

Held: In purchasing and using the smoke ball, Mrs Carlill had accepted the company's offer to pay 100*l*. should she contract influenza.

Judgment: LINDLEY LJ: . . . Then it is contended that it is not binding. In the first place, it is said that it is not made with anybody in particular. Now that point is common to the words of this advertisement and to the words of all other advertisements offering rewards. They are offers to anybody who performs the conditions named in the advertisement, and anybody who does perform the condition accepts the offer. In point of law this advertisement is an offer to pay 100*l*. to anybody who will perform these conditions, and the performance of the conditions is the acceptance of the offer . . .

---

[34] See note (3) to the *Land for Sale* case, *supra*, at 186; See also Article 2:201 PECL, *supra*, at 178 and the comments on that provision under C.
[35] 10 April 1981, NJ 1981, *Hofland* v. *Hennis*, annotated by CJHB.
[36] [1893] 1 QB 256. See also *supra*, **1.E.102.**

BOWEN LJ: . . . It was also said that the contract is made with all the world – that is, with everybody; and that you cannot contract with everybody. It is not a contract made with all the world. There is the fallacy of the argument. It is an offer made to all the world; and why should not an offer be made to all the world which is to ripen into a contract with anybody who comes forward and performs the condition? It is an offer to become liable to any one who, before it is retracted, performs the condition, and, although the offer is made to the world, the contract is made with that limited portion of the public who come forward and perform the condition on the faith of the advertisement. It is not like cases in which you offer to negotiate, or you issue advertisements that you have got a stock of books to sell, or houses to let, in which case there is no offer to be bound by any contract. Such advertisements are offers to negotiate – offers to receive offers – offers to chaffer, as, I think, some learned judge in one of the cases has said. If this is an offer to be bound, then it is a contract the moment the person fulfils the condition.

That seems to me to be sense, and it is also the ground on which all these advertisement cases have been decided during the century; and it cannot be put better than in Willes, J.'s, judgment in *Spencer* v. *Harding*. "In the advertisement cases," he says, "there never was any doubt that the advertisement amounted to a promise to pay the money to the person who first gave information. The difficulty suggested was that it was a contract with all the world. But that, of course, was soon overruled. It was an offer to become liable to any person who before the offer should be retracted should happen to be the person to fulfil the contract, of which the advertisement was an offer or tender. That is not the sort of difficulty which presents itself here. If the circular had gone on, 'and we undertake to sell to the highest bidder', the reward cases would have applied, and there would have been a good contract in respect of the persons." As soon as the highest bidder presented himself, says Willes, J., the person who was to hold the vinculum juris on the other side of the contract was ascertained, and it became settled.

A.L. SMITH LJ: . . . It was then said there was no person named in the advertisement with whom any contract was made. That, I suppose, has taken place in every case in which actions on advertisements have been maintained, from the time of *Williams* v. *Carwardine*, and before that, down to the present day. I have nothing to add to what has been said on that subject, except that a person becomes a persona designata and able to sue, when he performs the conditions mentioned in the advertisement.

Notes

(1) As discussed above,[37] the general rule in English law is that advertisements are invitations to treat. However, exceptions to the English rule may occur, as illustrated by *Carlill* v. *Carbolic Smoke Ball Co.* As we have seen in Chapter 1, in English law a distinction is made between so-called unilateral contracts and bilateral contracts. In summary, a unilateral contract can be characterized as a contract where only one party is bound: the party who has made the offer. The advertiser in *Carlill* v. *Carbolic Smoke Ball Co.* did not intend to create an obligation on anyone's part to use the smoke ball three times daily for two weeks, but indicated his intention to become bound to anybody who performed that act. Advertisements of unilateral contracts may be treated as offers in English law, as is shown by the present case, provided that they sufficiently show the offeror's willingness to be bound in the case of acceptance and that they are sufficiently clear as to the required performance.

[37] *Supra*, at 186, note 6.

(2) In France, the putting up of a reward or prize, which is of course an offer to the public, is probably considered a "real" offer in accordance with the general rule set out above.[39]

(3) In the American case of *Lefkowitz* v. *Great Minneapolis Surplus Store*,[40] a shop had published the following advertisement: "Saturday 9 A.M. Sharp 3 Brand New Fur Coats Worth to $100.00 First Come First Served $1 Each". The plaintiff was the first to present himself at the seller's store and demanded the coat as advertised, indicating his readiness to pay the sale price of $1. The shop refused to sell the coat to the plaintiff, stating that it was not bound by the advertisement. The court stated that the question whether, in any individual instance, a newspaper advertisement is an offer rather than an invitation to treat depends on the legal intention of the parties and the surrounding circumstances. The court held that the offer of the sale of the fur coat was clear, definite and explicit, and left nothing open for negotiation, and that the plaintiff was entitled to performance. It is not clear whether the English courts would have decided this case in accordance with *Partridge* v. *Crittenden* or *Carlill* v. *Carbolic Smoke Ball Co.*

Court of Appeal　　　　　　　　**2.E.10.**
Pharmaceutical Society v. *Boots*[41]

INVITATION TO TREAT

Self service pharmacy

Placing goods on a shop shelf merely constitutes an invitation to treat. No contract is therefore concluded when a customer takes the goods from the shelf to pay for them at the cash desk.

Facts: A chemist's "self-service" shop comprised one room around whose walls were shelves on which were laid out certain drugs and medicines specified in Part I of the Poisons List compiled under section 17 (1) of the Pharmacy and Poisons Act 1933. These preparations were wrapped in packages and containers with the prices marked on them. A customer entering the shop took a wire basket, selected any articles he required from the shelves, placed them in the basket, and carried them to a cashier at one of the two exits. The cashier then examined the articles the customer wished to purchase, stated the total price, and accepted payment. At this stage a registered pharmacist, who was authorized by the chemist to prevent the customer from buying any article if he thought fit, supervised the transaction. In order to decide whether the transaction took place "under the supervision of a registered pharmacist" as required by the provisions of section 18 (1) (a) (iii) of the Pharmacy and Poisons Act 1933, a question arose as to when the contract was concluded.

Held: The sale did take place under the supervision of a registered pharmacist.

Judgment: SOMERVELL LJ: . . . Is the invitation which is made to the customer to be regarded as an offer which is completed so that both sides are bound when the article is put into the receptacle, or is it to be regarded as a more organised way of doing what is already done in many types of shops—and a bookseller is, perhaps, the best example—namely, enabling customers to have free access to what is in the shop, to look at the different articles, and then, ultimately, having taken the one which they wish to buy, to come to the assistant and say: "I want this"? Generally speaking, the assistant will say: "That is all right", the money passes, and the transaction is completed. I agree entirely with what the Lord Chief Justice says and the reasons he gives for his conclusion that in the case of the

[39] *Supra*, at 186, note 1 and 2.
[40] 251 Minn. 188; 86 NW 2d 689 (1957).
[41] [1953] 1 All ER 482.

ordinary shop, although goods are displayed and it is intended that customers should go and choose what they want, the contract is not completed until the customer has indicated the article which he needs and the shopkeeper or someone on his behalf accepts that offer. Not till then is the contract completed, and, that being the normal position, I can see no reason for drawing any different inference from the arrangements which were made in the present case. The Lord Chief Justice expressed what I consider one of the most formidable difficulties in the way of the plaintiffs' case when he pointed out that, if they were right, once an article has been placed in the receptacle the customer himself is bound and he would have no right, without paying for the first article, to substitute an article which he saw later of the same kind and which he preferred. I can see no reason for implying from this arrangement any position other than that which the Lord Chief Justice found, namely, that it is a convenient method of enabling customers to see what there is for sale, to choose, and, possibly, to put back and substitute, articles which they wish to have, and then go to the cashier and offer to buy what they have chosen. . . .

Notes

(1) The decision given in the present case was repeated in *Fisher* v. *Bell*.[42] Thus, in the common situation of goods displayed in a shop and marked with a price, the intention of the seller is determined by means of a general rule:[43] the exhibition of goods in a shop-window or inside a shop—even a self-service shop—with a price attached does not constitute an offer to sell, but is merely an invitation to treat. However, exceptions to the general rule may follow from the special terms of a display or the circumstances in which it is made, and this may lead to the conclusion that the offeror intended to make a real offer.

(2) The reason for this rule given in the present case is that the consequence of the opposite view, in which the picking up of an article by a customer amounts to an acceptance, is undesirable, because the customer could not, on that view, change his mind and put the article back and substitute it by another. But this is not a valid reason for denying the display of priced goods the character of an offer to sell, because the acceptance of the buyer could be situated at a later moment in time, when he presents himself at the cash desk and pays for the things he has chosen.[44] The better reason to assume that the seller does not make a firm offer by displaying goods is that he wants to reserve the right to refuse to sell when a customer asks for the displayed thing, for example because the thing displayed in the shop-window was the last specimen. This argument, too, has been criticized however, as having no real application in the vast superstores of today.[45]

(3) In German law, variations on the common situation discussed above[46] may be treated differently. The display of priced goods in a shop-window, the display of price lists in a shop and the distribution of price lists are all regarded as a request to interested persons to make an offer;[47] However, there is controversy in German law about whether the display of goods in a self-service shop constitutes an offer. Some authors regard this as an offer that is accepted by the customer by presenting himself with the desired item at

---

[42] [1961] 1 QB 394.
[43] See Treitel, *Contract*, at 12; McKendrick, at 35.
[44] Treitel, *Contract*, at 12–13.
[45] McKendrick, *Contract*, at 34–5.
[46] *Supra*, at note (1).
[47] BGH 16.1.1980, NJW 1980.1388; Larenz, *AT* at 518; Medicus, *SAT* at 136; Flume, *Rechtsgeschäft* at 636.

the cash desk; others regard the customer who presents himself at the cash desk with the item he wants to buy as the person making the offer, because they want to reserve to the shop owner the right to refuse to conclude a contract. In Germany, it has been argued that, if these situations are not treated as "invitations to treat", there will be the risk of more acceptances than there are goods for sale.[48] As was observed above[49] in relation to the advertisement cases, this argument is not very strong, since such an offer may be assumed to implicitly contain a clause "as long as supplies/stock lasts". Indeed, in the case of a self service shop, there is no risk that the goods on display are not in stock.

Cour d'appel de Paris
14 December 1961[50]
and
Cass. civ. 1, 20 October 1964[51]

2.F.11–12.

ACCEPTANCE BY PLACING GOODS IN SUPERMARKET BASKET

Exploding lemonade bottle

A customer in a self-service store makes the contract by placing the goods selected in the basket provided, even though she does not have to pay for the goods until she leaves the store; and if she is subsequently injured by the goods her claim against the store will be in contract.[52] The manufacturer of the goods will not be liable if the accident was caused by the way the goods had been treated by the store, not by a defect in the goods.

Facts: Mme Dehen went to Supermag-Rennes' self-service store, and, having taken a basket provided by the store, put in it various items including a bottle of beer and a bottle of "Vittel-Delices". She then went to the checkout, where an employee of the supermarket took the items out of the basket. While Mme. Dehen waited for her total bill to be rung up she placed the items in her own bag. At this point the bottle of "Vittel-Delices" bumped gently against the bottle of beer and exploded, and either the bottle cap or a piece of glass struck Mme. Dehen in the right eye. She sued the supermarket and the producers of the lemonade, Vittel, in delict.

Held: Mme Dehen could recover from Supermag Rennes in contract but not against Vittel on the basis of Arts 1382–1384.

2.F.11.

(a) *Cour d'appel de Paris*

Judgment: THE COURT: . . .—Whereas . . . Mme Dehen has brought an action against Supermag-Rennes and Vittel . . . on the basis of Articles 1382, 1383 and 1384 Coded Civil, and on the basis of Articles 1641 *et seq*.
—Whereas Mme. Dehen is perfectly entitled to sue Supermag-Rennes but the latter's responsibility can only be contractual, even though the price is payable when the customer leaves the store.

---

[48] Medicus, *SAT* at 136;
[49] *Supra*, [0000].
[50] Gaz.Pal. 1962.1.135, JCP 1962.II.12547.
[51] DS 1965.62.
[52] NB Because of the principle of *non-cumul* in French law, this excludes the shop being liable in tort.

—Whereas when goods are purchased in a self service store, the sale takes place as soon as the customer, seeing an item marked with a price the client is prepared to accept, places the item in the basket or bag made available to her and which she is required to use until the goods are checked out by the employee at the till . . .

2.F.12.

(b) Cour de cassation

Facts: see above

Judgment: THE COURT:—Whereas however, seeing that, after pointing out correctly that the responsibility of Supermag-Rennes to the victim could only be contractual, the lower court held that the bottle of lemonade, which Mme. Dehen had taken from the shelf into her control, exploded when she placed it in her bag, where it bumped gently into a bottle of beer which was already in the bag; —Whereas the lower court held that the bottle was "abnormally warm" and that "the supermarket had failed to foresee, as it should have done, that fizzy drinks left carelessly near a heat source, could constitute a danger"; as against Vittel, the *cour d'appel* stated that the explosion could be accounted for by the circumstances in which Supermag-Rennes had made the sale, thereby implicitly but necessarily excluding both the good being dangerous in themselves and the theory that there was some defect in the bottle;
—Whereas on the basis of its findings of fact, the *cour d'appel* was entitled to allow the principal claim and reject the claim based on the *garantie*.

The appeal fails on both points, for these reasons, the appeal is dismissed.

Notes

(1) Tunc[53] makes the same objection to the reasoning of the court as led Somervell LJ in the *Boots* case to hold that the contract was not made until the checkout.

(2) If the claim was in contract, the store would be liable unless it could show a *cause étrangère*. Could it be that the court wanted to find a contract and that the reasoning is result-orientated?

(3) It seems to have been argued that there was no contract until the goods were paid for. This would mean that the customer could refuse to pay for any of the goods even if they had been rung up on the till. At what precise moment did Somervell LJ in the *Boots* case think the contract was made? Would this analysis not have provided a solution to the French case also?

(4) In Swiss law, the display of goods is regarded as the making of an offer:

Obligationenrecht

Article 7 3. The display of goods with price indication shall be considered as an offer.

(5) In another common situation, the sale on an auction, it was decided by the English Court of Appeal in *Payne* v. *Cave* [54] that the bidding of a buyer is an offer that is accepted by the auctioneer when he knocks down the hammer. In German law, the same view is adopted: the BGB provides

[53] RTD. civ. 1962.305.
[54] (1789) Term R 148, 100 ER 502.

§ 156: At an auction a contract is not concluded until the hammer falls. A bid ceases to be binding if a higher bid is made, or the auction is closed before the hammer falls.[55]

(6) In the common situation of an automatic car park with a ticket machine, it was said by Lord Denning in *Thornton* v. *Shoe Lane Parking*[56] that the offer is made when the proprietor of the machine holds it out as being ready to receive the money, and the acceptance takes place when the customer puts his money into the slot. As we have seen, the same view is generally adopted with regard to all slot machines in German law; see also Medicus,[57] who is of the opinion that putting money in the slot is the offer, which is accepted by the functioning of the machine. German authors point out, however, that the offer is necessarily limited to the content of the machine: when the machine is empty, no contract comes into existence by putting money in.

Final remarks

The problem of the distinction between the pre-contractual and the contractual phase is dealt with theoretically in the same way in the three legal systems. A distinction is made between statements constituting offers and statements that merely invite negotiations. First, in order to constitute an offer, the proposal must show the intention of the party who makes it to be bound in the case of acceptance. If that party makes a reservation as to his final decision to enter into a contract—e.g. "subject to confirmation"—then in general his proposal is not an offer. Furthermore, a proposal must contain the essential elements of the contract and be sufficiently definite.

In certain common situations the intention of the party making the proposal is determined by way of general rules which may differ between legal systems. Thus, for example, in French law an advertisement offering to sell a certain thing for a certain price is regarded as an offer, whereas in German and in English law such an advertisement is deemed an invitation to make an offer.

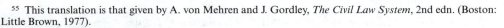

All three legal systems leave the final decision concerning the conclusion of the contract to the parties themselves in that no contract is concluded as long as elements that are considered essential by the parties or by one of them have not yet been agreed upon.

2.1.2.B. Requirements as to content

In French, English and German law it is generally assumed that, in addition to the "intention requirement", an offer must contain the essential elements of the contract.[58] An example of the law stating the essential elements of a contract is Article 1583 of the Code civil, which provides with regard to sale contracts that the sale is complete at the moment

[55] This translation is that given by A. von Mehren and J. Gordley, *The Civil Law System*, 2nd edn. (Boston: Little Brown, 1977).

[56] [1971] 1 All ER 686.

[57] Medicus, *SAT* at 136.

[58] F. Terré and Y. Lequette, *Grands arrêts de la jurisprudence civile – Obligations, contrats spéciaux, sûretés* (Paris: Dalloz, 2000) at 347; Terré, Simler and Lequette, para. 104; Larenz, *AT* at 517; Medicus, *SAT* at 135; Flume, *Rechtsgeschäft* at 635; Treitel, *Contract*, at 46–7.

the parties have reached an agreement on the thing sold and the price to be paid. An offer to enter into a sales contract must therefore, according to French law, at least mention the thing to be sold and the price to be paid. (It has however been decided that where an agreement—a "framework contract"—provides for further contracts to be made under it, the price need not be fixed in the first agreement: the *Alcatel* case.[59]) In contrast, under the Sale of Goods Act 1979, an agreement for the sale of goods may be binding as soon as the parties have agreed to buy and sell, the remaining details being determined by the standard of reasonableness or by law; section 8(2) of the Act provides that, if no price is determined by the contract, a reasonable price must be paid. Under English law therefore, a proposal to enter into a sales contract may amount to an offer even if it does not mention an (exact) price.

The question of the essential minimum that a proposal should include in order to make it an offer should be distinguished from the fact that, in some cases, a failure to agree some point will indicate that no contract was concluded. The latter question turns on whether the necessary "intention to be bound" was present: a proposal which mentions the thing to be sold and the price will not be an offer if the offeror does not intend the other party to be able to accept. According to French case law, if one of the parties makes it clear that he does not want to enter into a binding agreement before one or more other conditions of the contract is or are settled in a satisfactory manner, a contract does not come into existence before these additional matters are agreed upon.[60] English case law shows a similar picture: the question whether an agreement is a binding contract depends primarily on the intention of the parties and inferences on this intention may be drawn both from the importance of a matter left over for further agreement, and from the extent to which the parties have acted on the agreement.[61] This is the same in German law by virtue of the following provision:

BGB   **2.G.13.**

§ 154: So long as the parties have not agreed on all points of a contract upon which agreement is essential, according to the declaration even of one party, the contract is, in case of doubt, not concluded. . . .[62]

Compare also Article 2:103 (2) of the PECL and Article 2.13 of the Unidroit principles.[63]

2.1.2.C. REVOCABILITY OF AN OFFER

Principles of European Contract Law   **2.PECL.14.**

Article 1:303: **Notice**

      (1) Subject to paragraphs (4) and (5), any notice becomes effective when it reaches the addressee . . .

---

[59] Cass. Ass. plén. 1 December 1995, JCP 1995.II.22.565, annotated by Ghestin.
[60] Cass. civ. 3e, 2 May 1978, D. 1979.317, annotated by Schmidt-Szalewski and Cass. civ. 3e, 14 January 1987, D. 1988.80, annotated Schmidt-Szalewski.
[61] Treitel, *Contract*, at 53.
[62] Translated by von Mehren & Gordley, op. cit., *supra* note 55, at 193.
[63] *Supra*, at 178.

(5) A notice has no effect if a withdrawal of it reaches the addressee before or at the same time as the notice.

Article 2:202: **Revocation of an Offer**

(1) An offer may be revoked if the revocation reaches the offeree before it has dispatched its acceptance or, in cases of acceptance by conduct, before the contract has been concluded under Article 2:205(2) or (3).

(2) An offer made to the public can be revoked by the same means as were used to make the offer.

(3) However, a revocation of an offer is ineffective if:

> (a) the offer indicates that it is revocable; or
> (b) it states a fixed time for its acceptance; or
> (c) it was reasonable for the offeree to rely on the offer as being irrevocable and the offeree has acted in reliance on the offer.

Unidroit Principles   **2.INT.15.**

Article 2.3: (*Withdrawal of offer*)

1. An offer becomes effective when it reaches the offeree.

2. An offer, even if it is irrevocable, may be withdrawn if the withdrawal reaches the offeree before or at the same time as the offer.

Article 2.4: (*Revocation of offer*)

1. Until a contract is concluded an offer may be revoked if the revocation reaches the offeree before it has dispatched an acceptance.

2. However, an offer cannot be revoked

> a. if it indicates, whether by stating a fixed time for acceptance or otherwise, that it is irrevocable; or
> b. if it was reasonable for the offeree to rely on the offer as being irrevocable and the offeree has acted in reliance on the offer.[64]

RG, 25 October 1917[65]   **2.G.16.**

EFFECTIVE OFFER CANNOT BE WITHDRAWN

Delivery to a housemaid

An effective offer cannot be withdrawn. An offer which has been received by the offerees employee but has not come to the attention of the offeree is effective, and cannot therefore be withdrawn.

Facts: On 19 and 20 November 1915 the plaintiff requested, by way of newspaper advertisements, the submission of offers for the supply of military drill textiles. In response, Messrs B on 20 November offered him "without engagement or obligation", according to sample, pure linen drill approximately 84 cm in width at a price of 0.80 marks per metre, "pure net, prompt cash, approximately 20,000 m available for immediate delivery". The plaintiff replied on 22 November, having on that day received Messrs B's letter, stating that he accepted the offer of 20,000 m and requesting confirmation by telegram. Messrs B wired him at 5.15 p.m. on the same day in the following terms: "Organised only on the basis of telegraphic transfer of 1000 marks today, balance payable cash on delivery". That telegram was delivered at 7 p.m. to the plaintiff's residence, the plaintiff being out at the time. However, Messrs B then came to a different decision and asked the telegraph office to return their telegram. The telegraph office sent an official wire to the St. office, requesting the latter to stop the telegram sent to the

---

[64] See also CISG Articles 2.15 and 2.16, which are identical to these provisions.
[65] RGZ 91, 60.

plaintiff. However, since that telegram had already been delivered, it arranged for the telegraph messenger to get the housemaid of the plaintiff, who was still out of the house, to hand it back.

Held: The defendant was not entitled to withdraw the offer.

Judgment: . . .

2. The decision in the present case is founded on the import of § 130 BGB. The telegram sent by Messrs B, which was subsequently taken back, contained a contractual offer made to the plaintiff, and thus a declaration of intent which had to be received in order to be effective. It became effective, and the offer thus became binding (§§ 145, 146 BGB), at the moment in time when it reached the plaintiff. A statement contained in a letter, to which a telegraphic communication must be regarded as equivalent, is deemed to reach its recipient upon being delivered to the latter's address, even where it is handed to a member of the recipient's family or to a domestic servant, and irrespective of whether the recipient is at home or not; he is thereby given the opportunity of taking cognisance of its contents, this being an essential element of the concept of a communication "reaching" its recipient (RGZ, Vol. 50, p. 191, 194, Vol. 56, p. 262, Vol. 60, p. 334). It does not matter, therefore, whether it actually comes to the knowledge of the recipient; what matters is that it is placed at his disposal, so that he is given the opportunity of taking cognizance of it. It is for that reason, as stated in the decision of the court below, that the second sentence of § 130(1) additionally provides that the withdrawal of a declaration of intent needing to be received by its addressee will be effective only if it reaches the recipient before or at the same time as the initial declaration of intent; in such circumstances, the time at which the communication actually comes to the knowledge of its recipient is wholly immaterial. According to those principles, the offer made in the present case by Messrs B to the plaintiff reached him when it was handed, in his absence, to his housemaid, with the result that the party by whom the telegram was sent was bound by his contractual offer on the terms contained therein. The withdrawal contained in the second telegram was too late, since at the time when it was delivered, or rather could and should have been delivered, that is to say, when the telegraph messenger arrived at the plaintiff's residence bearing the withdrawal telegram, the proposal concerning implementation of the contract had already reached the plaintiff.

In opposition to this, the appellant relies, nevertheless, on the view occasionally advanced by certain academic legal authors, which the *Landgericht* [Regional Court] has likewise seen fit to adopt in its judgment, to the effect that it would be contrary to the principle of good faith if the recipient of a contractual offer were able to rely on that offer to his benefit, and could derive rights from it, notwithstanding that the contractual offer, despite having reached him earlier, only actually came to his knowledge at the same time as the withdrawal of that offer. However, that view is not compatible with the clear provision contained in the second sentence of § 130(1), which cannot be excluded. The sole decisive factor, as regards both the sender and the recipient, is the time at which the communication reached the latter; by contrast, the time at which it actually came to his knowledge is immaterial, as regards both the offer and the withdrawal thereof. . . .

Notes

(1) The German case cited above[66] is concerned with the question when an offer made to an absent person becomes effective. This question is of relevance under German law because any declaration, including an offer, may be retracted *before* it has become effective. In accordance with the terminology of the PECL, CISG and the Unidroit principles,

---

[66] *Supra*, at 195–6.

such a retraction will be described as a "withdrawal". The term "revocation" can thus be reserved for retraction of the offer *after* it has become effective, also in accordance with PECL, CISG and the Unidroit principles. The question of the revocability of an offer that is made orally to a present person or over the telephone does not arise, since such an offer is generally assumed to lapse if it is not accepted immediately[67]—unless the offeror intended it to remain valid for a longer time. Of greater importance is the question of the revocability of an offer when a contract is to be concluded *inter absentes*.

(2) The German Code contains a general provision on the moment any declaration directed to an absent person becomes effective:

BGB

§ 130: 1. A declaration of intention to another, if it is made to another in his absence, is effective at the moment when it reaches him. It does not become effective if a withdrawal[68] reaches him previously or simultaneously.

In the cited case the *Reichsgericht* states that, in accordance with the concept of *zugehen* (reaching) that it is not necessary that the offeree has actually been informed of the offer; it is sufficient that the letter or telegram containing the offer has been delivered at his house. Until that moment, the offer can be withdrawn by retracting it from the post or by sending a second letter or telegram that reaches the offeree before or at the same time as the offer; after that moment withdrawal is no longer possible, even if the offeree is informed of the withdrawal at the same moment as of the offer itself. The same decision was given in RG 8 February 1902.[69]

(3) The possibility of *withdrawal* of an offer is of particular importance in German law, because once the offer has reached the offeree, it cannot in principle be revoked: under § 145 BGB; an offeror is bound by his offer unless he has excluded this engagement (see the next note).

(4) In German law, although the main rule is that an offeror is bound by his offer, the offeror may exclude the binding force of the offer under § 145 BGB. He may do this by using terms such as *freibleibend, ohne obligo* or *Zwischenverkauf vorbehalten*.[70] As has been seen in 2.1.2.A.,[71] there is some uncertainty about the legal effect of such terms. It is certain, however, that a statement containing such terms may be revoked before it is accepted.

---

[67] Zweigert and Kötz, at 364; see also *infra*, at 207.
[68] According to the terminology adopted here.
[69] RGZ 50, 191.
[70] Medicus, *SAT* at 137; Flume, *Rechtsgeschäft* at 642.
[71] See the *Aeroplane Charter* case, *supra*, at 183–4.

OFFER OPEN FOR CERTAIN PERIOD

Chalet for sale

Where it is expressly or implicitly understood that an offer is to remain open for a certain period, the offer cannot be withdrawn within that period without incurring liability.

Facts: By letter of 11 August 1954, Isler informed Chastan that he was willing to sell to the latter a chalet owned by him, at a price of 2,500,000 francs. From the judgment, it appears that Chastan had written to Isler, saying that he planned to visit the chalet on the 15 or 16 August, and that Isler apparently approved this arrangement in his letter. Having visited the chalet four days later, Chastan notified Isler by telegram the following day that he accepted that offer. On 17 August 1954 he confirmed that acceptance by letter, stating that he was willing to pay the purchase price in cash upon the signing of the transfer deed. Chastan served formal notice on Isler on 6 September 1954, requiring the latter to accept the purchase price and to hand over the keys; Isler did not comply with that notice, whereupon Chastan brought legal proceedings. In the proceedings, Isler alleged that he could not have sold the chalet to the plaintiff on 16 August 1954, since, as at that date, he had already sold it to Puy. Puy intervened in the proceedings, stating that the sale of the property to him had been concluded at the beginning of August and that it had been formally completed by a private contract in writing on 14 August 1954, that act having been accompanied by a payment on account of one million francs.

Held: Chastan succeeded in his claim.

Judgment: . . .—Whereas whilst an offer may in principle be revoked at any time prior to its acceptance, that is not the position where the person making it has expressly or impliedly undertaken not to revoke it before a certain date;
—Whereas in the present case, the contested judgment, having acknowledged that the letter of 11 August 1954 constituted "merely an offer to sell" which could "in principle be revoked at any time prior to being accepted", goes on to state: "however, Isler, knowing from a letter from Chastan dated 9 August that the latter was proposing to visit the chalet on 15 or 16 August, and having authorised him to do so in his reply of 11 August, tacitly undertook to keep his offer open during the period thus envisaged, that is to say, until after the proposed visit had taken place", and that Isler could not therefore have withdrawn from the transaction on 14 August without "incurring liability" . . .
—Whereas it follows that the contested judgment did not infringe the legislation referred to in the appellant's pleadings and is justified in law.

Notes

(1) In French law, an offer is in principle revocable. The *Cour de cassation* held in a decision of Cass. civ. 1re, 3 February 1919:[73]

As an offer is not in itself binding on the offeror, it may in general be revoked so long as it has not been validly accepted.

This point of view can be explained theoretically by the fact that French law traditionally does not attribute binding force to a unilateral act.

(2) In practice, the rigid principle of revocability is not maintained, because it would lead to insecurity and injustice. The addressee of an offer may incur costs in reliance on the offer (e.g. travelling costs to examine the offer), or turn down other offers, or change

---

[72] D. 1959.1.33
[73] D.P. 23.I.126.

his position, for example by resigning from his job or by terminating his tenancy.. French case law has therefore strongly mitigated the principle of revocability and, in practice, has reversed it. If an offer expressly contains a period within which it has to be accepted, the offeror has the obligation to keep the offer open during that period.[74] Further, as the *Chalet for Sale* case shows, if the offer does not expressly contain a period for its acceptance, it may have to be implied that the offeror tacitly promised to keep his offer open during a certain period. Whether or not an offer implicitly contains a period for acceptance is a matter of fact that has to be decided by the lower courts.[75] In the French case cited here, the fact that the owner of the chalet had agreed on the offeree visiting the chalet on a certain date led to the assumption that his offer tacitly contained a period lasting at least until that date.

(3) Some French authors address a further category: offers that do not contain any period, even implicitly. They are of the opinion that such offers have to be maintained during a reasonable period: Malaurie and Aynès[76] admit an exception to this rule in the case of an offer to the public; Ghestin[77] rejects a distinction between offers to the public and offers to one or more particular persons.[78] The length of this period is determined as a matter of fact by the lower courts and depends on the circumstances of the case.

(4) The irrevocability of an offer does not lead to the same results in French law and in German law. It seems to follow from the *Chalet for Sale* case that, in French law, the consequence of the obligation to keep the offer open during a certain period is not that a revocation of the offer lacks effect, but that the offeror is liable to pay damages for the loss the offeree has suffered from the untimely revocation. French authors are of the opinion that these damages may be awarded *in natura* in the form of the conclusion of the contract,[79] but there is no case law to this effect. Given the relative ease with which an implicit promise not to revoke the offer can be established, these damages play an important role in compensating losses arising from the revocation of an offer. In German law on the other hand, the consequence of the binding force of an offer is that its revocation has no effect: even after the revocation the offeree can still accept and thus conclude a contract. The same is true for Dutch law; and also, it would seem, under PECL, CISG and the Unidroit Principles.

(5) In French law an offer can be effectively revoked without communicating the fact of the revocation to the offeree: for example, an offer to sell goods will be effectively revoked through a sale of the goods to a third party whether or not the offeree knows of the sale. This rule is in contrast to German law and, as we will see, English law.

---

[74] See e.g. Cass. civ., 10 May 1968, Bull. civ. III.209.
[75] See also the French cases mentioned in 2.1.2.C.
[76] Malaurie and Aynès, para. 384.
[77] Ghestin at 276–8.
[78] See also Terré, Simler and Lequette, para. 109.
[79] Ghestin, at 274.

Court of Appeal
Dickinson v. *Dodds*[80]

REVOCABILITY OF OFFER

Offer left over until Friday

An offer to sell property may be revoked before acceptance without any formal notice to the person to whom the offer is made. It is sufficient if that person has actual knowledge that the person who made the offer has done some act inconsistent with the continuance of the offer, such as selling the property to a third person.

Facts: The defendant, the owner of property, signed a document which purported to be an agreement to sell the property to the plaintiff at a fixed price. But a postscript was added, which he also signed—"This offer to be left over until Friday 9 A.M.". In the afternoon of the Thursday, the plaintiff was informed by a Mr. Berry that the defendant had been offering or agreeing to sell the property to Thomas Allan. Thereupon the plaintiff, at about half-past seven in the evening, went to the house of Mrs. Burgess, the mother-in-law of the defendant, where he was then staying, and left with her a formal acceptance in writing of the offer to sell the property. According to the evidence of Mrs. Burgess this document never in fact reached the defendant, she having forgotten to give it to him.

On the following (Friday) morning, at about seven o'clock, Berry, who was acting as agent for the plaintiff, found the defendant at the Darlington railway station, and handed to him a duplicate of the acceptance by the plaintiff, and explained to the defendant its purport. He replied that it was too late, as he had sold the property. A few minutes later the plaintiff himself found the defendant entering a railway carriage, and handed him another duplicate of the notice of acceptance, but the defendant declined to receive it, saying, "You are too late. I have sold the property".

Held: The document amounted only to an offer, which might be revoked at any time before acceptance, and that a sale to a third person which came to the knowledge of the person to whom the offer was made was an effectual revocation of the offer.

JUDGMENT: JAMES LJ: The document, though beginning "I hereby agree to sell," was nothing but an offer, and was only intended to be an offer, for the Plaintiff himself tells us that he required time to consider whether he would enter into an agreement or not. Unless both parties had then agreed there was no concluded agreement then made; it was in effect and substance only an offer to sell. The Plaintiff, being minded not to complete the bargain at that time, added this memorandum— "This offer to be left over until Friday, 9 o'clock A.M., 12th June, 1874." That shews it was only an offer. There was no consideration given for the undertaking or promise, to whatever extent it may be considered binding, to keep the property unsold until 9 o'clock on Friday morning; but apparently Dickinson was of opinion, and probably Dodds was of the same opinion, that he (Dodds) was bound by that promise, and could not in any way withdraw from it, or retract it, until 9 o'clock on Friday morning, and this probably explains a good deal of what afterwards took place. But it is clear settled law, on one of the clearest principles of law, that this promise, being a mere nudum pactum, was not binding, and that at any moment before a complete acceptance by Dickinson of the offer, Dodds was as free as Dickinson himself. Well, that being the state of things, it is said that the only mode in which Dodds could assert that freedom was by actually and distinctly saying to Dickinson, "Now I withdraw my offer." It appears to me that there is neither principle nor authority for the proposition that there must be an express and actual withdrawal of the offer, or what is called a retractation. It must, to constitute a contract, appear that the two minds were at one, at the same moment of time, that is, that there was an offer continuing up to the time of the acceptance.

---

[80] (1876) 2 Ch. D463.

If there was not such a continuing offer, then the acceptance comes to nothing. Of course it may well be that the one man is bound in some way or other to let the other man know that his mind with regard to the offer has been changed; but in this case, beyond all question, the Plaintiff knew that Dodds was no longer minded to sell the property to him as plainly and clearly as if Dodds had told him in so many words, "I withdraw the offer." This is evident from the Plaintiff's own statements in the bill.

The Plaintiff says in effect that, having heard and knowing that Dodds was no longer minded to sell to him, and that he was selling or had sold to some one else, thinking that he could not in point of law withdraw his offer, meaning to fix him to it, and endeavouring to bind him," I went to the house where he was lodging, and saw his mother-in-law, and left with her an acceptance of the offer, knowing all the while that he had entirely changed his mind. I got an agent to watch for him at 7 o'clock the next morning, and I went to the train just before 9 o'clock, in order that I might catch him and give him my notice of acceptance just before 9 o'clock, and when that occurred he told my agent, and he told me, you are too late, and he then threw back the paper." It is to my mind quite clear that before there was any attempt at acceptance by the Plaintiff, he was perfectly well aware that Dodds had changed his mind, and that he had in fact agreed to sell the property to Allan. It is impossible, therefore, to say there was ever that existence of the same mind between the two parties which is essential in point of law to the making of an agreement. I am of opinion, therefore, that the Plaintiff has failed to prove that there was any binding contract between Dodds and himself.

Notes

(1) English law is completely opposite to German law with respect to the revocability of offers: offers are freely revocable. Further, unlike French case law, English case law holds that offers are revocable regardless of whether they contain a time limit for their acceptance. Theoretically this point of view is based on the English doctrine of consideration.[81] No binding obligation can arise for the offeror to keep his offer open, even if he expressly fixes a period during which his offer may be accepted, since there is no consideration from the other party for such a promise. As Best CJ said in *Routledge* v. *Grant*:[82]

Here is a proposal by the Defendant to take property on certain terms; namely that he should be let into possession in July. In that proposal he gives the plaintiff six weeks to consider; but if six weeks are given on one side to accept an offer, the other has six weeks to put an end to it.

Compare also the case of *Byrne* v. *Van Tienhoven*.[83]

(2) It should be noted that an offer can be made irrevocable by an agreement between offeror and offeree in English law; the agreement will normally be made by deed to overcome the problem of consideration. In this case the offeree may accept the offer despite any purported revocation by the offeror: *Mountford* v. *Scott*.[84] However such "option agreements" are rare outside sales of land. US law goes further. UCC § 2–205 provides that if written offers relating to commercial sale contracts are stated to be binding, they may not be withdrawn during the prescribed period or, if no period is prescribed, for a reasonable period not exceeding three months.

(3) The more general question of when the offer becomes effective may also arise in English law, for example, where there is an issue whether the period of time for acceptance

---

[81] On which see Chapter 1.
[82] (1828) 4 Bing 653.
[83] (1880) 5 CPD 344.
[84] [1975] Ch. 258.

of an offer has expired—so that the offer has lapsed.[85] In English law, the two options are (a) the moment that the offer was dispatched and (b) the moment it was received by the offeree.[86] The answer is probably the same as that under German law: the moment the offer reaches the offeree. The CISG and the Unidroit principles distinguish between the moment the offer becomes effective[87] and the moment at which a period for acceptance begins to run.[88] In French law these questions do not seem to be of much practical importance.

(4) Like German law, and in contrast to French law, English law is to the effect that an offer can be revoked only through communication of the revocation to the offeree.[89]

Court of Appeal **2.E.19.**
Daulia v. *Four Millbank Nominees*[90]

REVOCABILITY OF UNILATERAL CONTRACT

Written contract, oral contract

A unilateral contract cannot be revoked once the offeree has begun performance of the unilateral condition.

Facts: The defendants were mortgagees of a portfolio of properties which, the mortgagor being in default, they were entitled to sell. The plaintiffs were anxious to purchase the properties and made several unsuccessful offers. However, on 21 December 1976, the parties agreed terms and further agreed to exchange contracts the next day. When the plaintiffs attended the defendant's offices on 22 December to exchange contracts the defendants, who had in the meantime found another purchaser at a substantially increased price, refused to complete the sale. The plaintiffs brought an action against the defendants claiming damages for breach of contract. The plaintiffs alleged that on 21 December an agent of the defendants' had promised the plaintiffs that if the plaintiffs procured a banker's draft for the deposit, attended at the defendants' offices at 10 o'clock the next morning and there tendered to the defendants the plaintiff's part of the contract engrossed and signed together with the banker's draft, the defendants would enter into a contract ("the written contract") with the plaintiffs for the sale of the properties. The plaintiffs further alleged that the agent's promise and the plaintiffs' performance of the conditions stipulated constituted a contract ("the oral contract") and that by refusing to accept the plaintiffs' tender of the engrossed and signed contract and banker's draft the defendants were in breach of the oral contract.

Held: The plaintiff's claim succeeded.

Judgment: GOFF LJ: The concept of a unilateral or "if" contract is somewhat anomalous, because it is clear that, at all events until the offeree starts to perform the condition, there is no contract at all, but merely an offer which the offeror is free to revoke. Doubts have been expressed whether the offeror becomes bound so soon as the offeree starts to perform or satisfy the condition, or only when he has fully done so. In my judgment, however, we are not concerned in this case with any such problem, because in my view the plaintiffs had fully performed or satisfied the condition when they presented themselves at the time and place appointed with a banker's draft for the deposit and their part of the written contract for sale duly engrossed and signed, and then retendered the same, which I understand to mean proffered it for exchange. . . .

---

[85] Treitel, *Contract*, at 16; see further 2.1.2.D, *infra*, at 206.
[86] See the similar problem, but of more practical importance, as to the moment at which the acceptance becomes effective, 2.1.3.B, *infra*, at 218.
[87] See Articles 15 and 2.3 respectively, *infra*, at 195.
[88] Articles 20 and 2.8 para. 1 respectively, cited in 2.1.2.D., *infra*, at 207.
[89] See *Byrne* v. *Van Tienhoven*, *infra*, at 222–3.
[90] [1978] 2 All ER 557.

Whilst I think the true view of a unilateral contract must in general be that the offeror is entitled to require full performance of the condition which he has imposed and short of that he is not bound, that must be subject to one important qualification, which stems from the fact that there must be an implied obligation on the part of the offeror not to prevent the condition becoming satisfied, which obligation it seems to me must arise as soon as the offeree starts to perform. Until then the offeror can revoke the whole thing, but once the offeree has embarked on performance it is too late for the offeror to revoke his offer.

Buckley LJ: . . . I agree with Goff LJ that the defendants could not withdraw their offer once the plaintiffs had embarked on those acts.

In my opinion, the re-amended statement of claim is capable of supporting a conclusion that a contract was made on 22nd December 1976 under which the defendants became bound to enter into a written agreement of sale of the properties to the plaintiffs on the terms which, as alleged in para 7 of the re-amended statement of claim, had been finally agreed on the previous day.

Notes

(1) The principle of free revocability in English law may cause particular hardship to an offeree who has partly performed the act required under a unilateral contract.[91] In such cases English courts have decided that the offeror can no longer revoke once the offeree has started to perform. *Daulia* v. *Four Millbank Nominees* is an example of this rule, as is *Errington* v. *Errington*.[92] In *Errington* v. *Errington* a father had bought a house for his son and daughter-in-law, paying part of the price (£250) in cash and borrowing the rest (£500) from a building society on the security of the house, the loan being repayable with interest by instalments over a period. The father told the daughter-in-law that the £250 was a present to her and her husband, handed the building society book to her, and said that if and when she and her husband had paid all the instalments the house would be their property. The daughter-in-law paid the instalments as they fell due. Then the father died and his widow claimed the house. It was held that the father's promise was a unilateral contract a promise of the house in return for their act of paying the instalments which could not be revoked by him once the couple entered on performance of the act, but which would cease to bind him if they left it incomplete and unperformed. Lord Denning said that the father expressly promised the couple that the property should belong to them as soon as the mortgage was paid, and impliedly promised that, so long as they paid the instalments to the building society, they should be allowed to remain in possession. Thus, the obligation not to revoke was regarded as stemming from an implied promise not to revoke.

(2) In American law the principle of free revocability used to prevail as in English law.[93] American law, as English law, also allows an exception to the main rule in the case of unilateral contracts:

---

[91] See for the notion of a unilateral contract 2.1.2.A., note under *Carlill* v. *Carbolic Smoke Ball Co, supra*, at 188.
[92] [1952] 1 All ER 149.
[93] 64 F 2d 344, 346 (2d Cir. 1933). See *James Baird Co.* v. *Gimbel Bros. Inc*; see also the Restatement of Contracts § 35.

§ 45: If an offer for a unilateral contract is made, and part of the consideration requested in the offer is given or tendered by the offeree in response thereto, the offeror is bound by a contract, the duty of immediate performance of which is conditional on the full consideration being given or tendered within the time stated in the offer, or, if no time stated therein, within a reasonable time.

However, the harsh effects of the rule of free revocability in American law appear to have been mitigated, even in relation to bilateral contracts. In *Drennan* v. *Star Paving Co*,[94] a general contractor, who was preparing to compete for the award of a construction contract, solicited bids from various subcontractors for the paving work to be done on the project. A subcontractor submitted the lowest bid and the general contractor relied upon it in computing his own bid for the entire project. After the contract had been awarded to the general contractor, the subcontractor revoked his bid, claiming error in computation. The court held that the offeree's reasonably foreseeable change of position in reliance upon an offer for a bilateral contract provides a basis for implying a subsidiary promise by the offeror not to revoke the offer. Of this case, it has been written:[95]

2.US.21.

Williston concludes that an offer is also a promise, albeit a conditional one, and that therefore the doctrine of promissory estoppel is applicable, presumably to make the offer irrevocable until the offeree has had a reasonable opportunity to accept it. On the other hand, in *James Baird Co.* v. *Gimble Bros., Inc.*, a case not factually dissimilar to the instant one, it was held that promissory estoppel is not applicable to an offer for a bilateral contract. Although the court stated that "an offer . . . is not meant to become a promise until a consideration has been received," it would seem that a better statement of the rationale for holding the doctrine of promissory estoppel inapplicable to offers is that an offer, being a promise conditional upon acceptance, is not reasonably relied upon until that condition has occurred.

Even if the doctrine of promissory estoppel is held not applicable to the offer itself, an offer can be irrevocable because of an enforceable express or implied subsidiary promise not to revoke. As to offers for unilateral contracts, which offers may not be capable of being accepted by the offeree without substantial preparation, Section 45 of the *Restatement of Contracts* states in effect that upon partial performance by the offeree, the offer becomes irrevocable during the time stated in the offer or, if no time is stated therein, for a reasonable time. Although comment *b* to this section suggests that the offer is irrevocable because of a subsidiary promise not to revoke for which the consideration is the offeree's partial performance, the comment's reference to section 90 raises the possibility that the promise not to revoke may be a gratuitous promise which becomes enforceable by virtue of the doctrine of promissory estoppel.

The court in the instant case, analysing from the *Restatement* rule relating to offers for unilateral contracts, stated that the offeree's reasonably foreseeable change of position in reliance upon an offer for a bilateral provides a basis for implying a subsidiary promise by the offeror not to revoke the offer. While noting that detrimental reliance upon an offer for a bilateral contract differs

---

[94] 51 Cal. 2d 409, 333 P. 2d 757 (1958); 59 Colum.L.Rev. 355 (1959), 279.
[95] "Subcontractor's offer for bilateral contract held irrevocable because of contractor's foreseeable reliance", 59 Columbia Law Review 355.

from reliance upon an offer for a unilateral contract in that the latter reliance usually manifests itself in part performance which serves as consideration for the implied promise not to revoke, the court stated that the reference made to section 90 in section 45 of the *Restatement* indicated that a promise not to revoke could be considered gratuitous and enforceable by virtue of the doctrine of promissory estoppel. Since in the instant case the contractor could reasonably have been expected to rely upon the offer of the subcontractor and did so rely, as corroborated by the fact that he included the name of the subcontractor in the submission of his bid for the main contract, the court held the subcontractor bound by an implied promise to give the contractor a reasonable opportunity to accept the offer.

This development in American case law has been laid down in § 87 paragraph 2 of the Restatement 2nd, providing that an offer is to be regarded as irrevocable if, as the offeror should reasonably have expected, it induces action or forbearance of a substantial character on the part of the offeree. In such a case the offer is to be regarded as binding only "to the extent necessary to avoid injustice". Like French law, American law therefore uses the idea of an implicit promise not to revoke as the basis for liability, but imposes liability on the basis of an estoppel rather than a tort.

On this issue, the approach of PECL,[96] CISG[97] and the Unidroit Principles[98] strongly resemble the solution adopted in the French and American case-law: revocability is the main rule, but the exceptions seem to be more important than the rule itself—although, as noted, the practical results under French law and the various Principles are different.[99]

In summary, the German system—irrevocability as a main rule—and the English system—revocability as a main rule—hold opposite views on the revocability issue. The French system is in its practical outcome very near to the German system. In the PECL, CISG and in the Unidroit principles, both views have been established: revocability as the main rule and irrevocability as the exception that, in practice, plays a more important part than the main rule itself.

The following excerpt from Zweigert and Kötz contains a strong argument for the binding force of an offer.[100]

2.G.22.

The critic is forced to conclude that on this point the German system is best. It is true that in practice the differences between the German system and the Common Law are slighter than might at first glance appear. . . . Even so, the German system is superior. Experience shows that its results are practical and equitable; the offeree can act with assurance in the knowledge that his acceptance will bring about a contract. It also makes sense to put the risk of any changes in supplies and prices on the offeror: it is he who takes the initiative, it is he who invokes the offeree's reliance, and so it must be for him to exclude or limit the binding nature of his offer, failing which it is only fair to hold him bound.

[96] See Article 2:202 (3), *supra*, at 195.
[97] See Article 16, *supra*, at 195, n. 64.
[98] See Article 2.4, *supra*, at 195.
[99] See also Article 6:219 para. 1 of the Dutch Civil Code: "An offer may be revoked, unless it includes a term for acceptance, or irrevocability results otherwise from the offer", Article 1328 (first sentence) and Article 1329 (first sentence) of the Italian CCi: "The offer may be revoked as long as the contract has not been concluded".
[100] Zweigert and Kötz, 2nd edn. (1987), at 388–9. (This passage is not in the 3rd edn—Ed.).

However, the following extract, which summarizes the results of an empirical survey of construction contractors operating under English law, might be thought to support the common law position. The scenario being discussed is that of the subcontractor ("sub") who offers a tender for a subcontract and later withdraws it, but not before the general contractor—the "general"—has entered into a binding contract with the employer on the basis of the tender—the very scenario which occurred in *Drennan* v. *Star Paving Co.*

2.US.23.

. . . The infrequency of the problem of withdrawal undoubtedly influences attitudes towards the introduction of legal sanctions to control it. But it may be that the informal control methods that already exist make legal regulation unnecessary. At least it is important to observe that the potential which exists for making use of the legal system has not been exploited. Generals have either not devised standard tender forms or allow subs to ignore them. They do not use option contracts or bid bonds and they do not close a deal as soon as possible so as to create a contract and threaten legal sanction to prevent withdrawal. Resort to a court to determine rights and liabilities was not mentioned as a possible remedy. Instead the sanctions discussed were informal: re-negotiation and applying economic pressure; arbitration by a third party such as a quantity surveyor or architect; and as an ultimate deterrent, the severing of trade relations between the respective firms . . . [The] legal solutions were rejected either as impractical, easily avoided and difficult to enforce, or as unfair and too inflexible in not making allowance for the several excuses which contractors recognised as good reasons for non-performance . . .[101]

If the reality is as this extract suggests, there would appear to be a strong argument in favour of the American solution: in general, offers are not binding, but the courts have the power (through the doctrine of estoppel) to correct an injustice in the particular case. On the other hand, as we saw in the last section, it seems that the doctrine of estoppel would not necessarily extend to provide a remedy in this scenario under English law, for it can be invoked as a defence to a claim but not as a cause of action. The doctrine of estoppel is therefore an important area in which the different common law jurisdictions have thus far reached different conclusions.

As for when a revocation of an offer becomes effective, see 2.1.3.C.

2.1.2.D. LAPSE OF OFFER

Principles of European Contract Law   **2.PECL.24.**

Article 2:206: *Time Limit for Acceptance*
> (1) In order to be effective, acceptance of an offer must reach the offeror within the time fixed by it.
> (2) If no time has been fixed by the offeror acceptance must reach it within a reasonable time.
> (3) In the case of an acceptance by an act of performance under Article 2:205(3), that act must be performed within the time for acceptance fixed by the offeror or, if no such time is fixed, within a reasonable time.

[101] See Lewis, "Contracts between Businessmen: Reform of the Law of Firm Offers" (1982) 9, Brit J. Law Soc., 153.

Article 2:207: *Late Acceptance*
(1) A late acceptance is nonetheless effective as an acceptance if without delay the offeror informs the offeree that he treats it as such.
(2) If a letter or other writing containing a late acceptance shows that it has been sent in such circumstances that if its transmission had been normal it would have reached the offeror in due time, the late acceptance is effective as an acceptance unless, without delay, the offeror informs the offeree that it considers its offer as having lapsed.

Unidroit Principles **2.INT.25.**

Article 2.5: (*Rejection of offer*)
An offer is terminated when a rejection reaches the offeror.

Article 2.7: (*Time of acceptance*)
An offer must be accepted within the time the offeror has fixed or, if no time is fixed, within a reasonable time having regard to the circumstances, including the rapidity of the means of communication employed by the offeror. An oral offer must be accepted immediately unless the circumstances indicate otherwise.

Article 2.8: (*Acceptance within a fixed period of time*)
(1) A period of time for acceptance fixed by the offeror in a telegram or a letter begins to run from the moment the telegram is handed in for dispatch or from the date shown on the letter or, if no such date is shown, from the date shown on the envelope. A period of time for acceptance fixed by the offeror by means of instantaneous communication begins to run from the moment that the offer reaches the offeree.
(2) . . .

CISG **2.INT.26.**

Article 18: 2. . . . An acceptance is not effective if the indication of assent does not reach the offeror within the time he has fixed or, if no time is fixed, within a reasonable time, due account being taken of the circumstances of the transaction, including the rapidity of the means of communication employed by the offeror. An oral offer must be accepted immediately unless the circumstances indicate otherwise.

Article 17: An offer, even if it is irrevocable, is terminated when a rejection reaches the offeror.

Article 21: *identical to Article 2.7 Unidroit Principles*

Cass. civ. 3e, 10 May 1972[103]   **2.F.27.**

Lopez/Le Baste

Where an offer is not accepted within ten months and within that time the offeree has communicated with the offeror in terms inconsistent with an intention to accept the offer, the offer will not be capable of acceptance.

Facts: Lopez had purchased from the "Le Baste" property company an apartment forming part of a block of flats constructed by that company. On 17 May 1967 Lopez made an offer to the manager of the company, to the effect that he was willing "to surrender his rights in consideration of the sum of 3,725 francs". The company accepted that offer on 16 March 1968. In a letter dated 17 August 1968, Lopez stated that he was revoking his offer to surrender his rights.

Held: The offer was not capable of acceptance in March 1968.

Judgment:—Whereas the court hearing the case at second instance, which has unfettered discretion in assessing whether an offer is implicitly made on the basis that it is to be accepted within a reasonable period, states: "given the rapidity with which the parties habitually replied to each other's correspondence . . . Lopez could not reasonably have foreseen that the manager of the property company would delay for ten months before responding to the letter containing his most recent demands, notwithstanding that he had stated that he looked forward to receiving a prompt reply . . . as regards the negotiations concerning the repurchase of Lopez' rights, it would have been understandable for Le Baste to have asked for an extended period to think the matter over if Lopez' demands concerning the repurchase price had differed substantially from the proposals which had been made to him".

—Whereas in actual fact, Lopez had only demanded an additional sum of forty thousand old francs; as Moreover, having received no response within a reasonable period to his two letters, Lopez was legitimately entitled to infer, upon receiving from the property company in December 1967 a communication, signed by the manager, inviting him to attend the general meeting of the company with a view to the regularisation of the allotment of the participating shares, that the counter-proposal made by him on 17 May 1967 had simply been rejected and that the invitation addressed to him constituted an unequivocal confirmation of that rejection"; lastly, on a date subsequent to 16 March 1968, Le Baste offered Lopez, by letter and by communication served by a process-server, a "type F 5" apartment;

—Whereas the cour d'appel considered therefore, without distorting the meaning of the documents submitted to it, that the acceptance dated 16 March 1968 "appeared nugatory and worthless"; . . .

Chancery Division   **2.E.28.**
Manchester Diocesan Council v. Commercial Investment[104]

The Council for Education

Where an offer is made in terms which fix no time limit for acceptance, the offer must be accepted within a reasonable time. "Reasonableness" should be assessed in the light of both the circumstances existing at the time of the offer and the circumstances arising thereafter.

[103] Bull. civ. III.297.
[104] [1969] 3 All ER 1593.

Facts: A freehold property was vested in the plaintiff, a diocesan council for education. Part of the property was vested in the plaintiff under a scheme whereby the property could be sold subject "to the approval of the purchase price" by the Secretary of State for Education and Science. In February 1963 the plaintiff's surveyor and the defendant company's surveyor started negotiations for the sale of the property by the plaintiff to the defendant company. Late in 1963 the plaintiff decided to sell the property by tender. Particulars and conditions of sale were prepared and these incorporated a form of tender. The conditions required, *inter alia*, that tenders be sent to the plaintiff's surveyor by 27 August 1964 and stipulated that the sale was subject to the approval of the purchase price by the Secretary of State. Clause 4 provided: "The person whose tender is accepted shall be the purchaser and shall be informed of the acceptance of his tender by letter sent to him by post addressed to the address given in the tender . . .". On 25 August 1964 the defendant company completed the form of tender and stated thereon: "and we agree that in the event of this offer being accepted in accordance with the above conditions . . . we will pay the said purchase price and carry out and complete the purchase in accordance with the said conditions . . .". This was sent on the following day to the plaintiff's surveyor. On 1 September the plaintiff's surveyor informed the defendant company's surveyor that he would recommend acceptance of the defendant company's offer and that he would write again as soon as he had formal instructions. On 14 September the defendant company's surveyor replied to the effect that he looked forward to receiving formal acceptance of the offer and he named the solicitors acting for the defendant company. This letter was acknowledged by the plaintiff's solicitor on 15 September when he also stated that the "sale has now been approved" by the plaintiff and that instructions had been given to obtain the approval of the Secretary of State. The approval of the Secretary of State was obtained on 18 November. On 23 December the plaintiff's solicitors wrote to the defendant company's solicitors and, after reciting that the offer by tender had been accepted by the plaintiff subject to the consent of the Secretary of State, added that the consent had been forthcoming and they concluded therefore that the contract was binding on both parties. The defendant company's solicitors replied that they did not agree that there was any subsisting binding contract. On 7 January 1965 the plaintiff's solicitors wrote to the defendant company at the address given by it in the form of tender giving formal notification of acceptance of its offer.

Held: The plaintiff succeeded in its claim that a valid contract had been formed.

Judgment: BUCKLEY J: . . . If I am right in thinking that there was a contract on 15th September 1964 that disposes of the case but, in the case I should be held to be wrong in that view, I will now consider the other point in the case and will for this purpose assume that no contract was made at that date. On this basis no contract can have been concluded before 7th January 1965. The defendant company contend that, as the tender stipulated no time within which it must be accepted, it was an implied term of the offer that it must be accepted, if at all, within reasonable time. It is said that acceptance on 7th January was not within a reasonable time.

It has long been recognised as being the law that, where an offer is made in terms which fix no time limit for acceptance, the offer must be accepted within a reasonable time to make a contract. . . . There seems, however, to be no reported case in which the reason for this is explained.

There appear to me to be two possible views on methods of approaching the problem. First, it may be said that by implication the offer is made on terms that, if it is not accepted within a reasonable time, it must be treated as withdrawn. Alternatively, it may be said that, if the offeree does not accept the offer within a reasonable time, he must be treated as having refused it. On either view the offer would cease to be a live one on the expiration of what in the circumstances of the particular case should be regarded as a reasonable time for acceptance. The first of these alternatives involves implying a term that if the offer is not accepted within a reasonable time, it shall be treated as withdrawn or lapsing at the end of that period if it has not then been accepted; the second is based on an inference to be drawn from the conduct of the offeree, that is, that having failed to accept the offer within a reasonable time he has manifested an intention to refuse it. If, in the first alternative, the time which the offeror is to be treated as having set for acceptance is to be such a time as is reasonable at the date of the offer, what is reasonable must depend on circumstances then existing and reasonably likely to arise during the continuance of the offer; but it would be not unlikely that the offeror and offeree would make different assessments of what would be reasonable even if, as might quite possibly not be the case, they based those judgments on identical known and anticipated circumstances. No doubt a court could resolve any dispute about this, but this approach clearly involves a certain degree of uncertainty about the precise terms of the offer. If on the other hand the time which the offeror is to be treated as having set for acceptance is to be such a time as turns out to be reasonable in the light of circumstances then existing and of circumstances arising thereafter during the continuance of the offer, whether foreseeable or not, an additional element of uncertainty is introduced. The second alternative on the other hand involves simply an objective assessment of facts and the determination of the question whether on the facts the offeree should in fairness to both parties be regarded as having refused the offer.

It does not seem to me that either party is in greater need of protection by the law in this respect than the other. Until his offer has been accepted it is open to the offeror at any time to withdraw it or to put a limit on the time for acceptance. On the other hand, the offeree can at any time refuse the offer or, unless he has been guilty of unreasonable delay, accept it. Neither party is at a disadvantage. Unless authority constrains me to do otherwise, I am strongly disposed to prefer the second alternative to the first . . .

I have dealt with this part of the case at some length because, if the first alternative were the correct view of the law and if what is reasonable had to be ascertained as at the time of the offer, the subsequent conduct of the parties would be irrelevant to the question how long the offer should be treated as remaining open. In my opinion, however, the subsequent conduct of the parties is relevant to the question, which I think is the right test, whether the offeree should be held to have refused the offer by his conduct.

In my judgment the letter of 15th September 1964 excludes the possibility of imputing to the plaintiff a refusal of the offer. If that letter does not itself constitute an effective acceptance, it clearly discloses an intention to accept from which there is nothing to suggest a departure before 7th January 1965. Accordingly, if no contract was formed earlier, I am of opinion that it was open to the plaintiff to accept it on 7th January and that the plaintiff's letter of that date was effectual to bind the defendant company contractually.

BGB[105]   **2.G.29.**

§ 146: An offer ceases to be binding if it is declined by the offeror, or if it is not accepted in due time according to §§ 147 to 149.

§ 147: An offer made to a person who is present may only be accepted there and then. This applies also to an offer made by one person to another on the telephone. An offer made to a person who is not present may be accepted only within the time the offeror may expect to receive an answer under ordinary circumstances.

§ 148: If the offeror has fixed a period of time for acceptance of the offer, the acceptance may take place only within that period.

Notes

(1) An offer will lapse if it is rejected by the offeree, even during the period fixed for acceptance.[106] In the *Lopez/La Baste* case, the Cour d'appel had not only decided that a reasonable period for the acceptance had expired before the offer was accepted, but also that a rejection of the offer had taken place before the acceptance. This could in itself have been a sufficient ground for its decision. Similarly, for English law, see the reasoning

---

[105] Translated by Von Mehren & Gordley, op. cit. *supra* note 55, at 193.
[106] See Malaurie and Aynès, para. 386.

of Buckley J in the *Manchester Diocesan Council* case;[107] the case of *Hyde* v. *Wrench*[108] illustrates that a counter offer will be treated as a rejection for this purpose. For German law, see § 146 BGB.

(2) The questions whether and when an offer lapses if it has been neither accepted nor revoked are dealt with by the French courts analogously to the question of the revocability of an offer. If the offer expressly contains a period for acceptance, the offer lapses when that period has expired without an acceptance taking place. An acceptance after the expiration of the period has no effect. If the offer does not expressly state a time for its acceptance, a reasonable time is implied either from the tacit will of the offeror or from other circumstances of the case.[109] Whether an offer implicitly contains a period for its acceptance and how long this period is is decided by the lower courts under a marginal supervision of the Cour de cassation.[110]

(3) This is a point on which the different jurisdictions studied have reached the same results. In English law, an offer that contains a time limit for its acceptance lapses if it has not been accepted within that time,[111] and an offer that does not fix a time limit for its acceptance lapses if it has not been accepted within a reasonable period.[112] What is a reasonable period depends on the circumstances of the case, and the *Manchester Diocesan Council* case held that this should take into account not only the circumstances at the time the offer is made, but also what happened after the offer was made. This is because one crucial factor is whether the offeree has rejected the offer, and this can only take place after the offer has been made. In the present case, because of his conduct in the period between the making of the offer and the final acceptance (the writing of several letters indicating his willingness to accept), the offeree could not be regarded as having silently rejected the offer.

(4) German law on this point is governed by § 146, § 147 sentence 2 and § 148 BGB. § 149 BGB deals with the situation where the acceptance has been dispatched in time and normally would have reached the offeror in time, but as the result of a delay has reached the offeror after the period for acceptance has expired. In such a situation the offeror must give notice of the delay to the acceptor, who would otherwise rely on his acceptance being in time. If the offeror fails to give such notice, the late acceptance will be regarded as timely.

(5) The opportunity to put a time limit on the validity of an offer is important in German law, where an offer is irrevocable until it lapses. In French law, although the offeror may limit the period of validity of his offer by fixing a time for acceptance and thus protect himself against unreasonably late acceptances, this period for acceptance will serve at the same time as a "no revocation period".[113] In view of the broad freedom to revoke in English law, there seems to be less need than in other systems for the protection of the offeror against unreasonably late acceptances, and the *Manchester Diocesan Council* case shows that an acceptance is not easily considered to be late.

---

[107] See also Treitel, *Contract*, at 41–2 and McKendrick, *Contract*, at 44.

[108] Cit. in 2.1.3.C. *infra* at 227.

[109] See Malaurie and Aynès, para. 386; Terré, Simler and Lequette, para. 189.

[110] Decisions equivalent to the present one are Cass. civ. 3ᵉ, 20 May 1992, Bull. civ. II.164; Cass. civ., 8 February 1968, Bull. civ. III.52; Cass. civ., 21 October 1975, Bull. civ. III.302; Cass. com., 6 February 1973, Bull. civ. IV.65.

[111] Treitel, *Contract*, at 41; McKendrick, *Contract*, at 52–3.

[112] Treitel, *Contract*, at 41; *Cheshire & Fifoot* at 62.

[113] As has been seen in 2.1.2.C, *supra*, at 199.

(6) As a result of the traditional view that the offer cannot exist without the will of the offeror, the French courts used to decide that an offer also lapses if the offeror dies. However, it seems that the Cour de cassation has recently begun to have doubts about this point of view. In 1983 it gave a decision to the opposite effect in the case of the death of the offeror:[114] However, in 1989, the Cour de cassation returned to the former point of view and decided that an offer for a sale had lapsed as a consequence of the death of the offeror. The consequences of the death of the offeror are unclear in English law as well. In *Dickinson* v. *Dodds*,[115] discussed above, Lord Mellish stated that it is admitted law that, if a man who makes an offer dies, the offer cannot be accepted after he is dead. However, a continuing guarantee of a bank overdraft is not terminated merely by the death of the guarantor—*Bradbury* v. *Morgan*.[116]

(7) There is no French case-law on the consequences of the offeror losing his legal capacity before the acceptance. Most authors hold the view that the offer lapses when the offeror loses his legal capacity before acceptance.[117] In English law, the supervening incapacity of the offeror also leads to the lapse of the offer.[118] In German law the opposite view is adopted as the main rule:

BGB   **2.G.30.**

§ 153: The conclusion of a contract is not prevented by the death or incapacity, prior to acceptance, of the offeror, unless the intention of the offeror appears to have been otherwise.[119]

The same is stated in Article 6:222 of the Dutch Civil Code.

(8) At an auction sale, the offer made by each bidder lapses as soon as a higher bid is made, so that the auctioneer can no longer accept the next highest bid if a higher bid is made and revoked.[120]

2.1.3. ACCEPTANCE

In relation to the doctrine of acceptance, there is again a central requirement that a communication be intended to operate as an acceptance. However, in this section, we focus on three issues: the forms in which an acceptance may be made, whether that acceptance must be communicated to the offeror in order to take effect, and whether the terms of the acceptance must mirror those of the offer exactly.

[114] Cass. civ. 3e, 9 November 1983, Bull. civ. III.222, 168; JCP 1984, IV.24; D. 1984, IR.174.
[115] [1876] 2 Ch. D 463.
[116] (1862) 1 H. & C. 249.
[117] Ghestin, at 281–2.
[118] Treitel, *Contract*, at 43.
[119] Trans. Von Mehren & Gordley, op. cit, *supra*, note 55, at 193.
[120] See Treitel, *Contract*, at 11; see also § 156 BGB, *supra*, at 193.

2.1.3.A. FORM OF ACCEPTANCE

An acceptance need not take any particular form of words. Indeed, an acceptance may be by conduct alone,[121] and exceptionally, silence. It is with these last two situations with which we are concerned in this subsection.

Principles of European Contract Law   **2.PECL.31.**

Article 2:204: *Acceptance*
    (1) Any form of statement or conduct by the offeree is an acceptance if it indicates assent to the offer.
    (2) Silence or inactivity does not in itself amount to acceptance.

Unidroit Principles   **2.INT.32.**

Article 2.6: (*Mode of acceptance*)
    (1) A statement made by or other conduct of the offeree indicating assent to an offer is an acceptance. Silence or inactivity does not in itself amount to acceptance.
    . . .
    (3) However, if, by virtue of the offer or as a result of practices which the parties have established between themselves or of usage, the offeree may indicate assent by performing an act without notice to the offeror, the acceptance is effective when the act is performed.

CISG   **2.INT.33.**

Article 18: 3. However, if, by virtue of the offer or as a result of practices which the parties have established between themselves or of usage, the offeree may indicate assent by performing an act, such as one relating to the dispatch of the goods or payment of the price, without notice to the offeror, the acceptance is effective at the moment the act is performed, provided that the act is performed within the period of time laid down in the preceding paragraph.[122]

House of Lords[123]   **2.E.34.**
Brogden v. *Directors of The Metropolitan Railway Company*

ACCEPTANCE BY CONDUCT

Supply of coal

The conduct of two parties may establish a binding contract between them, although the agreement has not been formally executed by either.

Facts: B. had for some years supplied the M. Railway Company with coals. It was eventually suggested by B. that a contract should be entered into between them. After their agents had met together the terms of

---

[121] See Treitel, *Contract*, at 17, McKendrick, *Contract*, at 42, Larenz, *AT* at 530 ff.; Medicus, *SAT* at 141–3.
[122] Article 18. 1 is identical to Article 2.6.1 Unidroit.
[123] 2 App.Cas. 666.

213

agreement were drawn up by the agent of the M. Company and sent to B. B. filled up certain parts of it which had been left in blank, and introduced the name of the gentleman who was to act as arbitrator in case of differences between the parties, wrote "approved" at the end of the paper, and signed his own name. B.'s agent sent back the paper to the agent of the M. Company, who put it in his desk, and nothing farther was done in the way of a formal execution of it. Both parties for some time acted in accordance with the arrangements mentioned in the paper, coals were supplied and payments made as therein stated, and when some complaints of inexactness in the supply of coals, according to the terms stated in the paper, were made by the M.Company, there were explanations and excuses given by B., and the "contract" was mentioned in the correspondence, and matters went on as before. Finally disagreements arose, and B. denied that there was any contract which bound him in the matter.

Held: These facts, and the actual conduct of the parties, established the existence of such a contract, and there having been a clear breach of it B. must be held liable upon it.

Judgment: LORD BLACKBURN: I have always believed the law to be this, that when an offer is made to another party, and in that offer there is a request express or implied that he must signify his acceptance by doing some particular thing, then as soon as he does that thing, he is bound. If a man sent an offer abroad saying: I wish to know whether you will supply me with goods at such and such a price, and, if you agree to that, you must ship the first cargo as soon as you get this letter, there can be no doubt that as soon as the cargo was shipped the contract would be complete, and if the cargo went to the bottom of the sea, it would go to the bottom of the sea at the risk of the orderer. So again, where, as in the case of *Ex parte Harris*, a person writes a letter and says, I offer to take an allotment of shares, and he expressly or impliedly says, If you agree with me send an answer by the post, there, as soon as he has sent that answer by the post, and put it out of his control, and done an extraneous act which clenches the matter, and shews beyond all doubt that each side is bound, I agree the contract is perfectly plain and clear.

But when you come to the general proposition which Mr Justice Brett seems to have laid down, that a simple acceptance in your own mind, without any intimation to the other party, and expressed by a mere private act, such as putting a letter into a drawer, completes a contract, I must say I differ from that. It appears from the Year Books that as long ago as the time of Edward IV, Chief Justice Brian decided this very point . . . I take it, my Lords, that that, which was said 300 years ago and more, is the law to this day, and it is quite what Lord Justice Mellish in *Ex parte Harris* accurately says, that where it is expressly or impliedly stated in the offer that you may accept the offer by posting a letter, the moment you post the letter the offer is accepted. You are bound from the moment you post the letter, not, as it is put here, from the moment you make up your mind on the subject.

But my Lords, while, as I say, this is so upon the question of law, it is still necessary to consider this case farther upon the question of fact. I agree, and I think every Judge who has considered the case does agree, certainly Lord Chief Justice Cockburn does, that though the parties may have gone no farther than an offer on the one side, saying, Here is the draft,—(for that I think is really what this case comes to,)—and the draft so offered by the one side is approved by the other, everything being agreed to except the name of the arbitrator, which the one side has filled in and the other has not yet assented to, if both parties have acted upon that draft and treated it as binding, they will be bound by it. When they had come so near as I have said, still it remained to execute formal agreements, and the parties evidently contemplated that they were to exchange agreements, so that each side should be perfectly safe and secure, knowing that the other side was bound. But, although that was what each party contemplated, still I agree (I think the Lord Chief Justice Cockburn states it clearly enough), "that if a draft having been prepared and agreed upon as the basis of a deed or contract to be executed between two parties, the parties, without waiting for the execution of the more formal instrument, proceed to act upon the draft, and treat it as binding upon them, both parties will be bound by it. But it must be clear that the parties have both waived the execution of the formal instrument and have agreed expressly, or as shewn by their conduct, to act on the informal one." I think that is quite right, and I agree with the way in which Mr Herschell in his argument stated it, very truly and fairly. If the parties have by their conduct said, that they act upon the draft which has been approved of by Mr Brogden, and which if not quite approved of by the railway company, has been exceedingly near it, if they indicate by their conduct that they accept it, the contract is binding.

Notes

(1) The speech of Lord Blackburn indicates that in English law there is a general requirement that an acceptance must be communicated to the offeror before it is effective.[124]

(2) The case is also clear authority that acceptance may take place by conduct, and in such cases, conduct that amounts to an acceptance will often consist in acts of performance (at least where these are known to the other party or show that the offeree is irrevocably committed to the contract). In relation to unilateral contracts, acceptance will always be by performance.

(3) An offer may state that it can only be accepted in a certain way. Whether such a prescription of the mode of acceptance is binding and prevents a contract from being completed by an acceptance in any other form is a question of construction of the offer in the light of the circumstances of the case. In *Manchester Diocesan Council* v. *Commercial Investment* (cited in **2.1.2.D.**) a tender for the purchase of property contained the condition that the company making the tender had to be informed of an acceptance of its tender by letter sent to it by post addressed to the address given in the tender, which was the address of the company. The owner of the property sent a letter of acceptance to the company's surveyor. Buckley J said:

It may be that an offeror, who by the terms of his offer insists on acceptance in a particular manner, is entitled to insist that he is not bound unless acceptance is affected or communicated in that precise way, although it seems probable that, even so, if the other party communicates his acceptance in some other way, the offeror may by conduct or otherwise waive his right to insist on the prescribed method of acceptance. Where, however, the offeror has prescribed a particular method of acceptance, but not in terms insisting that only acceptance in that mode shall be binding, I am of opinion that acceptance communicated to the offeror by any other mode which is no less advantageous to him will conclude the contract.

Cass. civ., 25 May 1870[125]   **2.F.35.**

FAILURE TO RESPOND TO LETTER

The accidental investor

Silence on the part of a person alleged to be bound by an obligation cannot suffice, in the absence of any other factor, to constitute proof that he is bound by the alleged obligation.

Facts: The banking firm Robin et Cie was instructed to procure from investors subscriptions for shares in the Société des Raffineries Nantaises. It entered in the list of subscribers the name of Mr Guilloux, a customer of the bank, assigning twenty shares to him. Robin et Cie do not appear to have received from Mr Guilloux any

---

[124] This issue is discussed further in **2.1.3.B**, *infra*, at 218.
[125] D.P. 70.1.257, S. 70.1.341.

215

formal order to that effect; but they wrote to him a letter in the following terms: "Dear Sir, we have debited you the sum of 2,500 francs by way of initial payment for the twenty shares in Raffineries Nantaises for which you have subscribed; please find enclosed the vouchers relating thereto." No reply to that letter was received. The Société des Raffineries Nantaises brought proceedings against Mr Guilloux and the—by that stage—insolvent firm of Robin et Cie, claiming payment of the outstanding sums due in respect of the twenty shares subscribed for.

Held: The Société's claim failed.

Judgment:—Whereas the contested judgment, in which it was held that the appellant was bound by the subscription undertaken in his name for twenty shares in the Société des Raffineries Nantaises, was based solely on the fact that the appellant did not reply to the letter by which Robin et Cie, acting on instructions to place the shares, had advised him that his name had been entered in the list of subscribers and that they had effected on his behalf the initial payment due in respect of the total amount of those shares;
—Whereas in law, silence on the part of a person alleged to be bound by an obligation cannot suffice, in the absence of any other factor, to constitute proof that he is bound by the alleged obligation;
—Whereas in ruling to the contrary, the contested judgment infringed the abovementioned provisions of the Code Napoléon; . . .

Note

As a rule, silence or inactivity does not amount to acceptance,[126] even when the offer states that it may be accepted by silence. In English law, this is established by the case of *Felthouse* v. *Bindley*.[127] The obvious justification for this is that an offeree should not be forced by an offer to take trouble and incur expense to reject it so as to avoid being bound. Compare Unidroit Principles Article 2.6(3) and CISG Article 18(3).[128]

RG, 1 February 1926[129]   **2.G.36.**

SILENCE CAN CONSTITUTE ACCEPTANCE

Alcohol for sale

Where an offer is made in terms which accord with an offeree's prior proposal, the offer can be accepted by silence.

Facts: On Wednesday, 10 December 1924, the plaintiff sent a telegram to the defendant in the following terms: "(We) offer, without engagement, ready for shipment, 3,300 litres of alcohol, neutral, high-proof, 4.55 [marks] per litre of alcohol free on rail, payment to be made in cash in advance by telegraphic transfer. Sample on its way by express delivery. Reply by wire." The defendant replied by wire on the same day: "Bank already closed. Settlement will be made tomorrow. (We) await express sample."

Held: The defendant's reply constituted an offer, and the contract had been accepted by the plaintiff's silence.

Judgment: The *Landgericht* [Regional Court] found that the first telegram contained an offer made by the plaintiff and that the second telegram constituted acceptance of that offer. The contested judgment draws attention, by contrast, to the qualifying words "without engagement". According

---

[126] See for English law Treitel, *Contract*, at 30, McKendrick, *Contract*, at 45 and for German law Medicus, *SAT* at 143–5; Flume, *Rechtsgeschäft* at 660.
[127] (1862) 11 CB (NS) 869.
[128] *Supra*, at 213.
[129] JW 26.2674.

to the prevailing view of the law, the effect of that qualification is such that the statement made constitutes not an offer but a request addressed to the other party, asking it to communicate an offer containing and setting out certain specific matters, which must be accepted in order to be effective . . . The appellate court concurred with that view. It regarded the defendant's telegram as amounting merely to an offer which still needed to be accepted by the plaintiff. However, it took the view that, in the present case, such acceptance could also take place tacitly, by silence on the part of the plaintiff. That court considered that such tacit acceptance had taken place by virtue of the fact that the plaintiff raised no objection of any kind to the offer during the period in which the defendant might under normal circumstances have expected to receive an answer from the plaintiff (§ 147(2) BGB). The appellate court held that, since the only appropriate method of replying was by wire, the period in question expired at 12.00 noon on Thursday, 11 December. It considered that the contract came into existence at that time on that day. There are no grounds in law for doubting the correctness of that finding. The defendant's offer read: "Bank already closed. Settlement will be made tomorrow." According to the interpretation applied by the appellate court, that meant that the purchase price would be remitted telegraphically on the following day. That interpretation, which was already advocated by . . . in the proceedings at first instance, is in itself entirely feasible. It does not appear to be vitiated by any error of law, and is consequently binding on the court hearing the appeal on a point of law. According to the interpretation in question, the defendant may logically be deemed to have replied to the plaintiff to the following effect: "we agree to your proposal in every respect. Consequently, we hereby make to you the offer that you want, and will tomorrow remit the purchase price telegraphically—without first waiting to receive from you confirmation that it is accepted. We would have remitted the purchase price today, but the bank was already closed." The appellate court could even have inferred from this that the defendant was waiving the obligation on the part of the plaintiff requiring the latter to state that it accepted the offer (first sentence of § 151 BGB). Still less can there be said to be any grounds for doubting that the contested judgment concerns one of those cases in which an offer is accepted by silence. The particular factors justifying such deemed acceptance are to be found in the fact that the defendant's offer accorded in every respect with the non-binding proposal previously put forward by the plaintiff, together with the urgency attaching—according to both parties—to the transaction, and the unconditional assurance given by the defendant in its telegram that it would transmit the purchase price telegraphically on the following day. It follows that the defendant needed to send a wire only if it agreed that the plaintiff, instead of sending any answer, should proceed without delay with the packing and shipment of the goods . . .

Notes

(1) In all three legal systems there are exceptions to the rule that silence cannot constitute an acceptance,[130] the most important ones being the existence of a course of dealing between the parties or a usage according to which silence amounts to acceptance and the situation in which the offer has been solicited by the offeree—as in the *Alcohol for Sale* case and BGH, 8 April 1957.[131] In English law it may be that the offeror who has said that the offer may be accepted by silence is bound by an acceptance by that means, but the offeree is not.[132]

(2) The comment on Article 2.6 of the Unidroit Principles makes it clear that the exception in cases of an existing course of dealing or usage also apply under paragraph 1

---

[130] See Treitel, *Contract*, at 31.
[131] NJW 1957.1105.
[132] Treitel, *Contract*, at 32–3.

of that Article—where only the main rule is set forth; cf. the words "in itself" in the second sentence of that paragraph. Compare also the American Restatement:

Restatement of Contract **2.US.37.**

§ 69: (1) Where an offeree fails to reply to an offer, his silence and inaction operate as an acceptance in the following cases only:

(a) where an offeree takes the benefit of offered services with reasonable opportunity to reject them and reason to know that they were offered with the expectation of compensation;

(b) where the offer has stated or given the offeree reason to understand that assent may be manifested by silence or inaction, and the offeree in remaining silent or inactive intends to accept the offer;

(c) where, because of previous dealings or otherwise, it is reasonable that the offeree should notify the offeror if he does not intend to accept.

2.1.3.B. A REQUIREMENT OF COMMUNICATION?

Principles of European Contract Law **2.PECL.38.**

Article 2:205: *Time of Conclusion of the Contract*
(1) If an acceptance has been dispatched by the offeree the contract is concluded when the acceptance reaches the offeror.
(2) In the case of acceptance by conduct, the contract is concluded when notice of the conduct reaches the offeror.
(3) If by virtue of the offer, of practices which the parties have established between themselves, or of a usage, the offeree may accept the offer by performing an act without notice to the offeror, the contract is concluded when the performance of the act begins.

Unidroit Principles **2.INT.39.**

Article. 2.6: (*Mode of acceptance*)
(1) . . .
(2) An acceptance of an offer becomes effective when the indication of assent reaches the offeror.

Article 2.4: (*Revocation of offer*)
(1) Until a contract is concluded an offer may be revoked if the revocation reaches the offeree before it has dispatched an acceptance.
(2) . . .

Article 2.10: (*Withdrawal of acceptance*)
An acceptance may be withdrawn if the withdrawal reaches the offeror before or at the same time as the acceptance would have become effective.

CISG **2.INT.40.**

Article 23: A contract is concluded at the moment when an acceptance of an offer becomes effective in accordance with the provisions of this Convention.

Article 24   For the purposes of this Part of the Convention, an offer, declaration of acceptance or any other indication of intention "reaches" the addressee when it is made orally to him or delivered by any other means to him personally, to his place of business or mailing address or, if he does not have a place of business or mailing address or, if he does not have a place of business or mailing address, to his habitual residence.

Article 161: Until a contract is concluded an offer may be revoked if the revocation reaches the offeree before he has dispatched an acceptance.[133]

As we have seen, the general rule in English law is that an acceptance must be communicated to the offeror. However, where an offer invites acceptance by conduct, as in Lord Blackburn's example of shipping cargo in *Brogden,* it often expressly or impliedly waives the requirement that acceptance must be communicated, though it seems that some act on the part of the offeree clearly committing him to performance—such as shipping the goods—is still necessary. Further, where acceptance takes place by performance of a unilateral contract, communication of acceptance is hardly ever required.[134] In *Carlill* v. *Carbolic Smoke Ball Co,* Lindley LJ said:

Unquestionably, as a general proposition, when an offer is made, it is necessary in order to make a binding contract, not only that it should be accepted, but that the acceptance should be notified. But is that so in cases of this kind? I apprehend that they are an exception to that rule, or, if not an exception, they are open to the observation that the notification of the acceptance need not precede the performance. This offer is a continuing offer. It was never revoked, and if notice of acceptance is required—. . .—. . . the person who makes the offer gets the notice of acceptance contemporaneously with his notice of the performance of the condition. If he gets notice of the acceptance before his offer is revoked, that in principle is all you want. I, however, think that the true view, in a case of this kind, is that the person who makes the offer shews by his language and from the nature of the transaction that he does not expect and does not require notice of the acceptance apart from the notice of the performance.

In German law, this issue is dealt with as a part of a more general question: when does a declaration of intention that is directed to another person (*empfangsbedürftige Willenserklärung*) become effective? According to § 130 paragraph 1 BGB a declaration of intention that is directed to an absent person becomes effective when it "reaches" that person. This provision applies to offers,[135] revocations of offers, acceptances and other declarations. Thus, in German law the contract is concluded when the acceptance "reaches" the offeror. On the concept of reaching (*zugehen*), see the *Delivery to a Housemaid* case;[136] as that case illustrates, a communication may reach a person without being communicated to them. Zweigert and Kötz suggest that the limits of the concept of reaching can be determined by reference to the idea of a "sphere of influence"; for example, a man may not prevent an acceptance from reaching him by refusing to collect it from his mail box, for it has already reached his "sphere of influence".[137]

A different outcome would probably be reached under the Unidroit Principles. According to the comment on Article 2.6, an acceptance by mere conduct becomes, just

---

[133] Article 22 CISG is identical to Article 2.10 Unidroit.
[134] Treitel, *Contract,* at 36; McKendrick, *Contract,* at 50.
[135] In relation to offers, see the *Delivery to a Housemaid* case, **2.1.2.B,** *supra,* at 195–6.
[136] Discussed *supra* at 195–6.
[137] See also Medicus, *SAT* at 142; Flume, *Rechtsgeschäft* at 657.

as any other acceptance, effective only when notice thereof reaches the offeror. The comment states that in cases where the conduct will of itself give notice of acceptance to the offeror within a reasonable period of time, special notice to this effect is not necessary. However, the use of the smoke ball in *Carlill* v. *Carbolic Smoke Ball Co*. would not have sufficed for this purpose. See the American Restatement 2d:

Restatement of Contracts   **2.US.41.**

§ 54: (1) Where an offer invites an offeree to accept by rendering a performance, no notification is necessary to make such an acceptance effective unless the offer requests such a notification.
(2) If an offeree who accepts by rendering a performance has reason to know that the offeror has no adequate means of learning of the performance with reasonable promptness and certainty, the contractual duty of the offeror is discharged unless
    (a) the offeree exercises reasonable diligence to notify the offeror of acceptance, or
    (b) the offeror learns of the performance within a reasonable time, or
    (c) the offer indicates that notification of acceptance is not required.

Cass. civ., 21 December 1960[138]   **2.F.42.**

MATTER FOR DISCRETION OF LOWER COURTS

Chomel

The question whether a contract has been concluded is a question of fact, and is therefore a matter for the unfettered discretion of the lower courts.
Judgment:—Whereas the appellant, Chomel, contests the judgment of the cour d'appel (Aix, 5 June 1958) by which it dismissed his claim to be entitled to rely on a [contractual] term agreed in correspondence between Roqueta and him, on the ground that it had not been proved that Roqueta, which had proposed that term, had received his letter agreeing to it before revoking its offer;
—Whereas the acceptance operated, as soon as it took place, to render the contract definitive and binding, and an offeror cannot revoke such an offer once it has been accepted;
—Whereas however, in deciding that Roqueta was entitled to revoke its offer at any time up until it received Chomel's acceptance, the court adjudicating on the substance of the case was merely exercising its unfettered discretion to construe the intentions of the parties; it follows that the appellant's plea is unfounded; . . .

Cass. com., 7 January 1981[139]   **2.F.43.**

DISPATCH OF ACCEPTANCE

L'Aigle/Comase

An acceptance by letter is effective upon dispatch, and not upon receipt.

Facts: On 10 June 1975 Messrs L'Aigle sent a purchase offer, valid for 30 days, to Messrs Comase. The latter company accepted it on 3 July, but was unable to prove that its acceptance reached the offeror before 10 July.

[138] D. 1961.I.417 annotated by Ph. Malaurie.
[139] Bull. civ. IV.14; RTD civ. 1981.849, annotated by F. Chabas.

220

Having failed to fulfil its obligations, L'Aigle sought to avoid the liability which it had incurred, by maintaining that the contract had not been concluded. It argued that a contract became definitive and binding only upon receipt by the offeror of acceptance of his offer; since it had not been proved by its opponent that such acceptance had indeed taken place within the time-limit stipulated in the offer, that offer had lapsed and it had not been possible for the contract to come into existence.

Held: A contract had been concluded.

Judgment: . . .—Whereas the appellant, Société L'Aigle, contests the judgment of the cour d'appel ordering it to pay damages to Société Comase by way of compensation for the loss suffered by the latter as a result of the wrongful termination by the said Société L'Aigle of the abovementioned agreement, on the ground that Société Comase had accepted the offer made within the time-limit laid down;

—Whereas according to the appellant, it is for the party seeking performance of an obligation to prove the same, and it is therefore for Société Comase to furnish evidence showing that it communicated its acceptance to Société L'Aigle before 10 July 1975; as the appellant further argues that, by basing its decision solely on its consideration of a letter from Société Comase dated 3 July 1975 (produced to the court in evidence), which could not have reached Société L'Aigle until after 10 July, the cour d'appel reversed the burden of proof, and that it was for Société Comase to prove that the letter was received before the time-limit expired, and not for Société L'Aigle to prove the contrary; as the appellant additionally maintains that, by failing, moreover, to investigate whether the letter reached its addressee by 10 July, the cour d'appel robbed its decision of any legal basis;

—Whereas however, in the absence of any stipulation to the contrary, the written communication of 10 June 1975 was intended to become definitive and binding not upon receipt by Société L'Aigle of Société Comase's acceptance but upon the despatch of that acceptance by Société Comase; the appellant's plea to the contrary is unfounded; . . .

King's Bench   **2.E.44.**
Adams v. *Lindsell*[140]

POSTAL RULE

Two days late

An acceptance by post is effective when it is sent, not when it is received.

Facts: The defendants by letter offered to sell to the plaintiffs certain specified goods, receiving an answer by return of post; the letter containing the offer being misdirected, the answer notifying the acceptance of the offer arrived two days later than it ought to have done; on the day following that when it would have arrived if the original letter had been properly directed, the defendants sold the goods to a third person. The defendants contended that until the plaintiff's answer was actually received, there could be no binding contract between the parties; and before then, the defendants had retracted their offer, by selling the goods to other persons.

Held: A contract had been concluded between the plaintiffs and the defendants.

Judgment: The court said that if that were so, no contract could ever be completed by the post. For if the defendants were not bound by their offer when accepted by the plaintiffs till the answer was received, then the plaintiffs ought not to be bound till after they had received the notification that the defendants had received their answer and assented to it. And so it might go on ad infinitum. The defendants must be considered in law as making, during every instant of the time their letter was travelling, the same identical offer to the plaintiffs; and then the contract is completed by

---

[140] (1818) 1 B. & Ald. 681, 106 ER 250.

the acceptance of it by the latter. Then as to the delay in notifying the acceptance, that arises entirely from the mistake of the defendants, and it therefore must be taken as against them, that the plaintiff's answer was received in course of post.

Common Pleas Division   **2.E.45.**
Byrne v. *Van Tienhoven*[141]

R<small>EVOCATION OF OFFER MUST BE COMMUNICATED</small>

Acceptance sent before revocation received

An offer is effectively revoked when the fact of the withdrawal is communicated to the offeree, and the mere posting of a notice of revocation will not suffice for this purpose. Once an offer has been accepted by dispatch of a letter of acceptance, the offer cannot be revoked.

Facts: By letter of 1 October the defendants wrote from Cardiff offering goods for sale to the plaintiffs at New York. The plaintiffs received the offer on the 11th and accepted it by telegram on the same day, and by letter on the 15th. On 8 October the defendants had posted to the plaintiffs a letter withdrawing the offer. This letter reached the plaintiffs on the 20th.

Held: The offer had not effectively been revoked before it had been accepted, and a binding contract had therefore been formed.

Judgment: L<small>INDLEY</small> J: There is no doubt that an offer can be withdrawn before it is accepted, and it is immaterial whether the offer is expressed to be open for acceptance for a given time or not: *Routledge* v. *Grant*. For the decision of the present case, however, it is necessary to consider two other questions, viz.: 1. Whether a withdrawal of an offer has any effect until it is communicated to the person to whom the offer has been sent? 2. Whether posting a letter of withdrawal is a communication to the person to whom the letter is sent?

It is curious that neither of these questions appears to have been actually decided in this country. As regards the first question, I am aware that Pothier and some other writers of celebrity are of opinion that there can be no contract if an offer is withdrawn before it is accepted, although the withdrawal is not communicated to the person to whom the offer has been made. The reason for this opinion is that there is not in fact any such consent by both parties as is essential to constitute a contract between them. Against this view, however, it has been urged that a state of mind not notified cannot be regarded in dealings between man and man; and that an uncommunicated revocation is for all practical purposes and in point of law no revocation at all. This is the view taken in the United States: see *Tayloe* v. *Merchants Fire Insurance Co.* cited in Benjamin on Sales, pp. 56–58, and it is adopted by Mr. Benjamin. The same view is taken by Mr. Pollock in his excellent work on *Principles of Contract*, ed. ii, p. 10, and by Mr. Leake in his *Digest of the Law of Contracts*, p. 43. This view, moreover, appears to me much more in accordance with the general principles of English law than the view maintained by Pothier. I pass, therefore, to the next question, viz., whether posting the letter of revocation was a sufficient communication of it to the plaintiff. The offer was posted on the 1st of October, the withdrawal was posted on the 8th, and did not reach the plaintiff until after he had posted his letter of the 11th, accepting the offer. It may be taken as now settled that where an offer is made and accepted by letters sent through the post, the contract is completed the moment the letter accepting the offer is posted: *Harris' Case*; *Dunlop* v. *Higgins*, even although it never reaches its destination. When, however, these authorities are looked at, it will be seen that they are based upon the principle that the writer of the offer has expressly or impliedly assented to

---

[141] (1880) 5 CPD 344.

treat an answer to him by a letter duly posted as a sufficient acceptance and notification to himself, or, in other words, he has made the post office his agent to receive the acceptance and notification of it. But this principle appears to me to be inapplicable to the case of the withdrawal of an offer. In this particular case I can find no evidence of any authority in fact given by the plaintiffs to the defendants to notify a withdrawal of their offer by merely posting a letter; and there is no legal principle or decision which compels me to hold, contrary to the fact, that the letter of the 8th of October is to be treated as communicated to the plaintiff on that day or on any day before the 20th, when the letter reached them. . . .

Before leaving this part of the case it may be as well to point out the extreme injustice and inconvenience which any other conclusion would produce. If the defendants' contention were to prevail no person who had received an offer by post and had accepted it would know his position until he had waited such a time as to be quite sure that a letter withdrawing the offer had not been posted before his acceptance of it. It appears to me that both legal principles, and practical convenience require that a person who has accepted an offer not known to him to have been revoked, shall be in a position safely to act upon the footing that the offer and acceptance constitute a contract binding on both parties . . .

Notes

(1) If the parties conclude the contract in each other's presence, normally no question arises with regard to the need for communication of the acceptance. The same is true when the parties are in different places and use an instantaneous means of communication, such as the telephone. But if the parties use a slower means of communication such as the post, these two moments are necessarily separated by a period of time. These cases therefore raise a question whether the acceptance must be communicated to the offeree.

(2) The question whether the acceptance must be communicated to the offeree is also of crucial importance for another purpose: to determine the moment at which the acceptance becomes effective and thus at which moment the contract comes into being. This issue can be of importance in several respects, for example, if a new Act has come into force or to determine the beginning of periods e.g. of prescription (limitation). An important consequence of the conclusion of a sale contract in French law is the transfer of the ownership and the risk of the thing sold. The moment at which the acceptance becomes effective therefore also affects the point at which risk in the goods is transferred to the buyer. In the case-law, the question at which moment the acceptance takes effect arises in most of the cases for the purpose of determining whether the offer has lapsed by that time (**2.1.2.C.**) or to determine the moment from which the offeror can no longer revoke his offer (**2.1.2.B.**).

(3) Four possible moments have been suggested for the conclusion of a contract when the acceptance takes place by letter: (a) the moment the letter containing the acceptance is written (externalization theory); (b) the moment at which the letter of acceptance is posted (expedition or dispatch theory); (c) the moment the letter is received by the offeror (reception theory); and (d) the moment the offeror is informed of the content of the letter (actual-notice theory). The externalization theory and the actual-notice theory are rather impractical: it is often impossible to establish at which the moment the letter of acceptance was written or read. On the other hand, the time of dispatch and the time of receipt can be determined objectively. Moreover, when the actual-notice theory is followed the offeror could postpone the conclusion of the contract by leaving the letter of

acceptance unopened. Italian law seems to have adopted the actual-notice theory in Article 1326 of the Italian CC: The contract is made at the moment at which the party who has made the offer knows of the other party's acceptance; but in practice receipt is regarded as knowledge in Italian law unless the offeror can prove that "without his fault, he was prevented from taking notice" (Articles 1328, 1334, 1335 of the Italian CC).

(4) The French *Cour de cassation* has in a large number of decisions adopted the view that the point at which a contract is effective is a matter of fact that is purely within the discretion of the lower courts: see the *Chomel* case. However, in the *L'Aigle/Comase* case, the *Cour de cassation* expressly adopted the dispatch theory. The lower courts seem to apply—indiscriminately—either the dispatch theory or the reception theory, according to the exigencies of the equity in each case.[142] French doctrine is divided between the two theories. Some authors, including Starck, Roland and Boyer,[143] are of the opinion that, in view of the important practical consequences, the matter should be settled by legislation to put an end to the uncertainty caused by the inconsistent case-law of the *Cour de cassation*.

(5) In English law, an acceptance by letter becomes effective the moment the letter is posted. Apart from the two cases cited above, this was also confirmed in *Henthorn* v. *Fraser*.[144] Similarly, an acceptance by telegram takes effect when the telegram is communicated to a person authorized to receive it for transmission to the addressee.[145] This rule applies only when it is reasonable to use the post as a means of communicating acceptance (*Henthorn* v. *Fraser*[146]) and the offeror can explicitly or implicitly exclude the "postal rule" in his offer.[147] The "postal rule" in English law applies only for the purposes of determining whether an offer can still be revoked, whether a contract has been concluded if the acceptance is lost or delayed in the post—this consequence is criticized by, for example, McKendrick[148]—and whether the contract takes priority over another contract relating to the same subject-matter. The English case law does not provide examples of other consequences that might be drawn from the rule. In particular, it has never been decided that an acceptor cannot withdraw his acceptance after it has been posted, for example by sending a telex message that reaches the offeror earlier than or at the same time as the letter of acceptance.

(6) In English law, an important function of the "postal rule" is that it limits the offeror's power to revoke:[149] once the letter containing the acceptance is posted, the offeror can no longer revoke, since at that moment a contract has been concluded. This function of the rule is reinforced by the rule that the revocation of an offer becomes effective only when it has reached the offeree.[150] Thus, a revocation will come too late to prevent the contract from being completed if it reaches the offeree after he has posted his letter or telegram of acceptance. In the comment on Article 2.4 of the Principles it

---

[142] Terré and Lequette, at para. 164.
[143] B. Starck, H. Roland and L. Boyer, *Obligations*, Vol. 2: *Contrat*, 5th edn. (Paris: Litec, 1995) at 139.
[144] [1892] 2 Ch. 27.
[145] Treitel, *Contract*, at 24; See *Brinkibon* v. *Stahag Stahl* [1982] 1 All ER 293.
[146] [1892] 2 Ch. 27.
[147] Treitel, *Contract*, at 25, McKendrick, *Contract*, at 47–50.
[148] McKendrick, *Contract*, at 48–9.
[149] See Treitel, *Contract*, at 27–8, McKendrick, *Contract*, at 49.
[150] See *Byrne* v. *Van Tienhoven* and *Stevenson, Jaques & Co.* v. *McLean* (1880) 5 QB 346.

is said that this solution may cause some inconvenience to the offeror who will not always know whether or not it is still possible to revoke the offer, but that it is justified in view of the legitimate interest of the offeree in the time available for revocation being shortened.

(7) However, the problem does not necessarily have to be dealt with in this way, and different issues—termination of the offeror's power to revoke, loss or delay of the acceptance in the post, withdrawal of acceptance, etc.—may be separated in time. For example, under the CISG and the Unidroit Principles[151] the moment at which the contract is concluded—when the acceptance reaches the offeror, Article 18 paragraph 2 resp. article 2.6 paragraph 2—is separated from the moment from which the offeror can no longer revoke, when the acceptance is dispatched, Article 16 paragraph 1 resp. 2.4 paragraph 1.[152]

(8) In German law, the problem is dealt with in accordance with the general concept of "reaching".[153] Further, § 130 paragraph 1 BGB states that a declaration does not become effective if a withdrawal reaches the other party before or at the same time as the declaration.[154]

(9) The approach of PECL, CISG and the Unidroit Principles, according to which an acceptance is effective to form the contract upon receipt but upon dispatch to terminate the offeror's power to revoke, is the most similar to English law. However, whereas in English law it is not completely certain what the consequences of the "postal rule" are—apart from terminating the offeror's power to revoke upon the dispatch of the acceptance—, under PECL, CISG and the Unidroit Principles the acceptance is effective upon receipt for all purposes other than terminating the offeror's power to revoke.

In summary, this issue is approached differently in the different jurisdictions studied. It can be seen that the moment at which an acceptance is effective is not the subject of clear rules in French law. English law establishes a general requirement of communication, but that requirement is subject to important exceptions, and the law thus takes an essentially pragmatic stance ultimately not dissimilar from the French position. In German law, on the other hand, one orderly approach is followed with regard to all related questions: an acceptance becomes effective upon receipt.

These different approaches can be traced back to the rules on revocability of offers. In English law, the dispatch rule is justified because in combination with the receipt rule for the revocation of offers, it provides the offeree with some protection against revocation of the offer. In German law, where offers are, as a main rule, irrevocable,[155] there is less need to advance the moment at which the acceptance becomes effective.

---

[151] *Supra*, at 218.
[152] See also Article 3:37 para. 3 and Article 6:219 para. 2 of the Dutch Civil Code.
[153] Discussed *supra*, at 219.
[154] See Article 22 CISG and Article 2.10 Unidroit Principles, *supra*, at 218.
[155] See **2.1.2.C.**, at 197.

2.1.3.C. Acceptance that deviates from the offer

(1) General

Principles of European Contract Law   **2.PECL.46.**

Article 2:208: *Modified Acceptance*
   (1) A reply by the offeree which states or implies additional or different terms which would materially alter the terms of the offer is a rejection and a new offer.
   (2) A reply which gives a definite assent to an offer operates as an acceptance even if it states or implies additional or different terms, provided these do not materially alter the terms of the offer. The additional or different terms then become part of the contract.
   (3) However, such a reply will be treated as a rejection of the offer if:
      (a) the offer expressly limits acceptance to the terms of the offer; or
      (b) the offeror objects to the additional or different terms without delay; or
      (c) the offeree makes its acceptance conditional upon the offeror's assent to the additional or different terms, and the assent does not reach the offeree within a reasonable time.

Unidroit Principles   **2.INT.47.**

Article 2.11: 1. A reply to an offer which purports to be an acceptance but contains additions, limitations or other modifications is a rejection of the offer and constitutes a counter-offer.
   2. However, a reply to an offer which purports to be an acceptance but contains additional or different terms which do not materially alter the terms of the offer constitutes an acceptance, unless the offeror, without undue delay, objects to the discrepancy. If the offeror does not object, the terms of the contract are the terms of the offer with the modifications contained in the acceptance.

CISG   **2.INT.48.**

Article 19: 1. A reply to an offer which purports to be an acceptance but contains additions, limitations or other modifications is a rejection of the offer and constitutes a counter-offer.
   2. However, a reply to an offer which purports to be an acceptance but contains additional or different terms which do not materially alter the terms of the offer constitutes an acceptance, unless the offeror, without undue delay, objects orally to the discrepancy or dispatches a notice to that effect. If he does not so object, the terms of the contract are the terms of the offer with the modifications contained in the acceptance.
   3. Additional or different terms relating, among other things, to the price, payment, quality and quantity of the goods, place and time of delivery, extent of one party's liability to the other or the settlement of disputes are considered to alter the terms of the offer materially.[156]

---

[156] Article 19 para. 1 CISG is identical to Article 2.11 Unidroit.

Rolls Court   **2.E.49.**
Hyde v. Wrench[157]

COUNTER OFFER IS REJECTION OF OFFER

Farm for sale

A counter-offer amounts to a rejection of the original offer, and the original offer cannot thereafter be accepted.

Facts: The defendant on 6 June offered in writing to sell his farm for £1000; but the plaintiff offered £950, which the defendant on 27 June, after consideration, refused to accept. On the 29th the plaintiff by letter agreed to give £1000, but there appeared to be no assent on the part of the defendant, though there had been no revocation of the first offer.

Held: No contract had been formed.

Judgment: LORD LANGDALE: Under the circumstances stated in this bill, I think there exists no valid binding contract between the parties for the purchase of the property. The defendant offered to sell it for £1000, and if that had been at once unconditionally accepted, there would undoubtedly have been a perfect binding contract; instead of that, the plaintiff made an offer of his own, to purchase the property for £950, and he thereby rejected the offer previously made by the defendant. I think that it was not afterwards competent for him to revive the proposal of the defendant, by tendering an acceptance of it; and that, therefore, there exists no obligation of any sort between the parties; . . .

Queen's Bench Division   **2.E.50.**
Stevenson, Jaques & Co. v. *McLean*[158]

INQUIRY AS TO ALTERNATIVE TERMS

Warrants for iron

A mere inquiry whether the offeror would accept particular terms does not amount to a counter-offer and thus a rejection of the original offer.

Facts: The defendant, being possessed of warrants for iron, wrote from London to the plaintiffs at Middlesborough asking whether they could get him an offer for the warrants. Further correspondence ensued, and ultimately the defendant wrote to the plaintiffs fixing 40s. per ton, net cash, as the lowest price at which he could sell, and stating that he would hold the offer open until the following Monday. The plaintiffs on the Monday morning at 9.42 telegraphed to the defendant: "Please wire whether you would accept forty for delivery over two months, or if not, longest limit you could give." The defendant sent no answer to this telegram, and after its receipt on the same day he sold the warrants, and at 1.25 pm telegraphed to plaintiffs that he had done so. Before the arrival of his telegram to that effect, the plaintiffs having at 1 pm found a purchaser for the iron, sent a telegram at 1.34 to the defendant stating that they had secured his price. The defendant refused to deliver the iron, and thereupon the plaintiffs brought an action against him for non-delivery thereof.

Judgment: LUSH J: . . . It is apparent throughout the correspondence, that the plaintiffs did not contemplate buying the iron on speculation, but that their acceptance of the defendants's offer depended on their finding some one to take the warrants off their hands. All parties knew that the

---

[157] (1840) 3 Beav. 334.
[158] (1880) 5 QB 346.

227

market was in an unsettled state, and that no one could predict at the early hour when the telegram was sent how the prices would range during the day. It was reasonable that, under these circumstances, they should desire to know before business began whether they were to be at liberty in case of need to make any and what concession as to the time or times of delivery, which would be the time or times of payment, or whether the defendant was determined to adhere to the terms of his letter; and it was highly unreasonable that the plaintiff's should have intended to close the negotiation while it was uncertain whether they could find a buyer or not, having the whole of the business hours of the day to look for one. Then, again, the form of the telegram is one of inquiry. It is not "I offer forty for delivery over two months," which would have likened the case to *Hyde* v. *Wrench*, where one party offered his estate for 1000l., and the other answered by offering 950l. Lord Langdale, in that case, held that after the 950l. had been refused, the party offering it could not, by then agreeing to the original proposal, claim the estate, for the negotiation was at an end by the refusal of his counter proposal. Here there is no counter proposal. The words are, "Please wire whether you would accept forty for delivery over two months, or, if not, the longest limit you would give." There is nothing specific by way of offer or rejection, but a mere inquiry, which should have been answered and not treated as a rejection of the offer . . .

BGB   **2.G.51.**

§ 150: . . .

(2) An acceptance with amplifications, limitations or other alterations is deemed to be a refusal coupled with a new offer.[159]

Note

(1) A statement that purports to be an acceptance but changes the terms of the offer is in reality a counter-offer: for example, an offer to supply goods that is "accepted" by an order for their supply and installation.[160] The rule according to which the terms of the acceptance must correspond to those of the offer is referred to in the common law as the "mirror-image rule". *Hyde* v. *Wrench* shows that a counter-offer is regarded in English law as a rejection of the original offer.[161] *Stevenson, Jaques & Co.* v. *McLean* shows that whether a communication is a counter-offer or a mere request for information depends on the intention with which it was made, objectively assessed.

(2) The "mirror-image rule" is also to be found in Article 1326 of the Italian CC and section 59 of the American Restatement 2nd. A variation on the mirror image rule can be found in the *Principles of European Contract Law*. Under Article 2:208, an acceptance need not mirror the offer precisely, but it must not "materially alter the terms of the offer" of the offer. Paragraph C of the Comment on the Article explains that "a term is material if the offeree knew or as a reasonable person in the same position as the offeree should have known that the offeror would be influenced in its decision as to whether to contract or as to the terms on which to contract". See also Unidroit Principles Article 2.11 and CISG Article 19,[162] and Article 6:225 paragraph 2 of the Dutch Civil Code:

---

[159] Translated by Von Mehren & Gordley, op. cit. at 193, n. 55. See also Malaurie and Aynès, para. 389.
[160] Treitel, *Contract*, at 18 and 41; see also McKendrick, *Contract*, at 27.
[161] With the result that the original offer lapses, as has been seen in **2.1.2.D**, *supra*, at 210–11.
[162] Cit. at the beginning of this section, *supra* at 226.

BW **2.NL.52.**

Article 6.225: 2. Unless the offeror objects to the differences without delay, where a reply intended to accept an offer only deviates from the offer on points of minor importance, the reply is considered to be an acceptance and the contract is formed according to the latter".

(2) The "battle of the forms"

Principles of European Contract Law **2.PECL.53.**

Article 2:209: *Conflicting General Conditions*
(1) If the parties have reached agreement except that the offer and acceptance refer to conflicting general conditions of contract, a contract is nonetheless formed. The general conditions form part of the contract to the extent that they are common in substance.
(2) However, no contract is formed if one party:
    (a) has indicated in advance, explicitly, and not by way of general conditions, that it does not intend to be bound by a contract on the basis of paragraph (1); or
    (b) without delay, informs the other party that it does not intend to be bound by such contract.
(3) General conditions of contract are terms which have been formulated in advance for an indefinite number of contracts of a certain nature, and which have not been individually negotiated between the parties.

Unidroit Principles **2.INT.54.**

Article 2.22: Where both parties use standard terms and reach agreement except on those terms, a contract is concluded on the basis of the agreed terms and of any standard terms which are common in substance unless one party clearly indicates in advance, or later and without undue delay informs the other party, that it does not intend to be bound by such a contract.

Court of Appeal **2.E.55.**
Butler Machine Tool Co. Ltd. v. *Ex-cell-O Corpn. Ltd*[163]

Different approaches to the battle of the forms

The tear-off acknowledgement slip

On one approach to the battle of the forms, it is not necessary to look only at an offer and an acceptance when considering whether a contract has been agreed. As an alternative, all of the relevant documentation should be construed together to discern whether a harmonious interpretation can be achieved.

---

[163] [1979] 1 All ER 965.

Facts: On 23 May 1969, in response to an enquiry by the buyers, the sellers made a quotation offering to sell a machine tool to the buyers for £75,535, delivery to be in ten months' time. The offer was stated to be subject to certain terms and conditions which "shall prevail over any terms and conditions in the Buyer's order". The conditions included a price variation clause providing for the goods to be charged at the price ruling on the date of delivery. On 27 May the buyers replied by placing an order for the machine. The order was stated to be subject to certain terms and conditions, which were materially different from those put forward by the sellers and which, in particular, made no provision for a variation in price. At the foot of the buyer's order there was a tear-off acknowledgement of receipt of the order stating that "We accept your order on the Terms and Conditions stated thereon". On 5 June the sellers completed and signed the acknowledgement and returned it to the buyers with a letter stating that the buyer's order was being entered "in accordance" with the seller's quotation of 23 May. When the sellers came to deliver the machine they claimed that the price had increased by £2,892. The buyers refused to pay the increase in price and the sellers brought an action claiming that they were entitled to increase the price under the price variation clause contained in their offer. The buyers contended that the contract had been concluded on the buyer's rather than the seller's terms and was therefore a fixed-price contract. The judge upheld the seller's claim on the ground that the contract had been concluded on the basis that the seller's terms were to prevail since they had stipulated that in the opening offer and all subsequent negotiations had been subject to that. The buyers appealed.

Held: A contract had been concluded by the parties.

Judgment: [LAWTON LJ and BRIDGE LJ applied the ordinary rules for counter-offers. This meant that the order of 27 May constituted a counter-offer because it referred to the general conditions of the buyers which were materially different from those used by the sellers. This counter-offer of the buyers was accepted by the sellers by the acknowledgement and letter of 5 June; the reference to the original offer served only to identify the transaction and not to reintroduce the terms of the sellers. Therefore a contract was concluded on the terms and conditions of the buyers. Lord Denning adopted a different approach]:

LORD DENNING MR: . . . If those documents are analysed in our traditional method, the result would seem to me to be this: the quotation of 23 May 1969 was an offer by the sellers to the buyers containing the terms and conditions on the back. The order of 27 May 1969 purported to be an acceptance of that offer in that it was for the same machine at the same price, but it contained such additions as to cost of installation, date of delivery and so forth, that it was in law a rejection of the offer and constituted a counter-offer. That is clear from *Hyde* v. *Wrench*. As Megaw J said in *Trollope & Colls Ltd* v. *Atomic Power Constructions Ltd*: ". . . the counter-offer kills the original offer". The letter of the sellers of 5 June 1969 was an acceptance of that counter-offer, as is shown by the acknowledgement which the sellers signed and returned to the buyers. The reference to the quotation of 23 May 1969 referred only to the price and identity of the machine . . .

In many of these cases our traditional analysis of offer, counter-offer, rejection, acceptance and so forth is out-of-date. . . . The better way is to look at all the documents passing between the parties and glean from them, or from the conduct of the parties, whether they have reached agreement on all material points, even though there may be differences between the forms and conditions printed on the back of them. As Lord Cairns LC said in *Brogden* v. *Metropolitan Railway Co*:

> ". . . there may be a *consensus* between the parties far short of a complete mode of expressing it, and that *consensus* may be discovered from letters or from other documents of an imperfect and incomplete description."

Applying this guide, it will be found that in most cases when there is a "battle of forms" there is a contract as soon as the last of the forms is sent and received without objection being taken to it. That is well observed in *Benjamin on Sale*. The difficulty is to decide which form, or which part of which form, is a term or condition of the contract. In some cases the battle is won by the man who fires the last shot. He is the man who puts forward the latest terms and conditions: and, if they are not objected to by the other party, he may be taken to have agreed to them. Such was *British Road Services Ltd* v. *Arthur V Crutchley & Co Ltd* per Lord Pearson; and the illustration given by

Professor Guest in Anson's Law of Contract where he says that "the terms of the contract consist of the terms of the offer subject to the modifications contained in the acceptance". That may however go too far. In some cases, however, the battle is won by the man who gets the blow in first. If he offers to sell at a named price on the terms and conditions stated on the back and the buyers orders the goods purporting to accept the offer on an order form with his own different terms and conditions on the back, then, if the difference is so material that it would affect the price, the buyer ought not to be allowed to take advantage of the difference unless he draws it specifically to the attention of the seller. There are yet other cases where the battle depends on the shots fired on both sides. There is a concluded contract but the forms vary. The terms and conditions of both parties are to be construed together. If they can be reconciled so as to give a harmonious result, all well and good. If differences are irreconcilable, so that they are mutually contradictory, then the conflicting terms may have to be scrapped and replaced by a reasonable implication.

In the present case the judge thought that the sellers in their original quotation got their blow in first; especially by the provision that "These terms and conditions shall prevail over any terms and conditions in the Buyer's order". It was so emphatic that the price variation clause continued through all the subsequent dealings and that the buyer must be taken to have agreed to it. I can understand that point of view. But I think that the documents have to be considered as a whole. And, as a matter of construction, I think the acknowledgement of 5th June 1969 is the decisive document. It makes it clear that the contract was on the buyer's terms and not on the seller's terms: and the buyer's terms did not include a price variation clause . . .

BGH, 26 September 1973[164]   **2.G.56.**

TERMS NOT AGREED BUT CONTRACT NEVERTHELESS CONCLUDED

The heat-retaining silo

Whilst particular terms and conditions may not be incorporated into a contract following a battle of the forms, the parties may be estopped from denying that a contract has in fact been concluded.

Facts: On 1 December 1969 the defendant, using its own order form which referred in the standard way to its "terms and conditions of purchase" printed overleaf, ordered a heat-retaining silo to be delivered by 15 April 1970. Clause 1 of the terms and conditions of purchase provided as follows:

> "Orders given by us . . . are placed on the basis of our terms and conditions of purchase. Where the contractor's standard-form terms and conditions provide otherwise, they shall be valid only if they are confirmed by us in writing."

The essence of clause 3 of the terms and conditions of purchase was that the statutory rules were to apply decisively to any claim for compensation for failure to comply with the deadline for delivery. Thereafter, on 5 January 1970, the plaintiff sent the defendant a detailed "confirmation of order", in which—likewise referring in the standard way to its attached "terms and conditions of sale and delivery"—it accepted the order on the basis that delivery was to be effected by no later than "middle to end April 1970". However, according to the plaintiff's terms and conditions of sale and delivery, the particulars concerning the delivery deadline were only approximate and non-binding; liability to pay compensation for late delivery was excluded.

By letter of 22 April 1970, the defendant, referring expressly to its order form, gave the plaintiff formal notice of default by the latter and announced that, in the event of failure by the plaintiff to effect delivery by 30 April 1970, it would claim compensation. The equipment was delivered at the end of June 1970 and put into operation by the defendant. The defendant withheld from the agreed purchase price of approximately DM 90,000 the sum of DM 27,450 by way of recompense for the damage caused by the delay.

Held: The defendant had not accepted the plaintiff's terms and conditions in passively receiving the conditions set out in the plaintiff's confirmation of order or in acceptance of delivery, but a contract had nevertheless been concluded between the parties.

[164] BGHZ 61.282.

231

Judgment: (a) As is apparent *inter alia* from § 362 HGB, silence does not in principle constitute consent, even in legal dealings between commercial traders (BGHZ 1, 353, 355). In particular, in a settled line of case-law—relating, it is true, to disputes which did not concern letters of confirmation passing between commercial traders, the Bundesgerichtshof has declined to construe the mere passive receipt, without objection, of a modified confirmation of order as constituting tacit acceptance thereof (BGHZ 18, 212, 216; judgment of 12 February 1952—I ZR 98/51 = LM BGB § 150, para. 2; judgment of 14 March 1963—VII ZR 257/61 = WM 1963, 528 = LM BGB § 150, para. 6) . . .

2. It follows that the plaintiff's terms and conditions of sale and delivery were not incorporated into the contract merely by virtue of the passive receipt by the defendant, without objection, of the confirmation of order dated 5 January 1970. Nor, however, is the plaintiff entitled to rely in that connection on the fact that the defendant subsequently accepted the equipment and put it into operation. It is true that, in certain circumstances, where a modified confirmation of order is sent and the purchaser takes delivery of the goods without raising any objection, that may be regarded as constituting tacit acceptance by the purchaser of the modified contract (§ 150(2) BGB), with the result that he is deemed to have consented to the seller's general terms of business, as referred to—particularly where the seller has clearly stated at a previous juncture that he is prepared to effect delivery only on his own terms (see the judgment of the BGH of 17 September 1954—I ZR 18/53 = LM BGB § 150, para. 3 = BB 1954, 882, and the judgment of 14 March 1963—VII ZR 257/61 = WM 1963, 528 = LM BGB § 150, para. 6 = NJW 1963, 1248). The present case does not, however, involve any passive receipt, taking place without any objection being raised, which could be construed as amounting to tacit acceptance. On the contrary, the defendant gave notice by letter of 22 April 1970, in which it referred to its written order of 1 December 1969, that it proposed to claim compensation for failure to comply with the delivery deadline . . .

3. The fact that, because the plaintiff accepted the defendant's order of 1 December 1969 only in a modified form and the defendant did not accept the new terms proposed by the plaintiff at all, neither the defendant's terms and conditions of purchase nor the plaintiff's terms and conditions of sale and delivery were therefore incorporated into the contract does not mean, however, that no contract came into existence. The application of § 150(2) BGB is subject to the principle of good faith (judgment of the BGH of 12 February 1952—I ZR 98/51, cited above). In the present case, neither of the parties has at any time called in question, either before or during the dispute, the fact that a legally effective purchase contract was concluded. They performed the contract—the plaintiff by delivering the equipment and the defendant by accepting delivery of it and by paying at least part of the purchase price, although it was already quite clear at that point that there was a dispute as to whose terms of business had been incorporated into the contract. In so doing, they made it clear that, as far as they were concerned, the determination of the matter in issue did not affect the existence of the contract itself. Consequently, in accordance with the principle of good faith, both parties must be deemed to be estopped from pleading that the contract never came into existence (judgment of the Chamber of 25 June 1957—VIII ZR 257/56 = WM 1957, 1064, not reproduced in that respect in LM BGB § 150, para. 5; Krause BB 1952, 996, 998).

BGH, 20 March 1985[165]   **2.G.57.**

CONFLICTING CLAUSES AND ADDITIONAL CLAUSES

Oven-timing clocks

Where a contract has been concluded but the parties each seek to rely on their standard terms, and the court is seeking to identify the terms of the contract, a party is not necessarily bound by a term which does not conflict with his own terms.

Facts: On 27 October 1980 the bankrupt debtor ordered from the plaintiff, on the terms and conditions of purchase printed on the reverse side of the order form, certain time-switch clocks to be installed in electric ovens. Clause 16 of those terms and conditions of purchase was in the following terms: "Diverging terms of business. By accepting our order, the supplier declares that he consents to these terms and conditions of purchase. In the event that our order is confirmed by the supplier on terms which diverge from our terms and conditions of purchase, the latter shall nevertheless apply, even where we do not raise any objection. Consequently, divergent terms shall apply only where they have been expressly acknowledged by us in writing. If the supplier does not consent to the foregoing way of proceeding, he shall be obliged forthwith to indicate his disagreement in a specific letter to that effect. In such cases, we reserve the right to cancel the order, without thereby entitling the supplier to make any claim whatever against us. Our terms and conditions shall also apply to future transactions, even where no express reference is made to them, provided solely that they have already been received by the customer." On 11 February 1982 the bankrupt debtor placed a supplementary order with the plaintiff for the supply of further energy-regulating devices. The plaintiff confirmed the order, referring to its General Terms and Conditions of Delivery and Payment, which provided that the transaction was to be governed exclusively by its written confirmation of order in conjunction with the said General Terms and Conditions of Delivery and Payment. Clause 7 of those Terms and Conditions contained an extended and wide-ranging retention of title provision in respect of delivered goods.

Held: Whilst a contract had been concluded, it was not possible to conclude that the bankrupt debtor intended, by means of its preventive clause, to exclude only those of the plaintiff's terms and conditions of sale which conflicted with its own terms and conditions of purchase, and not also to exclude the plaintiff's additional clauses.

Judgment: . . . The appellate court further concluded, correctly, that the bankrupt debtor did not declare, even tacitly, that it consented to the global incorporation into the contract of the plaintiff's General Terms and Conditions. A finding that the bankrupt debtor tacitly submitted to be bound by the plaintiff's terms and conditions of sale would conflict with the unequivocal statement contained in its own terms and conditions of purchase, to the effect that it contracted solely on its own terms and that it was to be deemed to have agreed to the application of divergent conditions appearing in the confirmation of order only if it had acknowledged in writing that those divergent conditions were to apply. . . . In view of the anticipatory objection by the bankrupt debtor, clearly expressed in the preventive clause contained in its terms and conditions, to the application of the plaintiff's General Terms and Conditions, such a change of mind on the bankrupt debtor's part cannot, in the absence of any new supervening circumstances, be held to have taken place and cannot, in particular, be inferred from the fact that the bankrupt debtor raised no fresh objection to the plaintiff's terms and conditions of sale and accepted delivery of the goods without reservation—as the appellate court rightly accepted, that point not having been challenged in the appeal on a point of law (see the judgment of the Chamber, WM 1977, 451 [452]) . . .

(aa) Where—as in the present case—a contract has come into existence without any agreement being reached as to the application of the general terms and conditions of either of the parties, that does not mean that, in such circumstances, the corresponding optional law is to apply in its entirety, and without exception, in place of the rules and stipulations laid down in the general terms and

---

[165] NJW 1985.1838.

conditions in question (see Bunte, ZIP 1982, 449 [450], setting out the relevant opinions on the issue; Wolf, in Wolf-Horn-Lindacher, *AGB-Gesetz*, § 2, note 77; Ulmer, in Ulmer-Brandner-Hensen, *AGB-Komm.*, 4th edition, § 2, note 101; Erman-Hefermehl, *BGB*, 7th edition, § 2 AGB-Gesetz, note 48). On the contrary, the parties may be deemed to have intended to apply those stipulations diverging from or supplementing the optional law which were contained in the general terms and conditions of both the parties, which were framed in similar or identical forms of wording and which both parties accordingly wished to see incorporated into the contract.

(bb) However, such a manifest consensus is lacking where the general terms and conditions of one of the parties contain "additional" stipulations which are not matched by corresponding, equivalent provisions contained in the terms and conditions of the other party, e.g.—as in the present case—a retention of title clause. The question whether, in such a case, it is possible to infer—even where no consensus is manifestly apparent from the general terms and conditions of both of the parties—that one of the parties tacitly agreed to the inclusion in the contract of the additional stipulations unilaterally laid down by the other party will depend on the wishes of the party opposing those stipulations, which are to be ascertained in the light of the other circumstances of the case (see Ulmer, § 2, note 104; Löwe-Graf von Westphalen-Trinkner, *AGB-Gesetz*, § 2, note 47). In the present case, however, it is not possible to conclude that the bankrupt debtor intended, by means of its preventive clause, to exclude only those of the plaintiff's terms and conditions of sale which conflicted with its own terms and conditions of purchase, and not also to exclude the plaintiff's additional clauses. . . .

Notes

(1) Lord Denning in the *Butler Machine Tool* indicates briefly three approaches to resolve the problem of the so-called "battle of forms". The traditional approach, which was adopted in that case by Lawton and Bridge L JJ, is to consider the communications between the parties as offers and counter-offers, in accordance with the "mirror-image rule".[166] Each communication in which a party refers to its own standard terms and conditions operates as a rejection of the other party's standard terms and conditions, and as a counter offer. In this approach the party who has made the last reference to its own terms and conditions often wins the battle—"last shot-doctrine"—, because its counter-offer is accepted by the conduct of the other party when that party carries out the contract for example by shipping the ordered goods or by taking delivery.[167]

(2) According to the Bundesgerichtshof in the *Heat Retaining Silo* case, the mere fact that A clearly believes a contract has been concluded for example by sending a reminder does not establish that the terms and conditions of the party that "fired the last shot" have been accepted by the other party. Rather, the Bundesgerichtshof requires that the other party actually performs its part of the contract or takes delivery of the goods ordered. However, since in that case the dispute about the terms of the contract had already arisen at the moment of delivery, the buyer's taking delivery could not operate as an acceptance of the sellers terms and conditions. Furthermore, as is shown by the *Oven Timing Clocks* case, if A's standard terms and conditions include a condition fending off B's terms and conditions, A's performance cannot be construed as an acceptance of B's terms and conditions. Thus, in German law an acceptance by conduct of the terms and conditions of the party who "fired the last shot" is not easily assumed—compare also 10 June 1974.[168]

---

[166] *Supra*, at 230.
[167] See for acceptance by conduct **2.1.3.A.**, *supra*, at 213 ff.
[168] BB 1974.1136.

(3) An objection raised to the "last shot-doctrine" is that it is arbitrary to give prece-dence to the terms and conditions of the party that happens to have "the last word" in the process of concluding the contract.

(4) Another way to resolve the problem could be to let the terms and conditions of the offeror prevail, unless they are expressly rejected by the acceptor: the "first blow" rule. The underlying idea is then that the party making the last communication has the last chance to clear up the matter; if he does not do this and enters into the contract without making his acceptance expressly conditional on acceptance of his own terms and condi-tions, he knowingly takes the risk of being bound to the other party's terms and condi-tions.[169] The German Bundesgerichtshof has followed this approach more than once. In this approach, in which an exception is made to the "mirror image" rule, the question remains on what terms and conditions the contract is concluded.

(5) An objection that is raised to both of the two approaches mentioned above is that one party should not be given control where, in reality, the parties are in disagreement on relevant terms.[170]

(6) This objection is met by a third approach, according to which the terms and con-ditions of both parties in so far as they can be reconciled are included in the contract, whereas the conflicting terms and conditions are left out—the "knock-out rule", adopted in Article 2.22 of the Unidroit Principles,[171] and by § 2–207(3) of the American UCC.[172] Any gaps in the contract will have to be filled by suppletive rules of law, usage, trade prac-tices etc. This approach was followed by the Bundesgerichtshof in the second of the two German cases here cited, where, as has been noted, the "last shot-doctrine" could not be applied in the absence of an acceptance by conduct. While applying the "knock-out rule", the BGH had to decide, however, not about a *conflicting* term, but about the inclusion in the contract of an *additional* term of the seller about reservation of property after deliv-ery, and which was not dealt with at all in the terms and conditions of the buyer. The BGH held that the inclusion in the contract of additional terms of one party depended on the will of the other party, which had to be determined having regard to the circum-stances. One of those circumstances was that the buyer's conditions fended off any devi-ating terms and conditions of the other party, and from this condition, the BGH deduced that the buyer did not assent to the incorporation of *any* other term, whether or not it conflicted with the buyer's own terms. It would seem more logical, however, to say that a condition that is different from the suppletive rules that would apply in its absence con-flicts with the terms of the offer if the offer does not address the subject in question.

(7) The case-law of the BGH shows a tendency towards an innovative and more real-istic approach to the battle-of-forms problem. Instead of giving precedence to the terms and conditions of one party, the BGH is prepared to place the terms and conditions of both parties on an equal footing and substitute the conflicting terms by suppletive rules of law. French case law adopts the German solution. A similar attempt has been made in the United States with § 2–207 of the UCC (Uniform Commercial Code). The provision is applicable only to sale contracts and constitutes a departure from the traditional rule

---

[169] See Von Mehren, op. cit. at 96.
[170] *Ibid.*, at 100.
[171] *Supra*, at 229.
[172] *Infra*, at 236.

that offer and acceptance have to be a mirror image of one another. The rationale of section § 2–207 is that a rigid application of the "mirror-image rule" with regard to sale contracts is contrary to practice, because of the increasing use of standard forms with
pre-printed terms and conditions. However, the provision requires a creative construction
in order to reach the "knock out" result:

Uniform Commercial Code   **2.US.58.**

§ 2–207: (1) A definite and reasonable expression of acceptance or a written confirmation which is
sent within a reasonable time operates as an acceptance even though it states terms additional to or different from those offered or agreed upon, unless acceptance is expressly
made conditional on assent to the additional or different terms.
(2) The additional terms are to be construed as proposals for addition to the contract.
Between merchants such terms become part of the contract unless:
  (a) the offer expressly limits acceptance to the terms of the offer;
  (b) they materially alter it; or
  (c) notification of objection to them has already been given or is given within a reas-
      onable time after notice of them is received.
(3) Conduct by both parties which recognises the existence of a contract is sufficient to
establish a contract for sale although the writings of the parties do not otherwise establish
a contract. In such case the terms of the particular contract consist of those terms on
which the writings of the parties agree, together with any supplementary terms incorporated under any other provisions of this Act.

By virtue of subsection (1), a contract may be concluded in spite of a "battle of
the terms" without a contrived "acceptance by conduct" of the "last shot" terms and conditions of the other party. Even an acceptance that does not truly mirror the offer can
conclude the contract, unless the acceptor has made his acceptance expressly conditional
on the offeror's assent to his additional and different terms. On the other hand, subsection (2) seems to adopt the "first blow" rule, according to which the offeror's terms and
conditions prevail; only terms and conditions contained in the acceptance and that do *not*
materially alter the offer become part of the contract (subsection 2.b.). Moreover, under
subsections 2.a and c, the offeror has the power to reject additional terms contained in
the acceptance. The provision does not therefore remove the objection that it is unrealistic and undesirable to give one party control where the parties are not agreed as to the
terms and conditions.

(8) The supporters of the "knock out-rule" have tried to construe subsection (2) in a
more innovative way.[173] They say that, since this subsection mentions only "additional
terms" and not "conflicting" terms of the acceptance, the latter are not covered by the
subsection. Therefore, if the acceptance contains conflicting terms, the offeror's terms do
not prevail. In such a case the conflicting terms and conditions contained in offer and
acceptance knock each other out, and gaps in the contract must be filled by suppletive
rules of law (the "knock out-rule"). This innovative reading of subsection (2) was applied
in *Daitom Inc.* v. *Pennwalt Corp.*[174]

[173] See Von Mehren, op. cit. at 97–9.
[174] 741 F 2d 1569 (10 Cir. 1984).

(9) The knock-out rule is adopted expressly in subsection 3 of the UCC provision. However, the provision applies only when no contract has been concluded on the basis of subsection (1), because there was no "definite and reasonable expression of acceptance" or because the acceptance was expressly made conditional on the offeror's assent to the additional and conflicting terms in the acceptance. In English law, Lord Denning made an effort to introduce an approach very similar to the knock out rule in the *Butler Machine Co* case,[175] but his Lordship's preference for looking at the documentation as a whole has been rejected by the House of Lords in *Gibson* v. *Manchester CC*.[176]

2.2. PRE-CONTRACTUAL GOOD FAITH

2.2.1. INTRODUCTION

The formation of a contract is often preceded by lengthy negotiations. Frequently, an offer and an acceptance cannot be identified. Today, especially with regard to major deals, there rather is "a gradual process in which agreements are reached piecemeal in several rounds with a succession of drafts".[177] Therefore, especially in modern trade, the classical rules on offer and acceptance appear to be insufficient to govern the process of formation of contract. The first to recognize this was Rudolph von Jhering. In a famous article of 1861 he maintained that a party might be liable for fault in negotiations.[178] His view was that a party who induces another to rely on the conclusion of a valid contract could be liable for *culpa in contrahendo*. It is often thought that Jhering proposed a liability for broken off negotiations. However, in that article he did not say a word about disappointing negotiations; he dealt exclusively with situations where at least one party thought that a valid contract was concluded.

The history of liability for broken off negotiations started in the shadow of Vesuvius. In 1906, the Neapolitan magistrate Gabriele Fagella published an article[179] in which he distinguished three stages in negotiations: the period before any offer has been drafted, the period during which an offer is drafted, and the period after an offer has been made. The novelty of Fagella's theory was that he accepted that a negotiating party could be liable in all these stages, including the period before an offer is made. The importance of Fagella's theory was recognised by the French comparative lawyer Raymond Saleilles. In an article entirely dedicated to Fagella's theory he endorsed his ideas and elaborated them on some points.[180] Only a few years after the BGB came into force, the German

---

[175] Cit. *supra*, at 229–231.

[176] [1979] 1 WLR 294.

[177] E. A. Farnsworth, "Pre-contractual Liability and Preliminary Agreements: Fair Dealing and Failed Negotiations" [1987] Columbia Law Review 217, at 218.

[178] R. von Jhering, "Culpa in contrahendo oder Schadensersatz bei nichtigen oder nicht zur Perfection gelangten Verträgen", Jahrbücher für die Dogmatik des heutigen römischen und deutschen Privatrechts", 1861.IV.1.

[179] G. Fagella, "Dei periodi precontrattuali e dell loro vera ed esatta costruzione scientifica", in *Studi Giuridici in onore di Carlo Fadda*, vol. III, at 271.

[180] R. Saleilles, "De la responsabilité précontractuelle; à propos d'une étude nouvelle sur la matière", RTD civ. 1907.697.

Reichsgericht adopted a general doctrine of *culpa in contrahendo*, using it, however, to solve a very different problem from those for which Jhering had proposed his theory.[181] The Italian Civil Code of 1942 was the first code to contain a specific provision on pre-contractual good faith.[182] Today, most systems accept a general duty of pre-contractual good faith. Although in most countries the brutal interruption of advanced negotiations is seen as the paradigmatic instance of negotiating contrary to good faith, the role of pre-contractual good faith is far from limited to that. In many systems the duty of pre-contractual good faith is applied in several other situations.

Legal scholars often emphasize that an intense regulation of the stage of formation is not without risk. Farnsworth warns of a "chilling effect".[183] This chapter will examine the balance the major European legal systems have found between freedom and respect for the interest of the other party in negotiations.

2.2.2. A GENERAL DUTY OF PRE-CONTRACTUAL GOOD FAITH

The civil codes in many of the jurisdictions studied contain clear provisions establishing a general duty of pre-contractual good faith. A number of those provisions are set out below. However, there is an immediate contrast between the civil law jurisdictions and the common law, for as we shall see, the common law imposes no general duty of pre-contractual good faith.

Principles of European Contract Law   **2.PECL.59.**

Article 2:301: Negotiations Contrary to Good Faith
> (1) A party is free to negotiate and is not liable for failure to reach an agreement.
> (2) However, a party who has negotiated or broken off contrary to good faith is liable for the losses caused to the other party.
> (3) It is contrary to good faith, in particular, for a party to enter into or continue negotiations with no real intention of reaching an agreement with the other party.

Unidroit Principles   **2.INT.60.**

Article 2.15: Negotiations in bad faith
> (1) A party is free to negotiate and is not liable for the failure to reach an agreement.
> (2) However, a party who negotiates or breaks off negotiations in bad faith is liable for losses caused to the other party.
> (3) It is bad faith, in particular, to enter or continue negotiations when intending not to reach an agreement with the other party.

Note
Both sets of Principles contain a provision on pre-contractual good faith: Article 2:301 PECL and Article 2.15 Unidroit. In addition to that, the Comments make clear that many

---

[181] *Infra* at 250.
[182] *Infra* at 240.
[183] Farnsworth, *supra*, note 177.

of the other rules, like those imposing a duty to inform, are based on the general duty of pre-contractual good faith. Compare Article 197 of the Greek Civil Code,[184] Article 227, Section 1, of the Portuguese Civil Code and Article 227 of the Spanish Código Civil.[185]

Code civil   **2.F.61.**

Article 1134: Contracts . . . must be performed in good faith.

Notes

(1) Article 1134 section 3 of the draft *Code civil* read as follows: "[*Les conventions*] *doivent être contractées et exécutées de bonne foi.*" However, the word "*contractées*" was struck out because Portalis found it superfluous.[186]

(2) Article 1134 does not relate to pre-contractual negotiations, but to the performance of contracts. However, today the courts and most contemporary French authors recognize a general duty of pre-contractual good faith.[187]

(3) In Belgium, the Civil Code does not establish a general duty of pre-contractual good faith. As we will see, liability for bad faith in pre-contractual dealings is rather dealt with on the basis of Articles 1382 and 1383 on liability for fault.[188]

BGB-KE (Draft Civil Code) II   **2.G.62.**

§ 305: A relationship imposing obligations within the meaning of Paragraph 241(2) BGB-KE may arise at the stage of, and by virtue of, negotiations with a view to the conclusion of a contract.

§ 241: A relationship imposing obligations on the parties thereto may, having regard to the content and nature thereof, be such as to require each party to take into special consideration the rights and legal interests of the other party. Such a relationship may be limited thereto.

Notes

(1) In Germany the Reichsgericht had already accepted that by taking up negotiations parties enter into a legal relationship (*Rechtsverhältnis*), similar to a contractual relationship, that gives rise to several duties between the negotiating parties, for example depending on the case, duties not to harm the other party's person or property, to provide her with certain types of information and not to break off very advanced negotiations. These duties will be discussed extensively in this chapter. The violation of such a duty makes a party liable for *culpa in contrahendo*.[189] The Bundesgerichtshof has proceeded on the same lines.[190] With regard to the dogmatic basis of these pre-contractual

---

[184] See Stathopoulos, *Contract law in Hellas* (The Hague-London-Boston/ Athens: Kluwer, 1995) para. 84.

[185] L. Díez-Picazo and A. Gullón, *Sistema de derecho civil*, Vol. II (Madrid: 1995), at 68.

[186] See P.A. Fénet, *Recueil complet des travaux préparatoires du Code civil, discussions, motifs, rapports et discours*, Book 3, title 3, at 54.

[187] See Malaurie and Aynès, para. 379; P. Jourdain, "Rapport Français", in *La bonne foi*, Travaux de l'Association Henri Capitant, vol. XLIII 1992 (Paris: 1994) at 131.

[188] See the Belgian *Glassmakers* case, *infra*, at 246.

[189] See Reichsgericht, 7 December 1911, cit. at 291.

[190] See e.g. BGH, 10 July 1970, cit. at 252. Compare for Austria: Koziol, Welser, *Grundriß des bürgerlichen Rechts, Vol. I Allgemeiner Teil des Schuldrechts* (Wien: Manz, 1995) at 204.

duties several suggestions have been made by legal doctrine (for example *Treu und Glauben*; the *Vertrauensprinzip*) but none of them can be said to have been generally accepted. It has been argued that the cases dealt with by the doctrine of *culpa in contrahendo* are so disparate in character that they cannot be said to have a common basis.[191] Nevertheless, the Law Reform Commission, contrary to the advice of Medicus,[192] has proposed the introduction of a common statutory basis for all pre-contractual duties: § 305 II BGB-KE.[193] This article refers to § 241 II BGB-KE,[194] also new, that should provide a statutory basis for the duty of care (*Schutzpflicht*) in any legal relationship (*Rechtsverhältnis*).

(2) In the Netherlands the Hoge Raad has decided, in words very similar to those of the German Bundesgerichtshof that parties starting negotiations enter into a legal relationship that is dominated by good faith, which requires them to take each other's interests into account.[195] Although this was a case on mistake, the doctrine is now, as in Italy, virtually always applied in cases concerning broken off negotiations.

Codice civile   2.I.63.

Article 1337: *Pre-contractual negotiations and liability.* During the course of the negotiations and in the formation of the contract, the parties must act in good faith.

Note

Under this Article of the Codice civile, there is a general duty to negotiate in accordance with good faith. Good faith here means objective good faith.[196] Therefore subjective good faith, for example in breaking off negotiations, is no excuse.[197] The duty to negotiate in accordance with good faith essentially means that a party has to take the other party's interest into account.[198] According to legal scholars this general duty is the basis for several more specific duties, such as a duty of confidentiality, a duty to inform,[199] but the courts have applied Article 1337 only in cases concerning broken off negotiations. See Article 1338 CC (Italy), which is generally seen as a *lex specialis* of Article 1337.[200]

---

[191] *Münchener Kommontar*, Vol. 2, Vor § 275 (Emmerich), para. 59; Soergel, *Bürgerliches Gesetzbuch mit Einführungsgesetz und Nebengesetzen*, 12th. edn. (Stuttgart/Berlin/ Köln/Mainz: 1990), § 275, para. 120. See on the collocation of the protection of so-called *vertragsfremde Rechtsgüter*, *infra*, **2.2.3.G** at 291.

[192] D. Medicus, *Verschulden bei Vertragsverhandlungen, Gutachten und Vorschläge zur Überarbeitung des Schuldrechts*, Vol. I (Köln: Haymanns, 1981) at 485.

[193] *Supra*, at 239.

[194] *Supra*, at 239.

[195] See HR, 15 November 1957.

[196] See e.g. Cass. it., 11 May 1990, n. 4051, at 261.

[197] See Sacco, *Il contratto*, Vol. II (Torino: UTET, 1993), at 235.

[198] See Bianca, *Il contratto* (Milano: Giuffrè, 1987) para. 78.

[199] See e.g. Trabucchi, *Istituzioni di Diritto Civile*, 34th edn. (Padova: CEDAM, 1993) para. 281.

[200] See Bianca, op. cit, para. 78, and see *infra* at 284.

House of Lords   **2.E.64.**
Walford v. *Miles*[201]

No duty of pre-contractual good faith

The lock-out agreement

A contract to negotiate is unenforceable for a lack of certainty, and it is not possible to make good that uncertainty by implying into the agreement a duty to conduct pre-contractual negotiations in good faith. Such a duty would be repugnant to the adversarial position of the parties during the negotiations.

Facts: In 1986, the respondents decided to sell their photographic processing business and premises. The appellants entered into negotiations with the respondents, and reached an agreement in principle for the sale of the business. The parties also made a "lock out" agreement, under which the respondents agreed to terminate and/or to refuse to enter into negotiations with any other party for the sale of the business. Under this agreement, the appellants were obliged to provide a letter from their bank confirming that the bank would provide them with a loan to facilitate the purchase, which they duly did. The respondents nevertheless sold the business to a third party, and the appellants brought an action against the respondents for breach of the lock-out agreement. The appellants alleged that the lock-out agreement was a collateral contract, the consideration for which was the provision of the letter and the continuation of negotiations. The appellants also argued that to give business efficacy to the agreement it must have contained an implied term that, so long as the respondents desired to sell the business and the premises, the respondents would continue to negotiate in good faith with the appellants. The appellants claimed that the business was in fact worth £1m more than they had agreed to pay, and claimed damages for the difference in value between the price agreed and the true value.

Held: The trial judge held that there was a collateral agreement and that this agreement had been repudiated by the appellants. He therefore ordered that the damages for the alleged loss of opportunity be assessed. He also awarded £700 damages for wasted expenditure arising from pre-contractual misrepresentations. A majority of the Court of Appeal upheld the award of £700, but reversed the decision on the collateral contract point, holding that the agreement alleged was no more than an agreement to negotiate and was therefore unenforceable. The House of Lords upheld the decision of the Court of Appeal.

Judgment: LORD ACKNER: The justification for the implied term . . . was that in order to give the collateral agreement "business efficacy", Mr Miles was obliged to "continue to negotiate in good faith." It was submitted to the Court of Appeal and initially to your Lordships that this collateral agreement could not be made to work, unless there was a positive duty imposed upon Mr. Miles to negotiate. It was of course conceded that the agreement made no specific provision for the period it was to last. It was however contended, albeit not pleaded, that the obligation to negotiate would endure for a reasonable time, and that such time was the time which was reasonably necessary to reach a binding agreement. It was however accepted that such a period of time would not end when negotiations had ceased, because all such negotiations were conducted expressly under the umbrella of "subject to contract". The agreement alleged would thus be valueless if the alleged obligation to negotiate ended when negotiations as to the terms of the "subject to contract" agreement had ended, since at that stage the Miles would have been entitled at their whim to refuse to sign any contract.

Apart from the absence of any term as to the duration of the collateral agreement, it contained no provision for the Miles to determine the negotiations, albeit that such a provision was essential. It was contended by Mr Naughton (counsel for the appellants) that a term was to be implied giving the Miles a right to determine the negotiations, but only if they had "a proper reason". However in order to determine whether a given reason was a proper one, he accepted that the test was not an objective one—would a hypothetical reasonable person consider the reason a reasonable one? The

---

[201] [1992] 2 AC 128.

241

test was a subjective one—did the Miles honestly believe in the reason which they gave for the termination of the negotiations? Thus they could be quite irrational, so long as they behaved honestly.

Mr. Naughton accepted that as the law now stands and has stood for approaching 20 years, an agreement to negotiate is not recognised as an enforceable contract. This was first decided in terms in *Courtney and Fairbairn Ltd* v. *Tolaini Brothers (Hotels) Ltd*. [1975] 1 W.L.R. 297 . . . The decision in *Courtney's* case [1975] 1 W.L.R. 297 was followed by the Court of Appeal in *Mallozzi* v. *Carapelli S.p.a* [1976] 1 Lloyd's Rep. 407. . . . The decision that an agreement to negotiate cannot constitute a legally enforceable contract has been followed at first instance in a number of relatively recent cases; . . .

Before your Lordships it was sought to argue that the decision in *Courtney's* case [1975] 1 W.L.R. 297 was wrong. Although the cases in the United States did not speak with one voice your Lordships' attention was drawn to the decision of the United States' Court of Appeal, Third Circuit, in *Channel Home Centers, Division of Grace Retail Corporation* v. *Grossman* (1986) 795 F. 2d 291 as being "the clearest example" of the American cases in the appellants' favour. That case raised the issue whether an agreement to negotiate in good faith, if supported by consideration, is an enforceable contract. I do not find the decision of any assistance. While accepting that an agreement to agree is not an enforceable contract, the Court of Appeal appears to have proceeded on the basis that an agreement to negotiate in good faith is synonymous with an agreement to use best endeavours and as the latter is enforceable, so is the former. This appears to me, with respect, to be an unsustainable proposition. The reason why an agreement to negotiate, like an agreement to agree, is unenforceable, is simply because it lacks the necessary certainty. The same does not apply to an agreement to use best endeavours. This uncertainty is demonstrated in the instant case by the provision which it is said to be implied in the agreement for the determination of the negotiations. How can a court be expected to decide whether, *subjectively*, a proper reason existed for the termination of negotiations? The answer suggested depends upon whether the negotiations have been determined "in good faith." However the concept of a duty to carry on negotiations in good faith is inherently repugnant to the adversarial position of the parties when involved in negotiations. Each party to the negotiations is entitled to pursue his (or her) own interest, so long as he avoids making misrepresentations. To advance that interest he must be entitled, if he thinks it appropriate, to threaten to withdraw from further negotiations or to withdraw in fact, in the hope that the opposite party may seek to reopen the negotiations by offering him improved terms. Mr. Naughton, of course accepts that the agreement upon which he relies does not contain a duty to complete the negotiations. But that still leaves the vital question—how is a vendor ever to know that he is entitled to withdraw from further negotiations? How is the court to police such an "agreement?" A duty to negotiate in good faith is as unworkable in practice as it is inherently inconsistent with the position of a negotiating party. It is here that the uncertainty lies. In my judgment, while negotiations are in existence either party is entitled to withdraw from those negotiations, at any time and for any reason. There can be thus no obligation to negotiate until there is a "proper reason" to withdraw. Accordingly a bare agreement to negotiate has no legal content.

Notes

(1) *Walford* v. *Miles* affirms that under English law there is no such thing as a general duty to negotiate in good faith. The point arose by virtue of the appellants' submission that the lock-in agreement could be rendered sufficiently certain by the implication of a duty to continue the negotiations in good faith. The House of Lords took the occasion to make clear by a single speech in very strong terms that English law does not know an obligation to negotiate in good faith.[202] This decision has met with criticism in England[203] and abroad.[204]

---

[202] See further on this case *infra* at 241–2.

[203] See e.g. McKendrick, *Contract*, at 62; contrast however, Treitel, *Contract*, at 57, who finds it entirely appropriate.

[204] See e.g. van Erp, "The Formation of Contracts", in *Towards a European Civil Code*, at 117.

(2) Scots law on this point is similar to English law—compare MacQueen and Thomson:[205]

> The general principle is that when parties are negotiating a contract they are at arms' length in the sense that each has to look after its own interests, and has no obligations to the other party short of telling lies (misrepresentations), practising deception (fraud), coercing the other party into entering the contract (force and fear), or exploiting a special relationship one has with the other party quite separately from the contract under negotiation (undue influence).

2.2.3. DEFINING PRE-CONTRACTUAL GOOD FAITH

What kinds of conduct are regarded as contrary to good faith? This chapter will discuss: (A) negotiating without intending to conclude a contract; (B) conducting parallel negotiations; (C) breaking off negotiations; (D) knowingly concluding an invalid contract; (E) not giving adequate information; (F) disclosing confidential information; (G) causing physical harm to the other party in the course of negotiations.

2.2.3.A. NO INTENTION TO CONCLUDE A CONTRACT

Principles of European Contract Law   **2.PECL.65.**

Article 2:301: *Negotiations Contrary to Good Faith*
(3) It is contrary to good faith, in particular, for a party to enter into or continue negotiations with no real intention of reaching an agreement with the other party.

Unidroit Principles   **2.INT.66.**

Article 2.15: *Negotiations in bad faith*
(3) It is bad faith, in particular, to enter or continue negotiations when intending not to reach an agreement with the other party.

Illustration No 1 to Article 2.15. A learns of B's intention to sell its restaurant. A, who has no intention whatsoever of buying the restaurant, nevertheless enters into lengthy negotiations with B for the sole purpose of preventing B from selling the restaurant to C, a competitor of A's. A, who breaks off negotiations when C has bought another restaurant, is liable to B, who ultimately succeeds in selling the restaurant at a lower price than offered by C, for the difference in price.

Cass. it., 28 January 1972[206]   **2.I.67.**

NEGOTIATING WITHOUT SERIOUS INTENT MAY BE CONTRARY TO GOOD FAITH

Niki

In considering whether a party is in breach of the duty of pre-contractual good faith, a court should look at the seriousness of the intentions of the party in conducting the negotiations, and not the fact that the party might not in fact have been able to comply with its duties under the contract.

[205] MacQueen and Thomson, *Contract Law in Scotland* (Edinburgh: Butterworths, 2000), para. 2.89.
[206] No. 199, Foro it. 1972.I.2088; Giur. it. 1972.I.1.1315.

Facts: The company Italtelecine s.r.l. reached a preliminary agreement with the company Cineriz di Angelo Rizzoli concerning the co-production of a film on the subject of Niki, the copyright in which it held. Although a date had already been fixed for signing the contract, Cineriz had put off signing it on various pretexts and had then let it be known that it no longer wished to proceed. The plaintiff therefore sought an order requiring Cineriz to perform the obligations imposed by the contract or, in the alternative, to pay damages on account of the latter having incurred extra-contractual liability.

Held: The Cassazione held that the Corte d'appello should have examined the seriousness of the intentions which prompted Cineriz to enter into negotiations, its good faith in continuing them and any justification for the grounds on which it suddenly broke them off.

Judgment: Pre-contractual liability, whilst not having hitherto gained unanimous acceptance amongst jurists, is founded on the solid base of the legal importance which it is recognised as possessing at the stage of negotiations. The real problem, which has given rise to some uncertainty, *inter alia* in the case-law, arises from the need to reconcile the obligation to pay compensation for having broken off the negotiations with the parties' recognised freedom to conduct legal transactions, on the basis of which they do not assume any obligation until such time as they can be seen to have reached a consensus. And the difficulty is increased by the fact that the obligation on both parties to conclude a contract (Article 1351 of the Civil Code), or even that incumbent on one of them alone (Article 1329 of the Civil Code), cannot arise without there being some appropriate manifestation of a direct wish to enter into a legal transaction involving the assumption of the commitment to fulfil the stipulations of a future contract. As this Court has previously confirmed (Cass., 10 October 1962, no 2919), it can never be possible to claim, on account of pre-contractual liability, compensation in any specific form, namely the conclusion of the contract with a view to which the negotiations which were subsequently broken off took place.

Even though the legislature fully respected the freedom of the parties to conduct legal transactions, it was prompted, by the need to offer those parties some protection during the negotiation stage, to enact the provisions contained in Article 1337 of the Civil Code. [. . .]

That said, it seems clear that subject-matter of the protection afforded by Article 1337 of the Civil Code is not the same as that which the party concerned intended to achieve by concluding the contract; it relates to an earlier stage and is represented by the legitimate expectation not so much that the negotiations would come to fruition (otherwise the result would be to encumber the freedom of the parties to negotiate) as that they would be conducted fairly and with propriety on an equal footing, and that one party would not, because of reservations or even because of a less than serious attitude and a lack of genuine intent, have involved the other party in negotiations (which he did not wish to bring to a conclusion), thus preventing the second party in the meantime from entering into an agreement with others.

And the expectation of the party who considers himself aggrieved cannot be regarded as a mere hope that the deal will be closed; rather—since it is legally important—it must be examined in relation to the conduct of the other party, because it is only where one party first causes the other to entertain a firm conviction that it will be possible to conclude a contract and then, after monopolising the latter's attention regarding the matter in hand, so that he does not seek other possible opportunities, and then withdraws without any justification, that there can be any question of lack of good faith in objective terms and the possibility of pre-contractual liability.

In this case the Corte d'appello, having established, in its appraisal of the facts, which is not open to challenge, that the parties had conducted serious negotiations concerning assignment of the copyright relating to Niki, reaching the final stage and setting the date on which the contract was to be signed, ought not then, illogically, to have considered the clauses of the not-to-be-signed contract and reached the conclusion that the latter, by itself, could not have provided Italtelecine with the benefits which it had in mind (production of the film) since it was linked with other arrangements for co-production agreements which were to follow, in respect of which Italtelecine could not yet claim any expectations. Instead, more simply, the court should have examined the seriousness of the intentions which prompted Cineriz to enter into the negotiations, its good faith in continuing them and any justification for the grounds on which it suddenly broke them off.

No reference to the lack of any certainty as to the possibility of securing the expected benefits from the contract could—contrary to the erroneous view taken by the Corte d'appello—have been of any great importance regarding impropriety and lack of good faith in the negotiations; and that, essentially, was the error which—as already stated—cause the Corte d'appello to stray from the proper course of inquiry.

Notes

(1) In most European legal systems it is held to be contrary to pre-contractual good faith to enter into negotiations without having any intention of making a contract.[207] If a party, for example, enters into negotiations for the sole purpose of obtaining knowledge of business secrets of the other party or for the sole purpose of preventing him from contracting with a competitor of the first party, he is liable. In the latter case the liability will amount to the lost opportunity to contract with the competitor (in such a case under German law liability can be based on § 826 BGB (*sittenwidrige vorsätzliche Schädigung*).[208] At common law, the same result would be reached, but through the doctrine of fraud. In an American case the lessor conducted negotiations with the lessee for renewal of the lease in order to have the premises occupied during negotiations with a third party for their sale. Here damages for lost opportunities included the profits lost due to the loss of the lessee's principal customer, which would not have occurred had the lessee concluded a contract with a third party instead of entering into these deceiving negotiations.[209] In another American case the defendant had advertised for bids, although having already decided to give the contract to one candidate.[210]

(2) Not only actual absence of intention to conclude a contract can lead to liability, but also negligence in beginning negotiations: see the *Niki* case.[211] See, as another example, RGZ 143, 219, 19 January 1934, where a party entered into negotiations while knowing that he would not be able to comply with conditions put by the other party for concluding a new contract (i.e. providing sufficient securities) and thus provoked unnecessary expense for the other party. In English law, there may be liability for the tort of negligence if pre-contractual representations are made without due care.[212]

(3) It is equally contrary to good faith to continue negotiations after having lost the intention to conclude the contract. A party who protracts negotiations after having decided that he will not conclude any contract with this partner is liable for expenses and lost opportunities.[213]

[207] See art. 2:301, section 3, PECL; 2.15, section 3 Unidroit; Terré, Simler and Lequette, para. 177; Bianca, op. cit., para. 79; Medicus, op. cit. *supra* note 192, at 495; Hondius, "General Report", in *Pre-contractual Liability; Reports to the XIIIth Congress International Academy of Comparative Law, Montreal, Canada 18–24 August 1990* (Deventer/Boston: 1991) at 16–17; Lando, Denmark, in *Pre-contractual Liability* op. cit., at 117–18.
[208] See Medicus, op. cit. *supra*, note 192, at 495.
[209] *Markov* v. *ABC Transfer & Storage Co.*, 76 Wash. 2d 388, 457 P 2d 535 (1969).
[210] *Heyder Products Co.* v. *United States*, 140 F Supp. 409 (Ct.Cl.1956).
[211] Cit. *supra*, at 244.
[212] See *Box* v. *Midland Bank Ltd* [1979] 2 Lloyds Rep. 391 (the decision was overturned on appeal on a different point [1981] 1 Lloyd's Rep. 434). Liability will depend, *inter alia*, on whether the criteria for the recovery of purely economic losses are satisfied in the particular case: see V. Gerven, *Tort Law* 2.4.1.
[213] See Weber, "Haftung für in Aussicht gestellten Vertragsabschluß", *AcP* 192 (1992), 390–435, at 396; Terré, Simler and Lequette, para. 177; Brunner, annotation under Plas/Valburg, HR 18 June 1982, NJ 1983, 723.

(4) The liability discussed here rests on the same principle as liability for inducing the other party into concluding a contract, while knowing that it will be invalid:[214] it is contrary to good faith to induce another party into negotiations on something one knows to be incapable of realisation.[215]

2.2.3.B. PARALLEL NEGOTIATIONS

Cour d'appel de Liège, 20 October 1989[216]   **2.B.68.**

PARALLEL NEGOTIATIONS NOT CONTRARY TO GOOD FAITH

The Belgian glassmakers

A party which conducts negotiations with more than one party with a view to securing the most advantageous terms and conditions does not act contrary to good faith.

Facts: In September 1977, four Belgian glass companies agreed to meet their usual supplier of carbonate of soda, Solvay, the following January to fix prices as from the following April. However, the glassmakers were dissatisfied with the terms offered by Solvay and agreed in principle to purchase carbonate of soda from the United States company FMC. At the request of FMC, the glassmakers signed a letter of intent dated setting out the duration of the contract, the quantities and the price structure. Workers at the Solvay plant learned that negotiations with FMC had reached an advanced stage, and held a high profile demonstration in the presence of the Minister for Economic Affairs. The Minister subsequently ordered the glass industry federation (which had been party to the negotiations between the glassmakers and FMC) and its members not to take any decision regarding any orders for carbonate of soda from abroad, and asked it to open negotiations with Solvay. FMC wrote to the glassmakers stating that it regarded the parties as legally bound by the sale/purchase contract contained in the letter of intent, and that it had started to take the necessary steps to be able to make deliveries as from 1 April 1978. However, soon afterwards the glassmakers announced that they were terminating the negotiations with FMC and signed supply contracts with Solvay for a five-year period. FMC sued the glassmakers, claiming an order requiring the glassmakers to cease acting in breach of the contract which it alleged had been concluded and damages for failure to fulfil the obligation to negotiate in good faith with a view to the conclusion of the contract (*culpa in contrahendo*).

Held: The cour d'appel de Liège held that the glassmakers had not acted contrary to good faith.

Judgment:—Whereas FMC alleges that the glass-making companies suddenly and prematurely broke off the negotiations for the conclusion of contracts for the supply of carbonate of soda, which were already at a very advanced stage.

—Whereas the overriding principle applying in a market economy is that of freedom of negotiation, the corollary of which is the freedom to enter, or to decline to enter, into a contract; the breaking-off of negotiations does not in itself give rise to liability, even if it results in damage; however, the circumstances in which they are broken off may be such as to give rise to fault within the meaning of Article 1383 of the Civil Code; . . . The breaking-off of negotiations cannot be regarded as giving rise to fault where it occurs for a valid reason, in particular where the party breaking them off does so in order to contract with another party offering more advantageous conditions (Planiol and Ripert, t. VI, no 33, final part; J. Schmidt, "La sanction de la faute précontractuelle", *Rev. Trim. Dr. Civ.*, 1974, p. 53, no 10); . . .

—Whereas it is apparent that Solvay and the glassmakers had previously agreed to meet during the course of the first quarter of 1978 in order to negotiate the prices which were to apply from 1 April; that circumstance, a normal one in a relationship of which FMC must have been aware (since it was

---

[214] See *infra*, **2.2.3.D**.
[215] Sacco, op. cit. *supra*, note 197 at 236.
[216] Revue de droit commercial belge, 1990, 521, annotated by X. Dieux.

seeking to take the place of the usual supplier), is not such as to establish in itself the existence of "parallel negotiations" between the glass-making companies and Solvay; in any event, the absence of any exclusivity clause in the documents exchanged, particularly in the letters of intent of 13 December 1977, meant that the glassmakers were free at the same time to carry on negotiations with one or more other suppliers; freedom to contract necessarily entails freedom to negotiate simultaneously or successively with more than one prospective partner with a view to finally securing the most advantageous contract (F. t'Kint, "Négociation et conclusion du contrat", in *Les obligations contractuelles*, Editions du Jeune Barreau de Bruxelles, 1984, p. 15, no 12);

—Whereas it is apparent, therefore, that in breaking off the negotiations, albeit that they had reached an advanced stage, in the circumstances described above, the glass-making companies did not commit any fault; they acted in the same way as any other normally diligent and prudent commercial company would have acted in similar economic and social circumstances.

Cour d'appel de Versailles, 5 March 1992[217]   **2.F.69.**

PARALLEL NEGOTIATIONS PERMITTED

A French, a British and a Belgian Company

In the absence of a memorandum of exclusivity prohibiting the vendor from entering into parallel negotiations, a vendor is free to conduct parallel negotiations with other parties.

Facts: In 1988, the French company Gallay decided to hive off its renovation division, and entered into negotiations with the Belgian company Alvat. The directors of the two companies met a number of times in order to "give concrete form to that project", and various documents were exchanged during the course of the negotiations. At a meeting held on 21 March 1989, Alvat learned that Gallay was conducting parallel negotiations with the British company Blagden. The Belgian company thereupon broke off the negotiations and sued the French company, seeking an order for specific performance of the transfer, which it regarded as having already been constituted, and claiming damages on a joint and several basis from the French company and the British company.

Held: Alvat's claim failed.

Judgment: *On the alleged fault on the part of Gallay in the conduct of the negotiations*:—Whereas the company Alvat Belgïe complains, first, that Gallay negotiated with other parties at the same time as it was conducting negotiations with Alvat and, second, that it wrongfully broke off the negotiations with the latter.

—Whereas it must be recalled, first of all, that Gallay never undertook not to conduct parallel negotiations with other parties concerning the transfer of the Rhodarec shares.

—Whereas, if Alvat Belgïe had wished to negotiate on an exclusive basis, it could, as is normal in such matters, have insisted upon the signature of a memorandum of exclusivity prohibiting the vendor from negotiating with any other prospective purchaser pending a decision by Alvat.

—Whereas in the present case, not only was there no such agreement, but it is also clearly apparent from the documents produced by Alvat Belgïe that those documents were intended for any prospective purchaser.

—Whereas the note from Gallay dated 10 February 1989 is headed "Search for a partner" and this establishes thus, at the very least, that the negotiations were open to any potential purchaser and that the appellant was not the victim of any unfair stratagem.

—Whereas nor was there any wrongful act on the part of Gallay in its discontinuance of the negotiations with Alvat Belgïe at the beginning of April 1989.

---

[217] RTD civ. 1992.753, annotated by J. Mestre; Bull. Joly, 1992.636 annotated by J. Schmidt.

Notes

(1) In most European legal systems conducting parallel negotiations is in itself not considered to be contrary to good faith. As a matter of fact, it is very common in practice, and indeed essential to a market economy, to compare different proposals and to choose the most advantageous one—see *The Belgian Glassmakers* case.[218]

(2) If a party wishes an exclusive right to negotiate with one other party excluding all others he will have to bargain for it. See *A French, a British and a Belgian Company*.[219] In English law, there has been some doubt about the enforceability of exclusive negotiation clauses. In *Walford* v. *Miles*[220] a lock-out agreement was held unenforceable for lack of certainty. However, in a later case such an agreement, which was limited to a period of two weeks, was held to meet the requirement of certainty.[221]

(3) In principle, a party is not under an obligation to inform the other party spontaneously that he is also negotiating with others.[222] Therefore, in principle, a negotiating party cannot expect to be the only one dealing with his partner.

(4) However, it is contrary to good faith actually to lead the other party to believe that he is negotiating exclusively.[223]

(5) Of course, it is also contrary to good faith for a party who is conducting parallel negotiations to continue negotiations with one party after having decided to conclude the contract with another party. This follows from the rule, discussed above,[224] that it is contrary to good faith to continue negotiations with a party whilst no longer having the intention to conclude a contract with him.

2.2.3.C. BREAKING OFF NEGOTIATIONS

No party is under a duty to reach an agreement. However, in exceptional cases a party may be liable for breaking off negotiations in a manner contrary to good faith. In this section we discuss both the general freedom to break off negotiations and the cases in which liability is imposed for breaking off negotiations in bad faith. We also discuss the remedies available in cases of such liability.

(1) The freedom to break off negotiations

Principles of European Contract Law   **2.PECL.70.**

Article 2:301: *Negotiations Contrary to Good Faith*
               (1) A party is free to negotiate and is not liable for failure to reach an agreement.

---

[218] *Supra*, at 246, and see e.g. Hondius, op. cit., at 17; Farnsworth, op. cit, at 279; Terré, Simler and Lequette, para. 177.
[219] *Supra*, at 247.
[220] *Supra*, at 241.
[221] See *Pitt* v. *PHH Asset Management Ltd* [1994] 1 WLR 327. This seems to be in line with American law, where such clauses are accepted as long as they contain a time limit. See Farnsworth, op. cit., at 279.
[222] See Cour d'appel de Pau, 14 January 1969, D. 1969.716.
[223] See Hondius, op. cit., at 17.
[224] *Supra*, at 2.2.3.A.

Article 2.15: *Negotiations in bad faith*
    (1) A party is free to negotiate and is not liable for the failure to reach an agreement.

Notes

(1) In the absence of a pre-contract, a negotiating party is under no duty to reach an agreement. The logical consequence of this rule is that every negotiating party is free to break off negotiations at any stage.[225] This freedom is a consequence of the freedom of contract and party autonomy. It is essential to a market economy. If a party risks being held liable if negotiations do not lead to a contract he will be less willing to enter into negotiations.

(2) In exceptional circumstances a party who has broken off negotiations can be held liable.[226] This liability is sometimes conceived as an exception to the rule that a party is always free to break off.[227] However, the better view seems to be that liability of a party who has broken off negotiations in a manner contrary to good faith is not liability for breaking off—this would amount to *Kontrahierungszwang*—, but for inducing the other party's reliance that a contract would be concluded. See for example Bianca:[228]

The conduct of the negotiations does not involve any obligation to contract. A party to those negotiations retains the power to withdraw any proposal which he may have made, or his acceptance of any proposal made to him, until such time as the contract is concluded, and the exercise of such power does not in itself constitute a breach of any obligation to behave in a given way. Instead, such liability as he may incur will derive from his having fraudulently or culpably led the other party to harbour a confident and reasonable belief that the contract would be concluded.

(3) If breaking off itself became unlawful at a certain point in the negotiations, this would imply that the party who breaks off at that point should compensate the expectation interest, since the damage caused by the breaking off (the unlawful act) consists in the non-conclusion of the contract and, as a consequence, in the loss of the profit that would have been made with it.[229] Such an extensive liability, however, is generally rejected by the legal systems.[230] An exception is Dutch law, where expectation damages can be recovered, and there indeed the Hoge Raad has accepted that there is a point in the negotiations from which parties are no longer free to break off.[231] Inconsistent in this respect is the terminology of the Comment to Article 2.15 of the Unidroit Principles,[232] which says that at a certain point a party may no longer be free to break off negotiations, but limits damages to the reliance interest.

---

[225] See e.g. Palandt-Heinrichs § 276, para. 72; Terré, Simler and Lequette, para. 177; Cian and Trabucchi, op. cit., under art. 1337, at 1057; Stathopoulos, op. cit., para. 86.

[226] The circumstances in which this liability may arise will be discussed extensively in section 2.

[227] See e.g. Ghestin, para. 329.

[228] Bianca, op. cit., para. 79; See also e.g. Larenz, *SAT* at 108; P. van Ommeslaghe, Rapport Général, in *La bonne foi,* op. cit., at 32; BAG, 7 June 1963, NJW 1963, 1843; JZ 1964, 324; Cour d'appel de Liège, 20 October 1989, *supra,* at 246.

[229] See Bianca, op. cit, para. 79.

[230] *Infra,* at 251–2.

[231] *Infra,* at 262.

[232] *Infra,* at 252.

(2) Liability for breaking off negotiations

In most legal systems, there are exceptional cases in which a party who breaks off negotiations in a manner contrary to good faith may be liable. This liability is not conceived in the same way in all legal systems. Is a party who breaks off negotiations in a manner contrary to good faith liable in tort, in contract or should a *sui generis* liability be recognized? Moreover, the extent of the recovery varies among the systems. The question of the nature of liability for breaking off negotiations—tort, contract, *sui generis*—is relevant for at least two reasons. First, most systems have different regimes for tort liability and contractual liability. For example, usually the periods of prescription (limitation) vary.[233] Secondly, this question is relevant for qualification in private international law; the conflict rule for torts might lead to applicability of a different legal system from the conflict rule for contracts, and the jurisdiction rules also usually differ.[234]

We examine the general tests which are applied in the various systems for establishing liability below, under (b). A comparison of the different approaches will be made and the availability of the remedy of specific performance in some jurisdictions will be dealt with under (c) and (d) respectively. First, however, we will explain a fundamental distinction with regard to the extent of liability, the distinction between the reliance (negative) interest and the expectation (positive) interest.

(a) Measure of Damages: Reliance (Negative) Interest v. *Expectation (Positive) Interest*

Jhering, *Culpa in Contrahendo* (1861)[235]   **2.G.72.**

The interest of the purchaser may be regarded, for the purposes of the relationship under consideration in this context, as being twofold in nature: first, as an interest in the maintenance of the contract, and thus in its performance; on this basis, the purchaser would receive the monetary equivalent of everything which he would be entitled to receive had the contract been validly concluded; and, second, as an interest in the non-conclusion of the contract; on this basis, he would be entitled to receive what he would have had if the apparent fact of the conclusion of the contract had never arisen. This distinction, which I propose for the sake of brevity to refer to as a positive and a negative interest in the contract, may be clarified by a number of examples.

However, the conclusion of the supposed contract may also have resulted in the plaintiff having foregone some profit, possibly by reason of his having, on account of the conclusion of that contract, rejected some other opportunity or omitted in good time to seek such an opportunity. . . . In certain circumstances, the negative interest may be as great as the positive one. In [such] cases, a plaintiff is entitled to receive precisely what he would have been able to claim if the contract had been performed, but for a totally different reason.

Note
With regard to damages, a distinction is generally drawn between the reliance (negative) interest and the expectation (positive) interest. This distinction was introduced by Jhering

---

[233] See e.g. Cass. it., 11 May 1990, No. 4051, discussed *infra*, at 285.
[234] Compare, under the Brussels Convention, ECJ Case C–26/91, *Jur.* I–3967 (Handte/TMCS).
[235] Op. cit. *supra* note 178, at 16 and 20.

in his discussion of liability for concluding an invalid contract.[235a] Recovery of the expectation interest gives the plaintiff the financial equivalent of what he would have had if a valid contract had been concluded, including the profit he would have made with that contract. Recovery of the reliance interest means that the plaintiff gets the financial equivalent of what he would have had if no negotiations had taken place. Thus he can recover the expenses he incurred—travelling, drafting contract etc. But reliance damages are not limited to that. Farnsworth has emphasized that they may also include recovery for lost opportunities, i.e. the loss a party made by not concluding an alternative contract with a third party due to the fact that he was engaged in negotiations with this party.[236] See for example the Swiss case of *Escophon AG* v. *Bank in Langenthal,*[237] where the plaintiff could recover two months' profit which it would have made had it concluded the credit agreement with another bank, and the American case *Markov*,[238] where lost opportunities included the profits lost due to the leaving of his principal customer, which would not have occurred had the plaintiff concluded a contract with a third party instead of entering into deceptive negotiations. The case of *The Giuliana*[239] shows that the lost opportunity to conclude a contract with a third party does not necessarily have to be an opportunity to conclude a contract of the same type. The distinction was criticized by Fagella,[240] who found it anti-juridical. He favoured an approach which is similar to what today in French law is known as the *théorie de la perte d'une chance* (loss of a chance). However, except for in French law,[241] today this distinction is very common in all legal systems.

(b) The Test for Liability and the Extent of Liability in the Various Systems

Principles of European Contract Law   **2.PECL.73.**

Article 2:301: *Negotiations Contrary to Good Faith*
          (2) However, a party who has negotiated or broken off negotiations contrary to good faith is liable for the losses caused to the other party.

Unidroit Principles   **2.INT.74.**

Article 2.15: *Negotiations in bad faith*
          (2) However, a party who has negotiated or broken off negotiations in bad faith is liable for the losses caused to the other party.

[235a] See on this problem *infra*, 2.7.3.D.
[236] Farnsworth, op. cit, at 225 ff; See, earlier, Jhering, op. cit., at 21, with regard to liability for concluding an invalid contract.
[237] Swiss Bundesgericht, 6 February 1979, BGE 105.II.75.
[238] *Supra*, note 209.
[239] Discussed *infra*, at 260.
[240] *Supra*, note 179.
[241] Discussed *infra*, at 256.

Notes

(1) The Comment on Article 2.15 of the Unidroit Principles says: "even before [an offer is made], or in a negotiating process with no ascertainable sequence of offer and acceptance, a party may no longer be free to break off negotiations abruptly and without justification. When such a point of no return is reached depends of course on the circumstances of the case, in particular the extent to which the other party, as a result of the conduct of the first party, had reason to rely on the positive outcome of the negotiations, and on the number of issues relating to the future contract on which the parties have already reached agreement".

(2) Under Article 2.15 of the Unidroit Principles and Article 2:301 PECL the party who breaks off negotiations contrary to good faith is liable for losses caused to the other party. The Comment on Article 2.15 Unidroit Principles explains that "losses" include expenses incurred during the negotiations and lost opportunities. However, the expectation interest may not be recovered.

(3) Neither the wording of Article 2.15 of the Unidroit Principles and Article 2:301 PECL nor the Comment on Article 2.15 of the Unidroit Principles indicates which regime is applicable to liability for breaking off negotiations. Since the Principles do not deal with torts, delictual liability seems excluded. However, as said above, the application of the contractual regime seems inappropriate here. Therefore, it seems, the most suitable solution would be here to adopt a *sui generis* liability for violation of the duty of precontractual good faith.

BGH, 10 July 1970[242]   **2.G.75.**

EXPECTATION OF CONTRACT INDUCED AND NO GOOD REASON FOR BREAKING OFF

The letter

Once a party has induced or encouraged in another a confident expectation that a contract will be concluded, the breaking off of negotiations without good reason will give rise to liability to compensate the other for damage suffered as a result of his reliance on the expectation.

Held: The criteria governing liability for breaking off contractual negotiations were not satisfied in the case, and the decision of the appellate court was upheld.

Judgment:

1. Even at the stage when negotiations are being conducted with a view to the conclusion of a contract, each party to those negotiations owes to the other party, in view of the relationship of trust created by the negotiations, which is analogous to that existing in a contractual relationship, a duty to have reasonable regard for the legitimate interests of that other party. This includes an obligation on each party not to break off the negotiations without good reason once that party has induced or encouraged in the other party a confident expectation that the contract will definitely come into existence. A culpable breach of that duty may give rise, on the basis of the doctrine of *culpa in contrahendo*, to liability to compensate the other party for the damage suffered by him as a result of his reliance on that expectation (judgments of the Chamber of 4.3.1955, V ZR 66/54, BB 55, 429; of 14.7.1967, V ZR 120/64, NJW 67, 2199, in each case with additional supporting mater-

---

[242] LM § 276 [Fa] BGB No. 34, NJW 1970.1840

ial; see also the BGH judgment of 6.2.1969, LM No 28 re § 276 (Fa) BGB = WM 69, 595; OLG *Munich*, NJW 68, 651). Those principles also apply to negotiations concerning contracts for the sale of land, which must, in accordance with § 313 BGB, be judicially or notarially recorded in an official document. The fact that the parties had not yet agreed all the details of the contract to be concluded does not of itself preclude liability in damages (see the judgment of the Chamber of 4.3.1955, cited above).

2. However, the criteria giving rise to liability in damages on those grounds are not established in the present case. (. . .)

b) . . . Where, in the course of contractual negotiations, a person states that he is willing to conclude a contract containing detailed specific provisions and thereby arouses or promotes in the other party a firm expectation that the contract will definitely come into existence, that person is not bound by that statement for an unlimited period of time, even if, and in so far as, a claim may lie against him, as described above, on account of *culpa in contrahendo*. Not only *his* conduct, but also that of the *other party*, must be judged in the light of the principle of good faith (§ 242 BGB). In accordance with that principle, the other party must, in particular, obtain clarification from him within a reasonable time as to whether or not he intends, for his part, to conclude a contract containing the provisions proposed. . . .

c) If, in accordance with the foregoing, the passage of time resulted in the plaintiff ceasing to be bound by the statement in her letter of 31.3.1965 that she was willing to conclude a contract, the fact that she may additionally have withdrawn from it for non-pertinent reasons is immaterial. In that respect too, it is necessary, however, to concur with the appellate court as regards the decisive points . . .

BGH, 25 November 1992[243] 2.G.76.

EXCEPTIONALLY, POSITIVE INTEREST MAY BE RECOVERED

Oolitic stones

A party is entitled to compensation in the measure of the positive interest if he can establish that, had the correct tendering procedure been followed, he would certainly have been awarded the contract.

Facts: The plaintiff was engaged in the extraction and sale of natural stones. The defendant, represented by the HM waterways authority, invited the plaintiff, in the context of a call for tenders limited to six tenderers, to submit, in compliance with certain regulations, an offer for the supply of stones for hydraulic structures. According to the "practical directions" contained in the regulations, the contracting authority was to proceed in accordance with the Terms and Conditions for the Award of Contracts (VOL/A). The invitation to tender provided that the material to be used was to be rubble for use in hydraulic structures consisting of basalt, greywacke or hard sandstone. The plaintiff submitted a tender for the supply of basalt stones at a price of DM 237,430.65. Apart from the plaintiff, two other tenderers responded to the invitation to tender. Messrs B submitted an offer for the supply of oolitic stones not corresponding with the requirements of the invitation to tender at a price of DM 118,349.10, together with an expert's report on the testing of such stones to establish their suitability for their intended purpose, and a third company, made an incomplete offer. Messrs B. were awarded the contract. The plaintiff brought proceedings against the defendant for breach of pre-contractual obligations claiming compensation for loss of profits. The claimant asserted that the defendant was bound to adhere to the provisions of the VOL/A and that it should have awarded the contract to the plaintiff.

Held: The Bundesgerichtshof upheld the appellate court's finding that the plaintiff was entitled to compensation in the measure of the positive interest.

[243] NJW 1993.520

Judgment: . . . This Court concurs with the appellate court's finding that the plaintiff is entitled to claim compensation in respect of its positive interest if it would definitely have won the contract had the procedure for awarding it been properly followed . . . It is true that the burden of proof rests on the tenderer, who must show that it would have been awarded the contract had it not been for the breach by the contracting entity of its obligations. However, in cases such as the present one, that burden is discharged by the plaintiff if it can show that, had the terms of the invitation to tender been adhered to, and had the award been properly made in accordance with § 25(3) VOL/A, the contract would have been concluded with the plaintiff (see, by way of example, OLG Düsseldorf BauR 1986, 107, 111; Feber BauR 1989, 553, 557). On that basis, this Court, hearing the appeal on a point of law, must find in favour of the plaintiff: neither of the other two tenderers should have been taken into account in the procedure which followed. Messrs B. should have been left out of consideration on account of its having submitted an ancillary offer excluded by § 25(1)(1)(g) VOL/A, and the third company should have been turned down on account of the absence of material price details as required by § 25(1)(1)(a) VOL/A. . . . There can be no question of taking into consideration any other circumstances precluding consideration of the plaintiff's offer.

Notes

(1) The mere lengthy prolongation of the negotiations or the mere fact of knowing that the other party has already made significant expenses does not make a party liable for breaking off negotiations.[244]

(2) Under German law only a party who by his fault has made the other party believe that a contract will certainly be concluded, but then without a good reason (*ohne triftigen Grund*) or from non pertinent motives (*sachfremde Erwägungen*) breaks off the negotiations, is liable, to the extent of the reliance interest. Liability is based on the doctrine of *culpa in contrahendo* as it was developed by the German courts: on liability for the violation of a pre-contractual duty, especially the duty to take the interests of the other party into consideration and the duty to inform see the *Letter* case.[245] However, as we have seen, the doctrine of *culpa in contrahendo* as originally proposed by Jhering did not extend to broken negotiations, and was rather limited to the knowing conclusion of an invalid contract.

(3) Some authors, like Ballerstedt, Canaris and Larenz, have maintained a different view.[246] According to these scholars liability for breaking off negotiations should not be based on the doctrine of *culpa in contrahendo*, because in their opinion the absence of a duty to conclude a contract implies that breaking off negotiations can never constitute a fault. Therefore, liability should not be based on the violation of a pre-contractual duty but on the protection of reliance (*Vertrauenshaftung*). In this view there is a strong analogy with liability ex § 122 BGB.[247] This approach has been adopted by some of the Bundesgerichtshof's Senates,[248] but it has not convinced the other Senates nor the majority of scholars.

[244] See BGH, 14 July 1967 and earlier RGZ 24 February 1931, 132, 26, 28 (the cost of a draft contract made by a notary).

[245] *Supra*, at 252; See, earlier, BGH LM § 276 (Fa) BGB Nr. 3; MDR 1954, 346 (16 March 1954); for a more recent example BGH ZIP 1988, 88 (21 September 1987).

[246] See Larenz, *SAT* at 108.

[247] See on this provision **3.G.40**, *infra* at 344.

[248] See BGH, LM § 276 (Fa) BGB Nr. 28 = WM 1969, 595 (6 February 1969); BGH, NJW 1975, 1774 (12 June 1975) and, more recently, BGH, LM §276 (Fa) Nr. 102 = NJW-RR 1989, 627 = ZIP 1989, 514 (22 February 1989).

(4) The most important difference between these approaches is that only in the *culpa in contrahendo* approach is fault required. However, the practical importance of this difference appears to be rather limited since it is hard to imagine a case where a party who breaks off negotiations without a good reason after having made the other party believe that a contract will certainly be concluded has not committed a fault. As regards the other two elements for liability, these are the same in both approaches: a party is liable only if (i) he has made the other party believe that a contract will certainly be concluded and (ii) he has broken off negotiations without having a good reason.

(5) As for the nature of liability, in Germany liability for breaking off negotiations, like any liability for *culpa in contrahendo*, is dealt with by the rules of contractual liability (§§ 276 ff. BGB).[249] Compare Austria.[250] As a matter of fact, the very reason why the courts have developed the doctrine of *culpa in contrahendo* lies in the shortcomings of German tort law.[251] Under tort law pure economic loss is not recoverable unless the damage is caused intentionally—see § 823 paragraph 1 and § 826 BGB. For broken-off negotiations this implies that, in principle, recovery for expenditure or lost opportunities would be impossible. Moreover, in tort there is no real vicarious liability. Finally, the period of prescription for tort-based actions is rather short. On all these points contractual liability is much more favourable for the plaintiff. That is why the German courts construed the relationship of mutual trust which is similar to a contractual relationship (*vertragsähnliches Vertrauensverhältnis*) which allowed them to apply the contractual regime in the case of *culpa in contrahendo*.[252] It should be remembered here that some scholars, followed by some senates of the Bundesgerichtshof, have argued that broken off negotiations are not a case of *culpa in contrahendo* but of protection of reliance. This view implies that § 123 BGB should be applied by analogy instead of the rules on contractual liability.

(6) As for the extent of liability, in German law a party who breaks off negotiations in a manner contrary to pre-contractual good faith duties is liable to repair the reliance interest.[253] In practice, in most cases reliance damages consist in expenses, but lost opportunities may be recovered as well. See for example BAG NJW 1963, 1843; JZ 1964, 324 (7 June 1963), where the plaintiff could recover the wages he would have had if he had not given up his current position in justified reliance on the successful outcome of negotiations for a new job. Unlike in case of application of §§ 122, 179, 307, liability here is not limited to the level of the expectation interest.[254] Expectation damages are not awarded, because a negotiating party is under no duty to contract.[255] A different rule would amount to *Kontrahierungszwang*.[256] In some *culpa in contrahendo* cases other than those concerning broken-off negotiations positive damages have been awarded. This was so in the *Oolitic Stones* case,[257] in the field of public bidding, where it was certain that a

---

[249] See e.g. BGH, 10 July 1970, cit at 252.
[250] See Posch, op. cit., at 46.
[251] See von Mehren, "The Formation of Contract", in *International Encyclopedia of Comparative Law* (1992), Volume VII *Contracts in General*, chapter 9, para. 121.
[252] See also at 250.
[253] See e.g. BGH, 10 July 1970.
[254] See e.g. Palandt-Heinrichs, op. cit., § 276, para. 100.
[255] See e.g. BGH LM § 276 (Fa) BGB Nr. 28; WM 1969, 595 (6 February 1969).
[256] See *Münchener Kommontar*, paras 165 and 207.
[257] *Supra*, at 253.

contract would have been concluded had the tenderee not violated its pre-contractual duties;[258] also in a case where an insurer had failed to inform the insured correctly about which countries were covered by his insurance;[259] and also in a case where a party had not informed the other party about a form requirement. In these cases the expectation interest was justified by the purpose of the duty concerned.[260] The law reform will not bring any change on this point. From the fact that § 305 BGB-KE refers only to the duty of care in § 241, which aims exclusively at protecting the obligee's present patrimonial position,[261] the conclusion can be drawn that the expectation interest will not be protected under the new law either. Compare the English case of *Blackpool & Fylde Aero Club* v. *Blackpool Borough Council*.[262]

Cass. Com., 20 March 1972[263]   **2.F.77.**

LIABILITY FOR BREAKING OFF NEGOTIATIONS ABRUPTLY AND WITHOUT LEGITIMATE REASON IN ADVANCED STAGE

The Hydrotile machine

Delictual liability for pre-contractual bad faith will be imposed where a party intentionally keeps another in a state of protracted uncertainty and then breaks off advanced negotiations without legitimate reason, knowing that the other has incurred considerable expense.

Facts: Société des Etablissements Gerteis entered into negotiations in April 1966 with Société Etablissements Vilber-Lourmat, the exclusive distributor in France of machines for the production of concrete pipes. The machines were manufactured by the American company Hydrotile Machinery Co. After a trip to the United States by Robert Gerteis to see the machines in operation, Société Gerteis asked Société Vilber-Lourmat for further information before choosing one of various kinds of machines manufactured by Hydrotile. Société Vilber-Lourmat did not reply to that letter. Société Gerteis subsequently learned that the American manufacturer had sent an estimate on to Vilber-Lourmat but the latter had not forwarded it to Société Gerteis. Vilber-Lourmat subsequently sold a Hydrotile machine to a competitor of Société Gerteis, and that contract of sale contained a clause under which Vilber-Lourmat undertook not to sell a similar machine in an area including the east of France for a period of 42 months following delivery of the machine ordered by the company Les Tuyaux Centrifugés. Société Gerteis commenced proceedings for damages against Société Vilber-Lourmat.

Held: The Cour de cassation upheld the Cour d'appel's decision in favour of Société Gerteis.

Judgment: On the two appeal grounds taken together:—Whereas the affirmative judgment now before this Court is criticised because it found against Société Vilber-Lourmat and upheld the accusations made against that company, whereas, according to the appeal, by referring to reciprocal commitments binding the two parties before negotiations were broken off, and to the fact that the discussions had progressed further than the pre-contractual stage, whilst at the same time affirming the decision of the lower court, which had held that the breaking off of negotiations by Société Vilber-Lourmat constituted a fault committed at the pre-contractual stage, falling within the scope of Article 1382 of the Civil Code, the Cour d'appel does not let it be known whether it considered that that company had incurred contractual liability or delictual liability; thus, by not clarifying the

---

[258] See also BGHZ 49, 77 (16 November 1967); for a Danish case see Lando, op. cit., at 118; contrast the American case *Heyder Products*, at *supra* note 210..

[259] BGH 108, 200 (4 July 1989).

[260] See Palandt-Heinrichs, op. cit, para. 101.

[261] *Supra*, at 239.

[262] [1990] 1 WLR 1995.

[263] Bull. civ. IV.93; JCP 1973.II-17543, annotated by J. Schmidt; RTD civ. 1972.722, annotated by G. Durry.

basis of its decision, the Cour d'appel did not provide it with a proper legal foundation, and, moreover, the affirmative judgment under appeal is not justified on the basis of either contractual liability or delictual liability; the Cour d'appel cannot, without distorting the terms of the dispute, base its decision on the contractual liability of Société Vilber-Lourmat, since Société Gerteis expressly confined itself to seeking an order against that company pursuant to Article 1382 of the Civil Code and, moreover, the grounds relied on by the court of first instance likewise do not justify the conclusion that the breaking off was improper; it is contradictory to say that negotiations were abruptly broken off whilst at the same time noting that Société Vilber-Lourmat was being dilatory, and that there was no legitimate reason for such breaking off, as likewise claimed, which has not been proved, since the Cour d'appel accepted as valid the exclusivity clause in the sale contract for a Hydrotile machine and did not respond to the submissions of Société Vilber-Lourmat, which contended that it had received a firm order for that high-technology machine, together with a payment on account from a company already specialising in the manufacture of concrete pipes;

—Whereas, however, the judgment under appeal, accepting submissions put to the court, noted that Société Vilber-Lourmat had deliberately not passed on the final estimate from the American manufacturer intended for Société Gerteis and, without legitimate reason, abruptly and unilaterally broken off the negotiations with that company which were at an advanced stage, and that company had already, to the other's knowledge, incurred considerable expense; as and it intentionally kept that company in a state of protracted uncertainty, thereby infringing the rules of good faith in commercial relations; the Cour d'appel, which certainly did not hold that Société Vilber-Lourmat had been in breach of contract, noted that Société Vilber-Lourmat had itself stated that, before committing itself to its other customer, it had made a last inquiry as to the intentions of Gerteis, but it did not produce the least proof of this, and in any event it was clear that such drawn-out negotiations could not be broken off by a mere telephone call;

—Whereas the court of first instance was therefore correct to declare that there had been "an improper breaking off of negotiations" by Société Vilber-Lourmat; having regard to the foregoing, and without considering the other pleas, which need not be examined, the Cour d'appel, without erring in the manner alleged in the appeal, was entitled to find that Société Vilber-Lourmat had incurred delictual liability and the finding against that company was therefore justified;

—Whereas none of the grounds of appeal can therefore be upheld.

Cass. civ. 3e, 3 October 1972[264]   **2.F.78.**

INTENTION TO CAUSE HARM NOT REQUIRED

Monoprix

Liability for pre-contractual bad faith does not require negotiations to have been broken off with an intention to cause harm to the other party.

Facts: The building company "Résidence Bonaparte" had a property complex built in Ajaccio which included, on the ground floor and in the basement, premises for commercial use. Société Anonyme des Monoprix expressed the intention to purchase those premises if the building company made certain alterations to them, and thus became involved in the construction and fitting out of the premises (by providing plans drawn up by its experts). The protracted discussions between the two companies were broken off by Monoprix as it established itself in other premises.

Held: Résidence Bonaparte's appeal before the Cour de cassation succeeded.

[264] Bull. civ. III.491.

Judgment:—Under Articles 1382 and 1383 of the Civil Code;—Whereas Société Civile Immobilière Résidence Bonaparte seeks an order requiring Société des Monoprix to pay it damages for misusing the right to break off sales negotiations, and the contested judgment, in dismissing the application on the ground that it had not been alleged that the defendant company caused all or any of the alterations to be carried out solely for the purpose of causing harm, states as a principle of law that "in the absence of a special agreement to the contrary, alterations to property by or with the authority of the owner thereof in the course of sales negotiations in order to render it suitable for the potential purchaser are carried out at the risk and peril of the owner. Consequently, even if there is no legitimate reason for it, a refusal by that potential purchaser to conclude the sale after the alterations have made it more difficult to sell the property to other persons does not cause him to incur quasi-delictual liability" and "the position could be different only where those alterations were brought about by the potential purchaser solely with the intention of causing harm".
—Whereas by giving judgment to that effect, even though delictual liability provided for in the above mentioned articles of the Civil Code may be held to exist in the absence of any intention to cause harm, the Cour d'appel infringed those provisions.

Notes

(1) In France there are only a few cases on this subject. Nevertheless, some rules can be inferred from those cases: although both parties have the right to break off negotiations at any stage, a party who abuses that right can be liable in tort. Compare Belgian law.[265] Only a *faute patente, indiscutable* may constitute a fault in negotiating.[266]

(2) With regard to the general concept of abuse of right, there has been a debate in France ever since the days of Ripert and Josserand concerning the question whether for an abuse of a right it is necessary that the defendant intended to harm the victim. This general debate has influenced the discussion on the specific question of liability for breaking off negotiations. In the *Monoprix* case,[267] the Cour d'appel had declined liability, holding that the constructor had acted at his own risk and that even though there was no valid ground which could justify Monoprix's breaking off, there was no abuse of right since it was not established that Monoprix had intended to harm the constructor. However, this very harsh decision was reversed by the Cour de cassation which held that for liability an intention to harm was not required. In a later case the Cour de cassation held that a prospective seller who eventually could not sell his land because he appeared not to be, as he thought, the sole owner would be liable only if he had intended to harm the prospective buyer or if he had been in bad faith.[268] The Cour de cassation (*chambre commerciale*) had already referred to the concept of good faith on an earlier occasion. It then held that it is contrary to good faith in commerce to break off negotiations all of a sudden without a legitimate reason (*rompre sans raison légitime, brutalement et unilatéralement, les pourparlers*), after having kept the other party deliberately in uncertainty.[269] And in a recent case again a party was held liable because it had brutally and unilaterally broken off very advanced negotiations and had not respected a duty of good faith which prevails in international trade.[270]

[265] See J. Herbots, *Contract Law in Belgium* (Deventer-Boston/Bruxelles: Bruylant, 1995) para. 190.
[266] Cour d'appel de Pau, 14 January 1969, D. 1969.716.
[267] *Supra*, at 257.
[268] Cass. civ. 1re, 12 April 1976, Bull. civ. I.122; Def. 1976.31434.5. 389, annotated by J.-L. Aubert.
[269] Cass. com., 20 March 1972 see *supra*, at 256.
[270] Cass. com., 22 April 1997, RTD Civ. 1997.651 annotated by J. Mestre.

(3) Most authors conclude from these cases that a party is liable for breaking off negotiations not only if he intended to harm the other party, but also if he acted in bad faith.
It is bad faith in particular to break off negotiations all of sudden, without a good reason, at a point where the other party could reasonably expect the conclusion a contract.[271]

(4) As regards the nature of liability, In France, pre-contractual liability is tort liability. There is a *communis opinio* on this point.[272]

(5) As regards the extent of liability, in France the distinction between reliance interest and expectation interest is not known as such. A party who is liable for breaking off
negotiations has to compensate the other party for its losses. This means in the first place
that he has to pay his expenses.[273] In addition to that, according to some authors the victim can recover the loss of the chance to conclude the contract that the parties negotiated
on, relying on the concept of *perte d'une chance*.[274]

Cass. it., 17 June 1974[275]   **2.I.79.**

EXPECTATION ON CONTRACT INDUCED AND UNJUSTIFIED WITHDRAWAL

The installation of machinery

*Liability to compensate a party to the extent of the negative interest for withdrawing from negotiations
without due cause after having caused the other party reasonably to expect that the contract would be
concluded.*

Held: The appeal to the Cassazione was upheld.

Judgment: . . .—By his second plea in law, the appellant, in alleging breach and misapplication of
Article 1337 of the Civil Code and failure to state reasons concerning decisive aspects of the dispute, maintains: (a) that, since there is nothing in the circumstances complained off constituting
conduct in breach of good faith, a decision establishing pre-contractual liability was inappropriate
. . .

These allegations must also be rejected. As observed earlier, the appeal court founded its judgment on *culpa in contrahendo*, referring to the letter of 5 August 1967, in which the plaintiff was
asked to arrange for installation of the machinery ordered. In fact, this Court shares the lower
court's view that that document unequivocally caused the addressee to entertain expectations to the
effect that he was entitled to rely on the other party's performing its obligation if it persuaded him
to incur expenditure in order to install the machines ordered.

It has already been held (Cass, 9 December 1957, No 4619) pursuant to Article 1337 of the Civil
Code that if, in the course of negotiations, one party caused the other reasonably to expect that the
contract would be concluded and then withdrew without due cause, he is required to pay compensation to the extent of the negative interest, that is to say for expenses incurred in contemplation of
conclusion of the contract. In this case there is: both (a) the expectation, arising from the abovementioned letter; and (b) unjustified withdrawal by the contracting party from the negotiations, in

---

[271] See e.g. Jourdain, op. cit, at 128; Terré, Simler and Lequette, para. 177; Malaurie and Aynès, para. 379;
Ghestin, para. 330; J. Schmidt-Szalewski, France, in: *Pre-contractual Liability*, op. cit, at 150.

[272] See e.g. Cass. com., 20 March 1972, *supra* at 256; Schmidt, op. cit., at 148; Malaurie and Aynès, para. 379.
See, for Spain, Díez-Picazo and Gullón, op. cit., at 69, and for Belgium, Herbots, op. cit, para. 193.

[273] See e.g. Cass. civ. 1re, 12 April 1976, *supra* note 268.

[274] See e.g. Terré, Simler and Lequette, para. 177.

[275] No. 1781, Foro padano 1975.I.80, annotated by Prandi; Temi, 175.408, annotated by Fajella.

259

that the low price—a matter well known to the addressee of the offer since August 1967 when the letter giving rise to the expectation was sent—cannot be regarded as a valid reason for not bringing the matter to a conclusion; (c) and damage limited to the *id quod interest contractum non fuisse*, namely the expenditure incurred with a view to completion of the transaction. . . .

Cass. it., 12 March 1993[276]   **2.I.80.**

LOSS OF OPPORTUNITY OF DIFFERENT KIND OF CONTRACT

The Giuliana

Reliance losses include not only expenses but also the loss of opportunities to conclude a contract with a third party, which may be of a different kind

Facts: S.r.l. Noleggi Imprese Marittime (NIM) entered into negotiations with s.n.c. Approvvigionamento Acqua Navi (SAAN) for the purchase of the motor vessel *Giuliana*. Expecting to sell the vessel to SAAN, NIM declined to hire the vessel to a third party, Total. However, the sale to SAAN did not take place, and NIM commenced proceedings before the Tribunale di Livorno, alleging that the deal was not completed as a result of SAAN's conduct in breach of good faith and thus seeking compensation.

Held: The Corte d'appello di Firenze awarded NIM damages for the loss of the hire to Total; the Cassazione dismissed the appeal.

Judgment: In its only ground of appeal . . . SAAN essentially complains that the Florence Court treated as negative interest, for which compensation should be paid to NIM, the loss suffered by the latter from the decision not to conclude with the Total company a contract for the hire of the motor vessel *Giuliana*, having regard to the sale of that vessel to SAAN. The appellant contends, however, that the negative interest can extend only to the loss of benefit arising from the fact that it declined, or allowed to fall through, in expectation of conclusion of the contract which did not come to fruition, other opportunities to conclude contracts identical or similar to the one not concluded, with the result that, in this case, calculation of the compensation payable to NIM could not include the financial loss suffered by the latter through failure to hire the *Giuliana* to Total, the latter contract being neither identical nor similar to the sale contract for which there had been negotiations between the appellant and NIM. . . .

The appeal is unfounded. Liability by way of *culpa in contrahendo* is non-contractual liability and, in accordance with the rules in Articles 1223 and 2056 of the Civil Code, covers the direct and immediate consequences of conduct characterised by law as unlawful as a result of breach of the general duty imposed by Article 1337 of the Civil Code to act in good faith in the stage preparatory to the contract.

It follows that if the damage eligible for compensation under Article 1337 of the Civil Code covers only the interest in not having commenced negotiations which were to come to nothing (negative contractual interest), thereby differing from the interest in performance of the contract (positive contractual interest), such damage nevertheless includes, in terms both of *damnum emergens* and *lucrum cessans*, all the harmful effects which are an immediate and direct consequence of non-conclusion of the contract, as a result of unlawful conduct by one of the parties.

Therefore, there is no reason to exclude from the compensation due under Article 1337 of the Civil Code financial loss deriving from the decision not to conclude a contract of different subject-matter from that for which the negotiations which did not come to fruition were carried out if the failure to conclude the first contract is seen to be the direct and immediate consequence of the con-

---

[276] No. 2973, Foro Italiano, I. 956.

duct of the other party, who broke off those negotiations when they had reached such a stage as to create a reasonable expectation that they would have a positive outcome.

Notes

(1) Under Italian law a party is liable if he breaks off negotiations without a good reason after having induced in the other party the justified reliance that a contract would be concluded.[277] Fault is not required.[278] This rule, like most other questions concerning pre-contractual liability, was settled in Italy as early as in the 1940s.[279]

(2) As regards the nature of liability, in Italy there is a consistent line of cases where it has been decided that pre-contractual liability is liability in tort. See for example Cass. it., 11 May 1990, n. 4051, *Foro It.* 1991, I, 184, note D. Caruso, *Note in tema di danni pre-contrattuali*, where the consequence of applicability of the tort regime was that the plaintiff had lost his action as a result of the short prescription period for actions in tort, whereas under the contract regime he would certainly have been successful since there was no doubt about the merits of his case. Some prominent Italian scholars, like Mengoni and Galgano, have maintained that the basis should be contractual, but the majority seems to agree with the Cassazione.[280]

(3) As regards the extent of liability, under Italian law only the reliance interest can be recovered, not the expectation interest: see Cass. it., 20 August 1980.[281] The explanation for this lies in the non-contractual nature of the liability:[282] if someone breaks off negotiations in a manner contrary to good faith the law does not reproach him for not having concluded the contract but for having given the other party the impression that a contract would be concluded.[283] Reliance losses include expenses as well as the loss of opportunities to conclude a contract with third parties.[284] Such an alternative contract does not necessarily have to be identical or even similar to the one parties were negotiating. It is sufficient that the plaintiff has interrupted the negotiations for a contract because he relied on the conclusion of a contract with the defendant: see for example the case of *The Giuliana*[285] where the plaintiff could recover the profits that he would have made from a lease of his boat, but which he did not conclude in the light of the expected sale to the defendant.

---

[277] See *The installation of machinery* case, *supra*, at 259.
[278] See Sacco, op. cit., 235.
[279] See Nanni, *La buona fede contrattuale, I grandi orientamneti della giurisprudenza civile e commerciale* (Padova: CEDAM, 1988) at 4.
[280] See Cian and Trabucchi, op. cit., at 1058.
[281] No. 4942, Mass. Foro it. 1980.78
[282] See e.g. Cass., 12 March 1993, n. 2973, *supra*, at 260.
[283] See Sacco, op. cit., at 256.
[284] See e.g. Cass., 20 August 1980, n. 4942.
[285] *Supra*, at 260.

HR, 18 June 1982[286]   **2.NL.81.**

RIGHT TO BREAK OFF NEGOTIATIONS MAY BE LOST WHERE NEGOTIATIONS ARE ADVANCED

The Dutch swimming pool

If a party was justified in relying on the expectation that some sort of contract would in any event result from the negotiations, the act of the other party in breaking them off may in itself be regarded as contrary to good faith. In such a situation, an obligation to pay compensation in the positive interest may exist.

Facts: At a meeting in June 1974, the Municipal Council of Valburg decided on the construction of an indoor swimming pool and resolved to make HFL 1,312,000 available for the building costs. Plas submitted an offer for the construction of an indoor swimming pool. A Council committee then decided to examine Plas' offer, along with offers submitted by three other contractors. Thereafter, the committee requested one of the three previous tenderers and Plas to adapt their plans and to submit priced tenders. In December 1974, Plas submitted an adapted offer priced in the sum of HFL 1,300,000. At a meeting of the Mayor and the Council held on 9 January, the Mayor stated on behalf of the Municipal Executive that Plas' tender was the lowest, that his plan was acceptable to the Municipality, that the Council should make a decision about it and that a few adjustments still needed to be made concerning various points of detail. At the close of a subsequent meeting of the Council at which the construction of the swimming pool was not an item appearing on the agenda, a councillor stated that Arns BV had a plan for the construction of the swimming pool which was HFL 156,000 cheaper than Plas' plan, and distributed documentation concerning the Arns plan to those present. The Arns plan was adopted by the Council at a meeting in March 1975. Plas brought an action, seeking, as his principal claim, performance of an agreement which he submitted had come into existence; in the alternative, he claimed damages for default; and in the further alternative, he claimed damages for the breaking off of negotiations. The Rechtbank (District Court) allowed his claim, but the Gerechtshof (Regional Court of Appeal) set that judgment aside and dismissed all his claims. Plas appealed to the Hoge Road (Court of cassation).

Held: Plas' appeal was allowed.

Judgment:
3. Findings in relation to the plea advanced:
. . . 3.4 The fourth part of the plea is also well founded. In the fourth of its grounds of judgment, the Regional Court of Appeal based its findings on the legal rule that the obligation to pay compensation on account of conduct in pre-contractual dealings which does not accord with the duty to act in good faith "extends no further than a requirement to make good the costs and damage incurred which the other party would not have suffered if the pre-contractual relationship had not arisen", and that it cannot therefore include an obligation to compensate for lost profits. However, the law generally affords no support for such a rule. It is not impossible that negotiations concerning a contract may reach such an advanced stage that the act of breaking them off must in itself be regarded, in the prevailing circumstances, as a breach of good faith, on the basis that the parties may be assumed mutually to have relied on the expectation that some sort of contract would in any event result from the negotiations. In such a situation, it may also be legitimate to find that an obligation exists to pay compensation for lost profits.

3.5 The fifth and sixth parts of the plea are directed against the fifth and sixth grounds of the judgment appealed against, in which the Regional Court of Appeal held that no compensation was payable in respect of the costs and damage incurred by Plas prior to the discussion on 9 January 1975, because it followed from Plas' arguments that the pre-contractual relationship on which his claim for compensation was based arose in the course of, and as a result of, that discussion, and because Plas never maintained that the Council was not free, prior to that date, to withdraw from the negotiations. The objections to this which are advanced in the fifth and sixth parts of the plea are well founded.

---

[286] NJ 1983,723, annotated by Brunner; AA 32 1983.758, annotated by Van Schilfgaarde.

The Regional Court of Appeal's finding that Plas at no time asserted that the Council was not free, prior to 9 January 1975, to withdraw from the negotiations must be considered in conjunction with the District Court's ruling that, following the discussion on that date, the Council was no longer entitled to break off the negotiations. In omitting to deal with the objection raised against that ruling by the Council, the Regional Court of Appeal clearly assumed that the ruling in question was correct. However, if the Council was no longer able, after 9 January 1975, to withdraw from the negotiations, it is impossible to see why a breach of its obligations should not result in the Council being required to make good costs which had already been incurred before 9 January 1975 in the context of the negotiations held prior to that date. Such a requirement to pay compensation might even arise if the negotiations had not yet reached the stage at which the Council was no longer able in good faith to break them off but had nevertheless already advanced to the point that the act of breaking them off resulted, in the circumstances, in its no longer being free to walk away from them without assuming responsibility, wholly or in part, for the expenses incurred by Plas.

Notes

(1) Since the *Plas/Valburg* case,[287] the Dutch courts distinguish three stages in the negotiating process. At a first stage both parties are entirely free to break off negotiations. At a second stage a party is still free to break off negotiations, but if he does so he has to pay the expenses the other party has incurred. Finally, at a third stage parties are no longer free to break off negotiations. This is the case where the other party may reasonably believe that some contract of the type the parties were negotiating will be concluded or if other circumstances of the case make breaking off unacceptable.[288] If a party breaks off at that third stage, he is liable in damages, which may even amount to the expectation interest.[289] Also he may be ordered to continue negotiations.[290] However, in a recent case,[291] the Hoge Raad seems to have limited its *Plas/Valburg* doctrine. In that case it held that the other party is not liable in all cases where a party was justified in expecting the imminent conclusion of a contract, because in determining whether there is liability that other party's interests must also be taken into account; moreover a change of circumstances during the negotiations may provide a justification as well. This decision, of course, raises the question whether a (new) better offer from a third party may justify breaking off negotiations even in that stage.

(2) In the third stage breaking off is in itself contrary to good faith. In other words, in opposition to other systems, under Dutch law the advanced stage of negotiations can actually make a party lose his right to break off negotiations. Thus Dutch law has replaced the clear-cut distinction between contract and no-contract by a gradual process where at a very advanced stage of negotiations a party can claim to be put financially into the position as if a contract were concluded.[292]

(3) As regards the nature of liability: the Dutch Hoge Raad has based its "three stages rule" on tort and good faith alternatively and sometimes on both.[293] Especially in the

---

[287] *Supra* note 213.
[288] See HR, 23 October 1987, NJ 1988, 1017, annotated Brunner (VSH/Shell).
[289] *Supra*, at 251.
[290] *Infra*, at 275.
[291] HR, 14 June 1996, NJ 1997.481, annotated by HJS (De Ruiterij/Ruiters).
[292] See Van Schilfgaarde, annotation under Plas/Valburg, *supra* note 213.
[293] For a decision based on tort see e.g. HR, 13 February 1981, NJ 1981, 456, annotated by Brunner (Heesch/Reijs).

most recent ones the Hoge Raad has based liability directly on good faith.[294] The drawback of such a "third way" approach to liability would be in most systems that the code provides for only two regimes of liability (contract and tort) and therefore acceptance of a new third regime by the courts would lead to considerable uncertainty. However, in the Netherlands this approach is possible since the Dutch code provides for a single regime for any type of liability—see Articles 6: 95 ff. and 3: 310 BW. See also Greek law, where the Civil Code has adopted a "tripartite system" of delictual, pre-contractual and contractual liability.[295]

(4) As regards the extent of liability, if a party breaks off negotiations in the so-called second stage, as said above, he must reimburses the other party's expenses. A party who breaks off negotiations in the third stage, where breaking off is no longer allowed, is liable for the expectation interest. This was first accepted in the *Plas/Valburg* case.[296] The principle has been repeated in every later case on breaking off negotiations.[297] However, it should be added that there has not been a case yet where expectation damages actually were awarded. The Dutch rule can be explained by the fact that in Dutch law in the so-called third stage, which begins at the moment the other party could reasonably expect that a contract will be concluded[298] breaking off itself is unlawful—contrary to good faith. The damage caused by this unlawful act—i.e. the breaking off—is the non-conclusion of the contract, since at that stage of the negotiations the contract would have been concluded if the negotiations had not been broken off. Thus the fact that Dutch courts accept expectation damages when negotiations are broken off in the third stage is just a logical consequence of considering their breaking off itself at a certain point unlawful—contrary to good faith. The *Plas/Valburg* case has been commented upon by several foreign authors, like Farnsworth, Sacco, Van Ommeslaghe. Most of them disapprove off the Dutch rule.[299]

Privy Council   **2.E.82.**

Att.-Gen. of Hong Kong v. *Humphreys Estates (Queen's Gardens)*[300]

ENCOURAGING BELIEF THAT ONE WILL NOT WITHDRAW MAY LEAD TO ESTOPPEL

Humphreys estates

In order to establish liability where pre-contractual negotiations are broken off, a party must establish a binding estoppel in his or her favour. It is therefore necessary to establish, first, that the other created or encouraged a belief or expectation on the part of the claimant that he or she would not withdraw from the agreement in principle, and secondly, that the claimant relied on that belief or expectation.

Facts: The defendants, as representatives of the government of Hong Kong, and a group of companies, which included the plaintiff company (HKL), entered into negotiations for the government to acquire 83 flats in premises owned by the group in exchange for the grant of a Crown lease of government property to the group

---

[294] See e.g. HR, 16 June 1995, NJ 1995.705, annotated by Stein.
[295] Stathopoulos, op. cit., para. 84.
[296] *Supra*, note 213.
[297] See e.g. recently HR, 24 November 1995, NJ 1996.162.
[298] See *supra*, at 263.
[299] See e.g. van Ommeslaghe, op. cit., at 34.
[300] [1987] 1 AC 114.

with the right to develop it and the group's adjoining property. In January 1981 an agreement in principle was reached "subject to contract", providing that the terms could be varied or withdrawn and that any agreement was subject to the necessary documents giving legal effect to the transaction being executed and registered. The group permitted the government to take possession of the flats. After spending money on them, the government had, by August 1981, moved senior civil servants into the flats, and disposed of the residences they formerly occupied. Although a draft licence was prepared giving the group the right to terminate the government's occupation of the flats, it was never executed. However, the government granted the group a licence, expressed to be revocable at any time without notice, to enter its property and allowed the group to demolish the existing buildings in preparation for redevelopment. By August 1982 the group had paid the government $103,865,608, being the agreed difference in value between the two properties, and the basic terms of the agreement in principle had been agreed and had been substantially performed. The requisite documents were drafted but they were not executed because in April 1984 the group decided to withdraw from the negotiations and the plaintiff gave notice to the government determining its licence to occupy the flats.

Held: In the High Court the judge ordered, *inter alia*, that the first defendant should pay $103,865,608 to the plaintiff and that the plaintiff was entitled to possession of the flats. The judge dismissed the defendants' counterclaim holding that the plaintiff was not estopped from requiring the government to deliver up possession. The Court of Appeal of Hong Kong dismissed the defendants' appeal and the defendants appealed to the Privy Council, where their appeal was dismissed.

Judgment: LORD TEMPLEMAN: By February 1984 there was no difficulty in the court devising an order for specific performance of the agreement in principle provided that the agreement had become binding by estoppel. . . .

Their Lordships accept that the government acted to their detriment and to the knowledge of HKL in the hope that HKL would not withdraw from the agreement in principle. But in order to found an estoppel the government must go further. First the government must show that HKL created or encouraged a belief or expectation on the part of the government that HKL would not withdraw from the agreement in principle. Secondly the government must show that the government relied on that belief or expectation. Their Lordships agree with the courts of Hong Kong that the government fail on both counts. . . .

Their Lordships accept that there is no doubt that the government acted in the confident and not unreasonable hope that the agreement in principle would come into effect. As time passed and more and more actions were undertaken in conformity with the proposals contained in the agreement in principle, the government's hopes strengthened. It became more and more unlikely that either the government or HKL would have a change of heart and would withdraw from the agreement in principle. But at no time did HKL indicate expressly or by implication that they had surrendered their right to change their mind and to withdraw. That right, expressly reserved and conferred by the government, was to withdraw at any time before "document or documents necessary to give legal effect to this transaction are executed and registered." HKL did not encourage or allow a belief or expectation on the part of the government that HKL would not withdraw. . . .

In the present case the government acted in hope that a voluntary agreement in principle expressly made "subject to contract" and therefore not binding would eventually be followed by the achievement of legal relationships in the form of grants and transfers of property. It is possible but unlikely that in circumstances at present unforeseeable a party to negotiations set out in a document expressed to be "subject to contract" would be able to satisfy the court that the parties had subsequently agreed to convert the document into a contract or that some form of estoppel had arisen to prevent both parties from refusing to proceed with the transactions envisaged by the document. But in the present case the government chose to begin and elected to continue on terms that either party might suffer a change of mind and withdraw.

Court of Appeal   2.E.83.
J.T. Developments v. *Quinn*[301]

ESTOPPEL CAN GIVE RISE TO LEASE

The coffee shop

Renovation work done on the faith of an assurance by an agent of the lessor that a new lease would be granted to tenants was capable of giving rise to an estoppel, the appropriate remedy for which might be the grant of the new lease.

Facts: The defendants, Mr and Mrs Quinn, were the tenants of a coffee shop under a lease which was due to expire on 24 June 1989. In October 1988, their landlords served notice under section 25 of the Landlord and Tenant Act 1954 terminating the tenancy. The notice informed the tenants that if they did not wish to give up possession they could serve a counter-notice on the landlords within two months and apply to the court for a grant of a new tenancy which the landlords would not oppose. The defendants did not respond to this notice, and were not therefore entitled to apply to the court for a new tenancy. In November 1988, the landlords' surveyor, Mr Clayton, visited the shop. Mr Quinn told Mr Clayton that the Quinns were planning to make improvements to the kitchen. Subsequently in January 1989, there was a telephone conversation between Mr Clayton and Mr Quinn, in which Mr Clayton stated that his employers were prepared to grant a new tenancy to Mr Quinn on the same terms as those contained in a tenancy recently granted by the landlords to a Mr Maclucas in respect of a nearby shop. In January and February 1989, Mr Quinn carried out the kitchen improvements. Mr Clayton visited the property in February 1989, to measure the square footage to calculate the amount of rent under any new tenancy. In March 1989, Mr Clayton told Mr Quinn that the rent would be the same as that paid by Mr Maclucas. However, the landlords sold the shop to the plaintiffs on 23 June 1989. The plaintiffs issued proceedings for possession.

Held: The trial judge refused to grant an order for possession. He held that the telephone conversation in January 1989 constituted an oral agreement to grant a new tenancy on the same terms as the new tenancy granted to Maclucas. Alternatively, he held that the landlords had made a sufficiently clear representation that they would grant a new tenancy and the defendants had relied upon that representation by carrying out the kitchen work. The landlords were therefore estopped from going back upon that representation. The Court of Appeal dismissed the plaintiffs' appeal.

Judgment: RALPH GIBSON LJ: The issue of estoppel raised questions which I have found to be difficult. I have in the course of considering the case hesitated long before reaching a final conclusion and I have changed my mind as to what is the right conclusion more than once. . . .

One distinction between promissory and proprietary or equitable estoppel, which has been regarded as established, is that a promissory estoppel cannot create any new cause of action where none existed before: see Halsbury's Laws of England: *Combe* v. *Combe*. In this case, it is common ground that the defendants have asserted a right in equity by agreement or estoppel to a new lease of their shop and have not merely denied the plaintiffs' right to possession. It is clear that, by whatever name it is called, the defendants have set out to prove such an equity as gives rise to that cause of action. The defendants, in short, rely upon the principle, expounded and illustrated in the authorities considered by Lord Templeman in *Att-Gen of Hong Kong* v. *Humphreys Estate* upon which a litigant, who is led to believe he will be granted an interest in land, and who acts to his detriment in that belief, is enabled to obtain that interest. The principle has generally been known in those authorities as proprietary or equitable estoppel.

The statement of the principle in a dissenting speech by Lord Kingsdown in *Ramsden* v. *Dyson* has been held to state the law correctly: *Inwards* v. *Baker* and was to the following effect:

"The rule of law applicable to the case appears to me to be this: if a man, under a verbal agreement with a landlord for a certain interest in land, or, what amounts to the same thing, under an expectation created or encouraged by the landlord, that he shall have a certain interest, takes possession of such land, with the consent of the landlord, and upon the faith of such promise or expectation, with the knowledge of the landlord,

[301] (1991) 62 P. & C.R. 33.

266

and without objection by him, lays out money upon the land, a court of equity will compel the landlord to give effect to such promise or expectation. . . ."

The law requires that a representation, if it is to provide the basis for an estoppel, be clear and unequivocal and that it be intended to be relied upon. The evidence of Mr Quinn, which the judge accepted, was that Mr Clayton said: "Mr Quinn would get a new tenancy on the same terms as Mr Maclucas." In one sense, there is nothing unclear or equivocal about that statement: it shows plainly the intention of the landlords. If I am right, however, in holding that no concluded agreement was made or intended to be made by the parties to that conversation, then the representation was, and would be understood as being, that Mr Quinn would get a new tenancy on the same terms as Mr Maclucas if, after Mr Quinn went and looked at the Maclucas lease, the parties were still in agreement to that effect. Nothing was said, it seems, about what was going to be done next or how long Mr Quinn would have to find out what he wanted to know about the Maclucas lease. The parties were, and knew that they were, negotiating the terms of a new lease which both sides probably expected would be completed. Nothing, however, was expressly stated to suggest that the parties had committed themselves in any way so as to deprive either side of the right to withdraw from the negotiations. On the judge's view, Mr Quinn's answer in the January conversation was equally plain: namely that he was in agreement that he would take the new lease. Each side, however, according to basic principles of our law of contract, was free to withdraw even if to his knowledge the other side believed that a binding contract would be made. The decisive question in this case, of course, is whether the landlords by what was said in the January conversation had imposed upon themselves the obligation of not departing from their statement of intention without giving notice to Mr Quinn and before Mr Quinn had within their knowledge acted to his detriment in reliance upon the statement made by Mr Clayton. . . .

It must be asked, therefore, in this case first whether any representation made by Mr Clayton in the January conversation can fairly be held to have created or encouraged an expectation in Mr Quinn, before anything further was done towards the agreeing or granting of a new lease, and without any further acts on the part of the landlords, that he would have a new lease of the shop: and, secondly, whether the work done by Mr Quinn in the shop in January and February was done upon the faith of that expectation and with the knowledge of Mr Clayton.

As to the first question, I have been reluctant to accept that Mr Clayton's statements to Mr Quinn can properly be held to have been a clear and unequivocal assurance, which Mr Quinn was entitled to regard as intended by Mr Clayton to be acted upon by Mr Quinn, so as to provide the basis for an equitable estoppel. . . . Secondly, my reluctance has been based upon the belief that there is a risk of injustice to a landlord if an unconfirmed and disputed statement in a telephone conversation, coupled with the expenditure of a sum of money upon premises of which the tenant is in occupation under an existing tenancy, can form the basis of a right to a new 18-year lease. I have reminded myself, however, that I have only read the papers and I have not had the benefit of seeing and hearing Mr Clayton and Mr Quinn. There is no suggestion, as I have said, that the judge misdirected himself in his approach to the primary issues of fact. If Mr Quinn spent £2,100 on the shop in reliance upon a clear promise made by Mr Clayton to him it would be unjust to let the landlords go back on that promise. Giving full effect, therefore, to the judge's findings of primary fact, and to the evidence of Mr Quinn upon which in particular Mr Rimer based his submissions, I have finally reached the conclusion that the assurance given by Mr Clayton was capable of providing the basis for the estoppel alleged. . . .

The second and last question remains for consideration: was it open to the judge to hold that the work done in the shop by Mr Quinn in January and February 1989 was done upon the faith of that expectation and with the knowledge of Mr Clayton? . . . The judge held, as I have said, that Mr Clayton, from what he had been told in November 1988, knew that the defendants would be staying and carrying out the works. With that knowledge he gave to Mr Quinn the assurance which, if

I am right, was to the effect that the defendants could, if they wanted it, have a new lease on the Maclucas terms. Mr Quinn, as the judge found, proceeded to spend £2,100 in January and February 1989 in the belief, founded upon the assurance which he had been given, that he could have a new lease on those terms. I do not think that this case is so clear that this court should hold that the judge could not properly regard it as within the principle applied by the court in *Crabb* v. *Arun District Council*.

I would dismiss the plaintiff's appeal.

High Court of Australia   **2.AUS.84.**
Waltons Stores (Interstate) Ltd v. *Maher*[302]

COMPENSATION AWARDED ON BASIS OF ESTOPPEL

The supermarket renovation

Where an estoppel is established in respect of pre-contractual negotiations, the court may order a payment of compensation in the expectation or positive measure in lieu of specific performance of the contract.

Facts: In September 1983 Waltons Stores (Interstate) Ltd. and the Mahers entered into negotiations with a view to Waltons leasing the Mahers' property at Nowra. The property required considerable work in order to be suitable for Waltons' purposes, and it was intended that the Mahers would carry out this work by 5 February 1984. In October 1983, Waltons' solicitor sent a form of lease to the Mahers' solicitor, and the Mahers' solicitor subsequently informed Waltons' solicitor on November 1 that the Mahers had begun to demolish the old building on the site. On 7 November, the Mahers' solicitor told Waltons' solicitor that, if Mr Maher was to have sufficient time to make the necessary preparations for Waltons' takeover, it was essential that the agreement be concluded within the next day or so. The Mahers' solicitor also said that Mr Maher did not want to demolish a new brick part of the old building until it was clear that there were no problems with the lease. Waltons' solicitor sent the Mahers' solicitor an amended lease with a covering letter stating that he would let Mr Maher know the next day whether Waltons disagreed with any of the amendments incorporated in the redraft. Neither on the next day nor at all did Waltons' solicitor inform the Mahers' solicitor that Waltons disagreed with any of the amendments. On 11 November the Mahers' solicitor forwarded to Waltons' solicitor "by way of exchange" the lease executed by the Mahers. Thereafter the Mahers began to demolish the new part of the old building. On or about 21 November Waltons had second thoughts about proceeding with the lease, and having ascertained from its solicitors that for want of an exchange of parts it was not bound to proceed, instructed them to "go slow". On 10 December Waltons became aware that the demolition had commenced. The Mahers began the building work in accordance with plans approved by Waltons in early January, but on 19 January, their solicitor received a letter from Waltons' solicitor saying that Waltons did not intend to proceed with the lease. The building was by then about 40 per cent complete. Between 11 November 1983 and 19 January 1984 Waltons' solicitor had not communicated with the Mahers' solicitor, and retained the copy of the lease signed by the Mahers. The Mahers commenced proceedings in the Supreme Court of New South Wales for a declaration that there was in existence a valid and enforceable agreement for a lease, an order for specific performance and alternatively damages in lieu thereof.

Held: Kearney J gave judgment for the Mahers for damages in lieu of specific performance, and Waltons' appeal to the Court of Appeal (Glass, Samuels and Priestley JJ A) was dismissed (1986) 5 NSWLR 407. Waltons appealed, by special leave, to the High Court, where the appeal was dismissed.

Judgment: MASON CJ and WILSON J:

20. This brings us to the doctrine of promissory estoppel on which the respondents relied in this Court to sustain the judgment in their favour. . . .

30. One may . . . discern in the cases a common thread which links them together, namely, the principle that equity will come to the relief of a plaintiff who has acted to his detriment on the basis of

---

[302] 164 CLR 387 (1987).

a basic assumption in relation to which the other party to the transaction has "played such a part in the adoption of the assumption that it would be unfair or unjust if he were left free to ignore it": per Dixon J. in *Grundt*, at p 675; see also Thompson, at p 547. Equity comes to the relief of such a plaintiff on the footing that it would be unconscionable conduct on the part of the other party to ignore the assumption. . . .

32. Because equitable estoppel has its basis in unconscionable conduct, rather than the making good of representations, the objection, grounded in *Maddison* v. *Alderson*, that promissory estoppel outflanks the doctrine of part performance loses much of its sting. . . .

34. The foregoing review of the doctrine of promissory estoppel indicates that the doctrine extends to the enforcement of voluntary promises on the footing that a departure from the basic assumptions underlying the transaction between the parties must be unconscionable. As failure to fulfil a promise does not of itself amount to unconscionable conduct, mere reliance on an executory promise to do something, resulting in the promisee changing his position or suffering detriment, does not bring promissory estoppel into play. Something more would be required. *Humphreys Estate* suggests that this may be found, if at all, in the creation or encouragement by the party estopped in the other party of an assumption that a contract will come into existence or a promise will be performed and that the other party relied on that assumption to his detriment to the knowledge of the first party. *Humphreys Estate* referred in terms to an assumption that the plaintiff would not exercise an existing legal right or liberty, the right or liberty to withdraw from the negotiations, but as a matter of substance such an assumption is indistinguishable from an assumption that a binding contract would eventuate. . . .

36. All this may be conceded. But the crucial question remains: was the appellant entitled to stand by in silence when it must have known that the respondents were proceeding on the assumption that they had an agreement and that completion of the exchange was a formality? The mere exercise of its legal right not to exchange contracts could not be said to amount to unconscionable conduct on the part of the appellant. But there were two other factors present in the situation which require to be taken into consideration. The first was the element of urgency that pervaded the negotiation of the terms of the proposed lease. As we have noted, the appellant was bound to give up possession of its existing commercial premises in Nowra in January 1984; the new building was to be available for fitting out by 15 January and completed by 5 February 1984. The respondents' solicitor had said to the appellant's solicitor on 7 November that it would be impossible for Maher to complete the building within the agreed time unless the agreement were concluded "within the next day or two". The outstanding details were agreed within a day or two thereafter, and the work of preparing the site commenced almost immediately.

37. The second factor of importance is that the respondents executed the counterpart deed and it was forwarded to the appellant's solicitor on 11 November. The assumption on which the respondents acted thereafter was that completion of the necessary exchange was a formality. The next their solicitor heard from the appellant was a letter from its solicitors dated 19 January, informing him that the appellant did not intend to proceed with the matter. It had known, at least since 10 December, that costly work was proceeding on the site.

38. It seems to us, in the light of these considerations, that the appellant was under an obligation to communicate with the respondents within a reasonable time after receiving the executed counterpart deed and certainly when it learnt on 10 December that demolition was proceeding. It had to choose whether to complete the contract or to warn the respondents that it had not yet decided upon the course it would take. It was not entitled simply to retain the counterpart deed executed by the respondents and do nothing: cf. Thompson, at p 547; *Olsson* v. *Dyson* (1969) 120 CLR 365, at p 376. The appellant's inaction, in all the circumstances, constituted clear encouragement or inducement to the respondents to continue to act on the basis of the assumption which they had made. It was unconscionable for it, knowing that the respondents were exposing themselves to detriment by

acting on the basis of a false assumption, to adopt a course of inaction which encouraged them in the course they had adopted. To express the point in the language of promissory estoppel the appellant is estopped in all the circumstances from retreating from its implied promise to complete the contract. . . .

BRENNAN J:

23. Parties who are negotiating a contract may proceed in the expectation that the terms will be agreed and a contract made but, so long as both parties recognise that either party is at liberty to withdraw from the negotiations at any time before the contract is made, it cannot be unconscionable for one party to do so. Of course, the freedom to withdraw may be fettered or extinguished by agreement but, in the absence of agreement, either party ordinarily retains his freedom to withdraw. It is only if a party induces the other party to believe that he, the former party, is already bound and his freedom to withdraw has gone that it could be unconscionable for him subsequently to assert that he is legally free to withdraw. . . .

25. The unconscionable conduct which it is the object of equity to prevent is the failure of a party, who has induced the adoption of the assumption or expectation and who knew or intended that it would be relied on, to fulfil the assumption or expectation or otherwise to avoid the detriment which that failure would occasion. The object of the equity is not to compel the party bound to fulfil the assumption or expectation; it is to avoid the detriment which, if the assumption or expectation goes unfulfilled, will be suffered by the party who has been induced to act or to abstain from acting thereon. . . .

27. But there are differences between a contract and an equity created by estoppel. A contractual obligation is created by the agreement of the parties; an equity created by estoppel may be imposed irrespective of any agreement by the party bound. A contractual obligation must be supported by consideration; an equity created by estoppel need not be supported by what is, strictly speaking, consideration. The measure of a contractual obligation depends on the terms of the contract and the circumstances to which it applies; the measure of an equity created by estoppel varies according to what is necessary to prevent detriment resulting from unconscionable conduct. . . .

29. . . . There is no logical distinction to be drawn between a change in legal relationships effected by a promise which extinguishes a right and a change in legal relationships effected by a promise which creates one. Why should an equity of the kind to which *Combe* v. *Combe* refers be regarded as a shield but not a sword? The want of logic in the limitation on the remedy is well exposed in Mr David Jackson's essay "Estoppel as a Sword" in (1965) 81 Law Quarterly Review at pp 241–243.

30. Moreover, unless the cases of proprietary estoppel are attributed to a different equity from that which explains the cases of promissory estoppel, the enforcement of promises to create new proprietary rights cannot be reconciled with a limitation on the enforcement of other promises. If it be unconscionable for an owner of property in certain circumstances to fail to fulfil a non-contractual promise that he will convey an interest in the property to another, is there any reason in principle why it is not unconscionable in similar circumstances for a person to fail to fulfil a non-contractual promise that he will confer a non-proprietary legal right on another? It does not accord with principle to hold that equity, in seeking to avoid detriment occasioned by unconscionable conduct, can give relief in some cases but not in others. . . .

32. The qualifications proposed bring the principle closer to a principle the object of which is to avoid detriment occasioned by non-fulfilment of the promise. But the better solution of the problem is reached by identifying the unconscionable conduct which gives rise to the equity as the leaving of another to suffer detriment occasioned by the conduct of the party against whom the equity is raised. Then the object of the principle can be seen to be the avoidance of that detriment and the satisfaction of the equity calls for the enforcement of a promise only as a means of avoiding the detriment and only to the extent necessary to achieve that object. So regarded, equitable estoppel

does not elevate non-contractual promises to the level of contractual promises and the doctrine of consideration is not blown away by a side-wind. Equitable estoppel complements the tortious remedies of damages for negligent mis-statement or fraud and enhances the remedies available to a party who acts or abstains from acting in reliance on what another induces him to believe. . . .

35. . . . Having elected to allow Mr Maher to continue to build, it was too late for Waltons to reclaim the initial freedom to withdraw which Waltons had in the days immediately following 11 November. As the Mahers would suffer loss if Waltons failed to execute and deliver the original Deed, an equity is raised against Waltons. That equity is to be satisfied by treating Waltons as though it had done what it induced Mr Maher to expect that it would do, namely, by treating Waltons as though it had executed and delivered the original Deed. It would not be appropriate to order specific performance if only for the reason that the detriment can be avoided by compensation. The equity is fully satisfied by ordering damages in lieu of specific performance. The judgment of Kearney J. is supported by the first basis of estoppel. . . .

Notes

(1) In *Walford* v. *Miles*,[303] the plaintiffs asserted that, in order to give "business efficacy" to the agreement of 17 March, it was necessary to imply a term that the defendants were obliged to continue the negotiations in good faith, with the result that they were entitled to terminate the negotiations only if they, subjectively, had a "proper reason" for doing so. This argument was rejected. The House of Lords held that either party is entitled to withdraw from negotiations, at any time and for any reason. See also *Humphreys Estates*[304] where the Privy Council gave much weight to the fact that the agreement in principle was "subject to contract" and that none of the parties had given up their right to withdraw from the negotiations.

(2) However, in some specific cases the doctrine of estoppel can give relief. Generally, estoppel can be used only as a shield, not as a sword. In other words, the doctrine of estoppel cannot be used to create a new cause of action. However, this is not true for a specific type of estoppel which is known as proprietary estoppel. On the basis of this doctrine a promisee who to his detriment has relied upon the landowner's promise that the landowner will grant him an interest in the land can be entitled to be brought into the position he expected.[305]

(3) In the traditional view this form of relief is restricted to cases where the promisee is induced to believe that he will acquire rights in the promisor's land. However, it has been argued that this restriction cannot be justified.[306] The only possible objection to accepting a cause of action in a case of detrimental reliance upon other promises is that it would be irreconcilable with the doctrine of consideration. However, in the Australian decision in *Waltons Stores (Interstate) Ltd* v. *Maher*,[307] Brennan J has shown that allowing promissory estoppel to give rise to a cause of action does not necessarily undermine the doctrine of consideration. The reason for this is that the object of the principle of promissory estoppel is not to make a promise binding, which would require consideration, but to avoid a detriment. In other words, since the doctrine of promissory estoppel

---

[303] *Supra*, at 241.
[304] *Supra*, at 264.
[305] See e.g. *J.T. Developments* v. *Quinn supra*, at 266.
[306] See McKendrick, *Contract*, at 117; contrast Treitel, *Contract*, at 123 and 134–5.
[307] *Supra*, at 268.

protects only the reliance interest and not the expectation interest no consideration is required.[308] When could the promissory estoppel come into play? Mere reliance on a promise to do something, resulting in the promisee changing his position or suffering detriment, is not sufficient. Something more is required. According to Mason CJ and Wilson J in *Waltons Stores* this "may be found, if at all, in the creation or encouragement by the party estopped in the other party of an assumption that a contract will come into existence or a promise will be performed and that the other party relied on that assumption to his detriment to the knowledge of the first party".

(4) In American law the doctrine of promissory estoppel is well established.[309] It has been applied in a case of broken off negotiations by the Supreme Court of Wisconsin.[310] It should however be added that this case seems to be rather isolated in American law.[311]

(5) In some specific situations other general doctrines may help in cases of broken off negotiations. Depending on the circumstances of the case there may be negligent misrepresentation or a ground for restitution or even a preliminary contract. In *Blackpool & Fylde Aero Club* v. *Blackpool Borough Council*,[312] the defendant had invited a number of parties including the plaintiff to tender for a concession according to a certain procedure. The defendant, in violation of the procedure it had proclaimed, had failed to consider the plaintiff's tender (it had not cleared the letterbox). It was held liable in damages; according to Bingham LJ on the basis of an—implied—contract: the Council had offered properly to consider tenders and the Club had accepted it.

(6) As regards the extent of liability, in *Walford* v. *Miles* the House of Lords denied the plaintiffs' claim for expectation damages (loss of the profit they would have had from buying a company worth £3 million for £2 million). However, it should be remembered that the trial judge had already, on the basis of misrepresentation, awarded compensation for expenses incurred in the negotiations and in the preparation of contract documents. It is doubtful whether a continental European court would have come to a different result in this case.[313] On the contrary, it seems likely that it would agree with Treitel[314] that the actual result in this case is entirely appropriate on the facts. McKendrick has argued that an eventual introduction of a cause of action based on promissory estoppel into English law following the example of American law and Australian law would not undermine the doctrine of consideration because this action would give right to recovery only of the reliance interest. This would follow from the object of the principle of estoppel which is to prevent a detriment.[315] This view seems indeed to be confirmed by the American case *Red Owl,*[316] where the plaintiff merely got relief for the expenses he had incurred. However, the result of *Waltons* seems to be different. Although the Australian High Court adopted the view that the object of the equity was to avoid detriment, the court held that the appellant was estopped from

---

[308] See McKendrick, *Contract*, at 118.
[309] See e.g. s. 90 of the Restatement (Second) of Contract.
[310] *Hoffman* v. *Red Owl Stores*, 26 Wis 2d 683, 133 N.W. 2d 267 (1965).
[311] See Farnsworth, op. cit., at 238; Von Mehren, op. cit., para. 124.
[312] [1990] 1 WLR 1995.
[313] See Kötz, *Europäisches Vertragsrecht* at 61.
[314] Treitel, *Contract*, at 57.
[315] *Supra*, note 308.
[316] *Supra*, note 310.

retreating from its implied promise to complete the contract and awarded damages in lieu of specific performance. It is clear that the interest protected here is the expectation interest, since protection of the reliance interest would have been limited to recovery of the expenses made in demolishing the old building and in building 40 per cent of the new one.

(c) Comparison

(1) Comparing the rules of the Principles, Germany, France, Italy and the Netherlands, the test for liability for breaking off negotiations appears to be the same. See also Austria and Spain.[317] The two decisive elements are: (1) the negotiations have come to a point where the other party, induced by the defendant, could reasonably expect that a contract would be concluded; (2) there is no good reason for breaking off. In England, a party who breaks off negotiations is not liable unless he made a misrepresentation or the negotiations dealt with rights in land.[318] However, the Australian (*Waltons Stores*) and American (*Red Owl*) examples show that the English position is not the only one possible under Common Law. The test applied in *Waltons Stores* is similar to the one applied in continental European systems. In most European systems liability for breaking off negotiations is based on tort and in most systems liability is limited to the reliance interest.

(2) As regards the first element of the test (the provocation of reliance), the mere hope for a contract is not sufficient.[319] First, the other party must have relied on the conclusion of the contract. In Germany it is even necessary that the other party believed that the conclusion of the contract was certain.[320] The period in which a party can rely on the expectation provoked by the other is not unlimited in time, because he himself is also under a duty to behave according to good faith. Therefore, he has to make clear within a reasonable time what he intends to do.[321] Secondly, the reliance must have been justified in the circumstances. Thirdly, the reliance must have been induced by a representation, silence or conduct of the other party, for example, by telling him that he can give up his current position,[322] or by asking him to prepare a tender which requires more costs than are normal in that field of business,[323] or by inviting or allowing him to start to perform the prospective contract without warning him about the risk that the contract will eventually not be concluded.[324] See, as examples, BGH 19 October 1960,[325] where a negotiating party allowed the other party to start to rebuild premises destroyed during the war on the land which he expected to lease, the French Monoprix case[326] and the English proprietary estoppel cases.[327]

---

[317] See Posch, op. cit., at 48 and Díez-Picazo and Gullón, op. cit., at 69, respectively.

[318] It is a different question whether the plaintiff may have a restitutionary (*quantum meruit*) claim based on work done in anticipation of a contract: see e.g. *British Steel Corp* v. *Cleveland Bridge Co*, **1.E.61**, *supra* at 83.

[319] See e.g. Cass. it., 28 January 1972, n. 199, *supra* at 243. See also, with regard to proprietary estoppel, *Att.-Gen. of Hong Kong* v. *Humphreys Estates*, *supra* at 264.

[320] See e.g. BGH, 14 July 1967, NJW 1967, 2162.

[321] BGH, 10 July 1970, *supra* at 252.

[322] See BAG, 7 June 1963, NJW 1963, 1843; JZ 1964, 324.

[323] See Lando, op. cit., at 121.

[324] See BGHZ 71, 386 [8 June 1978]; Cass. it., 17 June 1974, *supra* at 259.

[325] LM BGB § 276 (Fa) No. 11; NJW 61.169; MDR 1961.49.

[326] *Supra*, at 257.

[327] *Supra*, at 264–8.

It should be noted that in many cases objective circumstances, like the long duration of the negotiations or the very advanced stage they had reached, seem to be decisive, rather than actual reliance.[328] The Italian Cassazione has even held that there can be liability only if the parties have taken all essential elements of the contract into consideration.[329] *In casu*, the fact that in previous exchange contracts 30 per cent of the buildings built on the land had always been given in exchange for the property in the land was considered to be irrelevant, since for the present contract the counter-performance had not explicitly been taken into consideration yet. Although this decision is regarded by some authors as particularly harsh in its effects,[330] the need for an agreement on all essential points seems to be approved by most Italian legal scholars.[331] Conversely, the German Bundes-gerichtshof does not require agreement an all essential points.[332]

(3) As regards the second element, a good reason for breaking off will readily be accepted. A better offer from a third party can be sufficient.[333] The disloyal behaviour of the other party, for example his unexpectedly raising new unjustified conditions, can also justify termination of the negotiations, even if they were in a very advanced stage.[334] However, reasons that have nothing to do with the negotiations cannot justify the breaking off.[335] Saleilles held that breaking off must "be possibly justified by an economic interest".[336]

(4) Can a party ever be liable for breaking off negotiations if the negotiations were conducted in view to a formal contract? A formal contract is a contract which is binding only if a certain formal requirement is met. A statutory provision may for example require a certain type of contract to be concluded in writing. See, for example, in England, for the sale of land, section 2 of the Law of Property (Miscellaneous Provisions) Act 1989. Sometimes a form requirement may also consist of authentication by a notary. See, for example, in Germany, for the sale of land, § 313 BGB, and, for the foundation of a company, § 2 GmbHG. It has been suggested that breaking off negotiations over such a contract can never make a party liable because the other party is never justified in relying on the imminent conclusion of such a contract, since he should know that there will be no binding contract before the formal requirement is met. Moreover, it has been argued that liability would undermine the purpose of the form requirement, which is often protection of a party from his own over-hasty decisions. However, the German BGH has held that a party who breaks off negotiations can be liable even if the contract could be effective only after complying with a formal requirement.[337] The reason is that the party who broke off is not liable for the breaking off itself but for inducing the other party to believe

---

[328] See e.g. Rennes, 29 April 1992, JCP, 1993, éd G, IV, 1520, Juris Data, No. 048674; Riom, 10 June 1992. See also the Comment to art. 2.15 Unidroit.

[329] Cass. it., 22 October 1982, No. 5492, GI 1984.I.1.1.

[330] See e.g. Nanni, op. cit., at 8.

[331] See Bianca, op. cit., para. 79; contrast, however, Sacco, op. cit., at 233.

[332] See BGH, 10 July 1970, cit. at 252; see also the American case *Red Owl*, where agreement on all essential details was not held necessary for liability on the basis of promissory estoppel.

[333] See Cour d'appel de Liège, 20 October 1989, *supra* at 246; See also Palandt, op. cit., para. 72; Sacco, op. cit., at 234; Schmidt, op. cit., at 53; cf, earlier, Saleilles, op. cit. at 718.

[334] See Nanni, op. cit., at 64.

[335] See BGH, 7 February 1980, 76, 343–351, NJW 1980.1683.

[336] Saleilles, op. cit., at 718–19.

[337] See e.g., with regard to negotiations about the sale of land, BGH, 10 July 1970 cit at note 321, and, with regard to negotiations concerning the foundation of a company, BGH 21 September 1987, ZIP 1988.88, WM 1988.163.

that a contract would be concluded. Therefore liability does not undermine the form requirement.[338] Medicus has disapproved of these decisions in very strong terms.[339] He suggests that in cases where the result would be really unbearable § 242 BGB could bring a solution. Under English law, the statutory provision which requires most contracts for the sale or disposition of an interest in land to be made in writing (section 2 of the Law of Property (Miscellaneous Provisions) Act 1989) does not exclude the operation of the doctrine of proprietary estoppel.[340] In other countries this question does not seem to have led to any disputes yet.[341]

(5) Is liability for breaking off negotiations possible if the person who by his statements or conduct caused the reliance had no power to conclude a binding contract on behalf of the party, for example a company or a municipality, that he represented in the negotiations? The German Bundesgerichtshof has decided that lack of power of an agent does not exclude liability. Again the explanation lies in the character of liability for broken off negotiations. The fault lies in inducing reliance, not in refusing to conclude the contract.[342] Therefore, although the defendant cannot be bound by a person who has no power to conclude a contract on his behalf, this does not exclude his responsibility for the fault of those conducting negotiations on his behalf (§ 278).[343] In the Swiss case of *Escophon AG* v. *Bank in Langenthal,*[344] it was exactly the circumstance that neither the head office nor the branch had ever informed the plaintiff that any contract would require the head office's approval which made their eventual breaking off contrary to good faith.

(6) In France, if both negotiating parties are professionals, breaking off will lead to liability only in very exceptional cases, because the costs of unsuccessful negotiations are supposed to be part of the parties' general expenses, which they can incorporate in the price in contracts resulting from other, successful negotiations.[345]

(d) Order for Specific Performance
In some systems liability in damages is not the only remedy. There a party can be ordered to continue negotiations or even to conclude the contract.

Gerechtshof Amsterdam, 7 May 1987[346]   **2.NL.85.**

<small>COURT MAY ORDER THAT NEGOTIATIONS SHOULD BE CONTINUED</small>

De Ziener

The duty of pre-contractual good faith may give rise to a duty to continue negotiations, and where that duty is not complied with, a court may order that the relevant negotiations should take place.

---

[338] See BGH, 14 July 1967.
[339] Medicus, op. cit. *supra*, note 192, at 499.
[340] See *Yaxley* v. *Gotts* [2000] Ch. 162.
[341] See for liability for concluding an invalid contract **2.2.3.D.**
[342] See Medicus, op. cit., at 501.
[343] See e.g. BAG, 7 June 1963, and BGH, 20 September 1984, 92, 164; NJW 1985.1779.
[344] *Supra*, at note 237.
[345] See Ghestin, para. 330; Schmidt, op. cit., at 150. See, however, Com., 22 April 1997, RTD civ. 1997.651 annotated by J. Mestre, where both parties were professionals. Liability here may be explained by the fact that it could be said that a valid contract had been concluded. Compare Mestre's observation.
[346] NJ 1988.430.

275

Facts: In 12 October 1983, the film director Du Mee wrote to the widow of Simon Vestdijk expressing the wish to make a film of Vestdijk's novel "De Ziener". Mrs Vestdijk granted Du Mee an option expiring on 1 June 1984. Following the expiry of the option period, Du Mee sent his initial script of "De Ziener" to Mrs Vestdijk. Mrs Vestdijk wrote to Du Mee, informing him that a number of matters relating to the script needed to be resolved, and referred him to the publishing house De Bezige Bij in relation to these matters. In April 1985 the director of De Bezige Bij wrote to Du Mee informing him that he had been granted a further option for the film rights to De Ziener until 2 April 1986. The letter stated "We will be pleased, towards the end of the option period, to enter into more specific consultations with you concerning the contract and related matters of detail". In March 1986, Du Mee requested a one year extension of the option period, in view of the fact that he had not succeeded in arranging finance for the film. By a letter dated 24 April, De Bezige Bij stated that Mrs Vestdijk had not given a positive reaction to the request for an extension, and that that she was willing to give him until 15 May 1986 to produce a modified plan. On 11 May, Du Mee sent Mrs Vestdijk a new version of the script. However, on 27 May 1986, Mrs Vestdijk wrote to Du Mee informing him that the modified plan had not inspired in her any confident expectation that an extension of the option would lead to acceptable results. She was therefore unwilling to extend the option, and stated that it had terminated with effect from 15 May 1986. Du Mee brought proceedings seeking, (a) an order restraining the defendants from taking steps to prevent him from filming "De Ziener" and from carrying out the preparatory work required for the filming, (b) an order prohibiting the defendants from entering into negotiations concerning the filming of "De Ziener" with any person other than Du Mee and/or from giving any third party the right to film "De Ziener", and (c) an order requiring the defendants, or at least De Bezige Bij, within two days after service of the judgment to enter into reasonable consultations with Du Mee with a view to bringing into existence an agreement concerning the filming of "De Ziener". The President of the Amsterdam Rechtbank (District Court) dismissed the claims.

Held: On appeal, Du Mee succeeded in his claims under (b) and (c) above.

Judgment: . . . 4.5 The fourth plea is likewise well founded. As discussed in 4.3 above, Du Mee was entitled to assume, when seeking an extension of the option period, that, in the event of that request being refused, he would be given an opportunity to hold discussions with regard to a definitive contract taking immediate effect. De Bezige Bij did not give him that opportunity, choosing instead the middle course of confirming, by letter of 29 April 1986, the information, already given earlier in oral form, that Mrs Vestdijk had "not given a positive reaction" to Du Mee's request for an extension, and giving Du Mee, on behalf of Mrs Vestdijk, the opportunity of submitting a "modified plan or scenario" before 15 May 1986. Du Mee proceeded on that basis. De Bezige Bij's conduct was not in itself contrary to the principle of good faith.

4.6 However, following receipt of the second script, Mrs Vestdijk again indicated that she was "unable to give a positive reaction" to Du Mee's request for an extension of the option in respect of the film rights. She gave two reasons for this. First, she was not satisfied with either the first or the second version of the script. The second reason given by her was stated to be Du Mee's conduct in relation to the statement made by Mr Hamming of De Bezige Bij in his letter of 24 April 1986 that Mrs Vestdijk regarded it as most important that Du Mee should in the near future hold an exchange of views with her. There existed no obligation *per se* on the second and third defendants to extend the term of the option. However, the reasons given in Mrs Vestdijk's letter of 27 May 1986, as described above, did not justify the refusal, implicitly expressed in that letter and subsequently maintained, to negotiate with regard to the materialisation of a definitive contract. The first reason was inadequate, since Mrs Vestdijk, as is apparent from her letter of 2 April 1983, had already accepted the first script and, according to the contents of her letter of 27 May 1986, the second script differed from the first only in so far as one or two things in it had been altered, added or omitted. The second reason was inadequate . . . [because] given that the defendants were aware of the considerable importance which Du Mee attached to the conclusion of a definitive contract, the second and third defendants were under a duty to act in good faith by proceeding to enter into reasonable consultations with the appellant to that end.

4.7 It follows from the considerations set out above that the judgment appealed against must be set aside. The claim should be allowed. The Court considers in that regard that the first version of the script was accepted by Mrs Vestdijk, so that there can be no further debate concerning the script beyond what the appellant has stated in the second complete paragraph on p. 6 of his statement of grounds of appeal. The claim made under (b) falls to be allowed in the manner hereinafter set out. The claim made under (a) cannot be allowed, since no definitive contract ever materialised. In view of the relative significance of the matter to the parties, the Court proposes to limit the penalty to HFL 200,000 per breach.

Notes

(1) Under Dutch law a party who breaks off negotiations at a stage where this is no longer allowed[347] can be ordered to continue negotiations. See *De Ziener*,[348] where the widow of a writer was ordered to continue negotiations concerning the right to make a film on the basis of a famous novel.[349] According to some scholars, a party may even be ordered actually to conclude the contract.[350]

(2) In England, in a case of proprietary estoppel, the landowner may actually be compelled to grant the right in his land he has led the other party to expect he will obtain. See for example *Humphreys Estate* (per Lord Templeman),[351] where the Privy Council held that there was no difficulty in the court devising an order for specific performance provided that HKL was estopped from withdrawing from the negotiations. In the present case the Privy Council held that no estoppel could be established since the government had failed to show that HKL had encouraged a belief that they would not withdraw from the agreement in principle and that the government had relied on that belief. The Privy Council gave much weight to the fact that the agreement in principle was "subject to contract" and that none of the parties had given up their right to withdraw from the negotiations. Indeed in *J.T. Developments* v. *Quinn*,[352] where no such words had been used, proprietary estoppel was found. In view of these cases it seems likely that in *Walford* v. *Miles* specific performance could have been sought on the basis of proprietary estoppel, if the appropriate detrimental reliance could have been established—improvement to the promisor's land or conferment of some other benefit on him is, however, not a necessary condition.[353]

(3) In most other systems the remedies for broken off negotiations are limited to damages.[354] In Germany, the Bundesgerichtshof has held that a party who has broken off negotiations in a manner contrary to good faith cannot be ordered to continue negotiations or actually to conclude the contract.[355] Medicus finds German law inconsistent. He raises the question why a party at a certain point of the negotiations may rely on the conclusion of a contract but is denied the right to claim the actual conclusion of the contract or to claim expectation damages.[356] In France an order to conclude the contract, which there would be seen as damages *in natura*, is not admitted either,[357] nor is it in Italy.[358]

---

[347] See, on this so-called third stage, *supra*, at 263.

[348] *Supra*, at 275.

[349] See also Gerechtshof Arnhem, 14 November 1983, NJ 1984.499 (negotiations concerning the take over of a company).

[350] See Van Schilfgaarde, annotation under Plas/Valburg, AA 32 (1983) 758.

[351] *Supra*, [0000].

[352] (1991) 62 P. & C.R. 33 (Court of Appeal), *supra*, [0000].

[353] See Treitel, at 125.

[354] See Hondius, op. cit., at 23–4.

[355] See BGH, 19 October 1960, LM BGB § 276 (Fa) no. 11; NJW 61.169; MDR 1961.49.

[356] Medicus, op. cit., at 498.

[357] See e.g. Jourdain, op. cit., at 131; Terré, Simler and Lequette, para. 177.

[358] See Cass. it., 28 January 1972, No. 199, at [0000].

2.2.3.D. KNOWINGLY ENTERING AN INVALID CONTRACT

A party who knows or should know that a contract will be invalid, but nevertheless concludes it without warning the other party may be liable to pay reliance damages. This liability differs from liability for breaking off negotiations[359] in that here an agreement is reached. See Bianca:[360]

> Whilst in the case of unjustified withdrawal the party is involved in fruitless negotiations, here he is involved in a fruitless stipulation. Specifically, the person concerned is adversely affected as regards his contractual freedom in that the fraudulent or negligent conduct of the other party has led him to stipulate a contract which is invalid or inoperative.[361]

Liability for concluding an invalid contract was first recognized by Rudolph von Jhering in a famous article in 1861.[362] He stated that invalidity means that a party has no right to performance, but does not exclude recovery of reliance damage caused by the fault of the other party.[363] Jhering rejected a tort-based liability for negligently failing to give accurate information, because this would imply an unacceptable expansion of liability.[364] It is therefore perhaps ironic that, as we saw, the doctrine proposed by Jhering as an alternative has been invoked as the basis for extensive liabilities different in kind from those which he contemplated—that is, liability for breaking off negotiations.

Whereas in Jhering's view the fault lay in concluding a contract which one knows to be invalid,[365] in the approach of Article 1338 CC it. and of the German Bundesgerichtshof[366] the fault lies in the violation of a duty to inform. Compare § 878 ABGB, as it is interpreted by the Austrian Oberster Gerichtshof.[367] Bianca shares Jhering's view:[368]

the injurious act is not the failure to disclose the causes of invalidity or ineffectiveness but stems directly from the conclusion of the invalid or ineffective contract by the person who is or ought to be aware of those causes.

However, it may be objected that a party who concludes a contract which he knows to be invalid, after having informed the other party, is not at fault. In any case, it is submitted that the practical importance of this difference in conception is rather limited.

Unidroit Principles **2.INT.86.**

Article 2.15: *Illustration no. 2 to art. 2.15*

A, who is negotiating with B for the promotion of the purchase of military equipment by the armed forces of B's country, learns that B will not receive the necessary export licence from its own governmental authorities, a pre-requisite for permission to pay B's fees. A does not reveal this fact to B and finally concludes the contract, which,

---

[359] *Supra*, at **2.2.3.C.**
[360] Bianca, op. cit., at 174.
[361] See also Medicus, op. cit. *supra*, note 192, at 504.
[362] *Supra*, note 178.
[363] *Ibid.* at 32.
[364] *Ibid.* at 12.
[365] *Passim.* at 34.
[366] See *infra*, at 284 and 282 respectively.
[367] See Posch, "Austria" in *Pre-contractual Liability*, op. cit. *supra*, note 207, at 46.
[368] Bianca, op. cit., at 174.

however, cannot be enforced by reason of the missing licences. A is liable to B for the
costs incurred after A had learned of the impossibility of obtaining the required
licences.

Note

In systems which are not, like German law, dominated by the will theory, contracts are
less threatened with invalidity for defect of consent.[369] Therefore, there the use of the doctrine of *culpa in contrahendo* is much more limited. Whereas in Germany a party who has
concluded a contract under mistake can avoid it independently of whether the other party
knew better, that other party when he relied on the validity of the contract having to be
protected by an action for reliance damages, under, for example, the Unidroit Principles
the other party's reliance would make the contract incapable of being avoided—see
Article 3.5 of the Unidroit Principles. Therefore, in these systems—see also for example
in the Netherlands—this liability would, if ever, at most be of use in case of invalidity for
illegality or lack of form. The second illustration to Article 2.15 of the Unidroit
Principles[370] shows a case where a party who knows that the contract will be unenforceable and does not inform the other party about this fact acts contrary to good faith and
is, therefore, liable.

RGZ, 5 April 1922[371]   **2.G.87.**

LIABILITY FOR CAUSING MISUNDERSTANDING IN NEGOTIATIONS

Two sellers

*A party who negligently expresses himself in such a way as to bring about misunderstanding in the mind
of the other party and which prevents a contract from coming into existence may bear the burden of
liability for the loss and damage suffered as a result.*

Facts: Two parties had been so inept in their telegraphic communications with each other that a contract
appeared to have been concluded for the purchase of 100 kg of tartaric acid. It subsequently transpired that
each of them wished to sell the goods.

Held: Overturning the decision of the Oberlandesgericht (Court of Appeal), the RGZ held that the plaintiff
was not entitled to compensation for his loss of profit as a result of the defendant's failure to purchase the
acid.

Judgment: This case therefore involves a real absence of *consensus ad idem*. Each of the parties used
words which appeared to suit the other party's purposes, but they attached to those words a meaning which prevented any agreement from being reached. Consequently, no purchase agreement
came into existence. . . . It follows that the plaintiff cannot claim performance of the contract.

The question arises, however, whether the circumstances of the case, as described, are such as to
allow a claim for compensation to be made. . . . In the event that a contract fails to materialise, the
statute permits a claim to be made, in a good many factual instances, with regard to the negative
contractual interest (for damage suffered on account of reliance on a declaration, known as
Vertrauensschaden): that is the position, for example, under § 122 (avoidance of a declaration of

---

[369] See on this chapter III on validity, *infra*, **3.2.1**.
[370] *Supra*, at 278.
[371] RGZ 104.205.

intent on account of mistake), § 179 (absence of power of representation on the part of an ostensible representative), § 307 (an intentional or reckless promise to do something which cannot be done), and § 309 (conclusion of an illegal contract). The question whether those principles can be extended to cover similar cases is the subject of controversy and disagreement. . . .

On those grounds, and out of considerations of fairness and certainty in dealings between parties, it is justifiable to apply the same principles to the present case, involving what may be termed a hidden lack of consent. This because it is indeed in accordance with the concept of fairness, and with the requirements of certainty in dealings with other parties, to impose upon a party who negligently expresses himself in such a way as to bring about misunderstanding in the mind of the other party the burden of liability for the loss and damage suffered as a result.

BGH, 29 January 1965[372]   **2.G.88.**

L<small>IABILITY FOR NOT INFORMING ABOUT FORM REQUIREMENT</small>

The Housing Association

A failure on the part of a commercial company to ensure that a contract concluded with private individuals complies with the necessary formalities represents a breach of the company's duty to conduct pre-contractual negotiations with care, and can give rise to a claim to compensation for the loss suffered as a result.

Facts: The plaintiff, a non-profit-making housing undertaking, and the defendants, a married couple, entered into a private written agreement in which the defendants undertook to acquire as purchasers a single-family residence. The document concluded with the statement that "this undertaking shall be replaced by a final contract (the purchase contract) to be concluded during the construction period or once the single-family terraced house has been completed". The house was thereafter constructed and the defendants moved in, but no contract validly complying with the requisite formalities was ever executed; nor was ownership of the property ever transferred. Differences of opinion arose between the parties. In the course of those disagreements, the plaintiff declared that, since the defendants had by their conduct destroyed the underlying relationship of trust, it regarded itself as no longer bound by the agreement and was withdrawing from it. The plaintiff brought proceedings claiming the surrender and return of the property with vacant possession in return for payment of approximately DM 10,000; that sum was calculated on the basis of the payments of the purchase price made by the defendants less compensation of DM 250 per month for the use of the property which the plaintiff claimed from the defendants in respect of the period from the time when they moved into the house to the commencement of the action. The Landgericht (Regional Court) dismissed the claim. The plaintiff's appeal to the Oberlandesgericht (Higher Regional Court) was rejected.

Held: The Bundesgerichtshof dismissed the plaintiff's claim, and awarded the defendants compensation for the loss they had suffered.

Judgment: . . . It is impossible to see how the defendants, if ordered to surrender possession of the property, should be supposed to survive solely on what the plaintiff is willing to pay to them by way of a *quid pro quo* pursuant to § 273 BGB. In particular, the answer to that question does not emerge from the extracts from the works of academic legal authors cited in the judgment appealed against. . . . Those extracts merely deny that a compensation claim can take the form of an application for "performance" of a purchase contract which is invalid for want of legal form, i.e. the purchaser is not entitled to circumvent §§ 823 and 826 BGB by demanding conveyance of the property informally sold to him. A different question arises, however, as to whether, and to what extent, the defendants, if ordered to surrender possession of the property, are entitled to claim compensation from the plaintiff for *culpa in contrahendo*.

---

[372] NJW 65.813.

PRE-CONTRACTUAL GOOD FAITH

There can be no doubt, according to the findings made by the court adjudicating on the facts, that the criteria for such a compensation claim (§ 276 BGB) are fulfilled in the present case. The plaintiff, a non-profit-making housing undertaking, caused the defendant couple, who had applied to it trustingly with a view to acquiring a house to be built for occupation by them, to enter into an agreement which was void under §§ 313 and 125 BGB, by submitting to them for signature a document which it had itself drafted; the defendants believed, on the basis of that document, that all the necessary formalities had been completed and that, provided they performed the obligations incumbent on them, they would be duly registered in the land register as the owners of the property. By failing to draw to the defendants' attention the need to have the matters agreed judicially or notarially recorded in an official document, the plaintiff failed to act in accordance with the duty of care which had been established by the initiation of contractual negotiations between the parties. . . . The plaintiff's failure to explain to the parties with whom it was negotiating the formal requirements in respect of the pre-contractual agreement also constitutes fault on the part of the plaintiff. If, as the plaintiff maintains, it was really "completely unaware of the nullity of the contract", it should have been expected, as a commercial company and a non-profit-making housing undertaking, to seek proper legal advice, before concluding such contracts for the sale of real property with prospective purchasers, on the formal requirements needing to be complied with in that regard. . . .

As regards the quantum of the compensation payable to the defendants, it may be assumed from the findings of fact made in the judgment appealed against that, had they been aware that the financial burden facing them, which would exhaust their entire resources over a period of many years, did not give rise to any legally effective counter-obligation to sell the house to them, they would never have involved themselves in the conclusion of the private written pre-contractual agreement but would have demanded that the matter be formally documented by a notary. In those circumstances, it may naturally be supposed that the purchase contract would have come into existence in valid form without the behaviour on the plaintiff's part rendering it liable to pay compensation. The Court would then be faced with one of those cases in which performance of the contract may legitimately be claimed; the defendants would be entitled to be placed in the position which they would have occupied if the contract had been legally effective (RGZ 151, 357; Soergel-Schmidt, BGB 9, Aufl. Vorbem. 18 vor § 275; Soergel-Siebert, *loc. cit.*, § 242, note 222). That does not mean, however, that there exists any entitlement to claim relief in the form of the conclusion of a purchase contract fulfilling the requisite formal requirements, or even the conveyance of the property, since that would constitute a claim not for compensation but for performance of a contract, and would result in the nullification of the formal requirements laid down in § 313 BGB (judgment of the adjudicating Chamber of 4.3.1955, V ZR 66/54, WM 55, 728, 729 = BB 55, 429; Staudinger-Weber, *loc. cit.*, § 242, note A 788; see the different view expressed by Soergel-Siebert, *loc. cit.*). Instead, the plaintiff is liable to indemnify the defendants by paying them such monetary compensation as will enable them, after they have surrendered and returned the property, and taking into account the prices currently payable for real property and building materials and current salary levels, as well as their own financial resources at the material time (1957), to acquire a house of equivalent value.

EXCEPTIONALLY NOT PERMITTED TO RENEGE ON ASSURANCE THAT CONTRACT IS VALID

The employer's signature

Having assured the other party to the contract that the contract is valid, a party is not permitted to rely on the invalidity of the contract in defence to a claim on the contract.

Facts: The defendant sold the plaintiff a piece of real property. Upon concluding the contract in that regard, which required to be in notarial form, the defendant induced the plaintiff, a former employee, to forego compliance with the requirement of notarial form, on the grounds of its significance and standing and on the basis of an indication to the effect that a contract under private law was normally regarded as equivalent to a notarial one.

Held: The plaintiff was able to enforce the contract.

Judgment: In the present case, the fundamental idea expressed in the judgment of the Reichsgericht [Supreme Court of the German Reich] in RGZ 153, 59, necessarily results in the conclusion that the defendant is obliged, in accordance with the principle of good faith, to abide by the contract under private law dated 20 June 1958. The appellate court found that, upon the conclusion of the contract, the managing partner of the defendant firm, where the plaintiff had received his training as a businessman, allayed the plaintiff's concerns about the need for the involvement of a notary by pointing out, with a certain vanity, that the contract bore his signature. When the plaintiff, beset by doubts, pointed out that no human being lives for ever, the managing partner of the defendant firm further stated that he had also signed the contract in the name of the defendant firm and that the contract was therefore equivalent to a notarial contract. In accordance with this, the defendant also stated, in its subsequent letter to the plaintiff of 15 February 1963, that it was accustomed to honouring its obligations irrespective of whether those obligations had been assumed in oral, written or notarial form. In so doing, the defendant set great store by its significance and standing, and indicated in such emphatic terms that it was accustomed in its business to fulfil its commitments, that it effectively promised to perform the contract despite the defective form of the latter, so that it cannot repudiate the same without breaching the principle of good faith. Its subsequent reliance on the argument that the defective form of the contract renders it null and void constitutes an inadmissible exercise of its legal rights, irrespective of the fact that the plaintiff was not mistaken as to the formal requirements of that contract.

Notes

(1) In the BGB, Jhering's theory[374] has not been codified as such. Instead, the BGB contains several specific provisions on liability in many of the situations in relation to which Jhering developed his *culpa in contrahendo* theory. See for example § 122, reliance on a contract that is invalid as a result of *Mangel der Ernstlichkeit* (§ 118), *Irrtum* (§ 119), *falsche Übermittlung* (§ 120); § 179, reliance on a contract concluded by an agent who had no power of agency; § 307, reliance on a contract that is invalid for *unmögliche Leistung* (§ 306); § 309, which declares § 307 applicable in case the contract relied on is invalid for illegality (*Gesetzwidrigkeit*). These articles give the party that relied innocently on the validity of the contract the right to reliance damages, which are limited to the extent of

---

[373] BGHZ 48.396.
[374] See *supra*, at 250.

the expectation interest. However, under the BGB, in some of these cases—see for example § 122—fault is not required. There the underlying principle is no longer the doctrine of *culpa in contrahendo*, but the reliance principle. The *Reichsgericht*, first, and the *Bundesgerichtshof*, later, have expanded fault liability for concluding an invalid contract to other ineffective contracts.[375] By now a general rule can be formulated: "Where a party culpably fails to inform the other party about facts and matters which prevent the valid implementation of the transaction, that party is liable in respect of the negative interest, as limited by the positive interest".[376]

(2) The Bundesgerichtshof has in particular held that under certain circumstances, most often relating to the qualities of the parties, a negotiating party might have a duty to disclose about the presence of a form requirement. Liability for *culpa in contrahendo* here might extend to the expectation interest if in the absence of violation of this duty a valid contract would have been concluded. However, damages *in natura* leading to a duty to conclude a valid contract or even to transfer property are inadmissible because this would undermine the form requirement. See for example *The Housing Association* case,[377] where it was held that a common use flats company should inform the buyer about the formal requirement (§ 313). Most legal scholars reject this decision, because awarding expectation damages implies compulsion to contract and because, in their view, it equally undermines the form requirement.[378] In addition to this, in cases of extreme hardship, i.e. in cases where upholding the formal requirement would lead to an unbearable result (*unertragbaren Ergebnis*), invocation of the invalidity of the contract is held to amount to an abuse of right, contrary to good faith (§ 242 BGB), and is therefore inadmissible. See for example *The Employer's Signature*[379] where the plaintiff knew of the formal requirement but had been convinced by his former boss that his signature had the same value.[380]

(3) The question, discussed here, whether a party who concludes a contract which he knows will be invalid for lack of form, is liable, differs from the question, discussed at 274, whether a form requirement can exclude liability for breaking off negotiations. Here the negotiations have not been broken off but the parties have reached an agreement. However, the same argument invoked there for explaining that a form requirement for the conclusion of the contract does not exclude liability for breaking off negotiations, i.e. that liability would not frustrate the scope of the form requirement, is used here by the Bundesgerichtshof to justify liability.

(4) The duty to inform may include a duty to be informed oneself in order to be able to inform. Note *The Housing Association* case,[381] where it was held that a common use flats company should inform the buyer about the formal requirement, its own ignorance not serving as an excuse.[382]

[375] See the leading case *Two sellers*, *supra*, at 279.
[376] See Medicus, *SAT* para. 108.
[377] *Supra*, at 280.
[378] See e.g. Larenz, *SAT* at 114; see also Medicus, *Bürgerliches Recht*, 17th. edn. (Köln/Berlin/Bonn/München: Haymanns, 1996), para. 185, who for this reason rejects any liability for *culpa in contrahendo* in this type of cases; see earlier Jhering, *supra*, [0000].
[379] *Supra*, at 282.
[380] Compare Swiss law; See e.g. Merz, *Vertrag und Vertragsschluß* (Freiburg: 1988) para. 133.
[381] *Supra*, at 280.
[382] See also e.g. Bianca, op. cit., at 174.

(5) Many codes contain a specific provision that makes liable a party who concludes a contract on behalf of another party without being entitled to represent that party.[383]

Codice civile **2.I.90.**

Article 1338: *Knowledge of ground of invalidity*
> A party who knows or should have known of a ground of invalidity of a contract and did not inform the other party thereof shall be required to compensate for the damage suffered by the latter through his reliance, without fault on his part, upon the validity of the contract.

Cass. it., 28 May 1954[384] **2.I.91.**

LIABILITY ONLY RELATES TO VOID OR VOIDABLE CONTRACTS

The export licence

The liability provided for in Article 1338 of the Civil Code presupposes that the relevant contract is void or voidable. No liability under Article 1338 of the Civil Code therefore attaches to a party who concludes a contract of sale without informing the foreign contracting party of the need for an export licence.

Facts: An Italian buyer had concluded a contract with a foreign seller without informing him that a licence would be required for the importation of the goods. After the conclusion of the contract the buyer applied for the licence, but failed to obtain it. The *Corte d'appello* had held the buyer liable *ex* Article 1338.

Held: The decision below was annulled and the case remitted for consideration in accordance with principles laid down by the Cassazione.

Judgment: The judgment must therefore be annulled . . . and the case referred for further consideration to another court of the same level, which shall observe the following legal principles:

The liability provided for in Article 1338 of the Civil Code presupposes that an invalid contract is concluded, that is to say one which is void or voidable.

A contract for the purchase of goods to be imported from a foreign country is perfectly valid, notwithstanding that an appropriate licence for importation is required from the administrative authority which constitutes a *condicio iuris* for the efficacy of the transaction.

Therefore, there can be no liability under Article 1338 of the Civil Code attaching to an Italian contracting party who concluded the sale contract before applying for such a licence, without informing the foreign contracting party of the need for such a licence.

If the buyer subsequently applies for a licence and fails to obtain it for reasons not attributable to him, he bears no liability for the consequent ineffectiveness of the contract.

---

[383] See e.g § 179 BGB; art. 1398 CC it.; 3: 70 BW.
[384] No. 1731, Giust. Civ. 1954.1269.

Cass. it. (Sez. Un.), 11 February 1982[385]   **2.I.92.**

IGNORANTIA LEGIS NON EXCUSAT

Price prescription

Where all persons are deemed to possess a knowledge of the law, no liability in contrahendo may arise in relation to a failure to comply with that a certain rule.

Facts: The public administration had determined the transfer price for a residence in an inexpensive municipal building at a level lower than that prescribed by the relevant legal provisions. Having declared the contract void, the Court of cassation declared that in such circumstances there could be no liability *in contrahendo* on the part of the public administration.

Held: The Cassazione upheld the decision.

Judgment: The contested judgment, in fact, applied in a wholly proper manner the rule repeatedly laid down by this Supreme Court (a typical example being judgment No 2325 of 11 July 1972) that there can be no liability for *culpa in contrahendo* where the ground of invalidity of the transaction, although known to one of the parties but not disclosed by him, derives from a legal provision which must irrebuttably be deemed to be known by all persons subject to law.

Cass. it., 10 May 1950[386]   **2.I.93.**

RELIANCE ON CONTRACT CONCLUDED IN DISRESPECT OF FORM REQUIREMENT NOT PROTECTED

Signed with a cross

Where a claimant ought to have known that a contract for the transfer of immovable property is subject to a requirement of writing, he or she cannot claim compensation for culpa in contrahendo from the other party for a failure to disclose this requirement.

Facts: Morgese had concluded with La Greca a pre-contract for the sale of land. Morgese had signed the document by drawing a cross. Article 1351 jo. 1350 require that such a contract should be concluded in writing and as a result, the contract was invalid. La Greca subsequently claimed compensation from Morgese.

Held: La Greca's claim failed.

Judgment: And in fact, if a private document must be taken to mean any document not attested by a public officer, provided that it is signed by its author, it seems clear that the document at issue, lacking a signature by Morgese and, therefore, an essential requirement prescribed for it to constitute a private document, cannot be regarded as such ...

In the second ground of appeal, the breach is alleged of fundamental legal principles, and of Article 360(3) of the Code of Civil Procedure, it being alleged that the Court, closing its eyes to the reality of things, wrongly ruled out any pre-contractual liability on the part of Morgese, which had been upheld and accepted by the first court. It is submitted in that connection that as a result of the production of the instructions to sell, conclusion of the negotiations, receipt of part of the agreed price, transfer of possession of the property, drafting of the instrument of sale, participation therein of the guarantor and the commitment to sign an officially attested instrument by 15 January 1948, Morgese caused to arise in the appellant the legitimate expectation that the contract, which had already been essentially concluded, would be formally perfected.

[385] No. 835, Giust. civ. 1982.1238.
[386] No. 1205, Foro it. 1950.I.1307.

But that criticism likewise cannot be upheld . . . Article 1338, which imposes the obligation to disclose the existence of any defects, also raises a question of diligence, in the sense that it is not permissible to seek compensation for damage from another party who, being aware of the defects, did not disclose them, where the aggrieved party failed to make any enquiries in that regard, thus manifestly being at fault. And since, it is claimed, La Greca could not have been unaware of the fact that, for the transfer of immovable property, a written document is required *ad substantiam*, and that a document not signed by all the parties to the agreement constituting its subject-matter does not bring into being a valid act-in-the-law, it follows that La Greca, having incurred fault itself, could not claim compensation for the damage which it claimed to have suffered.

Notes

(1) The Italian Civil Code has dedicated a specific provision to the problem of *culpa in contrahendo*: Article 1338.[387] This provision is generally accepted to be a *lex specialis* of Article 1337.[388] According to most authors "*invalidità*" includes: any type of ineffectiveness including nullity (*nullità*); "voidability" (*annullabilità*); partial nullity (*nullità parziale*); inefficacy (*inefficacia*); non-existence (*inesistenza*).[389] However, the Cassazione has refused to apply Article 1338 to invalidity as a result of a statutory provision, holding that a citizen who does not know the law does not rely innocently.[390] In particular, the Cassazione has held that reliance on a contract that is not concluded in the required form cannot be protected.[391] This view has been criticized by most legal scholars who find it an unacceptable fiction to suppose that every citizen should know the law.[392] Furthermore, they argue, all invalidity is ultimately based on statute.[393] Referring to the *Export Licence*,[394] Sacco says:[395]

In the circumstances, the illegality of the contract—owing to some extravagant provision intended to sabotage international trade—is converted into a trap in order to allow the shrewd Italian contracting party to dupe with impunity the foreign, Nordic contracting party, who, as such, is trusting and slow-thinking."

There is, however, general agreement that a minor cannot be held liable for not informing the other party about his incapacity,[396] for the obvious reason that such a rule would undermine the protection of the minor.[397]

(2) Liability is limited to the reliance interest, i.e. losses as a result of preparing or starting performance and lost opportunities. In other words, the expectation interest cannot be recovered.[398] It is generally held that the recovery of the reliance interest cannot exceed the expectation interest.[399]

---

[387] *Supra*, at 284.
[388] See Cian and Trabucchi, under Article 1338, at 1059.
[389] *Ibid.*
[390] See the *Price Prescription* case, *supra*, at 285.
[391] See the *Signed with a Cross* case, *supra*, at 285.
[392] See Cian and Trabucchi, op. cit, at 1059.
[393] Sacco, op. cit., at 574.
[394] *Supra*, at 284.
[395] Sacco, op. cit., at 573.
[396] See Cian and Trabucchi, op. cit, at 1059.
[397] See Sacco, op. cit., at 571.
[398] *Ibid.*, 575.
[399] Contrast with Sacco, op. cit., at 576.

2.2.3.E. DUTY TO GIVE ADEQUATE INFORMATION

One of the most important specific duties based on the general duty to negotiate in good faith is the duty that negotiating parties may have to inform each other adequately about material facts.[400] A negotiating party violates this duty if he either gives the other party incorrect information or does not inform him about a material fact which he is under a duty to disclose. As regards the type of information that may be the object of this duty, a distinction can be made between information about the object of the prospective contract and information about the effects of the prospective contract. The first type, which in practice is by far the most important, is information that would influence the formation of the will of the negotiating party. Violation of this duty might therefore lead to a *vice de consentement*, the effect of which may be invalidity for fraud or mistake. Moreover, the party who has violated his duty to give adequate information of this type may be liable. The second type of information is information about the effect that the contract the parties are going to conclude will have. It may happen that, although parties have reached entire agreement, nevertheless their consensus does not have the effect the parties expected, because it is invalid, for example in the case of a form requirement. If one party knew or should have known from the outset that the contract would be invalid he may be liable. This is the type of case that Jhering had in mind when he developed his theory of *culpa in contrahendo*.[401]

Since invalidity usually is the most important consequence of violation of a duty to inform of the first type, cases regarding this duty will be discussed in the chapter on Error, Fraud and Misrepresentation.[402] In the second type of case, however, invalidity is not a consequence of violation of the duty to inform adequately, but the object. Therefore this duty has been dealt with in this chapter.[403] Finally, there is a third type of information that a negotiating party might be under a duty to give in the course of negotiations: information about his true intentions. If a party negotiates with *arrière-pensées* this may make him liable since conducting negotiations without having a true intention to conclude a contract is contrary to good faith. This problem has been dealt with in section 2.2.3.A.[404] A similar duty is the duty for a negotiating party to disclose that he has no power to conclude the contract.[405]

2.2.3.F. DUTY OF CONFIDENTIALITY

Principles of European Contract Law **2.PECL.94.**

Article 2:302: *Breach of Confidentiality*
> If confidential information is given by one party in the course of negotiations, the other party is under a duty not to disclose that information or use it for its own purposes whether or not a contract is subsequently concluded. The remedy for breach

---

[400] See e.g. Comment to art. 2.15 Unidroit.
[401] See Jhering, op. cit.
[402] See 3.2.1. *infra*.
[403] See 2.2.3.D.
[404] See *supra*, at 243.
[405] See e.g. the Swiss *Bank in Langenthal* case, discussed *supra*, at 251 and 275.

of this duty may include compensation for loss suffered and restitution of the benefit received by the other party.

Article 2.16: *Duty of Confidentiality*
Where information is given as confidential by one party in the course of negotiations,
the other party is under a duty not to disclose that information or use it improperly
for its own purposes, whether or not a contract is subsequently concluded. Where
appropriate, the remedy for breach of that duty may include compensation based on
the benefit received by the other party.

Court of Appeal   **2.E.96.**
Seager v. *Copydex Ltd.*[406]

CONFIDENTIALITY PROTECTED UNDER RULES OF EQUITY

Invisigrip

*The rules of equity offer protection against the use of private information provided in confidence dur-
ing the course of pre-contractual negotiations.*

Facts: An inventor made and sold a type of patented carpet grip, the marketing rights to which the defendant
company was negotiating for. The inventor attempted to interest the defendants in an alternative device which
he had created and which was not patented. Information relating to the alternative product was given in confidence. The defendant company was not at the time interested. Subsequently, negotiations regarding marketing
the patented grip having broken down, the defendant company applied for a patent in respect of a carpet grip
very similar to the alternative device, giving the name of the assistant general manager as inventor, and which
it called the "Invisigrip". It maintained that this grip was its own idea. The inventor brought proceedings against
the company for breach of confidence.

Held: The plaintiff succeeded in his claim to damages.

Judgment: LORD DENNING, MR: . . . I start with one sentence in the judgment of Lord Greene, MR,
in *Saltman Engineering Co., Ltd.* v. *Campbell Engineering Co., Ltd.*:

> "If a defendant is proved to have used confidential information, directly or indirectly obtained from the plain-
> tiff, without the consent, express or implied, of the plaintiff, he will be guilty of an infringement of the plain-
> tiff's rights."

To this I add a sentence from the judgment of Roxburgh, J, in *Terrapin, Ltd.* v. *Builders' Supply Co.
(Hayes), Ltd., Taylor Woodrow, Ltd. & Swiftplan, Ltd.*, which was quoted as correct by Roskill, J,
in *Cranleigh Precision Engineering Co., Ltd.* v. *Bryant*:

> "As I understand it, the essence of this branch of the law, whatever the origin of it may be, is that a person
> who has obtained information in confidence is not allowed to use it as a springboard for activities detrimen-
> tal to the person who made the confidential communication, and springboard it remains even when all fea-
> tures have been published or can be ascertained by actual inspection by any member of the public."

The law on this subject does not depend on any implied contract. It depends on the broad principle of equity that he who has received information in confidence shall not take unfair advantage of
it. He must not make use of it to the prejudice of him who gave it without obtaining his consent.
The principle is clear enough when the whole of the information is private. The difficulty arises

---

[406] [1967] 2 All ER 415.

when the information is in part public and in part private. As for instance in this case, a good deal of the information which the plaintiff gave to the defendant company was available to the public, such as the patent specification in the Patent Office, or the "Klent" grip, which he sold to anyone who asked. But there was a good deal of the other information which was private, such as, the difficulties which had to be overcome in making a satisfactory grip; the necessity for a strong, sharp tooth; the alternative forms of tooth; and the like. When the information is mixed, being partly public and partly private, then the recipient must take special care to use only the material which is in the public domain. He should go to the public source and get it: or, at any rate, not be in a better position than if he had gone to the public source. He should not get a start over others by using the information which he received in confidence. At any rate, he should not get a start without paying for it. It may not be a case for injunction, but only for damages, depending on the worth of the confidential information to him in saving him time and trouble. . . .

Cass. com., 3 October 1978[407]   2.F.97.

PROTECTION UNDER RULES OF UNFAIR COMPETITION

The Maine tunnel

Information obtained during the course of pre-contractual negotiations may be treated as confidential whether or not the relevant party has obtained a patent for that information. Mis-use of the information may thus give rise to liability.

Facts: Rousset, who perfected a process for putting up concrete buildings, lodged a patent application in June 1971. At the end of 1971, he offered that procedure to the company entrusted with building the Maine tunnel, Soc. Les Chantiers Modernes which, after visiting the plant where the components for that process were manufactured and examining a preliminary plan, did not take up Rousset's offer. In September 1972, Rousset discovered that his plan had been used for construction of the tunnel.

Held: Rousset succeeded in his claim based on unfair competition, and this judgment was upheld on appeal.

Judgment: . . .—Whereas the Cour d'appel is criticized for upholding the unfair competition proceedings brought by Rousset against Soc. Les Chantiers Modernes even though, according to the appeal, in the first place, no wrongful act constituting unfair competition is committed by a person who merely uses a process which is in the public domain; as in this case the construction company could have misappropriated the engineer's process during the discussions which it had with him only if that procedure had been original and could therefore have been appropriated. By not therefore considering whether the process which the engineer claimed as his was original, the Cour d'appel deprived its decision of any legal basis, and secondly, in its appeal submissions the construction company claimed, on the basis of the expert's report ordered by the first court, that there was nothing original about the engineer's process and that it was in the public domain. It inferred from this that the company had not committed any wrongful act of any kind by using it. By not responding to submissions whose relevance is clear from the foregoing considerations, the Cour d'appel failed to give a reasoned decision.

—Whereas however, the purpose of the unfair competition proceedings was to ensure protection for a person who cannot, in the circumstances, claim an exclusive right, as in the case of Rousset who was granted a patent only subsequently, and therefore the trial court was under no obligation to seek to establish whether or not the process of which he was the originator lacked novelty and fell within the public domain. By stating that documents produced to it proved that Les Chantiers

---

[407] D. 1980.55, annotated by J. Schmidt-Szalewski.

289

Modernes had, during negotiations with Rousset, appropriated technical data provided by him and without his authorisation improperly used the methods which had thus come to its knowledge, the Cour d'appel, which responded to the submissions by saying, rightly, that their contention, as regards the patentability of Rousset's invention, was inadmissible, was right, having regard to those findings, to find that the company had engaged in unfair competition. Neither limb of the ground of appeal can be upheld. . . .

Notes

(1) In the course of negotiations a party may have an interest in disclosing certain information regarding the object of the transaction, such as technical details, to the other party in order to convince him to conclude the contract. If these details are related to an idea which is protected by a patent, there is no risk for him in doing so since any infringement of his patent would make the other party liable. If, however, the information is not protected by such a right, he has an interest in concluding an agreement of confidentiality. In a situation where a party expressly declares that the given information is to be considered as confidential, receiving the information can be regarded as implicitly agreeing to treat it as confidential. In such a case disclosing it or using it for one's own purposes would constitute breach of contract.[408]

(2) In the absence of a patent or an agreement a party, in principle, is under no obligation to treat information obtained during negotiations as confidential. However, under certain circumstances it can be contrary to good faith for the receiving party to disclose information given by the other party, or to use it for his own purposes. In other words, the duty of pre-contractual good faith can imply a duty to treat information obtained during negotiations as confidential.[409] Such a duty of confidentiality is recognized in most countries. See for example *Seager* v. *Copydex*[410] and *The Maine Tunnel* case.[411] In some systems this duty is based on the general duty of pre-contractual good faith;[412] in English law it is based on a principle of equity (see Lord Denning in *Seager* v. *Copydex*).

(3) Under what circumstances does such a duty of confidentiality exist? According to the Comment on Article 2.16 of the Unidroit Principles the particular nature of the information or the professional qualifications of the parties can give rise to a duty of confidentiality. Instances of potentially confidential information which can be obtained during negotiations are: know-how; commercial strategies; lists of clients or suppliers; balance sheets which are more elaborate than those available to the public; the results of an audit or a due diligence investigation.[413] As regards the qualification of the parties, the main reason for a duty of confidentiality is, of course, them (or the third party, in case of disclosure) being (potential) competitors.

(4) There are essentially two distinct ways in which a party can violate his duty of confidentiality: first, by divulging the information to the public; secondly, by using it for his own purposes. The latter was the case in both the *Invisigrip* and *The Maine tunnel* case.[414]

---

[408] See Comment on art. 2.16 Unidroit.
[409] See Comment on art. 2.16 Unidroit.
[410] *Supra*, at 288.
[411] For a Danish case see Lando, op. cit., at 120.
[412] See Comment; van Ommeslaghe, op. cit., para. 15; Sacco , op. cit., at 246; Malaurie and Aynès, para. 379.
[413] See van Ommeslaghe, op. cit., para. 15.
[414] *Supra*, at 289.

(5) The principal remedy for violation of this duty is damages. Article 2.16 of the Unidroit Principles and Article 2:302 PECL say that damages may include recovery of the benefit the other party received by breaching his duty. The Commenton Article 2.16 of Unidroit says that such a compensation may be awarded even if the injured party has not suffered any loss. Furthermore, the injured party may also seek an injunction.[415]

(6) If a party enters into negotiations for the sole purpose of obtaining knowledge of another company's secrets, he not only is liable for an eventual breach of a duty of confidentiality, but he also has to reimburse the other party for the expenses incurred in negotiating.[416] The plaintiff's lost opportunities then will often be identical to the losses caused by the defendant's violation of his duty of confidentiality.

2.2.3.G. Non contract related interests

RG, 7 December 1911[417]   2.G.98.

PHYSICAL DAMAGE OCCASIONED DURING NEGOTIATIONS WITHIN PRE-CONTRACTUAL
DUTY OF CARE

Linoleum roll

Where a shop assistant causes a customer to sustain physical injury during the course of negotiations conducted with a view to the conclusion of a contract between the customer and a shop, the shop proprietor is liable under the doctrine of culpa in contrahendo for the injury.

Facts: Having already made various purchases in the defendant's department store, the defendant entered the linoleum department in order to buy a linoleum floor covering. She explained this to the shop assistant W., who was serving there, and selected from the samples produced by the latter the one corresponding to the floor covering which she wished to buy. In seeking to get out the roll indicated by the plaintiff, W. placed two other rolls slightly to one side. The rolls fell down, hit the plaintiff and her child, who had moved closer, and dragged them both to the ground. The purchase of the floor covering was not concluded because the plaintiff claimed to be too agitated as a result of the fall.

Held: The decision in favour of the plaintiff was upheld.

Judgment: The appellate court's view that the defendant is liable on the basis of § 278 BGB for W.'s fault cannot, contrary to the criticism expressed in the appeal on a question of law, constitute an objection in law, and is consistent with the case-law of the adjudicating Chamber. W. was representing the defendant (§ 164 BGB, § 54 BGB) in the purchase negotiations with the plaintiff. The plaintiff had asked for a linoleum roll to be produced, wishing to inspect it and to purchase it. W. acted in accordance with that request, with a view to concluding a sale. The request for the production of the roll, and the agreement to that request, were aimed at bringing about a sale, and thus at the conclusion of a legal transaction. This was not a merely *de facto* operation, such as an act done as a favour; a legal relationship existed between the parties with a view to the conclusion of a sale. That relationship was in the nature of a contractual relationship, and gave rise to legal obligations, inasmuch as the vendor and the prospective purchaser both assumed, upon the production and inspection of the goods, the duty to have regard for, and to exercise care in relation to, each other's health and safety and property. . . .

---

[415] See Comment.
[416] *Supra*, **2.2.3.C**.
[417] RGZ 78, 239.

The defendant used W. for the purpose of performing the obligation owed to the prospective purchaser, as described above, and is therefore responsible for his fault. The legal idea underlying § 278 BGB is fully applicable in this case, namely the principle that, where a person is himself liable to perform an obligation the fulfilment of which requires the exercise of care, and uses an assistant to that end, he is answerable for the careful performance of that obligation by the assistant, and accordingly the other party, for whose benefit the obligation is to be performed, must not be placed in a worse position by reason of the fact that the party owing the obligation does not perform it himself but instructs an assistant to perform it. It would be contrary to the general sense of justice if, in the event of damage being caused to prospective purchasers as a result of carelessness on the part of an employee of a business in producing or presenting goods for the purposes of their being inspected, sampled or tried out, etc., the proprietor of the business with whom the prospective purchaser intended to conclude the purchase were liable only as provided for by § 831 BGB and not unconditionally, and if the injured party were thus constrained, for the purposes of discharging the burden of proof, to have recourse to the employee, who will, more often than not, prove to be without financial means.

Notes

(1) Under German law vicarious liability for personal injury to customers in a shop is dealt with by the doctrine of *culpa in contrahendo*. Compare Austrian, Greek and Portuguese law.[418] The reasoning is as follows. The customer and the shop keeper by taking up negotiations enter into a relationship of mutual trust which is similar to a contractual relationship (*vertragsähnliches Vertrauensverhältnis*). This relationship gives rise to a duty of care, the violation of which constitutes *culpa in contrahendo* leading to contractual liability (§ 276 ff. BGB). See for example the *Linoleum Roll* case,[419] and BGHZ 66, 51 (28 January 1976), where a supermarket was held liable when a child of a customer, who accompanied her mother, slipped on a vegetable leaf, which lay on the floor (in the latter case the child was protected by the *culpa in contrahendo* doctrine in combination with the doctrine of *Vertrag mit Schutzwirkung zugunsten Dritter*). This reasoning, of course, is rather artificial, since quite often no real negotiations take place between the shopkeeper and the customer. Moreover, it gives rise to several questions, such as whether a shopkeeper can be liable if it is established that the injured person did not intend to buy anything in the shop where he fell.[420]

(2) It would be much more rational to deal with the protection of *Vertragsfremde Rechtsgüter* under tort law. However, this has proved to be impossible, due to shortcomings in German tort law. The most important of these is the absence of a real vicarious liability.[421] Therefore in cases like the *Linoleum Roll* case,[422] the shop owner would not be held liable for the fault of his servant if he were able to prove that he exercised due care in selecting and supervising the servant. Since the rules on contractual liability contain a provision on vicarious liability (§ 278 BGB) the Reichsgericht developed the *culpa in contrahendo* construction in order to be able to apply the contractual regime. Other short-

---

[418] See Posch, op. cit., at 49, Stathopoulos, op. cit., para. 86, and A. Varela, *Das Obrigações em Geral*, 6th edn. (Lisboa: 1996), para. 67 respectively.
[419] *Supra*, at 291.
[420] See von Mehren, op. cit., para. 28.
[421] *Ibid.*, para. 27.
[422] *Supra*, at 291.

comings of German tort law were: the absence of a general clause, very short delays for prescription of tort claims, unfavourable burden of proof, no recovery for pure economic loss.[423]

(3) In other systems, where tort law does not put such limitations on the plaintiff, this type of cases is usually dealt with by tort law.[424]

(4) The doctrine has met with general criticism. Today practically all scholars agree that the duties of care (*Schutzpflichten*) are *Verkehrspflichten*, i.e. they arise independently of whether there is a special relationship, and therefore should be dealt with by tort law.[425] In his *Gutachten* Medicus concludes:[426]

In accordance with what is said in Part IV above, the law of torts applying to the infringement of legal interests extraneous to the contract, which has developed as a result of greater familiarity with the duties imposed by dealings with the world at large, also extends to cover the stage at which negotiations are being conducted with a view to the possible conclusion of a contract. The only exception to this, as the law presently stands, concerns liability on the part of assistants; however, this lacuna in the law of torts should be closed by the reform which is proposed. It follows that the scope of fault in contractual negotiations, as discussed here, should no longer extend to cover legal interests extraneous to the contract.

However, according to Larenz, some *Schutzpflichten* exist only where there is a special relationship (*Sonderverbindung*):[427]

There is nowadays a widespread opinion, that under § 831—tending to the—reversal of the onus of proof, the cases of breach of a precontractual duty of care should only be dealt with under the law of torts, since in those cases it is a general obligation of security which is infringed, which does not affect only the other negotiating partner. It may be so in the Linoleum-roll case and in the Banana case; in other cases, a superior duty of care should be established on the basis of the special relationship.

Larenz seems to have convinced the Law Reform Commission, since it proposes the introduction of a new § 241 section 2 BGB-KE, that should provide a statutory basis for the duty of care (*Schutzpflicht*) in any legal relationship (*Rechtsverhältnis*), which is also applicable to a pre-contractual relationship (§ 305 section 2 BGB-KE)[428] and which should be distinguished from *Verkehrs(sicherungs)pflichten*.[429]

---

[423] Medicus, op. cit., at 489.
[424] See e.g. von Mehren, op. cit., para. 28; Hondius, op. cit., at 20–1.
[425] See e.g. Schlechtriem, *SAT*, para. 22 ff.; Soergel and Wiedemann, op. cit., § 275, para. 111.
[426] Medicus, op. cit., at 494.
[427] Larenz, *SAT*.
[428] See also *supra*, at 239.
[429] See Abschlußbericht, at 114.

CHAPTER THREE
VALIDITY

Introduction

Chapter 3 considers various situations in which the apparent agreement which has been reached by the parties will not be treated as fully effective for a variety of reasons.

In the first section the problem is that the contract involves illegality, either in the strict sense or in the sense of *"ordre public"* involving some infringement of public order or immorality. Illegality, in this broad meaning, is recognised in each system, but the extent of the control over what the parties may do and its technical rules vary from one jurisdiction to an other.

The second group of causes of invalidity deal with the classical defects of consent (*vices du consentement*) which cover mistake and misrepresentation, fraud and non-disclosure; and threats, which have been set in a separate section along with the modern notion of abuse of circumstances and the discussion of the question of laesio (the setting aside of a contract simply because the performances to be rendered by each party are not of equal value).

The last section reflects the more recent movement to protect consumers, here in the form of the special rules governing unfair clauses in contracts. 0

3.1. IMMORAL AND ILLEGAL CONTRACTS

3.1.1. INTRODUCTION

A contract may be invalid or unenforceable despite the fact that it was made freely and voluntarily by parties who knew what they were doing. If a mafia boss hires a hit-man to kill the police chief, no judge will order the hit-man to perform the contract specifically, or the mafia boss to pay the agreed price even though the parties' agreement was based on a serious intention to be bound and was not tainted by fraud, duress, misrepresentation or mistake. All legal systems reserve the right to declare a contract void if it is legally or morally offensive, contrary to public policy or *"ordre public"* or involves the commission of an unlawful act. Where a statute expressly prohibits a party from making a contract of a certain description it is clear that no court will uphold it. In most cases, however, the bounds of the permissible are not clearly defined, and it is then for the judge to test the circumstances of the case in order to discover whether, by the current standards of morality and public policy, it should be enforced or not.

In this task, continental judges get little help from the words of the civil codes. In most cases the codes simply provide that contracts offending against a statutory prohibition, good faith, or public policy are void.

§ 134: A juristic act which is contrary to a statutory prohibition is void, unless a contrary intention appears from the statute.

§ 138: (1) A juristic act that is contra bonos mores is void

(2) A juristic act is also void when a person takes advantage of the distressed situation, inexperience, lack of judgmental ability or grave weakness of will of another to obtain the grant, or promise of pecuniary advantages for himself or a third party which are obviously disproportionate to the performance given in return.

BW   **3.NL.2.**

Article 3:40: (1) A juridical act which by its content or necessary implication is contrary to good morals or public order is null.

(2) Violation of an imperative statutory provision entails nullity of the juridical act; if, however, the provision is intended solely for the protection of one of the parties to a multilateral juridical act, the act may only be annulled; in both cases this applies to the extent that the necessary implication of the provision does not produce a different result.

(3) Statutory provisions which do not purport to invalidate juridical acts contrary to them are not affected by the preceding paragraph.

Note

See also § 879 of the Austrian Civil Code. It is noteworthy that Swiss law draws a distinction between contracts which are illegal or immoral—Article 20 of the Swiss Law of Obligations—and those which are in breach of Article 27(2) of the Swiss Civil Code, which provides that "no one may alienate his liberty or restrict it to a degree inconsistent with law or morals".

Code civil   **3.F.3.**

Article 6:   Agreements between individuals may not derogate from laws concerning public order or good morals.

Article 1131: An obligation based on a false or illicit cause is without effect.

Article 1133: Cause is illicit when it is prohibited by law or is contrary to good morals or public order.

Note

Under Article 6 of the French Civil Code, the parties are forbidden to derogate by way of an agreement from laws concerning public order or good morals. A contract is contrary to "public order" if it violates statutory or judge-made rules protecting the political, social and economic order of the state. On the other hand, the term "good morals" is given a more restricted meaning in France than in Germany and other countries since a

---

¹ This translation is that given by A. von Mehren and J. Gordley, *The Civil Law System*, 2nd edn. (Boston: Little Brown, 1977).

contract will be invalid as offending the "*bonnes mœurs*" only when it tends to promote sexual immorality or is inconsistent with basic principles of family life. The French and Italian codes link the problem with the concept of "*cause*" or "*causa*". Thus Article 1131 of the French Civil Code provides that an obligation based on an illicit cause is void and then defines in Article 1133 a "cause" as one prohibited by law or contrary to good morals or public order.[2]

   The texts of the Civil Codes on contracts which conflict with good morals, public order or legal prescriptions are all couched in very broad terms and need to be fleshed out by reference to court decisions. Writers who try to put the cases into some sort of order invariably add that the categories they adopt are neither exhaustive nor mutually exclusive. Among the contracts potentially invalid as illegal or immoral are bargains harmful to the administration of justice, contracts intended to defraud third parties, agreements inducing a party to breach its contract with another or to commit an unlawful act, and many others. Here we shall deal only with cases involving agreements adversely affecting basic principles of family life and sexual morality (**3.1.2.**), contracts which improperly restrict a person's economic liberties and are therefore in "restraint of trade" (**3.1.3.**) and contracts allegedly invalid as being in breach of an express or implied statutory prohibition (**3.1.4.**). Normally, the invalidity of a contract will be pleaded as a defence to an action for the payment of the contractually agreed price or for damages resulting from the breach of a contractual duty. It is a quite different question to be discussed below in section **3.1.5.** whether a party to an illegal or immoral contract must give back what he received under it.

3.1.2. CONFLICTS WITH PRINCIPLES OF SEXUAL MORALITY AND FAMILY LIFE

The ideas of what is immoral change in the course of time, and behaviour which would have been regarded as utterly repulsive twenty years ago may be tolerated with equanimity, if not eagerly endorsed, by law nowadays. In the Australian case *Andrews* v. *Parker*,[3] Stable J said:[4]

Surely, what is immoral must be judged by the current standards of morality of the community. What was apparently regarded with pious horror when the cases were decided would, I observe, today hardly draw a raised eyebrow or a gentle "tut-tut" . . . George Bernard Shaw's Eliza Doolittle (circa 1912) thought the suggestion that she have a bath in private with her clothes off was indecent, so she hung a towel over the bathroom mirror. One wonders what she would have thought and said to the suggestion that she wear in public one of today's minuscule and socially accepted bikinis, held miraculously in place apparently with the aid of providence, and, possibly, glue.

It would seem, for example, that a prostitute's claim for the agreed price would still be regarded as unenforceable in most, if not all, legal systems. Other contracts made by prostitutes for the known purpose of furthering their business will be viewed these days with more tolerance than in the past.

---

[2] See also Articles 1343, 1418 para. 2 of the Italian Civil Code.
[3] [1973] Qd R. 93.
[4] *Ibid*. at 104.

Court of Appeal   3.E.4.
Pearce v. *Brooks*[5]

CONTRACT PROMOTING SEXUAL IMMORALITY ILLEGAL

The curiously-constructed carriage

A contract for the supply of a thing which it is known will be used for an immoral purpose is illegal and gives rise to no cause of action.

Facts: Coachbuilders sought to recover the hire payable for a "curiously constructed" horse-drawn carriage which they knew that the defendant, a prostitute, intended to use to attract customers.

Held: At first instance Bramwell B put the following question to the jury: 1. Did the defendant hire the brougham for the purpose of her prostitution? 2. If she did, did the plaintiffs know the purpose for which it was hired. The jury answered both questions affirmative and the judge directed a verdict for the defendant. The plaintiffs' appeal was dismissed.

Judgment: POLLOCK CB: I have always considered it as settled law, that any person who contributes to the performance of an illegal act by supplying a thing with the knowledge that it is going to be used for that purpose, cannot recover the price of the thing so supplied . . . Nor can any distinction be made between an illegal and an immoral purpose; the rule which is applicable to the matter is, *Ex turpi causa non oritur actio*, and whether it is an immoral or an illegal purpose in which the plaintiff has participated, it comes equally within the terms of that maxim, and the effect is the same; no cause of action can arise out of either the one or the other . . .

If, therefore, this article was furnished to the defendant for the purpose of enabling her to make a display favourable to her immoral purposes, the plaintiffs can derive no cause of action from the bargain . . .

Civ. 1re, 4 December 1956[6]   3.F.5.

IMMORAL PURPOSE MUST BE AGREED

La maison de tolérance

A lease of a house used for prostitution is illegal only if the parties have agreed to its use for that purpose.

Facts: R granted M. and Mme B a lease, with an option to purchase, in 1919; in 1929 the lease was extended until 1965. R having died, her residuary legatees argued that the lease was void.

Held: By the court of first instance and the appeal court, that the lease should not be annulled on the basis of immoral cause. The Cour de cassation upheld the decision.

Judgment: *On the first appeal ground*:—Whereas the appellants contest the decision of the court below, itself upholding an earlier decision, made by a lower court, refusing to annul, on the grounds of immorality or illegality, the lease, accompanied by a promise to sell, granted to Mr and Mrs Bony on 1 July 1919 by Mrs Royan, who is now deceased and represented in these proceedings by her residuary legatees, Mr and Mrs Cahen, together with the act of 16 December 1926 extending the aforementioned lease until 1965.

[5] (1866) LR 1 Ex. 213.
[6] JCP 1957.II.10008 annotated by J. Mazeaud.

—Whereas the appellants argue that a contract is void, even where its subject-matter is not the establishment of a licensed brothel, if it is contemplated, at least by one of the parties thereto, that it should serve as a means of achieving that immoral and illegal end.

—Whereas however, in the case of a contract alleged to be illegal, it is only the obligations of the parties which are relevant; as the court adjudicating at first instance found that "no evidence whatever has been adduced to show that, when the lease was entered into, and when it was subsequently extended by agreement between the parties, they agreed that the demised premises should be used as a brothel";

—Whereas the Cour d'appel, in inferring from those findings, which were made by the trial court in the exercise of its unfettered discretion, that the subject-matter of the contract was not illegal, did not infringe any of the legislative provisions referred to in the plea. . . .

On those grounds, the appeal is dismissed . . .

Note

In cases of this type *cause* is taken by the French courts as the *motif déterminant* (principal motive) without which the contract would not have been concluded. It is a disputed question whether the *motif déterminant* must be shared by both parties. This was the view taken by the court in this case; indeed it went so far as to say that the lessee's use of the property as a brothel must have been "agreed" (*convenu*) by the parties. Other cases and many writers regard it as sufficient that the improper *motif déterminant* of one party is known to the other. At any rate, a contract will be held valid if one party knows nothing about the improper motivation which induced the other to enter into it. It may be said in support of this rule that the innocent party must be protected. But this is persuasive only in cases in which the innocent party relies on the validity of the contract. In this case, however, the innocent lessor wanted to annul the contract and recover his property from the lessee. The dismissal of his action meant that the lessee was allowed to remain in possession of the property and to continue using it for an improper purpose. On this ground the decision may be criticized.[7] Another approach would have been to treat the contract as invalid and then to ask whether there were any plausible reasons to bar the lessor's restitutionary claim.[8]

BGH, 8 January 1975[9]   **3.G.6.**

A LEASE OF PREMISES FOR A BROTHEL NO LONGER UNENFORCEABLE FOR IMMORALITY

Homes for "working girls"

A lease of premises which the lessor knows are to be used as a brothel is not necessarily unenforceable on the ground of immorality.

Facts: The plaintiff was the lessor of a block of apartments which he knew were let by the lessee to prostitutes on a commercial basis. He brought an action for unpaid rent against the lessee.

Judgment: The view expressed by the appellate court—namely that contracts for the purchase or letting of brothels are, without qualification, immoral and consequently void because they promote

---

[7] See e.g. Terré, Simler and Lequette, para. 344.
[8] See *infra* **3.1.5**, at 326 *et seq*.
[9] BGHZ 63, 365.

illicit sexual practices and usufruct—does not, in the light of the matters of public policy at issue here, bear scrutiny. The attitude amongst broad sections of the public towards sexual issues may be seen to have altered; and that change is such as to prompt, in the assessment *inter alia* of the immorality of transactions relating to prostitution, . . . a move away from the earlier decisions of the highest courts. The legislature has taken that change in attitude into account in amending the law on sexual offences. Whereas, under the law previously applicable to the procuration of women for prostitution, a person committed an offence if he habitually or for reasons of self-interest aided and abetted illicit sexual practices by providing or procuring the opportunity for engagement therein, and in particular by running a brothel or similar establishment, the constituent elements of an offence under § 180a StGB [the Penal Code] are now such that, in cases concerning the maintenance or running of a business in which persons engage in prostitution, those persons must be kept in a state of personal or economic dependence, or the exercise of prostitution must be promoted by measures going beyond the mere provision of accommodation or premises and the incidental services normally connected therewith . . .

However, exemption from penal sanctions and tolerance on the part of the authorities do not mean that immorality cannot constitute an element of transactions concerning prostitution . . . If that were the case, the object pursued by the measures adopted by the legislature and by the authorities would not be fully achieved, since the rules laid down by civil law would be left out of account. The reduction of the threat of penal sanctions is intended to enable "working girls" to find some form of supervised accommodation and to escape from the disastrous influence and power of pimps. The tolerance of prostitution on the part of the authorities is designed to promote improved supervision of such girls from a medical and police standpoint, that being an indispensable requirement for effectively combating the spread of sexual diseases. . . . [Agreements for the leasing of brothels] are immoral, and thus void, only where the lessor demands excessively high rents from the prostitutes concerned, thereby economically exploiting them. That is also the position if he restricts their independence and forces them to carry on their activities. An agreement for the letting of a brothel will also be void, however, where a rent is agreed which is manifestly out of all proportion to the objective rental value of the demised premises, since such an excessive—not to say, usurious—rent can generally only be obtained if the prostitutes are being charged a disproportionately high sum in consideration of the provision of the accommodation.

Civ. 1re, 11 February 1986[10]   **3.F.7.**

GIFT TO FUTURE WIFE NOT ILLICIT

The mistress he married

A gift to a woman who was at the time the donor's mistress but whom he intended to marry, and later did marry, after his first marriage had been dissolved, was not illicit.

Facts: Adrien Hess, a married man, had given a sum of money to his mistress, Mme Ferrand, for the purchase of an apartment. After having divorced his wife he married Mme Ferrand and lived with her in the apartment for many years. After his death his first wife brought an action against Mme Hess-Ferrand's heir, alleging that the transaction was void for immorality and that the apartment formed no part of her estate.

Held: The claim was dismissed.

Judgment: . . .—Whereas having found that Adrien Hess and Mme Ferrand had known each other for fourteen years and had lived together for twelve years, and that, following the dissolution of the

[10] Bull. I.21. A further step was taken by Cass.civ.1, 3 Feb. 1999, J.C.P.1999.II.10.083, annotated by Billiau and Loiseau: the gift made with the purpose of maintaining an adulterous relationship is no longer considered as immoral.

marriage between M. Hess and his first wife, they had got married and had lived together in the apartment acquired in 1954 until the death of the second Mme Hess (formerly Mme Ferrand), that is to say, for eighteen years, the court adjudicating at first instance considered, in the unfettered exercise of its discretion, that the pecuniary gift made by Adrien Hess to the woman who had for a long time been his consort and whom he proposed to marry, could not be regarded as motivated by a desire to win her favours or to maintain an illicit sexual relationship.

—Whereas having thus rejected the claim that the gift was unlawful, the court hearing the case at second instance was not required to rule on the plea that the allegedly immoral nature of the transaction was to be inferred from the lease taken by Mme Ferrand from Adrien Hess; as nor was it obliged to consider whether that lease was itself founded on an illegal basis.

—Whereas the contested decision is legally justified on that account.

—Whereas the appeal ground is unfounded as regards the first three branches thereof . . .

BGH, 12 January 1984[11]   3.G.8.

LOAN NOT EXCLUSIVELY FOR SEXUAL MOTIVES IS VALID

A loan for love, not sex

A loan on favourable terms to a woman with whom the lender was having an illicit affair was not necessarily unenforceable if it was not primarily intended as payment for sexual favours.

Facts: After the plaintiff had broken off a sexual relationship with a married woman he brought an action against her and her husband who had known about the liaison for the repayment of a loan he had granted them on very favourable conditions.

Held: The appeal court held the loan agreement immoral and void. The Bundesgerichtshof sent the case back for further findings.

Judgment (citations omitted): . . . According to the case-law of the BGH, gifts made *inter vivos*, like disposals made on the death of the donor, are not to be regarded as immoral on the ground that there has been an extra-marital relationship—and, in particular, an adulterous sexual relationship—between the donor and the donee. § 138 BGB is concerned not with the penalization of immoral behaviour but merely with the question of the possible immorality of a transaction. No significance attaches, in principle, to the motives which may have prompted a testator to depart, when providing for the disposal of his estate, from the statutory order applying to succession on intestacy; his wishes must in principle be respected, even where his motives are not commendable. That applies not only to testamentary dispositions but also to transactions *inter vivos*. According to the system of values laid down by the BGB, paramount significance must attach to the principle of contractual and testamentary freedom. However, that principle is qualified by § 138 BGB. In the context of the requisite assessment of the overall nature of a transaction, significance may attach to the impropriety of the mentality of one or more of the parties, if that mentality finds expression in the transaction. Thus, a benefit bestowed for no consideration at all, or for virtually no consideration, must as a general rule be regarded as immoral if it is solely intended as a reward for the grant of sexual favours or to induce the donee to enter into or continue a sexual relationship. If the motives for which the benefit is conferred without consideration are not exclusively sexual, and if it is not prompted by other, respectable or neutral motives, then the decisive factors will depend on the other circumstances, including, in particular, any effects which the transaction may have on third parties. It is not clear from the contested judgment whether the appellate court, in

---

[11] NJW 1984.2150.

considering the loan agreement between the parties, proceeded on the basis of those legal criteria. The possibility cannot be excluded that it wrongly found, as a matter of law, that the conditions laid down by § 138 BGB had been satisfied merely because, amongst a multiplicity of motives, the greatest weight attached to the sexual relationship between the plaintiff and the second defendant. At all events, the findings of fact made by the appellate court are not sufficient to justifying assessing the entire transaction as immoral. It is true that a benefit was conferred for no consideration, since the loan was granted on the basis that no interest was payable and repayment was to be effected in very small instalments over a period of 15 years; moreover, the loan was to terminate prematurely in the event of the plaintiff's death. According to the findings of the appellate court, however, that benefit was not so exclusively characterized, from the plaintiff's standpoint, by improper motives that the transaction was to be regarded as immoral on that ground alone.

Cass., Ass. plén. 31 May 1991[12]   **3.F.9.**

WIFE OF BIOLOGICAL FATHER MAY NOT ADOPT CHILD BY SURROGATE MOTHER

The surrogate mother: France

The wife of a childless couple who arranges that another should bear the husband's child and surrender it on birth is not permitted to adopt the child.

Facts: In order to remedy their childlessness, a married couple had recourse to the Alma Mater association, since wound up. In accordance with a well-established practice, that association put the couple in touch with a woman who agreed to bear a child on their behalf. That child was conceived by artificial insemination, using the husband's sperm. The child, a girl, was declared as having been born on 7 February 1988 to LG, her biological father, who acknowledged her as his progeny. The name of the mother was not stated, her biological mother having given birth to her under the name of X. The wife of LG then lodged an application for full adoption.

Held: The Paris Tribunal de Grande Instance dismissed that application on 26 June 1989. Its decision was overturned by the Paris Cour d'appel (15 June 1990, J.C.P. 1991.II.21563). An appeal to the Cour de cassation was lodged by the Procureur Général (Attorney General) on the ground that a point of law of general interest was in issue.

Judgment: The Court:—*As regards the appeal brought before the Cour de cassation by the Procureur Général on a point of law of general interest*—Under Articles 6 and 1128 of the Civil Code, together with Article 353 thereof;
—Whereas an agreement whereby a woman undertakes, whether or not free of charge, to conceive and bear a child, with a view to abandoning it on its birth, is contrary both to the public policy principle of the inalienability of the human body and to that of the inalienability of a person's status. According to the contested judgment (Paris, 1re Ch. C., 15 June 1990), which overturned the decision of the court below, Mme X . . ., the wife of M. Y . . ., was incurably sterile, and her husband therefore gave his sperm to another woman who, after being artificially inseminated, bore and produced the child thus conceived; as upon being born, that child was declared as being the child of Y . . ., without its maternal affiliation being stated.
—Whereas in the context of pronouncing the adoption of the child by Mme Y . . ., the [contested] judgment states that, as matters currently stand with regard to scientific practice and morality, surrogate motherhood must be regarded as lawful and as not contrary to public policy, and that that adoption is in accordance with the interests of the child, who has been accepted and brought up in the home of M. and Mme Y . . . practically since its birth.

---

[12] D. 1991.417 with report by Chartier and annotated by Thouvenin.

—Whereas in so ruling, notwithstanding that the adoption was merely the final stage in an entire process designed to enable a couple to receive into their home a child conceived pursuant to a contract involving its abandonment at birth by its mother, and that that process, which violated the principles of the inalienability of the human body and of personal status, thus constituted an abuse of the institution of adoption, the cour d'appel infringed the abovementioned legislative provisions.

On those grounds, the Court quashes the contested judgment . . . but only in the interests of establishing the law and without referring the case back for further adjudication.

OLG Hamm, 2 December 1985[13]   **3.G.10.**

SURROGACY AGREEMENT ILLEGAL

The surrogate mother: Germany

An arrangement for surrogate motherhood is illicit and the money paid to the surrogate mother is not recoverable even if the surrogate mother's husband succeeds in claiming the child as his own.

Facts: No children had been born to the applicant and his wife. By written agreements dated 29 November and 18 December 1981, the applicant undertook to pay the respondent DM 27 000 if she would carry a child procreated by him to full term and hand it over, following its birth, for adoption by the applicant and his wife. After the respondent had been inseminated with the applicant's sperm, she bore a child which was immediately handed over to the applicant and his wife. Since the respondent was also married, the adoption could not proceed until the illegitimacy of the child had been established in proceedings brought by the respondent's husband. Those proceedings were duly brought by the husband—as likewise agreed between the parties—but they were dismissed, since it was established with virtually 100 per cent certainty that the child was his own. The applicant thereupon claimed repayment of the DM 27 000 together with reimbursement of the further costs incurred by him.

Held: The court held that the agreement was void.

Judgment: . . . As stated above, the agreements of 29 November and 18 December 1981 form an economic whole. The entire scheme of the contract exhibits the characteristics of a contract for work and services: the respondent was to carry to term and give birth to a child engendered by the applicant. He for his part was to pay her a sum by way of remuneration; although this was described as a "voluntary payment", it was, from an economic standpoint, in the nature of consideration. The payment was clearly not intended merely to compensate the respondent for additional expenditure incurred by her during her pregnancy; the arrangement that the agreed sum was not to be paid until the child was handed over shows in itself that it was intended to represent contractual consideration. Contracts of this kind are rightly described as "trading in human lives at prices equivalent to the cost of a medium-range car" (Lauff-Arnold, *Zeitschrift für Rechtspolitik* 1984, 282). The form taken by the contract concealed the critical danger that the child, after being handed over, would continue—even though that may not have been the intention—to retain the characteristics of an item of merchandise. As far as the respondent was concerned, the child was not a wished-for or heaven-sent relative and future member of her family and household, but someone who was to be removed immediately by the applicant. Within the respondent's household, therefore, there was no prospect of any real human devotion of the kind on which a tiny child is dependent from the start of its existence; on the contrary, the respondent had to take care, as far as possible, to avoid building up any deep-seated emotional bond with the child, so as to be able to separate herself from it quickly and painlessly. On the other hand, there was no guarantee that the child would be accepted into the applicant's family as if it were,

---

[13] NJW 1986.781.

genetically, their own offspring. It is true that the agreement of 18 December 1981 expressly stated—along the lines of an exclusion of warranty—that "the child [could] not, as a matter of principle, be rejected". Notwithstanding that, there were grounds for fearing that the child's prospects of development might from the outset be jeopardised if it failed, wholly or partially, to live up to the applicant's expectations, since it is natural that a child who has been "acquired" for a considerable financial outlay may be regarded differently from a child who is genetically one's own, whether or not its arrival in this world is a wished-for event. It was impossible to rule out the danger that the child might form the subject of a price/performance comparison. Moreover, the fact of taking the child over might possibly give rise to problems in the applicant's marriage, which could in turn adversely affect the child. It is impossible to foresee, for example, whether the state of the marriage and the emotional condition of the other spouse would be such as to enable her in the long term to put up with the existence in the family of a child who was not her own without any conflict or severe emotional upset occurring; moreover, it is uncertain what effects on the husband's attitude to the marriage might result from his consciousness of sharing the genetic parenthood with another woman (see in that regard BGHZ 87, 169 = NJW 1983, 2073).

Nor was there any certainty with regard to the destiny of the child from a legal standpoint. It is true that the respondent undertook in the agreement of 18 December 1981 to make "an irrevocable declaration of renunciation following the establishment of pregnancy, releasing the child for adoption". However, that declaration, quite apart from being void under § 138 BGB, was in any event ineffective, since consent to adoption cannot be given until the child is eight weeks old (§ 1747(3)(1) BGB). Conversely, even if a valid and effective consent to the adoption had been given, there was no guarantee that the applicant and his wife would adopt the child as their own. The decision as to whether an adoption is to take place lies with the *Vormundschaftsgericht* [Guardianship Court] (§ 1752(1) BGB). An adoption order may only be made if it is in the interests of the child and if there are grounds for anticipating the development of a parent-child relationship between the adoptive parent and the child (§ 1752(1) BGB). Thus there can be no certainty in advance that the intended adoption will take place.

3.1.3. CONTRACTS IN RESTRAINT OF TRADE

Contracts unduly fettering a person's freedom in the future to carry on his trade, business or profession will be struck down by the courts as being "in restraint of trade" or contrary to public policy. Many cases falling under this heading are dealt with by special legislation on restrictive trade practices, monopolies, resale price maintenance etc. Under Article 85 of the Treaty of Rome agreements "which have as their object or effect the prevention, restriction or distortion of competition within the common market" are void unless special exemption is granted by the Brussels authorities. We shall here focus on cases which may be void not only because they are inimical to the public interest in freedom of trade and unfettered competition but also in order to protect an economically weaker or inexperienced party against unconscionable contract terms.

Schroeder Music Publishing Co. v. *Macaulay*[14]

CONTRACT TO TAKE SONGWRITER'S COMPOSITIONS IN RESTRAINT OF TRADE

The young songwriter's contract

A contract which binds a young songwriter to a publisher, giving the latter an exclusive right to publish the composer's songs for a long period but imposing no duty to promote them is void as being in restraint of trade.

Facts: An unknown songwriter, aged 21, entered into an agreement with music publishers in their "standard form" whereby the publishers engaged his exclusive services during the term of the agreement and the songwriter assigned to the publishers the full copyright for the whole world in all his musical compositions during the term. If the total royalties during the term exceeded £5,000, the agreement was automatically extended for a further five years; otherwise, the agreement was to remain in force for five years. The publishers could terminate the agreement at any time by one month's written notice but no such right was given to the songwriter. The publishers had the right to assign the agreement, but the songwriter agreed not to assign his rights under the agreement without the publishers' prior written consent. The songwriter brought an action claiming, *inter alia*, a declaration that the agreement was contrary to public policy and void.

Held: Plowman J made the declaration sought, and his judgment was affirmed by the Court of Appeal and the House of Lords

Judgment: LORD REID: . . .

The public interest requires in the interests both of the public and of the individual that everyone should be free so far as practicable to earn a livelihood and to give to the public the fruits of his particular abilities. The main question to be considered is whether and how far the operation of the terms of this agreement is likely to conflict with this objective. The respondent is bound to assign to the appellants during a long period the fruits of his musical talent. But what are the appellants bound to do with those fruits? Under the contract nothing. If they do use the songs which the respondent composes they must pay in terms of the contract. But they need not do so. As has been said they may put them in a drawer and leave them there.

No doubt the expectation was that if the songs were of value they would be published to the advantage of both parties. But if for any reason the appellants chose not to publish them the respondent would get no remuneration and he could not do anything. Inevitably the respondent must take the risk of misjudgment of the merits of his work by the appellants. But that is not the only reason which might cause the appellants not to publish. There is no evidence about this so we must do the best we can with common knowledge. It does not seem fanciful and it was not argued that it is fanciful to suppose that purely commercial consideration might cause a publisher to refrain from publishing and promoting promising material. He might think it likely to be more profitable to promote work by other composers with whom he had agreements and unwise or too expensive to try to publish and popularise the respondent's work in addition. And there is always the possibility that less legitimate reasons might influence a decision not to publish the respondent's work . . .

Any contract by which a person engages to give his exclusive services to another for a period necessarily involves extensive restriction during that period of the common law right to exercise any lawful activity he chooses in such manner as he thinks best. Normally the doctrine of restraint of trade has no application to such restrictions: they require no justification. But if contractual restrictions appear to be unnecessary or to be reasonably capable of enforcement in an oppressive manner, then they must be justified before they can be enforced.

[14] [1974] 3 All ER 616.

In the present case the respondent assigned to the appellants "the full copyright for the whole world" in every musical composition "composed created or conceived" by him alone or in collaboration with any other person during a period of five or it might be 10 years. He received no payment (apart from an initial £50) unless his work was published and the appellants need not publish unless they chose to do so. And if they did not publish he had no right to terminate the agreement or to have copyrights re-assigned to him. I need not consider whether in any circumstances it would be possible to justify such a one-sided agreement. It is sufficient to say that such evidence as there is falls far short of justification. It must therefore follow that the agreement so far as unperformed is unenforceable.

I would dismiss this appeal.

[The other law lords delivered judgments to the same effect.]

Note

Suppose that there exists fierce competition in the UK between music publishing companies and that, despite this competition, all agreements made with young and unknown songwriters have for many years been couched in terms quite similar to those before the court in *Schroeder*'s case. Would it not follow from the House of Lords' holding that music publishing companies will refrain in the future from making any contracts with young songwriters so that they will be worse off than if the agreement had been upheld?[15]

BG, 23 May 1978[16]

3.G.12.

MANAGEMENT CONTRACT EXCESSIVE RESTRICTION ON PERSONAL FREEDOM

The jazz singer

A "management contract" under which a young singer places her entire career in her manager's hands for a period which the manager can extend indefinitely is an excessive restriction on the singer's personal freedom and contrary to Article 27 ZGB.

Facts: The defendant was a young woman who, after having been trained by the plaintiff for seven months in the art of singing jazz and popular songs, had entered into a "management contract" with her. In an action brought by the plaintiff for the payment of a contractually agreed penalty the defendant argued that the management contract was void under Article 27 paragraph 2 of the Swiss Civil Code which provides that an agreement is void by which a person "divests himself of, or restricts, his liberty to an extent contrary to the law or morality".

Held: The contract was void.

Judgment: . . . The defendant assigned to the plaintiff . . . the right to conclude, on the latter's own responsibility, contracts relating to appearances and the release of records, to delegate to a recognized agency responsibility for arranging appearances of all kinds, and for the plaintiff to collect fees and royalties herself. The defendant covenanted not to appear in public without the plaintiff's consent, not to enter into any contracts relating to artistic matters, to comply with all instructions given by the plaintiff, to accept all titles offered, to perform contracts relating to appearances, to meet deadlines and to remain sufficiently independent as to be in a position to make herself available when required. She further covenanted to notify the plaintiff of enquiries and offers received by her and not to conduct any negotiations in relation thereto, as well as to give immediate notice

---

[15] For an interesting discussion of *Schroeder*'s case from the viewpoint of an economic analysis of law see Trebilcock, "An Economic Approach to Unconscionability" in B. Reiter and J. Swan (eds.), *Studies in Contract Law* (Toronto: Butterworths, 1980) at 379.

[16] BGE 104.II.108.

of any absence lasting several days and of any change of address. Her right to share in decision-making concerning appearances was limited to matters regarding the repertoire, which was to be determined jointly; in the event of any difference of opinion, however, the decision was to lie with the plaintiff alone. Thus the defendant placed herself, as regards her plans to carve out a career as a pop singer, entirely in the hands of the plaintiff, and relinquished all power to make her own decisions. She was required to submit to restrictions not only in the sphere of her artistic activities but also with regard to the entire way in which she led her life, since she had to be available whenever the plaintiff needed her. Consequently, her freedom to lead a meaningful private life was substantially restricted, and her ability to engage in any other occupational activity or training was rendered, if not non-existent, at least fraught with extreme difficulty.

Clearly, the continuation of such a commitment against the defendant's wishes infringed her personal rights. The contract provided for its premature termination within the first two years only if both parties consented thereto and only in the event that the defendant's artistic abilities proved insufficient for the achievement of a "positive success", in particular if the efforts to secure a recording contracts within that period failed to bear fruit. In addition, the contract could be terminated if the defendant permanently discontinued her artistic activities. In both cases, however, the defendant was required to pay the plaintiff "all costs relating to expenditure of money and time by the management since the commencement of the contract", which would potentially impose a severe financial burden on the defendant.

Even after the fixed contractual term of five years had elapsed, the defendant did not automatically win unqualified freedom. In the event that notice to terminate the contract was not given six months prior to its expiry date, it was to be tacitly extended for a further year. And if, at the end of the contract, the defendant were offered a more favourable contract by a third party, the plaintiff was to have the preferential right "to conclude within 14 days an equivalent contract".

The imposition of such a mass of obligations on a 22-year-old, who could hardly yet have formed any clear ideas as to her future professional and artistic career, amounts to a severe restriction of personal freedom and is thus incompatible with Article 27 ZGB [Swiss Civil Code].

Note

If a trader agrees to buy certain goods he thereby necessarily limits or restricts his freedom to enter into another contract buying the same goods from somebody else. Clearly, this agreement is not invalid as being in restraint of trade. But suppose that the same trader agrees to buy certain goods from a seller and to refrain from buying them from anybody else for a term of 5, 10 or 20 years? Should this "exclusive dealing agreement" be struck down as an undue fetter on the trader's freedom to carry on his business as he pleases? What if the seller shows good reasons why a "tie" of a certain duration is needed for the commercial viability of the operation?

House of Lords   **3.E.13.**
Esso Petroleum Co. Ltd. v. *Harper's Garage (Stourport) Ltd.*[17]

21-YEAR EXCLUSIVE PETROL DISTRIBUTION AGREEMENT IN RESTRAINT OF TRADE

The English solus agreement

A contract between a petrol company and a filling station which binds the latter to selling the company's fuel for five years is reasonable but one for twenty-one years is void as being in restraint of trade.

---

[17] [1968] AC 269.

Facts: The respondents, the owners of two filling stations, agreed to purchase their total requirements of motor fuels exclusively from the appellants at their list prices in force on the date of delivery. The agreement for "Mustow Green Garage" was to remain in force for four years and five months, the one for "Corner Garage" for twenty-one years. The appellants had lent the respondents £7,000 for the purpose of acquiring the land on which the "Corner Garage" was being operated and of carrying out constructional work thereon. When the respondents started to sell another brand of petrol at their filling stations the appellants sought injunctions restraining the respondents from buying or selling motor fuels other than those of the appellants.

Held: The solus agreement in respect of Mustow Green garage was upheld, but in respect of Corner Garage, the agreement was held to be void.

Judgment: LORD REID: . . . It is I think well established that the court will not enforce a restraint which goes further than affording adequate protection to the legitimate interests of the party in whose favour it is granted. This must I think be because too wide a restraint is against the public interest. It has often been said that a person is not entitled to be protected against mere competition. I do not find that very helpful in a case like the present. I think it better to ascertain what were the legitimate interests of the appellants which they were entitled to protect and then to see whether these restraints were more than adequate for that purpose.

What were the appellant's legitimate interests must depend largely on what was the state of affairs in their business and with regard to the distribution and sale of petrol generally. And those are questions of fact to be answered by evidence or common knowledge.

When petrol rationing came to an end in 1950 the large producers began to make agreements, now known as *solus* agreements, with garage owners under which the garage owner, in return for certain advantages, agreed to sell only the petrol of the producer with whom he made the agreement. Within a short time three-quarters of the filling stations in this country were tied in that way and by the dates of the agreements in this case over 90 per cent had agreed to ties. It appears that the garage owners were not at a disadvantage in bargaining with the large producing companies as there was intense competition between these companies to obtain these ties. So we can assume that both the garage owners and the companies thought that such ties were to their advantage. And it is not said in this case that all ties are either against the public interest or against the interests of the parties. The respondents' case is that the ties with which we are concerned are for too long periods.

The advantage of the garage owner is that he gets a rebate on the wholesale price of the petrol which he buys and also may get other benefits or financial assistance. The main advantages for the producing company appear to be that distribution is made easier and more economical and that it is assured of a steady outlet for its petrol over a period. As regards distribution, it appears that there were some 35,000 filling stations in this country at the relevant time, of which about a fifth were tied to the appellants. So they only have to distribute to some 7,000 filling stations instead of to a very much larger number if most filling stations sold several brands of petrol. But the main reason why the producing companies want ties for five years and more, instead of ties for one or two years only, seems to be that they can organise their business better if on the average only one-fifth or less of their ties come to an end in any one year. The appellants make a point of the fact that they have invested some £200 millions in refineries and other plants and that they could not have done that unless they could foresee a steady and assured level of sales of their petrol. Most of their ties appear to have been made for periods of between five and 20 years. But we have no evidence as to the precise additional advantage which they derive from a five-year tie as compared with a two-year tie or from a 20-year tie as compared with a five-year tie.

The Court of Appeal held that these ties were for unreasonably long periods. They thought that, if for any reason the respondents ceased to sell the appellants' petrol, the appellants could have found other suitable outlets in the neighbourhood within two or three years. I do not think that that is the right test. In the first place there was no evidence about this and I do not think that it would be practicable to apply this test in practice. It might happen that when the respondents ceased to sell their petrol, the appellants would find such an alternative outlet in a very short time. But, looking to the fact that well over 90 per cent. of existing filling stations are tied and that there may be great difficulty in opening a new filling station, it might take a very long time to find an alternative. Any estimate of how long it might take to find suitable alternatives for the respondents' filling station could be little better than guesswork.

I do not think that the appellants' interest can be regarded so narrowly. They are not so much concerned with any particular outlet as with maintaining a stable system of distribution throughout the country so as to enable their business to be run efficiently and economically. In my view there is sufficient material to justify a decision that ties of less than five years were insufficient, in the circumstances of the trade when these agreements were made, to afford adequate protection to the appellants' legitimate interests.

But the Corner Garage agreement involves much more difficulty. Taking first the legitimate interests of the appellants, a new argument was submitted to your Lordships that, apart from any question of security for their loan, it would be unfair to the appellants if the respondents, having used the appellant's money to build up their business, were entitled after a comparatively short time to be free to seek better terms from a competing producer. But there is no material on which I can assess the strength of this argument and I do not find myself in a position to determine whether it has any validity. A tie for 21 years stretches far beyond any period for which developments are reasonably foreseeable. Restrictions on the garage owner which might seem tolerable and reasonable in reasonably foreseeable conditions might come to have a very different effect in quite different conditions: the public interest comes in here more strongly. And, apart from a case where he gets a loan, a garage owner appears to get no greater advantage from a 20-year tie than he gets from a five-year tie. So I would think that there must at least be some clearly established advantage to the producing company—something to show that a shorter period would not be adequate—before so long a period could be justified. But in this case there is no evidence to prove anything of the kind.

LORD WILBERFORCE: . . . The doctrine of restraint of trade (a convenient, if imprecise, expression which I continue to use) is one which has throughout the history of its subject-matter been expressed with considerable generality, if not ambiguity. The best-known general formulations, those of Lord Macnaghten in *Nordenfelt* and Lord Parker of Waddington in *Adelaide*, adapted and used by Diplock LJ in the Court of Appeal in the *Petrofina* case, speak generally of all restraints of trade without any attempt at a definition. Often we find the words "restraint of trade" in a single passage used indifferently to denote, on the one hand, in a broad popular sense, any contract which limits the free exercise of trade or business, and, on the other hand, as a term of art covering those contracts which are regarded as offending a rule of public policy. Often, in reported cases, we find that instead of segregating two questions, (i) whether the contract is in restraint of trade, (ii) whether, if so, it is "reasonable", the courts have fused the two by asking whether the contract is in "undue restraint of trade" or by a compound finding that it is not satisfied that this contract is really in restraint of trade at all but, if it is, it is reasonable. A well-known text book describes contracts in restraint of trade as those which "unreasonably restrict" the rights of a person to carry on his trade or profession. There is no need to regret these tendencies: indeed, to do so, when consideration of this subject has passed through such notable minds from Lord Macclesfield onwards, would indicate a failure to understand its nature. The common law has often (if sometimes unconsciously) thrived on ambiguity and it would be mistaken, even if it were possible, to try to crystallise the rules of this, or any, aspect of public policy into neat propositions. The doctrine of restraint of trade is one to be applied to factual situations with a broad and flexible rule of reason. . . .

This does not mean that the question whether a given agreement is in restraint of trade, in either sense of these words, is nothing more than a question of fact to be individually decided in each case. It is not to be supposed, or encouraged, that a bare allegation that a contract limits a trader's freedom of action exposes a party suing on it to the burden of justification. There will always be certain general categories of contracts as to which it can be said, with some degree of certainty, that the "doctrine" does or does not apply to them. Positively, there are likely to be certain sensitive areas as to which the law will require in every case the test of reasonableness to be passed: such an area has long been and still is that of contracts between employer and employee as regards the period after the employment has ceased. Negatively, and it is this that concerns us here, there will be types of contract as to which the law should be prepared to say with some confidence that they do not enter into the field of restraint of trade at all.

How, then, can such contracts be defined or at least identified? No exhaustive test can be stated-probably no precise non-exhaustive test. But the development of the law does seem to show that judges have been able to dispense from the necessity of justification under a public policy test of reasonableness such contracts or provisions of contracts as, under contemporary conditions may be found to have passed into the accepted and normal currency of commercial or contractual or conveyancing relations. That such contracts have done so may be taken to show with at least strong prima force that, moulded under the pressures of negotiation, competition and public opinion, they have assumed a form which satisfies the test of public policy as understood by the courts at the time, or, regarding the matter from the point of view of the trade, that the trade in question has assumed such a form that for its health or expansion it requires a degree of regulation. Absolute exemption for restriction or regulation is never obtained: circumstances, social or economic, may have altered, since they obtained acceptance, in such a way as to call for a fresh examination: there may be some exorbitance or special feature in the individual contract which takes it out of the accepted category: but the court must be persuaded of this before it calls upon the relevant party to justify a contract of this kind.

Some such limitation upon the meaning in legal practice of "restraints of trade" must surely have been present in to the minds of Lord Macnaghten and Lord Parker. They cannot have meant to say that any contract which in whatever way restricts a man's liberty to trade was (either historically under the common law, or at the time of which they were speaking) prima facie unenforceable and must be shown to be reasonable. They must have been well aware that areas existed, and always had existed in which limitations of this liberty were not only defensible, but were not seriously open to the charge of restraining trade. Their language, they would surely have said, must be interpreted in relation to commercial practice and common sense.

[LORDS MORRIS, HODSON and PEARCE agreed that the shorter agreement was valid but the longer one void.]

BGH, 31 March 1982[18]   **3.G.14.**

INDEFINITE TIE OVER FILLING STATION CONTRARY TO PUBLIC POLICY

The German solus agreement

An exclusive distribution agreement between a petrol company and a filling station which gives the former the effective right to renew the contract indefinitely is void as contrary to public policy.

Facts: An exclusive distribution agreement between a filling station and a petrol company was terminable on notice, but gave the petrol company the right to renew the agreement on the same terms as might be offered by any other company.

---

[18] BHGZ, 83.313.

Held: The contract was held to be void by the Bundesgerichtshof.

Judgment: In 1952 the defendants, owners of a filling station, had agreed to purchase all their requirements of motor fuels exclusively from the plaintiffs. The agreement was to remain in force until 31 December 1977, *i.e.* for 25 years. Clause 9 provided that while the defendants were free to buy motor fuels from other sources for the period commencing on 1 January 1978 the plaintiffs had an option to enter into a contract on the same terms as any agreement that might be offered to the defendants by another supplier. When the defendants refused to inform the plaintiffs of the contents of a contract they had made with such other supplier an action for damages was brought against them.

The appellate court correctly approached the case on the basis that Clause 9 of the contract results in the imposition on the defendants of a commitment *vis-à-vis* the plaintiff which is unlimited in time, since it makes it impossible for the defendants to terminate their contractual relationship with the plaintiff against the latter's will. It is true that the parties fixed a date—31 December 1977—on which the contract was to expire, provided notice to terminate it had been given in good time. However, as regards the defendants' commitment to the plaintiff, that arrangement was decisively restricted by Clause 9 of the contract, since the power irrevocably conferred on the plaintiff by that clause, enabling it to intervene in any offer made by a third party and to continue the contractual relationship on the terms contained in that offer, make it impossible for the defendants to break free from the plaintiff, despite having given a valid and effective notice to terminate the contract. Accordingly, the defendants are bound to the plaintiff for an unlimited period of time—possibly extending over 30, 40 or 50 years—as long as the plaintiff wishes to continue the contractual relationship, albeit on terms offered by third parties.

A contract of that sort, whereby the continuation of the contractual relationship is dependent on the wishes of the oil company alone and the filling-station owner is precluded in perpetuity from breaking free from a specific contracting party, constitutes an unjustifiable restriction on the economic freedom of movement and autonomy of the filling-station owner in the choice of a new contracting party following the expiry of the term of the contract; it thus results, as the appellate court correctly states, in the filling-station owner being bound to the oil company in a manner incompatible with the concept of fair business dealings. Thus Clause 9 of the contract is contrary to public policy (§ 138 BGB) and to the fundamental ideas on which the law is based, which must be respected in the present case. The Bundesgerichtshof has in the past been prepared to confirm the validity of contracts pursuant to which—as in the present case—the filling-station operator makes the site available for the sale of the company's petroleum products and the company assumes responsibility for the construction of the filling-station buildings, the procurement of petrol pumps and the acquisition of other technical equipment, even where the duration of the contract in question has been 10, 20 or 25 years. However, even in contracts of that duration, it is impossible to justify an arrangement such as that in the present case, which completely excludes the possibility of breaking free from a commitment to a specific contracting party. Recognition of the validity of long-term filling-station contracts having a duration of 10, 20 or 25 years is based on the consideration that oil companies invest substantial amounts of capital over many years in setting up and fitting out the filling-station, whether it is the company itself which effects the necessary installations and places the filling-station at the disposal of the person operating it, or whether it grants the latter a long-term loan in order to set up the filling-station. In all such cases, the intention is, as a general rule, that the capital invested should gradually be repaid from the receipts of the filling-station's business. That necessitates a long-term commitment by the filling-station operator to the contract and to the oil company, since it is only on that basis that the company can be sure that its capital will, over time, yield interest and be amortised from the profits of the filling-station. If the commitment were to last only for a few years, oil companies would no longer be willing, as a general

311

rule, to make long-term capital investments—to the detriment of filling-station operators, who have an interest in concluding such contracts. As a general rule, therefore, there can be no objection in principle to an arrangement whereby the parties to a filling-station contract declare that the matters agreed between them are to be incapable of termination throughout the duration of a reasonable period fixed by reference to amortisation considerations—which, in the present case, having regard to the contractual term stipulated by the plaintiff itself, should not extend beyond 31 December 1977. Where the filling-station owner is bound to the oil company for any longer period, as per Clause 9 of the contract in the present case, there can be no inherent grounds for such a commitment, since it cannot be justified either from the standpoint of reasonable amortisation or on the basis of any other considerations.

Note

A question arising frequently in this group of cases is whether a restraint which is invalid for excessive duration may be cut down to size by the court. The same problem must be solved in cases where there is a clause in a contract for the sale of a business or in an employment contract under which the seller or the employee promise not to engage in competition with the buyer or, after the end of the employment, with the former employer. If the clause as written is found unlawful as regards its duration, geographical area and/or subject-matter, must the court strike it down *in toto* or has it a power to reduce the clause to its reasonable scope and then to apply it in that form?

Cass. soc., 21 October 1960[19]

3.F.15.

Excessive restraint may be reduced

The sugar broker

A clause which places an excessive restriction on an ex-employee competing with his old firm may nonetheless be enforced to prevent him working from a direct competitor situated in the same town as his ex-employer.

Facts: Mermilliod was engaged in October 1951 by the firm of Borione & Cie, sugar brokers, without any particular job title, to visit sugar factories and refineries and, generally, to devote himself to the satisfactory operation and development of the business of that firm. The contract between the parties contained a non-competition clause which provided that, in the event of its termination by either of the parties, for whatever reason, Mermilliod, who acknowledged that he had hitherto had no knowledge of that business sector, would refrain for a period of ten years following his departure from joining any competitor of Messrs Borione and from operating in competition with that firm. Messrs Borione brought an action for damages against Mermilliod who, having resigned, joined the firm of Berger & Cie, sugar agents.

Held: The lower court held that the clause was completely ineffective. The Cour de cassation held that the clause was ineffective only in so far as it was too wide in time or geographical coverage and could be enforced to prevent the employee going to work, immediately after his employment, for a direct competitor.

Judgment: *On the sole appeal ground*:—Under Article 1134 of the Civil Code and Article 7 of the Law of 20 April 1810;—Whereas according to the wording of the first of those provisions, agreements legally entered into are to be binding on the persons concluding them.

—Whereas it appears from the recitals and grounds set out in the contested judgment that Mermilliod was engaged in October 1951 by the firm of Borione & Cie, sugar brokers, without any particular job title, to visit sugar factories and refineries and, generally, to devote himself to the

---

[19] JCP 1960.II.11886 (first case).

satisfactory operation and development of the business of that firm; as the contract between the parties contained a non-competition clause which provided that, in the event of its termination by either of the parties, for whatever reason, Mermilliod, who acknowledged that he had hitherto had no knowledge of that business sector, would refrain for a period of ten years following his departure from joining any competitor of Messrs Borione and from operating in competition with that firm.

—Whereas Messrs Borione brought an action for damages against Mermilliod who, having resigned, joined the firm of Berger & Cie, sugar agents.

—Whereas the court below considered, in holding that the employment contract was void and ineffective, and in dismissing Messrs Borione's claim, that the non-competition clause was unlawful, since it did not limit geographically the prohibition agreed to by Mermilliod, and further ruled that the promise made to Mermilliod by one of the partners in Messrs Borione, to the effect that the clause would not be enforced against him, constituted a fraudulent practice which had invalidated his consent.

—Whereas however, a non-competition clause is in principle lawful and should be annulled only in so far as it impairs freedom to work on account of its temporal and geographical scope and as regards the nature of the activities of the person to whom it applies.

—Whereas in the present case, the clause in issue was capable of being held valid at least in so far as it prohibited Mermilliod, in consideration of the apprenticeship of which he had had the benefit, from placing himself, on the day following his departure, at the service of a direct competitor of his former employer, established in the same city. . . .

—Whereas in declaring the non-competition clause unlawful, and in holding the employment contract to be void and ineffective, the contested judgment consequently misapplied and thus infringed the legislative provisions referred to above, and the court below failed to provide any legal basis for its decision.

On those grounds, the Court quashes and annuls the judgment delivered by the Tribunal Civil de la Seine and refers the case back to the Tribunal de Grande Instance de Versailles.

BGH, 16 and 17 September 1974[20]   **3.G.16.**

PERIOD OF TIE MAY BE REDUCED TO REASONABLE FIGURE

The 24-year beer tie

A tie on a restaurant requiring it to purchase all its beer from the plaintiff for twenty-four years was excessive, but a sixteen-year tie would have been reasonable and the penalty for breach of the tie should be adjusted accordingly.

Facts: The defendants, owners of a restaurant, had agreed in 1954 to buy all their requirements of beer and non-alcoholic beverages exclusively from the plaintiff, a brewery, for a period of twenty-four years ending on 31 October 1978. The defendants terminated the agreement on 31 October 1964, *i.e.* after ten years The plaintiff brought an action against the defendants relying on a clause in the contract providing that in the event of a termination prior to 31 October 1978 the defendants were to pay a penalty of 15% of the amount they would have paid for purchases of beer and non-alcoholic beverages during the remainder of the agreed contract period.

Held: The Bundesgerichtshof held that the penalty should be assessed for the period that would have been justified.

Judgment (citations omitted): [The court stated that the contract period of twenty-four years was excessive under the circumstances, and continued] . . . The fact that, in the present case, a twenty-four-year tie was, under any circumstances, contrary to public policy does not, however, preclude

---

[20] NJW 1974.2089.

the maintenance of the contract—none of the other contents of which were objectionable—on the basis that it should be for such shorter term as might still be regarded as reasonable, having regard to the services already rendered and yet to be rendered by each of the parties. The assessment needing to be carried out in that regard is, as a general rule, a matter for the trial court. In the present case, however, no further clarification is needed on that point. The appellate court has assessed the essential points at issue here—albeit partially in a different connection—as regards the reasonableness of the rights and obligations assumed by both sides. In the particular circumstances of this case, this Chamber can determine this question itself. Having regard to the fact that—in addition to the considerations put forward concerning the contravention of public policy—the defendants were required to procure all their beer supplies from the brewery, and were thus not permitted to obtain even small amounts of special beer from any other brewery, together with the fact that they were obliged to run their inn primarily as an establishment selling beer and were therefore limited in their ability to cater for changes in public taste, as well as the fact that they had, in addition, to live with the fear that, in the event of a downturn in business forced on them by the consequent decline in turnover, they would face a demand for immediate repayment of a loan granted to them at a relatively unfavourable rate of interest, a term running for a total of 16 years, that is to say, until 31 October 1970, would appear to be justifiable. There is no evidence to suggest that the contracting parties would have chosen not to enter into a contract at all rather than to conclude these contracts for a term of such shorter duration. Consequently, the appellate court should have imposed the contractual penalty only in respect of the period from 1 November 1964 (the date on which the beer procurement was discontinued) to 31 October 1970, i.e. for a period totalling six years.

A powerful argument against the technique of cutting objectionable restraints down to size has been made by the House of Lords in the following case.

House of Lords   3.E.17.
Mason v. *Provident Clothing & Supply Co. Ltd.*[21]

EXCESSIVE TIE WHOLLY UNENFORCEABLE

Employment within 25 miles of London

A clause preventing an ex-employee from working for any firm carrying on a similar business to the employer's within 25 miles of London was unreasonable when the employee had worked only in one branch. The clause was completely ineffective and the employee could not be prevented from working for a competitor close by.

Facts: The respondent, a clothing and supply company, entered into an employment contract with the appellant employee which provided that he should not within three years after the termination of his engagement "enter into any employment with other firms carrying on a business similar to that of the plaintiffs within 25 miles of London". The appellant was attached to the respondent's Islington branch and, after having been dismissed by it, entered into an employment contract with another company based in Islington which carried on a similar business. The respondent brought an action against the appellant for liquidated damages as provided in the agreement. It was argued on its behalf that even if the clause were found to be too wide in its geographical scope it surely covered the situation at hand in which the defendant had taken up employment with a competitor doing business around the corner.

Held: The House of Lords rejected the appellant's argument.

___
[21] [1913] AC 724.

314

Judgment: LORD MOULTON: . . . It was suggested in the argument that even if the covenant was, as a whole, too wide, the Court might enforce restrictions which it might consider reasonable (even though they were not expressed in the covenant), provided they were within its ambit. My Lords, I do not doubt that the Court may, and in some cases will, enforce a part of a covenant in restraint of trade, even though taken as a whole the covenant exceeds what is reasonable. But, in my opinion, that ought only to be done in cases where the part so enforceable is clearly severable, and even so only in cases where the excess is of trivial importance, or merely technical, and not a part of the main purport and substance of the clause. It would in my opinion be *pessimi exempli* if, when an employer had exacted a covenant deliberately framed in unreasonably wide terms, the Courts were to come to his assistance and, by applying their ingenuity and knowledge of the law, carve out of this void covenant the maximum of what he might validly have required. It must be remembered that the real sanction at the back of these covenants is the terror and expense of litigation, in which the servant is usually at a great disadvantage, in view of the longer purse of his master. It is sad to think that in this present case this appellant, whose employment is a comparatively humble one, should have had to go through four Courts before he could free himself from such unreasonable restraints as this covenant imposes, and the hardship imposed by the exaction of unreasonable covenants by employers would be greatly increased if they could continue the practice with the expectation that, having exposed the servant to the anxiety and expense of litigation, the Court would in the end enable them to obtain everything which they could have obtained by acting reasonably. It is evident that those who drafted this covenant aimed at making it a penal rather than a protective covenant, and that they hoped by means of it to paralyse the earning capabilities of the man if and when he left their service, and were not thinking of what would be a reasonable protection to their business, and having so acted they must take the consequences.

I am of opinion, therefore, that the appeal should be allowed and the action dismissed, with all such costs as by the rules of the Courts are payable in the case of a defendant who, as in the present case, appeals *in forma pauperis*.

Court of Appeal   **3.E.18.**
Goldsoll v. Goldman[22]

CLAUSE MAY BE SEVERED

Imitation jewellery

A clause which is unreasonably broad but which contains distinct restrictions, some of which are reasonable and some unreasonable, may be severed and the reasonable parts enforced.

Facts: Both parties were dealers in imitation jewellery. In a contract for the sale of his firm the defendant agreed that he would not for a period of two years directly or indirectly carry on a similar business in the "U.K. and the Isle of Man or in France, the U.S., Russia, or Spain, or within 25 miles of Potsdamer Strasse, Berlin, or St. Stefans Kirche, Vienna". The plaintiff alleged that the defendant had acquired an interest in a business selling imitation jewellery from shops in London.

Held: Neville J held that while the agreement was too wide in area, that part of it which prohibited carrying on business in the UK was severable from the rest and was not too wide. The defendant's appeal against the decision of Neville J granting an injunction was dismissed.

Judgment: KENNEDY LJ: . . . The doctrine of severability has been admitted by the Courts, and while I am far from saying that I do not see the force of the great objections brought forward by *Lord Moulton* in *Mason* v. *Provident Clothing and Supply Co.* and by *Neville J*. in this case, it is of no use

---

[22] [1915] 1 Ch. 292.

315

going into that, because it has been held in decisions binding on this Court that, if words are used in a covenant such as admit of severability by mentioning different areas, we must sever the covenant so as to limit its operation to an area which is not too large. Moreover, if ever there was a case of severability we have it here, for countries are specified which may be treated as representing the United Kingdom as distinguished from foreign countries. There is therefore no sound objection to holding, as Neville J. has, that severed in that way there is a reasonable part of the covenant which ought to be enforced in favour of the plaintiffs.

[SWINFEN EADY LJ and LORD COZENS-HARDY MR delivered judgments to the same effect. Appeal dismissed.]

Note
In *Atwood* v. *Lamont*,[23] the appellant, who had been employed as a tailor's cutter, entered a covenant not to act in any one of a long list of trades including that of tailor. It was argued that the court should simply strike out the references to the other trades and enforce the covenant against him acting as a tailor. The court refused to do so on the ground that in reality this was not a series of separate covenants but a single covenant which should stand or fall as a whole. As it was much too wide it was wholly unenforceable.

3.1.4. CONTRACTS FORBIDDEN BY STATUTE

The cases in this section deal with contracts alleged to be invalid or unenforceable as being contrary to a statutory prohibition. No serious problem arises in cases in which the statute explicitly makes some contract illegal and unenforceable. The more frequent and more difficult cases are those where a statute merely prohibits some activity, requires a licence for those wishing to engage in that activity, or prescribes a certain manner in which the activity must be carried out, but says nothing on the validity of a contract performed in a way prohibited by the statute. Thus if, contrary to a statutory prohibition, a shop owner sells his wares on a Sunday, a carrier overloads his lorry or a quack gives legal advice without being duly licensed as an attorney, he may be punished. But it is a wholly different question whether the contracts should be held unenforceable so that the shop owner, the carrier and the quack would be unable to sue for the agreed price, and the other parties to the contracts unable to claim damages for a breach of the contract.

---

[23] [1920] 3 KB 571 (CA).

Court of Appeal   **3.E.19.**
Re Mahmoud v. *Ispahani*[24]

PROHIBITED CONTRACT UNENFORCEABLE BY EITHER PARTY

Sale of linseed oil without licence

Where statute forbids the making of a contract without a licence and one party does not have the required licence, the contract is unenforceable by or against him, even if he has told the other party that he does have a licence.

Facts: By the Seeds, Oils and Fat Order 1919 licences were necessary for either the sale or purchase of linseed oil. The plaintiff sold linseed oil to the defendant. The plaintiff had a licence. Before entering into the contract he asked the defendant whether he had a licence and the defendant said he had. He had not. The defendant later refused to accept delivery and on being sued for damages for non-acceptance argued that the contract was illegal.

Held: The Court of Appeal overturned the first instance decision, holding that the contract was illegal under the Order and therefore unenforceable.

Judgment: BANKES LJ: . . . The first question is, What is the true construction of the Order of June 19, 1919? Clause 1 provides: "Until further notice a person shall not either on his behalf or on behalf of any other person buy or sell or otherwise deal in. . . . any of the articles specified in the schedule hereto"—which included linseed oil—"whether situated within or without the United Kingdom, except under and in accordance with the terms of a licence issued by or under the authority of the Food Controller." The language of the clause is clear. It makes it legal, on the part of the buyer and of the seller, to enter into a contract prohibited by the clause. [The Lord Justice also read clauses 2, 3 and 4.] It is not material to consider, for the purpose of deciding this case, whether or not the respondent has been guilty of an offence under the Order. It is said, as I understand it, that, provided a person complies with the requirements of clause 3 and asks for information which would be "for the purpose of satisfying them or him that the provisions of this Order have not been contravened," all the requirements of the Order have been complied with. That is not my view of the Order. I think clause 1 makes such a contract as this illegal. Clause 3 is an additional requirement for securing that persons shall not enter into these contracts; but when one is considering what is the effect of non-compliance with clause 1, it seems to me to be immaterial whether they do or do not make the inquiries. The Order is a clear and unequivocal declaration by the Legislature in the public interest that this particular kind of contract shall not be entered into. The respondent had a licence; the appellant had no licence. The respondent contends that, as he had a licence, the appellant cannot be heard to say that in the circumstances he had not a licence. I cannot assent to that proposition. I do not think there is any authority for it, and as the language of the Order clearly prohibits the making of this contract, it is open to a party, however shabby it may appear to be, to say that the Legislature has prohibited this contract, and therefore it is a case in which the Court will not lend its aid to the enforcement of the contract.

I say nothing upon the question whether the respondent may have a remedy in some other form of action against the appellant, who is said to have deceived him by making a deliberately false statement. That does not arise in this case.

ATKIN LJ: I agree. It is admitted that the Order . . . has the effect of a statute, and the contention is that by that Order the contract in this case was prohibited. When the Court has to deal with the

---

[24] [1921] 2 KB 716.

317

question whether a particular contract or class of contract is prohibited by statute, it may find an express prohibition in the statute, or it may have to infer the prohibition from the fact that the statute imposes a penalty upon the person entering into that class of contract. In the latter case one has to examine very carefully the precise terms of the statute imposing the penalty upon the individual. One may find that the statute imposes a penalty upon an individual, and yet does not prohibit the contract if it is made with a party who is innocent of the offence which is created by the statute. . . . Here it appears to me to be plain that this particular contract was expressly prohibited by the terms of the Order which imposes the necessity of a compliance with the licence. With great respect to the learned judge, I think the underlying fallacy in his judgement is that he has not directed his attention to the terms of the licence or to the terms of the order which says that no sale shall be made unless it complies with the terms of the licence . . .

The only other contention that I desire to refer to is the suggestion that there is something in the nature of an estoppel is this case. It seems to me that, when once it is appreciated that this prohibition is imposed for the public benefit, and is obviously made with the intention that the persons who are left in control of these goods shall not only be entitled to deal with them if they are licensed by the proper authority and if they act in accordance with the terms of that licence, it would reduce the legislation to an absurdity to say that, notwithstanding such a statutory prohibition, if the seller is deceived into believing that his purchaser has a licence, he may then hand over the goods to that lying purchaser free from any restrictions whatever and leave him in control of the goods. The absurdity is made still greater when one appreciates that, if two rogues each mutually deceive one another, apparently the legislation could be given the go-by altogether, and there would be unrestricted dealings in these particular commodities between such persons under contracts giving enforceable rights between one and the other. I cannot conceive that that can be the law, and I think that the express statutory prohibition prevents that state of law arising.

Notes

(1) Bankes LJ said that it was "shabby" for the defendant, a self-confessed liar, to rely upon his own illegality as a defence against the plaintiff's claim. While it is clear that the defendant was not liable in damages for the breach of his contractual duty to accept the linseed oil, it is not so clear whether he might not be liable on other grounds. On what grounds might the plaintiff succeed, and what would be the measure of damages?[25]

(2) If a statute prohibits both parties from concluding a contract and makes both parties liable to penalties the contract itself will normally be viewed as impliedly forbidden and void. However, in exceptional cases, a court may come to the conclusion that it would be unjust to allow a party to rely on the invalidity. This position was taken by the German Bundesgerichtshof in the following case.

BGH, 23 September 1982[26]   **3.G.20.**

ILLEGAL CONTRACT WHICH HAS BEEN CARRIED OUT MAY GIVE RISE TO CLAIM

Illegal building labour

A contract under which the parties agree to use illegal labour and which has been carried out may be enforced by one party to the extent of recovering excess charges paid to the other.

---

[25] *Supra*, at 2.2.3.D.
[26] BGHZ 85.39 (citations omitted).

Facts: By a contract of 16 January 1978 the defendant had agreed to build a house for the plaintiff for a price of DM 146.949,50. After the completion of the house it turned out that the plaintiff, who had paid DM 143.000, to the defendant, was liable for another DM 45.000,—to various suppliers of building materials with whom the defendant had placed orders on behalf of the plaintiff. In a suit brought by the plaintiff the defendant moved for a dismissal on the ground that the contract of 16 January 1978 was invalid. He relied on the fact that the house had been built, as was known to both parties, with the help of clandestine workers which was forbidden by a statute.

Held: The plaintiff could recover from the defendant builder the amount which the plaintiff had become liable to pay the suppliers.

Judgment: 1. . . . The question whether the commission, in the context of a transaction, of a breach of a statutory prohibition renders the transaction void falls to be determined in accordance with the object and purpose of the prohibition concerned. Where no express provision has been made in that regard, the answer will depend on whether it would be incompatible with the object and purpose of the prohibiting legislation to accept without demur the statutory rule infringed by the transaction and to allow it to stand.

The Law on the combating of clandestine labour . . . contains no provision expressly prohibiting clandestine labour. However, the object and purpose of the statute, together with the penalties in the form of fines provided for in §§ 1 and 2 thereof, indicate that the statute constitutes prohibiting legislation and that a transaction which infringes it is to be regarded as void pursuant to § 134 BGB.

The Law on the combating of clandestine labour is intended to combat the high level of unemployment in many occupational sectors, to prevent businesses, especially craft trades, from being jeopardised by wage and price undercutting and to protect customers who place contracts against loss and damage resulting from the provision of low-quality services and the improper use of raw materials. In addition, the statute is designed to prevent a diminution in tax revenues and a detrimental effect on the level of contributions received by the social insurance and unemployment insurance authorities. . . . §§ 1 and 2 of the statute provide, subject to certain conditions, for the imposition of fines on both persons engaging in clandestine work and those commissioning it. In so providing, the statute seeks, to all intents and purposes, to prohibit clandestine working and generally to prevent the exchange of services between the person commissioning the work and the unregistered person performing it. Thus, the prohibition of clandestine working is aimed not only at the person by whom the work is carried out but also at the person who commissions it. The fines provided for in §§ 1 and 2 of the statute provide in themselves significant grounds for supposing that the intention of the legal order is to refuse to recognise the validity of a contract which disregards the prohibition of clandestine working. Above all, the *aim* of the statute, namely to prevent clandestine working, can only be achieved if contracts which infringe it are regarded as invalid in law.

2. . . . Exceptionally, however, the invalidity of the contract under § 134 BGB does not, in the present case, mean that the plaintiff has no claim against the defendant for indemnification in respect of the sums due to the suppliers of materials which exceeded the fixed price agreed, since the defendant's plea that the contract was invalid violates, in the particular circumstances of the present case, the principle of good faith (§ 242 BGB).

[The Court pointed out that the contract price of DM 146.949,50 was a guaranteed price and that the defendant had given an implied promise to save the plaintiff harmless from any extra expense. The Court then continued:]

. . . The defendant arranged for the plaintiff's building project, apart from the garage and the fitting of the doors, to be carried out to a large extent by clandestine workers, as the parties had planned. The plaintiff paid the agreed "fixed price", apart from a sum of DM 3,949.50, corresponding more or less to the value of the garage and the uninstalled doors. Thus the contract was almost performed almost in its entirety *by both parties*. Moreover, neither of the parties wishes the restitution of the consideration furnished by them. Were the defendant, in this situation, to succeed with his plea alleging the nullity of the contract, he would be able to shift onto the plaintiff the risk, assumed by him in the contract, of his being able to adhere to the agreed "fixed price". He would thus free himself, at the plaintiff's expense, from an obligation pertaining to him, notwithstanding that the contract has, for the rest, been performed by both parties, and that is settled. He would thereby be able unilaterally to exploit the nullity of the contract to his advantage, even though, in concluding it, he likewise infringed the Law on the combatting of clandestine labour. Furthermore, the plaintiff, instead of the defendant, would not only have to assume the risk of adhering to the fixed price but would not even be able to check whether the defendant expended the whole of the sum paid over to him on the construction of the house. Clandestine workers do not, as a general rule, issue invoices and receipts. That was the position here. In cases of this kind, the person commissioning the building works would therefore have to rely, as regards the amounts paid to the clandestine workers, on the information provided by the person dealing with them. The latter could secure additional advantages by making false statements. Nor would it be possible to subject the value of the work carried out by the clandestine workers to an evaluation, since there are no "usual" prices for the labour of clandestine workers. The person commissioning the works would be in an almost completely unprotected position *vis-à-vis* the person to whom they were entrusted.

All in all, therefore, the plaintiff would be placed at an intolerable disadvantage, and the defendant would be unjustifiably better off, if the latter were allowed to succeed with his defence that the contract was invalid notwithstanding the fact that *both* parties acted unlawfully in agreeing that clandestine labour was to be used for the construction works and despite the fact that the offence committed by the defendant is rather more heinous than that of the plaintiff. The object of the Law on the combating of clandestine labour, namely to protect businesses engaged in craft trades and consumers by preventing work and services from being provided by clandestine labour, is not such as to require that the plaintiff be denied, in the particular circumstances of this case, the right to indemnification. The services of the clandestine workers have already been provided. Consequently, it is no longer possible, in the present case, to satisfy the protective purpose which the statute is designed to serve. Settlement of the outstanding aspects of the (void) contract, namely payment of the sums due for the materials supplied and indemnification of the plaintiff in respect of claims by the suppliers of those materials, can no longer jeopardise the protection of craft trades which the Law on the combating of clandestine labour is intended to ensure. The present case is not concerned with assessing the consequences arising from the prohibited use of clandestine labour but with settling the outstanding aspects of a void legal relationship, which is not essentially different from the settlement of matters under a valid contract.

3. . . . It follows that the defendant cannot rely, by way of defence against the plaintiff's claims, on the nullity of the contract. He must be ordered to repay to the plaintiff the sum which the latter has expended, or has yet to expend, in settlement of invoices rendered by the suppliers of materials or other firms.

Notes

(1) If it was the policy of the statute to deter owners and building contractors from entering into such agreements, the best deterrent would have been to deprive the plaintiff of contractual claim for the extra expense. Do you agree?

(2) In many cases a statute merely prohibits one party from entering into a contract. Sometimes the statute provides that contracts may be entered into or performed by that party only if it has obtained a licence or authorization by the government or if the contract is performed in a way defined by the statute. In *Phoenix General Insurance Co. of*

Greece SA v. *Adas*,[27] Kerr LJ described the test to be used in cases of a "unilateral prohibition" as follows:

Where a statute merely prohibits one party from entering into a contract without authority and/or imposes a penalty on him if he does so (i.e. a unilateral prohibition) it does not follow that the contract itself is impliedly prohibited so as to render it illegal and void. Whether or not the statute has this effect depends on considerations of public policy in the light of the mischief which the statute is designed to prevent, its language, scope and purpose, the consequences for the innocent party, and any other relevant considerations.

In that case, however, the relevant statute prohibited the "business of effecting or carrying out of contracts of insurance" without authorization. The Court of Appeal, obiter, accepted the correctness of an earlier decision,[28] that this meant that neither party could enforce any contract of insurance made without authorization. The result was, of course, very dangerous for the insured, who would be left without cover, and it was later reversed by statute: Financial Services Act 1986, section 132.

(3) In the following French case very little is said on the reasons which led the court to its conclusion. What might the court have said if it had used the test laid down by Kerr LJ?

Cass. civ. 1re, 15 February 1961[29]   **3.F.21.**

CONTRACT TO PAY BROKERAGE FEE NOT ILLEGAL

The bailiff's commission

Although it was a disciplinary offence for a bailiff to accept a fee for arranging a sale, the contract to pay the fee was not therefore illegal.

Facts: L, a bailiff arranged for property to be sold to M, who gave the bailiff a promissory note in payment of commission. Arranging a sale would constitute a commercial act by the bailiff, and bailiffs were at the time prohibited from engaging in commercial activity. M argued that the promissory note was unenforceable on the grounds of illegality.

Held: The cour d'appel held that obligation was founded on an illegal basis, but the Cour de cassation quashed this decision.

Judgment: *On the first branch of the first appeal ground*:—Whereas it appears from the statements contained in the contested judgment that on 30 January 1954 Lancroux sold to Mabru, through the intermediary of L. . . ., bailiff, of Souillac, a hotel/restaurant business situated in that locality; as on the same day, Mabru handed to L. . . ., as remuneration for his services and by way of commission, a promissory note by which he undertook to pay to the bearer of that note the sum of 162 500 francs.

—Whereas the appellant's complaint concerns the declaration by the cour d'appel that the obligation thus accepted and assumed was void on the ground of illegality; as according to the appellant, at the time when that obligation came into being, bailiffs were not prohibited from acting as brokers in the sale of businesses, which is not in any event a commercial activity.

---

[27] [1987] 2 All ER 152, 176.
[28] *Bedford Insurance Co. Ltd.* v. *Instituto de Ressurgos do Brasil* [1985] QB 966.
[29] Bull. civ. I.105.

321

—Whereas first of all, however, the fifth paragraph of Article 632 of the Commercial Code provides that all brokerage operations are deemed to constitute commercial acts; as second, it is clear from Articles 39, 40 and 41 of the Decree of 14 June 1813, which was in force at the material time, that bailiffs are prohibited from engaging in any commercial activity, whether because that prohibition results from the actual wording of the aforementioned Article 41 or because such activities are regarded as incompatible with the professional dignity of such ministerial officers.

—Whereas the appeal ground is consequently unfounded as regards the first branch thereof.

—Whereas the first branch of the first appeal ground must therefore be rejected.

As to the second branch of that appeal ground, however:—Under Articles 39, 40 and 41 of the Decree of 14 June 181;—Whereas although those articles prohibit bailiffs from engaging in any commercial activity, they merely state that such activities are incompatible with the duties of a bailiff, and provide only for the imposition of penalties in the form of disciplinary measures.

—Whereas the cour d'appel considered, as the grounds for its declaration that the obligation assumed by Mabru in favour of the bailiff L. . . . on 30 January 1954 was void, that that obligation was founded on an illegal basis.

—Whereas however, the brokerage operation in issue, which consisted of bringing the parties together and providing for L. . . . to be remunerated for his expenses and efforts, was not in itself, and on that account alone, founded on any illegal basis; it merely rendered that ministerial officer liable to the imposition of the disciplinary sanctions provided for in such cases.

—Whereas in ruling as it did, the cour d'appel infringed the legislative provisions referred to above. . . .

BGH, 26 November 1980[30]   **3.G.22.**

PURPOSE OF STATUTE NOT FURTHERED BY HOLDING CONTRACT ILLEGAL

Pre-auction bid

A statute forbidding auctioneers to take bids made before the auction begins unless they are in writing signed by the buyer is designed to prevent fraud by the auctioneer and if the auctioneer wrongly allows a bid which was sent in by unsigned telegram that does not render the contract of sale illegal.

Facts: A German statute (§ 34 VI No. 3 of the Trade Act) forbids auctioneers to take into consideration bids submitted by a party not physically present at the auction unless the pre-auction bid is in writing and signed by the bidder. A painting was knocked down by the plaintiff auctioneer to the defendant on the basis of a pre-auction bid which had been sent by telegram only and did not comply with the statutory form requirement. The defendant bidder argued that there was no contract his bid being invalid under the statute.

Held: The claim was dismissed and the contract upheld.

Judgment: . . . (a) Under § 134 BGB, a transaction which breaches a statutory prohibition is void only if the statute does not provide otherwise. It follows, according to settled case-law, that the question whether the breach renders the prohibited transaction void depends on the object and purpose of the prohibiting legislation. If the prohibition applies only to one of the contracting parties, the transaction will not, as a general rule, be void. However, in certain particular cases, a breach of even a unilateral prohibition will render the transaction void, especially where it would otherwise be impossible to achieve the protection aimed at by the statute in question.

---

[30] NJW 1981.1204 (citations omitted).

(b) § 34b VI No 3 GewO (Trade Regulation) expressly prohibits "the auctioneer" from bidding or purchasing auctioned items on behalf of another person unless there exists a written offer made by that other person. Thus, the only person to whom the prohibition applies is the auctioneer; in the event of an infringement, it is solely on him that a fine may be imposed.

The legislative provision in issue does not prohibit the auctioneer from acting on behalf of third parties under any circumstances whatever; it only prohibits him from so acting in the absence of evidence of authority in the form of a written offer which is accordingly verifiable in the context of the auction. Consequently, the object and purpose of the provision in question is not to exclude bidders who are not physically present at the auction from participating in it. On the contrary, the aim of the provision is merely, in the interests of ensuring the transparency of the auction, to prevent the auctioneer from secretly taking part in it himself—as he is in any case prohibited from doing by § 34b VI No 1 GewO—or from feigning the existence of bids by third parties in order to push up the price. There is nothing in the legislation to suggest, as the applicant maintains and as the appellate court accepted, that, in addition, bidders who are not present are to be protected against the consequences of over-hasty bidding; nor does that contention correspond to the particular circumstances of an auction. The course taken by an auction is frequently such as to force absent bidders to make rapid decisions which need to be given oral expression, for example, where the question arises as to whether to exceed the upper limit which one had intended to place on of one's own bids. Such circumstances do not, however, provide any grounds for accepting that the purpose of the statute is to protect absent bidders against oral bidding instructions. The protection which the prohibition laid down by the legislation is intended to provide is not such as to give rise in such circumstances to the inference that, because the offer made was unwritten, the bid, and its acceptance on the fall of the hammer, must necessarily be void, since, if the aim of the legislation is merely to prevent the auctioneer from participating in the auction himself and from feigning the existence of offers from absent bidders, there is no need, for the purposes of protecting either the principal on whose behalf the bid is made or the other bidders, for a declaration that bidding instructions which actually exist but which have merely not been given in writing are void.

Adequate sanctions are available against the auctioneer, in the form of the imposition of fines and the suppression or suspension of auctions held in breach of the statutory prohibition. In those circumstances, there is no need to determine the question whether that result would have been justified, because there existed in the present case a telegram containing the name, address and intended offer of the bidder, so that the breach of the prohibition related at most to a matter of external form—namely, the absence of a personal signature—whereas the protective purpose of the statute was fully satisfied.

Queen's Bench   **3.E.23.**
St. John Shipping Corp. v. *Joseph Rank Ltd.*[31]

OVERLOADING OF SHIP DOES NOT RENDER CONTRACT FOR CARRIAGE OF GOODS ILLEGAL

The overloaded ship

The fact that a shipowner has overloaded the ship does not entitle the owner of goods carried to refuse to pay the freight, at least if it was not intended when the contract was made that the ship should be overloaded.

---

[31] [1957] 1 QB 267.

Facts: The defendants chartered the plaintiff's ship to carry grain from the USA to the UK. During the voyage the ship was overloaded in contravention of the Merchant Shipping (Safety and Load Line Conventions) Act 1932. On arrival in the UK the Master was convicted and fined the maximum fine of £1,200. The defendants paid part of the freight but withheld a sum equivalent to the extra freight earned by the overloading. They argued that the plaintiffs could not recover the freight as they had illegally performed the charterparty.

Held: The defendants must pay the freight in full.

Judgment: DEVLIN J: . . . It is a misfortune for the defendants that the legal weapon which they are wielding is so much more potent than it need be to achieve their purpose. Believing, rightly or wrongly, that the plaintiffs have deliberately committed a serious infraction of the Act and one which has placed their property in jeopardy, the defendants wish to do no more than to take the profit out of the plaintiff's dealing. But the principle which they invoke for this purpose cares not at all for the element of deliberation or for the gravity of the infraction, and does not adjust the penalty to the profits unjustifiably earned. The defendants cannot succeed unless they claim the right to retain the whole freight and to keep it whether the offence was accidental or deliberate, serious or trivial. The application of this principle to a case such as this is bound to lead to startling results. Mr Wilmers does not seek to avert his gaze from the wide consequences. A shipowner who accidentally overloads by a fraction of an inch will not be able to recover from any of the shippers or consignees a penny of the freight . . . . Carriers by land are in no better position; again Mr Wilmers does not shrink from saying that the owner of a lorry could not recover against the consignees the cost of goods transported in it if in the course of the journey it was driven a mile an hour over its permitted speed. If this is really the law, it is very unenterprising of cargo owners and consignees to wait until a criminal conviction has been secured before denying their liabilities. A service of trained observers on all our main roads would soon pay for itself. An effective patrol of the high seas would probably prove too expensive, but the maintenance of a corps of vigilantes in all principal ports would be well worth while when one considers that the smallest infringement of the statute or a regulation made thereunder would relieve all the cargo owners on the ship from all liability for freight.

Of course, as Mr Wilmers says, one must not be deterred from enunciating the correct principle of law because it may have startling or even calamitous results. But I confess I approach the investigation of a legal proposition which has results of this character with a prejudice in favour of the idea that there may be a flaw in the argument somewhere. . . .

. . . There are two general principles. The first is that a contract which is entered into with the object of committing an illegal act is unenforceable. The application of this principle depends upon proof of the intent, at the time the contract was made, to break the law; if the intent is mutual the contract is not enforceable at all, and, if unilateral, it is unenforceable at the suit of the party who is proved to have it. This principle is not involved here. Whether or not the overloading was deliberate when it was done, there is no proof that it was contemplated when the contract of carriage was made. The second principle is that the court will not enforce a contract which is expressly or impliedly prohibited by statute. If the contract is of this class it does not matter what the intent of the parties is; if the statute prohibits the contract, it is unenforceable whether the parties meant to break the law or not. A significant distinction between the two classes is this. In the former class you have only to look and see what acts the statute prohibits; it does not matter whether or not it prohibits a contract; if a contract is deliberately made to do a prohibited act, that contract will be unenforceable. In the latter class, you have to consider not what acts the statute prohibits, but what contracts it prohibits; but you are not concerned at all with the intent of the parties; if the parties enter into a prohibited contract, that contract is unenforceable . . ..

Two questions are involved. The first—and the one which hitherto has usually settled the matter—is: does the statute mean to prohibit contracts at all? But if this be answered in the affirmative, then one must ask: does this contract belong to the class which the statute intends to prohibit? For example, a person is forbidden by statute from using an unlicensed vehicle on the highway. If one asks oneself whether there is in such an enactment an implied prohibition of all contracts for the use of unlicensed vehicles, the answer may well be that there is, and that contracts of hire would be unenforceable. But if one asks oneself whether there is an implied prohibition of contracts for the carriage of goods by unlicensed vehicles or for the repairing of unlicensed vehicles or for the garaging of unlicensed vehicles, the answer may well be different. The answer might be that collateral contracts of this sort are not within the ambit of the statute.

The relevant section of the Act of 1932, section 44, provides that the ship "shall not be so loaded as to submerge" the appropriate loadline. It may be that a contract for the loading of the ship which necessarily has this effect would be unenforceable. It might be, for example, that the contract for bunkering at Port Everglades which had the effect of submerging the loadline, if governed by English law, would have been unenforceable. But an implied prohibition of contracts of loading does not necessarily extend to contracts for the carriage of goods by improperly loaded vessels. Of course, if the parties knowingly agree to ship goods by an overloaded vessel, such a contract would be illegal; but its illegality does not depend on whether it is impliedly prohibited by the statute, since . . . there is an intent to break the law. The way to test the question whether a particular class of contract is prohibited by the statute is to test it in relation to a contract made in ignorance of its effect.

In my judgment, contracts for the carriage of goods are not within the ambit of this statute at all. A court should not hold that any contract or class of contracts is prohibited by statute unless there is a clear implication . . . that the statute so intended. If a contract has as its whole object the doing of the very act which the statute prohibits, it can be argued that you can hardly make sense of a statute which forbids an act and yet permits to be made a contract to do it; that is a clear implication. But unless you get a clear implication of that sort, I think that a court ought to be very slow to hold that a statute intends to interfere with the rights and remedies given by the ordinary law of contract. Caution in this respect is, I think, especially necessary in these times when so much of commercial life is governed by regulations of one sort or another, which may easily be broken without wicked intent. Persons who deliberately set out to break the law cannot expect to be aided in a court of justice, but it is a different matter when the law is unwittingly broken. To nullify a bargain in such circumstances frequently means that in a case—perhaps of such triviality that no authority would have felt it worth while to prosecute—a seller because he cannot enforce his civil rights, may forfeit a sum vastly in excess of any penalty that a criminal court would impose; and the sum forfeited will not go into the public purse but into the pockets of someone who is lucky enough to pick up the windfall or astute enough to have contrived to get it. It is questionable how far this contributes to public morality.

Court of Appeal   **3.E.24.**
Archbolds (Freightage) Ltd. v. *S. Spanglett Ltd.*[32]

CONTRACT OF CARRIAGE ENFORCEABLE BY GOODS OWNER THOUGH LORRY UNLICENSED

Stolen whisky

Although a road haulier commits a crime by carrying goods in an unlicensed lorry, this does not prevent the owner of the goods to be carried from recovering if the carrier allows them to be stolen.

Facts: The defendants, furniture manufacturers, owned a number of vans with "C" licences under the Road and Rail Traffic Act 1933, which allowed them to carry their own goods, but did not permit them to transport goods of others for reward. The defendants nevertheless agreed to carry a load of whiskey for the unsuspecting

---

[32] [1961] 1 QB 374.

plaintiffs. The whiskey was stolen during the transport. When the plaintiffs brought a claim for damages defendants pleaded the illegality of the contract as their van did not have a proper licence under the Act.

Held: Upholding the decision of Slade J at first instance, the Court of Appeal held that the plaintiff could enforce the contract.

Judgment: PEARCE LJ: . . . If a contract is expressly or by necessary implication forbidden by statute, or if it is ex facie illegal, or if both parties know that though ex facie legal it can only be performed by illegality or is intended to be performed illegally, the law will not help the plaintiffs in any way that is a direct or indirect enforcement of rights under the contract. And for this purpose both parties are presumed to know the law.

The first question, therefore, is whether this contract of carriage was forbidden by statute. [The judge discussed *J. Dennis & Co. Ltd.* v. *Munn* [1949] 2 K.B. 327 and *Re Mahmoud* (*supra* p.) . . . and concluded that] the carriage of the plaintiff's whiskey was not as such prohibited; the statute merely regulated the means by which carriers should carry goods. Therefore this contract was not expressly forbidden by the statute.

Was it then forbidden by implication? The Road and Rail Traffic Act, 1933, section 1, says: "no person shall use a goods vehicle on a road for the carriage of goods . . . except under licence", and provides that such use shall be an offence. Did the statute thereby intend to forbid by implication all contracts whose performance must on all the facts (whether known or not) result in a contravention of that section?

The object of the Road and Trail Traffic Act 1933, was not (in this connection) to interfere with the owner of goods or his facilities for transport, but to control those who provided the transport, with a view to promoting its efficiency. Transport of goods was not made illegal but the various licence holders were prohibited from encroaching on one another's territory, the intention of the Act being to provide an orderly and comprehensive service. Penalties were provided for those licence holders who went outside the bounds of their allotted spheres. These penalties apply to those using the vehicle but not to the goods owner. Though the latter could be convicted of aiding and abetting any breach, the restrictions were not aimed at him. Thus a contract of carriage was, in the sense used by Devlin J, [in *St. John Shipping Co.* v. *Joseph Rank Ltd.*, *supra*] "collateral", and it was not impliedly forbidden by the statute.

This view is supported by common sense and convenience. If the other view were held it would have far reaching effects. For instance, if a carrier induces me (who am in fact ignorant of any illegality) to entrust goods to him and negligently destroys them, he would only have to show that (though unknown to me) his licence had expired, or did not properly cover the transportation, or that he was uninsured, and I should then be without a remedy against him. Or, again, if I ride in a taxicab and the driver leaves me stranded in some deserted spot, he would only have to show that he was (though unknown to me) unlicensed or uninsured, and I should be without remedy. This appears to me to be an undesirable extension of the implications of a statute.

[SELLERS and DEVLIN LJJ delivered concurring judgments.]

3.1.5. RESTITUTION OF BENEFITS CONFERRED UNDER AN IMMORAL OR ILLEGAL CONTRACT

If an agreement is immoral or illegal and therefore void no party can sue on it either for specific performance or for damages resulting from a breach. But suppose that the agreement has been performed: Is a party entitled to recover the money paid or the property delivered under it? In cases where the plaintiff is guilty of clearly outrageous or shocking behaviour the answer must be no. Many such cases were discussed even in Roman law. Thus it was held that a person cannot reclaim a bribe paid to a judge or witness, or hush-money paid to a person who caught him *in flagranti* or the price paid for an immoral act. The general rule was that money cannot be recovered if both the payor and the payee, by paying and accepting the money, have contravened elementary principles of morality: *in pari delicto potiorem esse possessorem*.[33]

In the civil law the problem is discussed in the context of the law of restitution. While a performance made pursuant to a void contract is generally recoverable as not being based on a valid *"causa"*, such restitutionary claim will be barred when the performance was made and accepted for an immoral purpose or in contravention of a rule of public policy.[34] In France the courts invoke the principle *"nemo turpitudinem suam allegans auditur"*, and in England the principle is that *"ex turpi causa non oritur actio"* or—in the words of Lord Mansfield—that "no court will lend its aid to a man who founds his cause of action upon an immoral or illegal act".[35]

This principle makes sense in cases involving serious crimes and other grave infringements of the moral code. But it is very doubtful whether all restitutionary claims should be denied in cases in which the agreement, forbidden though it is, runs counter merely to one of the many modern, morally indifferent statutory prohibitions. Indeed, it has been held by French courts that restitution shall be denied if the agreement is immoral (*convention immorale*), but generally allowed if the agreement is simply illegal (*convention seulement illicite*).

Cass. com., 27 April 1981[36]   **3.F.25.**

KNOWLEDGE OF ILLEGAL USE OF PREMISES INVALIDATES GUARANTEE

Brothel closed down

The purchaser of a bar who knew when she bought it that it had been used for immoral purposes and that criminal investigations were under way had no action against the vendor when the authorities closed the establishment down and withdrew its licence.

Facts: R sold F the business of a bar which she had used as a brothel. F knew this and that a criminal investigation was under way. F re-sold the business to P. When the authorities closed down the bar and revoked its licence, F had to reimburse and pay damages to P. She then brought an action against R on the *garantie*.

Held: The cour d'appel held the claim on the *garantie* was inadmissible. This decision was affirmed.

Judgment: . . . THE COURT: *On the first appeal ground*:—Whereas according to the statements contained in the contested judgment (Nîmes, 20 June 1979), Mme Roux, who ran a public house known as the Bar des As, and who was at the material time being prosecuted for living on the earnings of prostitution on account of acts committed in that establishment, sold that business on 29 July 1975 to Mme Fonzo, who, having worked with the vendor, was aware of the situation; as on 18 October 1975 Mme Fonzo resold the business to Mme Plasson;

---

[33] *Papinian* D. 12.5.7.pr.
[34] See e.g. Art. 2033 of the Italian Civil Code, § 817 sect. 2 German Civil Code, Art. 66 Swiss Obligations Law, Art. 6: 211 Dutch Civil Code.
[35] *Holman* v. *Johnson* (1775) 1 Cowp. 341, 98 ER 1120.
[36] D.S. 1982.51 annotated by Ph. Le Tourneau.

—Whereas on 24 October 1975 the tribunal correctionnel [regional criminal court] imposed on Mme Roux the sentence of, *inter alia*, closure of the establishment for three months and withdrawal of the licence.

—Whereas as a result, Mme Plasson brought proceedings against Mme Fonzo for rescission of the sale of 18 October 1975 and damages.

—Whereas Mme Fonzo herself brought an action against Mme Roux, who had died in the interim and who had been succeeded by her son M. Roux, in which she sought an order requiring the defendant, first, to indemnify her in respect of the consequences of any order that might be made against her in favour of Mme Plasson and, second, to pay her, in addition to damages, a sum corresponding to the sale price stipulated by the deed of 18 October 1975; as she further applied for a declaration that the sale of 29 July 1975 was void.

—Whereas the cour d'appel declared the sale of 18 October 1975 to be void and ordered Mme Fonzo to pay various sums to Mme Plasson by way of reimbursement and damages; as it dismissed however Mme Fonzo's action to enforce a guarantee.

. . .*On the second appeal ground*:—Whereas the appellant further complains of the dismissal by the contested judgment of Mme Fonzo's claim for enforcement of the guarantee against Mme Roux on the ground that she was already aware, when entering into the contract, of the risks arising from the criminal proceedings then pending, that, underestimating those risks, she believed that she could resell the business, which she had bought cheaply, at a higher price, that the contract concerned was of an aleatory nature, the effect of which depended on a hypothetical and uncertain future event, and that, not having been the victim of any fraud, nor deceived as to the essential characteristics of the property sold, she had to bear any losses flowing from her speculation.

—Whereas the appellant argues that, since a vendor remains bound by any guarantee given to the purchaser, even where it is established that the latter was aware, at the time of the sale, of the risk to which he was exposed, the cour d'appel, in refusing to allow the guarantee claim made by a purchaser who had not stated that she was buying at her own risk and peril, nor agreed to any clause excluding the guarantee in question, manifestly infringed Article 1626 of the Civil Code.

—Whereas however, it is clear from the statements contained in the [contested] judgment that Mme Fonzo was aware of the immoral acts of Mme Roux;

—Whereas, given the turpitude respectively attaching to each of the parties, Mme Fonzo's claim to enforce a guarantee must automatically be declared inadmissible.

On those grounds, the Court dismisses the appeal.

Cour d'appel Aix, 28 March 1945[37]   **3.F.26.**

RESTITUTION OF MONEY PAID

Potage créole

Sum paid in performance of an obligation void for illegality may be recovered.

Facts: D sold P 150,000 cases of Potage Créole, a new food product which had not been approved by the authorities. P sought to recover the money it had paid.

Held: The price paid by the buyer could be recovered.

Judgment:—Whereas it is necessary and appropriate to adopt the grounds set out in the judgment of the court adjudicating at first instance, which correctly applied the principles of law to the facts of the case; as it is not denied by either of the parties that the sale of the 150,000 cases of "Potage

[37] Gaz. Pal. 1945.2.12.

Créole" was void, since it was contrary to the Law of 17 June 1942, which prohibits the sale of any new product intended for human consumption before that product receives official approval
—Whereas the "Potage Créole" has never been officially approved and its sale was unlawful.
—Whereas Société Soprodis, Pichon & Guimard and Établissements Bancey have no basis for their argument that the claim for restitution should be disallowed because payment for the goods was made in full knowledge of the circumstances and without any error on the part of the payor.
—Whereas the payment in question was made in performance of an unlawful obligation which was, as such, void; as and such a payment, made on an invalid basis, operates, irrespective of any error, to vest in Société Nationale the right to claim restitution.
—Whereas nor is it possible to accept the appellants' submission that Société Nationale should be refused the right to bring its claim in the courts on the ground that it participated in the illicit sale in full knowledge of the circumstances.
—Whereas it is true that the case-law on which they rely does indeed debar a person who claims that an agreement is void for immorality from bringing an action on that agreement, the position is not the same where the agreement is merely prohibited by law or contrary to public policy, as the case may be, and not actually immoral.
—Under Articles 1131 and 1133 of the Civil Code, a person who has paid sums in pursuance of obligations which are void for illegality may bring proceedings for their repayment.
—Whereas a sum of money paid in performance of a void obligation is not due, and moneys which have been paid without being due may be the subject of proceedings for restitution . . .
   On those grounds, the court confirms the contested judgment.

Note
To support the conclusion of the court in the preceding judgment one might also have argued that the prohibition was primarily directed to the defendant who, as a producer and seller of foodstuffs, was under a clear statutory duty to obtain the governmental authorization prior to marketing his products while the plaintiff, as buyer, was not equally to blame though he knew or had reason to know about the defendant's breach of his statutory duty. Indeed, many courts have held that restitution should be denied only if the parties are "*in pari delicto*". If it was primarily the defendant who was guilty of the illegality or immorality, the relatively innocent plaintiff should be allowed to reclaim. This principle is used in several different types of case. For example, a plaintiff is not "*in pari delicto*" with the defendant if he was induced to enter the agreement by the defendant's representation that it was lawful, nor if the defendant has exploited his difficulty, simplicity, or inexperience, and the same is true if the prohibitory law which renders the contract invalid was designed to protect a special class of persons which includes the plaintiff.

Privy Council   **3.E.27.**
Kiriri Cotton Co. Ltd. v. *Dewani*[38]

RESTITUTION IN FAVOUR OF PARTY TO BE PROTECTED

Key-money

Where a payment is rendered illegal in order to protect one of the parties from exploitation by the other, the first party may recover any sum paid.

[38] [1960] AC 192.

Facts: The appellant company let a flat at Kampala, Uganda, to the respondent and received from him a "premium" of 10,000 Shillings in contravention of the Uganda Rent Restriction Ordinance though neither party thought that he was doing anything illegal. When the respondent had gone into possession he discovered the illegality of the "premium" and brought an action to recover it.

Held: The Ugandan court allowed recovery. The Privy Council dismissed the landlords' appeal.

Judgment: LORD DENNING (delivering the judgment of the Privy Council): . . . The most important thing to observe is that the Rent Restriction Ordinance was intended to protect tenants from being exploited by landlords in days of housing shortage. One of the obvious ways in which a landlord can exploit the housing shortage is by demanding from the tenant "key-money". Section 3 (2) of the Rent Restriction Ordinance was enacted so as to protect tenants from exploitation of that kind. This is apparent from the fact that the penalty is imposed only on the landlord or his agent and not upon the tenant. It is imposed on the person who "asks for, solicits or receives any sum of money," but not on the person who submits to the demand and pays the money. It may be that the tenant who pays money is an accomplice or an aider and abettor . . . but he can hardly be said to be *in pari delicto* with the landlord. The duty of observing the law is firmly placed by the Ordinance on the shoulders of the landlord for the protection of the tenant: and if the law is broken, the landlord must take the primary responsibility. Whether it be a rich tenant who pays a premium as a bribe in order to "jump the queue" or a poor tenant who is at his wit's end to find accommodation, neither is so much to blame as the landlord who is using his property rights so as to exploit those in need of a roof over their heads.

Seeing then that the parties are not *in pari delicto*, the tenant is entitled to recover the premium by the common law.

Notes

(1) In English law a party is not entitled to restitution merely because the contract is illegal. Rather, illegality may be used as a defence by either party to any action for restitution by the other, on the *in pari delicto potior est conditio possidentis* principle referred to by Lord Denning. However, there are at least two exceptions. The first is where the contract was rendered illegal for the protection of one of the parties, as in this case; then the party to be protected can recover.

(2) The other is when the party seeking restitution has "repented" before the contract has been fully executed. The scope of the second exception, and particularly whether there must be genuine repentance or whether it suffices that, for whatever reason, the claimant no longer wishes to go on with the contract, is unclear.[39]

BGH, 23 November 1959[40] **3.G.28.**

RESTITUTION UNLESS WILFUL BREACH OF PUBLIC POLICY

The struggling fur trader

A borrower who has taken out an illegal loan which he is then required to repay may set off by way of restitution the interest he has paid to the lender, unless he has committed a wilful breach of public policy.

---

[39] See Treitel, *Contract* at 455–7; Law Commission No. 154, *Illegal Transactions: a Consultation Paper* (1999), paras 2.49–2.56.

[40] Lindenmaier/Möhring, *Nachschlagewerk der Rechtsprechung des Bundesgerichtshofs*, § 817 BGB No· 12.

Facts: The defendant had got into serious financial trouble. He had applied for and received various loans from the plaintiff at an exorbitant interest rate which rendered the agreements void under § 138 German Civil Code. When the plaintiff brought an action the defendant sought to set off a counterclaim for the restitution of the interest paid.

Held: The lower court dismissed the defendant's counterclaim on the ground that he knew or ought to have known that his financial breakdown was inevitable and than an artificial prolongation of his struggle might harm other unsuspecting creditors. The Bundesgerichtshof disagreed and allowed the defendant's counterclaim.

Judgment (citations omitted): . . . Those statements do not bear legal scrutiny. It may be doubtful whether the defendant objectively infringed the rules relating to public policy . . . However, there is no need to adjudicate on that issue, since, in any event, the subjective criteria laid down by the second sentence of § 817 BGB are not fulfilled. That provision divests a creditor of his right to claim, or at least to enforce a claim, based on the general rules relating to unjust enrichment. Whether the justification for that rule lies in the fact that the creditor should be punished for his contravention of public policy and morality, or whether the rule is regarded as justified on the ground that the State should deny the creditor the protection of the law because the State must itself be protected against abusive recourse to the courts by persons who have broken the law, the fact remains that it is always necessary, on account of the severe and harsh consequences for the creditor, that he must have committed a wilful breach of public policy. Such reprehensibility in the mind of the lender cannot generally be said to exist where a borrower has, out of necessity, taken out a loan at an excessively high rate of interest and has paid that interest in order, once again for reasons of necessity, to receive a further loan at an excessively high interest rate. The defendant had got into serious financial difficulties, arising primarily, according to the findings of the appellate court, from the fact that he owned a large warehouse at a time when there was a fall in prices in the fur trade of some 25% to 30%. The defendant was no longer able to obtain a bank loan, but was dependent on credit. He hoped to be able to overcome the difficulties affecting his business by means of the loan granted by the plaintiff. He did not manage to do so; in the spring of 1955 an out-of-court settlement was concluded, and the defendant has stated that his business undertaking has since then been the property of a bank. However, where a trader has been forced by financial difficulties to take out a loan at an excessively high rate of interest in order thereby to avoid the collapse of his business, even where that hope is not essentially fulfilled, and his recourse to the loan increases the risk of collapse of the business or operates to make the extent of the losses flowing from its possible collapse even greater, he does not generally act in deliberate contravention of public policy or morality; consequently, he should not be punished by a refusal to allow him to claim restitution of the interest paid on an unlawful basis or denied the legal protection afforded by the State, as if he had wilfully broken the law. Nor can there be any objective justification for allowing a lender who has granted a loan on unethical or usurious terms to retain, as a matter of principle, the interest paid to him by a borrower who took out that loan because he was in severe financial difficulties.

Court of Appeal and House of Lords   **3.E.29.**
Tinsley v. *Milligan*[41]

No RELIANCE ON ILLEGALITY

House put in one owner's name only

Even though one joint owner of a house had the house registered in the other owner's name only so as to defraud the social security authorities, the first joint owner may recover her share provided she can do so without relying on the illegal transaction.

[41] [1992] Ch. 310 (CA); [1994] 1 AC 340 (HL).

Facts: The plaintiff and the defendant were two single women who had formed a joint business venture to run lodging houses. Using funds generated by their business they purchased a house in which they lived together. Although it was their understanding that they were to own the house in equal shares it was registered in the sole name of the plaintiff. The reason was that the defendant, with the connivance of the plaintiff, wanted to defraud the Department of Social Security (DSS) by misrepresenting herself to be a person without financial means and thus to make false claims to housing benefits on the DSS. Subsequently the defendant repented of the frauds and disclosed to the DSS that the benefits she had received over a number of years were based on a fraudulent statement of her financial position. A quarrel between the parties led to the plaintiff moving out, leaving the defendant in occupation. Thereafter the plaintiff gave the defendant notice to quit and in due course brought proceedings against the defendant claiming possession and asserting sole ownership of the property. The defendant counterclaimed for an order for sale and for a declaration that the property was held by the plaintiff on trust for the parties in equal shares.

Held: The judge at first instance dismissed the plaintiff's claim and allowed the counterclaim. The plaintiff's appeal was dismissed by the Court of Appeal, which applied a test of whether allowing recovery would shock the public conscience and held that it would not. The House of Lords disapproved this approach but affirmed the decision on the ground that the defendant held the plaintiff's share of the house on a resulting trust which was not tainted by the illegality.

[In the Court of Appeal]

Judgment: [NICHOLLS LJ discussed a number of cases emphasizing that recently a more flexible approach had been used and that, in the words of Bingham LJ in *Saunders* v. *Edwards* [1987] 1 WLR 116, the courts have "to steer a middle course between two unacceptable positions. On the one hand it is unacceptable that any court of law should aid or lend its authority to a party seeking to pursue or enforce an object or agreement which the law prohibits. On the other hand, it is unacceptable that the court should, on the first indication of unlawfulness affecting any aspect of a transaction, draw up its skirts and refuse all assistance to the plaintiff, no matter how serious his loss nor how disproportionate his loss to the unlawfulness of his conduct." He then continued:]

These authorities seem to me to establish that when applying the "*ex turpi causa*" maxim in a case in which a defence of illegality has been raised, the court should keep in mind that the underlying principle is the so-called public conscience test. The court must weigh, or balance, the adverse consequences of granting relief against the adverse consequences of refusing relief. The ultimate decision calls for a value judgement . . .

If that approach is applied in the present case I have no doubt as to the answer. There has been illegal conduct of which the court should take notice. For years both parties, the plaintiff and the defendant, participated in the defendant presenting fraudulent benefit claims to the DSS. They shared the use of the benefits paid. The house was put in the plaintiff's sole name for a fraudulent purpose. That was not an essential step in the parties' dishonest activities. The defendant could still have said, untruthfully, that she was a lodger paying rent even if her name had been on the title deeds. But keeping her name off the deeds made detection of her fraud less likely. Furthermore, to a limited extent the fraudulently obtained benefits went in maintaining the very asset, to a half-share in which the defendant is laying claim. The benefits were a part, although only a small part, of the parties' total joint income used to defray their living expenses, including mortgage interest. That is one side of the story. It constitutes a powerful case for the court not now aiding the defendant in her efforts to obtain a half-share of the proceeds of sale of the house. Fraudulent claims for housing and other benefits are all too prevalent. Nothing should be done which will encourage people to make fictitious transfers of property for fraudulent purposes. They should not think that they have nothing to lose thereby, because in due course a soft-hearted court will help them recover their property, and do no more than rap their knuckles with some forthright comments about their past misbehaviour.

The other side is that at the time it was bought and put in the plaintiff's sole name, [the house] belonged beneficially to both parties. The equity had been provided by both of them. To refuse to grant relief to the defendant would be, in a very real sense, to deprive the defendant of her own property, and to give it to the plaintiff, her co-venturer in this fraudulent activity. Further, the sum involved is not significant. To these parties it is substantial. Still further, and in my view of considerable importance, the defendant has come clean and told the DSS what has been going on.

Balancing these considerations I have no doubt that, far from it being an affront to the public conscience to grant relief in this case, it would be an affront to the public conscience not to do so. Right thinking people would not consider that condemnation of the parties' fraudulent activities ought to have the consequence of permitting the plaintiff to retain the defendant's half-share of this house. That would be to visit on the defendant a disproportionate penalty, in the circumstances as they are now. That was the view taken by [the judge below.] I agree with him.

[LLOYD LJ concurred in the result, RALPH GIBSON LJ dissented. Appeal dismissed.]

The Plaintiff appealed to the House of Lords. The "public conscience test" of Nicholls LJ found no favour with the Law Lords. LORD GOFF, with whom LORD KEITH agreed, said:

[T]he adoption of the public conscience test, as stated by Nicholls LJ, would constitute a revolution in this branch of the law, under which what is in effect a discretion would become vested in the court to deal with the matter by the process of a balancing operation, in place of a system of rules, ultimately derived from the principle of public policy enunciated by Lord Mansfield CJ in *Holman* v. *Johnson*, 1 Cowp. 341, which lies at the root of the law relating to claims which are, in one way or another, tainted by illegality.

Note
The appeal was nevertheless dismissed by a majority. They took the view that the defendant could enforce her property rights provided that to do so did not involve relying on the illegal transaction. The leading speech was made by Lord Browne-Wilkinson. In his view the defendant was able, without having to plead or rely on an illegality, to avail herself of a rule under which property standing in the sole name of A will be held by A in trust for both A and B if both parties have contributed the purchase price of the property and if there was a common understanding by A and B that they were to own the property equally—this is termed a "resulting" trust. Lord Lowry and Lord Jauncey concurred.

3.2. FRAUD, MISTAKE AND MISREPRESENTATION

3.2.1. GENERAL INTRODUCTION

This Section and Section 3.3 deal with topics which in many European legal systems are linked together under the general heading of "defects of consent". According to the legal and moral theory dominant on the continent in the nineteenth century, the parties to an agreement could be bound only to the extent that they had so willed.[42] Explaining the nature of this "willing", Kant stated that:[43]

---

[42] See Zweigert and Kötz at 401.
[43] Kant, *Die Metaphysik der Sitten: Der Rechtslehre* (Königsberg: 1797), para. 20.

Through a contract I obtain the promise of the other party (but not that which is promised), and yet something does accrue to my possessions; I become the possessor, through acquisition, of an active obligation upon the freedom and capability of the other party.

The preconditions of such a valid alienation of individual freedom are, consistent with the notion of human freedom itself, voluntariness and adequate knowledge. In the absence of these features the consent of the contracting party is unacceptably flawed or simply non-existent. At least in the civilian systems, this theory remains at the core of the rules defining and delimiting the impediments to contract formation represented by error and fraud. Under the German BGB an individual's engagement in *Rechtsgeschäfte* (legal transactions) is an emanation of that individual's private autonomy. Thus, a declaration of will is voidable where the party making the declaration has done so under the influence of a mistake (§ 119 BGB) or where he has been deceived by the other party or certain third persons (§ 123 BGB). Similarly Article 1109 of the French Code Civil provides that there is no valid consent if the consent was only given as the result of error, was extorted by violence or was the result of fraud.

English law does not have an overarching structure linking the equivalent topics of mistake, duress and misrepresentation, but we will see that in practice the courts frequently treat them as parallel doctrines to the extent that a solution derived from one doctrine is applied by analogy to another.

However, in each of the three systems there are other doctrines which impinge on what, in functional terms, seem to be cases of fraud or mistake. The first point is that some of the grounds giving rise to a defect in consent are also civil wrongs. Which rule applies depends on the remedy the plaintiff is seeking. If she has been tricked into making a contract and has suffered losses as a result, she may seek to avoid the contract on the ground of fraud and also seek damages. In French or German law, whereas *rescission* would be given on the basis of one of the Articles referred to above, *damages* would be available under the general provisions on civil responsibility (Article 1382 of the Code Civil, § 829 BGB). In English law, fraud is both a ground for rescission of a contract and a tort which gives rise to damages.

Secondly, in each system the rules on defects of consent occupy only part of the ground. This is particularly so in cases where there has been a mistake but no fraud. We shall see that the fact that a "mistake" of some sort has been made by one or both parties may mean, not that the mistaken party may avoid the contract, but that there is no contract at all because they never reached an agreement—as it is put in French, there is an *erreur obstacle*—or the agreement is void for impossibility. Further, we will see that in English law the doctrine of mistake is very narrow, but is supplemented by a liberal doctrine of misrepresentation.

Returning to the central notion of defects of consent, it would be incorrect to seek the origins of the various current rules on error and fraud in subjectivist, will-centred theories alone. The nature and extent of remedies available in these cases is also determined by an objective evaluation of the needs of a functioning market and, thus, of the wider society. Especially in the case of errors confined to one of the parties, an unlimited right to rescind the contract would pose an unacceptable threat to the security of transactions and the functioning of the market. In English law, which notably privileges objective over subjective interpretation and external over internal phenomena as relevant to the creation of contractual obligations, very little ground has been conceded to doctrines of unilateral mistake where this has not resulted from the conduct of the other party.

It would be wrong to suggest that the continental systems are monolithically subjectivist and the common law objectivist. Elements of each approach are to be found in each system. This is nowhere more evident than in the BGB Articles on interpretation. Thus § 133 BGB states that the party's true intention must be sought without regard to the literal meaning of his declaration, which seems to be pure will theory; but § 157 BGB says that contracts shall be interpreted according to the requirements of good faith. § 157 seems to favour what is called the declaration theory—i.e. the expectations reasonably engendered by the declaration should be protected.

Similarly, in civilian systems only certain types of error are deemed sufficiently potent and significant in law to lead to the annulment of the contract. Relief for mistake may also be cut down in scope or simply rendered superfluous by the range of warranties expressly agreed by the parties or implied into the contract by the law of sale.

Although requiring as a causal element the error of one of the contracting parties, cases of fraud—like cases of violence[44]—are dealt with separately from and more severely than cases of mistake. In this regard continental law adopts the general position of English law in premising relief not solely upon the state of mind of the erring party, but also upon the conduct of the other party. The "victim" in such cases benefits from the sanctioning of his fraudulent opponent. This may be a reflection of the serious moral harm embodied in the manipulative use of another for one's own ends. A more instrumental justification would highlight the real threat posed by fraud and the fraudulent to the operation of the market.

The strength of the latter argument within the legal discourse of a particular jurisdiction will also be seen to determine the extent to which the legal system demands that one party take positive steps to disclose relevant information to the other party. A system which wishes to encourage the production of valuable information may be reluctant to define silence as fraudulent conduct. Other systems seem to place a greater weight on the moral issues involved in keeping silent when the other party is ignorant of some crucial fact.[45]

3.2.2. FRAUD

Principles of European Contract Law   **3.PECL.30.**

Article 4:107: *Fraud*

(1) A party may avoid a contract when it has been led to conclude it by the other party's fraudulent representation, whether by words or conduct, or fraudulent non-disclosure of any information which in accordance with good faith and fair dealing it should have disclosed.

(2) A party's representation or non-disclosure is fraudulent if it was intended to deceive.

---

[44] See *infra* section 3.3., at 430 ff.
[45] Section 3.2.4, *infra* at 409.

(3) In determining whether good faith and fair dealing required that a party disclose particular information, regard should be had to all the circumstances, including:
  (a) whether the party had special expertise;
  (b) the cost to it of acquiring the relevant information;
  (c) whether the other party could reasonably acquire the information for itself; and
  (d) the apparent importance of the information to the other party.

Article 4:117: *Damages*

(1) A party who avoids a contract under this Chapter may recover from the other party damages so as to put the avoiding party as nearly as possible into the same position as if it had not concluded the contract, provided that the other party knew or ought to have known of the mistake, fraud, threat or taking of excessive benefit or unfair advantage.

(2) If a party has the right to avoid a contract under this Chapter, but does not exercise its right or has lost its right under the provisions of Articles 4:113 or 4:114, it may recover, subject to paragraph (1), damages limited to the loss caused to it by the mistake, fraud, threat or taking of excessive benefit or unfair advantage. The same measure of damages shall apply when the party was misled by incorrect information in the sense of Article 4:106.

(3) In other respects, the damages shall be in accordance with the relevant provisions of Chapter 9, Section 5, with appropriate adaptations.

3.2.2.A. FRAUD AS A GROUND FOR AVOIDANCE OF A CONTRACT

Code civil   **3.F.31.**

Article 1116: Fraud is a ground for nullity of an agreement when the conduct (manoeuvres) of one of the parties is such that it is evident that, without this conduct, the other party would not have contracted.

Fraud will not be presumed and must be proved.

BGB   **3.G.32.**

§ 123: (1) Whoever has been induced to make a declaration of will by fraud or unlawfully by threats may rescind the declaration.

(2) If a third party was guilty of the fraud, a declaration which was required to be made known to another person may be rescinded only if the latter knew or should have known of the fraud. Insofar as a person other than the one to whom the declaration was required to be made has acquired a right directly through the declaration, the declaration may be rescinded as against him if he knew or should have known of the fraud.

The classic definition of fraud in English law is found in the judgment of Lord Herschell in *Derry* v. *Peek*:[46]

I think the authorities sustain the following propositions: First, in order to sustain an action of deceit, there must be proof of fraud, and nothing short of that will suffice. Secondly, fraud is proved

---

[46] (1889) 14 App Cas 337, H.L, at 374.

when it is shown that a false representation has been made (1) knowingly, or (2) without belief in its truth, or (3) recklessly, careless whether it be true or false. Although I have treated the second and third as distinct cases, I think the third is but an instance of the second, for one who makes a statement under such circumstances can have no real belief in the truth of what he states . . . Third, if fraud be proved, the motive of the person guilty of it is immaterial. It matters not that there was no intention to cheat or injure the person to whom the statement was made.

Derry v. *Peek* was an action for damages for the tort of deceit, rather than for rescission of the contract. At common law "rescission" (avoidance) was also available where there had been fraud in the sense defined in the case. We will see later[47] that the rule in equity was that rescission might be given for even "innocent", i.e. non-fraudulent, misrepresentation.[48]

It should be noted that in some systems fraud is seen as a particular kind of mistake, but one which has been provoked deliberately so that some of the normal restrictions on avoidance for mistake do not apply.

3.2.2.B. PARTICULAR ISSUES

(1) The requirement of dishonesty

Fraud requires an intention to deceive the other party.[49] In none of the three systems does it seem to be a requirement for rescission that the fraudulent person intended to cause loss to the other.[50]

(2) The type of conduct covered

In the continental systems, in many cases of fraud the victim would also be able to avoid the contract for mistake; a serious mistake by one party may be a ground for avoidance. In contrast, we shall see that in English law a mistake by one party (other than a mistake in declaration[51]) is not normally a ground for avoidance, though relief could be given for misrepresentation. This may be one reason why, in the continental systems, the kind of conduct which may be fraudulent is broadly defined (for example the French Civil Code speaks of *manœuvres*). Although in French and German law the starting point was that there was no duty to disclose facts that the other party did not know,[52] it is now established that keeping silent about some matter of which you know the other party is ignorant may in some circumstances amount to fraud. In contrast, in English law it is still the case that only the making of a false representation of fact amounts to fraud. This includes false representations by conduct—gestures as "a nod or a wink or a shake of the head or

---

[47] *Infra*, at 400.
[48] On the distinction between common law and equity see *supra*, at 11, n. 25.
[49] England: *Derry* v. *Peek*, *supra*; France: Malaurie and Aynès, para. 414; Germany: Larenz, *AT* para. 20 IVa.
[50] England: *Brown Jenkinson & Co. Ltd.* v. *Percy Dalton (London) Ltd* [1957] 2 QB 621; France, Ghestin para. 561; Germany: BGH NJW 1974.1505.
[51] See *section* 3.2.3.B, *infra* at 347.
[52] Malaurie and Aynès, para. 415; B.S. Markesinis, W. Lorenz and G. Dannemann,, *The German Law of Obligations*, Vol I: *The Law of Contracts and Restitution* (Oxford: Clarendon, 1997) at 209.

a smile",[53] or covering up defects[54]—but there must be some positive action: in English law mere failure to disclose a fact cannot be fraud.

This difference is so fundamental and seems to lead to such different results that it is explored in a separate subsection on non-disclosure.[55] In the rest of this section we will assume that the fraud consisted of a positive representation such as a false statement of fact.

(3) The apparent importance of the matter to which the fraud relates

Because of the moral opprobrium which attaches to fraud—in all the systems, fraud is in many situations a criminal offence—contracts may be avoided on this ground under much less strict conditions than on the other grounds. Accordingly, the rules which follow should be contrasted with those for mistake.[56]

Thus, French and German law each have a general rule that a contract may not be avoided because of a mistake which is only as to the value of the thing bought or sold. This rule does not apply when the mistake has been brought about by fraud.[57]

Another restriction on relief for mistake is that it will not be given if the mistake is in some way not central to the contract. Thus in German law, relief on the ground of mistake is usually not granted, for example, in cases of errors of motive unless the error is as to some characteristic of the subject matter which is regarded as essential; in French law, it is not granted where errors are not as to an "essential" substance of the subject matter.[58] In contrast, in all the systems relief will be given for any fraudulent statement even if it was only as to a matter of motive.[59] It is necessary only that the person fraudulently given the wrong information was mistaken as a result and was influenced by her mistake in entering the contract.[60]

However, all the laws exclude general commendation, "mere puffs", from counting as fraud. See for example Dutch law:

BW   **3.NL.33.**

Article 3:44(2): . . . Representations in general terms, even if they are untrue, do not as such constitute fraud.

Presumably this is because it is felt that no reasonable person would be influenced by such sales talk. In some English cases sellers got away with quite misleading claims (for example stating that land was "fertile and improvable" when it was in fact a useless marsh,[61] or

---

[53] *Walters* v. *Morgan* (1861) 3 De GF & J 718, 723.
[54] *Baglehole* v. *Walters* (1811) 3 Camp. 154.
[55] See section 3.2.4, *infra* at 409.
[56] *Infra*, at 367 ff.
[57] Malaurie and Aynès, para. 416; Larenz, *AT* §20 IVa.
[58] *Infra*, at 369 and 376.
[59] See e.g. RGZ 81, 13; See also Kötz, *European Contract Law* at 196.
[60] *Ibid.*; Malaurie and Aynès, para. 417.
[61] *Dimmock* v. *Hallett* (1866) LR 2 Ch.App. 21.

that silver-plated spoons were "equal to Elkington's 'A' "—a well-known brand of good quality—when in fact they were of much inferior quality.[62]

In one class of case the German courts have not been willing to allow rescission on grounds of fraud notwithstanding the importance of the statement, and the deceitful intention of the other party in making it. Where an employee is pregnant at the time of an interview it has been held that she may withhold this information from her prospective employer and may even respond untruthfully if questioned about it.[63] This "right to lie" is clearly conceded to job applicants on grounds of policy and in particular in implementation of EC law on sex discrimination.[64]

(4) The influence of the fraud

No relief will be given if the false information did not influence the recipient, for example because she did not read it or did not believe it. But at least in English and German law, it need not have been the only factor which influenced the decision to enter into the contract.[65]

In French law a distinction has sometimes been drawn between determinant fraud (*dol principal*) and incidental fraud (*dol incident*). The idea seems to be that if the victim of the fraud would have entered the contract anyway, though on different terms, this was only *dol incident* and the victim may not avoid the contract but only claim damages. However the distinction has been rejected by both jurisprudence and doctrine.[66]

(4) Avoidance

As mentioned above,[67] the victim of fraud can usually avoid the contract and recover damages; alternatively, she may claim damages without avoidance.

In some systems—for example, German law—, avoidance for mistake etc. must be claimed within a short time.[68] With fraud, the seriousness of the conduct is seen as a reason for not prejudicing the victim. Thus avoidance will not be prevented simply through the lapse of time until after the fraud has been discovered. § 124 II BGB provides specifically that rescission must take place within one year of the discovery of the fraud; under § 124 III BGB, there is an upper limit of thirty years from the date of the relevant declaration of will. In practice in Germany relief may be sought on the basis of *culpa in contrahendo* even when there has been fraud. This gives rise to problems over the period for avoidance.[69] In France the period is five years from the date of discovery: Art 1304 C.civ.

(5) Fraud By Third Persons

So far we have assumed that the fraud was committed by the other party to the contract. A recurring problem is that a fraud by a third party has induced the plaintiff to make a

---

[62] *R* v. *Bryan* (1857) 7 Cox's Crim.Cas. 312.
[63] BAG, NJW 1993.1154.
[64] See Case C–177/88 *Dekker* v. *VJV Centrum*, [1990] ECR I–3941 (ECJ).
[65] *Edgington* v. *Fitzmaurice* (1885) 29 Ch.D 459; RGZ 77, 309.
[66] See Cass. com. 14 March 1972, D. 1972, annotated by J. Ghestin.
[67] *Supra*, at 334.
[68] See *infra*, at 381.
[69] *Infra*, at 406.

contract with the defendant. Where there is a relationship of principal and agent between the defendant and the fraudulent third party, the former will be responsible for the latter's acts according to normal principles of agency; relief will also be given where they were accomplices. This does not meet all the problems, however, as the fraud may have been committed by a third person who was not an agent of either party nor an accomplice. As this problem also arises in relation to other kinds of invalidity, such as duress and unfair advantage-taking, it is dealt with later.[70]

3.2.2.C. DAMAGES FOR FRAUD

We have already noted,[71] that in all three systems fraud is a ground of tortious or delictual liability as well as a ground for avoidance of a contract.

Code civil **3.F.34.**

Article 1382: Any human act which causes damage to another obliges the person through whose fault it occurred to make reparation.

BGB **3.G.35.**

§ 823: 1) A person who wilfully or negligently, unlawfully injures the life, body, health, freedom, property or other right of another is bound to compensate him for any damage arising therefrom.
(2) The same obligation is placed upon a person who infringes a statute intended for the protection of others. If according to the provisions of the statute, an infringement of this is possible even without fault, the duty to make compensation arises only in the event of fault.
§ 826: A person who wilfully causes damage to another in a manner contrary to public policy is bound to compensate the other for damage arising therefrom.

For English law, see *Derry* v. *Peek*.[72] See also Article 4:117 PECL.[73] In all three national laws, fraud may give rise to liability even if it did not result in the conclusion of a contract.

Generally, fraud which gives a right to avoid the contract will also give rise to liability in damages. However, there is one exception under German law: a party seeking damages as well as avoidance on grounds of fraud must show an intention to deceive. Under § 823 II BGB[75] in connection with § 263 StGB (German Penal Code) damages may be sought for loss resulting from the violation of a protective statute, in this case the criminal code provision on fraud. Intention is a requirement of the latter offence. Alternatively damages may be sought under § 826 BGB[76] for harm inflicted *contra bonos mores* and this has to be wilfully done, i.e. with intention. In this case, the intention must be specifically to cause

---

[70] Section 3.3.6, *infra* at 487.
[71] *Supra*, at 334.
[72] *Supra*, note 46.
[73] *Supra*, at 336.
[75] *Supra*, at 336.
[76] *Supra*.

harm or loss. Oblique intention suffices—i.e. it suffices that the maker of the statement knew there was a possibility that harm would result and made the statement nonetheless. Naturally, the intention to cause harm includes the lesser intention to deceive the other party. In cases where only negligence, as opposed to intention, is shown damages may be available on the basis not of § 123 BGB, but of the doctrine of *culpa in contrahendo*.[77]

(1) Concurrence of actions

A buyer who has been induced by fraud to buy defective goods may also have a remedy for latent defect or non-performance. There may also be an overlap between the grounds for such remedies and mistake.[78] German law provides that in cases of mistake the buyer is confined to the remedies for latent defects (§§ 459 *et seq.*) where the risk has already passed.[79] By contrast in cases of fraud the buyer may choose between on the one hand rescission under § 123 BGB and damages under §§ 823, 826 BGB, and on the other hand the remedies for latent defects, whereby the availability of damages is more limited.[80]— English and French law allow a choice in all cases.

(2) The measure of damages

Because fraud is an intentional wrong, many systems of law provide more generous damages than for unintentional wrongs. For example, in English law, the normal rule which limits damages to losses which were foreseeable (the "remoteness" rule) does not apply to fraud (*Doyle* v. *Olby*;[81] and contributory negligence is not a defence: *Alliance & Leicester Building Society* v. *Edgestop Ltd*.[82] Similarly in German law contributory negligence does not apply to fraud.[83] Other rules on damages may also apply differently to actions for fraud than they do in actions based on negligence.[84]

While French law has no special rules on the way in which damages for fraud are to be calculated, leaving it to the proper appreciation of the judge, English and German law provide that the damages are to be calculated in a different way from damages for breach of contract.

In German law a claim for damages arising from fraud must based on the delict provisions of the Civil Code, §§ 823 II, 826 BGB. The measure of damages is therefore the negative interest. A party must be put in the position in which he would have been had he not relied on the other party's statement(s). Generally he may not seek to be put in the position in which he would have been if the other party's statements had been true, i.e. recovery of the positive/ expectation interest.[85] Exceptionally, a buyer may recover the expectation interest where the ground for seeking rescission under § 123 BGB was a fraud

---

[77] *Infra*, at 352.
[78] *Infra*, at 394 ff.
[79] *Infra*, at 408.
[80] RGZ 96, 156.
[81] [1969] 2 QB 158, CA. For the remoteness rule see *infra* at 821.
[82] [1993] 1 WLR 1462, Ch.D.
[83] BGH NJW 1971, 1975 (1978).
[84] See *Chitty*, para. 6–045–6–066 ff.
[85] *Münchener Kommentar* under § 123, para. 30.

of the seller as to the quality of the goods.[86] In English law it is also established that in an action for damages for fraud the victim's damages are to be measured by her negative interest. As Collins MR put it in *McConnel* v. *Wright*:[87]

It is not an action for breach of contract, and, therefore, no damages in respect of prospective gains which the person contracting was entitled to expect to come in, but it is an action of tort—it is an action for a wrong done whereby the plaintiff was tricked out of certain money in his pocket; and therefore, prima facie, the highest limit of his damages is the whole extent of his loss and that loss is measured by the money which was in his pocket . . .

In *Doyle* v. *Olby (Ironmongers) Ltd*[88] the Court of Appeal cited this statement with approval and pointed out that the plaintiff in a fraud case may recover for consequential "out of pocket" losses—in that case, money wasted trying to run a business which the fraud led him to buy but which was not in fact viable.

In *East* v. *Maurer*[89] the defendants owned two hair salons in Bournemouth. The plaintiff agreed to buy one of them for £20,000 after the defendant had stated that he would be opening another salon abroad and had no intention of working at the other salon in Bournemouth save in cases such as staff shortages caused by illness. This was untrue and he in fact worked full-time at the other Bournemouth salon. The plaintiffs found the business at the salon they had bought fell away very rapidly and, though they worked hard and made various investments in new equipment, they did not manage to make it profitable. Ultimately they sold the salon for £7,500. The court of first instance found that the defendant had committed fraud. The Court of Appeal held that the out-of-pocket losses could include the profit which the plaintiffs would have made if they had not bought the business which was the subject of the fraud but had bought another business of a similar kind in the same area. The plaintiffs should not, however, be awarded the profits they would have made if the false information they had been given was in fact true.

(3) Misleading advertising

In all the systems, additional controls have been placed on false or misleading advertising. These may take the form of criminal prohibitions, as with the English Trade Descriptions Act 1968 and Consumer Protection Act 1987, or operate via competition law:

UWG (Law against Unfair Competition) **3.G.36.**

§ 1: Any person who, in the course of business activity and for purposes of competition, commits acts which offend good morals, may be enjoined and held liable in damages.

Note
Under § 3 UWG misleading advertising is included among "acts which offend good morals". § 13a UWG gives buyers who were induced by misleading advertising the right to rescind the contract. § 13 VI No.1 UWG also gives the buyer a right to damages where

[86] RGZ 103, 154 (160).
[87] [1903] Ch. 546, 554.
[88] [1969] 2 QB 158.
[89] [1991] 2 All ER 733.

the advertiser knew that the statements were misleading.

Typically these laws take a broad definition of the type of statements which may mislead consumers:

Act of 27 December 1973 **3.F.37.**

Art. 44.1: Any advertisement comprising, in any form whatever, any representation, indication or appearance which is false or liable to mislead shall be prohibited where such representation, indication or appearance relates to one or more of the following: the existence, nature, composition, essential qualities, level of useful constituents, type, origin, quantity, manner and date of manufacture, properties, price or conditions of sale of goods or services forming the subject-matter of the advertisement, the conditions in which they are to be used, the results which may be expected from using them, the purpose for which or methods by which they are to be sold or provided as services, the scope of the obligations assumed by the advertiser or the identity, qualifications or capabilities of the manufacturer, of the retailers, of the promoters or of the providers thereof.

Note

Does this enactment set a higher standard for statements made to consumers? See Cass. crim., 21 May 1984:[90] advertisement showing suitcase being run over by a bulldozer not likely to mislead consumers as to their strength: "One mustn't treat consumers as imbeciles".[91]

In Germany, statute also provides relief to consumers in some cases where misleading statements have been made by the vendor of a product.

Misleading advertising is now the subject of an EC Directive, 84/450.[92] Article 4(1) obliges Member States to "ensure that adequate and effective means exist for the control of misleading advertising in the interests of consumers as well as competitors and the general public", and goes on to provide that persons or organisations regarded under national law as having a legitimate interest in prohibiting misleading advertising shall be enabled to bring proceedings, including to stop the use of the advertisements.[93]

3.2.3. MISTAKE

3.2.3.A. MISTAKE IN GENERAL

This section deals with a variety of situations which have in common the fact that one or both parties have entered the contract under some "mistake", using that word in the broadest sense—some misapprehension about the subject matter of the contract or the circumstances, or as to the terms of the contract. It is important to note that there may be a mistake in this broad sense even if the case would not be dealt with by the relevant

---

[90] RTD. com. 1985.379
[91] Malaurie and Aynès, para. 414, note 4.
[92] [1984] OJ L250/17.
[93] For an account of this and other attempts at EC legislation in this area, see S. Weatherill, *EC Consumer Law and Policy* (London: Longman, 1997), chapter 6.

legal system under that rubric. As we will see, sometimes relief for "mistake" will be given on some other ground and sometimes relief will be refused altogether even though one or both parties have made a mistake.

Principles of European Contract Law   **3.PECL.38.**

Article 4:103: *Fundamental Mistake as to Facts or Law*

    (1) A party may avoid a contract for mistake of fact or law existing when the contract was concluded if:

        (a) (i) the mistake was caused by information given by the other party; or

             (ii) the other party knew or ought to have known of the mistake and it was contrary to good faith and fair dealing to leave the mistaken party in error; or

             (iii) the other party made the same mistake,

    and

        (b) the other party knew or ought to have known that the mistaken party, had it known the truth, would not have entered the contract or would have done so only on fundamentally different terms.

    (2) However a party may not avoid the contract if:

        (a) in the circumstances its mistake was inexcusable, or

        (b) the risk of the mistake was assumed, or in the circumstances should be borne, by it.

Article 4:104: *Inaccuracy in Communication*

    An inaccuracy in the expression or transmission of a statement is to be treated as a mistake of the person which made or sent the statement and Article 4:103 applies.

In addition to English, French and German law, this section considers Dutch law which has a different approach from that of the others.

    Each of the four systems has a doctrine of mistake which plays a central role in such situations. The three civil codes have articles on mistake:

Code civil   **3.F.39.**

Article 1109: There is no valid consent if the consent was only given as the result of error, was extorted by violence or was the result of fraud.

Article 1110: Error is a cause of nullity of an agreement only when it goes to the very substance of the object of the agreement.

              It is not a ground of nullity when it relates only to the person with whom a party intends to contract, unless the consideration of that person was the principal purpose of the agreement.

Article 1117: An agreement entered into as the result of error, violence or fraud is not absolutely void; there is merely an action for nullity or for rescission in accordance with Section VII of chapter V of the present title.

BGB   **3.G.40.**

§ 119: (1) A person who, when making a declaration of intention, is in error as to its content, or did not intend to make a declaration of such content at all, may avoid the declaration if it

344

may be assumed that he would not have made it with knowledge of the facts and with reasonable appreciation of the situation.

(2) An error as to those characteristics of a person or thing which are regarded in business as essential is regarded in the same way as an error as to the content of a declaration.

§ 122: (1) If a declaration of intent is void under § 118, or avoided under §§ 119, 120, the declarant shall, if the declaration was required to be made to another party, compensate that party, or otherwise any third party, for the damage which the other party has sustained by relying on the validity of the declaration, not, however, beyond the value of the interest which the other or the third party has in the validity of the declaration.

(2) The obligation to compensate does not arise if the injured party knew the ground of the nullity or rescission or did not know of it due to negligence (should have known of it).

BW   3.NL.41.

Article 6:228: 1. A contract which has been entered into under the influence of error and which would not have been entered into had there been a correct assessment of the facts, can be annulled:

a.   if the error is imputable to information given by the other party, unless the other party could assume that the contract would have been entered into even without this information;

b. if the other party, in view of what he knew or ought to know regarding the error, should have informed the party in error;

c.   if the other party in entering into the contract has based himself on the same incorrect assumption as the party in error, unless the other party, even if there had been a correct assessment of the facts, would not have had to understand that the party in error would therefore be prevented from entering into the contract.

2. The annulment cannot be based on an error as to an exclusively future fact or an error for which, given the nature of the contract, common opinion or the circumstances of the case, the party in error should remain accountable.

English law too recognizes "mistake", but it divides mistake up into several categories, each with different rules: *unilateral* mistake, where one party enters the contract under a misapprehension; *common* mistake, where the parties share the misapprehension; and *mutual* mistake, where the parties simply misunderstand one another's proposals—what on the continent is often referred to as *dissensus*. The relevant cases will be excerpted or described in the sections that follow.

There are very significant differences even between the civil law doctrines. For example, the French Code Civil and, to a lesser extent, the BW make it clear that the mistake must be serious if the contract is to be annulled, whereas the German BGB contains no such restriction. However, the liberality of § 119 is counterbalanced by § 122, under which the avoiding party may have to compensate the other for his reliance losses.

There are even greater differences between the civil law doctrines and the common law. The doctrines of mistake in English law have a very narrow application. While the English rules concerning mistakes and misunderstandings about what are the terms of the contract apply in a reasonably broad fashion[94] in relation to other mistakes, such as mistakes

---

[94] For details see section 3.2.3.B, *infra* at 347.

as to the qualities of the subject matter or the circumstances surrounding the contract, the doctrines are confined to cases in which the mistake was shared by the parties.[95] However, English law has a highly developed doctrine of *misrepresentation*. This is a development of the doctrine of fraud and permits a party to avoid a contract when she has been misled by what the other party has told her, even if the other party acted without fault. In practice this covers many of the cases which are dealt with as mistake on the continent.

One major difference we noted earlier. A mere failure to disclose information cannot amount to fraud or misrepresentation in English law. The combination of this rule and the fact that mistakes as to the subject matter are relevant in English law only if they are shared[96] means that English law is very unlikely to give relief when one party has entered a contract under a self-induced misapprehension (even if it is excusable) as to the subject matter or the circumstances and the other party does not make the same mistake.

This difference does not seem to be just the result of technique, but also to reflect the differences mentioned in the introduction to this section.[98] Common law places great emphasis on the appearance of agreement, in order to protect the reasonable expectations of the other party. We shall see that it tends to confine relief to situations in which the other party's beliefs were not reasonable or where to some extent he himself caused the misapprehension. Continental systems have traditionally placed more emphasis on the will of the contracting party and are sometimes prepared to give relief when the resulting contract does not reflect what the party willed, though this liberality may be counterbalanced by greater willingness to award damages—on a delictual or other basis—to a party who loses as a result of a mistake which was the other party's fault, or which was not the first party's fault.

The comparison of the different laws is made even more difficult by the already mentioned fact that, in each system, situations which fall within the general heading of "mistake" are actually dealt with not just by doctrines of mistake and—in English law—misrepresentation but by other doctrines also. We shall see that there is a complex interplay involving, for example, rules of *objet*, *cause*, impossibility, *culpa in contrahendo*, offer and acceptance, interpretation, and responsibility for defects. This makes it essential to adopt a functional approach, in which we take characteristic situations rather than doctrines as our starting point.

We will start by considering cases in which there is, broadly speaking, some kind of communication problem between the parties so that one party is under a misapprehension as to what he or the other is agreeing to (**3.2.3.B.**). Then we consider the related case in which a party is under a mistake as to the identity or attributes of the other party (**3.2.3.C.**). Thirdly (**3.2.3.D.**), we will turn to look at cases where the misapprehension relates to other aspects of the subject matter or the circumstances. For that purpose, it is helpful to divide up situations according to how the misapprehension arose and the state of mind of the other party. We therefore consider cases of (i) shared mistake (ii) induced mistake and (iii) self-induced mistake.

---

[95] See section 3.2.3.D, *infra* at 367.
[96] *Infra*, at 384.
[98] *Supra*, at 333 ff.

3.2.3.B. MISTAKES AND MISUNDERSTANDINGS AS TO THE TERMS

In this section we consider two types of case: first, those in which there is some kind of misunderstanding as to what the terms of the contract are. Under 1(a) we consider cases in which the parties agree on the same thing, but use the wrong words to express their agreement, and under (1)(b), cases in which they appear to agree but their agreement is only apparent, not real. Secondly, we consider cases where one party appears to agree to contractual terms to which she does not in fact mean to agree.

In English, French and German law there is some uncertainty over how far any of the cases are to be dealt with under the rubric of mistake, and how far by a combination of the rules of offer and acceptance and of interpretation. This is most clear in the first category, misunderstandings.

(1) Misunderstandings as to the terms of the Contract

(a) Shared misunderstanding as to the meaning of the words used in the Contract

What if both parties are under the same misapprehension as to the meaning of their contract? For the continental systems this is really a case of interpretation of the agreement. In French law, Code civil Article 1156 will apply:

Code civil   **3.F.42.**

Article 1156: In [interpreting] agreements the common intention of the parties should be sought, rather than taking the literal meaning of the terms agreed.

RG, 8 June 1920 II (Ziv.)[99]   **3.G.43.**

COMMON INTENTION

Shark meat

Where the parties are agreed on a particular obligation but use the wrong word to describe it, their common intention will prevail.

Facts: On 18 November 1916 the defendant sold the plaintiff approximately 214 barrels of "*haakjöringsköd*" shipped ex steamship *Jessica* at 4.30 marks per kilo cif Hamburg net cash against bill of lading and insurance policy. At the end of November the plaintiff paid the defendant, on delivery of the documents, the purchase price calculated in the provisional invoices. Upon arrival in Hamburg, the goods were distrained upon, and shortly thereafter taken over, by Zentral-Einkaufsgesellschaft mbH of Berlin. The plaintiff asserted that the goods had been sold to it as whale meat, whereas they were shark meat. As whale meat, they would not have been subject to distraint. It claimed that the defendant, which had delivered goods not in conformity with the contract, was consequently liable to reimburse to it the difference between the purchase price and the considerably lower price paid by the Zentral-Einkaufsgesellschaft upon taking over the goods. It sought payment of 47,515.90 DM. . . .

Held: The Landgericht (Regional Court) held that there was a binding contract for the sale of whale meat and that the plaintiff could therefore claim the difference in price. The plaintiff's appeal to the Oberlandesgericht (Higher Regional Court) was rejected, as was his further appeal to the *Reichsgericht*.

---

[99] RGZ 99.147.

Judgment: On those grounds:

As the Oberlandesgericht (Higher Regional Court) rightly found, both parties erroneously assumed, upon the conclusion of the contract of 18 November 1916, that the goods constituting the subject-matter of the contract, and specified therein—namely, 214 barrels of haakjöringsköd loaded on board the steamship *Jessica*—were whale meat, whereas in reality they were shark meat and, as such, correctly described by the Norwegian word "haakjöringsköd", the meaning of which the parties did not know. However, that finding does not justify the view that what had been sold, namely haakjöringsköd, was also what had been delivered, and that it was open to the plaintiff, following delivery to it of the goods in the form of the handing over of the bill of lading, to avoid the contract under § 119 II BGB on account of mistake as to the essential commercial characteristics of the specific goods sold. On the contrary, it follows from that finding that both of the parties wished to contract in respect of whale meat, but that, in stating their contractual intention, they had erroneously used the term "haakjöringsköd", which did not correspond to that intention. Consequently, the legal relationship existing between them must be assessed in the same way as if they had used the expression "whale meat", which did reflect their intention (RGZ 61, 265). Accordingly, what was to be delivered under the contract was whale meat, and the plaintiff, having received delivery of shark meat, was constrained to seek the remedies provided for in §§ 459ff. BGB (RGZ 61, 171). This is because the goods delivered did not possess the characteristic of being whale meat, and even though that characteristic was not, perhaps, "warranted" within the meaning of § 459 II BGB, it was nevertheless so essential that its absence constituted a material defect within the meaning of § 459 I BGB. Thus the plaintiff was justified in avoiding the contract and it is consequently entitled to claim from the defendant a sum—the amount of which remains to be determined—equivalent to the purchase price paid to the defendant less the price allowed to it by the Zentral-Einkaufsgesellschaft upon the goods being taken over by the latter (see §§ 467, 346 ff. BGB)

Notes

(1) Although "*haakjöringsköd*" meant shark meat, the Reichsgericht upheld the parties' shared, but mistaken, understanding that it meant whale meat. On the facts of the case therefore the defendants had failed to deliver whale meat and were liable to pay damages under the law of sale (§§ 459 BGB *et seq.*)The amount of damages here was the difference between the contract price and the price paid by the state board which had seized the meat—during the First World War.

(2) This case demonstrates clearly the persistence after the enactment of the BGB of the older principle of *falsa demonstratio non nocet*—"a false description does not vitiate if the thing or person has been sufficiently described".

The result in English law appears to be the same. Even though it normally insists on an objective stance, it will not insist on upholding the letter of the contract against what the parties really meant. This is clearest with written documents, which can be "rectified". Rectification is a remedy usually used when the parties have reached an agreement and have then incorporated it into a written document, but by mistake the written document does not record accurately what they agreed. In order to protect themselves for the future—for example, if the mistake is in a lease, which might be assigned to another tenant who would not know what the original agreement was—, a party may apply to the court for correction, or *rectification* of the document.[100] However, the English Court of

---

[100] See Treitel, *Contract* at 296–301.

Appeal has held that the fact that each party had the same intention is irrelevant if neither had disclosed this to the other: *New Hampshire Ins. Co* v. *MGN Ltd.*[101]

Principles of European Contract Law   **3.PECL.44.**

Article 5:101: *General Rules of Interpretation*
   (1) A contract is to be interpreted according to the common intention of the parties
   even if this differs from the literal meaning of the words.

(b) Misunderstandings/dissensus/mutual mistake

Court of Exchequer   **3.E.45.**

Raffles v. *Wichelhaus*[102]

UNRESOLVABLE AMBIGUITY PREVENTS CONTRACT

The Peerless

*Where the parties to an agreement each hold equally reasonable but different understandings as to a
term of the contract, no binding contract will come into existence.*

Facts: See the report.

Report:
Declaration. For that it was agreed between the plaintiff and the defendants to wit, at Liverpool,
that the plaintiff should sell to the defendants, and the defendants buy of the plaintiff, certain
goods, to wit, 125 bales of Surat cotton, guaranteed middling fair merchant's Dhollorah, to arrive
ex "Peerless" from Bombay; and that the cotton should be taken from the quay, and that the defendants would pay the plaintiff for the same at a certain rate, to wit, at the rate of 17'/4d per pound,
within a certain time then agreed upon the arrival of the said goods in England. Averments: that
the said goods did arrive by the said ship from Bombay in England to wit, at Liverpool, and the
plaintiff was then and there ready, and willing and offered to deliver the said goods to the defendants, &c. Breach: that the defendants refused to accept the said goods or pay the plaintiff for them.

   Plea. That the said ship mentioned in the said agreement was meant and intended by the defendants to be the ship called the "Peerless", which sailed from Bombay, to wit, in October; and that the
plaintiff was not ready and willing and did not offer to deliver to the defendants any bales of cotton which arrived by the last mentioned ship, but instead thereof was only ready and willing and
offered to deliver to the defendants 125 bales of Surat cotton which arrived by another and different ship, which was also called the "Peerless", and which sailed from Bombay, to wit in December.

Demurrer,[103] and joinder therein.
Milward [counsel for plaintiff], in support of the demurrer. The contract was for the sale of a number of bales or cotton of a particular description, which the plaintiff was ready to deliver. It is

---

[101] *The Times*, 25 July 1995.
[102] (1864) 2 H & C 906.
[103] A "demurrer" was a form of pleading by which one party responded to the other's case by saying that,
even if what the other party alleged were true, it would not give him a cause of action or have the legal effect he
claimed.

349

immaterial by what ship the cotton was to arrive, so that it was a ship called the "Peerless". The words "to arrive ex 'Peerless'," only mean than if the vessel is lost on the voyage, the contract is to be at an end. [POLLOCK CB. It would be a question for the jury whether both parties meant the same ship called the "Peerless".] That would be so if the contract was for the sale of a ship called the "Peerless"; but it is for the sale of cotton on board a ship of that name. [POLLOCK CB. The defendant only bought that cotton which was to arrive by a particular ship. It may as well be said, that if there is a contract for the purchase of certain goods in warehouse A, that is satisfied by the delivery of goods of the same description in warehouse B.] In that case there would be goods in both warehouses; here it does not appear that the plaintiff had any goods on board the other "Peerless". [MARTIN B. It is imposing on the defendant a contract different from that which he entered into. POLLOCK CB. It is like a contract for the purchase of wine coming from a particular estate in France or Spain, where there are two estates of that name.] The defendant has no right to contradict by parol evidence a written contract good upon the face of it. He does not impute misrepresentation or fraud, but only says that he fancied the ship was a different one. Intention is of no avail, unless stated at the time of the contract. [POLLOCK CB. One vessel sailed in October and the other in December.] The time of sailing is no part of the contract.

Mellish [opposing counsel] (Cohen with him), in support of the plea. There is nothing on the face of the contract to shew that any particular ship called the "Peerless" was meant; but the moment it appears that two ships called the "Peerless" were about to sail from Bombay there is a latent ambiguity, and parol evidence may be given for the purpose of shewing that the defendant meant one "Peerless" and the plaintiff another. That being so, there was no consensus ad idem, and therefore no binding contract. He was then stopped by the Court.

Per Curiam [The Court]: There must be judgment for the defendants.

Notes

(1) There is in fact a good deal of debate over the exact ground on which this case was decided, as the court did not give reasons. The court did not accept the seller's argument that the mistake was of no relevance; it simply decided that "parol evidence"—i.e. evidence from outside the document—could be admitted to see what the intention was. If the parties meant the same ship, the contract would be for cotton from that ship; if they meant different ships, then presumably the court thought there would be no contract because, as counsel for the defendants argues, there would be no *consensus ad idem*. That suggests that the court was thinking that a subjective *consensus ad idem* was needed for a contract; but, as we shall see in more detail later, this is not the approach now taken by common law, which looks primarily at the objective appearance of agreement.[104]

(2) Even though common law now takes an objective approach, it seems the result would be that there was no contract. Each party takes a different view of which ship was meant; and, if neither was unreasonable, there is no reason to prefer one party's view to the other. The contract is too ambiguous to be enforced.

(3) The case also suggests the fluidity of the borderline between mistake and other doctrines. English textbooks usually deal with this case under the rubric of mistake; but it is frequently pointed out that the contract is simply void for uncertainty.[105]

Dutch law would deal with such a case in the same way as English law:

---

[104] See Gilmore, *The Death of Contract* (Columbus, Ohio: Ohio State Univ. Press, 1974) at 35–44.
[105] See e.g. Treitel, *Contract* at 282.

BW   **3.NL.46.**

Article 3:33: A juridical act requires an intention to produce juridical effects, which intention has manifested itself by a declaration.

Article 3:35: The absence of intention in a declaration cannot be invoked against a person who has interpreted another's declaration or conduct in conformity with the sense which he could reasonably attribute to it in the circumstances, as a declaration of a particular tenor made to him by that other person.

Applying these Articles, if neither party's view was unreasonable, there is no reason to permit one party to rely on what he understood by the other's declaration, so there is no contract.

Cass. civ.1re, 28 November 1973[106]   **3.F.47.**

FAILURE TO AGREE PRICE PREVENTS CONTRACT

Bottle-openers

A contract of sale will not come into existence unless a price for the contract has been agreed.

Facts: The sellers intended to sell bottle-openers at 550 Francs per thousand, the buyers to buy at 55 Francs per thousand. The buyers refused to pay the higher price.

Held: The lower court held the buyers liable but the Cour de cassation referred the case back for re-hearing.

Judgment: THE COURT: *On the first branch of the appeal ground*:—Under Article 7 of the Law of 20 April 1810 applicable to the case;—Whereas the Régie communale des Sources Nessel has been sued by Messrs Eurogadget for payment in respect of 60 000 bottle openers which, according to the plaintiff, were sold to the defendant at a price of 0.55 francs each, i.e. 550 francs per thousand.
—Whereas the defendant asserted that its consent had been vitiated by an error in respect of the basic price agreed, and contended that the contract should be declared void; as it was nevertheless ordered to pay the sum claimed from it, on the ground, in particular, that an error as to the price cannot be relied on in support of a plea that the contract should be annulled.
—Whereas however, in the claims advanced by it in the appeal proceedings, the Régie maintained that it had been induced into the erroneous belief that the agreed price was 55 francs per thousand and that a "fundamental misunderstanding" had thus arisen between the parties;
—Whereas in not dealing with that ground, the appellate court (cour d'appel, Colmar, 11th Chamber, 23 December 1971) failed to fulfil the requirements of the abovementioned provision.
   On those grounds, the Court sets aside the contested judgment and refers the case back to the cour d'appel de Colmar for a rehearing before a differently composed bench.

From the Note
Speaking of error on the identity of the object, Planiol said: "There is no consent because there is no agreement; it is a misunderstanding not a contract (*Traité élémentaire de droit civil*, Vol. 2, para. 1052) . . .
(1) This judgment does not question in the least what authors traditionally teach and what the Cour de cassation has traditionally admitted without question, that an error of value has no effect

---

[106] D. 1975.21 annotated by R. Rodière.

on the validity of a contract save in those very limited circumstances when the law allows a party to demand rescission on the ground of *lésion*.[107]

This judgment does not contradict that. The error here related to the chose, on the performance due from the party who under the agreement was the buyer . . .

(2) Our judgment does not involve art. 1110 Code civil and, even if the Court does not point to the text which the judges should base their decision on, it in fact based its censure not on art. 1110 but on art 1108 Code civil:

> "Four conditions are needed for a valid agreement: The consent of the party who undertakes an obligation (. . .)"

Before enquiring into the validity of consent one must ask whether it existed (Planiol, *op. cit.*, para. 1047; Carbonnier, para. 12). Also Planiol, before noting that there are immaterial errors, recognises, in addition to the error envisaged by art. 1110 which affects the validity of consent, that there may be *erreurs-obstacles* which mean that there is no consent (see also L. Josserand, *Cours de droit civil positif*, vol. 2, para. 61). . .

BGB **3.G.48.**

§ 155: If the parties to a contract which they regard as concluded have in fact not agreed upon a point upon which an agreement should have been arrived at, that which is agreed upon is valid if it may be assumed that the contract would have been concluded without a settlement of the point.

See the *Two sellers* case.[108]

Notes

(1) The *Tartaric Acid* case was a case of "total dissensus" beyond that contemplated in § 155 BGB. The latter allows enforcement of the contract only where the parties had reached agreement on the *essentialia negotii*. This was clearly not the case here. The Reichsgericht held that the parties had, on an objective interpretation, been at cross-purposes in their offers and that no contract had therefore been formed between the parties.

(2) This case is also a leading case on *culpa in contrahendo*. The plaintiffs were allowed to recover damages for losses suffered in reliance upon the existence of a contract, since the defendants were found to have been more at fault for the misunderstanding which arose.

(3) How much difference to the outcome of such cases does it make whether a subjective or an objective approach is taken? It may make a difference when one party's interpretation was objectively unreasonable. In cases in which each party's interpretation was equally reasonable, there is mutual misunderstanding and there is no contract whichever approach is taken.

The dissensus situation does not seem to be discussed in PECL or the Unidroit Principles but it is thought that the result would be same as in the national laws: no contract would be formed.

---

[107] See section 3.3.3, *infra* at 455.
[108] **2.G.71**, *supra* at 250.

(2) Mistake by one party

At this point the difference between the legal systems remarked on in the introduction to this section becomes more significant. In French law, the starting point is that the creation of the contract requires an agreement in a subjective sense—the parties must actually intend the same thing. In English law this is not required: it suffices that one party reasonably thinks that the other party has agreed. A classic statement of the "objective principle" is that of Blackburn J in *Smith* v. *Hughes*:[109]

> If whatever a man's real intention may be, he so conducts himself that a reasonable man would believe that he was assenting to the terms proposed by the other party, and that other party upon that belief enters into the contract with him, the man thus conducting himself would be equally bound as if he had intended to agree to the other party's terms.

Compare BW Article 3:35.[110]

German law seems to adopt an intermediate position, favouring a complex solution over the "bright line rule" of English law. As has been seen[111] there seems to be a tension in the BGB between objective and subjective standards of interpretation. This is, however, largely resolved in favour of the objective approach. Thus, even under § 133 BGB, the "intention" to be established is the communicated intention. Accordingly, in legal writing and in the cases, the declaration theory predominates over the will theory in relation to the formation and interpretation of contracts. This reliance-based liability may seem to be undercut, even if only in a qualified manner, by the relatively wide possibility of avoiding for mistake contracts held—objectively—to have been formed. But the objectivist position is again partially restored by obliging the party seeking avoidance of the contract under § 119 BGB to pay reliance damages to the other party under § 122 BGB, at least where the latter was unaware of the mistake.[112]

PECL seems to take an objective approach. First, intention is to be judged objectively:

Principles of European Contract Law   **3.PECL.49.**

Article 2:102: *Intention.* The intention of a party to be legally bound by contract is to be determined from the party's statements or conduct as they were reasonably understood by the other party.

Secondly, Articles 4:103 and 4:104,[113] which between them apply to this situation, limit relief to cases in which

(a)   (i) the mistake was caused by information given by the other party; or
        (ii) the other party knew or ought to have known of the mistake and it was contrary to good faith and fair dealing to leave the mistaken party in error; or
        (iii) the other party made the same mistake . . .

---

[109] (1871) LR 6 QB 597 at 607. See **3.E.78**, *infra* at 411.
[110] *Supra*, at 351.
[111] *Supra*, at 335.
[112] For analysis of these rules in terms of the allocation of risk, see *Alternativ Kommentar zum Bürgerlichen Gesetzbuch* (Neuwied: Luchterhand, 1987) under §119 BGB, para. 1–6.
[113] *Supra*, at 344.

In this section, we focus on the following situations:

(a) cases in which one party had no intention of contracting at all, for example the case of the person who visits a wine auction in Trier, waves to a friend and finds that by local custom his wave indicated that he was bidding on the wine being auctioned and that the wine in question has been "knocked down" to him;

(b) (i) "Slips of the pen"—for example you write £103 when you meant £130; and
(ii) cases where you used the wrong word—for example the tourist in Cologne who orders a "*halver Hahn*", meaning thereby a half chicken, when in Cologne a "*halver Hahn*" is a kind of cheese sandwich.

We will see that, whilst two situations dealt with under (b) are generally treated in the same way, a distinction is drawn between them in German law. Cases in which you sign a document which omits or includes terms which you thought would be included or not included are also dealt with in the same way as the cases under (b).

(a) The Mistaken Party did Not Intend to Enter Any Transaction at All: The Trier Wine Auction Case

It follows from what was stated in (a) above that in the *Trier Wine Auction* situation, no contract would result in French law, as there was no intention to enter any legal act. In contrast, in English law, provided the auctioneer reasonably believed that the buyer was bidding on the wine and accepted the bid in that belief, there would be a contract; and there would probably be no relief even on the ground of mistake, since the rules of English law on mistakes of this kind seem simply to be restatements of the original position: that what reasonably appears to the other party to be an offer or acceptance, and which the other believes to be such, is binding. This is illustrated by the cases on offer and acceptance such as *Kleinwort Benson Ltd* v. *Malaysia Mining Corp Bd*[114] and *Carlill* v. *Carbolic Smoke Ball Company*,[115] which look almost exclusively at what the parties said rather than what they may have intended to say.[116]

The *Trier Wine Auction* case is a famous "textbook" example in Germany. Commentators originally took the position that there was no subjective intention to perform a juristic act (*Erklärungsbewusstsein*) and therefore no legally significant declaration of intention which could go to constitute a contract. Avoidance would not be an issue in this case, since there is in effect nothing to avoid. Furthermore there would be no obligation on the "mistaken" party to make compensation under § 122 BGB.

However, recent doctrine and case-law have taken a more objective approach:

[114] [1989] 1 WLR 179; **1.E.72**, *supra* at 102.
[115] [1893] 1 QB 256; **1.E.103**, *supra* at 142.
[116] *Supra*, at 124. It is also illustrated by a parody of English law based on another famous parody of English manners, *Alice in Wonderland* by Lewis Carroll (the pen-name of the mathematician C.L.Dodgson): you may like to look at this in "A Lawyer's Alice" by Williams, 12 Cambridge LJ 171, 171–172.

BGH, 7 June 1984[117]   3.G.50.

CONTRACT MAY ARISE WHERE SUBJECTIVE INTENTION IS ABSENT

The bank guarantee

To form a valid contract, it does not matter whether the party communicating an intention to be bound by a contract actually had the will to make, or was even conscious of making, a declaration aimed at a legal transaction.

Facts: A savings bank wrote to the plaintiffs, a firm of steel contractors, stating that it had undertaken to guarantee the debts of one of the firm's customers. The firm subsequently sought to enforce the guarantee on the basis that a contract had been formed. The defendant bank admitted that by stating that it had given a guarantee it had made an incorrect statement of fact, but it claimed that it had had no subjective intention to perform a juristic act in sending the letter, only to give a representation of factual circumstances.

Held: The BGH held that the letter could be understood objectively as constituting the undertaking itself, and that a contract had been formed. Normally the defendants could have sought avoidance for mistake under § 119 I BGB and they would also have been liable to pay the plaintiffs reliance damages under § 122 BGB. However, the Court held that they had lost this right because of undue delay in claiming it.

Judgment (references omitted):
(a) This present Senate, starting from the considerations of the Second Civil Senate, has arrived at the conclusion that, in order for the obligation to provide a guarantee to be valid, it does not matter whether or not those representing the defendant, when signing and despatching their letter of 8 September 1981, actually had the will to make, or were even conscious of making, a declaration aimed at a legal transaction. In conformity with the view expressed by Bydlinski (JZ 1975, 1) and Kramer (*MünchKomm* § 119 Rdn. 81 *et seq.*), the following considerations are decisive for this result. The concept of declaration of intention (*Willenserklärung*) is not defined in §§ 116 *et seq.* BGB. More particularly, no argument against the view of this Court can be found in the wording of § 119 BGB. The fact that a party did not want to make "a declaration of this content" is not only true for a party which intended a legal transaction with a different content, but also for a party which did not want to make any declaration aimed at a legal transaction. It cannot be concluded from § 118 BGB that not being conscious of making a declaration (or the lack of will to do business) will always make a declaration void without any need for a rescission. If a party consciously makes a declaration, but without wanting to be bound, while expecting that this would be recognized (as is required by § 118 BGB), voidness corresponds with this party's intention. There is no need to grant to this party a choice, i.e. either to uphold the declaration with corresponding duties and rights, or to rescind this declaration under § 119 BGB. This situation cannot be compared to a declaration which was made without the awareness that it could be understood as constituting a legal transaction. Such a declaration is much closer to a declaration which is affected by a mistake, but which was aimed at a legal transaction. A party who declares to buy, but who actually means to sell, is in a situation very similar to that of a person who gives a signal which commonly indicates purchase, but who does not even think of buying. In both situations, it seems adequate to leave the choice to the declaring party, whether it wants to rescind under § 119 I BGB and compensate for reliance damage under § 122 BGB, or else to let this declaration stand and receive any counter-performance which might be due, and which might make the situation more profitable to him than a one-sided obligation to compensate for reliance damage.

This choice also does away with the concern that, without awareness of making a declaration, there is no self-determined shaping of one's freedom of contract, which cannot be replaced by a person's responsibility for his acts. The law on declarations of intention is not built on

[117] BGHZ 91.324.

355

self-determination by subjects of legal rights alone. In §§ 119, 157 BGB, it also protects the reliance of the recipient of the declaration, as well as certainty in trade, by binding the declaror to consequences which he had not intended, as well as—and this should be considered as equal—to legal consequences which this party was not conscious of instigating. By granting the declaror, who in both situations did not intend the legal consequences which were actually expressed by his declaration, the right to either destroy these consequences *ab initio* by way of rescission (§ 142 (1) BGB), or else to uphold them, the concept of self-determination is given sufficient consideration.

On the other hand, in cases where the awareness of making a declaration is lacking, a declaration of intention exists only if it can as such be attributed to the party who actually makes the declaration. In order for the declaration to be attributed to a party it is necessary that this party, if he had exercised the care which is necessary in social intercourse, could have realised, and avoided, that his declaration or conduct should have been understood by the recipient as a declaration of intention in accordance with good faith and with due regard to trade practice.[118]

(b) The Mistaken Party Intended to Enter a Contract but Stated the Terms He Intended Incorrectly ("Slips of the Pen" and the "Halver Hahn" Case)

Errors of this type are also known as communication errors. The party concerned fails to convert his intentions into the sign or formulation which he wished to use as a means of communication. He, for example, mistypes, misspells, enters relevant figures in the wrong column or misunderstands the terms which he uses. The consequences of such errors will vary depending on whether or not the other party was aware of the mistake.

(i) The Other Party is Aware of What was Actually Intended

It is easiest to start with the simple case in which you write offering to sell your hi-fi for £103, when you meant to write £130. If the other party knew that there had been an error and also what was meant—for example, if the other party knew you meant £130, but tried to take advantage of the slip by accepting your offer without pointing out the error—it is probable that, in all three systems, there would be a contract at £130.

In German law this case would be treated like one of *falsa demonstratio non nocet*—"false description does not vitiate if the thing is sufficiently described".[119] The other party was not misled and there is a good contract for £130. The situation seems not to be discussed in French law in either case-law or doctrine, but the result is probably the same: as a matter of interpretation it can be said that the parties had a common intention to deal at £130 and it would be bad faith for the non-mistaken party to try to argue that the price was less than this.

Queen's Bench **3.E.51.**
Hartog v. Colin & Shields[120]

BUYER MAY NOT ACCEPT OFFER HE KNOWS TO CONTAIN A MISTAKE

Hare skins

Where a party takes up an offer which he or she knows has been made in error, he or she will not be able to claim on the contract.

[118] Translation by G. Dannemann. Reproduced by kind permission of the translator.
[119] *Münchener Kommentar*, under §119 BGB, para. 49.
[120] [1939] 3 All ER 233.

Facts: The defendants offered to sell the plaintiff a quantity of Argentine hare skins at 10¼d per lb. This was an error for 10¼d per piece. In the trade, such skins were always sold by the piece; and there are about three pieces to the pound, so that the defendants' offer was the equivalent of 3¼d per piece, whereas three weeks earlier the quoted price had been 10¼d per piece. The plaintiff purported to accept the offer and, when the defendants refused to deliver, brought this action.

Held: The plaintiff's claim was dismissed.

Judgment: SINGLETON J: In this case, the plaintiff, a Belgian subject, claims damages against the defendants because he says they broke a contract into which they entered with him for the sale of Argentine hare skins. The defendants' answer to that claim is: "There really was no contract, because you knew that the document which went forward to you, in the form of an offer, contained a material mistake. You realised that, and you sought to take advantage of it."

Counsel for the defendants took upon himself the onus of satisfying me that the plaintiff knew that there was a mistake and sought to take advantage of that mistake. In other words, realising that there was a mistake, the plaintiff did that which James LJ in *Tamplin* v. *James* described as "snapping up the offer". It is important, I think, to realise that in the verbal negotiations which took place in this country, and in all the discussions there had ever been, the prices of Argentine hare skins had been discussed per piece, and later, when correspondence took place, the matter was always discussed at the price per piece, and never at a price per pound. . . .

I am satisfied . . . from the evidence given to me, that the plaintiff must have realised, and did in fact know, that a mistake had occurred. . . .

There was an absolute difference from anything which had gone before—a difference in the manner of quotation, in that the skins are offered per pound instead of per piece.

I am satisfied that it was a mistake on the part of the defendants or their servants which caused the offer to go forward in that way, and I am satisfied that anyone with any knowledge of the trade must have realised that there was a mistake. . . .

The offer was wrongly expressed, and the defendants by their evidence, and by the correspondence, have satisfied me that the plaintiff could not reasonably have supposed that that offer contained the offerers' real intention. Indeed, I am satisfied to the contrary. That means that there must be judgment for the defendants.

Notes

(1) "10¼d" and "10¾d" were English currency before decimalization ("d" means pence, from *denarii*).

(2) The judge seems to accept the argument that there was no contract; but in fact all that he had to decide was that there was no enforceable contract *at 10¾d per lb*. Whether there was in fact a binding contract at 10¾d per piece is unclear; but cases involving the equitable remedy of rectification suggest there was one. In addition to the cases discussed earlier in which the written document does not reflect the common agreement of the parties,[121] the remedy can also be used when the document does not reflect what one party intended and the other party knows this but does not point it out: *Thomas Bates & Son Ltd* v. *Wyndham's (Lingerie) Ltd*.[122] This presupposes that the underlying contract is valid.

It is conceiveable that the other party knows that you have made a slip, and again tries to take advantage by accepting the offer you appeared to make, without knowing what you meant—£113? £123? In English law there is no authority on this point but the

[121] *Supra*, at 348.
[122] [1981] 1 All ER 1077, CA.

probable result is that there is no contract: the other party cannot reasonably rely on what you have said but there is no other basis for determining the terms. Dutch law appears similar: see BW Article 3:35.[123] The same result would follow in French law simply on the basis that there was no consensus (compare the case in the next sub-section). In German law this point has not been fully clarified. What commentary there is prefers to dispose of the question under §§ 119, 122 II BGB.[124] Examples of such cases follow in the next sub-section.

Principles of European Contract Law   **3.PECL.52.**

Article 5:101: *General Rules of Interpretation*
(1) A contract is to be interpreted according to the common intention of the parties even if this differs from the literal meaning of the words.
(2) If it is established that one party intended the contract to have a particular meaning, and at the time of the conclusion of the contract the other party could not have been unaware of the first party's intention, the contract is to be interpreted in the way intended by the first party.
(. . .)

(ii) The Other Party is Unaware of the Mistake
It is in this case that the legal systems seem to differ considerably.

Cass. com., 15 February 1961[125]   **3.F.53.**

ERREUR OBSTACLE

Wine to Algiers

Where one party intends one price and the other another, the mistakes prevents there being an effective agreement and no contract is formed.

Facts: The parties were negotiating the sale of a large quantity of wine. Originally it was envisaged that the wine would be delivered at Cherchell but the buyers, Orazzi, refused this, and offered to share in the cost of transport to Algiers. The sellers, Tirat, demanded the sum of 60 francs per hectolitre. The buyers were not willing to pay this sum and sent a telegram intending to offer 30 francs per hectolitre but in fact offering 300 francs. The sellers accepted this, delivered the wine and billed the buyers accordingly and the buyers paid, but later they realised the mistake and demanded repayment. The cour d'appel of Montpellier gave judgment for the buyers and the sellers appealed, arguing (1) that the error was one of value not one of substance; (2) that the contract was valid until annulled, so that the buyers could not claim that the payment was invalid; and (3) that when the buyers paid the 300 francs they were accepting an offer from the sellers.

Held: The appeal was dismissed.

Judgment:—Whereas it is apparent from the statement of facts in the contested judgment (Montpellier, 16 October 1957) and from the introductory part thereof, Marius Tirat et Cie ("Tirat") was to deliver 2,000 hectolitres of Algerian wine FOB to the purchaser, Orazzi et Fils ("Orazzi"); as it was envisaged that delivery would take place at Cherchell, but this was refused by Orazzi which offered to share the cost of haulage from Cherchell to Algiers; this offer was set out

---

[123] *Supra* at 351.
[124] See *Münchener Kommentar*, § 122 BGB, para. 10.
[125] Bull. civ. III.91.

in a telegram agreeing to pay 300 francs a hectolitre; as after acceptance and delivery by Tirat, Orazzi claimed that the figure of 300 francs was the result of material error and that the true figure was 30 francs; accounts which were drawn up on the basis of the first figure were in the end reduced to 335,162 francs and Orazzi drew a bill of exchange on Tirat for that amount, which was dishonoured and protested.

—Whereas Tirat then sued the purchasers for damages for the loss caused by a bill of exchange improperly presented and then protested, whereupon Orazzi counter-claimed for payment of the bill; as subsequently, the court of first instance in its contested judgment recognised that a mistake had been made and dismissed the claim in the main proceedings and upheld Orazzi's counterclaim.

—Whereas the appellant challenges the judgment inasmuch as it held that the agreement as to haulage charges was invalid by reason of a substantial mistake, on the ground that it incorrectly showed the sum of 300 francs instead of 30 francs, whereas, it argues, first, a mistake as to value is not a material mistake and in any event the court failed to explain its reasoning concerning the claims made by Tirat on that point; as second, a voidable act remains valid until declared void by the court and there was consequently no legal basis for the bill of exchange, which was presented before any annulment and, finally, as it was possible to remedy the curable nullity arising from a mistake, the findings in the judgment establish that Orazzi had confirmed the contract by accepting without demur the agreement reached on the offer of 300 francs and the accounts presented.

—Whereas however, it is stated in the judgment that, for the reasons set out, the figure of 300 francs per hectolitre in Orazzi's telegram could only be the result of a material mistake; as Orazzi proposed or believed it was proposing 30 francs, that is to say half of what Tirat had asked for; there was no agreement as to the amount of the consideration; "that, since the parties' intentions differed as a result of a misunderstanding, it was not possible for an agreement to be formed"; as accordingly the Court, first, did not have to declare a contract void for a mistake as to the properties of its subject-matter and was not required to answer any arguments put forward on that point; as second, having found that no agreement had been concluded concerning the division of haulage costs, it could not find that there was no legal basis for the bill of exchange which was based on market terms and the abovementioned offer of 30 francs.

—Whereas finally, the last part of the plea based on confirmation of the correspondence between the parties, arising from the attitude subsequently adopted by Orazzi, was not raised in the grounds of Tirat's appeal, as inserted in the introductory parts; it is new, and it is a mixture of fact and law and, as such, inadmissible.

—Whereas no branch of the appeal ground can therefore be upheld.

On those grounds, the Court dismisses the appeal against the judgment of the cour d'appel, Montpellier, of 16 October 1957.

Notes

(1) Presumably the sellers should have been aware that the telegram from the buyers contained an error, as the sellers had already made an offer at 60 francs, one-fifth of the price offered in the telegram. However, nothing is made of this point and it seems that the result would have been the same even if the buyers had had no reason at all to suspect a mistake.

(2) This case seems to have been decided on the basis of *erreur-obstacle*, i.e. that the error prevented the formation of a contract, just as in the cases of *dissensus* discussed earlier. In practice, despite what Rodière wrote in his note of 1975,[126] French courts will often give relief in such cases on the basis of error as to the substance.[127]

---

[126] *Supra*, at 351.
[127] As to which see *infra*, at 367.

AVOIDANCE FOR MISTAKE AS TO CONTENT OF DECLARATION

Toilet paper

Where in a written statement of offer a technical term is incorrectly used the declaration of intention may be avoided; a claim for performance of the contract will not be upheld.

Facts: The defendant assistant principal of a girls' secondary school ordered from the plaintiff, as the school's representative, "25 Gros Rollen" (25 gross rolls) of toilet paper. In that connection, the defendant signed an order form filled out by the plaintiff's representatives, which contained, amongst other detailed provisions, the indication "Gros = 12×12". When the plaintiff sought to deliver the goods, the girls' school refused to accept the overwhelming majority of them. The plaintiff then claimed against the defendant and served a default summons on her, which she contested. In addition, she gave notice of avoidance of the transaction. She denied having been aware of the meaning of the quantitative term "Gros". Instead, she maintained that she had ordered only 25 double packs of toilet paper, which the school had, moreover, accepted and paid for. Admittedly, the term "Gros" had been specified when the order was placed. However, the representatives had referred to that term in the context of the measurement specification 12 x 12, relating to the manner of packaging.

Held: The plaintiff's claim for payment of the price of the toilet paper was unsuccessful.

Judgment:

Grounds . . .

The plaintiff has no claim against the defendant under § 179 BGB. It is true that the school represented by the defendant did not authorise the greater part of the transaction. However, the defendant is under no obligation to perform the contract, because it was effectively avoided by the defendant. In expressing her intention, the defendant committed an error consisting of what she actually said (§ 119 I BGB). On no account did she wish to buy $25 \times 12 \times 12 = 3,600$ rolls of toilet paper, merely 25 large (*große*) rolls. Although the plaintiff maintains that the defendant had known exactly what meaning was to be attached to her statement, that cannot be assumed as a fact. It runs totally counter to normal experience of life that a person representing a school which can only be described as a small institution should in one fell swoop order 3,600 rolls of toilet paper each containing 1,000 sheets—a quantity which would have met the school's requirements for a period of several years. Quite apart from the fact that this is scarcely conceivable for reasons relating to the budgetary accounts, which are normally compiled annually, the difficulty of storing such a quantity of goods alone necessitates the conclusion that there can be no question of any conscious intention to proceed in that manner. Nor does the argument that the defendant must, as a teacher, have been familiar with the meaning of the unit of quantity used necessarily indicate that she was aware of its meaning. Quite apart from the fact that it has not been established which subjects she taught, the quantitative term "Gros" is nowadays completely uncommon and obsolete, with the result that it can no longer be regarded as definitely falling within the ambit of the curriculum. Nor does the indication "Gros = 12×12" provide any clarification in that regard, since it does not necessarily enable the number of rolls to be identified but may quite easily be intended to signify other units of measurement, particularly having regard to the spelling mistakes made by the plaintiff's representatives on the order form.

---

[128] NJW 1979.721.

Notes

(1) § 119 I BGB does not require that the recipient of the mistaken declaration knows or has any reason to know of the mistake. Where he does not the declarant will have to compensate him under § 122 I BGB.[129] Having regard to the findings of the court in the above case it can be assumed that the seller of the toilet rolls did have reason to know of the mistake. Accordingly he would have been prevented from claiming reliance damages (§ 122 II BGB).

(2) The above judgment and the example of the man who ordered a *halver Hahn* in Cologne[130] are cases where the declarant clearly intended to make the declaration which they made, but were mistaken as to its meaning. German doctrine refers to this as an *Inhaltsirrtum* and it is specifically provided for in § 119 I BGB first alternative, which allows avoidance where a "person who is in error as to the content".

(3) By contrast where there is a "slip of the pen", such as occurred in the French "bottle-openers" case,[131] the declarant "did not intend to make a declaration with that content at all"(§ 119 I BGB, second alternative). This is referred to as an *Erklärungsirrtum* and it will equally lead to avoidance. A modern example is provided by OLG Hamm, 8 January 1993,[132] in which a slip in filling in a computerized version of a life insurance contract resulted in a sum which was intended to be paid as a single lump sum was stated to be payable annually.

Court of Appeal   **3.E.55.**

Centrovincial Estates plc v. *Merchant Investors Assurance Co Ltd*[133]

No relief for unilateral mistake once unambiguous offer is accepted

Current market rent

The offeror under a bilateral contract cannot withdraw an unambiguous offer, after it has been accepted in the manner contemplated by the offer, merely because he has made a mistake which the offeree neither knew nor could reasonably have known at the time when he accepted it.

Facts: The plaintiffs had let some floors of an office building to the Food, Drink and Tobacco Industry Training Board (FDTITB), which had in turn underlet one floor to the defendants at a rental of £68,320 per year. The underlease contained provisions for increasing the rent after four years to the then current market value; if the parties could not reach agreement on what this figure should be the matter would be referred to the assessment of an independent surveyor. Later FDTITB intended to surrender its lease so that the defendants would become direct tenants of the plaintiffs. A firm of solicitors, acting on behalf of both the plaintiffs and FDTITB, wrote to the defendants inviting the defendants to accept £65,000 as the current market value for the purpose of the review. The defendants wrote back agreeing. The solicitors then claimed that their letter had contained a mistake and the figure they had intended was £126,000.

It was disputed whether the defendants knew or ought to have known that the figure of £65,000 was a mistake. This could only be resolved by a full trial, but the plaintiffs sought a declaration that no agreement had been reached and asked for summary judgment (i.e. claimed that they were entitled to the declaration even without proving the defendant knew or should have known of the mistake).

---

[129] *Supra*, at 345.
[130] *Supra*, at 354.
[131] *Supra*, at 351.
[132] NJW 1993.2321; Markesinis, Lorenz and Dannemann, op. cit., at 199 and extracted at 246.
[133] [1983] Com. LR 158, CA.

361

Judgment: Slade LJ On the face of it, the letter of the 22nd June 1982 constituted a formal, unequivocal and unambiguous offer made to the defendants on behalf of the plaintiffs, with an intent to create legal relations, to agree that the "current market rental value" of the demised premises, for the purpose of sub-paragraph A of the rent review provision, was £65,000 per annum. On the face of it, the letter of the 23 June 1982 constituted a formal, unequivocal and unambiguous acceptance of that offer by the defendants. The plaintiffs' solicitors indeed assert that they erroneously inserted the figure of £65,000 in the letter of the 22 June 1982 in substitution for the figure of £126,000, which they had intended to insert; and like the learned Judge we are prepared to accept the truth of this assertion for the purpose of dealing with the present application. But in the absence of any proof, as yet, that the defendants either knew or ought reasonably to have known of the plaintiffs' error at the time when they purported to accept the plaintiffs' offer, why should the plaintiffs now be allowed to resile from that offer? It is a well-established principle of the English law of contract that an offer falls to be interpreted not subjectively by reference to what has actually passed through the mind of the offeror, but objectively, by reference to the interpretation which a reasonable man in the shoes of the offeree would place on the offer. It is an equally well-established principle that ordinarily an offer, when unequivocally accepted according to its precise terms, will give rise to a legally binding agreement as soon as acceptance is communicated to the offeror in the manner contemplated by the offer, and cannot thereafter be revoked without the consent of the other party. Accepting, as they do, that they have not yet proved that the defendants knew, or ought reasonably to have known, of their error at the relevant time, how can the plaintiffs assert that the defendants have no realistic hope of establishing an agreement of the relevant nature by virtue of the two letters of the 22 and 23 June 1982? Mr Richard Scott in answer has submitted an argument to the following effect. The "agreement" envisaged by sub-paragraphs A and B of the rent review provision is a genuine agreement, a real meeting of the minds. In the present case there was no real meeting of the parties' minds because of the plaintiffs' error. True it is that their intentions would have fallen to be judged objectively, according to their external manifestation, if the defendants had not only purported to accept the offer but had further altered their position as a result. However, so the argument runs, the general rule that the intentions of an offeror must be judged objectively is based on estoppel. Accordingly, if the person who has accepted the offer has not altered his position in reliance on the offer, no such estoppel arises. In the present case, it is submitted, the critical fact is that the figure of £65,000 was lower than the rent currently payable under the Lease immediately before the 25 December 1982. In these circumstances, it is said, the defendants in agreeing that figure, did not alter their position in any way. Because of sub-paragraph E of the rent review provision, the current rent of £68,320 would have continued to be payable after the 25 December 1982, notwithstanding the agreement. In all the circumstances, it is submitted, the plaintiffs, having proved their error at the relevant time, were at liberty to withdraw the offer contained in the letter of the 22 June 1982, even after it had been accepted, and they duly did so at the end of June 1982. We understand from the learned Judge's judgment that an argument on much the same lines was submitted to him on behalf of the plaintiffs and that, though he regarded it as novel and surprising, he was in the end convinced by it.

[SLADE LJ went on to explain that Mr Scott had accepted that this argument must fail if there was consideration for the agreement. As there was consideration, this concluded the question.]

Nevertheless, we should perhaps attempt to explain briefly (albeit *obiter*) why, quite apart from questions of consideration, we respectfully differ from the learned Judge on the question of mistake, as a matter of broad principle. The nature of the apparent contract concluded by the two letters of the 22 and 23 June 1982 is what is sometimes called a "bilateral contract". It was concluded

362

by (a) an offer by the plaintiffs to treat £65,000 as the "current market rental value" of the premises for the purpose of the Lease if the defendants would promise to accept that figure as that value, followed by (b) the giving of a promise by the defendants in those terms. Where the nature of an offer is to enter into a bilateral contract, the contract becomes binding when the offeree gives the requested promise to the promisor in the manner contemplated by the offer; the mutual promises alone will suffice to conclude the contract. In our opinion, . . . it is contrary to the well established principles of contract law to suggest that the offeror under a bilateral contract can withdraw an unambiguous offer, after it has been accepted in the manner contemplated by the offer, merely because he has made a mistake which the offeree neither knew nor could reasonably have known at the time when he accepted it. And in this context, provided only that the offeree has given sufficient consideration for the offeror's promise, it is nothing to the point that the offeree may not have changed his position beyond giving the promise requested of him. For these reasons we think that the plaintiffs' submissions based on mistake cannot, as matters stand, suffice to negative the existence of the apparent agreement of the parties to treat £65,000 as the current market rental value for the purpose of the Lease and to deprive the defendants of the right to defend this action on the basis of such agreement, though we are not, of course, saying that the plea of mistake as formulated in the statement of claim will not succeed at the trial.

. . . [We] have allowed this appeal and given the defendants unconditional leave to defend the action . . .

Notes

(1) Thus in English law a mistake in an offer or other contractual document is irrelevant where the other party had no reason to know of the mistake. This is an application of the objective principle i.e. the mistaken party is simply bound by what he said or wrote.

(2) Slade LJ's dictum suggests that an offeree may not be able to rely on an offer which he ought to know contains a mistake, even though he was not in fact aware of that. Actual decisions in England do not go so far: in fact the rectification cases[134] have refused relief in cases on unilateral mistake unless the other party had actual knowledge of the error, or suspected it and took deliberate steps to prevent the mistaken party from noticing his own error (*Commission for New Towns* v. *Cooper (Great Britain) Ltd*).[135] Canadian authority is more liberal, giving relief when the mistake should have been apparent: see *McMaster University* v. *Wilchar Construction Ltd.*[136]

(3) Occasionally, a party who has made such a mistake is given some relief in that the court may refuse to grant specific performance against him, even if it is one of the situations in which specific performance would normally be granted.[137] But the protection given to the mistaken party in this way is limited. First, there are many cases in which specific performance has been granted despite the mistake.[138] Secondly, even if it is refused, the party remains liable for damages for non-performance and there have been cases in which these have been claimed after specific performance was refused.[139]

---

[134] *Supra*, at 357.
[135] [1995] Ch. 259, Ch.D.
[136] (1971) 22 DLR (3d) 9, (aff'd (1973) 69 DLR (3d) 400n.
[137] We will see later that in English law specific performance is rarely ordered except for contracts for the sale of land, *infra*, at 680.
[138] E.g. *Tamplin* v. *James* (1880) 15 Ch. D 215. The circumstances in which it may be refused are discussed in *Stewart* v. *Kennedy* (1890) 15 App. Cas. 75, 105 and Treitel, *Contract* at 291–292.
[139] *Wood* v. *Scarth* (1855) 2 K & J 33 and (1858) 1 F & F 293.

(4) We saw above (the *Toilet Paper* case)[140] that in German law, two situations—(a) using a word you did not intend and (b) using the word you intended but under a misapprehension as to its meaning—are distinguished. We noted also that § 119 I BGB applies the same result to both—the mistaken party may avoid the contract. The two situations also seem to be treated in the same way by English law. For example, a typical rectification case is where the parties have written that one will pay the other "£1,000 free of tax" (which would mean that the payer pays £1,000 and the payee has to pay the tax), when what they meant is that the payer should pay such as sum after deduction of tax will amount to £1,000—see *Van der Linde* v. *Van der Linde*,[141] though there rectification was denied on other grounds.

However, it must be noted that the discussion in note (1), outlining the position where the other party has no knowledge of the mistake, also applies where the mistake is one as to the content of the declaration. Thus there is a fundamental difference between English and German law. In the *halver Hahn* case, the German buyer may avoid the contract even if the seller did not know of the mistake, whereas in England rectification will be granted only if the change would give the document the meaning which was intended by both parties, or if it is what one party meant and the other knew that.[142]

(5) It should be noted that in English law a unilateral mistake which is known to the other party is a ground for relief only when the mistake relates to what the terms of the contract are. If the mistake is one as to motive, mistake is not relevant (though there may be relief for misrepresentation).[143] For a case showing this see *Smith* v. *Hughes*.[144] This can produce nice distinctions: in the Canadian case of *Imperial Glass Ltd* v. *Consolidated Supplies Ltd*[145] a glazing subcontractor put in a bid for a job at far too low a figure because an assistant had misplaced a decimal point in calculating the area of wall involved. The court held that this was not a mistake about the terms of the contract, but only about the motives for it, so that the offeree could accept the bid even though he knew of the mistake. Presumably the result would have been different if the calculations had formed part of the subcontractor's bid. In the *McMaster* case cited in note (2) above, the University could not accept a contractor's bid when it should have known that the contractor had by mistake omitted a price escalation clause. German law draws a similar distinction between errors in declaration and errors in motive, but will allow relief for either kind of error.[146]

(3) Comparative summary

Thus we find a good deal of common ground:

> (a) In cases in which the parties use the wrong word to express their common intention, the contract will be interpreted to give effect to their actual intention (at least in so far as they had expressed it to each other[147]).

---

[140] *Supra*, at 360.
[141] [1947] Ch 306.
[142] *Supra* at 357 and 363.
[143] *Supra*, 346.
[144] **3.E.78**, *infra* at 411.
[145] (1960) 22 DLR (2d) 759, BC, CA.
[146] *Supra*, at 345.
[147] See this caveat for English law, *supra*, at 349.

(b) In cases of dissensus, in which neither party's interpretation is more reasonable that the other's, there will be no contract.

(c) Where there is either a slip of the pen, or the wrong word is used, by one party and the other party knows what was meant, the contract will again be interpreted as to give effect to the intention of the first party.

But if in either of the situations in (c) the other party does not know that there has been a mistake, the outcomes are rather different. In German law a party who by mistake understates the price, for example, may avoid the contract, whereas in English law the party is bound by what he wrote unless the other party actually knows that the offer contains a mistake. However, it must be remembered that in Germany the mistaken party will be liable under § 122 BGB to compensate the other for her reliance losses unless she knew or ought to have known of the mistake. French law in this case seems different again, though perhaps closer to the German position than to the English. It does seem to discuss the case of *Inhaltsirrtum*, but in the case of *Erklärungsirrtum* the result is that there is no contract because there is no consensus—though, as noted earlier, the courts in practice may avoid the contract under Article 1110 rather than rely on *erreur-obstacle*. In principle, the mistaken party who was careless might have to compensate the buyer on a delictual basis under Article 1382 of the Code civil.

The Principles of European Contract Law will enforce the contract in case (a). In case (b) there will not be a contract. In case (c)(i) there will be a contract on the terms intended by the mistaken party. In case (c)(ii) there will be a binding contract and it will not be avoidable on the grounds of mistake, since Article 4:103 limits relief to cases in which the other party either knew or ought to have known of the mistake, or shared it or caused it.

3.2.3.C. MISTAKE AS TO THE PERSON

A common problem is that a party is mistaken as to whom he is dealing with, or mistaken as to some attribute of that person—for example whether he is creditworthy. Consider the following examples:

(1) A wishes to sell his car privately for cash. He is approached by B, a rogue, who pretends that he is someone else (usually a well-known person whom A has heard of but never met), and so persuades A to let him take the car away against a cheque. The cheque turns out to be worthless but, before the fraud is discovered, B has sold the car to an innocent third party, C.

(2) A wishes to employ the house painter, F. Müller, who has previously proved himself to be a satisfactory tradesman. While searching the telephone book, he sees two painters of this name and chooses the wrong one, offering him the job.

(3) Again A wishes to employ a certain painter, F. Müller, and chooses the number correctly, offering him the job. He is mistaken in his belief, however, that it was F. Müller who had previously done work for him. It was in fact P. Müller.

(4) A meets a man on the street whom he erroneously believes to the painter F. Müller. He offers him the work.

The solutions to these examples are complex because more than one doctrine may come into play. First, the error may prevent any contract coming into existence at all because there is no sufficient agreement. Secondly, the mistake may be a ground on which the contract may be avoided on the ground of mistake as to the substance.

In English law, we shall see in the next part that the doctrine of mistake as to the substance plays a very limited role: it applies only to cases in which both parties make the same mistake—so-called "common mistake". It is possible to conceive of cases in which both parties might be mistaken as to the attributes of one of them—for example both employer and employee mistakenly think that the employee does not need a work permit—but there have been no such cases reported.

Even in English law, if one party entered a contract under a mistake as to the identity or attributes of the other, the contract may be avoided if the mistake results from a misrepresentation—for example fraud—by the non-mistaken party. Thus in example (1), A would have been able to rescind the contract on the ground of fraud—except that on the facts of the example, the acquisition of rights over the property by an innocent third party means that the right to rescind would have been lost and A cannot get back the car.

This result could be avoided if A could show that the contract was void for mistake. However, the only case in English law in which "mistake as to the person" operates is one in which the mistake as to identity prevents a contract coming into existence. If A makes an offer which is open only to B, but mistakenly addresses it to C, C may not be able to accept it. However, under the objective principle used in English law, it will be necessary to show that C knew or should have known that the offer was not open to him to accept— see *Ingram* v. *Little*.[148] Once again, there is doubt whether this is the result of a separate doctrine of mistake here or flows simply from the rules of offer and acceptance. It is possible that in example (1), A could show that B knew the offer was open only to the person A though he was dealing with. This has sometimes been held in cases of offers made in correspondence—for example *Cundy* v. *Lindsay*;[149] but when the parties are dealing with each other face to face, there is a strong presumption that A meant to deal with the person he was speaking to and that his mistake is not as to identity: *Lewis* v. *Avery*.[150]

In the remaining examples there would not be any relief in English law. The contract would not be voidable for fraud, since[151] English law does not recognize fraud except where one party has actively misled the other. In none of the remaining examples did the second party mislead A. Nor would the contract be void for mistake in English law, since in none of them did the non-mistaken party have any reason to think that A meant to deal with anyone else.

Article 1110 of the French Code Civil allows mistake as to the person as a ground on nullity when the "consideration of the person was the principal cause of the agreement". Attributes as well as identity may be sufficiently fundamental.

German law would deal with each of these sample situations differently. In example (1), the contract could be avoided for fraud under § 123 BGB; but further, in both examples (1) and (2), it might be avoided for mistake. (Note that in example (1), the innocent party C would be protected by the rules on moveable property where he had acquired the item in good faith (§§ 932ff BGB).) On an objective interpretation (§§ 133,157 BGB) the

---

[148] [1960] 3 All ER 332.
[149] (1878) 3 App. Cas. 459, HL.
[150] [1972] 1 QB 198, CA.
[151] As we saw earlier, *supra*, at 337, and see further *infra*, at 410.

declaration of will amounts to an offer to contract with the person in fact spoken to. There was, however, a divergence between this expression and A's actual intention. He made an error as to the content of his declaration of intention (*Inhaltsirrtum*). The latter may therefore be challenged under § 119 I 1st Alternative BGB.

In example (3), by contrast, A intended to contract with the person to whom the declaration of will was addressed. There can, therefore, be no avoidance under § 119 I 1st Alternative BGB. A's error is merely one of motive: a mistake as to an attribute of the person with whom he contracted. Was this an essential attribute within § 119 II BGB? Personal attributes which are of direct relevance to the purpose of the transaction are likely to be held by German courts to be essential. (For example, credit-worthiness will not be an essential attribute in a contract of sale where payment is by cash. It will be however, where payment is by cheque or a guarantee contract is at issue.[152]) It is doubtful whether there was such direct relevance in example (3).

In the final case, it is generally held that there is no error under either § 119 I 1st Alternative BGB or § 119 II BGB. The other party has been sufficiently identified by his physical presence. There is no error as to the content of the declaration; A intends to contract with the person before him. It may be possible to seek avoidance under § 119 II BGB if the person encountered on the street was not a painter, i.e. if there were an error as to an essential attribute of that person.

Dutch law treats mistaken identity or attributes as a kind of mistake falling under BW 6:228.

3.2.3.D. MISTAKE AS TO THE SUBJECT MATTER OR CIRCUMSTANCES

In the last part we looked at cases in which the misapprehension or misunderstanding was about what was being agreed between the parties. In this part we look at cases in which the parties have agreed in the same terms, but one or each of them is under some misapprehension as to the nature of the subject matter of the contract, or some relevant circumstance. Under what conditions will this give rise to relief under the various systems?

In both French and German law, this is the central ground of the doctrine of mistake— although the relevant provision in the BGB appears rather as an afterthought, added in the second draft to qualify the rule that mistakes as to motive were never relevant, only mistakes as to declaration.[153] In each system, a party who has entered a contract under a mistake as to, for example, the essential qualities of the subject matter of the contract will be able to avoid the contract.

We also noted earlier that in each system there are complications, in that what seem in functional terms to be cases of mistake may be dealt with under other doctrines, for example absence of *cause* or impossibility. These will lead to the conclusion, not that the contract may be avoided (*nullité relative*) but that there never was a contract (*nullité absolue*). Conversely, it may be that the legal system precludes any argument based on mistake by allocating the risk to one or other party. The typical example of this is where the seller of property is responsible for defects in it, even if he did not know of the defect.

---

[152] RGZ 90.206.
[153] *Infra*, 376.

Leaving such complications aside for the moment and concentrating on avoidance for mistake, in the traditional code systems the key question is, as we suggested in the introduction, a subjective one: was the party claiming relief making the contract under a sufficiently serious misapprehension that the contract should be set aside? It is true that in neither French nor German law will a mistake give a right to avoidance unless both parties would have regarded the matter to which the mistake related (for example, the age of a piece of furniture sold) as being essential; but the questions of how the mistake arose—for example, was it through incorrect information given by the other party or was it self-induced?—and the situation of the other party—did she know of the mistake or did she share it?—were of lesser importance, at least as far as avoidance of the contract was concerned.

The structure of English law is quite different. Mistake is a ground for relief only when (1) it is fundamental and (2) both parties make the same mistake (this book follows the modern custom of calling this "common" mistake, though the leading case[154] refers to it as "mutual" mistake). However, English law readily gives relief when one party has misled the other into entering the contract by giving incorrect information—even if this was done without fault. Relief is not under the doctrine of mistake but that of misrepresentation. In other words, the Common Law looks to the position of both parties and, with the limited exception of common mistake, insists on some misleading behaviour on the part of the other party before avoidance will be allowed (the "objective approach").

We shall see that the more modern Netherlands Civil Code and the international restatements take a "mixed" approach: a shared mistake may give a rise to avoidance but normally a mistake by one party alone will not do so unless the other party either caused the mistake or knew or should have known of it.

Even in the traditional civil systems, however, much depends on the remedy sought. *Avoidance* is based on the plaintiff's subjective mistake; but if the plaintiff wants *damages*, she will normally have to show either (i) some fault on the other party's part (*culpa in contrahendo*, *responsabilité delictuelle*) or (ii) that the defendant is contractually liable—having expressly undertaken that what the plaintiff believed to be true would in fact be true, or being responsible under the general law (for example implied terms, *garantie*) to the same effect.

In practice, these differing grounds do not always lead to differing remedies. In other words, even though either (i) fault on the defendant's part or (ii) the defendant's contractual liability is most often invoked in order that the plaintiff may claim damages, either ground can sometimes also lead to avoidance of the contract. First, in German law avoidance may on occasion be granted on the basis of *culpa in contrahendo* as well as on the ground of mistake. Secondly, the remedies under (ii) may well include avoidance or its functional equivalent (for example *action rédhibitoire*, *Wandlung*).

Again there are marked differences between the civil and common law systems. On (i), all systems recognize that there may be liability for fault. However, the civil systems have for some time accepted that keeping silent may amount to fault where there was a duty to disclose. The common law is much more reluctant to impose duties on parties and has never recognized any general obligation to disclose pertinent facts. This difference seems

---

[154] *Infra*, at 384.

so fundamental that it is considered in a separate section, section **3.2.4**.[155] On (ii), in contract, the common law seems readier to hold that a party has expressly undertaken that something stated about the subject matter will be true, and also to impose more extensive contractual liabilities by the implication of terms into the contract.[156]

It will be obvious that this is a complex subject: in each system there is a variety of doctrines which overlap, while the concepts used differ markedly between civil and common law. To try to make the material simpler, we first give a general account of the law of mistake in French, German, English and Dutch law. This account will be interrupted by a note on various complications which affect French and German law, and one which has "spilled over" into English law. We then set out one general exception to the rules on mistake, where relief on the basis of mistake is excluded because contractual liability is imposed on one party despite her mistake. After this, we compare the way in which two different species of mistake are dealt with in the different jurisdictions: (i) shared mistakes; and (ii) induced mistakes.

Following on from the discussion of mistake, we discuss the related issue of non-disclosure under **3.2.4** and the adaptation of contracts under **3.2.5**. We end this section by comparing the treatment of mistake and the related doctrines in the national laws and in the international restatements.

(1) Mistake in general: French and German law

Look again at the principal texts: French Code Civil Articles 1110 and 1117, BGB §§ 119, 122; Netherlands BW Article 6:228; PECL Article 4:103.[157]

Cass. civ., 23 November 1931[158]   **3.F.56.**

MISTAKE AS TO ESSENTIAL CHARACTERISTIC OF THING SOLD

The Villa Jacqueline

A party who has entered a contract under a mistake as to an essential quality of the thing sold may have the contract declared null. Essential qualities may include matters affecting the party's intended use of the property when this was known to the other party.

Facts: A villa which had been advertised as having grounds of 7,800 square metres was bought by the plaintiffs, who (as the seller was aware) intended to divide the ground into separate lots and re-sell them. The buyers discovered that the true area was only 5,119 square metres, which was too little for their scheme to be practical, and they claimed that the contract was null on the ground of mistake.

Held: The lower courts held the contract void on the ground of mistake and the Cour de cassation agreed.

Judgment: THE COURT: . . . *On the sole appeal ground*:—Whereas on 13 June 1924 Mr Beltinissin sold to Mr and Mrs Crozillac by private document property known as the "Villa Jacqueline", without mentioning the area, for FF 36 000, payable by the end of July 1924 at the latest, subject to the

---

[155] *Infra*, at 409.
[156] *Infra*, at 571 ff.
[157] *Supra*, at 344–345.
[158] D.P.1932.1.129, annotated by L. Josserand; Gaz.Pal. 1932.1.96.

369

condition that the sale would be set aside and a car, pledged as security, forfeited to the vendor if by that date the sale had not been confirmed by notarial act and the price paid in full.

—Whereas the appeal challenges the judgment (Bordeaux, 24 June 1926) in so far as, on the application of the purchasers, it declared the contract void on the ground of mistake as to area, regarded as an essential property of the thing sold.

—Whereas in accordance with Article 1619 of the Civil Code, deficiency in the area of a piece of land can give rise only to a reduction in price where the shortfall is greater than 5%, that is not the case where the deficiency in area makes the land unfit for its intended use, known to the parties, for the purpose of which it was purchased.

—Whereas in that case area actually becomes an essential property of the subject matter of the contract, and mistake as to such a property makes Article 1110 of the Civil Code applicable; as it is clear from the grounds of the judgment that the information given by Mr Beltinissin to the agencies instructed to sell the villa or appearing in newspaper advertisements gave the area of the land sold as 7,800 square metres, whereas it was only 5,119 at most.

—Whereas for Mr and Mrs Crozillac, who purchased the property for the sole purpose (as the vendor was aware) of dividing it into lots and reselling it, the stated area was an essential condition of the contract.

—Whereas furthermore, the judgment notes that the vendor, deliberately and in bad faith, misled the purchasers and by so doing invalidated their consent. In those factual circumstances, the judgment, which interpreted the agreement in accordance with the intentions of the contracting parties and without distortion, could validly hold, without infringing the statutory provisions referred to in the ground of appeal, that the mistake went to the very essence of the thing which was the subject-matter of the contract and declare the contract void.

On those grounds, the Court dismisses the appeal.

From the Note

On the facts the area of the land stated became, because of the buyer's plans (known to the seller), a substantial quality of the object of the contract; from that moment a mistake as to this quality brought into play article 1110: the contract must be annuled, at the buyer's request, for error as to the substance. In this way the Court of cassation overcame the obstacle of arts 1617 et seq. . . .

1. Mistake leads to the nullity of the contract not only when it is as to the substance, in the strict sense of the word, as to the matter of which the object is composed, but, much more generally, when it relates to the substantial qualities, that is to say, essential qualities, in consideration of which the parties were dealing with one another . . .

. . . These may be objective or subjective . . .

Objective qualities are those which, without necessarily having a material character, without being "substantial" in the etymological sense of the word, are nonetheless embodied in the object of the obligation and identified with it . . . he who thinks he is buying a Corot and in fact is paying dear for a copy, is the victim of an error of substance . . .

But it goes much further when we consider what we call error as to the subjectively substantial qualities. These are those, of infinite variety, which are attached to the object by the contracting party from such and such an angle, according to what he desires . . .

2. Always, for a mistake to lead to nullity of the contract, the case law demands that another condition be fulfilled . . . the seller must know that the buyer think she is buying a Corot . . . on the facts of this case, the seller knew the use to which the buyers intended to put the land; the judgment stressed that point twice: the purposes "was known to the two parties"; the buyer's purpose was known to the vendor. The mistake . . . must be shared, "agreed" or be error *ex pacto*. The formula is not rigorously precise, or at least, it could be made more precise: *the case law does not require that*

370

the seller have fallen into the same error as the buyer; it is enough that he knew of the conditions in which the buyer thought he was dealing, the belief in which he is abused. This proven – and it is obviously for the buyer, who seeks annulment, who has to prove it – the vendor finds himself in a dilemma: either he was himself in good faith, he thought the painting was a Corot, . . . or that the land had the stated area, and so there is shared mistake . . . and the contract must fall by virtue of art. 1110; or the seller knew the truth, and in this case he has committed fraud by his silence, his failure to disclose, his misleading statements, actual fraud which justifies the application of art. 1116.

Notes

(1) The Note refers to Article 1617, which provides:

Code civil   **3.F.57.**

Article 1617: If a sale of land was made with an indication of the contents by reference to the area, the seller is obliged to deliver to the buyer, if the latter demands it, the area indicated. If this is not possible or if the buyer does not demand it, the seller must grant a proportionate reduction in price.

In the *Villa Jacqueline* case the seller could not deliver the area of land indicated; and a proportionate reduction in the price would not have been satisfactory for the buyers because the deficiency in area meant that the land was insufficient for the development they intended. Thus the deficiency in area went to "the very substance of the object", as required by Article 1110. The case would presumably have been different if the buyers had intended simply to live in the villa. The error must have been "*la considération déterminante*" for the party seeking relief and a decision which failed to ask whether this was the case has been quashed.[159]

(2) The Note indicates that some matters go to the substance in an objective sense, others only in a subjective way. The defendant will be deemed to know the importance of a matter which goes to the substance in an objective sense, whereas if the matter is only subjectively important to the particular buyer, the buyer may have to show that the defendant was aware of this (as in the *Villa Jacqueline* case). If a matter is determining and this is known to the other party (either because it is objectively substantial or because the importance of it was known to the other party), this suffices to make it substantial for the purposes of Article 1110.

(3) The Note suggests that the seller was caught in a dilemma: either he had made the same mistake, so that relief is being given on the ground of shared (or "common") mistake; or he knew of the mistake and therefore was guilty of fraud in not pointing it out to the buyer. On the facts of the case this seems correct but in other situations there may be a third possibility. Suppose the seller had not stated the area of the land but the buyer had had it measured by a surveyor who had made a mistake. The seller would know that the area was important to the buyer but might not know that the buyer had been given an incorrect figure. It seems that in principle relief might be given. However, the court might take the line that the buyer was taking the risk. Thus it was held that there was no error

---

[159] Cass. civ., 17 November 1930, S.19321.17; D.P.1932.1.161, annotated by A. Breton; Gaz.Pal.1930.2.1031, annotated by J.-Ch. Laurent.

371

of substance when a dressmaker who bought material discovered that what he had bought was furnishing fabric.[160] Even though the seller knew the buyer's purpose, the latter as a professional should have known the material was unsuitable and bought it "*à ses risques et périls*".

(4) If the mistaken party was seriously at fault, the error may be described as *inexcusable* and relief denied.[161]

(5) It must be shown that the error related to an essential characteristic of the thing sold, not merely as to the motive for buying it. And a mistake simply as to the thing's value is not enough:[162]

An error as to motive which is not, at the same time, an error as to the substantial qualities of the thing sold is inoperative, even if the motive was determining for one party and this was known to the other party. That is not enough to make it an element of the contract: for that there must be a common intention of the parties.

The sole fact that there has been an error as to value does not suffice to justify annulation—otherwise this would lead to rescission for general *lésion*. Obviously, when there is an error as to substance there is always error as to value; but the opposite is not always true.

However, the price may be relevant to what is to be expected and this in turn may amount to a substantial quality of the object: see Cass. civ., 29 November 1968[163] (a holiday villa which was said to be comfortably equipped was let at 6,000FF a month; in fact it was in very poor repair and next to a noisy construction site; if held that the lessee was justified in assuming *un standing en rapport* with the high price, the finding of error of substance was justified.)

(6) The effect of an operative mistake is of *nullité relative*; in other words, only the party whose consent as vitiated can rely on the error: see Article 1117.[164] Article 1304 sets a time limit of five years from the date of discovery of the error. If the conditions are established, a court is bound to grant a decree of nullity; compare the case of *résolution* for non-performance.[165]

(7) Cass. civ., 29 November 1968[166] shows that where there is fault on the part of the non-mistaken party (or his agent), the mistaken party may recover damages. On the facts of the case, the owner and his agent "could not have been ignorant of the bad state of the villa or of the construction site". "This is not a question of error as to the substance but one of responsibility."[167] The basis of liability is considered to be the same as that for pre-contractual fault.[168] If the loss were partly the victim's own fault, in principle the damages could be reduced.

(8) The Note to the case goes on to suggest that if the party who has avoided the contract was mistaken through his own fault, he might be made liable in damages for any loss he has caused the other party.[169] This is the position taken by doctrine, but in practice it

[160] Cass. com., 4 July 1973, B. IV.238; D. 1974.538, annotated by Ghestin.
[161] See Malaurie and Aynès, para. 411: "*la loi ne protège pas les imbéciles*".
[162] See Malaurie and Aynès, para. 410. See also German law, *infra*, at 380.
[163] Gaz.Pal. 1969. II.63.
[164] *Supra*, at 344.
[165] *Infra*, at 748.
[166] See note (5), *supra*.
[167] See Malaurie and Aynès, para. 406.
[168] Nicholas at 110.
[169] Cf. § 122 BGB.

seems that this sanction is not demanded. Instead the normal sanction is to refuse *annulation* for error.[170]

Cass. civ., 13 December 1983[171]   **3.F.58–59.**
and
Cour d'appel, Versailles, 7 January 1987[172]

SELLER OF PAINTING WRONGLY ATTRIBUTED MAY AVOID CONTRACT

The Poussin

Where a party has been advised that a painting is not the work of a particular painter and therefore believes that the painting was painted by another, the party will be mistaken as to an essential attribute of the thing sold and will therefore be entitled to avoid the contract.

Facts: The St. Arromans owned a painting of Olympus and Marsyas which family tradition held to be by Poussin; but they were advised by an art dealer that it was of the school of Carracci and worth only some 1500FF. They sold it to a dealer for 2200FF but the National Museum exercized its right of pre-emption and shortly afterwards exhibited the painting as a Poussin. The St.Arromans sought to have the contract of sale set aside for mistake.

Held: In 1972, the St. Arromans succeeded at first instance on the grounds that there was no meeting of minds on the thing to be sold, the sellers intending to sell a painting of the school of Carracci and the buyer intending to buy a Pousssin (D.1973, 410, note J.Ghestin and Ph.Malinvaux). Advocate-general Gulphe later described this decision as a remarkable instance of Article 1110 being applied to protect a seller rather than a buyer.

The cour d'appel of Paris reversed this decision on the ground that it was not proven that the painting was by Poussin and therefore the error had not been established (D. 1976, 325, conclusions Cabannes; JCP 1976 II 18358, Note Lindon). That decision was in turn quashed by the Cour de cassation on the basis that the court had not enquired whether the consent of the sellers was not vitiated by an erroneous conviction that the work *could not be* by Poussin. The case was remitted to the cour d'appel of Amiens.

The court at Amiens also found against the St.Arromans, on the ground that at the time of sale the sellers had serious doubts whether the painting was by Poussin.

Before the Cour de cassation on its second consideration of the "Poussin case", M.Gulphe argued that the contract should be avoided. The authenticity of a painting is established as being a "substantial quality" within Article 1100 and

> [i]n this case, the determining cause of the sale of the disputed picture, the substantial quality, as far as the sellers were concerned, has a negative quality. It is claimed that the contract is null because the picture was sold by its owners in the certainty that they were not dealing with a picture by [Poussin].

He noted that the court at Amiens had found that at least the seller's agents were convinced that the painting *could not be* by Poussin, and therefore the court should have considered the application of Article 1110, but the court had not applied that Article on the ground that the attribution was not established at the time of sale. He noted:

> "The Amiens judgment adopts the doctrinal theory that a seller cannot annul a sale because of an error he has made unless there is fraud on the part of the buyer."

Once again the decision was reversed (see below), and in 1987 the sale was finally annulled by the Cour d'appel of Versailles (also below). The picture was returned to Mme. St.Arroman (her husband had died by this stage) and she refunded the 2200FF. Later she sold the painting to a Swiss gallery for 7,400,000FF.

---

[170] See Ghestin, para. 522.
[171] JCP 1984.II.20186.
[172] Gaz. Pal. 1987.34.

Cass. civ., 13 December 1983 **3.F.58.**

Judgment: *On the sole appeal ground in law*:—Under Article 1110 of the Civil Code;—Whereas Mr and Mrs Saint-Arroman sold a painting by public auction through Messrs Maurice Rheims, Philippe Rheims and René Laurin which family tradition had it was the work of Nicolas Poussin; as however, Robert Lebel, the expert called in by the auctioneers attributed it to the school of Carracci, with the result that it was listed as such in the sale catalogue with the owners' consent and sold for FF 2 000 on 21 February 1968;
—Whereas the Réunion des Musées Nationaux ("RMN") exercised its right of pre-emption and then exhibited the painting as an original work by Nicolas Poussin;
—Whereas Mr and Mrs Saint-Arroman brought an action to have the contract of sale set aside on the ground of mistake as to the essential property of the thing sold, but the cour d'appel, ruling after a previous judgment had been quashed and the case referred to it, rejected the claim on the grounds that, while at the time of the sale Mr and Mrs Saint-Arroman were convinced . . . that the painting at issue could not be by Poussin, neither the assignment of the painting in the Louvre to Poussin by order of 20 March 1968, nor the article by Mr Rosenberg in the *Revue du Louvre* which appeared in 1969, nor yet the fact that the painting was exhibited in the Louvre in the name of Poussin, gives rise to any implication or contains any evidence concerning the origin of the work either before or at the same time as the sale, and liable as such to influence the vendors' consent if at that time they or their agents had been aware of it.
—Whereas similarly, RMN observed in its pleadings that in short, and in spite of its own actions after acquiring the painting, there was no absolute certainty as to the origin of the work.
—Whereas the cour d'appel declared that "it is irrelevant whether the Réunion des Musées Nationaux maintained, or subsequently corrected, its opinion concerning the attribution of the painting to Poussin, since the mistake must be determined on the day of sale".
—Whereas by so deciding, and by denying Mr and Mrs Saint-Arroman the right to rely upon evidence subsequent to the sale in order to prove that there had been a mistake on their part at the time of the sale, the cour d'appel has infringed the abovementioned provision.
—Whereas the question of the validity of the sale and the question of the liability of the auctioneers and the expert are necessarily interdependent, the provision in the contested judgment concerning their liability must consequently be quashed, pursuant to Article 624 of the new Code of Civil Procedure.
On those grounds, the Court quashes the judgment given between the parties on 1 February 1982 by the cour d'appel, Amiens, and remits the matter to the cour d'appel, Versailles.

Cour d'appel, Versailles, 7 January 1987 **3.F.59.**

Judgment:—Whereas where works of art are sold by public auction from a catalogue containing authentication by an expert, the attribution of the work is for both seller and buyer an essential property of the thing sold;
—Whereas the seller's conviction as to the attribution is determined on the basis of the information given in the sale catalogue which includes a definition of the essential features and real nature of the object he is selling;
—Whereas in this case, the painting sold on 21 February 1968 was described in the catalogue as follows: "Carracci (school of), Bacchanalia. Large canvas. 1.03 m high, 0.87 m wide"; as this description, which thus defines the nature of the thing that is the subject-matter of the contract, contains no allusion to the existence of a possible attribution of the work to Nicolas Poussin or even to his school, to his style or manner, whereas it is, however, the custom in cases of uncertainty as to the creator of a work of art to use terms such as "signed by . . . attributed to . . . school of

... style ... *genre* ... manner"; as in the absence of any such expressions, to state merely "School of Carracci", to which it is undisputed that Nicolas Poussin never belonged, excludes an attribution to the latter and leaves no doubt;

—Whereas accordingly it is proved that when the sellers concluded the contract they were convinced that the painting was not by Nicolas Poussin and were sure only that it was to be attributed to the school of Carracci.

—Whereas it is immaterial that in their documents Mr and Mrs Saint-Arroman acknowledged that an old family tradition attributed the work at issue to Nicolas Poussin since, on the one hand, it is only what they actually believed at the moment of the sale which must be taken into account and, on the other, laymen as they were, they could not be criticised for falling in with the decisive opinion given by Mr Lebel, a well-known expert, and confirmed by Maître Rheims, an auctioneer and valuer of high renown, or for allowing themselves to be persuaded that their family tradition was incorrect and that the work could not be by Nicolas Poussin;

—Whereas the assertion of the auctioneer and the expert that Mr and Mrs Saint-Arroman concealed that family tradition from them cannot be regarded as proved to be true. It is made by parties with an interest in the outcome of the dispute, it is entirely unsubstantiated and is not supported by any evidence; as moreover, it is scarcely probable that Mr and Mrs Saint-Arroman, in selling their painting at the best possible price, should not have told their agents of its attribution according to the family tradition, just as it strains credulity that the prudent professionals that the agents were should have failed to question the sellers about any knowledge they might have as to the painter of the work which they put into the hands of the agents to sell; as the plea alleging that Mr and Mrs Saint-Arroman were grossly negligent in failing to reveal to Maître Rheims and Mr Lebel what they knew of the painter has no factual basis;

—Whereas the authenticity of the painting's attribution to the artist Nicolas Poussin remains uncertain, in the light of opinions given by eminent experts which are as peremptory as they are contradictory, and while the Court, in the absence of decisive proof, cannot resolve that point, this division among the experts cannot mean, as the Minister for Culture argues, that Mr and Mrs Saint-Arroman's mistake is not allowable as it relates to certain persons' opinions concerning attribution and not to attribution itself;

—Whereas this divergence does not precisely make it impossible for the work to be "a genuine Poussin", it supports Mrs Saint-Arroman's claim relying on the mistake which she and her husband made of selling the painting under the erroneous belief that it absolutely could not be the work of that painter, especially since at the same time, according to the evidence in the case, when the RMN exercised its right of pre-emption over the work it was, if not certain that the painting was by Poussin, at least persuaded that its origin was other than that stated in the catalogue; as if that were not so, it is inexplicable that the RMN, according to its own pleadings, was authorized to pay up to FF 40,000 by way of pre-emption, a sum 25 times greater than the estimate of FF 1,500 suggested by the expert, Mr Lebel;

—Whereas in addition, a fortnight after the sale an article by Jacques Thuillier, a Poussin specialist, was putting forward the painting as a work of Poussin's discovered by the Louvre's young conservation team, a view which the RMN shared at first instance but abandoned on appeal for the purposes of its own case;

—Whereas in order to resist (to no purpose) Mrs Saint-Arroman's action, the Minister for Culture objects that the mistake she pleads is in fact a mistake as to value and accordingly cannot render the sale void, because loss consisting of inadequate consideration cannot give rise to rescission of a contract for the sale of personal property; as the Minister argues that a distinction must be drawn between financial mistake arising from an incorrect economic assessment of correct facts, and mistake as to the qualitative value of the thing which, as in this instance, is only the result of a mistake as to an essential quality, in which case the mistake must be regarded as a mistake relating to the essential nature of the subject matter of the contract;

—Whereas there is no need otherwise to follow the parties into the details of their arguments; it must held that in believing that they were selling a canvas of the school of Carracci, of indifferent quality, that is to say, under the mistaken conviction that it could not be a work by Nicolas Poussin, when it is possible that the work is his, Mr and Mrs Saint-Arroman made a mistake relating to the essential nature of the thing transferred which was crucial to their consent, which they would not have given if they had been aware of the facts; as accordingly, the contested judgment must be upheld in so far as it annulled the sale of 21 February 1968 on the basis of Article 1110 of the Civil Code and, in addition, it must be ordered that the painting be returned to Mrs Saint-Arroman and that her undertaking to refund the sum received of FF 2,200 be formally recorded.

—Whereas Mrs Saint-Arroman's claim against Messrs Rheims and Laurin and the heirs of Mr Lebel is in the nature of a plea in the alternative, there is no need to adjudicate.

On those grounds, and having regard to the judgment of the Cour de cassation of 13 December 1983, the Court, in formal session in open court, confirms all the provisions of the judgment under appeal and, in addition, extends its effects to the Minister of Culture, orders the painting in dispute to be returned to Mrs Saint-Arroman, [and] formally records Mrs Saint-Arroman's undertaking to refund the proceeds of sale, that is to say, FF 2,200 . . . [The court held that there was no need to give a ruling on an alternative claim against Messrs Rheims and Laurin and the heirs of Mr Lebel.]

The Court orders the Réunion des Musées Nationaux and the Minister of Culture to pay both the costs of the appeal incurred before the cours d'appel of Paris and Amiens and those incurred before the cour d'appel, Versailles, and also the costs of the judgments quashed . . .

Notes

(1) If the non-mistaken party's conduct can be described as *fautive*, the mistaken party may claim damages on the basis of Article 1382 as well as avoid the contract for error.

(2) In German law this case might have been seen as a mere error of motive along the same lines as the error in the *Mozart Notebooks* case.[173] Even if § 119 II BGB had applied, the sellers would still have to pay damages under § 122 BGB unless the court's suspicions about the knowledge of the RMN's buyers crystallized into a definitive finding.

BGB   **3.G.60.**

§ 119(2): An error as to those characteristics of a person or thing which are regarded in business as essential is regarded in the same way as an error as to the content of a declaration.

AG Coburg, 24 April 1992[174]   **3.G.61.**

MISTAKE OF VALUE IRRELEVANT

Mozart notebooks

Where a party mistakenly includes in a lot for sale an item she had meant to reserve because of its value, there is no mistake as to the declaration under § 119 I BGB and no mistake as to the essential characteristics of the thing sold under § 119 II BGB. The buyer is not under an obligation to disclose the fact that the bundle includes a valuable item.

[173] *Infra.*
[174] NJW 1993.938.

Facts: The seller sold a bundle of miscellaneous notebooks for 10 DM, not realizing that she had included in the bundle a notebook by Mozart. She had intended to set this aside and sold the bundle without knowing exactly what was in it.

Held: She could not avoid the contract nor recover compensation for fraud by the buyer.

Judgment: The parties are in dispute concerning the return of antiquarian music note-books. On 13 October 1991 the defendant acquired from the plaintiff in a public "flea market", for the sum of 10 DM, various music note-books, sheets of music and musical periodicals. On 16/17 October 1991 the local press reported on a "sensational Mozart find" having "considerable rarity value" which the defendant had made in the flea market, whereupon the plaintiff declared, by letter dated 18 October 1991 which reached the defendant by 20 October at the latest, that she was avoiding, as against the defendant, the contract "relating to the collection of manuscript sheet music (by, *inter alia*, Mozart) handed over to you on 13 October 1991, by reason of mistake" and demanded the return of the items handed over in return for reimbursement of the purchase price. The plaintiff maintains that on 12 October 1991, as the owner of a great many music note-books, including *inter alia* the note-books and sheets forming the subject-matter of the claim, she sorted out and extracted from her stock the items produced prior to 1906, since these were not intended to be sold, and gathered all the rest together with a view to selling them in the flea market. She claims that, for inexplicable reasons, the items sorted out and extracted by her clearly got mixed up again with the items intended for sale, in some manner which she is unable to ascertain in detail, and that she was unaware on 13 October 1991 that the older items were included amongst the goods laid out on the stand in the flea market. When the defendant purchased the note-books and other similar items from her, she was certainly aware that he was buying note-books, but she did not notice which particular note-books were involved. The defendant considers that the plaintiff's mistake is not one which justifies avoidance of the contract.

Grounds:

. . . II.1. The plaintiff's assertion that, for inexplicable reasons, the items initially sorted out and extracted by her got mixed up again with the items intended for sale is irrelevant in all the circumstances of the present case. The rules relating to transactions and declarations of intent are fundamentally inapplicable to the actual acts falling to be considered in this matter, so that, for that reason alone, there can be no question of any avoidance of the contract. In so far as the contract and/or the transfer of ownership may have been indirectly influenced by this, avoidance of the contract and of the transfer of ownership on the ground of mistake cannot be legally justified, if only because the plaintiff's possible mistake or aberration could not have related to the declarations of intent themselves, but concerned only the circumstances surrounding the events leading up to the making of those statements.

2. There was patently no error made as regards the act of making the statements (§ 119 I second alternative BGB). The plaintiff wished to bind herself under a sale contract and to transfer to the defendant ownership of the goods which were relinquished to him.

3. There was no question of any mistake as to the content of the statements (§ 119 I first alternative BGB). The plaintiff was completely in the picture as to the meaning and legal consequences of the sale obligation into which she was objectively entering, and as to the transfer of ownership to the defendant. The subject-matter of the transaction, in the eyes of the plaintiff and the defendant, was the note-books handed over to the latter.

4. In so far as it was in fact open to the plaintiff to assume that the "packets of note-books handed over to the defendant" contained only the "flea market items" which she had got ready the day before, when they in fact also contained the note-books at issue in the present case, the plaintiff cannot be said to have made a mistake, since according to her own statements she did not notice which

particular note-books were involved; as a result of her conscious nonchalance in that regard, she made her contractual declaration, committing herself to the contract and to the transfer of owner-ship, in the conscious knowledge that she did not know precisely what inference was to be drawn from the objective circumstances (a contract of sale in respect of, and the transfer to the defendant of ownership in, certain note-books selected by the latter) as to the content of the items in question. Accordingly, the plaintiff cannot claim that, unknown to her, she was unaware of the actual facts asserted.

5. Nor can there be any question of an error as to ownership within the meaning of § 119 II BGB. The characteristics of a thing or matter include the already existing factual or legal relationships and connections with the surrounding circumstances, in so far as these can be seen, upon consideration of the commercial aspects of the specific transaction in question, to have any significance as regards questions of valuation or usabililty, and in so far as they directly characterise the thing or matter. The value of the antiquarian note-books in terms of their origin, age, state of preservation and rarity, which emerges only indirectly from a consideration of the transaction, does not constitute a characteristic within the meaning of § 119 II BGB; consequently, a possible mistake on the part of the plaintiff as to the actual value of the note-books handed over to the defendant for 10 DM is irrelevant in the present case.

6. Nor, lastly, can there be any question of avoidance of the contract and of the transfer of ownership pursuant to § 123 I BGB. Even if the defendant had recognised the value of what the plaintiff claims to be the "find", and had deliberately failed to disclose this to the plaintiff, the defendant cannot be said to have wilfully deceived the plaintiff, since the defendant was under no obligation to give the plaintiff any information or indication in relation to the fact not disclosed at the time (the tangible or intangible value of the note-books discovered). It is basically up to the parties to a contract to look after their own interests, and there exists no general duty, in the context of contractual or pre-contractual negotiations, to disclose all circumstances which might significantly affect the decision of the other party. Moreover, it is in the nature of a typical public flea market that anyone in such a market—even a person possessing no commercial experience—can offer to buy or sell or acquire objects of every kind and degree of quality at prices which are not solely calculated to result in a profit. It follows that the principle of good faith does not require the attention of offerors who possibly lack commercial experience to be drawn to what may be the far greater value of an object offered for sale, in order to prevent such offerors from entering into what may, from a commercial standpoint, be a significantly disadvantageous transaction to which they have not given sufficient thought.

7. Nor, clearly, can there be said to have been a lack of consensus between the parties. The declarations of intent made by each of them, as described in the statement of facts provided by the plaintiff, tally with each other. The existence of a possible mutual mistake by the parties concerning the declaration made by the other party (possible hidden lack of agreement) has not been substantiated by the pleas advanced and is not otherwise apparent.

Notes

(1) In German law the class of mistakes as to the substance or attributes of some thing or person has been interpreted in two ways. According to the first they normally amount to only insignificant errors of motive.[175] The nineteenth century writings of Zitelmann have influenced this position. His analysis of the process of contracting posited a prior and necessarily distinct phase wherein the party was influenced by one or several motives. Only thereafter was an intention formed and communicated to the other party. A

---

[175] Larenz, *AT* para. 20 II b.

textbook example of this distinction is where a proud father purchases a ring in ignorance of the cancellation of his daughter's wedding. Zitelmann—and indeed most contemporary systems—would hold that the father cannot avoid since his mistake was as to a motivating factor. His intention to purchase this ring from this jeweller was in no way flawed by mistake. He intended to make a declaration of will and one with this particular effect. He did this successfully. Errors as to the attributes, rather than the identity of a thing or person are also made at the earlier stage and thus amount to errors of motive. According to this theory § 119 II BGB makes an exception to this where the mistake was as to an attribute considered essential in business. The distinction between significant and insignificant errors is therefore drawn on the basis of whether the attribute has a direct influence on the value of the item and is of special significance for contracts of that type—for example the authenticity of a "Ming vase".[176] The definition in section II.5 of the above judgment reflects this approach.

(2) The foregoing approach has been criticized on the basis that it does not yield clear criteria defining exactly which mistakes will actually lead to avoidance. As such it threatens the security of transactions and unfairly puts the risk of (some) purely subjective errors of motive on the other party. A second, less objective, more context-dependent approach was therefore developed by Flume.[177] It is demonstrated in the reasoning of the following case.

BGH, 18 December 1954, II ZR[178] **3.G.62.**

<small>BUYER'S PURPOSE NOT "ESSENTIAL CHARACTERISTIC" UNLESS PART OF CONTRACT</small>

The ultrasonic device

The buyer's purpose does not amount to an "essential characteristic" of the goods within § 119 II BGB unless it has been agreed between the parties.

Facts: A doctor bought an "ultrasonic device" which had no technical defects but which was not suitable for its purpose. The seller sued for the contract price. The doctor claimed inter alia that he had been mistaken as to an essential characteristic of the device that the contract could therefore be avoided.

Held: Both the lower courts upheld the plaintiff's claim. The BGH dismissed the defendant's appeal, holding that as the device's suitability had not been "raised to being an element of the contract", no challenge could be made under § 119 II BGB.

Judgment: The plaintiff is claiming the sum of 6,367 DM, being the purchase price payable for an ultra-sound machine delivered to the defendant doctor in September 1949. The defendant used the machine and, by letter of 31 December 1949, placed it once again at the disposal of the seller. He contested the claim for the purchase price inter alia on the following ground: his personal experiences with the machine, which had been immediately confirmed by specialist colleagues, had shown that it in no way constituted a machine having any therapeutic value. It did not fulfil the full range of functions which it was claimed to possess. Even though the electrophysical machine revealed no technical defects, it was not suitable for its purpose as warranted; at any rate, treatment using the machine had produced results which were harmful and must be regarded as completely negative.

---

[176] RGZ 124.115.
[177] See generally, Flume, *Eigenschaftsirrtum und Kauf* (Darmstadt: 1975).
[178] BGHZ 16.54.

Grounds [extract]:

2. The court hearing the appeal on a point of law also examined whether the defendant's objections were capable of substantiating a plea of avoidance on the ground of mistake. They are not . . .

According to settled case-law, the value of an object cannot as such be deemed to constitute a characteristic of that object within the meaning of § 119 II BGB. . . . Consequently, the possible commercial utilization of an object is not *per se*, and on its own, a characteristic of that object which is of the essence of the transaction. That concept covers only such factual and legal relationships as are capable of characterising the object itself, and does not include circumstances which can only indirectly affect an assessment of it. . . . Even if it were possible to assume that the fitness of the ultra-sound machine for treating certain types of illnesses constitutes an intrinsic element of the object itself, it could nevertheless only be regarded as an essential characteristic of the transaction if the conceptions entertained in that regard by the defendant or by both the contracting parties were elevated to the status of elements going to the very contents of the contract itself. It has not been shown, however, that that was the case.

Notes

(1) It is stated in the above case that an attribute is essential only where its presence was provided for in the contract itself. More recent case-law has relaxed this requirement somewhat. The newer criterion is, thus, that the assumption must have been recognizably at the basis of the challenging party's entry into the agreement, without being necessarily contained in the contract.[179]

(2) It is stated in both of the above cases that the price or value of an item is not considered to be an essential attribute within § 119 II BGB. Why, as a matter of common sense, might this be so?

(3) An assumption as to the course of future events will not be considered to be significant within § 119 II BGB. Thus, it has been held that a declaration disclaiming an inheritance under a will in 1982 could not be avoided in 1990 because the declarant had mistakenly assumed that property mentioned in the will would remain under the control of the government of the German Democratic Republic.[180]

(4) The error must have been causative of the decision to enter into the contract such as it was. Causation in this regard is tested both subjectively—i.e. from the perspective of the mistaken party herself—and objectively. The latter allows courts to refuse avoidance of the contract where the mistaken facts would only have influenced a wilful or foolish individual. This requirement seems superfluous in cases coming within § 119 II BGB.

(5) A declaration of intention which proceeded from an error and which it is sought to set aside must be challenged through a further declaration of intention directed to the other party to the contract (§ 143 BGB). The subsequent declaration of intention may be a notice to the other party, or be constituted by conduct which unequivocally indicates an intention to avoid. § 142 BGB provides that rescission is of retrospective effect, i.e. the contract (or other juristic act) is void *ex tunc*. The German courts have made exceptions to this *ex tunc* rule, chiefly in the case of labour contracts and other ongoing contractual

---

[179] BGHZ 88.240.
[180] See LG Berlin, NJW 1991.1238.

relationships, and ordered the contract avoided *ex nunc* only. This may be justified by the difficulty of making restitution of benefits on avoidance of such contracts.[181]

(6) A challenge to a declaration made under the influence of a mistake, within § 119 BGB, must be made "without culpable delay" upon discovery of the grounds for challenge (§ 121 BGB). The period may be very short—in the *Bank Guarantee* case,[182] the right was lost in two weeks. How can this be rationalized on the basis of allocation of risk? In any case the right to challenge expires when thirty years have elapsed from the date of the impugned declaration of intention.

(7) The right to avoid under § 119 BGB (both sections) is not lost by the mistaken party, even though contributory negligence has been shown on his part. However, as we have seen, the other party is afforded a measure of protection by § 122 BGB. He may thereby claim reliance damages (*negative Interesse*) from the mistaken party where the latter opts to avoid. This right in its turn is conditional upon his having had no knowledge or possibility of knowing of the error. Thus the risk of "accidental misapprehensions" is allocated to the party who was best placed to avoid it. In contrast, there no such provision for compensation under § 123 BGB where there was fraud.

(2) Complications: absence of objet/cause and impossibility

At this stage we need to consider a complication. In at least French and German law there are a number of situations which involve a sort of mistake and in which the contract will be ineffective, but which are dealt with under doctrines other than mistake: for example lack of *objet*, lack of *cause* or impossibility. For example, suppose the parties agree to the sale of a car which, unknown to either party, has just been destroyed in a fire.

(a) Absence of Objet or of Cause in French Law
In French law, where there is a contract to sell specific goods which have ceased to exist, the contract will be void for lack of *objet* and so no question will arise of annulling it for mistake. This approach, which derives from Roman law, is also found in other systems, for example English law.[183]

In a French case M agreed with R (as was legally permissible) to do R's military service in R's place. Unknown to either of them, R was not liable for service. It was held that M's obligation lacked *objet* and R's lacked *cause*.[184]

b) Initial Impossibility in German Law
In the BGB mistakes as to the existence of the subject matter of the contract are dealt with not by §§ 119 *et seq.* BGB, but in the general part of the law of obligations under the rules on initial impossibility: §§ 306 *et seq.* BGB. Cases where the subject matter does not exist at the time of the contract are termed cases of objective impossibility. By contrast, where the contract debtor is not able to perform his obligations, though another might be able to do, the situation is deemed to be one of subjective impossibility.

---

[181] Termination of contracts in general is discussed more fully *infra* at 792.
[182] *Supra*, at 355.
[183] *Infra*, at 382–383.
[184] Req. 30 July 1873, S. 1873.1.448, D. 1873.1.330. See also **1.F.97**, *supra* at 135.

There will be objective impossibility where the performance physically cannot be rendered, for example where the item promised has perished by the time of the contract. (Also included in this category are cases where performance is technically (or physically) possible, but so unacceptably burdensome as to be as good as impossible, for example a contract to find a ring at the bottom of the ocean.) Subjective impossibility is instanced where one party promises to another a piece of art which he has already sold. This type of impossibility is also known more accurately as "incapability".

§ 306 BGB states that "a contract, performance of which is objectively impossible, is void". In such cases the law on unjustified enrichment in §§ 812ff BGB applies and restitution of benefits may be required. However, where one party knew or should have known of the initial objective impossibility she is obliged to pay reliance damages to the other party. This obligation is not incurred where the other party herself knew or should have known of the impossibility (§ 307 BGB).

By contrast, where the initial impossibility is subjective only, the contract is not void. Rather the contract debtor must pay expectation damages to the contract creditor. Some writers have argued that there should be a claim for damages only where there was some fault on the part of the contract debtor. However, a fault requirement has generally been rejected both by commentators and in the case-law. This means that where both parties were in error as to the subjective impossibility the contract debtor will nonetheless be required to pay damages.[185]

c) Cases Where the Goods Have Ceased to Exist in English Law

There is also a rule of English law that, if there is a contract to sell goods but, unknown to either party, the goods have already ceased to exist, the contract is void. The precise foundation of this rule, and its relationship to the rather limited doctrine of common mistake in English law, is not wholly clear.

The doctrine of common mistake in English law seems to be a relatively recent innovation, a nineteenth century importation from civil law.[186] During the first half of the century various cases which are now seen as involving common mistake were decided without invoking any such doctrine. Perhaps the best known is *Couturier* v. *Hastie*.[187] A c.& f. contract (rather like a cif contract but without the insurance element) had been made for a cargo of corn that both parties assumed was in existence. In fact the corn had begun overheating and the captain of the ship had unloaded and sold it (the normal practice). The sellers argued that the buyers must still take up the shipping documents and pay the price. If it had been the case that the goods had been damaged or lost after the contract had been made, then at least in modern law the buyer would indeed have been obliged to pay—the risk would have passed as from shipment and the buyer would be expected to claim on the insurance, if any. But the House of Lords affirmed the decision of the Exchequer Chamber that on the actual facts the buyer did not have to pay. The contract was one "for the sale of a cargo supposed to exist", not "for goods lost or not lost". The word mistake does not occur in the judgments, nor is there any discussion of whether

---

[185] On the German doctrine of *clausula rebus sic stantibus* see *infra*, at 397.
[186] See Simpson (1975) 91 LQR 247, 269.
[187] (1856) 5 HL Cas. 673.

the contract was void—the only point decided was that the seller could not require the buyer to perform.

The most obvious source for the doctrine of mistake is *Kennedy* v. *Panama, etc Royal Mail Co.*[188] The plaintiff had bought some shares relying on a statement that the company had obtained a valuable contract to carry mail for the New Zealand government. This would now be treated as an innocent misrepresentation.[189] But the case was argued and decided on purely common law grounds, and the question was simply whether there had been a total failure of consideration so that the plaintiff could get his money back.[190] Again, this is something different from mistake, but in deciding that there had not been a total failure of consideration Blackburn J drew on Roman law principles. He referred to the Roman doctrine of *error*, under which a mistake as to substance would invalidate a contract but a mistake merely as to quality would not; and said that the misunderstanding about the shares went only to quality, so that there was no total failure of consideration. It is easy to see how this could be interpreted as saying that a mistake as to substance will make the contract void for mistake, as it did in Roman law. At any rate, by the end of the century *Couturier* v. *Hastie* was considered to have been decided on the ground that the contract was void, and this solution was adopted by the Sale of Goods Act 1893, now replaced by the following provision:

Sale of Goods Act 1979   **3.E.63.**

Section 6: Where there is a contract for the sale of specific goods, and the goods without the knowledge of the seller have perished at the time when the contract is made, the contract is void.

This seems to be very close to the French rule that a contract of sale cannot be valid without an object. However, English law does not have the requirement of *objet*, and generally the problem of a contract about a non-existent item seems to have been treated by English courts as a question of mistake—for example, *Galloway* v. *Galloway*[191], in which a separation agreement between parties who mistakenly thought themselves validly married was held to be void for common mistake.

In contrast, more recent codes do not treat a contract as automatically void because it is impossible, for example in Dutch law the debtor can set aside the contract under BW Articles. 6:265 *et seq.*[192] See also the Greek Code civil, Articles 362–364 and the PECL:

Principles of European Contract Law   **3.PECL.64.**

Article 4:102: *Initial Impossibility*
A contract is not invalid merely because at the time it was concluded performance of the obligation assumed was impossible, or because a party was not entitled to dispose of the assets to which the contract relates.

[188] (1867) LR 2 QB 580 at 587.
[189] *Infra*, at 400.
[190] See further *infra* at 803.
[191] (1914) 30 TLR 531.
[192] See Hartkamp and Tillema, *Contract Law in the Netherlands* (The Hague/Boston: Kluwer, 1995), para. 93.

383

Nor do the Principles adopt a principle of *cause*.

(3) Mistake in general (resumed)

While the case of the contract for something which did not exist was thus covered in English law, there remained two questions: (1) does English law have a general doctrine of mistake or is it limited to cases of *res extincta*? (2) is a contract for specific goods which do not exist always void? But first we should consider the basic authorities on mistake as to the substance in English law.

House of Lords   **3.E.65.**
Bell v. *Lever Bros*[193]

COMMON MISTAKE AS TO ESSENTIAL QUALITIES OF SUBJECT MATTER

The golden handshakes

A common mistake which makes the subject-matter of a contract essentially different from what the parties supposed renders the contract void.

Facts: Two company directors, D'Arcy Cooper and Bell, agreed to leave their posts early in exchange for generous compensation which was paid to them by the company. The company later discovered that the directors had committed certain breaches of duty which (though the directors did not appreciate this) meant that they could have been dismissed without notice or compensation. The company sought to recover the money paid to the directors, claiming that the money should be repaid and damages for fraud.

Held: The jury found that the directors were not guilty of fraud. The court of first instance held that the compensation agreement was void for what it called mutual mistake, and the Court of Appeal agreed. The House of Lords reversed this decision. (There was an issue whether the plaintiffs had pleaded "mutual" (i.e. common) mistake, or only unilateral mistake, which would not be a sufficient ground (see *supra*, at 346). Lord Atkin held that this point need not be decided as the claim on mutual mistake failed in any event.)

Judgment: LORD ATKIN: . . . In the view that I take of the whole case it becomes unnecessary to deal finally with the appellants' complaint that the points upon which the plaintiffs succeeded were not open to them. I content myself with saying that much may be said for that contention.

Two points present themselves for decision. Was the agreement of March 19, 1929, void by reason of a mutual mistake of Mr. D'Arcy Cooper and Mr. Bell? . . . The rules of law dealing with the effect of mistake contract appear to be established with reasonable clearness. If mistake operates at all it operates so as to negative or in some cases to nullify consent. The parties may be mistaken in the identity of the contracting parties, or in the existence of the subject matter of the contract at the date of the contract, or in the quality of the subject matter of the contract. These mistakes may be by one party, or by both, and the legal effect may depend upon the class of mistake above mentioned. Thus a mistaken belief by A. that he is contracting with B., whereas in fact he is contracting with C., will negative consent where it is clear that the intention of A. was to contract only with B. So the agreement of A. and B to purchase a specific article is void if in fact the article had perished before the date of sale. In this case, though the parties in fact were agreed about the subject matter, yet a consent to transfer or take delivery of something not existent is deemed useless, the consent is nullified. As codified in the Sale of Goods Act the contract is expressed to be void if the seller was in ignorance of the destruction of the specific chattel. I apprehend that if the seller with

---

[193] [1932] AC 161.

knowledge that a chattel was destroyed purported to sell it to a purchaser, the latter might sue for damages for non-delivery though the former could not sue for non-acceptance, but I know of no case where a seller has so committed himself. This is a case where mutual mistake certainly and unilateral mistake by the seller of goods will prevent a contract from arising. Corresponding to mistake as to the existence of the subject-matter is mistake as to title in cases where, unknown to the parties, the buyer is already the owner of that which the seller purports to sell to him. The parties intended to effectuate a transfer of ownership: such a transfer is impossible: the stipulation is naturali ratione inutilis. This is the case of *Cooper* v. *Phibbs* (l), where A. agreed to take a lease of a fishery from B., though contrary to the belief of both parties at the time A. was tenant for life of the fishery and B. appears to have had no title at all. To such a case Lord Westbury applied the principle that if parties contract under a mutual mistake and misapprehension as to their relative and respective rights the result is that the agreement is liable to be set aside as having proceeded upon a common mistake. Applied to the context the statement is only subject to the criticism that the agreement would appear to be void rather than voidable. Applied to mistake as to rights generally it would appear to be too wide. Even where the vendor has no title, though both parties think he has, the correct view would appear to be that there is a contract: but that the vendor has either committed a breach of a stipulation as to title, or is not able to perform his contract. The contract is unenforceable by him but is not void.

Mistake as to quality of the thing contracted for raises more difficult questions. In such a case a mistake will not affect assent unless it is the mistake of both parties, and is as to the existence of some quality which makes the thing without the quality essentially different from the thing as it was believed to be. Of course it may appear that the parties contracted that the article should possess the quality which one or other or both mistakenly believed it to possess. But in such a case there is a contract and the inquiry is a different one, being whether the contract as to quality amounts to a condition or a warranty, a different branch of the law. The principles to be applied are to be found in two cases which, as far as my knowledge goes, have always been treated as authoritative expositions of the law. The first is *Kennedy* v. *Panama Royal Mail Co.*

In that case the plaintiff had applied for shares in the defendant company on the faith of a prospectus which stated falsely but innocently that the company had a binding contract with the Government of New Zealand for the carriage of. mails. On discovering the true facts the plaintiff brought an action for the recovery of the sums he had paid on calls. The defendants brought a cross action for further calls.

. . . The Court came to the conclusion in that case that, though there was a misapprehension as to that which was a material part of the motive inducing the applicant to ask for the shares, it did not prevent the shares from being in substance those he applied for.

The next case is *Smith* v *Hughes*, the well known case as to new and old oats (see *infra* at 411).

. . .

The Court ordered a new trial. It is not quite clear whether they considered that if the defendant's contention was correct, the parties were not ad idem or there was a contractual condition that the oats sold were old oats. In either case the defendant would succeed in defeating the claim.

In these cases I am inclined to think that the true analysis is that there is a contract, but that the one party is not able to supply the very thing whether goods or services that the other party contracted to take; and therefore the contract is unenforceable by the one if executory, while if executed the other can recover back money paid on the ground of failure of the consideration.

We are now in a position to apply to the facts of this case the law as to mistake so far as it has been stated. It is essential on this part of the discussion to keep in mind the finding of the jury acquitting the defendants of fraudulent misrepresentation or concealment in procuring the agreements in question. Grave injustice may be done to the defendants and confusion introduced into the legal conclusion, unless it is quite clear that in considering mistake in this case no suggestion of fraud is admissible and cannot strictly be regarded by the judge who has to determine the legal issues raised. The agreement which is said to be void is the agreement contained in the letter of 19 March 1929, that Bell would retire from the Board of the Niger Company and its Subsidiaries, and that in consideration of his doing so Levers would pay him as compensation for the termination of his agreements and consequent loss of office the sum of £30,000 in full satisfaction and discharge of all claims and demands of any kind against Lever Brothers, the Niger Company or its subsidiaries. The agreement which, as part of the contract was terminated, had been broken so that it could be repudiated. Is an agreement to terminate a broken contract different in kind from an agreement to terminate an unbroken contract, assuming that the breach has given the one party the right to declare the contract at an end? I feel the weight of the plaintiffs' contention that a contract immediately determinable is a different thing from a contract for an unexpired term, and that the difference in kind can be illustrated by the immense price of release from the longer contract as compared with the shorter. And I agree that an agreement to take an assignment of a lease for five years is not the same thing as to take an assignment of a lease for three years, still less a term for a few months. But, on the whole, I have come to the conclusion that it would be wrong to decide that an agreement to terminate a definite specified contract is void if it turns out that the agreement had already been broken and could have been terminated otherwise. The contract released is the identical contract in both cases, and the party paying for release gets exactly what he bargains for. It seems immaterial that he could have got the same result in another way, or that if he had known the true facts he would not have entered into the bargain. A. buys B.'s horse; he thinks the horse is sound and he pays the price of a sound horse; he would certainly not have bought the horse if he had known as the fact is that the horse is unsound. If B. has made no representation as to soundness and has not contracted that the horse is sound, A. is bound and cannot recover back the price. A. buys a picture from B.; both A. and B. believe it to be the work of an old master, and a high price is paid. It turns out to be a modern copy. A. has no remedy in the absence of representation or warranty. A. agrees to take on lease or to buy from B. an unfurnished dwelling-house. The house is in fact uninhabitable. A. would never have entered into the bargain if he had known the fact. A. has no remedy, and the position is the same whether B. knew the facts or not, so long as he made no representation or gave no warranty. A. buys a roadside garage business from B. abutting on a public thoroughfare: unknown to A., but known to B., it has already been decided to construct a byepass road which will divert substantially the whole of the traffic from passing A.'s garage. Again A. has no remedy. All these cases involve hardship on A. and benefit B., as most people would say, unjustly. They can be supported on the ground that it is of paramount importance that contracts should be observed, and that if parties honestly comply with the essentials of the formation of contracts—i.e., agree in the same terms on the same subject-matter—they are bound, and must rely on the stipulations of the contract for protection from the effect of facts unknown to them.

This brings the discussion to the alternative mode of expressing the result of a mutual mistake. It is said that in such a case as the present there is to be implied a stipulation in the contract that a condition of its efficacy is that the facts should be as understood by both parties—namely, that the contract could not be terminated till the end of the current term. The question of the existence of conditions, express or implied, is obviously one that affects not the formation of contract, but the investigation of the terms of the contract when made. A condition derives its efficacy from the consent of the parties, express or implied. They have agreed, but on what terms. One term may be that unless the facts are or are not of a particular nature, or unless an event has or has not happened, the contract is not to take effect. With regard to future facts such a condition is obviously contractual. Till the event occurs the parties are bound. Thus the condition (the exact terms of which need not here be investigated) that is generally accepted as underlying the principle of the frustration cases is contractual, an implied condition. Sir John Simon formulated for the assistance of your Lordships a proposition which should be recorded: "Whenever it is to be inferred from the terms of a contract or its surrounding circumstances that the consensus has been reached upon the basis of a particular contractual assumption, and that assumption is not true, the contract is avoided: i.e., it is void ab initio if the assumption is of present fact and it ceases to bind if the assumption is of future fact".

I think few would demur to this statement, but its value depends upon the meaning of "a contractual assumption," and also upon the true meaning to be attached to "basis," a metaphor which may mislead. When used expressly in contracts, for instance, in policies of insurance, which state that the truth of the statements in the proposal is to be the basis of the contract of insurance, the meaning is clear. The truth of the statements is made a condition of the contract, which failing, the contract is void unless the condition is waived. The proposition does not amount to more than this that, if the contract expressly or impliedly contains a term that a particular assumption is a condition of the contract, the contract is avoided if the assumption is not true. But we have not advanced far on the inquiry how to ascertain whether the contract does contain such a condition. Various words are to be found to define the state of things which make a condition. "In the contemplation of both parties fundamental to the continued validity of the contract," "a foundation essential to its existence," "a fundamental reason for making it," are phrases found in the important judgment of Scrutton LJ in the present case. The first two phrases appear to me to be unexceptionable. They cover the case of a contract to serve in a particular place, the existence of which is fundamental to the service, or to procure the services of a professional vocalist, whose continued health is essential to performance. But "a fundamental reason for making a contract" may, with respect, be misleading. The reason of one party only is presumedly not intended, but in the cases I have suggested above, of the sale of a horse or of a picture, it might be said that the fundamental reason for making the contract was the belief of both parties that the horse was sound or the picture an old master, yet in neither case would the condition as I think exist. Nothing is more dangerous than to allow oneself liberty to construct for the parties contracts which they have not in terms made by importing implications which would appear to make the contract more businesslike or more just. The implications to be made are to be no more than are "necessary" for giving business efficacy to the transaction, and it appears to me that, both as to existing facts and future facts, a condition would not be implied unless the new state of facts makes the contract something different in kind from the contract in the original state of facts. Thus, in *Krell* v. *Henry* (*infra*, at 612), Vaughan Williams LJ finds that the subject of the contract was "rooms to view the procession": the postponement, therefore, made the rooms not rooms to view the procession. This also is the test finally chosen by Lord Sumner in *Bank Line* v. *Arthur Capel & Co.*, agreeing with Lord Dunedin in *Metropolitan Water Board* v. *Dick Kerr*, where, dealing with the criterion for determining the effect of interruption in "frustrating" a contract, he says: "An interruption may be so long as to destroy the identity of the work or service, when resumed, with the work or service when interrupted."

We therefore get a common standard for mutual mistake and implied conditions whether as to existing or as to future facts. Does the state of new facts destroy the identity of the subject matter as it was in the original state of fact?

To apply the principle to the infinite combinations of facts that arise in actual experience will continue to be difficult, but if this case results in establishing order into what has been a somewhat confused and difficult branch of the law it will have served a useful purpose:

I have already stated my reasons for deciding that in the present case the identity of the subject-matter was not destroyed by the mutual mistake, if any, and need not repeat them . . .

Notes

(1) Because the mistake made in this case seems serious, yet relief was denied, some commentators argued that English law still does not go beyond giving relief in the cases of *res extincta* and *res sua*, and that it does not have a general doctrine of mistake as to substance. But the most recent judicial opinion has rejected this: see the judgment of Steyn J in *Associated Japanese Bank (International) Ltd* v. *Crédit du Nord SA*,[194] preferring Lord Atkin's broader formula.

[194] [1989] 1 WLR 255.

(2) Lord Atkin says that the mistake must make the thing "essentially different"; and the examples he gives make it clear that this is interpreted strictly. Many of the cases in which he says there will be no operative mistake are ones in which the mistake would be sufficiently serious to ground relief in French or German law. This strictness may be the counterpart of the relative generosity of English law in allowing rescission under the doctrine of misrepresentation.[195]

(3) It may be that Lord Atkin was too restrictive in some of his examples. Treitel argues persuasively that in Lord Atkin's example of the contract for the picture which the parties mistakenly thought to be by an Old Master, the contract might be void for mistake, as the thing bought and sold would be essentially different from what the parties believed they were buying and selling.[196] The parties would not say they had just bought and sold "a picture of . . ." but "a Rembrandt". However, Treitel accepts the other examples.

(4) In the last two large paragraphs extracted above, Lord Atkin seems to admit that English courts can reach the same results as under the doctrine of mistake by using the doctrine of implied conditions. It will be seen later that the English courts will imply into a contract terms which they consider the parties must have intended. Some implied terms place an obligation on one party (for example *The Moorcock*[197]) but others may be conditions—i.e. a term[198] to the effect that, unless and until something occurs, a contractual obligation will not come into effect.[199] In this context the argument would be that the operation of the contract was conditional on the facts being as the parties believed them to be. On occasions the courts decide what look like mistake cases without ever mentioning mistake but instead relying on an implied condition: for example *Financings Ltd* v. *Stimpson*.[200] This raises two questions. The first is whether English law really recognizes a separate doctrine of common mistake. It has been argued that the "implied condition" approach leaves no room for an independent doctrine of mistake.[201] The second is that the implied condition approach gives the court greater flexibility: for example in *Financings* the contract was found to be void for failure of an implied condition precedent even though the "mistake" seems not to have been sufficiently serious to give relief under the doctrine of common mistake, cf. the examples in the previous note.

(5) Lord Atkin does not discuss the question of what will happen if one party was at fault, in the sense that he ought to have known the truth. This problem arose graphically in the Australian case of *McRae* v. *Commonwealth Disposals Commission*.[202] The Disposals Commission purported to sell to a salvage contractor the wreck of an oil tanker lying on the Jourmand Reef, the position of which was stated; but when the contractor's salvage expedition arrived it could find no reef at such a location, let alone a

---

[195] *Infra*, at 403.

[196] Treitel, *Contract* at 268–269.

[197] **4.E.25**, *infra* at 585.

[198] Note that in English law "term" is used in a quite different sense from "*termes*" in French law. The English terms may include both obligations and conditions, whereas a French *terme* is something which is bound to occur, like the passage of time and therefore excludes conditions which are not bound to occur. See Nicholas at 158–9.

[199] This would be a condition "precedent". It is also possible that the occurrence of the event will bring a contractual obligation to an end, in which case the condition is said to be "subsequent".

[200] [1962] 1 WLR 1184; see also P. Atiyah, *Essays on Contract* (Oxford: Clarendon, 1989), chap. 9.

[201] See Smith, (1994) 110 LQR 400 and *Chitty*, para. § 5–000.

[202] (1950) 84 CLR 377 (High Ct).

wreck and the contractor sued for non-delivery. The Disposals Commission argued that the contract was void for mistake but the High Court rejected the argument. *Couturier* v. *Hastie*[203] had not decided that a contract for non-existent goods was necessarily void, merely that the buyer did not have to pay; and the Australian equivalent of the Sale of Goods Act section 6 did not apply since the goods had never existed. The Commission had contracted that there was a tanker in the location specified and was liable for non-delivery. In the *Associated Japanese Bank* case Steyn J said:[204]

. . . [There] is a requirement which was not specifically discussed in *Bell* v. *Lever Bros. Ltd.* What happens if the party who is seeking to rely on the mistake had no reasonable grounds for his belief? An extreme example is that of the man who makes a contract with minimal knowledge of the facts to which the mistake relates but is content that it is a good speculative risk. In my judgment a party cannot be allowed to rely on a common mistake where the mistake consists of a belief which is entertained by him without any reasonable grounds for such belief: *McRae* v. *Commonwealth Disposals Commission.* That is not because principles such as estoppel or negligence require it, but simply because policy and good sense dictate that the positive rules regarding common mistake should be so qualified. Curiously enough this qualification is similar to the civilian concept where the doctrine of error in substantia is tempered by the principles of culpa in contrahendo.

The similarity noted by the judge should not be taken too literally, however. Suppose the parties agree to the sale of a picture which both parties believed, based on their own judgement, to be by an artist "of the school of Constable" but not by Constable himself; but the seller should know from documents he (but not the buyer) has seen that the picture is almost certainly by Constable himself and so worth much more than the sale price. In English law the effect is to prevent the seller avoiding the contract. In contrast, in German law the seller may avoid the contract but will have to compensate the buyer under § 122 BGB.

(6) In English law the doctrine of mistake as to the subject matter or as to the circumstances is strictly limited to "common mistake" i.e. cases where both parties make the same mistake. "Unilateral" mistake is recognized only when it is a mistake as to the terms of the contract which prevents there being a proper agreement.[205] However, a large number of contracts are set aside for what looks like a kind of mistake under the doctrine of misrepresentation.[206]

(7) If there is an operative common mistake under the common law principle described in *Bell* v. *Lever Bros.*, the effect is that the contract is void. Compare the next case.

Court of Appeal   **3.E.66.**
Solle v. *Butcher*[207]

CONTRACT ENTERED UNDER COMMON FUNDAMENTAL MISTAKE VOIDABLE

A new flat?

A contract which the parties have entered into under a common and fundamental misapprehension as to the facts is voidable in equity.

[203] *Supra*, at 382.
[204] [1989] 1 WLR 255 at 268.
[205] See *supra* at 364.
[206] *Infra*, at 400.
[207] [1950] 1 KB 671.

Facts: The defendant was the landlord of a flat which was let to the tenant at a rent which was controlled. The landlord made various improvements which would have given him the right to increase the rent from £140 to approximately £250, as long as he served a special notice. He did not do this because the parties both considered that the work done meant that the old rent for the flat would no longer apply as it would constitute a new flat within the meaning of the rent-control legislation. Instead he simply let the flat to the tenant for seven years at £250 a year. After some months of paying the new rent the tenant claimed that the flat was still subject to the old rent figure and demanded repayment of the difference. It was by then too late for the landlord to serve a notice of increase.

Held: The old rent did still apply but the contract had been entered under a shared fundamental mistake and could be set aside. The tenant was given the choice of leaving or paying £250 a year.

Judgment: LORD DENNING: . . . In this plight the landlord seeks to set aside the lease. He says, with truth, that it is unfair that the tenant should have the benefit of the lease for the outstanding five years of the term at 140*l*. a year, when the proper rent is 250*l*. a year. If he cannot give a notice of increase now, can he not avoid the lease ? The only ground on which he can avoid it is on the ground of mistake. It is quite plain that the parties were under a mistake. They thought that the flat was not tied down to a controlled rent whereas in fact it was. In order to see whether the lease can be avoided for this mistake it is necessary to remember that mistake is of two kinds: first, mistake which renders the contract void, that is, a nullity from the beginning, which is the kind of mistake which was dealt with by the courts of common law; and, secondly, mistake which renders the contract not void, but voidable, that is, liable to be set aside on such terms as the court thinks fit, which is the kind of mistake which was dealt with by the courts of equity. Much of the difficulty which has attended this subject has arisen because, before the fusion of law and equity, the courts of common law, in order to do justice in the case in hand, extended this doctrine of mistake beyond its proper limits and held contracts to be void which were really only voidable, a process which was capable of being attended with much injustice to third persons who had bought goods or otherwise committed themselves on the faith that there was a contract. In the well-known case of *Cundy* v. *Lindsay*, Cundy suffered such an injustice. He bought the handkerchiefs from the rogue, Blenkarn, before the Judicature Acts came into operation. Since the fusion of law and equity, there is no reason to continue this process, and it will be found that only those contracts are now held void in which the mistake was such as to prevent the formation of any contract at all.

Let me first consider mistakes which render a contract a nullity. All previous decisions on this subject must now be read in the light of *Bell* v. *Lever Bros. Ltd*. The correct interpretation of that case, to my mind, is that, once a contract has been made, that is to say, once the parties, whatever their inmost states of mind, have to all outward appearances agreed with sufficient certainty in the same terms on the same subject matter, then the contract is good unless and until it is set aside for failure of some condition on which the existence of the contract depends, or for fraud, or on some equitable ground. Neither party can rely on his own mistake to say it was a nullity from the beginning, no matter that it was a mistake which to his mind was fundamental, and no matter that the other parts knew that he was under a mistake. A fortiori, if the other party did not know of the mistake, but shared it. The cases where goods have perished at the time of sale, or belong to the buyer, are really contracts which are not void for mistake but are void by reason of an implied condition precedent, because the contract proceeded on the basic assumption that it was possible of performance. So far as cases later than *Bell* v. *Lever Bros. Ltd*. are concerned, I do not think that *Sowler* v. *Potter* can stand with *King's Norton Metal Co. Ltd*. v. *Edridge*, which shows that the doctrine of French law as enunciated by Pothier is no part of English law. Nor do I think that the contract in *Nicholson and Venn* v. *Smith Marriott* was void front the beginning.

Applying these principles, it is clear that here there was a contract. The parties agreed in the same terms on the same subject-matter. It is true that the landlord was under a mistake which was to him fundamental: he would nor for one moment have considered letting the flat for seven years if it means that he could only charge *140l.* a year for it. He made the fundamental mistake of believing that the rent lie could charge was not tied down to a controlled rent; but, whether it was his own mistake or a mistake common to both him and the tenant, it is not a ground for saying that the lease was from the beginning a nullity. Any other view would lead to remarkable results, for it would mean that, in the many cases where the parties mistakenly think a house is outside the Rent Restriction Acts when it is really within them, the tenancy would be a nullity, and the tenant would have to go; with the result that the tenants would not dare to seek to have their rents reduced to the permitted amounts lest they should be turned out.

Let me next consider mistakes which render a contract voidable, that is, liable to be set aside on some equitable ground. Whilst presupposing that a contract was good at law, or at any rate not void, the court of equity would often relieve a party from the consequences of his own mistake, so long as it could do so without injustice to third parties. The court, it was said, had power to set aside the contract whenever it was of opinion that it was unconscientious for the other party to avail himself of the legal advantage which he had obtained: *Torrance* v. *Bolton* per James LJ.

The court had, of course, to define what it considered to be unconscientious, but in this respect equity has shown a progressive development. It is now clear that a contract will be set aside if the mistake of the one party has been induced by a material misrepresentation of the other, even though it was not fraudulent or fundamental; or if one party, knowing that the other is mistaken about the terms of an offer, or the identity of the person by whom it is made, lets him remain under his delusion and concludes a contract on the mistaken terms instead of pointing out the mistake. That is, I venture to think, the ground on which the defendant in *Smith* v. *Hughes* would be exempted nowadays, and on which, according to the view by Blackburn J of the facts, the contract in *Lindsay* v. *Cundy*, was voidable and not void; and on which the lease in *Sowler* v. *Potter* was in my opinion, voidable and not void.

A contract is also liable in equity to be set aside if the parties were under a common misapprehension either as to facts or as to their relative and respective rights, provided that the misapprehension was fundamental and that the party seeking to set it aside was not himself at fault.... [The] House of Lords in 1867 in the great case of *Cooper* v. *Phibbs*, affirmed the doctrine there acted on as correct. In that case an uncle had told his nephew, not intending to misrepresent anything, but being in fact in error, that he (the uncle) was entitled to a fishery; and the nephew, after the uncle's death, acting in the belief of the truth of what the uncle had told him, entered into an agreement to rent the fishery from the uncle's daughters, whereas it actually belonged to the nephew himself. The mistake there as to the title to the fishery did not render the tenancy agreement a nullity. If it had done, the contract would have been void at law from the beginning and equity would have had to follow the law. There would have been no contract to set aside and no terms to impose. The House of Lords, however, held that the mistake was only such as to make it voidable, or, in Lord Westbury's words, " liable to be set aside " on such terms as the court thought fit to impose; and it was so set aside.

The principle so established by *Cooper* v. *Phibbs* has been repeatedly acted on: see, for instance, *Earl Beauchamp* v. *Winn*, and *Huddersfied Banking Co. Ltd.* v. *Lister*. It is in no way impaired by *Bell* v. *Lever Bros. Ltd.*, which was treated in the House of Lords as a case at law depending on whether the contract was a nullity or not. If it had been considered on equitable grounds, the result might have been different. In any case, the principle of *Cooper* v. *Phibbs* has been fully restored by *Norwich Union Fire Insuarance Society Ltd.* v. *William H. Price, Ltd.*

Applying that principle to this case, . . . [on] the defendant's evidence, which the judge preferred, I should have thought there was a good deal to be said for the view that the lease was induced by an innocent material misrepresentation by the plaintiff. It seems to me that the plaintiff was not merely expressing an opinion on the law: he was making an unambiguous statement as to private rights; and a misrepresentation as to private rights is equivalent to a misrepresentation of fact for this purpose: *MacKenzie* v. *Royal Bank of Canada*. But it is unnecessary to come to a firm conclusion on this point, because, as Bucknill LJ has said, there was clearly a common mistake, or, as 1 would prefer to describe it, a common misapprehension, which was fundamental and in no way due to any fault of the defendant; and *Cooper* v. *Phibbs* affords ample authority for saying that, by reason of the common misapprehension, this lease can be set aside on such terms as the court thinks fit. . . .

What terms then should be imposed here? If the lease was set aside without any terms being imposed, it would mean that the tenant would have to go out and would have to pay a reasonable sum for his use and occupation. That would, however not just be to the tenant. It is similar to a case where a long lease is made at the full permitted rent in the common belief that notices of increase have previously been served, whereas in fact they have not. In *Cooper* v. *Phibbs*, as in this, when the lease is set aside terms, must be imposed so as to see that the tenant is not unjustly evicted.

. . . if the mistake here had not happened a proper notice of increase would have been given and the lease would have been executed at the full permitted rent. I think this court should follow these examples and should impose terms which will enable the tenant to choose either to stay on at the proper rent or to go out.

In my opinion, therefore, the appeal should be allowed. The declaration that the standard rent of the flat is 140*l*. per annum should stand. An order should be made on the counter claim that, on the landlord giving the undertaking which I have mentioned, the lease be set aside. An account should be had to determine the sum payable for use and occupation. The tenant's claim for repayment of rent and for breach of covenant should be dismissed, In respect of the tenant's occupation during the rescinded lease and licence, he will be liable to pay a reasonable sum for use and occupation. That sum should, *prima facie*, be assessed at the full amount permitted by the Acts, not, however, exceeding £250 a year. Mesne profits as against a tresspasser are assessed at the full amount permitted by the Acts, even though notices of increase have not been served, because that is the amount lost by the landlord. The same assessment should be made here because the sums payable for use and occupation are not rent, and the statutory provisions about notices of increase do not apply to them. All necessary credits must, of course, be given in respect of past payment, and so forth.

BUCKNILL LJ delivered a concurring judgment.

JENKINS LJ (dissenting): . . . The learned county court judge in the passage I have just quoted said that "both parties for some obscure reasons imagine that the Rent Acts did not apply" and that he did not think "they ever addressed their minds to the materials question of the identity. This was criticised as contrary to the evidence. I do not agree. I think the learned county judge, who had himself formed a clear opinion to the effect that the reconstructed flat was in substance the same dwelling house as the original flat, described the reason why the parties did not appreciate this and the consequent continued application of the standard rent of £140 as "obscure" but accounted for it by concluding that the parties formed the view that the alterations and improvements prevented the old standard rent from applying without really directing their minds to the material question whether the, notwithstanding all the alterations and improvements, the flat proposed to be let to the tenant was not, after all, substantially the same dwelling house as the flat formerly let to Mr. Howard Taylor. I see nothing in the evidence inconsistent with this explanation of the mistake, but, whether the parties failed to ask themselves the right question or, having asked it, although wrongly, I find it impossible to hold that a mutual mistake of the character here involved affords a good ground of recission. The landlord meant to grant and the tenant meant to take the lease in the terms in which the lease was actually granted of the premises which the lease actually granted was compromised. They all knew the material facts bearing on the effect of the Rent Restriction Acts on a lease of these premises, but they mutually misapprehend the effect which in that state of facts those

Acts would have on such a lease. This is a mistake of law of a kind which, so far as I am aware, has never yet been held to afford good ground for recission. It is a question of private right affecting the basis of the contract entered into: see *Cooper* v. *Phibbs*; but simply a mistake as to the effect of certain public statutes on the contract made being in all respects precisely the contract the parties intended to make . . .

Notes

(1) The correctness of this case has been much discussed, since (i) the existence of a separate equitable doctrine was not mentioned in *Bell* v. *Lever Bros.* and (ii) it is far from clear when a mistake will be sufficiently "fundamental" to give rise to relief in equity yet not make the thing contracted for "essentially different" so that the contract is void at common law.[208] However, the courts have on several occasions applied the equitable doctrine and the Court of Appeal has held that it is bound to follow the decision until it is reversed by the House of Lords: *West Sussex Properties Ltd.* v. *Chichester District Council* (unreported, July 2000).

(2) It is not clear how far the requirements of the equitable doctrine are less stringent than those of the common law doctrine. Some of the decisions seem more lenient than anything contemplated by Lord Atkin (for example *Grist* v. *Bailey*,[209] in which the seller of a house was allowed to rescind the contract of sale when she discovered that a tenant in the house was not, as the parties had thought, entitled by statute to remain in possession: but this case was recently doubted: see *William Sindall Ltd.* v. *Cambridgeshire CC*[210]).

(3) The effect of a fundamental common mistake in equity is that either party may seek to avoid the contract—but, as *Solle* v. *Butcher* shows, the court may allow rescission only "on terms"—which is a form of adaptation of the contract.[211]

BW   3.NL.67.

Article 6:228:   1. A contract which has been entered into under the influence of error and which would not have been entered into had there been a correct assessment of the facts, can be annulled:
   a. if the error is imputable to information given by the other party, unless the other party could assume that the contract would have been entered into even without this information;
   b. if the other party, in view of what he knew or ought to know regarding the error, should have informed the party in error;
   c. if the other party in entering into the contract has based himself on the same incorrect assumption as the party in error, unless the other party, even if there had been a correct assessment of the facts, would not have had to understand that the party in error would therefore be prevented from entering into the contract.
   2. The annulment cannot be based on an error as to an exclusively future fact or an error for which, given the nature of the contract, common opinion or the circumstances of the case, the party in error should remain accountable.

[208] See Cartwright (1987) 103 LQR 594.
[209] [1967] Ch. 532.
[210] [1994] 1 WLR 1016, 1035.
[211] See further section 3.2.5, *infra* at 422.

Notes

(1) Article 6:228 seems generous in allowing relief even though the mistake is not as to the substance of the thing contracted for. It suffices that the mistake concerns facts or circumstances which are essential to the mistaken party (in the sense that he would not have entered the contract on the same terms or at all had he known the truth), even if the facts or circumstances are extrinsic to the contract. However, there is no relief if, at the time of the contract, the other party did not know and had no reason to know that the facts or circumstances were essential to the mistaken party.[212]

(2) However, it is narrower than French or German law in restricting the scope of error for which relief will be given by paragraphs (a)–(c).

(3) Article 3:49 provides:

Where a juridical act is subject to annulment, it can be annulled either by extrajudicial declaration or by judgment.

(4) The mistaken party may be able to claim damages from the other if the latter was at fault under the general rule relating to unlawful acts: Article 6:162. The damages will not include loss of expectation.

(4) Qualification of the mistake doctrine: mistakes and obligations imposed by law

In all the systems there are cases in which one or both parties entered the contract under some misapprehension about the subject matter, and might therefore be able to invoke error, but where the law also provides that one party has a particular responsibility under the contract which has been breached as a result of the mistake. A typical example of the problem arises with sale of goods when the goods turn out to be defective. Usually neither the buyer nor the seller will have known this fact, and the parties will both therefore be mistaken as to the condition of the goods. However, the laws of the jurisdictions studied each impose certain obligations on the seller of goods in relation to their condition.

Under French law, the seller is subject to the *garantie des vices cachés*; in German law, to § 459 BGB which applies when—and only when—risk in the goods has passed to the purchaser; in Dutch law, to BW Articles 6:74ff and 7:21ff.; and in English law, provided the seller was selling in the course of a business, to the Sale of Goods Act (SGA) 1979 section 14. These regimes are discussed further below.[213] However, for present purposes, the question is how the claims of both the buyer and the seller on grounds of mistake interrelate with the particular obligations and liabilities of the seller.

German law has a rule that mistake does not apply to cases within § 459 BGB. In BGH, 14 December 1960,[214] a case in which the defendant had bought some property which he

---

[212] See Hartkamp and Tillema, op. cit., para. 80.
[213] *Infra*, at 662–666. It should be remembered that there are significant differences between the regimes: of particular relevance here are (i) the range of application, in that the French *garantie* and § 459 BGB apply to sales of property generally while in English law the seller's liability is confined to sales of goods made in the course of a business (in sales of land the doctrine of *caveat emptor* applies); and (ii) the remedies available. In French and German law the disappointed buyer may claim only return of the price or a reduction of price, unless the seller knew of the defect or warranted its absence; whereas in English law the seller is liable for damages in all cases where SGA 1979 s.14 applies.
[214] BGHZ 34, 32.

then discovered to be in the path of a planned by-pass, when sued for the price he sought to avoid the contract under § 119 II BGB. The BGH said:

The starting-point in that regard is the case-law of the Reichsgericht, as confirmed by the Bundesgerichtshof and extensively approved in the works of academic legal authors, according to which the provisions of § 459ff. BGB constitute special rules precluding the application of §119 II BGB. . . . That view is substantiated by the fact that the object aimed at by the rules on rescission, which finds expression, in particular, in the short limitation periods laid down by § 477 BGB—namely, in the interests of securing the certainty needed in the dealings between the parties, to enable sale transactions to proceed smoothly and within a relatively short period of time—would not be achieved if, by reason of some defect in the subject-matter of the sale within the meaning of § 459ff. BGB constituting at the same time an essential characteristic of the transaction within the meaning of § 119 II BGB, avoidance were possible under the latter provision.

Under § 477 BGB the limitation period for actions to enforce obligations as to quality in the sale of goods is six months after delivery in the case of moveable property and one year after transfer in the case of real property. As the BGH states, this limitation period would be undermined if avoidance for mistake under § 119 BGB were permitted, since the latter type of claim expires only thirty years after the relevant declaration of will (§ 121 BGB).

Where it is the seller rather than the buyer who is seeking to rely on § 119 II BGB, the relationship of § 119 II BGB with §§ 459ff BGB is somewhat different. The seller will not be allowed to escape his obligations under the law of sale by claiming that he was in error as to the presence of an essential attribute of the object of sale if that attribute is one which he is taken by law to have guaranteed to the buyer. The existence of these obligations depends upon the continued existence of the contract, so if the seller could avoid the contract for mistake it could evade its obligations under §§ 459ff. Only where the buyer is not seeking to rely on § 459ff BGB will the seller be allowed to invoke § 119 II BGB.[215]

In the other Civil Law systems the disappointed buyer may choose between remedies on the *garantie* (for example French Code Civil Articles 1641–1649), or for non-performance, and seeking to avoid the contract for error. This may give the plaintiff extra time in which to seek a remedy, since claims on the *garantie* must be brought within *un bref délai* (French Code Civil Article 1648). Dutch law also allows the buyer a choice but the rules on limitation are the same: BW 7:23. The question of choice does not seem to arise in English law since there would be no advantage in the buyer seeking a remedy for mistake rather than one for breach of the implied terms under the SGA; but alternative claims for breach and misrepresentation are common.

The other possibility is that the seller tries to avoid liability on the *garantie* or for breach by arguing mistake. In English law it is thought that the court would hold that the defect could not make the performance essentially different as the risk of a defect is placed by law on the seller.[216]

There is also the possibility of overlap between error and a remedy against the seller for non-performance of some express undertaking he gave.[217]

---

[215] BGH, NJW 1988.2597.
[216] See *Chitty* paras 5-024–5-026.
[217] E.g. the English case of *Dick Bentley Productions Ltd* v. *Harold Smith (Motors) Ltd* [1965] 1 WLR 623 CA (undertaking as to condition of car sold); see *infra* at 407.

(5) Application of mistake: shared mistake

Suppose both the parties have entered the contract on an incorrect assumption about the subject matter or the circumstances ("common" mistake); neither has been influenced by incorrect information given by the other (this situation is considered under (6)[218]). For example:

(a) A wants to sell an area of waste land to B, who wishes to subdivide it for building a housing development. As neither of them knows how much land there is and thus whether B can build enough houses to make it profitable at the price A is asking, they agree to employ a surveyor who tells them that 50 houses can be built. B agrees to buy the land for £1m. In fact the area is only enough for 40 houses and B would not have paid more than £750,000 had he known this.

(b) C sells D a picture of Salisbury Cathedral; both of them assume (from the previous history of the painting, etc.) that it is by the famous artist John Constable. In fact, many years ago there was a wrong attribution and the painting is by one of Constable's sons, a much less gifted artist whose paintings command only very modest prices.

(c) E goes to an auction of the contents of a country house owned by F's estate. The auction is very informal. E bids on a picture which pleases her eye and buys it for 500FF. She then discovers that it is a lost Caravaggio and worth 10m FF.

Can D, B or F's executors obtain relief under any of the systems of law we have considered?

In French law, case (a) closely resembles the case of the *Villa Jacqueline*,[219] save that here both parties share in the mistake. This would not affect the outcome. Case (b) also seems to be a case of error as the substance and relief would be given. Case (c) might be treated differently; the seller's failure to discover the provenance of the picture might be treated as inexcusable and relief be denied on that ground.

In English law, it is doubtful whether the doctrine of mistake would apply in any of the three cases. In case (a), the error does not seem to make the thing contracted for "essentially different" within the strict test laid down in *Bell* v. *Lever Bros.*[220] It is possible that the court might be persuaded to set the contract aside on the ground of mistake under the equitable jurisdiction developed by *Solle* v. *Butcher*;[221] the scope of this is unclear and controversial. Alternatively, it might be possible for the buyer to persuade the court that the contract as a whole was conditional on the area of land being adequate for fifty houses (see *Financings Ltd.* v. *Stimpson*[222]). The contract in case (b) might be void at common law, but there are dicta in *Bell* v. *Lever Bros.*[223] to the contrary: see Note 3.[224] In case (c) it seems likely that the court would say that the estate, by selling without getting an expert opinion, was taking the risk that the picture might be an Old Master and thus

[218] *Infra*, at 400.
[219] *Supra*, at 369.
[220] *Supra*, at 386.
[221] *Supra*, at 389.
[222] *Supra*, at 388.
[223] *Supra*, at 386.
[224] *Supra*, at 388.

refuse relief: see Note 5.[225] (Relief would not be given on the ground of misrepresentation, as neither party seems to have relied on anything stated by the other party, but on
what they were told by a third party. The rules on misrepresentation are covered in the
next subsection.)

In Dutch law it seems that relief would be given in cases (a) and (b) under BW 6:228
litt. c. In case (c) it is possible that the seller would be denied relief under paragraph 2,
because, according to the *communis opinio*, the risk of a mistake relating to the value of
a thing sold should be borne by the seller.[226] But this view is now disputed by Dutch
authors, especially if the buyer is a professional and the seller is not.

In German law, the solution to the three examples give earlier might be as follows. In
cases (a) and (b), relief could be given on the ground of mistake. B could probably claim
that his mistake as to the capacity of the land was an error concerning a fundamental
attribute which formed the basis of the contract and that he is therefore entitled to avoid
under § 119 II BGB. C could make a similar claim as regards case (b). By contrast it is
hard to see how F can claim that he was in error as to anything apart from the value of
the painting. As an unexceptional error of motive (i.e. one which had not been made the
basis of, much less part of the contract) it could not justify avoidance. F's case seems as
little likely to suceed as the seller in the "Mozart notebooks" case.[227]

In German law many cases of shared mistake are dealt with under the doctrine of
clausula rebus sic stantibus rooted in § 242 BGB instead of § 119 II BGB. This more flexible doctrine has been used by German courts to allow for revision of contracts in the
light of supervening circumstances fundamentally different from those envisaged or
assumed by the parties at the time of contracting.[228] Revision is similarly permissible
where circumstances assumed to be present at the time of formation were in fact absent.
The basis of the contract, which is said in such cases to have "collapsed" or be "absent",
may be objective—external to the contract itself, as in the period of drastic inflation in
the 1920s—or subjective—where the parties were both in error as to a fundamental fact
at the time of contracting. The following case, involving a shared error is an example of
the absence of the subjective basis of a contract:

BGH, 13 November 1975[229]   **3.G.68.**

SHARED MISTAKE—ADAPTATION OF THE CONTRACT

Match-fixing

*A contract formed under a shared misapprehension which goes to the basis of the contract can be
adapted or set aside having regard to the requirements of good faith.*

Facts: On 24 June 1971 the defendant, a football club in the *Bundesliga* (Federal League), reached agreement
with the plaintiff, a club in the *Regionalliga* (third division league), regarding the transfer of W., a semi-
professional player. Unknown to either party, W. had accepted a bribe on the occasion of the defendant's

---

[225] *Supra*, at 388.
[226] HR, 19 June 1959, NJ 1960.59.
[227] *Supra*, at 376.
[228] See chap. 5 on Supervening Events, *infra*, esp. at 630 ff.
[229] NJW 1976.565.

Bundesliga match against Arminia Bielefeld on 29 May 1971. At the beginning of August 1971 W., who had in the meantime played in three games for the plaintiff, made a confession. He was dismissed by the plaintiff without notice. The Deutscher Fußballbund (DFB = German Football Association) imposed a ban on him. The plaintiff, which had purported to avoid the transfer agreement, claimed from the defendant reimbursement of the transfer fee paid by it.

Held: The lower courts allowed the claim. The defendant's appeal to the BGH on a point of law was dismissed.

Judgment:

Grounds (extract):

II.2 (b). . . . [W]here two football clubs, such as the parties in the present case, agree to the payment of a transfer fee in order to fulfil one of the mandatory conditions laid down by the rules of the DFB, namely the requirement that a player must obtain a licence to play for the club acquiring him, they are to be deemed, upon any reasonable assessment of their reciprocal interests, to be attaching to their willingness to contract the fundamental precondition that the player must possess no personal qualities which render him, on an objective basis, unfit for the grant of a player's licence.

3. The court hearing the appeal on questions of fact and law bore in mind the fact that not every impairment of the basis of the transaction is necessarily significant in legal terms. In view of the overriding importance attaching, under the law of contract, to the principle of contractual good faith, a plea alleging a fundamental violation of the basis of the transaction will only exceptionally be admissible, where it appears unavoidable in order to avoid a result which would be intolerable, incompatible with the requirements of law and equity and thus incapable, according to the principle of good faith, of being ascribed to the party concerned. . . . Where a football player accepts a bribe whereby he is to "fix" the result of a game, he commits a serious breach of the recognised rules of the sport and of the principles of sportsmanship. As a general rule, he ceases to be eligible to receive the authorisation to play issued in respect of DFB clubs. From a legal standpoint, the payment of a transfer fee ceases to be of any relevance . . . [A]n agreement relating to the payment of a transfer fee can only be meaningful if the player fulfils the personal criteria which such an agreement necessarily entails, namely the condition that he is eligible, under the rules of the DFB, for the grant to him of the requisite player's licence. That condition is not, in principle, fulfilled in the case of a player who, in return for the payment of a sum of money, has been prepared to act deceitfully in order to influence the results of sporting competitions.

Thus there can be no inherent legal justification for any compensatory adjustment of the financial position as between the clubs which were parties to the transfer agreement. From an objective standpoint, the player personally charged with such a serious offence is no longer of any value to his former club, since the discovery of his lack of entitlement to play results, to all intents and purposes, in his being ineligible to play for any club. According to the principle of good faith, there appears to be no justification for an order requiring the transferor club to be compensated for a loss which it would have suffered even if the player had not moved to another club, and imposing on the transferee club the corresponding burden of paying such compensation despite the fact that, in the absence of the requisite player's licence, it can have no further use for the player, either in sporting or financial terms. In those factual circumstances, the basis of the transaction has been frustrated in such a way that the club liable to pay can no longer be deemed to be bound by the transfer agreement, which was concluded in ignorance of the bribery. Nor can there be any doubt that, if the factual position in the present case had been known, not only would the plaintiff have refrained from concluding an agreement but so too would any other club.

4. The court hearing the appeal on questions of fact and law also acted correctly, from a legal standpoint, in determining the extent of the risks confronting each of the parties. As regards the legal consequences of the absence or extinction of the basis of the transaction, particular significance attaches to the way in which the risk fell to be apportioned, as the appellant has correctly pointed out. It is acknowledged in the relevant case-law that circumstances which manifestly fall, in

accordance with the purpose of the contract, within the ambit of the risks faced by only one of the parties do not in principle entitle that party to plead that the basis of the transaction has been impaired. . . . However, that is not the position in the present case.

. . .

(b) The court hearing the appeal on questions of fact and law recognised that any transfer agreement concluded in the field of professional football necessarily entails a certain element of risk. It referred to the general risk, applying in every case, that a player who has been "bought" by a club may not live up to the expectations which it is hoped that he will fulfil—in particular, that his performance as a player may not be what is expected of him. Such conceptions and expectations basically fall outside the ambit of the circumstances which are capable of influencing a transfer agreement reached in accordance with the principle of good faith. The risk that the full extent and significance of an injury suffered by a player before his move to another club may not become clear until after that move may possibly be regarded as typical of that type of contract. Nowadays, participation in competitive sports, including, in particular, professional football, invariably involves, as experience has shown, the risk of an injury which only manifests itself fully at some later date. The prejudice attributable to such an injury, or the cessation of the footballer's ability to play which necessarily results from it, has a direct effect only on the *actual* employment of the player with his new club. This involves a risk which must normally be borne by the (new) employer. The question whether, in such cases, it is solely the transferee club which has to bear the risk of the possibly fruitless expenditure of the transfer fee does not need to be decided in the present case, any more than does the example, also given by the court below, of a player who commits a criminal act outside the context of his sports activities which initially remains undiscovered but which results, following his transfer to another club, in the loss of his player's licence.

. . .

(d) In determining the apportionment of the risk, the court below placed decisive emphasis on the extent to which the alleged misconduct of the player affects the essence of his intrinsic relationship with the club employing him. It considered that the obligation owed by a semi-professional player to his club is, in essence, such as to require him to play for his club and not against it, and accordingly placed the risk of breach of that obligation on the club employing him, even in the event that the player subsequently moves to another club. Those considerations are unimpeachable in law. The court below correctly placed the risk at the door of the defendant, as the club which, in the circumstances of this particular case, was "closer to the situation" than the plaintiff. The bribery of the player W. in the context of the defendant's *Bundesliga* match in Bielefeld on 27 May 1971, which constitutes the cause of the impairment of the contractual basis of the transfer agreement, falls within the ambit of the risks to be borne by the defendant, and not only because of the point in time at which it occurred. On the contrary, the player's misconduct is directly connected with his sports activities as an employee of the defendant. In view of that circumstance, there can be no question, applying the principle of good faith, of that risk being transferred to the plaintiff.

5. The court below held that the legal consequence of the absence of the basis of the transaction was such as to entitle the plaintiff to rescind the contract; accordingly, it allowed a claim for repayment in full of the transfer sum paid. That decision is similarly unimpeachable in law.

(a) However, the absence or extinction of the basis of a transaction does not automatically result in the total elimination of the contractual relationship. On the contrary, there can only be any question of one or both of the contracting parties being released from their contractual obligations in so far as this is required by the application of the principle of good faith. It follows that the primary question to be asked is whether the contract can be adapted to fit the actual facts of the situation in a form which takes into account the legitimate interests of both parties. . . . The court below bore those principles in mind. No objection can raised on legal grounds to its finding that, having regard to the worthlessness, in practical terms, of the consideration furnished by the defendant, namely the premature release of the player W., there could be no question of any adaptation of the contract, and, in particular, that, in view of the unambiguousness of the way in which the risk fell to be apportioned, there could be no question of both parties being ordered to bear the pecuniary loss proportionately between them.

Note
In this case the Court recognized a right in the purchasing club to withdraw from the contract and seek recovery of the transfer fee (§§ 327, 346 BGB). The more usual remedy will be the adaptation of the agreement in the light of the changed circumstances.[230]

Normally a mistaken party will have to seek avoidance under § 119 BGB rather than under the general principle of § 242 BGB. The latter, and in particular the doctrine of collapse of the basis of the contract, however allows an adjustment of the rights and liabilities of the parties more in consonance with objective fairness and the allocation of risk under the contract than the regime of unilateral avoidance and—possible—compensation established by § 119, 122 BGB.

(6) Application of mistake: induced mistake

In the jurisdictions studied, this situation may be dealt with under a variety of doctrines. We consider the different approaches in turn.

(i) Avoidance for mistake
In practice, many cases which in civil law are dealt with under the doctrine of mistake are ones in which one party has stated what he thinks to be the facts and the other has believed him; that is why the other party has entered the contract under a misapprehension. An example is the case of the *Villa Jacqueline*.[231] Of course, if the party making the statement knew that what he was saying was untrue and intended to deceive the other, there is fraud; but if he did not know, relief can be given for mistake. In German law, an error caused by the other party but without fraud may amount to an error as to an attribute considered essential in business within § 119(2) BGB, allowing the first party to avoid the contract.

(ii) Rescission for misrepresentation
In principle, in English law the contract might be void or voidable for mistake in this situation if the error was sufficiently fundamental; but in practice this will not be argued. This is because it is so difficult to show that a contract is void for mistake, whereas there is an easily available remedy for misrepresentation:

---

[230] Adaptation and other remedies are discussed more fully in 3.2.5 *infra*, at 422.
[231] *Supra* at 369.

Court of Appeal   3.E.69.
Redgrave v. *Hurd*[232]

CONTRACT MAY BE AVOIDED FOR INNOCENT MISREPRESENTATION

The elderly solicitor's practice

Facts: The plaintiff, an elderly solicitor, advertised for a younger partner who would not object to buying the plaintiff's house as well as to joining the plaintiff in practice. The plaintiff told the defendant that the practice brought in about £300 a year. The plaintiff showed the defendant summary accounts showing business of about £200 a year and said that the rest related to other business not summarized but which was referred to in a bundle of other papers. This he pointed out to the defendant but the defendant did not examine it. In fact examination of these other papers would have revealed that there was almost no other business. The defendant signed an agreement to purchase the house; this agreement made no reference to the agreement over the practice. When the defendant discovered the truth about the practice he refused to complete the purchase of the house. The plaintiff brought an action for specific performance and the defendant counter-claimed for rescission and damages.

Held: Fry J held that the defendant, having had the opportunity to check the truth of what he had been told but not having taken it, must be taken not to have relied on the representations, and granted specific performance. The Court of Appeal reversed this decision. Although the defendant's counter-claim for damages must fail because he had not pleaded that the plaintiff knew that the statements he was making were untrue, he was still entitled to rescind the agreement on the ground of innocent misrepresentation.

Judgment: JESSEL MR: As regards the rescission of a contract, there was no doubt a difference between the rules of Courts of Equity and the rules of Courts of Common Law—a difference which of course has now disappeared by the operation of the Judicature Act which makes the rules of equity prevail. According to the decisions of Courts of Equity it was not necessary, in order to set aside a contract obtained by material false representation, to prove that the party who obtained it knew at the time when the representation was made that it was false. It was put in two ways, either of which was sufficient. One way of putting the case was, "A man is not to be allowed to get a benefit from a statement which he now admits to be false. He is not to be allowed to say, for the purpose of civil jurisdiction, that when he made it he did not know it to be false; he ought to have found that out before he made it". The other way of putting it was this: "Even assuming that moral fraud must be shown in order to set aside a contract, you have it where a man, having obtained a beneficial contract by a statement which he now knows to be false, insists upon keeping that contract. To do so is a moral delinquency: no man ought to seek to take advantage of his own false statements". The rule in equity was settled, and it does not matter on which of the two grounds it was rested. As regards the rule of Common Law there is no doubt it was not quite so wide. There were, indeed, cases in which, even at Common Law, a contract could be rescinded for misrepresentation, although it could not be shewn that the person making it knew the representation to be false. They are variously stated, but I think, according to the later decisions, the statement must have been made recklessly and without care, whether it was true or false, and not with the belief that it was true . . .

There is another proposition of law of very great importance which I think it is necessary for me to state, because, with great deference to the very learned Judge from whom this appeal comes, I think it is not quite accurately stated in his judgment. If a man is induced to enter into a contract by a false representation it is not a sufficient answer to him to say, "If you had used due diligence you would have found out that the statement was untrue. You had the means afforded you of

---

[232] (1881) 20 Ch.D 1.

discovering its falsity, and did not choose to avail yourself of them". I take it to be a settled doctrine of equity, not only as regards specific performance but also as regards rescission, that this is not an answer unless there is such delay as constitutes a defence under the Statute of Limitations. That, of course, is quite a different thing. Under the statute delay deprives a man of his right to rescind on the ground of fraud, and the only question to be considered is from what time the delay is to be reckoned. It had been decided, and the rule was adopted by the statute, that the delay counts from the time when by due diligence the fraud might have been discovered. Nothing can be plainer, I take it, on the authorities in equity than that the effect of false representation is not got rid of on the ground that the person to whom it was made has been guilty of negligence. One of the most familiar instances in modern times is where men issue a prospectus in which they make false statements of the contracts made before the formation of a company, and then say that the contracts themselves may be inspected at the offices of the solicitor. It has always been held that those who accepted those false statements as true were not deprived of their remedy merely because they neglected to go and look at the contracts. Another instance with which we are familiar is where a vendor makes a false statement as to the contents of a lease, as, for instance, that it contains no covenant preventing the carrying on of the trade which the purchaser is known by the vendor to be desirous of carrying on upon the property. Although the lease itself might be produced at the sale, or might have been open to the inspection of the purchaser long previously to the sale, it has been repeatedly held that the vendor cannot be allowed to say, "You were not entitled to give credit to my statement". It is not sufficient, therefore, to say that the purchaser had the opportunity of investigating the real state of the case, but did not avail himself of that opportunity.

. . . [T]he learned Judge came to the conclusion either that the Defendant did not rely on the statement, or that if he did rely upon it ho had shown such negligence as to deprive him of his title to relief from this court. As I have already said, the latter proposition is in my opinion not founded in law, and the former part is not founded in fact; I think also it is not founded in law, for when a person makes a material representation to another to induce him to enter into a contract, and the other enters into that contract, it is not sufficient to say that the party to whom the representation is made does not prove that he entered into the contract, relying upon the representation. If it is a material representation calculated to induce him to enter into the contract, it is an inference of law that he was induced by the representation to enter into it, and in order to take away his title to be relieved from the contract on the ground that the representation was untrue, it must be shown either that ho had knowledge of the facts contrary to the representation, or that ho stated in terms, or showed clearly by his conduct, that he did not rely on the representation.

Notes

(1) This case is a leading example of the difference in English law between the rules of common law and the rules of equity, the latter of which would provide additional remedies when the common law appeared to be deficient.[233] As we saw earlier,[234] the common law permitted rescission in cases of fraud; but, as Jessel MR remarks, in the nineteenth century the common law courts started to insist on a narrow definition of fraud involving dishonesty. This may have been justified by the fact that at common law fraud would also give rise to liability in damages. The Courts of Equity could grant only rescission and perhaps for that reason would allow a remedy even in cases of "innocent" misrepresentation.

(2) In other respects the requirements for misrepresentation were the same as for fraud: the plaintiff must have entered the contract in reliance on a false statement of a material

---

[233] *Supra*, at 11, note 25.
[234] *Supra*, at 337.

fact by the other party to the contract. (As we noted earlier, in English law there is no remedy for fraud or misrepresentation if a party merely keeps silent about a pertinent fact.)

(3) This meant that rescission for misrepresentation was very readily available: the incorrect information did not have to relate to a substantial matter so long as the reasonable person would see it as having some relevance, and it did not have to be the only thing the plaintiff relied on in deciding to enter into the contract.[235] Equitable remedies are frequently given only at the court's discretion; but, strangely, it seems that if the requirements set out in the previous note were met, rescission for misrepresentation would always be given. Thus the buyer of a house who had been told by the seller that the drains were in good order would be able to rescind the contract even if only one drain was not in good order. This rule was potentially inconvenient and unjust. It was tempered by a rule that, when land or houses were sold, the right to rescind was lost when the "completion"—i.e. the transfer of ownership, which in English practice would take place some time after contract—had taken place. This rule was equally unjust and in 1967 both were changed by statute. The fact that the contract has been performed is no longer a bar to rescission (Misrepresentation Act 1967, section 1); but in cases other than fraud the court is given power to refuse rescission and award damages instead:

Misrepresentation Act 1967   **3.E.70.**

Section 2(2): Where a person has entered a contract after a misrepresentation has been made to him otherwise than fraudulently, and he would be entitled, by reason of the misrepresentation, to rescind the contract, then, if it is claimed, in any proceedings arising out of the contract, that the contract has been or ought to be rescinded, the court or arbitrator may declare the contract subsisting and award damages in lieu of rescission, if of opinion that it would be equitable to do so, having regard to the nature of the misrepresentation and the loss that would be caused by it if the contract were upheld, as well as to the loss that rescission would cause to the other party.

In *William Sindall Ltd* v. *Cambridgeshire* CC[236] a land developer claimed rescission on the ground of an alleged misrepresentation about a sewer crossing the site. The court held that on the facts there not been any misrepresentation; but it went on to say that it would have refused rescission, because the main reason for the developer seeking to rescind appeared to be that the value of site had fallen by millions of pounds through a general slump in property values.

(5) The right to rescind is not only subject to the court's discretion; it may be lost in a number of ways including affirmation or the lapse of quite a short time, even if the fact that there had been a misrepresentation was not discovered within that period: see *Leaf* v. *International Galleries Ltd*.[237] The case of *Bernstein* v. *Pamson Motors Ltd*[238] suggests that the time may be only a few weeks from the making of the contract.[239]

---

[235] *Supra*, at 339.
[236] [1994] 1 WLR 1016.
[237] [1950] 2 KB 86.
[238] [1987] 2 All ER 220.
[239] See 6.4.9, *infra* at 806.

(iii) Liability in Tort or Delict for Damages

Principles of European Contract Law   **3.PECL.71.**

Article 4:106: *Incorrect Information*
> A party which has concluded a contract relying on incorrect information given it by the other party may recover damages in accordance with Article 4:117(2) and (3) even if the information does not give rise to a fundamental mistake under Article 4:103, unless the party which gave the information had reason to believe that the information was correct.

Misrepresentation Act 1967   **3.E.72.**

Section 2(1): Where a person has entered into a contract after a misrepresentation has been made to him by another party thereto, and as a result thereof he has suffered loss, then, if the person making the misrepresentation would be liable to damages in respect thereof had the misrepresentation been made fraudulently, that person shall be so liable notwithstanding that the misrepresentation was not made fraudulently, unless he proves that he had reasonable grounds to believe, and did believe up to the time the contract was made that the facts represented were true.

Note

(1) Where one party has given misleading information to the other, and the party who gave the information, though not fraudulent, was at fault, English law provides for damages. The law on this point has developed relatively recently. For many years rescission was the only remedy available for innocent—i.e. non-fraudulent—misrepresentation. After the case of *Hedley Byrne & Co. Ltd.* v. *Heller & Partners Ltd.*[240] it became arguable that, if the misrepresentor was shown to be negligent, the misrepresentee could recover damages in tort, but this was not confirmed until the case of *Esso Petroleum Co. Ltd.* v. *Mardon*.[241]

(2) Before that decision, the 1967 Act also created liability in damages when the misrepresentor, though honest and therefore not guilty of fraud, had no reasonable grounds for believing that what he said was true. The drafting of this section, with its "fiction of fraud", seems very curious: it was probably written in this way in order to avoid having to state all the basic requirements for liability in misrepresentation.[242] It has some interesting consequences. First, the measure of damages is the same as for fraud i.e. loss of expectation is not included.[243] Secondly, the rule that any loss caused by the fraud may be recovered, even if it was not foreseeable, applies also to what is essentially liability for negligence under this section. See *Royscott Trust Ltd* v. *Rogerson*.[244] This consequence of the fiction of fraud may not have been intended, and the decision has been criticized.[245]

Although statutory, liability under section 2(1) is essentially tortious. Other systems also provide—in addition to the possibility of avoidance for mistake—delictual remedies when one party has misled the other. In French law the general rule for tortious liability applies:

---

[240] [1964] AC 465.
[241] [1968] 1 QB 801.
[242] See note (2) *supra* at 402.
[243] *Supra*, at 341.
[244] [1991] 2 QB 267.
[245] See *Chitty* paras 6-069–6-070.

404

Code civil   **3.F.73.**

Article 1382: Any human act which causes damage to another obliges the person through whose
fault it occurred to make reparation.

Similarly in Dutch law: the fact that one party has given the other incorrect information
is one of the heads under which the contract may be avoided under Article 6:228, and if
there was fault damages may be recovered from the party at fault under Article 6:162.[246]
We noted earlier[247] that in German law an error caused by the other party but without
fraud may amount to an error as to an attribute considered essential in business within §
119 II BGB, allowing the first party to avoid the contract. Should this be the case, the
avoiding party will be freed from his obligation to pay reliance damages to the other party
under § 122 BGB if the other party knew or should have known of the mistake. The
express provisions of the BGB give no right to avoid where an error which does not come
within § 119 BGB has been caused by the mere negligence or "innocent" conduct of the
other party. Since, by definition, the actions of the other party will not be intentional so
as to come within § 826 BGB, the code itself gives no right to damages in such cases—in
the absence of a protective law, violation of which would under § 823 II BGB ground an
action in delict.

The alternative for the erring party is to make out a case of *culpa in contrahendo* and to
seek restoration of the *status quo ante* as per § 249 BGB. Liability in *culpa in contrahendo*,
which has already been discussed,[248] is imposed in cases of harm done in the bargaining
process, whether intentionally or carelessly (§ 276 BGB). Negligently caused error leading
to entry into the contract is a clear example of such harm. The usual remedy for *culpa in
contrahendo* is an award of the negative interest in damages under § 249 BGB.[249]

This may not be adequate, however, where a contract has in fact been formed. As well
as seeking reliance damages, the misled party may raise the fault of the other party as a
defence to an action for enforcement of the contract. He can thereby be freed from his
unfairly burdensome contractual obligations.[250] Where the buyer—or contractor in the
case of a work contract—wishes to retain the other party's performance the BGH has on
occasion ordered a reduction in the price payable corresponding to the negative interest.[251]

A line must be drawn between cases in which the plaintiff may rely on *culpa in contrahendo* and cases covered by §§ 459 ff. BGB. Since *culpa in contrahendo* is a "supplementary" doctrine, it is relevant only where the Code itself provides no appropriate remedies.
Such a claim may thus, for example, be precluded by the availability of remedies in the law
of sale (§§ 459ff BGB). As will be seen in the next subsection, these cover defects in the
thing itself, including the absence of qualities the seller explicitly promised. Carelessly
given information about other factors is, by contrast, not covered. In such cases it will be

---

[246] *Supra*, at 394.
[247] *Supra*, at 400.
[248] *Supra*, at 237.
[249] See *Münchener Kommentar*, under § 275 BGB, para. 194.
[250] BGH NJW 1962.1196.
[251] BGH JZ 1989.592.

open to the plaintiff to raise a claim in *culpa in contrahendo*. (As we have already noted[252] a claim for avoidance on the ground of fraud under § 123 BGB is not precluded by the availability of remedies in the law of sale arising out of the same set of facts. This is because, by contrast with § 119 BGB, the policy of the law as embodied in § 123 BGB is of greater importance than the preservation of §§ 459ff BGB as *lex specialis*.)

The application of *culpa in contrahendo* raises problems of limitation in connection with § 123 BGB. A declaration which it is sought to avoid for fraud must be challenged within a year of discovery of the deception and in any case no later than thirty years after the declaration was made (§ 124 BGB). A claim for rescission under *culpa in contrahendo* may be raised, however, at any time up to thirty years from the time of the wrongdoing (§ 195 BGB). Thus, the limitation period laid down in § 124 BGB may be undercut even in cases of mere negligence. It has, thus, been strongly argued that, by analogy, the limitation period for misstatement amounting to *culpa in contrahendo* should be confined at least to that provided for in § 124 BGB.[253]

(iv) Liability for Breach of Contract

There is another possibility to consider. If one party has made a statement to the other about the subject matter of the contract, in some systems he may become liable for breach of contract (non-performance) if what he says turns out to be incorrect.

Suppose that the seller of goods indicates that a particular item corresponds to the buyer's description of what he wants, or the seller's own description of what it is he has to sell. If the goods do not correspond, the seller will in French law be guilty of *inexécution* of the contract and the buyer may seek *résolution*.

Code civil **3.F.74.**

Article 1604: Delivery is putting the thing sold into the control and possession of the buyer.

From this it is deduced that the buyer need not accept something different from what he was sold.

In German law the seller may be liable under § 459ff BGB. These will be relevant where a defect in the thing itself is at issue. Certain of the remedies under §§ 459ff BGB are themselves contingent upon there having been a representation—amounting to a warranty—by the buyer to the seller. Thus:

BGB **3.G.75.**

§ 459: The seller also warrants that, at the time the risk passes, the thing has the promised qualities.

The remedies available for breach of this warranty are wider than those where the implied obligation as to quality under § 459 I BGB is breached:

---

[252] *Supra*, at 341.
[253] See Larenz, *SAT* para. 9I.

§ 463: If a promised quality in the thing sold was absent at the time of purchase, the purchaser may demand compensation for non-performance, instead of cancellation [of the contract] or reduction [of the contract price].

In English law the seller will be in breach of the implied term that the goods will correspond to their description (SGA 1979, section 13). However, there will not be breach of section 13 simply because some statement made by the seller about the goods turns out to be incorrect. Section 13 has been held to apply only where the statement identifies the type of goods sold, and the goods actually supplied are of a different commercial description. See *Reardon Smith Line Ltd.* v. *Hansen-Tangen*;[254] *T & J Harrison* v. *Knowles and Foster*[255] (parties negotiating about sale of identified ships; sellers' statement of carrying capacity did not form part of description within section 13). But this restrictive approach is counterbalanced by another principle. A statement about the goods, even if it does not affect the commercial description of the goods, may amount to an express promise: see *Dick Bentley Productions Ltd.* v. *Harold Smith Motors Ltd.*[256] Again, if the statement turns out to be untrue there will be a breach of contract; in other words, the seller is treated as giving a guarantee that what he said is true. In principle such a promise could be as to some essential characteristic of the goods on which the parties agree, so that there would be both a breach of an express term and a breach of the implied term that the goods will correspond to the description; but in practice the reported cases are principally about statements relating to the goods but falling outside section 13—statements which in French law might fall under Article 1604 of the Code civil and which in German law would presumably fall under § 459 II BGB.

Principles of European Contract Law   **3.PECL.76.**

Article 6:101: *Statements giving rise to Contractual Obligations*
> (1) A statement made by one party before or when the contract is concluded is to be treated as giving rise to a contractual obligation if that is how the other party reasonably understood it in the circumstances, taking into account:
>> (a) the apparent importance of the statement to the other party;
>> (b) whether the party was making the statement in the course of business; and
>> (c) the relative expertise of the parties.
> (2) If one of the parties is a professional supplier which gives information about the quality or use of services or goods or other property when marketing or advertising them or otherwise before the contract for them is concluded, the statement is to be treated as giving rise to a contractual obligation unless it is shown that the other party knew or could not have been unaware that the statement was incorrect.
> (3) Such information and other undertakings given by a person advertising or marketing services, goods or other property for the professional supplier, or by a person in earlier links of the business chain, are to be treated as giving rise to a contractual obligation on the part of the professional supplier unless it did not know and had no reason to know of the information or undertaking.

---

[254] [1976] 1 WLR 989.
[255] [1910] 1 KB 608.
[256] [1965] 1 WLR 623.

The recent EC Directive on certain aspects of the sale of consumer goods and associated guarantees of 25 May 1999 is in rather similar terms:

Directive 1999/44/EC **3.EC.77.**

Article 2: Consumer goods are presumed to be in conformity with the contract if they:
(a) comply with the description given by the seller and possess the qualities of the goods which the seller has held out to the consumer as a sample or model;
(b) are fit for any particular purpose for which the consumer requires them and which he made known to the seller at the time of conclusion of the contract and which the seller has accepted.
(c) are fit for the purposes for which goods of the same type are normally used;
(d) show the quality and performance which are normal in goods of the same type and which the consumer can reasonably expect, given the nature of the goods and taking into account any public statements on the specific characteristics of the goods made about them by the seller, the producer or his representative, particularly in advertising or on labelling.

Article 3: There shall be deemed not to be a lack of conformity for the purposes of this Article if, at the time the contract was concluded, the consumer was aware, or could not reasonably be unaware of, the lack of conformity, or if the lack of conformity has its origin in materials supplied by the consumer.

Article 4: The seller shall not be bound by public statements, as referred to in paragraph 2(d) if he:
—shows that he was not, and could not reasonably have been, aware of the statement in question,
—shows that by the time of conclusion of the contract the statement had been corrected, or
—shows that the decision to buy the consumer goods could not have been influenced by the statement.

(v) Comparison of the Different Remedies for Mistake Induced by the Other Party
What practical difference will it make whether the plaintiff seeks remedies on the basis of mistake, misrepresentation or non-performance? For example, a private motorist sells a car which is five years old but which he has owned for only two years. During the negotiations he tells the buyer that the car has travelled 50,000 miles. He believes this to be true; when he bought it, it had 20,000 miles on the odometer and he has done 30,000 more. The buyer pays £5,000 for the car. The car's engine is severely damaged when the timing chain breaks; the chain should have been changed after 60,000 miles. The buyer discovers that the car has done more like 130,000 miles but the first owner had turned the odometer back. A car of the relevant age which had done only 30,000 miles would have been worth £6,000; the actual car was worth only £2,000 when it was delivered and the engine will cost £1,500 to repair.

Remedies based on non-performance would entitle the buyer to purchase a car of the same make and age, but which had done only 50,000 miles, at the seller's expense—or at least to claim the equivalent sum in damages. (These remedies would not be available in German law if the property had passed; the defects regime in BGB § 459 would apply, and this would allow only rescission or price reduction.[257] However the non-performance

---

[257] *Infra*, at 662.

remedies might apply if the buyer discovered the truth before property had passed by delivery.)

Remedies based on mistake—in French law, or German law if property in the goods had not passed—or on misrepresentation—in English law—would probably allow the buyer to avoid the contract; but he would not recover the additional cost of buying a car which had done only 50,000 miles—under German law in this case the buyer would have to pay the seller damages (§ 122) as the seller did not know of mistake.

If the buyer were to keep the car—or if it was held that he had lost the right to avoid the contract, for example through the lapse of time—the question of his entitlement to damages for the cost of repairs to the engine would arise. The outcome would normally depend on whether the seller was at fault. Arguably he was not at fault on the facts given.

Remedies under the special regimes applying to defects in goods sold in French and German law would lead to much the same results as remedies based on mistake or misrepresentation. However, as noted, in German law the mistake regime cannot not apply if the property has passed.

In French law the buyer could at most recover the price. However, if the seller were not a private person but a professional, he would be presumed to know of the defect and therefore would be liable in damages.[258] In German law the buyer would be confined to remedies in the law of sale which have priority over the more general rules on *culpa in contrahendo* and mistake. If he could show that there was a guarantee or wrongful concealment he would be entitled to damages. The former may be possible on the facts. Otherwise he would be entitled only to cancellation of the contract (*Wandlung*) or reduction of the purchase price (*Minderung*).

3.2.4. NON-DISCLOSURE

Suppose a party enters the contract on some assumption about the substance of the contract or the circumstances which is incorrect. This is not because he is relying on information given by another; his misapprehension is "self-induced". We have seen that in the Civil Law jurisdictions, the mistaken party may be able to avoid the contract on the basis of mistake, albeit that he or she may come under a duty to compensate the other party for losses resulting from his or her mistake—under, for example, Article 1382 of the Civil Code or § 122 of the BGB. However, in this section we consider whether the result is any different where the other party either knows of the misapprehension but does not point it out or does not know that the first party is mistaken but should have known.

To some extent, all the systems indirectly place at least professional sellers under an obligation to disclose any defect in the goods of which they are aware—or be liable for it. Thus in English law, a seller who is selling in the course of a business is liable under the Sale of Goods Act 1979, section 14(2) (as amended) if the goods are not of satisfactory quality—except as regards any defect which was drawn to the buyer's attention. In French law the *garantie* applies only to *vices cachés*, not to ones which were pointed out by the seller. Under § 460 BGB a seller is not responsible for a defect in the thing sold if the

---

[258] *Infra*, at 665.

purchaser knew of the defect at the time of entering the contract. Thus if the seller knows of a defect, he must point it out or be liable. Furthermore a seller will be liable to pay damages where he fraudulently concealed the defect from the buyer (§ 463 1 BGB).

These "indirect" obligations of disclosure are fairly limited in that they relate only to sale of property—in English law only to the sale of goods—and only to certain characteristics of the items sold. There may be many other facts which are crucial to a party's decision whether to enter into a contract for the purchase of goods, let alone other types of contract where there may not be similar obligations.

It is in relation to more general duties of disclosure that the various systems produce radically different solutions. We will see later that in French and German law various doctrines supplement the doctrine of mistake to produce wide-ranging duties of disclosure. Thus in French law the plaintiff may be able to base a claim on *dol par réticence*, and it is argued that there is a general duty of disclosure. In German law, fraud and *culpa in contrahendo* are both possible bases of relief.

In contrast, under the common law, with its objective approach and its reluctance to impose duties to act on parties, there may be no remedy at all. We have seen that the common law does not recognize fraud by silence, and that mistake will not apply unless either (1) the mistake was about the terms of the contract, so that there was no agreement, or (2) it was shared. The following case shows that under the objective approach of the Common Law, the seller is under no obligation to bring to the buyer's attention the fact that he has made a mistaken assumption as to the subject matter of the contract.

(1) Common law

Queen's Bench   **3.E.78.**
Smith v. *Hughes*[259]

NO OBLIGATION TO DISCLOSE RELEVANT FACTS

Old oats or new oats?

A seller of goods is under no duty to point out to the buyer that the latter is mistaken as to a characteristic of the goods sold (assuming that the goods are of satisfactory quality within what is now section 14 SGA).

Facts: The plaintiff, a farmer, offered the defendant, a race horse trainer, a quantity of oats. The defendant's manager looked at a sample of the oats and agreed to buy them, but when the oats were delivered he refused to pay for them on the ground that he had been under the impression that the oats were "old", i.e. last season's oats, whereas the oats delivered were "green", i.e., this season's oats. The defendant had no use for green oats. There was a conflict of evidence on whether the word "old" had been used in the negotiations.

Held: The trial judge directed the jury that if the word old had been used they should find for the defendant; and also they should find for the defendant if nothing was said about the oats being old but if the plaintiff believed that the defendant believed that he was contracting for old oats. The jury found for the defendant and the plaintiff appealed. The Court of Appeal held that the first part of the judge's direction was correct (there would have been a contractual promise, or at least a representation, that the oats were old); but that the second part was incorrect. As it was not possible to tell on which ground the jury had found for the defendant, there must be a new trial.

[259] (1871) LR 6 QB 596.

Judgment: COCKBURN CJ: . . . [We] must assume that nothing was said on the subject of the defendant's manager desiring to buy old oats, nor of the oats having been said to be old; while, on the other hand, we must assume that the defendant's manager believed the oats to be old oats, and that the plaintiff was conscious of the existence of such belief, but did nothing, directly or indirectly, to bring it about, simply offering his oats and exhibiting his sample, remaining perfectly passive as to what was passing in the mind of the other party. The question is whether, under such circumstances, the passive acquiescence of the seller in the self-deception of the buyer will entitle the latter to avoid the contract. I am of opinion that it will not.

I take the true rule to be, that where a specific article is offered for sale, without express warranty, or without circumstances from which the law will imply a warranty—as where, for instance, an article is ordered for a specific purpose—and the buyer has full opportunity of inspecting and forming his own judgment, if he chooses to act on his own judgment, the rule caveat emptor applies. If he gets the article he contracted to buy, and that article corresponds with what it was sold as, he gets all he is entitled to, and is bound by the contract. Here the defendant agreed to buy a specific parcel of oats. The oats were what they were sold as, namely, good oats according to the sample. The buyer persuaded himself they were old oats, when they were not so; but the seller neither said nor did anything to contribute to his deception. He has himself to blame. The question is not what a man of scrupulous morality or nice honour would do under such circumstances. The case put of the purchase of an estate, in which there is a mine under the surface, but the fact is unknown to the seller, is one in which a man of tender conscience or high honour would be unwilling to take advantage of the ignorance of the seller; but there can be no doubt that the contract for the sale of the estate would be binding . . .

Now, in this case, there was plainly no legal obligation on the plaintiff in the first instance to state whether the oats were new or old. He offered them for sale according to the sample, as he had a perfect right to do, and gave the buyer the fullest opportunity of inspecting the sample, which practically, was equivalent to an inspection of the oats themselves. What, then, was there to create any trust or confidence between the parties, so as to make it incumbent on the plaintiff to communicate the fact that the oats were not, as the defendant assumed them to be, old oats? If, indeed, the buyer, instead of acting on his own opinion, had asked the question whether the oats were old or new, or had said anything which intimated his understanding that the seller was selling the oats as old oats, the case would have been wholly different; or even if he had said anything which shewed that he was not acting on his own inspection and judgment, but assumed as the foundation of the contract that the oats were old, the silence of the seller, as a means of misleading him, might have amounted to a fraudulent concealment, such as would have entitled the buyer to avoid the contract. Here, however, nothing of the sort occurs. The buyer in no way refers to the seller, but acts entirely on his own judgment.

[The remainder of the judgment is concerned with the possibility that the seller intended to sell the oats as they were but knew that the buyer thought he was buying them with a warranty that they were old. In this case there would be a misunderstanding as to the terms of the contract and no contract might result (see *supra*, at 356). This should have been explained to the jury (in the nineteenth century, it was still common for contract cases to be tried by jury) in clearer terms, and a new trial on this point was ordered.]

Note
Cockburn CJ refers to the question whether there was any relationship of trust between the parties. English law does recognize a duty to disclose when there is a "relationship of confidence" between the parties, for example where one is the other's solicitor.[260] There

---

[260] *Infra*, at 474.

are a limited number of other cases in which even according to the Common Law a party does have a duty to disclose in English law. The most obvious example is the exceptional case of the contract of insurance. This is described as a contract "of the utmost good faith"; the insured must disclose any fact which is material in the sense that it may influence the reasonable insurer in deciding whether or not to accept the risk or on what terms. Similarly, there is a duty of disclosure in some family arrangements such as agreements over the division of a deceased family member's property; and sureties must be told of unusual risks related to the loan they are guaranteeing.[261] There are numerous examples of duties to disclose imposed by statute in particular situations, for example under Consumer Credit Act 1974 and Financial Services and Markets Act 2000.

In the Civil Law systems the position is very different. There may be relief simply on the basis of the doctrine of mistake, in accordance with the rules set out above—see for example the *Poussin* case.[262] However, we have seen that even under the subjective approach of the civil law jurisdictions, the doctrine of mistake operates within significant limits. It is therefore notable that relief may be available on two alternative bases. First, in contrast to the common law, it has been recognized that a failure to point out the mistake may amount to fraud if it is dishonest. Secondly, there is some recognition of a duty to disclose which may give rise to liability in damages even though there was no fraud.

(2) France

(a) Non-Disclosure as Fraud
At one time the French courts appeared to deny that a mere failure to disclose a pertinent fact to the other party could amount to fraud: for example Cass. civ., 30 May 1927.[263] But doctrine was critical of this approach. As Breton argued in his note to that case, mere silence is capable of provoking an error; the fact that it is an "absence of action" does not deprive it of causal effect, as in the context things would have been different if the party accused of fraud had spoken out. The word manœuvre is capable of covering reticence. and while an abstention, keeping silent, is often morally indifferent, it is not always so. He quotes Ripert:

What is true is that in the majority of contracts there is a conflict of interests between the parties. Each has to look after his own interests and should therefore make himself informed. There is then nothing wrong with not giving the other party information he could have found for himself. But the situation changes and silence becomes culpable if one of the parties has an obligation in conscience to speak out rather than take advantage of the other's ignorance.

Cass. Civ.3, 2 October 1974[264] **3.F.79.**

SILENCE AMOUNTING TO DECEIT

The pig farm

Deceit may take the form of silence on the part of a contracting party who conceals from the other party a fact which, had it been known by the latter party, would have caused him not to enter into the

---

[261] See *Chitty* para. 44-033.
[262] *Supra*, at 373.
[263] Gaz. Pal. 1927.2.338; S.1928.1.105, annotated by Breton.
[264] Bull. civ. III.330; D.1974, IR.252; RGLJ 1975.669, annotated by Blanc.

contract. Since the consent of the innocent party was induced by the error brought about by the deceit, that error can be taken into consideration, even if it does not go to the substance of the thing forming the subject-matter of the contract.

Facts: By a simple contract of 6 October 1970, Marcel Jacob, acting as agent for Mr and Mrs Paul Jacob, purchased from Mr and Mrs Goutailler a dwelling-house and some land for the sum of 95,000 francs, of which he paid on account the sum of 10,000 francs. That agreement, which was subject, in particular, to the condition precedent of the grant to Mr and Mrs Jacob by a financial organization of a loan of 60,000 francs, was to be drawn up in the form of a notarial deed by no later than 1 December 1970. It was stipulated that Mr and Mrs Jacob were to take the property subject to all servient easements of whatever kind which might encumber the land sold and that, in the event of default on the part of the purchasers, the vendors would be entitled to require completion of the sale or to retain the sum paid on account by way of penalty. On 22 April 1971 Marcel Jacob informed the notary that it had not been possible to obtain the loan envisaged and that, having just learned of the imminent establishment of a piggery containing 400 pigs within a distance of 100 metres from the house, he was withdrawing from the sale; he stated that, had he been informed of this, his son Paul would never have agreed to purchase such a country house, given the drawbacks and the unpleasant smells involved, especially during the holiday period at the height of the summer. That disagreement between the purchasers and the vendors remained unresolved, and the latter consequently sold the house and land to a third party for the sum of 80,000 francs.

Held: Mr and Mrs Goutailler were ordered to repay to Mr and Mrs Paul Jacob the sum of 10,000 francs paid on account. The Goutailler's appeal was rejected.

Judgment: *On the two appeal grounds taken together*: [the court stated the facts as above, and continued:]
—Whereas the contested judgment is challenged on the basis of a appeal ground that it renders inapplicable, on the ground of fraudulent non-disclosure on the part of the vendors, the clause in the contract excluding any guarantees in respect of the servient easements; as according to the appellants, no evidence was adduced establishing any wrongful intention on the part of the vendors;
—Whereas the appellants contend, moreover, that the non-disclosure, which was not accompanied by any stratagems designed to mislead the other party to the contract, does not constitute deceit within the meaning of Article 1116 of the Civil Code, because the vendor's knowledge of the perfectly proper establishment of the piggery did not involve or signify the adoption of any such stratagems or any ignorance on the part of the purchaser, *a fortiori* since that piggery, which is located on neighbouring land, does not constitute an easement and does not affect any substantial feature of the property sold;
—Whereas it is further argued that, by failing to rule on the question whether Mr and Mrs Jacob would have proceeded with the purchase if they had been aware of the situation, the court below did not examine whether the conduct imputed to the vendor had been the determining factor which caused them to sign the agreement, and did not establish any causal connection between the alleged fraudulent non-disclosure on the part of the vendor and the consent given by the purchasers.
—Whereas the contested judgment is further criticized on the ground that it refused to apply the clause in the contract whereby, in the event of default by the purchasers, the vendors were to be entitled to retain the sum paid on account by way of penalty; according to the appellants, the terms of the synallagmatic promise to sell the property . . . expressly provided that the purchasers were to take the property sold in its existing condition and subject to all servient easements of whatever kind which might encumber the property in question, and further that, in the event of default on the part of the purchasers, the vendors were to be entitled either to demand completion of the sale or to retain the sum paid on account by way of penalty.
—Whereas however, deceit may consist and take the form of silence on the part of a contracting party who conceals from the other party a fact which, had it been known by the latter party, would have caused him not to enter into the contract.
—Whereas the consent of the innocent party was induced by the error brought about by the deceit, that error can be taken into consideration, even if it does not go to the substance of the thing forming the subject-matter of the contract.

—Whereas the cour d'appel observes that, upon being informed of the purchasers' objection regarding the establishment of the piggery, Mr Goutailler, far from protesting his own ignorance of it, pointed out the date of the prefectorial order authorizing its establishment and simply claimed that Mr Jacob "was deemed to have been aware of it" and that the latter had agreed to buy subject to all servient easements encumbering the property sold; as the court below also found that Mr Goutailler, knowing of the proposed establishment of that noxious and insanitary undertaking, which was bound to have a seriously adverse effect on the enjoyment of a country house situated in the immediate vicinity, not only mentioned nothing about it to his purchaser but also took care to ensure, upon the conclusion of the contract of 6 October 1970, that it contained a clause excluding guarantees, the entire value of which lay "in the fact that he was the only person aware of the situation".

—Whereas on the basis of those findings, it was open to the cour d'appel, without falling foul of the criticisms raised by the appellants, to infer that the vendor's non-disclosure was fraudulent in nature and that it had induced the purchasers, who were city-dwellers seeking a house in the country, to make an error in relation to an element which determined the giving of their consent.

—Whereas that defective consent affected the validity of the contract, the court below was right to refuse to allow the vendors to profit from the terms of that contract, which they persisted in trying to apply to their advantage, with a view to attempting to secure for themselves the benefit of their own non-disclosure and to retain the payment on account made by the victims of their fraudulent conduct.

—Whereas it follows that, on the aforementioned grounds alone, the cour d'appel has justified its decision in law and that the appellant's grounds are unfounded.

On those grounds, this Court dismisses the appeal.

Notes

(1) The essence of *dol* is an error, either created by the defendant or of which he takes deliberate advantage. Seeking a remedy for fraud rather than for mistake may be advantageous, however, for the reasons suggested earlier;[265] in particular, if the defendant was fraudulent the plaintiff will have to show that the error went to the substance of the thing contracted for.

(2) The development of the notion of *dol par réticence* is described in Legrand[266] and Ghestin.[267]

(3) Doctrine and jurisprudence frequently link fraud by non-disclosure to a duty to disclose. Is there always such a duty? In some situations it is said that the plaintiff has a duty to inform himself. Ghestin notes, after discussing various decisions, that "It remains that this principle is difficult to apply, as the divergent decisions in different areas show".[268]

(b) A Duty of Disclosure Beyond Cases of Fraud?
French law has many examples of duties of disclosure imposed by statute[269] and of contractual—as opposed to pre-contractual—obligations to give information to the other

---

[265] *Supra*, at 338.
[266] Legrand (1986) 6 Oxford JLS 322.
[267] Ghestin paras. 566–568; See also Simler, Lequette and Terré, para. 225.
[268] Ghestin para. 571.
[269] See a list of examples given by Fabre-Magnan "Duties of Disclosure and French Contract Law", in Beatson and Friedmann (eds.), *Good Faith and Fault in Contract Law* (Oxford: Clarendon, 1995), 99–120 at 100.

party. Writers, notably Ghestin,[270] have argued for the existence of a general duty to disclose independent of error or fraud. There have been a number of cases in French law in which the courts have imposed liability for non-disclosure without reference to either fraud or mistake: Legrand summarizes:[271]

A pre-contractual obligation of information would thus be imposed by the court where there exists:
—an information asymmetry flowing from the status of the party, one being a *professionel* and the other a *profane*;
—a legitimate dependence or reliance by the *profane* on the *professionel*;
—a fact relating to the object of the contract which is known, or ought to be known, by the *professionel* to be material to the *profane's* decision to enter into the contract at all or to do so on different terms.

(3) Germany

German law also recognizes that a party to a contract will be under an obligation to make disclosure of certain important facts to the other party. Obligations of this sort are imposed under a number of provisions of the code (§§ 123, 460, 463 BGB) and under the doctrine of *culpa in contrahendo*. It should be remembered first, however, that if the fact which should have been disclosed was one relating to an essential attribute of a thing or person, it will be possible to avoid the contract under § 119 II BGB. But, since the category of essential attributes is limited,[272] and having regard to the very brief limitation period for taking such claims (§ 121 BGB), one of the aforementioned alternatives is often preferred.

(a) Non-Disclosure as Fraud

As we saw above, it is a requirement of any claim for avoidance under § 123 BGB that the challenging party has been deceived by the conduct of her contract-partner or by certain other third parties. Silence will be sufficient as conduct where there was a duty to disclose. When will such a duty arise?

The German courts have been particularly keen to impose a duty to make disclosure in cases arising from the sale of used cars and other vehicles, as the following case shows:

BGH, 3 March 1982[273] **3.G.80.**

SIGNIFICANT DAMAGE TO VEHICLE MUST BE DISCLOSED

The used lorry

A seller of a vehicle must disclose to the buyer the fact that the vehicle has suffered significant damage in an accident, but need not disclose that the vehicle has a replacement engine, nor the seller's doubts about the accuracy of the odometer reading.

[270] In Harris and Tallon (eds), *Contract Law Today: Anglo-French Comparisons* (Oxford: Clarendon, 1989) at 151.
[271] Legrand, op. cit., at 336–8.
[272] *Supra*, at 380.
[273] NJW 1982.1386.

Facts: On 8 November 1978 the plaintiff purchased from the defendant, for the sum of DM 54,880, a second-hand lorry which had been fitted with a replacement engine and a replacement gearbox by the person who had owned it prior to the vendor. The plaintiff took delivery of the lorry on 9 November 1978. The written sale contract, which was entitled "Invoice" and which was not drawn up on the basis of a printed form, provided *inter alia*: "bought as seen . . . guaranteed for 6 months or 100,000 km—kilometres covered: 421,861". By a letter from his lawyer dated 16 March 1979, the plaintiff avoided the contract on the ground of wilful deceit, claiming that the vehicle had covered a greater number of kilometres than had been indicated.

Held: The Landgericht (Regional Court) dismissed the plaintiff's claim, by which he sought an order for repayment of the purchase price, compensation for expenditure incurred by him and the return of bills of exchange in respect of the purchase price which had not yet matured. The plaintiff's appeal to the Oberlandesgericht (Higher Regional Court), in which he also pleaded fraudulent non-disclosure of a rear-end collision, was likewise dismissed. The plaintiff's further appeal on a point of law resulted in the judgment of the court below being set aside and in the case being referred back to the lower court.

Judgment: . . . II.2.(a) According to the settled case-law of the Bundesgerichtshof, where the seller of a second-hand lorry is aware of a defect or of an earlier accident, he is in principle under a duty to inform the buyer of it, even if the latter does not ask about it. If he fails to do so, he will be liable for wilful deceit. According to the findings of the appellate court, the husband of the proprietor of the defendant firm, who acted on behalf of the defendant in the sale, gave the plaintiff no such indication, although he was aware that during the course of being driven by the previous owner to the place where it was to be delivered to the defendant, the lorry had been involved in a rear-end collision in which the front bumper, at least, had been damaged and had had to be replaced.

(b) However, the duty of disclosure is not completely unlimited in its scope. Since its justification is founded on the special characteristics of the second-hand vehicle trade, and since the purchaser's knowledge of defects and accidents suffered by the vehicle in question has a decisive influence on his decision to buy, he does not need to be informed of an accident which was so slight that it could not, on any reasonable view, influence his decision to buy. However, in the case of cars, the adjudicating Senate has hitherto recognised as falling into that category of "trifling damage" only very minor external (paintwork) damage, and has held that it does not include other (bodywork) damage, even where such latter damage had no far-reaching consequences and the repair cost amounted (as it did in a 1961 case) to only DM 332.55 (BGH NJW 1967, 1222).

(c) In the case of lorries, however, it is legitimate to treat even more extensive damage as "trifling", since the undamaged condition of the vehicle, including its bodywork, and the external appearance which that lends to the vehicle, does not as a general rule matter so much with commercial vehicles as it does with cars. Nevertheless, the criterion applying in the case of load-carrying or commercial vehicles is that defects which amount to more than merely visible and external damage, and which affect the condition of the vehicle in a more far-reaching way, must be excluded from the "trifling" category.

That is not the position in the present case. It is not necessary to decide whether the damage caused to the front bumper constitutes of itself a danger to other parts which necessarily renders the accident more than merely "slight". The appellant rightly complains that the court below failed to take full account of the plaintiff's assertions and of the summary of the evidence concerning the extent of the damage. In his grounds of appeal, the plaintiff had maintained that, as a result of the rear-end collision—which initially was untruthfully denied by the defendant—several of the blades of the viscosity ventilating fan [*Viskolüfter*] were missing. The husband of the proprietor of the defendant firm, who gave evidence as a witness to the accident, stated in that regard that, in the course of the rear-end collision which occurred during a transportation journey, damage had been sustained not only to the bumper but also to the ventilation fan and the radiator. The court below did not deal with that statement. If, in fact, parts of the engine such as the fan and the radiator were damaged, there can be no question, even in the case of a lorry, of mere "trifling" damage which does not need to be disclosed, since the risk of further adverse consequences would be so considerable for any purchaser that the decision as to whether to inform the buyer of the accident and of the main aspects of the repairs can no longer be left to the discretion of the seller.

. . .

III.3.(b) [It is not] possible to accept the appellant's submission that the defendant should at least have disclosed his doubts regarding the conformity of the reading on the tachometer with the total distance actually covered by the vehicle and the installation of a replacement engine and a replacement gearbox. It is not necessary to decide whether an assertion of wilful deceit concerning the possibly material circumstances relating to the distance covered by a lorry necessarily falls to be rejected where the actual distance covered is not declared. At all events, the defendant has not breached any duty of disclosure in that regard. Even in the second-hand vehicle trade, the vendor is under no duty—save in so far as, exceptionally, he takes it upon himself to give advice to the purchaser, which was not the position in this case—to inform the other party to the contract of all facts and/or considerations affecting the value to be placed upon the vehicle. Depending on the ambit of those facts and/or considerations, his duty of disclosure is also conditioned by the extent to which the purchaser is himself capable of gaining knowledge of them, and also by the latter's conduct, particularly as regards any interest manifested by him in individual facts and matters. The plaintiff, who was not completely lacking in experience of transport vehicles, was (or should have been) as aware as the defendant that the tachometer reading did not necessarily provide a reliable indication of the distance which the lorry had actually covered. If he had regarded that distance as an important factor, then he should have asked about it. The same consideration applies as regards the replacement engine and the replacement gearbox, from the presence of which in the vehicle no convincing conclusions can be drawn as to its having covered a given number of kilometres where—as is not disputed between the parties—the date of, and the reason for, their installation in the lorry were not known. Even the appellant does not question the fact that the installation of such replacement parts does not in itself indicate the existence of any defects requiring to be disclosed.

Notes

(1) A party may expect disclosure in accordance with the requirements of good faith and fair practices in accordance with § 242 BGB. Both the circumstances of the concrete transaction and the type of contract involved will be relevant to the identification of such duties. The BGH refers to the "special features of the used car market" as justifying an extensive duty of disclosure in these cases. It is not quite clear what these "features" are—perhaps the difficulty for buyers of discovering defects in used vehicles.

(2) The drafters of the BGB avoided including any general rule on positive duties of disclosure. They preferred instead to leave precision of § 123 BGB in this sense to future courts on the basis of the good faith provision of § 242 BGB.[274] What are the advantages of such a solution? What are the disadvantages?

(3) In spite of this prescribed casuistry, some tendencies are evident in the case law:[275]

(a) Questions must be answered truthfully;
(b) A partial concealment is as good as a lie;
(c) An imbalance in skill or access to information leading to significant reliance on the part of the challenging party is likely to lead to a duty to disclose;
(d) Increasing complexity of the transaction is also likely to lead to such a duty.

---

[274] See *Motive zu dem Entwurf eines Bürgerlichen Gesetzbuches für das Deutsche Reich*, Vol. 1: *Allgemeiner Teil* (1888) at 208.
[275] See *Münchener Kommentar* under § 275 BGB, para. 80.

(4) Not everything known to one party must be disclosed to the other, only those facts which would indicate to the other party that his purpose in entering into the contract is likely to be thwarted. Is there any reason of economic policy for denying a wider duty to disclose?

In certain cases the German courts have found that there is no obligation to disclose information.

BGH, 13 July 1988[276]   **3.G.81.**

NON-DISCLOSURE WHICH DOES NOT AMOUNT TO FRAUD

The doctor's practice

A doctor who sells his practice on the basis that it has a turn over of a certain amount is not required to disclose the type of patients which he had.

Facts: The defendant sold his doctor's practice to the plaintiff for 75,000 DM, of which the plaintiff had already paid half. In the advertisement of sale he had stated *inter alia* that the practice generated a turnover of about 465,000 DM per year and that it was very possible that this would increase in the future. After the plaintiff took over the business it soon became apparent that the figure of 465,000 DM had been significantly composed of the fees of a relatively small number of private, fee-paying patients. There was a risk in the future that these patients would desert the practice. The plaintiff claimed that the defendant had deceitfully concealed the patient-profile of the practice. He accordingly sought to avoid the contract on the basis within § 123 BGB and the return of the 75,000 DM which he had paid.

Held: At first instance the Landgericht upheld the plaintiff's claim. This decision was upheld by the Oberlandesgericht. The defendant's appeal to the BGH was successful.

Judgment: I. The court hearing the appeal on the facts regarded the plaintiff's claim for payment as well founded in accordance with §§ 812, 818 and 123 of the BGB. It held that, upon the conclusion of the contract for the transfer of the practice, the defendant had fraudulently misrepresented to the plaintiff the extent of his income from his activities as a doctor in the private sector. It further ruled that the claim for a declaration was justified, since the defendant had made further, exaggerated representations.

. . . [T]he appellate court below exaggerated the scope of the obligations imposed by the duty to provide information. Such a duty, breach of which may constitute fraudulent misrepresentation, has been inferred by case-law from the specific legal relations existing between negotiating parties in cases where, having regard in particular to the possible frustration of the purpose of the contract, non-disclosure of the facts would be contrary to the principle of good faith and where the party to whom the representations were made was entitled, according to the accepted view, to expect to be informed of the fact concealed. . . . That principle also applies to negotiations for contracts of sale. However, it does not extend so far as to require the vendor, of his own accord, to enlighten the purchaser in relation to all facts and matters which may of significance for the purposes of creating in the latter an intention to contract. On the contrary, it is necessary to have regard to the opposing principle that a person concluding a contract must satisfy himself as to whether or not that contract is advantageous to him. This is something to which the other party may adjust his conduct; consequently, he is not required to draw attention to facts and matters which he may expect to be asked about if any weight is attached to them by the first party. . . .

The facts on which the appellate court below based its decision are insufficient to warrant any conclusion that the defendant was required to provide the plaintiff, without being asked, with

[276] NJW 1989.763.

information concerning the very substantial level of fees attributable to individual patients. The situation might be different if, for example, only two or three patients likely to pass away in the near future had accounted for an annual fee income of approximately DM 370,000, alternatively DM 270,000, out of a total of DM 465,000. . . . Such an extreme situation has not been found to exist in the present case; nor, indeed, has it been alleged. True, a practice with only a few patients individually paying very high amounts in fees clearly involves greater risks for a purchaser than a practice based predominantly on patients whose care is funded by a health insurance scheme. If, in such circumstances, even just one patient withdraws his custom from the purchaser, this may in itself result in very considerable financial loss. However, it is for the prospective purchaser to obviate such risks. The vendor is entitled to assume that the purchaser reckons on being able himself to provide medical care in such a way as to retain the loyalty to the practice of the majority of the patients. A different assessment might be necessary if there existed, for example, certain specific links or ties (e.g. as a result of kinship or on account of particular indulgence shown to inveterate patients). No such finding was made by the appellate court below; nor did it find that there had been any contravention of the law relating to doctors' fees. It simply accepted, without making any corresponding findings of fact, that the defendant had received income which could not have been earned by a subsequent proprietor of the practice on the basis of compliance with the law relating to doctors' fees. Nor does the finding of the appellate court below that the defendant had not operated any proper medical filing system warrant any inference with regard to the duty to provide information. The appellate court below made that assessment on the basis of the testimony of the witness S., even though she had seen only about 100 of the total of 800 file index cards which existed. The information contained on the cards available related merely to prescription details and, at most, blood pressure levels; they did not, however, contain any proposals for treatment or results of analyses. It is not clear how the plaintiff could have gained any information concerning the very substantial levels of fees attributable to a small number of patients from a comprehensively maintained patient filing system as conceived by the appellate court below, even if he had inspected all of the files and index cards concerned. In order to gain a proper picture of the fee structure, the course of action which he should have taken was not to look through 800 file index cards but instead to pose the appropriate question to the defendant. The plaintiff has not asserted that he asked any such question.

3. Since the finding made by the appellate court below to the effect that the plaintiff had effectively rescinded the contract on account of fraudulent misrepresentation concerning the fee structure cannot be valid, it follows that there can be no basis for its conclusion that the contract was consequently void in law, that the defendant should be ordered, pursuant to §§ 812 and 818 of the BGB, to repay the purchase price instalment of DM 75,000 which had already been paid and that he was not entitled to receive payment of the balance of the purchase price . . . For the purposes of determining whether the defendant was obliged to provide the plaintiff with information concerning the fee structure, the rules applying to a claim in damages for *culpa in contrahendo* are the same as those applying under § 123 BGB to the application for a declaration of entitlement to avoid the contract.

Note
If the deceitful concealment was as to a defect in property sold then § 123 BGB will be displaced by the special rules on sale, in particular § 463 BGB which would allow damages in such a case.

(b) Culpa in contrahendo
As with § 123 BGB, there may be liability in *culpa in contrahendo* where a contracting party has breached a duty to make disclosure as opposed to actively causing a mistake. We have already seen that fault in the contracting process may be constituted by negligent

as well as fraudulent conduct. The instances recognized in the academic writing and case-law as giving rise to a duty to disclose under *culpa in contrahendo* are largely similar to those under § 123 BGB.[277] The appropriate allocation of the risk of a particular eventuality is very often decisive in this matter. Although a tendency to expand the duty has been observed,[278] there is no general obligation to make disclosure. Only those things need be disclosed which are recognizably of crucial significance to the entry of the other party into the contract.

There will frequently be a duty (under both *culpa in contrahendo* and § 123 BGB) on the offeror, or those acting on his behalf, to advise the offeree of the true content and legal significance of his offer.

BGH, 16 January 1991[279] **3.G.82.**

No duty to disclose former employee's untrustworthiness

The tax advisors

The seller of a business is under no duty to disclose problems with an employee to a buyer where these problems lie in the past and where the buyer has made his own investigations of the matter.

Facts: The plaintiff bought from the defendant a company which specialized in tax advice. Among the employees of the company was one N. a former partner, who had been accused of unacceptable practices by the local chamber of tax advisors. Having had cause to dismiss N., the plaintiff sought alternatively reduction of the purchase price damages under the law of sale or damages for *culpa in contrahendo* from the defendant. In relation to the latter the plaintiff claimed that the defendant should have disclosed N.'s tendency to criminal behaviour.

Held: The Landgericht rejected the claim. The Oberlandesgericht held for the plaintiff on the grounds that there had been a culpable failure to disclose. The defendant's appeal to the BGH was successful.

Judgment: II. The findings of the appellate court below do not stand up to scrutiny in all respects.

(aa) A claim for *culpa in contrahendo* will exist where the vendor has made negligent statements or been guilty of non-disclosure, regarding attributes inherent in the thing sold. . . . Contrary to the view taken by the court hearing the appeal on the facts, the special rules concerning warranties do not exclude even as regards attributes in respect of which an assurance could have been given but was not given liability based on *culpa in contrahendo* for merely negligent breach of a duty of disclosure. . . .

. . . However, such liability is eliminated by reason of the fact that the defendant did not breach any duty of disclosure; consequently, the question of causality and fault does not arise. In negotiations with a view to the conclusion of a contract of sale, a duty of disclosure exists *inter alia* where the concealment of facts would be contrary to the principle of good faith and the party to whom statements are addressed was entitled, according to the accepted view, to expect to be informed of the fact concealed. . . . The court hearing the appeal on the facts linked the duty of disclosure to the factual circumstances which had prompted the defendant, some two years prior to the contractual negotiations with the plaintiff, to address a serious reprimand to N. . . . and to advise him to "give some thought, with the minimum of delay, to a solution to [the problems affecting] the employment relationship". The court below makes no findings with regard to the possibility that, following the

---

[277] *Supra*, at 417.
[278] Larenz, *SAT* para. 9 I.
[279] NJW 1991.1223.

official warning given to him N. may again have given cause for complaint or that he and the defendant may have come close to dissolving the employment relationship. The very passage of time militates against any conclusion that the defendant was under a duty to provide information *a fortiori* since the matter involved facts the unsolicited revelation of which might have been precluded by considerations with regard to N.'s personal rights. The fact that the plaintiff, as a tax adviser, possesses business skills constitutes a material factor as regards the information which he was entitled to expect to be given. . . . Moreover, that circumstance must be considered in conjunction with the fact that the plaintiff not only took over N. as an employee of the practice but also when concluding the contract with the defendant, offered to sell N. a share in the business. The plaintiff's proposed association with N. as a co-owner of the business should have prompted him on his own initiative to seek such information concerning N by means of enquiries made of the defendant, for example, or by inspecting the documents made available to him, or by requesting particulars, as to obviate any need to rely on unsolicited disclosure by the defendant. Having regard to the specific facts which the court below omitted to assess, it cannot be said that any duty to provide information existed with regard to the formal warning letter.

Note

(1) The German courts have identified duties of disclosure in certain cases coming under the following headings:

—where one party is or should be aware that the other is or may be under a misapprehension as to the content and legal and economic significance of the agreement which they are about to enter into;[280]
—where one party is aware of a formal requirement of validity of the contract or performance of the obligations thereunder which has not been satisfied;[281]
—where one party knows of circumstances which threaten his or her ability to meet his or her obligations;[282]
—where one party knows of circumstances which make it unlikely that the objective of the contract can be attained—although generally a buyer takes the risk of the thing sold not being suitable for his further purposes.[283]

(2) The usual consequence of a finding of *culpa in contrahendo* is an award of damages in the amount of the negative interest. Exceptionally the expectation interest may be awarded if it can be shown that the party claiming would have entered into a contract on better terms, as opposed to not entering into the contract at all. In addition the contract may be adjusted to change terms which have resulted from the *culpa in contrahendo*.

(4) Netherlands

BW **3.NL.83.**

Art.6:228: 1. A contract which has been entered into under the influence of error and which would not have been entered into had there been a correct assessment of the facts, can be annulled: . . .

[280] BGH NJW 1968.986.
[281] BGHZ 6.330 (333); 16.334 (336).
[282] RGZ 132.305 (309); BGHZ 56.81 (88).
[283] BGH NJW 1970.653 (655).

b. if the other party, in view of what he knew or ought to know regarding the error, should have informed the party in error; . . .

3.2.5. ADAPTATION OF CONTRACTS

This part covers two related questions:

(1) What is the outcome where one party offers to perform the contract in the way the other party had thought would be the case when he entered it?
(2) If one party has a *prima facie* right to avoid the contract, but the court thinks it can reach a fair result by adjusting the terms of the contract, can it do so and refuse to permit avoidance?

The most obvious example of (1) is where there is a mistake over the terms of the contract: for example I make a mistake and offer to sell you my house for £120,000 when I meant to write £130,000. Assuming I have a right to escape from the contract, should I still be entitled to escape if, when you hear that there has been a mistake, you offer to pay the larger amount?

The same sort of problem can arise where the mistake is about the circumstances: for example, a flooring contractor employed to floor a large building makes a fundamental mistake about the amount of work needed. This mistake should have been known to the other party so the contractor has the right to avoid the contract. The employer offers to release the contractor from the extra work without any reduction in the payment. Can the contractor avoid the contract?

Principles of European Contract Law **3.PECL.84.**

Article 4:105: *Adaptation of Contract*
(1) If a party is entitled to avoid the contract for mistake but the other party indicates that it is willing to perform, or actually does perform, the contract as it was understood by the party entitled to avoid it, the contract is to be treated as if it had been concluded as the that party understood it. The other party must indicate its willingness to perform, or render such performance, promptly after being informed of the manner in which the party entitled to avoid it understood the contract and before that party acts in reliance on any notice of avoidance.
(2) After such indication or performance the right to avoid is lost and any earlier notice of avoidance is ineffective.
(3) Where both parties have made the same mistake, the court may at the request of either party bring the contract into accordance with what might reasonably have been agreed had the mistake not occurred.

In this situation neither French nor English law seems to prevent the mistaken party from relying on the mistake to escape the contract. In German law, if the other party offers to perform the contract in the manner intended by the mistaken party it is held that it would be contrary to good faith (§ 242 BGB) to allow the latter to avoid. The contract, as intended, remains valid and enforceable. Were the mistaken party to insist on avoidance, a claim of *venire contra factum proprium* could be raised against him, i.e. a party cannot enforce a right if he would, thereby, be acting inconsistently with his previous conduct.[284] This is expressly provided for in relation to avoidance for mistake in the Swiss Code (Article 25 II OR).[285]

Dutch law has a specific provision:

BW **3.NL.85.**

Art. 6:230: The power to annul a contract on the basis of Articles 228 and 229 lapses when the other party timely proposes a modification to the effects of the contract which adequately removes the prejudice which the person entitled to the annulment suffers by the continuance of the contract.

In situation (2), some systems seem to have limited powers of adjustment. Thus under the English equitable doctrine of mistake, the court may "set aside the contract on terms",[286] which may have the practical effect of adjusting the contract.

In German law, even where the relevant grounds are made out, avoidance may be viewed by the court as unfair having regard to § 242 BGB. As will be seen,[287] in such cases the contract may be adapted if its continued application would be in the interests of both parties. Accordingly, the performance required of either or both parties may be adjusted to reflect the "true" basis of the contract. The remedies under *culpa in contrahendo* were also seen to be more flexible than that of avoidance under § 119 BGB. In relation to defects, the BGB provides that the contract price may be reduced in proportion to the extent to which an item sold or work carried out is defective: § 462 BGB, § 634 BGB. This will include cases where the party seeking these remedies was in error as to the presence of the defect.[288]

BW **3.NL.86.**

Article 6:230: (2) Furthermore, instead of pronouncing the annulment the judge may, upon the demand of one of the parties, modify the effects of the contract so as to remove this prejudice.

3.2.6. COMPARATIVE SUMMARY: MISTAKE AND THE INTERNATIONAL RESTATEMENTS

It is useful to compare the national laws we have considered with each other and to the provisions of the international restatements of contract law, particularly the Principles of European Contract Law and the Unidroit Principles.

---

[284] RGZ 102.87.
[285] See also, Article 1432 of the Codice Civile and *Münchener Kommentar* under § 119 BGB, para. 129.
[286] *Supra*, at 389.
[287] *Infra*, at 630 ff.
[288] RGZ 103.154 (159); BGH NJW 1977.1538 (1539).

All four legal systems covered in this section allow a party to escape a contract which he has entered into on the ground of a mistake as to the subject matter or circumstances, but under rather different conditions and sometimes under doctrines other than mistake.

First, the mistake may prevent there being a contract at all under separate doctrines: in French law because the contract lacks *objet* or *cause*; in German law because it is objectively impossible.[289] English law probably reaches a similar result where the contract is for the sale of goods which have already ceased to exist. These rules are not reflected in the more recent Dutch code, and they are explicitly rejected by PECL Article 4:102[290] and Unidroit Article 3.3.

A contract may also be void on the ground of mistake under the English doctrine at common law. However, the mistake must be very serious and the doctrine is very restrictive in that the mistake must be shared by both parties. The equitable doctrine treats the contract as voidable rather than void, but it also requires that the mistake be shared by the parties and seems to apply only to equally fundamental mistakes.

In contrast the continental systems all permit a party who has entered a contract on the basis of a mistake to avoid it on more liberal bases. While in French law the mistake must relate to an essential quality of the subject-matter, or in German law to a characteristic considered essential in business, these notions seem to be applied less strictly than the common law's requirement that the mistake "render the thing essentially different" or the equitable doctrine's requirement of "fundamental" mistake.[291] Further, neither system requires that the mistake be shared. The matter to which the mistake relates must be something which, to use broad terms, both parties would recognize as being important;[292] but neither system requires that the defendant has to have made the same mistake.

Nonetheless, the practical importance of these differences must not be exaggerated. In cases of shared("common") mistake, while French and German law seem to allow avoidance more readily than English law will find the contract void or voidable for mistake, we saw that English courts can avoid the requirement that the mistake be essential or fundamental by the device of the implied condition precedent, so that if the facts are not as assumed there is again no contract.[293] But, secondly, cases of "pure" shared mistake are relatively rare. Much more frequent are cases where the parties do indeed share the same misapprehension, but this is because the plaintiff has relied on incorrect information given him—without fraud[294]—by the other party. Here the differences between the continental and common law systems are very slight. In the continental systems, the contract may be avoided for mistake, in England, it may be avoided for misrepresentation. Indeed the doctrine of misrepresentation may be the more liberal, as the matter misrepresented need not be of particular importance, though the court now has power to refuse to

---

[289] *Supra*, at 381.

[290] *Supra*, at 383.

[291] *Supra*, at 388 and 393.

[292] *Supra*, at 372 and 380.

[293] The fact that this approach and the common law doctrine of mistake both lead to the contract being void rather than voidable seems to have little practical importance in the cases. The question is most likely to be relevant when a third party is affected, but none of the reported cases seems to involve third parties.

[294] Of course if the party giving the information was dishonest, in all systems the contract is voidable for fraud; but not if the party was honestly mistaken. *Supra*, at 337.

permit rescission on this or other grounds.[295] Thus in this situation the chief difference between the Common Law and the Civil Law systems is simply the ground on which avoidance is permitted. Both PECL (Article 4:103[296]) and Unidroit (Article 3.5[297]) adopt the continental approach.

There are of course differences between the French and German approaches. Perhaps the most noticeable is that in French law the mistake must relate to a substantial quality of the thing sold, and this must have been determining for the avoiding party; while German law is possibly a little more liberal, in that any characteristic which affects the value of the property seems to be treated by the courts as falling within § 119 II BGB. However, this is balanced by the obligation to pay reliance damages under § 122 BGB. It may be that the differences between the two systems are not really significant.

Dutch law is also generous in that the circumstances about to which one party is mistaken are broadly defined; but relief under BW Article 6:228 is precluded if the other party did not know and had no reason to know of the importance of the fact to the party seeking to avoid the contract.[298]

Where the party giving the incorrect information was at fault, even if the conditions for avoidance on the ground of mistake have not been met, all four systems will allow the recovery of damages.[299] PECL Article 4:106[300] is to the same effect. Unidroit does not have a parallel provision; damages may be recovered only if the contract could have been avoided for mistake:

<table>
<tr><td>Unidroit Principles</td><td>3.INT.87.</td></tr>
</table>

Article 3.18: Irrespective of whether or not the contract has been avoided, the party who knew or ought to have known of the ground of avoidance is liable for damages so as to put the other party in the same position in which it would have been if it had not concluded the contract.

Compare the rather more elaborate provision of PECL:

<table>
<tr><td>Principles of European Contract Law</td><td>3.PECL.88.</td></tr>
</table>

Article 4:117: *Damages*
(1) A party who avoids a contract under this Chapter may recover from the other party damages so as to put the avoiding party as nearly as possible into the same position as if it had not concluded the contract, provided that the other party knew or ought to have known of the mistake, fraud, threat or taking of excessive benefit or unfair advantage.
(2) If a party has the right to avoid a contract under this Chapter, but does not exercise its right or has lost its right under the provisions of Articles 4:113 or 4:114, it may recover, subject to paragraph (1), damages limited to the loss caused to it by the

---

[295] Misrepresentation Act 1967, s.2(2), *supra*, at 403.
[296] *Supra*, at 344.
[297] *Infra*, at 427.
[298] *Supra*, at 393–394.
[299] *Supra*, at 404 ff.
[300] *Supra*, at 404.

> mistake, fraud, threat or taking of excessive benefit or unfair advantage. The same
> measure of damages shall apply when the party was misled by incorrect information
> in the sense of Article 4:106.
> (3) In other respects, the damages shall be in accordance with the relevant provi-
> sions of Chapter 9, Section 5, with appropriate adaptations.

The second paragraph is intended to prevent a party who has not avoided the contract
from recovering damages that would pass to the other party the loss caused by a fall in
value in the property transferred unrelated to the misrepresentation: see Comment C.

The cases in which real differences between the systems emerge are those in which one
party has made a mistake which the other party does not share, but which is not the result
of any untrue statement by the latter. Here we saw that French and German law will allow
avoidance on the ground of mistake, provided the normal conditions as to the importance
of the mistake are satisfied. Further, if the defendant was aware of the plaintiff's mistake
and does not point it out, he will be guilty of fraud if good faith requires that he say something. Also in Germany there are, and in France there are argued to be, general duties of
disclosure in the absence of fraud. In contrast, English law does not give a remedy for mistake in these circumstances, does not recognize that keeping silent may amount to fraud
and has only limited duties of disclosure.

Perhaps an even more striking difference between the systems lies in the case in which
one party enters the contract under a self-induced misapprehension about which the
other party does not know, and has no reason to know. Here there is no element of dishonesty or reproachable behaviour on the part of the second party, and there is no question of liability in damages under any of the systems; but in principle French and German
law may each allow relief, provided that the mistake was one as to the substance or sufficiently essential. However, it should be said that in both systems this statement needs
qualification. In French law the mistaken party's error may be branded *inexcusable* and
relief be denied altogether. In German law relief on the ground of mistake is precluded
where the rules on defects in property sold (§§ 459ff BGB) apply, and the mistaken party
who avoids the contract may have to pay negative interest damages to the other under §
122 BGB. The Dutch BW is perhaps less clear on this point. Article 6:228 limits relief to
cases in which the mistake was caused by incorrect information, was shared or in which:

BW   **3.NL.89.**

Article 6:228: b. . . . the other party, in view of what he knew or ought to know regarding the error,
should have informed the party in error; . . .

This may at first sight seem to suggest that the other party must have known, or have had
reason to know, of the mistake; but Hartkamp and Tillema[301] deny that this is necessary,
though pointing out that knowledge would be relevant to a claim for damages under BW
Article 6:162.[302]

---

[301] Hartkamp and Tillema, op. cit., para. 80.
[302] *Supra*, at 394.

It will be seen that the PECL limit relief for mistake under Article 4:103 to cases where:

Principles of European Contract Law   **3.PECL.90.**

Article 4:103: ... (i) the mistake was caused by information given by the other party; or
(ii) the other party knew or ought to have known of the mistake and it was contrary to good faith and fair dealing to leave the mistaken party in error; or
(iii) the other party made the same mistake,

...

The corresponding provision of Unidroit is slightly broader:

Unidroit Principles   **3.INT.91.**

Article 3.3: (1) A party may only avoid a contract for mistake if when the contract was concluded the mistake was of such importance that a reasonable person in the same situation as the party in error would have contracted only on materially different terms or would not have contracted at all if the true state of affairs had been known, and
(a) the other party made the same mistake, or caused the mistake, or knew or ought to have known of the mistake and it was contrary to reasonable commercial standards of fair dealing to leave the mistaken party in error, or
(b) the other party has not at the time of avoidance acted in reliance on the contract.
(2) However, a party may not avoid the contract if
(a) it committed the mistake with gross negligence, or
(b) the mistake relates to a matter in regard to which the risk of mistake was assumed or, taking into account all the relevant circumstances, should be borne by the mistaken party.

Article 3.3 (1) (b) permits avoidance by a party whose unilateral mistake was unknown to and not caused by the other party, provided that the latter has not relied on the contract. This has parallels in some European laws, see PECL Article 4: Note 6), but was not adopted as part of the Principles.

On the question of fraud by silence, the Principles of European Contract Law quite clearly reject the common law approach:

Principles of European Contract Law   **3.PECL.92.**

Article 4:107: *Fraud*
(1) A party may avoid a contract when it has been led to conclude it by the other party's fraudulent representation, whether by words or conduct, or fraudulent non-disclosure of any information which in accordance with good faith and fair dealing it should have disclosed.
(2) A party's representation or non-disclosure is fraudulent if it was intended to deceive.
(3) In determining whether good faith and fair dealing required that a party disclose particular information, regard should be had to all the circumstances, including:
(a) whether the party had special expertise;
(b) the cost to it of acquiring the relevant information;

(c) whether the other party could reasonably acquire the information for itself; and

(d) the apparent importance of the information to the other party.

Readers may be interested in considering two related questions. The first is why the common law has such a different attitude towards non-disclosure. Is it simply an accident of history? Can it be explained by the typical cases which are heard by the courts in the different countries. English contract law is often dominated by cases between commercial businesses operating at arm's length, where perhaps good faith would not require disclosure; possibly the English rule is aimed primarily at such cases but is applied, too broadly, to all cases. Or may the difference reflect underlying philosophies about law and the role of the legal system? Secondly, what should the law on self-induced mistake and non-disclosure be?[303]

One argument made by Kronman and Rudden is an economic one. Consider the example (somewhat out of date, perhaps, but the point is still valid) given by Cockburn CJ in his judgment in *Smith* v. *Hughes*:[304] the buyer of land knows that there is coal under the land and also knows that the sellers do not know this. Should the buyer have to reveal its knowledge? An argument against imposing a duty of disclosure on the buyer is that it will have discovered the coal only through a costly investigation. If it has to reveal its information, it will lose its advantage and it will no longer be worthwhile investing in costly investigations. That however would be inefficient.

But even if the efficiency argument is accepted, should the coal company be allowed to buy the land at its normal agricultural value when it is worth so much more? Is the additional value of the land once it is known to contain coal in direct proportion to the cost of exploration? If the cost of exploration is less than the increased value, is there any way in which the court might allow the oil company some advantage, so as to encourage it to search for oil, yet have to pay something extra to X?

You may like to consider Ghestin's account of an unpublished decision.[305]

Sometimes, however, the information to be obtained may call for a very substantial investigation and therefore justify an exceptional profit. A case decided by the Tribunal de Grand Instance of Paris on 6 March 1985 (unpublished) provides a good illustration. The Congregation of the Sisters of Saint Charles du Puy had sold the contents of an attic to a dealer for 6,800 francs. Among the objects sold was a picture which was later acquired for 4,000 francs by a young picture restorer. After patient restoration and considerable research, particularly in Italy, he established that the painting was a genuine work of the Italian painter Lorenzo Lotto. He then sold this Carrying of the Cross to the State, for the Louvre, for 3,250,000 francs. The court rejected a claim of ownership made by the Congregation, but opened the way to a solution which, on the one hand, would allow the sellers to invoke their mistake—provided that in the circumstances it was excusable—and thus to obtain the annulment of the initial and the subsequent sales, and, on the other hand, allow the

[303] Pieces worth reading include Kronman, "Mistake, Disclosure, Information and the Law of Contracts" (1978) 7 J Law & Society 1 (extracts, in *Beale, Bishop and Furmston* 3rd ed. pp 468–469); Kronman, "Contract Law and Distributive Justice" (1980) 89 Yale LJ 472 (extracts, BBF 3rd ed. pp 716–718); Rudden, "Le juste et l'inefficace pour un non-devoir de renseignements" RTD civ. 1985.91; Fabre-Magnan, op. cit. at 99–120; *Alternativ Kommentar zum BGB*, under § 119 BGB, paras. 27–30.

[304] *Supra*, at 411.

[305] Ghestin in *Contract Law Today*, op. cit., at 159.

"discoverer" to retain a significant part of the value added to the painting as recompense for his "work" and his "perspicacity". The legal basis for this solution could be authorized management of another's affairs (gestion d'affaires), as it is now understood by the jurisprudence.

Further Reading

—*Alternativ Kommentar zum BGB*, Vol. I: *Allgemeiner Teil* (various authors) (Neuwied: Luchterhand, 1987);

—H. Beale, "The Europeanisation of Contract Law" in R. Halson (ed.), *Exploring the Boundaries of Contract Law* (Aldershot: Dartmouth, 1996) at 23–47;

—*Chitty*, chapters 5 (mistake) and 6 (misrepresentation);

—M. Fabre-Magnan, "Duties of Disclosure and French Contract Law" in J. Beatson and D. Friedmann (eds.), *Good Faith and Fault in Contract Law* (Oxford: Clarendon, 1995) at 99–120;

—M. Fabre-Magnan, "Defects of Consent in Contract Law" in *Towards a European Civil Code* at 219–237;

—W. Flume, *Eigenschaftsirrtum und Kauf* (Darmstadt: 1948);

—Ghestin, paras. 490–548;

—D. Harris and D. Tallon (eds.), *Contract Law Today: Anglo-French Comparisons* (Oxford: Clarendon, 1989), chapter 4;

—A. Hartkamp and M.M. Tillema, *Contract Law in the Netherlands* (The Hague/Boston: Kluwer, 1995), paras. 71–84;

—H. Kötz, chapter 10;

—A. Kronman, "Mistake, Disclosure, Information and the Law of Contracts" (1978) 7 J Law & Society 1;

—A. Kronman, "Contract Law and Distributive Justice" (1980) 89 Yale LJ 472;

—Larenz, *AT*;

—Larenz, *SAT*;

—P. Legrand (1986) 6 Oxford JLS 322;

—E. McKendrick, *Contract* at 67–72 (agreement mistakes), 253–65 (duty to disclose), 234–53 (misrepresentation) and 289–299 (common mistake);

—Malaurie and Aynès, paras. 402–412;

—B.S. Markesinis, W. Lorenz and G. Dannemann, *The German Law of Obligations*, Vol I: *The Law of Contracts and Restitution* (Oxford: Clarendon, 1997) at 197–206;

—*Münchener Kommentar zum BGB*;

—B. Nicholas, at 83–100;

—B. Rudden, "Le juste et l'inefficace pour un non-devoir de renseignements" RTD civ. 1985.91;

—G. Treitel, *Contract*, chapters 8 (mistake) and 9 (misrepresentation);

—C. Witz, *Droit privé allemand*, Vol. I: *Actes juridiques, droits subjectifs* (Paris: Lictec);

—K. Zweigert and H. Kötz, at 411–28.

3.3. THREATS AND ABUSE OF CIRCUMSTANCES

3.3.1. INTRODUCTION

Principles of European Contract Law   **3.PECL.93.**

Article 1:102: *Freedom of Contract*
(1) Parties are free to enter into a contract and to determine its contents, subject to the requirements of good faith and fair dealing, and the mandatory rules established by these Principles.
(2) The parties may exclude the application of any of the Principles or derogate from or vary their effects, except as otherwise provided by these Principles.

Article 4:108: *Threats*
A party may avoid a contract when it has been led to conclude it by the other party's imminent and serious threat of an act:
(a) which is wrongful in itself, or
(b) which it is wrongful to use as a means to obtain the conclusion of the contract, unless in the circumstances the first party had a reasonable alternative.

Article 4:109: *Excessive Benefit or Unfair Advantage*
(1) A party may avoid a contract if, at the time of the conclusion of the contract:
(a) it was dependent on or had a relationship of trust with the other party, was in economic distress or had urgent needs, was improvident, ignorant, inexperienced or lacking in bargaining skill, and
(b) the other party knew or ought to have known of this and, given the circumstances and purpose of the contract, took advantage of the first party's situation in a way which was grossly unfair or took an excessive benefit.
(2) Upon the request of the party entitled to avoidance, a court may if it is appropriate adapt the contract in order to bring it into accordance with what might have been agreed had the requirements of good faith and fair dealing been followed.
(3) A court may similarly adapt the contract upon the request of a party receiving notice of avoidance for excessive benefit or unfair advantage, provided that this party informs the party which gave the notice promptly after receiving it and before that party has acted in reliance on it.

Article 4:111: *Third Persons*
(1) Where a third person for whose acts a party is responsible, or who with a party's assent is involved in the making of a contract:
(a) causes a mistake by giving information, or knows of or ought to have known of a mistake,
(b) gives incorrect information,
(c) commits fraud,
(d) makes a threat, or
(e) takes excessive benefit or unfair advantage,
remedies under this Chapter will be available under the same conditions as if the behaviour or knowledge had been that of the party itself.

430

(2) Where any other third person:
   (a) gives incorrect information,
   (b) commits fraud,
   (c) makes a threat, or
   (d) takes excessive benefit or unfair advantage, remedies under this Chapter will be available if the party knew or ought to have known of the relevant facts, or at the time of avoidance it has not acted in reliance on the contract.

"Parties are free to enter into a contract and to determine its contents, subject to the requirements of good faith and fair dealing. . . ." Article 1:102(1) of the PECL expresses a universally accepted doctrine of contract law: that of freedom of contract (see Article 1.1 of the UP). Article 6:111 of the PECL adds another, albeit implicitly: "A party is bound to fulfil its obligations even if performance has become more onerous, whether because the cost of performance has increased or because the value of the performance it receives has diminished"—namely, the binding character of contracts (*pacta sunt servanda*; cf. explicitly Article 1.3 of the UP: "A contract validly entered into is binding upon the parties . . .").

In the continental legal systems, both doctrines are closely linked with the notion of party autonomy, in that a person may conclude a contract if he so wishes and is legally bound to a contract if he so wills. However, in terms of the will theory, a party's will may be defective in a number of ways, as in the case where the party was mistaken, or deceived or threatened by the other party (or a third person). These instances are known to civilian lawyers as the "defects of consent" ("*Willensmängel*", "*vices du consentement*"). As a general rule, a defect of consent, existing at the moment of conclusion of the contract, affects the validity of the contract. As the previous section shows, even systems which do not recognize the will theory, such as the Common Law, accept that in some circumstances a party's consent may not have been validly given, though in such systems the concentration may be more on the acts of the other party (for example that he gave inaccurate information) than on the subjective state of mind of the claimant.

This section first examines the question whether and, if so, under what conditions, a contract is rendered voidable at the instance of a party who entered into the contract under the influence of a threat (**3.3.2**). Clearly, not all threats are actionable in law as some threats are part of everyday (business) life. For instance, if A is negotiating to buy a car from B, who is a car dealer, and A threatens that if B does not reduce the price, A will instead buy a car from C, and B does reduce the price, B cannot then avoid the contract with A on the ground of threat. In order to distinguish threats which render a contract voidable from those which do not, legal systems give specific rules. Thus, the continental jurisdictions are concerned only with psychological constraints (**3.3.2.A**) but do not restrict their doctrines of threat to particular means or objects of pressure, as was traditionally the case in English law (**3.3.2.B**). All legal systems agree that a threat must be illegitimate in order to render a contract voidable (**3.3.2.C**). Furthermore, the jurisdictions discussed require—in one way or another—that the threatened party entered into the contract as a result of the threat (**3.3.2.D**) and that the threat is sufficiently serious and imminent as to determine the will of a reasonable person or the party in question (**3.3.2.E**).

This section then turns to the question whether a contract may be avoided simply on the ground that in terms of substance it is very unfair—for example, the buyer is being charged far more than the property is worth, or the seller is receiving much less (**3.3.3**). This is often referred to by the Roman name, *laesio enormis*. It will be seen that the legal systems rarely give relief on this ground alone—it should perhaps be noted that *laesio enormis* is an independent doctrine and not as such directly related to the core matter of this section, *viz.* threats and abuse of circumstances; it is included in this section, however, mainly for purposes of exposition.

The situation changes, however, if the unfairness to the one party is the result of his predicament, inexperience, dependence, etc., having been abused by the other party—for instance, in a case where A is in urgent need of medication and B supplies him with the medication at excessive prices. This type of case, in which there is both an abuse of circumstances and a gross disproportion in the mutual performances—an excessive (dis)advantage—, is here referred to as "qualified *laesio enormis*" (the phrase is borrowed from the 1968 report on the validity of international sales contracts by the Max-Planck Institute in Hamburg). The legal systems deal with this issue by applying rather different doctrines, notwithstanding that the end result is often the same (**3.3.4**).[306]

There follows a section which considers whether an abuse of a party's circumstances may give that party the right to avoid the contract even if the resulting contract is not excessively disadvantageous to him, or if the disadvantage is other than financial or if there is no disadvantage at all (**3.3.5**). In other words, is relief for abuse of circumstances limited to cases of qualified *laesio enormis*, or is there a broader doctrine designed to ensure true freedom of choice?

Lastly, it will be considered whether a contract is voidable where it has been made as the result of a threat or abuse of circumstances not by the other party to the contract, but by a third person (**3.3.6**).

3.3.2. THREATS

Principles of European Contract Law   **3.PECL.94.**

Article 4:108: *Threats*

A party may avoid a contract when it has been led to conclude it by the other party's imminent and serious threat of an act:
(a) which is wrongful in itself, or
(b) which it is wrongful to use as a means to obtain the conclusion of the contract, unless in the circumstances the first party had a reasonable alternative.[307]

Code civil   **3.F.95.**

Article 1109: Where consent is given solely by reason of mistake, or is extorted by threat or obtained by fraud, it shall not constitute valid consent.

---

[306] Contracts in restraint of trade and unfair terms will not be discussed in this section, as they are covered by sections **3.1** and **3.4**, *supra* at 304 and *infra* at 494 respectively.
[307] See also Art. 3.9 UP, which is in similar terms.

Article 1111: Any threat brought to bear against the party who has contracted the obligation shall constitute a ground of nullity, even where it has been brought to bear by a party other than the party for whose benefit the agreement was made.

Article 1112: (1) Threat exists where it is such as to make an impression on a reasonable person and may instil in him the fear of exposing his person or his material possessions to substantial and imminent harm.
(2) Regard shall be had in that connection to the age, sex and condition of the persons concerned.

Article 1113: Threat shall constitute a ground of nullity of the contract not only where it has been brought to bear against the contracting party but also where it has been brought to bear against his or her spouse or relatives in the descending or ascending line.

Article 1114: Fear inspired by feelings of awe at the consequences of disobeying a parent or other relative in the ascending line shall not of itself, in the absence of threat, constitute a sufficient ground for annulment of the contract.

BGB   **3.G.96.**

§ 123: [Voidability on account of deceit or threat]
(1) Where a person has been induced by wilful deceit or unlawful threat to make a declaration of intent, that person may avoid the statement in question . . .

BW[308]   **3.NL.97.**

Article 3:44: (1) A juridical act may be annulled when it has been entered into as a result of threat, fraud or abuse of circumstances.
(2) A person who induces another to execute a certain juridical act by unlawfully threatening him or a third party with harm to his person or property, makes a threat. The threat must be such that a reasonable person would be influenced by it . . .

3.3.2.A. VIS COMPULSIVA AS OPPOSED TO VIS ABSOLUTA

In the jurisdictions of continental Europe a distinction is made between physical compulsion (*vis absoluta*) and psychical pressure (*vis compulsiva*). Where actual physical force is used to compel a party to enter into a contract, for example if one party takes the other party's hand and makes him sign a document, there is no freedom of choice and, as a consequence, no contract comes into being ("void contract"). In the case of psychological pressure, on the other hand, the threatened party does have a choice, albeit between what he considers to be the lesser of two evils (*coactus volui, tamen volui*). However, his consent to enter into the contract is defective because of the pressure put on him: he consents because he fears the consequences of not entering into the contract. The contract is therefore voidable at the instance of the threatened person. The continental doctrines of threat are concerned only with cases of psychological pressure.[309]

---

[308] [Translation by Mackay and Haanappel.]
[309] See e.g. Larenz, *AT* at 700; Terré, Simler and Lequette, paras 234 ff.; Zweigert and Kötz, at 428; Max Planck Institut, *Die materielle Gültigkeit von Kaufverträgen. Ein rechtsvergleichender Bericht* (Berlin/Tübingen: 1968) at 123.

433

In English law the distinction between *vis absoluta* and *vis compulsiva* appears to be irrelevant. In fact, the common law concept of duress to the person is said to consist of actual or threatened physical violence. In either case the contract is voidable.[310] It may be that the case of the person whose hand is literally forced would be dealt with under another doctrine, that of *non est factum*.[311] If so, the contract would be absolutely void.

3.3.2.B. THE MEANS OF COMPULSION

At one time the common law concept of duress was restricted to actual or threatened violence to, and unlawful constraint of, the person of the contracting party ("duress to the person"; for an example see *Barton* v. *Armstrong*).[312] Unlawful detention of another's goods, or threats of such detention, did not constitute duress.[313] In *The "Siboen" and the "Sibotre"*,[314] Kerr J rejected this stern concept of duress. His opinion has been accepted in later cases.

Queen's Bench Division   **3.E.98.**
North Ocean Shipping Co. Ltd. v. *Hyundai Construction Co., Ltd*[315]

ECONOMIC DURESS

The "Atlantic Baron"

An agreement to alter the terms of an existing contract entered into as the result of a threat by one party to break the terms of the existing contract if the alteration is not agreed to, may be voidable on the grounds of duress if the party threatened had no practical alternative but to give in to the threat.

Facts: On 10 April 1972 a shipbuilding company agreed to build a ship (The "Atlantic Baron") for the owners at a fixed price in US dollars, payable in five instalments. The shipbuilders opened a letter of credit by way of security for repayment of the instalments in the event of their default in the performance of the contract. After payment of the first instalment, the US dollar devalued by 10%. The shipbuilders threatened not to deliver the ship unless the owners would agree to increase the remaining instalments by 10 %. The owners asserted that there was no legal ground for the shipbuilders' claim but on 28 June 1973 they agreed (by telex) to pay the additional 10%, "without prejudice" to their rights, as they were afraid to lose a very lucrative contract for the charter of the ship, which at that time they were negotiating with Shell. In turn, the owners requested the shipbuilders to increase the letter of credit by 10%, which the shipbuilders did. The owners paid the remaining instalments, including the 10% increase, without protest and in November 1975 the shipbuilders delivered the ship. Some eight months later the owners claimed the return of the additional 10% paid on the last four instalments; they argued that they did not make the claim earlier because they feared that the delivery of sister ship might be affected, but in arbitration this fear was found to be groundless. For their claim the owners asserted that there had been no consideration for their promise to pay the extra 10% and that they had entered into that agreement under duress.

Held: It was held (1) that the shipbuilders had given consideration for the owners' promise to pay the additional 10% by increasing the letter of credit by corresponding percentage and (2) that the shipbuilders' threat to break the original contract unless the owners agreed to increase their payments, amounted to economic duress. The

---

[310] See Treitel, *Contract* at 375; McKendrick, *Contract* at 352. Contrast: *Restatement of the Law (Second), Contracts 2d*, §174 ("When Duress by Physical Compulsion Prevents Formation of a Contract") and §175 ("When Duress by Threat Makes a Contract Voidable").
[311] See Treitel, *Contract* at 301 ff.
[312] [1976] AC 104, cited in **3.3.2.D**, *infra* at 447.
[313] E.g. *Skeate* v. *Beale* (1840) 11 Ad. & E 983.
[314] [1976] 1 Lloyd's Rep. 293.
[315] [1979] 1 QB 705.

agreement of 28 June 1973 was therefore voidable; it was found, however, that the owners, by paying the increased instalments without protest and by waiting for eight months before bringing their claim, had affirmed the agreement.

Judgment: MOCATTA J.: . . . Having reached the conclusion that there was consideration for the agreement made on June 28 . . . 1973, I must next consider whether even if that agreement, varying the terms of the original shipbuilding contract of 10 April 1972, was made under a threat to break that original contract and the various increased instalments were made consequently under the varied contract, the increased sums can be recovered as money had and received [a restitutionary remedy for unjust enrichment].

[The judge then considered the English case law and literature, as well as a number of Australian cases, especially the jugdment of Isaacs J in *Smith* v. *William Charlick Ltd.* (1924) 34 CLR 38, as to the question whether the doctrine of duress is limited to either duress to the person of the contracting party or to goods.]

Before proceeding further it may be useful to summarise the conclusions I have so far reached. First, I do not take the view that the recovery of money paid under duress other than to the person is necessarily limited to duress to goods falling within one of the categories hitherto established by the English cases. I would respectfully follow and adopt the broad statement of principle laid down by Isaacs J. cited earlier and frequently quoted and applied in the Australian cases. Secondly, from this it follows that the compulsion may take the form of "economic duress" if the necessary facts are proved. A threat to break a contract may amount to such "economic duress". Thirdly, if there has been such a form of duress leading to a contract for consideration, I think that contract is a voidable one which can be avoided and the excess money paid under it recovered.

I think that the facts found in this case do establish that the agreement to increase the price by 10 per cent. Reached at the end of June 1973 was caused by what may be called "economic duress". The Yard [i.e. the respondent shipbuilders] were adamant in insisting on the increased price without having any legal justification for so doing and the owners realised that the Yard would not accept anything other than an unqualified agreement to the increase. The owners might have claimed damages in arbitration against the Yard with all the inherent unavoidable uncertainties of litigation, but in view of the position of the Yard vis-à-vis their relations with Shell it would be unreasonable to hold that this is the course they should have taken: see *Astley* v. *Reynolds* (1731) 2 Str. 915. The owners made a very reasonable offer of arbitration coupled with security for any award in the Yard's favour that might be made, but this was refused. They then made their agreement, which can truly I think be said to have been made under compulsion, by the telex of 28 June without prejudice to their rights. I do not consider the Yard's ignorance of the Shell charter material. It may well be that had they known of it they would have been more exigent.

If I am right in the conclusion reached with some doubt earlier that there was consideration for the 10 per cent. Increase agreement reached at the end of June 1973, and it be right to regard this as having been reached under a kind of duress in the form of economic pressure, then what is said in *Chitty on Contracts*, 24th ed. (1977, vol. 1, para. 442, p. 207 . . . is relevant, namely, that a contract entered into under duress is voidable and not void:

> ". . . consequently a person who has entered into a contract under duress, may either affirm or avoid such contract after the duress has ceased; and if he has so voluntarily acted under it with a full knowledge of all the circumstances he may be held bound on the ground of ratification, or if, after escaping from the duress, he takes no steps to set aside the transaction, he may be found to have affirmed it. . . ."

On the other hand, the findings of fact in the special case [arbitration] present difficulties whether one is proceeding on the basis of a voidable agreement reached at the end of June 1973, or whether such agreement was void for want of consideration, and it were necessary in consequence to establish that the payments were made involuntarily and not with the intention of closing the transaction.

I have already stated that no protest of any kind was made by the owners after their telex of June 28, 1973, before their claim in this arbitration on 30 July 1975, shortly after in July of that year the *Atlantic Baroness*, a sister ship of the *Atlantic Baron*, had been tendered, though, as I understand it, she was not accepted and arbitration proceedings in regard to her are in consequence taking place. There was therefore a delay between 27 November 1974, when the *Atlantic Baron* was delivered and 30 July 1975, before the owners put forward their claim.

The owners were, therefore, free from the duress on 27 November 1974, and took no action by way of protest or otherwise between their important telex of 28 June 1973, and their formal claim for return of the excess 10 per cent. paid of 30 July 1975, when they nominated their arbitrator. One cannot dismiss this delay as of no significance, though I would not consider it conclusive by itself. I do not attach any special importance to the lack of protest made at the time of the assignment, since the documents made no reference to the increased 10 per cent. However, by the time the *Atlantic Baron* was due for delivery in November 1974, market conditions had changed radically, as is found in paragraph 39 of the special case [the decision of the abitrators] and the owners must have been aware of this. The special case finds in paragraph 40, as stated earlier, that the owners did not believe that the Yard would have refused to deliver the vessel or the *Atlantic Baroness* and had no reason so to believe. . . . after careful consideration, I have come to the conclusion that the important points here are that since there was no danger at this time in registering a protest, the final payments were made without any qualification and were followed by a delay until 31 July 1975, before the owners put forward their claim, the correct inference to draw, taking an objective view of the facts, is that the action and inaction of the owners can only be regarded as an affirmation of the variation in June 1973 of the terms of the original contract by the agreement to pay the additional 10 per cent. In reaching this conclusion I have not, of course, overlooked the findings in paragraph 45 of the special case, but I do not think that an intention on the part of the owners not to affirm the agreement for the extra payment not indicated to the Yard can avail them in the view of their overt acts. As was said in *Deacon* v. *Transport Regulation Board* [1958] V.R. 458, 460 in considering whether a payment was made voluntarily or not: "No secret mental reservation of the doer is material. The question is—what would his conduct indicate to a reasonable man as his mental state." I think this test is equally applicable to the decision this court has to make whether a voidable contract has been affirmed or not, and I have applied this test in reaching the conclusion I have just expressed . . .

Notes

(1) Lord Goff of Chieveley has stated that the limitation in *Skeate* has been "discarded, and it is now accepted that economic pressure may be sufficient to amount to duress" (*Dimskal Shipping Co. S.A.* v. *I.T.F.* (*The "Evia Luck"*)[316]). Hence, today, both duress to the person and duress to goods may entitle a party to avoid a contract.[317]

(2) This type of duress had earlier been recognized in American law.[318]

(3) It is also to be noted that where pressure is exercised which did not amount to duress at common law because the pressure did not involve an element of physical violence, relief was previously granted in equity on the ground of "actual" undue influence. In the case of *Williams* v. *Bayley*,[319] for instance, where a contract was obtained by a threat of prosecution for a criminal offence, it was held that the contract was not enforceable in equity. Theses cases might now be decided on the basis of economic duress.[320]

[316] [1992] 2 AC 152, 165.
[317] See McKendrick, *Contract* at 352.
[318] See e.g. Dawson, "Economic Duress—An Essay in Perspective", 45 Mich.LR 253 (1947).
[319] (1866) LR 1 HL 200.
[320] The doctrine of undue influence is discussed in **3.3.4** and **3.3.5**, *infra* at 471 and 485.

(4) *The "Siboen" and the "Sibotre"*[321] was a case of economic compulsion as the plaintiffs exerted commercial pressure on the defendants by threatening them with breach of contract—yet the plea of duress failed because the pressure was acceptable and had not vitiated the defendant's consent. See *North Ocean Shipping Co. Ltd.* v. *Hyundai Construction Co. Ltd.*[322] (*The "Atlantic Baron"*[323]); *Pao On* v. *Lau Yiu Long.*[324] Another example of economic duress can be found in the case of *Universe Tankships Inc. of Monrovia* v. *International Transport Workers Federation* (*The "Universe Sentinel"*),[325] where the defendants had "blacked" a ship owned by the plaintiffs, preventing it from leaving port. In order to obtain the lifting of the blacking, the plaintiffs agreed to comply with the defendants' demand to pay a contribution to a general welfare fund for sailors. The plaintiffs feared catastrophic financial consequences if they would not submit because the ship was off-hire under a time charter while the blacking continued.

(5) The civil law systems take a rather broad view of the means and object of threat. For instance in French law, a threat with any kind of harm directed against the person or the property of the contracting party may constitute "*violence*" (Article 1112 CC: "*exposer sa personne ou sa fortune à un mal*"). The nature of the threatened harm may be physical, moral or pecuniary.[326] For code provisions similar to Article 1112 CC, see Article 1435 of the Italian CC ("*esporre sè o i suoi beni a un male*"), Article 3:44 II BW ("*enig nadeel in persoon of goed*") and Article 30 I of the Swiss Code of Obligations ("*an Leib und Leben, Ehre oder Vermögen mit . . . Gefahr bedroht*"). §123 I BGB does not mention the means or object of "*Drohung*", but, according to some authors,[327] any kind of harm, material or immaterial, may suffice.[328]

(6) Like the civil law jurisdictions, Article 4:108 of the PECL—and equally Article 3.9 UP—does not restrict threat to any particular means or object. Comment A to Article 4:108 reads:

It is not only threats of physical violence or damage to property which constitute wrongful threats. A threat to inflict economic loss wrongfully, e.g. by breaking a contract, can equally constitute duress.

> *Illustration 2*: X owes a large debt to Y. Knowing that Y desperately needs the money, X tells Y that he will not pay it unless Y agrees to sell X a house which Y owns at a price well below its market value. Faced with bankruptcy, Y agrees. X then pays the debt. Y may avoid the contract to sell the house.

In practice the threat of a breach of contract is often used in an attempt to secure re-negotiation of the same contract. In this case the re-negotiation agreement may be avoided.

> *Illustration 3*: C has agreed to build a ship for D at a fixed price. Because of currency fluctuations which affect various subcontracts, C will lose a great deal if the contract price is not changed and it threatens not to deliver unless D agrees to pay 10% extra. D will suffer serious harm if the contract is not performed. D pays the extra sum demanded by C. D may recover the extra sum paid.

---

[321] [1976] 1 Lloyd's Rep. 293.
[322] [1979] 1 QB 705.
[323] Cit. *supra* at 434.
[324] [1980] AC 614.
[325] [1983] AC 366; cit. in **3.3.2.C** at 444.
[326] See Terré, Simler and Lequette, 5th edn. (1996), at 192–3; Malaurie and Aynès, at 250–1.
[327] Palandt-Heinrichs, under §123 BGB, para. 3 aa.
[328] For a French and a Dutch case of economic threat see: Cass. com., 28 May 1991, Bull. civ. IV.180; D. 1992. 166 annotated by Morvan; HR 27 March 1992, NJ 1992.377.

Under both Article 4:108 PECL and Article 3.9 UP a threat may consist of an act or omission.

(7) Can a contract be avoided on the ground of threat if the pressure was directed against a third person? Article 1113 of the French CC puts "*violence*" to the contracting party on a par with "*violence*" against certain close relatives (husband, wife, descendants and ascendants) of the contracting party. Cf. Article 1436(1) of the Italian CC. Article 1113 is interpreted either as establishing a legal presumption that a threat to these close relatives did constrain the contracting party or merely as giving examples.[329] The latter interpretation leaves it to the judge to decide whether a threat against a third person did in fact constrain the contracting party. Cf. Article 1436(2) of the Italian CC. In either interpretation, the list of third persons in Article 1113 is not exhaustive: a threat against any third person may entitle the contracting party to avoid the contract. The decisive test is whether the threat against a third person established a "*contrainte déterminante*" for the contracting party.[330] The same rule applies in Dutch law.[331] Equally in German law, a threat against a third person may consitute "*Drohung*" in the sense of §123(1) BGB.[332] See for example BGHZ 25, 217 (threat to prosecute the husband of the contracting party).[333] The English courts have held that pressure directed against a third person may amount to (actual) undue influence (see for example *Williams* v. *Bayley*:[334] threat to prosecute the son of the contracting party; *Kaufman* v. *Gerson*:[335] threat to prosecute the husband of the contracting party). Some English authors are of the opinion that the third person need not necessarily be related to the contracting person, and that the third person may even be a total stranger to him.[336]

3.3.2.C. THREAT MUST BE ILLEGITIMATE

Cass. civ. 1re, 3 November 1959[337]   **3.F.99.**

THE ILLEGITIMACY OF A THREAT

The inexperienced widow

A threat of exercising a right is illegitimate if the person threatening is thus trying to achieve a goal, such as the conclusion of a contract, for which his right is not given.

Facts: On 15 March 1947 Mrs Y, a widow, successfully bid at auction to acquire the house in which she had always lived. Two days later Mr X, a business agent, obtained from Mrs Y her agreement to withdraw from her acquisition of the property, in the form of a mandate in his favour authorising a declaration that she had been

[329] See Terré, Simler and Lequette, para. 237.

[330] See **3.2.2.C.** *infra* at 340.

[331] See Art. 3:44 II BW and Asser and Hartkamp, *Verbintenissenrecht*, Vol. II, 10th edn. (Zwolle: 2001) para. 208.

[332] See Palandt-Heinrichs, under §123 BGB, para. 3 aa.

[333] In **3.2.2.C.** *infra* at 340.

[334] (1866) LR 1 HL 200.

[335] [1904] 1 KB 591.

[336] See *Chitty* para. §7–008; H. McGregor, *Contract Code (Drawn up on behalf of the English Law Commission)* (London, 1994) at 221 (comment to s. 562). See also *Restatement of the Law (Second), Contracts 2d*, Comment to §176 and illustration 5.

[337] D. 1960.187 annotated by G. Holleaux; RTD civ. 1960.295 annotated by H. and L. Mazeaud.

acting in the auction on his behalf. Mr X thus took her place as the successful bidder. Mrs Y sought to avoid her declaration on the ground of *"violence"* (threat): she had given in to Mr X's threat that he would exercise his right *"de surenchérir"* (see below, note 2). The contested judgment was challenged by Mr X on the ground that it annulled the said declaration as having been vitiated by *"violence"* despite the fact that the Cour d'appel had not established the existence of coercion on the part of Mr X, that it had not taken into account the true statement that he had the right to make a higher bid and that Mrs Y, a capable woman in possession of her faculties, had freely signed an advantageous agreement.

Held: The Cour de cassation dismissed the appeal.

Judgment:—Whereas the appellate court noted the unremitting steps taken by Mr X in relation to Mrs Y, together with his repeated threats that he would outbid her and that, having successfully bid for the property, he would immediately evict her if she did not agree to withdraw and let him take her place as the successful bidder in return for a promise to provide her with accommodation for a further two years and to pay her 25,000 francs; as it found that on 17 March, in the course of one of his final visits to the home of Mrs Y, whom he found alone, Mr X at last succeeded in overcoming her resistance and got her to sign the document which he had brought with him, already prepared, under pressure of the same threats which he had previously used, in order to instil in that inexperienced woman "such fear as to rob her of her free will and to override her consent, which she would not otherwise have given" to an act which would deprive her of a house which she had acquired only in order to be able to continue living in it.

—Whereas the contested judgment further states that, although Mr X undoubtedly had the right to submit a higher bid and, in the event of his bid being successful, to institute eviction proceedings, the existence of that right "was nevertheless incapable of rendering the compulsion exerted by him lawful, since Mr X, who had no right or entitlement capable of justifying his claim to require the signature of a declaration that Mrs Y had been acting on his behalf or her withdrawal in his favour, was not seeking to assert a legitimate right".

—Whereas having regard to those absolute findings and assessments, the contested judgment, which contains a sufficient statement of reasons, constitutes justification in law for the decision of the appellate court.

Notes

(1) French case law and legal doctrine agree that a threat must be illegitimate to render a contract voidable on the ground of *"violence"*. The Code civil does not contain an express provision on this point, but some authors argue that it follows (*e contrario*) from Article 1114 (mere *metus reverentialis* (reverential fear), without more, does not render the contract voidable).[338] Threats of physical violence (*"voies de fait"*) are always illegitimate; threats of exercise of a right (for example legal action; *"voies de droit"*), on the other hand, are legitimate, unless the exercise of a right amounts to abuse of right (*"abus de droit"*). The Cour de cassation once put it thus in: Cass.civ.3^e, 17 January 1984, Bull. civ. III, no. 13

". . . the threat of recourse to legal action constitutes violence within the meaning of Article 1111 et seq. only if there is an abuse of the right to resort to such action, either because it is exercised for a purpose other than the achievement of its proper objective or because it is used in order to obtain a promise or an advantage which is unrelated or disproportionate to the essential obligation owed."

(2) In the case of Cass. civ. 1re, 3 November 1959,[339] X had a right *"de surenchérir"*, i.e. a right to outbid others at auction. This right may be exercised even within ten days

[338] See e.g. Malaurie and Aynès, at para. 427; Nicholas, at 107.
[339] D. 1960.187; cit. *supra* at [0000].

after the last and highest bid has been made (in this case by Y).[340] If X had asserted that right, he would have been legally entitled to force Y to leave the house. However, X threatened Y that he would exercise his right *"de surenchérir"* in order to obtain from Y a declaration that she had been acting in the auction on X's behalf (which X in fact did obtain, thus depriving Y of her own rights in the house). As the right *"de surenchérir"* is not given for this purpose, X was guilty of abuse of right, rendering the threat illegitimate.[341]

(3) In the case of Cour d'appel de Paris, 31 May 1966,[342] a woman who was caught shoplifting in a branch of the Monoprix firm agreed to pay 5,000 francs to the firm in order to induce it to refrain from taking proceedings against her. As the 5,000 francs was far greater than the amount of the firm's loss, it was held that there was abuse of right.

(4) Apart from abuse of right, a threat to exercise a right may also be illegitimate if it is accompanied by illegitimate means of pressure. See Cass. soc., 8 November 1984[343] (threat of a strike coupled with (threats of) physical violence).

BGH, 23 September 1957[344]   **3.G.100.**

THE ILLEGITIMACY OF A THREAT

The threatened wife

If the means and the purpose of the exerted pressure are in themselves legitimate, the threat may nevertheless be illegitimate depending on whether the person threatening has a legitimate interest in achieving the result he is after and whether, according to all right-thinking persons, the threat constitutes a reasonable means to achieve that result. Furthermore, a threat is illegitimate only if the person making the threat knows or should know the facts rendering the threat to be contrary to morality (bonos mores).

Facts: The plaintiff bank had business dealings with the firm H, the proprietor of which was the defendant's husband; the defendant had an interest in the undertaking by virtue of having invested in it. On 11 November 1953 the plaintiff concluded an agreement with the firm. The defendant acted as guarantor for the performance of the obligations owed by the firm to the plaintiff. After composition proceedings had been instituted in respect of the assets of the firm H, a settlement was duly reached; however, it was not performed by the defendant's husband. The plaintiff then brought an action against the defendant under the guarantee. The defendant pleaded in her defence that the guarantee she had provided was a nullity, since she allegedly had avoided it pursuant to § 123 BGB. She argued that the deputy director of the plaintiff had threatened her that criminal proceedings for "kite flying" (jobbing in bills) would be brought against her husband unless she guaranteed his debts; as a result, she had been induced into signing the deed of guarantee.

Held: The Bundesgerichtshof set aside the decision of the appellate court, dismissing the plaintiff's claim, because it had applied a wrong standard in deciding whether the threat, which was lawful in its means and object, was illegitimate. The Bundesgerichtshof formulated the test which should have been applied and referred the case back to the appellate court.

Judgment: "(a) The answer to the question as to the criteria which must be fulfilled in order to render a threat unlawful where the means and the objective of the pressure exerted are in themselves

---

[340] See Malaurie, Aynès and Gautier, *Les contrats spéciaux*, 13th edn. (Paris: Cujas, 1999) at 137.
[341] Cf. the note by Holleaux: "The objective pursued by the perpetrator of the violence was an objective other than the normal purpose to be achieved by exercising the right which he may have possessed. There was thus an abuse."
[342] Gaz. Pal. 1966.2.194; RTD civ. 1967.147, annotated by J. Chevallier.
[343] Bull. civ. V.423.
[344] BGHZ 25.217.

permissible cannot be made to depend solely on whether the party making the threat is legally entitled to require the threatened person to provide the declaration in question. If he is so entitled, the threat will not normally be tainted by unlawfulness; however, there are also cases in which, notwithstanding the absence of such legal entitlement, the threat cannot be held to be unlawful. The contrary view, regularly expressed in the past and still found even today in the works of certain academic jurists, according to which a threat must invariably be unlawful in the absence of such entitlement, must be rejected, as has been shown in later decisions of the Reichsgericht . . . and in decisions of the Bundesgerichtshof . . . The Senate concurs with that conclusion.

According to those decisions, it is necessary first of all to examine whether the person making the threat has a legitimate interest in achieving the result sought after by him and whether, in the view of all fair-minded and right-thinking persons, the threat constitutes a reasonable means of achieving that result . . . In the assessment which those decisions require to be carried out, it is necessary to have regard to all circumstances which characterize the events which occur. It is true that these include, most importantly, the question whether the person making the threat has a right to the objective which he is seeking to achieve. Even where he does not possess such a right, however, his conduct may appear justified in the particular circumstances of the case. This may be taken into account *inter alia* where, despite the fact that the legal order does not confer on the creditor any enforceable right, considerations of public policy indicate that the debtor should fulfil his obligations. Where, in such circumstances, the means employed by the creditor in making the threat are in themselves permissible, his conduct will still be capable, in the absence of any other aggravating factors, of being regarded as compatible with public policy and hence as not unlawful.

(b) Those principles also apply to a threat to lay an information leading to a criminal prosecution which—in the opinion of the creditor, at any rate—is justified.

A creditor cannot be debarred from requiring the debtor to make good the damage done to him by the latter's criminal act on the basis that, unless the debtor does so, he may expect such information to be laid . . . Such a threat must be regarded as a reasonable means of achieving its purpose; its justification is to be found in the relationship between the criminal act and the claim asserted.

That assessment is not altered by the fact that the case may involve a relationship between the creditor and a third party. Even where the creditor has no legal claim against that third party in substitution for his claim against the debtor, the threat may nevertheless, depending on the circumstances of the case, be regarded as permissible. That will be the position, for example, where the third party has participated, in a manner which does not fall foul of the criminal or civil law, in the criminal act giving rise to the damage suffered, or where he has gained some advantage from it. The question of illegitimacy cannot be answered solely by reference to the concerns of the person threatened; the interests of the creditor also have to be taken into account. From the creditor's point of view, it may seem morally justifiable in such a case for him to threaten the third party—by whom he may also feel himself to have been prejudiced, or whom he may consider to have profited from the criminal act—with the laying of an information against the person who committed that act unless the third party also takes reasonable steps to make good the damage suffered.

Thus it is invariably necessary to weigh up all the circumstances in their entirety. The possibility cannot be excluded, even in a case such as that described by way of example above, that a threat to procure the institution of criminal proceedings may be unlawful. It is true that this will most frequently be the case where there exists an inherent connection between the criminal act and the claim asserted by the creditor; however, it is possible to envisage other situations involving competing interests in which such a threat may be justified.

. . . The criminal acts allegedly committed by the husband in the present case are said to have consisted of the issue and acceptance of what are known as "kites" (fictitious bills), by means of which, it is claimed, he sought to obtain capital for his firm. The defendant's involvement in the firm was not insignificant; she had placed DM 36,000 at the disposal of the firm H. and had entered into a deficiency guarantee in favour of the firm Ho. in the sum of DM 24,000. Given those circumstances, there may be grounds for thinking that she too benefitted, even if only indirectly, from the conduct in which her husband is alleged to have engaged and from the discounting of the bills by the plaintiff, to its detriment. In accordance with the statements made above, that factor should not be left out of account in the assessment of the question whether the threat was unlawful; it should at least have been discussed.

[About the material requirements of applicability of § 123 BGB :]

(b) . . . As has already been mentioned above, it is also necessary, in considering whether the avoidance was permissible pursuant to § 123 BGB on the ground of the issue of a threat, to have regard to the interests of both parties. The primary consideration must of course be the need to protect the freedom of decision of the person to whom the threat is made; however, the fact that that person may have been prevented from exercising such freedom by the acts of another is not enough to render § 123 BGB applicable . . . There must also exist, on the part of the creditor, some intrinsic attitude of a particular kind which necessarily characterises his conduct as an unlawful threat within the meaning of § 123 BGB.

It is on that basis that the Reichsgericht arrived at its decision. It pointed out, first of all, that the person issuing the threat must be conscious of the pressure exerted by him, and that his intention must be to compel the performance of an act by bending the will of the other party . . . There appears to be no dispute in that regard . . .

It must not be forgotten that avoidance pursuant to § 123 BGB on account of the issue of a threat is permissible only where there also exist, in relation to the unlawfulness of that threat, certain intrinsic elements underlying and prompting the conduct of the person by whom the threat is made. As has been emphasised above, it is not only the interests of the person whose freedom of action has been taken away that must be taken into consideration; the question must always be asked as to whether, and to what extent, the person issuing the threat also deserves protection. He should unreservedly be given that protection where his attitude in the matter accords with the principles established by the legal order . . .

It follows that a creditor will be protected against avoidance where, in issuing his threat, he proceeds without fault on the basis of facts which do not appear to render his conduct impermissible. By contrast, such protection must invariably be denied, having regard to what amounted at the time to the overriding interests of the person threatened, where the person exerting the pressure correctly appreciated the facts but drew the wrong legal conclusions from them. In such circumstances, the person issuing the threat will have deviated in his intentions from the fundamental requirements which the law imposes on all persons, and will consequently be forced to accept a finding that his conduct was impermissible and thus unlawful . . .

It follows that it is necessary to adhere to the following rule: in order for a finding of unlawfulness to be made within the meaning of § 123 BGB, it must be established that the creditor is, or should be, aware of the facts characterising his threat as contrary to morality; culpable ignorance is thus equivalent to knowledge of the facts. Under no circumstances can the illegitimacy of the threat be precluded by an incorrect legal assessment of the facts on the part of the creditor . . .

The judgment must therefore be set aside, and the case must be referred back to the appellate court.

Notes

(1) German law appears to take a somewhat different approach to the requirement of illegitimacy—unlawfulness. In accordance with §123(1) BGB a contract can be avoided if a party was illegitimately induced, by a threat, to enter into the contract (*"widerrechtlich*

durch Drohung bestimmt worden").[345] The emphasis is thus on the illegitimate nature of the inducement. It could be argued, however, that if the inducement is illegitimate, the *"Drohung"* itself is also illegitimate. In any event, it is not unusual for German courts and legal authors to relate the requirement of illegitimacy to the *"Drohung"*.[346]

(2) The illegitimacy of the threat may arise from the means of the pressure (i.e. the threatened harm; *"Widerrechtlichkeit des Mittels"*), its purpose (*"Widerrechtlichkeit des Zweckes"*) or the relation between means and purpose of the pressure (*"Widerrechtlichkeit der Mittel-Zweck-Relation"*).[347] The threat is always illegitimate if the means of the pressure is illegitimate, even though the purpose of the pressure may well be legitimate, for example if a promissee is threatened with physical violence by his promissor to pay his debt. *Vice versa*, the threat is also illegitimate if the purpose of the pressure is illegitimate, although the means of the pressure may be legitimate, for example if A threatens B with legal action (to which A is legally entitled) in order to induce B to enter into an illegal or immoral contract. In this type of case, however, the contract will generally be void on the ground of illegality (§134 BGB) or immorality (§138 BGB).[348] Finally, in the case of *"Widerrechtlichkeit der Mittel-Zweck-Relation"* (also known as *"Inadäquanz von Mittel und Zweck"*), both the means and the purpose of the pressure are legitimate, yet the threat is illegitimate because it is illegitimate to use this particular means to this particular end. The Bundesgerichtshof has repeatedly held that the decisive test is

> . . . whether the person issuing the threat has a legitimate interest in achieving the result sought after by him and whether, in the view of all right-thinking persons [or: in accordance with the principle of good faith], the threat constitutes a reasonable means of achieving that result,

taking into consideration all the circumstances of the case, especially the interests of both parties.[349] If A, who suffered damage as a result of a criminal act by B, threatens B with criminal prosecution to compensate him for his injury, the threat is not illegitimate as it does not constitute an *"unangemessenes Mittel"*. The position will be different, however, if A threatens B with criminal prosecution to make B pay a debt which B indeed owes to A, but which is wholly unrelated to B's criminal act. In this case the threat does constitute an *"unangemessenes Mittel"*.[350]

The question whether the exerted pressure must be illegitimate in order to render the contract voidable on the ground of duress was orginally of no great importance in English law, as the only form of duress recognized was that to a person,[351] where the

---

[345] Cf. Art. 29 I of the Swiss OR.

[346] See Larenz, *AT* at 701; *Palandt*, under §123 BGB, para. 3 b; BGHZ 25, 217, 219, cit. *supra*, 440; BGH, NJW 1983.384.

[347] See Flume, *Allgemeneier Teil des Bürgerlichen Rechts*, Vol. II: *Das Rechtsgeschäft*, 4th edn. (Berlin: 1992) at 535 ff, Larenz, *AT* at 701 ff.; Soergel and Hefermehl, *Bürgerliches Gesetzbuch*, Vol. I: Allgemeiner Teil (Stuttgart: 1987), under §123 BGB, para. 44 ff.; Markesinis, Lorenz and Dannemann,, *The German Law of Obligations*, Vol I: *The Law of Contracts and Restitution* (Oxford: Clarendon, 1997) at 210–11.

[348] See Köhler, *BGB. Allgemeiner Teil*, 23rd edn. (München: Beck, 1996) at 152; Soergel-Hefermehl, op. cit., under §123 BGB, para. 46.

[349] Cf. BGH 2, 287, 297, cit. in **3.3.2.D** *infra* at 448; BGHZ 25, 217, 220, 221, cit. *supra* at 440; BGH, NJW 1982.2301, 2302; BGH, NJW 1983.384, 385.

[350] See BGHZ 25, 217, 220–222, sit. *supra* at 440, also dealing with the question whether there can be *"Inadäquanz von Mittel und Zweck"* if the threat with criminal prosecution is directed against a third party.

[351] See *supra* under **3.3.2.B.**

threat is in its nature illegitimate. In the early cases of "economic duress" the test applied by the courts was whether there was a "coercion of the victim's will" such as to "vitiate his consent"?[352] But this was not consistent with the explanation of duress given in cases in which duress was argued as a defence to a criminal charge.[353] Therefore the "vitiation of consent" test met with strong disapproval[354] and several authors have argued that, instead, greater emphasis should be placed upon the nature of the pressure.[355]

House of Lords   **3.E.101.**

Universe Tankships Inc. of Monrovia v. International Transport Workers Federation[356]

THE ILLEGITIMACY OF A THREAT

The "Universe Sentinel"

Whether a threat is (il)legitimate depends on the nature of the threat and the nature of the demand.

Facts: The defendants had "blacked" a ship owned by the plaintiffs, preventing it from leaving port. In order to obtain the lifting of the blacking, the plaintiffs agreed to comply to the defendants" demand to pay a contribution to a general welfare fund for sailors. The plaintiffs feared catastrophic financial consequences if they did not submit because the ship was off-hire under a time charter while the blacking continued.

Judgment: LORD SCARMAN [dissenting, though not on this point]: . . . It is, I think, already established law that economic pressure can in law amount to duress; and that duress, if proved, not only renders voidable a transaction into which a person has entered under its compulsion but is actionable as a tort, if it causes damage or loss: *Barton* v. *Armstrong* [1976] A.C. 104 and *Pao On* v. *Lau Yiu Long* [1980] A.C. 614. The authorities upon which these two cases were based reveal two elements in the wrong of duress: (1) pressure amounting to compulsion of the will of the victim; and (2) the illegitimacy of the pressure exerted. There must be pressure, the practical effect of which is compulsion or the absence of choice. Compulsion is variously described in the authorities as coercion or the vitiation of consent. The classic case of duress is, however, not the lack of will to submit but the victim's intentional submission arising from the realisation that there is no other practical choice open to him. This is the thread of principle which links the early law of duress (threat to life and limb) with later developments when the law came also to recognise as duress first the threat to property and now the threat to a man's business or trade. The development is well traced in *Goff and Jones, The Law of Restitution*, 2nd ed. (1978), chapter 9.

The absence of choice can be proved in various ways, e.g. by protest, by the absence of independent advice, or by a declaration of intention to go to law to recover the money paid or the property transferred: see *Maskell* v. *Horner* [1915] 3 K.B. 106. But none of these evidential matters goes to the essence of duress. The victim's silence will not assist the bully, if the lack of any practicable choice to submit is proved. The present case is an excellent illustration. There was no protest at the time, but only a determination to do whatever was needed as rapidly as possible to release the ship. Yet nobody challenges the judge's finding that the owner acted under compulsion. . . .

---

[352] See e.g. Kerr J in *The "Siboen" and the "Sibotre"* [1976] 1 Lloyd's Rep. 293.
[353] See the speeches of Lord Wilberforce and Lord Simon of Glaisdale in *Lynch* v. *DPP for Northern Ireland* [1975] 1 All ER 913, 926, 938.
[354] See, in particular, Atiyah, "Economic Duress and the 'Overborne Will' ", (1982) 98 LQR 197.
[355] See e.g. McKendrick, *Contract* at 354.
[356] [1983] AC 366.

The real issue in the appeal is, therefore, as to the second element in the wrong duress: was the pressure applied by the I.T.F. in the circumstances of this case one which the law recognises as legitimate? For, as Lord Wilberforce and Lord Simon of Glaisdale said in *Barton* v. *Armstrong* [1976] A.C. 104, 121D: "the pressure must be one of a kind which the law does not regard as legitimate."

As the two noble and learned Lords remarked at p. 121D, in life, including the life of commerce and finance, many acts are done "under pressure, sometimes overwhelming pressure": but they are not necessarily done under duress. That depends on whether the circumstances are such that the law regards the pressure as legitimate.

In determining what is legitimate two matters may have to be considered. The first is as to the nature of the pressure. In many cases this will be decisive, though not in every case. And so the second question may have to be considered, namely, the nature of the demand which the pressure is applied to support.

The origin of the doctrine of duress in threats to life and limb, or to property, suggests strongly that the law regards the threat of unlawful action as illegitimate, whatever the demand. Duress can, of course, exist even if the threat is one of lawful action: whether it does so depends upon the nature of the demand. Blackmail is often a demand supported by a threat to do what is lawful, e.g. to report criminal conduct to the police. In many cases, therefore, "What [one] has to justify is not the threat, but the demand . . .": see *per* Lord Atkin in *Thorne* v. *Motor Trade Association* [1937] A.C. 797, 806 . . .

Appeal allowed.

Notes

(1) This approach forces the courts to distinguish between legitimate and illegitimate pressures. In *The "Universe Sentinel"*[357] Lord Scarman held that a threat may be illegitimate either because what is threatened is unlawful, such as a threat to commit a tort or a crime, or because the threat is unlawful in its demand (purpose), even though the thing threatened may be lawful, such as a blackmailer's threat to report a person's criminal conduct to the police to make him enter into a contract.[358] As a general rule, threats to enforce contractual rights are not illegitimate. For example, in *CTN Cash and Carry Ltd.* v. *Gallaher Ltd.*,[359] it was held that the defendants' threat to withdraw the plaintiff's credit facilities—as the defendants were entitled to—did not amount to duress, even though the withdrawal would have seriously prejudiced the plaintiffs' business.

(2) On threats to exercise a right, the Italian *Codice Civile* and the Swiss *Obligationenrecht* contain an express provision. Article 1438 of the Italian CC provides: "A threat to exercise a right may only constitute a ground for annulling the contract where its objective is to gain an unfair advantage" ("*La minaccia di far valere un diritto può essere causa di annulamento del contratto solo quando è diretta a conseguire vantaggi ingiusti*"). Article 30 II OR appears to take a more restrictive approach: "Apprehension that a right may be exercised shall be taken into account as a material factor only if the predicament of the person threatened has been exploited in order to extort from him the concession of some excessive advantage" ("*Die Furcht vor der Geltendmachung eines Rechtes wird nur*

---

[357] *Supra.*
[358] See Cartwright, *Unequal Bargaining. A Study of Vitiating Factors in the Formation of Contracts* (Oxford: Clarendon, 1991) at 165–6; Treitel, *Contract* at 375–6; McKendrick, *Contract* at 354–7.
[359] [1994] 4 All ER 714.

dann berücksichtigt, wenn die Notlage des Bedrohten benutzt worden ist, um ihm die Einräuming übermäßiger Vorteile abzunötigen").

(3) Threats of a breach of contract may amount to illegitimate pressure. *When* they do so has been a topic of debate in England. Some authors argue that a threat to break a contract constitutes illegitimate pressure if the threat was made in bad faith.[360]

(4) Also in Dutch law, a threat is illegitimate—in the sense of Article 3:44 II BW—if either the threatened act is itself unlawful or if the purpose of the threat (with an otherwise lawful act) is unlawful.[361]

(5) Article 4:108 PECL recognizes that not every threat to break a contract is illegitimate. Comment B to the Article reads:

Not Every Warning of Non-performance Amounts to a Threat: If one party genuinely cannot perform the contract unless the other party promises to pay an increased price and the first party simply informs the second of this fact, the second party cannot later avoid any promise it makes to pay a higher price. The first party's statement was merely a warning of the inevitable; there is no threat within the meaning of this Article.

Illustration 4: A employs B to build a road across A's farmland at a fixed price. A finds that the land is much wetter than either party had realised and A will literally be bankrupt before it has performed the contract at the original price. A informs B of this and B agrees to pay an increased price. Although B had no real choice, it cannot avoid the agreement to pay the increased price.

Like the jurisdictions discussed, art. 4:108 PECL furthermore recognises that a threat of an act which is itself lawful may nonetheless be illegitimate as a way of obtaining the desired end. Comment C reads:

C. Threats Which It is Wrongful to Use to Obtain the Promise: Even a threat to do something lawful may be illegitimate if it is not a proper way of obtaining the benefit sought, as in blackmail.
Illustration 5: E threatens his employer F that he will reveal to F's wife F's affair with his secretary unless F increases E's wages. F complies. He may avoid the agreement to pay E the higher wages.[362]

(6) Subjective requirements concerning the party making the threat are unknown to most legal systems. In their comparative report on the validity of international sales contracts, the authors of the Max-Planck Institut explained: "The personal requirements of the perpetrator of the threat are thus of such minor significance, because all legal systems attach primary importance to the subjective circumstances of the person threatened". (*"Die inneren Voraussetzungen in der Person des Drohenden haben deswegen eine so geringe Bedeutung, weil alle Rechtsordnungen die subjektiven Verhältnisse des Bedrohten in den Vordergrund rücken"*, at 134). Yet, in BGHZ 25, 217, 223–5,[363] the Bundesgerichtshof held that, in the sense of §123 BGB, *"Drohung"* is illegitimate only if the party exerting the pressure knows that his conduct amounts to a threat. It also held: "In order for a finding of unlawfulness to be made within the meaning of §123 BGB, it must be established that the creditor is, or should be,

---

[360] See e.g. Birks, *An Introduction to the Law of Restitution* (Oxford: Clarendon, 1994) at 183. For an extensive discussion of the nature of threats amounting to duress, see *Chitty* para. 7–023 ff. See also *Restatement of the Law (Second), Contracts 2d*, §176 ("When a Threat is Improper") and the Comments and Illustrations; McGregor, op. cit., s. 562 ("Improper pressure").

[361] See e.g. HR 8 January 1999, NJ 1999.342; Asser and Hartkamp, op. cit., para. 207.

[362] See also Art. 3.9 UP, Comment 2.

[363] *Supra*, at 440.

aware of the facts characterizing his threat a contrary to morality. . . ." (*"Zur Annahme der Widerrechtlichkeit im Sinne des §123 BGB bedarf es der Feststellung, daß der Gläubiger die Tatsachen kennt oder kennen muß, die seiner Drohung den sittlich anstößigen Charakter geben . . ."*). On this point, however, the decision has been strongly criticized by many authors. They argue that §123 BGB aims at protecting the *"freie Willensentschließung"* of the threatened party, irrespective of the other party's good faith.[364]

3.3.2.D. CAUSATION

A party will not be permitted to avoid a contract on the ground of duress unless she was in fact influenced by the threat—in other words unless there was some causal link between the threat and the contract which the claimant seeks to set aside. Some legal systems require, in addition, that the threat be such that the claimant was not acting unreasonably in giving in to it—thus it must, for example, be serious and imminent.[365]

Privy Council (on appeal from New South Wales)   **3.E.102.**
Barton v. *Armstrong*[366]

THREAT MUST BE A FACTOR

Death threats

A party who entered into a contract after he was threatened with death by the other party may avoid the contract for duress unless the other party shows that the threat was of no influence on the first party's decision to make the contract.

Facts: Barton, a managing director of a public company, executed on its behalf a deed by which the company agreed to pay $140,000 to Armstrong, its chairman, and to purchase Armstrong's shares in the company for $180,000, in order to get Armstrong off the board of the company. It was established that Barton acted as he did partly for commercial reasons, but the court also found that Armstrong had threatened Barton to have him killed if he did not make the arrangements. Barton later tried to avoid the deed for duress.

Held: The Court of Appeal of the Supreme Court of New South Wales held that the onus was on Barton to show that he would not have signed the deed but for the threats, and Barton had failed to discharge that onus. The Privy Council, by a majority, recommended that an appeal be allowed.

Judgment: LORD CROSS OF CHELSEA [delivering the majority judgment]: Their Lordships turn now to consider the question of law which provoked a difference of opinion in the Court of Appeal Division. It is hardly surprising that there is no direct authority on the point, for if A threatens B with death if he does not execute some document and B, who takes A's threat seriously, executes the document it can be only in the most unusual circumstances that there can be any doubt whether the threats operated to induce him to execute the document. But this is a most unusual case and the findings of fact made below do undoubtedly raise the question whether it was necessary for Barton in order to obtain relief to establish that he would not have executed the deed in question but for the threats . . . There is an obvious analogy between setting aside a disposition for duress or undue influence and setting it aside for fraud . . .

---

[364] See e.g. Flume, op. cit., at 539; Larenz, *AT* at 703–4; Soergel and Hefermehl, op. cit., under §123 BGB, para. 51.

[365] The second requirement is discussed in **3.3.2.E**, *infra* at 451.

[366] [1976] AC 104.

"Once make out that there has been anything like deception, and no contract resting in any degree on that foundation can stand": *per* Lord Cranworth LJ in *Reynell* v. *Sprye* (1852) 1 De G.M. & G. 660, 708 . . . Their Lordships think that the same rule should apply in cases of duress and that if Armstrong's threats were "a" reason for Barton's executing the deed he is entitled to relief even though he might well have entered into the contract if Armstrong had uttered no threats to induce him to do so . . .

If Barton had to establish that he would not have made the agreement but for Armstrong's threats, then their Lordships would not dissent from the view that he had not made out his case. But no such onus lay on him. On the contrary it was for Armstrong to establish, if he could, that the threats which he was making and the unlawful pressure which he was exerting for the purpose of inducing Barton to sign the agreement and which Barton knew were being made and exerted for this purpose in fact contributed nothing to Barton's decision to sign. The judge has found that during the 10 days or so before the documents were executed Barton was in genuine fear that Armstrong was planning to have him killed if the agreement was not signed. His state of mind was described by the judge as one of "very real mental torment" and he believed that his fears would be at end when once the documents were executed. It is true that the judge was not satisfied that Vojinovic had been employed by Armstrong but if one man threatens another with unpleasant consequences if he does not act in a particular way, he must take the risk that the impact of his threats may be accentuated by extraneous circumstances for which he is not in fact responsible. It is true that on the facts as their Lordships assume them to have been Armstrong's threats may have been unnecessary; but it would be unrealistic to hold that they played no part in making Barton decide to execute the documents. The proper inference to be drawn from the facts found is, their Lordships think, that though it may be that Barton would have executed the documents even if Armstrong had made no threats and exerted no unlawful pressure to induce him to do so the threats and unlawful pressure in fact contributed to his decision to sign the documents and to recommend their execution by Landmark and the other parties to them. It may be, of course, that Barton's fear of Armstrong had evaporated before he issued his writ in this action but Armstrong—understandably enough—expressly disclaimed reliance on the defence of delay on Barton's part in repudiating the deed.

[LORD WILBERFORCE and LORD SIMON OF GLAISDALE (dissenting on the ground that it was not open to the court to review findings of fact made in the courts below)]: The next necessary step would be to establish the relationship between the illegitimate means used and the action taken. For the purposes of the present case (reserving our opinion as to cases which may arise in other contexts) we are prepared to accept, as the formula most favourable to the appellant, the test proposed by the majority, namely, that the illegitimate means used was a reason (not *the* reason, nor the *predominant* reason nor the *clinching* reason) why the complainant acted as he did. We are also prepared to accept that a decisive answer is not obtainable by asking the question whether the contract would have been made even if there had been no threats because, even if the answer to this question is affirmative, that does not prove that the contract was not made because of the threats.

BGH, 14 June 1951[367]   **3.G.103.**

THREAT MUST BE A FACTOR

The young mother

For a declaration of will (a "Rechtsgeschäft", such as a contract) to be voidable on the ground of threat it must be shown that the threat was a decisive factor for the threatened party to make the declaration.

[367] BGHZ 2.287.

Facts: On 4 March 1948 the plaintiff had given birth to a child, fathered on her by a married man. The man was already father of three legitimate (*"eheliche"*) children. As early as on the day after the birth the plaintiff's mother sought to persuade her that she should give up the child, reproaching her for having brought shame on the family by having a relationship with a married man. The plaintiff's mother further told her that her father had expressed thoughts of suicide and that she could only return to the family home if she were to part from the child. On 20 March the plaintiff signed a document (*"Einwilligungserklärung"*) giving up the child up for adoption. Nine months later the plaintiff sought to avoid the *"Einwilligungserklärung"* on the ground of, among other things, the threat exercised by her mother.

Held: Considering the plaintiff's age, her financial independence, the fact that she had had independent advice and that two weeks had passed before she signed the document, there was no causal link between the mother's threat and the plaintiff's decision to give up her child for adoption.

Judgment: In order for the plaintiff's declaration to be voidable on the ground of an unlawful threat, the plaintiff must have given her consent under pressure from her mother. The threat must have caused her to make the declaration. Thus it is necessary to show that, in the absence of the threat, the plaintiff would not have provided the declaration, or that she would not have provided it at the time when she did, or that she would have provided it in a different form. It is sufficient in that regard for the threat to have been a decisive factor in conjunction with other motivating factors (Palandt, *loc. cit.*, § 123, note 4, with supporting arguments).

As regards this point, the following findings of the appellate court are of significance: it is stated, in the context of the unlawfulness of the threat, that the plaintiff's mother had not shielded her from all external influences. The officials working in the youth welfare office in M., namely the witnesses B. and H., had allegedly had the opportunity of exerting an influence on the plaintiff, and had stated that, in their view, she should not give up the child. The plaintiff was old enough and financially independent, so that she was not constrained, by virtue of having no choice in the matter, to accede to the wishes of her mother; and she may, in making her decision, have taken into account the views which had been expressed by the witnesses. If, notwithstanding the counter-effect exerted by the statements of both the witness S. and the two officials, she acted in accordance with her mother's wishes in the matter, that can only mean, according to the court below, that she preferred to come to an understanding with her parents and to provide her child with the opportunity of a future without the stigma of illegitimacy caused by adultery than to sacrifice her feelings, as a daughter, for her mother. Those statements signify that, taking into consideration the plaintiff's age and financial independence, and having regard to the influence exerted by the abovementioned witnesses, the pressure which her mother brought to bear on the plaintiff no longer influenced her decision, and, by contrast, that the plaintiff reached her decision to agree to the adoption of her child after herself weighing up the pros and cons of the matter. That means, however, that there can be no causal connection between the threat made by the plaintiff's mother and the decision made by the plaintiff, particularly having regard to the fact that a period of some two weeks elapsed between the issue of the threat by the mother and the signature of the declaration by the plaintiff. If the threat ceased to constitute one of the deciding factors which led the plaintiff to give her consent, and if, instead, she decided of her own free will between continuing to live with her parents and continuing to live with her child, then there can be no possibility in law of avoiding that consent. The element of unlawful manipulation of the will of the person making the declaration, constituting a necessary criterion for the application of § 123(1) BGB, is lacking.

Notes

(1) The threat must have induced the threatened party to conclude the contract. In other words, if the contract is to be avoided on the ground of threat, the requirement of causation has to be met. This rule applies in all legal systems. In many civil codes the requirement follows from the wording of the relevant provisions. See for example § 123(1)

BGB ("*zur Abgabe einer Willenserklärung durch . . . Drohung bestimmt worden*"); Article 3:44 I and II BW ("A juridical act . . . entered into as a result of threat"; "A person who induces another to execute a certain juridical act by unlawfully threatening him"). See also Article 3.9 UP ("led to conclude the contract by . . . threat") and Article 4:108 PECL. The problem of causation does not often arise. One explanation is, that if the threat was of a serious and imminent nature it will be only in rare cases that the threat did not induce the threatened party to enter into the contract.[368]

French textbooks do not discuss the problem of causation under a separate heading. Rather, causation is dealt with together with the requirement of a "*mal considérable et présent*": the threat must be sufficiently serious as to determine the threatened party's consent.[369]

In German textbooks, on the other hand, the issue of the serious nature of the threat tends to merge into a discussion of the requirement of causation. In establishing the causative link between the threat and the conclusion of the contract, the German courts apply a subjective test.[370] In BGHZ 2, 287[371] it was held that the plaintiff had not signed the document as a result of her mother's threats. The Bundesgerichtshof took into consideration the plaintiff's age and economic independence, the fact that she had had independent advice and that she had taken two weeks to make her decision. Also the court stated as a general rule that the requirement of causation is met if the threatened party would not have concluded the contract at all, or would have done so at another moment, or on different terms, but for the threat. The same rule applies in Dutch law.[372]

(2) In the decision cited above the Bundesgerichtshof furthermore held that it suffices if the threat was *a* motive for the threatened party to conclude the contract.[373] In *Barton* v. *Armstrong*,[374] which was a case of duress to the person, the Privy Council also held that the threat need be only *a* reason (not even the predominant or clinching reason) for the conclusion of the contract. It remains to be seen, however, whether the English courts will apply the same rule in cases of economic duress.[375] However, in *Dimskal Shipping Co. S.A.* v. *I.T.F.* (*The "Evia Luck"*),[376] Lord Goff said simply that the illegitimate economic pressure need have been only "a significant cause". While the rule applied in duress to the person (that it is necessary for the party who made the threat to show that it had no causative effect) may not apply to economic duress.[377] it appears from Lord Goff's statement that the causal requirement may not be anything more than that the threat influenced the decision.[378]

---

[368] See the speech of Lord Cross of Chelsea in *Barton* v. *Armstrong* [1976] AC 104, 118, *supra*, at 447. See also Max-Planck Institut, op. cit., at 129.

[369] See in **3.3.2.E**, *infra*, at 451.

[370] Cf. RG JW 1929.242.

[371] *Supra*, at 448.

[372] See Asser and Hartkamp, op. cit., paras. 177, 208.

[373] See *Palandt*, under §123 BGB, para. 4.

[374] [1976] AC 104, *supra*, at 447.

[375] See Cartwright, op. cit., at 168. §175 of the *Restatement of the Law (Second), Contracts 2d*, appears to be less generous than the rule laid down in *Barton*, since Comment *c* reads: "A party's manifestation of assent is induced by duress if the duress substantially contributes to his decision to manifest his assent", at 478.

[376] [1992] 2 AC 152, 165.

[377] See next note.

[378] See *Chitty* paras 7-015–7-022 and further **3.3.2.E**, note 4, *infra* at 453.

(3) Which party has to prove whether the threat induced the conclusion of the contract? In most jurisdictions, the general rule is that the onus of proof rests with the party seeking to avoid the contract.[379] In *Barton*'s case the onus of proof was placed on the party who had made the illegitimate threats (i.e. Armstrong). It is not clear whether this is the general rule in English law. In this particular case, however, there was much to be said for placing the onus on Armstrong. Cartwright[380] explains: "Once it is shown that the defendant acted wrongly in applying unlawful pressure, he ought to have the (very difficult) burden of disproving the causal relationship between the pressure and the contract; the law favours the innocent party over the wrongdoer". Interestingly, a similar approach was taken by the Dutch Hoge Raad in several tort cases.[381] As suggested in the note above, this very stringent rule of English law may not apply outside duress to the person.[382]

3.3.2.E. SERIOUS AND IMMINENT THREAT

Cass. com., 30 January 1974[383]   **3.F.104.**

THREAT MUST BE SUFFICIENTLY SERIOUS

The former shop director

A contract cannot be avoided on the ground of "violence" (threat) if the threat was not sufficiently serious to determine the threatened party's consent.

Facts: Ms Ceytère, a former shop director, entered into a contract with M and Mme Tournaire, owners of the shop, whereby Ms Ceytère agreed to pay a debt to Etablissements Claritex for the supply of goods she had ordered in her capacity as shop director. Mrs Tournaire had made it clear in a letter that if Ms Ceytère did not settle the debt, criminal proceedings would be undertaken against her on account of her improper behaviour as a shop director.

Held: The appellate court had dismissed Ms Ceytère's claim for avoidance of the contract on the ground of "*violence*" (i.e. the threat with criminal prosecution), because the court was of the opinion that Ms Ceytère had not been influenced by the threat, having regard to, among other things, her experience as a business woman and her age. The Cour de Cassation upheld that decision.

Judgment:—Whereas first, the cour d'appel found that Mlle Ceytère, confronted by Mme Tournaire's letter of 3 October 1969 with the option either of settling the Claritex debt herself or of facing criminal and civil proceedings on account of irregularities discovered in her managerial activities, possessed sufficient experience of business matters, and was old enough, to resist intimidation and to avoid succumbing to irrational fears of criminal prosecution;
—Whereas the judgment further observes that that letter made so little impression upon her that she waited for three months before replying to it, and that she was so sure of having the upper hand that she attached precise terms to her acceptance of the arrangement by giving Mme Tournaire a

---

[379] See *Max Planck Institut (1968)*, op. cit., at 129. See for French law e.g. Terré, Simler and Lequette, para. 242; Marty and Raynaud, *Les obligations*, 2nd edn. (Paris: Dalloz, 1988) at 170; for German law e.g. *Palandt* under §123 BGB, para. 6; BGH, NJW 57.988.

[380] Cartwright, op. cit. at 155.

[381] See Asser and Hartkamp, op. cit., I, para. 434 a.

[382] See *Chitty*, paras 7-016–7-018.

[383] D. 1974.382.

deadline of forty eight hours in which to confirm her final agreement; as Mlle Ceytère therefore gave her undertaking with full knowledge of the facts and in a state of total lucidity.
—Whereas on those grounds, the cour d'appel considered, in the exercise of its sovereign discretion, that Mlle Ceytère's consent had not been vitiated by any constraint . . .
On those grounds, this Court dismisses the appeal.

Notes

(1) Not all threats, not even all illegitimate threats, will justify the avoidance of a contract. Some Civil Codes of the European continent expressly provide that a threat (or its means) must be imminent and serious. See for example Article 1112(1) of the French CC (*"un mal considérable et présent"*), Article 1267(2) of the Spanish CC (*"un mal imminente y grave"*), Article 30 I of the Swiss OR (*"mit einer nahen und erheblichen Gefahr bedroht"*). Article 1112 CC is interpreted thus: that the threat, considering its seriousness and imminence, must have determined the consent of the threatened party to conclude the contract.[384] In fact, this interpretation seems to imply a test of causation: did the threat cause the threatened party to enter into the contract?[385]

(2) Whether the threat was sufficiently serious to determine the threatened party's consent can be established in two different ways: by applying either a subjective test—did the threat in fact constrain this person?—or an objective test—was the threat such as to constrain a reasonable person? Article 1112 CC is self-contradictory on this point as it provides for the former test in paragraph (1) and for the latter in paragraph (2). However, both the courts and legal doctrine have adopted the subjective test. See for example Terré, Simler and Lequette:[386]

"The decisive factor in the case-law is the application [of the test] *in concreto*. The courts examine whether the party claiming nullity was *in fact* influenced by fear. This gives rise to a legal individualisation of threat [*"violence"*]. The threshold beyond which threat becomes a ground of nullity may vary from one individual to the next, depending on that individual's strength of character, age, sex, social position, etc".

Thus, in the case of Cass. com., 30 January 1974,[387] Miss Ceytère failed to avoid the contract on the ground of *"violence"* because she was experienced and old enough to resist the threat with criminal prosecution. Moreover, Miss Ceytère had waited three months before answering Mrs Tournaire's letter and she had accepted Mrs Tournaire's offer under precise conditions. On these facts the court concluded that Miss Ceytère's consent had not been determined by the threat. Contrast for example Cass. civ. 3re, 19 February 1969[388] and Cass. civ. 1re, 3 November 1959,[389] in which case it was established that Y, who was a widow, had signed the document:

---

[384] See e.g. Terré, Simler and Lequette, para. 241; Marty and Raynaud, op. cit., at 165.

[385] Cf. for Spanish law, Díez-Picazo and Gullón, *Sistema de derecho civil*, Vol. II, 7th edn. (Madrid: 1995) at 60: ". . . the threat must constitute a determining factor prompting the declaration of intent; there must exist a causal link between it and the consent given" (*"la amenaza debe ser determinante de la declaración de voluntad, debe existir un enlace causal entre ella y el consentimiento emitido"*). On causation see **3.3.2.D.**, *supra* at [0000].

[386] At 198.

[387] D. 1974.382, *supra* at 451.

[388] Bull. civ. III.119.

[389] D. 1960.187, *supra* in **3.3.2.C**, at 438.

". . . under pressure of the same threats which he [X, the party threatening] had previously used, in order to instil in that inexperienced woman "such fear as to rob her of her free will and to override her consent, which she would not otherwise have given . . .".[390]

As far as the imminence of the threat is concerned, Jacques Ghestin[391] is of the opinion that Article 1112 CC's requirement of a "*mal présent*" is an inaccurate translation of the Roman concept of *metus praesens*. The requirement should be understood thus, that the threatened party's fear exists at the moment of conclusion of the contract. See Marty and Raynaud:[392] "the wording of the text means that the constraint must instil fear at the time when the consent is given" ("*le texte veut dire que la contrainte doit inspirer la crainte au moment du consentement*").

(3) Article 3:44 II, second sentence, of the Dutch Civil Code provides that the threat must be such that a reasonable person would be influenced by it. Hence, in Dutch law, the objective test appears to prevail. Arthur Hartkamp, however, argues that Article 3:44 II BW should not be interpreted as laying down an objective test. Yet, in Hartkamp's opinion, the test is not wholly subjective either: the courts have to ascertain in each individual case whether the threat was such that this person *could* be influenced by it, taking into consideration all the circumstances of the case, such as that person's age, experience, character, physical and mental condition, etc. (thus, within the category of the inexperienced, for example, it must be established whether this particular person could reasonably have been influenced by the threat).[393] Unlike the old Dutch Civil Code (in Article 1360 I), Article 3:44 II BW does not require that the threat (or what is threatened) is imminent.

(4) It has already been noted[394] that in English law it is unclear what is the causal requirement in cases of economic duress: need the threat have been merely one factor, as in duress to the person,[395] or must it have had some greater influence? In *The Universe Sentinel*[396] Lord Scarman identified two elements of the concept of duress, one of which was the "pressure amounting to compulsion of the will of the victim". There is compulsion of the victim's will, still according to Lord Scarman, if the pressure was so great that it gave the victim no other choice but to act as he did.[397] This appears to be comparable to the requirement in French and Dutch law, that the threat must have been sufficiently serious to determine the consent of the threatened party. In establishing whether the pressure was so great as to leave the victim no other choice, the English courts take a number of factors into consideration: whether the party alleged to have been coerced did or did not protest; whether he did or did not have an alternative course open to him, such as an adequate legal remedy; whether he was independently advised; and whether after entering into the contract he took steps to avoid it.[398] These factors seem to imply that the test applied is an objective, rather than a subjective one. But contrast *Scott* v. *Sebright*,[399] a

---

[390] See also Cass. com., 28 May 1991, Bull.civ. IV.180; D. 1992.166.
[391] Ghestin at 571.
[392] At 165.
[393] See Asser and Hartkamp, op. cit., II, para. 208.
[394] See **3.3.2.D**, note 2.
[395] See *Barton* v. *Armstrong*, *supra* in **3.3.2.D** at 447.
[396] Extracted *supra* in **3.3.2.C.**, at 444.
[397] See Cartwright, op. cit., at 163.
[398] See *Pao On* v. *Lau Yiu Long* [1980] AC 614, 635; *The "Siboen" and the "Sibotre"* [1976] 1 Lloyd's Rep. 293.
[399] (1886) 12 PD 21.

case of duress to the person in which Butt J held:[400] "It has sometimes been said that in order to avoid a contract entered into through fear, the fear must be such as would impel a person of ordinary courage and resolution to yield to it. I do not think that is an accurate statement of the law". Butt J then applied a subjective test, taking into account the sex, age, mental condition and inexperience of the threatened person.[401]

(5) § 123(1) BGB does not provide that the threat must be imminent and serious. However, this does not mean that the seriousness and the imminence of the threat are irrelevant in German law. Soergel-Hefermehl explains:[402] "However, the gravity of the threatened harm must also have been sufficient, in accordance with § 123, to place the person making the declaration in a position of constraint, since otherwise, by virtue of the lack of a causal link, there will exist no ground for upholding a submission that the contract has been avoided" ("*Doch muß die Schwere des Übels auch nach § 123 ausgereicht haben, den Erklärenden in eine Zwangslage zu versetzen, da sonst wegen mangelnder Kausalität kein Grund für die Zulassung einer Anfechtung vorliegt*"). The test to establish the causal link between the threat and the conclusion of the contract is a subjective one.[403] As for the imminent nature of the threat, it could be argued that it is also a requirement in German law since "*Drohung*" is defined as "An announcement of the prospect of some future harm . . .; not, however, the exploitation of some existing harm" ("*Ankündigung eines künftigen Übels . . . nicht aber die Ausnutzung eines bestehenden Übels*").[404]

(6) Under Article 3.9 UP the threat must have been so imminent and serious as to leave the threatened party no reasonable alternative but to conclude the contract on the terms proposed by the other party. As in English law, probably the availability of an adequate legal remedy will qualify as such, as will, to give another example, the availability on the market of the goods or services bargained for.[405] The Comment to Article 3.9 UP does not discuss "reasonable alternative"; it does state that the "imminence and the seriousness of the threat must be evaluated by an objective standard, taking into account the circumstances of the individual case". It is not surprising that the test to be applied is an objective one since the Unidroit Principles lay down general rules for—international—commercial contracts, which are generally concluded between parties who have been negotiating at arm's length. An objective test, being stricter than an subjective test, therefore seems more appropriate.

Under Article 4:108 PECL also the threat must have been imminent and serious—it is not clear from the wording of Article 4:108 whether the test to be applied is a subjective or an objective one; further, the contract may not be avoided if the complaining party had a reasonable alternative.

The comment explains: "E. No Reasonable Alternative: Relief will not be given if a party gave in to a threat when it had a perfectly good alternative—e.g. it could have found someone else to do the work, or could have obtained an order forcing the other party to do it. If there was a reasonable alternative, that suggests that the threat was not the real

[400] At 24.
[401] See *Chitty* paras. 7-015–7-022.
[402] Under §123 BGB, para. 41.
[403] See *supra* **3.3.2.D**, note 1, at 449.
[404] Cf. BGHZ 2, 287, 295, in **3.3.2.D**, at 448.
[405] See also *Restatement of the Law (Second), Contracts 2d*, §175, Comment *b* and the Illustrations.

reason for the threatened party agreeing to the demand. The burden of proving that the party had a reasonable alternative rests on the party which made the threat."

3.3.3. *LAESIO ENORMIS*

Can a contract be avoided on the ground of *laesio enormis*, i.e. if there is a gross disproportion between the mutual performances?

Code civil   **3.F.105.**

Article 1674: If the seller has agreed to a price which undervalues the immoveable by more than seven-twelfths, he may demand rescission of the sale, even if in the contract he has explicitly given up such a right of rescission or has declared the difference in value to be a gift.

Article 1675: In order to estimate whether there is *lésion* of more than seven-twelfths, the relevant value is the value of the immoveable at the time of sale and in its condition at that time.

In the case of an option to sell *lésion* should be calculated on the value at the date the option was exercised.

Notes

(1) Article 1674 CC embodies one of three cases of "*lésion*" (*laesio enormis*) admitted by Article 1118 CC (the others concern minors and partition among heirs). Although Article 1677 requires that "the facts alleged are sufficiently plausible and serious that '*lésion*' may be presumed" ("*les faits articulés seraient assez vraisemblables et assez graves pour faire présumer la lésion*"), it appears that this relates only to the alleged value of the immoveable, which will be judged by a panel of three experts (Article 1678). It has been held by the courts that the test is purely objective in that "*lésion*" is a ground for rescission "in and by itself, independently of the circumstances which may have accompanied it or given rise to it".[406]

(2) It should be noted that the doctrine of "*lésion*" is of very narrow application since it is a ground for rescission only where specified by law as in the case mentioned in note 1, *viz.* sale of land. Under the French doctrine of "*violence (morale)*" a gross inequality in the mutual performances cannot in itself render the contract voidable.[407] None of Dutch, English or German law recognize a disparity in value alone as a ground of invalidity.[408] But see §§ 934, 935, 1060 ABGB laying down a doctrine of *laesio enormis* which actually goes further than the French.[409]

---

[406] Req. 28 December 1932, S. 1933.1.377 annotated by Torat; D. 1933.1.87, rapport Dumas; See Nicholas at 139 and Ghestin at 762 ff.
[407] See **3.3.4.A**, note 1, *infra* at 469.
[408] See *infra* at 458 and **3.3.4.A** at 460.
[409] See Kötz, *European Contract Law* at 130–1.

BGH, 24 January 1979[410] **3.G.106.**

LAESIO ENORMIS IS IN ITSELF NOT A GROUND OF INVALIDITY

The pool/billiards equipment

A (gross) disparity in value between the performances does not in itself render the contract void for being contrary to bonos mores (§ 138 BGB)

Facts: On 24 January 1973 the plaintiff and the defendant, who at that time was running a hotel and restaurant business, concluded an agreement headed "Rental Agreement" in respect of pool/billiards equipment. Under that agreement, the defendant was required, with effect from a date four weeks after the installation of the equipment, to pay a monthly rental sum of DM 285 plus value added tax at the rate applying from time to time. The agreement contained the following clause: "After 42 months the equipment becomes the property of the hirer". In total, the defendant had to pay DM 13,386.70 (42 x DM 285 plus 11% VAT). Upon the installation of the equipment on 1 February 1973, the defendant received a crossed cheque for DM 2 000. Altogether, the plaintiff was obliged to provide the equipment, which had a market value of DM 3252.30, and to make a cash payment of DM 2000 (adding up to DM 5,242.30). There was therefore a disparity between the value of the defendant's performance and the plaintiff's of almost 250%. By letter of 14 February 1973 the defendant declared that he regarded the contract as void under § 138 BGB.

Held: According to the Bundesgerichtshof, the appellate court rightly held that, despite the disparity in value between the performances, the agreement was not contrary to *bonos mores* (public policy), since there was no usury in the sense of § 138 (2) BGB nor a reprehensible motive on the part of the plaintiff which, coupled with the disparity, could have rendered the agreement void under § 138 (1) BGB.

Judgment: I. The court hearing the appeal on questions of law and fact examined whether the contract was contrary to public policy and consequently void pursuant to § 138 BGB.

1. The appellate court correctly ruled that the circumstances of the case did not amount to usury. The defendant did not plead necessity or carelessness on his part; moreover, the Landgericht, to whose statements the higher appellate court referred, rightly found that there had been no carelessness. Nor could the defendant's submission that he lacked experience of life generally and business matters in particular be regarded as a valid plea of "inexperience". Even if he did not possess adequate specialist knowledge in relation to the market price and profitability of the billiards equipment, that did not mean that a finding of inexperience on the part of the defendant was appropriate, since, as the appellate court rightly stated, such inexperience cannot be held to exist where the party to the contract in issue merely lacks experience and business knowledge of a specific area of life or commercial activity . . .

2. The appellant on a point of law wrongly considers that the difference in value between the billiards equipment and the consideration to be furnished by the defendant is so disproportionate that § 138(1) BGB must necessarily be applicable. The view is unanimously expressed in the case-law of the Reichsgericht (RGZ 150, 1 [4]; 165, 1 [14]) and of the Bundesgerichtshof (Senat, NJW 1957, 1274 = LM § 138 [Ba] BGB Nr. 2; BGH; WM 1969, 1256 et seq.) that, in the case of an obvious disproportion between consideration and performance in a contract, that contract is void as contrary to public policy where the motives of the party benefitting from the contract are shown to have been reprehensible, particularly in the event of conscious exploitation of the predicament of the other party (see BGH, WM 1971, 857 et seq.). In that regard, the fact that the relationship between consideration and performance is particularly disproportionate may necessarily prompt the conclusion that there has been conscious or grossly negligent exploitation of some factual circumstance restricting the freedom of action of the other party to the contract (RGZ 150, 1 [6]; Senat, WM 1969, 1256 et seq.; WM 1966, 832 [835]). The appellate court did not misconstrue or misapply those

[410] NJW 1979.758.

principles. Its refusal to conclude, solely on the basis of the disproportion which it found to exist between the consideration to be furnished by the defendant and the performance incumbent on the plaintiff (the value of the former being some two and a half times as great as that of the latter), that the plaintiff's motives were reprehensible fell within the scope of its discretion as the court adjudicating on the facts . . .

The appellant on a point of law is admittedly correct in his submission that it was not open to the court hearing the appeal on questions of fact and law to proceed, in its examination of the disproportionate relationship between consideration and performance, on the basis of the loan amount specified in the loan application. Instead, it is necessary to have regard to the objective value (market value: BGH, LM § 138 [Ba] BGB Nr. 1) of all the obligations to be fulfilled by the parties pursuant to the rental agreement of 24 January 1973, rather than those obligations which in fact subsequently fell to be performed (BGH, WM 1977, 399). Accordingly, the defendant was required to pay DM 13,286.70 in 42 monthly instalments of DM 285 each plus 11% value added tax, whilst the plaintiff for his part was obliged in return to make a cash payment of DM 2,000 and to provide equipment having, according to the findings made in another connection by the court hearing the appeal on questions of fact and law, a market value of DM 3,252.30. It follows, therefore, that the court hearing the appeal on questions of fact and law was correct in its assessment of the respective values in question, notwithstanding that it left out of account the fact—working in the plaintiff's favour—that the obligation to be performed by the defendant was spread over a period of 42 months and that, to a considerable extent, allowance should therefore be made for this.

The question whether, in the event of a disparity of some 250% between the value of the consideration and that of the performance, it must be concluded that the motives of the party benefitting from the transaction must necessarily be reprehensible cannot be mechanically determined solely by reference to the degree of disparity in terms of the figures involved. The answer will depend on the facts of each individual case. In this connection, the court hearing the appeal on questions of fact and law was not bound to find that the plaintiff's motives had been reprehensible and, in particular, to conclude that the plaintiff had been actuated by an unscrupulous and exaggerated pursuit of profit since it has not been shown that the profit is purely and simply reflected in terms of the expense factors contained in the net cash price of DM 6,850 calculated by the plaintiff. As far as what may be termed the subjective aspect of the matter is concerned, the answer will depend not so much on the objective market value to be ascertained by means of experts' reports as on the value of the performance from the plaintiff's point of view (see Senat, judgment of 2.2.1960—VIII ZR 200/59, p. 16) and on the profit-reducing expense factors needing to be taken into account.

The court hearing the appeal on questions of fact and law was also correct in rejecting the argument that, regardless of whether he was driven by a censurable pursuit of profit, the plaintiff was actuated by reprehensible motives because he exploited the defendant's troublesome predicament. Nor has the appellant indicated that that was the position. The defendant was clearly prompted to enter into the transaction by a possible exaggerated expectation of profit—which was not subsequently fulfilled—without undertaking (as, being a businessman, he could quite easily have done) an examination of the objective relationship between the value of the consideration and that of the performance. Where it is open to the adversely affected party himself to calculate the advantages and disadvantages of the transaction, and he nevertheless enters into it (particularly where his reasons for doing so are speculative) without properly protecting his interests, notwithstanding that he should necessarily have been expected to weigh those interests up, then there cannot be said to have been any exploitation of a factor restricting the freedom of action of the other party to the contract. Nor has it been shown that an exaggerated expectation of profit on the part of the defendant was brought about by any particular incorrect statement made by the plaintiff. Moreover, the defendant's further submission in this regard, that the events relating to the cheque for DM 2,000 should not have been left out of account, fails to fulfil the specific criteria governing the application of

§ 138(1) BGB, since, according to the findings of the court hearing the appeal on questions of fact and law, which deal correctly, from a legal standpoint, with the issue of avoidance on the ground of wilful deceit, and which have not been individually challenged by the appellant, it cannot be assumed that the defendant was misled concerning his obligation to repay that sum in the context of the monthly rental payments.

Notes

(1) In German law, an obvious disproportion ("*auffälliges Mißverhältnis*") between the performance and counter-performance does not in itself render a contract void under §138(1) BGB (nor, of course, under §138(2) BGB as paragraph (2) expressly requires the exploitation ("*Ausbeutung*") of one of the enumerated weaknesses in addition to the obvious inequality).[411] In BGHZ 80, 153,[412] it was decided[413] that not even a particularly gross disparity can in itself void the contract. For the contract to be *contra bonos mores* (contrary to public policy) under §138(1) BGB, a further requirement has to be met. This requirement is a subjective one. On several occasions, the Bundesgerichtshof has held that if there is an obvious disparity in the mutual performances, the contract is *contra bonos mores* and therefore void under §138(1) BGB if the advantaged party displayed a reprehensible attitude ("*verwerfliche Gesinnung*"), for example by deliberately exploiting the disadvantaged party's weaker economic position.[414] However, the terms of the contract alone may "suffice . . . to indicate a transaction in the nature of exploitation which is contrary to public policy": BGHZ 80, 153 (below, 3.3.4.A); cf. BGH, NJW 1979, 758 (above). Thus, the reprehensible attitude may be inferred from the contractual imbalance. See **3.3.4.A** for further details.

(2) In Dutch law an inequality in the mutual performances does not in itself render a contract voidable under Article 3:44 IV BW; there must be an abuse by the one party of the circumstances in which the other party finds himself. Yet the inequality may be a relevant factor in establishing whether the one party should have refrained from promoting the conclusion of the contract.[415]

(3) Equally English law has no doctrine of *laesio enormis*. In order for there to be a contract in English law, there must consideration of some economic value, but this is satisfied without the consideration being "adequate".[416] Inadequacy of consideration is a ground for relief but only when coupled with other factors such as undue influence or unconscionable behaviour. These doctrines are dealt with in the next section.[417] As with German and Dutch law, it must be said that on occasion the additional requirements which have to be met for the doctrine of unconscionability to be satisfied may be inferred from the gross undervalue.[418]

(4) The nearest English law comes to *laesio enormis* is that under section 137 of the Consumer Credit Act 1974 the English courts may reopen a credit agreement if it finds a

---

[411] See Larenz, *AT* at 755; Soergel and Hefermehl, op. cit., under §138 BGB, para. 73; *Palandt*, under §138 BGB, para. c; BGH, NJW 1979.758, *supra* at 456; BGHZ 87, 309, 317, 318.

[412] *Infra*, at 460.

[413] Overruling OLG Stuttgart, NJW 1979.2409.

[414] Cf. e.g. BGH, NJW 1979.758, *supra* at 456.

[415] See **3.3.4.A**, note 5, *infra* at 470 and **3.3.5**, *infra* at 485.

[416] See *supra* at 140 ff.

[417] **3.3.4.B–D**, *infra* at 471–478.

[418] See *infra* at 478, note (4).

credit bargain "extortionate", as for instance in the case where the bargain "requires the debtor . . . to make payments . . . which are grossly exorbitant" (section 138(1)(a). Section 138(2)–(4) lays down the relevant factors for determining whether or not a credit bargain is "extortionate"; many of them relate to the circumstances in which the credit agreement was made and some of the cases have stated that the creditor must have taken advantage of the debtor.[419] The mentioned sections of the Act read as follows:

s. 137 (1) If the court finds a credit bargain extortionate it may reopen the credit agreement so as to do justice between the parties.

s. 138 (1) A credit bargain is extortionate if it—

    (a) requires the debtor or a relative of his to make payments (whether conditionally, or on certain contingencies) which are grossly exorbitant, or

    (b) otherwise grossly contravenes ordinary principles of fair dealing.

(2) In determining whether a credit bargain is extortionate, regard shall be had to such evidence as is adduced concerning—

    (a) interest rates prevailing at the time it was made,

    (b) the factors mentioned in subsection (3) to (5), and

    (c) any other relevant considerations.

(3) Factors applicable under subsection (2) in relation to the debtor include—

    (a) his age, experience, business capacity and state of health; and

    (b) the degree to which, at the time of the making the credit bargain, he was under financial pressure, and the nature of that pressure.

(4) Factors applicable under subsection (2) in relation to the creditor include—

    (a) the degree of risk accepted by him, having regard to the value of any security provided;

    (b) his relationship to the debtor; and

    (c) whether or not a colourable cash price was quoted for any goods or services included in the credit bargain.

(5) Factors applicable under subsection (2) in relation to a linked transaction include the question how far the transaction was reasonably required for the protection of debtor or creditor, or was in the interest of the debtor.

(5) In accordance with the jurisdictions discussed above, an (excessive) benefit does not in itself seem to suffice to render a contract voidable under Article 4:109 PECL.[420] The provision requires that the one party knew or ought to have known of the other party's weak bargaining position and, in addition, that he abused that position by either taking advantage of it in a grossly unfair manner or by taking an excessive benefit.

Unidroit Principles   **3.INT.107.**

Article 3.10: *Gross disparity*

    (1) A party may avoid a contract or an individual term of it if, at the time of the conclusion of the contract, the contract or term unjustifiably gave the other party an excessive advantage. Regard is to be had, among other factors, to

        (a) the fact that the other party has taken unfair advantage of the first party's dependence, economic distress or urgent needs, or of its improvidence, ignorance, inexperience or lack of bargaining skill, and

        (b) (b) the nature and purpose of the contract . . .

---

[419] See *Chitty* para. 38-316 and Treitel, *Contract* at 389–90, with references to case-law.
[420] See *supra*, 430.

Note

Article 3.10 UP appears to be more generous in this respect. It allows a party to avoid a contract if, at the moment of conclusion of the contract, there is a gross disparity between the performance and counter-performance which gives one party an unjustifiably excessive advantage. As to the requirement of an "excessive advantage" Comment 1 reads: "What is required is that the disequilibrium is in the circumstances so great as to shock the conscience of a reasonable person". Apart from being excessive, the advantage must also be "unjustifiable". Whether it is, depends on an evaluation of all the relevant circumstances of the individual case. According to Comment 2 an excessive advantage may be unjustifiable *without* there being an abuse of the other party's weak bargaining position. Comment 2 explains: "Whether this is the case will often depend upon the nature and purpose of the contract. Thus, a contract term providing for an extremely short period for giving notice of defects in goods or services to be supplied may or may not be excessively [read: unjustifiably] advantageous to the seller or supplier, depending on the character of the goods or services in question". From this comment it appears therefore that under Article 3.10 UP, contrary to the legal systems discussed above and Article 4:109 PECL, an unjustifiably excessive advantage taken by the one party may sometimes in itself render a contract voidable.

3.3.4. ABUSE OF CIRCUMSTANCES AND EXCESSIVE BENEFIT: QUALIFIED *LAESIO ENORMIS*

Can a contract be avoided on the ground of what is here called qualified *laesio enormis*, i.e. if the one party took an excessive advantage by abusing the situation in which the other party found himself?

3.3.4.A. GENERAL DOCTRINES: CONTINENTAL LAW

BGB   **3.G.108.**

§ 138 [Transactions contrary to public policy; usury]
    (1) A transaction which is contrary to public policy is void.
    (2) In particular, a transaction by which a person exploits the position of constraint in which another person finds himself, or the inexperience, lack of discernment or substantial weakness of will of that other person, in order, for his own benefit or that of a third party, to procure the promise of, or to obtain, a pecuniary advantage in return for the provision of a service which is markedly disproportionate to such provision, is void.

BGH, 12 March 1981[421]   **3.G.109.**

QUALIFIED LAESIO ENORMIS IS A GROUND OF INVALIDITY

The disproportionate loan agreement

If there is a marked disproportion between the mutual performances and if the advantaged party had the intention—which may be inferred from the circumstances of the case—to exploit the disadvantaged

---

[421] BGHZ 80.153.

party's economically weaker position, a contract is contrary to public policy and void (under § 138 (1) BGB).

Facts: The defendant was "jointly liable" for the repayment of a loan taken out in March 1976 by her then fiancé, through a credit broker, with B. Bank. The "total loan" amounted to DM 20 325.70. That sum was made up of the following:

1. Sum paid out	12,000.00 DM
2. Credit broker's commission	600.00 DM
3. Extraneous expenses, inquiries, etc.	50.00 DM
4. Insurance premium covering inability to pay the residual debt due in the event of death or incapacity	1,210.00 DM
5. Monthly loan charges amounting to 0.95% of the "amount financed" (DM 13,860, representing the sum of items 1 to 4), totalling	6,188.50 DM
6. 2% handling charge, application fee, collection expenses arising from the "amount financed"	277.20 DM
	20,325.70 DM

The total sum was repayable in 47 monthly instalments from 1 May 1976. The debtors fell into arrears with the repayment instalments. The plaintiff applied for an order requiring the defendant to pay the sum of money due under the contract. The defendant applied for the claim to be dismissed, asserting that the loan contract was contrary to public policy.

Held: The contract is void for being contrary to public policy (§ 138 (1) BGB) because there is not only an obvious disproportion between the performances given, for one thing, the fact that the monthly loan charge of 0.95% exceeded the predominant market rate of 0.33% considerably, but also an intention on the part of the lender to exploit the borrower's weaker financial position. This reprehensible attitude of the lender can be inferred from the circumstances of this case, such as the disparity between the mutual performances

Judgment: The judgment given in the appeal on questions of fact and law stands up to the test applied to it in the appeal on a point of law. The loan agreement on which the plaintiff bases its claims against the defendant as a jointly liable party is contrary to public policy and void (§ 138(1) BGB).

I. 1. However, it is not possible in law to uphold the view expressed by the appellate court, to the effect that a loan agreement providing for part payment or payment by instalments will only be contrary to public policy on the ground of a "particularly serious disparity" between consideration and performance where the effective annual interest rate demanded by the bank exceeds the normal market rate of interest by more than 100%.

(a) It is true that § 138 BGB imposes restrictions on contractual freedom, particularly as regards the way in which the contract is formulated, with a view to preventing abuse of that freedom. However, § 138 is not designed to restrict the subjective assessment by the parties to the contract of the equilibrium between consideration and performance by rendering such assessment subject to the application of objective "standard prices" established by the courts, such as the fixing of a maximum interest rate applicable to consumer credit transactions. . . .

(b) The appellate court is incorrect in its attempts to draw support for its findings from the rules contained in a foreign system of law, namely Austrian law (§ 934 ABGB), and to establish a connection with legal principles which have applied in the past (the *ius commune* concept of *laesio enormis*). The legislature was aware of the provisions of Austrian law and the *ius commune* when it decided against the adoption of a statutory rule whereby, in the absence of abuse of contractual freedom, particularly as regards the way in which the contract is formulated, a contract is rendered contrary to public policy by the existence of an objective disparity, albeit a substantial disparity, between consideration and performance. . . . Thus it has also been acknowledged in the relevant case-law that, in order for a transaction to be held contrary to public policy within the meaning of § 138(1) BGB, there must also exist, in addition to a marked objective disparity between consideration and performance, a subjective factual element, in particular a reprehensible motive on the part of the creditor (BGB NJW 1951, 397; 1957, 1274). Otherwise, the concept of *laesio enormis*, which was eliminated from the Civil Code, would find itself being reintroduced. . . .

(c) It is likewise apparent from the way in which the law has developed since the entry into force of the Civil Code that credit transactions which provide for a rate of interest in excess of a given rate are not to be regarded as contrary to public policy solely because of the high level of interest charged, and that regard must also be had to the other circumstances of the case . . .

It is true that, according to the current view of the law, the function of § 138 BGB is to secure compliance not only with the moral principles underlying the assessment of legal and social issues but also with the essential principles and basic norms of the law relating to abuse of contractual freedom (see BGHZ 68, 1, 4). It is not possible, however, even taking into account the notions of consumer protection expressed in the various different rules, to infer from the prevailing legal order any principles or norms suggesting that a credit transaction must be held contrary to public policy pursuant to § 138 BGB solely because it provides for a high rate of interest, and without having any regard to the other circumstances of the case . . .

2. Moreover, as the appellant has rightly argued, the alternative grounds advanced in support of its judgment by the appellate court, to the effect that the criteria laid down by § 138(2) BGB in respect of usury are fulfilled, are erroneous in law.

The appellate court bases its alternative reasoning on the argument that the factual criteria established by a rule such as that contained in § 138(2) BGB, involving "factual elements varying as to the limits imposed on them", are fulfilled even where one of the elements in question (in the present case, the marked disparity between consideration and performance) is "abundantly fulfilled" but another element which is equally essential (in this case, the inexperience of the party contracting with the lender) is "insufficiently fulfilled" or fulfilled "only to a limited extent" (the so-called "heap of sand" proposition).

That view, which has also been the subject of criticism in the works of academic legal authors . . ., cannot be upheld. A transaction will be usurious within the meaning of § 138(2) BGB only if *all* of the factual elements constituting usury are fulfilled. It is true that a serious disparity between consideration and performance may provide compelling grounds for supposing that the party benefitting from that objective disparity between consideration and performance has consciously, or with gross negligence, exploited, contrary to public policy, some factor restricting the freedom of action of the other party (see BGH WM 1969, 1255, 1257). However, the appellate court made no findings of fact justifying the conclusion that—assuming there to have been a substantial disparity between consideration and performance—the plaintiff did actually exploit any youthful inexperience on the part of the defendant, who was not yet 20 years old at the time when the contract was concluded. It is apparent even from the significance attached by the court below to what it found to have been "artful deceit" in respect of the interest rate that there are no grounds for finding that a usurious transaction took place within the meaning of § 138(2) BGB. The question is therefore whether the findings of fact arrived at by the appellate court are sufficient to establish the existence of a transaction in the nature of usury which is contrary to public policy pursuant to § 138(1) BGB.

II. 1. In its case-law, the adjudicating Senate has assessed credit agreements providing for the grant of loans at a high rate of interest, and for part payment or payment by instalments, in the light of the principles governing transactions in the nature of usury as contemplated by § 138(1) BGB. According to those principles, a loan agreement is void, as the Senate has previously held on a number of occasions (*inter alia* in its judgment of 9 November 1978—III ZR 21/77 = NJW 1979, 805, and, most recently, in its judgment of 10 July 1980—III ZR 177/78 = NJW 1980, 2301, accompanied in each case by supporting arguments), if there exists a marked disparity between the consideration provided by the lender and the obligations imposed on the borrower in consequence of the unilateral formulation of the contract, and if the lender consciously exploits to his own advantage the economically weaker position of the borrower and the latter's inferior bargaining power at the time when the terms and conditions of the loan are fixed. The same considerations apply where the lender, acting in a manner which, from an objective standpoint, is contrary to public policy, irresponsibly closes his eyes to the fact that the borrower is agreeing to terms and conditions which will place a heavy burden on him only because he is in a financially weaker position. The contents and purpose of the loan agreement, together with all the other circumstances surrounding the transaction, must be assessed as a whole. That overall assessment must take into account the consideration and performance obligations laid down by the contract, together with any other rules by which it is governed, including the lender's standard terms and conditions of business (BGH judgment of 25 October 1979—III ZR 182/77 = NJW 1980, 445, 446). Particular weight must be given in that regard to the relationship between the consideration for the loan, the interest payable and the main service provided by the lender, namely the transfer, for a given period of time, of the ability to utilize a capital sum.

2. Those principles underlying the assessment of such cases do not preclude the possibility that the relationship between consideration and performance which is found to exist by the court examining the facts will suffice on its own to indicate a transaction in the nature of exploitation which is contrary to public policy. The Bundesgerichtshof has previously considered, in individual cases concerning commercial loans, the question whether a given rate of interest justifies the conclusion that the transaction is in the nature of exploitation and contrary to public policy. It has confirmed, in relation to transactions involving a particularly high interest rate (rates of 40% or more, for example, and certainly in the case of rates of 50% or more), that such contracts are contrary to public policy. . . . In so doing, it has taken into account, to a considerable extent, the risk incurred by the lender in handing over the money . . .

3. (a) A comparison of market rates represents an appropriate means of examining, in accordance with the requirements referred to above (II 1), whether there exists a marked disparity between consideration and performance; by means of such a market comparison, it is possible to ascertain what constitutes the customary and economically acceptable consideration which is normally to be provided in return for a loan, and to compare that norm with the credit agreement in issue, in order to verify whether the latter is contrary to public policy (judgments of the Senate of 10 July 1980, *loc. cit.*, of 17 April 1980—III ZR 96/78 = NJW 1980, 2076, and of 10 April 1980—III ZR 59/79 = NJW 1980, 2074). In that connection, the adjudicating Senate has hitherto not concentrated solely on the interest rates charged by the finance houses but has also taken into account the whole of the market for loans repayable in instalments involving the lending of comparable sums for comparable periods (judgments of 10 April 1980 and 17 April 1980, *loc. cit.*, with supporting arguments). That was also the basis on which the court below proceeded. It considered, for the purposes of comparison, the "predominant" rate of interest indicated in the monthly reports of the Deutsche Bank, which covers not only the rates charged by the finance houses but also those charged by the general clearing banks. The use of such material for comparative purposes by courts adjudicating on the facts has previously been approved by this Senate (see the judgments of 17 April 1980, *loc. cit*, and 10 July 1980 *loc. cit.*) . . .

III. 1. According to the findings of the court below, the loan repayable in instalments to which the defendant committed herself constituted a loan *arranged through an intermediary* which provided for *insurance cover* in respect of the outstanding residue in the event of the death or incapacity of the borrower. For the purposes of assessing whether the transaction is contrary to public policy, and in the context of the market comparison to be carried out to that end, that circumstance must be taken into account, in accordance with the requirement that all the circumstances of the matter be weighed generally in the balance. The fact that a legally independent brokerage agreement may exist between the intermediary negotiating the loan and the borrower and, in particular, the fact that, in the present case, the insurance contract covering residual indebtedness which was concluded between the plaintiff and the insurer was legally independent of the loan agreement, is not decisive. For the purposes of assessing whether a credit agreement constitutes a transaction in the nature of exploitation which is contrary to public policy and infringes § 138(1) BGB, the terms and conditions imposed by, and attributable to, the lender must be taken into account, together with "all the objective circumstances" in which the transaction came to be effected. . . . The requirement that regard must be had to all the circumstances characterizing the contract involves, in essence, consideration of the purpose and economic significance of the individual acts of consideration and performance in the relationship between the parties, rather than of the outward legal form which the lending bank chooses to attach to the standard commercial operations involved.

In accordance with the requirement that an overall assessment be carried out, proper weight must be given in the market comparison, first of all, to the remuneration payable by borrowers in consideration of the placing of capital sums at their disposal for utilization by them, together with the interest and/or credit charges payable, in credit transactions involving the lending of comparable sums for comparable periods. Other credit charges imposed on the borrower by the lender, such as application fees, must also be included in the assessment. It is true that such costs do not constitute interest charges in the legal sense of the term; they are not a *quid pro quo* for the use of the capital sum in the sense of being dependent on, and referable to, the term of the loan and constituting monetary consideration. However, the fact that the lender may include those costs relating to the provision and grant of the loan as part of the interest constituting the consideration for the use of the capital sum, and that they place a burden on the borrower similar to that imposed by credit charges, conclusively indicates that they must be taken into account. For the bank, interest and credit charges are in a certain sense "interchangeable". For the borrower, higher interest payments and lower credit charges (or *vice versa*) may ultimately mean, depending on the way in which the other terms of the contract are formulated, that he is required to bear the same financial burden for a loan of the same amount (see the judgments of the Senate of 10 July 1980, *loc. cit.*, and of 10 April 1980, *loc. cit.*, accompanied in each case by supporting arguments).

2. The *arrangement fees* imposed on the borrower and financed by the bank, which were clearly indicated by the latter in the loan agreement, likewise constitute remuneration for the procurement or grant of the sum loaned, and are not, therefore, interest charges within the civil law meaning of the term. They must be included as a factor in the overall assessment of the matter, in order to ascertain the total cost of the loan to the borrower. According to the past case-law of the Senate, regard must be had in that context to the purpose which they serve and the advantage which they are intended to give to one or other of the contracting parties (see the judgments of the Senate of 9 November 1978, *loc. cit.*, of 11 January 1979—III ZR 119/77 = NJW 1979, 808, and of 29 June 1979, *loc. cit.*; (. . .)).
. . .

3. As the Senate has previously held, the cost imposed on the borrower of the *insurance cover in respect of residual indebtedness* arranged for him by the plaintiff must also be taken into account in the overall assessment of all the circumstances of the matter, and likewise in the comparison of the terms and conditions of the various different credit institutions (see the judgments of the Senate of 11 January 1979, 29 June 1979, 10 April 1980, 17 April 1980 and 10 July 1980, cited above . . .

IV. The findings of the court below and the uncontested facts of the case are such as to justify a conclusive decision in the matter.

The "predominant" rate of interest shown in the monthly reports of the Deutsche Bank, which the court below took into account in its assessment of the case, represents the average rate of interest, disregarding the top 5% of the credit institutions charging the highest rates and the bottom 5% charging the lowest rates. At the time when the contract was concluded, the predominant rate was 0.33% per month, whilst the monthly rate charged by the plaintiff was 0.95% of the original amount of the loan. That rate diverges considerably—indeed, markedly—from the rate charged by the majority of credit institutions, and thus, in addition, from the normal rate payable for loans repayable in instalments which are not negotiated through an intermediary. The fact that the loan at issue in the present case was of an amount higher than, and was granted for a term longer than, the loans covered by the monthly reports of the Deutsche Bank is immaterial in that regard. The normal commercial interest rate for such a loan might well be lower on account of the reduced administrative expense of granting a larger loan for a longer term. Even if the cost burden imposed on the borrower, particularly in respect of the charges for the negotiation of the loan through an intermediary, which were clearly indicated to him, and the cost of the insurance cover in respect of residual indebtedness, represented the normal commercial remuneration payable for the service rendered by the credit broker and for the insurance protection provided by the insurer, there would still be a marked disparity between consideration and performance as regards the cost of the loan by comparison with the cost of loans from other credit institutions. The general reference made to increased refinancing costs and administrative expenses is not enough to invalidate the indication, suggested by the circumstances of the case, that the transaction involved a marked disparity.

There are in addition further elements which indicate that the transaction constituted exploitation contrary to public policy within the meaning of § 138(1) BGB, namely an unreasonable accumulation of excessive cost burdens imposed in the event of the borrower falling into arrears. In anticipation of such an event, the plaintiff sought, even at the time when the transaction was held to be contrary to public policy, to impose on the borrowers corresponding charges payable in arrears situations, including a fee, described by the plaintiff itself as a "contractual penalty", of 5% due in the event of its having to assert its claims by the institution of legal proceedings, and agreement to a default fee of 1.5% per month over and above the credit charges, without there having been at the time any tacit agreement, as is normally the case in the sector concerned, providing for the reimbursement of unused credit charges in the event of the loan falling due. The imposition of a charge analogous to a penalty in the event that it becomes necessary to resort to legal proceedings is liable not only to place an excessive burden on the borrowers but also to deter them from seeking to safeguard their rights by allowing matters to reach the stage of a lawsuit.

Where a borrower is in a weaker financial position, contractual terms providing for the situation which is to apply in the event of his falling into arrears assume considerable significance. The danger exists that, upon falling into arrears, and faced with the mounting claims of the lender, he will fall into even heavier debt. This also applies with regard to the defendant, who, following her apprentice's final examination, worked as an assistant in a photographic laboratory and who, by assuming responsibility for the repayment of the loan, took on what was for her the substantial commitment of monthly instalment payments in excess of DM 400.

As a result of the form which it took, the entire contract is in the nature of a transaction contrary to public policy, and is void (see the judgment of the Senate of 9 November 1978, *loc. cit.*, accompanied by supporting arguments) . . .

Notes

(1) As has already been noted in **3.3.3**, a contract is void under §138(2) BGB for being *contra bonos mores* if one of the weaknesses enumerated in that provision has been exploited ("*Ausbeutung*") and if, in addition, the contract entailed an obvious disproportion ("*auffälliges Mißverhältnis*") between the performance and the counter-performance. Cf. Article 21 I OR; § 879 II (4) ABGB; Article 179 of the Greek CC; Article 1448 of the Italian CC. This type of case is commonly known as "*Wucher*"(usury). Whether or not the requirement of "*auffälliges Mißverhältnis*" has been met in a particular case must be decided by comparing the objective (market) value of the mutual performances at the moment of conclusion of the contract and by taking into account all the relevant circumstances of the individual case.

(2) As regards the obvious nature of the inequality Larenz and Wolf[422] write: "There may only by said to be a "striking" disparity where the disparity is so great that it patently goes beyond the limits of what is justifiable in all the circumstances" ("*Von einem 'auffälligen' Mißverhältnis wird man nur dann sprechen können, wenn das Mißverhältnis so groß ist, daß die Grenzen dessen, was sich nach den gesamten Umständen gerade noch rechtfertigen läßt, eindeutig überschritten sind*").[423]

(3) "*Ausbeutung*" is the exploitation of a weakness, enumerated in §138(2) BGB, on the part of the other party. The party exploiting the weakness must have had knowledge of the weakness and of the obvious disparity. Constructive knowledge does not suffice, nor is an intention to exploit required See for example BGH, 8 July 1982.[424] The weaknesses enumerated in §138(2) BGB are discussed in detail by Soergel-Hefermehl.[425] If in a particular case the requirements of §138(2) BGB have not been fulfilled, the contract may be void under paragraph (1) of §138 BGB (as a "*wucherähnliches Geschäft*", a "usury-like contract") which lays down the general rule on juristic acts, such as contracts, contrary to *bonos mores*. The courts have held that a contract is void under paragraph (1) of §138 BGB if there is an obvious disproportion between the mutual performances and the advantaged party displayed a reprehensible attitude ("*verwerfliche Gesinnung*") by either deliberately exploiting the weaker economic position of the disadvantaged party, or by grossly negligently failing to realize that the disadvantaged party entered into the contract only because of his predicament.[426] It should be noted, however, that the subjective requirement of a "*verwerfliche Gesinnung*" is in a sense fictitious[427] since the courts are prepared to infer the reprehensible attitude from the objective circumstances of the individual case—especially from (the extent of) the disparity.[428] As the courts have brought the "*wucherähnliche Geschäfte*" under the sphere of application of §138(1) BGB, para.(2) of §138 BGB has lost much of its practical importance.

Req., 27 April 1887[429]   **3.F.110.**

EXTORTIONATE SALVAGE

The "Rolf"

The abuse by the one party of the other party's state of necessity, which has led that party to enter into an onerous (salvage) agreement renders the agreement voidable on the ground of "violence" as the consent to enter into the agreement is not freely given.

---

[422] Larenz, *AT*, at 761.
[423] See also *Palandt*, under §138 BGB, para. 4 bb; Soergel and Hefermehl, under § 138 BGB, para. 74; BGH, NJW 1979.758, cit. in **3.3.3** at 456; for a "*Ratenkreditvertrag*", extensively, BGHZ 80, 153, 162 ff. *supra* at 460.
[424] NJW 1982.2767, 2768; See also *Palandt*, under §138 BGB, para. 74; Soergel and Hefermehl, under §138 BGB, para. 82; Larenz, *AT* at 762.
[425] Under §138 BGB, paras. 78–81.
[426] See e.g. BGHZ 80, 153, 160–161, *supra* at 460.
[427] See *Münchener Kommentar* (*Mayer-Maly*), under § 138 BGB, para. 102.
[428] Cf. e.g. BGH, NJW 1979.758, in **3.3.3**, at 456; BGHZ 80, 153, 161, *supra* at 460; Soergel and Hefermehl, under § 138 BGB, para. 73.
[429] D. 1888.1.263; S. 1887.1.372

Facts: On 22 September 1886 Mr Fleischer, captain of the steamship *Rolf*, which had run aground on the sands of the bay at the mouth of the Seine and was on the point of being lost, together with her cargo, agreed to a price of 18,000 francs fixed by the captain of a tug as the value of the provision of salvage and towage services. It was only through this agreement that Mr Fleischer could avoid a total loss of the *Rolf* and the cargo. However, upon being subsequently sued for payment of the agreed sum, Mr Fleischer argued that the agreement was void on the ground that it was vitiated by an absence of freely given consent on his part.

Held: On 13 October 1886 the Rouen *Tribunal de commerce* (Commercial Court) accepted that argument and ordered Mr Fleischer to pay to the tug owner, Mr Lebret, the sum of 4,190 francs by way of recompense for the towage services provided. On appeal by Mr Lebret, the *Cour de Rouen* on 10 December 1886 upheld that judgment. Mr Lebret appealed to the Cour de Cassation, but again his appeal was rejected.

Judgments: [In the Cour de Rouen (appellate court)]:—Whereas at the time when the agreement in issue was concluded, Fleischer, the master of the *Rolf*, could have been in no doubt that, unless he received prompt assistance, his vessel, which was aground on the sand, would, upon the arrival of the next high tide, become fatally submerged and would be lost, and further that his only chance of salvation lay in being refloated by Delamer, the master of the tug *Abeille No 9*, who had been the only person to answer his distress signals and to offer his services.

—Whereas in requiring in advance, as the price of the salvage and towage, one twentieth of the value of the vessel and its cargo, namely a sum of approximately 18,000 francs, Delamer had abused the desperate situation in which the master of the *Rolf* found himself; as having tried in vain to get him to accept less harsh terms, Fleischer was constrained and forced to submit as a matter of necessity to the agreement imposed on him; since his consent was not freely given, the agreement, which is vitiated as a matter of principle, is not merely rescindable but voidable in its entirety; as it must be declared null and void.

—Whereas leaving the contract to one side, however, the owner of the *Abeille No 9* is entitled to be rewarded for the service rendered by his tug to the *Rolf*. In order to determine the level of remuneration to which he is entitled, it is appropriate to some extent to take into account the value of the vessel and her cargo, which were saved, but regard must also be had, primarily and above all, to the efforts deployed and the risks faced or run by the salvor; as the value of the *Rolf* and her cargo was not less than 363,000 francs; however, the *Abeille No 9*, sailing on 22 September between the hours of half past five and seven o'clock in the evening, was drawing little water in a sufficient depth of sea and was exposed to no serious danger.

—Whereas although she remained stationary until about half past three in the morning, at anchor in the Seine estuary and within range of the *Rolf*, waiting for the tide to enable her to bring assistance to the *Rolf*, that wait involved merely a waste of time without any risk; as the refloating, which was commenced at twenty past three in the morning of 23 September and completed less than three quarters of an hour later in normal conditions, caused the *Abeille* to suffer no accident or damage apart from the insignificant breakage of a towing cable, for which Captain Fleischer offered to pay.

—Whereas although the tug's engine had to be run on full power, it did not exceed its capacity; and it has not been alleged that it suffered any deterioration as a result.

—Whereas it is necessary to encourage salvage operations as a beneficial activity, and, having regard to the circumstances, generously to reward those undertaking them, they must nevertheless not be allowed to become a means of exploiting the perils or misfortunes faced by others.

—Whereas the sum awarded to Lebret by the court at first instance is adequate, even taking into account the contingent stipulation whereby nothing was to be payable in the event of an unsuccessful outcome, etc.

[In the Cour de Cassation]: *Judgment*: *On the sole appeal ground alleging misuse of powers, infringement of Article 1134 of the Civil Code and misapplication of Articles 1109, 1111 et seq. of that Code*:—Under Article 1108 of the Civil Code, the consent of the person assuming the obligation is an essential condition governing the validity of an agreement.

—Whereas such consent is not freely given, and is given only out of fear instilled by some substantial and present ill to which the person or chattel concerned is exposed, a contract entered into in those circumstances is vitiated by a defect rendering it voidable.

—Whereas the contested judgment found that the master of the *Rolf* assumed the obligation at issue only in order to save his ship, which would otherwise have swiftly become fatally submerged and lost.

—Whereas that obligation was assumed as a result of constraint and by force of circumstance. Having sought in vain to secure less onerous terms, the master of the *Rolf* was forced as a matter of necessity to enter into the agreement which the master of the *Abeille No 9*, exploiting the desperate situation in which the former found himself, imposed on him.—Whereas in consequently declaring that agreement void, the appellate court neither misused its powers nor infringed or misapplied any of the abovementioned articles.

On those grounds, the Court dismisses the appeal.

Note

Cases of salvage were later dealt with by statute; see L.67–545 of 7 July 1967 (replacing a statute of 1916).

Cass. soc., 5 July 1965[430]   **3.F.111.**

EXTORTIONATE LABOUR CONTRACT

A pressing need for money

A (labour) contract which is disadvantageous for the the one party is voidable on the ground of "violence" if that party's consent to enter into the agreement is not freely given because of his urgent need for money.

Facts: Pursuant to a contract dated 22 January 1959, Mr Maly was engaged for six months on a probationary basis as a salesman by Frameco, a manufacturer of concrete products, on terms whereby he was to receive a 3% commission on the net price of direct and indirect sales. As he had to move from Paris to Grenoble, he resigned on 21 September 1959. At that time Mr Maly was in urgent need of money to provide medical treatment for his sick child. On 12 October 1959 he entered into a new agreement with I.M.A.C., a firm, whereby he was, with the authorization of Frameco, to sell the same product as an independent operator and was to receive a commission of 1.5% on direct sales only; this arrangement was to have retroactive effect. On 17 February 1960 Mr Maly sued I.M.A.C., seeking an order requiring that company to pay commission on the basis on the agreement of 22 January 1959.

Held: The Cour de Cassation upheld the decision of the appellate court that the contract of 12 October 1959 was to be declared void on the ground of "*violence*" as Mr Maly's consent, given, among other things, his pressing need of money, had been constrained.

Judgment:—Whereas the contested judgment is challenged in that (a) it declared the agreement of 12 October 1959 void on the ground that it was vitiated by "violence", (b) it held that the relationship between the parties continued to be governed by the agreement of 22 January 1959 and (c) it appointed an expert to calculate the commission due, on the grounds that Maly had had certain doubts as to the enforceability against I.M.A.C. of the agreement entered into with Frameco and that Maly had only agreed to accept the conditions laid down in the agreement of 12 October 1959 because of the constraint in which he found himself.

---

[430] Bull. civ. IV.545.

—Whereas according to the appellant, it is patently clear that Maly at all times worked on behalf of I.M.A.C., that it was that company which paid him his commission and which he sued for payment of the commission provided for under the original agreement, and that he could not therefore have been unaware that that agreement could if necessary be enforced against I.M.A.C.; as furthermore, the legal status of a salesman is such that he is required to exercise his profession on an exclusive and steadfast basis, and the contested judgment, which did not examine the question whether, as is contended by I.M.A.C., Maly had sold goods for a competitor, provided no legal basis for the decision delivered by the court below; as lastly, the appellant contends that the findings in the contested judgment do not adequately establish, first, that the rate of commission was not reduced in pursuance of an agreement between the parties and, second, that the contract of 12 October 1959 was entered into in circumstances of compelling constraint amounting to "violence".

—Whereas the contested judgment found, however, that, at the time of his resignation, Maly, who was required to leave Paris and take up residence in Grenoble with a sick child, was in pressing need of money, that his employer refused to perform the obligations imposed by the initial contract, that he was faced with the alternative of either bringing what might prove to be protracted proceedings or agreeing to the immediate receipt of a reduced sum by consenting to pursue his activities on draconian terms which involved a considerable reduction in the rate of commission and the renunciation of social benefits, etc., one of those terms being unlawful and their provisions as a whole being inequitable; As the complaint that Maly had effected sales for a competitor undertaking—which Maly contested, stating that the company had agreed to his carrying out such operations on an occasional basis—was not levelled against him by the company at the time of his departure, the company having, on the contrary, expressed its regret at seeing him go, and was only raised in the course of the proceedings; as moreover, he had not exerted any influence on the signature of the second agreement.

—Whereas in inferring from this that Maly's consent had been vitiated by intellectual "violence" ["*violence morale*"] and that the contract of 12 October 1959 was void, the contested judgment provided a legal basis for the decision therein contained.

Notes

(1) French law has been struggling with the question whether or not a contract is voidable on the ground of "*violence*", in the sense of the Code Civil, if the constraint of the will of the one party (the plaintiff) did not arise from a threat exercised by the other party, but from the external circumstances in which the one party found himself, such as a state of necessity or economic dependence. The courts and authors are divided over this issue.[431] Relevant cases are few but there are decisions in which a contract was held to be voidable because of "*violence*"—in this context often referred to as "*violence morale*"—arising from a state of necessity ("*état de necessité*"). The courts seem to require that the other party has gained an excessive advantage by abusing the state of necessity (when an advantage can be said to be excessive, the courts have not specified; it appears that all the relevant circumstances of the case, such as the market value, are to be taken into consideration).[432] The above cited case of *The "Rolf"* illustrates this position: the Cour de cassation upheld the decision of the appellate court that the agreement was voidable because of "*violence (morale)*" as the captain of fhe *Rolf*, which was in danger of being lost unless it was pulled of the sandbank on which it had grounded, gave in to the captain of the tug

---

[431] For a discussion see Terré, Simler and Lequette, paras 239–240; Nicholas, at 108–10.
[432] See e.g. Ghestin, at 568.

and agreed to pay a price which, as the trial court had found, was four times the reasonable figure.[433] Another example in point is the case of Cass. soc., 5 July 1965,[434] in which a contract of employment was declared void as the employee (the disadvantaged party) entered into the contract of 12 October 1959 under a pressing need for money occasioned by the illness of his child—although the Cour de cassation did not explicitly consider whether in this case there was an abuse of the father's state of necessity, it did speak of the "draconian terms" of the contract from which it might have inferred an abuse. See for a more restrictive approach however, Cass.com, 20 May 1980,[435] which was a case of economic dependence.

(2) It should be noted that in some cases of qualified *laesio enormis*, the courts have held a contract to be voidable on the ground of *"dol"* (fraud).[436]

(3) The French legislature has dealt with particular cases of *"état de necessité"* and *"dépendance économique"*. See for example L.72–1137 of 22 December 1972 (Article 7; abuse of weakness or ignorance in case of doorstep sales) and Ordonnance no. 86–1234 of 1 December 1986 (Article 8; prohibition of *"l'exploitation abusive"* by an enterprise or group of enterprises of a dominant market position or a state of economic dependence on the part of an *"entreprise cliente ou fournisseur"*).

(4) Interestingly, the Belgian courts and legal authors have developed a doctrine of qualified *"lésion"* based on the doctrine of *"cause licite"* and/or the doctrine of *culpa in contrahendo*. On this Belgian doctrine of qualified *"lésion"*, Jacques Herbots writes:[437]

"The doctrine requires two elements: first a serious disproportion between the terms of the contract. But this is not sufficient. Moreover there must be an exploitation of one of the parties, a taking advantage of the needs, weaknesses, emotions or ignorance of one of the parties, or an abuse of a dominant position".[438]

(5) In Dutch law, in a case of qualified *laesio enormis*, the contract is voidable under Article 3:44 IV BW as there has been an abuse of circumstances and the excessive disadvantage should have prevented the one party from prompting the other party to enter into the contract.[439]

3.3.4.B. SPECIFIC DOCTRINES: UNDUE INFLUENCE IN ENGLISH LAW

It is in English law that it is least clear whether there is any equivalent to what is here called qualified *laesio enormis*. Certainly there are certain doctrines which lean in that direction, notably "undue influence" and the rules on "unconscionable bargains". However the former is distinctly limited in its application while the latter, though of ancient origin, is of uncertain scope in modern law. An attempt by Lord Denning MR to formulate a broad doctrine of inequality of bargaining power was firmly rejected by the House of Lords.

[433] See the English salvage case of *The Port Caledonia and The Anna* [1903] P 184.
[434] Bull. civ. IV.545, *supra* at 468.
[435] Bull. civ. IV.212 (quashing Cour d'appel de Paris, 27 September 1977, D. 1978.690).
[436] See e.g. Kötz, *European Contract Law* at 132, with references to case law.
[437] *Contract Law in Belgium* (1995), 129.
[438] With references to Cass., 25 November 1977, Arr. Cass., 1978.343 and Comm. Brussels, 16 April 1974, B.R.H., 1974. 229.
[439] See **3.3.3**, note 2, *supra* at 458 and **3.3.5**. *infra* at 484.

Court of Appeal **3.E.112.**
Bank of Credit and Commerce International S.A. v. *Aboody*[440]

UNDUE INFLUENCE

The trusting wife

A contract is voidable on the ground of undue influence only if the contract is shown to be manifestly disadvantageous to the influenced party (as to actual undue influence, this part of the decision was later overruled by the House of Lords; see below, note 4).

Facts: The defendants, Mr and Mrs Aboody, who were husband and wife, were directors and shareholders of a family company (Eratex) which had exceeded the prescribed limits of its overdraft at the plaintiff bank. The company's liabilities to the bank were secured by guarantees given by the defendants and by charges on the wife's house signed by her. After the company had collapsed, owing the bank nearly £890,000, the bank brought an action to enforce its securities. The wife challenged the validity of the guarantees and the charges on the ground, *inter alia*, that they were obtained by the (actual) undue influence on the part of the husband.

Held: Even though the wife had been induced to enter into the security transactions by the undue influece of her husband, the security transactions are not voidable because it is not established that the transactions were manifestly disadvantageous to her.

Judgment: [SLADE LJ]: *Issue (1)* We now turn to consider the point of law which constitutes the first ground of appeal, namely that a party who proves that a transaction was induced by the actual exercise of undue influence is entitled to have it set aside without also proving that the transaction was manifestly disadvantageous to him or her.

Ever since the judgments of this court in *Allcard* v. *Skinner* (1887) 36 Ch D 145 a clear distinction has been drawn between (1) those cases in which the court will uphold a plea of undue influence only if it is satisfied that such influence has been affirmatively proved on the evidence (commonly referred to as cases of "actual undue influence" and, in argument before us, as "class 1' cases); (2) those cases (commonly referred to as cases of "presumed undue influence", and, in argument before us, as "class 2" cases) in which the relationship between the parties will lead the court to presume that undue influence has been exerted unless evidence is adduced proving the contrary, e.g. by showing that the complaining party has had independent advice . . .

There are well-established categories of relationship, such as a religious superior and inferior and doctor and patient where the relationship as such will give rise to the presumption (frequently referred to in argument before us as "class 2a" cases). The relationship of husband and wife does not as such give rise to the presumption: see *National Westminster Bank plc.* v. *Morgan* [1985] AC 686 at 703 and *Bank of Montreal* v. *Stuart* [1911] AC 120. Nor does the normal relationship of banker and customer as such give rise to it. Nevertheless, on particular facts (frequently referred to in argument as "class 2b" cases) relationships not falling within the class 2a category may be shown to have become such as to justify the court in applying the same presumption . . .

In the majority of reported cases on undue influence successful plaintiffs appear to have succeeded in reliance on the presumption. If on the facts both pleas are open to him, a plaintiff in such a case may be well advised to rely on actual and presumed undue influence cumulatively or in the alternative.

In the present case, however, no doubt after carefully considered advice, no attempt has been made to plead or submit that Mrs Aboody is entitled to the benefit of any presumption. Her case throughout has been pleaded and argued on the footing that it is a class 1 case, so that the onus falls

---

[440] [1990] 1 QB 923.

upon her to establish undue influence—an onus which, subject to the question of manifest disadvantage, the judge considered that she had discharged.

In the court below it appears to have been more or less conceded on behalf of Mrs Aboody that the House of Lords in *National Westminster Bank plc.* v. *Morgan* [1985] A.C. 686 considered that the same principle applies (that manifest disadvantage must be shown before a transaction will be set aside for undue influence) whether the case falls within class 1 or class 2, though her counsel there submitted that, in so far as the relevant part of Lord Scarman's speech was directed to cases of actual undue influence, it was no more than a weighty dictum. In this court, in his very attractive argument on behalf of Mrs Aboody, Mr Wadsworth QC has made no such concession. He has submitted that, in referring to the concept of disadvantage in *Morgan*, their Lordships were not concerned with or directing their minds to cases of actual undue influence at all, and that there is no reason on principle or authority why manifest disadvantage should have to be shown in such cases.

[The court considered the authorities and held that manifest disadvantage must be shown whether the undue influence is presumed or actual.]

Issue (2): Since Mrs. Aboody's claim in the present case is based exclusively on undue influence, it thus becomes necessary to consider whether, contrary to the judge's view, she has shown that all or any of the six transactions were manifestly disadvantageous to her. The judge explained the sense which he attached to the concept of manifest disadvantage as follows:

> "I regard 'victimisation' (the word used by Lindley L.J.) and 'unfair advantage' (the words used by Lord Scarman) to be examples of the creation of a disadvantage and I would hold that a disadvantage would be a manifest disadvantage if it would have been obvious as such to any independent and reasonable persons who considered the transaction at the time with knowledge of all the relevant facts." . . .

We can see no good reason to disagree with the judge's explanation of the concept of manifest disadvantage, and merely add these observations. We accept Miss Williamson's submission that the overall disadvantageous nature of a transaction cannot be said to be manifest if it only emerges after a fine and close evaluation of its various beneficial and detrimental features. It must be obvious. We also accept that its nature has to be judged in the circumstances subsisting at the date of the transaction, though, as Mr Wadsworth pointed out, subsequent events may conceivably throw light on what could reasonably have been foreseen as at that date.

Whenever a guarantee or charge is given, there is always the risk that the guarantee may be called in or the charge enforced. Therefore, as Miss Williamson submitted, the question whether the assumption of such a risk is manifestly disadvantageous to the giver must depend on the balance of two factors, namely, (a) the seriousness of the risk of enforcement to the giver, in practical terms; and (b) the benefits gained by the giver in accepting the risk. The judge, after a full and careful examination of the background to each of the six transactions, carried out this balancing exercise and came to the conclusion that as a matter of fact no manifest disadvantage had been shown . . .

In the end, we can see no sufficient grounds for disagreeing with his conclusion that on balance a manifest disadvantage has not been shown by Mrs Aboody in respect of any of the six transactions.

Issue (3): Our conclusions on issues (1) and (2) must lead to the dismissal of this appeal. Nevertheless, though this is not necessary for our decision, we propose to say something about the allegation of actual undue influence in case (contrary to our view) either (a) as a matter of law manifest disadvantage does not have to be shown in an action where a party is relying on actual undue influence, or (b) manifest disadvantage has on the evidence been shown in the present instance . . .

Lindley LJ in *Allcard* v. *Skinner* said that no court has ever attempted to define undue influence. Lord Scarman gave a warning against any attempt at comprehensive definition in *National Westminster Bank plc.* v. *Morgan* [1985] AC 686 at 709. We heed this warning. Nevertheless, for the purpose of dealing with issue (3), it is necessary briefly to consider what has to be shown if an allegation of actual undue influence is to be made out.

Leaving aside proof of manifest disadvantage, we think that a person relying on a plea of actual undue influence must show: (a) that the other party to the transaction (or someone who induced the transaction for his own benefit) had the capacity to influence the complainant; (b) that the influence was exercised; (c) that its exercise was undue; (d) that its exercise brought about the transaction. We will consider condition (d) under issue (4). On the evidence there appears to be no doubt that conditions (a) and (b) are satisfied. The findings of the judge show that Mrs Aboody at the invitation of her husband was habitually prepared to sign documents relating to the affairs of Eratex without considering their contents because she trusted him. They also show that he invited her to enter into the first five transactions. The present issue, therefore, resolves itself to the question whether the exercise of Mr Aboody's influence was on the facts undue . . .

As will have been seen from *Morgan*'s case, the essence of the law of undue influence is to provide a remedy in cases in which, by the exercise of influence, proved by evidence or presumed, unfair advantage has been taken by another. If, contrary to our view, the five transactions were manifestly disadvantageous to Mrs Aboody, we do not see how it could be disputed that unfair advantage had been taken of her by her husband. In this context we cite a brief passage from the judgment:

"There was more than a situation of trust; there was actual influence founded on that trust and he used it intentionally. He intended and knew that without any discussion or consideration of risk she would sign security documents for a series of increasingly large overdrafts of the company. He never offered her any choice of her own. She was deprived altogether of the free use of any independent and informed judgment in the transaction. He never mentioned risk at all even if he thought it was a slight one. The only judgment that she could be said to have exercised was her mistaken judgment of Mr Aboody and his business capacity and probity.'

When one couples with these findings the fact that it was Mr Aboody who suggested to his wife that she should enter into the first five transactions, the unfair advantage taken of her by him became apparent. If he had positively misrepresented to her the extent of the risks involved, a plea based on misrepresentation might well have been available to her. The mere fact that in order to get his own way he chose deliberately to say nothing as to the risks, rather than to misrepresent them, would not, in our judgment, save his conduct from being unconscionable or absolve him from a charge of actual undue influence, bearing in mind that it was he who invited her to enter into them. On the particular facts of this case we think it could fairly be said that Mrs Aboody's mind was in effect "a mere channel through which the will of [Mr Aboody] operated": compare the observations of Jenkins and Morris L.JJ. in *Tufton* v. *Sperni* [1952] 2 TLR 516, 530, 532 . . .

In the present case, as Mr Wadsworth submitted, the evidence and findings of the judge show that Mr Aboody, in inducing his wife to enter into the six transactions, deliberately acted so as to conceal matters from her in a way which prevented her from giving proper detached consideration to her independent interests in transactions which involved substantial risks to her. The mere fact that Mr Aboody may have had no intention to injure her does not save his conduct from being unconscionable. If, contrary to our view, (a) as a matter of law manifest disadvantage did not have to be shown in a case where a party is relying on actual undue influence, or (b) manifest disadvantage had on the evidence been shown in the present case, we would have found actual undue influence on the part of Mr Aboody proved in respect of each of the six transactions. However, no manifest disadvantage having been established, we agree with the judge that the plea of actual undue influence must fail.

[The court then considered issues of causation and the bank's knowledge of any undue influence.]

Notes

(1) The meaning of the phrase "undue influence" is not exactly clear.[441] In the *Restatement of the Law (Second), Contracts 2d*, §177(1), undue influence is defined as follows: "Undue influence is unfair persuasion of a party who is under the domination of the person exercising the persuasion or who by virtue of the relation between them is justified in assuming that that person will not act in a manner inconsistent with his welfare".

(2) In English law, as in other common law jurisdictions, undue influence is traditionally divided into two categories: actual undue influence ("class 1") and presumed undue influence ("class 2").[442]

(3) The requirements of actual undue influence were stated by the Court of Appeal in the *Aboody* case:[443] "Leaving aside proof of manifest disadvantage, we think that a person relying on a plea of actual undue influence must show that (a) the other party to the transaction (or someone who induced the transaction for his own benefit) had the capacity to influence the complainant; (b) the influence was exercised; (c) its exercise was undue; (d) its exercise brought about the transaction". Actual undue influence involves some unfair and improper conduct by the one party (or a third person; see **3.3.6**) *vis-à-vis* the other party. The exerted pressure need not necessarily consist of active coercion or a threat (as in the case of duress), but may also consist of more subtle forms of influence;[444] As to the requirement of the influence being "undue", Cartwright writes:[445]

"It is taking advantage of a superior position . . ., in a way which equity does not regard as fair. For influence to be "undue", it is not, however, necessary for it to be accompanied by malign intent: the party exerting the influence may not intend to cause any detriment to the influenced party, and may believe that the contract which is entered into as a consequence of the influence is justifiable".[446]

(4) The decision by the Court of Appeal in *Aboody*'s case that even in actual undue influence cases the claimant must show manifest disadvantage was overruled by the House of Lords in *C.I.B.C. Mortgages Plc.* v. *Pitt*.[447]

(5) In cases of presumed undue influence the relationship between the parties is thought to give rise to a presumption of undue influence. Cases of presumed undue influence can be divided into two categories.[448] The first category consists of relationships which, as a matter of law, raise the presumption that undue influence has been exercised ("class 2A"). Relationships recognized as such include those between parent and child,[449] solicitor and client[450] and religious adviser and disciple;[451] not recognized as such is the relationship between husband and wife[452] or the normal business relationship between

---

[441] See McKendrick, *Contract* at 367.

[442] See *Bank of Credit and Commerce S.A.* v. *Aboody* [1990] 1 QB 923, 953, *supra* at 471; the classification of cases of undue influence by the Court of Appeal in *Aboody* was adopted by the House of Lords in *Barclays Bank Plc.* v. *O'Brien* [1994] 1 AC 180, 189–90 (speech of Lord Browne-Wilkinson); See McGregor, Contract Code, s. 563.

[443] *Supra*, at 471.

[444] See Treitel, *Contract* at 377; Cartwright, op. cit., at 172–4.

[445] At 17.

[446] See *Aboody*, *supra* at 471, at 968, 970.

[447] [1994] 1 AC 200; see **3.3.5.**, *infra* at 485.

[448] See *Aboody*, *supra* at 471, at 953.

[449] E.g. *Powell* v. *Powell* [1900] 1 Ch. 243.

[450] E.g. *Wright* v. *Carter* [1903] 1 Ch. 27.

[451] E.g. *Allcard* v. *Skinner* (1887) 36 Ch.D 145.

[452] E.g. *Bank of Montreal* v. *Stuart* [1911] AC 120.

bank and customer.[453] The second category involves cases in which the plaintiff shows that there was *de facto* a relationship under which he reposed trust and confidence in the other party ("class 2B").[454]

(6) In cases of presumed undue influence the plaintiff does not have to show that undue influence has been exercised; he does have the obligation, however, of proving manifest disadvantage. In *Aboody*, the Court of Appeal agreed with the explanation of the concept of manifest disadvantage given by the judge of first instance: "a disadvantage would be a manifest disadvantage if it would have been obvious as such to any independent and reasonable persons who considered the transaction at the time with knowledge of all the relevant facts", but "the overall disadvantageous nature of a transaction cannot be said to be manifest, if it only emerges after a fine and close evaluation of its various beneficial and detrimental features. It must be obvious".[455] See *Barclays Bank plc.* v. *Coleman*,[456] where the Court of Appeal held (1) that the fact that the disadvantage must be clear and obvious does not mean that it must be large or even medium-sized, but that it may be small, (2) that an objective view must be taken of it and (3) that that view must be taken as at the date of the conclusion of the contract.

(7) The presumption of undue influence, once it has arisen, may be rebutted by showing that the plaintiff acted independently of any influence. The most usual way of rebutting the presumption is to show that the plaintiff had independent and competent advice before entering into the contract.[457]

(8) An example of "class 2B" undue influence is provided by *Lloyd's Bank Ltd* v. *Bundy*.[458] In that case the defendant was an elderly farmer who was not well versed in business matters. His son formed a plant hire company. Father, son and the company were customers of the same plaintiff bank. The son's company was in financial difficulties. The defendant had already given a guarantee and a charge for £7,500 over his farmhouse (his only asset) to secure the company's overdraft. On that occasion the defendant had been advised by his solicitor that this was the most he could afford to commit to his son's business. The company's affairs got worse and a assistant bank manager and the son went to see the defendant. The assistant manager told the defendant that the bank could allow the company's overdraft to increase only if the defendant increased the guarantee and charge to £11,000. The defendant signed the form of guarantee and charge. There was evidence that the assistant manager knew that the defendant was relying on him for advice and that the house was the defendant's only asset; he did not explain the company's position in full to the defendant. The plaintiff bank proceeded to enforce the charge and sought possession of the farmhouse. The majority of the Court of Appeal decided that the defendant could set aside the charge on the basis of presumed undue influence by the bank. It should have been obvious to the bank that the defendant was trusting the manager to advise him and so a confidential relationship had been shown on the facts. Sir Eric Sachs said:

---

[453] E.g. *National Westminster Bank Plc.* v. *Morgan* [1985] AC 686.

[454] For examples see *Re Craig* [1971] Ch. 95 (in which an elderly widower had employed a young woman as his secretary and companion) and *Lloyd's Bank Ltd.* v. *Bundy* [1975] 1 QB 326, discussed in note 8, *infra*.

[455] At 965.

[456] [2000] 1 All ER 385, 400.

[457] For further details see Treitel, *Contract* at 382; Cartwright, op. cit., at 185–7. See also McGregor, op. cit., s. 563 para. 3 and at 223.

[458] [1975] 1 QB 326; See also **3.3.4.D** at 478.

[O]nce the existence of a special relationship has been established, then any possible use of the relevant influence is, irrespective of the intentions of the persons possessing it, regarded in relation to the transaction under consideration as an abuse—unless and until the duty of fiduciary care has been shown to be fulfilled or the transaction is shown to be truly for the benefit of the person influenced. This approach is a matter of public policy . . .

Having discussed the nature of the issues to which the county court should have directed his mind, it is now convenient to turn to the evidence relating to the first of them—whether the special relationship has here been shown to exist at the material time . . .

The situation was thus one which to any reasonably sensible person, who gave it but a moment's thought, cried aloud Mr Bundy's need for careful independent advice. Over and above the need any man has for counsel when asked to risk his last penny on even an apparently reasonable project, was the need here for informed advice as to whether there was any real change of the company's affairs becoming viable if the documents were signed. If not, there arose questions such as, what is the use of taking the risk of becoming penniless without benefitting ayone but the bank? Is it not better both for you and your son that you, at any rate, should still have some money when the crash comes? Should not the bank at least bind itself to hold its hand for some given period? The answers to such questions could only be given in the light of a worth-while appraisement of the company's affairs—without which Mr Bundy could not come to an informed judgment as to the wisdom of what he was doing.

No such advice to get an independent opinion was given; on the contrary, Mr Head [the assistant bank manager] chose to give his own views on the company's affairs and to take this course, though he had at trial to admit: "I did not explain the company's affairs very fully as I had only just taken over." . . .

On the above recited facts, the breach of the duty to take fiduciary care is manifest.[459]

(9) Undue influence renders a contract voidable,[460] although the courts and legal doctrine tend to speak of "granting relief" or "setting aside the contract".

3.3.4.C. SPECIFIC DOCTRINES: UNCONSCIONABILITY AND OTHER RULES IN ENGLISH LAW

Court of Appeal   3.E.113.
Crédit Lyonnais Bank Nederland NV v. Burch[461]

UNCONSCIONABLE ADVANTAGE-TAKING

The junior employee's flat

For a bank to take as security for a business's debts a charge over a flat belonging to a junior employee of the company with no stake in the business, knowing that the employee had refused to take independent advice, may be unconscionable conduct entitling the employee to set aside the charge.

Facts: The defendant, Miss Burch, had given a guarantee and charged her flat to secure the borrowings of her employer's company. She was a junior employee of the company with no stake in its future. She had been advised by the bank to seek independent advice but had said she had no need of it.

---

[459] Extracts from Lord Denning MR's judgment in this case will be found in **3.3.4.D**, *infra* at 478.
[460] See Cartwright, op. cit., at 192; See also *Restatement of the Law (Second), Contracts 2d*, §177 (2).
[461] [1997] 1 All ER 144.

Held: The charge could be set aside on the ground of undue influence by the employer of which the bank had constructive notice (on this point see below, **3.3.6**). The charge might also have been set aside on the basis of unconscionable conduct by the bank.

Judgment: NOURSE L.J.: On that state of facts it must, I think, have been very well arguable that Miss Burch could, directly against the bank, have had the legal charge set aside as an unconscionable bargain. Equity's jurisdiction to relieve against such transactions, although more rarely exercised in modern times, is at least as venerable as its jurisdiction to relieve against those procured by undue influence. In *Fry* v. *Lane, re Fry, Whittet* v. *Bush* (1889) 40 Ch D 312 at 322, [1886–90] All ER Rep 1084 at 1089, where sales of reversionary interests at considerable undervalues by poor and ignorant persons were set aside, Kay J, having reviewed the earlier authorities, said:

> The result of the decisions is that where a purchase is made from a poor and ignorant man at a considerable undervalue, the vendor having no independent advice, a Court of Equity will set aside the transaction. This will be done even in the case of property in possession, and *a fortiori* if the interest be reversionary. The circumstances of poverty and ignorance of the vendor, and absence of independent advice, throw upon the purchaser, when the transaction is impeached, the onus of proving, in Lord Selbome's words, that the purchase was "fair, just, and reasonable".

Lord Selborne LC's words will be found in *Earl of Aylesford* v. *Morris* (1873) LR 8 Ch App 484 at 491, [1861–73] All ER Rep 300 at 303. The decision of Megarry J in *Cresswell* v. *Potter* [1978] 1 WLR 255 at 257 where he suggested that the modern equivalent of "poor and ignorant" might be a member of the lower income group . . . less highly educated", demonstrates that the jurisdiction is in good heart and capable of adaptation to different transactions entered into in changing circumstances. See also the interesting judgment of Balcombe J in *Backhouse* v *Backhouse* [1978] 1 All ER 1158 at 1165–6, [1978] 1 WLR 243 at 250–252, where he suggested that these cases may come under the general heading which Lord Denning MR referred to in *Lloyds Bank Ltd* v. *Bundy* [1974] 3 All ER 757 at 765, [1975] QB 326 at 339 as "inequality of bargaining power".

A case based on an unconscionable bargain not having been made below, a decision of this court cannot be rested on that ground . . .

Notes

(1) Outside the doctrine of undue influence, equity can give relief against what are often called "unconscionable bargains" in cases in which the one party, being in a strong position, has exploited a weakness of the other party. One category of these cases involves transactions at (considerable) undervalue by poor and ignorant persons[462] and expectant heirs.[463]

(2) So far, the courts have failed to define the basis of their jurisdiction in this area and it is therefore not exactly clear which requirements have to be met if relief is to be granted.[464] Cartwright, however, emphasizes:[465] "that neither an unfair bargain, nor an inequality between the parties' bargaining positions, of themselves, vitiate a contract. What is required is an abuse of that inequality, which may be shown by the existence of an unfair bargain". See Lord Brightman in *Hart* v. *O'Connor*,[466] who held:

---

[462] See e.g. *Fry* v. *Lane* (1888) 40 Ch.D 312; *Cresswell* v. *Potter* [1978] 1 WLR 255.
[463] See e.g. *Earl of Aylesford* v. *Morris* (1873) 8 Ch. App. 484. For the other categories of cases, see Beale, Bishop and Furmston, at 803 ff.
[464] See McKendrick, *Contract* at 372.
[465] Cartwright, op. cit., at 215.
[466] [1985] AC 1000, 1017–18.

Equity will relieve a party from a contract which he has been induced to make as a result of victimisation. Equity will not relieve a party from a contract on the ground only that there is contractual imbalance not amounting to unconscionable dealing.[467]

(3) In *Boustany* v. *Piggott*[468] the Privy Council set aside a lease on the ground of unconscionability. Lord Templeman, delivering the judgment of the Privy Council, agreed in general terms with the submissions of counsel for the appellant:[469] (1) there must be unconscionability in the sense that objectionable terms have been imposed on the weaker party in a reprehensible manner; (2) "unconscionability" refers not only to the unreasonable terms but to the behaviour of the stronger party, which must be morally culpable or reprehensible; (3) unequal bargaining power or objectively unreasonable terms are no basis for interference in equity in the absence of unconscionable or extortionate abuse where, exceptionally and as a matter of common fairness, "it is unfair that the strong should be allowed to push the weak to the wall"; (4) a contract will not be set aside as unconscionable in the absence of actual or constructive fraud or other unconscionable conduct; and (5) the weaker party must show unconscionable conduct, in that the stronger party took unconscientious advantage of the weaker party's disabling condition or circumstances.

(4) In *Crédit Lyonnais Bank Nederland NV* v. *Burch*[470] Millett LJ pointed out that it would be necessary to show that the bank had imposed the objectionable terms in a morally objectionable manner, but said that impropriety might be inferred from the terms of the transaction itself in the absence of an innocent explanation.

(5) English law also has a special rule allowing agreements for salvage to be adjusted if the salvor has charged an extortionate fee: *The Port Caledonia and The Anna*.[471] This rule is not one of Common Law but of Admiralty Law, which in turn came from the Roman *ius commune*.

(6) As noted previously, English legislation allows the re-opening of credit agreements in circumstances which amount to qualified *laesio enormis*: see the Consumer Credit Act 1974, section 137.[472]

3.3.4.D. AN ATTEMPT AT A GENERAL DOCTRINE IN ENGLISH LAW

Court of Appeal   **3.E.114.**
Lloyds Bank v. Bundy[473]

A GENERAL PRINCIPLE OF INEQUALITY OF BARGAINING POWER

Mr. Bundy's farm

For the facts and the decision of the majority of the Court of Appeal, namely that the defendant could set aside the charge on the ground of presumed undue influence by the bank, see above **3.3.4.B**, note 8. Lord Denning

[467] Cf. also *Alec Lobb* v. *Total Oil GB Ltd.* [1985] 1 All ER 303. Equity thus seems to focus primarily on the unconscionable conduct of the stronger party ("procedural unfairness").
[468] (1995) 69 P.& C.R. 298.
[469] At 303.
[470] [1997] 1 All ER 144, 153; see *supra* at 476.
[471] [1903] P 184; in **3.3.4.A**, note 1, at 470.
[472] **3.3.3**, note 4, at 459.
[473] [1975] 1 QB 326.

reached the same conclusion but on broader grounds. What follows here is Lord Denning's attempt to infer from the case law a general principle that English law grants relief in cases of "inequality of bargaining power".

Judgment: LORD DENNING MR:
The general rule

Now let me say at once that in the vast majority of cases a customer who signs a bank guarantee or a charge cannot get out of it. No bargain will be upset which is the result of the ordinary inter-play of forces. There are many hard cases which are caught by this rule. Take the case of a poor man who is homeless. He agrees to pay a high rent to a landlord just to get a roof over his head. The common law will not interfere. It is left to Parliament. Next take the case of a borrower in urgent need of money. He borrows it from the bank at high interest and it is guaranteed by a friend. The guarantor gives his bond and gets nothing in return. The common law will not interfere. Parliament has intervened to prevent moneylenders charging excessive interest. But it has never interfered with banks.

Yet there are exceptions to this general rule. There are cases in our books in which the court will set aside a contract, or a transfer of property, when the parties have not met on equal terms—when the one is so strong in bargaining power and the other so weak—that, as a matter of common fair-ness, it is not right that the strong should be allowed to push the weak to the wall. Hitherto those exceptional cases have been treated each as a separate category in itself. But I think the time has come when we should seek to find a principle to unite them. I put on one side contracts or transac-tions which are voidable for fraud or misrepresentation or mistake. All those are governed by set-tled principles. I go only to those where there has been inequality of bargaining power, such as to merit the intervention of the court.

The categories

The first category is that of "duress of goods." A typical case is when a man is in a strong bar-gaining position by being in possession of the goods of another by virtue of a legal right, such as by way of pawn or pledge or taken in distress. The owner is in a weak position because he is in urgent need of the goods. The stronger demands of the weaker more than is justly due: and he pays it in order to get the goods. Such a transaction is voidable. He can recover the excess: see *Astley* v. *Reynolds* (1731) 2 Stra. 915 and *Green* v. *Duckett* (1883) 11 Q.B.D. 275. To which may be added the cases of "colore officii," where a man is in a strong bargaining position by virtue of his offical position or pub-lic profession. He relies upon it so as to gain from the weaker—who is urgently in need—more than is justly due: see *Pigott's* case cited by Lord Kenyon C.J. in *Cartwright* v. *Rowley* (1799) 2 Esp. 723, 723–724; *Parker* v. *Bristol and Exeter Railway Co.* (1851) 6 Exch. 702 and *Steele* v. *Williams* (1853) 8 Exch. 625. In such cases the stronger may make his claim in good faith honestly believing that he is entitled to make his demand. He may not be guilty of any fraud or misrepresentation. The inequal-ity of bargaining power—the strength of the one versus the urgent need of the other—renders the transaction voidable and the money paid to recovered back: see *Maskell* v. *Horner* (1915) 3 K.B. 106.

The second category is that of the "unconscionable transaction." A man is so placed as to be in need of special care and protection and yet his weakness is exploited by another far stronger than himself so as to get his property at a gross undervalue. The typical case is that of the "expectant heir." But is applies to all cases where a man comes into property transferred to him: see *Evans* v. *Llewellin* (1987) 1 Cox 333. Even though there be no evidence of fraud or misprestation, never-theless the transaction will be set aside: see *Fry* v. *Lane* (1888) 40 Ch.D. 312, 322 where Kay J. said:

> "The result of the decisions is that where a purchase is made from a poor and ignorant man at considerable undervalue, *the vendor having no independent advice*, a court of equity will set aside the transaction".

This second category is said to extend to all cases where an unfair advantage has been gained by an unconscientious use of power by a stronger party against a weaker: see the cases cited in

Halsbury's Laws of England, 3rd ed., vol. 17 (1956), p. 682 and, in Canada, *Morrison* v. *Coast Finance Ltd.* (1965) 55 D.L.R. (2d) 710 and *Knupp* v. *Bell* (1968) 67 D.L.R. (2d), 256. The third category is that of "undue influence" usually so called. These are divided into two classes as stated by Cotton L.J. in *Allcard* v. *Skinner* (1887) 36 Ch.D. 145, 171. The first are those where the stronger has been guilty of some fraud or wrongful act—expressly so as to gain some gift or advantage from the weaker. The second are those where the stronger has not been guilty of any wrongful act, but has, through the relationship which existed between him and the weaker, gained some gift or advantage for himself. Sometimes the relationship is such as to raise a presumption of undue influence, such as parent over child, solicitor over client, doctor over patient, spiritual advisor over follower. At other times a relationship of confidence must be proved to exist. But to all of them the general principle obtains which was stated by Lord Chelmsford L.C. in *Tate* v. *Williamson* (1866) 2 Ch.App. 55, 61:

> "Wherever two persons stand in such a relation that, while it continues, confidence is necessarily reposed by one, and the influence which naturally grows out of that confidence is possessed by the other, and this confidence is abused, or the influence is exerted to obtain an advantage at the expense of the confiding party, the person so availing himself of his position will not be permitted to retain the advantage, although the transaction could not have been impeached if no such confidential relation had existed".

Such a case was *Tufton* v. *Sperni* (1952) 2 T.L.R. 516.

The fourth category is that of "undue pressure." The most apposite of that is *Williams* v. *Bayley* (1866) L.R. 1 H.L. 200, where a son forged his father's name of which they were both customers. The bank said to the father, in effect: "Take your choice—give us security for your son's debt. If you do take that on yourself, then it will all go smoothly: if you do not, we shall be bound to exercise pressure". Thereupon the father charged his property to the bank with payment of the note. The House of Lords held that the charge was invalid because of undue pressure exerted by the bank. Lord Westbury said, at pp. 218–219:

> "A contract to give security for the debt of another, which is a contract without consideration, is above all things, a contract that should be based upon the free and voluntary agency of the individual who enters into it".

Other instances of undue pressure are where one party stipulates for an unfair advantage to which the other has no option but to submit. As where an employer—the stronger party—has employed a builder—the weaker party—to do work for him. When the builder asked for payment of sums properly due (so as to pay his workmen) the employer refused to pay unless he was given some added advantage. Stuart V.-C. said: "Where an agreement, hard and inequitable in itself, has been exacted under circumstances of pressure on the part of the person who exacts it, this court will set it aside": see *Ormes* v. *Beadel* (1860) 2 Giff. 166, 174 (reversed on another ground, 2 De G.F. & J. 333) and *D. & C. Builders Ltd.* v. *Rees* (1966) 2 Q.B. 617, 625.

The fifth category is that of salvage agreements. When a vessel is in danger of sinking and seeks help, the rescuer is in a strong bargaining position. The vessel in distress is in urgent need. The parties cannot be truly said to be on equal terms. The Court of Admiralty have always recognised that fact. The "fundamental rule" is

> "if the parties have made an agreement, the court will enforce it, unless it be manifestly unfair and unjust; but if it be manifestly unfair and unjust, the court will disregard it and decree what is fair and just".

See *Akerblom* v. *Price* (1881) 7 Q.B.D. 129, 133, per Brett L.J., applied in a striking case *The Port Caledonia and The Anna* (1903) P. 184, when the rescuer refused to help with a rope unless he was paid £1,000.

The general principles:

Gathering all together, I would suggest that through all these instances there runs a single thread. They rest on "inequality of bargaining power." By virtue of it, the English law gives relief to one who, without independent advice, enters into a contract upon terms which are very unfair or transfers property for a consideration which is grossly inadequate, when his bargaining power is grievously impaired by reason of his own needs or desires, or by his own ignorance or infirmity, coupled with undue influences or pressures brought to bear on him by or for the benefit of the other. When I use the word "undue" I do not mean to suggest that the principle depends on proof of any wrongdoing. The one who stipulates for an unfair advantage may be moved solely by his own self-interest, unconscious of the distress he is bringing to the other. I have also avoided any reference to the will of the one being "dominated" or "overcome" by the other. One who is in extreme need may knowingly consent to a most improvident bargain, solely to relieve the straits in which he finds himself. Again, I do not mean to suggest that every transaction is saved by independent advice. But the absence of it may be fatal. With these explanations, I hope this principle will be found to reconcile the cases.

Notes

(1) Lord Denning's new doctrine did not find favour with other judges and was rejected by the House of Lords in *National Westminster Bank Plc.* v. *Morgan*.[474] Lord Scarman said:

> Lord Denning MR believed that the doctrine of undue influence could be subsumed under a general principle that English courts will grant relief where there has been "inequality of bargaining power" (p. 339). He deliberately avoided reference to the will of one party being dominated or overcome by another. The majority of the court did not follow him; they based their decision on the orthodox view of the doctrine as expounded in *Allcard* v. *Skinner*, 36 Ch.D. 145. The opinion of the Master of the Rolls, therefore, was not the ground of the court's decision, which was to be found in the view of the majority, for whom Sir Eric Sachs delivered the leading judgment.
>
> Nor has counsel for the respondent sought to rely on Lord Denning MR's general principle: and, in my view, he was right not to do so. The doctrine of undue influence has been sufficiently developed not to need the support of a principle which by its formulation in the language of the law of contract is not appropriate to cover transactions of gift where there has been no bargain. The fact of an unequal bargain will, of course, be a relevant feature in some cases of undue influence. But it can never become an appropriate basis of principle of an equitable doctrine which is concerned with transactions "not to be reasonably accounted for on the ground of friendship, relationship, charity, or other ordinary motives on which men act" (Lindley LJ in *Allcard* v. *Skinner*, at p. 185). And even in the field of contract I question whether there is any need in the modern law to erect a general principle of relief against inequality of bargaining power. Parliament has undertaken the task—and it is essentially a legislative task—of enacting such restrictions upon freedom of contract as are in its judgment necessary to relieve against mischief: for example, the hire-purchase and consumer protection legislation, of which the Supply of Goods (Implied Terms) Act 1973, Consumer Credit Act 1974, Consumer Safety Act 1978, Supply of Goods and Services Act 1982 and Insurance Companies Act 1982 are examples. I doubt whether the courts should assume the burden of formulating further restrictions.

See also Lord Scarman's speech in *Pao On* v. *Lau Yiu Long*.[475] Some authors, on the other hand, have shown not to be dismissive and do seem to favour a general doctrine of inequality of bargaining power or unconscionability.[476] Whether any general doctrine in

---

[474] [1985] 1 AC 687.
[475] [1980] AC 614, 634–5; Treitel, *Contract*, at 384–5.
[476] See e.g. McKendrick, *Contract* at 361–2; D. Capper, "Undue Influence and Unconscionability: a Rationalisation" (1998) 114 LQR 479

this field will be recognized in English law in the near future is uncertain. Until then, English law will pursue its piecemeal treatment of this type of case.[477]

(2) A general doctrine of unconscionability has made its way into Australian and Canadian and American law.[478]

(3) A doctrine of unconscionability, based on the eighteenth century English cases but now very much broader, is well-established in the United States.

Uniform Commercial Code   **3.US.115.**

§2–302: Unconscionable Contract or Clause
(1) If the court as a matter of law finds the contract or any clause of the contract to have been unconscionable at the time it was made the court may refuse to enforce the contract, or it may enforce the remainder of the contract without the unconscionable clause, or it may limit the application of any unconscionable clause as to avoid any unconscionable result . . .

Restatement of the Law (Second), Contracts 2d   **3.US.116.**

§208: Unconscionable Contract or Term
If a contract or term thereof is unconscionable at the time the contract is made a court may refuse to enforce the contract, or may enforce the remainder of the contract without the unconscionable term, or may so limit the application of any unconscionable term as to avoid any unconscionable result . . .

3.3.4.E. INTERNATIONAL RESTATEMENTS

Draft Uniform Law on the Substantive Validity   **3.INT.117.**
of International Contracts for the Sale of Goods
(Max Planck Institut, 1968)

Article 17: Where a person has been induced, as a result of improper exploitation of his personal or business circumstances, to conclude a contract pursuant to which, at the time of its conclusion and performance, there is a marked disparity between the consideration and performance to be respectively provided by the parties, that contract may be avoided on the ground of abuse of the circumstances.

Principles of European Contract Law   **3.PECL.118.**

Article 4:109: *Excessive Benefit or Unfair Advantage*
(1) A party may avoid a contract if, at the time of the conclusion of the contract:
(a) it was dependent on or had a relationship of trust with the other party, was in economic distress or had urgent needs, was improvident, ignorant, inexperienced or lacking in bargaining skill, and

---

[477] See *supra* **3.3.4.C**.

[478] See e.g. Enman, "Doctrines of Unconscionability in Canadian, English and Commonwealth Contract Law" (1987) 16 AALR 191; the Australian case of *Commercial Bank of Australia Ltd.* v. *Amadio* (1983) 151 CLR 447, cited in Beale, Bishop and Furmston, at 807–9.

(b) the other party knew or ought to have known of this and, given the circumstances and purpose of the contract, took advantage of the first party's situation in a way which was grossly unfair or took an excessive benefit . . .

COMMENTS

B. *Weakness or Need Essential*

It would create too much uncertainty if a party could escape from a contract, even if it is disadvantageous to him, when there is no apparent reason why he did not look after his own interests better when agreeing. Relief should only be available when the party can point to some weakness, disability or need on his part to explain what happened. This may include the fact that he had a confidential relationship with the other party and was relying on the other to advise him, if this meant that he was not exercising his own independent judgement.

C. *Knowledge of Party Obtaining Advantage*

It would also create too much uncertainty to upset contracts which are one-sided when there was no reason for the party who gains the advantage to know that the other party was in a weaker position. It is only when he should know that the other party is not in a position to safeguard his own interests that the stronger party should have to have regard to the weaker party's interests.

D. *Excessive Advantage*

The article applies where the advantage gained by one party is demonstrably excessive in comparison to the "normal" price or other return in such contracts. The fact that a shortage of supply has led to generally high prices is not a ground for the application of this Article, even if the sudden price increase has allowed one party to make an abnormally high profit.

Illustration 1: During a sudden cold snap during early summer the price of tomatoes increases dramatically. B agrees to buy tomatoes from A at the increased price. B cannot avoid the contract under this Article even though it discovers that A had bought the tomatoes at a much lower price earlier in the summer and had kept them in cold store.

Where however a party takes advantage of another's ignorance or need to make a particularly one-sided contract, this Article will apply.

Illustration 2: X, an uneducated person with no business experience, is left some property. He is contacted by Y who offers to buy it for a sum much less than it is actually worth, telling X that he must sell quickly or he will lose the chance. X agrees without consulting anyone else. X may avoid the contract.

Illustration 3: U and her family are on holiday abroad when they are involved in a car crash and U's husband is badly hurt. He urgently needs medical treatment which is not locally available. V agrees to take the man by ambulance to the nearest major hospital, charging approximately five times the normal amount for such a journey. U is so worried that she agrees without getting other quotations; she does not discover until later that she has been overcharged. She may obtain relief.

Illustration 4: as the last Illustration. U realises that V is demanding an extortionate price but his is the only ambulance available. She may obtain relief.

Unidroit Principles **3.INT.119.**

Article 3.10: *Gross disparity*

(1) A party may avoid the contract or an individual term of it if, at the time of the conclusion of the contract, the contract or term unjustifiably gave the other party an excessive advantage. Regard is to be had, among other factors, to

483

       (a) the fact that the other party has taken unfair advantage of the first party's
           dependence, economic distress or urgent needs, or of its improvidence, igno-
           rance, inexperience or lack of bargaining skill, and
       (b) (b) the nature and purpose of the contract . . .

Note

It will be seen that the PECL and the UP have some significant differences. Article 3.10
UP may, as argued above,[479] in some cases allow avoidance when there is simple *laesio
enormis*, whereas Article 4:109 PECL is confined to qualified *laesio enormis* in that the
one party must have abused some weakness of the other party's situation. On the other
hand, it seems to be essential for avoidance under Article 3.10 UP that there be excessive
advantage, whereas Article 4:109 PECL requires that the other party took an excessive
benefit *or* took advantage of the one party's situation in a grossly unfair manner. It is
argued below[480] that this formula may have a wider reach than that of Article 3.10 UP.

3.3.4.F. CAUSATION

The undue influence, *"violence morale"* or "abuse of circumstances" exercised by the one
party must have caused the other party to enter into the contract. In French and Dutch
law the general test of causation applied in cases of threat[481] is also applicable in cases of
"violence morale" and "abuse of circumstances". In the case of presumed undue influence, the party presumed to have exercised the influence must show that his conduct did
not cause the contract to be concluded—rebuttal of the presumption. As regards the case
of actual undue influence, the Court of Appeal in *Aboody*[482] held that equity will not give
relief if "on balance of probabilities the complainant would have entered into the transaction in any event".[483] According to Cartwright,[484] however, this does not specify the
test of causation, nor the burden of proof. It could thus be argued that the test of causation applied in cases of duress is also applicable in a case of actual undue influence.

    It seems that in German law causation is not a separate requirement under §138 BGB
(anyhow, it is not discussed as such in the textbooks and commentaries on §138 BGB).
Apparently, for instance in the case of *"Wucher"*, the requirements of *"Ausbeutung"* and
"auffälliges Mißverhältnis" suffice to render a contract contrary to *bonos mores*.

    Also under Article 3.10 UP and Article 4.109 PECL any requirement of causation
appears to be absent which is probably due to the fact that these provisions focus primarily on the excessive nature of the advantage taken by the other party.

3.3.5. OTHER ABUSE OF CIRCUMSTANCES

Can a contract be avoided in a case where the one party has abused the situation in which
the other party found himself, but (a) where the contract is not excessively disadvantageous

---

[479] In **3.3.3**, *supra* at 460.
[480] At 486.
[481] See **3.3.2.D** at 449–50.
[482] **3.3.4.B** at 471.
[483] See **3.3.2.D** at 473.
[484] Cartwright, op. cit., at 188.

to the latter party—i.e. there is no gross disproportion in the mutual performances—or (b) where the disadvantage is of a nature other than financial, or (c) where there is no disadvantage at all?

In Dutch law, a contract may be voidable for abuse of circumstances in the sense of Article 3:44 IV BW.[485] if the one party promotes the conclusion of the contract even though he knows or ought to know that the other party enters into the contract because of the circumstances he finds himself in, which should have prevented the first party from promoting the conclusion of the contract. It is not required that the contract is grossly disadvantageous to the other party. In fact, the Hoge Raad has recently held that disadvantage is not a constituent element whatsoever; see HR 5 February 1999.[486] This decision is in tune with the wording of Article 3:44 IV BW—which does not mention disadvantage, and it could be argued that to require disadvantage is unnecessary because the fact that the consent of the abused party has been constrained by the abuse itself should suffice to render the contract voidable.[487] Even though excessive disadvantage is not a constituent element, it may be taken into account in establishing whether or not the one party should have refrained from promoting the conclusion of the contract—he should have if he knew or ought to have known that the contract is disadvantageous to the other party.[488] In the context of abuse of circumstances, "disadvantage" is to be understood in the broad sense of the word: it not only includes material or financial disadvantage, but also immaterial—subjective—disadvantage.[489] Art. 3:44 IV BW does not give an exhaustive account of the circumstances which may be abused; thus, an abuse of someone's economic dependence may also render the contract voidable.

In English law, the decision by the Court of Appeal in *Aboody's* case[490] that even in actual undue influence cases the claimant must show manifest disadvantage was overruled by the House of Lords in *C.I.B.C. Mortgages Plc.* v. *Pitt*.[491] Lord Browne-Wilkinson said:

My Lords, I am unable to agree with the Court of Appeal's decision in *Aboody*. I have no doubt that the decision in *Morgan* does not extend to cases of actual undue influence. Despite two references in Lord Scarman's speech to cases of actual undue influence, as I read his speech he was primarily concerned to establish that disadvantage had to be shown, not as a constituent element of the cause of action for undue influence, but in order to raise a presumption of undue influence with Class 2. That was the only subject matter before the House of Lords in *Morgan* and the passage I have already cited was directed solely to that point. With the exception of a passing reference to *Ormes* v. *Beadel* (1860) 2 Gif. 166, all the cases referred to by Lord Scarman were cases of presumed undue influence. In the circumstances, I do not think that this House can have been intending to lay down any general principle applicable to all claims of undue influence, whether actual or presumed.

Whatever the merits of requiring a complainant to show manifest disadvantage in order to raise a Class 2 presumption of undue influence, in my judgment there is no logic in imposing such a requirement where actual undue influence has been exercised and proved. Actual undue influence

---

[485] See *supra* at 433.
[486] RvdW 1999, 27.
[487] See Lord Browne-Wilkinson in *Pitt's* case, *supra* at note 447.
[488] See Asser and Hartkamp, op. cit., II, paras. 214–216; see also **3.3.3**, note 2, *supra* at 458.
[489] See HR 29 May 1964, NJ 1965.104; HR 13 June 1975, NJ 1976.98; Asser and Hartkamp, op. cit, II, para. 215.
[490] *Supra* at 471.
[491] [1994] 1 AC 200.

is a species of fraud. Like any other victim of fraud, a person who has been induced by undue influence to carry out a transaction which he did not freely and knowingly enter into is entitled to have that transaction set aside as of right. No case decided before *Morgan* was cited (nor am I aware of any) in which a transaction proved to have been obtained by actual undue influence has been upheld nor is there any case in which a court has even considered whether the transaction was, or was not, advantageous. A man guilty of fraud is no more entitled to argue that the transaction was beneficial to the person defrauded than is a man who has procured a transaction by misrepresentation. The effect of the wrongdoer's conduct is to prevent the wronged party from bringing a free will and properly informed mind to bear on the proposed transaction which accordingly must be set aside in equity as a matter of justice.

I therefore hold that a claimant who proves actual undue influence is not under the further burden of proving that the transaction induced by undue influence was manifestly disadvantageous: he is entitled as of right to have it set aside.

I should add that the exact limits of the decision in *Morgan* may have to be considered in the future. The difficulty is to establish the relationship between the law as laid down in *Morgan* and the long standing principle laid down in the abuse of confidence cases *viz.* the law requires those in a fiduciary position to enter into transactions with those to whom they owe fiduciary duties to establish affirmatively that the transaction was a fair one: see for example *Demerara Bauxite Co. Ltd.* v. *Hubbard* [1923] A.C. 673; *Moody* v. *Cox* [1917] 2 Ch. 71 and the discussion in the *Aboody* case [1990] 1 Q.B. 923, 962–964. The abuse of confidence principle is founded on considerations of general public policy, viz. that in order to protect those to whom fiduciaries owe duties *as a class* from exploitation by fiduciaries *as a class*, the law imposes a heavy duty on fiduciaries to show the righteousness of the transactions they enter into with those to whom they owe such duties. This principle is in sharp contrast with the view of this House in *Morgan* that in cases of presumed undue influence (a) the law is not based on considerations of public policy and (b) that it is for the claimant to prove that the transaction was disadvantageous rather than for the fiduciary to prove that it was not disadvantageous. Unfortunately, the attention of this House in *Morgan* was not drawn to the abuse of confidence cases and therefore the interaction between the two principles (if indeed they are two separate principles) remains obscure: see also "The Limits of Undue Influence", David Tiplady (1985) 48 M.L.R. 579; *Wright* v. *Carter* [1903] 1 Ch. 27.

As to manifest disadvantage not needing to be shown in "abuse of confidence cases",[492] Article 4:109 PECL[493] does not require abuse of circumstances to have resulted in manifest disadvantage in the sense of "excessive benefit", as the Article states that the other party must have taken advantage of the complaining party's situation "in a way which was grossly unfair *or* took an excessive benefit" (emphasis supplied). The Comment states:

E. *Grossly Unfair Advantage*
The Article may apply even if the exchange is not excessively disparate in terms of value for money, if grossly unfair advantage has been taken in other ways. For example, a contract may be unfair to a party who can ill afford it even if the price is not unreasonable.

Illustration 5: X, a widow, lives with her many children in a large but dilapidated house which Y, a neighbour, has long wanted to buy. X has come to rely on Y's advice in business matters. Y is well aware of this and manipulates it to his advantage: he persuades her to sell it to him. He offers her

---

[492] See also McKendrick, *Contract* at 358, and Comment *b* to §177, *Restatement of the Law (Second), Contracts 2d* (the unfairness of the transaction is only a factor to be taken into account in determining whether there was unfair persuasion but it is not in itself "controlling").
[493] *Supra* at 482.

the market price but without pointing out to her that she will find it impossible to find anywhere else to live in the neighbourhood for that amount of money. X may avoid the contract.

3.3.6. THREATS OR ABUSE OF CIRCUMSTANCES BY THIRD PERSONS

Can a contract between A and B be avoided on the ground that B entered into the contract under a threat or abuse of circumstances exercised by C, a third person who is not a party to the contract?

French Civil Code **3.F.120.**

Article 1111: Any threat brought to bear against the party who has contracted the obligation shall constitute a ground of nullity, even where it has been brought to bear by a party other than the party for whose benefit the agreement was made.

Note

In French law, B may avoid a contract on the ground of *"violence (morale)"* exercised by C, regardless of whether A was in good faith, i.e. whether A knew or ought to have known of the threat or abuse by C. See Article 1111 CC;[494] Article 1268 of the Spanish CC; Article 1434 of the Italian CC. Also in German law, B is entitled to avoid the contract in a case where C exerted a threat, even though A was in good faith.[495] The position taken by French and German law is explained by Kötz:[496]

German law and the Romanistic systems regard the contractor's will as more strongly vitiated by duress than by deceit, so allow avoidance even as against a party in good faith.

However, in BGH, NJW 1994, 1341, 1343, in which case a father (C) had acted *contra bonos mores* by having his daughter (B) provide security for his debts in favour of a bank (A), the Bundesgerichtshof held that the guarantee (*"Bürgschaft"*) may be void under § 138(1) BGB if the bank knew that the main debtor had *contra bonos mores* and illegally influenced the personal guarantee or if the bank had in full knowledge endorsed such behaviour.

Swiss Code of Obligations **3.CH.121.**

Article 29: (2) Where the threat is issued by a third party and the threatened party does not wish to keep to the contract, the latter shall, in so far as may be consistent with principles of fairness, compensate the other party to the contract if that other party neither knew nor should have known of the threat.

Note

Swiss law also entitles B to avoid the contract even if A was in good faith. In that case, however, B must compensate A for his reliance damages if equity so requires.[497] The same rule seems to apply in Greek law.[498]

---

[494] See Terré, Simler and Lequette, para. 238; Ghestin at 567; Nicholas at 108.
[495] See Palandt-Heinrichs, under § 123 BGB, para. 3 (with reference to BGH, NJW 1966.2399); Larenz, *AT* at 701.
[496] Kötz, *European Contract Law*, at 213.
[497] See von Tuhr and Peter, *Allgemeiner Teil des Schweizerischen Obligationenrechts*, Vol. I, 2nd edn. (Zürich: 1979) at 328–9.
[498] See Stathopoulos, *Contract Law in Hellas* (Deventer: Kluwer, 1995) at 107.

Article 3:44: (5) If a declaration has been made as a result of threat, fraud or abuse of circumstances on the part of a person who is not party to the juridical act, this defect cannot be invoked against a party to the juridical act who had no reason to assume its existence.

Note
Under Article 3:44 V BW, B is not entitled to avoid the contract if A was in good faith. To the same effect, §875 ABGB.[499] The rule laid down in Article 3:44 V BW applies to cases of threat as well as abuse of circumstances by C.

House of Lords **3.E.123.**
Barclays Bank plc v. *O'Brien*[500]

CONSTRUCTIVE NOTICE

Matrimonial home

A creditor which takes a security from a surety whom he knows is in a relationship with his debtor such that undue influence or some other wrong is a substantial risk, and where the giving of the security is on its face not to the surety's financial advantage, will be treated as having constructive notice of any misrepresentation or undue influence by the debtor unless the creditor has warned the surety to take independent advice.

Facts: The defendants, Mr and Mrs O'Brien, who were husband and wife, agreed to execute a mortgage of their matrimonial home as security for overdraft facilities extended by the plaintiff bank to the husband's company. The branch manager of the bank had sent the documents to another branch with the instruction to make sure that both defendants were fully aware of the nature of the documents and that, if in doubt, they should consult their solicitor before signing. This instruction was neglected and the wife signed without reading the document. She relied on her husband's false representation that the security was limited to £60,000 and would last only three weeks. When the company's overdraft exceeded £154,000 the bank sought to enforce the security. The wife claimed the avoidance as against the bank of the security transaction on the ground of the misrepresentation by her husband.

Held: The wife's appeal was dismissed by the judge in first instance, but allowed by the Court of Appeal. The House of Lords dismissed the bank's appeal holding that, given the circumstances of the case (see below), the bank had had constructive notice of the husband's misrepresentation.

Judgment: LORD BROWNE-WILKINSON:
"*Undue influence, misrepresentation and third parties*
Up to this point I have been considering the right of a claimant wife to set aside a transaction as against the wrongdoing husband when the transaction has been procured by his undue influence. But in surety cases the decisive question is whether the claimant wife can set aside the transaction, not against the wrongdoing husband, but against the creditor bank. Of course, if the wrongdoing husband is acting as agent for the creditor bank in obtaining the surety from the wife, the creditor will be fixed with the wrongdoing of its own agent and the surety contract can be set aside as against the creditor. Apart from this, if the creditor bank has notice, actual or constructive, of the undue influence exercised by the husband (and consequentially of the wife's equity to set aside the transaction)

[499] See Koziol and Welser, *Grundriß des bürgerlichen Rechts*, Vol. I, 10th edn. (Wien: Mainz, 1995) at 137.
[500] [1994] 1 AC 180.

the creditor will take subject to that equity and the wife can set aside the transaction against the creditor (albeit a purchaser for value) as well as against the husband: see *Bainbrigge* v. *Browne* (1881) 18 Ch. D. 188 and *Bank of Credit and Commerce International S.A.* v. *Aboody* [1990] 1 Q.B. 923, 973. Similarly, in cases such as the present where the wife has been induced to enter into the transaction by the husband's misrepresentation, her equity to set aside the transaction will be enforceable against the creditor if either the husband was acting as the creditor's agent or the creditor had actual or constructive notice.

[Lord Browne-Wilkinson then discussed cases decided on the basis of a "special equity" in favour of wives derived from the Privy Council case of *Turnbull* v. *Duval* [1902] AC 429]

Conclusions
Wives . . .

In my judgment, if the doctrine of notice is properly applied, there is no need for the introduction of a special equity in these types of cases. A wife who has been induced to stand as a surety for her husband's debts by his undue influence, misrepresentation or some other legal wrong has an equity as against him to set aside that transaction. Under the ordinary principles of equity, her right to set aside that transaction will be enforceable against third parties (e.g. against a creditor) if either the husband was acting as the third party's agent or the third party had actual or constructive notice of the facts giving rise to her equity. Although there may be cases where, without artificiality, it can properly be held that the husband was acting as the agent of the creditor in procuring the wife to stand as surety, such cases will be of very rare occurrence. The key to the problem is to identify the circumstances in which the creditor will be taken to have had notice of the wife's equity to set aside the transaction . . .

Therefore, in my judgment a creditor is put on inquiry when a wife offers to stand surety for her husband's debts by the combination of two factors: (a) the transaction is on its face not to the financial advantage of the wife; and (b) there is a substantial risk in transactions of that kind that, in procuring the wife to act as surety, the husband has committed a legal or equitable, wrong that entitles the wife to set aside the transaction.

It follows that, unless the creditor who is put on inquiry takes reasonable steps to satisfy himself that the wife's agreement to stand surety has been properly obtained, the creditor will have constructive notice of the wife's rights.

What, then are the reasonable steps which the creditor should take to ensure that it does not have constructive notice of the wife's rights, if any? Normally the reasonable steps necessary to avoid being fixed with constructive notice consist of making inquiry of the person who may have the earlier right (ic the wife) to see if whether such right is asserted. It is plainly impossible to require of banks and other financial institutions that they should inquire of one spouse whether he or she has been unduly influenced or misled by the other. But in my judgment the creditor, in order to avoid being fixed with constructive notice, can reasonably be expected to take steps to bring home to the wife the risk she is running by standing as surety and to advise her to take independent advice. As to past transactions, it will depend on the facts of each case whether the steps taken by the creditor satisfy this test. However for the future in my judgment a creditor will have satisfied these requirements if it insists that the wife attend a private meeting (in the absence of the husband) with a representative of the creditor at which she is told of the extent of her liability as surety, warned of the risk she is running and urged to take independent legal advice. If these steps are taken in my judgment the creditor will have taken such reasonable steps as are necessary to preclude a subsequent claim that it had constructive notice of the wife's rights. I should make it clear that I have been considering the ordinary case where the creditor knows only that the wife is to stand surety for her husband's debts. I would not exclude exceptional cases where a creditor has knowledge of further facts which render the presence of undue influence not only possible but probable. In such cases, the creditor to be safe will have to insist that the wife is separately advised . . .

Other persons

I have hitherto dealt only with the position where a wife stands surety for her husband's debts. But in my judgment the same principles are applicable to all other cases where there is an emotional relationship between cohabitees. The "tenderness" shown by the law to married women is not based on the marriage ceremony but reflects the underlying risk of one cohabitee exploiting the emotional involvement and trust of the other. Now that unmarried cohabitation, whether heterosexual or homosexual, is widespread in our society, the law should recognise this. Legal wives are not the only group which are now exposed to the emotional pressure of cohabitation. Therefore if, but only if, the creditor is aware that the surety is cohabiting with the principal debtor, in my judgment the same principles should apply to them as apply to husband and wife.

In addition to the cases of cohabitees, the decision of the Court of Appeal in *Avon Finance Co Ltd* v. *Bridger* [1985] 2 All ER 281 shows (rightly in my view) that other relationships can give rise to a similar result. In that case a son, by means of misrepresentation, persuaded his elderly parents to stand surety for his debts. The surety obligation was held to be unenforceable by the creditor inter alia because to the bank's knowledge the parents trusted the son in their financial dealings. In my judgment that case was rightly decided: in a case where the creditor is aware that the surety reposes trust and confidence in the principal debtor in relation to his financial affairs, the creditor is put on inquiry in just the same way as it is in relation to husband and wife.

Summary

I can therefore summarise my views as follows. Where one cohabitee has entered into an obligation to stand as surety for the debts of the other cohabitee and the creditor is aware that they are cohabitees: (1) the surety obligation will be valid and enforceable by the creditor unless the suretyship was procured by the undue influence, misrepresentation or other legal wrong of the principal debtor; (2) if there has been undue influence, misrepresentation or other legal wrong by the principal debtor, unless the creditor has taken reasonable steps to satisfy himself that the surety entered into the obligation freely and in knowledge of the true facts, the creditor will be unable to enforce the surety obligation because he will be fixed with constructive notice of the surety's right to set aside the transaction; (3) unless there are special exceptional circumstances, a creditor will have taken such reasonable steps to avoid being fixed with constructive notice if the creditor warns the surety (at a meeting not attended by the principal debtor) of the amount of her potential liability and of the risks involved and advises the surety to take independent legal advice. . . .

The decision of this case

Applying those principles to this case, to the knowledge of the bank Mr and Mrs O'Brien were man and wife . . .

Unfortunately Mr Tucker's [the branch manager of the bank] instructions were not followed and to the knowledge of the bank (through the clerk at the Burnham branch) Mrs O'Brien signed the documents without any warning of the risks or any recommendation to take legal advice. In the circumstances the bank (having failed to take reasonable steps) is fixed with constructive notice of the wrongful misrepresentation made by Mr O'Brien to Mrs O'Brien. Mrs O'Brien is therefore entitled as against the bank to set aside the legal charge on the matrimonial home securing her husband's liability to the bank.

For these reasons I would dismiss the appeal with costs.

[The other members of the House agreed.]

Notes

(1) In English law, in a case where undue influence has been exerted by C, equity will not grant relief to B against A, if A, at the moment of conclusion of the contract, was in

good faith and gave value.[501] As a general rule, equity will grant relief, however, if A had actual or constructive "notice"—knowledge—of the undue influence exercised by C, or if C acted as an "agent" for A. See for example *Bank of Credit and Commerce International S.A.* v. *Aboody*.[502] The above cited case of *O'Brien* elaborates and extends the point of constructive knowledge.

(2) In *C.I.B.C. Mortgages Plc.* v. *Pitt*,[503] which was heard with *O'Brien's* case, the husband had exercised undue influence. Although the court held that in a case of actual undue influence it was not necessary for the claimant to show manifest disadvantage in order to be able to set aside a transaction as against the party (her husband) who had used the undue influence, the position *vis-à-vis* the bank was different. The bank would be put on notice, and therefore would have to give a warning, only if the arrangement on its face appeared to be disadvantageous to her. In that case the arrangement was a loan to the husband and wife. In fact the husband used the money for speculating on the stock market, but on its face it was a loan to the couple to enable them to buy a holiday home, so it was apparently advantageous to the wife. For a case of undue influence by an employer over his employee and where constructive notice of the bank was accepted along the lines set out in *O'Brien*, see *Crédit Lyonnais Bank Nederland NV* v. *Burch*;[504] contrast *Barclays Bank plc.* v. *Coleman*.[505]

(3) *O'Brien* was a case of misrepresentation by the husband, *Pitt* one of undue influence. In a case of duress exercised by C, B may avoid the contract if he proves that A knew or had constructive notice of the duress.[506]

Draft Uniform Law on the Substantive Validity   **3.INT.124.**
of International Contracts for the Sale of Goods
(Max Planck Institut, 1968)

Article 18: (2) Paragraph (1) shall apply *mutatis mutandis* where the threat for which the other party to the contract is responsible is issued by a third party.
(3) Where the threat is issued by a third party for whose acts the other party to the contract is not responsible, the threatened party may avoid the contract. However, if the other party to the contract neither knew nor should have known of the threat, the threatened party must compensate him in accordance with the principles of fairness.

Note
This draft takes the same position as Swiss and Greek law.[507]

---

[501] See e.g. *Coldunell Ltd.* v. *Gallon* [1986] QB 1184; Treitel, *Contract* at 386–7.
[502] [1989] 1 QB 923, 971–3; See *supra* at **3.3.4.B**.
[503] [1994] 1 AC 200.
[504] [1997] 1 All ER 144, **3.3.4.C.** *supra* at 476.
[505] [2000] 1 All ER 385. See further Treitel, *Contract* at 386–9; Cartwright, op. cit., at 188–92. See also *Restatement of the Law (Second), Contracts 2d*, §177 (3) and Comment c.
[506] E.g. *Talbot* v. *Von Boris* [1911] 1 KB 854; *Kesarmal s/o Letchman Das* v. *Valliappa Chettiar (N.K.V.) s/o Nagappa Chettiar* [1954] 1 WLR 380; see also *Restatement of the Law (Second), Contracts 2d*, §175 (2), Comment *e* and Illustrations 10 and (110), or if the conditions laid down in *O'Brien's* case are satisfied.
[507] See *supra* at 487.

Article 4:111: *Third Persons*
> (1) Where a third person for whose acts a party is responsible, or who with a party's assent, is involved in the making of a contract:
>> (a) causes a mistake by giving information, or knows of or ought to have known of a mistake,
>> (b) gives incorrect information,
>> (c) commits fraud,
>> (d) makes a threat, or
>> (e) takes excessive benefit or unfair advantage,
>
> remedies under this Chapter will be available under the same conditions as if the behaviour or knowledge had been that of the party itself.
> (2) Where any other third person:
>> (a) gives incorrect information,
>> (b) commits fraud,
>> (c) makes a threat, or
>> (d) takes excessive benefit or unfair advantage,
>
> remedies under this Chapter will be available if the party knew or ought to have known of the relevant facts, or at the time of avoidance it has not acted in reliance on the contract.

Notes

(1) Article 4:111 PECL—and Article 3.11 UP, which is a very similar provision—appears to be influenced by Anglo-American law as it makes a distinction between cases where A is responsible for C—C acting as an "agent" for A—and cases where A is not responsible for C.[508]

(2) For cases in which the party is not responsible for the third person the PECL comment:

B. *Remedies Where Fraud, etc. by a Third Person for Whom Party is not Responsible.*
A party cannot be fixed with the consequences of improper or careless behaviour of a third person for whom it is not responsible and who does not fall into the other categories mentioned in Comment A. But it should not be allowed to enforce a contract which it knows or should know was concluded only through such behaviour by a third person, if, had it behaved in the same way itself, the other party to the contract could have a remedy under the provisions of this chapter.

Illustration 2: A bank lends money to a husband's business on the strength of a charge, signed by the wife, over the family home. The charge is very much against the wife's interest and the husband has procured the wife's signature by duress. The bank ought to know that it is most unlikely that the wife would sign voluntarily and the bank cannot enforce the charge. It should have made enquiries to ensure that the wife was acting freely.

The party should also be liable for damages under Article 4:117 if it knows of the ground for avoidance, or if it knows that the other party has been given incorrect information by a third person but does not inform the other party that the information is incorrect.

(3) Also, the element of reliance in Article 4:111 PECL (and paragraph (2) of Article 3.11 UP) appears to be borrowed from American law.[509] According to Comment 2 to

---

[508] Cf. *supra* and *Restatement of the Law (Second), Contracts 2d*, §175 (2), Comment e.
[509] See *Restatement of the Law (Second), Contracts 2d*, §175 (2) and §177 (3).

Article 3.11(2) UP, the exception to the rule that B may avoid the contract only if A is in good faith, is justified because if A has not acted in reliance on the contract, A does not need protection.

Further Readings
—C. Asser and A. Hartkamp, *Verbintenissenrecht*, Vol. I, 11th edn. (Zwolle: 2000);
—C. Asser and A. Hartkamp, *Verbintenissenrecht*, Vol. II, 10th edn. (Zwolle: 2001);
—P. Atiyah, "Economic Duress and the 'Overborne Will'" (1982) 98 LQR 197;
—P. Birks, *An Introduction to the Law of Restitution* (Oxford: Clarendon, 1994);
—D. Capper, "Undue Influence and Unconscionability: A Rationalisation" (1998) 114 LQR 479;
—J. Cartwright, *Unequal Bargaining. A Study of Vitiating Factors in the Formation of Contracts* (Oxford: Clarendon, 1991);
—H. Beale (gen. ed.), *Chitty on Contracts*, 28th edn. (London: Sweet & Maxwell, 1999);
—J. P. Dawson, "Economic Duress—An Essay in Perspective", 45 Mich.LR 253 (1947);
—L. Díez-Picazo and A. Gullón, *Sistema de derecho civil*, Vol. II, 7th edn. (Madrid: 1995);
—U. Drobnig, "Substantive Validity" (1992) 40 AJCL 634;
—S. E. Enman, "Doctrines of Unconscionability in Canadian, English and Commenwealth Contract Law" (1987) 16 AALR 191;
—M. Fabre-Magnan, "Defects of Consent in Contract Law" in *Towards a European Civil Code*, at 219;
—W. Flume, *Allgemeneier Teil des Bürgerlichen Rechts*, Vol. II: Das Rechtsgeschäft, 4th edn. (Berlin: 1992);
—J. Ghestin, *Traité de droit civil—La formation du contrat*, 3rd edn. (Paris: LGDJ, 1993);
—J. Herbots, *Contract Law in Belgium* (Brussels: Bruylant,1995);
—H. Koziol and R. Welser, *Grundriß des bürgerlichen Rechts*, Vol. I, 10th edn. (Wien: Mainz, 1995);
—H. Köhler, *BGB. Allgemeiner Teil*, 23rd edn. (München: Beck, 1996);
—H. Kötz and A. Flessner, *European Contract Law*, Vol. I, transl. by T. Weir (Oxford: Clarendon, 1997);
—K. Larenz and M. Wolf, *Allgemeiner Teil des bürgerlichen Rechts*, 8th edn. (München: Beck, 1997);
—Ph. Malaurie and L. Aynès, *Cours de droit civil—Les obligations*, 10th edn. (Paris: Cujas, 1999)
—Ph. Malaurie, L. Aynès and P.-Y. Gautier, *Contrats Spéciaux*, 13th edn. (Paris: Cujas, 1999);
—G. Marty and P. Raynaud, *Les obligations*, 2nd edn. (Paris: Dalloz, 1988);
—H. McGregor, *Contract Code (Drawn up on behalf of the English Law Commission)*, (London: 1994);
—E. McKendrick, *Contract Law*, 4th edn. (Basingstoke: Macmillan, 2000);
—B. Nicholas, *The French Law of Contract*, 2nd edn (Oxford: Clarendon, 1992);
—Max Planck Institut, *Die materielle Gültigkeit von Kaufverträgen. Ein rechtsvergleichender Bericht* (Berlin/Tübingen: 1968);

—H. Soergel and W. Hefermehl, *Bürgerliches Gesetzbuch*, Vol. I: *Allgemeiner Teil* (Stuttgart: 1987);

—M. P. Stathopoulos, *Contract Law in Hellas* (Deventer: Kluwer, 1995);

—F. Terré, Ph. Simler and Y. Lequette, *Droit civil—Les obligations*, 5th edn. (Paris: Dalloz, 1996);

—G. Treitel, *The Law of Contract*, 10th edn. (London: Sweet & Maxwell, 1999);

—A. von Tuhr and H. Peter, Allgemeiner Teil des Schweizerischen Obligationenrechts, Vol. I, 2nd edn. (Zürich: 1979);

—R. Zimmermann, *The Law of Obligations. Roman Foundations of the Civilian Tradition* (Oxford: Clarendon, 1993);

—K. Zweigert *et al.* "Der Entwurf eines einheitlicen Gesetzes über die materielle Gültigkeit internationaler Kaufverträge über bewegliche Sachen" (1968) 32 RabelsZ 201;

—K. Zweigert and H. Kötz, *Introduction to Comparative Law*, 3rd edn., transl. by T. Weir (Oxford: Clarendon, 1998).

3.4. UNFAIR CLAUSES

3.4.1. INTRODUCTION

The principle of "freedom of contract" has traditionally been of paramount importance in the different countries considered in this casebook, but it no longer has an exclusive hold over the law of contract across Europe. Since the 1960s, and perhaps earlier, contract law has been seen to reflect a new principle, described by Zweigert and Kötz as "contractual justice".[510] Contractual justice is not confined to *procedural* fairness (the way in which the conclusion of the contract took place), but also relates to *substantive* fairness—the very content of the contract.[511]

Central to the development of "contractual justice" has been the recognition of particular forms of protection for consumers, and this has functioned as a catalyst for the development of more profound controls on unfair contract terms. One of the most obvious ways to foster contractual justice is the protection of a contracting party against unfair clauses, and particularly *exclusion* and *limitation* clauses. Exclusion (sometimes called *exemption*) clauses and limitation clauses are terms of a contract which *exclude* some right which one of the parties would otherwise have had under the law, or which *reduce* the remedies available to him.[512] The need for control is particularly pressing when these contractual provisions are part of "standard term" contracts which have not been negotiated by the parties in the particular case.

[510] Zweigert and Kötz, at 331.

[511] See von Mehren, *International Encyclopedia of Comparative Law*, op. cit., 1982, Vol. VII: *Contracts in General*, chapter 1, at 72.

[512] See for a survey of the different clauses: BBF3 at 837–8.

In order to control contract terms, the courts used, at least until recently, a number of general doctrines of private law. First, the doctrine of "offer and acceptance" has been used, whereby a party is required to show that the (standard) terms in question have been incorporated into the contract in the particular case.[513] Secondly, an unfair clause may be vitiated by misrepresentation, duress or undue influence.[514] Thirdly, the courts in some countries have developed doctrines to prevent such clauses applying where a contract has been breached in a particular way.[515] Fourthly, rules of construction can be used, for example the rule that ambiguous clauses are to be construed against the party putting them forward (the *contra preferentem* rule).[516] Finally, the content of a contract term may conflict with "public policy", "good morals" or "reasonableness and equity", and may therefore be inapplicable.[517]

However, more overt forms of review of unfair terms have also developed in both the Civil Law and Common Law countries. Originally, in several Civil Law jurisdictions (such as Germany and the Netherlands), the general requirement of contractual "good faith" was invoked as the basis of review. Today, the review of unfair contract terms is based upon specific statutory provisions. Indeed, since 1993, a European Community directive has provided for common standards across the Community in the control of unfair terms in consumer contracts. Thus, in contrast to the other parts of this casebook, this section deals to a large extent with statutory materials.[518] However, the general doctrines discussed above remain applicable in this context, and are of particular importance when the statutory rules do not apply (for example, where the subject-matter of the contract or the status of the parties involved takes it outside the statutory schemes).

This section follows a more or less historical sequence, starting with the "indirect" controls through the general law; then considering selected national legislation; next, the impact of the Directive on Unfair Terms in Consumer Contracts; and, finally, compares some key features of the protection now available against unfair terms in the different countries studied. The section thus traces the development of controls on unfair contract terms in Europe, and shows that there was in fact considerable convergence between the different systems even before the European Directive was introduced.

---

[513] See **3.4.2.A**, *infra* at 496 ff.
[514] See **3.4.2.B**, *infra* at 502 ff.
[515] See **3.4.2.C**, *infra* at 502 ff.
[516] See **3.4.2.D**, *infra* at 505 ff. and also chap. 4, *infra* at 568 ff.
[517] See **3.4.2.E**, *infra* at 509 ff.
[518] See for a survey of legislative developments with regard to unfair contract terms in consumer transactions before the harmonisation in the EC by the directive: Hondius, *Unfair Terms in Consumer Contracts* (Utrecht: 1987).

3.4.2. CONTROLS UNDER THE GENERAL LAW

3.4.2.A. INCORPORATION TESTS

Court of Appeal **3.E.126.**

Interfoto Picture Library Ltd v. *Stiletto Visual Programmes Ltd*[519]

REASONABLE NOTICE

Unusual charges for keeping pictures

A party who wishes to rely on a clause in standard conditions of contract which have not been signed by the other party must give the other reasonable notice of the existence of the terms at or before the time the contract is made and, if the term is unusual or onerous, must take steps to bring the particular term to the other party's attention.

Facts: The plaintiffs ran a photographic transparency lending library. Following a telephone inquiry by the defendants, the plaintiffs delivered to them 47 transparencies together with a delivery note containing nine printed conditions. Condition 2 stipulated that all the transparencies had to be returned within 14 days of delivery otherwise a holding fee of £5 a day plus VAT would be charged for each transparency retained thereafter. The defendants, who had not used the plaintiffs' services before, did not read the conditions and returned the transparencies four weeks later whereupon the plaintiffs invoiced the defendants for £3,783.50. The defendants refused to pay and the plaintiffs brought an action to recover that sum. The judge gave judgment in favour of the plaintiffs for the amount claimed.

Held: Allowing the appeal, the Court of Appeal held that the plaintiffs were not entitled to rely on Condition 2 of the contract because (per DILLON LJ) Condition 2 had never been made a term of the contract or (per BINGHAM LJ) the defendants were relieved of any liability under the clause. The plaintiff was therefore entitled only to an award assessed quantum meruit.

Judgment: DILLON LJ: . . . There was never any oral discussion of terms between the parties before the contract was made. In particular there was no discussion whatever of terms in the original telephone conversation when Mr. Beeching made his preliminary inquiry. The question is therefore whether condition 2 was sufficiently brought to the defendants' attention to make it a term of the contract which was only concluded after the defendants had received, and must have known that they had received, the transparencies and the delivery note.

This sort of question was posed, in relation to printed conditions, in the ticket cases, such as *Parker* v. *South Eastern Railway Co.* (1877) 2 C.P.D. 416, in the last century. At that stage the printed conditions were looked at as a whole and the question considered by the courts was whether the printed conditions as a whole had been sufficiently drawn to a customer's attention to make the whole set of conditions part of the contract; if so the customer was bound by the printed conditions even though he never read them.

More recently the question has been discussed whether it is enough to look at a set of printed conditions as a whole. When for instance one condition in a set is particularly onerous does something special need to be done to draw customers' attention to that particular condition? In an obiter dictum in *J. Spurling Ltd.* v. *Bradshaw* [1956] 1 W.L.R. 461, 466 (cited in Chitty on Contracts, 25th ed. (1983), vol. 1, p. 408) Denning L.J. stated:

> "Some clauses which I have seen would need to be printed in red ink on the face of the document with a red hand pointing to it before the notice could be held to be sufficient."

[519] [1989] QB 433.

Then in *Thornton* v. *Shoe Lane Parking Ltd.* [1971] 2 Q.B. 163 both Lord Denning MR and Megaw LJ held as one of their grounds of decision, as I read their judgments, that where a condition is particularly onerous or unusual the party seeking to enforce it must show that that condition, or an unusual condition of that particular nature, was fairly brought to the notice of the other party. . . . [W]hat their Lordships said was said by way of interpretation and application of the general statement of the law by Mellish LJ in *Parker* v. *South Eastern Railway Co.*, 2 C.P.D. 416, 423–424 and the logic of it is applicable to any particularly onerous clause in a printed set of conditions of the one contracting party which would not be generally known to the other party.

Condition 2 of these plaintiffs' conditions is in my judgment a very onerous clause. The defendants could not conceivably have known, if their attention was not drawn to the clause, that the plaintiffs were proposing to charge a "holding fee" for the retention of the transparencies at such a very high and exorbitant rate.

At the time of the ticket cases in the last century it was notorious that people hardly ever troubled to read printed conditions on a ticket or delivery note or similar document. That remains the case now. In the intervening years the printed conditions have tended to become more and more complicated and more and more one-sided in favour of the party who is imposing them, but the other parties, if they notice that there are printed conditions at all, generally still tend to assume that such conditions are only concerned with ancillary matters of form and are not of importance . . .

In the present case, nothing whatever was done by the plaintiffs to draw the defendants' attention particularly to condition 2; it was merely one of four columns' width of conditions printed across the foot of the delivery note. Consequently condition 2 never, in my judgment, became part of the contract between the parties.

BINGHAM LJ: In many civil law systems, and perhaps in most legal systems outside the common law world, the law of obligations recognises and enforces an overriding principle that in making and carrying out contracts parties should act in good faith. This does not simply mean that they should not deceive each other, a principle which any legal system must recognise; its effect is perhaps most aptly conveyed by such metaphorical colloquialisms as "playing fair," "coming clean" or "putting one's cards face upwards on the table." It is in essence a principle of fair and open dealing. In such a forum it might, I think, be held on the facts of this case that the plaintiffs were under a duty in all fairness to draw the defendants' attention specifically to the high price payable if the transparencies were not returned in time and, when the 14 days had expired, to point out to the defendants the high cost of continued failure to return them.

English law has, characteristically, committed itself to no such overriding principle but has developed piecemeal solutions in response to demonstrated problems of unfairness. Many examples could be given. Thus equity has intervened to strike down unconscionable bargains. Parliament has stepped in to regulate the imposition of exemption clauses and the form of certain hire-purchase agreements. The common law also has made its contribution, by holding that certain classes of contract require the utmost good faith, by treating as irrecoverable what purport to be agreed estimates of damage but are in truth a disguised penalty for breach, and in many other ways.

The well known cases on sufficiency of notice are in my view properly to be read in this context. At one level they are concerned with a question of pure contractual analysis, whether one party has done enough to give the other notice of the incorporation of a term in the contract. At another level they are concerned with a somewhat different question, whether it would in all the circumstances be fair (or reasonable) to hold a party bound by any conditions or by a particular condition of an unusual and stringent nature . . .

The tendency of the English authorities has, I think, been to look at the nature of the transaction in question and the character of the parties to it; to consider what notice the party alleged to be bound was given of the particular condition said to bind him; and to resolve whether in all the circumstances it is fair to hold him bound by the condition in question. This may yield a result not very different from the civil law principle of good faith, at any rate so far as the formation of the contract is concerned . . .

The crucial question in the case is whether the plaintiffs can be said fairly and reasonably to have brought condition 2 to the notice of the defendants. . . . In my opinion the plaintiffs did not do so. They delivered 47 transparencies, which was a number the defendants had not specifically asked for. Condition 2 contained a daily rate per transparency after the initial period of 14 days many times greater than was usual or (so far as the evidence shows) heard of. For these 47 transparencies there was to be a charge for each day of delay of £235 plus value added tax. The result would be that a venial period of delay, as here, would lead to an inordinate liability. The defendants are not to be relieved of that liability because they did not read the condition, although doubtless they did not; but in my judgment they are to be relieved because the plaintiffs did not do what was necessary to draw this unreasonable and extortionate clause fairly to their attention. I would accordingly allow the defendants' appeal and substitute for the judge's award the sum which he assessed upon the alternative basis of quantum meruit.

Notes

(1) The "reasonable notice test" was laid down by the Court of Appeal in *Parker* v. *South Eastern Railway Co Ltd.*[520] It is not sufficient that the plaintiff knew that there was writing on a ticket or notice (in that case, a ticket was given when luggage was deposited in a left-luggage office and a notice was located outside the office); according to the majority,[521] he must know or have been given reasonable notice that the writing contained conditions. Thus, if the plaintiff might reasonably have thought that a ticket given to him was simply a receipt for his payment, he is not bound by terms in the ticket: see *Chapelton* v. *Barry UDC*[522] (P was given a ticket when he hired a deck-chair; he was not bound by the conditions on the ticket). The *Interfoto* case confirmed earlier suggestions that it may not suffice to give the plaintiff general notice that the contract contains conditions; if the conditions contain any term which is particularly onerous, the plaintiff may have to be given fair notice of the existence of that term.

(2) In the *Interfoto* case, Dillon and Bingham LJJ adopted slightly different approaches. Dillon LJ held that, in the light of the plaintiff's failure to give the defendants reasonable notice of the onerous term, the term had not been incorporated into the contract. Bingham LJ expressed his conclusion slightly differently, holding that the failure to afford reasonable notice entitled the defendants to relief from liability under the clause. In this approach, Bingham LJ appears to have been substantially influenced by the fact that, in continental jurisdictions, the plaintiffs' conduct might have been held contrary to the principle of good faith,[523] thereby entitling the defendants to relief from the clause. However, it seems that the approach of Dillon LJ adheres more closely to the authorities relied upon by the court.

(3) Under the "reasonable notice" test, it follows that the notice must be given before the contract is made.[524]

---

[520] (1877) 2 CPD 416.
[521] Bramwell LJ dissented on this point.
[522] *Chapelton* v. *Barry UDC* [1940] 1 KB 532.
[523] See *infra* at 509.
[524] See *Thornton* v. *Shoe Lane Parking Ltd* [1971] 2 QB 163 (*supra*, at 497).

(4) Terms in notices, tickets etc. may also be incorporated by a previous course of dealing on those terms, even if on the occasion in question the terms were not referred to.[525] However, for this purpose there must have been a course of previous dealing between the parties[526] and the terms in question must have been used consistently in previous contracts.[527]

(5) In contrast, if the condition has been brought to the plaintiff's attention, it will be incorporated into the contract. The same is true if the plaintiff has signed the contract, even if she has not read the document and the clause was in "regrettably small print"; in the absence of fraud, misrepresentation or possibly mistake, the clause will form part of the contract.[528]

Cass. civ. 1re, 4 July 1967[529]   **3.F.127.**

LIMITATION OF LIABILITY CLAUSE BINDING ONLY IF ACCEPTED BY INJURED PARTY

Tragic flying lesson

A limitation of liability clause not contained in a written contract will be binding on the other party only if it is shown that he knew of it.

Facts: At the end of a flying lesson provided by the aeroclub, the instructor gave the pupil a demonstration of low-level flying. The aircraft touched a high-tension electricity line and crashed, killing both pupil and pilot. The pupil's widow brought an action against the aeroclub. The club argued that its liability was limited by a statute of 2 March 1957 applicable to aerial transport, or by a notice which referred to the limitation of liability set out in this law and which therefore became part of the contract.

Held: By the Court of Appeal, that this was not a contract of transport by air, as it was not intended to convey the pupil from one place to another; that the pupil was still not a regular passenger even if the tuition had ended; and that the club had failed to prove that the pupil knew of the notice. The Cour de cassation agreed with the Court of Appeal. On the notice point it said:

Judgment: THE COURT:—Whereas it is complained that the lower court, by requiring that the Aeroclub prove that the victim knew of the notice referring to the law of 1957, reversed the burden of proof . . .
—Whereas however by seeing that the limitation of liability clause must have been intended by the parties, under the normal rules of formation of agreements; and thus it was for the club or its insurer to prove the agreement between the parties on which they seek to rely . . .
. . . —[The] ground of appeal must be struck out . . .

---

[525] See *Henry Kendall & Sons* v. *William Lillico & Sons Ltd* (appeals from *Hardwick Game Farm* v *Suffolk Agricultural and Poultry Producers Assoc.*) [1969] 2 AC 31.
[526] See *Hollier* v. *Rambler Motors (AMC) Ltd* [1972] 2 QB 7 (three or four times over a period of five years not sufficient).
[527] *McCutcheon* v. *David MacBrayne Ltd* [1964] 1 WLR 165, H.L.
[528] *L'Estrange* v. *Graucob Ltd* [1934] 2 KB 394, CA (the legibility of the clause will be relevant if it can be challenged under legislation as unfair or unreasonable, see below, **3.4.3.A** and **3.4.4.**, *infra* at 513 and 521 respectively.
[529] Bull. civ. I..248; JCP 67.II.15234.

Cass. civ. 1re, 3 June 1970[530]   **3.F.128.**

<small>REGULAR PASSENGER TAKEN TO KNOW OF CONDITIONS</small>

Air passenger in a hole

A regular passenger on an airline that has always publicized its conditions of carriage will be taken to know of them.

Facts: M. Maché travelled with Air France from Orly to Palma de Majorca where, with the other passengers, he was directed by an Air France employee to make his way by a short cut to the airport building. On the way he caught his foot on a broken paving stone and fell into a shaft, injuring himself seriously. He sued Air France.

Held: By the lower court, that the employee had been negligent in not checking that the short cut he had directed passengers to take was safe; but that the company was protected by the limitation of liability clause in its general conditions. On these points the Cour de cassation agreed.

Judgment: THE COURT: *On the first appeal ground, taken in its various branches*:—Whereas the findings of the judgment appealed against were that Maché, who had flown on 29 March 1958 with Air France from Orly to Palma de Majorca, had been directed with the other passengers from the deboarding area to the airport buildings by an employee of the company; as in the course of this walk, Maché caught his foot on a broken paving stone and fell into a shaft, injuring himself seriously; as the Court of Appeal had found that the accident had resulted from the carelessness of the employee of Air France who, contrary to his employer's instructions, had pointed out a short cut without first having reconnoitred it, so that the victim could bring himself within the provisions of at. 1147, Code civil; as it had however held that the carrier could invoke the limitation of liability clause contained in its general conditions of carriage of passengers; as it is complained that the court so decided when, on the one hand, it had not answered the various points made by Maché showing that he could not have accepted the purported limitation of liability clause without knowing of it; and as, on the other hand, according to the judgment, since it accepted that Maché had never been in the places in which the carrier displayed the conditions, the judgment appealed against could not, without contradicting itself and reversing the burden of proof, justify its decision that he knew of them and accepted them;

—Whereas, however, the lower court held that the report of an officer of a *huissier* that, since it was first set up, the company Air France had always displayed its conditions for the carriage of passengers in public places; as the limitation of liability clauses is referred to under para. 2(b) of the conditions for contracts of transport; as the general conditions themselves state, in para. 3, that the liability of the carrier for injury is limited to 125,000 gold francs, or the equivalent; that it stressed the fact that Maché was a frequent air traveller;

—Whereas, without contradicting itself or reversing the burden of proof, and taking into account the points supposedly ignored, the cour d'appel had been within its powers to decide that Maché "could not have been ignorant of the existence of the clause concerned";

—Whereas therefore the first appeal ground must be rejected.

. . .

Notes

(1) In French law, in principle it is for the party which wishes to rely on the clause to show that the other party accepted it, i.e. knew of it at the time the contract was made.

---

[530] Bull. civ. I.190; D. 1971.373.

(2) However, as the second case shows, the party's knowledge may be deduced from the circumstances, particularly from prior dealings between the parties.

(3) Malaurie and Aynès[531] note that the French law is rather similar to the English law on notices, such as tickets or signs, which are not part of any document signed by the parties. They remark that German law looks at the substance of the clause more than the manner of acceptance.

BGH, 4 June 1970[532]   **3.G.129.**

UNEXPECTED TERMS CONTRARY TO GOOD FAITH

"Greedy accountant"

A clause which is surprising and which is merely incorporated by reference is not consistent with good faith.

Facts: The defendant transferred all his tax matters to the plaintiff under a mandate. The plaintiff subsequently confirmed the oral agreement in writing, pointing to his general terms of service with regard to the carrying out of his duties and the calculation of his remuneration. The standard terms incorporated a clause saying that the standard terms of trade agreed by the profession (ALLGO) would apply unless the plaintiff's terms provided to the contrary. The defendant did not respond to this letter, however he sought to revoke the mandate before the plaintiff had completed his work under it. The plaintiff pointed to one of the standard terms of ALLGO which was to the effect that anyone who revoked a mandate prematurely without good reason was liable to pay in full, incompleteness of the work notwithstanding.

Held: A clause which makes a contracting partner liable to payment in full for premature revocation of a mandate, without regard to the service actually provided, is contrary to good faith and was consequently, as it was not part of the individually negotiated contract but merely incorporated by reference, ineffective.

Judgment: . . . It is settled by the courts that the person who relies on standard terms of trade assumes for himself control over freedom of contract as far as the content of the contract is concerned, and is consequently obliged at the stage of framing those standard terms of trade to look to the reasonable protection of the interests of his future contractual partners. If he protects only his own interests, then he abuses freedom of contract, which to this extent is limited by § 242. Standard terms of trade can therefore lose their legal force, insofar as they contain disproportionate or surprising terms, in which the abusive furthering of one-sided interests at the expense of the other party is apparent and which, when the interests of those usually taking part in such transactions are weighed up, offend principles of fairness.

If provisions of dispositive law are based not only on the facilitation of transactions, but also on an immanent principle of fairness, then reasons must be evident when provisions in the form of standard terms of trade depart from this, calling into question the principle of fairness on which dispositive law is based while at the same time passing themselves off as being in accordance with principles of law and justice in the field they regulate. The justice content of the dispositive norms framed by the legislature can vary. The stronger it is, the more stringently must the ability to contract out of good morals and good faith by means of standard terms of trade be scrutinised. The requirements of day-to-day legal transactions, which take place under the tyranny of standard terms of trade, demand that these terms stay within the boundaries of what fair and just-minded individuals would think reasonable. The contracting party, who has submitted himself to the

---

[531] Malaurie and Aynès, at 377.
[532] BGHZ 17, 1, 3.

501

Standard Terms set up by the other party, can be held to have agreed only to such terms as one can reckon with as a matter of fairness and justice. (BGHZ 41, 151, 154; 38, 183, 185; 33, 216, 219; 22, 90, 94; compare Fischer Anm. LM Nr 1 relating to AGB and BB 1957, 481, 486)

The provision which falls to be considered in the present case, §17 ALLGO, does not satisfy the requirements which have been worked out by the VIII and II Senates and which the present Senate has adopted (compare, for instance, BGH 48, 264, 268; 52 171, 178; NJW 1963, 1148). . . . [Further extracts from this case, on the question of whether the substance of the clause was in conformity with good faith, will be found below.[533]]

3.4.2.B. MISREPRESENTATION ETC.

In the English case of *Curtis* v. *Chemical Cleaning and Dyeing Co Ltd*,[534] the plaintiff took a wedding dress to be cleaned by the defendants. She was asked to sign a document which exempted the defendants from liability "for any damage howsoever arising". The plaintiff asked why she had to sign and was told that it was because the defendants could not accept responsibility for damage to beads or sequins on the dress. The plaintiff then signed the document. The dress was returned to her with a stain on it that had not been there before, and the defendants denied liability, relying on the clause. The Court of Appeal held that the statement made to the plaintiff misrepresented the effect of the clause and therefore the defendants could not rely on the clause. A similar result would have been reached in France and Germany, but on the basis of the plaintiff's—subjective—mistake.[535]

Whilst *Curtis* is a straightforward application of the doctrine of misrepresentation, one can readily envisage that parties will fail accurately to explain the effect of their exclusion or limitation clauses, and that the doctrine may therefore assume particular importance in this context.

3.4.2.C. NATURE OF THE BREACH OF CONTRACT

As mentioned above, legal controls on the use of unfair terms have been particularly concerned with the use of exclusion and limitation clauses. The type of control considered in this section applies particularly where one party is in breach of contract and seeks to rely on a limitation or exclusion clause to reduce his or her liability.

Civ. com., 15 June 1959[536]   **3.F.130.**

DOL OU FAUTE LOURDE

Rotting vegetables

A clause seeking to exclude liability for breach of contract will be disregarded where the relevant breach of contract occurred intentionally (dol) or resulted from gross negligence (faute lourde).

---

[533] *Infra* at 509.
[534] [1951] 1 KB 805, CA.
[535] See *supra* at 347 ff..
[536] Capitant, Terré and Lequette, *Les Grands arrêts de la jurisprudence civile*, 10 th edn. (Paris: Dalloz, 1994), n° 96.

Facts: SICOMA contracted with Cherenque to import and transport some fresh vegetables from Spain to France. For the transport, Cherenque contracted a refrigerated car from STEF. All of the mentioned parties are companies. On arrival, the temperature was more than 40°C and the goods were damaged. Cherenque sought recovery for the damages she had to pay to SICOMA. The contract between Cherenque and SICOMA contained an exclusion clause with regard to the temperature in the regrigerated car, especially in so far as the condition of the goods on delivery are concerned.

Held: The judgment of the cour d'appel, to the effect that the clause should be disregarded, was set aside.

Judgment: THE COURT:—Under Article 1134 of the Civil Code;
—Whereas where a party seeks to avoid liability by relying on a clause exempting him from liability which is contained in the contract and accepted by the other party, that clause is inapplicable only if there has been intentional fault or gross negligence on the part of the party invoking it;
—Whereas in merely stating, as a ground for disregarding the clause in question, that the contract was badly performed, without making any finding of intentional fault or gross negligence on the part of STEF, the cour d'appel failed to provide a legal basis for its decision;
  On those grounds, and without there being any need to examine any of the other aspects of the appeal grounds advanced, this Court hereby sets aside the judgment appealed against . . .

Notes
  (1) Thus, an exemption clause cannot be invoked by a contractor who is guilty of intentional fault or gross negligence ("*dol ou faute lourde*").
  (2) Furthermore, according to French law an exclusion of liability arising from the law of torts is void, because these rules are deemed to be of public policy.
  (3) With regard to clauses excluding liability for hidden defects, such a contractual exemption clause used by a professional seller is void under Article 1643 of the Code civil (because a professional seller is presumed to have knowledge of the hidden defect) *unless* the buyer himself knew of the defect or is himself a merchant dealing in goods of that kind and who does not therefore need protection.

Court of Appeal 3.E.131.
Karsales v. *Wallis*[537]

DOCTRINE OF FUNDAMENTAL BREACH

The Buick

A breach which goes to the root of the contract disentitles the party from relying on the exempting clause.

Facts: A buyer agreed to buy a Buick car on credit terms. The buyer had seen the car at a dealer's at which time it was in good condition. Under the credit arrangement, the car was sold by the dealer to a finance company who in turn agreed to sell it to the defendant. When it was delivered by the dealer, it was in very poor condition and was incapable of self-propulsion. The finance company, which was quite unaware of what had happened and had never seen the car, claimed the price from the buyer, relying on a clause in the contract which stated that it was not responsible for the condition of the car.

Held: Overturning the decision at first instance, the Court of Appeal held that the finance company was not entitled to rely on the exemption clause.

---

[537] [1956] 1 WLR 936.

Judgment: . . . DENNING LJ: [T]he law about exempting clauses has been much developed in recent years, at any rate about printed exempting clauses, which so often pass unread. Notwithstanding earlier cases which might suggest the contrary, it is now settled that exempting clauses of this kind, no matter how widely they are expressed, only avail the party when he is carrying out his contract in its essential respects. He is not allowed to use them as a cover for misconduct or indifference or to enable him to turn a blind eye to his obligations. They do not avail him when he is guilty of a breach which goes to the root of the contract. The thing to do is to look at the contract apart from the exempting clauses and see what are the terms, express or implied, which impose an obligation on the party. If he has been guilty of a breach of those obligations in a respect which goes to the very root of the contract, he cannot rely on the exempting clauses . . .

The principle is sometimes said to be that the party cannot rely on an exempting clause when he delivers something "different in kind" from that contracted for, or has broken a "fundamental term" or a "fundamental contractual obligation," but these are, I think, all comprehended by the general principle that a breach which goes to the root of the contract disentitles the party from relying on the exempting clause. In the present case the lender was in breach of the implied obligation that I have mentioned. When the defendant inspected the car before signing the application form, the car was in excellent condition and would go: whereas the car which was subsequently delivered to him was no doubt the same car, but it was in a deplorable state and would not go. That breach went, I think, to the root of the contract and disentitles the lender from relying on the exempting clause.

Notes

(1) Denning's judgment is an example of the so-called "substantive" doctrine of fundamental breach (the other LJJ decided the case on interpretation of the clause). The result of this doctrine was that a person who committed a breach of a "fundamental term"—apparently meaning a condition of the contract[538]—or a fundamental breach— apparently meaning a serious breach of an innominate term[539]—is precluded from relying on any exemption clause.[540]

(2) In *Suisse Atlantique* v. *NV Rotterdamsche Kolen Centrale*[541] (discussed further *infra*) this doctrine was disapproved by both the Court of Appeal and the House of Lords, but some doubts about its validity remained until the decision in *Photo Production Ltd.* v. *Securicor Transport Ltd.*

House of Lords   **3.E.132.**
Photo Production Ltd. v. *Securicor Transport Ltd*[542]

NO SUBSTANTIVE DOCTRINE OF FUNDAMENTAL BREACH

The bored security guard

The questions whether, and to what extent, an exclusion clause is to be applied to a fundamental breach are simply a matter of construction of the contract.

---

[538] See *infra* at 736.
[539] See *infra* at 765.
[540] See on the doctrine of fundamental breach: *Chitty*, para. 14–020 ff.; Treitel, *Contract*, at 212–13 and 747.
[541] [1967] 1 AC 361.
[542] [1980] 1 All ER 556.

Facts: While carrying out a night patrol at the factory of Photo Production, an employee of Securicor, a security company, deliberately lit a small fire which got out of hand. The factory and stock inside, together valued at £615,000, were completely destroyed. Photo Production sued Securicor for damages on the ground that they were liable for the act of their employee. Securicor pleaded, *inter alia*, an exemption clause in the contract, to the effect that Securicor was not responsible for damage caused its employee unless that damage could have been avoided through due diligence on the part of the company or the employee had been acting in the course of his employment when he or she caused the damage.

Held: In the Court of Appeal, Lord Denning held that Securicor were in fundamental breach of contract, and that they were not therefore entitled to rely on the exclusion clause. In doing so, his Lordship stated that he was applying the decision of the House of Lords in *Suisse Atlantique*. Allowing the appeal, the House of Lords held that Securicor were entitled to rely on the exclusion clause.

Judgment: LORD WILBERFORCE: My Lords, whatever the intrinsic merit of [the] doctrine [of fundamental breach], . . . it is clear to me that so far from following this House's decision in the *Suisse Atlantique* it is directly opposed to it and that the whole purpose and tenor of the *Suisse Atlantique* was to repudiate it . . .

I have no second thoughts as to the main proposition that the question whether, and to what extent, an exclusion clause is to be applied to a fundamental breach, or a breach of a fundamental term, or indeed to any breach of contract, is a matter of construction of the contract. Many difficult questions arise and will continue to arise in the infinitely varied situations in which contracts come to be breached—by repudiatory breaches, accepted or not, by anticipatory breaches, by breaches of conditions or of various terms and whether by negligent, or deliberate action or otherwise. But there are ample resources in the normal rules of contract law for dealing with these without the superimposition of a judicially invented rule of law.

. . . The doctrine of "fundamental breach" in spite of its imperfections and doubtful parentage has served a useful purpose. There was a large number of problems, productive of injustice, in which it was worse than unsatisfactory to leave exception clauses to operate. Lord Reid referred to these in the *Suisse Atlantique* case [1967] 1 A.C. 361, 406, pointing out at the same time that the doctrine of fundamental breach was a dubious specific. But since then Parliament has taken a hand: it has passed the Unfair Contract Terms Act 1977. This Act applies to consumer contracts and those based on standard terms and enables exception clauses to be applied with regard to what is just and reasonable. It is significant that Parliament refrained from legislating over the whole field of contract. After this Act, in commercial matters generally, when the parties are not of unequal bargaining power, and when risks are normally borne by insurance, not only is the case for judicial intervention undemonstrated, but there is everything to be said, and this seems to have been Parliament's intention, for leaving the parties free to apportion the risks as they think fit and for respecting their decisions.

Note

Whilst the *Securicor* case is clear authority that there is no place for the doctrine of fundamental breach in English law, this is true only of the *substantive* doctrine. As we will see in the next section, a particular rule of *construction* remains applicable to breaches of fundamental terms, and will be of significance if, for example, if the statutory controls on unfair terms do not apply to the disputed clause.

3.4.2.D. INTERPRETATION

The interpretation—or construction—of unfair clauses is the most important mechanism for controlling the effect of these terms under the general law. The principal rule of construction in the systems studied is the *contra preferentem* rule: if a clause is not expressed clearly and without ambiguity, it will be interpreted against the party trying to rely on it, and thus may be held so as not to apply in the particular circumstances which have arisen.[543]

An exclusion or limitation clause may in effect deprive one party of any benefit under the contract, as where a term purports to exclude all liability for breach of contract. This inconsistency between the primary contractual obligation and the exclusion clause can be resolved using the *contra preferentem* rule, as illustrated by English law. In a case after *Photo Productions*,[544] the House of Lords ruled that a distinction should be drawn between the interpretation of clauses which *exclude* liability altogether and those which only *limit* liability to a certain sum. Exclusion clauses are subjected to the strictest standards of *contra preferentem* interpretation, whereas limitation clauses are construed less strictly, for the reason that a party is more likely to have agreed to a limitation of his legal right than the complete exclusion of it.[545] Similarly, whilst the House of Lords in the *Suisse Atlantique* case ruled out the "substantive" doctrine of fundamental breach,[546] they ruled that the *contra preferentem* rule should be applied to fundamental breaches of contract as follows: the more serious the breach, the less likely it is that the parties intended to exclude or limit liability for that breach.[547] Cooke and Oughton remark:[548]

The decision in *Photo Production* should not be taken to mean that the doctrine of fundamental breach is now irrelevant, for there may be cases in which an exclusion clause is construed so as not to apply to a particular breach. While the Unfair Contract Terms Act 1977 may have rendered the doctrine obsolete in certain respects, there are contracts to which the Act does not apply, in which case the doctrine can play a constructive part.

Nevertheless, as illustratated by the following case, there remains a key difference between the "substantive" and "construction" doctrines of fundamental breach; under the latter, but not the former, a clearly worded exclusion or limitation clause may apply even to breaches of conditions of the contract:

Court of Appeal and House of Lords   **3.E.133.**
George Mitchell (Chesterhall) Ltd. v. *Finney Lock Seeds Ltd.*[549]

EXCLUSION CLAUSES AND LIMITATION CLAUSES

Cabbage seeds

Where an exclusion or limitation clause clearly applies to a given situation, it is not open to the courts to put a strained interpretation on that clause so as to diminish its effects.

Facts: George Mitchell (Chesterhall) Ltd. ordered a quantity of Dutch winter cabbage seeds from Finney Lock Seeds Ltd., a company of seed merchants. Owing to errors by the suppliers and employees of Finney Lock

---

[543] See also chapter 4, *infra* at 568 ff.
[544] *Supra*, at 504.
[545] See *Ailsa Craig Fishing Co. Ltd.* v. *Malvern Fishing Co. Ltd.* [1983] WLR 964, 970, (*infra* at 508).
[546] *Supra* at 504.
[547] See also the accounts of Lord Denning and Lord Bridge in the *George Mitchell* case, *infra* at 507.
[548] Cooke and Oughton, *The Common Law Of Obligations* (London: Butterworths, 1993) at 400.
[549] [1983] QB 284 and [1983] 2 AC 803.

Seeds, the seeds were in fact not of this variety but were autumn cabbage seeds. The resulting crop proved to be worthless. In an action by the farmer for wasted expenditure and loss of anticipated profits, the seller of the seeds relied on a clause in its standard conditions of sale which provided that, if the seeds sold or agreed to be sold did not comply with the express terms of the contract or proved defective in varietal purity, the seller's liability was limited to the replacement of the seeds or a refund of the price paid.

Held: In the Court of Appeal, a majority (Oliver and Kerr LJJ, Lord Denning dissenting on this point) held that, properly construed, the limitation clause did not protect the sellers from the consequences of their own negligence because the wrong kind of seed had been supplied. The House of Lords, overturned the decision of the Court of Appeal, holding that the limitation clause clearly applied to the breach of contract which had occurred.

Judgment of the Court of Appeal: LORD DENNING *The heyday of freedom of contract*: None of you nowadays will remember the trouble we had—when I was called to the Bar—with exemption clauses. They were printed in small print on the back of tickets and order forms and invoices. They were contained in catalogues or timetables. They were held to be binding on any person who took them without objection. No one ever did object. He never read them or knew what was in them. No matter how unreasonable they were, he was bound. All this was done in the name of "freedom of contract". But the freedom was all on the side of the big concern which had the use of the printing press. No freedom for the little man who took the ticket or order form or invoice. The big concern said, "Take it or leave it". The little man had no option but to take it. The big concern could and did exempt itself from liability in its own interest without regard to the little man. It got away with it time after time. When the courts said to the big concern, "You must put it in clear words," the big concern had no hesitation in doing so. It knew well that the little man would never read the exemption clauses or understand them.

It was a bleak winter for our law of contract . . .

The secret weapon: Faced with this abuse of power—by the strong against the weak—by the use of the small print of the conditions—the judges did what they could to put a curb upon it. They still had before them the idol, "freedom of contract." They still knelt down and worshipped it, but they concealed under their cloaks a secret weapon. They used it to stab the idol in the back. This weapon was called "the true construction of the contract." They used it with great skill and ingenuity. They used it so as to depart from the natural meaning of the words of the exemption clause and to put upon them a strained and unnatural construction . . .

Fundamental breach: No doubt has ever been cast thus far by anyone. But doubts arose when in this court—in *Karsales (Harrow) Ltd. v. Wallis* [1956] 1 W.L.R. 936—we ventured to suggest that if the big concern was guilty of a breach which went to the "very root" of the contract—sometimes called a "fundamental breach"—or at other times a "total failure" of its obligations—then it could not rely on the printed clause to exempt itself from liability. This way of putting it had been used by some of the most distinguished names in the law. Such as Lord Dunedin in *W. S. Pollock Co. v. Macrae*, 1922 S.C.(H.L.) 192; by Lord Atkin and Lord Wright in *Hain Steamship Co. Ltd. v. Tate Lyle Ltd.* (1936) 41 Com.Cas 350, 354 and 362–363 respectively and by Devlin J. in *Smeaton Hanscomb Co Ltd. v. Sassoon I. Setty, Son Co. (No. 1)* [1953] 1 W.L.R. 1468, 1470. But we did make a mistake—in the eyes of some—in elevating it—by inference—into a "rule of law." That was too rude an interference with the idol of "freedom of contract." We ought to have used the secret weapon. We ought to have said that in each case, on the "true construction of the contract" in that case, the exemption clause did not avail the party where he was guilty of a fundamental breach or a breach going to the root. That is the lesson to be learnt from the "indigestible" speeches in *Suisse Atlantique Société d'Armement Maritime S.A. v. N.V. Rotterdamsche Kolen Centrale* [1967] 1 A.C. 361.

Judgment of the House of Lords: LORD BRIDGE OF HARWICH: . . . In his judgment, Lord Denning MR traces, in his uniquely colourful and graphic style, the history of the courts' approach to contractual clauses excluding or limiting liability . . . My Lords, in considering the common law issue, I will resist the temptation to follow that fascinating trail, but will content myself with references to the two recent decisions of your Lordships' House commonly called the two Securicor cases: *Photo Production Ltd.* v. *Securicor Transport Ltd.* [1980] A.C. 827 ("Securicor 1") and *Ailsa Craig Fishing Co. Ltd.* v. *Malvern Fishing Co. Ltd.* [1983] 1 W.L.R. 964 ("Securicor 2").

Securicor 1 gave the final quietus to the doctrine that a "fundamental breach" of contract deprived the party in breach of the benefit of clauses in the contract excluding or limiting his liability. Securicor 2 drew an important distinction between exclusion and limitation clauses. This is clearly stated by Lord Fraser of Tullybelton, at p. 105:

> "There are later authorities which lay down very strict principles to be applied when considering the effect of clauses of exclusion or of indemnity: see particularly the Privy Council case of *Canada Steamship Lines Ltd.* v. *The King* [1952] A.C. 192, 208, where Lord Morton, delivering the advice of the Board, summarised the principles in terms which have recently been applied by this House in *Smith* v. *UMB Chrysler (Scotland) Ltd.*, 1978 S.C.(H.L.) 1. In my opinion these principles are not applicable in their full rigour when considering the effect of conditions merely limiting liability. Such conditions will of course be read contra proferentem and must be clearly expressed, but there is no reason why they should be judged by the specially exacting standards which are applied to exclusion and indemnity clauses."

My Lords, it seems to me, with all due deference, that the judgments of the learned trial judge and of Oliver LJ on the common law issue come dangerously near to re-introducing by the back door the doctrine of "fundamental breach" which this House in *Securicor 1* [1980] A.C. 827, had so forcibly evicted by the front. The learned judge discusses what I may call the "peas and beans" or "chalk and cheese" cases, sc. Those in which it has been held that exemption clauses do not apply where there has been a contract to sell one thing, e.g. a motor car, and the seller has supplied quite another thing, e.g. a bicycle. I hasten to add that the judge can in no way be criticised for adopting this approach since counsel appearing for the appellants at the trial had conceded "that if what had been delivered had been beetroot seed or carrot seed, he would not be able to rely upon the clause": [1981] 1 Lloyd's Rep. 476, 479. Different counsel appeared for the appellants in the Court of Appeal, where that concession was withdrawn.

In my opinion, this is not a "peas and beans" case at all. The relevant condition applies to "seeds." Clause 1 refers to seeds "sold" and "seeds agreed to be sold." Clause 2 refers to "seeds supplied." As I have pointed out, Oliver LJ concentrates his attention on the phrase "seeds agreed to be sold." I can see no justification, with respect, for allowing this phrase alone to dictate the interpretation of the relevant condition, still less for treating clause 2 as "merely a supplement" to clause 1. Clause 2 is perfectly clear and unambiguous. The reference to "seeds agreed to be sold 'as well as to' seeds sold" in clause 1 reflects the same dichotomy as the definition of "sale" in the Sale of Goods Act 1979 as including a bargain and sale as well as a sale and delivery. The defective seeds in this case were seeds sold and delivered, just as clearly as they were seeds supplied, by the appellants to the respondents. The relevant condition, read as a whole, unambiguously limits the appellants' liability to replacement of the seeds or refund of the price. It is only possible to read an ambiguity into it by the process of strained construction which was deprecated by Lord Diplock [1980] A.C. 827, 851C in *Securicor 1* and by Lord Wilberforce in *Securicor 2* [1983] 1 W.L.R. 964, 966G.

In holding that the relevant condition was ineffective to limit the appellants' liability for a breach of contract caused by their negligence, Kerr LJ applied the principles stated by Lord Morton of Henryton giving the judgment of the Privy Council in *Canada Steamship Lines Ltd.* v. *The King* [1952] A.C. 192, 208. The learned Lord Justice stated correctly that this case was also referred to by Lord Fraser of Tullybelton in *Securicor 2* [1983] 1 W.L.R. 964, 970. He omitted, however, to notice that, as appears from the passage from Lord Fraser's speech which I have already cited, the whole point of Lord Fraser's reference was to express his opinion that the very strict principles laid down in the *Canada Steamship Lines* case as applicable to exclusion and indemnity clauses cannot be applied in their full rigour to limitation clauses. Lord Wilberforce's speech contains a passage to the like effect, and Lord Elwyn-Jones, Lord Salmon and Lord Lowry agreed with both speeches. Having once reached a conclusion in the instant case that the relevant condition unambiguously limited the appellants' liability, I know of no principle of construction which can properly be applied to confine the effect of the limitation to breaches of contract arising without negligence on the part of the appellants. In agreement with Lord Denning MR, I would decide the common law issue in the appellants' favour.

Notes

(1) Having held that the clause, properly interpreted, did apply in the instant case, the House of Lords went on to consider whether the clause satisfied the statutory controls on unfair terms. This aspect of the decision is considered below at page 545.

(2) Whilst exemption clauses are construed strictly under English law, the House of Lords has emphasized that, since there are now statutory controls on unfair contract terms, there is no justification for placing a strained and artificial meaning upon the language of a clear and unambiguous clause so as to avoid the exclusion or restriction of liability contained in it. The *George Mitchell* case is an example of this. The House of Lords thus rejected an approach evident in some of the earlier case-law (as described by Lord Denning in the extract above) and which had developed in the absence of substantive controls on contractual terms.[550]

3.4.2.E. SUBSTANTIVE CONTROLS UNDER THE GENERAL LAW

In this section we consider the extent to which the courts in the various countries are empowered under the general law to review the terms of contracts simply on the basis of their substance.

BGB **3.G.134.**

§ 138: *Transactions contrary to public policy; usury*
(1) Any transaction which is contrary to public policy is void.
(2) In particular, a transaction by which a person exploits the position of constraint in which another person finds himself, or the inexperience, lack of discernment or substantial weakness of will of that other person, in order, for his own benefit or that of a third party, to procure the promise of, or to obtain, a pecuniary advantage in return for the provision of a service, is void.

§ 242: *Performance in accordance with the principle of good faith*
The debtor must perform his obligation in accordance with the requirements of good faith, taking into account the prevailing practice.

BGH, 4 June 1970[551] **3.G.135.**

[For the facts of this case see above, p. 501]

A clause allowing an accountant to charge the full fee when the client cancels his mandate before the accountant has done the work is contrary to good faith.

---

[550] See also *Chitty*, para. 14–005 ff.
[551] BGHZ 17, 1, 3

Judgment: The provision which falls to be considered in the present case, §17 ALLGO, does not satisfy the requirements which have been worked out by the VIII and II Senates and which the present Senate has adopted (compare, for instance, BGH 48, 264, 268; 52 171, 178; NJW 1963, 1148).

It cannot, however, be deemed unacceptable in any case that the content of a claim for complete remuneration in case of early revocation of the agency agreement "without justification" can and should be retained by the agent. Regulation of the issue of remuneration in the case of conflict arising, for which this principle is the starting point, is in no way alien to the law, which is shown by the Appeal Court's use of § 649 BGB, and also by § 615 BGB in the context of contracts of employment, though with the limitations contained in § 649 BGB, 2nd half sentence and § 615 BGB sentence 2 respectively. According to this principle, the clause which falls to be ruled on is not inherently contrary to the jurisprudence outlined.

The clause does not however accord with principles of good faith and good morals, because in setting the level of the remuneration claim of the agent in the case of early revocation of the mandate it pays no attention at all to the extent to which services have actually been provided at that point, but instead gives full remuneration even in the case where he has performed minimal or even no services at all, that is to say when the agreed payment bears absolutely no relation to the actual performance by the agent. Such regulation, which makes such an outcome possible, is contrary to good faith and good morals and represents an abusive pursuit of the self interest of one contracting party at the expense of the other, whose justifiable needs are entirely ignored.

§ 628 para 1 sentence 1 BGB relating to partial remuneration in case of premature termination of a contract of services is to be understood in the context of the unusual rights to termination of §§ 626, 627 BGB, which seek to facilitate its operation. Of interest here is only § 627 BGB, which ALLGO also leaves unaffected. In framing this provision, the legislature clearly takes account of the fact that, according to experience, there exists an interrelation between the remuneration payable to the terminated service provider and the exercise of the right to terminate in itself. If the remuneration payable, in spite of the fact that termination has occurred prematurely, bears no defensible relation to the actual services already provided, then termination under § 627 BGB is disproportionately impeded. This being the case, the legal intention underlying that provision is also called into question, which is to allow anyone, who can demand service of a higher kind from an independent third party on the basis of a special fiduciary relationship, to be bound to the agreement arrived at only for so long as the fiduciary relationship underlying this agreement subsists, irrespective of the fact whether the termination of that relationship is based upon a good reason or not.

The statutory provision of § 626 para 1 sentence 1 BGB therefore in no way rests upon considerations of mere practicality. Rather, it is there for the purpose of striking a just balance between the conflicting interests of the parties in the dispute at issue. The claimant cannot argue that in tax advisory professions special conditions obtain, which require the complete disapplication in favour of the agent of statutory provisions, even to argue that this is the just outcome in the instant case. Moreover, there is no sufficient reason in evidence which would justify the view that departures from statutory provisions by general terms of trade put to one side the principles of justice inherent in § 628 para 1 sentence 1 and completely disregard the justifiable interests of the principal.

Consequently a diverging provision in general terms of trade must, if it is intended to be in accordance with principles of good faith and good morals, protect the interests of the principal in case of premature termination of the mandate to the minimum standard according to the substance of the legal intention underlying the relevant statutory provision. An aspect of this is that the relation between the level of remuneration and the actual services provided must be within a spectrum which can be described as proportionate and which is defensible with regard to the unusual right to terminate granted to the principal by § 627 BGB. It is of lesser importance in which way this is achieved, whether through an added appendix containing an appropriate and general limitation of the general clause requiring full remuneration, or regulated from the start by means of a sensible sliding scale or breakdown of payments which orientates itself roughly along the lines of the separate services to be performed.

. . .

The possibilities of regulating the assessment of the level of remuneration payable in the instant case of a mandate terminated prematurely without legal reason, on the one hand by going on the original agreement that full remuneration should be paid, and on the other hand to have regard to the appropriate level in the light of the actual performance, are too many and varied for this court to construe §17 para 1 ALLGO in a supplemental way under § 157 BGB so as to give it a content which is in harmony with the requirements of content laid down in the case law outlined. The clause must therefore be ineffective in its entirety, without any judgment being made as to the effectiveness of the rest of ALLGO, which is not at issue in the present case, let alone as to the validity of the entire contract between the parties (BGHZ 51, 55, 57; 22, 90, 92). Moreover, the statutory provision which was ineffectively sought to be displaced, § 628 para 1 sentence 1 BGB, takes the place of the omitted contractual term.

Note

The German legal system was one of the first to develop a comprehensive and successful system of judicial review of standardized contracts.[552] The courts based their intervention on general principles of German contract law, such as the rule prohibiting contracts contrary to good morals (§ 138 BGB), which are held void, and the general reqirement of good faith (§ 242 BGB).

BW   **3.NL.136.**

Article 6.1.1.2: (1) A creditor and debtor must, as between themselves, act in accordance with the requirements of reasonableness and equity.
(2) A rule binding upon them by virtue of law, usage or a juridical act does not apply to the extent that, in the given circumstances, this would be unacceptable according to criteria of reasonableness and equity.

Article 6:248: (2) A rule binding upon the parties as a result of the contract does not apply to the extent that, in the given circumstances, this would be unacceptable according to criteria of reasonableness and equity.

Hoge Raad, 19 May 1967[553]   **3.NL.137.**

CRITERIA FOR ASSESSING REASONABLENESS AND EQUITY

Saladin/HBU

Whether a clause satisfies the requirements of 'reasonableness and equity' should be assessed by reference to criteria including those referred to in the judgment below.

Facts: After being advised by the Hollandsche Bank-Unie, a bank, Mr Saladin, a layman in financial affairs, bought shares in a Canadian company. The advice proved to be too optimistic. Saladin had to bear a loss of Dfl. 80,000. The bank pleaded an exception clause for negligent information and advice.

---

[552] See Von Mehren, op. cit., para. 79.
[553] NJ 1967.261 (G.J. Scholten).

Judgment: . . . The answer to the question as to the circumstances in which a party—such as the Bank in the present case—is debarred from relying on a term in a contract excluding him from liability for certain conduct, even where that conduct wrongfully prejudices the other party, may depend on the assessment of numerous factors, such as: the gravity of the fault, taking into account the nature and substance of the interests affected by the conduct in question, the nature and other contents of the agreement containing the term in issue, the social position of the parties and their mutual relationship, the way in which the term came into existence, and the extent to which the other party was aware of the effect of the term . . .

Notes

(1) In Dutch law a contract term does not apply to the extent that, in the given circumstances, this would be unacceptable according to criteria of reasonableness and equity (Articles 6.1.1.2 and 248(2) BW). An interpretation of the relevant circumstances is given in the *Saladin/HBU* case.

(2) These general rules of "good faith" may be invoked when Article 6.5.3 BW (standard term contracts[554]) is not applicable, particularly where a term is not part of standard terms or when the other party is a "large company" within the meaning of Article 6:235 BW.

We will also see that in France, the Cour de cassation granted the civil courts the autonomous power to annul unfair contract terms.[555] This decision built upon the existing statutory controls on unfair contract terms, but at that time the statutory controls were extremely limited. As we will see, the decision of the Cour de cassation transformed the nature of the controls under French law from a mere public law power, given effect through abstract review, to a power to declare unfair contract terms null and void in the course of civil proceedings. However, this decision is better considered in conjunction with the relevant legislation.

In England there was a single-handed attempt by Lord Denning to develop the overt review of unfair contract terms at common law. In *Lloyds Bank Ltd.* v. *Bundy*,[556] his Lordship expressed the view that English law contains a general doctrine of "inequality of bargaining power". The importance of such a doctrine in relation to the control of standard contract terms can readily be seen, but Lord Denning's view was explicitly rejected by the House of Lords in a later case.[557] In *Gillespie Bros. & Co Ltd.* v. *Roy Bowles Transport Ltd,*[558] his Lordship had previously suggested that the courts had the power to review contract terms on a yet more open-ended basis:

Thus we reach, after long years, the principle which lies behind all our striving the court will not allow a party to rely on an exemption or limitation clause in circumstances in which it would not be fair or reasonable to allow reliance on it; and, in considering whether it is fair and reasonable, the court will consider whether it was in a standard form, whether there was equality of bargaining power, the nature of the breach, and so forth.

---

[554] See *infra* at 515.

[555] Cf. also Cass. civ., 26 May 1993, D. 1993.568 annotated by Paisant. See Malaurie and Aynès, para. 612, Starck, Roland and Boyer, *Les Obligations*, vol. II: *Contrat*, 5th edn. (Paris: Litec, 1993), paras. 671 ff., and Terré, Simler and Lequette, para. 309–311.

[556] *Lloyds Bank Ltd.* v *Bundy* [1975] QB 326 (a case of undue influence: *supra* at 478.

[557] See *National Westminster Bank Ltd* v. *Morgan* [1985] AC 686; *supra* at 481.

[558] *Gillespie Bros. & Co Ltd* v *Roy Bowles Transport Ltd* [1973] 1 QB 400 at 416.

Lord Denning explained that the statutes enacted by Parliament (the Supply of Goods (Implied Terms) Act 1973 and Unfair Contract Terms Act 1977[559]) had influenced his thinking in this regard, and expressed the same view in the *George Mitchell* case, discussed above. It would appear that the broader view expressed by Lord Denning has never been explicitly rejected by the House of Lords. However, whilst it is undoubtedly true that the English courts can now review the fairness of many types of term under the legislation referred to, it is tolerably clear that Lord Denning's view does not represent the position at common law.[560]

3.4.3. LEGISLATIVE CONTROLS

In each of the three countries to be discussed in this section (England, France and Germany), controls developed by the courts at common law or under general provisions of the civil codes have been supplemented by legislation aimed specifically at unfair terms of various kinds. The legislation varies significantly in both the scope and the means of control employed.

3.4.3.A. GERMANY: THE AGBG OF 1976

AGBG (1976)[561]   **3.G.138.**

CHAPTER 1 SUBSTANTIVE PROVISIONS
Subchapter 1: General provisions
§ 1: *Definitions*
    (1) Standard contract terms are all those contractual provisions drawn up for a large number of contracts which one contracting party (the proponent) presents to the other contracting party for his assent. It makes no difference whether the stipulations are contained in a separate instrument or included in the contract itself, what their scope may be, what type of writing is used, or what the form of the contract may be.
    (2) Standard contract terms are not involved when and insofar as the contractual conditions are individually negotiated between the parties.

§ 2: *Contents of the Contract*
    (1) Standard contract terms become a component part of the contract only if the proponent upon the making of the contract
        (i) expressly brings them to the attention of the other party or, if this would be unduly difficult under the circumstances, he does so by a clearly visible notice posted at the place of making of the contract, and
        (ii) if the other party has had a reasonable chance to obtain knowledge of their content, and if the other contracting party agrees to their application.
    (2) The contracting parties may agree in advance to the application to a specific type of legal transaction of specific standard contract terms, upon compliance with the requirements mentioned in paragraph 1 above.

[559] See *infra* at 515 and 545.
[560] See the judgment of Lord Reid in *Suisse Atlantique Société d'Armement Maritime SA* v. *NV Rotterdamsche Kolen Centrale* [1967] 1 AC 361, 406, and Treitel, *Contract*, at 223.
[561] Translation by Nina Moore Galston.

§ 3: *Unusual Clauses*
Stipulations in standard contract terms which, according to the circumstances, particularly according to the external appearance of the contract, are so unusual that the contracting partner of the proponent need not anticipate them, do not become an integral part of the contract.

§ 4: *Precedence of Individually Agreed-Upon Provisions*
Individually agreed-upon provisions take precedence over standard contract terms.

§ 5: *Rules for Obscurity*
Uncertainty concerning the interpretation of standard contract terms is resolved against the proponent.

§ 6: *Legal Consequences of Exclusion and Invalidity*
(1) If standard contract terms are excluded from the contract or have become invalid either in whole or in part, the contract remains valid in other respects.
(2) To the extent that the contractual stipulations have been excluded from the contract or have become invalid, the content of the contract in governed by stautory provisions.
(3) A contract is invalid if compliance therewith, even with the modificaion provided for in paragraph 2, would subject one of the contracting parties to undue hardship.

§ 7: *Prohibition of Evasion*
This act shall be applied even if an attempt is made to evade its provisions.

Subchapter 2: Invalid Clauses
§ 8: *Limitations on Control over Contents*
Articles 9 through 11 govern only those stipulations in standard contract terms by which it is agreed to deviate from legal rules or their supplementary regulations.

§ 9: *General Clauses*
(1) Stipulations in standard contract terms are invalid if the contracting partner prejudices unreasonably the command of good faith.
(2) In case of doubt, an unreasonable prejudice is presumed if a stipulation
(i) cannot be reconciled with the fundamental idea underlying the legal rule from which it deviates, or
(ii) so limits essential rights or duties inherent In the nature of the contract that attainment of the purpose of the contract is jeopardized.

Notes

(1) Markesinis has said of the AGBG of 1976:[562]

The Act essentially turned some twenty years of case law into a statute. This belies common misconceptions about German law (shared by some German lawyers) that courts merely apply the statutes and that their decisions are not a source of law.

(2) As regards the subject-matter, the AGBG applies only to standard terms (§ 9(1)). Individually negotiated contracts have priority over standard terms (§ 4 AGBG).

(3) According to the general clause (*Generalklausel*) of § 9(1), a contract clause is not binding (*unwirksam* i.e. void) when the other party suffers an "undue advantage" (*unangemessene Benachteilung*) to such an extent as to be incompatible with good faith. (*Treu und Glauben*).

---

[562] Markesinis, Lorenz and Dannemann,, *The German Law of Obligations*, Vol I: *The Law of Contracts and Restitution* (Oxford: Clarendon, 1997), at 212.

(4) § 11 AGBG contains a "black list", a list of terms which are deemed to be not binding, and § 10 AGBG contains a "grey list", the terms in this list are not binding if they contain disproportionate elements.[563] Only consumers can directly invoke these lists (§24 AGBG). However, as we will see, the lists may be applied indirectly to commercial contracts.[564]

(5) According to § 13 ff AGBG an action to review a standard term cannot only be brought to a district court by an individual, but also by consumer groups or associations. The review in such a "class action" has an abstract character.

(6) See also Articles 6:231, 6:233, 6:236, 6:237; 6:240; 6:241, 6:243 of the BW, which are to similar effect.

3.4.3.B. ENGLAND: THE UNFAIR CONTRACT TERMS ACT 1977

Unfair Contract Terms Act 1977   **3.E.139.**

Introductory

Section 1: **Scope of Part I**
. . .
(3) In the case of both contract and tort, sections 2 to 7 apply (except where the contrary is stated in section 6(4)) only to business liability, that is liability for breach of obligations or duties arising—
   (a) from things done or to be done by a person in the course of a business (whether his own or another's); or
   (b) from the occupation of premises used for business purposes;
and references to liability are to be read accordingly . . .

Avoidance of liability for negligence, breach of contract, etc

Section 2: **Negligence liability**
(1) A person cannot by reference to any contract term or to a notice given to persons generally or to particular persons exclude or restrict his liability for death or personal injury resulting from negligence.
(2) In the case of other loss, or damage, a person cannot so exclude or restrict his liability for negligence except in so far as the term or notice satisfies the requirement of reasonableness.
(3) Where a contract term or notice purports to exclude or restrict liability for negligence a person's agreement to or awareness of it not of itself to be taken as indicating his voluntary acceptance of risk.

Section 3: **Liability arising in contract**
(1) This section applies as between contracting parties where one of them deals as consumer or on the other's written standard terms of business.
(2) As against that party, the other cannot by reference to any contract term—
   (a) when himself in breach of contract, exclude or restrict any liability of his in respect of the breach; or

---

[563] These provisions are set out *infra* at 538.
[564] See **3.4.5.B**, *infra* at 528. See extensively on the AGBG (in German): Umer, Brandner and Hensen, *AGB-Gesetz*, 8th edn. (Köln: Schmidt, 1997).

(b) claim to be entitled—
    (i) to render a contractual performance substantially different from that which was reasonably expected of him, or
    (ii) in respect of the whole or any part of his contractual obligation, to render no performance at all,
except in so far as (in any of the cases mentioned above in this subsection) the contract term satisfies the requirement of reasonableness.

Section 4: Unreasonable indemnity clause
(1) A person dealing as consumer cannot by reference to any contract term be made to indemnify another person (whether a party to the contract or not) in respect of liability that may be incurred by the other for negligence or breach of contract, except in so far as the contract term satisfies the requirement of reasonableness.
(2) This section applies whether the liability in question—
    (a) is directly that of the person to be indemnified or is incurred by him vicariously;
    (b) is to the person dealing as consumer or to someone else.

Liability arising from sale or supply of goods

Section 5: "Guarantee" of consumer goods
(1) In the case of goods of a type ordinarily supplied for private use or consumption, where loss or damage—
    (a) arising from the goods proving defective while in consumer use; and
    (b) results from the negligence of a person concerned in the manufacture or distribution of the goods;
liability for the loss or damage cannot be excluded or restricted by reference to any contract term or notice contained in or operating by reference to a guarantee of the goods.
(2) For these purposes—
    (a) goods are to be regarded as "in consumer use" when a person is using them, or has them in his possession for use, otherwise than exclusively for the purposes of a business; and
    (b) anything in writing is a guarantee if it contains or purports to contain some promise or assurance (however worded or presented) that defects will be made good by complete or partial replacement, or by repair, monetary compensation or otherwise.
(3) This section does not apply as between the parties to a contract under or in pursuance of which possession or ownership of the goods passed.

Section 6: Sale and hire-purchase
(1) Liability for breach of the obligations arising from—
    (a) section 12 of the Sale of Goods Act 1979 (seller's implied undertakings as to title, etc);
    (b) section 8 of the Supply of Goods (Implied Terms) Act 1973 (the corresponding thing in relation to hire-purchase),
cannot be excluded or restricted by reference to any contract term.
(2) As against a person dealing as consumer, liability for breach of the obligations arising from
    (a) section 13, 14 or 15 of the 1979 Act (seller's implied undertakings as to conformity of goods with description or sample, or as to their quality or fitness for a particular purpose);

(b) section 9, 10 or 11 of the 1973 Act (the corresponding things in relation, to hire-purchase);

cannot be excluded or restricted by reference to any contract term.

(3) As against a person dealing otherwise than as consumer, the liability specified in subsection (2) above can be excluded or restricted by reference to a contract term, but only in so far as the term satisfies the requirement of reasonableness.

(4) The liabilities referred to in this section. are not only the business liabilities defined by section 1(3), but include those arising under any contract of sale of goods or hire-purchase agreement.

Section 7: **Miscellaneous contracts under which goods pass**

(1) Where the possession or ownership of goods passes under or in pursuance of a contract not governed by the law of sale of goods or hire-purchase, subsections (2) to (4) below apply as regards the effect (if any) to be given to contract terms excluding or restricting liability for breach of obligation arising by implication of law from the nature of the contract.

(2) As against a person dealing as consumer, liability in respect of the goods' correspondence with description or sample, or their quality or fitness for any particular purpose cannot be excluded or restricted by reference to any such term.

(3) As against a person dealing otherwise than as consumer, that liability can be excluded or restricted by reference to such a term,. but only in so far as the term satisfies the requirement of reasonableness.

3(A) Liability for breach of the obligations arising under section 2 of the Supply of Goods and Services Act 1982 (implied terms about title etc in certain contracts for the transfer of the property in goods) cannot be excluded or restricted by references to any such term.

(4) Liability in respect of—

(a) the right to transfer ownership of the goods, or give possession; or

(b) the assurance of quiet possession to a person takin goods in pursuance of the contract,

cannot (in a case to which subsection (3A) above does not apply) be excluded or restricted by reference to any such term except in a far as the term satisfies the requirement of reasonableness.

Other provisions about contracts

Section 10: **Evasion by means of secondary contract**

A person is not bound by any contract term prejudicing or taking away rights of his which arise under, or in connection with performance of, another contract, so far as those rights extend to the enforcement of another's liability which this Part of this Act prevents that other from excluding or restricting.

. . .

Explanatory provisions[565]

Section 13: **Varieties of exemption clause**

(1) To the extent that this Part of this Act prevents the exclusion or restriction of any liability also prevents—

---

[565] Section 11, which defines "fair and reasonable", and Sched. 2, which sets out guidelines on reasonableness, are extracted in **3.4.5.C** *infra* at 544. Section 12, which defines "dealing as a consumer", will be found in **3.4.5.A** *infra* at 533.

(a) making the liability or its enforcement subject to restrictive or onerous conditions;

(b) excluding or restricting any right or remedy in respect of the liability, or subjecting a person to any prejudice in consequence of his pursuing any such right or remedy;

(c) excluding or restricting rules of evidence or procedure;

and (to that extent) sections 2 and 5 to 7 also prevent excluding or restricting liability by reference to terms and notices which exclude or restrict the relevant obligation or duty.

(2) But an agreement in writing to submit present or future differences to arbitration is not to be treated under this Part of this Act as excluding or restricting any liability.

Section 14: **Interpretation of Part I**

In this Part of this Act:

"business" includes a profession and the activities of any government department or local or public authority;

"goods" has the same meaning as in the Sale of Goods Act 1979;

"hire-purchase agreement" has the same meaning as in the Consumer Credit Act 1974;

"negligence" has the meaning given by section 1(1);

"notice" includes an announcement, whether or not in writing, and any other communication or pretended communication; and

"personal injury"" includes any disease and any impairment of physical or mental condition.

Notes

(1) The Unfair Contract Terms Act 1977 does not apply only to contract terms, but also to non-contractual notices which purport to exclude or restrict liability in tort. Nevertheless, the Act is concerned mainly with contractual liability. The Act does not seek to control unfair contract terms in general. For the most part, it applies only to exclusion and limitation clauses.

(2) The pattern of control exercized by the Act is very complex. With regard to the Act, Zweigert and Kötz[566] remarked: "This very complex enactment is hard enough for the English lawyer, let alone the foreigner, to understand". The three broad divisions of control—which may overlap[567]—are:

(a) contract terms which exclude or restrict liability for negligence;[568]

(b) contract terms which exclude or restrict liability for breach of certain terms implied by statute or common law in contracts of sale of goods, hire-purchase and in other contracts for the supply of goods; and

(c) contract terms contained in either (i) contracts with consumers or (ii) a party's written standard terms of business, and which exclude or restrict liability for breach of contract, or which purport to entitle one of the parties to render a contractual performance substantially different from that reasonably expected of him, or to render no performance at all.

---

[566] Zweigert and Kötz, *Introduction to Comparative Law*, 2nd edn., transl. by T. Weir (Oxford: Clarendon, 1987) at 366 (omitted from 3rd edn.).

[567] See *Chitty*, para. 14–058.

[568] See s. 1(1).

(3) The exclusion or restriction of liability may be rendered *absolutely ineffective*; or effective only in so far as the term satisfies the *requirement of reasonableness*:

(a) *Absolutely Ineffective*: for example, contract terms and notices excluding and limiting liability for death or personal injury resulting from negligence (section 2(1)); exclusion and limitation clauses contained in "guarantees" of consumer goods given by manufacturers, etc and purporting to exclude the manufacturer's liability for negligence (section 5); clauses in sale of goods and hire-purchase limiting the supplier's liability of the goods are not of the right type or quality (section 6(2)); the same for clauses in other contracts for the supply of goods to a consumer (section 7(2), (3a));

(b) *Requirement of Reasonableness*: for example, contract terms excluding or limiting liability for harm other than death or personal injury caused by negligence (section 2(2)); clauses in consumer contracts and standard form contracts (section 3); clauses in contracts for supply of goods to businesses purporting to exclude or limit the supplier's liability of the goods are not of the right type or quality (section 6(3) and section 7(3)); indemnity clauses in consumer contracts (section 4); clauses excluding liability for misrepresentation (section 8, which amends section 3 of the Misrepresentation Act 1967).

(4) Section 6 of the Act was not new legislation but replaced similar provisions in the Supply of Goods (Implied Terms) Act 1973. The only significant change from the 1973 legislation is that the "reasonableness" test has been changed from the test of "whether it was reasonable for a party to rely on the clause" to the test of "whether or not the clause was a fair and reasonable one to be included in the contract".[569] (The *George Mitchell* case,[570] was decided under the 1973 Act.)

3.4.3.B. FRANCE: THE LOI SCRIVENER

Loi Scrivener[571]   **3.F.140.**

Article 35: 1. In contracts between professionals and non-professionals or consumers, a decree of the *Conseil d'État* made on the advice of the Commission established by art. L. 132–2, may, taking into account the nature of the goods or services concerned, forbid, limit or regulate any clause dealing with a determined or determinable price, or its payment, with the quality of the thing or its delivery, with the allocation of risks, or with termination or modification of the agreement, where such clauses appear to be imposed on the non-professional or consumer by an abuse of economic power by the other party and to give the other party an excessive advantage.

2. Such abusive clauses, stipulated contrary to the preceding artice, are to be treated as of no effect.

---

[569] UCTA S. 11, *infra* at 544.
[570] *Supra* at 506 and *infra* at 545.
[571] Loi n°. 78–23.

Notes

(1) France, in contrast to most other legal systems in Europe, the overt examination of contract terms by civil courts is a recent development. Until recently the French civil courts had no general statutory mandate to examine the reasonableness of terms in (standard) contracts. The control had an administrative, public law, character. Article 35 of the *Loi Scrivener* of 10 January 1978 empowered the government to issue decrees prohibiting specified clauses in contracts between professionals and consumers. The only decree ever issued is decree n° 78–464 of 24 March 1978 (a kind of "black list'). The *Loi Scrivener* set up a "*Commission des clauses abusives*" with an advisory task towards the government and a task to make (non-binding) recommendations with regard to the suppression or modification of terms which the Commission regarded as unreasonable.

(2) In 1993 the *Loi Scrivener* was incorporated into a codification of French statutes on consumer protection, the *Code de la consommation*. Article 35 became Article L 132–1 of the Code.

(3) The provision set out above was effective in France until 1995, when the Code was revised again in order to satisfy the demands of the Community Directive on Unfair Terms In Consumer Contracts.[572]

Cass. civ., 14 May 1991[573]   **3.F.141.**

COURTS EMPOWERED TO REVIEW UNFAIR TERMS IN CIVIL PROCEEDINGS

Minit France

The civil courts are entitled to apply Article 35 of the Loi Scrivener to unfair contract terms in the course of civil proceedings, and to hold that an unfair term is null and void.

Facts: A consumer took his slides to a branch of Minit France, a photography shop, in order to get them printed as photographs. The slides were lost. The receipt contained an exclusion clause.

Held: The Cour de cassation held that the cour d'appel was right in considering the clause void.

Judgment: . . .—Whereas having observed that the clause appearing on the deposit receipt exonerated the laboratory from all liability in the event of loss of the slides, the court below, whose contested judgment indicates that a clause of that kind conferred an excessive advantage on Minit France and that that company was able, on account of its economic position, to impose it on its customers, rightly decided that that clause was unfair and must be deemed null and void;
—Whereas neither part of the appela ground can therefore be upheld;

Note

In this decision, the Cour de cassation took the view that the civil courts were entitled to invoke the ground of review set out in Article 35 of the *Loi Scrivener* to render unfair clauses inapplicable in the course of civil disputes. The decision therefore transformed the nature of the controls on unfair contract terms under French law.

---

[572] See *infra* at 521; Paisant, D. 1995, Chr., 99.
[573] D. 1991.449, annotated by J. Ghestin.

3.4.4. THE EFFECT OF THE EC DIRECTIVE ON UNFAIR TERMS IN CONSUMER CONTRACTS

3.4.4.A. THE EUROPEAN COMMUNITY DIRECTIVE

EC Directive 93/13/EEC of 5 April 1993   **3.EC.142.**
on Unfair Terms in Consumer Contracts[574]

Article 1:   1. The purpose of this Directive is to approximate the laws, regulations and administrative provisions of the Member States relating to unfair terms in contracts concluding between a seller or supplier and a consumer.
2. The contractual terms which reflect mandatory statutory or regulatory provisions
and the provisions or principles of international conventions to which the member
states or the community are party, particularly in the transport area, shall not be subject to the provisions of this directive.

Article 2:   For the purpose of this Directive:
(a) "unfair terms" means the contractual terms defined in article 3;
(b) "consumer" means any natural person who, in contracts covered by this directive,
is acting for purposes which are outside his trade, business or profession;
(c) "seller or supplier" means any natural or legal person who, in contracts covered by
this directive, is acting for purposes relating to his trade, business or profession, whether
publicly owned or privately owned.

Article 3:   1. A contractual term which has not been individually negotiated shall be regarded as
unfair if, contrary to the requirement of good faith, it causes a significant imbalance in
the parties' rights and obligations arising under the contract.
2. A term shall always be regarded as not individually negotiated where it has been
drafted in advance and the consumer has therefore not been able to influence the substance of the term, particularly in the context of a pre-formulated standard contract.
The fact that certain aspects of a term or one specific term have been individually negotiated shall not exclude the application of this article to the rest of a contract if an overall assessment of the contract indicates that it is nevertheless a pre-formulated standard
contract.
Where any seller or supplier claims that a standard term has been individually negotiated, the burden of proof in this respect shall be incumbent on him.
3. The Annex shall contain an indicative and non-exhaustive list of the terms which
may be regarded unfair.

Article 4:   1. Without prejudice to article 7, the unfairness of a contractual term shall be assessed,
taking into account the nature of the goods or services for which the contract was concluded and by referring, at the time of conclusion of the contract, to all the circumstances attending the conclusion of the contract and to all the other terms of the
contract or of another contract on which it is dependent.
2. Assessment of the unfair nature of the terms shall relate neither to the definition of
the main subject matter of the contract nor to the adequacy of the price and remuneration, on the one hand, as against the services or goods supplies in exchange, on the
other, in so far as these terms are in plain intelligible language.
. . .

---

[574] [1993] OJ L 095.

521

Article 6: 1. Member States shall lay down that unfair terms used in a contract concluded with a consumer by a seller or supplier shall, as provided for under their national law, not be binding on the consumer and that the contract shall continue to bind the parties upon those terms if it is capable of continuing in existence without the unfair terms.
2. Member States shall take the necessary measures to ensure that the consumer does not lose the protection granted by this directive by virtue of the choice of the law of a non-member country as the law applicable to the contract if the latter has a close connection with the territory of the Member States.

Article 7: 1. Member States shall ensure that, in the interests of consumers and of competitors, adequate and effective means exist to prevent the continued use of unfair terms in contracts concluded with consumers by sellers or suppliers.
2. The means referred to in paragraph 1 shall include provisions whereby persons or organisations, having a legitimate interest under national law in protecting consumers, may take action according to the national law concerned before the courts or before competent administrative bodies for a decision as to whether contractual terms drawn up for general use are unfair, so that they can apply appropriate and effective means to prevent the continued use of such terms.
3. With due regard for national laws, the legal remedies referred to in paragraph 2 may be directed separately or jointly against a number of sellers or suppliers from the same economic sector or their associations which use or recommend the use of the same general contractual terms or similar terms.

Article 8: Member States may adopt or retain the most stringent provisions compatible with the treaty in the area covered by this directive, to ensure a maximum degree of protection for the consumer.

Article 9: The Commission shall present a report to the European Parliament and to the Council concerning the application of this directive five years at the latest after the date in article 10.

Article 10: 1. Member States shall bring into force the laws, regulations and administrative provisions necessary to comply with this directive no later than 31 December 1994. They shall forthwith inform the Commission thereof. These provisions shall be applicable to all contracts concluded after 31 December 1994.
2. When Member States adopt these measures, they shall contain a reference to this directive or shall be accompanied by such reference on the occasion of their official publication. The methods of making such reference shall be laid town by the member states.
3. Member States shall communicate the main provisions of national law which they adopt in the field covered by this directive to the Commission.
. . .

Notes

(1) Member States were obliged to implement the Directive no later than 31 December 1994. The provisions of the Directive are applicable to all contracts concluded after that moment (Article 10 (1)).

(2) The Directive has a minimum character, which means that it allows Member States to grant consumers a higher level of protection than the Directive (Article 8). As we will see, some Member States have retained features of the pre-existing statutory controls on

unfair terms, and as a result offer protection wider in scope than that required by the Directive.

(3) The subject matter of the Directive is *standard terms* only; that is, terms in contracts that have not been individually negotiated (Article 3 (1)). The Directive does not apply to non-contractual notices. Looking at the scope of the Directive as a whole, it is notable that the provisions of the Directive extend only to contracts for the sale or supply of goods or services, and probably also to contracts for land.

(4) The standard for review is the "unfairness" of a clause. A contractual term is "unfair" if it (a) causes a *significant imbalance* in the parties' rights and obligations arising under the contract, which is (b) to the *detriment of the consumer* and (c) contrary to the requirement of *good faith* (Article 3(1)). Whether a term is "unfair" depends on all the circumstances attending the conclusion of the contract (Article 4(1)). The Annex to the Directive contains *an indicative* and non-exhaustive list of the terms which *may be regarded* as unfair (Article 3(3)).[575] The unfairness of a contract term shall not be related to the core provisions of the contract, such as the subject matter or the price (Article 4(2)).

(5) When a contractual term is regarded as "unfair", the term is not binding (Article 6(1)).

(6) Article 7 of the Directive requires that the Member States must ensure adequate and effective means to prevent the continued use of unfair terms in consumer contracts. These means have to include individual actions by persons or "class actions" by organizations having a legitimate interest under national law in protecting consumers, and which may be heard by (civil) courts or by competent administrative bodies. The review in a collective action has an "abstract" character; the judicial control is thus exercized independently of the validity of a term in any particular contract.

Joined Cases C–240/98 to C–244/98 ECJ[576]   **3.EC.143.**
Oceano Grupo Editorial SA v. *Rocio Murciano Quintero (and others)*

EX OFFICIO DECLARATION OF UNFAIRNESS

The Spanish Encyclopaedia

A national court has the power to determine of its own motion whether a term of a contract is unfair when making its preliminary assessment whether a claim should be allowed to proceed before the national courts.

Facts: The various defendants agreed to purchase encyclopaedias from the plaintiffs, with payment to be made in instalments. The contracts of sale contained clauses conferring jurisdiction over the contract on the courts in Barcelona where the plaintiffs had their principal places of business, but where none of the defendants were domiciled. In the event of default by the defendants, the plaintiff companies commenced summary proceedings for the recovery of the sums owed. In considering whether to allow these claims to go ahead, the national court took the view that the jurisdiction clauses were potentially incompatible with the Directive on Unfair Terms in Consumer Contracts. The national court therefore referred a question to the ECJ whether a national court might of its own motion raise the unfairness of a term under the Directive when making a preliminary assessment of whether a claim should be allowed to proceed.

---

[575] The annex is set out *infra* at 541–543.
[576] **To be published in [2000] ECR.**

Held: The court held that the jurisdiction clauses were unfair under sub-paragraph (q) of paragraph 1 of the Annex, and that the national court was empowered to raise the point of its own motion. (Only that latter point is dicussed in the extract below.)

Judgment: . . .

25. As to the question of whether a court seised of a dispute concerning a contract between a seller or supplier and a consumer may determine of its own motion whether a term of the contract is unfair, it should be noted that the system of protection introduced by the Directive is based on the idea that the consumer is in a weak position vis-à-vis the seller or supplier, as regards both his bargaining power and his level of knowledge. This leads to the consumer agreeing to terms drawn up in advance by the seller or supplier without being able to influence the content of the terms.

26. The aim of Article 6 of the Directive, which requires Member States to lay down that unfair terms are not binding on the consumer, would not be achieved if the consumer were himself obliged to raise the unfair nature of such terms. In disputes where the amounts involved are often limited, the lawyers' fees may be higher than the amount at stake, which may deter the consumer from contesting the application of an unfair term. While it is the case that, in a number of Member States, procedural rules enable individuals to defend themselves in such proceedings, there is a real risk that the consumer, particularly because of ignorance of the law, will not challenge the term pleaded against him on the grounds that it is unfair. It follows that effective protection of the consumer may be attained only if the national court acknowledges that it has power to evaluate terms of this kind of its own motion.

27. Moreover, as the Advocate General pointed out in paragraph 24 of his Opinion, the system of protection laid down by the Directive is based on the notion that the imbalance between the consumer and the seller or supplier may only be corrected by positive action unconnected with the actual parties to the contract. That is why Article 7 of the Directive, paragraph 1 of which requires Member States to implement adequate and effective means to prevent the continued use of unfair terms, specifies in paragraph 2 that those means are to include allowing authorised consumer associations to take action in order to obtain a decision as to whether contractual terms drawn up for general use are unfair and, if need be, to have them prohibited, even if they have not been used in specific contracts.

28. As the French Government has pointed out, it is hardly conceivable that, in a system requiring the implementation of specific group actions of a preventive nature intended to put a stop to unfair terms detrimental to consumers' interests, a court hearing a dispute on a specific contract containing an unfair term should not be able to set aside application of the relevant term solely because the consumer has not raised the fact that it is unfair. On the contrary, the court's power to determine of its own motion whether a term is unfair must be regarded as constituting a proper means both of achieving the result sought by Article 6 of the Directive, namely, preventing an individual consumer from being bound by an unfair term, and of contributing to achieving the aim of Article 7, since if the court undertakes such an examination, that may act as a deterrent and contribute to preventing unfair terms in contracts concluded between consumers and sellers or suppliers.

29. It follows from the above that the protection provided for consumers by the Directive entails the national court being able to determine of its own motion whether a term of a contract before it is unfair when making its preliminary assessment as to whether a claim should be allowed to proceed before the national courts.

3.4.4.B. IMPLEMENTATION OF THE DIRECTIVE BY MEMBER STATES

The Member States have approached the implementation of the Directive in different ways. For example, in France and Germany, the Directive has been implemented through amendments to the existing statutory controls on unfair contract terms. In Germany, two new sections have been added to the AGBG to ensure that the Act complies with the Directive. The new §12 is concerned with the conflict of laws, and is not reproduced here.

AGBG (1996)[577]   **3.G.144.**

§ 24a: With regard to contracts between a person acting in the course of its professional or business activity (seller or supplier) and a natural person who concludes the contract for the purpose which cannot be regarded as part of its trade or independent professional activity, the provisions of this act will apply in the following way:
1. standard contract terms are regarded as having been presented by the supplier unless they have been introduced by the consumer into the contract.
2. the §§ 5, 6, 8–12 must be applied to pre-formulated terms even if they are intended only for a single use and the consumer could not have any influence on their content because of the pre-formulation.
3. in determining unreasonable prejudice for the purposes of § 9 the circumstances at the time of the conclusion of the contract must be taken into account.

Note
(1) The new Act makes two important amendments to German law.[578] First, § 24a introduces a presumption that standard terms are to be treated as though they were introduced by the supplier unless they were introduced into the contract by the consumer, so that the AGBG applies even if the terms were drafted by a third party. Secondly, whilst the AGBG generally only applies to terms in multiple use, several provisions of the Act apply now even if the terms have been used only once.

(2) The amendments to the AGBG have not introduced any new rules on transparency as required by Article 4(2) of the Directive. Reich has noted that, in particular, § 3 of the AGBG is not included in the list of provisions applied to consumer contracts under § 24 (2). However, the concept of good faith under § 9 has been interpreted as requiring transparency in standard terms, and is likely to be interpreted to ensure conformity with the Directive.

France has also adapted its *Code de la consommation*:

Code de la consommation   **3.F.145.**

Article L. 132–1: Any clause contained in a contract concluded between a seller or supplier and a person who is not acting in the course of his trade, business or profession or a consumer shall be regarded as unfair if its object or effect is to create, to the detriment of that person or consumer, a significant imbalance in the rights and obligations of the parties to the contract.
Types of clauses which are to be regarded as unfair within the meaning of the first paragraph may be specified by decree(s) enacted by the *Conseil d'Etat* [Council of State] following delivery of an opinion issued by the committee established by Article L. 132–2.

---

[577] Translation by Norbert Reich.
[578] See Reich, "The Implementation of Directive 93/13/EEC on Unfair Terms in Consumer Contracts in Germany" (1997) 2 Eu. Rev. Priv. L. 165, at 169.

There shall be annexed to this Code an indicative and non-exhaustive list of clauses which, if they fulfil the conditions laid down in the first paragraph, are to be regarded as unfair. In any proceedings concerning a contract containing such a clause, the onus of proving the unfairness of the clause in question shall lie with the plaintiff .

These provisions shall be applicable irrespective of the form of the contract or the medium in which it appears. The foregoing shall apply *inter alia* to any purchase order, invoice, guarantee, delivery note or delivery order, ticket or coupon containing stipulations, whether or not the same have been freely negotiated, or references to general conditions drawn up in advance.

Without prejudice to the rules of construction laid down in Articles 1156 to 1161, 1163 and 1164 of the Civil Code, the unfairness of a clause shall be assessed by reference, at the time of conclusion of the contract, to all the circumstances attending the conclusion of the contract and to all the other terms of the contract. It shall also be assessed in the light of the clauses contained in another contract where the conclusion or performance of each of those two contracts is legally dependent on the conclusion or performance of the other.

Unfair clauses shall be deemed null and void.

Assessment of the unfair nature of any clause within the meaning of the first paragraph shall relate neither to the definition of the main subject-matter of the contract nor to the adequacy of the price or remuneration as against the goods sold or the service offered.

The contract shall continue in full force and effect as regards all provisions thereof apart from those held to be unfair, provided that it is capable of continuing in existence without the said unfair clauses.

The provisions of this Article are a matter of public policy.

Notes

(1) The new Article 132–1 of the Code, set out above, has thus replaced the provision ultimately derived from Article 35 of the *Loi Scrivener*, and has put the civil law control of unfair terms on a statutory footing in French law.

(2) The Annex to the *Code de la consommation* reproduces the blacklist set out in the annex to the Directive. The Annex to the Directive is set out at 541 below, and for this reason, the Annex to the Code is not also reproduced here.

In contrast to France and Germany, the Directive was implemented in England by a new statutory instrument, the Unfair Terms in Consumer Contracts Regulations 1994, now been replaced by the Unfair Terms in Consumer Contracts Regulations 1999.[579] (The regulations are not reproduced here, as they are nearly identical to the Directive itself.) Consequently, the UTCC Regulations 1999 now operate alongside the Unfair Contract Terms Act 1977, with the result that English law contains two separate schemes for the regulation of unfair contract terms. It is worth highlighting some of the key differences between the two schemes. First, the Regulations refer only to contract terms, whereas some provisions of the Act also apply to non-contractual notices which purport to exclude or limit liability. Secondly, the Regulations apply only to contract terms that have not been individually negotiated; in general (but see the partial exception of section

---

[579] See *supra*, at 27. The 1999 Regulations are considered in detail in *Chitty* chapter 15.

3(1)), the Act applies to individually negotiated contract terms. Thirdly, the Regulations apply only to consumer contracts (contracts concluded between professionals and consumers), whereas some provisions of the Act also apply where both parties are merchants (acting in the course of a business). Fourthly, the Act renders some clauses of no effect.

In contrast to France, Germany and the United Kingdom, the Dutch legislation took the view that Article 6.5.3 BW on standard term contracts was sufficient to satisfy the requirements of the Directive.

3.4.5. KEY ISSUES IN UNFAIR CONTRACT TERMS LEGISLATION

3.4.5.A. CONSUMERS AND NON-CONSUMERS

The "status" of the parties to a contract generally determines whether the courts are empowered to review its terms for unfairness (or the extent of the courts' powers of review). In a contractual relationship between two equally powerful commercial parties, there is widespread agreement that they can look after themselves. According to Guest:[580]

It can reasonably be argued that, in many commercial contracts where both parties are of equal bargaining power, such exclusion or restriction of liability does no more than apportion the risk between the parties, in respect of which one party will be expected to insure.

A different view is taken of the review of terms in contracts concluded between a professional seller or supplier and a consumer-purchaser ("consumer contracts"). Given the inferior bargaining power of the consumer, the courts are inclined to redress the contractual imbalance by protecting the consumer against onerous clauses. (Of course, controls on unfair contract terms generally respond to some substantive unfairness in the terms of the contract rather than simply an inequality of bargaining power.)

However, whilst consumers may require particular protection, a small business may also find itself dealing with a much more powerful and experienced party, as where the manager of petrol station deals with an oil company. These small businessmen arguably need the same protection as consumers. On the other hand, the need for consumer protection in certain situations is questionable; for example, where the consumer can be regarded as an expert in a certain field or where they enjoy professional advice.

In this section, we consider the influence of the status of the contracting parties in the review of unfair clauses. Two questions arise: (i) does legislation which protects "consumers" ever apply so as to protect a business"? (ii) does the legislation in the systems studied also apply to businesses, and if so, how?

AGBG   **3.G.146.**

§ 24: *Scope of application as regards the persons affected*
    The provisions of §§ 2, 10, 11 and 12 do not apply to Standard Business Conditions
    (1) which are applied as against a merchant if the contract falls within the scope of such merchant's business operations, or

---

[580] In *Chitty*, para. 14–001.

(2) which are applied as against a legal entity created under public law or a special legal authority.

§ 9 is to be applied in cases included under sentence 1 in so far as this leads also to the invalidity of contractual provisions designated in §§ 10 and 11; the usages and practices of the business community are thereby to be appropriately considered.

BGH, VII, 8 March 1984[581]   **3.G.147.**

APPLICATION OF AGBG TO CONTRACTS BETWEEN PROFESSIONALS

Foam insulation

Professional parties are in general equally prejudiced by terms shortening the generally applicable limitation period in relation to proceedings for breach of a construction contract, and are thus able to complain that such a term is contrary to § 9 AGBG.

Facts: A company charged a building company with the job of insulating two tanks, containing hot liquids, with polyether-foam. After a while the foam bubbled and cracked. The building company's standard terms included a provision that shortened the statutory limitation of the action based on quality and fitness for the purpose. A question arose whether, in the light of §24 (2) AGBG, that Act applies to a limitation clause in a standard contract concluded between professionals.

Held: The company was entitled to complain that the term was contrary to the AGBG.

Judgment: . . . The customs and usages applying in commercial dealings to which reasonable regard must (under § 24(2) AGBG) be paid in the context of the application of § 9 AGBG are not such as to permit the determination of this case in a way which diverges from § 11 no 10ff AGBG. Where a stipulation used in dealings with non-business people falls within one of the prohibitions laid down in § 11 AGBG, that indicates that, even if used in dealings between business people, it will place the party on whom it is imposed at an unreasonable disadvantage, unless, exceptionally, it is capable of being regarded as reasonable on account of the particular interests and requirements inherent in commercial business dealings. . . . However, the essential idea underlying the statutory rule diverged from (§ 9 II no 1 AGBG), namely that the relatively short periods prescribed by §§ 477, 638 BGB for bringing breach of warranty claims take reasonable account of the periods within which defects usually appear, and that any (further) shortening of the limitation periods would unreasonably prejudice the customer as regards defects which initially remain hidden, also applies in commercial dealings. . . .

In carrying on their trade or profession, business people are no less affected than non-business people by construction defects. The particular interests and requirements inherent in commercial business dealings, and the standards applying in such dealings, are irrelevant as regards the risk to which the customer is typically exposed where construction works are concerned. A business person is not generally in a position to detect hidden construction defects any earlier than a non-business person. It follows that, as a general rule, business people engaged in carrying on their trade or profession are also unreasonably prejudiced, in their capacity as customers, by a stipulation contained in standard terms and conditions which shortens the five-year limitation period (commencing on acceptance of the works) for bringing breach of warranty claims in respect of works done under a construction contract, and this is contrary to the requirements of good faith (§ 9 AGBG).

---

[581] NJW 1984.1750.

Notes

(1) As regards the parties covered, the AGBG applies whenever general terms have been used, even if both parties are merchants. According to § 24 AGBG transactions between merchants are exempted from certain provisions of the Act, such as the "grey list" of § 10 and the "black list" of § 11, with their automatic invalidation of standard terms of the specified types. These lists can be directly invoked by consumers only. However, the general clause—§ 9 AGBG—remains applicable in business transactions.

(2) The decision in the *Foam Insulation* case shows that, in general, when a merchant uses a clause which fails within one of the prohibited categories of §§ 10 and 11, the court will invoke § 9 in order to hold it invalid. The black and grey lists provide an indication that the contract terms contained therein are invalid (the so-called *Indizwirkung*).

Cass. civ. 1re, 28 April 1987[582]   **3.F.148.**

BUSINESS AS CONSUMER

Defective alarm

A business which is unfamiliar with the contents and technical subject matter of a contract is a consumer for the purposes of that contract.

Facts: Pigranel S.A., a housing bureau, bought an alarm system from Abonnement Téléphonique S.A. The alarm never functioned well. The contract contained an exclusion clause regarding the responsibility of Abonnement Téléphonique. The question arose as to whether the clause was valid in the light of Article 35 of the Loi Scrivener (now Article L. 132–1 Code la consommation), which presupposes that the relevant party is a "consumer".

Held: Pigranel was a consumer for the purposes of the contract.

Judgment: . . .—Whereas however on the first point, the cour d'appel considered that the contract concluded between Abonnement Téléphonique and Pigranel S.A. fell outside the ambit of the latter's professional competence; as Pigranel, as a company engaged in the business of estate agency, was unfamiliar with the highly specialised technology of alarm systems and was therefore as ignorant about the contents of the contract in issue as any other consumer would have been; —Whereas the cour d'appel rightly found that the Law of 10 January 1978 was applicable . . .

Cass., civ. 1re, 24 January 1995[583]   **3.F.149.**

NOT CONSUMER IF CONTRACT FORMS PART OF BUSINESS ACTIVITIES

Contract for electricity

Articles L. 132–1 and L. 133–1 of the Consumer Code do not apply to contracts for the supply of goods or services which directly relate to the business activity carried on by the party in receipt of them.

Facts: La Société Héliogravure Jean Didier, a printing business, contracted with EDF, the French electricity company which holds a monopoly position, for the supply of electricity. The question was whether the Société was a "consumer" for the purposes of the contract.

[582] D. 1988.1, annotated by Delebecque.
[583] D. 1995.327, annotated by Paisant.

Held: The Société was not a consumer for the purposes of the contract.

Judgment: . . .—Whereas, second, a consumer is a person who contracts outside his usual sphere of activity and his special field;

—Whereas contracts entered into with EDF are standard-form contracts which are not open to negotiation, because that public service enjoys a monopoly which places commercial customers, when they contract, in the same situation as any ordinary private individual;

—Whereas in finding that the Société Héliogravure Jean Didier, a printing firm, was a business user of electric energy and that it was thus not covered by the provisions of Law No 78–23 of 10 January 1978, the cour d'appel acted contrary to Article 35 of that Law and contrary to Article 2 of Decree No 78–464 of 24 March 1978;

—Whereas, however, the provisions of Article 35 of Law No 78–23 of 10 January 1978—now contained in Articles L. 132–1 and L. 133–1 of the Consumer Code—and of Article 2 of the Decree of 24 March 1978 do not apply to contracts for the supply of goods or services which directly relate to the business activity carried on by the party in receipt of them;

—Whereas on those substituted grounds, the decision is legally justified;

On those grounds, this Court dismisses the appeal.

Notes

(1) This case is also discussed below in Chapter 5.[584]

(2) Article L. 132–1 of the *Code de la consommation* applies to contracts concluded between professionals on the one side and non-professionals or consumers on the other side (*non-professionnels ou consommateurs*). Initially, in the *Defective Alarm* case, the Cour de cassation gave a very broad interpretation of the notion of "consumer" (or non-professional).[585] Whether or not a professional was considered to be a consumer depended on whether the professional was in the same state of ignorance (*le même état d'ignorance*) as every other consumer. In its 1995 judgment, the Cour de cassation uses a much narrower notion of consumer. The actual criterion is that if there is a direct relationship (*rapport direct*) between the contract matter and the professional activities of the buyer or client, the latter is not regarded as a consumer.

BW   **3.NL.150.**

Article 6.235: (1) The grounds of annulment referred to in articles 233 and 234 cannot be invoked by:

    a. a legal person as referred to in article 360 of Book 2 who, at the time of entering into the contract, has lastly made public its annual account, or a legal person in respect of whom, at that time, article 403 paragraph q of Book 2 has lastly been applied;

    b. a party to whom the provision of sub-paragraph a does not apply, if at the aforementioned time, fifty or more persons word there or if, at that time, a declaration pursuant to article 17a of the *Handelsregisterwet* shows that fifty or more persons work there.

(2) The ground of annulment referred to in article 233 *sub* a can also be invoked by a party for whom the general conditions have been used by a procurator, provided

---

[584] *Infra* at 596.

[585] Cf. also Cass. civ. 1re, 25 May 1992, D. 1993.87 (Nicolau): a housing bureau that bought an alarm system was judged to be a consumer. See also Malaurie and Aynès, para. 863 and Starck, Roland and Boyer, op. cit., para. 680 ff.

that the other party enter repeatedly into contracts to which the same or almost the same general conditions apply.

(3) The grounds of annulment referred to in articles 233 and 234 cannot be invoked by a party who uses the same or almost the same general conditions in its contracts repeatedly.

(4) The period referred to in article 52 paragraph 1 *sub* d of Book 3 commences upon the beginning of the day following the one on which the stipulation has been invoked.

Article 6.244: (1) A person acting in the course of a profession or business may not invoke a stipulation in a contract with a party who, using general conditions, has entered into contracts with its clients concerning the goods or services to which that contract applies, to the extent that invoking that stipulation would be unreasonable because of its close connection with a stipulation contained in the general conditions which, pursuant to this section, has been annulled or has been affected by a decision as referred to in article 240 paragraph 1.

(2) Where an action as referred to in article 240 paragraph 1 has been instituted against the user, he is entitled to implead that person in order to have it judicially declared that invoking a stipulation as referred to in the preceding paragraph would be unreasonable. Article 241 paragraphs 2, 3 *sub* c, 4 and 5, as well as articles 68, 69 and 73 of the Code Civil Procedure apply *mutatis mutandis*.

(3) Article 242 applies *mutatis mutandis* to the decision.

(4) Paragraphs 1—3 apply *mutatis mutandis* to earlier contracts pertaining to the aforementioned goods and services.

(See also Article 6:236 and Article 6:237 BW (the black and grey lists), not set out here for reasons of space. They are similar to the Directive.)

Explanatory Legislative Commentaries   **3.NL.151.**
on Article 6:236 of the New Dutch Civil Code

§ 5: The opening wording of Articles 3 and 4 (d) (Articles 6:236 and 6:237, ed.) limits the scope of those provisions, as already mentioned, to agreements in which the party other than the user is a consumer, that is to say, a person who, at the time of conclusion of the agreement, is not acting in the course of a profession or business. That limitation is prompted by the practical consideration that it is not possible, in our view, to review the entire area of agreements both parties to which are business persons in such a way as to justify making those agreements likewise subject to the provisions of Articles 3 and 4, or to part thereof.

The limitation should not be taken to indicate that we are of the opinion that there is no need in the world of business for protection of the kind offered by this draft legislation; . . ..
However, we are of the view that that need is adequately met by other provisions of the draft law, in particular Articles 2 and 6 (Arts. 6:232 and 6:240, ed.), which are also applicable to commercial transactions, and Article 10 (Art. 6:244, ed.). We would point out in that connection that Articles 3 and 4 are also designed to produce a certain normative effect, precisely by means of the operation, where necessary, of the unqualified rule contained in Article 2(2)(a) in the case, *inter alia*, of review of agreements between parties engaged in business. Moreover, Article 5(1) (Art. 6:239, ed.) makes it possible, by means of an Order in Council, to render stipulations in agreements between business persons subject to the presumption referred to in Article 4.

Notes

(1) In principle, the BW protects both consumers and merchants against unduly oner-ous clauses (Article 6:233). Large legal persons (companies, associations, governmental bodies) are not protected by this rule (Article 6:235 BW). However, they may invoke the general rules of reasonableness and equity (Articles 6:2(2) and 248(2) BW), which apply to all contracts.[586]

(2) Under Articles 6:236 and 237 BW, only consumers can profit directly from the spe-cial protection of the black and the grey lists. The notion of consumer in Articles 6:236 and 237 BW is a narrow one, and applies only to "a contract between a user and the other party, where the latter is a natural person not acting in the course of a business or pro-fession". However, the explanatory commentaries to the new Civil Code indicate that even in cases between merchants, the court may be inspired by the fact that a clause is mentioned in the black list or the grey list when considering whether a clause is un-reasonably onerous (see Article 6:233). On the limits on the protection afforded to mer-chants, see the decision in *The Shipyard De Schelde* case, below.

(3) A particular kind of protection of small businessmen is provided by Article 6:244 BW. It affords some protection to a dealer (retailer) who uses standard contract terms annulled or prohibited according to the previous Articles, but which are closely related to (general) conditions which he himself has been "forced" to accept by his seller, for exam-ple a producer. This seller in the previous link of the distribution chain is not allowed to invoke his contract terms in so far as this would be unreasonable for the retailer because of such a connection.

Hoge Raad, 31 December 1993[587]   **3.NL.152.**

BUSINESSES IN RELATED INDUSTRIES

The Shipyard De Schelde

In agreements between businesses in related industries, it is not unreasonable wholly or partially to exclude liability for serious fault on the part of subcontractors.

Facts: Matatag c.s., the owners of a ship, held the shipyard De Schelde responsible for the damage caused by an employee of its subcontractor. The shipyard referred to an exclusion clause in the contract. The shipowners for their part argued that the clause was not applicable, because that would be unacceptable according to criteria of reasonableness and equity (Articles 6:2(2) en 248 (2) of the Civil Code).

Held: The clause was not unreasonable.

Judgment: . . . 3.2. For the purposes of assessing the plea advanced, the following must be taken into consideration.

This case concerns an agreement between two businesses—a ship-owning company and a ship-yard—operating in industrial sectors which regularly have dealings with each other and in which the standardisation of agreements by the inclusion therein of general terms and conditions incor-porating exclusion of liability clauses is an everyday phenomenon. . . .

---

[586] See Hartkamp and Tillema, *Contract Law in the Netherlands* (The Hague/Boston: Kluwer, 1995) para. 114.
[587] NJ 1995.389 (Brunner).

After all, in the case of agreements of the type at issue here, concluded between business entities as indicated above, it cannot be said to be unacceptable, according to the criteria of reasonableness and fairness, to incorporate in the applicable general terms and conditions stipulations which wholly or partially exclude liability, even for serious fault on the part of persons engaged to carry out the work who are not members of the management of the business concerned, and then to rely on that exclusion in the event of loss or damage as suffered in the present case.

Unfair Contract Terms Act 1977   **3.E.153.**

Section 12: **Dealing as consumer**
>   (1) A party to a contract "deals as consumer" in relation to another party if—
>   (a) he neither makes .the contract in the course of a business nor holds himself out as doing so; and
>   (b) the other party does make the contract in the course of a business; and
>   (c) in the case of a contract governed by the law of sale of goods or hire-purchase, or by section 7 of this Act, the goods passing under or in pursuance of the contract are of a type ordinarily supplied for private use or consumption.
>   (2) But on a sale by auction or by competitive tender the buyer is not in any circumstances to be regarded as dealing as consumer.
>   (3) Subject to this, it is for those claiming that a party does not deal as consumer to show that he does not.

Court of Appeal   **3.E.154.**
R&B Customs Brokers Ltd. v. *United Dominions Trust Ltd*[588]

COMPANY CAN DEAL AS CONSUMER

The managing director's car

When a company purchases goods of a type in which it does not ordinarily deal and which are not for a purpose integral to the business, it may "deal as a consumer" within UCTA 1977, section 12.

Facts: R&B Customs Brokers purchased a car on credit from United Dominions Trust, a finance company, the car being supplied by a motor dealer. The car was for the personal and business use of a director. The roof of the car leaked, and the motor dealer failed to repair this defect. R&B Customs Brokers rejected the car and brought an action against United Dominions to recover the money paid under the sale agreement. United Dominions relied on an exclusion clause in the sale agreement.

Held: Under section 14(3) of the Sale of Goods Act 1979, there was to be implied into the contract of sale a condition that the car was reasonably fit for the particular purpose for which it had been purchased, namely, ordinary use upon the roads in England in English weather (not extracted); and that R&B had acted as a consumer when purchasing the car, and the implied term could not be excluded under section 6(2) of UCTA.

Judgment: DILLON LJ: . . . Two questions therefore arise, and success on either of them is sufficient for the company's purposes, viz.: (1) In entering into the conditional sale agreement with the defendants, was the company "dealing as consumer?" If it was, then, on the wording of the defendants' printed conditions, the condition 2(a) did not apply, no doubt because under section 6(2) of the Act of 1977 the liability could not be excluded. (2) If the company was dealing otherwise than as a consumer, does the defendants' condition 2(a) excluding liability under section 14(3) satisfy "the requirement of reasonableness".

---

[588] [1988] 1 All ER 847.

3.E.154.

. . . It is accepted that the conditions (b) and (c) in section 12(1) [of UCTA] are satisfied. This issue turns on condition (a). Did the company neither make the contract with the defendants in the course of a business nor hold itself out as doing so?

In the present case there was no holding out beyond the mere facts that the contract and the finance application were made in the company's corporate name, and in the finance application the section headed "Business Details" was filled in to the extent of giving the nature of the company's business as that of shipping brokers, giving the number of years trading and the number of employees, and giving the names and addresses of the directors. What is important is whether the contract was made in the course of a business.

In a certain sense, however, from the very nature of a corporate entity, where a company which carries on a business makes a contract, it makes that contract in the course of its business; otherwise the contract would be ultra vires and illegal. Thus, where a company which runs a grocer's shop buys a new delivery van, it buys it in the course of its business. Where a merchant bank buys a car as a "company car" as a perquisite for a senior executive, it buys it in the course of its business. Where a farming company buys a landrover for the personal and company use of a farm manager, it again does so in the course of its business . . .

We have been referred to one decision at first instance under the Act of 1977, *Peter Symmons Co.* v. *Cook* (1981) 131 N.L.J. 758, but the note of the judgment is too brief to be of real assistance. More helpfully, we have been referred to decisions under the Trade Descriptions Act 1968, and in particular to the decision of the House of Lords in *Davies* v. *Sumner* [1984] 1 W.L.R. 1301.

Under the Trade Descriptions Act 1968 any person who in the course of a trade or business applies a false trade description to goods is, subject to the provisions of the Act, guilty of an offence. . . . [I]t would, in my judgment, be unreal and unsatisfactory to conclude that the fairly ordinary words "in the course of business" bear a significantly different meaning in, on the one hand, the Trade Descriptions Act 1968, and, on the other hand, section 12 of the Act of 1977. In particular I would be very reluctant to conclude that these words bear a significantly wider meaning in section 12 than in the Trade Descriptions Act 1968.

I turn therefore to *Davies* v. *Sumner* [1984] 1 W.L.R. 1301. That case was not concerned with a company, but with an individual who had used a car for the purposes of his business as a self-employed courier. When he sold the car by trading it in part exchange for a new one, he had applied a false trade description to it by falsely representing the mileage the car had travelled to have been far less than it actually was. Lord Keith of Kinkel, who delivered the only speech in the House of Lords, commented, at p. 1304F, that it was clear that the transaction—sc. of trading in the car on the purchase of a new one—was reasonably incidental to the carrying on of the business, but he went on to say, at p. 1305:

"Any disposal of a chattel held for the purposes of a business may, in a certain sense, be said to have been in the course of that business, irrespective of whether the chattel was acquired with a view to resale or for consumption or as a capital asset. But in my opinion section 1(1) of the Act is not intended to cast such a wide net as this. The expression 'in the course of a trade or business' in the context of an Act having consumer protection as its primary purpose conveys the concept of some degree of regularity, and it is to be observed that the long title to the Act refers to 'misdescriptions of goods, services, accommodation and facilities provided in the course of trade.' Lord Parker C.J. in the *Havering* case [1970] 1 W.L.R. 1375 clearly considered that the expression was not used in the broadest sense. The reason why the transaction there in issue was caught was that in his view it was 'an integral part of the business carried on as a car hire firm.' That would not cover the sporadic selling off of pieces of equipment which were no longer required for the purposes of a business. The vital feature of the *Havering* case appears to have been, in Lord Parker's view, that the defendant's business as part of its normal practice bought and disposed of cars. The need for some degree of regularity does not, however, involve that a one-off adventure in the nature of trade, carried through with a view to profit, would not fall within section 1(1) because such a transaction would itself constitute a trade."

. . . Lord Keith emphasised the need for some degree of regularity, and he found pointers to this in the primary purpose and long title of the Trade Descriptions Act 1968. I find pointers to a similar need for regularity under the Act of 1977, where matters merely incidental to the carrying on of a business are concerned, both in the words which I would emphasise, "in the course of" in the phrase "in the course of a business" and in the concept, or legislative purpose, which must underlie the dichotomy under the Act of 1977 between those who deal as consumers and those who deal otherwise than as consumers.

This reasoning leads to the conclusion that, in the Act of 1977 also, the words "in the course of business" are not used in what Lord Keith called "the broadest sense". The reconciliation between that phrase and the need for some degree of regularity is, as I see it, as follows: there are some transactions, which are clearly integral parts of the businesses concerned, and these should be held to have been carried out in the course of those businesses; this would cover, apart from much else, the instance of a one-off adventure in the nature of trade where the transaction itself would constitute a trade or business. There are other transactions, however, such as the purchase of the car in the present case, which are at the highest only incidental to the carrying on of the relevant business; here a degree of regularity is required before it can be said that they are an integral part of the business carried on and so entered into in the course of that business.

Applying the test thus indicated to the facts of the present case, I have no doubt that the requisite degree of regularity is not made out on the facts. Mr. Bell's evidence that the car was the second or third vehicle acquired on credit terms was in my judgment and in the context of this case not enough. Accordingly, I agree with the judge that, in entering into the conditional sale agreement with the defendants, the company was "dealing as consumer." The defendants' condition 2(a) is thus inapplicable and the defendants are not absolved from liability under section 14(3).

It follows that it is unnecessary to decide whether, if the company had been dealing otherwise than as a consumer, the defendants' condition 2(a) excluding all liability under, inter alia, section 14(3) satisfied the requirement of reasonableness.

Notes

(1) It is necessary to recall that, in addition to the question whether one party is a consumer or not, UCTA generally applies only to "business liability", that is a liability which arises from some business or governmental activity, or from the possession of premises used for commercial or governmental purposes (see sections 1(3) and 14). Section 6 is an exception to this general requirement.

(2) Many provisions of the Act apply only when a party to a contract "deals as a consumer": see sections 3, 4 6(2) and 7(2). For this purpose, the cumulative conditions under section 12(1) of UCTA must be satisfied.

(3) In the *R&B Brokers* case, the Court of Appeal held that, for a purchase to be in the course of a business, it must be an integral part of the business, or, if only incidental thereto, be of a type regularly entered into. (In contrast, in *Stevenson* v. *Rogers*,[589] the Court of Appeal held that a person may *sell* in the course of a business even though the goods are not of a type he ordinarily sells, where a professional fisherman had sold a second-hand boat. The Court was clearly sceptical about the *R&B* case.)

(4) The burden of proof of dealing as a consumer rests on the party who claims that the other party does not deal as a consumer.[590]

(5) The Unfair Terms in Consumer Contracts Regulations 1999, which operate in parallel to the Act, adopt the narrower definition of consumer set out in the Directive, and discussed immediately below.

[589] [1991] 2 WLR 1064
[590] Section 12(3).

EC Directive 93/13/EEC of 5 April 1993   **3.EC.155.**
on Unfair Terms in Consumer Contracts[591]

Article 2: (b) "consumer" means any natural person who, in contracts covered by this directive, is acting for purposes which are outside his trade, business or profession, whether publicely owned or privately owned.

Case 361/89 ECJ   **3.EC.156.**
Criminal Proceedings against Di Pinto[592]

APPLICATION OF DIRECTIVE TO BUSINESSES

The Advertiser

The Directive on Canvassing does not extend protection to a businessman seeking to sell his business and who makes a contract for the advertisement of his business.

Facts: Mr Di Pinto was the manager of a company in France which published a periodical in which businesses were advertised for sale. After an initial approach through a telephone call, the company would send a representative to visit traders intending to sell their businesses. Orders for publication in the periodical had to be paid for immediately. Mr Di Pinto was accused of having violated a French law on the protection of consumers with regard to canvassing and door-to-door selling. He was convicted by the Cour d'appel in Paris. In the course of the appeal against that judgment two questions arose on the interpretation of Directive 85/577/EEC, a directive to protect the consumer in respect of contracts negotiated away from business premises. A reference was therefore made to the ECJ on this question.

Held: Mr Di Pinto's dealings with companies were not within the scope of the Directive.

Judgment:

14. In its first question, the Cour d' appel de Paris seeks in substance to ascertain whether a trader who is canvassed for the purpose of concluding an advertising contract concerning the sale of his business must be regarded as a consumer entitled to protection under the Directive.

15. It is necessary on this point to refer to article 2 of the Directive. It follows from that provision that the criterion for the application of protection lies in the connection between the transactions which are the subject of the canvassing and the professional activity of the trader: the latter may claim that the Directive is applicable only if the transaction in respect of which he is canvassed lies outside his trade or profession. Article 2, which is drafted in general terms, does not make it possible, with regard to acts performed in the context of such a trade or profession, to draw a distinction between normal acts and those which are exceptional in nature.

16. Acts which are preparatory to the sale of a business, such as the conclusion of a contract for the publication of an advertisement in a periodical, are connected with the professional activity of the trader; although such acts may bring the running of a business to an end, they are managerial acts performed for the purpose of satisfying requirements other than the family or personal requirements of the trader.

17. The Commission, which favours the application of the Directive in such a case, objects that a trader, when canvassed in connection with the sale of his business, finds himself in an unprepared state similar to that of an ordinary consumer. For that reason, it argues, traders ought also to be entitled to the protection which the Directive confers.

[591] [1993] OJ L95.
[592] [1991] ECR 1189.

18. That argument cannot be accepted. There is every reason to believe that a normally well-informed trader is aware of the value of his business and that of every measure required by its sale, with the result that, if he enters into an undertaking, it cannot be through lack of forethought and solely under the influence of surprise.

The answer to the first question must therefore be that a trader canvassed with a view to the conclusion of an advertising contract concerning the sale of his business is not to be regarded as a consumer protected by Directive 85/577.

Notes

(1) The EC Directive on Unfair Terms in Consumer Contracts is applicable only to consumer contracts, that is to say contracts between a (professional) seller or supplier and a consumer (Article 1(1)). A consumer can only be a natural person and not a legal person. Furthermore, he must act outside his trade, business or profession.

(2) In the *Di Pinto* case, the Court of Justice of the European Communities adopted a narrow conception of "consumer". It must be noted that Article 2 of Directive 85/577/EEC on Canvassing adopts the same definition of "consumer" as Article 2 of the Directive on Unfair Terms in Consumer Contracts. According to Article 2 of the Directive on Canvassing, "consumer" means a natural person who, in transactions covered by this Directive (canvassing), is acting for purposes which can be regarded as outside his trade or profession. In the *Di Pinto* case, the Court of Justice identified a relatively loose connection between the transaction and the trade or profession; a trader is regarded as a consumer only if the contract is made for family or personal requirements. The Court of Justice also took the view that the average, well-informed trader should be credited with a basic level of awareness.[593]

(3) The Court of Justice nevertheless went on to decide that the Directive on Canvassing did not prevent Member States from extending their national legislation to traders in the same position as that in the instant case. This point was decided under Article 8 of the Directive, which was clearly to this effect.

(4) It is therefore clear that the Directive has a notably narrower focus than the pre-existing legislation in some of the Member States. The *Di Pinto* case suggests that the Court of Justice may not be inclined to broaden its scope through a broad interpretation of the term "consumer".

3.4.5.B. NEGOTIATED AND NON-NEGOTIATED TERMS

(See the Directive on Unfair Terms in Consumer Contracts, Article 3; Code de la consommation, Article L. 132–1; and the language of the AGBG and the BW generally.)

Notes

(1) Article L 132–1 of the *Code de la consommation* applies to all contract terms, whether in individually negotiated or in standard term contracts. In the United Kingdom, the Unfair Contract Terms Act 1977 is also for the most part not limited to non-negotiated terms. Under the 1977 Act, the controls over clauses excluding or restricting liability for negligence (section 2 and, in guarantees, section 5); those dealing with similar

---

[593] See extensively on the notion of consumer in European Community law: Mortelmans and Watson (1995) *Tijdschrift voor Consumentenrecht* (4) 229 ff (in English).

clauses in contracts for the supply of goods (sections 6 and 7) and those dealing with indemnity clauses (section 4) and clauses excluding or restricting liability for misrepresentation (section 8) all apply whether the clause was negotiated or not. On the other hand, section 3 (on general liability for breach of contract) applies only to clauses in a party's written standard terms of business and in consumer contracts (where the vast majority of such clauses will in any event have been non-negotiated).

(2) In contrast, the language of the AGBG and the BW is worded so as to apply the relevant controls only to "standard terms" and "general conditions" respectively.

(3) Article 3 of the Directive also makes clear that the Directive is to apply only to standard term contracts.

(4) French and UK law are therefore wider in scope than the legislation in Germany and the Netherlands, and also than the Directive on Unfair Terms in Consumer Contracts (all of which are confined to standard terms). However, the Directive does cover non-negotiated terms which are not in writing—for instance, if a consumer is told of standard conditions when making a booking over the telephone.

3.4.5.C. BLACKLISTS AND GREY LISTS

AGBG   **3.G.157.**

§ 10: *Clauses prohibited subject to evaluation*
    In all standard contract terms the following in particular are invalid:
    (1) (Time-Limits for Acceptance and Performance)
    a stipulation by which the proponent prescribes unreasonably long or inadequately defined time-limits for the acceptance or refusal of an offer or the performance of in act;
    (2) (Extension of time-limit)
    a stipulation by which the proponent prescribes an unreasonably long or inadequately defined extension of time for his performance contrary to § 326 paragraph 1 of the civil code;
    (3) (Right to Withdraw)
    the grant of a right for the benefit of the proponent to withdraw without justification or adequate legal basis specified in the contract; this does not apply to long-term contractual relations;
    (4) (Provisions for Modification)
    the stipulation of a right for the benefit of the proponent to alter or deviate from the prescribed performance, unless the stipulation of the alteration or the deviation can be anticipated by the contracting partner, taking into consideration the interests of the proponent;
    (5) (Simulated Declarations)
    a stipulation according to which a performance or omission of a specified act by the contracting partner of the proponent is deemed the equivalent of the making of or the failure to make a declaration, unless
        (a) a reasonable time-limit for the making of an express declaration is granted to the contracting partner, and
        (b) the proponent undertakes in particular to bring to the attention of the contracting partner at the commencement of the time-limit the significance ascribed to his conduct;
    (6) (Fiction of Receipt of Notice)
    a stipulation which provides that a declaration by the proponent with special significance is deemed to have been received by the other party to the contract;

(7) (Settlement of Contracts)
a stipulation by which the the proponent, in the event that a contracting party withdraws or gives notice of withdrawal, claims

    (a) an unreasonably high compensation for the enjoyment or use of a thing or right or for the completed performance, or

    (b) an unreasonably high reimbursement for expenses;

§ 11: *Clauses Prohibited per se*:
In standard contract terms, site following are invalid:

(1) *Short-Term Price Increases*: a stipulation which prescribes an increase in the price of goods or services within four months from the date when the contract is made or is to be performed; this does not apply to goods or services which are to be delivered or performed over a period of time or to performances whose price is regulated by § 99 paragraph 1 or 2 number 2 of the act against unfair competition;

(2) *Right to Refuse Performance*: a stipulation by which

    (a) the right to refuse performance, which belongs to the contracting partner of the proponent according to § 320 of the civil code, is eliminated or restricted, or

    (b) a right of retention belonging to the contracting partner of the proponent and arising from the same contractual relationship is excluded or restricted, particularly if made dependent upon the acknowledgement of the existence of defects by the proponent;

(3) *Prohibition of Set-Off*: a stipulation by which the contracting partner of the proponent in deprived of his right to set off an undisputed or legally valid claim;

(4) *Notice, Grant of Time-Limit*: a stipulation by which the proponent is released from a statutory obligation to give notice to the other party to the contract, or to grant an additional time-limit for performance;

(5) *Deduction of Lump-Sum as Indemnity*: the agreement to a lump-sum claim for the proponent as indemnity or compensation for depreciation, if:

    (a) the lump sum exceeds the amount which in ordinary circumstances would be paid an compensation in the normal course of events or as the usual amount for depreciation, or

    (b) it eliminates proof by the other party to the contract that damage or depreciation did not occur or were substantially less than the lump sum provided for;

(6) *Penalty*: a stipulation by which payment of a penalty to the proponent is prescribed in the event of non acceptance or late acceptance of his performance, or in the event that the other party withdraws from the contract;

(7) *Limitation of Liability for Gross Negligence*: an exclusion of or limitation on liability for damages arising from a grossly negligent breach of contract by the proponent or a deliberate or grossly negligent breach of contract by a statutory agent or employee of the proponent; this applies also to damages for the violation of duties during the course of contract negotiations;

(8) *Default, Impossibility*: a stipulation by which, in the event of default by the proponent or impossibility of performance for which he is responsible

    (a) the right of the other party to rescind the contract is either excluded or limited or

    (b) the right to claim compensation is excluded or limited contrary to (7) above,

(9) *Partial Default, Partial Impossibility*: a stipulation which excludes the right of the other contracting party, in the event of partial non-performance by the proponent or partial impossibility of performance for which he is responsible, to claim compensation for the failure to perform the whole obligation or to cancel the whole contract, if partial performance of the contract is of no benefit to him;

(10) *Warranty*: a stipulation by which, in contracts providing for deliveries of newly produced goods and services,
- (a) (*Exclusion and Notice to Third Parties*)
  claims of warranty against the proponent, including contingent claims for repair and substitution relating to the whole or to a separate part, are excluded, are limited to the recovery of claims against third parties, or are made contingent upon the bringing of a prior legal action against third parties;
- (b) (*Limitation on repair*)
  claims of warranty against the proponent relating to the whole or to a separate part are limited to a right to repair or substitution if there is no express reservation of the right of the other contracting party to a reduction in compensation upon the failure of the repair or substitution or, it the subject of the warranty is not a construction contract, to demand rescission of the contract at his election;
- (c) (*Expenses of Repair*)
  the duty of the proponent warrantor to bear the expenses which are necessary to fulfil the purpose of the contract, particularly the costs of transport, tolls, and work and materials, is excluded or limited;
- (d) (*Withholding Correction of a Defect*)
  the proponent conditions the correction of a defect or the substitution of a defect-free item on prior payment of the whole price or of a sum disproportionately high in light of the nature of the defect;
- (e) (*Time-Limit for Notice of Defect*)
  the proponent sets a time-limit for notice of hidden defects which is shorter than the period of limitation for statutory warranties;
- (f) (*Limitation of Period of Warranty*)
  the statutory period of warranty is shortened.

(11) *Liability for Warranty of Quality*: a stipulation by which in a contract of sale, for work, or for work and materials, claims for indemnity against the proponent under §§ 463, 480 paragraph 2 and 635 of the civil code for breach of warranty of quality are excluded or diminished;

(12) *Duration of Term of Continuing Obligation*: in a contractual relation which has as its object regular deliveries of merchandise or the regular performance of services or work by the proponent,
- (a) a term of more than two years during which the contract is binding on the other party,
- (b) "a tacit extension of the term of the contract for more than a year is binding on the other party",
  the contract for more than a year is binding on the other party,
- (c) the other party is required to give notice of cancellation more than three months before the date of the express or tacit extension of the contract;

(13) *Change of Contracting Partner*: a stipulation in a contract of sale, for service, or for work in which a third party may take the place of the proponent with respect to the rights and duties under the contract, unless
- (a) the third party is mentioned by name, or
- (b) a right is granted to the other party to withdraw from the contract;

(14) *Liability of the Agent Entering into a Contract*: a stipulation by which the proponent imposes upon an agent who concludes a contract for the other party
- (a) without a proper express and separate statement, a personal responsibility or duty to indemnify, or

(b) in the case of an unauthorised agent, a responsibility greater than that provided for in § 179 of the civil code;

(15) *Burden of Proof*: a stipulation by which the proponent alters the burden of proof to the prejudice of the other contracting party, particularly one by which he

(a) imposes upon the latter the burden of proof of circumstances which fall within the scope of responsibility of the proponent;

(b) requires the other party to allege certain facts.

Subsection b does not apply to a separately signed acknowledgement;

(16) *Form of Notice and Explanation*: a stipulation by which a notice or explanation delivered to the proponent or to a third party is required to be in a form more exacting than the written form or dependent upon notice requirements.

. . .

Note

AGBG § 11 contains a list of clauses which are always invalid; § 10 a list which are "prohibited subject to evaluation". This paragraph appears to put the burden of proving the clause to be consistent with good faith on the proponent.

As we have seen, the Unfair Contract Terms Act 1977 also renders some clauses completely invalid whilst others may be valid if they are fair and reasonable.[594] Where a term is subject to a requirement of reasonableness, the Act explicitly places the burden of proof on the party claiming that a contract term or notice satisfies the requirement of reasonableness: section 11(5). The UTCCR 1999 follow the wording of the Directive so that who has the burden of proof is not clear.

The annex to the Code de la consomation reproduces the annex to the Directive, set out below. The effect of inclusion in the annex is that a term will be treated as unfair. Under Article 132–1 of the Code, the onus of proving that a term is unfair is upon the plaintiff. Given that the Article provides that certain terms are to be treated as unfair, this apparently means that the burden of proof is upon party seeking to rely on the clause. French law does not therefore adopt a "black list and grey list" approach.

Directive 93/13/EEC of 5 April 1993   **3.EC.158.**
on Unfair Terms in Consumer Contracts

Article 3: 3. The Annex shall contain an indicative and non-exhaustive list of the terms which may be regarded unfair.

ANNEX

Terms referred to in article 3 (3)

1. Terms which have the object or effect of:

(a) excluding or limiting the legal liability of a seller or supplier in the event of the death of a consumer or personal injury to the latter resulting from an act or omission of that seller or supplier;

(b) inappropriately excluding or limiting the legal rights of the consumer vis- à-vis the seller or supplier or another party in the event of total or partial non-performance or inadequate performance by the seller or supplier of any of the contractual obligations, including the option of offsetting a debt owed to the seller or supplier against any claim which the consumer may have against him;

---

[594] See *supra* at 519.

(c) making an agreement binding on the consumer whereas provision of services by the seller or supplier is subject to a condition whose realisation depends on his own will alone;

(d) permitting the seller or supplier to retain sums paid by the consumer where the latter decides not to conclude or perform the contract, without providing for the consumer to receive compensation of an equivalent amount from the seller or supplier where the latter is the party cancelling the contract;

(e) requiring any consumer who fails to fulfil his obligation to pay a disproportionately high sum in compensation;

(f) authorising the seller or supplier to dissolve the contract on a discretionary basis where the same facility is not granted to the consumer, or permitting the seller or supplier to retain the sums paid for services not yet supplied by him where it is the seller or supplier himself who dissolves the contract;

(g) enabling the seller or supplier to terminate a contract of indeterminate duration without reasonable notice except where there are serious grounds for doing so;

(h) automatically extending a contract of fixed duration where the consumer does not indicate otherwise, when the deadline fixed for the consumer to express this desire not to extend the contract is unreasonably early;

(i) irrevocably binding the consumer to terms with which he had no real opportunity of becoming acquainted before the conclusion of the contract;

(j) enabling the seller or supplier to alter the terms of the contract unilaterally without a valid reason which is specified in the contract;

(k) enabling the seller or supplier to alter unilaterally without a valid reason any characteristics of the product or service to be provided;

(l) providing for the price of goods to be determined at the time of delivery or allowing a seller of goods or supplier of services to increase their price without in both cases giving the consumer the corresponding right to cancel the contract if the final price is too high in relation to the price agreed when the contract was concluded;

(m) giving the seller or supplier the right to determine whether the goods or services supplier are in conformity with the contract, or giving him the exclusive right to interpret any term of the contract;

(n) limiting the seller' or supplier's obligation to respect commitments undertaken by his agents or making his commitments subject to compliance with a particular formality;

(o) obliging the consumer to fulfil all his obligations where the seller or supplier does not perform his;

(p) giving the seller or supplier the possibility of transferring his rights and obligations under the contract, where this may serve to reduce the guarantees for the consumer, without the latter's agreement;

(q) excluding or hindering the consumer's right to take legal action or exercise any other legal remedy, particularly by requiring the consumer to take disputes exclusively to arbitration not covered by legal provisions, unduly restricting the evidence available to him or imposing on him a burden of proof which, according to the applicable law, should lie with another party to the contract.

2. Scope of subparagraphs (g), (j) and (l)

(a) subparagraph (g) is without hindrance to terms by which a supplier of financial services reserves the right to terminate unilaterally a contract of indeterminate duration without notice where there is a valid reason, provided that the supplier is required to inform the other contracting party or parties thereof immediately.

(a) subparagraph (j) is without hindrance to terms under which a supplier of financial services reserves the right to alter the rate of interest payable by the consumer or due to the latter, or the amount of other charges for financial services without notice where there is a valid reason, provided that the supplier is required to inform the other contracting party or parties thereof at the earliest opportunity and that the latter are free to dissolve the contract immediately;

Subparagraph (j) is also without hindrance to terms under which a seller or supplier reserves the right to later unilaterally the conditions of a contract of indeterminate duration, provided that he is required to inform the consumer with reasonable notice and that the consumer is free to dissolve the contract.

(c) subparagraph (g), (j) and (l) do not apply to:

—transactions in transferable securities, financial instruments and other products or services where the price is linked to fluctuations in stock exchange quotation or index or a financial market rate that the seller or supplier does not control;

—contracts for the purchase or sale of foreign currency, traveller's cheques or international money orders denominated in foreign currency;

(d) subparagraph (l) is without hindrance to price-indexation clauses, where lawful, provided that the method by which prices vary is explicitly described.

Note

The EC Directive contains in the Annex contains what Article 3(3) describes as "an indicative and non-exhaustive list of the terms which may be regarded unfair". This list may be of somewhat limited effect, for there is no clause clearly to the effect that terms on the list are to be deemed unfair unless the contrary is shown by the business which uses them. The AGBG and the *Code de la consommation* nevertheless appear to have applied a presumption against the party seeking to rely on the clause. The UTCC Regulations follow the Directive.

3.4.5.E. "FAIR", "REASONABLE", IN ACCORDANCE WITH "GOOD FAITH"

Directive 93/13/EEC of 5 April 1993   **3.EC.159.**
on Unfair Terms in Consumer Contracts

Article 3: 1. A contractual term which has not been individually negotiated shall be regarded as unfair if, contrary to the requirement of good faith, it causes a significant imbalance in the parties' rights and obligations arising under the contract.

Article 4: 1. Without prejudice to article 7, the unfairness of a contractual term shall be assessed, taking into account the nature of the goods or services for which the contract was concluded and by referring, at the time of conclusion of the contract, to all the circumstances attending the conclusion of the contract and to all the other terms of the contract or of another contract on which it is dependent.

The Unfair Terms in Consumer Contracts Regulations 1999 adopt the precise wording of the Directive. However, the Unfair Contract Terms Act 1977 applies a different test, considered below.

(See also Code de la consommation, Article L. 132–1.[595])

---

[595] *Supra* at 525.

Notes

(1) The standard for review in the renewed Article L. 132–1 of the *Code de la consomma-tion* is similar to the one in the European Directive. A contractual term is unfair ("abusive") if it causes a significant imbalance (*déséquilibre significatif*) in the parties' rights and obliga-tions arising under the contract, to the detriment of the non-professional or consumer. Under the former Article 35 of the *Loi Scrivener*, an "abuse of economic power" by the pro-fessional (*abus de puissance économique*) was required. However, the change is relatively insignificant, because the Cour de cassation decided that an abuse of economic power of a professional is inherent in standard term contracts concluded between professionals and consumers.[596] (In contrast to the Directive, the provision in the French code does not men-tion the requirement of good faith; it is said that this vague concept has no additional value.[597])

(2) Whether a term is "unfair" depends on all the circumstances attending the conclu-sion of the contract (Article L 132–1, al. 5). The Annex to the *Code de la consommation* also contains an indicative and non-exhaustive list of the terms which can be regarded as unfair, as discussed above. The onus of proof of unfairness lies on the plaintiff (Article L 132–1, al 3).

(See AGBG, § 9.[598])

Unfair Contract Terms Act 1977 **3.E.160.**

Explanatory provisions

Section 11: *The "reasonableness" test*

(1) In relation to a contract term, the requirement of reasonableness for the purposes of this Part of this Act, section 3 of the Misrepresentation Act 1967 and section 3 of the Misrepresentation Act (Northern Ireland) 1967 is that the term shall have been a fair and reasonable one to be included having regard to the circumstances which were, or ought reasonably to have been, known to or in the contemplation of the parties when the contract was made.

(2) In determining for the purposes of section 6 or 7 above whether a contract term satisfies the requirement of reasonableness, regard shall be had in particular to the mat-ters specified in Schedule 2 to this Act; but this subsection does not prevent the court or arbitrator from holding, in accordance with any rule of laid, that a term which pur-ports to exclude or restrict any relevant liability is not a term of the contract.

(3) In relation to a notice (not being a notice having contractual effect), the require-ment of reasonableness under this Act is that it should be fair and reasonable to allow reliance on it, having regard to all the circumstances obtaining when the liability arose or (but for the notice) would have arisen.

(4) Where by reference to a contract term or notice a person seeks to restrict liability to a specified sum of money, and the question arises (under this or any other Act) whether the term or notice satisfies the requirement of reasonableness, regard shall be had in particular (but without prejudice to subsection (2) above in case of contract terms) to—

---

[596] Cass. 1e civ, 6 January 1994, D. 1994. S.209 annotated by Delebecque.
[597] See Paisant, D. 1995.100.
[598] *Supra* at 513.

(a) the resources which he could expect to be available to him for the purpose of meeting the liability should it arise; and

(b) how far it was open to him to cover himself by insurance.

SCHEDULE 2
"GUIDELINES" FOR APPLICATION OF REASONABLENESS TEST

The matters to which regard is to be had in particular for the purposes of sections 6(3), 7(3) and (4), 20 and 21 are any of the following which appear to be relevant—

(a) the strength of the bargaining positions of the parties relative to each other, taking into account (among other things) alternative means by which the customer's requirements could have been met;

(b) whether the customer received an inducement to agree to the terms, or in accepting it had an opportunity of entering into a similar contract with other persons, but without having to accept a similar term;

(c) whether the customer knew or ought reasonably to have known of the existence and extent of the term (having regard, among other things, to any custom of the trade and any previous course of dealing between the parties);

(d) where the term excludes or restricts any relevant liability if some condition is not complied with, whether it was reasonable at the time of the contract to expect that compliance with that condition would be practicable;

(e) whether the goods were manufactured, processed or adapted to the special order of the consumer.

Notes

(1) The Guidelines contained in Schedule 2 of the Act are brought forward from the earlier Supply of Goods (Implied Terms) Act 1973. Technically they apply only to cases falling within sections 6 and 7 (see section 11(2)), but the courts also take these factors into account in other cases: for example *Rees Hough Ltd* v. *Redland Reinforced Plastics Ltd*;[599] *Phillips Products Ltd* v. *Hyland*.[600]

Court of Appeal and House of Lords **3.E.161.**
George Mitchell (Chesterhall) Ltd. v. *Finney Lock Seeds Ltd.*[601]

REASONABLENESS

Defective cabbage seed

The following factors are relevant in assessing whether it is reasonable to rely on a limitation clause: (i) the fact that the supplier does in practice pay compensation to some customers who have suffered the same loss as the purchaser irrespective of the clause; (ii) the fact that supplier could insure against such losses without materially increasing the price of the goods; (iii) the fact that the goods supplied were of no value to the purchaser.

Facts: See above.[602]

---

[599] (1984) 27 Building LR 136.
[600] [1987] 2 All ER 620, CA.
[601] [1983] QB 284 and [1983] 2 AC 803.
[602] *Supra* at 506.

Held: In addition to finding that the seller was not entitled to rely on the clause, the Court of Appeal unanimously found that it was not reasonable for the sellers to rely on the clause under the Supply of Goods (Implied Terms) Act 1973. Having overturned the decision of the Court of Appeal on the first point, the House of Lords upheld the decision on the reasonableness point.

Judgment of the Court of Appeal: LORD DENNING: . . .

The Supply of Goods (Implied Terms) Act 1973

In any case the contract for these cabbage seeds was governed by s 4 of the Supply of Goods (Implied Terms) Act 1973: see now s 55(4) as set out in para II of Sch I to the Sale of Goods Act 1979. That section says that in the case of a contract of sale of goods any terms "is . . . not enforceable to the extent that it is shown that it would not be fair or reasonable to allow reliance on the term". That provision is exactly in accord with the principle which I have advocated above. So the ultimate question, to my mind, in this case is just this: to what extent would it be fair to reasonable to allow the seeds merchants to rely on the limitation clause?

Fair and reasonable

There is only one case in the books so far on this point. It is *R W Green Ltd* v *Cade Bros Farm* [1978] I Lloyd's Rep 602. There Griffith J held that it was fair and reasonable for seed potato merchants to rely on a limitation clause which limited their liability to the contract price of the potatoes. That case was very different from the present. The terms had been evolved over twenty years. The judge said (at 607): "They are therefore not conditions imposed by the strong upon the weak; but rather a set of trading terms upon which both sides are apparently content to do business." The judge added (at 608): "No moral blame attaches to either party; neither of them knew, nor could be expected to know, that the potatoes were infected." In that case the judge held that the case was fair and reasonable and that the seed merchants were entitled to rely on it.

Our present case is very much on the borderline. There is this to be said in favour of the seed merchants. The price of this cabbage seed was small: £192. The damages claimed are high: £ 61,000. But there is this to be said on the other side. The clause was not negotiated between persons of equal bargaining power. It was inserted by the seed merchants in their invoices without any negotiation with the farmers.

To this I would add that the seed merchants rarely, if ever, invoked the clause. Their very frank director said: "The trade does not stand on the strict letter of the clause . . . Almost invariably when a customer justifiably complains, the trade pays something more than a refund." The papers contain many illustrations where the clause was not invoked and a settlement was reached.

Next, I would point out that the buyers had no opportunity at all of knowing or discovering that the seed was not cabbage seed, whereas the sellers could and should have known that it was the wrong seed altogether. The buyers were not covered by insurance against the risk. Nor could they insure. But, as to the seed merchants, the judge said ([1981] I Lloyd's Rep 476 at 480):

> "I am entirely satisfied that it is possible for seedsmen to insure against this risk. I am entirely satisfied that the cost of so doing would not materially raise the price of seeds on the market. I am entirely satisfied that the protection of this clause for the purpose of protecting against the very rare case indeed , such as the present, is not reasonably required. If and in so far as it may be necessary to consider the matter, I am also satisfied that it is possible for seedsmen to test seeds before putting them on to the market."

To that I would add this further point. Such a mistake as this should not have happened without serious negligence on the part of the seed merchants themselves or their Dutch suppliers. So serious that it would not be fair to enable them to escape responsibilities for it.

In all the circumstances I am of opinion that it would not be fair or reasonable to allow the seed merchants to rely on the clause to limit their liability.

I would dismiss the appeal accordingly.

Judgment in the House of Lords:

LORD BRIDGE: . . . This is the first time your Lordships' House has had to consider a modern statutory provision giving the court power to override contractual terms excluding or restricting liability, which depends on the court's view of what is "fair and reasonable." The particular provision of the modified section 55 of the Act of 1979 which applies in the instant case is of limited and diminishing importance. But the several provisions of the Unfair Contract Terms Act 1977 which depend on "the requirement of reasonableness," defined in section 11 by reference to what is "fair and reasonable," albeit in a different context, are likely to come before the courts with increasing frequency. It may, therefore, be appropriate to consider how an original decision as to what is "fair and reasonable" made in the application of any of these provisions should be approached by an appellate court. It would not be accurate to describe such a decision as an exercise of discretion. But a decision under any of the provisions referred to will have this in common with the exercise of a discretion, that, in having regard to the various matters to which the modified section 55 (5) of the Act of 1979, or section 11 of the Act of 1977 direct attention, the court must entertain a whole range of considerations, put them in the scales on one side or the other, and decide at the end of the day on which side the balance comes down. There will sometimes be room for a legitimate difference of judicial opinion as to what the answer should be, where it will be impossible to say that one view is demonstrably wrong and the other demonstrably right. It must follow, in my view, that, when asked to review such a decision on appeal, the appellate court should treat the original decision with the utmost respect and refrain from interference with it unless satisfied that it proceeded upon some erroneous principle or was plainly and obviously wrong.

. . . [I]t is common ground that the onus was on the respondents to show that it would not be fair or reasonable to allow the appellants to rely on the relevant condition as limiting their liability. It was argued for the appellants that the court must have regard to the circumstances as at the date of the contract, not after the breach. . . . But, in any event, the language of subsections (4) and (5) of that section is clear and unambiguous. The question whether it is fair or reasonable to allow reliance on a term excluding or limiting liability for a breach of contract can only arise after the breach. The nature of the breach and the circumstances in which it occurred cannot possibly be excluded from "all the circumstances of the case" to which regard must be had.

My Lords, . . . I turn to the application of the statutory language to the circumstances of the case. Of the particular matters to which attention is directed by paragraphs (a) to (e) of section 55 (5), only those in (a) to (c) are relevant. As to paragraph (c), the respondents admittedly knew of the relevant condition (they had dealt with the appellants for many years) and, if they had read it, particularly clause 2, they would, I think, as laymen rather than lawyers, have had no difficulty in understanding what it said. This and the magnitude of the damages claimed in proportion to the price of the seeds sold are factors which weigh in the scales in the appellants' favour.

The question of relative bargaining strength under paragraph (a) and of the opportunity to buy seeds without a limitation of the seedsman's liability under paragraph (b) were inter-related. The evidence was that a similar limitation of liability was universally embodied in the terms of trade between seedsmen and farmers and had been so for very many years. The limitation had never been negotiated between representative bodies but, on the other hand, had not been the subject of any protest by the National Farmers' Union. These factors, if considered in isolation, might have been equivocal. The decisive factor, however, appears from the evidence of four witnesses called for the appellants, two independent seedsmen, the chairman of the appellant company, and a director of a sister company (both being wholly-owned subsidiaries of the same parent). They said that it had always been their practice, unsuccessfully attempted in the instant case, to negotiate settlements of farmers' claims for damages in excess of the price of the seeds, if they thought that the claims were "genuine" and "justified." This evidence indicated a clear recognition by seedsmen in general, and the appellants in particular, that reliance on the limitation of liability imposed by the relevant condition would not be fair or reasonable.

Two further factors, if more were needed, weight the scales in favour of the respondents. The supply of autumn, instead of winter, cabbage seeds was due to the negligence of the appellants' sister company. Irrespective of its quality, the autumn variety supplied could not, according to the appellants' own evidence, be grown commercially in East Lothian. Finally, as the trial judge found, seedsmen could insure against the risk of crop failure caused by supplying the wrong variety of seeds without materially increasing the price of seeds.

My Lords, even if I felt doubts about the statutory issue, I should not, for the reasons explained earlier, think it right to interfere with the unanimous original decision of that issue by the Court of Appeal. As it is, I feel no such doubts. If I were making the original decision, I should conclude without hesitation that it would not be fair or reasonable to allow the appellants to rely on the contractual limitation of their liability.

I would dismiss the appeal.

Note

This case was decided not under UCTA 1977, but under the Supply of Goods (Implied Terms) Act 1973 (now superseded by UCTA). The earlier Act used the test not of whether it was reasonable to incorporate the clause into the contract, but whether it was reasonable for the seller to rely on the clause.

House of Lords   **3.E.162.**
Smith v. *Eric S. Bush*[603]

SURVEYOR'S DISCLAIMER UNREASONABLE

The building society surveyor

It is unreasonable for a surveyor employed by a building society to value a property to disclaim liability for negligence towards the ultimate purchasers of the property when the property is a modest one and the surveyor should know that the purchaser will rely on the surveyor's report as showing that there were no serious problems with the property rather than arranging their own survey at extra cost.

Facts: In order to purchase a house, Mrs Smith applied for a mortgage to the Abbey National Building Society. An inspection report of the house was needed. The Abbey National instructed the firm Eric S. Bush to carry out the valuation. The application form filled in by Mrs Smith and the report of Eric S. Bush contained a disclaimer of responsibility for the condition of the property. Eighteen months after Mrs Smith entered the contract, bricks from the chimney collapsed and fell through the roof into the loft and the main bedroom and ceilings on the first floor. Mrs Smith claimed that the surveyor was liable because he did not exercise reasonable skill and care in carrying out the valuation.

Held: The House of Lords held that the disclaimer was not fair and reasonable under the Unfair Contract Terms Act 1977 and must be held ineffective. The surveyor was therefore liable in tort to the purchaser (who was not a party to the contract between surveyor and building society).

Judgment: LORD GRIFFITHS: . . . I believe that it is impossible to draw up an exhaustive list of the factors that must be taken into account when a judge is faced with this very difficult decision. Nevertheless, the following matters should, in my view, always be considered.

1. Were the parties of equal bargaining power. If the court is dealing with a one-off situation between parties of equal bargaining power the requirement of reasonableness would be more easily discharged than in a case such as the present where the disclaimer is imposed upon the purchaser who has no effective power to object.

[603] [1990] 1 AC 831.

2. In the case of advice would it have been reasonably practicable to obtain the advice from an alternative source taking into account considerations of costs and time. In the present case it is urged on behalf of the surveyor that it would have been easy for the purchaser to have obtained his own report on the condition of the house, to which the purchaser replies, that he would then be required to pay twice for the same advice and that people buying at the bottom end of the market, many of whom will be young first-time buyers, are likely to be under considerable financial pressure without the money to go paying twice for the same service.

3. How difficult is the task being undertaken for which liability is being excluded. When a very difficult or dangerous undertaking is involved there may be a high risk of failure which would certainly be a pointer towards the reasonableness of excluding liability as a condition of doing the work. A valuation, on the other hand, should present no difficulty if the work is undertaken with reasonable skill and care. It is only defects which are observable by a careful visual examination that have to be taken into account and I cannot see that it places any unreasonable burden on the valuer to require him to accept responsibility for the fairly elementary degree of skill and care involved in observing, following-up and reporting on such defects. Surely it is work at the lower end of the surveyor's field of professional expertise.

4. What are the practical consequences of the decision on the question of reasonableness. This must involve the sums of money potentially at stake and the ability of the parties to bear the loss involved, which, in its turn, raises the question of insurance. There was once a time when it was considered improper even to mention the possible existence of insurance cover in a lawsuit. But those days are long past. Everyone knows that all prudent, professional men carry insurance, and the availability and cost of insurance must be a relevant factor when considering which of two parties should be required to bear the risk of a loss. We are dealing in this case with a loss which will be limited to the value of a modest house and against which it can be expected that the surveyor will be insured. Bearing the loss will be unlikely to cause significant hardship if it has to be borne by the surveyor but it is, on the other hand, quite possible that it will be a financial catastrophe for the purchaser who may be left with a valueless house and no money to buy another. If the law in these circumstances denies the surveyor the right to exclude his liability, it may result in a few more claims but I do not think so poorly of the surveyor's profession as to believe that the floodgates will be opened. There may be some increase in surveyors' insurance premiums which will be passed on to the public, but I cannot think that it will be anything approaching the figures involved in the difference between the Abbey National's offer of a valuation without liability and a valuation with liability discussed in the speech of my noble and learned friend, Lord Templeman. The result of denying a surveyor, in the circumstances of this case, the right to exclude liability, will result in distributing the risk of his negligence among all house purchasers through an increase in his fees to cover insurance, rather than allowing the whole of the risk to fall upon the one unfortunate purchaser.

I would not, however, wish it to be thought that I would consider it unreasonable for professional men in all circumstances to seek to exclude or limit their liability for negligence. Sometimes breathtaking sums of money may turn on professional advice against which it would be impossible for the adviser to obtain adequate insurance cover and which would ruin him if he were to be held personally liable. In these circumstances it may indeed be reasonable to give the advice upon a basis of no liability or possibly of liability limited to the extent of the adviser's insurance cover.

In addition to the foregoing four factors, which will always have to be considered, there is in this case the additional feature that the surveyor is only employed in the first place because the purchaser wishes to buy the house and the purchaser in fact provides or contributes to the surveyor's fees. No one has argued that if the purchaser had employed and paid the surveyor himself, it would have been reasonable for the surveyor to exclude liability for negligence, and the present situation is not far removed from that of a direct contract between the surveyor and the purchaser. The evaluation of the foregoing matters leads me to the clear conclusion that it would not be fair and reasonable for the surveyor to be permitted to exclude liability in the circumstances of this case. I would therefore dismiss this appeal.

It must, however, be remembered that this is a decision in respect of a dwelling house of modest value in which it is widely recognised by surveyors that purchasers are in fact relying on their care and skill. It will obviously be of general application in broadly similar circumstances. But I expressly reserve my position in respect of valuations of quite different types of property for mortgage purposes, such as industrial property, large blocks of flats or very expensive houses. In such cases it may well be that the general expectation of the behaviour of the purchaser is quite different. With very large sums of money at stake prudence would seem to demand that the purchaser obtain his own structural survey to guide him in his purchase and, in such circumstances with very much larger sums of money at stake, it may be reasonable for the surveyors valuing on behalf of those who are providing the finance either to exclude or limit their liability to the purchaser.

Notes

(1) The criterion of "reasonableness" (UCTA 1977 section 11(1)) does not materially differ from the concept of "good faith", although the latter is not a fundamental feature of English contract law as it is in many continental jurisdictions.[604]

(2) In *George Mitchell*, Lord Bridge stated clearly his view that the question of "reasonableness" is really a matter of impression for the trial judge. It is therefore difficult to state any rules about how the tests will be applied. However, the cases set out above provide some indication of factors which the courts clearly will take into account, such as which party could more easily insure[605] or whether the customer had a choice[606] etc.

3.4.6. PUBLIC LAW CONTROLS

Directive 93/13/EEC of 5 April 1993   **3.EC.163.**
on Unfair Terms in Consumer Contracts

Article 7: 1. Member states shall ensure that, in the interests of consumers and of competitors, adequate and effective means exist to prevent the continued use of unfair terms in contracts concluded with consumers by sellers or suppliers.

2. The means referred to in paragraph 1 shall include provisions whereby persons or organisations, having a legitimate interest under national law in protecting consumers, may take action according to the national law concerned before the courts or before competent administrative bodies for a decision as to whether contractual terms drawn up for general use are unfair, so that they can apply appropriate and effective means to prevent the continued use of such terms.

3. With due regard for national laws, the legal remedies referred to in paragraph 2 may be directed separately or jointly against a number of sellers or suppliers from the same economic sector or their associations which use or recommend the use of the same general contractual terms or similar terms.

It has already been noted that the French *Loi Scrivener* was originally designed, not to affect the private rights of parties *inter se*, but to prohibit the use of abusive clauses. The

---

[604] See Atiyah, *The Sale of Goods*, op. cit., at 315.

[605] *George Mitchell* and *Smith* v. *Bush*, *supra* at 548, and also *Phillips Products Ltd* v. *Hyland* [1987] 2 All ER 620.

[606] *Smith* v. *Bush* and *Phillips* v. *Hyland*.

Commission has been retained under the amended legislation. Under the following provisions of the *Code de la comsommation*, consumer associations also have the right to challenge unfair terms in civil proceedings:

Code de la consommation   **3.F.164.**

Aritcle L. 421–1: Duly registered associations whose object is expressly stated in their articles of association to be the defence of the interests of consumers may, if authorized so to do, exercise the rights conferred on plaintiffs in civil proceedings in relation to matters causing direct or indirect prejudice to consumers as a whole . . .

Article L. 421–2: Where a consumer association of the type referred to in Article L. 421–1 is acting in the circumstances specified in that article, it may apply to the civil court adjudicating on the civil action, or to the criminal court adjudicating on the civil action, for an order against the defendant or accused, accompanied where appropriate by the sanction of a penalty payment or payments, requiring any measure to be taken with a view to restraining any unlawful acts or removing an unlawful term or clause from the contract or type of contract proposed to consumers. . . .

Article L. 421–6: A consumer association of the type referred to in Article L. 421–1 may apply to a civil court for an order, accompanied where appropriate by the sanction of a penalty payment or payments, requiring the removal of unfair terms or clauses from standard-form agreements habitually proposed by sellers or suppliers to consumers and/or from agreements of that kind which are intended for consumers and which are proposed by professional organisations to their members.

The German AGBG of 1976 also created a public law control on the use of unfair standard terms in addition to the civil law control:

AGBG   **3.G.165.**

Chapter 3: Procedure
§ 13: *Claims for Discontinuance and Retraction*
   (1) One who applies or re-commences the application to legal transactions of stipulations in standard contract terms which are invalid under §§ 9 through 11 of this Act may have a claim for discontinuance or retraction brought against him.
   (2) Claims for discontinuance and for retraction may be brought only
      1. by associations with legal capacity whose statutory duty it is to protect the interests of the consumer by giving information and advice, if these associations have as members other associations active in this sphere, or at least 75 natural persons;
      2. by associations with legal capacity to advance commercial interests; or
      3. by chambers of industry and commerce or chambers of artisans.
   (3) The associations mentioned in paragraph (2) (1) may not advance claims for discontinuance and retraction if the standard terms are applicable against a merchant and the contract belongs within the scope of his business or if the standard contract terms are recommended for application exclusively between merchants.

(4) Claims within paragraph (1) must be brought within two years commencing with the time when the claimant has acquired knowledge of the application or recommendation of invalid standard contract terms and, even without such knowledge, within four years commencing with the time of the application or recommendation.

Note

Consumer organisations are thus empowered to act under the Law on Standard Contracts. They can obtain a written assurance from the business and take proceedings if the assurance is broken. This has proven to be an extremely effective control.[607]

In England there was before 1994 no equivalent to these procedures, even for the limited range of unfair clauses[608] falling within the Unfair Contract Terms Act 1977. Under the Fair Trading Act 1973 (Part III), the Director-General of Fair Trading has the power to act against traders who persist in a course of conduct which is detrimental or unfair to consumers. However, this idea is presently defined in terms of a breach of the civil or criminal law, and thus will not even cover the use of blacklisted terms unless there is legislation specifically prohibiting their use. Part II of the Act does contain powers to issue regulations banning the use of clauses if they amount to "consumer trade practices which adversely affect the interests of consumers", and in accordance with this power, the Consumer Transactions (Restrictions on Statements) Order 1976[609] makes it a criminal offence to include in a consumer contract of sale an exclusion clause which would automatically be void under UCTA section 6. However, the Part II procedure has a number of serious defects and has given rise to few prohibitions.[610]

When the Directive on Unfair Terms in Consumer Contracts was first implemented in the UK, the power to take action was given only to the Director-General of Fair Trading. Despite warnings that this would fail to satisfy Article 7 of the Directive,[611] some commentators took the view that these powers of the Director General of Fair Trading satisfied the requirements of the Directive.[612] The Office of Fair Trading has in fact been very active in obtaining assurances that unfair terms in contracts will be removed by the businesses responsible for them. In any event, regulation 11 of and schedule 1 to the 1999 Regulations now give the power to take action to a much wider range of authorities (including local trading standards officers) and to the Consumers Association.

3.4.7. CONCLUDING REMARKS

One of the most important and innovative developments in private law in this century has been the judicial review of unfair contract terms. Although the principle of freedom of contract remains of paramount importance, this freedom is subject to restrictions. This is

---

[607] See Micklitz, RIDC 1989.101; Hondius, *Unfair Terms in Consumer Contracts* (Utrecht: Molengraaf Institute for Private Law, 1987), at 184.
[608] Primarily exclusion and limitation of liability clauses, see *supra* at 518.
[609] SI 1976/1813, as amended. by SI 1978/127.
[610] See Beale in Beatson and Friedmann, *Good Faith and Fault in Contract Law* (OUP, 1995), at 253.
[611] See *ibid.*, at 256–9.
[612] See Guest in *Chitty* (27th ed., 1994), para. 14–104.

especially true where the freedom of contract is monopolized by one of the contracting parties with a stronger bargaining position and for that reason may easily lead to contractual injustice. Nowadays this role of the courts is commonly accepted, even in countries, such as France, where the protection of weaker parties against unfair terms effectively imposed by stronger parties has traditionally been a feature of administrative law.

The use by the courts of open-ended concepts, such as good morals or good faith, has in some countries been replaced by legislation which specifically empowers the courts to review unfair contract terms. This legislation is sometimes of general application and is sometimes restricted to standard terms or particular contracts (such as sale of goods or insurance contracts). The most recent development in this story is the EC Directive on Unfair Terms in Consumer Contracts, which has given rise to a partial harmonization of the laws in the Member States and thus created a minimum level of consumer protection against unfair clauses in standard terms. In the EU, the review of unfair standard terms may occur through an individual action before the civil courts, or through a public action (United Kingdom and France) or collective action (Germany, France, and the Netherlands). The collective or public review of contract terms has an inevitably abstract character.

Clauses that are individually negotiated and clauses in contracts between professional parties are outside the scope of the Directive. The availability of review for such clauses therefore remains a matter for the Member States. We have seen that, in addition to general concepts such as good faith, a number of other general doctrines of contract law are used to control the effect of unfair contract terms, notably the law relating to the formation of contracts and the rules on interpretation. In the application of these more general contract law rules, the courts in any Member State may derive inspiration from particular legislation (the so called *Indizwirkung* of the indicative list of unfair clauses for contracts between large companies and small businessmen) as well as, evidently, from case law in other Member States. However, some Member States, notably Germany and the UK, do have legislative controls over unfair clauses used in contracts between businesses, and under UCTA 1977, the control is not limited to standard contractual terms.

The Principles of European Contract Law subject any term which has not been individually negotiated to a test of good faith and fair dealing (Article 4:110), and provide that any clause exempting or limiting liability, negotiated or not, may be relied on only it is not contrary to good faith to do so (Article 8:109). It is therefore arguable that the Principles accurately reflect an emerging common law of Europe on the treatment of unfair contract terms.

Principles of European Contract Law   **3.PECL.166.**

Article 4:110: *Unfair Terms not Individually Negotiated*
> (1) A party may avoid a term which has not been individually negotiated if, contrary to the requirements of good faith and fair dealing, it causes a significant imbalance in the parties' rights and obligations arising under the contract to the detriment of that party, taking into account the nature of the performance to be rendered under the contract, all the other terms of the contract and the circumstances at the time the contract was concluded.
> (2) This Article does not apply to:
>> (a) a term which defines the main subject matter of the contract, provided the term is in plain and intelligible language; or to

553

(b) the adequacy in value of one party's obligations compared to the value of the obligations of the other party.

Article 8:109: *Clause Excluding or Restricting Remedies*
Remedies for non-performance may be excluded or restricted unless it would be contrary to good faith and fair dealing to invoke the exclusion or restriction.

CHAPTER FOUR
INTERPRETATION AND CONTENTS

Words are not always understood as intended. The meaning of a verbal statement depends essentially on what the parties making and receiving it think it means, but since what people think depends on their personal knowledge, experience, preferences, concerns and interests, the author of the statement and its addressee can easily think it means different things. If the statement forms part of a contract, it must be given a single meaning binding on both parties. The process of educing such a meaning is called interpretation.[1]

Interpretation is also needed when the parties have failed to provide for a contingency which they would have covered had they thought of all the problems which might arise as the contract proceeded. Contracts are almost always incomplete in this sense. There are several reasons for this. In finalizing their agreement negotiators tend to concentrate on their respective undertakings and ignore the many things that may go wrong—that a party may perform late, in the wrong place, in the wrong way, or not at all. They often make no provision for the incidence or consequences of such breaches of contract, because they think them unlikely to occur, because they reckon on reaching some agreement if they do, or because they are reluctant to hamper the negotiations by questioning the other party's readiness and ability to perform. It may, indeed, be simply impossible for the parties to conceive and provide for all the possible respects in which performance may prove defective, especially if the contract is to last a long time. The true reason for the incompleteness of most contracts is, however, an economic one, namely that negotiation can cost more than it saves: if there is only one chance in 100 that a particular risk of losing 500 will eventuate, it makes no sense to invest more than five in negotiating with a view to casting this risk on the other party. The expense of regulating breaches of contract in detail is justified only where large sums of money are involved or where, though each individual contract may be of low value, the party makes so many of them that it is worth the effort and expense to work out a detailed regime, usually in the form of "general conditions of business", to be put to the other party. Only then are contracts even relatively "complete". But in fact no contract has ever been really complete, for even when the parties and their legal advisers have taken every care in drafting a contract, experience shows that it will still contain ambiguities and omissions which the judge will have to deal with, a task he or she performs by applying "default rules" which the legal system has developed for the very purpose of filling such gaps, or by means of interpretation.[2]

---

[1] Cases in which the courts have tackled the problem of ascertaining the meaning of contractual words will be discussed *infra*, in section 1.

[2] Interpretation as a means of filling gaps in contract will be addressed *infra*, in section 2.

4.1. INTERPRETING CONTRACTUAL WORDS

4.1.1. GENERAL RULES

If contracting parties are agreed on what they said or wrote but differ on what it means, the process of interpretation may be guided by two different approaches. On one view, consistently with the principle of party autonomy that legal obligations arise from, and are justified by, the free will of the individual, precedence is given to the "will of the parties". The other view gives precedence to the external fact of the words in which the will has been expressed. After all, social and commercial intercourse requires that reliance be protected, and people rely on what others actually say, not on what they meant to say. One often comes across the statement that the common law, in the interest of commercial convenience and the security of transactions, looks to the external appearance of consent and is therefore based on what has been called the "expression theory", while the civil law, following the "will theory", is inclined to favour the true state of mind of the parties (see section **1.3.2.D** above). It is an open question whether this statement has any provable substance today.

Most civil codes hover between "objective" and "subjective interpretation":

Code civil   **4.F.1.**

Article 1156: In the analysis of an agreement, it is necessary to seek out the common intention of the contracting parties, rather than merely to concentrate on the literal meaning of the terms used.

Article 1135: Agreements impose obligations not only with respect to the express terms used but also as regards all the consequences which equitable principles, practice and custom or the law may attach to the obligation concerned in accordance with its nature.

BGB   **4.G.2.**

§ 133: In interpreting an expression of intention the real intention is to be ascertained without clinging to the literal meaning of the statement.

§ 157: Contracts are to be interpreted in accordance with the dictates of good faith taking into account normal commercial practice.

CISG   **4.INT.3.**

Article 8: (1) For the purposes of this Convention statements made by and other conduct of a party are to be interpreted according to his intent where the other party knew or could not have been unaware what that intent was.
(2) If the preceding paragraph is not applicable, statements made by and other conduct of a party are to be interpreted according to the understanding that a reasonable person of the same kind as the other party would have had in the same circumstances.
(3) In determining the intent of a party or the understanding a reasonable person would have had, due consideration is to be given to all relevant circumstances of the case

including the negotiations, any practices which the parties have established between themselves, usages and any subsequent conduct of the parties.[3]

If parties choose to use words in a distinctive sense, different from their usual meaning, everyone agrees that it is their intention rather than their expression that counts: *falsa demonstratio non nocet*. Thus it was held in the German leading case on the subject that if buyer and seller both use the word *Haakjöringsköd* to signify "whalemeat" when it properly denotes "sharkmeat", the contract is for whalemeat, and if the seller tenders sharkmeat the buyer can claim damages for non-performance.[4]

BGH, 23 February 1956[5] **4.G.4.**

Judgment: The appellate court states, on the basis, in particular, of the wording of the contract of 23 February 1949, that the meaning of the contract is rendered so contradictory by those words that it is impossible to ascertain what the contracting parties intended. According to the appellate court, it must be concluded from this that the contract never came into existence, since its contradictory contents do not permit any construction to be placed on the intention of the parties.

The appellant contests those statements, contending that, in making them, the appellate court wrongfully concentrated solely on the wording of the contract and omitted to attempt to ascertain the meaning which the contracting parties intended to give to the contract.

It is settled case-law, laid down at the highest judicial level, that a court may not concentrate, for the purposes of interpreting a contract, solely on its wording. That is the position, in any event, where the wording of the contract is not clear and unambiguous. In such a case, the court is required, in order properly to fulfil its interpretative task, to take into account all circumstances and factors which may be material for the purposes of construing the content of what is stated in the contract and the intention of the parties thereto. This involves consideration not only of the intended economic purpose of the contract but also of the meaning which the contracting parties themselves attached to the individual formulations which they chose to include in the contract. In that connection, it is basically necessary to proceed in accordance with the principle, derived from experience, that, even in the case of a contract couched in inadequate or contradictory terms, the contracting parties, in concluding the contract, were envisaging and pursuing a specific economic objective, and that they wished to express their intention by means of the words chosen by them. Consequently, it is only in quite exceptional circumstances that the interpretation of a contract may be regarded as impossible by reason of its totally contradictory or nonsensical content.

For the purposes of interpreting a contract, the meaning of its wording becomes wholly immaterial where the contracting parties have attached to a congruous, specific idea an incomplete, incorrect or even nonsensical term or expression which is not covered, either at all or without being supplemented, by the wording in question. In such a case, the content of the contract is deemed, regardless of the wording chosen, to be what the contracting parties actually intended. In that legal situation, the objective principles of law applying to the interpretation of contracts will be violated if the trial court, faced with a contract which is unclear or contradictory, purports to interpret it by considering and assessing only its written terms, thereby completely disregarding other material factors.

Only if the contradiction inherent in the wording remains unclarified and unresolved even after those further factors have been taken into consideration will it be legitimate for the court in its final

---

[3] A similar rule has been adopted in Arts. 4.1–4.3 UPCL.
[4] RG 8 June 1920, RGZ 99.147; see *supra*, at 347–9.
[5] BGHZ 20.109.

judgment to conclude, quite exceptionally, that an interpretation of the contract is impossible on account of its contradictory or nonsensical content.

Note

In rare cases it happens that a clause is utterly ambiguous in the sense that, despite one's best efforts at interpretation, no single meaning can be given to it, since the reasonable man would find either of two meanings equally plausible. If such a clause relates to an essential point of the transaction, the contract fails for want of agreement. In the famous English case of *Raffles* v. *Wichelhaus*[6] the plaintiff had sold the defendant 125 bales of cotton "to arrive ex *Peerless* from Bombay", and tendered cotton which arrived in Liverpool in December on a vessel of that name. The defendant refused to accept it and, when the seller claimed damages, offered evidence that he had in mind a quite different vessel also called *Peerless* which had sailed from Bombay and arrived in Liverpool in October. The court held that this would be a good defence and allowed the proof to be brought. The outcome of the case is unknown, but if one accepts that in the light of the actual evidence the reasonable observer would have been unable to determine which of the vessels the parties had agreed on, it would be right to hold that no contract had come about.[7]

Queen's Bench Division   **4.E.5.**
Vitol B.V. v. *Compagnie européenne des pétroles*[8]

INTERPRETATION IN THE LIGHT OF THE AGREEMENT AS A WHOLE

Agreed upon laydays

Words which are unclear or ambiguous must be given the interpretation which makes most sense in the light of the agreement as a whole and the circumstances.

Facts: Clause 7 of a contract for the sale of 500,000 barrels of crude oil provided that the parties were to agree, as to each month, on the range of days when the oil was to be lifted by the buyers ("lifting range"). Under clause 8 the buyers had to pay $ 36.75 per barrel. However, if the "official price" were to decrease by more than $ 0.75 per barrel the buyers had to pay the lower price (minus $ 0.10). The term "official price" was defined as "the price in force 7 days before the [first] day of the confirmed and agreed upon laydays". Laydays are the days permitted for the charterer to have the ship loaded; they begin to run once the ship has arrived and the charterer has been notified that she is ready to load. In early February the lifting range had been agreed by the parties to commence on 15 February. The buyers' ship arrived in the port of loading on 23 February, and this day was therefore the first layday. Since the "official price" had been reduced on 9 February to $ 35.25, i.e. by more than $ 0.75, the sellers invoiced the buyers at $ 36.75 on the ground that the terms "the confirmed and agreed upon laydays" referred to the agreed lifting range commencing on 15 February so that the price drop on 9 February had come too late to affect the shipment. The buyers contended that the clause referred to "laydays" so that the price change had occurred more than 7 days before the first layday (23 February).

Held: The arbitrators held that the clause must refer to the laydays, but the Queen's Bench Division held that it referred to the days of the "lifting period".

---

[6] (1864) 2 H & C 906.
[7] For further details of this case see *supra*, at 349.
[8] [1988] 1 Lloyd's Rep. 574.

558

Judgment: SAVILLE J: The approach of the English law to questions of the true construction of contracts of this kind is to seek objectively to ascertain the intentions of the parties from the words which they have chosen to use. If those words are clear and admit of only one sensible meaning, then that is the meaning to be ascribed to them—and that meaning is taken to represent what the parties intended. If the words are not clear and admit of more than one sensible meaning, then the ambiguity may be resolved by looking at the aim and genesis of the agreement, choosing the meaning which seems to make the most sense in the context of the contract and its surrounding circumstances as a whole. In some cases, of course, having attempted this exercise, it may simply remain impossible to give the words any sensible meaning at all, in which case they (or some of them) are either ignored, that is to say, treated as not forming part of the contract at all, or (if of apparent central importance) treated as demonstrating that the parties never really made an agreement at all, that is to say, had never truly agreed upon the vital terms of their bargain. In any of these cases, if it can be demonstrated that the parties were in fact agreed upon the terms of their bargain, but by mistake wrote them down wrongly, then the law allows the contract to be rectified so as to accord with what was in fact agreed.

Applying this approach to the present case, I take the view that the words in question themselves do not admit of only one clear or sensible meaning—for, while the word "laydays" would *prima facie* seem to refer to the laytime provisions of the contract, the words "confirmed and agreed upon" can hardly do so and seem instead to be referring to something that has to be settled between the parties as the contract progresses, the obvious candidate being the lifting range period in cl. 7.

The arbitrator appears to have concluded that, since the word "laydays" could only be a reference to the laytime provisions of the contract, the other words had simply to be ignored—to be treated, as he put it, as "surplus". However, if the phrase is read as a whole, I am of the view that this conclusion does not necessarily follow. The words "confirmed and agreed upon" qualify the word "laydays". *Prima facie*, therefore, the phrase is referring to laydays that are to be confirmed and agreed upon. That is not the case with the laytime provisions of the contract (that have already been agreed and are not subject to confirmation)—and it is much more in line with the days that are to be agreed or "reconfirmed" under cl. 7 for the period during which the vessel is to load. In short, reading the phrase as a whole, I see no undue difficulty in treating the qualifying words as altering the meaning that would ordinarily, in the absence of those words, be given to the word "laydays". That is not to say, of course that this meaning is thus automatically to be preferred to that adopted by the arbitrator; what is now to be done is to see which meaning makes most sense in the context of the contract and its surrounding circumstances as a whole.

On this aspect of the case it seems to me that the most sensible construction is that contended for by the sellers. The pricing provisions give the sellers an additional option if there is a certain fall in the official price; indeed, the arbitrator found that at the time the contract was made it was well known in the market that the official price was likely to fall. The parties were agreed that the option given to the sellers could only be exercised if the official price of Ekofisk was reduced by more than $ 0.75 seven days or more before the relevant date.

If the relevant date is the first day of the loading range, then as soon as this is settled the sellers will know that any official price reduction less than seven days before will be irrelevant, and can decide what to do with regard to any earlier price reduction of more than $ 0.75. If, on the other hand, the relevant date is the first day of laytime, the exercise of counting back cannot be done until after that uncertain date has arrived, so that for a period the sellers could be effectively deprived of their contractual right through simply not knowing whether or not it was or would be available to them.

In my view, the latter would not be as sensible a construction as the former, and accordingly I consider that the ambiguity in the phrase under discussion should be resolved in favour of the sellers. It follows, therefore, that I allow the appeal from this award.

TECHNICAL MEANING UNKNOWN TO ONE PARTY

Demand guarantee

A guarantee given by a layperson cannot be interpreted as a demand guarantee, even if that is what was asked of her, if the party seeking the guarantee must have known that the layperson would not understand the meaning of the phrase.

Facts: The defendant was the wife of a man whose business partner had borrowed money from the plaintiff. In order to secure the loan her husband had persuaded her to give the plaintiff a "demand guarantee" which is generally understood in the export trade to mean that the guarantor must pay immediately on demand and can raise defences to the claim only in a subsequent action for restitution. The defendant argued that she had no experience in the export or banking business and had therefore believed the guarantee to be a "simple" guarantee.

Held: The defendant's appeal was allowed; "guarantee" must be interpreted as "simple" guarantee.

Judgment: The interpretation depends primarily on the content of the deed of guarantee [citations omitted]. Even assuming that the plaintiff, in formulating its terms, deliberately chose a form of wording which is regularly used by banks for "demand" guarantees, it was not entitled, on that ground alone, to presume, upon receiving the declaration of guarantee, that the defendant intended to go so far as to shoulder liability under such a "demand" guarantee. From the point of view of the creditor, who arranged for the declaration of guarantee to be given and formulated its wording, the intention of the guarantor can only have been in accordance with what she understood the wording submitted to her to mean. Consequently, the plaintiff must accept the declaration of guarantee as having the meaning which, having regard to the circumstances characterising it, it must on an objective basis be understood as possessing, even if that meaning is contrary to its interests [citations omitted].

However, the wording of the agreement in issue ("The guaranteed sum shall become payable forthwith upon demand or upon this deed being first produced . . .") corresponds to the standard wording which has come to be used in banking transactions for "demand" guarantees. Such accessory circumstances, lying outside the ambit of the declaratory act, may be taken into account for the purposes of interpretation, in so far as they allow the recipient of the declaration to draw a conclusion as to its meaning [citations omitted]. That is not the position in the present case, since the plaintiff could not assume that the defendant knew or recognised the meaning attaching to the wording of the agreement in banking operations. It is only since the end of the 1970s that the concept of a "demand" guarantee—designed to meet the needs of an export-oriented economy—has been judicially recognised; it is used primarily as a means of security in foreign trade. In domestic transactions, it has acquired practical significance mainly in the context of the financing of groups of companies [citations omitted]. A "demand" guarantee is a typical type of banking transaction. It is little known outside banking circles. The plaintiff has not sought to argue that the defendant possessed any knowledge or experience with respect to credit security generally or in relation to areas in which "demand" guarantees are to be encountered in particular; nor has it submitted that the defendant, before assuming the guarantee obligation, was informed of the special characteristics of "demand" guarantees.

A person who possesses no particular knowledge of the field of credit security and who is, in particular, ignorant of the legal character of a "demand" guarantee cannot infer from the agreement an intention that the guarantor should be under an ongoing payment obligation which cannot be contested on the basis of any objection or defence arising from the principal debtor-creditor relationship (. . .)

[9] NJW 1992.1446.

House of Lords 4.E.7.
Charter Reinsurance Co. Ltd. v. *Fagan*[10]

MEANING DEPENDS ON CONTEXT

Sums actually paid

Words used in a contract must be interpreted in a way which makes sense in the context as a whole; the notion of "literal meaning" is unhelpful when words may mean different things in different contexts.

Facts: An insurance company (Charter) had entered into reinsurance contracts with reinsurers. Clause 2 (a) provided that the reinsurers would only be liable "if and when" the "net loss"" sustained by Charter exceeded a specified amount. Clause 2 (c) defined the term "net loss" as being "the sum actually paid" by Charter in settlement of losses or liabilities of its insureds. Charter went into liquidation being unable to pay its debts. The reinsurers did not dispute that all the requirements of a valid claim against them by Charter were present, save one: that Charter, because of its insolvency, had not "actually paid" anything on the reinsured claims.

Held: At first instance it was held that the reinsurer must pay. This decision was affirmed by the Court of Appeal and by the House of Lords.

Judgment: LORD HOFFMANN: My Lords, this appeal turns upon the construction of a standard clause known as the ultimate net loss (UNL) clause which is in common use in the London excess of loss reinsurance market. . . . The question is whether the words "actually paid" mean that the liability of the reinsurers is limited to the sum in respect of which Charter has discharged its liabilities in respect of the risks which it insured. Mr Sumption QC says that this is the natural meaning of the words. There is nothing in the context which requires them to be given a different meaning and that is the end of the matter.

I think that in some cases the notion of words having a natural meaning is not a very helpful one. Because the meaning of words is so sensitive to syntax and context, the natural meaning of words in one sentence may be quite unnatural in another. Thus a statement that words have a particular natural meaning may mean no more than that in many contexts they will have that meaning. In other contexts their meaning will be different but no less natural.

Take, for example, the words "pay". In many contexts, it will mean that money has changed hands, usually in discharge of some liability. In other contexts, it will mean only that a liability was incurred, without necessarily having been discharged. A wife comes home with a new dress and her husband says: "What did you pay for it?" She would not be understanding his question in its natural meaning if she answered, "Nothing, because the shop gave me 30 days credit". It is perfectly clear from the context that the husband wanted to know the amount of the liability which she incurred, whether or not that liability has been discharged.

What is true of ordinary speech is also true of reinsurance. In *Re Eddystone Marine Insurance Co., ex p Western Insurance Co.* [1892] 2 Ch. 423 the policy obtained the form of reinsurance clause then in common use—"and to pay as may be paid thereon". As in this case, the reinsured company was insolvent and could not pay its debts. Stirling J. said that the policy did not mean that the liability should have been discharged. They meant only that "the payment to be made on the reinsurance policy is to be regulated by that to be made on the original policy of insurance" (see [1892] 2 Ch. 423 at 427). In other words, the clause is concerned with the amount of liability and is indifferent to whether or not it has been discharged.

But, said Mr Sumption, there is the word "actually". Stirling J. might have been willing to accept that "paid" could in some artificial or figurative sense mean "liable to be paid". But the word

---

[10] [1996] 3 All ER 46.

"actually" was surely added to make it clear that money must have changed hands. "Actually paid" said Mr Sumption, meant actually paid.

One speaks of something being "actually" the case to point a contrast; perhaps with what appears to be the case, or with what might be the case, or with what is deemed to be the case. The effect of the word therefore depends upon the nature of the distinction which the speaker is wanting to make. This can appear only from the context in which the phrase is used. It is artificial to start with some contextual preconception about the meaning of the words and then see whether that meaning is somehow displaced. The context might indicate that the word was used to reverse the ruling in the *Eddystone* case and require the liability of the reinsured to have been discharged. On the other hand, it might suggest that a different contrast was intended.

To revert to my domestic example, if the wife had answered "Well, the dress was marked £ 300, but they were having a sale" and the husband then asked "So what did you actually pay?", she would again be giving the question an unnatural meaning if she answered, "I have not paid anything yet". It is obvious that the contrast which the husband wishes to draw is between the price as marked and the lower price which was charged. He is still not concerned with whether the liability has been discharged. This is not a loose use of language. In the context of the rest of the conversation, it is the natural meaning.

What then is the context? [After a thorough analysis of the history of reinsurance clauses in the London market Lord Hoffmann concluded that "actually paid" means "exposed to liability as a result of the insured loss". He continued:] I find further support for my view in the fact that the UNL clause has been thought suitable for use in the London excess of loss reinsurance market. There are certainly forms of reinsurance in which it may be commercially appropriate to make discharge of his liability by the reinsured a condition of the liability of the reinsurer. It may be, as in cases of mutual insurance, that the reinsurer has an interest in making certain that the reinsured maintains sufficient liquid assets to meet his liabilities. Or it may be a protection against fraudulent claims. But the London excess of loss market operates on the assumption that a reinsurance programme will relieve the insurer of the burden of having to pay claims covered by the reinsured layers. The regulation of insurers in this country uses a test of solvency which treats reinsurance cover as a proper deduction from the insurer's liabilities. None of this would make sense if the insurer had first to satisfy the claim out of his own resources before he could call upon his reinsurers to pay.

Mr Sumption suggested a stratagem which insurers might use to avoid having to pay the whole claim themselves. They could pay a part, even a very small part, of the reinsured liability and then, having to this extent actually paid, they could call upon the reinsurer to reimburse them. Having thus primed the pump, they could by successive strokes draw up the full amount from the reinsurance well. I cannot imagine that the parties could ever have contemplated such a strange procedure and one is bound to ask what commercial purpose the reinsurer could have expected to achieve by being able to insist upon it.

Considerations of history, language and commercial background therefore lead me to the conclusion that the word "actually" in the UNL clause is used to emphasise that the loss for which the reinsurer is to be liable is to be net and that the clause does not restrict liability to the amount by which the liability of the reinsured for the loss has been discharged. I think that this is the natural meaning of the clause . . . I would dismiss the appeal.

[LORD MUSTILL delivered a judgment to the same effect. LORD GOFF OF CHIEVELEY, LORD GRIFFITHS and LORD BROWNE-WILKINSON concurred.]

In France, courts and writers agree that interpretation must seek the "common intention" of the parties (Article 1156 C.civ.). But they also accept that in the normal case where no real common intention of the parties can be established the task of the judge is to ascertain what must, in the light of all the circumstances, be taken to be what the parties must reasonably have intended.

Normally, the Cour de cassation refuses to review the lower courts' interpretation of a contract since this is held to be within "*le pouvoir souverain des juges de fond*".[11] But it is otherwise where there is a clause which in the view of the Cour de cassation is "*claire et précise*", for then it will quash decisions of the lower courts which give it any other meaning, even on the ground of a supposed common intention of the parties. This rule was first laid down in 1872.

Cass. civ., 15 April 1872[12]	4.F.8.

CLEAR AND PRECISE MEANING

Discretionary Bonuses

An employee has no enforceable right to a promised bonus if the bonus was clearly stated to be discretionary.

Facts: The defendants had publicly announced that they would pay their employees a premium if certain conditions were met. When they discontinued the practice of paying the premium, relying on a clause in the announcement which gave them a power to do so, an employee brought an action.

Held: The *conseil des prud'hommes de Flers* [Flers Labour Court] held that the employee had a right to the bonus, but the Cour de cassation quashed the decision.

Judgment: THE COURT: Having regard to Article 1134 of the Civil Code . . . That article provides: "An agreement which is legally created shall bind the parties by whom it is made as if its terms were laid down by legislation". Where the wording of an agreement is clear and precise, a court may not misconstrue the obligations resulting from it or modify the stipulations which it contains. The clause relied on by the appellants in cassation as justifying their refusal to pay the premiums claimed by Pringault, pursuant to a management notice posted up in the factory of Messrs Veuve Foucauld & Colombe, expressly states: "it is understood that, whatever the circumstances may be, payment of the premium shall be and remain optional and discretionary". That clause, by which the company stipulates that it shall not be bound to pay the premium, is express and can be validly relied on in every case as against the workers in the factory. The *conseil des prud'hommes de Flers*, in seeking to justify the non-application of the clause at issue to the dispute before it, relied, first, on the fact that Pringault had carried out his work in accordance with the notice in question and, second, on the fact that he had previously been paid premiums. In paying those premiums, and in subsequently refusing to award them to Pringault, the appellants exercised the discretion which they had reserved unto themselves by the abovementioned clause, and of which they could avail themselves or decline to avail themselves as they wished. It follows that, in ordering Messrs Veuve Foucauld & Colombe to pay the premiums claimed by Pringault, the contested judgment formally infringed the provisions of Article 1134 of the Civil Code.

On those grounds, the Court quashes the judgment of the *conseil des prud'hommes de Flers* of 4 March 1870.

---

[11] Cass. sections réunies 2 February 1808 *Lubert*, S. Chron.
[12] DP 1872.1.176.

Cass. civ., 14 December 1942[13]   **4.F.9.**

CLEAR AND PRECISE MEANING

Codfish

An agreement which gave the seller a right to reduce the amount it had to deliver if a clearly stated event had occurred was entitled to rely on the clause even if the circumstances which gave rise to the stated event were not what had been anticipated.

Facts: The plaintiff had agreed to buy a certain quantity of codfish, subject to reduction by the seller if the fishmongers' association so decided. The association did so decide, and in accordance with that decision the seller delivered only half the quantity originally agreed. The buyer sued for damages on the basis that the seller, who had sufficient codfish in stock, could have delivered the full amount.

Held: The lower courts twice gave judgment for the buyer, apparently because the parties had originally assumed that a reduction would be authorized only if there were a drop in the catch, not just because of a sudden a rise in demand, as was the case. The Cour de cassation quashed both decisions, and the buyer's claim was dismissed. The clause in question being unambiguous, further investigation of the intention of the parties was excluded.

Judgment: THE COURT: Rovida brought proceedings against Vimeney for termination of the contract on the ground that it had not been performed in its entirety. The *cour d'appel* rightly acknowledged that "the clause in issue is sufficiently clear and precise, and plainly affords the vendor the right to impose on the purchaser a reduction in the quantities fixed by the contract, in reliance on the decision taken by the abovementioned Association". Nevertheless, it proceeded to award Rovida the damages claimed, on the following grounds: (a) that "it is necessary to determine the common intention of the parties from the facts and documents in the case"; (b) that the spirit of the clause is such as to shift from the vendor to the purchaser the burden of proof regarding impossibility of performance, and consequently to restrict the exercise of the right to cases in which performance is impossible; (c) consequently, that Rovida had established the lack of justification for the Association's decision by supplying proof that the fishing catch in 1928 was inadequate only in the light of the increase in consumer demand, and not in terms of the average catch during the previous five years; and (d) that Vimeney could have performed the Rovida contract by accepting Rovida's priority and by declining fresh orders from other customers at a substantially higher price. However, it was not possible for the *cour d'appel*, without contradicting itself, to rule that the clause in issue was clear, precise and lawful and at the same time to refuse to apply it in its exact terms. The courts below acknowledged that Vimeney was entitled to impose on the purchaser, in line with the fishing yield, a reduction in the unsecured contractual quantity, by reference to the "decision" of the Association, taken pursuant to the power of assessment vested in it by the contract, declaring a deficit in the 1928 fishing catch on the basis that it was insufficient to meet the increase in consumer demand; [yet the lower courts found for the buyer] on the pretext that the spirit of the clause, despite the general way in which it was formulated, was such as to permit a reduction only in the event of performance being absolutely impossible, and did not concern the loss which the fishing yield might cause the vendor to suffer. Since the clause was clear and required no interpretation, it was not open to the courts below to seek to justify their refusal simply to apply its terms by relying on a letter sent by Vimeney to its broker after the conclusion of the sale, in which it acknowledged that the Association's decision must be justified by a fishing deficit; that letter does not state how a "deficit" is to be defined, and the contested judgment formally acknowledges that Vimeney did not waive any of its rights in its correspondence. It follows that, in ruling as it did, the *cour d'appel* infringed the legislation referred to above.

[13] D. 1944.12 annotated by Lerebours-Pigeonnière.

On those grounds, the Court quashes the contested judgment and refers the case back to the cour d'appel de Poitiers.

Note

In cases in which the contractual words are ambiguous or vague the parties often argue that the courts should interpret them in the light of prior negotiations and should therefore admit evidence on what took place during such negotiations. In France such evidence is generally regarded as admissible. It is true that according to Article 1341 C.civ. the evidence of witnesses is inadmissible to show that there was an oral agreement before, during or after the conclusion of the written contract by which the import of that contract would be altered or varied. But the courts have always held that "*cette preuve peut cependant être invoquée pour interpréter un acte, s'il est obscur ou ambigu*".[14] The same position is taken in Germany: while there is a presumption that the contract as written is accurate and complete this presumption is rebuttable. English judges, on the other hand, seem to be reluctant to admit such evidence.

House of Lords   **4.E.10.**
Prenn v. Simmonds[15]

PRIOR NEGOTIATIONS DISREGARDED

When construing an agreement, any pre-contractual negotiations between the parties should not be taken into account with a view to resolving ambiguities of expression.

Judgment: LORD WILBERFORCE: In order for the agreement . . . to be understood, it must be placed in its context. The time has long passed when agreements, even those under seal, were isolated from the matrix of facts in which they were set and interpreted purely on internal linguistic considerations. There is no need to appeal here to any modern, anti-literal, tendencies, for *Lord Blackburn*'s well-known judgment in *River Wear Commissioners* v. *Adamson* (1877) 2 App. Cas. 743, 763 provides ample warrant for a liberal approach. We must, as he said, enquire beyond the language and see what the circumstances were with reference to which the words were used, and the object, appearing from those circumstances, which the person using them had in view.

Counsel . . . however, contended for even greater extension of the court's interpretative power. They argued that later authorities have gone further and allow prior negotiations to be looked at in aid of the construction of a written document. In my opinion, they did not make good their contention . . .

The reason for not admitting evidence of these exchanges is not a technical one or even mainly one of convenience (although the attempt to admit it did greatly prolong the case and add to its expense). It is simply that such evidence is unhelpful. By the nature of things, where negotiations are difficult, the parties' positions, with each passing letter, are changing and until the final agreement, although converging, still divergent. It is only the final document which records a consensus. If the previous documents use different expressions, how does construction of those expressions, itself a doubtful process, help on the construction of the contractual words? If the same expressions are used, nothing is gained by looking back; indeed, something may be lost since the relevant surrounding circumstances may be different. And at this stage there is no consensus of the parties to

---

[14] See e.g. Civ. 1e, 3 March 1969, DP 1969.477.
[15] [1971] 3 All ER 237.

565

appeal to. It may be said that previous documents may be looked at to explain the aims of the parties. In a limited sense this is true; the commercial, or business object, of the transaction, objectively ascertained, may be a surrounding fact . . . And if it can be shown that one interpretation completely frustrates that object, to the extent of rendering the contract futile, that may be a strong argument for an alternative interpretation, if that can reasonably be found. But beyond that it may be difficult to go; it may be a matter of degree, or of judgment, how far one interpretation, or another, gives effect to a common intention; the parties, indeed, may be pursuing that intention with differing emphasis, and hoping to achieve it to an extent which may differ, and in different ways. The words used may, and often do, represent a formula which means different things to each side, yet may be accepted because that is the only way to get "agreement" and in the hope that disputes will not arise. The only course then can be to try to ascertain the "natural" meaning. Far more, and indeed totally, dangerous is it to admit evidence of one party's objective—even if this is known to the other party. However strongly pursued this may be, the other party may only be willing to give it partial recognition, and in a world of give and take, men often have to be satisfied with less than they want. So, again, it would be a matter of speculation how far the common intention was that the particular objective should be realised.

In my opinion, then, evidence of negotiations, or of the parties' intentions, and *a fortiori* of Dr. Simmonds's intentions, ought not to be received, and evidence should be restricted to evidence of the factual background known to the parties at or before the date of the contract, including evidence of the "genesis" and objectively the "aim" of the transaction . . .

What if, during negotiations, the parties have clearly settled on one particular meaning of a word?

Queen's Bench Division   **4.E.11.**
The Karen Oltmann[16]

AGREED MEANING

The Karen Oltmann

Where the parties have agreed during negotiations that a word shall have a particular meaning, or where one party has put forward a particular meaning and the other party has acted on that, that meaning will prevail.

Facts: The owners of the *Karen Oltmann* let her on a timecharter to the charterers for two years but gave the charterers an option "to redeliver the vessel after 12 months' trading subject to giving 3 months' notice". After nineteen months the charterers gave three months' notice of their intention to redeliver the vessel on the ground that "after 12 months' trading" meant "at any time after the expiry of 12 months". The owners argued that the clause gave the charterers a choice of either twelve months (subject to three months' notice) or two years and sought to introduce as evidence a pre-contractual telex exchange supporting their view.

Held: The pre-contractual exchanges showed that the parties had agreed that the clause should have the meaning claimed by the owners.

Judgment: KERR J: The first question which arose at this point was whether this plea and the submissions founded on it entitled the Court to look at the exchange of telex messages. In my view they do. Take *Prenn* v. *Simmonds*, as an example. The issue in that case was whether the reference to "profits" in the contract meant the profits of the holding company only or the consolidated profits

---

[16] [1976] 2 Lloyd's Rep. 708.

of the whole group. If in the course of the negotiations one party had made anything in the nature of a representation to the other to the effect that references to "profits" were to be taken in one of these senses and not in the other, and the other party had thereupon negotiated on this basis, then extrinsic evidence to establish this representation would in my view clearly be admissible. Similarly, if it had been contended that the parties had conducted their negotiations on an agreed basis that the word "profits" was used in one sense only, although in the contract it was capable of having two senses, and that the contract had been executed on this basis, then I do not think that the Court would be precluded by authority from admitting extrinsic evidence to see whether or not this agreed basis could be established. Both these situations would be a long way from the attempts made in *Prenn* v. *Simmonds* and *Arrale* v. *Costain* [1976] 1 Lloyd's Rep. 98, to adduce extrinsic evidence to try to persuade the Court that one interpretation of the contract was in all the circumstances to be preferred to the other.

I think that in such cases the principle can be stated as follows. If a contract contains words which, in their context, are fairly capable of bearing more than one meaning, and if it is alleged that the parties have in effect negotiated on an agreed basis that the words bore only one of the two possible meanings, then it is permissible for the Court to examine the extrinsic evidence relied upon to see whether the parties have in fact used the words in question on one sense only, so that they have in effect given their own dictionary meaning to the words as the result of their common intention. Such cases would not support a claim for rectification of the contract, because the choice of words in the contract would not result from any mistake. The words used in the contract would *ex hypothesi* reflect the meaning which both parties intended.

In the present case, after some argument about these principles and the limits of the parol evidence rule, I decided to look at the pleaded telex messages, though Counsel for the charterers rightly submitted that I could only do so *de bene esse*. He was right about this, because if they did not support the owners' arguments on the lines discussed above, then I would have to put them out of mind and fall back on my construction as a matter of first impression.

I therefore turn to consider the pleaded telex exchanges. Although I do not consider that they support the allegation of an estoppel, I think that they clearly show that the words "after 12 months' trading" were used in an agreed sense. From start to finish the owners wanted maximum duration and certainty whereas the charterers wanted minimum duration and maximum flexibility. It is clear that both parties throughout used the word "after" in the sense of "on the expiry of" and not "at any time after the expiry of".

Some codes take pride in laying down maxims or rules of thumb to help the judges interpret contracts. Thus Article 1157 C.civ. tells us that one should prefer a reading of a clause which gives it some effect rather than none. If a clause is ambiguous one is to adopt the meaning *qui convient le plus à la matière du contrat* (Article 1158), or the sense which would be attributed to it in the place where the contract was drawn up (Article 1159). Where an expression is indefinite, its scope should be narrowed so as to cover only what the parties really intended (Article 1162), and individual clauses must be construed in the light of the contract as a whole (Article 1161), and so on. Such maxims are considered as were guidelines and play little part in court practice; it seems indeed that the judges cite them only to support a conclusion they have already reached on quite different grounds. The draftsmen of the BGB took a dim view of such maxims on the ground that it was no part of the legislator's task "to teach the judges practical logic".

4.1.2. THE "CONTRA PREFERENTEM" INTERPRETATION RULE

There is one rule of interpretation which does make sense and is widely used by the courts: Unclear contract terms are to be construed against the party who did the drafting and could have done it better ("*contra preferentem* rule"). It is right that the risk of ambiguity in a contract clause should be borne by the party who could more cheaply avoid it, and that is usually the party who selected or drafted the clause rather than the party to whom it was presented.

BGH, 19 March 1957[17]   **4.G.12.**

CONTRA PREFERENTEM

Gold Coast cocoa

A clause which is unclear in its scope will be interpreted against the party who was responsible for drafting the contract.

Facts: The plaintiffs had bought from the sellers 105 tons Gold Coast cocoa. The confirmation note was on a form supplied by the sellers' agents and provided:

> "Delivery: ex quay Hamburg
> Packaging: in sacks . . .
> Time of delivery: 25 tons in each of the months of July, August and September 1954. Subject to the goods being properly and punctually delivered to, and safely received by, the sellers from their own suppliers, and subject to any official measures taken by the authorities.
> Payment: net cash against invoice . . .
> Special terms and conditions: . . ."

The sellers argued that they were relieved from their duties to perform the contract under the clause "*Richtige und rechtzeitige Selbstbelieferung . . . vorbehalten*", since their own suppliers had become insolvent and failed to deliver the cocoa. The buyers brought an action for damages. In their view the clause was applicable only in the event of delay.

Held: The BGH held for the buyer.

Judgment: [The court stated reasons to hold for the buyers and clinched its argument as follows (citations omitted):] Moreover, it has always been a settled rule, established by the case-law relating to exemption clauses, that a seller who wishes to make his delivery obligation subject to reservations of a more or less extensive nature must signal his intention in a clear and unambiguous manner. As the *Reichsgericht* has pointed out, a clause rendering the transaction conditional on the seller himself taking delivery of the goods constitutes, and is regarded as, an exceptional phenomenon. The defendant's sale confirmation note provided an opportunity of giving clear expression to such an exception, and of securing total exoneration from the delivery obligation, by inserting the appropriate reservation either next to the heading "Delivery", or in the section headed "Special terms and conditions", or in the general provisions of the contract, for example, after the word "sells". Instead, it was inconspicuously inserted under the heading "Time of delivery" after the statement "25 tons in each of the months of July, August and September 1954". The effect of this—whatever the circumstances, and even upon careful scrutiny of the contract—was to leave the buyer in a state of uncertainty as to the scope of the intended exclusion of liability, which, providing as it purports to do for exoneration from the entire contractual risk in the event of non-performance by the seller's

---

[17] BGHZ 24.39.

supplier, was not something that the buyer should have expected to encounter at that point in the extensive confirmation document. The existence of any possibly justified doubt as to the scope of such an exemption—which, as is generally recognised, must always be narrowly construed—will necessarily result in its being interpreted against the party using such forms of wording, since that party is easily able, by arranging the layout of the document in an appropriate manner and by duly highlighting any wording requiring emphasis, to give clear expression to an agreement which is so far-reaching in its scope and which affects the entire contractual obligation. It follows that the defendant must accept the more obvious—and, from its point of view, less favourable—interpretation of its ambiguously framed conditions.

Court of Appeal   **4.E.13.**
Houghton v. Trafalgar Insurance Co. Ltd[18]

CONTRA PREFERENTEM

The overloaded car

A clause which is unclear in its scope will be interpreted against the party who was responsible for drafting the contract.

Facts: A policy of insurance covering a motor-car contained a provision excluding liability for damage "caused or arising whilst the car is conveying any load in excess of that for which it was constructed". At the time of the plaintiff's accident six persons were being conveyed in the car, although seating accommodation was only provided for five persons, and the insurers denied liability on the ground that a load in excess of that for which the car was constructed was being carried.

Held: At first instance, Gorman J decided against the insurers' contention and gave judgment for the plaintiff. The insurers appealed, but the appeal was dismissed.

Judgment: SOMERVELL LJ: If there is any ambiguity, since it is the defendants' clause, the ambiguity will be resolved in favour of the assured. In my opinion, the words relied on "any load in excess of that for which it was constructed", only clearly cover cases where there is a weight load specified in respect of the motor-vehicle, be it lorry or van. I agree that the earlier words in the clause obviously are applicable to an ordinary private car in respect of which there is no such specified weight load. But there was—and I think that it would have been inadmissible—no evidence whether this was a form which was used for lorries as well as for ordinary private motor-cars. I do not think that that matters. We have to construe the words in their ordinary meaning, and I think that those words only clearly cover the case which I have put. If that is right, they cannot avail the insurance company in the present case.

I would only add that the present suggestions of their application is, to me, a remarkable one. I think that it would need the plainest possible words if it were desired to exclude the insurance cover by reason of the fact that there was at the back one passenger more than the seating accommodation. All sorts of obscurities and difficulties might arise. I would like to add that if this or any other insurance company wishes to put forward a policy which will be inapplicable when an extra passenger is carried, I hope that they will print their provision in red ink so that the assured will have it drawn to his particular intention. For these reasons, in my opinion, this appeal should be dismissed.

[DENNING LJ and ROMER LJ concurred.]

---

[18] [1954] 1 QB 247.

569

Cour d'appel de Colmar, 25 January 1903[19] **4.F.14.**

Late completion of dwelling

A clause which is unclear in its scope will be interpreted against the party who was responsible for drafting the contract.

Facts: The defendant builder had undertaken to construct a house with three flats. Clause 13 of the contract gave him fifty days for the job, and clause 14 provided for the payment of a penalty in the case of delay. The words used were not clear as to whether the fifty-day-period was to apply for the construction of just one flat or of the whole building. The parties also disagreed on the relevance of an instruction by the employer's architect extending the time for the whole building to seventy-five days.

Held: The clause applied to the completion of just one dwelling; the attempt to order completion of the whole project within seventy-five days was contrary to good faith.

Judgment: THE COURT: As to the law: whereas having regard to Article 1134 of the Civil Code, according to which agreements are to be carried out in good faith, and Article 1162, which provides that "in the event of uncertainty, an agreement is to be construed against the party stipulating an obligation and in favour of the party entering into that obligation" . . . Whereas the second of those provisions is applicable with particular strictness to standard-form contracts, such as a detailed specification of works, which is not the outcome of free negotiation but comprises a whole series of stipulations imposed on a contractor. Whereas a penalty clause included in a specification of works is especially subject to that rule of interpretation, which is reinforced in such cases by the principle *odia restringenda*.

Whereas the penalty clause relied on by the respondent is ambiguous, since the phrase "in relation to a dwelling-house", contained in the annex, may be interpreted as meaning that the time allowed is to be multiplied by the number of individual dwellings. Whereas the wording in issue is as follows: "Art. 14: In the event of the works not being completed within the period prescribed, and without there being any need for the prior service of any formal default notice, there shall be deducted from the total due the sum of 5,000 old francs for each working day that the works remain uncompleted . . .—Annex to Art. 13. Time allowed for carrying out the works: the periods hereinafter specified shall in each case run from the time when instructions are given in accordance with the building trade practice. The table appearing below applies in relation to a dwelling-house: completion of fabric of building . . . 50 working days . . .."

Whereas in view of Article 1162 of the Civil Code, the uncertainty resulting from the poor-quality drafting of the specification of works, which was prepared by the respondent's representative, must be removed by the adoption of an approach favouring the contractor against whom the clause is to operate. Whereas it is immaterial that an instruction subsequently given by the architect expressly fixed a time-limit, this time of 75 days, for completion of the entire fabric; an instruction does not constitute an agreement since it is, by definition, a unilateral act. Whereas it can acquire the nature of an agreement only once it is expressly accepted by the party to whom it is addressed.

As to the facts: whereas, far from accepting the instruction in question, Gentner raised a protest, which was such as to preclude the signature which he appended to the document before returning it from being construed as an acceptance; whereas that signature appears, in all probability, to have been no more than an acknowledgement of receipt.

Whereas the claim made by Roesch or by his representative, alleging that the contractor was under an obligation to construct the fabric of three individual dwellings in 75 working days, is of a

[19] Gaz. Pal. 1963.I.277. Citations omitted.

draconian nature. Whereas it amounts to an invitation to carry out the work perfunctorily and to ignore the established rules of construction, which are modelled on the requirements of nature; whereas according to those requirements, a house in the course of construction must be given the time to settle; in particular, the site must be left to stand over the winter, in order to allow the frost to draw the moisture out from the walls, which are saturated with it. Whereas a person who disregards those rules is acting like a motorist who drives a new car at top speed without bothering with the essential business of running it in. Whereas to require the work to be carried out with excessive haste is contrary to the precepts inherent in a conscientious professional approach. It follows that such a claim is vitiated by bad faith . . .

Notes

(1) The last paragraph of the judgment shows clearly the Court's hostility to the substance of the penalty clause. However, in many cases, the courts, instead of striking down clauses as unfairly prejudicial to the customer, have preferred to achieve the same result by way of interpretative devices, such as the *contra preferentem* rule;[20] thus they avoid having to articulate the reasons for their hostility.[21]

(2) Now that special legislation on unfair contract terms has been enacted in nearly all European countries there is no need to use the *contra preferentem* rule in order to do indirectly what is better done directly by controlling the substance of contract terms. Article 5(2), of EC Directive of 5 April 1993 on Unfair Terms in Consumer Contracts[22] provides:

Where there is doubt about the meaning of a term, the interpretation most favourable to the consumer shall prevail.

4.2. SUPPLYING OMITTED TERMS

Even when one has ascertained the meaning of what the parties actually said, there is still room for interpretation: a problem may arise while the contract is under way for which the parties have provided no solution, either because they did not foresee the problem at all or foresaw it and failed to deal with it. The question is how to fill this gap in the contract, and whether interpretation can help.

In this situation the continental judge looks first to the civil and commercial codes and any special laws which contain rules intended to be applied by the court "in default" of a contractual agreement by the parties. In France these statutory rules, along with the glosses added by the courts, are called *règles supplétives*, in Germany *dispositives Recht*. Thus when parties to a sale in France have said nothing about the seller's liability for latent defects, the courts apply not only Article 1645 C.civ. which renders the seller who knows of the defect liable for all consequential loss due to it, but also the judge-made rule

---

[20] In French law the *contra preferentem* rule is in favour of the debtor in general and in synallagmatic contract against the one who can impose his conditions: the seller in the contract of sale (Art. 1602 C.civ.) and, *a pari*, the lessee. In relation to "*contrats d'adhésion*" it will be construed in favour of the one who did not write the contractual terms. This solution is systematic for consumer contracts (Art. L. 133–2 C.consomm.).

[21] See the statement by Lord Denning in *George Mitchell (Chesterhall) Ltd.* v. *Finney Lock Seeds Ltd.* [1983] 1 All ER 108 quoted *supra*, at 507.

[22] On this Directive see *supra*, at 521 *et seq*, **3.EC.142**.

which imputes such knowledge to all commercial distributors such as manufacturer, wholesaler and retailer.[23]

In England, too, gaps in agreed contractual structures are made good by recourse to general rules—"terms implied in law"—which apply unless the parties have provided otherwise, depending on the type of contract in issue. The Sale of Goods Act 1979 and the Supply of Goods and Services Act 1982 contain rules which were developed originally at common law and now perform for contracts of sale and services the same role as the corresponding suppletive rules in the continental civil codes. For example, under the Sale of Goods Act 1979,[24] the following terms will normally be implied: that the seller has the right to sell the goods (section 12); that the goods will correspond to their description (section 13); that, if the seller sells in the course of a business, the goods will be of satisfactory quality and, subject to certain conditions, will be reasonably fit for the particular purpose for which the buyer requires them (section 14); and that, if the goods were sold by sample, they will correspond to the sample (section 15). Statutory provisions of this kind are not nearly as common in England as in civil law jurisdictions, and in their absence English judges apply rules they themselves have developed in relation to the major types of contract such as employment contracts, tenancy agreements and contracts of insurance and carriage.

Thus, if a building contract is silent in the contractor's liability if the materials supplied by him turn out to be defective a term (warranty) would be implied so as to make the contractor liable in damages not only when reasonable inspection would have shown the materials to be defective but also in the case of a latent defect. This applied even where the contractor was instructed by the employer to use a certain type of material manufactured by one producer only.

House of Lords   **4.E.15.**
Young and Marten Ltd. v. *McManus Childs Ltd*[25]

CONTRACTOR IS STRICTLY LIABLE FOR THE QUALITY OF MATERIALS HE USES

Defective roofing tiles

A contractor employed to carry out building work and instructed to use a particular kind of material will, unless otherwise agreed, be liable for any defects in the material even if it could not have discovered the defect and has no claim against the manufacturer from which it obtained the defective materials.

Facts: The respondents, the employers, engaged a contractor to build a number of houses for sale. The contractor subcontracted the roofing to the appellants; the appellants were instructed to use a rather expensive type of tile called a "Somerset 13", manufactured only by Browne of Bridgwater. The appellants in turn subcontracted the work to Acme, who bought the tiles from Browne. The tiles were defective in a way that could not have been detected by any reasonable examination and the buyers of the houses recovered the cost of re-roofing them from the respondents. The respondents then brought in the appellants, arguing that the appellants were

---

[23] See *infra*, at 850; note that this situation might also be covered by the Product Liability Directive 85/374/EEC, see *Tort: Scope of Protection* at 389, **9.EC.109** and the Consumer Guarantees Directive 99/44/EC.
[24] This Act replaced the Sale of Goods Act 1893, which referred to "merchantable" rather than "satisfactory" quality.
[25] [1969] 1 AC 454.

liable to them on an implied warranty of quality. (For reasons which are not explained, the case was argued on the basis that the contractor had merely acted as agent for the employers in making the contract with the appellants, so that there was a direct contract between appellant and respondents, and the judgments discuss the situation as if the appellants were the contractors.) The appellants were unable to bring in Acme in turn, as they would normally have done, because the limitation period for their claim against Acme had expired.

Held: The appeal was dismissed; the respondents were liable for the defect.

Judgment: LORD REID: I take first the general question of the contractor's liability where the material which he is required to use can be obtained from any one of several suppliers and the choice of suppliers is left to him. There is no doubt that in every case he is bound to make a proper inspection of the material before using it, and he will be liable if the loss is caused by the use of material which reasonable inspection would have shown to be defective. The question is whether he warrants the material against latent defects.

There are, in my view, good reasons for implying such a warranty if it is not excluded by the terms of the contract. If the contractor's employer suffers loss by reason of the emergence of the latent defect, he will generally have no redress if he cannot recover damages from the contractor. But, if he can recover damages, the contractor will generally not have to bear the loss; he will have bought the defective material from a seller who will be liable under section 14(2) of the Sale of Goods Act, 1893, because the material was not of merchantable [now 'satisfactory'-Ed.] quality. And, if that seller had in turn bought from someone else, there will again be liability, so that there will be a chain of liability from the employer who suffers the damage back to the author of the defect. Of course, the chain may be broken because the contractor (or an earlier buyer) may have agreed to enter into a contract under which his supplier excluded or limited his ordinary liability under the Sale of Goods Act. But in general that has nothing to do with the employer and should not deprive him of his remedy. If the contractor chooses to buy on such terms, he takes the risk of having to bear the loss himself if the goods prove to be defective.

Moreover, many contracts for work and materials closely resemble contracts of sale: where the employer contracts for the supply and installation of a machine or other article, the supply of the machine may be the main element and the work of installation be a comparatively small matter. If the employer had bought the article and installed it himself, he would have had a warranty under section 14(2), and it would be strange that the fact that the seller also agreed to install it should make all the difference.

The speciality in the present case is that these tiles were only made by one manufacturer. So the contractor had to buy them from him or from someone who bought from him. Why should that make any difference? It would make a difference if that manufacturer was only willing to sell on terms which excluded or limited his ordinary liability under the Sale of Goods Act, and that fact was known to the employer and the contractor when they made their contract. For it would be unreasonable to put on the contractor a liability for latent defects when the employer had chosen the supplier with knowledge that the contractor could not have recourse against him. If the manufacturer's disclaimer of liability caused him to supply the goods at cheaper price, as in theory at least it should, the employer ought not to get the benefit of a cheap price as well as a warranty from the contractor.

A more difficult case would be where the employer and contractor had no reason to suppose, when they made their contract, that the manufacturer would refuse to sell subject to a seller's ordinary liability in respect of latent defects in their tiles. No doubt there will be some cases where, although the contractor had a right of recourse against the manufacturer, he cannot in fact operate that right. The supplier may have become insolvent, or, as in the present case, the action against the contractor may be so delayed that he has no time left in which to sue his supplier. But these cases must be relatively few and it would seem better that the contractor should occasionally have to suffer than the employer should very seldom have any remedy at all. It therefore seems to me that general principles point strongly to there being an implied warranty of quality in this case.

There is little assistance to be got from the earlier authorities . . .

In the present case one must sympathise with the appellants because, through no fault of their own, they have lost their right of ultimate recourse against the makers of these tiles. But, putting that aside, because the existence or non-existence of the warranty must be determined as at the date of the contract, this appears to me to be a clear case in which a warranty of quality must be implied. I would therefore dismiss the appeal.

LORD PEARCE: If the appellant's argument is correct, an employer has no redress for loss arising out of the use of material with latent defects, if he has ordered a particular kind of material. For it was not the employer but the contractor who bought from the manufacturer. The employer therefore cannot sue the manufacturer, unless it is possible to extend *Donoghue* v. *Stevenson* further than it has gone up to the present.

I see great difficulty in extending to an ultimate consumer a right to sue the manufacturer in tort in respect of goods which create no peril or accident but simply result in substandard work under a contract which is unknown to the original manufacturer. And if originally, as a term of his contract, the manufacturer limited his liability for defects, there seems no reason (where there is no peril or accident) why a third party should have better rights than the original purchaser. And, if his rights are the same, there is no need to introduce a rule which would cause various confusions and difficulties, since the same result can be achieved in the normal case by the third party procedure.

If, however, the employer can sue the contractor in respect of the faulty materials, then the contractor can in turn recover from the manufacturer, with whom the ultimate blame lies. This would follow the normal chain of liability which attaches to sales and sub-sales of goods.

Note

A German or French court would in such a case supply the omitted terms on the contractor's liability by reference to §§ 633, 635, BGB, Article 1792 of the French Civil Code. Note that since *Young and Marten Ltd.* v. *McManus Childs Ltd.* was decided in 1969 even terms to be implied in building contracts are now in statutory form under the Supply of Goods and Services Act 1982.

House of Lords   **4.E.16.**
Liverpool City Council v. *Irwin*[26]

IMPLIED TERM IN LEASE

Stairways and lifts

When a flat is in a tower block the landlord is under an implied obligation to use reasonable care to keep the common areas, such as stairways, lifts and rubbish chutes, in good repair.

Facts: The appellants were tenants of an apartment on the ninth floor of a 15 storey block containing some seventy dwelling units erected and owned by the respondents, a municipal corporation. Owing in part to vandalism, in part to non-co-operation by the tenants, and in part to inaction by the local authority, serious defects in the common parts of the building developed, including a continual failure of the lifts, lack of lighting on the stairs, dangerous condition of the staircase with unguarded holes giving access to the rubbish chutes, etc. The tenancy agreement imposed a number of obligations on the tenants but said nothing concerning the obligations of the respondents. When the appellants refused to pay rent the respondents sought an order for possession of their apartment, and the appellants counterclaimed alleging that the respondents had been in breach of an implied duty to keep the common parts of the block in repair and the lights in working order.

[26] [1976] 2 All ER 39.

Held: The landlords were under an implied obligation to take reasonable care to keep the common areas, such as stairways, lifts and rubbish chutes, in good repair; but there was no evidence that they had failed to use reasonable care.

Judgment: LORD WILBERFORCE: [After stating that the written tenancy agreement contained nothing on the obligations of the respondents his Lordship continued:] We have then a contract which is partly, but not wholly, stated in writing. In order to complete it, in particular to give it a bilateral character, it is necessary to take account of the actions of the parties and the circumstances. As actions of the parties, we must note the granting of possession by the corporation and reservation by it of the "common parts"—stairs, lifts, chutes etc. As circumstances we must include the nature of the premises, viz a maisonette for family use on the ninth floor of a high block, one which is occupied by a large number of other tenants, all using the common parts and dependent on them, none of them having any expressed obligation to maintain or repair them.

To say that the construction of a complete contract out of these elements involves a process of "implication" may be correct: it would be so if implication means the supplying of what is not expressed. But there are varieties of implications which the courts think fit to make and they do not necessarily involve the same process. Where there is, on the face of it, a complete, bilateral contract, the courts are sometimes willing to add terms to it, as implied terms; this is very common in mercantile contracts where there is an established usage; in that case the courts are spelling out what both parties know and would, if asked, unhesitatingly agree to be part of the bargain. In other cases, where there is an apparently complete bargain, the courts are willing to add a term on the ground that without it the contract will not work . . . This is, as was pointed out by the majority in the Court of Appeal, a strict test—though the degree of strictness seems to vary with the current legal trend, and I think that they were right not to accept it as applicable here. There is a third variety of implication, that which I think *Lord Denning* MR favours, or at least did favour in this case, and that is the implication of reasonable terms. But though I agree with many of his instances, which in fact fall under one or other of the preceding heads, I cannot go so far as to endorse his principle; indeed, it seems to me, with respect, to extend a long, and undesirable, way beyond sound authority.

The present case, in my opinion, represents a fourth category or, I would rather say, a fourth shade on a continuous spectrum. The court here is simply concerned to establish what the contract is, the parties not having themselves fully stated the terms. In this sense the court is searching for what must be implied. [His Lordship then stated the parties' legal positions and continued:]

My Lords, in order to be able to choose between these, it is necessary to define what test is to be applied, and I do not find this difficult. In my opinion such obligation should be read into the contract as the nature of the contract itself implicitly requires, no more, no less; a test in other words of necessity. The relationship accepted by the corporation is that of landlord and tenant; the tenant accepts obligations accordingly, in relation, *inter alia*, to the stairs, the lifts and the chutes. All these are not just facilities, or conveniences provided at discretion; they are essentials of the tenancy without which life in the dwellings, as a tenant, is not possible. To leave the landlord free of contractual obligation as regards these matters, and subject only to administrative or political pressure, is, in my opinion, totally inconsistent with the nature of this relationship. The subject-matter of the lease (high-rise blocks) and the relationship created by the tenancy demands, of its nature, some contractual obligation on the landlord . . .

It remains to define the standard. My Lords, if, as I think, the test of the existence of the term is necessity the standard must surely not exceed what is necessary having regard to the circumstances. To imply and absolute obligation to repair would go beyond what is a necessary legal incident and would indeed be unreasonable. An obligation to take reasonable care to keep in reasonable repair and usability is what fits the requirement of the case. Such a definition involves—and I think rightly—recognition that the tenants themselves have their responsibilities. What it is reasonable to expect of a landlord has a clear relation to what a reasonable set of tenants should do for themselves.

[The other Law Lords delivered speeches to the same effect.]

Note
In this case French and German courts would have supplied the omitted terms by reference to the relevant provisions of the French or German Civil Codes.

Code civil   4.F.17.

Article 1719: The lessor is bound, by the nature of the contract, and without there being any need for any special stipulation:
(1) to supply to the lessee the thing leased;
(2) to maintain that thing in such condition that it may be used for the purpose for which it has been let.

Article 1720: The lessor is bound to supply the thing in a good state of repair in every respect. He is obliged, throughout the period of the lease, to carry out all repairs to it which may become necessary, other than those which are the lessee's responsibility.

BGB   4.G.18.

§ 537: The lessee is entitled to withhold the rent, wholly or in part, if at the time when the thing leased is handed over to the lessee, it is vitiated by a defect which is such as to nullify or reduce its fitness for its intended use under the contract, or if such a defect comes into existence during the course of the lease . . .

Note
§ 538 entitles the lessee to claim damages if a defect as defined in § 537 exists at the time when the thing is handed over to him or if such defect develops during the lease. However, in the latter case, the lessee must show that the damages were caused by the lessor's negligent failure to take the care that would be expected from a reasonable lessor under the circumstances.

In employment contracts the obligations of the parties are left undefined in many cases and are settled by the courts through the device of the implied term. Thus it has been held that the employee is under an implied duty to use proper care in the performance of his duties, not to enter into competition with his employer, not to divulge or improperly use confidential information acquired in the course of his employment and, within certain limits, to disclose to the employer information harmful to the employer's interest. It has also been held that employees engaging in "go slow" or "work to rule" action are in breach of an implied duty to serve their employers faithfully with a view of promoting their commercial interests.[27] On the other hand, an employer is bound by an implied duty to take all reasonable care for the safety of the employee in the course of his or her work. It is probably safe to say, however, that English judges tend to be more reluctant in

---

[27] See *Secretary of Employment* v. *ASLEF* [1972] 2 QB 455, at 498, 508, and BGH, 31 January 1978, BGHZ 70.277.

implying employers' duties than their continental brethren. Thus it has been held by the House of Lords in *Lister* v. *Romford Ice and Cold Storage Co. Ltd.* [28] that an employer of a driver is under no implied duty to see to it that the driver is protected by insurance from any liability *vis-à-vis* third parties arising from his driving and that, accordingly, the employer, having paid the third party under the rules of vicarious liability, can recover from the employee the full amount.[29] The justice of this decision has little to commend itself since there are strong grounds for arguing that the rule on which it is based is unjustifiable in modern conditions, not only because of the disastrous effect it might have on labour relations if the employers, or their liability insurers as subrogees, were to enforce it against employees. In order to avoid a legislative reaction employers' liability insurers have entered into a "gentleman's agreement" not to take advantage of the *Lister* rule unless there was evidence of collusion or wilful misconduct.

Court of Appeal 4.E.19.

Reid v. *Rush & Tompkins Group plc*[30]

NO IMPLIED OBLIGATION TO WARN EMPLOYEE ABOUT INSURANCE

Dangers abroad

An employee who sends an employee abroad is not under an implied obligation to insure the employee against risks he may face because of the law of the country in which he is working, nor to warn him to insure himself.

Facts: The plaintiff was employed by the defendants as a quarry foreman on a project in Ethiopia. In the course of his employment the plaintiff, while driving along a bush road, was seriously injured when his vehicle collided with a lorry being driven in the opposite direction by an unidentified person. The sole cause of the accident was the negligence of the other driver but since the driver's identity was unknown the plaintiff was unable to recover against him and, furthermore, there was no compulsory third party motor insurance and no scheme to cover uninsured third parties in Ethiopia. The plaintiff brought an action against the defendants alleging that they were in breach of their duty of care as employers in failing either to insure the plaintiff against being injured in a traffic accident as the result of the negligence of a third party or to advise him to obtain such cover for himself.

Held: At first instance it was held that the plaintiff's claim disclosed no reasonable cause of action and should be struck out. The Court of Appeal dismissed the appeal.

Judgment: RALPH GIBSON LJ: [After stating that the defendants had given no implied undertaking to insure the plaintiff against risk of uncompensated injury caused to him by third parties while acting in the course of his employment in Ethiopia, his Lordship turned to the question whether there was an implied term in the contract of employment imposing on the defendants a duty to inform the plaintiff of the special risks involved and to advise him that he should himself obtain appropriate insurance cover, and said:]

It is clear, I think, that a new term can be implied by law into contracts of employment . . . It is, however, impossible, in my judgment, to imply in this case a term as a matter of law in the form contended for, namely a specific duty to advise the plaintiff to obtain specific insurance cover. Such a duty seems to me inappropriate for incorporation by law into all contracts of employment in the circumstances alleged. The length of time during which the servant will work abroad and the nature

---

[28] [1957] AC 555.
[29] The opposite result has been reached in Germany: see BAG, 9 August 1996, NJW 1966.2233.
[30] [1989] 3 All ER 228.

of his work may vary greatly between one job and another and hence the extent to which the servant would be exposed to the special risk. Further, having regard to the many different ways in which a servant working abroad may run the risk of uncompensated injury caused by the wrongdoing of a third party, apart from a traffic accident, it seems to me impossible to formulate the detailed terms in which the law could incorporate into the general relationship of master and servant a contractual obligation to the effect necessary to cover the plaintiffs claim. I have considered whether the implied term could be limited to the risk from injuries in a traffic accident, but then the question is raised whether the obligation should arise on any difference between the total protection provided in this country by compulsory third party insurance . . . on the one hand, and such protection as exists in the foreign country, on the other hand, or only on the total absence of the protection provided in this country. I have also considered whether the term could be expressed as follows: an employer who takes a person into his employment in this country for work to be done in a foreign country shall take reasonable care to provide sufficient information and warning to that servant with reference to any risk of suffering uncompensated injury in the course of his employment in the foreign country, caused through the fault of a third party, which risk would not be suffered in this country and of which a reasonable person would require to be informed before accepting such employment. For my part I am unable to accept that the court could properly incorporate such a term by law into contracts of employment. It seems to me that it would require of employers, many of whom may have no such resources of advice or experience as may be available to these defendants, and who may employ only one or two servants, to discover much information about foreign legal and social systems in order to decide whether such a term requires action on their part. The usefulness of the principle contended for seems to me, in social terms, to be plain enough; but to incorporate the duty by law into contracts of employment would, in my view, require, if it were to work fairly, exemptions and limitations which can only properly be achieved by legislation.

[NEILL LJ and MAY LJ agreed.]

Notes

(1) Compare the cost to the employer and to the employee of obtaining information on the risks involved and the availability and price of appropriate insurance. Is it not wasteful to impose that cost on the employee? Is it plausible to say that the employer's duty to give proper advice "can only properly be achieved by legislation"?

(2) English lawyers often divide implied terms into those "implied in law", and those "implied in fact". The difference between the two categories is not as clear in practice as it appears on paper, but its basis is that, in relation to the former category, the terms implied will usually be framed in such general expressions as to be applicable, failing contrary provision, to all contracts of a particular type. For this reason, terms implied in law will on the continent be supplied in most, but by no means in all, cases by provisions in the Civil Codes or some other statute laying down the basic framework of a particular type of contract. On the other hand, a term may be "implied in fact" where there is an apparently complete bargain but the parties have left open a particular point which calls for a "made to measure" solution since without it the contract will not work.

In the words of Lord Cross in *Liverpool County Council* v. *Irwin* [31]:

When it implies a term in a contract the court is sometimes laying down a general rule that in all contracts of a certain type—sale of goods, master and servant, landlord and tenant, and so on—some provision is to be implied unless the parties have expressly excluded it. In deciding

[31] See *supra*, at 574, **4.E.16.**

whether or not to lay down such a prima facie rule the court will naturally ask itself whether in the general run of such cases the term in question would be one which it would be reasonable to insert. Sometimes, however, there is no question of laying down any prima facie rule applicable to all cases of a defined type but what the court is being in effect asked to do is to rectify a particular—very often a very detailed—contract by inserting in it a term which the parties have not expressed. Here it is not enough for the court to say that the suggested term is a reasonable one the presence of which would make the contract a better or fairer one; it must be able to say that the insertion of the term is necessary to give—as it is put—"business efficacy" to the contract and that if its absence had been pointed out at the time both parties—assuming them to have been reasonable men—would have agreed without hesitation to its insertion.[32]

On the Continent, the statute book will not be of much use in cases of the latter category. If faced with a case of this type a German judge will ask if the gap in the contract can be filled by what is called "constructive interpretation" (*ergänzende Vertragsausle-gung*). The formula generally used is this: where the parties have omitted to say something, no default rule being supplied by a statute, the judge must "discover and take into account what, in the light of the whole purpose of the contract, the parties, as reasonable and fair-minded persons, would have said if they had regulated the point in question, acting pursuant to the requirements of good faith and good commercial practice". French courts actually decide in much the same way. Sometimes they say that the term to be implied is based on what the court, exercising its *"pouvoir souverain des juges de fond"*, thinks has been the "common intention of the parties". Sometimes they rely on Article 1135 of the French Civil Code which provides that the obligations imposed on the parties are not only those expressed in their agreement but also those which *"l'équité, l'usage ou la loi donnent à l'obligation d'après sa nature"*.

Unidroit Principles   4.INT.20.

Article 4.8: *(Supplying an omitted term)*
    (1) Where the parties to a contract have not agreed with respect to a term which is important for a determination of their rights and duties, a term which is appropriate in the circumstances shall be supplied.
    (2) In determining what is an appropriate term regard shall be had, among other factors, to
        (a) the intention of the parties;
        (b) the nature of the contract;
        (c) good faith and fair dealing;
        (d) reasonableness.

BGH, 18 December 1954[33]   4.G.21.

CONSTRUCTIVE INTERPRETATION

Exchange of doctors' practices

If it emerges that the contract does not provide for the situation which has occurred, including a situation which the parties had not considered, the court will fill the lacuna by constructive interpretation, supplying a term which the parties would have agreed had they considered the point.

---

[32] At 46–7.
[33] BGHZ 16.71.

579

Facts: The parties were two doctors who had agreed to exchange practices. The defendant found his new place of work not to his liking and intended to return and set up a new practice in his old town only nine months later. The plaintiff feared that the defendant's patients would flock back to him and sought an injunction. Since there was nothing in the contract on a "right to return", the question arose whether a term disallowing such return could be read into it.

Held: The defendant had no unqualified right to return to compete in private practice with the claimant. The case was sent back to the lower court to take further evidence on the local conditions, the type of the parties' patients, etc. and then to rule on the precise limits, as to time and location, of the defendant's right to return.

Judgment: § 157 BGB provides that in the interpretation of contracts due consideration is to be given to the principle of good faith and the prevailing practice. It is true that, according to that provision, the interpretation must be based—having regard to the purpose of the contract, the principle of good faith and the prevailing practice—on the discernible states of mind of the parties at the time when the contract was concluded. However, § 157 BGB requires the court to ascertain the entire content of the contract according to objective criteria. That task will be fulfilled only if the court also establishes the content of the contract as regards those points which have not been agreed by the parties, irrespective of whether they consciously dispensed with any detailed stipulations, whether the lacuna in the matters agreed existed from the outset or whether it only manifested itself at a later stage, as a result of subsequent developments. It may therefore also be necessary, in undertaking a constructive interpretation of the contract, to ascertain and take into account matters which the parties did not clarify but which, in view of the purpose of the contract as a whole, they would have clarified had they also settled the outstanding point when reaching their agreement, thereby observing, at the same time, the dictates of good faith and of the prevailing practice. This is conditional on the existence, within the actual context of the contract, of a lacuna needing to be filled, that is to say, one which is essential for the purposes of securing the purpose of the contract.

In the present case, the criteria for a constructive interpretation of the contract are fulfilled. According to the findings of the appellate court, the parties, when agreeing the terms on which the practices were to be exchanged, did not contemplate the possibility that one of them might soon return to the area in which he formerly practised; and they made no particular provision for that eventuality. Yet the facts of the case are clearly such that it needed to be catered for. Even if one concurs with the appellate court's view that the actual purpose of the exchange contract was limited to affording the possibility of carrying on the other party's practice by taking over that party's patient clientèle, there can be no serious doubt that such a possibility would be considerably impaired by the return of the former owner of the practice, if he were unable, either at all or at any rate immediately, to secure readmission to practise under a health insurance scheme. There is no need to determine the question whether, as the plaintiff maintained, a medical practice is generally speaking viable only if it produces income from the treatment of private patients as well as patients who are members of a health insurance scheme. It is indisputable that the parties both practised on a private basis and accordingly intended to continue to do so. However, there is bound to be a diminution in the income from the private practice if the patients within that practice are once again given the opportunity of going for treatment to the former owner of the practice, with whom they have built up, in some cases over a period of many years, a relationship of trust. Thus, the entire purpose of the contract would be substantially jeopardised if one of the parties were to return, only a short while after its conclusion, to the place in which he had formerly practised . . . In those circumstances, the appellate court should not simply have taken as the starting-point for its interpretation the mere fact that there was no agreement between the parties regarding the possible return by one of them to the place in which he had previously practised. Instead, it should have examined whether, and if so to what extent, the parties would have included in the contract a clause prohibiting them from returning to their former practice area if they had given any thought to that eventuality at the time. The contractual lacuna existing in that regard falls within the effective scope of the arrangements made between the parties. We are concerned here not with the creation of an additional obligation going beyond the essential content of the contract for the exchange of practices, but merely with the concrete enunciation of a collateral obligation which is closely connected with the purpose of the contract. Consequently, the filling of that lacuna would not result in an impermissible extension of the content of the contract . . .

The constructive interpretation of the contract which is possible—and, indeed, necessary—in the light of the above can in principle be provided by this Court itself, applying the objective criteria laid down in § 157 BGB. On the basis of the foregoing considerations, that interpretation must be that, upon a reasonable assessment of the purpose for which the practices were to be exchanged, the parties—had they given any thought in advance to the possibility of one of them returning to the immediate vicinity of his former practice—would have agreed to prohibit such a return within a given period of, say, 2 to 3 years following completion of the exchange of practices. This is because it is not generally possible, within such a period, for the successor to a practice to consolidate his relations with his predecessor's patients to such an extent that he need no longer fear any significant loss or damage as a result the latter's return. Within those parameters, therefore, the contract must in any event be deemed to include a stipulation prohibiting a return.
[Citations omitted.]

BGH, 25 June 1980[34]   **4.G.22.**

CONSTRUCTIVE INTERPRETATION TO AVOID RESULT
AT ODDS WITH PURPOSE OF CONTRACT

Redecoration

A term will be supplied by constructive interpretation only if not to do so would produce a result at odds with the purpose of the contract as agreed by the parties.

Facts: The parties had entered into an agreement for the lease of a restaurant providing that, upon its termination, the lessee was bound to carry out at his expense certain repair work designed to restore the premises to good condition. The lessee had failed to do so. The lessor then decided to rebuild the premises, and there was no dispute that the rebuilding would have destroyed the repair work if it had been carried out by the lessee. The lessor sued the lessee for the value of the repair work. The lessee's defence was that his failure to carry out the contractually agreed repair work had caused no loss to the lessor. Since the contract was silent on whether the lessor was to have such a claim the question was whether such a term could be implied.

Held: The lessor was not entitled to require the tenant to perform the obligation; at most he could claim the saving to the tenant through not having to do the work.

Judgment: The plaintiff's claim may . . . be substantiated if a constructive interpretation of the contract shows that the presumed intention of the parties must have been to allow the plaintiff, in the event of the demised premises being rebuilt, a pecuniary claim instead of an accrued entitlement to demand performance . . .

The parties agreed that the lessee was to carry out the decorative repairs. The contract is silent on the question whether the lessor was to be entitled to compensation in the event that, upon the lessee failing at the end of the lease to carry out the outstanding decorative repairs, the lessor were immediately to rebuild the demised premises in accordance with a decision which—as the appellate court found—he had already made prior to the termination of the lease, and the rebuilding resulted in the destruction of any decorative repairs which might have been carried out. There is, to that extent, a lacuna in the contract.

[34] BGHZ 77.301.

However, not every point which a contract omits to regulate is susceptible of resolution by means of a constructive interpretation. Where the parties to a contract make no stipulation regarding a given matter, it may generally be assumed that they are content to let the form which their contractual relationship is to take be governed by the provisions enshrined in statutory legislation. A contractual lacuna needing to be filled by interpretation exists only where the contract requires to be supplemented within its established framework or within the ambit of the matters on which the parties actually intended to agree. A judicial interpretation may not have the effect of extending the subject-matter of the contract, and must be supported by the contents of the contract. It must follow cogently and self-evidently from the entire context of the matters agreed, in such a way that, if the contract were not thus supplemented, the result would be manifestly at odds with the matters which, according to the contents of the contract, were actually agreed between the parties.

That may possibly be the position in the present case. It would be absurd for the lessor, having firmly decided to rebuild, to be stuck with having to demand the performance by the lessee of the latter's obligation to carry out the decorative repairs, as laid down in the contract, notwithstanding that, upon that obligation being performed, the work done would immediately be destroyed. On the other hand, however, it would clearly be at variance with the content of the contract—as a general rule, in any event—if the lessee were to be released from his obligation without having to pay any compensation in lieu, since the lessee's obligation, laid down in the lease, requiring him to carry out the decorative repairs represents, generally at any rate, part of the consideration due from the lessee in return for performance by the lessor . . . Consequently, in accordance with the principle of good faith and the prevailing practice, the intention of the contracting parties must be presumed to have been that the lessor should have a corresponding pecuniary entitlement in lieu of the right to require the decorative repairs to be carried out, which had become economically pointless (§ 157 BGB). That pecuniary entitlement consists of an amount equivalent to what the lessee would have had to spend in carrying out the requisite decorative repairs. The corresponding sum is payable by the lessee to the lessor.

The amount of such pecuniary entitlement will depend on the circumstances of each individual case. In particular, significance may attach to the question whether, according to the presumed intention of the parties, the lessor would have had to accept the decorative repairs being done by the lessee personally or by relatives or acquaintances of the lessee. If so, the sum due to the lessor may be less substantial than it would have been if the lessor could have insisted on the repair works being done by a professional workman.
[Citations omitted.]

Note
"Constructive interpretation" is also used by German courts in cases where a clause in a standard form contract is struck down as unfair and the question arises how the resulting gap is to be filled. Thus it was held in an action brought by a consumers' organization against **Daimler-Benz AG** that the defendants, as sellers of new cars, could not validly reserve a power to charge their buyer the price in force at the time of delivery regardless of the time that would elapse between the date of the contract and the time of delivery. In order to fill the gap the court supplied a term which upheld the sellers' right to charge the list price in force at the time of delivery but added a right for the buyer to cancel the contract if the difference between the two prices "substantially exceeds" the rise of the general costs of living between the two relevant dates.[35] Writers have criticized this

---

[35] See BGH, 1 February 1984, BGHZ 90.69.

decision on the ground that it is in conflict with a rule laid down in other German cases according to which courts cannot rewrite a clause, only strike it out *in toto*.[36]

Cour d'appel de Rouen, 29 November 1968 [37] **4.F.23.**

Delayed building work

A clause will be implied into a contract on the basis of Article 1160 CC only if the parties must have intended it to apply but omitted it unintentionally.

Facts: The parties had entered into a contract in 1957 under which the plaintiff building contractor had agreed to carry out certain work for a price. For various reasons, the work was not completed before 1967. The contractor asked the employer to pay a higher price computed on the price revision mechanism known in the industry as the "M.R.L. method". The employer paid only what had been agreed in 1957 contract.

Held: The lower court gave judgment for the plaintiff contractor on the ground that a clause entitling him to a price revision was to be implied on the basis of art. 1160 French Civil Code which empowers the court to read into a contract "*les clauses qui y sont d'usage, quoiqu'elles n'y soient pas exprimées*". The defendant appealed. The appeal was allowed.

Judgment: Whereas Article 1160 of the Civil Code authorises the implied inclusion in contracts of clauses which, although not expressly set out therein, are of the type customarily contained in such contracts. Whereas however, the sole purpose and effect which that provision can have is to modify the scheme of the contract by introducing into it, where the parties have said nothing on the point, a clause which alters the main elements of their rights and obligations. Whereas a clause may be said to be "customary" within the meaning of the abovementioned provision only if, first, its omission must be presumed to have been unintentional and the parties must be deemed to have intended in any event to apply it and, second, if it can be applied without the court having to stipulate factual matters the choice and determination of which lay with the parties alone and with regard to which the court may not substitute its own ideas of what the parties intended for those of the parties themselves. Whereas the omission of the price revision clause in the agreement between Guéry and Druart does not appear to be the result of mere inadvertence, since it has not been established, or even alleged, that Guéry enjoyed, in his contractual relations with his clients, the benefit of the possibility of a revision of the price. Whereas furthermore, in order for such a clause to be applied, it would be necessary to determine the revision dates and the matters capable of being revised, and to choose between the various possible methods of revision. Whereas it follows that, as a matter of law, there exists no basis on which Article 1160 of the Civil Code can apply. Whereas the court adjudicating at first instance believed that it could infer that adherence to the fixed prices had been abandoned in November 1957 from the fact that, by letter of 14 February 1959, Druart, without alluding to those initially agreed prices, proposed new prices, referring to "our meeting on 12 February 1959". Whereas however, the 1957 prices and the 1959 prices do not relate to the same works; the 1957 prices concern works in connection with flooring and skirting-boards, whilst the 1959 prices concern stairs and risers. Whereas consequently, the fixing in 1959 of prices relating to matters not provided for in 1957 does not signify any abandonment of the prices previously agreed. Whereas since no price revision was provided for, notwithstanding that it was clearly going to be a long time before the works were completed, the conclusion reached by the court below, based on the length

---

[36] There is authority for this rule in England too; see *Stewart Gill Ltd.* v. *Horatio Myer & Co. Ltd.* [1992] 2 All ER 257 and the discussion in Kötz, *European Contract Law*, chapter 8, at 149.
[37] D. 1969.146.

of time which elapsed between the prices being agreed and the works being completed, is wholly invalid. Whereas if Société Druart had intended to take precautions against a change in economic circumstances, it could have provided either for a maximum period for completion of the works or for the possibility of revision; but it did not at any juncture suggest a price revision, proceeding without reservation to carry out the works at Saint-Étienne-du-Rouvray whilst none the less reserving the right to include V.A.T. in its final account. Whereas it was only when that account was drawn up (on 4 March 1960) that it applied the simplified method of revision published by the Seine-Maritime M.R.L., which Guéry was unwilling to accept, since, despite the numerous demands made by Druart, it was not until 2 December 1961 that a bill of exchange for 3 452.70 francs was accepted, representing settlement of 95% of the price of the works; the difference of 5% did not correspond to the normal retention sum and does not explain the dispute regarding a possible revision. It follows that Druart's claim is unfounded and that the court below was wrong to allow it.

Cass. civ. 3e, 15 February 1972[38]   **4.F.24.**

REFERENCE TO A NON-EXISTENT FACTOR

Wage scale no longer published

Where the price in a contract is to be determined by reference to a price index which, during the course of the contract, ceases to be published, the court will substitute a closely equivalent scale.

Facts: Premises were sold to the appellants at a price payable over five years and to be adjusted by reference to a wage scale for a particular class of skilled worker. This scale ceased to be published.

Held: By the court of Caen, that the price should be adjusted by reference to the closest equivalent wage scale. The buyers' appeal was dismissed.

Judgment: THE COURT: As to the first plea advanced.—Whereas by a notarial act dated 28 February 1964, Mr and Mrs Couasse purchased a property for residential use and for use as premises in which to carry on a motor mechanic's business. Whereas the price was 85,000 francs, payable over five years. Whereas they are appealing against the ruling in the contested judgment (Caen, 3 June 1970) that the indexation clause provided for in the contract should apply, on the ground that the court below, having found that it was not possible to apply the literal terms of the clause in question, nevertheless proceeded arbitrarily to alter its terms by inserting "particulars other than those by reference to which the parties had contracted". Whereas however, having noted that the parties had taken as the indexation basis the index for a grade O P 4 skilled worker as published from time to time in the lists of standard occupational wages, the *cour d'appel* observed that that index did not exist and that no such lists of standard occupational wages were published. Whereas in seeking to determine the common intention of the parties by means of the requisite interpretation of the wording of the deed, the *cour d'appel* found that it was apparent from the evidence in the case that the contracting parties had intended, from the outset of their dealings, that the purchase price, payable over a term of years, should be coupled with, and subject to, a price adjustment clause linked to increases in the salary of a skilled worker in the highest grade, that a reference to a grade three skilled mechanic came closest to reflecting that occupational category, and that reference should be made to the written wording in which the variations in the index chosen appeared. Whereas in so ruling, the *cour d'appel* were merely exercising their unfettered discretion. The first plea must therefore be rejected.

[38] D. 1973.147 annotated by J. Ghestin.

Note

The Cour de Cassation, under cover of the "pouvoir souverain" of the lower court, a bold interpretation of the indexation clause, in order to save it. There is considerable debate in England about the conditions which must exist before the court may imply a term adding to or qualifying the express terms of an agreement. One test is to ask whether implying a term is necessary "to give such business efficacy to the transaction as must have been intended by both parties".

Court of Appeal   **4.E.25.**
The Moorcock[39]

TERM IMPLIED TO GIVE CONTRACT BUSINESS EFFICACY

The Moorcock

A term will be implied into a contract if the term is necessary in order to give "business efficacy" to the contract.

Facts: The defendants had agreed to let the plaintiff unload his ship at the defendant's jetty on the Thames. When the tide went out the ship inevitably settled and was holed because the river bed was uneven.

Held: By the court of first instance and the Court of Appeal, that a term must be implied that the berth was safe or that, if it was not, the defendant would warn the shipowner.

Judgment: BOWEN LJ: The defendants in this case are the owners of a wharf and jetty attached in the river Thames, and the only use to which it is put is holding out to ships facilities for loading and unloading alongside of it. There is only one berth where the ships can lie, and that is close alongside the jetty. The question which arises in this case is whether, when a contract is made to let the use of this jetty to a ship which can only use it, as is known to both parties, by her taking the ground, there is any implied warranty on the part of the wharfingers, and if so what is the extent of that warranty.

An implied warranty, or as it is called a covenant in law, as distinguished from an express contract or express warranty, really is in every instance founded on the presumed intention of the parties and upon reason. It is the implication which the law draws from what must obviously have been the intention of the parties, an implication which the law draws with the object of giving efficacy to the transaction and preventing such a failure of consideration as cannot have been within the contemplation of either of the parties. I believe that if one were to take all the instances, which are many, of implied warranties and covenants in law which occur in the earlier cases it will be seen that in all these cases the law is raising an implication from the presumed intention of the parties with the object of giving to the transaction such efficacy as both parties must have intended it should have. If that is so the reasonable implication which the law draws must differ according to the circumstances of the various transactions, and in business transactions what the law desires to effect by the implication is to give such business efficacy to the transaction as must have been intended by both parties; not to impose on one side all the perils of the transaction or to emancipate one side from all the burdens, but to make each party promise in law as much, at all events, as it must have been in the contemplation of both parties that he should be responsible for.

What did each party in the present case know? Because, if we are examining into their presumed intention, we must examine into their minds as to what the transaction was. Both parties knew that the jetty was let for the purpose of profit, and knew that it could only be used by the ship taking

---

[39] [1886–90] All ER 530.

the ground and lying on the ground. They must have known that it was by grounding that she would use the jetty. They must have known, both of them, that unless the ground was safe the ship would be simply buying an opportunity of danger and buying no convenience at all, and that all consideration would fail unless the ground was safe. In fact, the business of the jetty could not be carried on unless, I do not say the ground was safe, it was supposed to be safe. The master and crew of the ship could know nothing, whereas the defendants or their servants might, by exercising reasonable care, know everything. The defendants or their servants were on the spot at high and low tide, morning and evening. They must know what had happened to the ships that had used the jetty before, and with the slightest trouble they could satisfy themselves in case of doubt whether the berth was safe or not safe. The ship's officers, on the other hand, had no means of verifying the state of the berth, because, for ought I know, it might be occupied by another ship at the time the Moorcock got there.

The question is how much of the peril or the safety of this berth is it necessary to assume in order to get the minimum of efficacy to the business consideration of the transaction which the ship consented to bear, and which the defendants took upon themselves. Supposing that the berth had been actually under the control of the defendants, they could, of course, have repaired it and made it fit for the purpose of loading and unloading. It seems to me that *Mersey Docks Trustees* v. *Gibbs* shows that those who own a jetty, who take money for its use, and who have under their control the locus in quo, are bound to take all reasonable care to prevent danger to those using the jetty, either to make the berth good or else not to invite ships to go to the jetty, *i.e.* either to make it safe or to advise ships not to go there. But there is a distinction between that case and the present. The berth here was not under the actual control of the defendants . . .

Applying that modification, which is a reasonable modification, to this case, it may well be said that the law will not imply that the defendants, who had not control of the place, ought to have taken reasonable care to make the berth good, but it does not follow that they are relieved from all responsibility, a responsibility which depends not merely on the control of the place, which is one element as to which the law implies a duty, but on other circumstances. The defendants are on the spot. They must know the jetty cannot be safely used unless reasonable care is taken. No one can tell whether reasonable safety has been secured except themselves, and I think that, if they let out their jetty for use, they at all events imply that they have taken reasonable care to see that the berth, which is the essential part of the use of the jetty, is safe, and, if it is not safe, and if they have not taken such reasonable care, it is their duty to warn persons with whom they have dealings that they have not done so . . .

[FRY LJ agreed.]

Notes

(1) Since *The Moorcock* there have been a number of judicial attempts to describe the tests for implying terms. One which is often quoted is the "official bystander test" of MacKinnon LJ in *Shirlaw* v. *Southern Foundries*:[40]

Prima facie that which in any contract is left to be implied and need not be expressed is something so obvious that it goes without saying. Thus, if, while the parties were making their bargain, an officious bystander were to suggest some express provision for it in their agreement, they would testily suppress him with a common: Oh, of course.[41]

(2) In other cases terms have been implied without the judges worrying too much about any "test". In *Aerial Advertising Co.* v. *Batchelors Peas Ltd.*[42] a publicity firm

[40] [1939] 2 KB 206.
[41] At 227.
[42] [1938] 2 All ER 788,

was to advertise its client's wares by flying low over towns towing a streamer bearing the slogan "Eat Batchelor's Peas". It chose to fly over Manchester on Armistice Day when the crowds in the main square were observing the two minutes' silence. The public were scandalized, and the firm was held liable. Atkinson LJ did not bother with the "business efficacy test" or the "officious bystander test" but simply said:

There must be implied in that contract a term that the flying under the contract would be carried out with reasonable skill and reasonable care, having regard to the object of the contract, and, in whatever precise words the implied obligation is expressed, it must be, I think, certainly wide enough to exclude flying in a way which would bring the advertisers into hatred and contempt.[43]

In *British School of Motoring Ltd.* v. *Simms*[44] a woman caused an accident while taking her driving test in a car which belonged to the driving school but was not insured for her to drive. She was held liable for the damage caused by the accident but sought to recover it from the owners of the driving school on the basis of their breach of an implied duty to provide a car insured for her driving. Talbot J said:

It is pleaded that there was an implied term, because there is no evidence of any expressed term, that she would be covered for all insurance purposes by the driving school during the time she was in a vehicle provided by them for her driving lessons and test. I am prepared to accept that in such a contract as this is, in the absence of any expressed condition, there is an implied term that such a person going to a driving school will be covered by insurance in the motor car provided by the driving school. Therefore, there was a breach of contract by the driving school in providing her with a car which was not insured for her driving. She is entitled to damages which flow from that breach. The measure of those damages, in my opinion, is the damage she now has to pay which she would not have had to pay had she been properly insured.

(3) The "business efficacy" and "officious bystander" tests are all based on an attempt to ascertain what the parties would have agreed had they been put on notice at the time of contracting that there was a gap in their agreement. Similarly, the German BGH will supply a missing term by resorting to what is described as the "hypothetical" or "presumable" intention of the parties. It is arguable that the judges cling to this terminology only to cloak the fact that they are simply deciding on the rule which provides a reasonable and appropriate solution to the dispute.

English judges would not go that far. Summarizing the effect of *Liverpool County Council* v. *Irwin* on the law relating to terms to be implied in fact (on a "one-off" basis) Lord Denning said in *Shell U.K. Ltd.* v. *Lostock Garage Ltd.*:[45]

These are cases, not of common occurrence, in which from the particular circumstances a term is to be implied. In these cases the implication is based on an intention imputed to the parties from their actual circumstances . . . Such an imputation is only to be made when it is necessary to imply a term to give efficacy to the contract and make it a workable agreement in such manner as the parties would clearly have done if they had applied their mind to the contingency which has arisen . . . In such cases a term is not to be implied on the ground that it would be reasonable, but only when it is necessary and can be formulated with a sufficient degree of precision. [46]

---

[43] At 792.
[44] [1971] 1 All ER 317.
[45] [1977] 481.
[46] At 487–8.

(4) Economic analysis of law suggests that contracts are inevitably incomplete since the parties' "transaction cost" of negotiating every detail of their arrangements exceeds the benefit each party may expect to derive from such negotiations. For this reason, economic analysis also suggests that, in the absence of express terms, the courts should supply, as "implied terms", rules to which the parties would have agreed if negotiations had cost nothing, i.e. if the parties had had all the time and money in the world to work out a solution of the problem that would have left them both as well off as possible. Assuming that the parties in *The Moorcock* had been able to negotiate at no transaction cost they would have allocated the risk to that party who, at lower cost than the other side, would have been able to prevent it from materializing (and/or to cover it by insurance). Clearly, information about the condition of the river bed was accessible to the owners of the jetty at much lower cost than to the shipowner.

In the words of Bowen LJ :

The owners of the jetty, or their servants, were there at high tide and low tide, and with little trouble they could satisfy themselves, in case of doubt, as to whether the berth was reasonably safe. The ship's owner, on the other hand, had not the means of verifying the state of the jetty.[47]

It would follow that in an ideal world where negotiations cost nothing the jetty owner would have accepted the risk, and this is indeed the term that was implied by the court. The same analysis might be used in the following case.

Court of Appeal   **4.E.26.**
K.C. Sethia Ltd. v. *Partabmull Rameshwar*[48]

TERM NOT IMPLIED UNLESS BOTH PARTIES WOULD HAVE ACCEPTED IT

Jute quotas

A term excusing one party in certain circumstances will not be implied if the circumstances are partly within the control of that party, as it is not clear that the other party would have accepted the term.

Facts: The sellers had agreed to sell certain quantities of jute from India c.i.f. Genoa. The parties were aware of the fact that the export of jute from India was prohibited except under licence and that licences would be granted by the Indian Government under a "quota system". Under this system, shippers were required to choose as their basic year one of the years from 1937 and 1946, and were allotted a quota in regard to the countries to which they had shipped in their basic year and in proportion to the amount shipped to those countries in that year. The sellers chose as their basic year a year in which they had made no shipments to Italy, so they received no quota in Italy. Having obtained no licence the sellers did not deliver. The buyers claimed damages for breach of contract. The sellers contended that an implied term should be read into the contract providing that they were to deliver only "subject to quota". They relied on *The Moorcock* and on *Re Anglo-Russian Merchant Traders and John Batt & Co.* [1917] 2 KB 679 in which it had been held that British exporters of aluminium were not liable in damages if, despite the use of reasonable diligence, they had been unable to obtain a licence.

Held: The case went to arbitration, which gave an award in the buyers' favour. This was upheld by the court of first instance. The sellers appealed. The appeal was dismissed.

Judgment: JENKINS LJ: I agree that the appeal fails. In considering the question whether an implied term should be read into contracts such as those, there is, I think, a real and important distinction

---

[47] At 69.
[48] [1950] 1 All ER 51.

between circumstances such as those in *Re Anglo-Russian Merchant Traders and John Batt & Co. (London)*, where the commodity in question was a commodity all dealings in which were unlawful in the absence of a licence and circumstances such as those in the present case which concerns a commodity subject to control on a quota system under which individual dealers can lawfully deal with the commodity up to the amount of the quota allotted to them respectively. In cases of the former type, it is easy to imply a term to the effect that the transaction is subject to the necessary licence being obtained, for otherwise it would be manifest to both parties that the transaction could not be carried out at all, but in cases of the present type, while it is, no doubt, true that both parties know that the contract can only be met out of the seller's quota, the question whether the seller's quota will suffice for that purpose seems to me to depend on a variety of matters concerning the conduct of the seller's business, and, as such, matters peculiarly within his knowledge as opposed to that of the buyer. The seller will know which basic year he chose for the purpose of fixing his quota. He will know (as is material here) to which countries he exported, and, therefore, what quota he is likely to get, if any, for the particular country where the commodity, the jute, is to be delivered. The seller will further know, and he *prima facie* alone will know, what other contracts he has entered into or intends to enter into. These would, of course, affect the sufficiency or otherwise of his quota. Further, it must be presumed that he knows the market in which he deals, and knows the prospects, if necessary, of buying quota to supplement any deficiencies in his own, or, perhaps, of exchanging quota available for one country for quota available for another, and thus enabling himself to carry out his contract. In these circumstances, as it seems to me, *prima facie* the sufficiency of the seller's quota to meet any contract he enters into is a matter for him to see to, and any difficulties he may encounter as regards the sufficiency of his quota seem to me *prima facie* to be a business risk which he must accept in the absence of some provision to the contrary in the contract. Otherwise, it seems to me that these transactions would be unworkable.

One thing, I think, is clear about implied terms. I do not think that the court will read a term into a contract unless, considering the matter from the point of view of business efficacy, it is clear beyond a peradventure that both parties intended a given term to operate, although they did not include it in so many words. In the *Anglo-Russian Merchant Traders* case it was relatively easy to formulate the implied term. Here it seems to me that it is absolutely impossible to do so. An unqualified provision to the effect that the contract was subject to the quota being sufficient and to the seller using his best endeavours to obtain a sufficient quota, would, as it seems to me, be quite inadequate, for the reason my Lord has pointed out, that the sufficiency of quota depends not only on the amount of quota the seller is able to get but on the quantity of jute he is committed to deliver under the totality of contracts that he has entered into. The term would, therefore, have to include a provision dealing in some way or other with the situation in which the seller had, in fact, had sufficient quota to meet the particular contract, but not enough to meet that contract and all his other contracts. How the seller and the buyer are to be assumed to have wished to deal with that kind of situation, it is really quite impossible to say. For these reasons, in addition to those given by my Lords, I agree that this is not a case in which it is right, or, indeed, possible, to read into the contracts an implied term of the kind contended for by the sellers. The appeal, accordingly, fails, and should be dismissed.

[TUCKER LJ and SINGLETON LJ delivered judgments to the same effect.]

CHAPTER FIVE
SUPERVENING EVENTS IN THE LIFE OF CONTRACT

Between the moment the contract is made and its performance, events may occur which impede this performance.

This period between the making and the performance of the contract may be long or short. There are contracts—contracts for a number of performances or by instalments, or contracts for an indefinite period—which envisage lasting for some time—for example, a lease—but it can also happen that the performance of a contract which is due to be carried out quickly may be impeded by some unforeseen event: for example, when a picture has been sold its export might be forbidden.

The circumstances existing at the moment the contract was made will be radically changed if its performance is prevented, or at least rendered much more difficult, by, for example, a strike, an economic crisis, an embargo or a monetary devaluation. In a society such as ours, such situations are frequent.

It should be noted that we are dealing here only with non-performance which is not the responsibility of the debtor. If the non-performance is the responsibility of the debtor, the creditor can put in motion the different mechanisms which allow him to obtain performance *en nature*, if that is still possible, or a substitute for performance. We should note moreover the variations between the various national laws on the question of when a non-performance is the responsibility of the debtor.

The parties may also have foreseen the occurrence of these events and have in consequence introduced in their contracts adequate provisions, for example a rent indexation clause designed to overcome the consequences of monetary inflation.

If not, performance will be blocked by a cause which is outside the control of the parties: this is the hypothesis of *force majeure*.

There may also be the intermediate situation: unforeseen events do not make the performance impossible, but only much more burdensome than was envisaged at the time that the contract was made. The debtor may still perform but he is likely to ruin himself in doing so. The dividing line between the two situations is fluid and one may consider this situation more or less rigorously as being within the notion of impossibility (*force majeure*), notably from the economic point of view.

From the legal point of view, the question is who has to bear the risk of these changes in the initial situation. Also, in a synallagmitic contract, one must consider the repercussions on the counter-performance. The question becomes even more complicated when we are dealing with a contract which involves the transfer of property, where one talks also of the risk of the property perishing. The transfer of risk is further connected to the transfer of ownership (*res perit domino*) or sometimes to the delivery of the thing. For contracts in general, there is on one side the danger of laxity. It is important not to allow the debtor to escape his obligations too easily. That would be dangerous for the security of contract. But, on the other hand, there are considerations of equity. It would be unjust to overwhelm the debtor by making him bear all the consequences of unforeseen events.

We will consider in turn the consequences of impossibility of performance due to *force majeure*, revision of the contract in cases where performance has become much more onerous (*imprévision*) and lastly the clauses by which the parties seek to deal with the consequences of unforeseen events.

5.1. IMPOSSIBILITY OF PERFORMANCE

Principles of European Contract Law   **5.PECL.1.**

Article 8:108: *Excuse Due to an Impediment*

(1) A party's non-performance is excused if it proves that it is due to an impediment beyond its control and that it could not reasonably have been expected to take the impediment into account at the time of the conclusion of the contract, or to have avoided or overcome the impediment or its consequences.

(2) Where the impediment is only temporary the excuse provided by this Article has effect for the period during which the impediment exists. However, if the delay amounts to a fundamental non-performance, the creditor may treat it as such.

(3) The non-performing party must ensure that notice of the impediment and of its effect on its ability to perform is received by the other party within a reasonable time after the non-performing party knew or ought to have known of these circumstances. The other party is entitled to damages for any loss resulting from the non-receipt of such notice.

An event after the conclusion of the contract may make its performance impossible. How should this impossibility be defined? And what are the consequences both on the obligation performance of which has become impossible and, when one is dealing with a synallagmatic contract, on the counter-performance due from the other party?[1]

The answer varies in fairly clear ways according to the system considered: the French (*infra* **5.1.1.**), the German (*infra* **5.1.2.**) and the English (*infra* **5.1.3.**). We will then consider various texts from uniform laws (*infra* **5.1.4.**).

5.1.1. THE FRENCH SYSTEM

The position of French law on this question produces a clear division: it is all or nothing. Either there is total impossibility and the debtor is freed; or else he must perform the contract however onerous its performance has become. The civil jurisprudence—in contrast to the administrative jurisprudence—rejects the theory of *imprévision*. It refuses to give the judge the power to revise the contract even it has become ruinous for one of the parties.[2]

---

[1] On a question of terminology, the determination of who bears the risk of the loss or deterioration of a particular piece of property—particular because generic goods do not perish: *genera non pereunt*—brings in what one calls in French the theory of risks (in the plural) The word risk has a different and wider sense in English. It is useful to distinguish the two to avoid difficult confusions.

[2] See *infra*, at 627 ff.

The texts on the matter use different words to designate this impossibility: "*cause étrangère* which cannot be imputed to the debtor" (Article 1147 C.civ.), *force majeure* or *cas fortuit* (Article 1148 C.civ.) and *cas fortuit* (Article 1722 C.civ.). Nowadays doctrine agrees in considering that these terms mean the same thing. We will use the term *force majeure* since this is the most widely used and also the best known outside France.

Building on traditional law, the courts have constructed a theory of *force majeure* around two short Articles in the section of the C.civ. entitled "Damages Resulting from Non-Performance of an Obligation".[3] Several texts concern special contracts, the most important being Article 1722 C.civ. on leases.

Code civil **5.F.2.**

Article 1147: The debtor is liable, where appropriate, to pay damages, either because he has not performed an obligation or because he was late in performing, in all cases in which cannot prove that the non-performance resulted from a *cause étrangère* for which he was not responsible and also that there was no bad faith on his part.

Article 1148: There will be no damages when as the result of *force majeure* or *cas fortuit* the debtor has been prevented from delivering or doing that which he was obliged to deliver or do or has done that which was forbidden.

Article 1722: If, during the duration of the lease the thing leased is destroyed in its totality by *cas fortuit*, the lease is automatically rescinded. If it is only destroyed in part, the lessee can, according to the circumstances, demand either a diminution of the price or the rescission of the lease. In neither case will there be any liability for damages.

All these texts rest on a long tradition. They may be compared to those of the Italian Codice civile, whose Article 1218 is placed in Chapter 3, "Non-Performance of Obligations" and Article 1256 in Section 4 on "Supervening Impossibility not the Responsibility of the Debtor" of Chapter 4 "Discharge by Another Way than Performance".

Codice civile **5.I.3.**

Article 1218: *Responsibility of the debtor.* The debtor who does not exactly perform his obligation is bound to pay damages if he doesn't show that the non-performance or delay resulted from impossibility of performance caused by some event for which he was not responsible.

Article 1256: *Permanent impossibility and temporary impossibility.* The obligation is extinguished when performance becomes impossible for a reason which is not the responsibility of the debtor.
If the impossibility is only temporary, the debtor, as long as the impossibility lasts, is not responsible for delay in execution. In any event, the obligation will be extinguished if the impossibility lasts so long that, in the light of the nature of the obligation and of the object, the debtor cannot be considered as obliged to perform or when the creditor no longer has any interest in obtaining performance.

---

[3] C.civ. Section 4 of Chapter 3 on the "Effect of Obligations".

One may compare the two series of texts as to their meaning and their character in more or less detail. The comparison can be extended to the texts of the German BGB.[4]

The texts of the French Civil Code have had to be fleshed out by the case law, on the question of the definition of *force majeure* (*infra* **5.1.1.A.**) and its effects (*infra* **5.1.1.A.**) and this explains why certain solutions are not wholly clear.

5.1.1.A. THE DEFINITION OF *FORCE MAJEURE*

For an event to constitute *force majeure*, is traditionally necessary for it to be irresistible, unforeseeable and external to the debtor. The first two conditions allow a fairly large measure of appreciation to the judge. The courts sometimes speak of events which are normally irresistible, that is to say irresistible by the ordinary person exercising reasonable care.

The two conditions of *unforseeability* and *irresistibility* are connected and the following judgment of the first civil chamber of the Cour de cassation of 9 March 1994 gives interesting details on this subject.

Cass. civ. 1re, 9 March 1994[5]   **5.F.4.**

UNAVOIDABLE EVENT AND *FORCE MAJEURE*

The Saint-Tropez robbery

Impossibility of resisting the event in itself constitutes force majeure *where to foresee it does not enable its effects to be averted.*

Facts: At around 5 o'clock in the morning of 27 July 1985, four wrongdoers managed to gain access to the hotel "Résidence des Lices", Saint-Tropez, where they forced the staff under the threat of arms to open the safe, which they emptied. On 10 June 1986 Mr Montagnani, an Italian customer of the hotel, brought proceedings against the Hotel des Lices company ("the company") and the Concorde Group, its insurer, for recovery of the equivalent of LIT 32.850.000 and USD 1.030, which he said he had deposited in the hotel's safe.

Held: According to the findings of the lower court, the judgment appealed against (Aix-en-Provence, 9 April 1991), setting aside the lower court's decision, upheld that claim, taking the view that armed robbery of that kind did not constitute a case of *force majeure* for the purposes of Article 1954(1) of the Civil Code. The Cour de cassation approved.

Judgment: . . . *The first two branches of the sole appeal ground by the company and the first branch of the first ground of appeal of the Concorde Group, taken together*:—Whereas the company and its insurer criticise the judgment appealed against for finding there to have been no case of *force majeure* whereas, according to the appeal grounds, the cour d'appel which found that no resistance could have been offered to the armed robbery, ought to have considered whether that impossibility of resistance did not of itself constitute a case of *force majeure*; as by holding that the *hôtelier* ought to have carried out stricter controls of entries and exits and ought to have drawn up an inventory, in the presence of the parties concerned, of the items deposited, after finding there to have been violence and armed threats, the court of second instance, giving judgment on inoperative grounds, deprived its decision of any legal basis under Article 1954, al. 1, of the Civil Code; as unforeseeability is on the other hand a relative concept and not absolute in nature; as the judgment appealed

---

[4] See *infra*, at 502.
[5] Bull.civ. I.91; annotated by Viney JCP, 1994 I.3773; Jourdain, RTD civ. 1994.871.

against by considering that an armed robbery was not unforeseeable in a hotel in Saint-Tropez owing to its wealthy clientele, it did not attach sufficient weight to the normal unforeseeability of armed aggression carried out by ruse in the hotel, and again deprived its decision of any legal basis under the aforementioned provision;

—Whereas, however, although impossibility to resist the event constitutes in itself a case of *force majeure* where to foresee it does not enable its effects to be averted, the defendant must still have taken all the precautions necessary in order to avoid the occurrence of the event; as having found that the *hôtelier* or his agents and employees did not carry out a strict control of entries since the night watchman himself let in one of the wrongdoers who claimed to have an appointment with one of the hotel's customers, the cour d'appel was right in taking the view that the armed robbery in question did not constitute a case of *force majeure*, since not all the possible precautions necessitated by its foreseeability had been taken; . . .

Notes

(1) Article 1954, al. 1, cited by the Court provides: "Innkeepers or *hôteliers* shall not be liable in respect of thefts or injury occurring as a result of *force majeure* . . ."

(2) That judgment confirms and develops earlier case-law: impossibility of resisting the event in itself constitutes *force majeure* where to foresee it does not enable its effects to be averted. The rule is logical: if the event is unavoidable, even if it could be foreseen, it constitutes in itself a case of *force majeure*. In this case the court finds that armed robbery is impossible to resist. Certainly, it was foreseeable but the possible precautions "necessitated by its foreseeability" had not been taken. If those precautions had been taken, there would have been a case of *force majeure*, notwithstanding the foreseeability of the event.

(3) What is, then, the purpose of the unforeseeability test? Rather than a substantive criterion of *force majeure*, it is a condition of admissibility, a preliminary issue: could the event have been avoided by taking normal precautions? It would even be preferable to speak of inevitability rather than unforeseeability.[6]

Moreover, unforeseeability may be an indicator of the impossibility of averting the event: frequently, an event cannot be averted only because it was not foreseen. And it should be remembered that the latter factor is appraised only at the time when the contract was entered into.

It is also to be noted that the test applied by the Cour de cassation brings foreseeability into connection with the negligent conduct of the defendant, which was negligent by virtue of the fact that it did not take the precautions required by the damage foreseeably likely to occur.

(4) It is sometimes difficult to distinguish between *force majeure* and absence of fault. According to prevailing opinion, failure to fulfil obligations is not imputed to the defendant if it is not his fault, or if he is not liable under a law or legal act.[7]

b) The *event must be extraneous* to the defendant. This condition is more open to debate and is not always required by the case-law, for example, in the event of the defendant's illness. On the other hand, it is required when the event constitutes a failure on the part of persons for whom the defendant is liable or by materials used by him. A good example of this is strike action.

---

[6] See Jourdain, RTD civ. 1994.871.
[7] See also NBW Art. 6:75, *infra*, at 603 **5.NL.10**, where both fault and imputability are mentioned.

Cass. civ. 1re, 24 January 1995[8]   **5.F.5.**

STRIKE AND EXTRANEOUS CHARACTER OF THE EVENT

The EDF strike

A strike is an internal event except when it affects the public as a whole.

Facts: On 18 November 1992 the company, Héliogravure Jean Didier entered into a contract with the French public utility, Electricité de France ("EDF") for the supply of high-tension electric current. Complaining of interruptions in the supply in January 1987 and in 1988, it brought proceedings against EDF claiming payment of the sum of FR 784.230 by way of compensation for the loss caused by those interruptions. EDF countered that those interruptions were the result of a strike led by part of its staff, constituting a case of *force majeure*. EDF counterclaimed for payment of the sum of FR 567.084,49 being the amount of its invoice for the month of January 1987.

Held: The judgment appealed against (Cour d'appel de Douai 14 May 1992) dismissed the claim for compensation for the interruptions in the supply in January 1987, holding that the conflict situation had given rise, as far as EDF was concerned, to a situation of constraint constituting a case of *force majeure*. As regards the interruptions in the supply in 1988, the Cour d'appel considered that EDF had not adduced proof that these were interruptions within the meaning of Article XII(5) of the contract capable of being treated as cases of *force majeure*. It therefore calculated compensation in accordance with Article XII(3) which limited the amount of compensation to the user, save in the event of a finding of a serious fault, thus rejecting the arguments of Héliogravure Jean Didier that that clause should be deemed to be non-existent in pursuance of Article 35 of Act 78–23 of 10 January 1978 and Article 2 of Order 78–464 of 24 March 1978. Finally, offsetting the compensation thus calculated with the sum of FR 70.891,72, the amount due from Héliogravure Jean Didier, which the latter did not contest, it ordered Héliogravure Jean Didier to pay the amount of FR 496.192,77, together with interest as from 7 June 1990. The Cour de cassation upheld the decision.

Judgment: *On the three branches of the first appeal ground*:—Whereas Héliogravure Jean Didier criticises the contested judgment for deciding so, on the one hand, and according to the terms of the appeal ground, the cour d'appel infringed Article 16 of the NCPC [*Nouveau code de procédure civile*] by taking cognisance, of its own motion, without first requesting the parties to submit their own observations, of the argument that the strike by EDF employees constituted an extraneous event, on the ground that "when they collectively cease to render their services in pursuance of the right to strike conferred on them by the constitution and by legislation, they are no longer under the authority of the employer who has no means of compelling them to perform on his behalf the tasks necessary to satisfy users' needs"; as the fact that agents or employees take strike action does not in itself constitute an event extraneous to the undertaking necessary for a finding of *force majeure* such as to exempt the undertaking from liability; as by so deciding, the cour d'appel therefore infringed Article 1147 of the Civil Code; as, moreover, a general large scale strike in a nationalised public service is far from constituting an unforeseeable event; as, therefore, by declaring *force majeure* to be inapplicable solely on account of the abovementioned characteristics of strike action without making any actual findings as to unforeseeability, the lower court reached its decision without any legal basis under the abovementioned provision;

—Whereas, however, EDF claimed in its pleadings served on 5 February 1992 that the strike had been called by the large trade unions in order to protest against the wages policy in the public and nationalised sector and that it was unable either to forbid its staff to take strike action or decide on requisition measures, or recruit sufficiently well qualified temporary staff; as irrespective of the taking cognisance of arguments of its own motion, the cour d'appel which examined the circumstances of the case thus described in order to determine whether they revealed the existence of *force*

---

[8] D. 1995.237 annotated by G. Paisant.

majeure, noted that that public utility was unable in January 1987 to provide a continuous supply of electric current, as it was contractually obliged to do, to Héliogravure Jean Didier owing to large-scale strike action affecting the whole of the public and nationalised sector, and thus extraneous to the undertakings, and that EDF could not have foreseen this action, or avert it by satisfying the claims of its employees, in view of government control on decisions concerning wages; nor from a technical point of view could it overcome the problems associated with such action; the appeal is therefore without any ground;

On the two branches of the second appeal ground:—Whereas Héliogravure Jean Didier criticises also on this ground the judgment for deciding the case as it did, on the one hand, according to the terms of the plea ground, by relying on the fact that that company had available to it staff competent in the legal sector, which had in no way been contended on behalf of EDF, the cour d'appel infringed Article 7 NCPC; whereas, on the other hand, a consumer is a person who enters into a contract outside his usual sphere of activities and specialities; as the contracts entered into with EDF are standard-form of contracts which cannot be negotiated owing to the monopoly exercised by that public utility, which places consumers, when they enter into contracts, in the position of a mere individual; as by considering that Héliogravure Jean Didier, a printing company, was a professional user of electricity not entitled to avail itself of the provisions of Act 78–23 of 10 January 1978, the cour d'appel infringed Article 35 of that Law and Article 2 of Order 78–464 of 24 March 1978.
—Whereas, however, the provisions of Article 35 of Act 78–23 of 10 January 1978—now Articles L 132–1 and L 133–1 of the *Code de la consommation*—and Article 2 of the Order of 24 March 1978 do not apply to agreements for the supply of goods and services directly related to the business carried on by the other contracting party; as on those alternative grounds, the decision is legally justified,

On those grounds, the appeal is dismissed.

Notes

(1) A strike by employees of an undertaking does not normally constitute a case of *force majeure* even if it is unforeseeable and impossible to avert because it is an internal event for which the head of the undertaking must be called to account. It is otherwise where the strike, as in this case, affects the whole of the public and nationalized sector. On that account it is extraneous to the undertaking. And it is certainly impossible to avert since wages in that sector are determined by the government and not by the undertaking.

It is to be noted that foreseeability—which cannot be denied in this case—is not even raised because EDF could do nothing to avoid the strike.

(2) Another point of interest in this judgment is that it gives a new definition to the term business (*professionnel*) within the meaning of Article L 132–1, in the version contained in Act 95–96 of 1 February 1995 enacted in pursuance of Directive 93/13/EEC of 5 April 1993 on Unfair Terms in Consumer Contracts.[9] This legislation amends the earlier system for reviewing unfair terms in "contracts entered into between businesses and individuals or consumers". In this case the EDF contract contained a clause concerning compensation in the event of power cuts during 1988—whereas that clause was not in existence for 1987 in respect of which the new definition of *force majeure* was given—and that clause could fall under the purview of the rules on unfair terms in contracts between a business and an individual or consumers. The legislation contains no definition of these

---

[9] On this Directive see *supra*, at 521, **3.EC.142.**

terms. As is borne out by this judgment, the courts are moving towards a wide definition. A person who enters into a contract directly related to his business activities is not a consumer.[10]

The extraneous factor is linked to the warranty against internal defects, even those which may be undetected and unforeseeable. A tragic illustration of this is afforded by the liability incurred as a result of contamination by the AIDS virus following a blood transfusion.

Cass. civ. 1re, 12 April 1995 (2nd judgment)[11]   **5.F.6.**

INTERNAL AND UNDETECTABLE DEFECT OF A PRODUCT

The infected blood transfusion

The internal defect of a product, even undetectable, does not constitute an external event.

Facts: Following a blood transfusion the plaintiff was contaminated by the AIDS virus. She brought proceedings against both the clinic where the transfusion was given and the departmental transfusion centre which supplied the blood to the clinic.

Held: The centre and the clinic were jointly and severally liable. The Cour de cassation partially quashed the decision of the cour d'appel.

Judgment: . . .—Whereas after giving birth by ceaserian section at the Essonne Clinic, Marie-Laure Dupuy on 16 May 1984 received a transfusion of 3 globular concentrates from the departmental blood transfusion centre in Essonne; as she underwent a test on 27 February 1986 which showed she had been contaminated by the HIV virus; as she brought an action for a declaration of liability and damages against the centre, its insurer, La Mutuelle d'Assurance du corps médical français, and against the Essonne Clinic; as the plaintiff died of AIDS on 8 April 1992 and the proceedings were continued by her heirs; as the judgment appealed against, which upheld the judgment of the lower court, declared the centre and the clinic jointly and severally liable for damages resulting from the contamination;

On the single appeal ground . . . raised by the centre and its insurer:—Whereas the judgment appealed against is criticised for upholding the claim against the centre. By finding the centre to be liable owing to the presence of an undetectable virus in the blood given to Marie-Laure Dupuy, the cour d'appel disregarded the fact that the virus is undetectable and outside the responsibility of the blood transfusion centre and would have therefore infringed Article 1147 of the Civil Code.
—Whereas, however, the cour d'appel correctly held that an internal defect in blood, even if its undetectable, does not constitute for the supplying entity a cause which is extraneous to it, and that the obligations on blood transfusion centres as to the storage of blood and the supply thereof, over which they have a monopoly, do not relieve them of the duty to afford restitution in respect of the injurious consequences attributable to the supply of infected blood. It follows that that plea cannot be upheld.

However, on the first branch of the single appeal ground . . . lodged by the Essonne Clinic:
—Under Article 1147 of the Civil Code;
—Whereas in holding the Clinic to be liable, the judgment appealed against merely states that, owing to the trust necessarily placed in it by the patient, the Clinic is under an obligation to supply

---

[10] On this issue see *supra*, at 215 ff.
[11] JCP 1995. II.22467 annotated by P. Jourdain.

blood products which are not infected and, by supplying blood contaminated by the HIV virus, it incurred liability;

—Whereas by so holding, without examining whether the Clinic, which was simply under an obligation to show prudence and diligence in the administering of blood products supplied by a transfusion centre, was in a position to check the quality of the blood administered to Marie-Laure Dupuy, the decision of the cour d'appel had no legal basis in the abovementioned provision of the Civil Code;

On those grounds, and without there being any need to give a decision on the second and third branches of the appeal ground;

Dismisses appeal . . . lodged by the Essonne Departmental Blood Transfusion Centre;

Quashes the judgment given on 28 November 1991 between the parties by the Paris cour d'appel, but only in so far at it declares the Essonne Clinic liable for the damage suffered by Mr and Mrs Dupuy as a result of the blood transfusion received by Mrs Dupuy on 16 May 1984 . . .

Note

This decision deals with the liability of the blood transfusion centre and the clinic, and in a different manner as regards each of them. The victim's action against the blood transfusion centre is contractual in nature even if there is no direct relationship between the victim and the centre. That represents the application of settled case-law on the direct contractual action in the case of a series of contracts: the right of action on a warranty against latent defects is assigned together with the subject-matter of the contract.[12]

It may be noted that the courts had previously analysed the matter differently as a third party clause in favour of the recipient of the transfusion.[13] However the case may be, the transfusion centre is bound by an obligation as to the safety of the outcome of which it may be relieved only by an extraneous cause. But the "internal defect" of the blood, even if undetectable, does not constitute as regards the supplying entity a cause extraneous to it. That is the classic solution applicable to the warranty obligation for latent defects incumbent on the vendor who is irrebuttably presumed to know the defect of the thing he supplies and is applied by analogy to supplies of blood. One may also consider that to be a consequence of the condition that *force majeure* must be an external factor; yet an inherent defect is not an extraneous occurrence. On the other hand, the Cour de cassation considers that the clinic is bound by a simple duty of prudence and diligence—obligation as to means (*obligation "de moyens"*)—and that the Cour d'appel ought to have examined whether the clinic was in a position to check the quality of the blood, which seems rather unlikely.

It may be wondered how liability could be justified in such circumstances under Directive 85/374/EEC of 25 July 1985 on Product Liability[14]—now implemented in France by Act 98–389 of 19 May 1998.[15]

The expediency of introducing a special compensation scheme should also be studied.[16] A comparative study of the manner in which this sensitive problem is dealt with could be very illuminating.

[12] See Cass. civ. 1re, 9 October 1979, Bull.civ. I.241.

[13] Cass. civ. 1re, 17 December 1954, JCP 1955.II.8490 annotated by Savatier; D. 1995.269 annotated by Rodiere; see also on this judgment, *infra*, Chapter 7, at 891.

[14] [1985] OJ L 210/29, see van Gerven *et al.* (eds.), *Ius Commune Casebooks for the Common Law of Europe—Torts* (Oxford: Hart Publishing, 2000), **6.EC.33.**

[15] Now C.civ., Art. 1386–1 ff: see van Gerven *et al.* (eds.), *Ius Commune Casebooks for the Common Law of Europe—Torts* (Oxford: Hart Publishing, 2000), **6.F.37.**

[16] See Jourdain JCP 1995. II.22467.

5.1.1.B. EFFECTS OF *FORCE MAJEURE*

The debtor does not have to perform the obligation—obviously in the case of performance in kind, since it is by definition impossible—but also in the case of equivalent performance: he is not obliged to pay damages and interest.[17]

In the event of partial non-performance the debtor is relieved of his obligation only to the extent of the impossibility of performance, provided that performance of the remainder of the contract is still of sufficient interest to the creditor.[18] When impossibility of performance is momentary, the contract is merely suspended; it resumes effect on the disappearance of the obstacle provided that performance retains utility.[19]

In the case of a synallagmatic contract, the contract as a whole falls away and the other party is thus released from it—subject to the possibility of partially maintaining the contract in the event of partial non-performance—owing to the interdependence of obligations.

The detailed rules governing such disappearance of the contract are however uncertain.

For the most part the courts accept that disappearance occurs automatically by operation of law: release of the debtor automatically entails cancellation of the contract—wholly or in part. That is affirmed in particular by the judgment of 28 April 1982[20] in light of Article 1147 C.civ.: "An application for the judicial termination of the contract is not necessary in the case of impossibility of performance". That solution is also expressly provided for in Article 1722 C.civ. in regard to leases.[21]

However, other judgments—particularly from the First Civil Chamber of the Cour de cassation—rely on Article 1184 C.civ. which unambiguously lays down the need for an application for termination by the parties suffering from the non-performance, but gives no further particulars. There is to be found in a judgment of 2 June 1982[22] an unequivocal statement of principle: "It follows from that provision (Article 1184 C.civ.) that the termination of a synallagmatic contract may be declared in the event of non-performance of its obligations by one of the parties, even where such non-performance is not occasioned by fault, and whatever may be the ground which prevented that party from fulfilling its obligations, even where the party was so prevented by the act of a third party or by *force majeure*".

Similar uncertainty prevails in international instruments. Under Article 79(5) of the Convention on the International Sale of Goods (CISG), the disappointed creditor retains the right to exercise all his rights other than that of obtaining damages and interest; this is construed as enabling him to terminate the contract for non-performance. Under Article 26 CISG a declaration of termination of the contract is effective only if made by notification to the other party, the CISG having dispensed with judicial dissolution required under French law, at least in the case of unspecified non-performance. There is therefore no termination—even if performance of the contract is manifestly impossible—in the absence of such notification.[23]

---

[17] See Art. 1148 C.civ., *supra*, at 593, **5.F.2**
[18] The theory of partial nullity applied here: Tené, Simler, Leguette no. 395.
[19] See Cass. civ., 19 June 1923, DP 1920.I.94.
[20] Cass. comm., Bull.civ. 1982.IV.145.
[21] Which deals with the destruction of the property through *force majeure*.
[22] Cass. civ. 1re, Bull.civ. 1982.I.205.
[23] See also Art. 6.267 BW which also allows judicial termination.

More reasonably, the Principles of European Contract Law remove the need for notification and return to termination by operation of law in the event of total and permanent prevention of performance.[24]

It is instructive to compare the respective advantages of automatic termination, judicial termination and termination by unilateral declaration. It may also be wondered whether in practice the difference is important.

Finally, it is appropriate to set out the consequences of the occurrence of *force majeure* in the case of a contract transferring title to property. In French law this is termed the theory of risks. The onus of risks is linked to the transfer of property: *res perit domino*. Such transfer—at least for specific items—normally takes place solely by operation of the contract.[25] It follows that an alteration of the time of transfer of the property entails an alteration in the transfer of risk.

Cass. comm., 20 November 1979[26]   **5.F.7.**

RES PERIT DOMINO

The nickel-plating installation

It is for the owner of the goods to bear the risk of their destruction by force majeure.

Facts: A machine sold subject to reservation of title was destroyed by fire before it was fully paid for. The seller sued to recover the price.

Held: The Cour d'appel considered that the risk had been transferred to the buyer and thus set aside the judgment. This judgment was in turn set aside.

Judgment: *The first branch of the second appeal ground*:—Under Article 1134 of the Civil Code;
—Whereas the cour d'appel held that the risk arising from loss of the nickel-plating installation sold and delivered by the company Neochrome to Mecarex, but not fully paid for, which was caused by a fire in the workshops of Mecarex, was to be borne by the buyer on the ground that a clause in Neochrome's general conditions of sale provided that: "all equipment shall remain our property until payment in full by the purchaser; that clause being not a condition subsequent but a condition of termination";
—Whereas in so holding, the cour d'appel distorted the meaning of that clause which provided in a clear and precise manner that a transfer of title in the installation was to be suspended until full payment, thereby infringing the abovementioned provision;

On those grounds, and without there being any need to give a decision on the first appeal ground or on the second branch of the second appeal ground,

Sets aside in its entirety the judgment given on 14 October 1977 between the parties by the Colmar cour d'appel. . . .

Note

The Cour de cassation finds that the transfer of title was delayed until payment, the burden of risk remaining on the seller who retained title. For it to be otherwise it would have been necessary for there to have been a clause transferring risk to the buyer. Note also

---

[24] See Art. 9:303(4) PECL.
[25] See Art. 1138(2) C.civ.
[26] Bull.civ. IV.300; JCP 1981.II.19615 annotated by Ghestin.

application of the theory of distortion of the ordinary sense and meaning of clear and precise clauses in a contract, which enabled the Cour de cassation to intervene in spite of the sovereign power of the lower courts in matters touching the interpretation of contracts.

The Italian Codice civile is more explicit than the French Civil Code on the consequences of *force majeure*, and more specifically, in the case of contracts for the transfer of title as show Article 1463 ff. Codice civile.

Codice civile   **5.I.8.**

Article 1463: *Total impossibility*. In synallagmatic contracts, the party released by the occurrence of impossibility of performance may not require performance by the other party and must afford restitution of items already received, in accordance with the rules governing restitution [*ripetizione dell'indebito*].

Article 1464: *Partial impossibility*. Where performance by one party has become only impossible in part, the other party may reduce correspondingly performance of its obligation and may even withdraw from the contract if it does not have sufficient interest in its partial implementation.

Article 1465: *Contracts transferring or establishing title to property*. In contracts for the transfer of title to a specific thing, or establishing or transferring rights *in rem*, loss of the items for a reason not attributable to the vendor does not release the buyer from the obligation of performing his side of the bargain, although the thing contracted for has not been delivered to him.
The same shall apply where the effect of the transfer or creation of the right is postponed until after the expiry of a period of time certain.
If the thing to be transferred is a thing determined merely generically, the buyer is not released from the obligation to perform his side of the bargain, if the vendor has delivered the goods or they have been identified.
In any event the purchaser shall be released from his obligation, if the transfer is subject to a condition subsequent and impossibility of performance has occurred before that condition is met.

5.1.2. THE GERMAN SYSTEM

The concept of impossibility (*Unmöglichkeit*) plays an important role in German law but it presents specific features in the general theory of impossibility of performance. Various categories of impossibility may be distinguished (for example, initial, subsequent, objective, subjective, contemporary, definitive) and with regard to subsequent impossibility, impossibility attributable or not attributable to the debtor.

What is of interest to us here is subsequent impossibility not attributable to the debtor. We know that the BGB acknowledged only two causes of non-performance, namely impossibility of performance and delay.

As regards impossibility of performance, § 275 BGB provides for release of the debtor where he is not responsible for the supervening circumstances. In the case of a synallagmatic contract, § 323 governs the consequences of impossibility with regard to the other contracting party:

BGB[27]   **5.G.9.**

§ 275: The debtor is relieved from his obligation to perform if the performance becomes impossi-
       ble because of a circumstance for which he is not responsible and which occurred after the
       creation of the obligation.
       If the debtor after the creation of the obligation, becomes unable to perform, it is equivalent
       to a circumstance rendering the performance impossible.

§ 323: If the performance due from one party under a two-sided contract becomes impossible
       because of a circumstance for neither he nor the other party is responsible, he loses the claim
       to counterperformance; in case of partial impossibility the counter-performance is dimin-
       ished in conformity with §§ 472 and 473.

It is instructive to compare the wording of *Burgerlijk Wetboek* Article 6:74 and 6:75
which is quite similar.

BW   **5.NL.10.**

Article 6:74: (1) Every failure in the performance of an obligation obliges the debtor to repair the
            damage which the creditor suffers therefrom, unless the failure cannot be imputed to
            the debtor.
            (2) To the extent that performance is not already impossible, paragraph (1) only
            applies subject to the provisions of paragraph (2)[28] respecting the fault of the debtor.

Article 6:75: A failure in the performance cannot be imputed to the debtor if it does not result from
            his fault, and if he cannot be held accountable for it by law, juridical act or common
            opinion either.

5.1.2.A. THE CONCEPT OF IMPOSSIBILITY FOR WHICH THE DEBTOR IS RESPONSIBLE

The German notion is both broader and more flexible than French *force majeure*—
acknowledging for example economic impossibility.[29] It is to be noted also that § 275
BGB does not require the event to be unforseeable.

RG, 3 February 1914[30]   **5.G.11.**

EXCEPTIONAL CIRCUMSTANCES, GOOD FAITH AND PERFORMANCE

The bad harvest

*One cannot be required to do more than one can reasonably perform considering good faith require-
ments and exceptional circumstances.*

Facts: In June 1909 the defendant sold to the plaintiff 20.000 kg of sugar beet seed in respect of each of the
years 1910, 1911 and 1912 at the price of 26 Reichsmarks per 50 kg, to be delivered in February in each year. In

---

[27] The English translation of the BGB is that given by von Mehren and Gordley, *The Civil Law System*, 2nd
edn. (Boston, Mass.: Little Brown, 1977).
[28] The second para. of Section 9, Articles 6:81–6:87 deals with the debtor's default.
[29] See Zweigert and Kötz at 516 ff.
[30] RGZ 84.125.

February 1912 only 920 kg were delivered because in 1911, owing to the drought, only 933,35 quintals were harvested, instead of the 4,908 expected. Since the defendant was also committed to other purchasers he allocated the supplies of seeds on a pro rata basis to each of the customers ordering. The plaintiff disputed the allocation thus carried out (namely 46% of the contractually agreed quantity) and brought an action for performance of the contract and seeking judgment to be entered against the defendant for damages and interest.

Held: The Handelsgericht dismissed the plaintiff's action. The Oberlandesgericht set aside the judgment and upheld the claim. The defendant appealed to the Reichsgericht (RG) which quashed the appeal judgment.

Judgment: The RG approves the finding of the lower courts that the sugar beet seeds were generic. Consequently § 279 BGB was to be applied.

It is important to note that the order was for quality seed from the defendant's own cultivation. Consequently, the lower courts misdirected themselves as to the action and the rights of the parties, when they considered that the defendant was entitled in the event of need to supply substitute seed of the same quality as that provided for in the contract. Pursuant to the agreement entered into, the plaintiff was entitled to call for seed from the defendant's own personal cultivation. Inability to perform the contract releases the defendant only where, on the one hand, performance has become totally impossible and, on the other hand, on condition as a *sine qua non* that no fault could be attributed to the defendant under § 279 BGB.

The defendant is entitled to claim that in their appraisal of impossibility the Oberlandesgericht judges infringed the provisions of § 242.

It is common ground that the Summer of 1911 was marked by a drought of such extraordinary severity that harvests were very bad. Consequently, in light of the requirements of good faith laid down in § 242 and the exceptional circumstances supervening in 1911, the defendant cannot be required to do more than he can reasonably perform. Thus he was entitled to treat his customers on an equal footing and to sell his seeds on a pro rata basis in accordance with quantities ordered by each of them.

It should be declared that the plaintiff's action is ill-founded and that the appeal in revision by the defendant should be granted.

Note

It is to be noted first of all that since the case involved a limited generic quantity—the seeds produced by the seller—there could be no question of substitute purchasing in order to satisfy the order. The seller is released, according to the court, when performance is—reasonably—impossible and there is no fault. It therefore seems that, unlike French law, the concept of *force majeure* in German law is mingled with that of absence of fault. Reference is also made to good faith (§ 242) which further reinforces the subjective nature of impossibility.

5.1.2.B. THE EFFECTS OF IMPOSSIBILITY

The debtor is released and his side of the bargain can no longer be enforced or must be returned, as is illustrated by the two following decisions. Where impossibility is only temporary, the contract is suspended.

AG Mannheim, 20 October 1990[31]   **5.G.12–13.**
and
OLG Düsseldorf, 30 December 1964[32]

DISCHARGE BY IMPOSSIBILITY

In case of impossibility, the debtor is released of his obligations.

a) AG Mannheim, 20 October 1990   **5.G.12.**

The death of the conductor

Facts: A person bought three seats for a concert to be given by the Budapest Symphony Orchestra on 8 January 1990. The orchestra was to have been conducted by György Lehel. The name of the conductor was mentioned on the tickets. Owing to the conductor's death the orchestra was conducted by another person. The plaintiff and his friends did not go to the concert owing to the death of the conductor. The plaintiff brought an action for recovery of the price of the tickets. He stated that on the evening of the concert, after learning of the change of the programme, he wished to have the tickets taken back but this was refused him.

It was contended on behalf of the defendant that the plaintiff ought to have known that Lehel had died, since his death had occurred in September 1989. Moreover, the name of the new conductor had been widely publicized. Consequently, reimbursement of the price of the ticket ought to have been requested well before the date of the concert.

Held: The Mannheim Amtsgericht granted the claim for recovery of the price of the tickets.

Judgment: . . .The plaintiff substantiates his claim to recovery of the admission price of 3 tickets for the concert to be given on 8 January 1990. By acquiring admission tickets on which the name of Lehel was printed, the plaintiff entered into a contract with the defendant for the provision of works whose content was stipulated by what was printed on the tickets. If, at the time the tickets were bought, it was already known it was to be another conductor who would conduct the concert, the tickets ought to have given the name of the new conductor, and that name should have been superimposed. In the present case the bargain was not carried out, since the plaintiff and his friends did not go to the concert, the defendant not providing the services which he was bound to provide under the contract. Owing to the change in the conductor, the service offered no longer corresponds to the service agreed. More accurately it is a case of impossibility. Inasmuch as it is an impossibility for which neither of the parties is liable, § 323 BGB is applicable. Accordingly, the defendant is released from his obligation to perform his side of the bargain but has lost his right to call for performance by the other party guaranteed under § 323 (III) and by the provisions on unjust enrichment. Thus, the plaintiff may obtain recovery of the price of the tickets. . . .

b) OLG Düsseldorf, 30 December 1964   **5.G.13.**

The illuminated sign

Facts: A trader desired to advertise the name of her undertaking by means of an illuminated sign. In October 1961 she contacted a company specializing in such signs. After several proposals she ordered a sign which was to be mounted on the roof of her factory. During negotiations both parties agreed that such an installation in a protected area needed an administrative authorization which would not be easy to obtain. On 31 October 1961 the company confirmed the order at the price of DM 5.415,50. At the end of the letter of confirmation, under

[31] NJW 1991.1490.
[32] NJW 1965.761.

the signature, reference was made to the General Conditions of Sale and Delivery which contained a clause providing that the validity of the sales contract was not subject to the obtaining of any administrative authorization. On the same day, the selling company sought in its name and on behalf of the trader the administrative authorization required in order to install the sign. On 23 November 1961 the customer made an initial payment of DM 1.733. On 28 November 1961 the administrative authority refused the request for authorization. The trader brought an action in order to obtain reimbursement of the amount of DM 1.733.

Held: At first instance and on appeal the trader was successful. The Bundesgerichtshof dismissed the further appeal.

Judgment: . . . *Two grounds are raised in favour of the appeal in revision.*

The appellant considers that, inasmuch as the parties had thought that the authorisation would be granted, the contract was subject to a condition subsequent; thus §§ 323(I) and (IV) on impossibility and § 812 BGB on unjust enrichment were not applicable.

Moreover, the general conditions of sale provided that the contract was not subject to any administrative authorisation.

1.—*On impossibility*

The question arose as to whether the parties intended to make the contract subject to the condition subsequent of issue of the administrative authorisation.

According to the BGH, if the parties, on entering into the contract, seriously envisaged the possibility of not obtaining authorisation, then at that time the will to make the contract subject to a condition subsequent was not present. Thus the claim for recovery by the trader is admissible under §§ 323 (I) and (III) and 812 BGB. The provisions on impossibility must be applied.

Performance by the selling company (namely manufacture and sale of the sign) became legally impossible as a result of the refusal of the request for authorisation which represents a permanent obstacle to the installation of the sign.

The impossibility of performance is not attributable to either of the two parties. The mere fact that the selling company sought authorisation on behalf of the trader does not mean that on that account the risk was transferred. The company cannot be held responsible for the refusal of the request since it was instructed merely to seek authorisation. Nor is the impossibility to be borne by the trader on account of her refusal to change the sign and order another sign. Consequently, a case of impossibility is established.

2.—*Inclusion of general conditions in the contract*

The clause providing for the general conditions may not allow the burden of risk to be imposed on the appellant since in the present case the general conditions do not form part of the contract.

In fact, reference to the general conditions at the foot of the confirmation letter (under the signature) does not form part even of the confirmation letter but constitutes a mere reference to the general conditions appended. Mere reference is not sufficient according to principles established by the courts.

It is not sufficiently certain that the trader in fact had the intention to accept the general conditions which had the effect of providing for a transfer of risk. Thus the general conditions did not become an integral part of the contract since there were not two declarations of intent on that score. The requirements of trade are that there should be two express and unequivocal such declarations. The penalty for non-observance of this principle must be borne by the party seeking to rely on those general conditions. The contents of the letter of confirmation were so far removed from what the parties had succeeded in agreeing beforehand, that the selling company could not reasonably expect the trader's agreement.

The principle that silence maintained after receipt of a letter of confirmation is to be construed as acquiescence must be derogated from in such a situation since that principle developed by the courts is based on fair dealing. For that reason an exception must be allowed to it when a trader acts unfairly.

Thus, the impossibility of performance is not to be borne by either of the parties. Consequently, the selling company is released from its obligations and loses its right to its side of the bargain. Furthermore, since the trader has made a payment of DM 1.733, she is entitled to claim reimbursement under §§ 325 (I) and (II) and 812 BGB.

Note

These two decisions illustrate the application of § 323 BGB and the interdependence of obligations under a synallagmatic contract. Performance by one of the parties has become impossible: death of the conductor in one case—on the basis that, as found by the court, the personal identity of the conductor was an essential element of the contract[33]—, refusal of authorization in the other. In both cases valuable consideration was paid—the price of the ticket, a payment on account. Recovery lies under § 323 which governs the rules on unjust enrichment.[34]

German law acknowledges that there may be impossibility of performance although the event is not actually unforeseeable, and seems thus to follow current French law.[35] Also worthy of note in the second judgment is the discussion concerning the application of the clause in the general conditions of sale imposing on the customer the risk with regard to performance by it under the contract. According to the court, that clause was not incorporated into the contract because it was not in conformity with the very strict rules applied by the courts.[36] Nor were the rules—under German law—on the effects of a letter of confirmation observed. By way of conclusion, it may be observed that there is less reason to rely in German law on subsequent impossibility not attributable to the debtor, owing to wide acceptance of revision in the case of unforeseen circumstances, which frequently allows a contract to be saved.

5.1.3. THE ENGLISH SYSTEM

English law is situated between the French and German system. Impossibility of performance is perceived less narrowly than under French law, since it includes the notion of that which renders the contract "something radically different from that which was in the contemplation of the parties", which goes further than *force majeure*. But, unlike German law, English law declines to allow the courts to adapt contracts in the event of frustration.

The system has been built up in successive layers and does not necessarily form a coherent whole. Moreover, the terminology is fluid. One may speak of frustration of the purpose, of impossibility, of act of God, or of discharge by supervening illegality.[37]

---

[33] French law would doubtless here have applied a causal analysis: was the personal identity of the conductor a decisive reason for the contract?

[34] Here again French law would have applied the notion of *cause*: the price of the ticket, the making of a payment on account lost their purpose (*cause*).

[35] See *supra*, at 595.

[36] See § 2 of *Gesetz zur Regelung des Rechts der Allgemeinen Geschäftsbedingungen* (AGBG) on the inclusion of general conditions, discussed in Chapter 3, section 4, *supra*, 513 ff., **3.G.138.**

[37] See Treitel, *Contracts* at 805 ff.

5.1.3.A. THE CASES

The starting point is rigorous for the debtor. A person who has undertaken obligations must perform them whatever happens.

King's Bench   **5.E.14.**
Paradine v. *Jane*[38]

THE ABSOLUTE CONTRACT DOCTRINE

Prince Rupert's army

The undertaking by the contractual debtor is total and an inevitable accident cannot release him because he could have guarded against it in the contract.

Facts: A farmer was sued for the payment of arrears of rent. In his defence he stated that he had been ejected from his land for four years by Prince Rupert's army.

Held: He was ordered to pay.

Judgment: . . . It was resolved that the matter of the plea was insufficient, for although the whole army had been alien enemies, yet the defendant ought to pay his rent. And this difference was taken, that where the law creates a duty or charge, and the party is disabled to perform it without any default in him, and hath no remedy over, there the law will excuse him. As in the case of waste, if a house be destroyed by tempest or by enemies, the lessee is excused. . . But when the party by his own contract creates a duty or charge upon himself he is bound to make it good, if he may, notwithstanding any accident by inevitable necessity because he might have provided against it by his contract. And therefore, if the lessee covenants to repair a house, although it is burnt by lightning or thrown down by enemies, yet he ought to repair it: Anon YB 40 Edw 3, fo 6. The rent is a duty created by the parties upon the reservation, and had there been a covenant to pay it there would have been no question but the lessee must have made it good, notwithstanding the interruption by enemies, for the law would not protect him beyong his own agreement, no more than in the case of reparations. This reservation, then, being a covenant in law and whereupon an action of covenant has been maintained (as Rolle J has said) it is all one as if there had been an actual covenant. Another reason was added, that as the lessee is to have the advantage of casual profits, so he must run the hazard of casual losses and not lay the whole burden of them upon his lessor. *Richard le Taverner's Case* was cited for this purpose, that thought the land be surrounded or gained by the sea or made barren by wildfire, yet the lessor shall have his whole rent. And judgment was given for the plaintiff.

Note

This decision illustrates the doctrine of "*absolute contract*" which continued to apply until the judgment in *Taylor* v. *Caldwell* of 1863.[39] The undertaking by the contractual debtor is total and an "accident by inevitable necessity" cannot release him because he could have guarded against it in the contract. The judgment in *Taylor* v. *Caldwell* mitigated the rigour of that rule.

---

[38] (1647) Aleyn 26.
[39] See *infra*, at 609 **5.E.15.**

608

Queen's Bench 5.E.15.
Taylor v. Caldwell[40]

DISAPPEARANCE OF THE PERSON OR THE THING

The burnt music hall

Impossibility of performance resulting from the disappearance of the person or the thing releases the debtor in certain circumstances.

Facts: A hall was hired for a series of four concerts. Before the date set for the first concert, the hall was completely destroyed by a fire for which neither of the parties was responsible. The hirer sued for damages to cover the cost of wasted advertising.

Held: The contract had been discharged so that the defendant was not liable.

Judgment: BLACKBURN J.: In this case the plaintiffs and defendants had, on the 27 May, 1862, entered into a contract by which the defendants agreed to let the plaintiffs have the use of the Surrey Gardens and Music Hall on four days then to come, viz, the 17 June, 15 July, 5 August and 19 August, for the purpose of giving a series of four grand concerts, and day and night fêtes at the Gardens and Hall on those days respectively; and the plaintiffs agreed to take the Gardens and Hail on those days, and pay £700 for each day.

The parties inaccurately call this a "letting", and the money to be paid a "rent"; but the whole agreement is such as to shew that the defendants were to retain the possession of the Hall and Gardens so that there was to be no demise of them, and that the contract was merely to give the plaintiffs the use of them on those days. Nothing however, in our opinion, depends on this. The agreement then proceeds to set out various stipulations between the parties as to what each was to supply for these concerts and entertainment, and as to the manner in which they should be carried on. The effect of the whole is to shew that the existence of the Music Hall in the Surrey Gardens in a state fit for a concert was essential for the fulfilment of the contract,—such entertainment as the parties contemplated in their agreement could not be given without it.

After the making of the agreement, and before the first day on which a concert was to he given, the Hall was destroyed by fire. This destruction, we must take it on the evidence, was without the fault of either party, and was so complete that in consequence the concerts could not be given as intended. And the question we have to decide is whether, under these circumstances, the loss which the plaintiffs have sustained is to fall upon the defendants. The parties when framing their agreement evidently had not present to their minds the possibility of such a disaster and have made no express stipulation with reference to it, so that the answer to the question must depend upon the general rules of law applicable to such a contract.

There seems no doubt that where there is a positive contract to do a thing not, not in itself unlawful, the contractor must perform it or pay damages for not doing it, although in consequence of unforeseen accidents, the performance of his contract has become unexpectedly burdensome or even impossible. The law is so laid down in 1 Roll Abr 450, Condition (G), and in the note to *Walton* v. *Waterhouse*, and is recognised as the general rule by all the Judges in the much discussed case of *Hall* v. *Wright*. But this rule is only applicable when the contract is positive and absolute, and not subject to any condition either express or implied: and there are authorities which, as we think, establish the principle that where, from the nature of the contract, it appears that the parties must from the beginning have known that it could not be fulfilled unless when the time for the fulfilment of the contract arrived some particular specified thing continued to exist, so that, when entering

[40] (1863) 3B & S 826.

into the contract, they must have contemplated such continuing existence as the foundation of what was to be done; there, in the absence of any express or implied warranty that the thing shall exist, the contract is not to be construed as a positive contract, but as subject to an implied condition that the parties shall be excused in case, before breach, performance becomes impossible from the perishing of the thing without default of the contractor.

There seems little doubt that this implication tends to further the great object of making the legal construction such as to fulfil the intention of those who entered into the contract. For in the course of affairs men in making such contracts in general would, if it were brought to their minds, say that there should be such a condition. . . . There is a class of contracts in which a person binds himself to do something which requires to be performed by him in person; and such promises, eg promises to marry, or promises to serve for a certain time, are never in practice qualified by an express exception of the death of the party; and therefore in such cases the contract is in terms broken if the promisor dies before fulfilment. Yet it was very early determined that, if the performance is personal, the executors are not liable; *Hyde* v. *The Dean of Windsor*. See 2 Wms Exors 1560 5th edn, where a very apt illustration is given. "Thus", says the learned author, "if an author undertakes to compose a work, and dies before completing it, his executors are discharged from this contract: for the undertaking is merely personal in its nature, and, by the intervention of the contractor's death, has become impossible to be performed." For this he cites a dictum of Lord Lyndhurst in *Marshall* v. *Broadhurst*, and a case mentioned by Patteson J in *Wentworth* v. *Cock*. In *Hall* v. *Wright*, Crompton J, in his judgment, puts another case. "Where a contract depends upon personal skill, and the act of God renders it impossible, as, for instance, in the case of a painter employed to paint a picture who is struck blind, it may be that the performances might be excused."

It seems that in those cases the only ground on which the parties or their executors, can be excused from the consequences of the breach of the contract is, that from the nature of the contract there is an implied condition of the continued existence of the life of the contractor, and, perhaps in the case of the painter of his eyesight. In the instances just given, the person, the continued existence of whose life is necessary to the fulfilment of the contract, is himself the contractor, but that does not seem in itself to be necessary to the application of the principle; as is illustrated by the following example. In the ordinary form of an apprentice deed the apprentice binds himself in unqualified terms to "serve until the full end and term of seven years to be fully complete and ended", during which term it is covenanted that the apprentice his master "faithfully shall serve", and the father of the apprentice in equally unqualified terms binds himself for the performance by the apprentice of all and every covenant on his part. (See the form, 2 Chitty on Pleading, 370, 7th ed by Greening.) It is undeniable that if the apprentice dies within the seven years, the covenant of the father that he shall perform his covenant to serve for seven years is not fulfilled, yet surely it cannot be that an action would lie against the father? Yet the only reason why it would not is that he is excused because of the apprentice's death.

These are instances where the implied condition is of the life of a human being, but there are others in which the same implication is made as to the continued existence of a thing. For example where a contract of sale is made amounting to a bargain and sale, transferring presently the property in specific chattels, which are to be delivered by the vendor at a future day; there, if the chattels, without the fault of the vendor, perish in the interval, the purchaser must pay the price and the vendor is excused from performing his contract to deliver, which has thus become impossible.

That this is the rule of the English law is established by the case of *Rugg* v. *Minett*, where the article that perished before delivery was turpentine, and it was decided that the vendor was bound to refund the price of all those lots in which the property had not passed; but was entitled to retain without deduction the price of those lots in which the property had passed, though they were not delivered, and though in the conditions of sale, which are set out in the report, there was no express qualification of the promise to deliver on payment. It seems in that case rather to have been taken for granted than decided that the destruction of the thing sold before delivery excused the vendor from fulfilling his contract to deliver on payment.

This is also the rule in the civil law, and it is worth noticing that Pothier, in his celebrated Traité du contrat de vente (see part 4, ss 307 et seq; and Part 2, ch 1, s 1 art 4, a1) treats this as merely an example of the more general rule that every obligation de certo corpore is extinguished when the thing ceases to exist. See Blackburn on the Contract of Sale, p. 173.

It may, we think, be safely asserted to be now English law, that in all contracts of loan of chattels or bailments if the performance of the promise of the borrower or bailee to return the things lent or bailed, becomes impossible because it has perished, this impossibility (if not arising from the fault of the borrower or bailee from some risk which he has taken upon himself) excuses the borrower or bailee from the performance of his promise to redeliver the chattel.

The principle seems to us to be that, in contracts in which the performance depends on the continued existence of a given person or thing, a condition is implied that the impossibility of performance arising from the perishing of the person or thing shall excuse the performance; . . . but that excuse is by law implied, because from the nature of the contract it is apparent that the parties contracted on the basis of the continued existence of the particular person or chattel. In the present case, looking at the whole contract, we find that the parties contracted on the basis of the continued existence of the Music Hall at the time when the concerts were to be given; that being essential to their performance.

We think, therefore, that the Music Hall having ceased to exist, without fault of either party, both parties are excused, the plaintiffs from taking the gardens and paying the money, the defendants from performing their promise to give the use of the Hall and Gardens and other things. Consequently the rule must be absolute to enter the verdict for the defendants.

Note

Taylor v. *Caldwell* mitigates the rigour of the old principle by establishing the rule that, in contracts whose performance depends on the continued existence of a person (contracts *intuitu personae*) or of a thing, there is an implied condition that the impossibility of performance resulting from the disappearance of the person or the thing releases the debtor.

Noteworthy in this connection is the reference to Pothier's *Traité du contrat du vente*—rather than to the Civil Code—Napoleonic Code![41]—a practice which could usefully be revived in both directions.

The rule is limited but offers the means of extending it by application of the doctrine of implied term which can be and has been used for other contracts. The implied term was, however, abandoned in the case of "frustration", in particular by the judgment in *Davis Contractors Ltd.* v. *Fareham UDC*.[42] Frustration has however been developed on that legal basis, particularly in the judgments in the Coronation cases given following postponement of the Coronation of King Edward VII because of illness.

[41] See Art. 1722 C.civ. *supra*, at 593
[42] (1956); see *infra*, at 617, **5.E.18**.

Court of Appeal **5.E.16.**
Krell v. *Henry*[43]

FRUSTRATION AND ESSENTIAL FEATURE OF THE CONTRACT

The Coronation

A contract may be frustrated when its essential feature no longer exists.

Facts: Henry hired a room in order to watch the passing of the procession. The price agreed was £75. He paid £25 on account. Although the coronation was postponed, the hirer claimed payment of the remaining amount, that is £50. Henry counterclaimed for recovery of the payment on account.

Held: At first instance Henry was successful on both points. Krell's appeal was dismissed.

Judgment: VAUGHAN WILLIAMS LJ: . . . The real question is the extent of the application in English law of the principle of the Roman law which has been adopted and acted on in many English decisions, and notably in the case of *Taylor* v. *Caldwell* . . .

English law applies the principle not only to cases where the performance of the contract becomes impossible by the cessation of existence of the thing which is the subject-matter of the contract, but also to cases where the event which renders the contract incapable of performance is the cessation or non-existence of an express condition or state of things, going to the root of the contract, and essential to its performance. It is said, on the one side, that the specified thing, state of things, or condition the continued existence of which is necessary for the fulfilment of the contract, so that the parties entering into the contract must have contemplated the continued existence of that thing, condition, or state of things as the foundation of what was to be done under the contract, is limited to things which are either the subject-matter of the contract or a condition or state of things, present or anticipated, which is expressly mentioned in the contract. But, on the other side, it is said that the condition or state of things need not be expressly specified, but that it is sufficient if that condition or state of things clearly appears by extrinsic evidence to have been assumed by the parties to be the foundation or basis of the contract, and the event which causes the impossibility is of such a character that it cannot reasonably be supposed to have been in the contemplation of the contracting parties when the contract was made. In such a case the contracting parties will not be held bound by the general words which, though large enough to include, were not used with reference to a possibility of a particular event rendering performance of the contract impossible. I do not think that the principle of the civil law as introduced into the English law is limited to cases in which the event causing the impossibility of performance is the destruction or non-existence of some thing which is the subject-matter of the contract or of some condition or state of things expressly specified as a condition of it. I think that you first have to ascertain, not necessarily from the terms of the contract, but, if required, from necessary inferences, drawn from surrounding circumstances recognised by both contracting parties, what is the substance of the contract, and then to ask the question whether that substantial contract needs for its foundation the assumption of the existence of a particular state of things. If it does, this will limit the operation of the general words, and in such case, if the contract becomes impossible of performance by reason of the non-existence of the state of things assumed by both contracting parties as the foundation of the contract, there will be no breach of the contract thus limited. Now what are the facts of the present case? The contract is contained in two letters of 20 June which passed between the defendant and the plaintiff's agent, Mr Cecil Bisgood. These letters do not mention the coronation, but speak merely of the taking of Mr Krell's chambers, or, rather, of the use of them, in the daytime of

[43] [1902] 2 KB 740.

26 and 27 June, for the sum of £75, £25 then paid, balance £50 to be paid on 24 June. But the affidavits, which by agreement between the parties are to be taken as stating the facts of the case, shew that the plaintiff exhibited on his premises, third floor, 56A, Pall Mall, an announcement to the effect that windows to view the Royal coronation procession were to be let, and that the defendant was induced by that announcement to apply to the housekeeper on the premises, who said that the owner was willing to let the suite of rooms for the purpose of seeing the Royal procession for both days, but not nights, of 26 and 27 June. In my judgment the use of the rooms was let and taken for the purpose of seeing the Royal procession. It was not a demise of the rooms, or even an agreement to let and take the rooms. It is a licence to use rooms for a particular purpose and none other. And in my judgment the taking place of those processions on the days proclaimed along the proclaimed route, which passed 56A, Pall Mall, was regarded by both contracting parties as the foundation of the contract; and I think that it cannot reasonably be supposed to have been in the contemplation of the contracting parties, when the contract was made, that the coronation would not be held on the proclaimed days, or the processions not take place on those days along the proclaimed route; and I think that the words imposing on the defendant the obligation to accept and pay for the use of the rooms for the named days, although general and unconditional, were not used with reference to the possibility of the particular contingency which afterwards occurred. It was suggested in the course of the argument that if the occurrence, on the proclaimed days, of the coronation and the procession in this case were the foundation of the contract, and if the general words are thereby limited or qualified, so that in the event of the non-occurrence of the coronation and procession along the proclaimed route they would discharge both parties from further performance of the contract, it would follow that if a cabman was engaged to take some one to Epsom on Derby Day at a suitable enhanced price for such a journey, say £10, both parties to the contract would be discharged in the contingency of the race at Epsom for some reason becoming impossible; but I do not think this follows, for I do not think that in the cab case the happening of the race would be the foundation of the contract. No doubt the purpose of the engager would be to go to see the Derby, and the price would be proportionately high; but the cab had no special qualifications for the purpose which led to the selection of the cab for this particular occasion. Any other cab would have done as well. Moreover, I think that, under the cab contract, the hirer, even if the race went off, could have said, "Drive me to Epsom; I will pay you the agreed sum; you have nothing to do with the purpose for which I hired the cab," and that if the cabman refused he would have been guilty of a breach of contract, there being nothing to qualify his promise to drive the hirer to Epsom on a particular day. Whereas in the case of the coronation, there is not merely the purpose of the hirer to see the coronation procession, but it is the coronation procession and the relative position of the rooms which is the basis of the contract as much for the lessor as the hirer; and I think that if the King, before the coronation day and after the contract, had died, the hirer could not have insisted on having the rooms on the days named. It could not in the cab case be reasonably said that seeing the Derby race was the foundation of the contract, as it was of the licence in this case. Whereas in the present case, where the rooms were offered and taken, by reason of their peculiar suitability from the position of the rooms for a view of the coronation procession, surely the view of the coronation procession was the foundation of the contract, which is a very different thing from the purpose of the man who engaged the cab—namely, to see the race—being held to be the foundation of the contract. Each case must be judged by its own circumstances. In each case one must ask oneself, first, what, having regard to all the circumstances, was the foundation of the contract? Secondly, was the performance of the contract prevented? Thirdly, was the event which prevented the performance of the contract of such a character that it cannot reasonably be said to have been in the contemplation of the parties at the date of the contract? If all these questions are answered in the affirmative (as I think they should be in this case), I think both parties are discharged from further performance of the contract. I think that the coronation procession was the foundation of this contract, and that the

non-happening of it prevented the performance of the contract; and, secondly, I think that the non-happening of the procession, to use the words of Sir James Hannen in *Baily* v. *De Crespigny*, was an event "of such a character that it cannot reasonably be supposed to have been in the contemplation of the contracting parties when the contract was made, and that they are not to be held bound by general words which, though large enough to include, were not used with reference to the possibility of the particular contingency which afterwards happened."

The test seems to be whether the event which causes the impossibility was or might have been anticipated and guarded against. It seems difficult to say, in a case where both parties anticipate the happening of an event, which anticipation is the foundation of the contract, that either party must be taken to have anticipated, and ought to have guarded against, the event which prevented the performance of the contract. In both *Jackson* v. *Union Marine Insurance Co.* and *Nickoll* v. *Ashton* the parties might have anticipated as a possibility that perils of the sea might delay the ship and frustrate the commercial venture: in the former case the carriage of the goods to effect which the charterparty was entered into; in the latter case the sale of the goods which were to be shipped on the steamship which was delayed. But the Court held in the former case that the basis of the contract was that the ship would arrive in time to carry out the contemplated commercial venture, and in the latter that the steamship would arrive in time for the loading of the goods the subject of the sale.

I wish to observe that cases of this sort are very different from cases where a contract or warranty or representation is implied, such as was implied in *The Moorcock*, and refused to be implied in *Hamlyn* v. *Wood*. But *The Moorcock* is of importance in the present case as shewing that whatever is the suggested implication—be it condition, as in this case, or warranty or representation—one must, in judging whether the implication ought to be made, look not only at the words of the contract, but also at the surrounding facts and the knowledge of the parties of those facts. There seems to me to be ample authority for this proposition. Thus in *Jackson* v. *Union Marine Insurance Co.*, in the Common Pleas, the question whether the object of the voyage had been frustrated by the delay of the ship was left as a question of fact to the jury, although there was nothing in the charterparty defining the time within which the charterers were to supply the cargo of iron rails for San Francisco, and nothing on the face of the charterparty to indicate the importance of time in the venture; and that was a case in which, as Bramwell B. points out in his judgment at p. 148, *Taylor* v. *Caldwell* was a strong authority to support the conclusion arrived at in the judgment—that the ship not arriving in time for the voyage contemplated, but at such time as to frustrate the commercial venture, was not only a breach of the contract but discharged the charterer, though he had such an excuse that no action would lie . . .

I myself am clearly of opinion that in this case, where we have to ask ourselves whether the object of the contract was frustrated by the non-happening of the coronation and its procession on the days proclaimed, parol evidence is admissible to shew that the subject of the contract was rooms to view the coronation procession, and was so to the knowledge of both parties. When once this is established, I see no difficulty whatever in the case. It is not essential to the application of the principle of *Taylor* v. *Caldwell* that the direct subject of the contract should perish or fail to be in existence at the date of performance of the contract. It is sufficient if a state of things or condition expressed in the contract and essential to its performance perishes or fails to be in existence at that time. In the present case the condition which fails and prevents the achievement of that which was, in the contemplation of both parties, the foundation of the contract, is not expressly mentioned either as a condition of the contract or the purpose of it; but I think for the reasons which I have given that the principle of *Taylor* v. *Caldwell* ought to be applied. This disposes of the plaintiff's claim for £50 unpaid balance of the price agreed to be paid for the use of the rooms. The defendant at one time set up a cross-claim for the return of the £25 he paid at the date of the contract. As that claim is now withdrawn it is unnecessary to say anything about it. I have only to add that the facts of this case do not bring it within the principle laid down in *Stubbs* v. *Holywell Ry. Co.*; that in the case of contracts falling directly within the rule of *Taylor* v. *Caldwell* the subsequent impossibility does not affect rights already acquired, because the defendant had the whole of 24 June to pay the balance, and the public announcement that the coronation and processions would not take place on the proclaimed days was made early on the morning of 24 June, and no cause of action could accrue till the end of that day. I think this appeal ought to be dismissed.

Court of Appeal   **5.E.17.**
Herne Bay Steam Boat Co. v. *Hutton*[44]

FRUSTRATION AND ESSENTIAL FEATURE OF THE CONTRACT

The naval review

A contract may be frustrated when its essential feature no longer exists.

Facts: Hutton chartered a boat to take his friends to see the naval review and to take them round the naval fleet. The naval review was cancelled but the fleet remained in the offing. Hutton did not use the boat and the ship-owner sought payment of the amount due under the charter-party.

Held: This was refused at first instance. The Court of Appeal quashed the decision of the lower court.

Judgment: VAUGHAN WILLIAMS LJ: Mr Hutton, in hiring this vessel, had two objects in view: first, of taking people to see the naval review, and, secondly, of taking them round the fleet. Those, no doubt, were the purposes of Mr Hutton, but it does not seem to me that because, as it is said, those purposes became impossible, it would be a very legitimate inference that the happening of the naval review was contemplated by both parties as the basis and foundation of this contract, so as to bring the case within the doctrine of *Taylor* v. *Caldwell*. On the contrary, when the contract is properly regarded, I think the purpose of Mr Hutton, whether of seeing the naval review or of going round the fleet with a party of paying guests, does not lay the foundation of the contract within the authorities.

Having expressed that view, I do not know that there is any advantage to be gained by going on in any way to define what are the circumstances which might or might not constitute the happening of a particular contingency as the foundation of a contract. I will content myself with saying this, that I see nothing that makes this contract differ from a case where, for instance, a person has engaged a brake to take himself and a party to Epsom to see the races there, but for some reason or other, such as the spread of an infectious disease, the races are postponed. In such a case it could not be said that he could be relieved of his bargain. So in the present case it is sufficient to say that the happening of the naval review was not the foundation of the contract.

ROMER LJ: . . . In my opinion, as my Lord has said, it is a contract for the hiring of a ship by the defendant for a certain voyage, though having, no doubt, a special object, namely, to see the naval review and the fleet; but it appears to me that the object was a matter with which the defendant, as hirer of the ship, was alone concerned, and not the plaintiffs, the owners of the ship. The case cannot, in my opinion, be distinguished in principle from many common cases in which, on the hiring of a ship, you find the objects of the hiring stated. Very often you find the details of the voyage stated with particularity, and also the nature and details of the cargo to be carried. If the voyage is intended to be one of pleasure, the object in view may also be stated, which is a matter that concerns the passengers. But this statement of the objects of the hirer of the ship would not, in my opinion, justify him in saying that the owner of the ship had those objects just as much in view as

---

[44] [1903] 2 KB 683.

615

the hirer himself. The owner would say, "I have an interest in the ship as a passenger or cargo carrying machine, and I enter into the contract simply in that capacity; it is for the hirer to concern himself about the objects".

In the present case, with regard to the suggestion that there was something in the stipulation that the plaintiffs were to have the right on their part of placing ten persons on board, which would change the nature of the hiring, I need only say that there is nothing in that provision to lead the Court to treat the transaction otherwise than as an ordinary case of hiring a vessel: it does not make it in any sense a joint speculation or anything of that sort. The stipulation that the owners are "to have the right of ten persons above crew, on board" only amounts to this, that in the eye of the law the defendant as the hirer of the ship licenses the owner to send ten persons on board.

The view I have expressed with regard to the general effect of the contract before us is borne out by the following considerations. The ship (as a ship) had nothing particular to do with the review or the fleet except as a convenient carrier of passengers to see it: any other ship suitable for carrying passengers would have done equally as well. Just as in the case of the hire of a cab or other vehicle, although the object of the hirer might be stated, that statement would not make the object any the less a matter for the hirer alone, and would not directly affect the person who was letting out the vehicle for hire. In the present case I may point out that it cannot be said that by reason of the failure to hold the naval review there was a total failure of consideration. That cannot be so. Nor is there anything like a total destruction of the subject-matter of the contract. Nor can we, in my opinion, imply in this contract any condition in favour of the defendant which would enable him to escape liability. A condition ought only to be implied in order to carry out the presumed intention of the parties, and I cannot ascertain any such presumed intention here. It follows that, in my opinion, so far as the plaintiffs are concerned, the objects of the passengers on this voyage with regard to sight-seeing do not form the subject-matter or essence of this contract. . . .

STIRLING LJ: . . . It seems to me that the reference in the contract to the naval review is easily explained; it was inserted in order to define more exactly the nature of the voyage, and I am unable to treat it as being such a reference as to constitute the naval review the foundation of the contract so as to entitle either party to the benefit of the doctrine in *Taylor* v. *Caldwell*. I come to this conclusion the more readily because the object of the voyage is not limited to the naval review, but also extends to a cruise round the fleet. The fleet was there, and passengers might have been found willing to go round it. It is true that in the event which happened the object of the voyage became limited, but, in my opinion, that was the risk of the defendant whose venture the taking the passengers was. For these reasons I am unable to agree with the learned judge in holding that in the contemplation of the parties the taking place of the review was the basis for the performance of the contract, and I think that the defendant is not discharged from its performance.

Notes

(1) These two decisions given by the same court composed of the same judges may appear contradictory. In the first case, the spectacle of the procession is the essential feature of the contract. It is an implied term of the contract and the judges apply the rule in *Taylor* v. *Caldwell*, widely construed. The judgment alludes to the reasonably unforeseeable nature of the event when the contract was entered into. Finally, it should be noted that the defendant abandoned his claim for recovery of the payment on account.[45]

(2) The second judgment is justified in different terms by the judges. For some of them, attending the naval review was not the foundation of the contract since the excursion

---

[45] See *infra*, at 623.

round the fleet remained possible. It was also pointed out that a charter-party is solely for the making available of a vessel and does not concern the purpose of the voyage. Finally, it is suggested that it is not possible to discern what would have been the parties' intentions if they had considered the question. Commentators also emphasize that in justifying the difference in solution in the first judgment the hirer of the room was an ordinary person whereas the ship-owner was a professional.

(3) These solutions may be compared with those to which French law might have arrived by applying the theory of the object and the theory of the cause—"entering into the contractual sphere" according to the formula used by H. Capitant. The frustration route opened by *Taylor* v. *Caldwell* was to be pursued but the ground of action would change.

House of Lords   5.E.18.
Davis Contractor Ltd v. Fareham UDC[46]

Frustration defined

The 78 houses contract

For a frustration to occur, there must be such a change in the significance of the obligation that the thing undertaken would, if performed, be a different thing from that contracted for.

Facts: An undertaking contracted to build seventy-eight houses for a local authority within a period of eight months. In actual fact twenty-two months were required for completion chiefly owing to the lack of labour. The undertaking which was paid the contractual price sought additional compensation on the basis of unjust enrichment.

Held: The action was dismissed. There was no frustration.

Judgment: Lord Reid: . . . Frustration is regarded as depending on the addition to the contract of an implied term or as depending on the construction of the contract as it stands. . . .

I may be allowed to note an example of the artificiality of the theory of an implied term given by Lord Sands in *James Scott Sons Ltd.* v. *Del Sel*: "A tiger has escaped from a travelling menagerie. The milkgirl fails to deliver the milk. Possibly the milkman may be exonerated from any breach of contract; but, even so, it would seem hardly reasonable to base that exoneration on the ground that "tiger days excepted" must be held as if written into the milk contract."

I think that there is much force in Lord Wright's criticism in *Denny, Mott Dickson Ltd.* v. *James B. Fraser Co. Ltd.*: "The parties did not anticipate fully and completely, if at all, or provide for what actually happened. It is not possible, to my mind, to say that, if they had thought of it, they would have said: "Well, if that happens, all is over between us." On the contrary, they would almost certainly on the one side or the other have sought to introduce reservations or qualifications or compensations."

It appears to me that frustration depends, at least in most cases, not on adding any implied term, but on the true construction of the terms which are in the contract read in light of the nature of the contract and of the relevant surrounding circumstances when the contract was made.

Lord Radcliffe: . . . Before I refer to the facts I must say briefly what I understand to be the legal principle of frustration. It is not always expressed in the same way, but I think that the points which

---

[46] [1956] AC 696.

617

are relevant to the decision of this case are really beyond dispute. The theory of frustration belongs to the law of contract and it is represented by a rule which the courts will apply in certain limited circumstances for the purpose of deciding that contractual obligations, ex facie binding, are no longer enforceable against the parties. The description of the circumstances that justify the application of the rule and, consequently, the decision whether in a particular case those circumstances exist are, I think, necessarily questions of law.

It has often been pointed out that the descriptions vary from one case of high authority to another. Even as long ago as 1918 Lord Sumner was able to offer an anthology of different tests directed to the factor of delay alone, and delay, though itself a frequent cause of the principle of frustration being invoked, is only one instance of the kind of circumstance to which the law attends (see *Bank Line Ltd.* v. *Arthur Capel Co.*). A full current anthology would need to be longer yet. But the variety of description is not of any importance so long as it is recognised that each is only a description and that all are intended to express the same general idea. I do not think that there has been a better expression of that general idea than the one offered by Lord Loreburn in *F. A. Tamplin Steamship Co. Ltd.* v. *Anglo-Mexican Petroleum Products Co. Ltd*. It is shorter to quote than to try to paraphrase it: ". . . a court can and ought to examine the contract and the circumstances in which it was made, not of course to vary, but only to explain it, in order to see whether or not from the nature of it the parties must have made their bargain on the footing that a particular thing or state of things would continue to exist. And if they must have done so, then a term to that effect will be implied, though it be not expressed in the contract. . . . no court has an absolving power, but it can infer from the nature of the contract and the surrounding circumstances that a condition which is not expressed was a foundation on which the parties contracted." So expressed, the principle of frustration, the origin of which seems to lie in the development of commercial law, is seen to be a branch of a wider principle which forms part of the English law of contract as a whole. But, in my opinion, full weight ought to be given to the requirement that the parties "must have made" their bargain on the particular footing. Frustration is not to be lightly invoked as the dissolvent of a contract. Lord Loreburn ascribes the dissolution to an implied term of the contract that was actually made. This approach is in line with the tendency of English courts to refer all the consequences of a contract to the will of those who made it. But there is something of a logical difficulty in seeing how the parties could even impliedly have provided for something which ex hypothesi they neither expected nor foresaw; and the ascription of frustration to an implied term of the contract has been criticised as obscuring the true action of the court which consists in applying an objective rule of the law of contract to the contractual obligations that the parties have imposed upon themselves. So long as each theory produces the same result as the other, as normally it does, it matters little which theory is avowed (see *British Movietonews Ltd.* v. *London and District Cinemas Ltd.*, per Viscount Simon). But it may still be of some importance to recall that, if the matter is to be approached by way of implied term, the solution of any particular case is not to be found by inquiring what the parties themselves would have agreed on had they been, as they were not, forewarned. It is not merely that no one can answer that hypothetical question: it is also that the decision must be given "irrespective of the individuals concerned, their temperaments and failings, their interest and circumstances" (*Hirji Mulji* v. *Cheong Yue Steamship Co. Ltd*). The legal effect of frustration "does not depend on their intention or their opinions, or even knowledge, as to the event." On the contrary, it seems that when the event occurs "the meaning of the contract must be taken to be, not what the parties did intend (for they had neither thought nor intention regarding it), but that which the parties, as fair and reasonable men, would presumably have agreed upon if, having such possibility in view, they had made express provision as to their several rights and liabilities in the event of its occurrence" (*Dahl* v. *Nelson*, per Lord Watson).

By this time it might seem that the parties themselves have become so far disembodied spirits that their actual persons should be allowed to rest in peace. In their place there rises the figure of the fair and reasonable man. And the spokesman of the fair and reasonable man, who represents after all no more than the anthropomorphic conception of justice, is and must be the court itself. So perhaps it would be simpler to say at the outset that frustration occurs whenever the law recognises that without default of either party a contractual obligation has become incapable of being performed because the circumstances in which performance is called for would render it a thing radically different from that which was undertaken by the contract. *Non haec in foedera veni.* It was not this that I promised to do.

There is, however, no uncertainty as to the materials upon which the court must proceed. "The data for decision are, on the one hand, the terms and construction of the contract, read in the light of the then existing circumstances, and on the other hand the events which have occurred" (*Denny, Mott Dickson Ltd.* v. *James B. Fraser Co. Ltd.*, 25 per Lord Wright). In the nature of things there is often no room for any elaborate inquiry. The court must act upon a general impression of what its rule requires. It is for that reason that special importance is necessarily attached to the occurrence of any unexpected event that, as it were, changes the face of things. But, even so, it is not hardship or inconvenience or material loss itself which calls the principle of frustration into play. There must be as well such a change in the significance of the obligation that the thing undertaken would, if performed, be a different thing from that contracted for.

I am bound to say that, if this is the law, the appellants' case seems to me a long way from a case of frustration.

Note

This judgment highlights the artificiality of the implied term doctrine in relation to frustration. Thus, Lord Radcliffe's formula should be borne in mind:

Frustration occurs when ever the law recognises that, without default of either party, a contractual obligation has become incapable of being performed because the circumstances in which performance is called for would render it a thing radically different from that which was undertaken by the contract.

It may be wondered to what extent that formula differs from the definition in French law of *imprévision*[47] or from the German doctrine of *Wegfall der Geschäftsgrundlage*.[48]

Other judgments enable the scope of the doctrine of frustration to be determined.

Court of Appeal   **5.E.19.**
Ocean Tramp Tankers Corp. v. *VO Sovracht, The Eugenia*[49]

FORESEEABLE EVENT MAY FRUSTRATE THE CONTRACT IF NOT PROVIDED FOR

The Suez canal

For a contract to be frustrated, the event must bring about a fundamentally different situation from the one contemplated by the parties.

Facts: Under charter-party the vessel *Eugenia* was to undertake a voyage to the Indies via the Black Sea. The parties were aware of the risk of closure of the Suez Canal but had made no express contractual provision in that regard. On 25 October the *Eugenia* left Odessa for the Indies via the Suez Canal, which had been declared a danger zone. The charterer did not prevent it from doing so and the vessel was blocked in the Canal. The charterer relied on frustration.

[47] See *infra*, at 622 ff.
[48] See *infra*, at 630 ff.
[49] [1964] 2 QB 22.

Held: The Court of Appeal held that the charterer could not plead frustration.

Judgment: DENNING LJ: The second question is whether the charterparty was frustrated by what took place. The arbitrator has held it was not. The judge has held that it was. Which is right? One thing that is obvious is that the charterers cannot rely on the fact that the Eugenia was trapped in the canal; for that was their own fault. They were in breach of the war clause in entering it. They cannot rely on a self-induced frustration, see *Maritime National Fish Ltd.* v. *Ocean Trawlers Ltd.* But they seek to rely on the fact that the canal itself was blocked. They assert that even if the Eugenia had never gone into the canal, but had stayed outside (in which case she would not have been in breach of the war clause), nevertheless she would still have had to go round by the Cape. And that, they say, brings about a frustration, for it makes the venture fundamentally different from what they contracted for. The judge has accepted this view . . .

This means that once again we have had to consider the authorities on this vexed topic of frustration. But I think the position is now reasonably clear. It is simply this: if it should happen, in the course of carrying out a contract, that a fundamentally different situation arises for which the parties made no provision—so much so that it would not be just in the new situation to hold them bound to its terms—then the contract is at an end.

It was originally said that the doctrine of frustration was based on an implied term. In short, that the parties, if they had foreseen the new situation, would have said to one another: "If that happens, of course, it is all over between us." But the theory of an implied term has now been discarded by everyone, or nearly everyone, for the simple reason that it does not represent the truth. The parties would not have said: "It is all over between us." They would have differed about what was to happen. Each would have sought to insert reservations or qualifications of one kind or another. Take this very case. The parties realised that the canal might become impassable. They tried to agree on a clause to provide for the contingency. But they failed to agree. So there is no room for an implied term.

It has frequently been said that the doctrine of frustration only applies when the new situation is "unforeseen" or "unexpected" or "uncontemplated", as if that were an essential feature. But it is not so. The only thing that is essential is that the parties should have made no provision for it in their contract. The only relevance of it being "unforeseen" is this: If the parties did not foresee anything of the kind happening, you can readily infer they have made no provision for it: whereas, if they did foresee it, you would expect them to make provision for it. But cases have occurred where the parties have foreseen the danger ahead, and yet made no provision for it in the contract. Such was the case in the Spanish Civil War when a ship was let on charter to the republican government. The purpose was to evacuate refugees. The parties foresaw that she might be seized by the nationalists. But they made no provision for it in their contract. Yet, when she was seized, the contract was frustrated, see *W. J. Tatem Ltd.* v. *Gamboa*. So here the parties foresaw that the canal might become impassable: it was the very thing they feared. But they made no provision for it. So there is room for the doctrine to apply if it be a proper case for it. We are thus left with the simple test that a situation must arise which renders performance of the contract "a thing radically different from that which was undertaken by the contract," see *Davis Contractors Ltd.* v. *Fareham Urban District Council*, by Lord Radcliffe. To see if the doctrine applies, you have first to construe the contract and see whether the parties have themselves provided for the situation that has arisen. If they have provided for it, the contract must govern. There is no frustration. If they have not provided for it, then you have to compare the new situation with the situation for which they did provide. Then you must see how different it is. The fact that it has become more onerous or more expensive for one party than he thought is not sufficient to bring about a frustration. It must be more than merely more onerous or more expensive. It must be positively unjust to hold the parties bound. It is often difficult to draw the line. But it must be done. And it is for the courts to do it as a matter of law: see *Tsakiroglou & Co. Ltd.* v. *Noblee Thorl G.m.b.H* by Lord Simonds and by Lord Reid.

Applying these principles to this case, I have come to the conclusion that the blockage of the canal did not bring about a "fundamentally different situation" such as to frustrate the venture. My reasons are these:

(1) The venture was the whole trip from delivery at Genoa, out to the Black Sea, there load cargo, thence to India, unload cargo, and redelivery. The time for this vessel from Odessa to Vizagapatam via the Suez Canal would be 26 days, and via the Cape, 56 days. But that is not the right comparison. You have to take the whole venture from delivery at Genoa to redelivery at Madras. We were told that the time for the whole venture via the Suez Canal would be 108 days and via the Cape 138 days. The difference over the whole voyage is not so radical as to produce a frustration.

(2) The cargo was iron and steel goods which would not be adversely affected by the longer voyage, and there was no special reason for early arrival. The vessel and crew were at all times fit and sufficient to proceed via the Cape.

(3) The cargo was loaded on board at the time of the blockage of the canal. If the contract was frustrated, it would mean, I suppose, that the ship could throw up the charter and unload the cargo wherever she was, without any breach of contract.

(4) The voyage round the Cape made no great difference except that it took a good deal longer and was more expensive for the charterers than a voyage through the canal.

Note

In his judgment Lord Denning deals with three questions. The first is that frustration cannot be relied on when it is self-induced, that is to say it is the fault of the party relying on it. On the second question Lord Denning adopts an original approach because he considers that frustration may apply even if the event is foreseeable, so long as the basic criterion of something fundamentally different from that which was in the parties' contemplation is satisfied. It does not appear that this dictum by Lord Denning is universally accepted.[50] Finally, he examines whether the alteration is sufficiently important in order to render the contract radically different.

Court of Appeal **5.E.20.**

Staffordshire Area Health Authority v. *South Staffordshire Water Works Co.*[51]

INFLATION AND FRUSTRATION

The supply of water contract

In principle the disequilibrium brought about by inflation is not a case of frustration.

Facts: In a situation similar to that which gave rise to the celebrated French judgment in *Canal de Craponne*[52] a contract for the supply of water was entered into in 1919 "at all times hereafter" at a price which by 1975 had become derisory. The company sought rescission of the contract.

Held: The court refused to grant rescission. The Court of Appeal held that the contract could be ended.

---

[50] See McKendrick, *Contract* at 14–5.

[51] [1978] 3 All ER 769, CA.

[52] It will be noted that in the *Canal de Craponne* case a declaration of the nullity of the contract could have been sought on the ground that it was in breach of the perpetuity rule. Or one could have upheld its description as an easement (drawing rights) which would have legitimised the transaction.

Judgment: DENNING LJ: [From recent cases] . . . it is possible to detect a new principle emerging as to the effect of inflation and the fall in the value of money. In the ordinary way this does not affect the bargain between the parties. As I said in *Treseder-Griffin* v. *Co-operative Insurance Society Ltd.* [1956] 2 Q.B. 127, 144:

> "in England we have always looked upon a pound as a pound, whatever its international value . . . Creditors and debtors have arranged for payment in our sterling currency in the sure knowledge that the sum they fix will be upheld by the law. A man who stipulates for a pound must take a pound when payment is made, whatever the pound is worth at that time."

But times have changed. We have since had mountainous inflation and the pound dropping to cavernous depths. In the recent case of *Multi-service Bookbinding Ltd.* v. *Marden* [1978] 2 W.L.R. 535, 544, BrowneWilkinson J departed from some of the things I said in *Treseder-Griffin* for that very reason-because of 20 years' experience of continuing inflation. The time has come when we may have to revise our views about the principle of nominalism, as it is called.—Dr F A Mann in his book on *The Legal Aspect of Money*, 3rd ed. (1971) said, at p. 100:

> "If the trend" [of inflation] "which has clouded the last few decades continues some relief in the case of certain long-term obligations . . . will become unavoidable."

That was written in 1971. Inflation has been more rampant than ever since that time. Here we have in the present case a striking instance of a long term obligation entered into 50 years ago. It provided for yearly payments for water supplies at seven old pence per 1,000 gallons. In these 50 years, and especially in the last 10 years, the cost of supplying the water has increased twenty-fold. It is likely to increase with every year that passes. Is it right that the hospital should go on forever only paying the old rate of 50 years ago? It seems to me that we have reached the point which Viscount Simon contemplated in *British Movietonews Ltd.* v. *London and District Cinemas Ltd.* [1952] A.C. 166, 185. Speaking à propos of a depreciation of currency, he envisaged a situation where

> "a consideration of the terms of the contract, in the light of the circumstances existing when it was made, shows that they never agreed to be bound in a fundamentally different situation which has now unexpectedly emerged . . ."

When such a situation emerges, he went on to say:

> "the contract ceases to bind at that point-not because the court in its discretion thinks it just and reasonable to qualify the terms of the contract, but because on its true construction it does not apply to the situation."

That is the forerunner of the modern rule of construction.

So here the situation has changed so radically since the contract was made 50 years ago that the term of the contract "at all times hereafter" ceases to bind: and it is open to the court to hold that the contract is determined by reasonable notice.

Conclusion

I do not think that the water company could have determined the agreement immediately after it was made. That cannot have been intended by the parties. No rule of construction could sensibly permit such a result. But, in the past 50 years, the whole situation has changed so radically that one can say with confidence: "The parties never intended that the supply should be continued in these days at that price." Rather than force such unequal terms on the parties, the court should hold that the agreement could be and was properly determined in 1975 by the reasonable notice of six months. . . .

Note

The two other Appeal Court judges did not follow Lord Denning's reasoning, taking the view, on a construction of the parties' intentions, that the contract was a contract for an indefinite period which could be brought to an end after a reasonable period of notice.[53] In any event, it is not a matter in English law of revising a contract but solely of bringing it to an end. French law for its part declines to bring a contract to an end on the grounds of inflation.[54]

5.1.3.B. EFFECTS

Frustration causes the contract to disappear. The courts cannot alter it. It is generally accepted that the disappearance of the contract is by operation of law: *Hirjimulji* v. *Cheong Yue SS Co Ltd.*[55] Frustration may have limited effect when there is partial non-performance: *Sainsbury (HR&S) Ltd.* v. *Street.*[56] A grower contracted to sell 275 tonnes of oats from his holding, which, however, produced only 140 tonnes. The vendor was released in respect of 135 tonnes but had to deliver the 140 tonnes produced—the similarity of the facts with the German judgment, RG, 3 February 1914[57] should be noted.

However, the common law rule, as applied in particular in *Chandler* v. *Webster*,[58] excluded any restitution in respect of monies paid under the contract.

The judgment in *Fibrosa Spolka Akcyjna* v. *Fairbairn, Lawson, Combe, Barbour Ltd.*[59] changed the rule where there was a total failure of consideration but neither the new nor the old rule was thought to be satisfactory. Therefore, the legislature intervened.

Law Reform (Frustrated Contracts) Act 1943   **5.E.21.**

section 1: (1) Where a contract governed by English law has become impossible of performance or been otherwise frustrated, and the parties thereto have for that reason been discharged from the further performance of the contract, the following provisions of the section shall, subject to the provisions of section two of this Act, have effect in relation thereto.
(2) All sums paid or payable to any party in pursuance of the contract before the time when the parties were so discharged (in this Act referred to as "the time of discharge") shall, in the case of sums so paid, be recoverable from him as money received by him for the use of the party by whom the sums were paid, and, in the case of sums so payable, cease to be so payable:
Provided that, if the party to whom the sums were so paid or payable incurred expenses before the time of discharge in, or for the purpose of, the performance of the contract, the court may, if it considers it just to do so having regard to all the circumstances of the case, allow him to retain or, as the case may be, recover the whole or any part of the sums so paid or payable, not being an amount in excess of the expenses so incurred.
(3) Where any party to the contract has, by reason of anything done by any other party thereto in, or for the purpose of, the performance of the contract, obtained a valuable benefit (other than a payment of money to which the last foregoing subsection applies) before the time of discharge, there shall be recoverable from him by the said other party

---

[53] See Treitel, *Contract* at 822.
[54] See *infra*, at 627 ff.
[55] [1926] AC 497.
[56] [1972] 3 All ER 1127.
[57] See *supra*, **5.G.11.**
[58] [1904] 1 KB 493.
[59] [1943] AC 32.

such sum (if any), not exceeding the value of the said benefit to the party obtaining it, as the court considers just, having regard to all the circumstances of the case and, in particular:

    (a) the amount of any expenses incurred before the time of discharge by the benefited party in, or for the purpose of, the performance of the contract, including any sums paid or payable by him to any other party in pursuance of the contract and retained or recoverable by that party under the last foregoing subsection, and

    (b) the effect, in relation to the said benefit, of the circumstances giving rise to the frustration of the contract.

(4) In estimating, for the purposes of the foregoing provisions of this section, the amount of any expenses incurred by any party to the contract, the court may, without prejudice to the generality of the said provisions, include such sums as appears to be reasonable in respect of overhead expenses and in respect of any work or service performed personally by the said party.

(5) In considering whether any sum ought to be recovered or retained under the foregoing provisions of this section by any party to the contract, the court shall not take into account any sums which have, by reason of the circumstances giving rise to the frustration of the contract, become payable to that party under any contract of insurance unless there was an obligation to insure imposed by any express term of the frustrated contract or by or under any enactment.

(6) Where any person has assumed obligations under the contract in consideration of the conferring of a benefit by any other party to the contract upon any other person, whether a party to the contract or not, the court may, if in all the circumstances of the case it considers it just to do so, treat for the purposes of sub-section (3) of this section any benefit so conferred as a benefit obtained by the person who has assumed the obligations as aforesaid.

Note

The Act deals with restitution of money (section 1(2)) and of other benefits (section 1(3)). The latter text is particularly complex. Note the quasi-discretionary power given to the court, particularly by the proviso to section 1(1) and section 1(3) which, to some extent, makes up for the lack of power to revise the contract.

5.1.4. IMPOSSIBILITY OF PERFORMANCE IN INTERNATIONAL INSTRUMENTS

The United Nations Convention on the International Sale of Goods (CISG) of 11 April 1980, which has been adopted by fifty-seven States, provides for discharge as a result of impossibility of performance.

CISG   **5.INT.22.**

Article 79: (1) A party is not liable for a failure to perform any of his obligations if he proves that the failure was due to an impediment beyond his control and that he could not reasonably be expected to have taken the impediment into account at the time of the conclusion of the contract or to have avoided or overcome it or its consequences.

(2) If the party's failure is due to the failure by a third person whom he has engaged to perform the whole or a part of the contract, that party is exempt from liability only if:
    (a) he is exempt under the preceding paragraph; and
    (b) the person whom he has so engaged would be so exempt if the provisions of that paragraph were applied to him.
(3) The exemption provided by the article has effect for the period during which the impediment exists.
(4) The party who fails to perform must give notice to the other party of the impediment and its effect on his ability to perform. If the notice is not received by the other party within a reasonable time after the party who fails to perform knew or ought to have known of the impediment, he is liable for damage resulting from such non-receipt.

This text formed the point of departure for the Unidroit Principles[60] and for the Principles of European Contract Law:

Principles of European Contract Law   **5.PECL.23.**

Article 8:101:   *Remedies Available*
    (1) Whenever a party does not perform an obligation under the contract and the non-performance is not excused under Article 8:108, the aggrieved party may resort to any of the remedies set out in Chapter 9.
    (2) Where a party's non-performance is excused under Article 8:108, the aggrieved party may resort to any of the remedies set out in Chapter 9 except claiming performance and damages.
    (3) A party may not resort to any of the remedies set out in Chapter 9 to the extent that its own act caused the other party's non-performance.

Article 8:108:   *Excuse Due to an Impediment*
    (1) A party's non-performance is excused if it proves that it is due to an impediment beyond its control and that it could not reasonably have been expected to take the impediment into account at the time of the conclusion of the contract, or to have avoided or overcome the impediment or its consequences.
    (2) Where the impediment is only temporary the excuse provided by this Article has effect for the period during which the impediment exists. However, if the delay amounts to a fundamental non-performance, the creditor may treat it as such.
    (3) The non-performing party must ensure that notice of the impediment and of its effect on its ability to perform is received by the other party within a reasonable time after the non-performing party knew or ought to have known of these circumstances. The other party is entitled to damages for any loss resulting from the non-receipt of such notice.

Article 9:303:   *Notice of Termination*
    (1) A party's right to terminate the contract is to be exercised by notice to the other party.
    (2) The aggrieved party loses its right to terminate the contract unless it gives notice within a reasonable time after it has or ought to have become aware of the non-performance.

---

[60] See Art. 7.1.7.

(3) (a) When performance has not been tendered by the time it was due, the aggrieved party need not give notice of termination before a tender has been made. If a tender is later made it loses its right to terminate if it does not give such notice within a reasonable time after it has or ought to have become aware of the tender.

(b) If, however, the aggrieved party knows or has reason to know that the other party still intends to tender within a reasonable time, and the aggrieved party unreasonably fails to notify the other party that it will not accept performance, it loses its right to terminate if the other party in fact tenders within a reasonable time.

(4) If a party is excused under Article 8:108 through an impediment which is total and permanent, the contract is terminated automatically and without notice at the time the impediment arises.

These texts should be compared to each other and to the national solutions, especially on the conditions of impossibility, the mechanisms employed and the effects of excuse.

Conclusion

A fairly wide divergence in national laws may be noted. It may be wondered whether the international instruments have succeeded in harmonizing them. Certainly, the practical results are frequently identical in the case of absolute impossibility but, from a doctrinal point of view, the approach is not the same. As regards the manner in which the systems deal with the legal consequences of the occurrence of unforeseen but not completely insurmountable events, opposing points of view are much clearer.

5.2. HARDSHIP, *IMPREVISION*

Principles of European Contract Law **5.PECL.24.**

Article 6:111: *Change of Circumstances*

(1) A party is bound to fulfil its obligations even if performance has become more onerous, whether because the cost of performance has increased or because the value of the performance it receives has diminished.

(2) If, however, performance of the contract becomes excessively onerous because of a change of circumstances, the parties are bound to enter into negotiations with a view to adapting the contract or terminating it, provided that:

(a) the change of circumstances occurred after the time of conclusion of the contract,

(b) the possibility of a change of circumstances was not one which could reasonably have been taken into account at the time of conclusion of the contract, and

(c) the risk of the change of circumstances is not one which, according to the contract, the party affected should be required to bear.

(3) If the parties fail to reach agreement within a reasonable period, the court may:

(a) terminate the contract at a date and on terms to be determined by the court; or

(b) adapt the contract in order to distribute between the parties in a just and equitable manner the losses and gains resulting from the change of circumstances.

In either case, the court may award damages for the loss suffered through a party refusing to negotiate or breaking off negotiations contrary to good faith and fair dealing.

The nature of the question will be recalled. An unforeseen event occurring after the conclusion of the contract renders performance much more difficult. Performance remains possible but under far more onerous conditions than were envisaged when the contract was entered into. It is in that respect that an unforeseen event (*imprévision*) may be distinguished from *force majeure* which prevents any performance.

The point of departure is obviously observance of the binding force of the contract "which has the force of law" as between those who entered into it[61] and can be altered or dissolved prematurely only by common accord of the parties.

On the occurrence of extraordinary events—economic crisis, war—it is for the legislature to intervene, as happened after the two world wars, by conferring on the courts a provisional power of revision; for example, in France the Acts of 21 January 1918 and 22 April 1949; in Germany the law on assistance to contracts (*Vertragshilfgesetz*) of 26 March 1952, not to speak of permanent enactments for certain long-term transactions.[62]

It remains to be determined whether it is desirable to make this kind of provision permanent. Doctrinal controversy developed after the First World War—even if the French judgment of principle dates back to 1876[63]—and, following a famous German judgment of the 1920s,[64] judicial revision of the contract in the case of an unforeseen event has been allowed by the laws of several countries and in certain international instruments; these will be dealt with in section **5.2.2**. Others have, however, declined, on grounds of principle, to give courts the power to adjust the original contract—French and English law; these will be dealt with in section **5.2.1**.

5.2.1. LAWS WHICH DECLINE TO REVISE THE CONTRACT

5.2.1.A. FRENCH LAW

Introductory Note
The landmark judgment is that in *Canal de Craponne* of 6 March 1876,[65] in regard to an agreement of 1567 which fixed a charge for water at a rate which three centuries later had become derisory. That judgment set aside the judgment of a cour d'appel which had readjusted the charge. It is not certain that the factual situation was correctly assessed since it might rather have been a case of an easement.

The position adopted by the Cour de cassation was resumed after the First World War owing to the resulting monetary depreciation—500 per cent price inflation. An example of this may be seen in the judgment of the civil chamber of the Cour de cassation of

---

[61] See Art. 1134, al. 1, C.civ.
[62] Eg French Act of 25 March 1949 on revision of annuities.
[63] Cass. civ., 6 March 1876, *Canal de Craponne*, D. 1876.I.93.
[64] See *infra*, **5.G.26 and 27.**
[65] Cass. civ., 6 March 1876, *Canal de Craponne*, D. 1876.I.93.

6 June 1921 in factual circumstances very close to those of the contemporaneous judgment of the RG of 27 June 1922.[66] At the same time a doctrinal controversy sprang up which has lasted until the present day.

Cass. civ., 6 June 1921[67]   **5.F.25.**

IMPREVISION, EQUITY AND REVISION

The stock-rearing contract

No equitable consideration permits the courts to vary the contract.

Facts: Under a peculiar stock contract entered into in 1910, the farmer was required to leave the herd with capital of the same value as he had received, that value being fixed in the contract. The owner claimed a proportion of the added value resulting from monetary depreciation during the war.

Held: This claim was upheld by the cour d'appel. The judgment was set side.

Judgment: THE COURT:—By reference to Articles 1134 and 1826[68] of the Civil Code,
—Whereas agreements legally entered into have the force of law as regards those entering into them and that no consideration of equity allows the courts, where agreements are clear and precise, to amend on the pretext of interpretation the provisions contained therein;
—Whereas on 4 December 1910, Saint-Pé, a proprietor, entered into a stock-rearing contract with Bacou containing the following clause: "The capital taken over by the farmer amounts to 3.000 FRF for the beasts and 2.425 FRF for the herd, and it is in respect of this amount in cash or in kind, as the proprietor shall decide, which the farmer shall account on expiry of the agreement"; as that precise and clear clause derogated from the rules of the Civil Code on stock leases containing an estimate of the condition of the animals, solely inasmuch as it gave the lessor the right to opt at the end of the lease between payment in cash or restitution in kind but for the rest left the parties subject to the ordinary law; as, accordingly, the stock account was to be governed by Article 1826 of the Civil Code;
—Whereas under that provision, the farmer at the end of the lease is required to leave stock "equal in value to that which he received"; as, if there is a deficit he must pay it but any surplus belongs to him; as no distinction is made between the value added to the stock by the care and improvements of the farmer and that stemming from accidental circumstances; as it is apparent from Article 1826 read in conjunction with Article 1821 that the farmer shall "leave beasts equal in value to the estimated price of those he received"; as secondly, the law had in contemplation the actual value of the stock and not its potential for commercial exploitation; as the judgment therefore erred in holding that Bacou should share the entirety of the added value acquired by the stock and by the herd, instead of awarding it to Bacou.
—Whereas the cour d'appel asserts in vain that, in entering into the contract, the parties could not have foreseen the extraordinary increase in animal prices as a result of the First World War but merely a normal rise the maximum amount of which evidently corresponded to the highest price for stock during the period of the latest years prior to conclusion of the contract.
—Whereas by undertaking indeed to bear the risk of a future rise in prices of animals and herds, the counterpart of the risks likely to result from either a fall in those prices or fortuitous loss of the

---

[66] See *infra*, **5.G.25 and 27.**
[67] D.1921.I.73, with the report of Colin; S. 1921.I.193, annotated by Hugueney.
[68] This provision has been amended in 1941 and fixes now as the date at which the evaluation should take place the day the contact comes at an end.

animals entrusted to the farmer, Saint-Pé imposed upon himself a law from which he could not exempt himself by alleging that his forecasts had been wrong; as it was for him to restrict his commitment to a given amount; as by inferring however such restriction from circumstances concerning which the lease was silent, the judgment appealed against merely substituted a presumed agreement for the agreement expressed by the contracting parties; as in that regard it infringed the abovementioned legislation;

On those grounds the judgment is set aside.

Note

This judgment essentially follows the judgment in *Canal de Craponne*, setting aside the appeal decision which divided between the farmer and proprietor the added value resulting from the depreciation of the franc after the First World War, contrary to the clause in the contract which awarded that added value to the farmer.

It reaffirms the absolute nature of the contract as a "law" as between the parties, even if the projections of one of the parties turn out to be wrong. No "equitable consideration" permits the courts to vary the contract. It gives precedence to Article 1134, al. 1, C.civ.—the binding force of the contract—over Article 1134, al. 3—agreements are to be performed in good faith—and Article 1135—contract is binding as regards all the effects to which by its nature equity, usage or the law the obligation gives rise. Thus there is no *rebus sic stantibus* clause. The courts may not substitute a "presumed agreement" for the actual "agreement expressed" by the parties. Thus, one finds in the judgment the argument advanced in certain academic quarters that the courts are not well placed to intervene and that it is for the legislature to do so, or that it was for the proprietor to guard against the risk by inserting a clause in the contract to that effect. Indeed it has been maintained, in support of the Cour de cassation rigid stance, that that approach encourages the parties to make appropriate contractual provision.

On the other hand, the judgment is not based on the argument derived from the cause—disequilibrium in the contract—, nor on the economic argument, which appeared later, that in serial contracts the creditor when called upon to pay compensation in respect of an unforeseen event, a compensation indeed not foreseen by him, may for his part claim compensation from other contracting parties, and so on.

Belgian case-law is to the same effect as French case-law.[69]

Prevailing opinion now favours recognition of the moderating power of the courts, pursuant to Articles 1134, al. 3 and 1135 C.civ.. It is contrary to good faith and equity to impose the burden of unforeseen risks on one of the parties only. Certain recent decisions may be interpreted as going in that direction.[70]

For its part, decisions of the administrative courts, starting with the landmark judgment of the Conseil d'Etat of 30 March 1916, *Gaz de Bordeaux*[71] allows adjustment in the case of a contract whose "structure is absolutely overturned owing to exceptional circumstances". The public authorities are then liable to pay compensation such as to share equitably the exceptional burden. The ideas put forward to justify that stance are twofold.

[69] See Cass., 19 May 1921, Pas. 1921.I.380; Cass., 30 October 1924, Pas. I.565.
[70] See Cass. comm., 3 November 1992, Bull.civ. IV.338, annotated by Mestre at the RTD civ. 1993.124; see, however, a judgment reflecting the traditional view: Cass. comm., 18 December 1979, Bull.civ. IV.329.
[71] S. 1916.III.17, opinion by Chardenet, annotated by Hauriou.

First, the principle of the continuity of the public service: in the absence of an adjustment the public service secured under the contract would be interrupted. Secondly, the right of the person contracting with the public authorities to expect financial equilibrium within the contract.[72]

None the less, the question remains a sensitive one. The CISG deliberately refrained from laying down any provision in this regard and thus precludes revision in respect of unforeseen events (*imprévision*), according to the majority interpretation of Article 79 CISG, which does not mention revision.[73]

5.2.1.B. ENGLISH LAW

If one considers that the essential feature of the doctrine of the unforeseen event (*imprévision*) is the revising power which it gives to the courts, the question does not arise in English law. The existence of such a power has never been accepted, even in situations which undoubtedly constitute cases of *imprévision*, for example, the cases arising out of the closure of the Suez Canal. Nor does the intangibility of contract appear to be called in question in academic writings.

Lord Radcliffe, in the judgment in the *Davis Contractors* case,[74] approves the dictum of Lord Loreburn:

a court can and ought to examine the contract and the circumstances in which it was made, not of course to vary, but only to explain it, in order to see whether or not from the nature of it the parties must have made their bargain on the footing that a particular thing or state of things would continue to exist.

See also for a case turning on facts similar to those in the French *Canal de Craponne* judgment *Staffordshire Area Health Authority* v. *Staffordshire Staffs Waterworks Co*,[75] where even Lord Denning did not advocate revising the contract; but note that the Court of Appeal did release the parties in this case, and no doubt they then negotiated a new contract.

Contrary to the position under German law, disappearance of the contractual basis entails disappearance of the contract and not revision.

English law differs from French law, inasmuch as frustration is a more flexible notion than *force majeure*.[76]

5.2.2. RECOGNITION OF THE REVISING POWER: GERMAN LAW

Introductory Note
The point of departure is the same in German law as in French law: the contract must be performed, except in the case of absolute impossibility. Thus it was held in the judgment

[72] See de Laubadère, Venezia and Gaudemet, *Traité de droit administratif*, Vol. I, 15th edn. (Paris: LGDJ, 1999), para. 1072–6.

[73] See also in this connection decisions cited by Witz, *Les premières applications jurisprudentielles du droit uniforme de la vente internationale* (Paris: LGDJ, 1995), para. 87; Trib. Monza, 29 March 1993, Foro It. I.916–923; OLG Aix la Chapelle, 14 May 1993, RIW 1993.760.

[74] *Supra*, **5.E.18.**

[75] *Supra*, **5.E.20.**

[76] See *supra*, at 607 ff.

of the RG of 4 May 1915[77] that it is not possible to terminate the hiring of a circus arena on account of the war, which prevented normal operations, where there was no express or implied provision to that effect in the contract, since "good faith and commercial loyalty in no way justify transferring to the defendant the loss which the war has occasioned to the plaintiff".

It took the end of the war and the collapse of the Mark—no comparison between this and the fall in the French Franc—for the German courts, under the constraint of necessity, to abandon the strict conception of the binding force of the contract.

It is to be noted that the new events are of a monetary nature and that, in addition to the principle of the binding force of contract, at stake is also the principle of monetary nominalism, that is to say the principle that a monetary unit, for as long as it retains the same name, retains the same value, even if over time its real value (purchasing power) has changed. Since the debtor may discharge his obligations by means of a currency devalued to the extreme, the creditor alone bears the risk of devaluation. The question of the revision of the contract owing to unforeseen events thus also embraces the question of the revalorisation of pecuniary debts.

As from 1920 the Reichsgericht began slowly to accept revision, on justificatory grounds which have altered over time.

RG, 3 February 1922[78]   **5.G.26.**

REBUS SIC STAIIBUS

The 1919 inflation

In case of exceptional circumstances going to the roots of the contract, the judge is entitled to revise the contract and should try not to terminate it.

Facts: The defendant M and the trader B were owners of a partnership (*offene Handelsgesellschaft—oHG*). After dissolving the partnership, M entered into relations with the plaintiff R in order to save his investment. On 31 May 1919 a contract was entered into before a notary under which the defendant declared:
"1. Should I acquire land and buildings having been in the ownership of the partnership on the dissolution of the partnership at a price less than or equal to 600.000 RM, I shall cede to R such asset at the price at which I acquired it.
2. Should I acquire land and buildings having been in the ownership of the partnership at a price greater than 600.000 RM, I shall cede such asset to R for 600.000 RM. In such a situation he shall pay the sum of 600.000 RM and undertakes to pay one half of the surplus to B.
3. Should B acquire land and appurtenances at a price in excess of 600.000 RM, I shall retain the sum of 600.000 RM payable to me, any amount over and above 600.000 RM being payable to R."
    On behalf of the plaintiff, R's representative promised to pay the sale price on the transfer of the property. The contract also provided: "Should R acquire possession of the partnership, he will be in a position to employ M as a director and to guarantee him a salary to be contractually determined". R was bound by the contract until 31 December 1919.
    By letter dated 12 January 1920, R's representative informed M that he regarded himself as bound by the contract beyond 31 December 1919 and that the rights under the contract continued in force. Through his lawyer M stated that he was not interested.
    The plaintiff R brought an action for a declaration that:
—the contract of 31 December 1919 remained in force and that the defendant was still legally bound;

---

[77] ERGZ 397.
[78] RGZ 103.328.

—the rights of R continued to subsist in the event that a person other than the defendant M should become the owner of the partnership;

In support of the second claim, R asserted that since the partners M and B had not been able to agree on the liquidation of the partnership, the land should be sold at auction and that, moreover, the extension of the contract in such a case should be upheld.

Opposing the action, the defendant contended that the extension of the contract should be in notarial or judicial form and that the contract terminated on 31 December 1919.

Held: The Landgericht dismissed the action brought by R. The Oberlandesgericht (OLG) set aside that decision. The appeal in revision was upheld and the appeal judgment revised.

Judgment: . . . [On the application of the *clausula sic stantibus*:] The OLG considered that where it is sought to give the defendant the right to rescind the contract in order to palliate the alteration in economic circumstances, regard must be had to contract law. The RG criticises the OLG for being circumspect. By way of precaution it is necessary to lay down the limits within which the exception to the *clausula sic stantibus* may apply.

The RG considers that it is lawfully pleaded by the defendant that the amounts of 600.000 RM provided for in Clauses 1 to 3 are based on an approximate determination which is set too high, and the appropriate price should be 300.000 RM. It was acknowledged by the courts that the monetary depreciation since the Autumn of 1919 had very serious economic consequences.

The plaintiff for his part stated that the defendant was not in any way bound under the contract by an obligation to purchase which could subsequently have cost him more. Consequently, it should be held that performance was not rendered difficult but only that the proportion of the value of performance by the parties was altered.

The defendant's arguments were not lightly to be dismissed. it was a matter of verifying whether the contractual basis, according to Oertmann (1921), which is constituted by the parties' idea of the legal relationship on conclusion of the contract, has disappeared.

Accordingly, the decision appealed against must be set aside. The parties will have to enter fresh negotiations before the courts which will have to take account of the disappearance of the contractual basis. However, the courts must be careful to ensure that the defendant M does not avail himself of that opportunity to withdraw completely from his contractual obligations.

The courts must seek to maintain the contract whilst adapting it. That obligation arises from Article 232 concerning good faith.

RG, 27 June 1922[79]   **5.G.27.**

The farmer's stocks

Facts: By notarial deed of 17 August 1894 the defendant gave a lease over land for a period expiring on 1 July 1922. With regard to stock, the contract expressly referred to the provisions of §§ 587 to 589 BGB. The value of the whole of the stock for the purposes of valuation at the end of the contract was fixed at 113.802 RM.

The defendant considered that the plaintiff was required at the end of the lease to sell the stock for consideration in kind and for its actual value. The estimate of the value of the stock merely served to describe the different elements and gave only an indication of the state of those assets.

The plaintiff requested the court to declare that, on return of the stock, the component animals are to be assessed on the basis of their intrinsic value on the date of their return, and thus if the estimated value is greater or less than the original amount, in the former case the defendant is obliged to compensate the plaintiff on account of enrichment and in the latter case the opposite solution must be adopted. The courts trying the case on its merits upheld that claim.

Held: LG and OLG took the view that liquidation of stock at the end of the lease was governed by § 589 (III), without there being any need to take into consideration monetary depreciation which was foreseeable. The RG disapproved that reasoning.

[79] RGZ 104.394–402. The English translation is from von Mehren and Gordley, *The Civil Law System*, 2nd edn. (Boston, Mass.: Little Brown, 1977), at 1080–5.

Judgment: The presumption made by the OLG that the lessor could refuse the valuation is without foundation and is based on a manifest disregard of § 589 (III). Under that provision, the lessor may only refuse the taking into account by the farmer of elements of stock which are superfluous or have too high a value for the land. An increase in the value of the stock does not permit him to refuse the lease.

Moreover, the decision of the OLG is equitable neither under §§ 587 to 589 nor in light of the situation caused by the unhappy outcome of the war and the terrible fall in the German currency. § 589 must be understood as follows. The pecuniary valuation of the stock undertaken at the beginning of the lease by the lessor and the farmer must be compared to the value of the stock on its return. The initial valuation is not intended solely to determine the assets comprising the stock but is also to facilitate establishment of the starting value and value at the end of the contract.

Under §§ 588 and 589 (I) and (II), the stock belongs to the land and must remain there. That is true not only of stock items at the beginning of the contract but also of items acquired by the farmer during the lease. The latter become the property of the lessor by virtue of their incorporation into the contract (§ 588 (II)). On the other hand, if the strict application of those provisions required the lessor to incur considerable expenditure for stock maintenance, they would have to be disapplied.

The collapse of the German currency is so major that governing lease arrangements according to the provisions of § 589 (III) makes stock maintenance impossible. The gold mark which served as the basis for valuing the stock and the paper mark on the basis of which compensation is to be calculated are in no wise comparable, notwithstanding the financial parity established by the law.

Neither the legal provisions not contractual provisions enable the dispute to be resolved. The courts must be creative and deliver a judgment which accords with equity. The guiding principle must be that an equitable adjustment of the interests at stake must be made. The motives of the parties in light of the pre-war economic situation must be taken into consideration. In the present case, the extent of the stock was not in itself altered (that is to say neither increased nor diminished). Thus the lessor may not be obliged to pay sums greater than one million RM on return of the stock solely on account of the impressive rise in prices. The value of the stock increased by only 2%. It is that added value in respect of which an obligation arises for the lessor. The economic and legal principles elaborated by the RG must be observed by the courts trying the issues of fact. A decision taking into account the interests of the parties must be adopted.

The case is referred back to the OLG to apply these principles of adjustment.

Notes

These two decisions are the consequence of the devaluation of the Mark at the end of the First World War. One may note the similarity of the facts leading to the judgment of the RG of 27 June 1922[80] and to that of 22 December 1920—and the diametrically opposed result at which those of the Cour de cassation arrived.[81]

The two judgments of the RG recognize, on the one hand, judicial revision and consider that revision is preferable to rescission. The first judgment even encourages the parties to make appropriate contractual provision. On the other hand, those judgments are the first openly to acknowledge as the basis for that revision the Oertmann theory of the "disappearance of the contractual basis" (*Wegfall der Geschäftsgrundlage*). It would, then, be contrary to good faith to maintain the contract as it stands. The resemblance to the English Law doctrine of frustration is to be noted: the contract is no longer the same

[80] See *supra*, **5.G.27.**
[81] See *supra*, **5.F.28.**

as that which the parties initially entered into. But the outcome is different: English law does not acknowledge revision of the contract, but merely, in a proper case, its disappearance. And English law, *pace* Lord Denning, would certainly recognize that such circumstances would give rise to frustration of the contract.

Immediately after the Second World War a special law was enacted to regulate the monetary consequences on contracts of the German capitulation (*Vertragshilfgesetz* of 26 March 1952). The courts have continued to allow revision in cases not covered thereby.

BGH, 16 January 1953[82]   **5.G.28.**

REVISION OF THE CONTRACT

The Berlin blockade

According to the theory of the disappearance of the contractual basis, judges seek, on the basis of the respective interests of the contracting parties, to adapt the contract equitably.

Facts: The defendant, a company established in West Berlin which had for a long time conducted business relations with the plaintiff, ordered by letter dated 31 May 1948 600 drill hammers. It wished to take delivery of them as quickly as possible and said that it would organize a convoy to take delivery of the goods. Finally, it stated that payment would be made by its West German office. The drill hammers were ordered for the External Trade Administration in the Eastern zone for mining operations in that zone. That fact was known to the plaintiff. Between the issue and receipt of the order letter, the Berlin blockade occurred. It was to last from 24 June 1948 to 22 May 1949. Pursuant to the order the plaintiff initially manufactured 200 drill hammers and proposed to deliver them under cover of an invoice dated 30 November 1948. It went on to manufacture seventy-eight more hammers and started production of the remaining 326 hammers. The defendant neither took delivery of nor paid for those hammers. The plaintiff brought an action for payment under the order.

Held: The Oberlandesgericht (OLG) ordered the defendant immediately to pay on delivery of the drill hammers. The defendant's appeal was dismissed.

Judgment: . . . 1.—*Was delivery of the drill hammers a condition subsequent of the contract?*

In light of § 158 BGB neither the terms of the defendant's order nor acceptance by the plaintiff enable the view to be taken that validity of the contract depended on the possibility of delivery in the Eastern zone. In support of its claims the defendant contends that the hammers in question used old technology as far as the West German mining industry was concerned. When the plaintiff received the order the Berlin blockade had already occurred and it was impossible to determine when it would be lifted.

According to the plaintiff, to make the validity of the contract depend on that factual situation would have given rise to major and very heavy production costs. The plaintiff had no interest in making validity of the contract subject to the possibility of making deliveries in the Eastern zone. It was not in the plaintiff's interest to know how the defendant intended to use the drill hammers. Its sole interest in performance under the contract was in the taking of delivery of and payment for the hammers by the defendant under the terms of the contract. There is no expression of intention by the parties to make the purpose for which the hammers were to be used a condition subsequent entailing termination of the contract.

2.—*Performance of contractual obligations does not preclude specific legal provisions from prohibiting or limiting exports to the eastern zone.*

To the extent to which an unlawful circumvention of any export ban had not been included in the contract and the defendant did not take delivery of the goods at the place of performance specified

---

[82] MDR 1953.282.

in the contract, the appeal in *Revision* based on the fact that performance is contrary to § 134 BGB is inadmissible and ill-founded. Furthermore, performance of its obligations by the defendant has not become impossible.

The question arose whether the theory of economic impossibility might apply where performance had been rendered more difficult after creation of the contract to such an extent that foreseeable sacrifices were exceeded. That theory, which has been abandoned, was based on the legal consequences of impossibility. The RG then focussed on the contractual basis in light of § 242.

The problem remains that of the foreseeability of performance of the contract which falls to be resolved by taking into consideration the equity of the divergent interests of the parties in accordance with § 242 which allows the contract to be adapted to new circumstances, regard being had to the parties' interests and the principle of foreseeability.

The OLG correctly assessed foreseeability in regard to disappearance of the contractual basis under § 242 and in regard to economic impossibility.

Both the LG and the OLG considered that the contractual basis was the delivery and sale of the drill hammers. That analysis is legally questionable. Certainly the manufacturer will often know the purpose to which his products are to be put, but the purpose of the contract as far as the works contractor for buildings is concerned does not constitute the contractual basis as far as the two parties are concerned. Each party must bear the risk of the disappearance of the subjective purpose of the contract. The parties agreed, in spite of the existence of the blockade on the date when the contract was created, on the manufacture and delivery of drill hammers in the Eastern zone.

The expectation of the parties was not realised. The question arises whether the contractual basis existed on the creation of the contract. It was only after conclusion of the contract that it was agreed that the sale could not be realised. Consequently, that cannot entail nullity of the contract but its adaptation in accordance with the provisions of § 242.

Solution.—In order to adapt the contract, the contractual interests at stake must be determined. The defendant is obliged to pay the cost of the work representing 1/4 of the amount due and provided for *expressis verbis* by the contract.

Note

This judgment takes up again the theory of the disappearance of the contractual basis described by Oertmann, which had been to some extent discarded in earlier decisions where the theory of economic impossibility was applied instead.[83] According to that theory the courts had direct regard to the legal consequences of the occurrence of an economic event. According to the theory of disappearance of the contractual basis, the courts first seek to discern the initial basis of the contract and the parties' interests on creation of the contract. They will then seek, on the basis of the respective interests of the contracting parties, to adapt the contract equitably. The comparison may be made with the dicta of Lord Radcliffe.[84] The theory is to lead to adjustment of performance under the contract rather than to termination.

A more recent example provided by the German reunification—which has given a boost to the theory—well illustrates the pre-eminence of adaptation over disappearance of the contract.

---

[83] See RGZ 57.116; RGZ 94.45; RGZ 102.98.
[84] See *supra*, at 617–19.

BGH, 14 October 1992[85]   **5.G.29.**

GOOD FAITH

The German reunification

The theory of the disappearance of the contractual basis should be implemented in order to save the contract taking into account good faith requirements.

Facts: The parties are former state undertakings in East Germany which were transformed into private limited companies. Following an order by the predecessor in title of the plaintiff, VEB Berliner A. E. Fabrilx and following confirmation on 10 January 1990 by the predecessor in title of the defendant, VEB E. Export Import, a contract was entered into for the importation of a pressurised milling machine at an agreed price of 1,706,000 Ostmarks. Delivery of the machine was to form part of a reconstruction plan envisaged by the State. In respect of 1990 the financial needs for achievement of the plan were estimated at 7,675,000 Ostmarks which were to be borne as to 50% by means of a subsidy and as to the remainder by a loan from the defendant. On 14 December 1989 the plan which provided, *inter alia*, for the acquisition of the machine in question was approved by the Council of Ministers and included in the economic plan.

The machine supplied to the plaintiff by an Austrian manufacturer at a price of AS 2,644,259 was imported by the plaintiff on 27 March 1990, and the defendant took delivery of it on 26 April 1990. The Deutsche Aussenhandelsbank granted the defendant a loan of 1,706,000 Ostmarks. On 4 April 1990 the plaintiff called for payment of the agreed price. From April to June 1990 the defendant endeavoured to secure the financial aid provided for under the plan. It obtained only a part of the credit facility. On 27 June 1990 BS Bank AG advanced a loan of 376,806,90 Ostmarks. That sum was paid to the plaintiff on 29 June 1990. However, the defendant could secure no subsidy and was informed that it would not be receiving any additional credit facility.

The plaintiff brought an action for payment of the price laid down in the contract, the defendant being liable in the amount of DM 664,597 (1,706,000—376,806.90 = 1,329,193.90 Ostmarks = DM 664,597, following monetary union on 1 June 1990).

The defendant argued that it was not bound to pay the price inasmuch as the price was agreed before monetary union on the basis of State provisions. The Ostmark price could no longer be called for after entry into force of the Regulation of 25 June 1990. The initial price of the machine amounted to DM 376,806.90, the DM equivalent to the agreed price in Austrian schillings. The plaintiff's profit margin is 2.5% and the officially agreed exchange rate (*Richtungskoeffizienten*) 240% which does not form part of the price but is an official conversion method and, as such, a typical tool used by a centralised, planned economy to manipulate prices.

Held: The Commercial Chamber of the Berlin Landgericht upheld the claim. On appeal the Kammergericht set aside the decision at first instance and ordered the defendant to pay the amount of DM 451,346.55 together with interest at the rate of 28%. That decision was revised by the BGH.

Judgment: The BGH considers that the East German law cannot be applied inasmuch as the law on contracts was repealed on 1 July 1990.

The court below took the view that the defendant was entitled to a reduction in price under § 242 BGB which is applicable to contracts entered into before the entry into force of the BGB in the East German zone. It is of no relevance that the defendant was unable to secure credit. Certainly, it was provided in the contract that the acquisition would be financed as to 50% by a credit. However, a debtor may never plead refusal of a loan in support of financial difficulties. The decisive factor for the purposes of § 242 is that the defendant did not secure the subsidy provided for in the East Germany's budget. Both parties had in mind on the creation of the contract that the acquisition of the machine formed part of an economic plan and that it would be financed as to 50% by a subsidy.

As a result of the failure of the plan at the time the contract was entered into and of the consequent impossibility of seeking the subsidy, the contractual basis disappeared. With the disappearance of the subsidy corresponding to 50% of the investment, performance of the contract at the agreed price constitutes an unforeseeable burden for the defendant. After transformation of the parties into share-capital companies, the requirements of good faith make it inappropriate to allow such a burden to be imposed on the defendant.

[85] BGHZ 120.10.

The BGH recalls that the contractual basis is constituted by the intentions of the two parties respectively. In this case the intention to enter into legal relations was dependent upon the economic plan. Whilst the BGH was entitled to consider that refusal of aid did not amount to disappearance of the contractual basis, it should be emphasised that the defendant had no freedom of choice and had to implement the plan. On the adjustment of the contract the requirements of good faith have to be taken into account. It is a question as a matter of principle of upholding the contract as far as possible and of adapting it in the interests of the parties to the new circumstances.

Note

The German reunification has given rise to numerous decisions of which the 1992 judgment is a very good example. It renews the theory of disappearance of the contractual basis, whilst at the same time having direct regard to the principle of good faith in § 242 BGB.

The notion of disappearance of the contract as the ultimate remedy, to be used only if an adjustment is not possible, had already been used by the BGH in a judgment of 11 February 1958.[86] "Disappearance of the contractual basis must not lead systematically and as a matter of priority to cancellation of the contract but rather to an adaptation of the contractual obligations to the changed circumstances." That stance had already been adopted in the 1922 judgments. That adaptation may be made in various ways: lessening performance in kind, price reductions, postponement of due dates, or performance by instalments, compensation, etc.

Contrary to fears expressed, particularly by French academic writers, judicial revision in the event of disappearance of the contractual basis is not a threat to security of contract because the German courts use it conscientiously and with moderation. That is why the German model has been followed and codified in a number of national laws and adopted in certain harmonising instruments, which go further than the CISG.

The solutions adopted by the German courts have been formalized with slight variations by subsequent codes.

Codice civile[87] **5.I.30.**

Article 1467: *Synallagmatic contracts (corrispettive).* In continuing or periodic contracts, or where performance is deferred, if performance by one of the parties has become excessively onerous as a result of the occurrence of exceptional or unforeseeable events, the party liable for performance under such conditions may apply for termination of the contract which will entail the effects laid down in Article 1458.

Article 1468: *Contract with obligations on one of the parties only.* In the case mentioned in the preceding article, if the contract merely provides for performance by one of the parties, that party may apply for a lessening of performance or an alteration in the manner of performance which must be sufficient for the contract to proceed on an equitable basis.

Article 1469: *Speculative contract (contratto aleatorio).* The provisions of the preceding articles shall not apply to contracts which are speculative in nature or according to the intentions of the parties.

[86] NJW 1457.785.
[87] These Articles of the Italian *Codice civile* belong to Section III on *eccessiva onerosità* of Chapter XIV on "Termination of Contracts".

Article 6:258: (1) Upon the demand of one of the parties, the judge may modify the effects of a contract, or he may set it aside in whole or in part on the basis of unforeseen circumstances which are of such a nature that the co-contracting party, according to criteria of reasonableness and equity, may not expect that the contract be maintained in an unmodified form. The modification or the setting aside of the contract may be given retroactive force.

(2) The modification or the setting aside of the contract is not pronounced to the extent that the person invoking the circumstances should be accountable for them according for them according to the nature of the contract or common opinion.

(3) For the purposes of this article, a person to whom a contractual right or obligation has been transferred, is assimilated to a contracting party.

Principles of European Contract Law   **5.PECL.32.**

Article 6:111: *Change of Circumstances*

(1) A party is bound to fulfil its obligations even if performance has become more onerous, whether because the cost of performance has increased or because the value of the performance it receives has diminished.

(2) If, however, performance of the contract becomes excessively onerous because of a change of circumstances, the parties are bound to enter into negotiations with a view to adapting the contract or ending it, provided that:

(a) the change of circumstances occurred after the time of conclusion of the contract,

(b) the possibility of a change of circumstances was not one which could reasonably have been taken into account at the time of conclusion of the contract, and

(c) the risk of the change of circumstances is not one which, according to the contract, the party affected should be required to bear.

(3) If the parties fail to reach agreement within a reasonable period, the court may:

(a) end the contract at a date and on terms to be determined by the court; or

(b) adapt the contract in order to distribute between the parties in a just and equitable manner the losses and gains resulting from the change of circumstances.

In either case, the court may award damages for the loss suffered through a party refusing to negotiate or breaking off negotiations contrary to good faith and fair dealing.

These three provisions may usefully be compared as follows:

—conditions of unforeseeability (excessive burdens, criteria of reason and equity and reliance by the other party);

—implementing rules (obligation to renegotiate, proposal by defendant for equitable amendment of the provisions of the contract);

—result (rescission, amendment, retroactivity).[88]

---

[88] See also art. 388 of the Greek Civil Code and art. 6:21, 6:22 and 6:23 of the Unidroit Principles.

5.3. CLAUSES DEALING WITH SUPERVENING EVENTS

The parties may attempt by agreement to make provision for situations arising from the occurrence of "perturbing" events, despite the fact that they cannot know whether those events will arise. Such situations include monetary depreciation, strikes, embargoes, etc. Clauses of that type are particularly useful in long-term contracts, in which the circumstances existing at the time when the contract is entered into may well alter during the course of its term. They may assist in the determination of conditions in which situations of *force majeure* or unforeseen circumstances are to be deemed to have arisen, since those conditions are frequently uncertain. They may also be designed to regulate the consequences which such situations are to have in relation to the contract, by providing either that it is to cease to be effective or that its terms are to be adjusted. They enable the parties, in principle, to avoid having recourse to the courts. They must be distinguished from clauses which define the scope of the performance or consideration to be provided: there is no point in debating the effects which *force majeure* may have on a deadline which is stated in the contract to be for guidance purposes only. By the same token, they are different from clauses excluding liability or penalty clauses, which are applicable only in the event of failure to perform on the part of the party from whom performance is due.

Clauses dealing with supervening events are to be found, in particular, in international contracts;[89] however, they have also found their way into domestic legal systems, in which they are on occasion the subject of specific qualifications and prohibitions. Of these, the most strict are frequently requirements relating to public policy—or *ordre public*, for example, public policy in monetary matters.

Amongst the numerous types of clauses encountered in practice, those most often used are indexation clauses (*infra*, **5.3.1.**), *force majeure* clauses (*infra*, **5.3.2.**) and hardship or saving clauses (*infra*, **5.3.3.**).

5.3.1. INDEXATION CLAUSES

These clauses are designed to provide against future price changes, arising generally from disorders of a monetary nature. The circumstances arising have already been encountered in the context of unforeseen events. Numerous examples spring to mind, including the paper money (*assignats*) crisis in France during the Revolution, the plummeting of the German Mark in the aftermath of the First World War and the semi-permanent inflation which set in following the end of the Second World War. Exchange rate fluctuations may also be provoked by economic factors—as in the case of the oil crises—or political factors—such as the closure of the Suez Canal, the Gulf War, etc.

Such circumstances make it very difficult to determine with any certainty the price to be paid—for goods, services, etc.—under a long-term contract. The legal problems which

---

[89] See Fontaine (ed.), *Droit des contrats internationaux. Analyse et rédaction de clauses* (Paris: FEDUCI, 1989) which lists many such contracts.

may arise in relation to the determination of the price—involving, *inter alia*, the degree of certainty with which it can be determined, "open price" clauses, subsequent unilateral price determination, etc.[90]—have already been considered.

In addition, it is necessary to have regard to monetary issues, such as the principle of monetary nominalism—a pound remains a pound, whatever its purchasing power may be—and the system of legal tender and of the forced value of a currency. In addition, a distinction is universally drawn between the currency of account—which is used to evaluate the debt—and the currency of payment—which is used to discharge the debt.

Various clauses have been formulated in practice to provide for variations in the amount to be paid on the due date, depending on fluctuations in the price of gold, foreign exchange and economic indices, etc. Other, similar clauses provide for prices to vary in accordance with the most favourable terms offered by competitors or terms agreed to by other customers—competitive offer clauses, most-favoured-customer clauses, etc.

The lawfulness of such clauses, and especially of what are known as "monetary" clauses—linked to gold, gold values, foreign currencies, etc.—will depend on the degree of importance attached to public policy concerning monetary matters in a given country. At international level, the importance of public policy requirements is diminished, by force of circumstance. As we will see, the rules relating to indexation clauses differ according to the laws under consideration.

5.3.1.A. Indexation clauses under English law

Introductory Note
The validity of indexation clauses has been the subject of less debate than in other countries, doubtless because the pound sterling has proved to be a more stable currency than certain others. It is true that Lord Denning has stated that a clause linked to the value of gold in a domestic contract "is disturbing";[91] but his view was not shared by the other judges.

Chancery Division   **5.E.33.**
Multiservice Bookbinding v. *Marden*[92]

Index-link to foreign currency valid

Link to Swiss franc

A clause linking the amount of capital and interest to be due under a loan agreement to the value of the Swiss franc is not contrary to public policy.

Facts: A mortgage was granted in 1966 to secure capital and interest payments in respect of a debt which was index-linked to the value of the Swiss franc. That debt was repayable at the end of a term of ten years. Repayment was demanded in 1976; the validity of the clause was challenged on the ground that the value of the pound had fallen from twelve Swiss francs in 1966 to four Swiss francs in 1976. Two defences were advanced: the first, adopting Lord Denning's arguments, asserted that the clause was contrary to public policy, and the second maintained that it was unlawful by reason of the usurious rate applied by it.

---

[90] See *supra*, at 194.
[91] *Treseder Griffin* v. *Cooperative Insurance Society* [1958] 2 All ER 33.
[92] [1978] 2 All ER 489.

Held: The two defences were rejected. [Discussion of the second defence is not extracted here.]

Judgment: BROWNE-WILKINSON J: . . . I deal first with the question of public policy. The plaintiffs' case on this issue is based entirely on certain statements made by Denning LJ in *Treseder-Griffin* v. *Co-operative Insurance Society Ltd.* [1956] 2 QB 127. That case concerned the effect of a clause in a long lease which provided for the payment

> "yearly during the said term either in gold sterling or Bank of England notes to the equivalent value in gold sterling the rent of £1,900 . . . by equal quarterly payments . . ."

The main point at issue was one of construction, which does not touch the present case. But in the Court of Appeal, Denning LJ said, at pp. 144, 145:

> "This is the first case, so far as I know, to come before our courts where the parties have inserted a 'gold clause' in a domestic contract where all the parties are within our own country. In external transactions it is, of course, quite common for parties to protect themselves against a depreciation in the rate of exchange by means of a gold clause. But in England we have always looked upon a pound as a pound, whatever its international value. We have dealt in pounds for more than a thousand years—long before there were gold coins or paper notes. In all our dealings we have disregarded alike the debasement of the currency by kings and rulers or the depreciation of it by the march of time or events. This is well shown by the Case *de Mixed Moneys* (1604) Davies's Rep. 48. Creditors and debtors have arranged for payment in our sterling currency in the sure knowledge that the sum they fix will be upheld by the law. A man who stipulates for a pound must take a pound when payment is made, whatever the pound is worth at that time. Sterling is the constant unit of value by which in the eye of the law everything else is measured. Prices of commodities may go up or down, other currencies may go up and down, but sterling remains the same."

Then after referring to an example of that principle:

> "The principle which I have stated is so well established that it is disturbing to find a creditor inserting a gold clause in a domestic transaction. I am not altogether sure that it is lawful. In the United States gold clauses are declared by the joint resolution of Congress to be contrary to public policy: see *Rex* v. *International Trustee for the Protection of Bondholders Aktiengesellschaft* [1937] AC 500. In Canada they are rendered inoperative by the Gold Clauses Act 1937: see *New Brunswick Railway Co.* v. *British and French Trust Corporation Ltd.* [1939] AC 1. Many other countries have like legislation. In France, ever since the Franco-Prussian War, the Cour de cassation has ruled that gold clauses are invalid in the case of internal contracts for payments in France by the French people; but they are valid in the case of international payments, that is, which involve a traffic across international frontiers. Those countries do it, I suppose, to protect their own currencies. If we are now to hold gold clauses valid in England for internal payments, we may be opening a door through which lessors and mortgagees, debenture holders and preference shareholders, and many others, may all pass. We might find every creditor stipulating for payment according to the price of gold; and every debtor scanning the bullion market to find out how much he has to pay. What, then, is to become of sterling? It would become a discredited currency unable to look its enemy inflation in the face. That should not be allowed to happen."

MORRIS LJ, who with Denning LJ constituted the majority of the Court of Appeal on the construction point, expressed no view on the public policy point. Harman J, who dissented on the construction point, expressly said, at p. 163, that such a clause was not unlawful even in a domestic contract.

Mr Nugee, who appeared for the plaintiffs, contended that the remarks of Denning LJ formed a separate ground of decision which was binding on me. I cannot think that that is right. Denning LJ prefaced the material passage by the words, and I quote, at p. 145, "I am not altogether sure that it is lawful." These are not words of decision but of doubt. Therefore in my opinion Denning LJ's dictum is not strictly binding on me. But of course it carries great weight.

I have had the point elaborately argued before me by distinguished counsel, and after considering the arguments I do not feel that in 1977 I can declare that an index-linked money obligation is contrary to public policy.

The reasons which lead me to this view are as follows:

(1) If, as Denning LJ said, the evil to be guarded against is that sterling will become discredited, this evil will flow not only from indexing by reference to the price of gold or Swiss franc, but equally

from any other form of indexing, for example an obligation quantified by reference to the cost of living index. The evil lies in the revalorization of the pound sterling by reference to any other yardstick, not in the nature of the yardstick itself.

(2) Today a large number of obligations originally expressed in pounds sterling are varied by reference to an external yardstick. Long-term commercial contracts frequently include index linked obligations: so do many contracts of employment. The rent payable under certain leases has for centuries been made variable dependent upon the price of corn. More important, Parliament itself has authorised the linking of public service pensions to the cost of living and the issue of Savings Bonds similarly linked. It would be strange if Parliament had authorised transactions contrary to public policy.

(3) Denning LJ treated the process of index-linking as being a cause, not a symptom, of inflation. I know nothing of economics but it has been demonstrated to me that economists are not agreed that indexing has a deleterious effect in promoting inflation. It would, in my judgment, be wrong for the courts to declare that a particular class of transaction is against the public interest even though there is a body of better-informed opinion that takes the view that no harm is caused. It is for Parliament, with all its facilities for weighing the complex issues involved, to make a policy decision of this kind.

(4) It seems to me that, even if there are good grounds for saying that indexing causes inflation, there may well be counter-availing considerations which would have to be weighed. In any economy where there is inflation there are few inducements to make long-term loans expressed in a currency the value of which is being eroded. It is at least possible that, unless lenders can ensure that they are repaid the real value of the money they advanced, and not merely a sum of the same nominal amount but in devalued currency, the availability of loan capital will be much diminished. This would surely not be in the public interest.

(5) Shortly after 1956, the Cour de cassation in France reversed its policy referred to by Denning LJ and allowed index-linked obligations even in domestic contracts. Index-linked obligations were held valid by the High Court of Australia in *Stanwell Park Hotel Co. Ltd.* v. *Leslie* (1952) 85 CLR 189.

Therefore I feel unable to follow the obiter dictum of Denning LJ I need hardly say that I do so with considerable diffidence; but I receive some comfort from the fact that since he expressed his views, we have experienced 20 years of inflation and, on the somewhat analogous question whether a judgment of an English court can be expressed otherwise than in pounds sterling, he has departed from the nominalist principle which underlies his remarks in the *Treseder-Griffin* case [1956] 2 QB 127. In my judgment, clause 6 of the mortgage is not contrary to public policy. . . .

Notes

(1) See, to the same effect, also in relation to a mortgage loan: *National Building Society* v. *Registry of Friendly Societies*.[93]

(2) In *Multiservice Bookbinding* v. *Marden* the judge was prompted, not without some diffidence, to criticize Lord Denning. He considered that he was not bound by the latter's dictum, which was a statement of doubt and did not have binding force; and he took the view that there had been a change of circumstances over the course of twenty years. It is interesting to note the recourse had to comparative law, both by Lord Denning and by Browne-Wilkinson J Reference is made not only to the common law systems—in the United States, Canada and Australia—but also to the most recent French case-law.[94]

---

[93] [1983] 3 All ER 296.
[94] Browne-Wilkinson J cites indeed the 1957 reversal of precedent effected by the decision, *infra*, **5.E.33.**

The judge considered that there was nothing to preclude the use of indexation clauses in general and, in particular, the use of a clause linked to the value of a foreign currency, such as that at issue in the case under consideration. He took the view that, in 1977, public policy did not preclude such a clause, which had become necessary by reason of the depreciation in the value of the pound. He concluded, departing from the view expressed by Lord Denning, that index-linking was not a cause but a symptom of inflation. Moreover, it was hardly appropriate to condemn a practice which had become commonplace by virtue of general usage and which had even been adopted by the public authorities. In the judge's view, it was not for the courts—which maintain, in any event, a somewhat cautious approach to the extension of public policy by the creation of "new heads"—to declare such a practice to be unlawful; that is a matter solely for Parliament, which alone possesses the facilities for weighing all the issues involved. And, by contrast with what happened in France, the British Parliament has not intervened in the matter.

5.3.1.B. INDEXATION CLAUSES UNDER GERMAN LAW

Introductory Note
Germany has been the chief country to be hit by a wave of galloping inflation: it is this which has given rise to the formulation in German case-law of the doctrine of *Wegfall der Geschäftsgrundlage* or disappearance of the contractual basis—sometimes referred to as the doctrine of *clausula rebus sic stantibus*—, which entails the modification of the contract. Although the nominalist principle continues to be the underlying rule, it has been modified by that case-law.

In Germany, therefore, indexation clauses are less important than elsewhere. However, the aftermath of the Second World War saw the enactment, on 18 June 1948, of the Currency Act (*Währungsgesetz*), which reformed the monetary system and provided for the replacement of the Reichsmark by the new Deutschmark. Under that statute, indexation clauses were subjected to a system of control.

Währungsgesetz of 18 June 1948 **5.G.34.**

§ 3: Save where special authorisation is granted by the body empowered to control monetary policy, money-debts may not be contracted in any currency other than the German mark. The same rule shall apply to debts the amount of which in DM is to be linked to the exchange rate of another currency, to the price or quantity of fine gold or of other goods, or to the price of benefits or services.

This regime does not apply to legal transactions concluded between residents and non-residents.

The authorizations in question are issued by the Bundesbank. In 1978, it published, by way of guidance, a schedule of clauses for which authorization is required and of those for which it is not required. Practitioners in that sphere have gone to considerable lengths in their efforts to formulate clauses which circumvent the requirements laid down by the statute; they have been assisted in that regard by the applicable case-law, which has taken the view that the legislation must be narrowly construed, inasmuch as it constitutes a restriction on the principle of contractual freedom.[95]

[95] See BGH, 17 September 1954, BGHZ 14.306; BGH, 3 July 1981, BGHZ 81.135.

Certain clauses, regarded as excessively inflationary, cannot be authorized under any circumstances; these include indexation clauses linked to obligations relating to money trading or the capital markets—loans, insurance, etc.—"upwards only" clauses, and clauses based on the price of gold, the purchasing power of the DM, average wage levels or average pension levels. Other clauses may circumvent the need for authorization, depending on the classification applied to them.

BGH, 4 March 1964[96]   **5.G.35.**

RENT REVIEW BY THIRD PARTY VALID

"Performance proviso" clauses (*Leistungsvorbehalte*)

A clause which permits the rent of a building to be reviewed by a third party after five years if during that time there has been a significant change in economic circumstances is valid.

Facts: On 8 December 1954 the plaintiff let to the defendants, for a term of ten years, a shop having a surface area of 73.6 square metres, a cellar and some garages, at an annual rent of DM 5.340, together with DM 40 for the cellar and DM 70 for the garages. Clause 14 of the lease stipulated:

"Following the expiry of a period of five years, the parties may demand a rent review if the economic circumstances have altered appreciably in the interim. In the event that the parties are unable to reach agreement on the new rent, each party may appoint a Hamburg estate agent to act as arbitrator."

The defendants took up occupation of the premises on 27 July 1955. On 26 April 1960, the plaintiff's property manager, asserting that there had been an appreciable change of circumstances, demanded a higher rent pursuant to clause 14 of the contract. Upon that demand being contested by the defendants, the plaintiff brought an action for an order requiring the defendants to appoint an estate agent to act as arbitrator, in order that the new rent might be determined.

Held: The Landgericht allowed the plaintiff's claim. Its judgment was set aside by the Oberlandesgericht, and the latter court's decision was in turn reviewed by the Bundesgerichtshof.

Judgment: Discussion: According to the analysis applied by the Oberlandesgericht, clause 14 is to be construed as meaning that a new determination of the rent may be demanded by one of the parties only if it is established that there has been a significant change in the cost of living or an economic crisis. The question to be decided is what is meant by the term "significant change". The OLG interpreted clause 14 of the contract too restrictively. The intention of the parties was to provide for the possibility of modifying the contract in the event of an appreciable alteration in the economic circumstances. Contrary to the findings made by the OLG, such an alteration may occur even though the currency is stable and there has been no significant change in the cost of living index. For the purposes of assessing the scope and meaning of the phrase in issue, it is necessary to have regard to the fact that we are concerned here not with the letting of a residential dwelling but with commercial premises.

Where such a clause is contained in a commercial lease, it must take effect in the event of a substantial alteration in the economic situation as a whole, and not merely in relation to price stability and the cost of living. Between 1955 and 1960, the German economy expanded to an extraordinary extent.

Decision: Thus, on a proper construction of its meaning, clause 14 does not become operative solely in the event of a monetary crisis or a substantial alteration in the cost of living; the clause is clear, and does not allow of any other interpretation.

[96] NJW 1964.1021.

Note

The exemption from the need to obtain authorization was based on the fact that the rent review was not to occur automatically. In this case, the amount of the new rent was to be determined by a third party appointed by the parties. This could have been done by the parties themselves. It is interesting to note the statements made by the BGH concerning the correct way of assessing whether there had been a change of circumstances; this was to be considered in the light of the economic situation—which, in the present case, was booming—as a whole, and not merely by reference to the monetary situation and the cost of living—which were, in the present case, stable.

BGH, 6 December 1978[97]   **5.G.36.**

UNAUTHORISED CLAUSE MAY BE REPLACED IF PARTIES SO AGREED

Clause "to be adjusted by court"

A rent-review clause which will require adjustment after a short period is invalid without authorization. However, the parties may provide in the contract for the court to adjust it so as to validate it.

Facts: The plaintiff, who had constructed a building in 1972, let it to the defendant for commercial use until 31 December 1978. The parties agreed a rent of DM 80 per square metre. Clause 6 of the contract provided for indexation linked to the cost of living index. In addition, clause 20 contained a nullity provision, in the following terms: "In the event that any stipulation contained in this contract proves to be invalid, it shall be adjusted and adapted in such a way as to enable the object which it seeks to achieve to be attained as far as possible. The contract shall in any event remain valid as regards the remaining stipulations contained therein, without the stipulation impugned." The parties did not seek authorization for the indexation clause. The reference index having risen by over ten points, the plaintiff claimed a proportional increase in the rent from 1 April 1973 until 31 October 1974. In addition, the plaintiff applied for an order requiring the defendant to accept the transformation of the indexation clause into a "performance proviso" clause.

Held: The Landgericht and the Oberlandesgericht declared the claim to be admissible and well founded. The defendant's appeal on a point of law was dismissed.

Judgment: In order to be valid, the indexation stipulation contained in clause 6 of the contract, providing as it did for a genuine graduated scale, required the grant of authorisation by the central bank pursuant to the third sentence of § 3 of the Währungsgesetz. That authorisation could not be taken for granted, since the lease had been concluded for a term of less than ten years.

In view of the fact that the indexation clause was not capable of being valid, the OLG correctly examined whether there might be grounds for considering, by means of a supplementing interpretation of the contract, that the parties had intended to provide for the substitution of an alternative clause. According to the appellant, such an interpretation could not be validly applied, since the parties knew that the clause was invalid and that there was no prospect of its being authorised. The BGH does not share that view.

According to the OLG, the parties wished to be able subsequently to alter the amount of the rent. There is nothing to indicate whether the parties knew that the same goal, more or less, could equally well be attained by using either an indexation clause or a "performance proviso" clause, which did not require authorisation.

The BGH considers, having regard to the objective aimed at by the contract, that the parties intended to provide for a clause other than the indexation clause which would safeguard their interests and which would be valid. The substitution of a clause not requiring authorisation in place of

---

[97] NJW 1979.2250.

the indexation clause corresponds to the intentions of the parties, as is apparent from clause 20. The clause substituted by the OLG is in conformity with the interests of both parties, on the basis of a supplementing interpretation. It reflects the intention of the contracting parties as expressed in clause 6, and makes it possible for the rent to be varied in accordance with fluctuations in the cost of living index.

Inasmuch as the parties have been unable to reach agreement concerning the change to be made to the amount of the rent, the plaintiff is entitled to adjust it on the basis of the cost of living index (§§ 315, 316 BGB). Thus it should be adjusted having regard to equitable principles.

Note

It is interesting to note here the efforts made by the courts to save the contract. The initial "graduated scale" clause had not been authorized, and was incapable of being authorized in view of the excessively short term of the contract. However, the contract contained a clause providing for it to be salvaged in the event of the nullity of the clause at issue, and the courts applied to it a bold interpretation founded on equitable principles. One wonders, in the circumstances, what purpose was served by declaring the unauthorized clause to be null and void.

Another type of clause is the "*Spannungsklausel*", otherwise known as a "tension" clause or "divergence" clause.

BGH, 25 May 1977[98]   **5.G.37.**

"Tension clauses" (*Spannungsklausel*)

In the case of a continuing contract providing a "tension clause", a modification of the equivalence between the service provided could be demanded only if there was an imbalance between the obligations which formed part of a long-term phenomenon.

Facts: In 1972 the plaintiffs purchased from the defendant a single-occupation dwelling house. The supply of fuel for heating and hot water in the houses on the estate was provided by a business owned by the defendant. Paragraph L of the notarially recorded sale contract, dated 18 January 1972, provided: "Water and heating is to be supplied from a thermal boiler plant. The price per calorific unit shall correspond to that charged by the municipal boiler undertaking." The general terms and conditions of supply were to be such that the customer was not placed in a less advantageous position than if the supplies had been made from the municipal boiler, and were to be equivalent to the latter's terms. The prices charged for supplies were not to be higher than those charged by the municipal boiler undertaking. The municipal boiler undertaking supplied its customers with heating on the basis of a standard-form contract, at a price made up of a price relating to the annual provision of services and a price relating to the labour corresponding to the quantity of heat supplied. Each customer could choose one of two different tariffs. The standard-form contract contained a "tension" clause geared to the price of coal, the transport cost and the hourly rate of the employees concerned.

The parties disagreed as to the price to be charged for the provision of supplies to the plaintiff's house.

Held: The Landgericht ordered the defendant to supply the plaintiff, throughout the year, with hot water and heating at the rate charged by the municipality. The Oberlandesgericht upheld the judgment of the lower court and the appeal lodged on a point of law against its decision was dismissed. The BGH confirmed the decision.

Judgment: Under the contract concluded between the parties, the defendant is required to supply hot water and heating to the plaintiff at the price charged by the municipal boiler undertaking. The

---

[98] NJW 1977.2262.

defendant may free himself from that obligation by pleading, on the basis of the principles of good faith (§ 242 BGB), that the circumstances underlying the contract have ceased to exist. In support of his arguments, the defendant maintains that the oil crisis has brought about an increase in the price of raw materials which has imposed a very heavy financial burden; he further claims that the municipality uses coal, not fuel oil. The appellate court rightly took the view that, when the crisis came to an end, the prices of coal and of fuel oil were similar to those prevailing at the commencement of the contractual relationship. In the case of a continuing contract, a modification of the equivalence between the service provided could be demanded only if there was an imbalance between the obligations which formed part of a long-term phenomenon. Variations in the relative prices of coal and of fuel oil fall within the sphere of activities of the undertaking concerned, which must bear the risk in that regard, since that risk is not highly unreasonable. It should be noted, moreover, that it is open to the defendant to choose between two sources of heat production.

Note
The contract, which was of a relatively complex nature, contained a "tension" clause linking the price level to variations in the cost of similar goods or services: the "tension" between the two—in this instance, coal and fuel oil—was to remain constant. It is interesting to note the link with the doctrine of unforeseeability, which was also pleaded in this case—to no avail.

The highly liberal approach taken by the case-law has had the effect of restricting considerably the scope of those cases in which the authorization of the Bundesbank is required.

5.3.1.C. INDEXATION CLAUSES UNDER FRENCH LAW

Introductory Note
The history of indexation clauses has been far more chaotic under French law. In the aftermath of the paper money (*assignats*) crisis at the time of the French Revolution, the Civil Code formulated the principle of monetary nominalism in relation to loans, and this is regarded as applying to all money debts.

Code civil **5.F.38.**

Article 1895: The obligation resulting from the lending of money shall at all times be to pay, in numerical terms, the sum specified in the contract.
In the event that there occurs an increase or decrease in the value of cash prior to the time at which payment is to be made, the debtor shall be required to repay, in numerical terms, the sum lent, and repayment of that sum shall be effected only in the coin constituting legal tender at the time when the payment is made.

As we have seen, French law does not countenance any revaluation by the courts to allow for monetary depreciation.[99]

The approach adopted in relation to indexation clauses, whether or not linked to monetary factors, has fluctuated and varied over the years. The judgment in what has come to be known as the *Matter* doctrine—named after the *Avocat général* who proposed the

---

[99] See *supra*, at 627 ff.

decision adopted in the court's decision—recognized the validity of clauses linked to gold in international contracts, subject to the possible application of exchange control rules. In French domestic law, by contrast, the position was different: whilst clauses linked to the value of gold and of foreign currencies were in principle considered to be contrary to public policy, clauses providing for a graduated scale were regarded as valid, subject to certain reservations the scope of which was sometimes uncertain, especially in cases involving the lending of sums of money.[100]

Thereafter, the Cour de cassation, by a conscious reversal of precedent, lifted all restrictions.

Cass. civ. 1re, 27 June 1957[101]   **5.F.39.**

INDEX-LINKING IN DOMESTIC CONTRACT VALID

Guyot

A clause in a domestic loan agreement indexing the amount to be repaid under a loan to the price of corn is valid.

Facts: A loan of a sum of money was index-linked to the price of corn prevailing as at the date on which the debt was to be repaid. The debtor pleaded that the indexation clause was void.

Held: The court of first instance upheld the creditor's claim; the debtor's appeal against the judgment was dismissed.

Judgment: THE COURT—*On the two appeal grounds considered together*:—Whereas Mr Praquin, a grain trader, lent the sum of 350,000 francs to Mr and Mrs Guyot, who were farmers; as, according to the contract, that sum corresponded, at the time when the contract was concluded, to the value of 500 quintals of corn, and the borrowers were required to discharge the debt in seven annual instalments, the first six of which each were to correspond to the value of 70 quintals of corn and the seventh of which was to correspond to the value of 80 quintals by reference to the price of corn prevailing at the date when the instalments respectively fell due or were paid;
—Whereas the price of corn subsequently rose, and Mr and Mrs Guyot refused to pay the sum of 693.000 francs which represented, in consequence of the price increase, the first four instalments; they pleaded that the clause providing for a graduated scale was void. The contested judgment upholding the plaintiff's claim declared the clause to be valid, on the ground that there existed no provision permitting the loan to fall outside the system of ordinary law, under which such a graduated scale is lawful, where, as in the present case, that scale may move upwards or downwards and is therefore incapable of frustrating the operation of the applicable monetary laws, evidencing instead merely the parties' intention to provide against economic instability.
—Whereas the appellants criticise the conclusion reached by the cour d'appel, arguing that it disregarded the *ordre public* consideration inherent in the rule laid down by Article 1895 of the Civil Code, which provides that a person borrowing a sum of money is required only to repay, in numerical terms, the sum lent; they further maintain that the contested judgment infringes the monetary laws establishing the forced currency, since, in their submission, the clause in issue can only have been intended to frustrate the operation of those laws.
—Whereas, however, the clause at issue is not invalidated by the legislation in question;

---

[100] See Cass. civ., 3 June 1930, DP 1931.1.5; opinion by Matter, annotated by Savatier.
[101] D. 1957.649 annotated by Ripert.

648

—Whereas, first of all, the sole object of Article 1895 is to preclude, where the agreement is silent on the point, any revision by the courts of the terms on which the loan is to be repaid, in the event that application is made for such revision under Article 1892 on the ground that the "quality" of the currency has changed.

—Whereas in the case of a loan of money, the *ordre public* does not actually requires that the borrower should be protected against the free acceptance by him of the risk of an increase in the sum to be repaid, which is intended to preserve the purchasing power of the sum lent, on the basis that the sum repayable is to be assessed in relation to the cost of a commodity, since such borrowers are able to assume risks of similar magnitude when entering into other contracts.

—Whereas it is nor possible to claim that the mandatory nature of Article 1895 is justified by monetary principles which dictate its application on account of some threat allegedly posed to the stability of the currency by clauses providing for such increases, since, as matters stand, the effect of such clauses appears to be too uncertain to justify their being found to be void on the ground that they seriously undermine the security of the savings and credit system.

—Whereas, lastly, alleged *ordre public* consideration can hardly be reconciled with the provisions of Article 1897, concerning loans of commodities, which, in the event of an increase in the price of the commodity lent, requires the borrower in every case to bear the consequences of that increase, irrespective of its cause.

—Whereas the clause in issue rendered is not void by any monetary laws currently in force, since those laws cannot prevent variations in the purchasing power of the currency, which varies with the price of commodities, and cannot preclude the lenders concerned, any more than other creditors, from taking variations in purchasing power into account.

—Whereas, leaving aside the reasons stated by the cour d'appel concerning the reciprocity of the clause and the intention of the parties, which are immaterial, and the criticism of which by the appellant is therefore irrelevant, the contested decision is consequently legally justified.

On those grounds, the appeal is dismissed. . . .

Notes

(1) The position under the relevant case-law had previously been somewhat uncertain as regards money loans, the indexation of which was in some instances regarded as running directly counter to the principle of monetary nominalism, as expressly laid down by the Civil Code in relation to lending. The judgment in *Guyot* sweeps all those reservations aside. It construes Article 1895 on the basis that that provision is not of a mandatory nature. It further states that the threat posed by such indexation clauses to the stability of the currency is too uncertain. Some of the grounds of the judgment appealed against—concerning the reciprocity of the clause and the intention of the parties—which the Cour de cassation expressly disregards had been the subject of particular debate in the court below.

(2) The Belgian Cour de cassation had, moreover, already ruled to the same effect, in relation to a mortgage loan which was index-lined to the pound sterling. The reasons given by the Belgian court were somewhat different. [102]

—Whereas the court below, in stating the grounds on which its contested judgment was based, objected to the loan instrument of 7 August 1925 on the basis that it authorised the lenders to determine the value of the sum lent by reference to the pound sterling, a foreign currency, and that it thus indirectly derogated from the principle of the public interest allegedly enshrined in Article 1895 of the Civil Code.

[102] Cass., 12 May 1932, Pas. 1932.I.167.

—Whereas the clause objected to is designed to secure the lenders against the loss resulting from the possible depreciation of the franc against the pound sterling, so that, by virtue of its cause and its object, it governs legal relations which are different from those envisaged by Article 1895 of the Civil Code.

—Whereas consequently, that provision could not preclude the contracting parties, with a view to maintaining the equivalence of the consideration which each of them was to furnish to the other, from fixing the amount of the capital repayments and interest payments to be made on the due dates, in accordance with the terms complained of . . .

(3) The French legislature—which was authorized at that time to legislate in economic matters by way of orders—reacted immediately, by enacting Article 79–3 of the Order of 30 December 1958 (amended in 1959, 1970 and 1977).

Order of 30 December 1958 **5.F.40.**

Article 79–3: (Order 59–246 of 4 February 1959, Article 14): The provisions contained in any new articles of association, agreement or contract may not, save where they concern maintenance obligations, include any clause stipulating indexation based on the guaranteed minimum wage, the general level of prices or wages or the price of goods, products or services not directly related to the subject-matter of the articles, agreement or contract or to the activity carried on by one of the parties.

(Act 70–600 of 9 July 1970): Any clause contained in an agreement concerning a constructed building which provides for indexation based on variations in the national index of construction costs published by INSEE [*Institut national de la statistique et des études économiques* = National Economic Studies and Statistical Institute] shall be deemed to be directly related to the subject-matter of that agreement.

Any clause providing for such indexation which is contained in any currently existing articles of association, agreement or contract shall cease to have effect beyond the level reached on the last revaluation prior to 31 December 1958, where the provisions of the articles, agreement or contract in question directly or indirectly relate to reciprocal obligations to be performed successively.

(Act 70–600 of 9 July 1970): Any clause in an agreement relating to residential premises which provides for indexation based on the "rent and service charges" index used to determine general indices of retail prices shall be prohibited. The same rule shall apply in relation to any clause providing for indexation based on the rate of statutory increases laid down pursuant to Law No 48–1360 of 1 September 1948, unless the initial amount has been fixed in accordance with the provisions of that Law and of the legislation implementing it.

(Act 77–1457 of 29 December 1977): Where any clause in a continuing contract, in particular a contract relating to a lease or tenancy of any kind, provides for a period of variation of the index which is longer than the period elapsing between each review, that clause shall be deemed to be void.

It will be noted that, save in special cases—maintenance obligations—certain types of indexation are prohibited, whilst others are permissible only where they are "directly related to the subject-matter of the articles, agreement or contract or to the activity carried on by one of the parties".

For example, in the Cour de cassation case of 12 January 1988,[103] a loan of a sum of money was index-linked to the Swiss franc. The Cour de cassation found that the loan was of a domestic nature, and thus subject to the rules enacted in 1958–9.

The court said:

[S]ince it was accepted that the loan was of a domestic nature, the second-instance court rightly held that that contract was subject to Order 59–246 of 4 February 1959 amending the Order of 30 December 1958, which permits indexation only where the indexation in question is directly related to the subject-matter of the agreement or to the activity carried on by one of the parties and thus prohibits the fixing of the debt in a foreign currency, save where one of the contracting parties is a banker or financier. Consequently, the loan at issue could not validly relate to a sum of money expressed in Swiss francs. That loan is therefore unlawful as regards its subject-matter, and hence null and void.

The emphasis on the domestic character of the loan confirms that international contracts remain outside the scope of the legislation concerned—save that payment in France must be made in French francs, as the only currency in which obligations may be discharged, such clauses relating solely to the currency of account. The concept of international payment is also flexible, having been held to constitute a payment forming part of an international transaction.[104]

Consequently, the above judgment refused to countenance indexation based on a foreign currency—in the form of a foreign currency value clause—in a contract between private persons, save where one of the contracting parties—in particular, the lender—is a banker or financier, because in the latter case the indexation is directly related to that party's business.[105] Article 79 does not specify the manner in which unlawful indexation is to be penalized—save in the fourth subparagraph of Article 79–3: "shall be deemed to be void". The nullity is generally regarded as absolute, since the public interest is involved. That being the case, it is necessary to apply the general rule to the effect that it is only the offending clause which is to be deemed void, unless the inclusion of that unlawful clause was a determining factor in the conclusion of the contract.[106] It is not open to the courts, save by means of interpretation, to substitute a valid index in place of an index which is invalid or no longer effective.[107]

A comparative study of German, English and French law may raise questions of what is meant, first of all, by the concept of public policy.[108] Public policy in monetary matters provides a good illustration of the relativeness attaching to the concept at different times and in different places.

The question also arises whether the restrictive measures adopted by French law and German law have been particularly effective, given that they have been watered down by case-law and that practitioners have found ways of circumventing them.[109]

[103] Cass. civ. 1re, 12 January 1988, Rep. Défrénois 1989.169, annotated by P. Malaurie.
[104] Cass. civ. 1re, 13 May 1985, Bull.civ. I.146.
[105] See the judgment in *Multiservice Bookbinding* v. *Marden*, *supra*, at 640, **5.E.33**.
[106] See *supra*, 650.
[107] On the consequences arising from the invalidation of an indexation clause, see the passage relating to hardship clauses, and the judgment of the Paris cour d'appel of 28 September 1976, *infra*, at 655, **5.F.43**. Compare with Cass.civ.3, 15 Feb. 1972, *supra* **4.F.24**, on the possibility to replace a wage scale no longer published, by way of interpretation of the clause.
[108] See *supra* at 295 ff.
[109] See, by way of example in relation to French law, Dion and Thierache, "Faut-il abroger les ordonnances de 1958 et 1959 sur les indexations?", D. 1995, chron. 55.

5.3.2. *FORCE MAJEURE* CLAUSES

It is generally accepted, to a very considerable extent, that the parties may by agreement modify the rules applying under the ordinary law to cases of *force majeure*, either by extending them or by restricting them, and that they may even provide that *force majeure* is not to have the effect of releasing them from their obligations. We have already come across a clause of that type, in the judgment of the French Cour de cassation of 24 January 1995.[110]

Such modifications may relate to the definition of *force majeure*, particularly with a view to avoiding uncertainty concerning the circumstances in which it is to be deemed to exist, the procedure to be followed—for example, the notice to be given—and/or the effect which it is to have on the contract.

Such clauses have been very frequently used in international contracts, but they may also be found in domestic law, in which they appear to raise few problems save as regards their interpretation.[111]

The model *force majeure* (exemption) clause drawn up by the International Chamber of Commerce—text and commentary—illustrates the issues raised by that type of clause. It is not unreasonable to wonder in what respects it modifies the regimes applying under the various domestic legal systems.

ICC force majeure (exemption) clause[112]   **5.INT.41.**

Grounds of relief from liability

1. A party is not liable for a failure to perform any of his obligations in so far as he proves
   —that the failure was due to an impediment beyond his control; and
   —that he could not reasonably be expected to have taken the impediment and its effects upon his ability to perform into account at the time of the conclusion of the contract and
   —that he could not reasonably have avoided or overcome it or at least its effects.

2. An impediment within paragraph (1) above, may result from events such as the following, this enumeration not being exhaustive:
   a) war, whether declared or not, civil war, riots and revolutions, acts of piracy, acts of sabotage;
   b) natural disasters such as violent storms, cyclones, earthquakes, tidal waves, floods, destruction by lightning;
   c) explosions, fires, destruction of machines, of factories, and of any kind of installations
   d) boycotts, strikes and Lockouts of all kinds, go-slows, occupation of factories and premises, and work stoppages which occur in the enterprise of the party seeking relief;
   e) acts of authority, whether lawful or unlawful, apart from acts for which the party seeking relief has assumed the risk by virtue of other provisions of the contract; and apart from the matters mentioned in paragraph 3, below.

3. For the purposes of paragraph 1 above, and unless otherwise provided in the contract, impediment does not include lack of authorisations, of licences, of entry or residence permits, or of

---

[110] Cass. civ. 1re, 24 January 1995, *supra* at 596, **5.F.5**; see also Cass. comm., 8 July 1981, Bull.civ. IV.312.

[111] See, e.g., *Pagnan SpA* v. *Trada Ocean Transport SA* [1987] 3 All ER 564, which featured a combination of the provisions of the normal *force majeure* clause incorporating the general GAFTA conditions and of the clause making the vendor responsible for obtaining an export certificate.

[112] With the kind authorization of the International Chamber of Commerce.

approvals necessary for the performance of the contract and to be issued by a public authority of any kind whatsoever in the country of the party seeking relief

Duty to notify
4. A party seeking relief shall as soon as practicable after the impediment and its effects upon this ability to perform became known to him give notice to the other party of such impediment and its effects on his ability to perform. Notice shall be given when the ground of relief ceases.

5. The ground of relief takes effect from the time of the impediment or, if notice is not timely given, from the time of notice. Failure to give notice makes the failing party liable in damages for loss which otherwise could have been avoided.

Effects of grounds of relief
6. A ground of relief under this clause relieves the failing party from damages, penalties and other contractual sanctions, except from duty to pay interest on money owing as long as and to the extent that the ground subsists.

7. Further it postpones the time for performance, for such period as may be reasonable, thereby excluding the other party's right, if any, to terminate or rescind the contract. In determining what is a reasonable period, regard shall be had to the failing party's interest in receiving performance despite the delay. Pending resumption of performance by the failing party the other party may suspend his own performance.

8. If the grounds of relief subsist for more than such period as the parties provide (the applicable period to be specified here by the parties), or in the absence of such provision for longer than a reasonable period, either party shall be entitled to terminate the contract with notice.

9. Each party may retain what he has received from the performance of the contract carried out prior to the termination. Each party must account to the other for any unjust enrichment resulting from such performance. The payment of the final balance shall be made without delay.

Force Majeure clause—model reference clause
Parties who wish to incorporate this clause by reference in their contracts are recommended to use the following wording:
"The Force Majeure (Exemption) clause of the International Chamber of Commerce (ICC Publication n° 421) is hereby incorporated in this contract".

The influence of the CISG will also be noted.[113]

5.3.3. HARDSHIP CLAUSES

The contracting parties may envisage the occurrence of future events which disrupt the normal operation of the contract without rendering its performance impossible. International practitioners have likewise formulated a whole range of clauses dealing with such circumstances, to which different names have been applied—harshness clauses, saving clauses, renegotiation clauses, hardship clauses, unforeseeability clauses, etc.—and which provide for different outcomes: renegotiation of the contract, intervention by a third party—ombudsman, conciliator—etc. They are frequently combined with arbitration clauses.

[113] See *supra*, at 624, **5.INT.22**.

The International Chamber of Commerce has drawn up "drafting suggestions" in relation to such clauses, which may serve as a basis for discussion.

ICC drafting suggestions for hardship clauses[114]   **5.INT.42.**

Important: this is not a standard clause. It cannot be incorporated in a contract by reference.

1. Should the occurrence of events not contemplated by the parties fundamentally alter the equilibrium of the present contract, thereby placing an excessive burden on one of the parties in the performance of its contractual obligations, that party may proceed as follows:

2. The party shall make a request for revision within a reasonable time from the moment it becomes aware of the event and of its effect on the economy of the contract. The request shall indicate the grounds on which it is based.

3. The parties shall then consult one another with a view to revising the contract on an equitable basis, in order to ensure that neither party suffers excessive prejudice.

4. The request for revision does not of itself suspend performance of the contract.

The provision may then be continued with any one of the following four alternatives.

First alternative

5. If the parties fail to agree on the revision of the contract within a time-limit of 90 days of the request, the contract remains in force in accordance with its original terms.

Second alternative

5. Failing an agreement of the parties on the revision of the contract within a time-limit of 90 days of the request either party may refer the case to the ICC Standing Committee for the Regulation of Contractual Relations in order to obtain the appointment of a third person (or a board of three members) in accordance with the provisions of the rules for the regulation of contractual relations of the ICC. The third person shall give his opinion to the parties as to whether the conditions for revision provided in Paragraph 1 are satisfied. If so, he shall recommend an equitable revision of the contract which ensures that neither party suffers excessive prejudice.

6. The opinion and recommendation of the third person shall not be binding on the parties.

7. The parties will consider the third's person opinion and recommendation in good faith in accordance with Article 11 (2) of the said rules for the regulation of contractual relations. If the parties then fail to agree on the revision of the contract, the contract remains in force in accordance with its original terms.

Third alternative

5. If the parties fail to agree on the revision of the contract within a time-limit of 90 days of the request, either party may bring the issue of revision before the arbitral forum, if any, provided for in the contract, or otherwise the competent courts.

Fourth alternative

5. Failing an agreement of the parties on the revision of the contract within a time-limit of 90 days of the request either party may refer the case to the ICC Standing Committee for the Regulation of Contractual Relations in order to obtain the appointment of a third person (or a board of three members) in accordance with the provisions of the rules for the regulation of contractual

---

[114] With the kind authorization of the International Chamber of Commerce.

relations of the ICC. The third person shall decide on the parties behalf whether the conditions for revision provided in paragraph 1 are satisfied. It so he shall revise the contract on an equitable basis in order to ensure that neither party suffers excessive prejudice.

6. The decision of the third person shall be binding on the parties and shall be deemed to be incorporated in the contract.

Note

Paragraph 1 should be compared to cases of unforeseeability—where it is accepted that the contract may be revised on account of unforeseen circumstances.[115] There is a procedure for renegotiation (paragraphs 2 to 4). Four alternative solutions are proposed, in increasing order of the effects which they have (paragraph 5 *et seq.*).

Hardship clauses are starting to be used in domestic law.

Cour d'appel, Paris, 28 September 1976[116]   **5.F.43.**

RENEGOTIATION UNDER SUPERVISION OF THIRD PARTY ORDERED

Renegotiation of oil supply contract

A clause requiring the parties to consult one another in certain circumstances may be given effect by ordering negotiations under the supervision of a third party.

Facts: The indexation clause in a contract for the provision of oil concluded between EDF and Shell (France) was rendered inoperable (as the parties acknowledged) by the upheaval caused to the market by the oil crisis. The contract contained a saving clause, in the following terms: "In the event of an increase of six francs per tonne in relation to the initial value, the parties shall consult one another with a view to considering the alterations, if any, to be made to the contract (as regards the price or any other clause)". An attempt at conciliation proved abortive.

Held: The Paris tribunal de commerce declared that the contract had become null and void (ie had lapsed) in consequence of the cessation of existence of the price. The cour d'appel reversed the judgment.

Judgment: . . .—Whereas the so-called "saving" clause contained in the contracts provides that, in the event that the price of ordinary fuel oil delivered to its destination increases by more than six francs per tonne in relation to its initial value, the parties are to "consult one another with a view to considering the alterations, if any, to be made to the contract (as regards the price or any other clause)".
—Whereas it is not contested that prices have risen by more than the amount thus provided for. The contracting parties are therefore required, in accordance with the obligation entered into by them, to negotiate such modifications as may have become necessary.
—Whereas the failure of the attempt at conciliation which took place in 1974 did not put an end to that obligation, because, since that time and even now, the parties have manifestly declared their intention to continue to perform the agreements reached between them, the supplier by delivering fuel in return for sums "on account" of the price, and EDF by accepting deliveries on the basis of that reservation concerning the subsequent determination of the new price.
—Whereas the attitude jointly adopted by the contracting parties clearly shows that, far from wanting the agreements to lapse, they simply wish to adapt them to the new circumstances. Consequently, for the purposes of calculating the price and the variations in that price, it falls to them to substitute, in place of a reference mechanism which has ceased to operate or has become inapplicable, a formula

---

[115] See *supra*, **5.2.**, 626 ff.
[116] JCP 1979.II.18810, annotated by Robert.

that will ensure that EDF benefits, in respect of each category of fuel, from a reduced purchase price reflecting the exceptional magnitude of the supplies made to it, in terms of their volume and duration and taking into account the public service provided by that organisation, whilst leaving the oil company with an adequate profit margin; as before any ruling is given on the substance of the case, it is appropriate that the parties be ordered, in accordance with the obligation incumbent upon them, to conclude an agreement on that point, under the auspices of an observer.; as only if those negotiations fail to bear fruit will the Court, in the knowledge of the solutions proposed, declare whether the formula which might possibly be suitable on a financial level (fundamentally) modifies the stipulations laid down by the contracts currently existing and therefore precludes the Court from imposing it, or whether, on the other hand, it is restricted, in accordance with the wishes of the parties, and without altering the basic scheme of the contracts, to adapting the price to the fluctuations in the market and can thus be substituted by the Court of its own motion;

On those grounds; the Court, before giving any ruling as to the substance of the case:

—orders the parties to negotiate with a view to determining, by consent, the new prices of the different categories of fuel oil supplied to EDF and the formula or formulae applicable to variations in those prices; instructs Stéphane Thouvenot, of 74 Rue . . ., to attend the negotiations;

—and orders that, in the event of the failure of those negotiations to bear fruit, the case be referred back to the Court, within six months from the bringing of the proceedings before it, in order for a ruling to be given concerning the substance thereof;—costs reserved.

Note

This is a bold judgment—and it is a pity that the case was not brought before the Cour de cassation; first of all, from a procedural standpoint, in that the Paris cour d'appel decided to order the parties to re-open the negotiations—which was not something for which the parties had applied—under the auspices of an observer—for which the contract had not provided. The Paris cour d'appel even envisaged, not without a certain degree of inconsistency, the possibility of substituting, of its own motion, a formula limited, "without altering the basic scheme of the contracts, to adapting the price to the fluctuations in the market". Two factors played a part: the fact that the parties were continuing to perform the contract and EDF's "public service" function—which brings to mind the acceptance of revision, on account of unforeseen circumstances, of contracts concluded by administrative authorities[117]—notwithstanding that the case in question concerned a contract concluded under private law. The Paris cour d'appel justified its decision by interpreting the contract, thereby seeking to give effect to the real wishes of the parties. Ultimately the parties came to a settlement.

Under English law, it may be asked, echoing McKendrick,[118] what penalty is applicable, in the light of *Walford* v. *Miles*,[119] for failure to comply with the obligation to renegotiate. It may also be asked, with reference to the third alternative, what powers a court may have in the event that the *lex fori* does not authorize revision of the contract owing to unforeseen circumstances, as is the case with French law.

Comparisons may be drawn with "performance proviso" clauses or "tension" clauses under German law,[120] which are quite closely related, although inspired by different motives—requirement of Bundesbank authorisation.

---

[117] See *supra*, at 627.
[118] McKendrick, *Contract* at 232.
[119] [1992] 1 AC 128; *supra*, at 241, **2.E.64**.
[120] See *supra* at 646, particularly **5.G.37.**

Further Reading:
—Carbonnier, at 269–278 (on revision) and 294–302 (on *force majeure*);
—M. Fontaine, "Les clauses de hardship", DPCI 1976.7;
—M. Fontaine (ed.), *Droit des contrats internationaux. Analyse et rédaction de clauses* (Paris: FEDUCI, 1989);
—Ghestin, Jamin and Billiau, para 623 ff.
—Lando and Beale, at 322–8 (on hardship) and 379–85 (on excuse due to an impediment);
—Larenz, *SBT–1* at 97–103 and and 304–43 (on impossibility) and 170–4 (on indexation clauses);
—Malaurie and Aynès, *Obligations* para. 620 ff. (on hardship clauses), para. 827 ff. (on *force majeure* clauses) and para. 993 ff. (on indexation clauses);
—McKendrick, *Contract* para. 14–19 ff.;
—F. Mann, *The Legal Aspect of Money*, 5th edn (Oxford: Clarendon, 1992);
—D. Medicus, *SAT* at 177–89 (on impossibility in general) and 230–8 (on impossibility in synallagmatic contracts);
—P. van Ommerslaghe, "Les clauses de force majeure et d'imprévision dans les contrats internationaux", RDIDC 1980.7;
—B. Oppetit, "L'adaptation des contrats internationaux aux changements de circonstances: la clause de hardship", JDI 1974.794;
—R. Rodière and D. Tallon (eds.), *Les modifications du contrat au cours de son exécution en raison de circonstances monétaires* (Paris: Institut de droit comparé, 1986);
—Schlechtriem, *SAT* at 156–63 (on impossibilty) and 163–70 (on the *Wegfall der Geschäftgrundlage*),
—Terré, Simler and Lequette, para. 449 (on hardship clauses), para. 556 ff. (on *force majeure* clauses) para. 1230 ff. (on indexation clauses);
—G. Treitel, *Frustration and Force Majeure* (London: Sweet & Maxwell, 1994);
—Treitel, *Contract* at 805–863;
—Zweigert and Kötz at 516–36.

CHAPTER SIX
REMEDIES FOR NON-PERFORMANCE

In this chapter we consider the remedies which are available to a party when the other party has failed to perform its contractual obligations and the non-performance is not excused under one of the doctrines concerning "Supervening Events" which were treated in Chapter 5.[1] The remedies covered by the chapter are specific enforcement; withholding of performance; termination; and damages. The chapter also covers reduction of the price and restitutionary claims which may be available after termination.

6.1. FAULT AND THE NATURE OF THE DEBTOR'S OBLIGATION

INTRODUCTORY NOTE

This chapter assumes that the debtor is responsible for the non-performance. On the one hand this means that some obligation under the contract has not been performed. The fact that the creditor has not obtained what she hoped for does not necessarily mean that the debtor has failed to perform. A patient may not have been cured but, if the doctor has done all he should have with reasonable care and skill, the doctor will normally have fulfilled his contractual obligation. On the other hand, it means that if there has been some non-performance of an obligation, the non-performance was not excused. In Chapter 5 we saw that a party may be excused from its obligation to perform because some event, subsequent to the making of the contract and for which the party is not responsible, has made its performance impossible[2] or very much more onerous.[3] The present chapter assumes that there is no such excuse.

The question whether the debtor is responsible for the non-performance or whether he is excused is viewed in rather different terms in the continental and common law traditions. In the continental systems, the question is thought of primarily in terms of what remedies are available against the debtor.[4] For example, as we saw in Chapter 5,[5] if the debtor is excused because of some supervening event, the creditor will be able to withhold her own performance and terminate the contract but she will not be able to claim damages for non-performance. In the common law, in contrast, the question of the debtor's responsibility is viewed as substantive: has there been a breach of contract? If there has not, none of the normal remedies will apply.[6]

---

[1] *Supra* at 592.
[2] *Ibid.*
[3] *Supra* at 626 ff.
[4] See Treitel, *Remedies* at 7–8, para. 8.
[5] *Supra* at 600 ff. and 602 ff.
[6] It will be remembered that in English law, if the contract is frustrated, it is automatically discharged.

The most obvious case in which the debtor is responsible for the non-performance is where the debtor is at fault. It is true that the creditor will normally have the remedies which are to be described in this chapter against a debtor whose non-performance was, in a general sense, its own "fault". The converse, that the remedies will not be available if the debtor was not "at fault", does not follow. Each system is characterized by a significant number of obligations in contract in which there is to some extent "strict" liability, i.e. obligations which will be excused only if the debtor shows something more than that he was not at fault. It is also argued that in each system there are certain obligations which are absolute, in that no excuse for non-performance will be accepted. This is less clear; we will see that it depends on how the obligations in question are described.

6.1.1. THE GERMAN APPROACH

BGB   **6.G.1.**

§ 275: (1) The debtor is relieved from his obligation to perform if the performance becomes impossible because of a circumstance, for which he is not responsible, occurring after the creation of the obligation.
(2) The inability of a debtor to perform after the creation of an obligation is equivalent to subsequent impossibility of performance.

§ 276: (1) A debtor is responsible, unless it is otherwise proved, for wilful conduct and negligence. A person who does not exercise ordinary care acts negligently. The provisions of §§ 827, 828 apply.
(2) A debtor may not be released beforehand from responsibility for wilful conduct.

§ 278: A debtor is responsible for the fault of his legal representative and of persons whom he employs in performing his obligation, to the same extent as for his own fault. The provision of § 276 (2) does not apply.

§ 279: If a debt described by class is owed [generic obligation], and so long as delivery out of this class is possible, the debtor is responsible for his inability to deliver, even though no fault may be imputed to him.

§ 280: (1) Where performance becomes impossible because of a circumstance for which the debtor is responsible, the debtor shall compensate the creditor for any damage arising from the non-performance.
(2) [partial impossibility]

§ 282: If it is disputed whether the impossibility of performance is the result of a circumstance for which the debtor is responsible, the burden of proof falls on the debtor.

§ 284: (1) If after his obligation is due, the debtor does not perform after a warning from the creditor, he is in delay. Bringing an action for performance and service of a judicial order for payment are equivalent to a warning.
(2) [delay where date for performance is fixed by the calendar]

§ 285: The debtor is not in default so long as the performance does not take place because of a circumstance for which he is not responsible.

§ 323: (1) If the performance due from one party under a mutual contract becomes impossible because of a circumstance for which neither he nor the other party is responsible, he loses the claim to counter-performance; in case of partial impossibility the counter performance is diminished in accordance with §§ 472, 473 . . .

§ 324: (1) If the performance due from one party under a mutual contract becomes impossible because of a circumstance for which the other party is responsible, the first party retains his claim for counter-performance. He must, however, deduct what he saves in consequence of release from the performance, or what he acquires or wilfully omits to acquire by a different use of his labour . . .

§ 325: (1) If the performance due from one party under a mutual contract becomes impossible because of a circumstance for which he is responsible, the other party may demand compensation for non-performance, or withdraw from the contract . . .

§ 326: (1) If, in the case of a mutual contract, one party is in delay in performing, the other party may give him a reasonable period within which to perform his part with a declaration that he will refuse to accept the performance after the expiration of the period. After the expiration of the period he is entitled to demand compensation for non-performance, or to withdraw from the contract, if the performance has not been made in due time; the claim for performance is barred . . .

Notes

(1) In the German Civil Code, and in the case law of the BGH, breach of contract is not dealt with as such but is identified through three types of irregularity in performance: impossibility (§§ 275, 325), delay (§§ 284, 326) and positive breach (case law and doctrine). The debtor will be liable in each case only if he is found to be responsible for the irregularity.

(2) § 275 relieves the debtor of his obligation to perform, in the sense that he cannot be ordered to perform, in any case of supervening impossibility; it does not draw a distinction between objective impossibility and subjective impossibility. However whether the debtor was responsible for the impossibility will affect the creditor's right to damages. § 276 BGB states that the debtor will be responsible in cases of negligence or wilful conduct. Thus, the requirement of fault is in principle basic to contractual liability in Germany, though it must be noted that it is not the creditor who must prove fault but the debtor who must disprove it (§ 282 BGB).

(3) § 326 BGB provides that the creditor in a bilateral contract may seek damages for non-performance where the debtor is in delay as per § 284 and where he has failed to respond to a subsequent notice to perform. Alternatively the creditor may withdraw from the contract (*Rücktritt*). The fault requirement of § 285 is thus applicable in these cases.

(4) Liability in generic obligations under § 279 BGB is "strict". The debtor undertakes the risk of not being able to obtain the items sold on the market. It may be said that the debtor in entering such a contract undertakes to have the means to obtain the items sold on the open market. The obligation is strict, therefore, because of the general principle of German law that a debtor is always responsible for his own financial situation. Note that *a fortiori* a debtor of money will also be strictly liable for his failure to pay.[7]

(5) However, "strict" liability under § 279 BGB is not absolute. § 279 only refers to inability to deliver—i.e. subjective impossibility. Objective impossibility within § 275(1)

---

[7] See *Münchener Kommentar* under § 279 BGB, para. 5.

may still be raised as a defence to a claim for non-performance. Thus if the whole *genus* is exhausted or if the State seizes all items of the sort stipulated in the contract or prohibits trading in them—for example in time of war—, § 279 is subjected to a restrictive interpretation and the debtor will not be held liable.[8] Similarly if the debtor's supply was limited in the contract to one particular source (*Vorratsschuld*) he will not be liable if that source is exhausted—for example through destruction or theft—after the formation of the contract.

(6) In addition the doctrine of *Wegfall der Geschäftsgrundlage*, based on the principle of good faith in the performance of contractual obligations (§ 242 BGB), may exceptionally be applicable to allow relief of the debtor from obligations which have become disproportionately burdensome due to supervening circumstances.[9]

(7) The German law of sale also contains obligations of strict liability (*Garantiehaftung*) in relation to defects in goods.

BGB   6.G.2.

§ 459: (1) The seller of a thing warrants the purchaser that, at the time when the risk passes to the purchaser, it is free from defects which diminish or destroy its value or fitness for its ordinary use, or the use provided for in the contract. An insignificant diminution in value or fitness is not taken into consideration.

(2) The seller also warrants that, at the time the risk passes, the thing has the promised qualities.

§ 460: A seller is not responsible for a defect in the thing sold if the purchaser knew of the defect at the time of entering into the contract. If a defect of the kind specified in § 459(1) has remained unknown to the purchaser in consequence of gross negligence, the seller is responsible only if he has fraudulently concealed it, unless he has guaranteed that the thing is free from defect.

§ 462: On account of a defect for which the seller is responsible under the provisions of §§ 459, 460, the purchaser may demand annulment of the sale (cancellation; *Wandlung*), or reduction of the purchase price (reduction; *Minderung*).

§ 463: If a promised quality in the thing sold was absent at the time of the purchase, the purchaser may demand compensation for non-performance, instead of cancellation or reduction. The same applies if the seller has fraudulently concealed a defect.

Notes

(1) The seller's responsibility for defects in goods appears to be absolute: the seller cannot defeat a buyer's claim by showing that it was in no way his fault that the goods were "defective"—for example because no one could have discovered the defect. However, the buyer does not necessarily have the full range of remedies. In the absence of a promise that the goods have a particular quality or fraudulent concealment of a known defect (§ 463) the buyer's only remedies will be cancellation (*Wandlung*) and price reduction (*Minderung*) (§§ 459(1), 462 BGB).

---

[8] Larenz, *AT*, para. 21 I d.
[9] See *supra* at 632.

(2) The presence of particular qualities (§ 459(2) BGB) and thus also freedom from particular defects (§ 460 BGB) may be promised expressly or implicitly. Each case falls to be decided on an interpretation of the particular contract in accordance with §§ 133, 157 BGB.[10] Courts are more likely to find an implicit promise where there was particular reliance by the buyer on the seller's skill and knowledge, for example in sales of automobiles.[11] But the burden of proving that the seller made a promise, or fraudulently concealed the defect, is on the buyer.[12] Therefore the remedies of cancellation and price reduction are still of importance in the German law of sale.

(3) The buyer may choose damages only instead of—i.e. not as well as—reduction or cancellation (§ 463 BGB);[13] where damages are awarded this will be according to the expectation measure.

(4) The extent to which liability under § 459 BGB can be described as absolute is thus debatable. First, as mentioned in note (1), if the seller has not promised that the goods have a particular quality he will be liable only to refund or reduce the price. Secondly, if it is in fact possible to supply goods without the defect in question there is no objective impossibility. Thus the only case in which the seller will be fully liable even though he was in no way at fault and there is "objective" impossibility seems to be when he has promised that the goods have a particular quality which no such goods can have.

6.1.2. THE FRENCH APPROACH

Code civil   **6.F.3.**

Article 1137:   The obligation to take care of a thing, whether the agreement is for the benefit of one party only or for their common benefit, only obliges the party to take reasonable care (*apporter tous les soins d'un bon père de famille*).
This obligation is greater or less in relation to particular contracts, whose effects in this respect are stated in the relevant articles [of the Civil Code].

Article 1147:   The debtor is liable, where appropriate, to pay damages either for non-performance of an obligation, or for delay in performance, in any case in which he does not prove that the non-performance was due to an extraneous cause (*cause étrangère*) which cannot be imputed to him and that there was no bad faith on his part.

Malaurie and Aynès[14]   **6.F.4.**

Contradictory texts.—Does it suffice for a creditor who is the victim of a non-performance to show that the debtor has not performed, or has not done so properly; or must he show also that this was due to the imprudence, negligence or bad faith of the debtor? The Civil Code answers this with two contradictory texts, arts. 1137 and 1147 . . .

[10] See BGHZ 59.158.

[11] *Münchener Kommentar*, under § 459, para. 56.

[12] Contrast with French law, where a seller who knew of the defect is also liable in damages and there is a presumption that a professional seller knew of the defects in the goods, see *infra* at 665.

[13] Again compare French law, under which the buyer may seek damages in addition to these remedies under Article 1645: C.civ. *infra* at 665.

[14] Paras. 816–7.

Doctrinal distinction.—In 1928 [*sic*] René Demogue wrote that contractual responsibility always presupposes proof of fault, but that the proof was more or less easy according to whether the obligation was one of *moyens* or one of result.[15]

For him this distinction was not a *summa divisio* of obligations. It became that under the influence of MM. Mazeaud,[16] using different terminology (obligation of *prudence* and *obligation déterminée*); then, a third category was added, so that nowadays there are three: obligations *de moyens*, *de résultat* and *de garantie*. The distinction was rapidly adopted by the jurisprudence, which continues to refer to it despite the criticism which it has attracted.

Notes

(1) For some authors, "contractual fault" is just the non-performance of an *obligation de moyens*. For others, "*faute contractuelle*" is the non-performance of any kind of obligation, whether *de moyens* or *de résultat* and for them the notion of "faute contractuelle" is of no use.

(2) We have already seen an example of the distinction between *moyens* and *résultat* at work earlier, in the case of the exploding bottle of lemonade.[17] In comparison, the occupier of business premises is usually held to be under an obligation to take only reasonable care for the safety of its customers.[18]

(3) Nicholas makes the point that it is hard to know when the French courts will characterize the obligation as one *de moyens* and when one *de résultat*.[19] As he says, it is hard to see why a cinema owner and other occupiers are usually under only the first obligation while the operator of "dodgem" cars at a fairground is bound by an obligation of result in relation to the safety of customers, so that customer who was injured by the shock of a collision with another dodgem car could recover damages without showing fault on the part of the operator.[20]

(4) An example of *garantie* liability in French law is the case of a defect in goods sold.

Code civil   **6.F.5.**

Article 1641: The seller is bound by a guarantee against any hidden defect in a thing sold which renders it of no use for the intended purpose, or of less use for that purpose such that, had the buyer known of the defect, he would not have bought the thing or would only have bought it at a reduced price.

Article 1642: The seller is not responsible for defects which were apparent and which the buyer could have seen for himself.

Article 1643: He is responsible for hidden defects, even if he could not have known of them, unless, in such a case, he has stipulated that that he will not be liable on any guarantee.

Article 1644: In the cases covered by articles 1641 and 1643, the buyer has the choice of returning the thing and recovering the price or keeping the thing and recovering a proportion of the price, the proportion to be judged by experts.

[15] Demogue, *Traité des obligations*, Vol. V (Paris: A. Rousseau, 1925), para: 1237 ff.
[16] Mazeaud, Mazeaud and Tunc, *Traité théorique et pratique de la responsabilité civile contractuelle et délictuelle*, Vol. I, 6th edn. (Paris: Montchrestien, 1965), para. 103–2 ff.
[17] See **2.F.11–12**, *supra* at 191.
[18] See Cass. civ., 17 March 1947, D. 1947.1.269: a cinema owner is only obliged to use measures of prudence and reasonable care for the safety of spectators.
[19] Nicholas, at 54.
[20] Zweigert and Kötz, at 501 ff.

Article 1645: If the seller knew of the defect in the thing, he is liable for damages to the buyer in addition to returning the price.

Article 1646: If the seller did not know of the defect in the thing, he is only liable to return the price and to reimburse the buyer for expenses occasioned by the sale.

Note

Article 1643 makes it clear that absence of fault is no defence to liability under the *garantie*. On the other hand, in principle under Article 1645 and 1646 the seller is liable only to return the price—or part of it—and to pay the buyer's expenses, and not for damages, unless the seller knew of the defect. This principle is now heavily qualified, as there is an irrebuttable presumption that a professional seller knew of the defects.[21]

6.1.3. THE ENGLISH APPROACH

In English Law, the basic rule is often said to be that contractual liability is strict. In *Raineri* v. *Miles*,[22] Lord Edmund-Davies said:

In relation to a claim for damages for breach of contract, it is, in general, immaterial why the defendant failed to fulfil his obligations and certainly no defence to plead that he had done his best.[23]

The statement by Lord Edmund-Davies represents the traditional position of English law: liability to achieve what was promised is strict and thus it is no defence to show that the non-performance was caused by something outside the debtor's control—unless, as suggested earlier, the event frustrates the contract. Thus, for example, a seller of goods is liable for late delivery even if this was caused by an Act of God or industrial action; a builder is liable for failure to complete the work on time even if the delays were caused by unforeseeably bad weather; and so on. *Force majeure* which is not sufficiently serious to frustrate the contract is not a defence.[24]

However, three points must be noted. The first is that contracts very commonly contain clauses altering the general rule. Thus sale contracts frequently contain *"force majeure"* clauses excusing late delivery for reasons outside the seller's control; building contracts frequently contain "extension of time clauses" under which the employer must allow the contractor additional time for delays caused by bad weather, etc.[25]

The second point is that occasionally the courts have mitigated the strict rule that the debtor is liable even in the absence of fault, by holding that, as a matter of interpretation of the particular contract, a non-performance caused by something not the debtor's fault provides an excuse, so that the debtor is not liable in damages, even though the contract is not frustrated. The most common case is where an employee or person due to perform personal services is prevented from doing so temporarily by illness.[26] The result is clearly close to the French doctrine of *cause étrangère*.

---

[21] See Ghestin and Desché, para. 851 ff. and *infra* at 850.

[22] [1981] AC 1050.

[23] *Ibid.* at 1086.

[24] See section 1 of chapter 5 *supra* at 609 ff.

[25] See McKendrick, *Force Majeure and Frustration of Contract*, 2nd edn. (London: Lloyd's of London Press, 1995) and Treitel, *Frustration*.

[26] See the cases discussed *supra* at 610.

Thirdly, and most importantly, there are many contracts in which the debtor's obligation is not strict but only one to use reasonable care and skill. This is the general rule in contracts for services, as is provided by Supply of Goods and Services Act 1982, section 13.

Supply of Goods and Services Act 1982   **6.E.6.**

section 13: *Implied term about care and skill*

> In a contract for the supply of a service where the supplier is acting in the course of a business, there is an implied term that the supplier will carry out the service with reasonable care and skill.

Notes

(1) It would perhaps be more accurate to say that the obligation is one to see that reasonable care and skill are taken. This is because, if the debtor delegates performance to another (as is permissible unless the performance involves a personal element or the contract prohibits delegation), and the person to whom the work is delegated fails to use reasonable care and skill, the debtor will be liable, even though it itself used reasonable care in selecting the sub-contractor.

(2) Although the duty in contracts of service is usually only that described in section 13, it is possible that the debtor will be held to have warranted that it will achieve a particular result.[27] This is unusual; however; the English Court of Appeal has, for example, refused to find that a doctor who performed an operation to sterilize a man was promising that the man would be rendered permanently sterile, even though the doctor told the patient that the operation was "irreversible"; thus the doctor was not liable because the operation, which had been carried out properly, reversed itself naturally.[28]

(3) Even a debtor who is strictly liable may be able to rely on the doctrine of frustration. Thus although the contractor under a building contract is strictly liable to produce the building by the time stated, a building contract may be frustrated if extreme delays caused be external events make performance "radically different from what was originally contemplated".[29] In that sense liability is not absolute.

(4) But, as was mentioned earlier,[30] there are cases in which there may appear to be absolute liability because the doctrine of frustration will not apply. Thus under the Sale of Goods Act 1979 (as amended by the Sale and Supply of Goods Act 1994) section 14, the seller who sells in the course of a business is responsible for the goods being of satisfactory quality. If the goods are not satisfactory, not only is it no defence that the seller was not at fault, it is no defence that the defect could not have been discovered by any amount of skill and care.[31]

(5) Equally a seller of generic goods cannot rely on frustration when he cannot obtain the goods, even if this happens without his fault—for example because the sole source is

---

[27] For an example, see *infra* at 670.
[28] *Thake* v. *Maurice* [1986] QB 644; on the facts though, the doctor was held liable for negligence in failing to give the patient an warning of this possibility.
[29] *Metropolitan Water Board* v. *Dick Kerr & Co* [1918] AC 119, HL. See also *supra* at 619.
[30] *Supra* at 660.
[31] *Frost* v. *Aylesbury Dairy* [1905] 1 KB 608; *Kendall* v. *Lillico* [1969] 2 AC 31, 84.

unavailable because of the outbreak of war. The contract will be frustrated if the parties both contemplated that the seller would have to obtain the goods from that single source.[32] In other cases the seller is in effect treated as guaranteeing that it has, or will get, the goods, so that liability here also appears to be absolute.

(6) However, in neither case is the liability truly absolute. In the generic goods case, disappearance of the sole source does make the contract impossible if it was agreed that the goods should be obtained from there. In other situations other, similar goods might be obtained elsewhere, just as in the defective goods case, it is presumably possible to supply goods without the relevant defect.

6.1.4. COMPARATIVE OVERVIEW

Thus we can see that in some legal systems liability for non-performance is in principle usually based on fault. This is true of German law, but even here there are also some instances of liability without fault. These cases are seen as exceptional to the basic rule, but they are wide in scope. Thus liability for defects in goods sold and in services rendered under a work contract (*Werkvertrag*), as well as liability for failure to supply generic goods (§ 279 BGB) and the liability of the debtor for persons engaged to carry out his obligations (§ 278 BGB) is strict.

The other systems base liability on fault in relation to some obligations. Thus in French law, many obligations are only obligations to use reasonable care, *obligations de moyens*, and if the debtor has used reasonable care the fact that some result the parties hoped for has not come about does not mean that the debtor has failed to perform. Equally in English law a contracting party is often under a duty only to use reasonable care and skill, rather than undertaking that a particular result will be achieved. If reasonable care and skill have been used there will be no breach of contract by the debtor. For example, in neither system will a doctor be liable if she fails to cure a patient, provided the doctor has used reasonable care and skill. In such cases, provided the debtor has in fact done what he should with reasonable care and skill, there will no non-performance—and consequently the creditor will not have a remedy.

However, the absence of fault in a general sense does not always mean that the debtor is not responsible. Both English and French law are characterized by a significant number of obligations in contract in which there is to some extent "strict" liability—i.e. liability without fault. French law recognizes that some obligations are to bring about particular results—*obligations de résultat*. English law seems to go even further: English lawyers are accustomed to say that contractual liability is normally strict and that cases in which the debtor is obliged only to use reasonable care and skill are exceptional—in fact they are not at all uncommon.

This "strict" liability "without fault" is not necessarily absolute. In France a debtor who is under an *obligation de résultat* may be excused if his performance is prevented by a *cause étrangère* which is not imputable to him; in England, the debtor who is strictly liable may be discharged under the doctrine of frustration. In the exceptional cases of

---

[32] *Re Badische Co Ltd* [1921] 2 Ch. 331.

strict liability in German law mentioned a moment ago, the debtor is protected to an extent by the doctrine of *Wegfall der Geschäftsgrundlage* (§ 242 BGB); and even in cases of generic obligations a debtor will be excused in cases of objective impossibility (§ 275 I BGB). Similarly, though § 279 BGB provides that the debtor of generic goods is responsible "even though no fault may be imputed to him", he will be excused if delivery out of the genus is no longer possible. But each of these defences requires something more than the absence of fault, so that it makes sense to say that each system recognizes both liability based on fault and a stricter kind of liability.

We saw in Chapter 5 that in the three systems there is a further, still stricter or absolute type of liability. For example, in neither French nor English Law is an inability to obtain generic goods treated as, respectively, *cause étrangère* or frustration, and the debtor will be liable for non-performance even in such cases. In German law, the seller's liability for defects may be "guarantee" liability. Given the narrowness of this case, however, and the general applicability of the fault principle in the BGB, it may be observed that French and English law seem to produce more cases in which the debtor will be liable without fault than German law.

Indeed, if the seller's liability for defects under § 459 and § 463 is not treated as absolute, the net result seems to be that German law works with two categories, French and English law with three. In French law, if the obligation is one *de moyens*, the debtor is obliged only to use reasonable care; if the obligation is one *de résultat* the debtor will be liable if the result was not achieved, unless the debtor can show it was prevented from achieving the result by a *cause étrangère*; and in certain situations of *obligation de garantie*, even a *cause étrangère* is no defence. In English law, if the obligation is one to use reasonable care and skill, there will be no liability unless a failure to use care and skill is shown; if liability is strict, the debtor will be liable if the result promised has not been achieved, unless the debtor can prove discharge by frustration; and there are certain types of obligation to which the doctrine of frustration seems not to apply, so that in effect liability is absolute. A similar result appears to be reached in the Unidroit Principles.

Unidroit Principles   **6.INT.7.**

Article 5.4:   (*Duty to achieve a specific result; Duty of best efforts*)
(1) To the extent that an obligation of a party involves a duty to achieve a specific result, that party is bound to achieve that result.
(2) To the extent that an obligation of a party involves a duty of best efforts in the performance of an activity, that party is bound to make such efforts as would be made by a reasonable person of the same kind in the same circumstance.

Article 5.5:   (*Determination of kind of duty involved*)
In determining the extent to which an obligation of a party involves a duty of best efforts in the performance of an activity or a duty to achieve a specific result, regard shall be had, among other factors, to
(a) the way in which the obligation is expressed in the contract;
(b) the contractual price and other terms of the contract;
(c) the degree of risk normally involved in achieving the expected result;
(d) the ability of the other party to influence the performance of the obligation.

668

Article 7.1.7: (*Force majeure*)
>   (1) Non-performance by a party is excused if that party proves that the non-performance was due to an impediment beyond its control and that it could not reasonably be expected to have taken the impediment into account at the time of the conclusion of the contract, or to have avoided or overcome it or its consequences . . .

Notes

(1) Article 7.1.7(1) of Unidroit seems to imply that absence of fault is no defence if the party should have taken into account the risk which occurred, which seems to suggest that there are some risks which the party will be expected to bear, fault or no fault.

(2) The PECL contain an Article on *force majeure*, Article 8:108(1), which is almost identical to Unidroit Article 7.1.7(1). They do not contain any provisions on the distinction between *obligations de moyens* and *obligations de résultat*; it appears to have been considered that it was not possible to lay down useful general rules on which obligation would apply in which circumstances. But the distinction is discussed in the Comment to Article 6:102, where it is suggested that the relevant factors are exactly the same as those listed in Article 5.5 of Unidroit.

We noted earlier[33] that the effect of supervening impossibility is viewed differently between the systems. So, in the continental systems the excuse—for example *cause étrangère, nachträgliche Unmöglichkeit* (subsequent objective impossibility for which the debtor is not responsible)—is usually seen as affecting the remedies available to the creditor; the latter may not seek specific performance or damages but in principle retains the choice whether to terminate the contract or not. In the common law, the doctrine of frustration discharges the obligations of both parties automatically. A parallel difference applies to questions of fault. In common law, the question whether the debtor is strictly liable or has only to use reasonable care and skill is usually considered to be a question of what were the debtor's obligations, and is likely to be discussed under the rubric of "contents of the contract". In French and German law the question is more usually linked to the "legal effects" of a failure to perform, that is to the question of remedies.[34] This seems to make little practical difference.

It is also said that, though the systems have very different starting points, the practical results reached are surprisingly similar.[35] There is truth in this; and it is certainly the case that one system is in principle capable of reaching the same results as another. For example, all three systems recognize both obligations to produce a result and obligations to use reasonable care. But the hesitation of the Commission on European Contract Law to lay down general rules on *obligation de moyens* and *obligation de résultat* seems justified when it is seen that the systems by no means always categorize obligations in the same way—so the actual results even in everyday cases may be startlingly different. Two examples of these divergences follow.

---

[33] *Supra* at 659.
[34] See Treitel, *Remedies* at 7–8, para. 8.
[35] See Zweigert and Kötz, at 533 ff.

6.1.4.A. CONTRACTS OF CARRIAGE

The first example concerns contracts of carriage: what is the carrier's *obligation de sécurité*, its liability if the things or persons carried are damaged or injured? In respect of loss of or damage to the goods French law holds the carrier is under an *obligation de moyens*. However, French jurisprudence has established the principle that the safety of passengers is an *obligation de résultat*, so that the carrier will be liable for any injury which is not shown to result from a *cause étrangère*.[36] English law has the reverse rule: a carrier is under an obligation only to take reasonable care to prevent injury to passengers. Even more curiously, the old Common Law rule[37] was that a common carrier of goods was strictly liable for damage unless he could show that it was caused by one of a series of exceptions such as Act of God or act of a third party—a rule that seems very close to the French obligation of result. It is no doubt facile to suggest the difference between the two laws says something about the relative importance given to persons and possessions in the two countries! German law seems to be most protective of the creditor in contracts of carriage. Liability will be imposed on the carrier in every case of damage to goods or persons carried save where the latter was caused by an Act of God or the actions of the creditor.

6.1.4.B. CONSTRUCTION CONTRACTS

The second example is the contract to design and construct a building. In English law, the builder is strictly liable for the quality of the *materials* used. Thus in *Young & Marten* v. *McManus Childs*,[38] a building contractor was building houses and sub-contracted the roofing to the appellants, instructing them to use a particular brand of roofing tile. The appellants in turn sub-sub-contracted the work to Acme, who bought the tiles from the manufacturers. The batch of tiles supplied was not of satisfactory quality. It was held that the appellants were responsible even though they were in no way at fault and had no choice as to which kind of tile to use. In contrast, the contractor is liable for defective *work* only if it failed to use reasonable care and skill in virtue of section 13 of the Supply of Goods and Services Act 1982.[39] Similarly, an architect who designs the building will not be in breach of contract simply because the design is in some way defective; it must normally be shown that the architect was negligent. The designer will only be strictly liable in exceptional circumstances.

Court of Appeal **6.E.8.**

Greaves & Co (Contractors) Ltd v. *Baynham, Miekle & Partners*[40]

STRICT LIABILITY FOR DESIGN WORK

The structural engineer and the warehouse

Engineers employed by a contractor to design a building to meet a specified performance, as required by the "design and build" contract between the contractor and the employer, are liable even without fault if the design of the building fails to meet the specification.

[36] See **1.F.36–1.F.38**, *supra* at 42–45.
[37] See *Coggs* v. *Bernard* (1703) 2 Ld. Raym. 918; *Forward* v. *Pittard* (1785) 1 TR 27.
[38] **4.E.15**, *supra* at 572.
[39] See *supra* at 666.
[40] [1975] 3 All ER 99.

Facts: A firm of contractors entered a "design and build package deal" contract with an oil company to provide the company with a warehouse for storing large drums of oil. The defendants were employed by the contractors to design the warehouse. The oil drums were very heavy and would be moved around by fork-lift trucks. The warehouse was to be built in accordance with a new system of construction. The British Standards Institution had issued a circular warning designers of the effect of vibrations in such buildings, but the defendants read this as a warning merely about vibrations in general and did not allow for the random impulses set up by the fork-lift trucks. After a year the floor of the warehouse cracked and repairs costing £100,000 were required. The contractors were liable to bear this cost and brought an action seeking a declaration that the defendants were liable to reimburse them.

Held: The trial judge held that the defendants were in breach of an implied term that the design would be fit for its purpose. The defendants appealed. The Court of Appeal agreed that on the facts of the case the defendants were strictly liable, though it also decided that they had failed to use reasonable and skill in designing the building without allowing for the random impulses.

Judgment: LORD DENNING: . . . The law does not usually imply a warranty that he will achieve the desired result, but only a term that he will use reasonable care and skill. The surgeon does not warrant that he will cure the patient. Nor does the solicitor warrant that he will win the case. But when a dentist agrees to make a set of false teeth for a patient, there is an implied warranty that they will fit his gums: see *Samueis* v. *Davis* [1943] K.B. 526.

What then is the position when an architect or an engineer is employed to design a house or a bridge? Is he under an implied warranty that, if the work is carried out to his design, it will be reasonably fit for the purpose? Or is he only under a duty to use reasonable care and skill? This question may require to be answered some day as a matter of law. But in the present case I do not think we need answer it. For the evidence shows that both parties were of one mind on the matter. Their common intention was that the engineer should design a warehouse which would be fit for the purpose for which it was required. That common intention gives rise to a term implied *in fact*.

Notes

(1) This case has been interpreted as meaning that a professional who is given a specification of what is required is strictly responsible for achieving that specification.[41] However, the *Greaves* case has been treated by the courts as depending on its special facts, in particular the fact that the contractors who had employed the engineer were themselves working under a "package deal" contract under which they may have been obliged to produce a building that was fit for the employer's purposes.[42]

(2) An architect is often responsible for both designing the building and supervising its construction. Even if elements of the design work may involve strict liability, as the *Greaves* case may be interpreted as suggesting, the supervisory duties are—unless agreed otherwise—only duties to take reasonable care.

In French Law the result is different. The contract falls within a group known as *contrats d'entreprise*, in which the contractor is subject to strict liability in relation to the work as well as the materials used. In relation to building contracts there is now specific legislation which covers both builders and designers of buildings.

---

[41] See Treitel, *Remedies* at 27–30, para. 27.
[42] See *Hawkins* v. *Chrysler (UK) Ltd and Burne Associates* (1986) 38 BLR 36.

Code civil   **6.F.9.**
(Loi No. 78–12 of 4 January 1978)

Article 1792:   Every constructor of building work is fully responsible, as against the client or the purchaser of the building, for damage, even resulting from a defect in the sub-soil, which affects the structure of the building or which, because it affects one of its constituent parts or one of its items of equipment, renders it unfit for its purpose. This liability does not apply if the constructor proves that the damage was caused by a *cause étrangère*.

Article 1792–1:   The following are deemed to be constructors of building work:
(1) Every architect, developer, technician or other person linked by contract to the client;
(2) Any person who sells a building, after completion, which he has built or had built for him;
(3) Any person who, although dealing as an agent of the proprietor of the work, performs a task equivalent to a landlord.

In German law a builder's obligations are determined in the first instance by the provisions of the BGB relating to work contracts (*Werkverträge*). The rules governing work contracts are very similar to those governing the sale of goods in relation to remedies for defects.[43] In both cases the availability of certain remedies is dependent on whether the debtor was at fault or not.

BGB   **6.G.10.**

§ 633:   (1) The contractor is obliged to carry out the work in such a manner that it has the guaranteed attributes and that it is not subject to defects which negate or reduce its value or the usefulness for the purposes to which it would be put in the ordinary course of things or for those which were envisaged in the contract.
(2) If the work is not of this standard, the employer can require that the defect be cured. § 476a applies accordingly. The contractor is entitled to refuse to effect a cure if this would require disproportionate expenditure.
(3) If the contractor is in delay in removing the defect, the employer can cure it himself and demand restitution of the costs so arising.

§ 634:   (1) The customer may allot to the contractor a reasonable period for the removal of a defect of the kind specified in § 633 with a declaration that he will refuse the removal of the defect after the expiration of the period. If a defect has already appeared before the delivery of the work, the customer may fix the period forthwith (. . .) After the expiration of the period the customer may demand the annulment of the contract (cancellation; *Wandlung*), or reduction of the remuneration (reduction; *Minderung*), unless the defect has been removed in due time; the claim for removal of the defect is barred . . .

§ 635:   If the defect in the work is caused by a circumstance for which the debtor is responsible, the customer may demand compensation for non-fulfilment, instead of cancellation or reduction.

---

[43] See *supra* at 662.

§ 636: (1) If the work is wholly or in part not produced in due time, the provisions of §634(1) to (3), applicable to cancellation, apply *mutatis mutandis* (. . .)

§ 637: An agreement, whereby the obligation of the contractor as to responsibility for a defect in the work is released or limited, is void if the contractor fraudulently conceals the defect.

Notes

(1) As in the law of sale, a creditor may seek cancellation (*Wandlung*) or reduction of the purchase price (*Minderung*) on the basis of strict liability for defects. Note that, by contrast with a purchaser of goods, he has an automatic right to require the debtor to cure the defect before going over to these remedies (§ 633(2) BGB).[44]

(2) A further similarity is that damages for non-performance are made contingent upon the fault of the debtor (§ 635 BGB). The burden of disproving fault is on the debtor.[45]

(3) The obligation in work contracts is one of result. In this no distinction is made, unlike in English law, between liability for defective materials and liability for defective work. Work contracts are distinguished in this respect from service contracts (*Dienstverträge*). Under the latter the debtor is obliged to perform tasks, but does not bear the risk of the desired result not being achieved. Thus, both contracts of employment (*Arbeitsverträge*) and contracts with most professionals are classified as service contracts.[46] Occasionally, however, German law identifies hybrid or mixed service/work contracts in the manner of English law, for example where a supplier both makes equipment (work contract or, in English law, a sale contract) and installs it (service contract).[47]

(4) Contracts with architects form an exception to the foregoing. The architect's liability in relation to the drafting of the plan for a building is clearly strict. The supervisory tasks of the architect during the construction phase, on the other hand, seem to amount to service type obligations. Nonetheless, the BGH and academic commentators have held that the result-orientation of the planning stage predominates throughout. They hold, therefore, that the architect's contract is a work contract with corresponding liability for failure to achieve the result of a defect-free building in accordance with the plans.[48] Note, however, that the architect will only be liable for defects caused by his work.

Further Reading on remedies for non performance
—D. Harris and D. Tallon (eds.), *Contract Law Today: Anglo-French Comparisons* (Oxford: Clarendon, 1989), chapter 6;
—H. Kötz and A. Flessner, *European Contract Law*, Vol. II, transl. by T. Weir (forthcoming);
—Larenz, AT;
—Larenz, SBT-1;
—B.S. Markesinis, W. Lorenz and G. Dannemann,, *The German Law of Obligations*, Vol I: *The Law of Contracts and Restitution* (Oxford: Clarendon, 1997);

---

[44] Contrast with § 476a BGB, whereby the right to cure in sales must be agreed in advance.
[45] See *Münchener Kommentar* under § 635, para. 99.
[46] See Larenz, *SBT–I* , para. 52 I.
[47] See *Münchener Kommentar* under § 611, paras. 44–48.
[48] BGHZ 45.372; 83.131; Larenz, *SBT–I* , para. 53 I.

—K. Rebmann and F. Säcker (eds.), *Münchener Kommentar zum Bürgerlichen Gesetzbuch*, 4th edn. (München: Beck, 2000);

—D. Tallon, "Breach of Contract and Reparation of Damage" in *Towards a European Civil Code*, at 223–235;

—Treitel, *Remedies*;

—Zweigert and H. Kötz, chapters 35 and 36.

6.2. ENFORCEMENT *IN NATURA*

Principles of European Contract Law   **6.PECL.11.**

Article 9:101: *Monetary Obligations*

(1) The creditor is entitled to recover money which is due.

(2) Where the creditor has not yet performed its obligation and it is clear that the debtor will be unwilling to receive performance, the creditor may nonetheless proceed with its performance and may recover any sum due under the contract unless:

(a) it could have made a reasonable substitute transaction without significant effort or expense; or

(b) performance would be unreasonable in the circumstances.

Article 9:102: *Non-monetary Obligations*

(1) The aggrieved party is entitled to specific performance of an obligation other than one to pay money, including the remedying of a defective performance.

(2) Specific performance cannot, however, be obtained where:

(a) performance would be unlawful or impossible; or

(b) performance would cause the debtor unreasonable effort or expense; or

(c) the performance consists in the provision of services or work of a personal character or depends upon a personal relationship, or

(d) the aggrieved party may reasonably obtain performance from another source.

(3) The aggrieved party will lose the right to specific performance if it fails to seek it within a reasonable time after it has or ought to have become aware of the non-performance.

Article 9:103: *Damages Not Precluded*

The fact that a right to performance is excluded under this Section does not preclude a claim for damages.

In this section on literal enforcement of obligations we deal separately with enforcement of claims to money, such as a claim for the price, and enforcement of other obligations, such as to transfer property, to do something or not to do something (in French, *de donner, de faire ou de ne pas faire*). We start with obligations other than those to pay money.[49]

---

[49] For claims to money, see section **6.2.2**, *infra* at 717.

6.2.1. NON-MONETARY OBLIGATIONS

6.2.1.A. INTRODUCTORY NOTE

Each of the systems will in some circumstances ensure that the plaintiff gets the performance it has bargained for, rather than getting a substitute such as damages. The exact conditions under which this remedy will be given vary, as we will see. First we must note that the notion of "enforced performance"—in French *exécution en nature*—itself differs as between the systems. In the civil law systems, this phrase is used to cover not only the case in which the defendant is compelled to perform itself (*exécution forcée*) but also the case where the plaintiff is entitled to obtain performance by a third party at the defendant's expense (*exécution par un tiers*). The common law recognizes only the first situation as one of specific performance. If the plaintiff wants to get performance by a third party, the plaintiff is expected to terminate the original contract and to recover the cost of obtaining performance by a third party by way of a claim for damages. This is one reason why the common law remedy of specific performance appears to be much more limited than execution *in natura* in continental systems. We will see other differences between what is regarded as literal enforcement and what is regarded as a form of damages.

6.2.1.B. THE BASIC RULES

Code civil **6.F.11.**

Article 1138: The obligation to deliver the thing is perfected by the simple agreement of the contracting parties.
    It makes the creditor owner and puts the thing at his risk from the moment when it should have been delivered, even though the handing over has not yet been effected, unless the debtor is in delay in delivery, in which case the thing remains at the latter's risk.

Article 1142: Every obligation to do or not to do (*de faire ou de ne pas faire*), if it is not performed by the debtor, gives rise to damages.

Article 1143: Nonetheless the creditor has the right to demand that anything done in contravention of the contract be destroyed; and may have it destroyed at the debtor's expense, without prejudice to any right to damages.

Article 1144: The creditor may also, in a case of non-performance, be authorised to have the obligation performed at the debtor's expense. The latter may be ordered to pay the necessary costs of this in advance.

Cass. civ., 20 January 1953[50] **6.F.12.**

ORDER TO DELIVER EQUIVALENT GOODS

Inability to deliver goods

Where the defendant is obliged to deliver specified goods to the plaintiff but is unable to do so, the court may order him to deliver equivalent goods.

[50] JCP 1953 II.7677, annotated by P. Esmein.

Facts: The plaintiff had obtained an order that the defendant should deliver various goods to the plaintiff, their owner. The defendant claimed that he was unable to do so.

Held: The court of first instance had ordered the defendant to deliver goods of the same kind and value instead. The Cour de Cassation rejected his appeal.

Judgment: THE COURT: . . . *On the second appeal ground*:—Whereas by reason of Ailloud's alleged inability to deliver certain chattels as required by the judgment of 20 January 1947, it is asserted in the appeal that reparation of the resulting loss suffered by Plissonnier, their owner, should take the form of damages;

—Whereas the appellant submits that, in ordering him to deliver goods of the same kind and value, the contested judgment therefore infringed Article 1142 of the Civil Code.

—Whereas however, that provision is applicable only in the case of non-compliance with a personal obligation to do or refrain from doing something; it follows from the findings contained in the contested judgment that the fault giving rise to the loss consists, quite simply, in the unjustified retention of goods belonging to another;

—Whereas consequently, the provision relied on in the appeal is inapplicable in the present case, and in ruling that the delivery of equivalent, commonly available goods of the same kind is the best way of making good the loss, the cour d'appel was merely exercising its absolute discretionary power.

—Whereas it follows that the appeal ground is unfounded.

On those grounds, the Court dismisses the appeal.

Notes

(1) In the case of an obligation to deliver (*de donner*), the creditor is treated as having a right to take the property because he has become owner, and the court may make an order for possession to be enforced by an official. If transfer of ownership requires the execution of a formal document, the court's order will act as a substitute for this document.[51]

(2) Article 1142 reflects the general principle that the law should not force individuals to perform a specific act—*nemo praecise cogi potest ad factum*—and appears at first sight to mean that obligations to do or not to do will not be enforced specifically. Thus it seems to suggest that all cases of non-performance other than a failure to deliver specific property will merely give the creditor the right to damages, even where the debtor has promised to deliver generic goods. But this is misleading in several ways.

(3) First, the creditor may obtain performance at the debtor's expense under Article 1143 or 1144. This is treated as a form of *exécution en nature*.

(4) Alternatively the defendant may be ordered to deliver the article on pain of an *astreinte*.[52] If goods sold are not specific, it necessarily follows that the creditor will not become owner of them, and to obtain the goods he will either have to obtain an *astreinte* on the debtor or use Article 1144 to obtain equivalent goods at the debtor's expense.

(5) A third possibility is that a debtor who claims to be unable to deliver items of property as ordered may simply be ordered to provide equivalent items. In principle the Civil Code does not permit this but in practice it is done, as the case Cass civ. 20 January 1953[53] shows.[54]

[51] See Treitel, *Remedies* at 56–57, para. 50.
[52] See *infra* at 680.
[53] *Supra*.
[54] See Treitel, *Remedies* at 55–6, para. 49.

(6) Thus it is widely recognized in doctrine that Article 1142 is misleading, since in effect it is limited to cases where performance is no longer possible or where the courts will not grant execution *in natura* because the performance would require the personal skill of the debtor.[55]

The note to Cass. civ. 19 February 1970[56] says:

The least one can say of art. 1142 is that it is very badly drafted. It presents as an imperative rule what is no more than an option, though, it is true, the statistically dominant one.

(7) The defendant will not be made to perform an act which it had not undertaken to perform as one of its contractual obligations. Thus a railway company cannot be ordered to repair a customer's goods which the railway had damaged during the course of carriage.[57]

BGB	**6.G.13.**

§ 241: The effect of an obligation is that the creditor is entitled to claim performance from the debtor. Performance can also be constituted by an omission to act.

§ 249: Whosoever is obliged to provide compensation must restore the situation which would have existed if the circumstance giving rise to the obligation to make compensation had not occurred. If compensation is required to be made for injury to a person or damage to a thing, the creditor may demand instead of restitution in kind, the sum of money necessary for such restitution.

Zivilprozeßordnung (ZPO)	**6.G.14.**
(German Code of Civil Procedure)	

§ 887: (1) If the debtor does not fulfil his obligation to render performance, which can be rendered by a third party, the creditor is to be authorised on application by the procedural court [*Prozessgericht*] of first instance to have performance so rendered at the expense of the debtor.

(2) The creditor can at the same time require that the debtor be ordered to pay in advance such costs as will be incurred through obtaining performance; the right to seek retrospective payment if obtaining performance requires still greater expenditure is not thereby prejudiced.

(3) The execution procedure to obtain transfer or supply of an item is not subject to these provisions.

§ 888: (1) If an activity cannot be undertaken by a third party and if it is dependent exclusively on the will of the debtor, it is to be recognised on application to the procedural court of first instance, that the debtor is to be held to his performance through fine, or committal where this cannot be levied, or through committal. A single fine may not exceed the sum of 50,000 Deutschmarks. The provisions of the fourth section [of the ZPO] apply to committal.

(2) This provision is of no application in cases of a judgment to enter marriage, in cases of a judgment to engage in marital life and in cases of a judgment to provide services under a contract of service.

---

[55] See *infra* at 700.
[56] Gaz.Pal. 1970.1.282; quoted by Nicholas at 218.
[57] Cass. civ. 4 June.1924, S.1925.1.97, D.H. 1924.469, Gaz.Pal.1924.2.237.

Notes

(1) BGB § 241 refers only to the actual performance promised. However, as ZPO § 887 provides, this primary obligation may be enforced by judicially sanctioned performance by a third party.

(2) The creditor is never confined to the remedy of specific performance. ZPO § 893(1) provides that the right of the creditor to seek damages instead of enforced performance is not limited by the provisions governing the latter; note that the creditor who wishes to claim damages for non-performance from the debtor may first have to serve a notice demanding performance by a certain date (*Nachfrist*); and if the date has passed without performance, the creditor may not normally demand performance.[58]

(3) If there is a fixed date for performance of a commercial contract (i.e. if the contract is a *Fixgeschäft*) the presumption is in favour of damages or termination and therefore the creditor must put the debtor on notice of his intention to claim performance *in natura* immediately: § 376(1) second sentence HGB.

(4) § 249 BGB defines the nature of the obligation to make compensation (*Schadensersatz*). According to this, restoration of the *status quo ante* and not money damages is the normal rule. Thus an obligation to supply replacement goods, for example, would be characterized as compensation within § 249 BGB although, as Treitel notes, lawyers in other systems might understand this as a form of enforced performance.[59]

(5) German law allows a creditor to choose between compensation *in natura*—as per § 249 BGB first sentence—and money damages, or more exactly to "go over" to damages in certain cases, viz.: where person is injured or physical property is damaged—§ 249 BGB second sentence; after a notice period has expired (§ 250 BGB, § 510b ZPO); or where performance *in natura* is insufficient to compensate the creditor (§ 251(1) second sentence BGB). In cases of delay the claim for performance is extinguished on expiry of the notice period and the only remedies available are damages for non-performance or *Rücktritt*: § 326(1) second sentence BGB.[60]

In English Law, the Common Law courts at a very early date ceased to order the defendant to perform a contract literally and gave only monetary remedies such as damages. The courts of equity would grant specific performance, but only as a supplementary remedy when the remedy at Common Law was thought to be inadequate.

Vice-Chancellor's Court   **6.E.15.**
Falcke v. *Gray*[61]

SPECIFIC PERFORMANCE WHERE GOODS UNIQUE

Chinese vases

Where there is a contract to sell goods which are unique, specific performance may be ordered.

Facts: The defendant let her house to the plaintiff for six months, and gave him the option of purchasing at the end of the term certain articles of furniture at a valuation. Among the articles were what counsel described as

---

[58] See *infra* at 750 ff.
[59] Treitel, *Remedies* at 51, para. 44
[60] See further *infra* at 750 ff.
[61] (1859) 4 Drew 651.

"a couple of large Oriental jars, with great ugly Chinese pictures upon them". The valuer admitted that he was ignorant of the value of the vases, but a sum of £40 was eventually agreed on, although the defendant said in her evidence that she had been left the jars by a lady who had, she understood, been offered £100 for them by King George IV. The defendant was later offered £200 for the jars by a purchaser, to whom she had explained what had happened, and she accepted that offer. The plaintiff obtained an *ex parte* injunction against the defendant and the second purchaser, and then sought specific performance.

Held: The Vice-Chancellor expressed himself willing to grant specific performance, except for the fact that the price the purchaser had agreed to pay was inadequate. [This part of the decision would probably not be followed today].[62]

Judgment: THE VICE-CHANCELLOR (Sir R.T. Kindersley) [after stating the facts above]: The first ground of defence is that, this being a bill for the specific performance of a contract for the purchase of chattels, this Court will not interfere. But I am of opinion that the Court will not refuse to interfere simply because the contract relates to chattels, and that if there were no other objection the contract in this case is such a contract as the Court would specifically perform.

What is the difference in the view of the Court between realty and personality in respect to the question whether the Court will interfere or not? Upon what principle does the Court decree specific performance of any contract whatever? Lord Redesdale in *Harnett* v. *Yeilding* says: "Whether Courts of Equity in their determinations on this subject have always considered what was the original foundation for decrees of this nature I very much doubt. I believe that from something of habit, decrees of this kind have been carried to an extent which has tended to injustice. Unquestionably the original foundation of these decrees was simply this, that damages at law would not give the party the compensation to which he was entitled; that is, would not put him in a situation as beneficial to him as if the agreement were specifically performed". So that the principle on which a Court of Equity proceeds is this. A Court of law gives damages for the non-performance, but a Court of Equity says "that is not sufficient—justice is not satisfied by that remedy"; and, therefore, a Court of Equity will decree specific performance because a mere compensation in damages is not a sufficient remedy and satisfaction for the loss of the performance of the contract.

Now why should that principle apply less to chattels? If in a contract for chattels damages will be a sufficient compensation, the party is left to that remedy. Thus if a contract is for the purchase of a certain quantity of coals, stock &c, this Court will not decree specific performance, because a person can go into the market and buy similar articles and get damages for any difference in the price of the articles in a Court of law. But if damages would not be a sufficient compensation, the principle, on which a Court of Equity decrees specific performance, is just as applicable to a contract for the sale and purchase of chattels, as to a contract for the sale and purchase of land.

In the present case the contract is for the purchase of articles of unusual beauty, rarity and distinction, so that damages would not be an adequate compensation for non-performance; and I am of opinion that a contract for articles of such a description is such a contract as this Court will enforce; and, in the absence of all other objection, I should have no hesitation in decreeing specific performance.

Notes

(1) In the case of an obligation not to do something, the court may order an injunction. If it is merely an order not to do something in the future, it is termed "prohibitory"; whereas if it also requires the defendant to undo something which he has done in breach of contract, it is known as "mandatory".

(2) Neither specific performance nor a mandatory injunction will be granted if damages would be an adequate remedy. This is because these are in origin equitable remedies

---

[62] See Spry, *Equitable Remedies*, 3rd edn (London: Sweet & Maxwell,1984) at 186.

and the Lord Chancellor would normally grant a remedy only when the remedy at common law seemed inadequate.[63] However, with prohibitory injunctions the courts do not always insist on this. Where the defendant has undertaken expressly not to do a certain thing, the injunction may be issued even without showing that the breach is causing the plaintiff any loss at all.[64] The difference must not be exaggerated. First, even in the case of an express negative promise, the court will not make an order if this would have the practical effect of forcing the defendant to perform a contract which is not otherwise specifically enforceable.[65] Secondly, the court will not hold that the contract "impliedly" forbids a particular act, and then grant an injunction against doing that act, if the effect would also be to coerce performance.[66]

Thus in English Law, specific performance is a relatively unusual remedy, as normally if the plaintiff obtains damages it will be able to make a substitute transaction with a third party and be compensated for any other losses. The only case in which specific performance is regularly granted is in contracts for interests in land. This may be because each piece of land was regarded as unique, so that the plaintiff cannot go out and buy an equivalent.[67]

Principles of European Contract Law   **6.PECL.16.**

Article 9:102: *Non-monetary Obligations*
    (1) The aggrieved party is entitled to specific performance of an obligation other than one to pay money, including the remedying of a defective performance.
    (2) Specific performance cannot, however, be obtained where: . . .
        (d) the aggrieved party may reasonably obtain performance from another source.

6.2.1.C. MAKING THE DEFENDANT PERFORM

In French law, if a defendant refuses to obey a court order to perform, the public authorities will only employ force to recover a piece of moveable property or to evict the defendant from an immovable—and even then the authorities may exercise a discretion to refuse to act. More usually the court will order an *astreinte*, a monetary penalty for non-compliance.

Loi no 91–650 du 9 juillet 1991   **6.F.17.**
portant réforme des procédures civiles d'exécution
(French Act Reforming Enforcement Civil Procedures)

Article 33: Any court may, of its own motion or otherwise, order the payment of a penalty (*astreinte*) in order to ensure compliance with its decision.

---

[63] See *supra* at 11, note 25.
[64] *Marco Productions Ltd.* v. *Pagola* [1945] 1 KB 111 (express promise not to perform in competing theatre).
[65] For an example, see *infra* at 701, note 112.
[66] See *Chitty*, §§ 28-064–28-065.
[67] Nowadays, whatever its origin, the rule is inextricably linked to the notion of "equitable interests" in property, which result in a person who has merely agreed to take an interest in property being regarded for many purposes as the owner, even though there has been no conveyance of the property.

A court implementing such compliance may attach an order for payment of a penalty (*astreinte*) to a decision made by another court, if it appears necessary in the circumstances so to do.

Article 34: Penalties (*astreinte*) are independent of damages.

A penalty (*astreinte*) shall be provisional or definitive. It shall be regarded as provisional unless it is expressed to be definitive by the court imposing it.

No order shall be made imposing a definitive penalty (*astreinte*) until an order has first been made imposing a provisional penalty (*astreinte*) for such period as the court shall determine. In the event of non-compliance with any of the foregoing requirements, the penalty (*astreinte*) shall be levied on a provisional basis.

Article 35: A penalty (*astreinte*), whether provisional or definitive, shall be levied by the court implementing compliance with the decision, save where the court which ordered its imposition remains seised of the case or has reserved to itself the power to levy the same.

Article 36: Regard shall be had, in levying the amount of a provisional penalty (*astreinte*), to the conduct of the party to whom the order is addressed and to any difficulties encountered by that party in complying therewith.

The amount of a definitive penalty (*astreinte*) may not be altered upon the same being levied.

A provisional or definitive penalty (*astreinte*) shall be lifted, either wholly or in part, where it is established that the non-compliance, or delay in compliance, with the court's order results wholly or in part from some extraneous cause.

Article 37: The court's decision shall be automatically enforceable on a provisional basis.

Notes

(1) The *astreinte* condemns the debtor to pay a sum of money if he does not perform. It is often fixed at so much per day of delay. It does not give the creditor a direct right against the debtor; the creditor has to apply to the court to obtain the money. The *astreinte* is at first provisional, in the sense that when the defendant has performed, the judge may adjust the sum payable. If the defendant fails to perform, the *astreinte* may be made definitive; in this case there is no power to adjust it later.

(2) The money is payable to the plaintiff. When the *astreinte* was first developed in the late nineteenth century, its legal basis was uncertain and in some respects it was often treated as a form of damages. Thus for a period it was held that when the judge liquidated a provisional *astreinte*, the sum payable by the defendant should not exceed the plaintiff's loss.[68] Since 1972 the *astreinte* has had a legislative basis and it is clear that it is not compensation but a penalty payable to the plaintiff. The plaintiff may also recover damages.

Zivilprozeßordnung (ZPO) **6.G.18.**
(German Code of Civil Procedure)[69]

§ 890: (1) If the debtor breaches an obligation to refrain from an action or to tolerate an action, he is, on the application of the creditor, to be ordered by the court of first instance to pay a

[68] See Nicholas at 221–4; Cass. civ. 20 October 1959, S. 1959.225, D. 1959.537, annotated by Holleaux.
[69] See also ZPO §§ 887, 888, *supra* at 677.

fine for each infraction (in cases where this cannot be paid, to be detained) or to be detained for up to six months. A single fine may not exceed the amount of five hundred thousand Deutschmarks; the period of detention may not exceed two years.

(2) The order must be preceded by an appropriate warning which, if it is not contained in the judgment declaring the obligation, is to be issued by the court of first instance on application.

(3) On the application of the creditor, the debtor may also be ordered to provide security for such damage as may be caused by future infractions.

§ 894: (1) If the debtor is ordered to make a declaration of will, the declaration is taken as having been made as soon as the judgment is final [has legal force]. If the declaration of will is made conditional upon a counter-performance, it is effective as soon as an executable copy of the final judgment is issued in accordance with the provisions of §§ 726, 730.

(2) The provisions of the first section are not applicable in the case of an order to enter into marriage.

Notes

(1) By contrast to the *astreinte* procedure in French law, any fines levied under ZPO §§ 887, 888 are paid into court, not to the creditor.

(2) Detailed provisions are laid down in the ZPO in relation to the duration of custody where committal is ordered and prohibiting this measure where the health of the debtor would be endangered thereby (ZPO §§ 904–914, 906).

In English law the debtor who fails to obey an order of specific performance or an injunction will be in contempt of court. He may be imprisoned or fined; and if the defendant is a company, its assets may be sequestered and its directors imprisoned or fined. But in cases of transfer of land, the court will simply order that the land be transferred, and will if necessary execute any documents itself. The ease of this and the harshness of the sanction for contempt of court may explain why specific performance is given readily in land cases but so rarely in other situations.

6.2.1.C. PERFORMANCE BY A THIRD PARTY

Code civil   **6.F.19.**

Article 1143: Nonetheless the creditor has the right to demand that anything done in contravention of the contract be destroyed; and may have it destroyed at the debtor's expense, without prejudice to any right to damages.

Article 1144: The creditor may also, in a case of non-performance, be authorised to have the obligation performed at the debtor's expense. The latter may be ordered to pay the necessary costs of this in advance.

The creditor cannot have the work performed at the debtor's expense without first serving on the debtor a *mise en demeure* and obtaining a court order.[70] However, a court order is not required in cases of urgency or in commercial cases.[71]

---

[70] See Cass. civ. 3, 20 March 1991, Bull. civ. III.94.

[71] See Nicholas at 217; Treitel, *Remedies* at 56–7, para. 50; it is stated in the second edition of Zweigert and Kötz at 510 that a court order is not required as a matter of trade usage. This statement is not repeated in the 3rd edn.

BGB **6.G.20.**

§ 633: (1) The contractor is obliged to carry out the work in such a manner that it has the guaranteed attributes and that it is not subject to defects which negate or reduce its value or the usefulness for the purposes to which it would be put in the ordinary course of things or for those which were envisaged in the contract.

(2) If the work is not of this standard, the employer can require that the defect be cured. §476a applies accordingly. The contractor is entitled to refuse to effect a cure if this would require disproportionate expenditure.

(3) If the contractor is in delay in removing the defect, the employer can cure it himself and demand restitution of the costs so arising.

Notes

(1) In German law the obligation of the builder, arising under a contract for services (*Werkvertrag* BGB § 631(1)), would be enforceable under ZPO §887, i.e. performance could be rendered by a third party at the expense of the debtor. This right to demand full performance is unlimited where the creditor has not yet "accepted" the work (BGB § 640). Generally he may not demand full performance after this point, but he still retains a right to have any defects cured under BGB § 633(2).[72]

(2) Similarly to French Law, a set notice period must have expired—i.e. the contractor must be in delay—before the employer is entitled to have a third party remove the defect. It is also open to the employer, under BGB § 634(1), to accompany the setting of a notice period with a declaration that he will refuse any offer of cure thereafter. On expiry of the period he may choose between cancellation of the contract and reduction of the purchase price (BGB § 634(1) second sentence), or damages, provided in the latter case that the contractor is responsible for the defect (§ 635 BGB).

(3) Full performance may be demanded notwithstanding prior acceptance if an attempt at curing by repair would be inadequate to remove the defect.[73]

Thus both French and German Law require the creditor to obtain a court order authorizing performance by a third party (§ 887 ZPO—"*der Gläubiger [ist] von dem Prozessgericht . . . auf Antrag zu ermächtigen*"; Article 1144 "*Le créancier peut . . . être autorisé*"). This is not a requirement of English law; for example, if a builder has committed a serious breach of contract; the employer may terminate the contract by a simple notice to the builder.[74] The employer may then employ another builder to do the work and can recover any additional expense as damages. However, most building contracts of any complexity will contain provisions which in effect require the employer to give the contractor an opportunity to correct any defect before terminating the contract on this ground.

6.2.1.D. PRACTICAL EXAMPLES

(1) A Seller Fails to Deliver

A striking example of the differences between the Civil Law systems on the one hand and the Common Law on the other is provided by the case of a sale of goods contract under which the seller refuses to deliver the goods.

---

[72] We will return to the "disproportionate expenditure" point in § 633(2) BGB, *infra* at 690.

[73] See BGH 10 October 1985 BGHZ 96, 111, **6.G.32** *infra* 691.

[74] See *infra* at 790–791.

Code civil **6.F.21.**

Article 1610: If the seller fails to deliver within the time agreed between the parties, the buyer may choose between termination (*résolution*) of the sale or delivery of the item, provided the delay is due to the seller's default.

Note
The court may impose an astreinte on the seller until the property is delivered.[75]

BGB **6.G.22.**

§ 433: (1) By the contract of sale the seller of a thing is bound to deliver the thing to the purchaser and to transfer ownership of the thing. The seller of a right is bound to transfer the right to the purchaser and, if the right entitles one to the possession of a thing, to deliver the thing
. . .

Note
Performance of this primary obligation may be demanded in accordance with § 241 BGB.[76] It is enforceable under the provisions of § 883 ZPO which allow for the seizure of movable property.

In England, contracts for the sale of goods are specifically enforced only if the goods are unique or unobtainable. The rule is strictly applied. Thus in *Société des Industries Métallurgiques SA* v. *The Bronx Engineering Co Ltd.*[77] the sellers of a machine tool wrongly refused to deliver it, threatening to sell it instead to a third party. The Court of Appeal said that specific performance would not be available even though it would be nine months before the buyers could obtain a similar machine from any other supplier. However, it has been accepted that a contract for the sale of goods may be specifically enforced if a temporary shortage means that they are practically unavailable from any other source: *Sky Petroleum Ltd.* v. *VIP Petroleum Ltd.*[78]

(2) A Builder Fails to Complete the Work
If a builder fails to complete work under a construction contract, or fails to rectify defects in the work, it is common in French or German law for the employer to obtain enforcement *in natura*.[79] Either the employer may obtain an order that the builder shall do the work or, more usually, it may have the necessary work done by a third party at the original builder's expense. Again there is a contrast with English law. English courts will not usually grant specific performance of a building contract.

---

[75] Cass. com.12 December 1966, Bull.civ. 1966.II.424 (car) and Req. 18 November 1907, S. 1913.386 (land), both cited in Zweigert and Kötz, at 476, who point out that alternatively a *huissier* could be ordered to execute the judgment.
[76] See *supra* at 677.
[77] [1975] 1 Lloyd's Rep. 465, CA.
[78] [1974] 1 WLR 576 (during an oil crisis the defendants threatened to refuse to supply the plaintiffs, who would not be able to get oil from any other source; the court gave an injunction prohibiting the defendants from selling the oil to anyone else, thereby effectively forcing them to supply to the plaintiffs).
[79] For examples, see the cases extracted *infra* at 689 and 691.

However, the contrast between the common law and the continental systems may be more apparent than real. First, as suggested earlier, in English Law the employer may terminate the contract, employ another builder to do the work and then claim any extra cost incurred from the original builder in an action for damages. This is functionally equivalent to execution by a third party. Secondly, even if a French court orders the builder to finish the work on pain of an *astreinte*, the builder does not have to do the work himself; he can arrange for a third person to do it. Thus the principal difference between this and English law is as to who has to organize the replacement builder. Thirdly, there is one situation in which even in England a building contract may be specifically enforced. This is where the work is to be done on the defendant's own land, so that the plaintiff cannot simply employ another builder or do the work himself because that would involve trespassing on the defendant's land. Damages would not be an adequate remedy.[80]

(3) A Seller Delivers Goods Which Are Defective

At this point we encounter the special regimes which, as mentioned earlier,[81] apply in French and German law to defects in goods. Broadly speaking these provide that if the seller delivers goods which contain a defect which was not apparent to the buyer, the latter may claim either cancellation of the contract and a return (redhibition) of the price, or a reduction in price.[82] Under certain conditions the seller may also be liable in damages for any further loss to the buyer.[83]

There are differences between the regimes. One is that in German law the buyer may claim these remedies against the immediate seller, whereas in French law they may be claimed from any previous seller.[84] A second difference, which is of immediate relevance, is that in German law if the rules on defects in goods apply, other remedies are excluded. In French law this is not necessarily the case; for example, as we saw earlier,[85] a buyer who has received defective goods may have a choice between an action on the *garantie des vices cachés* and avoiding the contract for error. There may also be a choice between an action on the *garantie* and one for non-performance of the contract, but we will see that the overlap here is less.

BGB 6.G.23.

§ 480: The purchaser of a generic item may demand, instead of cancellation of the contract (*Wandlung*) or reduction of the purchase price (*Minderung*), that in place of the defective thing one free from defect be delivered to him. The provisions of §§ 464–466, § 467 sent. 1 and §§ 469, 470, 474–479, applicable to cancellation of the contract, apply *mutatis mutandis* to this claim.

Notes

(1) It is important to be aware that this right of the buyer to demand conforming tender is limited to sales of generic goods as defined in § 91, and § 279 BGB provides that the

---

[80] See *Wolverhampton Corp.* v. *Emmons* [1901] 1 KB 515.

[81] *Supra* at 662 and 664.

[82] When cancellation is permitted, and when only a reduction of price, is considered in the section on Termination, *infra* at 756–757.

[83] This was referred to *supra* at 662 and 665, and is considered further in section **6.5** on Damages, *infra* at 850.

[84] This is considered in detail in section 1 of chapter 7, *infra* at 887.

[85] *Supra* at 395.

685

vendor will be held responsible for supply for as long as the genus is not exhausted. Indeed he remains subject to his obligation to provide a thing of "average type and value": § 243(1) BGB.

(2) Where specific goods are sold, it is clearly not possible simply to order the delivery of conforming goods; any order would in effect be one to repair the goods and then to deliver them. In such cases a defect will as a rule give rise only to a right to cancel the contract or have the contract price reduced.[86] This is so since the supply of defective goods is held to be poor performance, but not non-performance. The latter would be constituted only by a failure to deliver or to pass unencumbered title to the buyer. Even in such contracts, however, the parties may agree a right to cure.

BGB   **6.G.24.**

§ 476a: If, in place of the right of the buyer to cancellation (*Wandlung*) or reduction of the purchase price (*Minderung*), a right to cure is agreed, the vendor must bear the cost of transport, material and work incurred for the purpose of curing . . .

The agreement of a right to cure, particularly through the general conditions of business, is in practice very common.

The recent Directive 1999/44/EC on certain aspects of the sale of consumer goods and associated guarantees of 25 May 1999 obliges Member States to provide consumers who have been sold defective goods with the right to "require the seller to repair the goods" (Article 3.2). This may necessitate a change in German law.

Code civil   **6.F.25.**

Article 1641: The seller is bound by a guarantee against any hidden defect in a thing sold which renders it of no use for the intended purpose, or of less use for that purpose such that, had the buyer known of the defect, he would not have bought the thing or would only have bought it at a reduced price.

Article 1642: The seller is not responsible for defects which were apparent and which the buyer could have seen for himself.

Article 1643: He is responsible for hidden defects, even if he could not have known of them, unless, in such a case, he has stipulated that that he will not be liable on any guarantee.

Article 1644: In the cases covered by Articles 1641 and 1643, the buyer has the choice of returning the thing and recovering the price or keeping the thing and recovering a proportion of the price, the proportion to be judged by experts.

Article 1645: If the seller knew of the defect in the thing, he is liable for damages to the buyer in addition to returning the price.

Article 1646: If the seller did not know of the defect in the thing, he is only liable to return the price and to reimburse the buyer for expenses occasioned by the sale.

---

[86] See § 462 BGB, *supra* at 758.

Note

In French law the buyer who has received "defective" goods may have a choice between a remedy on the basis of the hidden defect and one for non-performance, as the courts have interpreted the two notions in such a way that there is a considerable overlap—a defect may constitute a non-performance and *vice versa*. In such a case, the traditional view is that the remedies available will depend on whether or not the buyer has accepted the goods. If it has not accepted them, it may either bring an action on the *garantie* for cancellation of the contract, or it may seek the normal remedies for non-performance. Once the goods have been accepted, however, the buyer's only remedies will be under the *garantie*.[87] In either case, can the buyer in effect force the seller to perform by making it deliver proper goods or repair the ones which have been delivered? According to the traditional view:

—If the buyer has not accepted the goods, the Civil Code does not have specific provisions on the replacement of defective goods but the case is treated as one of non-delivery. It is clear that the buyer may purchase replacement goods at the seller's expense in accordance with Article 1144. Where the buyer needs the goods urgently this may be done without prior judicial authorization.[88] Alternatively the court might impose an *astreinte* on the seller until it delivers conforming goods.[89] It will then be up to the seller whether it repairs the goods originally tendered so that they conform to the contract, or purchases replacement goods and tenders these.
—If the goods have been accepted by the buyer, the buyer will not be able to get an order for repair or have the goods repaired at the seller's expense. This is because the remedies under the *garantie* are exclusive; and, as in German law, the seller is not treated as promising that the goods will be free from defect. The obligation is only to refund the price, in whole or in part, if the goods are defective.[90]

After some divergences between its divisions, the Cour de cassation decided in favour of a clear distinction between "garantie des vices cachés"—which renders the goods unfit for their usage—and non-conformity—which is the delivery of non-conforming goods.[91]

English law does not recognize explicitly the right of the buyer to either replacement of the goods or their repair. However the same practical result is reached in other ways. Though in English law the buyer has only the right to reject the goods and recover the money paid, or to claim damages, and cannot demand a replacement item from the seller, the seller may of course offer a replacement. The offer would be relevant to any question of mitigation of damages[92]—in other words, if the seller offered to replace the goods at no cost to the buyer, but the buyer unreasonably rejected this offer and bought replacement goods from a third party at a higher price, the buyer would not be entitled to recover damages for the additional cost of purchasing the replacement.[93] Similarly with repair: under the present law, the buyer who has received defective goods will usually have the

---

[87] Ghestin and Desché, paras. 718 and 762.
[88] See Ghestin, *Conformité et garanties dans le vente* (Paris: LGDJ, 1983) para. 187.
[89] Ghestin and Desché, para. 698.
[90] And in certain circumstances to pay damages, see *infra* at 850.
[91] Cass. civ. 1, 27 Oct. and 8 Dec. 1993, D. 1994.112; commentary by A. Bénabent, D. 1994. Chr.. 115.
[92] See *Payzu Ltd v. Saunders* [1919] 2 KB 581, CA.
[93] On mitigation see *infra* at 827.

right to claim the cost of having them repaired by a third party; this will be an element in the buyer's damages. The cost of repair will not be awarded when it exceeds the difference between the value of the goods as they are and that they would have if repaired, unless the goods are irreplaceable and have some particular sentimental value to the buyer.[94]

We noted above that Article 3(2) of Directive 1999/44/EC on certain aspects of the sale of consumer goods and associated guarantees of 25 May 1999 obliges Member States to provide consumers who have been sold defective goods with the right to "require the seller to repair the goods". The same Article also requires that the consumer be given a right to replacement of the goods. It is not clear whether Article 3(2) will necessitate a change in English Law for consumer sales. In their evidence to the House of Lords Select Committee, which was charged with considering a similarly-worded draft of the Directive, representatives of the European Commission indicated that, in their view, the present English law would comply with the Directive.[95]

BW   **6.NL.26.**

Article 7:21: 1. Where what has been delivered does not conform to the contract, the buyer may demand:
    (a) delivery of what is lacking;
    (b) repair of the thing delivered, provided that the seller can reasonably comply herewith;
    (c) replacement of the thing delivered, unless the deviation from what has been agreed to is too minor to justify this (. . .)
3. If, in a consumer sale, the seller has not performed his obligation to repair the thing delivered, within a reasonable period after a written notice to that effect from the buyer, the latter is entitled to have the repair done by a third person and to claim the costs thereof from the seller.

Principles of European Contract Law   **6.PECL.27.**

Article 9:102: *Non-monetary Obligations*
    (1) The aggrieved party is entitled to specific performance of an obligation other than one to pay money, including the remedying of a defective performance . . .[96]

6.2.1.E. COMPARATIVE SUMMARY ON BASIC RULES AND THE INTERNATIONAL RESTATEMENTS

Because of the differences in what is understood in the various systems by the phrase "specific performance", the differences between the systems may be less than appears at first sight. Nonetheless, the point remains that in French and German law specific enforcement is seen as a normal remedy for non-performance, while in the Common Law it is seen as exceptional—save in contracts for land. However, it is thought that practice,

---

[94] See *O'Grady* v. *Westminster Scaffolding Ltd* [1962] 2 Lloyd's Rep. 238 and *Darbishire* v. *Warren* [1963] 1 WLR 1067 (both tort cases) and *Ruxley Electronics and Construction Ltd.* v. *Forsyth* [1996] AC 344, **6.E.33** *infra* at 694.

[95] See 10th Report, Session 1996–97, Consumer Guarantees (HL Paper 57, March 1997), para. 97.

[96] See also Article 46(3) of CISG.

at least in Germany, reduces the differences still further, in that a creditor will not seek an order for performance if it is feasible to find a substitute.[97]

CISG appears to follow the continental approach. Article 46(1) allows a buyer to require performance by the seller of his obligations subject only to the buyer not having resorted to any remedy which would be inconsistent with this. PECL, in contrast, takes a more compromising approach which is thought to be more generous towards specific performance than the common law but more in line with practice on the continent, at least in the German system.

Principles of European Contract Law **6.PECL.28.**

Article 9:102: *Non-monetary Obligations*
> (1) The aggrieved party is entitled to specific performance of an obligation other than one to pay money, including the remedying of a defective performance.
> (2) Specific performance cannot, however, be obtained where . . .
>> (d) the aggrieved party may reasonably obtain performance from another source.[98]

6.2.1.F. LIMITATIONS ON SPECIFIC PERFORMANCE

(1) Impossibility

In none of the systems will the court make an order for performance when that is no longer possible, even if that was the debtor's fault. This is expressly provided for in German law.

BGB **6.G.29.**

§ 251: (1) Insofar as restitution is impossible or is insufficient to compensate the creditor, the person liable shall compensate him in money.
> (2) The person liable may compensate the creditor in money if restitution in kind is possible only through disproportionate outlays. The costs arising from the treatment of an injured animal are not disproportionate simply because they significantly exceed its value.

§ 325: If the performance due from one party under a bilateral contract becomes impossible because of a circumstance for which he is responsible, the other party may demand damages for non-performance, or withdraw from the contract . . .[99]

(2) Disproportionate Expense

Cass. civ., 17 November 1984[100] **6.F.30.**

DISPROPORTIONATE EXPENSE

The French swimming pool

Specific performance should not be refused simply on the ground that the inconvenience caused to the creditor by the non-performance is slight.

---

[97] See Zweigert and Kötz, at 484.
[98] Article 7.2.2 (c) Unidroit PCL is in similar terms.
[99] See PECL Article 9:102(2) (a), *supra* at 674.
[100] Not reported.

Facts: A contract for a swimming pool required it to be provided with four steps. It was built with only three. The employer sought an order that the defect should be corrected.

Held: The cour d'appel refused an order on the ground that it had not been shown that having only three steps caused any inconvenience. This decision was quashed.

Judgment: *In the matter of the appeal lodged by Mr Maurice Abou . . . seeking the setting aside of a judgment delivered . . . by the Aix-en-Provence cour d'appel (8th Chamber) in favour of Mr François Alessandra . . .* :—Whereas by his first appeal ground, Mr Abou complains of the dismissal by the contested judgment of his application for an order requiring Mr Alessandra to carry out the necessary works and to make the swimming pool and its appurtenances correspond with the contractual quotation of 26 December 1977, in particular as regards the number of steps providing access to the swimming pool in question, the said application having been dismissed on the ground that no evidence had been adduced showing that that deviation from the contract would render access to the pool more difficult and that the claim should not therefore be upheld.

—Whereas the appellant asserts that the cour d'appel refused to apply the terms of the contract signed by the two parties . . . and that, in the light of Article 1134 of the Civil Code, its decision thus has no legal basis . . .

—Whereas article 1184 of the Civil Code provides that where a party is owed an obligation which is not performed, that party may require the other party to perform the agreement where such performance is possible;

—Whereas in dismissing the application by the party who had commissioned the works for an order requiring the swimming pool to be fitted with four steps in conformity with the contract, instead of the three steps installed therein, the contested judgment found that no evidence had been adduced showing that that deviation from the contract would render access to the pool more difficult;

—Whereas in so ruling, without examining whether or not the installation could be altered so as to conform with the contract, the cour d'appel provided no legal basis for its decision.

On those grounds, the Court quashes and sets aside the contested judgment.

Note

The judgment appears to suggest that correction of the defect should be ordered unless it is impossible; the mere fact that the defect has not been shown to cause any inconvenience is not an adequate ground for refusing the order.

BGB   **6.G.31.**

§ 633: (1) The contractor is obliged to carry out the work in such a manner that it has the guaranteed attributes and that it is not subject to defects which negate or reduce its value or the usefulness for the purposes to which it would be put in the ordinary course of things or for those which were envisaged in the contract.

(2) If the work is not of this standard, the employer can require that the defect be cured. §476a applies accordingly. The contractor is entitled to refuse to effect a cure if this would require disproportionate expenditure.

(3) If the contractor is in delay in removing the defect, the employer can cure it himself and demand restitution of the costs so arising.

BGH, 10 October 1985[101]   **6.G.32.**

<small>REPLACEMENT ONLY PRACTICAL MEANS</small>

Insulated windows

A claim for performance of a contractor's obligation to remedy a defect complained of may be brought, even after acceptance of the work, if that is the only way in which such a defect or defects can be permanently eliminated.

Facts: In 1977 the plaintiff commissioned the defendant to install aluminium-framed windows and doors in the former's single-family residence at a cost of DM 21,607.04. Since the plaintiff required the smallest possible loss of heat (calorific value), the defendant proposed for the frames a construction having a calorific value of between 2.4 and 2.6. That proposal, together with the defendant's terms and conditions of supply and payment, formed the basis of the contract; for the rest, Part B of the VOB (*Verdingungsordnung für Bauleistungen* = contracting rules for the award of public works contracts) was to apply. By way of guarantee, Clause 9 of the terms and conditions of supply and payment provided *inter alia*: "Duly established defects shall be repaired or replaced free of charge; a reasonable time shall be deemed to be agreed for completion of the work required in that regard. All further claims, e.g. for damages, are excluded."

In 1977 the works carried out by the defendant were accepted. It subsequently became apparent that the actual calorific value of the window-frame and door-frame parts used was 3.8 (value per square metre). The plaintiff brought an action for an order requiring the defendant to perform his contractual obligation by replacing *all* the frames and casements of the windows and doors with new ones having a calorific value of between 2.4 and 2.6 and by carrying out all necessary ancillary work.

Held: By the *Landgericht* in Berlin and the *Kammergericht*, that the cost of replacing the windows was not disproportionate and that the work should be done. An appeal to the BGH was dismissed.

Judgment: . . . In support of his claim, [the plaintiff] pointed out that the inferior thermal insulation meant that additional heating was needed, and that it was giving rise to slight condensation on the profiles of the windows and doors which had resulted *inter alia* in the formation of mould on the wallpaper and plastering.

The defendant opposed the claim on the grounds that the replacement of all the windows and doors would require it to incur disproportionate and unreasonable expense, involving a cost price of approximately DM 22,000. In practical terms, this would mean carrying out the work again from scratch, which it was no longer obliged to do, the works having been accepted. Moreover, the state of technological development in 1977 was in fact such that a calorific value of between 2.4 and 2.6 for the frames could not at that time have been achieved. It maintained that the value and fitness of the windows and doors had suffered only an insignificant reduction as a result of the failure to conform to the calorific value indicated to the plaintiff in the offer made to the latter. The risk of the formation of mould arose only when the outside temperature was between –5 and –10 degrees centigrade—thus only on a few days in the year . . .

On those grounds:

III.2. The Chamber proposes to depart from its previous case-law, and henceforth to determine the point of law in issue, which is crucial to the outcome of, *inter alia*, the present case, by ruling that a claim for performance of a contractor's obligation which seeks an order requiring the works to be carried out again from scratch may invariably be brought if that is the only way in which the defects can be permanently eliminated, irrespective of whether the contract for the work is governed solely by the rules laid down in the *Bürgerliches Gesetzbuch* or whether Part B of the *Verdingungsordnung für Bauleistungen* applies to it.

---

[101] BGHZ 96.111

(a) In the judgments previously given, excessive attention has in general been paid to (what may be supposed to be) *notional* distinctions between the carrying out of the works again from scratch ["*Neuherstellung*"] and the making good of defects following completion of the works ["*Nachbesserung*"]. Insufficient regard has been had, by contrast, to the *purpose* of the elimination of defects, which occupies such a prominent place in the law relating to building contracts.

The word "*Nachbesserung*" does not appear in the relevant legislation or Part B of the *Verdingungsordnung für Bauleistungen*; instead, they merely speak of the elimination of a defect, for which a demand may be made (§§ 633, 634 BGB; §§ 4(7), 13 VOB/B). However, the *elimination* of defects, considered in terms of its natural meaning, merely signifies that defective workmanship must be replaced by workmanship which is free from defects, *in so far* as that is *necessary* in order to give rise *as a whole* to a work which is free from defects. The more far-reaching the defect, the greater the scope of the remedial work which may be demanded. Consequently, the comprehensive elimination of defects is intrinsically and *a priori* such that it may even necessitate the total replacement of previously defective workmanship by new, defect-free workmanship where that is the only way of successfully achieving the goal sought after by the elimination of the defects. In such a situation, and depending on the circumstances, the carrying out of the works again from scratch ["*Neuherstellung*"] means no more than the remedying of post-completion defects ["*Nachbesserung*"] on the largest possible—but also the requisite—scale. The remedying of post-completion defects which is such as to leave intact only a—possibly minimal—residual part of the work originally carried out frequently shifts seamlessly into the carrying out of the works again from scratch, where even that part of the work which has most recently been carried out needs to be replaced or done again. The distinction between such measures for the elimination of defects is one of scope, not of substance. To render the contractor's obligation to eliminate defects dependent on whether such elimination involves "*Neuherstellung*" or merely "*Nachbesserung*" entails problems of demarcation which cannot easily be overcome, and constitutes an approach which leads not infrequently to purely haphazard and thus unsatisfactory results . . .

The only proper approach to adopt is to treat the elimination of defects as covering *all* measures which are *necessary* in order to produce a work which, *taken as a whole*, is in conformity with the contract and is free from defects, even if that entails the total replacement of works which have already been carried out. In that connection, the amount which it costs to eliminate the defects by carrying out of the works again from scratch cannot constitute a material factor. It can be very expensive even to remedy individual defects by means of "*Nachbesserung*"; depending on the extent and scope of such defects, the cost of doing so may frequently far exceed the remuneration payable for the work as a whole. By contrast, it may be substantially cheaper for the contractor to carry out all of the work again from scratch than to remedy defects in the majority of the individual parts. Consequently, it must from the outset be open to the contractor, in accordance, at the very least, with the principle of good faith, to choose to remedy defects by carrying out the work again from scratch, provided that, in the circumstances prevailing, that is not unreasonable from the point of view of the client. . .

(e) For the purposes of weighing up the interests of the parties in circumstances involving the elimination of defects, priority must be given to the interest of the client/customer in the production of an end result which is *free from defects* and which it is the responsibility of the contractor to provide. The latter's interest in restricting his involvement in the matter, following acceptance of the works, to the construction as accepted by the client, and in being required only to remedy defects appearing in individual parts thereof, must take second place. Compared to the success of the project, which he is contractually bound to ensure, his own interest in the matter is less deserving of protection. It follows that the interest of the client/customer in the production of a work which is free from defects must prevail even where—indeed, particularly where—the nature, gravity and significance of the defects is such that the only way in which that objective can be achieved is by starting again from scratch and completely replacing all of the works which have already been carried out ["*Neuherstellung*"].

In those circumstances, the contractor is by no means deprived of all means of protecting himself against a demand by the client that he should carry out all the work again from scratch. Thus, he is only required to take such action if it is really *necessary* in order permanently to eliminate the defects, that is to say, if the remedying of defects in individual parts of the completed work would not suffice. Even where such remedial steps would suffice, the scope of his obligation to take those steps will depend on, and be restricted to, such measures as are necessary in order to produce an end result which is free from defects.

Where the client demands that the contractor should eliminate the defects by carrying out of the works again from scratch ["*Neuherstellung*"], that demand is subject to the further qualification that the contractor may refuse to eliminate a defect if it would be disproportionately expensive to do so. That restriction likewise applies to all claims for the remedying of post-completion defects ["*Neuherstellung*"] (§ 633(2) BGB, second sentence; § 13(6) VOB/B, first sentence). It is sufficient, as a general rule, to prevent inequitable results in individual cases . . .

3. In the present case, it is undeniable that the thermal insulation guaranteed by the defendant to the plaintiff in relation to the door-frames and window-frames can be achieved only by their total replacement (including the panes). That is tantamount to carrying out the work again from scratch. When the construction works were at the planning stage, the plaintiff set particular store by the provision of above-average insulation. Consequently, it was of decisive importance to him that the window-frames and door-frames should provide a high level of heat insulation. By contrast, the court below found, on the basis of an expert's report, that the windows and doors installed in the premises constituted, in terms of the insulation of the premises as a whole, "a significant weakness compromising the thermal insulation of the property to a considerable degree". In those circumstances, the plaintiff should not have to settle for the remedying of individual defects; instead, it will only be possible for the defendant to fulfil its obligation to produce an end result corresponding to the standard guaranteed by it, that is to say, work which is free from defects, if the windows and doors are replaced in their entirety. The plaintiff is entitled to demand that; in particular, he should not have to settle for a reduction in the price payable for the work. There is no need to examine the question of the extent of any entitlement which he may have to damages.

4. The court below rightly found, moreover, that the defendant was not entitled to refuse to take the remedial action demanded (in this instance, the carrying out of the works again from scratch) on the ground that it would involve disproportionate expense (§ 13(6) VOB/B).

It would only have been open to the defendant to refuse to take remedial action if, weighing up all the circumstances, the expense involved in eliminating the defects bore no reasonable relationship to the prospects of successfully eliminating them. That issue depends not solely on the amount of the costs arising, but on the relationship which such expense bears to the benefit accruing to the client as a result of the elimination of the defects. On that basis, the improvement to be achieved in the calorific value constituted a significant benefit for the plaintiff, since it would remove a substantial "weakness" in the thermal insulation of the building. The plaintiff wished, by means of the high level of thermal insulation sought after by him, *inter alia* to eliminate the long-term risk of the formation of mould during periods of frosty weather; consequently, the average number of days per year on which such mould is likely to form with the frames originally installed is not a material consideration.

Furthermore, as regards the resulting increase in heating costs, the plaintiff runs the risk, in the event of significant unexpected increases in those costs, of incurring a corresponding loss. It follows that, having regard to all the circumstances, the replacement of the windows and doors with new ones possessing the guaranteed calorific value is by no means out of all reasonable proportion to the expense to the defendant, which is calculated to involve a cost price of DM 22,000. The question of "disproportionality" does not depend on the amount required for the work.

Note

Both the right to have full performance and the right to demand a cure are limited by the proportionality requirement of BGB § 633(2), the former implicitly and the latter explicitly.

The disproportion point rarely arises in relation to specific performance in English law because specific performance is so rarely granted; but it arises in relation to the measure of damages.

House of Lords   **6.E.33.**

Ruxley Electronics and Construction Ltd v. *Forsyth*[102]

UNREASONABLE TO CURE DEFECT

The English swimming pool

When building work has been done defectively the plaintiff will not recover damages based on the cost of correcting the defect, even if he undertakes to use the damages to this end, if to do so would be unreasonable.

Facts: The defendant had contracted for a swimming pool 7'6" deep. In breach of contract the finished pool was only 6' deep and when the contractors sued for the price the defendant counter-claimed for the cost of deepening it. This would have involved total reconstruction. Before the Court of Appeal the defendant offered an undertaking to use any damages awarded on this basis for correcting the defect.

Held: The trial judge held that the depth was perfectly adequate for the-off-the-side diving which was all that was intended and that it would be unreasonable to reconstruct the pool. The plaintiff was therefore entitled only to damages for any difference in value between a 6' pool and a 7'6" one, plus £2,500 for loss of amenity. The Court of Appeal by a majority reversed this decision. The defendant could not reasonably mitigate the loss, for example by buying another house with a deeper pool. The reasonableness of his desire to reconstruct the pool was irrelevant if that was the only way in which the defendant could get what he had contracted for (Staughton LJ); or reconstruction was not unreasonable (Mann LJ). The House of Lords restored the first instance judgment.

Judgment: LORD JAUNCEY: . . . Mr McGuire for the appellants argued that the cost of reinstatement was only allowable where (1) the employer intended as a matter of probability to rebuild if damages were awarded, and (2) that it was reasonable as between him and the contractor so to do. Since the judge had found against the respondent on both these matters the appeal should be allowed. Mr.Jacob on the other hand maintained that reasonableness only arose at the stage when a real loss had been established to exist and that where that loss could only be met by damages assessed on one basis there was no room for consideration of reasonableness. Such was the case where a particular personal preference was part of the contractual objective—a situation which did not allow damages to be assessed on a diminution of value basis . . .

Damages are designed to compensate for an established loss and not to provide a gratuitous benefit to the aggrieved party from which it follows that the reasonableness of an award of damages is to be linked directly to the loss sustained. If it is unreasonable in a particular case to award the cost of reinstatement it must be because the loss sustained does not extend to the need to reinstate. A failure to achieve the precise contractual objective does not necessarily result in the loss which is occasioned by a total failure . . .

I take the example suggested during argument by my noble and learned friend, Lord Bridge of Harwich. A man contracts for the building of a house and specifies that one of the lower courses of brick should be blue. The builder uses yellow brick instead. In all other respects the house conforms to the contractual specification. To replace the yellow bricks with blue would involve

---

[102] [1996] AC 344.

694

extensive demolition and reconstruction at a very large cost. It would clearly be unreasonable to award to the owner the cost of reconstructing because his loss was not the necessary cost of reconstruction of his house, which was entirely adequate for its design purpose, but merely the lack of aesthetic pleasure which he might have derived from the sight of blue bricks. Thus in the present appeal the respondent has acquired a perfectly serviceable swimming pool, albeit one lacking the specified depth. His loss is thus not the lack of a useable pool with consequent need to construct a new one. Indeed were he to receive the cost of building a new one and retain the existing one he would have recovered not compensation for loss but a very substantial gratuitous benefit, something which damages are not intended to provide.

What constitutes the aggrieved party's loss is in every case a question of fact and degree. Where the contract breaker has entirely failed to achieve the contractual objective it may not be difficult to conclude that the loss is the necessary cost of achieving that objective. Thus if a building is constructed so defectively that it is of no use for its designed purpose the owner may have little difficulty in establishing that his loss is the necessary cost of reconstructing. Furthermore in taking reasonableness into account in determining the extent of loss it is reasonableness in relation to the particular contract and not at large. Accordingly if I contracted for the erection of a folly in my garden which shortly thereafter suffered a total collapse it would be irrelevant to the determination of my loss to argue that the erection of such a folly which contributed nothing to the value of my house was a crazy thing to do. As Oliver J. said in *Radford* v. *De Froberville* [1977] 1 W.L.R. 1262, 1270:

> "If he contracts for the supply of that which he thinks serves his interests—be they commercial, aesthetic or merely eccentric—then if that which is contracted for is not supplied by the other contracting party I do not see why, in principle, he should not be compensated by being provided with the cost of supplying it through someone else or in a different way, subject to the proviso, of course, that he is seeking compensation for a genuine loss and not merely using a technical breach to secure an uncovenanted profit."

However where the contractual objective has been achieved to a substantial extent the position may be very different.

It was submitted that where the objective of a building contract involved satisfaction of a personal preference the only measure of damages available for a breach involving failure to achieve such satisfaction was the cost of reinstatement. In my view this is not the case. Personal preference may well be a factor in reasonableness and hence in determining what loss has been suffered but it cannot per se be determinative of what that loss is.

My Lords, the trial judge found that it would be unreasonable to incur the cost of demolishing the existing pool and building a new and deeper one. In so doing he implicitly recognised that the respondent's loss did not extend to the cost of reinstatement. He was, in my view, entirely justified in reaching that conclusion. It therefore follows that the appeal must be allowed.

It only remains to mention two further matters. The appellant argued that the cost of reinstatement should only be allowed as damages where there was shown to be an intention on the part of the aggrieved party to carry out the work. Having already decided that the appeal should be allowed I no longer find it necessary to reach a conclusion on this matter. However I should emphasise that in the normal case the court has no concern with the use to which a plaintiff puts an award of damages for a loss which has been established. Thus irreparable damage to an article as a result of a breach of contract will entitle the owner to recover the value of the article irrespective of whether he intends to replace it with a similar one or to spend the money on something else. Intention, or lack of it, to reinstate can have relevance only to reasonableness and hence to the extent of the loss which has been sustained. Once that loss has been established intention as to the subsequent use of the damages ceases to be relevant.

The second matter relates to the award of £2,500 for loss of amenity made by the trial judge. The respondent argued that he erred in law in making such award. However as the appellant did not challenge it, I find it unnecessary to express any opinion on the matter.

LORD MUSTILL: My Lords, I agree that this appeal should be allowed for the reasons stated by my noble and learned friends, Lord Jauncey of Tullichettle and Lord Lloyd of Berwick. I add some observations of my own on the award by the trial judge of damages in a sum intermediate between, on the one hand, the full cost of reinstatement, and on the other the amount by which the mal-performance has diminished the market value of the property on which the work was done: in this particular case, nil. This is a question of everyday practical importance to householders who have engaged contractors to carry out small building works, and then find (as often happens) that performance has fallen short of what was promised. I think it proper to enter on the question here, although there is no appeal against the award, because the possibility of such a recovery in a suitable case sheds light on the employer's claim that reinstatement is the only proper measure of damage.

The proposition that these two measures of damage represent the only permissible bases of recovery lie at the heart of the employer's case . . .

In my opinion there would indeed be something wrong if, on the hypothesis that cost of reinstatement and the depreciation in value were the only available measures of recovery, the rejection of the former necessarily entailed the adoption of the latter; and the court might be driven to opt for the cost of reinstatement, absurd as the consequence might often be, simply to escape from the conclusion that the promisor can please himself whether or not to comply with the wishes of the promise which, as embodied in the contract, formed part of the consideration for the price. Having taken on the job the contractor is morally as well as legally obliged to give the employer what he stipulated to obtain, and this obligation ought not to be devalued. In my opinion however the hypothesis is not correct. There are not two alternative measures of damage, at opposite poles, but only one; namely, the loss truly suffered by the promisee. In some cases the loss cannot be fairly measured except by reference to the full cost of repairing the deficiency in performance. In others, and in particular those where the contract is designed to fulfil a purely commercial purpose, the loss will very often consist only of the monetary detriment brought about by the breach of contract. But these remedies are not exhaustive, for the law must cater for those occasions where the value of the promise to the promisee exceeds the financial enhancement of his position which full performance will secure. This excess, often referred to in the literature as the "consumer surplus" (see for example the valuable discussion by Harris, Ogus and Philips (1979) 95 LQR 581) is usually incapable of precise valuation in terms of money, exactly because it represents a personal, subjective and non-monetary gain. Nevertheless where it exists the law should recognise it and compensate the promisee if the misperformance takes it away. The lurid bathroom tiles, or the grotesque folly instanced in argument by my noble and learned friend, Lord Keith of Kinkel, may be so discordant with general taste that in purely economic terms the builder may be said to do the employer a favour by failing to install them. But this is too narrow and materialistic a view of the transaction. Neither the contractor nor the court has the right to substitute for the employer's individual expectation of performance a criterion derived from what ordinary people would regard as sensible. As my Lords have shown, the test of reasonableness plays a central part in determining the basis of recovery, and will indeed be decisive in a case such as the present when the cost of reinstatement would be wholly disproportionate to the non-monetary loss suffered by the employer. But it would be equally unreasonable to deny all recovery for such a loss. The amount may be small, and since it cannot be quantified directly there may be room for difference of opinion about what it should be. But in several fields the judges are well accustomed to putting figures to intangibles, and I see no reason why the imprecision of the exercise should be a barrier, if that is what fairness demands. My Lords, once this is recognised the puzzling and paradoxical feature of this case, that it seems to involve a contest of absurdities, simply falls away. There is no need to remedy the injustice of awarding too little, by unjustly awarding far too much. The judgment of the trial judge acknowledges that the employer has suffered a true loss and expresses it in terms of money. Since there is no longer any issue about the amount of the award, as distinct from the principle, I would simply restore his judgment by allowing the appeal.

[LORDS KEITH, BRIDGE and LLOYD delivered concurring judgments.]

Note
While the courts may disagree on what will constitute disproportionate expense (see the French and English swimming pool cases, above), it is thought that there is a general principle that specific performance should not be ordered if it would involve the debtor in expense or difficulty which would be disproportionate to the benefit the creditor would gain thereby. The PECL provide:

Principles of European Contract Law **6.PECL.34.**

Article 9:102: *Non-monetary Obligations*
> (1) The aggrieved party is entitled to specific performance of an obligation other than one to pay money, including the remedying of a defective performance.
> (2) Specific performance cannot, however, be obtained where:
>> (b) performance would cause the debtor unreasonable effort or expense; or
>> . . .[103]

(3) Effects on Third Persons or the Public

Cass. civ., 17 December 1963[104] **6.F.35.**

ILLICIT BUILDING TO BE DESTROYED DESPITE HOUSING SHORTAGE

Too many storeys

A housing shortage does not justify refusing to order the destruction of a building which has been built in breach of planning laws.

Facts: The defendant lessees had built more storeys on their apartment building than was permitted by the lease they had been granted. The owners demanded the demolition of the extra storeys.

Held: The Cour d'appel of Montpellier refused their demand, in the light of the interests of the tenants living there, and awarded damages instead. The owners appealed and the earlier decision was quashed.

Judgment: THE COURT: . . . *On the first branch of the second appeal ground*: . . .—Under Article 1143 of the Civil Code;
—Whereas the sole application made to the court adjudicating on the substance of the case was for an order requiring Parena and the Société Civile Immobilière La Rabelais to demolish the storeys of the building which they had constructed in breach of a provision contained in the specifications governing the erection of constructions on the land.
—Whereas although the contested judgment found that that provision had indeed been breached, it refused to order the demolition of the extra storeys and awarded the plaintiffs compensatory damages on the ground that it was necessary to safeguard the interests of the tenants living in those storeys.

---

[103] See also UPCL Article 7.2.2 (b).
[104] JCP 1964.II.13609, annotated by Blaevoelt; Gaz.Pal. 1964.1.158.

—Whereas the cour d'appel acknowledged that it would not be impossible to enforce the order for specific performance applied for, and that the plaintiffs had an interest in obtaining such an order, but nevertheless refused to make the order in question, for reasons relating to the interests of third parties; in so doing, it infringed the legislative provision referred to above.

[On those grounds, and without there being any need to rule on the second part of that plea, the Court quashes and sets aside the contested judgment.]

[From the note:] The facts are very simple. Parena and the Société Immobilière Le Rabelais had constructed on a parcel of land a building comprising more storeys than permitted by the specifications relating to that land. The owners of certain lots brought proceedings against them for an order requiring them to demolish the surplus storeys. The Montpellier cour d'appel, before which the case was brought, found that the provisions contained in the specifications had indeed been infringed, but refused to order the demolition sought and awarded the plaintiffs compensatory damages on the ground that it was necessary to safeguard the interests of the tenants of the dwellings located in those storeys. It is that judgment which is contested.

The 1st Civil Chamber of the Cour de cassation, ruling on the plea relating to Article 1143 of the Civil Code, held that the cour d'appel had infringed that article: although the cour d'appel acknowledged that it would not be impossible to enforce the order sought, and that the plaintiffs had an interest in obtaining such an order, it nevertheless refused to make the order in question, for reasons relating to the interests of third parties.

However, certain cours d'appel were in the habit of restricting the relief granted by them to awards of damages. In so doing, those courts invoked various considerations, such as the fact that "a demolition order would be disproportionate to the loss suffered", the fact that the permitted height of the building had not been significantly exceeded, the general need, in dealing with construction cases, to have regard to the crisis in the housing sector and, in certain cases, the fact that the builder had acted in good faith (. . .) The strict approach adopted by the Civil Chamber in applying the Civil Code is commendable, since it accords with the concern of the legislature to preserve the salubrity of certain premises by providing, in the town planning rules enacted by it, for the imposition of severe penalties for infringements of those rules.

Note

In the English case of *Wrotham Park Estates Co.* v. *Parkside Homes*,[105] developers acquired land subject to a restrictive covenant limiting the number of houses which could be built. In ignorance of the restriction, they built more houses than they were allowed to. Brightman J refused a mandatory injunction ordering destruction of the houses, as that would be "an unpardonable waste of much needed housing", and awarded damages instead.[106]

Such factors are not referred to in the international restatements.

(4) Contracts Involving Personal Services

The fact that a contract is for services does not prevent the court from granting execution *in natura*. First, in French or German Law it may be possible for the contract to be performed by a third person at the defendant's expense. Examples are the building contract cases (these are contracts for services and materials); or the contract to publish, which can be performed

---

[105] [1974] 1 WLR 798, Ch.D.
[106] On the way the judge calculated the damages, see *infra* at 857 ff.

by a third party in certain circumstances.[107] Secondly, in both those systems, and even in English Law on the rare occasions in which a contract for services and materials is specifically enforceable, the courts will not be concerned if the defendant can get someone else to do the work. It will different if only the defendant can perform the contract.

Cass. civ., 14 March 1900[108]   **6.F.36.**

ARTISTIC OBLIGATIONS

Lady Eden's portrait

Specific performance of a contract involving artistic or other personal services will not be granted.

Facts: Sir William Eden had commissioned James McNeill Whistler to paint a portrait of Lady Eden. The painting had been completed and exhibited, and Eden had tendered payment for it; but the parties fell out. Whistler refused to deliver the picture and painted the head of another woman in place of Lady Eden's. Mr [sic] Eden appealed to the Cour de cassation against the judgment delivered by the cour de Paris on 2 December 1897, reported in S. and P. 1900.2.201. The sole plea advanced by the appellant alleged infringement of Articles 1136, 1138, 1583, 1584, 1603 *et seq.*, 1787 and 1788 of the Civil Code, misapplication of Article 1142 of the Civil Code, the absence of any legal basis, a lack of reasons and infringement of Article 7 of the Law of 20 April 1810, in that, although the contested judgment acknowledged that Whistler had contracted with Sir William Eden to paint the portrait of Lady Eden, and that he had painted and completed that portrait, it refused to order that the portrait be delivered to the plaintiff, on the ground that the contract concluded between the parties had given rise only to a mere obligation to perform an act the remedy for the non-performance of which lay in damages; the appellant asserted that that contract in fact constituted an agreement for the sale of an object to be created in the future or for the provision of services in the form of work requiring the provider of those services to deliver the result of his labours, or, at the very least, that the contract imposed an obligation to hand something over, the effect of which was automatically to transfer ownership of the portrait to the plaintiff as soon as it was completed, or at least upon its being approved by Sir Eden [sic], prior to delivery thereof; the plaintiff further claimed that, even if Mr Whistler's obligation was merely to perform an act, the court adjudicating on the substance of the case should nevertheless have ordered specific performance, since the obligation in question was susceptible of specific performance and did not impose any constraint on the freedom of the party by whom it was owed.

Held: In the lower courts the plaintiff's action for delivery of the painting was dismissed, and an appeal was rejected.

Judgment: THE COURT:—Whereas an agreement whereby a painter undertakes to paint a portrait for an agreed sum constitutes a contract of a special kind, pursuant to which property in the picture does not pass to the person commissioning it until the artist presents that picture to his client and the picture is approved by the latter; as until that stage is reached, the painter retains control over his work, although he may not lawfully keep it for himself or dispose of it as a portrait to a third party, since the right to reproduce the features of the sitter has only conditionally been conferred on him with a view to completion of the contract and in the event of failure by the artist to fulfil his obligations, he will incur liability in damages.

—Whereas as is indicated in the findings made in the contested judgment, Whistler undertook to paint a portrait of Lady Eden but refused throughout to make that portrait available to the plaintiff, who had commissioned it; having exhibited the picture at the *Salon du Champ-de-Mars*, he made radical changes to the painting, replacing the head of Lady Eden with that of another person.

—Whereas it was held in the contested judgment, first, that, since the plaintiff had not become the owner of the picture, he was not entitled to require it to be delivered to him in its existing state and,

---

[107] E.g. OLG München MDR 1955.682.
[108] S. 1900.1.489.

699

second, that Whistler was liable, by way of damages, to return the price paid in advance and in addition, the contested judgment prohibited Whistler from making any use whatever of the canvas until such time as he had altered its appearance in such a way as to render it unrecognisable, in so ruling, the contested judgment, which is accompanied by a statement of reasons, did not infringe the legislative provision referred to by the appellant; on the contrary, it correctly applied the same.

[On those grounds, the Court dismissed the appeal.]

Notes

In English law a contract between an author and a publisher to publish a book was held not to be specifically enforceable, on the ground that co-operation between the parties would be necessary: *Malcolm* v. *Chancellor, Masters and Scholars of the University of Oxford.*[109]

§ 888(2) ZPO[110] precludes the enforcement of personal service obligations under a contract of service (*Dienstvertrag*), But it is notable that the carrying out of work under a contract for services (*Werkvertrag*) is not similarly excluded. Thus, as long as such an obligation could not be performed by a third party and is dependent solely on the will of the debtor it could be enforced. This raises the possibility that in German Law, unlike in English or French Law, an artist could be compelled to paint a picture under a contract for services. Of course the practical difficulties and the probably unsatisfactory nature of the end product has meant that such enforcement is rarely sought.

Principles of European Contract Law   **6.PECL.37.**

Article 9:102: *Non-monetary Obligations*
          (2) Specific performance cannot, however, be obtained where: (. . .)
              (c) the performance consists in the provision of services or work of a personal character or depends upon a personal relationship . . .[111]

(5) Employment Contracts

The traditional rule is that a contract of employment cannot be enforced specifically.

ZPO   **6.G.38.**

§ 888: . . .
          (2) This provision is of no application in cases of a judgment to enter marriage, in cases of a judgment to engage in marital life and in cases of a judgment to provide services under a contract of service.

Note

In England, the traditional position is that a contract of employment will not be specifically enforced at the suit of either party—not against the employee because of the interference with liberty, and not against the employer on the ground that an employer should not have

---

[109] *The Times*, 19 December 1990.
[110] See **6.G.38**.
[111] UPCL Article 7.2.2.(d) excludes enforcement of an obligation which requires "performance of an exclusively personal character".

to employ anyone against its will. Now the Trade Union and Labour Relations (Consolidation) Act 1992, section 236 provides that no court shall compel an employee to do any work by ordering specific performance of a contract of employment or by restraining the breach of such contract by injunction. The case law has turned around two questions.

The first is whether it is possible to restrain an employee who is threatening to do something forbidden by the contract, such as working for a competitor. In English law the answer rests on whether this would be tantamount to giving specific enforcement, since preventing the employee from working for any other employer might prevent them from having any income unless they came to work for the plaintiff.[112] In German Law the HGB provides for the agreement of such restrictive clauses in certain employment contracts (at §§ 74–75d) and the Federal Labour Court (BAG) has applied these to all employment contracts. These statutory rules and the case law of the BAG indicate a policy of confining and ameliorating the effects of such clauses. This is because the *Grundgesetz* (GG) guarantees freedom to choose and exercise one's profession or calling and to choose where to do so (Article 12 GG). Thus such clauses must be in writing; they must serve a legitimate business interest of the employer; they must not unfairly limit the scope for professional development of the employee; they may last no longer than two years; and the employer must pay compensation to the employee during the relevant period. The enforcement of such clauses through the agreement of penalties is also subject to review by the courts (§§ 339 ff BGB). While the employment contract subsists, the employee is of course subject to a *Nebenpflicht* not to compete.[113]

The second is whether employers can be restrained from dismissing employees wrongfully when in fact the employers—or at least the employees' immediate superiors who will have to work with them—still have trust in the employees and are themselves willing to employ them. As just stated, the traditional attitude was that neither specific performance nor an injunction would be given against the employer would be given any more than it would be against the employee.

Court of Appeal   **6.E.39.**
Powell v. *Brent London Borough Council*[114]

INJUNCTION TO RESTRAIN WRONGFUL DISMISSAL

Ms. Powell

Where an employer is perfectly willing to continue employing the plaintiff but as the result of pressure from a trade union threatens to dismiss her wrongfully, the court will issue an injunction to restrain the dismissal.

Facts: The plaintiff had applied for promotion to the post of Principal Benefits Officer. At interviews she was

---

[112] See *Lumley* v. *Wagner* (1852) 1 De GM & G 604 (which involved the opera singer Joanna Wagner), *Warner Bros* v. *Nelson* [1937] 1 KB 209, KB (which involved the film star Bette Davis) and *Page One Records Ltd* v. *Britton* [1968] 1 WLR 157 (which involved "The Trogs"). In addition the clause must not be in unreasonable restraint of trade: see section **3.1.3**, *supra* at 305 ff.

[113] See generally *Münchener Kommentar*, under § 611, para. 488.

[114] [1987] IRLR 466.

told that she had been selected and she reported to her new place of employment. It was then alleged that the selection procedure had not complied with the Borough's equal opportunities code of practice and she was instructed to return to her previous post. She refused. Although the Borough strongly opposed her continuing in her new job, it was stated that her superiors had complete confidence in her and that her return to her job would cause no friction with those with whom she would be working.

Held: Knox J refused an injunction but the Court of Appeal granted an interlocutory injunction (i.e. an temporary injunction pending trial of the action).

Judgment: RALPH GIBSON LJ: For my part on this issue I have reached the conclusion that the decision of Knox J. cannot stand. I have reached that conclusion with hesitation because it seems to me essentially unlikely for a plaintiff to be able to satisfy the court that, despite strenuous opposition by her employers to her continuing in her job, nevertheless there subsists the necessary confidence between her and her employers to justify the making of an injunction. The fact of the opposition is likely in my view to be a true indication of the absence of confidence, but as I said at the outset I think this is a most unusual case.

First I must state the principle which must, I think, guide our decision. It is clear to me that part of the basis of the general rule against specific performance of contracts of service is that mutual confidence is normally a necessary condition for the satisfactory working of a contract of service. If one party refuses to allow the relationship to continue the mutual confidence is almost certainly missing. Knox J referred to the judgment of Geoffrey Lane LJ in *Chappell* v. *Times Newspapers Ltd.* [1975] I.C.R. 145, 178–179.

For my part I am not able to derive much assistance from the words "complete confidence" for the purposes of this case. I prefer to state what I think the applicable principle to be in this way. Having regard to the decision in *Hill* v. *C. A. Parsons & Co. Ltd.* [1972] Ch. 305 and to the long-standing general rule of practice to which *Hill* v. *C. A. Parsons & Co. Ltd.* was an exception, the court will not by injunction require an employer to let a servant continue in his employment, when the employer has sought to terminate that employment and to prevent the servant carrying out his work under the contract, unless it is clear on the evidence not only that it is otherwise just to make such a requirement but also that there exists sufficient confidence on the part of the employer in the servant's ability and other necessary attributes for it to be reasonable to make the order. Sufficiency of confidence must be judged by reference to the circumstances of the case, including the nature of the work, the people with whom the work must be done and the likely effect upon the employer and the employer's operations if the employer is required by injunction to suffer the plaintiff to continue in the work.

Notes

(1) This case is exceptional in the sense that the employer had confidence in the employee and was bowing to union pressure. However this is not an uncommon situation in England.[115]

(2) Even if the employer may be made to reinstate an employee, it is not clear that the employer has to do more than pay her salary; it may not have to give her any work to do.

In *Bliss* v. *South East Thames Regional Health Authority*,[116] the trial judge had awarded the plaintiff orthopaedic surgeon damages for distress, frustration and vexation after the defendants had, in breach of contract, required him to submit to examination by a psychiatrist and, when he refused, suspended him from duty; but this part of the decision was reversed by the Court of Appeal. If an employer does something wrongful which results in the employee finding it harder to obtain new employment—such as running a disrep-

---

[115] See also *Hill* v. *CA Parsons* [1972] Ch. 305.
[116] [1987] ICR 700.

utable business, contrary to the implied obligation of trust and confidence—, "stigma" damages reflecting the increased difficulty may be awarded;[117] but the older decision of *Addis* v. *Gramophone Co. Ltd.*[118] still seems to preclude damages being awarded for the humiliation of dismissal.[119]

Cass. soc., 14 June 1972[120]   **6.F.40.**

REINSTATEMENT OF EMPLOYEE

M. Dal Poz

An employer which wrongly dismisses an employee without using the proper procedures will be ordered to re-instate the employee.

Facts: The employer had purported to dismiss M. Dal Poz, who was a trade union representative, without going through the required procedure to get the approval of the Inspecteur du Travail. Dal Poz claimed to be reinstated.

Held: The Court of Appeal could properly make such an order.

Judgment: A cour d'appel may, without contradicting itself, take the view that there is an urgent need to put an end to a contravention attributable to a company which has sought to take the law into its own hands by dismissing a trade union representative, and may provisionally order that the parties be placed in the positions previously occupied by them, without examining the merits of the substantive case or pre-judging its outcome.

THE COURT: *On the second appeal ground, which falls to be dealt with as a preliminary point*:— Whereas the appellant contests the judgment made by the cour d'appel, in the context of an application for interim measures, ordering the reinstatement of Dal Poz, a staff representative and a trade union representative, whom the Société Anonyme Comptoir des Revêtements Revet-Sol had dismissed, notwithstanding the refusal of the Inspecteur du Travail to sanction that dismissal, on the ground that such a dispute did not fall within the jurisdiction of the *conseil de prud'hommes* [works council], the competence of courts hearing applications for interim measures being restricted to disputes the power to hear and determine the merits of which is vested in the civil courts, and that of *conseils de prud'hommes* being limited to the power to hear and determine disputes arising between employers and their workers or employees;

—Whereas however, the court seised of the case at first instance, having declared itself to be competent in the matter, ordered that Dal Poz be provisionally reinstated in his employment, on pain of the imposition of a penalty in the event of non-compliance with that order;

—Whereas the cour d'appel, which has full jurisdiction both in civil matters and in industrial relations cases, and in which the power to hear and determine disputes is vested by the devolutionary effect of an appeal, was required to rule thereon, regardless of whether or not the court seised of the case at first instance possessed jurisdiction in respect of it. Consequently, the decision in the contested judgment rejecting the objection of lack of jurisdiction was justified.

On the first, third and fourth appeal grounds:—Whereas the Société Comptoir des Revêtements Revet-Sol further contests the order made in that judgment requiring Dal Poz to be reinstated in his employment on the grounds that, in dismissing that union representative on 20 October 1970, it had

---

[117] *Malik* v. *Bank of Commerce and Credit International SA (in liquidation)* [1998] AC 20, HL.
[118] [1909] AC 488.
[119] See further *infra* at 840 ff.
[120] D.73.114 annotated by N. Catala; JCP 72.1.17275, annotated by G. Lyon-Caen.

infringed the mandatory provisions of the law and had taken the law into its own hands by committing an act incapable of terminating the employment contract;

—Whereas the appellant maintains, first, that it was not open to the cour d'appel, without contradicting itself and doubly prejudicing the substance of the case, to rule on the meaning and scope of a fundamental legal rule and to give effect to that ruling in contested proceedings, thereby prejudging the outcome of the case; as second, it asserts that the performance of a contract of employment entails an obligation to perform an act, the only remedy for non-fulfilment of which is an award of damages; it further argues that there exists no legal rule requiring the reinstatement of a trade union representative who has been improperly dismissed, that the taking of the law into one's own hands, which is a material act having no connection with the application of any legislative provision, cannot result from the normal exercise of an employer's undeniable right to terminate a contract of employment subject to review by the courts; as lastly, the appellant maintains that, in a written pleading to which no reply was lodged, it asserted that the Law of 27 December 1968 did not require the reinstatement of a trade union representative and, moreover, that the employer had merely exercised its incontestable, legally recognized right to dismiss its employees;

—Whereas the contested judgment correctly states, however, that Dal Poz's claim merely sought an order for the continued performance of a contract of employment, the proper existence of which had not in itself been denied, and which the employer had purported to terminate by taking the law into its own hands, despite the fact that the right to terminate that contract unilaterally had been withdrawn by the Law of 27 December 1968 and notwithstanding that the employer had not obtained the prior assent of the Inspecteur du Travail;

—Whereas the cour d'appel was at liberty to conclude, without contradicting itself, that there was an urgent need to put an end to the contravention committed by the company, which had sought to take the law into its own hands, and provisionally to order that the parties be placed in the positions previously occupied by them, without examining the merits of the substantive case or pre-judging its outcome;

It follows that none of the criticisms directed against the contested judgment is well founded.

[On those grounds, the Court dismissed the appeal lodged against the judgment delivered on 27 May 1971 by the cour d'appel, Lyon.]

Bundesarbeitsgericht, 10 November 1955[121]   **6.G.41.**

R EINSTATEMENT OF EMPLOYEE

The Radiologist

An employer may be ordered to reinstate an employee who has been wrongly dismissed, even if this will require the employer to organize its operations in such a way as to provide her with work.

Facts: The plaintiff was a consultant radiologist who was appointed head of the X-ray department. After a re-organization of the department she was dismissed, the employer claiming that she did not fit the requirements of head of the new department.

Held: The Landesarbeitsgericht granted her an order for continuation of her employment as head of department and damages for loss suffered as the result of the employer's actions. An appeal to the Bundesarbeitsgericht was dismissed.

Judgment: The plaintiff had been a specialist in internal medicine since 1933 and a specialist in radi-

---

[121] NJW 1956.359.

ology and radiotherapeutics since 1937. From 1933 onwards she worked as an assistant doctor, and from 1943 onwards as a senior consultant, in the X-ray department of the R. Hospital. On 1 November 1947, having already worked for a long period as the acting chief physician in the absence of the incumbent of that post, she was appointed to the position of chief physician in charge of that department. In the course of the reconstruction of the R. Hospital, the X-ray department was accommodated in a newly constructed building, in the medical aspects of the design and organization of which the plaintiff participated to a considerable extent. On 10 December 1953 she was given notice of dismissal with effect from 30 June 1954, on the ground that she did not satisfy the requirements needed of the head of the newly completed radiology institute.

The plaintiff considered that her dismissal was unjustified, and brought proceedings for a declaration that the employment relationship was not terminated by the notice in question. She further claimed an order for the continuation of her employment as chief physician in charge of the radiology and radiotherapeutics department of the R. Hospital, together with a declaration that the defendant was liable to compensate her for all damage suffered by her as a result of the refusal to allow her to continue her activities as head of that department. The *Landesarbeitsgericht* (Higher Labour Court) allowed those claims. The defendant's appeal on a point of law against the judgment of the *Landesarbeitsgericht* was dismissed.

On those grounds: II. It is also necessary to concur with the finding of the *Landesarbeitsgericht* that, according to recent developments in the law, there exists in principle an obligation on employers to give their employees work to do. An employment relationship is a mutual relationship conferring personal rights which does not merely involve the provision of specified individual services—as in the case of a contract for services entered into by a self-employed person or a contract imposing similar obligations—but extends to cover the employee's entire being, and thus substantially shapes and dictates that employee's life and personality. Moreover, the respect and approval due to an employee as a human being are based not merely on the commercial value of his/her services (reflected in the amount of his/her remuneration) but also, to a considerable extent, on the manner in which he/she fulfils the tasks which he/she is called upon to perform. In the sphere of a person's working life, it is that, above all, which decisively confers on that person his/her value as a human being. It follows that the employer is obliged, not merely on the basis of his duty to act in good faith but also, and above all, in accordance with the obligation imposed on all persons by Articles 1 and 2 of the *Grundgesetz* (Basic Law), to refrain from any act which might be detrimental to the value of the employee and the free development of his/her personality. Both of those aspects of the employee's fundamental rights would be impaired were he/she expected, not merely on a temporary basis but possibly for years on end, to draw his/her salary without being able to carry on the activity pertaining to his/her previous profession. That would be tantamount to compelling the employee concerned to do nothing, and would result in his/her ceasing in any way to be a full member of the professional community and of society. Not only the general public, but also the overwhelming majority of employees who are conscious of their abilities and achievements, regard it as contemptible to draw a wage which has not been earned by the provision of corresponding services. Moreover, such a situation would mean that an employee who was prohibited, during the existing employment relationship, from offering his labour to anyone else would be prevented from continuing his/her professional activities and from maintaining and improving his professional skills—in other words, from developing his/her personality. The foregoing applies in particular in the case of senior employees or others fulfilling particularly important tasks, since a lengthy period with no work to do creates the impression that the services previously rendered by the employee must have been so inferior that the employer prefers to spend money than to be provided with those services.

Consequently, the employer's right, during the course of the existing contract, and subject to the continued payment of the employee's salary, to give the latter nothing to do must be restricted, unless the employee agrees, to a temporary period only, possibly amounting to the length of a notice period. In other cases, there must exist special reasons justifying such a regime, which must be subjected to careful scrutiny.

In the present case, however, there is no need to enquire further into the findings made in that regard by the *Landesarbeitsgericht*, since the defendant's contention that its refusal to provide the plaintiff with work is justified by overriding interests cannot be considered further. That contention merely repeats, in essence, the assertion, given as a reason for the plaintiff's dismissal, that, following the changes arising from the reconstruction of the X-ray department, she was no longer acceptable to the hospital. In the event, however, of its being definitively established that the employment relationship continues to exist, and that the plaintiff is entitled to continue her activities as chief physician in charge of the X-ray department of the R. Hospital, the defendant will be unable to escape from its obligation in that regard; it will be required, in those circumstances, to organize its operations in such a way as to enable the plaintiff to continue to carry on her activities. Only if that subsequently proves *de facto* to be impossible, for unforeseeable reasons which are not attributable to the defendant, will it be possible, in proceedings instituted on the basis of a fresh notice of dismissal, to examine the situation anew.

Note

K. Larenz[122] writes:

In a rejection of his services the employee may suffer a personal rejection or a setback, including a disadvantage in respect of his professional development. If, for example, an actor is engaged to act by the management of a theatre, it would have a serious impact on him if he were denied any acting roles. It is thus clear that many contracts of service have a "personal" character from the perspective of the employee. In such cases, the refusal of services offered would be a breach of the duty of good faith of the employer, unless it were justified for special reasons. Put positively, this means that the employer can, under certain circumstances be obliged under BGB §242 to take up the services offered to him and to engage the employee in an appropriate way. Thus in essence is the "obligation to engage (*Beschäftigungsanspruch*)".

English Law seems the most restrictive of the three laws, granting reinstatement to the employee only in exceptional circumstances, and even then taking a very mercenary attitude to the employment, so that the employee needs be protected only against financial loss. The international restatements (PECL, Unidroit) say nothing about employment contracts specifically.

(6) Obligations Requiring the Involvement of Third Parties

ZPO   **6.G.42.**

§ 888: (1) If an activity cannot be undertaken by a third party and if it is dependent exclusively on the will of the debtor, it is to be recognised on application to the procedural court of first instance, that the debtor is to be held to his performance through fine, or committal where this cannot be levied, or through committal. A single fine may not exceed the sum of fifty thousand Deutschmarks. The provisions of the fourth section [of the ZPO] apply to committal . . .

---

[122] Larenz, *SBT–I*, para. 52 II c

PERFORMANCE NOT DEPENDENT SOLELY ON WILL OF DEBTOR

The Mom and Pop Shop

Where the debtor will not be able to perform the contract without the co-operation of third parties who are not before the court, specific performance cannot be ordered.

Facts: The lease of a small shop required the tenants to carry on a grocery and dairy business. The lessor sought to enforce this obligation.

Held: By judgment of the *Amtsgericht* (Local Court) the defendants were ordered, on pain of the imposition by the court of such legally permissible fine or detention order as it might decide upon, to carry on their grocery and dairy produce business in S. Upon the continued refusal by the defendants to carry on the business in question, the plaintiff applied to the S. *Amtsgericht* for an order for the enforcement of the judgment in accordance with §890 ZPO; the court imposed on the defendants, jointly and severally, a fine in the sum of DM 2,000. On appeal by the defendants the *Landgericht* overturned this decision. The plaintiff's appeal the *Oberlandesgericht* was rejected.

Judgment: . . . in the circumstances of the case, the plaintiff's further special appeal cannot be allowed.

The defendants' non-compliance with the obligation imposed on them by the judgment of the S. *Amtsgericht*, requiring them to carry on a grocery and dairy produce business, can be penalized by enforcement measures only if that obligation involves an act to be performed by the defendants in person and is exclusively dependent on the will of the defendants, or alternatively if the claim is capable, like a claim to compel a person from refraining from doing something, of being enforced. Neither of those conditions is satisfied in the present case.

In the Senate's view, the obligation to carry on a grocery and dairy produce business in specified premises must be regarded as involving an act to be performed by the defendants in person. An act is fungible only if it is capable of being performed by a third party. That will be the position where, from the point of view of the party to whom the obligation is owed, it is commercially immaterial whether the act is performed by the other party himself or by a third person, and where, from the point of view of the party by whom the obligation is owed, the performance of the act is legally permissible. In the present case, it is doubtful whether the identity of the person carrying on the grocery business in her premises is commercially immaterial to the plaintiff. In the tenancy agreement, she expressly imposed on the defendants the obligation to carry on the grocery and dairy produce business. Furthermore, the operation of a grocery and dairy produce business involves so many different acts, such as buying, selling, the acquisition of advertising material and the maintenance of the shop premises, that, for that reason also, there can scarcely be any question of a third party being able to fulfil that obligation. Moreover, even if performance by another person were ordered, the operation of the business by a third party would conflict with the plaintiff's obligation to permit the defendants to use the premises. Consequently, the obligation to carry on a grocery and dairy produce business in premises let by the plaintiff to the defendants involves an act which may not be performed by another, within the meaning of § 888 ZPO. That does not mean, however, that enforcement is therefore possible under § 888 ZPO. That provision further stipulates that the performance of the act must be dependent exclusively on the will of the party obliged to perform it. The operation of a grocery and dairy produce business involves the conclusion of contracts with suppliers who deliver the goods to be sold in the business. Consequently, the operation of the business not only requires willingness on the part of the defendants to run it but also involves the

---

[123] NJW 1973.1135.

conclusion of contracts with the suppliers, who must be willing to contract with the defendants. Even if the suppliers are willing to enter into the relevant contracts, the operation of the business is dependent on circumstances which are not contingent solely upon the will of the defendants.

Nor, accordingly, can there can be any question of the imposition of a penalty under § 890 ZPO. The judgment ordering the defendants to operate a grocery and dairy produce business constitutes a decision requiring the defendants to perform an act. It is true that, in its judgment of 4 June 1962 the *Oberlandesgericht* Hamm considered that a claim for performance of an act pursuant to a long-term obligation was enforceable. However, that view is not shared by the Senate in the present case. The wording of § 890 ZPO does not cover the imposition of a penalty on the basis of a right to demand performance. § 890 ZPO is concerned only with claims for injunctive relief in the form of an order restraining a person from doing something. Enforcement of an order requiring a person, in mandatory terms, to perform an act is never permissible under § 890 ZPO; such an order may be enforced only pursuant to §§ 887 and/or 888 ZPO. The *Oberlandesgericht* Hamm purported, in its aforementioned decision, to have identified a lacuna in the legislation, consisting of the impossibility of applying any pressure in the form of a penalty to procure compliance with an order for the performance of an act incapable of being performed by anyone else, which is unenforceable under § 888 ZPO; in the Senate's view, however, that earlier finding does not justify the application of § 890 ZPO by analogy to claims for mandatory injunctive relief. It cannot be assumed in that regard that there exists any latent lacuna in the legislation which is capable of being filled by case-law. In providing, in § 888 ZPO, that a claim for the performance of an act may be enforced by the imposition of a penalty only where such performance is exclusively dependent on the will of the party required to perform it, the legislature was seeking to achieve a rational objective. A decision imposing a penalty under § 888 ZPO is not conditional on the existence of fault. Such a penalty constitutes an enforcement measure falling within the ambit of the civil law. By contrast, a penalty imposed under § 890 ZPO is in the nature of a criminal sanction. It is for the party to whom the obligation is owed, when instituting the proceedings, to have regard to the different enforcement possibilities. Where a claim for performance of an act is not enforceable by the imposition of a penalty, it is not the task of the court seised of the enforcement application to make that claim enforceable by treating it, by analogy, as if it were a claim to restrain a person from doing something. If enforcement of a claim for performance of an act cannot be ordered under § 888 ZPO, the only remedy available to the party to whom the obligation is owed is an award of damages pursuant to § 893 ZPO.

Note

It is not clear that other systems do not regard the co-operation of third parties as a problem. For example, compare the English cases in the next section.

(7) Problems with supervising long-term contracts

In the English cases it used frequently to be said that it is not possible to order specific performance of an obligation which is to be performed over a period of time, as the court has no mechanism for supervising the performance. Thus in *Ryan* v. *Mutual Tontine Westminster Chambers Association*[124] the court refused to order specific performance of a contract to provide portering services to an apartment. However the cases have not been consistent: for example contracts for building work have on occasion been enforced specifically if damages would not be an adequate remedy.[125]

---

[124] [1893] 1 Ch. 116.
[125] See *supra* at 685.

In *Giles Co.* v. *Morris*[126] Megarry J said:

One day, perhaps, the courts will look again at the so-called rule that contracts for personal services or involving the continuous performance of services will not be specifically enforced. Such a rule is plainly not absolute and without exception, nor do I think that it can be based on any narrow consideration such as difficulties of constant superintendence by the court. Mandatory injunctions are by no means unknown, and there is normally no question of the court having to send its officers to supervise the performance of the order of the court. Prohibitory injunctions are common, and again there is no direct supervision by the court. Performance of each type of injunction is normally secured by the realisation of the person enjoined that he is liable to be punished for contempt if evidence of his disobedience to the order is put before the court; and if the injunction is prohibitory, actual committal will usually so long as it continues, make disobedience impossible. If instead the order is for specific performance of a contract for personal services, a similar machinery of enforcement could be employed, again without there being any question of supervision by any officer of the court. The reasons why the court is reluctant to decree specific performance of a contract for personal services (and I would regard it as a strong reluctance rather than a rule) are, I think, more complex and more firmly bottomed on human nature. If a singer contracts to sing, there could be no doubt be proceedings for committal if, ordered to sing, the singer remained obstinately dumb. But if instead the singer sang flat, or sharp, or too fast, or too slowly, or too loudly, or too quietly, or resorted to a dozen of the manifestations of temperament traditionally associated with some singers, the threat of committal would reveal itself as a most unsatisfactory weapon: for who could say whether the imperfections of performance were natural or self-induced? To make an order with such possibilities of evasion would be vain; and so the order will not be made. However, not all contracts of personal service or for the continuous performance of services are as dependent as this on matters of opinion and judgment, nor do all such contracts involve the same degree of the daily impact of person upon person. In general, no doubt, the inconvenience and mischief of decreeing specific performance of most of such contracts will greatly outweigh the advantages, and specific performance will be refused. But I do not think that it should be assumed that as soon as any element of personal service or continuous services can be discerned in a contract the court will, without more, refuse specific performance. Of course, a requirement for the continuous performance of services has the disadvantage that repeated breaches may engender repeated applications to the court for enforcement. But so may many injunctions; and the prospects of repetition, although an important consideration, ought not to be allowed to negative a right. As is so often the case in equity, the matter is one of the balance of advantage and disadvantage in relation to the particular obligations in question: and the fact that the balance will usually lie on one side does not turn this probability into a rule. The present case, of course, is a fortiori, since the contract of which specific performance has been decreed requires not the performance of personal services or any continuous series of acts, but merely procuring the execution of an agreement which contains a provision for such services or acts.

---

[126] [1972] 1 WLR 307 at 318.

Co-operative Insurance Society Ltd. v. *Argyll Stores (Holdings) Ltd.*[127]

NO SPECIFIC PERFORMANCE OF "KEEP OPEN" COVENANT

Supermarket

A tenant will not be ordered to "keep open" a business.

Facts: The appellant defendants, Argyll Stores (Holdings) Ltd. ("Argyll"), decided in May 1995 to close their Safeway supermarket in the Hillsborough Shopping Centre in Sheffield because it was losing money. This was a breach of a covenant in their lease, which contained in clause 4(19) a positive obligation to keep the premises open for retail trade during the usual hours of business. Argyll admitted the breach. The landlords, Co-operative Insurance Society Ltd. ("C.I.S."), brought an action.

Held: The trial judge refused to order specific performance and the defendants consented to an order for damages to be assessed. The Court of Appeal [1996] Ch. 286, reversing the trial judge, ordered that the covenant be specifically performed. It made a final injunction ordering Argyll to trade on the premises during the remainder of the term (which would expire on 3 August 2014) or until an earlier subletting or assignment. The Court of Appeal suspended its order for three months to allow time for Argyll to complete an assignment which by that time had been agreed. After a short agreed extension, the lease was assigned with the landlord's consent. In fact, therefore, the injunction never took effect. The appeal to the House of Lords was substantially about costs, but the issue remained of great importance to landlords and tenants under other commercial leases.

Judgment: LORD HOFFMANN: My Lords,

1. The issue—In 1955 Lord Goddard CJ said:

> No authority has been quoted to show that an injunction will be granted enjoining a person to carry on a business, nor can I think that one ever would be, certainly not where the business is a losing concern:" *Attorney-General* v. *Colchester Corporation* [1955] 2 Q.B. 207, 217.

In this case his prediction has been falsified . . . [His Lordship stated the facts as above]

4. The settled practice
There is no dispute about the existence of the settled practice [of refusing to make an order to carry on a business] to which the judge referred . . .

But the practice has never, so far as I know, been examined by this House and it is open to C.I.S. to say that it rests upon inadequate grounds or that it has been too inflexibly applied.

Specific performance is traditionally regarded in English law as an exceptional remedy, as opposed to the common law damages to which a successful plaintiff is entitled as of right. There may have been some element of later rationalisation of an untidier history, but by the 19th century it was orthodox doctrine that the power to decree specific performance was part of the discretionary jurisdiction of the Court of Chancery to do justice in cases in which the remedies available at common law were inadequate. This is the basis of the general principle that specific performance will not be ordered when damages are an adequate remedy. By contrast, in countries with legal systems based on civil law, such as France, Germany and Scotland, the plaintiff is prima facie entitled to specific performance. The cases in which he is confined to a claim for damages are regarded as the exceptions. In practice, however, there is less difference between common law and civilian systems than these general statements might lead one to suppose. The principles upon which English judges exercise the discretion to grant specific performance are reasonably well settled and depend upon a number of considerations, mostly of a practical nature, which are of very general application. I have made no investigation of civilian systems, but a priori I would expect that judges take much the same matters into account in deciding whether specific performance would be inappropriate in a particular case.

---

[127] [1998] AC 1.

The practice of not ordering a defendant to carry on a business is not entirely dependent upon damages being an adequate remedy. In *Dowty Boulton Paul Ltd.* v. *Wolverhampton Corporation* [1971] 1 W.L.R. 204, Sir John Pennycuick V.-C. refused to order the corporation to maintain an airfield as a going concern because: "It is very well established that the court will not order specific performance of an obligation to carry on a business:" see p. 211. He added: "It is unnecessary in the circumstances to discuss whether damages would be an adequate remedy to the company:" see p. 212. Thus the reasons which underlie the established practice may justify a refusal of specific performance even when damages are not an adequate remedy.

The most frequent reason given in the cases for declining to order someone to carry on a business is that it would require constant supervision by the court. In *J. C. Williamson Ltd.* v. *Lukey and Mulholland* (1931) 45 C.L.R. 282, 297–298, Dixon J said flatly: "Specific performance is inapplicable when the continued supervision of the court is necessary in order to ensure the fulfilment of the contract."

There has, I think, been some misunderstanding about what is meant by continued superintendence. It may at first sight suggest that the judge (or some other officer of the court) would literally have to supervise the execution of the order. In *C.H. Giles & Co. Ltd.* v. *Morris* [1972] 1 WLR 307, 318 Megarry J said that "difficulties of constant superintendence" were a "narrow consideration" because:

> "there is normally no question of the court having to send its officers to supervise the performance of the order . . . Performance . . . is normally secured by the realisation of the person enjoined that he is liable to be punished for contempt if evidence of his disobedience to the order is put before the court . . ."

This is, of course, true but does not really meet the point. The judges who have said that the need for constant supervision was an objection to such orders were no doubt well aware that supervision would in practice take the form of rulings by the court, on applications made by the parties, as to whether there had been a breach of the order. It is the possibility of the court having to give an indefinite series of such rulings in order to ensure the execution of the order which has been regarded as undesirable.

Why should this be so? A principal reason is that, as Megarry J pointed out in the passage to which I have referred, the only means available to the court to enforce its order is the quasi-criminal procedure of punishment for contempt. This is a powerful weapon; so powerful, in fact, as often to be unsuitable as an instrument for adjudicating upon the disputes which may arise over whether a business is being run in accordance with the terms of the court's order. The heavy-handed nature of the enforcement mechanism is a consideration which may go to the exercise of the court's discretion in other cases as well, but its use to compel the running of a business is perhaps the paradigm case of its disadvantages and it is in this context that I shall discuss them.

The prospect of committal or even a fine, with the damage to commercial reputation which will be caused by a finding of contempt of court, is likely to have at least two undesirable consequences. First, the defendant, who ex hypothesi did not think that it was in his economic interest to run the business at all, now has to make decisions under a sword of Damocles which may descend if the way the business is run does not conform to the terms of the order. This is, as one might say, no way to run a business. In this case the Court of Appeal made light of the point because it assumed that, once the defendant had been ordered to run the business, self-interest and compliance with the order would thereafter go hand in hand. But, as I shall explain, this is not necessarily true.

Secondly, the seriousness of a finding of contempt for the defendant means that any application to enforce the order is likely to be a heavy and expensive piece of litigation. The possibility of repeated applications over a period of time means that, in comparison with a once-and-for-all inquiry as to damages, the enforcement of the remedy is likely to be expensive in terms of cost to the parties and the resources of the judicial system.

This is a convenient point at which to distinguish between orders which require a defendant to carry on an activity, such as running a business over or more or less extended period of time, and orders which require him to achieve a result. The possibility of repeated applications for rulings on compliance with the order which arises in the former case does not exist to anything like the same extent in the latter. Even if the achievement of the result is a complicated matter which will take some time, the court, if called upon to rule, only has to examine the finished work and say whether it complies with the order . . .

This distinction between orders to carry on activities and orders to achieve results explains why the courts have in appropriate circumstances ordered specific performance of building contracts and repairing covenants: see *Wolverhampton Corporation* v. *Emmons* [1901] 1 K.B. 515 (building contract) and *Jeune* v. *Queens Cross Properties Ltd.* [1974] Ch. 97 (repairing covenant). It by no means follows, however, that even obligations to achieve a result will always be enforced by specific performance. There may be other objections, to some of which I now turn.

One such objection, which applies to orders to achieve a result and a fortiori to orders to carry on an activity, is imprecision in the terms of the order. If the terms of the court's order, reflecting the terms of the obligation, cannot be precisely drawn, the possibility of wasteful litigation over compliance is increased. So is the oppression caused by the defendant having to do things under threat of proceedings for contempt. The less precise the order, the fewer the signposts to the forensic minefield which he has to traverse. The fact that the terms of a contractual obligation are sufficiently definite to escape being void for uncertainty, or to found a claim for damages, or to permit compliance to be made a condition of relief against forfeiture, does not necessarily mean that they will be sufficiently precise to be capable of being specifically enforced. So in *Wolverhampton Corporation* v. *Emmons*, Romer LJ said, at p. 525, that the first condition for specific enforcement of a building contract was that "the particulars of the work are so far definitely ascertained that the court can sufficiently see what is the exact nature of the work of which it is asked to order the performance" . . .

Precision is of course a question of degree and the courts have shown themselves willing to cope with a certain degree of imprecision in cases of orders requiring the achievement of a result in which the plaintiffs' merits appeared strong; like all the reasons which I have been discussing, it is, taken alone, merely a discretionary matter to be taken into account: see Spry, *Equitable Remedies*, 4th ed. (1990), p. 112. It is, however, a very important one . . .

There is a further objection to an order requiring the defendant to carry on a business, which was emphasised by Millett LJ in the Court of Appeal. This is that it may cause injustice by allowing the plaintiff to enrich himself at the defendant's expense. The loss which the defendant may suffer through having to comply with the order (for example, by running a business at a loss for an indefinite period) may be far greater than the plaintiff would suffer from the contract being broken . . .

It is true that the defendant has, by his own breach of contract, put himself in such an unfortunate position. But the purpose of the law of contract is not to punish wrongdoing but to satisfy the expectations of the party entitled to performance. A remedy which enables him to secure, in money terms, more than the performance due to him is unjust. From a wider perspective, it cannot be in the public interest for the courts to require someone to carry on business at a loss if there is any plausible alternative by which the other party can be given compensation. It is not only a waste of resources but yokes the parties together in a continuing hostile relationship. The order for specific performance prolongs the battle. If the defendant is ordered to run a business, its conduct becomes the subject of a flow of complaints, solicitors' letters and affidavits. This is wasteful for both parties and the legal system. An award of damages, on the other hand, brings the litigation to an end. The defendant pays damages, the forensic link between them is severed, they go their separate ways and the wounds of conflict can heal.

The cumulative effect of these various reasons, none of which would necessarily be sufficient on its own, seems to me to show that the settled practice is based upon sound sense. Of course the grant or refusal of specific performance remains a matter for the judge's discretion. There are no binding rules, but this does not mean that there cannot be settled principles, founded upon practical considerations of the kind which I have discussed, which do not have to be re-examined in every case, but which the courts will apply in all but exceptional circumstances . . .

6. Conclusion: I think that no criticism can be made of the way in which Judge Maddocks exercised his discretion. All the reasons which he gave were proper matters for him to take into account. In my view the Court of Appeal should not have interfered and I would allow the appeal and restore the order which he made.

Note

In German law the requirement of certainty of performance relates in the first instance to the creditor's application seeking enforcement. Thus, the court will refuse enforcement under ZPO §§ 887, 888, 890 if the application is not sufficiently specific.

(8) Hardship and Other Factors

ZPO   6.G.45.

§ 765a: (1) On the application of the debtor the court (of execution) may revoke, prohibit or temporarily suspend, either completely or in part, a measure of execution, if, in full consideration of the creditor's need for protection, the measure would lead to hardship *contra bonos mores* because of very particular circumstances. If the measure concerns an animal the court must take account of the responsibility of the person for that animal in its deliberations.

Notes

(1) § 765a ZPO applies to all forms of execution. In practice, however, it has been most frequently invoked where eviction under a lease agreement is sought.

(2) It is assumed that apart from in the most drastic and exceptional circumstances the creditor's interest in having the judgment enforced should prevail. Mere inconvenience or purely financial hardship on the part of the debtor probably will not be sufficient.

(3) In every case, even where the debtor claims that their life or health is at risk the court must weigh up the interests on both sides. The Federal Constitutional Court has held upon a number of occasions that, having regard to the right to life of the debtor (Article 2(2) 1 GG), lower courts must take into account suicide threats and the risks to old people from their infirmity where execution is sought.[128]

We have already noted above[129] that, as regards compensation in German law, there is a presumption that this will be *in natura* (§ 249 BGB) and that in contract, such compensation *qua* replacement can be viewed as the functional equivalent of enforcement in other systems. Two exceptions are made to this presumption.

---

[128] BVerfGE 52, 214; NJW 1991.3207.
[129] See *supra* at 678.

BGB **6.G.46.**

§ 251: (1) Insofar as restitution in kind is impossible or is insufficient to compensate the creditor, the person liable shall compensate him in money.
(2) The person liable may compensate the creditor in money if restitution in kind is only possible through disproportionate outlay.

OLG Hamm, 11 December 1946[130] **6.G.47.**

RESTITUTION IN KIND WHERE MONEY INADEQUATE

Shortage of horses

In considering whether restitution in kind would be a disproportionate burden upon the debtor a court should have regard to the fact that money damages would not adequately compensate the creditor.

Facts: Towards the end of March 1945 the third company of the Becker combat group was located in G. On 24 March 1945 it needed horses for the purposes of a sortie which it was to make in the direction of Wesel. At the instigation of the company commander and the sergeant-major, the witness Sp., who at that time was a non-commissioned officer in that unit of the German armed forces, procured from the plaintiff a dark chestnut mare belonging to the latter, which was harnessed to a wagon belonging to the company. On 26 March 1945 that mare was returned, but on 27 March it was once again requisitioned by the company, since the company was being forced to retreat by virtue of the military situation. On 27 March the mare was again collected from the plaintiff by the witness Sp., and was harnessed, along with a horse belonging to the witness Th., to an ammunition cart belonging to the company.

On 30 March 1945 the witness Sp. appeared, together with a severely lame mare, whose hind legs were not shod, at the defendant's farm. Sp. requested the latter to exchange that horse for a horse belonging to the defendant. The defendant stated that he was willing to do so. The defendant's horse was harnessed up, and Sp. departed with the wagon, leaving the lame mare at the defendant's farm.

Neither the plaintiff nor the defendant recovered the horses which they had made available for use by the army. In the autumn of 1945, the horse which Sp. had left at the defendant's farm died from meningitis at the defendant's sister's farm in Münster-St. Mauritz, whither the defendant had arranged for it to be taken.

The plaintiff pleaded in the proceedings as follows: in May 1945 he had made a total of three visits to the defendant's farm. Initially, after the plaintiff had described his horse to the defendant, the latter had stated that no such horse had ever been in his possession. Later on, the defendant had admitted that such a horse had been left by the army at his farm. However, that horse had been taken away again by a group of Poles. The defendant had produced in that regard a certificate signed by one of the Poles. The defendant refused to allow the plaintiff access to his stables. The plaintiff had therefore been forced to desist from making any further enquiries regarding the horse. It was not until January 1946 that he learned from a conversation with Sp. that his horse had in fact come to the defendant's farm.

Since, in his view, it appeared certain that the mare would have survived if the defendant had handed her over to him, the plaintiff claimed that the defendant was liable to compensate him for all the loss which he had suffered. According to the plaintiff, the horse in question had been a particularly valuable, five to six-year old breeding mare of a special class, the standard price for which was 2,600 Reichsmarks. The plaintiff claimed that the defendant was therefore liable to supply him with a horse of equivalent value, belonging to that special class, which should, as far as possible, be capable of use for breeding purposes. He also claimed that the defendant could render compensation in the form of the supply of a horse in that condition, since the defendant kept on his farm three load-bearing horses and a one and a half-year-old foal. The plaintiff claimed to have suffered further loss by reason of the fact that he had had to dispense with the horse's services in the context of the work to be carried out in the sowing season and at harvest time. In addition, he had invariably possessed three working horses on his farm, which was significantly larger than that of the defendant. Despite the most strenuous efforts, he had been unable to procure a replacement horse. He had had to spend the sum of 145 Reichsmarks just for the use of a tractor for mowing purposes—a course of action to which he had had to resort as a result of the loss of the horse.

[130] MDR 1947.100.

The plaintiff therefore claimed inter alia that the defendant should be ordered to supply to him a working horse, if possible a mare, of equivalent value to the heavy dark chestnut mare, aged between five and six years, belonging to the plaintiff, which had died in the defendant's custody in autumn 1945 (an animal of a special class for which the standard price was 2,600 Reichsmarks).

The defendant denied the plaintiff's account of the facts and contended that the claim should be dismissed.

Held: The *Landgericht* (Regional Court) found in favour of the plaintiff and made an order against the defendant in the terms sought. The *Oberlandesgericht* (Higher Regional Court) dismissed as unfounded the defendant's appeal against that judgment. In the grounds for its decision, it stated that the horse which had died was the plaintiff's horse and that the plaintiff had remained the owner of it. It further stated that the defendant was liable to compensate the plaintiff pursuant to §§ 990 and 826 BGB. The issue of the form which such compensation should take was dealt with as follows in the grounds of the judgment.

Judgment: § 249 BGB provides that a person liable to provide compensation must in principle be required to restore the situation to that which would have existed if the circumstance giving rise to such liability had not arisen. Thus the legislation lays down the principle that compensation is to take the form of restitution in kind, and it is only as an alternative measure, provided for by § 251 BGB, that it may be permitted, subject to the fulfilment of special conditions, to take the form of pecuniary damages. In accordance with the principle laid down by § 249 BGB, the plaintiff is therefore entitled to claim from the defendant restitution in kind, provided that that is at all feasible in the present case. However, restitution in kind does not mean that the situation must literally be restored to that which previously existed; it suffices for that situation to be restored in economic terms. Even though the horse does not constitute something which is capable of being replaced by exactly the same thing, nevertheless, it is not inconceivable that, where such a thing has been lost, restitution in kind, in the form of the provision of something of equivalent value, may be an appropriate remedy. In the present case, that must *a fortiori* be the position, since the defendant is himself a farmer and the owner of horses. He undeniably possesses four horses, whereas the plaintiff, whose farm is at least as large as that of the defendant, currently has only two horses at his disposal. If, however, the defendant is liable to furnish compensation, the means of discharging his liability must extend to cover the things which he has on his own farm. That must *a fortiori* be the position as matters currently stand, since in the present circumstances the payment of a sum of money cannot satisfy the plaintiff's entitlement. The defendant cannot rely on the fact that delivery of the horse would involve him in disproportionate expense. According to the tenor of § 251(2) BGB, regard may be had to the interests of a debtor only where that does not prejudice the legitimate interests of the creditor. It follows that § 251(2) BGB cannot be applicable where the needs of the debtor are opposed by corresponding needs of the creditor.

The approach taken by the legislation is in principle that the debtor is obliged to provide compensation for the totality of the loss in the form of restitution in kind. He is only entitled to provide compensation in the form of money where restitution which does not prejudice the interests of the creditor is only possible at disproportionate expense. There is no need to consider the question whether an order for restitution in kind may also be made where the debtor does not possess a thing capable of being supplied as a replacement; in the present case, the defendant possesses horses and can supply the plaintiff with one of those horses as a replacement for the latter's deceased mare. It may well be that the defendant normally keeps, and needs, four horses on his farm. However, since the plaintiff only has two horses on his farm at present, and that farm is at least as big as that of the defendant, it is entirely appropriate to require the defendant to compensate the plaintiff by providing the latter with one of his own horses. In so far as he cannot procure another horse elsewhere, he will have to make do with three horses; moreover, the Senate is convinced in that regard that, if he makes sufficient effort, he will be in a position to do so. The defendant's objection that it will not be possible for him to comply with the judgment given are unfounded; the judgment is to be enforced immediately by the removal of one of the defendant's horses.

Notes

(1) The substantive action here was clearly in tort, but the remedial question was decided under BGB § 251(2), which is applicable to contractual, as well as delictual liability.

(2) The decision of the plaintiff to opt for compensation *in natura* was almost certainly motivated by the inadequacy of almost any damages award given the great scarcity of livestock in the immediate post-war period.[131]

(3) German commentators agree that specific performance is not discretionary in the way it is in English law. The creditor has a right to claim performance, indeed without fault having been proved on the part of the debtor, under § 241 BGB. Only in exceptional cases[132] may relief from this be claimed.[133] The discretion mentioned in § 251(2) BGB relates only to cases where the debtor is "compensating"—for example a replacement vase is sought, but only money offered—rather than "performing" *stricto sensu*—for example the creditor seeks the original vase.

Court of Appeal   **6.E.48.**
Patel v. Ali[134]

HARDSHIP TO THE DEFENDANT

Seller becomes disabled

Specific performance of a contract may be refused where, as the result of events since the contract was made and not attributable to the plaintiff, the order would cause hardship to the defendant.

Facts: The vendor of a house had, since the sale (the performance of which had been much delayed for reasons not the fault of either party), become disabled and heavily dependent on her neighbours for help. If the vendor was forced to relinquish the house she would have to leave the neighbourhood as she could no longer afford to buy another property in the area (prices had risen), so she would lose her neighbours' support.

Held: Specific performance would not be granted against her.

Judgment: GOULDING J: It is not in dispute that, like other equitable relief, the specific performance of contracts is a discretionary remedy; but, in the ordinary case of a sale of land or buildings, the court normally grants it as of course and withholds it only on proof of special facts. The textbooks and reported decisions have long recognised hardship as one ground on which, in a proper case, a purchaser or vendor may be refused specific performance and be left to his right to damages for breach of contract at law. The difficulty is to determine within what limits hardship to a defendant can properly be said to justify this exercise of judicial discretion. There is no doubt that, in the majority of cases, the hardship which moves the court to refuse specific performance is either a hardship existing at the date of the contract or a hardship due in some way to the plaintiff. In the present case, neither of those conditions being satisfied, the plaintiffs rely strongly on that principle or practice, which is stated in varying terms in all the well-known textbooks. It is sufficient for me to cite a passage from Fry on Specific Performance, 6th ed. (1921), p. 199:

---

[131] See Zweigert and Kötz, at 472.
[132] As under ZPO, *supra* at 713.
[133] See Horn, Kötz and Leser, *German Private and Commercial Law—An Introduction* (Oxford: Oxford University Press, 1982) at 109.
[134] [1984] Ch. 283.

It is a well-established doctrine that the court will not enforce the specific performance of a contract, the result of which would be to impose great hardship on either of the parties to it; and this although the party seeking specific performance may be free from the least impropriety of conduct. The question of the hardship of a contract is generally to be judged of at the time at which it is entered into: if it be then fair and just and not productive of hardship, it will be immaterial that it may, by the force of subsequent circumstances or change of events, have become less beneficial to one party, except where these subsequent events have been in some way due to the party who seeks the performance of the contract. For whatever contingencies may attach to a contract, or be involved in the performance of either part, have been taken upon themselves by the parties to it. It has been determined that the reasonableness of a contract is to be judged of at the time it is entered into, and not by the light of subsequent events, and we have already seen that the same principle applies in considering the fairness of a contract.

However, the principle so stated cannot be erected into a fixed limitation of the court's equitable jurisdiction. It is recognised, both by Fry LJ in his book and in the argument of Mr Simpkiss for the plaintiffs in the present action, that the court has sometimes refused specific performance because of a change of circumstances supervening after the making of the contract and not in any way attributable to the plaintiff. One such case is *City of London* v. *Nash* (1747) 1 Ves. Sen. 11, 12 . . .

The important and true principle, in my view, is that only in extraordinary and persuasive circumstances can hardship supply an excuse for resisting performance of a contract for the sale of immovable property. A person of full capacity who sells or buys a house takes the risk of hardship to himself and his dependants, whether arising from existing facts or unexpectedly supervening in the interval before completion. This is where, to my mind, great importance attaches to the immense delay in the present case, not attributable to the defendant's conduct. Even after issue of the writ, she could not complete, if she had wanted to, without the concurrence of the absent Mr Ahmed. Thus, in a sense, she can say she is being asked to do what she never bargained for, namely to complete the sale after more than four years, after all the unforeseeable changes that such a period entails. I think that in this way she can fairly assert that specific performance would inflict upon her "a hardship amounting to injustice" to use the phrase employed by James LJ, in a different but comparable context, in *Tamplin* v. *James* (1880) 15 Ch.D. 215, 221. Equitable relief may, in my view, be refused because of an unforeseen change of circumstances not amounting to legal frustration, just as it may on the ground of mistake insufficient to avoid a contract at law.

In the end, I am satisfied that it is within the court's discretion to accede to the defendant's prayer if satisfied that it is just to do so. And, on the whole, looking at the position of both sides after the long unpredictable delay for which neither seeks to make the other responsible, I am of opinion that it is just to leave the plaintiffs to their remedy in damages if that can indeed be effective.

I have come to this conclusion without taking into account the welfare of the defendant's children except as involved in her own personal hardship. I much doubt whether, even in the present atmosphere of opinion on which Mr Briggs dwelt in his address, the interests of the children are material in their own right . . .

6.2.2. MONETARY OBLIGATIONS

In all the systems, a sum of money—typically the price—due under the contract may be recovered once it is due. Thus if the plaintiff has delivered goods to the defendant or performed services for him and has not been paid the agreed price by the time she should have received it, she may simply sue for the sum due. The mechanisms for enforcement differ but this question is procedural and outside the scope of this book.

Where the systems seem to differ is over the case in which the party who is ultimately to pay indicates, before he has received the other's performance and before the price is due, that he no longer wishes to receive the performance.

In the continental systems, it appears that the creditor may normally require the debtor to pay; whether he wishes to receive the services or take the goods in exchange is a matter for the debtor. This follows from the principle that the creditor can normally require performance. In English law, however, we have seen that the creditor is not normally able to make an unwilling debtor perform an obligation. Is it different if the obligation is simply one to pay money? The question will not arise if the defendant has to something else before the creditor can "earn" the price. for example, if the creditor is to paint the debtor's house, with payment due on completion, and the defendant refuses the creditor admission to the house, the creditor cannot earn the price without gaining admission—and if, as in English law, he will normally not get an order that the creditor must admit him, he will in practice be unable to sue for the price. Instead he will have to sue for damages[135] and he will be expected to take reasonable steps to mitigate his loss, for example by finding other work.

What if the creditor is able to perform without the debtor having to co-operate further?

House of Lords   **6.E.49.**
White & Carter (Councils) Ltd. v. *McGregor*[136]

CREDITOR MAY IGNORE REPUDIATION AND CONTINUE PERFORMANCE

Litter bins

Despite a repudiation of the contract by one party, the other may continue performance of his obligations under the contract if he is able to do so without the first party's co-operation, and then claim the payment due on completion.

Facts: The plaintiffs made bins for litter, which they supplied free of charge to local authorities; they made their money by placing advertisements on the bins. The defendants' sales manager entered into a contract for the defendant's business to be advertised in this way for three years. The same day the defendant repudiated the agreement, but the plaintiffs displayed the advertisements nonetheless and then claimed the price, which, under an "acceleration clause" stating that in the event of delay in payment the whole sum would become due immediately, was then due.

Held: The lower court held that the plaintiffs could not recover the full price, but the House of Lords (by a majority, LORDS REID, HODSON and TUCKER) reversed this decision.

Judgment: LORD REID: The general rule cannot be in doubt. It was settled in Scotland at least as early as 1848 and it has been authoritatively stated time and again in both Scotland and England. If one party to a contract repudiates it in the sense of making it clear to the other party that he refuses or will refuse to carry out his part of the contract, the other party, the innocent party, has an option. He may accept that repudiation and sue for damages for breach of contract, whether or not the time for performance has come; or he may if he chooses disregard or refuse to accept it and then the contract remains in full effect . . .

I need not refer to the numerous authorities. They are not disputed by the respondent but he points out that in all of them the party who refused to accept the repudiation had no active duties under the contract. The innocent party's option is generally said to be to wait until the date of performance and then to claim damages estimated as at that date. There is no case in which it is said that he may, in face of the repudiation, go on and incur useless expense in performing the contract

---

[135] As we will see in more detail section **6.5**, *infra* at in 811 ff.
[136] [1962] AC 413.

and then claim the contract price. The option, it is argued, is merely as to the date as at which damages are to be assessed. Developing this argument, the respondent points out that in most cases the innocent party cannot complete the contract himself without the other party doing, allowing or accepting something, and that it is purely fortuitous that the appellants can do so in this case. In most cases by refusing co-operation the party in breach can compel the innocent party to restrict his claim to damages. Then it was said that, even where the innocent party can complete the contract without such co-operation, it is against the public interest that he should be allowed to do so. An example was developed in argument. A company might engage an expert to go abroad and prepare an elaborate report and then repudiate the contract before anything was done. To allow such an expert then to waste thousands of pounds in preparing the report cannot be right if a much smaller sum of damages would give him full compensation for his loss. It would merely enable the expert to extort a settlement giving him far more than reasonable compensation.

The respondent founds on the decision of the First Division in *Langford Co. Ltd.* v. *Dutch*. There an advertising contractor agreed to exhibit a film for a year. Four days after this agreement was made the advertiser repudiated it but, as in the present case, the contractor refused to accept the repudiation and proceeded to exhibit the film and sue for the contract price. The Sheriff-Substitute dismissed the action as irrelevant and his decision was affirmed on appeal. In the course of a short opinion Lord President Cooper said:

> The pursuers could not force the defender to accept a year's advertisement which she did not want, though they could of course claim damages for her breach of contract. On the averments the only reasonable and proper course, which the pursuers should have adopted, would have been to treat the defender as having repudiated the contract and as being on that account liable in damages, the measure of which we are, of course, not in a position to discuss.

The Lord President cited no authority and I am in doubt as to what principle he had in mind . . .

We must now decide whether that case was rightly decided. In my judgment it was not. It could only be supported on one or other of two grounds. It might be said that, because in most cases the circumstances are such that an innocent party is unable to complete the contract and earn the contract price without the assent or co-operation of the other party, therefore in cases where he can do so he should not be allowed to do so. I can see no justification for that. The other ground would be that there is some general equitable principle or element of public policy which requires this limitation of the contractual rights of the innocent party. It may well be that, if it can be shown that a person has no legitimate interest, financial or otherwise, in performing the contract rather than claiming damages, he ought not to be allowed to saddle the other party with an additional burden with no benefit to himself. If a party has no interest to enforce a stipulation, he cannot in general enforce it: so it might be said that, if a party has no interest to insist on a particular remedy, he ought not to be allowed to insist on it. And, just as a party is not allowed to enforce a penalty, so he ought not to be allowed to penalise the other party by taking one course when another is equally advantageous to him. If I may revert to the example which I gave of a company engaging an expert to prepare an elaborate report and then repudiating before anything was done, it might be that the company could show that the expert had no substantial or legitimate interest in carrying out the work rather than accepting damages: I would think that the de minimis principle would apply in determining whether his interest was substantial, and that he might have a legitimate interest other than an immediate financial interest. But if the expert had no such interest then that might be regarded as a proper case for the exercise of the general equitable jurisdiction of the court. But that is not this case. Here the respondent did not set out to prove that the appellants had no legitimate interest in completing the contract and claiming the contract price rather than claiming damages; there is nothing in the findings of fact to support such a case, and it seems improbable that any such case could have been proved. It is, in my judgment, impossible to say that the appellants should be deprived of their right to claim the contract price merely because the benefit to them, as against claiming damages and re-letting their advertising space, might be small in comparison with the loss to the respondent: that is the most that could be said in favour of the respondent. Parliament has on many occasions relieved parties from certain kinds of improvident or oppressive contracts, but the common law can only do that in very limited circumstances. Accordingly, I am unable to avoid the conclusion that this appeal must be allowed and the case remitted so that decree can be pronounced as craved in the initial writ.

LORD MORTON OF HENRYTON [dissenting]: It is well established that repudiation by one party does not put an end to a contract. The other party can say "I hold you to your contract, which still remains in force." What then is his remedy if the repudiating party persists in his repudiation and refuses to carry out his part of the contract? The contract has been broken. The innocent party is entitled to be compensated by damages for any loss which he has suffered by reason of the breach, and in a limited class of cases the court will decree specific implement [the Scottish equivalent of specific performance]. The law of Scotland provides no other remedy for a breach of contract and there is no reported case which decides that the innocent party may act as the appellants have acted.

The present case is one in which specific implement could not be decreed, since the only obligation of the respondent under the contract was to pay a sum of money for services to be rendered by the appellants. Yet the appellants are claiming a kind of inverted specific implement of the contract. They first insist on performing their part of the contract, against the will of the other party, and then claim that he must perform his part and of pay the contract price for unwanted services. In my opinion, my Lords, the appellants' only remedy was damages, and they were bound to take steps to minimise their loss, according to a well-established rule of law. Far from doing this, having incurred no expense at the date of the repudiation, they made no attempt to procure another advertiser, but deliberately went on to incur expense and perform unwanted services with the intention of creating a money debt which did not exist at the date of the repudiation.

LORD HODSON: It is settled as a fundamental rule of the law of contract that repudiation by one of the parties to a contract does not discharge it . . .

It follows that if, as here, there was no acceptance, the contract remains alive for the benefit of both parties and the party who has repudiated it can change his mind but it does not follow that the party at the receiving end of the of the proffered repudiation is bound to accept it before the time for performance and is left to his remedy in damages for breach . . .

The true position is that the contract survives and does so not only where specific implement is available . . .

[LORD TUCKER agreed with the reasoning of Lord Hodson.]

Notes

(1) This case arose in Scotland but this is an area of law in which Scots and English law were treated by the House of Lords as being the same.

(2) The minority held that the repudiation by the defendant was a breach of contract which gave the plaintiff a right to damages but also a duty to take reasonable steps to mitigate the loss.[137] The plaintiff could not recover more than he would had he so mitigated.

(3) The majority decision was much criticized in England as being wasteful. If the plaintiffs had been claiming damages, they would have been under a duty to mitigate their loss[138]

---

[137] See further, *infra* at 827.
[138] *Ibid.*

by seeking other advertisers to take the space. It seems wrong that they should be able to evade this requirement by performing and then suing for the price. In effect, this amounts to giving specific performance of a type of contract which, in English law, would not normally be specifically enforceable.

(4) Lord Reid qualifies his decision by saying that the plaintiff must have a substantial and legitimate interest in claiming damages. Technically this was an *obiter dictum*, and neither of the other members of the majority mentioned it; but subsequent cases have adopted it.[139] In the *Clea Shipping* case[140] time-charterers of a ship stated that they had no use for her services, but the owners ignored this repudiation and kept the vessel anchored off Piraeus with a full crew and ready to sail as soon as the charterers gave an order. The charterers refused to pay the hire. The owner's action to recover it was rejected by Lloyd J, who held that the owners should have terminated the contract and sought alternative employment for the ship.

(5) In any event, the principle of *White & Carter* applies only when the plaintiff can perform without the defendant's co-operation. If he cannot and the defendant refuses to co-operate, the outcome will depend on whether the plaintiff can get an order of specific performance. If this is not available (as it will usually not be except in cases of sales of land: see above) the plaintiff will in practice have no choice but to terminate and sue for damages—in which case he will be under a duty to mitigate his losses. The courts have taken a narrow view of when a contract may be performed without the other party's co-operation; thus in the *Clea Shipping* case[141] Lloyd J suggested, without deciding, that the owners of a ship cannot perform a time-charter without the co-operation of the charterer.

(6) English law is not wholly consistent on this point. We have seen that normally a contract for the sale of goods is not specifically enforceable against the seller. By reason of the principle of mutuality, the seller cannot get an order of specific performance against the buyer. However, the Sale of Goods Act 1979, section 49(1) provides:

Where, under a contract of sale, the property in the goods has passed to the buyer and he wrongfully neglects or refuses to pay for the goods according to the terms of the contract, the seller may maintain an action against him for the price of the goods.

The property in the goods may pass to the buyer before they have been delivered: SGA 1979, section 18 rule 1. This means that the seller may sue for the price even though the buyer has not yet received the goods and does not want them. The rule is criticized by English writers.[142]

(7) Continental European legal systems do not at first sight seem to have equivalent restrictions upon claims for payment. However there are a number of situations in which the same practical result, that the aggrieved party cannot carry on regardless of the other's desires, is reached by specific provisions. Thus in German law, in a *Diensvertrag* or a *Werkvertrag* the customer or employer is entitled to cancel the contract on payment of the agreed payment less the expenses saved by the other party (BGB §§ 615, 649); and in

---

[139] See *Attica Sea Carriers Corp.* v. *Ferrostaal Poseidon Bulk Reederi GmbH, The Puerto Buitrago* [1976] 1 Lloyd's Rep. 250; *The Odenfeld* [1978] 2 Lloyd's Rep. 357, 374; and *Clea Shipping Corp.* v. *Bulk Oil International Ltd, The Alaskan Trader* [1984] 1 All ER 129.

[140] *Clea Shipping Corp.* v. *Bulk Oil International Ltd, The Alaskan Trader* [1984] 1 All ER 129.

[141] *Ibid.*

[142] E.g. Atiyah and Adams, *Sale of Goods*, 9th edn. (London: Pitman, 1995) at 435–6.

French law the employer can cancel a *contrat d'entreprise* unilaterally upon payment of damages to the other party (C.civ. Article 1794).[143] Belgian law recognizes that the creditor must also terminate when to insist on performance would be contrary to good faith or an abuse of right.[144]

Principles of European Contract Law   **6.PECL.50.**

Article 9:101: *Monetary Obligations*

    (1) The creditor is entitled to recover money which is due.

    (2) Where the creditor has not yet performed its obligation and it is clear that the debtor will be unwilling to receive performance, the creditor may nonetheless proceed with its performance and may recover any sum due under the contract unless

        (a) it could have made a reasonable cover transaction without significant effort or expense; or

        (b) performance would be unreasonable in the circumstances.

Further readings on enforcement in natura:

—K. Larenz, *Schuldrecht—Allgemeiner Teil*, 14th edn. (München: Beck, 1987);

—Ph. Malaurie and L. Aynès, *Cours de droit civil—Les obligations*, 10th edn. (Paris: Cujas, 1999), paras. 1010–1204;

—K. Rebmann and F. Säcker (eds.), *Münchener Kommentar zum Bürgerlichen Gesetzbuch*, 4th edn. (München: Beck, 2000);

—B. Nicholas, *The French Law of Contract*, 2nd edn. (Oxford: Clarendon, 1992), at 216–24;

—G. Treitel, *Remedies for Breach of Contract* (Oxford: Clarendon, 1988), chapter 3;

—K. Zweigert and H. Kötz, *Introduction to Comparative Law*, 3rd edn., transl. by T. Weir (Oxford: Clarendon, 1998), chapter 35.

6.3. WITHHOLDING PERFORMANCE

6.3.1. AN INTRODUCTION TO WITHHOLDING PERFORMANCE AND TERMINATION

In this section and section 6.4.[146] we consider the remedies of withholding performance and termination of the contract. By "withholding of performance" we mean a party's right to refuse to perform some or all of its obligations until the other party has performed its obligations, or at least until it is willing to perform them. "Termination" means

---

[143] See Treitel, *Remedies* at 126–8, § 107.

[144] See Cass. 16 Jan. 1986, Arr.Cass. n°317, RW 1987–88, 1470 annotated by Oevelen, RGDC/TBBR 1987.130.

[146] *Infra* at 744.

the right to refuse to accept further performance by the other party, and to refuse to perform one's own counter-obligations, on a permanent basis—in other words, to escape from the contract.[147] In most of the systems considered, the two remedies are linked.

Including the right to withhold performance until the other party has performed (*exceptio non adimpleti contractus*) in this chapter involves a broad definition of "remedies". Not all of the systems would define the right to withhold performance as a remedy, but we deal with it in this chapter because it seems to us to fulfil a function as a temporary remedy.

We describe the remedies of withholding performance and termination as "linked" for at least two reasons. First, withholding performance is usually a prelude to seeking some other remedy, and (especially in those systems in which specific performance is not readily granted) very often that other remedy will be termination. When party A has not performed its part of a contract, frequently party B will withhold its performance as a temporary measure; if A's default continues, B will terminate the contract. Secondly, in some legal systems the two remedies are linked conceptually, in that the justification for allowing B to withhold its performance is partly the same as that given for ultimately allowing B to terminate the contract—though for B to be entitled to terminate, additional factors, such as the expiry of the time for performance, will have to be present.

In other systems there is more of a contrast between the two sets of rules. This is particularly so in French law. In principle, in French law termination (*résolution*) is a judicial act.

Code civil **6.F.51.**

Article 1184: In synallagmatic contracts, a resolutory condition is always implied for the case where one of the two parties does not fulfil his obligations.

In this case, the contract is not terminated automatically. The party to whom the obligation which has not been performed is owed has the choice of forcing the other party to perform, where this is possible, or of demanding termination and damages. Termination must be ordered by a court and may, according to the circumstances, be granted subject to a delay in favour of the debtor.

In contrast, if the necessary grounds exist, withholding of performance can be done unilaterally by the creditor. However even in French law the two "remedies" are seen as linked, as the performances due from each side are interdependent, each being the *cause* of the other.

In German law, termination is an act of the creditor rather than of the court, but it is frequently necessary for the creditor to give formal notice before termination, allowing

---

[147] There is a marked lack of consistency over the correct terminology in the English cases and doctrine. Some judges and authors refer to "repudiation", some to "rescission", some to "termination". We prefer to describe the process of ending a contract because of a non-performance by the other party as "termination". This is to avoid confusion. "Refusal to perform" and "repudiation" are also used to mean *wrongful* refusals to perform a contract. "Rescission" is also used to describe the process of avoiding a contract on the grounds of invalidity (e.g. for fraud), which in English law (and some other laws) has a different effect from termination for breach.

the debtor a further chance to perform, whereas formal notice is not required for withholding of performance. In English law both withholding of performance and termination may be exercised unilaterally and, in most cases, without prior warning.

There is another theme which you may wish to consider as you read through the sections on withholding of performance and termination. This is the extent to which the rules are influenced by what each legal system seems to consider as the "primary remedy" for breach of contract.[148] It is arguable that the conceptual "primacy" of specific performance in the civil law systems has a considerable impact on the rules to be considered now.

6.3.2. WITHHOLDING OF PERFORMANCE

Principles of European Contract Law   **6.PECL.52.**

Article 9:201:   *Right to Withhold Performance*

> (1) A party which is to perform simultaneously with or after the other party may withhold performance until the other has tendered performance or has performed. The first party may withhold the whole of its performance or a part of it as may be reasonable in the circumstances.
>
> (2) A party may similarly withhold performance for as long as it is clear that there will be a non-performance by the other party when the other party's performance becomes due.

6.3.2.A. BASIC RULES

In this section we start by considering when party A will have a right to withhold performance because party B has not performed his obligations under a straightforward synallagmatic contract—i.e. a contract in which each party's obligations are exchanged for the other, as expressed by the maxim *do ut des*.[149] Later we consider related rights, such as the *droit de rétention, Zurückbehaltungsrecht* or the lien, which may apply within individual non-synallagmatic contracts or, indeed, to situations involving several contracts or none at all.

Carbonnier[150]   **6.F.53.**

It is a principle recognised in case-law that in synallagmatic contracts both obligations must be performed at the same time. Each party may demand performance of the obligation due to him only if he offers to perform his side of the bargain. Conversely, he may withhold performance if his contractual partner does not offer performance. This refusal is manifested by an *exception*—in the procedural sense of the term—, namely that of non-performance of the contract (*exceptio non adimpleti contractus*). It stems from the interdependence of the obligations under a synallagmatic contract. Furthermore, it is not always easy to distinguish this objection from the right of retention

---

[148] See *supra*, **6.2.**

[149] See the definitions in Article 1102 C.civ. The same idea is expressed in the phrases *trait pour trait, Zug um Zug.*

[150] Carbonnier at 338–9, para. 194.

which comes under the law of credit (a kind of guarantee whereby the creditor who holds or possesses an asset belonging to the debtor may refuse to give it up as long as he has not been paid)
. . .

The objection of non-performance is provided for only in a few miscellaneous texts—for example Articles 1612 and 1653. However, in order to confer general scope on the objection, it is possible to base an *a fortiori* argument on Article 1184: it is better to permit withholding of performance than for there to be a retroactive repudiation with its sequel of restitution.

(1) Principle

The courts have allowed the objection of non-performance in cases other than those provided for by legislation (for example tenant may refuse to pay rent if he does not have free enjoyment of the rented premises; the lessor may refuse to carry out repairs if rents are not paid to him). It is the notion of the synallagmatic contract which determines the scope of this principle: the objection is admissible in the case of all genuine synallagmatic contracts; and even in imperfectly synallagmatic contracts (argued from Article 1948: but is this not rather a right of retention?) The exception is further extended to the converse synallagmatic case of the parties when a contract has been avoided or terminated: the two obligations to make restitution must be performed *trait pour trait*.

(2) Restrictions

The courts dismiss the objection where it appears to them to be invoked in cases where it is contrary to the obligation of good faith binding the contracting parties. For example, a tenant may not refuse to pay his rent on the pretext that the landlord has failed to carry out necessary repairs to the building. It would not be in keeping with the principle of good faith to object to non-performance of a relatively secondary obligation (and moreover one which is not liquidated) in order to escape from a fundamental obligation. It is only obligations of the same importance which must be performed on a reciprocal basis. Under the lease the tenant, by virtue of the fact that he is in enjoyment of the rented premises, already benefits from performance sufficient to balance his obligation to pay the rent.[151]

Code civil   **6.F.54.**

Article 1612: The seller is not bound to deliver the thing, if the buyer does not pay the price and the seller has not agreed to give the buyer credit.

Notes

(1) The *exception* applies to the case where the two parties are due to perform simultaneously. If party A is to perform before party B, B may refuse to until A has done so simply because B's performance is not yet due; B need not resort to the *exception*.

(2) French authors frequently stress that the *exception* is a self-help remedy, not directly subject to control of the court but which enables the creditor to put pressure on the debtor for example.[152] The same authors remark[153] that *doctrine* usually sees the basis of the theory being *cause*; *jurisprudence* more commonly links it to *connexité* [154] and to good faith.

[151] On the *droit de rétention* referred to by Carbonnier see *infra* at 743.
[152] Malaurie and Aynès, para. 720–1.
[153] *Ibid.*, para. 722.
[154] The notion that obligations are connected, so that, for instance, one debt may be set off against another; see Malaurie and Aynès, para. 1074.

(3) It is also sometimes remarked that the creditor may exercise the *exception* without giving the debtor a *mise en demeure*, which is normally necessary before the creditor can claim damages or terminate the contract.[155]

(4) Carbonnier refers to the coercive effect of the exception. All the systems in some circumstances allow a party who has received a performance which is defective and therefore worth less than it should have been, to reduce the price that he agreed to pay for the performance.[156] Equally, if the non-performance causes a loss, the creditor may be able to deduct the damages to which he is entitled from any payment due. In a way these solutions look like withholding performance; but they are different. They provide a permanent solution rather than just a temporary one, and the creditor is entitled to reduce the price only in proportion to the reduction in value of the performance he has received, or to deduct the actual amount of his loss. If he is entitled to withhold performance, however, he may be entitled to withhold the whole of his performance. It is this which gives withholding of performance its coercive effect. Restrictions on the amount the creditor may withhold will be considered later.[157]

BGB   **6.G.55.**

§ 320: (1) Whoever is bound by a synallagmatic contract may refuse to perform his part until the other party has performed his part, unless the former party is bound to perform his part first. If the performance is to be made to several persons, the part due to one of them can be refused until the entire counter-performance has been effected. The provision of s. 273(3) does not apply.

(2) If one side has performed in part, the counter-performance may not be refused to the extent that the refusal would be, in the circumstances, contrary to good faith, especially in view of the disproportionate triviality of the remaining part.

§ 322 (1) If one party brings an action for the performance due to him under a mutual contract, the enforcement of the other party's right to refuse performance until the counter-performance has been made, has the effect only that a court may order the other party to make his performance contemporaneously.

(2) If the party bringing the action has to perform first he may, if the other party is in default in acceptance, bring an action for performance after receipt of the counter-performance.

(3) The provision of § 274(2) applies to compulsory execution.

Notes

(1) German law distinguishes between the "genetic" and the "functional" synallagma. It is the second which we are concerned with here, where under a valid contract one party's obligation to perform is contingent upon the other's readiness and willingness to do likewise. ("Genetic synallagma" denotes the fact that A's obligations under the contract will fall away if B's obligation is held not to exist, for example, where B's declaration of will is avoided.)

---

[155] See Cass. com., 27 January 1970, JCP 1970.II.16554, annotated by A. Huet.
[156] See *infra* at 850.
[157] See *infra*, **6.3.2 D**, *infra* at 738.

(2) It may seem that the basis of the *exceptio* in BGB § 320 is simply that no duty to perform has yet arisen (*Einwendung*). The prevailing view, however, is that it is a defence (*Einrede*) which must be raised by the party against whom judgment is sought for the performance of the corresponding obligation.[158]

(3) The BGB has a separate paragraph, § 273, on right of retention (*Zurückbehaltungsrecht*).[159] It also has special rules, including a form of *exceptio*, for cases of defects in property sold.[160]

<table>
<tr><td align="center">*King's Bench*</td><td align="right">**6.E.56.**</td></tr>
<tr><td align="center">Kingston v. Preston[161]</td><td></td></tr>
</table>

CONDITIONS PRECEDENT AND CONCURRENT CONDITIONS

Giving security

A contractual obligation may be independent of the other party's obligation; or one party's obligation may be a condition precedent to, or a concurrent condition of, the other's obligation.

Facts: The plaintiff agreed to serve the defendant for a year and a quarter in the defendant's business as a silk-mercer, and the defendant agreed that at the end of the period he would convey the business and the stock in trade to the plaintiff and the defendant's nephew. The stock in trade was to be paid for over a period of time, and the plaintiff agreed to provide security for these payments. The plaintiff claimed that the defendant had failed to convey the business; the defendant pleaded that the plaintiff had failed to provide the promised security.

Held: The giving of the security was a condition precedent to the defendant's obligation to convey the business.

Judgment: LORD MANSFIELD: There are three kinds of covenants:
1. Such as are called mutual and independent, where either party may recover damages from the other, for the injury he may have received by a breach of the covenants in his favour, and where it is no excuse for the defendant, to allege a breach of the covenants on the part-of the plaintiff.
2. There are covenants which are conditions and dependant, in which the performance of one depends on the prior performance of another, and, therefore, till this prior condition is performed, the other party is not liable to an action on his covenant.
3. There is also a third sort of covenants, which are mutual conditions to be performed at the same time; and, in these, if one party is ready, and offered, to perform his part, and the other neglected, or refused, to perform his, he who was already, and offered, has fulfilled his engagement, and may maintain an action for the default of the other; though it is not certain that either is obliged to do the first act.

[His Lordship then proceeded to say that the dependence, or independence, of covenants was to be collected from the evident sense and meaning of the parties, and that, however transposed they might be in the deed, their precedence must depend on the order of time in which the intent of the transaction requires their performance. In the case before the Court, it would be the greatest injustice if the plaintiff should prevail: the essence of the agreement was that the defendant should not trust to the personal security of the plaintiff, but, before he delivered up his stock and business, should have good security for the payment of the money. The giving of such security, therefore,

---

[158] Treitel, *Remedies*, at 316–7, para. 238.
[159] This is considered in more detail in **6.3.2.F**, *infra* at 742.
[160] These are considered in **6.3.2.E**, *infra* at 740.
[161] (1773) 2 Doug KB at 689–91.

must necessarily be a condition precedent. Judgment was accordingly given for the defendant, because the part to be performed by the plaintiff was clearly a condition precedent.]

Sale of Goods Act 1979   6.E.57.

Section 28: Unless otherwise agreed, delivery of the goods and payment of the price are concurrent conditions, that is to say, the seller must be ready and willing to give possession of
the goods to the buyer in exchange for the price and the buyer must be ready and willing to pay the price in exchange for possession of the goods.

Note
English law explains the right to withhold performance in terms of conditional obligations. Although it is possible for the two obligations to be entirely independent of each
other, so that each must perform irrespective of the other's failure, this is uncommon.
Normally party A is only obliged to perform:

(1) if party B is to perform first, when B has done so (B's performance is a "condition
precedent" to A's obligation); or
(2) if A and B are to perform simultaneously, when party B is ready and willing to do perform (the performances are "concurrent conditions" of each other).

Thus in a contract of sale, as section 28 states, the buyer need not pay until the seller has
the goods ready and the seller need not deliver until the buyer is ready to pay.[162]

It is important to note that to say that B's performance is a condition precedent to A's
obligation to perform, or a concurrent condition of it, is different from saying that the
operation of the contract, or of one of its terms, is conditional on the occurrence of some
event which is—wholly or partly—outside the control of the parties. The latter is sometimes called a "suspensive" condition. An example would be a contract which is to come
into effect only if the Government grants an export licence. The difference is that, in the
example just given, neither party will be liable to the other if the condition fails to occur
because the licence is refused (though there may be liability if one party brings about the
refusal of the licence by, for example, not submitting a proper application). In the cases
we are considering in this chapter, although B's performance is a condition of A's obligation, B is *obliged* to perform. If he fails, he will normally be in breach of contract and
liable for damages. To make this clear, sometimes this type of condition is called "promissory", whereas the type of condition involved in the case of the contract dependent on
the grant of the licence is termed "contingent".[163]

---

[162] There is a complication, however, caused by the fact that in the English law of sale, property may pass
before the goods are delivered, so that the goods belong to the buyer even though they remain in the seller's possession. The seller may still refuse to deliver the other party's property until the buyer tenders the price for the
goods (unless the seller has agreed to deliver on credit). The Sale of Goods Act 1979, s. 39 describes this as the
seller's "lien or right to retain the goods". If the buyer's default continues the seller may, after giving notice to
the buyer, re-sell the goods: s. 48(3). This has the effect of terminating the contract of sale and re-vesting the
property in the seller: *R. V. Ward* v. *Bignall* [1967] 1 QB 534, CA. English law recognizes liens in other situations
also. Thus a person who has been employed to repair goods may refuse to re-deliver them to their owner them
until he has been paid for the work done ("the repairer's lien": see Goode, *Commercial Law*, 2nd edn. (London:
Penguin, 1995) at 668–9.

6.3.2.B. THE ORDER OF PERFORMANCE

(1) Introductory Note
In the simplest cases the right to withhold performance is the simple result of the order
of performance—either an order which was agreed expressly in the contract or one which
is applicable to the contract under the relevant rules of law. Thus if a sales contract provides for payment in cash on delivery, it seems self-evident that the seller does not have to
deliver unless he is going to be paid. The right to deliver follows simply from the fact that
the seller is not obliged to perform until the buyer does so. *A fortiori* the case where under
the contract, A is to perform first; B is not obliged to perform until A has done so. On a
simple reading, BGB § 320, the French jurisprudence referred to by Carbonnier and the
English doctrine of conditions are no more than reflections of this.

   This seems to be confirmed by the details of the doctrine. Thus in German law, BGB
§ 320 does not apply simply because the contract as a whole involves an exchange of
undertakings. It is necessary that the obligation performance of which is to be withheld
be synallagmatic with the obligation which the other party has not yet performed. We will
consider one example of this later, when we see that a minor obligation of the contract
may not be synallagmatic with other obligations under the same contract—so that non-
performance of the minor obligation does not justify withholding performance of the
rest.[164] Another example of non-synallagmatic obligations can be found in a contract of
agency. The agent may be obliged to render accounts to the principal and the principal
may have to indemnify the agent for expenses incurred; but it has been held that the two
obligations are not synallagmatic, so that the agent cannot refuse to account because he
has not been paid his expenses.[165] There may, however, be a "right of retention" even in
this case.[166]

   The English notion that some "covenants" may be "independent" of each other also
seems to reflect the same idea that, if there is to be a right to withhold performance of one
obligation because of non-performance of the other, the obligations must be synallagmatic. Thus in *Taylor* v. *Webb*[167] du Parcq J held that a landlord must repair the leased
premises even if the tenant was in arrears with the rent, as the two obligations were independent.

(2) Establishing the Order of Performance
In order to apply such principles to decide whether party A is entitled to withhold its performance until B has performed, it will first be necessary to determine the order in which
the parties are to perform. For instance, the provisions which allow sellers to refuse
to deliver and buyers to refuse to pay until the other is ready to perform assume that
payment is to be made on delivery. Obviously the seller who has agreed that the buyer
may pay after a period of credit cannot refuse to deliver merely because the buyer is not

---

[163] See Treitel, *Remedies*, at 259–61, para. 198. For a case which turned on which type of condition was
involved, see *Trans-Trust SPRL* v. *Danubian Trading Co Ltd* [1952] 2 QB 297.
[164] See *infra* at 732 ff.
[165] See *Münchener Kommentar*, under § 662 BGB, para. 5.
[166] See **6.3.2.F**, *infra* at 742.
[167] [1937] 2 KB 283.

prepared to pay at the time of delivery.[168] Indeed withholding performance by a party bound to perform in advance is expressly precluded by the wording of § 320 I BGB.

The order of performance will determine the extent to which one party will have to extend credit to the other. If the performances can be exchanged simultaneously, no extension of credit by either will be necessary. This may be why, when the parties have not expressly agreed the order of performance, the three systems seem to have some presumption in favour of simultaneous exchange. This is clear in the Common Law[169] and may be deduced in French and German Law.[170] However, all three systems depart from this when simultaneous performance would be impractical—for example, in a contract for building work it would hardly be sensible to require the employer to pay a builder as each brick is laid. In such cases it will have to be decided which party is to perform first.

"Work first, payment later" is the norm in service contracts and work contracts. This is explicit in the BGB (§§ 614, 641). Frequently, however, there are contrary customs—such as for contracts to see theatre performances. In addition the parties may, of course, contract out of or reverse legal rules or customary stipulations in favour of advance performance.[171]

Principles of European Contract Law   **6.PECL.58.**

Article 6:110: *Order of performance*

(1) To the extent that the performances of the parties can be rendered simultaneously, the parties are bound to render them simultaneously unless the circumstances indicate otherwise.

(2) To the extent that the performance of only one party requires a period of time, that party is bound to render its performance first, unless the circumstances indicate otherwise.

Note

It will also be necessary to decide *how much* of one party's performance is due before the other's obligation arises—must the first party perform the whole of his obligation, or is he entitled to the counter-performance "bit by bit"?

In English law the question is put thus: is the obligation entire or severable? Again to reduce the amount of credit that must be advanced, there is a presumption in favour of severability. Thus unless agreed otherwise, a contract for employment is treated as severable by the day, so that at the end of each day the employee will have earned a day's pay.[172] However, if there is no way of apportioning the price to the various tasks to be carried out under the contract it will be treated as entire. Thus a builder's obligation under a

---

[168] The situation in which the buyer may never be able to pay is considered *infra* at 740.

[169] See Treitel, *Remedies*, at 279–81, para. 214.

[170] *Ibid.*, § 220.

[171] See the discussion of this in Gernhuber, *Handbuch des Schuldrechts*, Vol. VIII (Tübingen: Mohr, 1989) at 354–7.

[172] See Apportionment Act 1870, s. 2; in practice it is usually agreed that payment will be deferred until the end of the week or month.

simple contract for building work where the price is stated as a single ("lump") sum is entire, so that the builder is not entitled to any payment until the work is finished.[173]

6.3.2.C. WITHHOLDING WHEN THE OTHER PARTY HAS PERFORMED BUT HAS DONE SO DEFECTIVELY, OR HAS NOT PERFORMED SOME OF HIS OBLIGATIONS

Evidently, a party may be entitled to withhold its performance even if the other has not totally failed to perform, provided that the non-performance is of some essential obligation. Thus if a seller tenders goods which are obviously defective, the buyer need not take them or pay for them. Does *any* failure to perform by party A justify party B in withholding his performance, or must the failure be a serious one?

In German Law two principles apply. The first deals with the case in which a particular obligation has not been performed and looks at its importance. The second considers rather the case in which an obligation has been performed defectively.

On the first, German Law employs a number of tests in order to distinguish obligations which are synallagmatic from those which are not. First, the main obligations (*Hauptpflichten*) for the contract type will be taken to be in a synallagmatic relationship. These are the obligations which are considered essential to the existence of a contract of the particular type. Thus in contracts of sale, the obligation of the seller to supply the buyer with the goods (§ 433 I BGB) and the obligation of the buyer to pay the purchase price (§ 433 II BGB) are *Hauptpflichten*. In contrast, the obligation of the buyer to take delivery is not normally a main obligation but a collateral obligation (*Nebenpflicht*).[174] Further, protective duties (*Schutzpflichten*), as implied by the law on positive breach of contract, will not be in synallagmatic relationship. The agreement of the parties may make an obligation a main one, even where it is not typically so.[175]

On the second idea, § 320(2) BGB is explicit:

If one side has performed in part, the counter-performance may not be refused to the extent that the refusal would be, in the circumstances, contrary to good faith, especially in view of the disproportionate triviality of the remaining part.

---

[173] *Sumpter* v. *Hedges* [1898] 1 QB 673, **6.E.106**, *infra* at 804. In practice, builders cannot afford to extend this much credit to employers, and therefore in England large building contracts usually provide for the value of the work carried out to be certified at monthly intervals. The employer must pay the value of these "interim certificates", less previous payments and a "retention percentage", within thirty days of the date of the certificate. Recently a scheme has been provided by statute: see Housing Grants, Construction and Regeneration Act 1996 (c.53) ss. 109–113. German law and practice on building contracts have developed in a rather similar fashion. BGB §641 states that payment in a contract for work is to be made on acceptance of the completed work. But, if the work is accepted in parts then payment must be made on each separate acceptance. Furthermore, advance, instalment and completion payments on presentation of certificates attesting to the progress of building work are provided for specifically in Part B of the General Conditions for Construction Works (*Verdingungsordnung für Bauleistungen*) which may be adopted into the contract by the parties; see Lorenz, *International Encyclopaedia of Comparative Law— Specific Contracts for Work on Goods and Building Contracts* (Tübingen: Mohr, 1971) at 117–18, paras. 6–7. Similarly, in leases the basic rule is that the rent is to be paid at the end of the period of the lease, or at the end of such time intervals as the rent is calculated by (Germany, BGB § 551; England, *Coomber* v. *Howard* (1845) 1 CB 440), though very frequently the parties agree on payment in advance.

[174] The obligation of the lessor to allow the use of the property to the lessee (§ 535 1 BGB) and the obligation of the lessee to pay rent (§ 535 2 BGB) are *Hauptpflichten*. By contrast, neither the obligation of the lessor to make good any expenditure by the lessee on the property (§ 547 BGB) nor that of the lessee to return the property at the end of the lease (§ 556 I BGB) is a main obligation. As merely collateral obligations (*Nebenpflichten*), they are not, therefore, in synallagmatic relationship.

[175] See Gernhuber, op. cit., at 322–5.

Notes

(1) The German courts understand the *exceptio* as a means of compelling perform-ance and, therefore, interpret § 320 (2) BGB narrowly.[176] They take account of the fact that it is often where the outstanding performance, or the size of the defect, is quite small that the other party is least willing to make up the difference. There is no sense therefore in which the performance withheld must be equivalent (in value or otherwise) to the performance outstanding.[177]

(2) It is accepted that defective performance is tantamount to part performance within the terms of § 320 (2) BGB.

(3) Apart from the breach itself, in determining the requirements of good faith, a court may consider the general circumstances of the case including the length of the delay in performing and the deterioration of relations between the parties. Even if §320 (2) BGB is applicable A may withhold a part of his own performance sufficient to compel B to perform.

Cass. com., 30 January 1979[178]   **6.F.59.**

No WITHHOLDING FOR MINOR NON-PERFORMANCE

Defective computer

The lessee of defective equipment is entitled to suspend payment of rentals only if the breach commit-ted by the lessor is of a sufficient magnitude.

Facts: According to the judgment appealed against (Paris, 25 March 1977), SEFCO, an IT company working on accounting and management, used equipment hired or sold by the company, Honeywell Bull, which main-tained that equipment subject to a monthly payment. By letters of 26 September and 30 October 1968 contain-ing an exclusivity clause, Honeywell Bull agreed that SEFCO could rescind the contract in the event that a Honeywell installation were used by an IT company located in the same geographical area as SEFCO. In spite of difficulties in regard to monthly payments, and although SEFCO alleged that Honeywell Bull equipped a competing company, SEFCO nevertheless on 31 December 1971 entered into a contract under which Honeywell Bull sold it a computer which to be operational depended on hired equipment; it was provided that that con-tract was to replace all earlier contracts. In 1972 fresh difficulties led Honeywell Bull to rescind the maintenance and leasing contract in respect of which periodic payments had not been paid and to sue SEFCO on 4 October 1972 for payment of the sums due. SEFCO counterclaimed for damages and interest in respect of the loss which it alleged it had suffered owing to the need to reconvert its equipment.

Held: The defects in the equipment were not serious enough to justify withholding of the rental payments.

Judgment: . . . :—Whereas the judgment appealed against is also criticised for ordering SEFCO, the lessee of two magnetic disc units which it considered to be defective, to pay the entirety of the rentals; whereas, according to the appeal, the objection of non-performance applies to defective performance in the same way as it does to total non-performance; as the lessee of defective equip-ment is therefore, it is submitted, entitled to suspend payment of rentals, especially where, as in the present case, it ceased payments only a long time after noting the difficulties that had occurred.

—Whereas in finding that the H1200 unit and discs, although not a brilliant performer, had shown itself to be viable for SEFCO which used it until 1973, the court of appeal made clear that, although

---

[176] See BGH NJW 1958.706.
[177] See Gernhuber, op. cit., at 343–6.
[178] Bull.civ. 1979.IV.41.

defective performance of the contract allowed that undertaking to raise the objection of non-performance, the deficiencies found were not, however, sufficient to warrant withholding performance even if that withholding occurred only after a long period of difficulties; and therefore the plea is unfounded. . . .

On those grounds: The appeal against the judgment delivered on 25 March 1977 by the court of appeal, Paris, is dismissed.

Note

It has already been pointed out that French doctrine tends to see the *exception d'inexécution* as linked to good faith. Malaurie and Aynès say:

For the exception to be relied on there must be a serious non-performance and good faith on the part of the party invoking it.[179]

A tenant cannot normally withhold rent on the ground of the landlord's failure to carry out repairs, but may do so if the defects prevent the premises being used safely.[180]

In English law the question of how serious a non-performance must be to justify the other party withholding performance, and the closely related question of how serious a breach of contract must be to entitle the innocent party to terminate the contract, have caused great difficulty and complexity. Different though related rules have been developed in different contractual situations. In contracts for work in which one party is to perform the work in advance of payment, and has not completed it or has done some of it defectively, the courts have applied a doctrine known as the doctrine of substantial performance.

Court of Appeal   **6.E.60.**
Hoenig v. *Isaacs*[181]

SUBSTANTIAL PERFORMANCE

Defects in a flat

Once building work has been substantially completed the employer must pay the contract price but may deduct damages, including the cost of having any defects in the work put right.

Facts: The defendant employed the plaintiff to decorate and furnish the defendant's flat for £750. The work was finished bar some defects in a bookcase and a wardrobe, which would cost about £55 to rectify, and the defendant moved into the flat, but he refused to pay the outstanding balance of the contract price.

Held: The court of first instance held that the balance of the price must be paid subject to any counter-claim for damages. The Court of Appeal dismissed the employers' appeal.

Judgment: SOMERVELL LJ: Each case turns on the construction of the contract. In *Cutter* v. *Powell* the condition for the promissory note sued on was that the sailor should proceed to continue and do his duty as second mate in the ship from Jamaica to the port of Liverpool. The sailor died before the ship reached Liverpool and it was held his estate could not recover either on the contract or on a quantum meruit. It clearly decided that his continuing as mate during the whole voyage was a condition precedent to payment. It did not decide that if he had completed the main purpose of the

---

[179] Malaurie and Aynès, para. 724.
[180] *Ibid.*, para. 722; Nicholas at 215, citing Cass. civ., 21 February 1927, DH 1928.82 and Cass. soc. 10 April 1959, D 1960.61.
[181] [1952] 2 All ER 176.

contract, namely, serving as mate for the whole voyage, the defendant could have repudiated his liability by establishing that in the course of the voyage the sailor had, possibly through inadvertence,
failed on some occasion in his duty as mate whereby some damage had been caused.

The learned official referee regarded *H Dakin & Co Ltd* v. *Lee* laying down that the price must be
paid subject to set-off or counterclaim if there was a substantial compliance with the contract. I
think on the facts of this case where the work was finished in the ordinary sense, though in part
defective, this is right. It expresses in a convenient epithet what is put from another angle in the Sale
of Goods Act. 1893. The buyer cannot reject if he proves only the breach of a term collateral to the
main purpose. I have, therefore, come to the conclusion that the first point of counsel for the
defendant fails.

The learned official referee found that there was substantial compliance. Bearing in mind that
there is an appeal on fact, was there evidence on which he could so find? The learned official referee
having, as I hold, properly directed himself, this becomes, I think, a question of fact. The case on
this point was, I think, near the border line, and if the finding had been the other way I do not think
we could have interfered . . .

DENNING LJ: This case raises the familiar question: Was entire performance a condition precedent
to payment? That depends on the true construction of the contract. In this case the contract was
made over a period of time and was partly oral and partly in writing, but I agree with the official
referee that the essential terms were set down in the letter of 25 April, 1950. It describes the work
which was to be done and concludes with these words:

> "The foregoing, complete, for the sum of £750 net. Terms of payment are net cash, as the work proceeds: and
> balance on completion."

The question of law that was debated before us was whether the plaintiff was entitled in this action
to sue for the £350 balance of the contract price as he had done. The defendant said that he was
only entitled to sue on a quantum meruit. The defendant was anxious to insist on a quantum
meruit, because he said that the contract price was unreasonably high. He wished, therefore, to
reject that price altogether and simply to pay a reasonable price for all the work that was done. This
would obviously mean an inquiry into the value of every item, including all the many items which
were in compliance with the contract as well as the three which fell short of it. That is what the
defendant wanted. The plaintiff resisted this course and refused to claim on a quantum meruit. He
said that he was entitled to the balance of £350 less a deduction for the defects.

In determining this issue the first question is whether, on the true construction of the contract,
entire performance was a condition precedent to payment. It was a lump sum contract, but that
does not mean that entire performance was a condition precedent to payment. When a contract
provides for a specific sum to be paid on completion of specified work, the courts lean against a
construction of the contract which would deprive the contractor of any payment at all simply
because there are some defects or omissions. The promise to complete the work is, therefore, construed as a term of the contract, but not as a condition. It is not every breach of that term which
absolves the employer from his promise to pay the price, but only a breach which goes to the root
of the contract, such as an abandonment of the work when it is only half done. Unless the breach
does go to the root of the matter, the employer cannot resist payment of the price. He must pay it
and bring a cross-claim for the defects and omissions, or, alternatively, set them up in diminution of
the price. The measure is the amount which the work is worth less by reason of the defects and omissions, and is usually calculated by the cost of making them good: see *Mondel* v. *Steel*; *H Dakin &
Co Ltd.* v. *Lee* and the notes to *Cutter* v. *Powell* in *Smith's Leading Cases*, 13th edn, vol 2, pp 19–21.
It is, of course, always open to the parties by express words to make entire performance a condition
precedent. A familiar instance is when the contract provides for progress payments to be made as

the work proceeds, but for retention money to be held until completion. Then entire performance is usually a condition precedent to payment of the retention money, but not, of course, to the progress payments. The contractor is entitled to payment pro rata as the work proceeds, less a deduction for retention money. But he is not entitled to the retention money until the work is entirely finished, without defects or omission . . . But . . . I think this contract should be regarded as an ordinary lump sum contract. It was substantially performed. The contractor is entitled, therefore, to the contract price, less a deduction for the defects. . .

ROMER LJ: The position is, I think, in some respects analogous to a case where a man agrees to sell land and, before completion, finds that he is unable to make title to a small part of it which is of no great significance in relation to the whole. In such a case the vendor can substantially perform what he has agreed to do but cannot perform it wholly, and the Court of Chancery has never hesitated to grant specific performance at this instance against the purchaser subject to a proper and reasonable deduction being made in the purchase price. It would not, however, make such an order if it resulted in the purchaser getting something substantially less than or different from what he had bargained for. . . . I am, accordingly, of the opinion, as already indicated, that the learned official referee fell into no error of law and that this appeal fails.

Notes

(1) The effect of this rule is that exact performance is not a condition precedent to the employer's obligation to pay; the condition precedent is that the work be substantially completed. The employer may deduct from the price damages for the builder's failure complete. Usually the damages will be the cost of having the work finished by another builder, but for an exception see the *Ruxley* case.[182]

(2) As the judgment notes, the doctrine of substantial performance, that the price is earned once the work is substantially complete, is the general rule, but the parties may provide that the work must be done exactly as a condition precedent to payment.

(3) In *Hoenig* v. *Isaacs* the employer offered to pay a reasonable sum for the work done. If the employer had been right that the work had not been substantially completed, it seems that he would not have been *obliged* to pay anything at all.[183]

(4) There is some debate in English law whether the doctrine of substantial performance applies only when the work has been completed but some of it has been done defectively, or also when some of the work has not been done at all. Treitel[184] explains *Hoenig* v. *Isaacs* by saying that the obligation to complete the work was entire, but the obligation as to its quality was not. He continues:

In relation to "entire obligations", there is no scope for the doctrine of "substantial performance".[185]

The courts have applied the doctrine in cases in which some element of the work had simply not been done.[186]

---

[182] See *supra* at 694.
[183] There are dicta in *Hoenig* v. *Isaacs* to the effect that the employer would have to pay something on a restitutionary basis ("guantum meruit", meaning simply "however much it is worth"). They are not extracted here and they seem to be inconsistent with the generally accepted rule in English law; see *infra* at 804.
[184] Treitel, *Contract*, at 729–30.
[185] See McKendrick, *Contract*, at 427.
[186] E.g. *Dakin* v. *Lee* [1916] 1 KB 566.

In English Law there is second approach, which is applied to contracts in general. This is to ask whether the term which has not been performed was a "condition", going "to the root of the contract", or only a "warranty".

In *Wallis, Son & Wells* v. *Pratt & Haynes*,[187] Fletcher Moulton LJ explained the distinction thus:

A party to a contract who has performed or is ready and willing to perform his obligations under that contract is entitled to the performance by the other contracting party of all the obligations which rest upon him. But from a very early period of our law it has been recognised that such obligations are not all of equal importance. There are some which go so directly to the substance of the contract, or, in other words, are so essential to its very nature, that their non-performance may fairly be considered by the other party as a substantial failure to perform the contract at all. On the other hand, there are other obligations which, though they must be performed, are not, so vital that a failure to perform them goes to the substance of the contract. Both clauses are equally obligations under the contract, and the breach of any on of them entitles the other party to damages. But in the case of the former class he has the alternative of treating the contract as being completely broken by the non-performance, and (if he takes proper steps) he can refuse to perform any of the obligations resting upon himself and sue the other party for a total failure to perform the contract.

This usage has been followed in the codification of the law of the contract of sale in the Sale of Goods Act. . . .

Note that Fletcher Moulton LJ uses the words "refuse to perform" in the same sense as we have used "terminate". He refers to conditions as giving rise to a right to refuse to perform and to sue for damages for total failure to perform. He is assuming that the time for performance has expired. Before that time, the buyer would normally not be entitled to terminate, but it would be able to withhold payment until the seller was ready and willing to perform those terms which are conditions of the contract. It could not, however, withhold its performance merely because the seller had not performed a warranty.

The distinction between conditions and warranties is taken up in the Sale of Goods Act 1979:

Sale of Goods Act 1979   **6.E.61.**

Section 11: (2) Where a contract of sale is subject to a condition to be fulfilled by the seller, the buyer may waive the condition, or may elect to treat the breach of condition as a breach of warranty and not as a ground for treating the contract as repudiated.
(3) Whether a stipulation in a contract of sale is a condition, the breach of which may give rise to a right to treat the contract as repudiated, or a warranty, breach of which may give rise to a claim for damages but not to a right to reject the goods and treat the contract as repudiated, depends in each case on the construction of the contract; and a stipulation may be a condition, though called a warranty in the contract.

We will see that the English courts have found the distinction between conditions and warranties to be too rigid to produce satisfactory results in all cases. The decisions have

---

[187] [1910] 2 KB 1003. The actual question in this case was about whether an exclusion clause applied to a breach of condition. The clause excluded liability for any "warranty". Was it effective to exclude liability when the breach was one of a term stated by the Sale of Goods Act 1893, s. 13, to be a condition, even though the buyers had accepted the goods and thus lost their right to terminate the contract? The majority held that it was, but the dissenting judgment of Fletcher Moulton LJ. was approved by the House of Lords [1911] AC 394.

all concerned attempts by one party to terminate the contract, and therefore we consider them in the next section.

The English law on withholding of performance seems to operate rather less subtly than the French or German rules. On the one hand, since there is no doctrine of good faith, a party may be able to withhold a performance worth a great deal more than the obligation that the other party has not performed.[188] On the other hand, the fact that English law decides whether a party may withhold its performance by the same criteria as whether it may, if the other's non-performance continues, terminate the contract may reduce the availability of withholding of performance in English law compared to the continental systems. A slight breach—i.e. one which is not a breach of condition, nor sufficiently serious to justify termination under the rules just mentioned—, cannot give rise to a right to withhold performance. The good faith test of French and German law seems more flexible.

Principles of European Contract Law **6.PECL.62.**

Article 9:201: *Right to Withhold Performance*

(1) A party which is to perform simultaneously with or after the other party may withhold performance until the other has tendered performance or has performed. The first party may withhold the whole of its performance or a part of it as may be reasonable in the circumstances.

COMMENT

B. *Non-performance need not be fundamental*

Where the obligations of the two parties are to be performed simultaneously a party's non-performance need not be fundamental in order to entitle the other party to withhold its own performance. But it is not necessarily appropriate for a party to be entitled to withhold the whole of its performance if the obligations not performed by the other party are not fundamental. In the common law countries the right to withhold performance is restricted to cases where the contract expressly or impliedly makes the obligations conditional upon one another and to cases of fundamental non-performance; in other cases the aggrieved party must perform its obligations in full (though if the non-performance is a breach it may have a claim for damages). Other systems are more flexible, permitting withholding of performance as a way of coercing the non-performing party even where the non-performance is minor, provided that the amount withheld is not wholly disproportionate and the withholding party acts in good faith. It is this approach which is adopted by this Article, which must be read together with Article 1:201 (Good Faith and Fair Dealing).

Illustration 3: A agrees to buy a new car from B, a dealer. When A comes to collect the car he finds it has a scratch on the bodywork. He may refuse to accept the car or pay any part of the price until the car is repaired.

Illustration 4: The same except that the car is to be shipped to A's home in another country, where B has no facilities. Since it would be unrealistic to expect B to repair the scratch, it would be contrary to good faith for A to withhold more than the cost of having the car repaired locally.

In some cases the aggrieved party cannot practicably withhold part of its performance—for instance, many obligations to perform a service must realistically be performed in full or suspended in full. The aggrieved party may only withhold its performance in full if in the circumstances that

---

[188] The rules mentioned in the previous paragraph and to be described in more detail later, *infra* at 765, were developed to deal with this and the parallel problem in the context of termination of a contract on the pretext of a slight breach.

is not unreasonable. However, it may be expressly provided in the contract that a performance is made reciprocal to the other performance.

6.3.2.D. WITHHOLDING PERFORMANCE WHEN THE BUYER HAS BEEN SUPPLIED WITH DEFECTIVE GOODS

(1) Introductory Note

A buyer who has been supplied with defective goods may wish to refuse to pay for them, or even to refuse to accept them at all, unless either the goods are properly repaired or the seller provides goods which are not defective.

In English law the case of defective goods is treated in the same way as other breaches of contract and, indeed, the rules on sale of goods were used to illustrate the general rules on when an aggrieved party may withhold its performance. However we saw earlier that French and German Law have special regimes governing defective goods. How do these govern the question of withholding performance?

BGB **6.G.63.**

§ 478: (1) If the buyer has notified the seller of the defect or forwarded notice thereof to him before the claim for cancellation or reduction is barred by prescription, he may, even after the expiration of the period of prescription, refuse to pay the purchase price, insofar as he would be entitled to do so by reason of cancellation or reduction (. . .)

(2) If the seller has fraudulently concealed the defect, notice (. . .) is not necessary.

§ 479: The claim for compensation may be set off after the expiration of the period of prescription only if the buyer has previously performed one of the acts specified in § 478. This limitation does not arise if the seller has fraudulently concealed the defect.

Notes

(1) The general provisions of §§ 320 ff BGB apply only before the goods are transferred to the buyer. Thereafter he can only seek the specific remedies laid down in the law of sale.[189]

(2) § 478 BGB represents a lightening of the burden upon the buyer which results from the short (six month) limitation period of § 477 BGB within which he must seek cancellation (*Wandlung*) or price reduction (*Minderung*). As long as he has not yet paid and has notified the seller of the defect within the period he does not have to choose a specific remedy. Instead of withholding the whole purchase price he may opt for *Wandlung* whereby he comes under a duty to return the goods. If he opts for *Minderung* he withholds part of the purchase price corresponding to the extent of the defect.[190] By analogy a buyer is also allowed to withhold the purchase price where a right to cure has been agreed in accordance with § 476a BGB.

(2) § 478 BGB creates a right to withhold, but not to recover performance. Thus, a buyer may not rely on it to obtain a return of the purchase price where he has already paid in full or in part, for example, where he has paid a deposit on the goods.

---

[189] §§ 459 ff BGB; see *supra* at 662.
[190] See *Münchener Kommentar*, under § 478 BGB, para 6.

(3) § 479 BGB allows buyer who has a right to claim damages (for example under § 463 BGB or for positive breach) to withhold payment of the purchase price, or part thereof by way of set off against that claim.[191]

(4) §§ 478 and 479 BGB are also applicable as regards the remedies for defects in work contracts (§ 639 I BGB).

In French Law, as we saw earlier, the delivery of "defective" goods may amount to a non-performance of the contract and render the seller liable under the *garantie*; and in such circumstances the buyer's rights in French law will depend on whether it has accepted the goods. If it has not done so, then it may treat the tender of defective goods as a non-performance and may rely on the *exception d'inexécution* in the usual way.[192] If the buyer has accepted the goods then it may rely only on its remedies under the *garantie*. There is some dispute, as the seller's obligation on the *garantie* is strictly speaking not a contractual one, but it seems that the buyer may rely on the exception and refuse to pay the price or a proportionate part of it,[193] provided of course that the defect is sufficiently serious.

How would the three laws deal with Illustrations 3 and 4 to PECL Article 9:201, the case of the scratch on the new car?[194]

In English law, the right to withhold performance is co-extensive with the right to terminate. It is possible that the scratch might mean that the car was not of satisfactory quality under Sale of Goods Act 1979, section 14(2) (as amended). If so, the buyer would be entitled to reject the car in either situation. If the scratch did not result in the seller being in breach of section 14(2), the buyer could not withhold performance in either case. The buyer could, however, deduct the cost of having the scratch repaired (i.e. the damages he suffers) from the price to be paid.

In German Law, if the car had not yet been transferred to the buyer (as in Illustration 3) §§ 320ff BGB would apply, allowing a right to withhold performance, but subject to an exception on grounds of proportionality as per §320 II BGB. As regards Illustration 4 the first question to be asked is whether the defect (i.e. the scratch) is so insignificant[195] as to take it outside the scope of remedies in the law of sale. Accepting a defect in the car, the buyer may withhold the purchase price and thereafter opt for *Wandlung* or *Minderung*, or claim damages for non-performance within § 463 BGB. Where the buyer opts for *Minderung* only an amount corresponding to the diminution in value of the car may be withheld. In the case of *Wandlung* the buyer could withhold the whole price and require the seller to bear the cost of recovering the goods. As the shipping to another country was agreed the seller would seem obliged to bear the cost in this case. Note that the buyer has a completely free choice as between the two remedies: he is not obliged to choose *Minderung* where this would be more proportionate.

In French Law it seems that the principle of good faith would result in the two cases in Illustrations 3 and 4 being solved in the same way as under PECL.

---

[191] See *ibid.*, § 479 BGB.
[192] See Ghestin, *Conformité et garantie dans la vente* (Paris: LGDJ, 1983), para.. 146 ff.
[193] See Treitel, *Remedies*, at 300–2, para. 230.
[194] *Supra* at 737–738.
[195] See § 459 I 2 BGB.

6.3.2.E. DEFAULT CAN BE ANTICIPATED

As set out in **6.3.2.B.** above, the logic of the right to withhold performance may simply be that A's performance is not due until either B has performed—where B is to perform in advance—or is ready and willing to do so—when B is to perform simultaneously. But what of the case where it is A who is to perform in advance, but he is unwilling to do so because he believes that B will fail to reciprocate? The simple logic of *trait pour trait* or *Zug um Zug* will not assist here.

BGB **6.G.64.**

§ 321: If a person is obliged by mutual contract to perform his part first, he may, if after the conclusion of the contract a significant deterioration in the financial position of the other party occurs whereby the claim for the counter-performance is endangered, refuse to perform his part until the counter-performance is made or security is given for it.

Notes

(1) The deterioration referred to in § 321 BGB must have occurred after the formation of the contract. If it occurred before, then the appropriate remedy is rescission for mistake or fraud under §§ 119 II, 123 BGB,[196] where applicable. Only deterioration in the particular party's situation will be considered, not general deterioration in the economic climate, though the doctrine of *clausula rebus sic stantibus* may be invoked in such cases (§ 242 BGB).

(2) The policy embodied in § 321 BGB has been summed up by one author as follows:

The undertaking of a duty to perform in advance represents a granting of credit. Whoever provides credit must rely upon the other party to a heightened degree. The law protects this reliance in cases of subsequent deterioration in the finances of the other party . . .[197]

Neither English nor French Law has a general provision, but in some cases they reach a similar result by a slightly different means. Both systems, and also German Law, recognize, in addition to the right to withhold performance, a right of retention or lien. As we saw earlier, in some cases this operates in more or less the same way as the right to withhold performance: for example, the English Sale of Goods Act 1979, section 39.[198] In some ways, however, the seller's right of lien and retention may go beyond what would be possible under the simple notion of withholding performance. The situation we are considering, of the party who is to perform first but who anticipates a default by the other, is one of them.

Sale of Goods Act 1979 **6.E.65.**

Section 41: (1) Subject to this Act, the unpaid seller of goods who is in possession of them is entitled to retain possession of them until payment or tender of the price in the following cases:–

    (a) where the goods have been sold without any stipulation as to credit

    (b) where the goods have been sold on credit but the term of credit has expired;

    (c) where the buyer becomes insolvent . . .[199]

[196] See *supra*, at 344 and 336.
[197] Larenz, *SAT*, para. 15 I.
[198] See *supra* at 728.
[199] It will be noted that (c) applies even when the seller had agreed to deliver on credit.

Code civil   **6.F.66.**

Article 1613: Even if he has agreed to deliver goods on credit, [the seller] is not obliged to deliver if, since the contract of sale was made, the buyer has become bankrupt, or is in such financial embarrassment that the seller is in imminent danger of not being paid, unless the buyer provides security for payment.

Note

This provision antedates the courts' recognition of the *exception d'inexécution*, and may thus be seen as an example of the right of retention which French law also recognizes. Thus neither English nor French Law has a general provision dealing allowing a party to withhold his performance because he fears that the other will not perform when the time comes.

Principles of European Contract Law   **6.PECL.67.**

Article 9:201: *Right to Withhold Performance*
    (1) . . .
    (2) A party may similarly withhold performance for as long as it is clear that there will be a non-performance by the other party when the other party's performance becomes due.

Article 8:105: *Assurance of Performance*[200]
    (1) A party which reasonably believes that there will be a fundamental non-performance by the other party may demand adequate assurance of due performance and meanwhile may withhold performance of its own obligations so long as such reasonable belief continues.
    (2) Where this assurance is not provided within a reasonable time, the party demanding it may terminate the contract if it still reasonably believes that there will be a fundamental non-performance by the other party and gives notice of termination without delay.[201]

6.3.2 F. NON-PERFORMANCE OF OTHER CONTRACTS

A frequent practical problem is that there is a series of contracts between the parties, and A wishes to withhold performance under a contract it has not yet performed because B has not yet performed an earlier one, for example has not yet paid for goods received earlier. Is this permissible?

In German law, the right to withhold performance under § 320 BGB will not apply unless the obligations which, on the one side, have not been performed and, on the other, are consequently being withheld, are synallagmatic, i.e. exchanged one for the other. Thus § 320 BGB cannot be used in a number of situations. One is where the contract imposes obligations which are imperfectly synallagmatic.[202] Another, and this is the one which is to be discussed here, is where the obligations in question arise under different contracts.

---

[200] This provision is modelled on a rule found in the US Uniform Commercial Code § 2–609 on the "right to adequate assurance of performance".
[201] See further *infra* at 782.
[202] We saw earlier (*supra*, at 729) that in a contract of agency, under which the agent is obliged to render accounts to the principal and the principal has to indemnify the agent for expenses incurred, it has been held that

Although § 320 BGB does not apply to such cases, there is a general right of retention. This is described as a right of lien but is a good deal wider since it is not limited to the withholding of the other party's property:

BGB **6.G.68.**

§ 273: (1) If the debtor has a matured claim against the creditor arising from the same legal relationship upon which his own obligation is based, he may, unless a contrary intention appears from the obligation, refuse to effect the performance due from him until the performance due to him is effected (right of retention).
(2) Whoever is obliged to hand over an object has the same right, if he has a claim due on account of disbursements incurred in connection with the object, or on account of any damage caused to him by it, unless he has acquired the object by an unlawful wilful act.
(3) The creditor may avoid the exercise of the right of lien by giving security. The giving of security by way of guarantee is barred.

§ 274: (1) As against the claims of the creditor the only effect of the enforcement of the right of lien is that the debtor is ordered to perform on receipt of the performance due to him (contemporaneous performance).
(2) By virtue of such a judgment the creditor may pursue his claim by means of compulsory execution without effecting the performance due from him if the debtor is in default with is acceptance.

Notes

(1) This allows a party to withhold performance of his obligation under one contract if the other party is in default under a separate contract, provided that there is a "connection" between the two obligations. The BGH has stated fairly loosely that the latter should be "a natural, internal economic connection, based upon a single factual relationship" such that "to enforce one claim without regard the other would be against good faith".[203]

(2) If §§ 273–274 are compared to §§ 320–322, it will be seen that the procedure is different. §§ 320–322 look to performance and the creditor whose claim is properly met by a defence that the debtor is withholding performance will get a judgment for performance conditional upon himself performing. Under § 273, in contrast, the creditor may defeat the debtor's right of retention either by performing or by giving the debtor security—so that, at the end of the day, the debtor may have to be content with having a (secured) money claim against the creditor rather than having actual performance.

the two obligations are not synallagmatic, so that the agent cannot refuse to account because he has not been paid his expenses. It seems that the distinction in German law between synallagmatic obligations to which §§ 320–322 apply and non- synallagmatic is parallel to the English distinction between covenants which are conditions (concurrent or precedent) and "independent" covenants: see *supra* at 727. There is no right to withhold your performance because the other party has not performed if his obligation is independent. However how different will the outcome be? Take the case referred to earlier, *Taylor* v. *Webb* [1937] 2 KB 283, in which it was held that a landlord must repair the leased premises even if the tenant was in arrears with the rent, as the two obligations were independent. The tenant will not be able to get an order of specific performance against the landlord; he will have to claim damages for the cost of repairs and other loss. This may then be deducted from the rent due, as it is permissible to set off against one another counter-claims arising from the same transaction.

[203] BGHZ 64.122 (124); 47.157 (167).

French Law, though it applies the *exception d'inexécution* in contracts which it treats as imperfectly synallagmatic,[204] insists that it applies only to performances under the same contract.

English law has no general rule allowing a party to withhold performance under a contract because another contract has not been performed. However, in English law a lawyer may exercise a lien over documents belonging to the client until the client has paid the lawyer's fees, even if the documents retained are not connected to the work for which the fee is due.[205] Furthermore, such a "general lien" may be created expressly by contract and such clauses are common in sales.[206]

It should also be noted that all the systems, under differing conditions, allow claims arising out of the same or different contracts to be "set off" against one another. This is particularly important when one party has become insolvent.[207]

Further readings on withholding performance:

—K. Larenz, *Schuldrecht—Allgemeiner Teil*, 14th edn. (München: Beck, 1987);
—J. Gernhuber, *Handbuch des Schuldrechts*, Vol. VIII: *Das Schuldverhältnis* (Tübingen: JCB Mohr (Paul Siebeck), 1989);
—Ph. Malaurie and L. Aynès, *Cours de droit civil—Les obligations*, 10th edn. (Paris: Cujas, 1999), paras. 721–6;
—K. Rebmann and F. Säcker (eds.), *Münchener Kommentar zum Bürgerlichen Gesetzbuch*, 4th edn. (München: Beck, 2000);
—B. Nicholas, *The French Law of Contract*, 2nd edn. (Oxford: Clarendon, 1992), at 213–16;
—G. Treitel, *Remedies for Breach of Contract* (Oxford: Clarendon, 1988), chapter 8.

---

[204] For example a contract of deposit is initially unilateral, imposing no obligation on the depositor (in common law terms, it is a gratuitous arrangement). Nonetheless, the depositor will be liable to indemnify the depositee for expenses incurred in conserving the property (C.civ. Article 1947), so the contract is treated as imperfectly synallagmatic. The *exception d'inexécution* applies and the depositee may retain the property until he is indemnified by the depositor (Malaurie and Aynès, para. 723). It does not seem to draw the same distinction between types of obligation within what is, overall, a synallagmatic contract; the *exception d'inexécution* applies to all the obligations.

[205] See Goode, *Commercial Law*, 2nd edn. (London: Penguin, 1995) at 668.

[206] E.g.: "The Company shall be entitled, without prejudice to its other rights and remedies, either to terminate wholly or in part any or every contract between itself and you or to suspend any further deliveries under any or every such contract in any of the following events:
(a) if any debt is due and payable by you to the Company but is unpaid;
(b) . . .
(c) if you have failed to take delivery of any goods under any contract between you and the Company otherwise than in accordance with your contractual rights."

[207] Suppose A owes B £1,000 under contract No. 1 and B owes A £1,500 under contract No. 2. A becomes bankrupt. If there were no right of set-off, B will have to pay £1,000 to A and then prove in the bankruptcy for the £1,500. He will probably get only a small proportion of the amount. If he can set off the two debts, however, he may retain £1,000 and need only prove for the balance of what he is owed. For English law see Goode, *Legal Problems of Credit and Security*, 2nd edn. (London: Sweet & Maxwell, 1988) chapter VI. In Germany set off (*Aufrechnung*) is regulated in §§ 387 ff. BGB. In France set off (*compensation*) is regulated by Article 1289 ff. C.civ; see Toledo, "La compensation conventionnelle" RTD civ. 2000.265.

6.4. TERMINATION

Article 8:103: *Fundamental Non-Performance*
A non-performance of an obligation is fundamental to the contract if:
(a) strict compliance with the obligation is of the essence of the contract; or
(b) the non-performance substantially deprives the aggrieved party of what it was entitled to expect under the contract, unless the other party did not foresee and could not reasonably have foreseen that result; or
(c) the non-performance is intentional and gives the aggrieved party reason to believe that it cannot rely on the other party's future performance.

Article 8:106: *Notice Fixing Additional Period for Performance*
(1) In any case of non-performance the aggrieved party may by notice to the other party allow an additional period of time for performance.
(2) During the additional period the aggrieved party may withhold performance of its own reciprocal obligations and may claim damages, but it may not resort to any other remedy. If it receives notice from the other party that the latter will not perform within that period, or if upon expiry of that period due performance has not been made, the aggrieved party may resort to any of the remedies that may be available under chapter 9.
(3) If in a case of delay in performance which is not fundamental the aggrieved party has given a notice fixing an additional period of time of reasonable length, it may terminate the contract at the end of the period of notice. The aggrieved party may in its notice provide that if the other party does not perform within the period fixed by the notice the contract shall terminate automatically. If the period stated is too short, the aggrieved party may terminate, or, as the case may be, the contract shall terminate automatically, only after a reasonable period from the time of the notice.

Article 9:301: *Right to Terminate the Contract*
(1) A party may terminate the contract if the other party's non-performance is fundamental.
(2) In the case of delay the aggrieved party may also terminate the contract under Article 8:106(3).

Article 9:302: *Contract to be Performed in Parts*
If the contract is to be performed in separate parts and in relation to a part to which a counter-performance can be apportioned, there is a fundamental non-performance, the aggrieved party may exercise its right to terminate under this Section in relation to the part concerned. It may terminate the contract as a whole only if the non-performance is fundamental to the contract as a whole.

Article 9:303: *Notice of Termination*
(1) A party's right to terminate the contract is to be exercised by notice to the other party. . . .

744

As mentioned earlier,[208] the legal systems differ in the means by which a contract may be terminated. This has a marked effect on the substance of the law: for example, English law, in which termination is an informal act of the aggrieved party, contains much more detailed rules on when termination is permitted than does French law, which in principle requires a court decision and which leaves a great deal to the appreciation of the judge.

6.4.1. THE MEANING OF TERMINATION

Although in each system the basic notion of termination seems similar—as suggested at the start of section **6.3**,[209] the idea of escaping from the contract—there are quite significant differences in the detailed conceptions of what is involved. The principal difference is whether the process is seen as essentially retrospective, that is, to undo what has taken place so far; or essentially only prospective, that is, for the future.

In French law, for example, *résolution* is seen as retrospective; the contract is treated almost as if it had been annulled and there will have to be mutual restitution of benefits. Where performance takes place over a period of time—*contrats à exécution échelonée* (such as. a lease or an employment contract)—it may be impractical to restore the benefits received and then the contract may simply be terminated for the future. It is common to distinguish this process from *résolution* by terming it *résiliation*. It seems that considerations other than the ease of restitution may also enter the decision whether to grant *résolution* or only *résiliation*.[210] However, there are important differences from the case of nullity: after *résolution* the aggrieved party will have an action for damages for breach of contract and may enforce a penalty clause against the other party.

In contrast, in English law termination is seen as essentially prospective: the aggrieved party is entitled to refuse to accept the other's performance in the future and itself to refuse to perform. Termination does not necessarily lead to a restitution of benefits transferred but, in practice, may lead to the undoing of what has been done. The aggrieved party must act consistently; it cannot, for example, both refuse to perform its part and keep the counter-performance it has received when it is able to return it. Thus a buyer who has received defective goods and wishes to refuse to pay for them will normally have to reject them and allow the seller to take them away.[211] But a party who has received services before justifiably terminating the contract may simply refuse to pay. As we shall see in section **6.4.9.C** below,[212] the party in breach will not usually have a claim in restitution. The aggrieved party will usually claim damages, but he may be permitted instead, subject to quite stringent conditions, to claim in restitution for the value of the benefits he has conferred on the other party, and he may be subject to restitution in favour of the party in breach.[213]

---

[208] *Supra* at 723.
[209] *Supra* at 722–723.
[210] See further *infra* at 798 ff.
[211] If the contract is for a number of goods of which only some are defective, the buyer may reject the whole quantity or keep the ones that are in accordance with the contract and reject the rest, in which case it must pay for the goods kept at the contract rate: SGA 1979 ss. 30 and 35A (inserted by Sale and Supply of Goods Act 1994, s. 3).
[212] *Infra* at 795.
[213] This is explored in **6.4.9**, *infra* at 792–809.

German law recognizes termination in both senses. As in French law, if contractual obligations are to be performed over an extended period (*Dauervertrag*), a party will in general be permitted to terminate only with effect *ex nunc*. This is known as *Kündigung*.[214] It should be noted that *Kündigung* is available in two types of case: first, where it is sought to bring the contract to an end in normal circumstances and, secondly, where it is sought to terminate owing to a breach of contract. We are, of course, concerned only with the latter case here.

Termination must be understood broadly as the "winding down" of the contract at the election of the creditor. This "winding down" is achieved in two main ways: (1) a claim for damages for non-performance, or (2) a declaration of termination (*Rücktritt*). For example, in relation to late performance the BGB provides for the availability of both these remedies:

BGB **6.G.70.**

§ 326: (1) If, in the case of a mutual contract, one party is in delay in performing, the other party may give him a reasonable period within which to perform his part with a declaration that he will refuse to accept the performance after the expiration of the period. After the expiration of the period he is entitled to demand compensation for non-performance, or to withdraw from the contract, if the performance has not been made in due time; the claim for performance is barred . . .

In both cases the main performance obligations of the contract are converted into "secondary" obligations. In the case of the creditor opting for termination (*Rücktritt*) these are obligations to make restitution of performance(s) already rendered under the contract. The BGB contains special rules (§§ 346–356) governing the "winding down" of the contract in this manner. In the case of damages for non-performance, the main performance obligation is converted into an obligation imposed on the debtor to pay damages. The creditor is no longer obliged to perform and may claim damages in the amount of the difference between the value of the two parties' performance—the so-called "difference theory".[215] Alternatively, where the creditor has an interest in doing so, he may go ahead and perform his own obligations, in which case he can claim the full value of the other party's performance—"Surrogation/Exchange method".[216]

Whether the creditor opts for *Rücktritt* or for damages, he may claim damages for breach of collateral obligations (*Nebenpflichten*) and positive breach, as well as damages for delay not amounting to non-performance (§ 286 I BGB), in addition to either restitution (in the case where he opts for *Rücktritt*) or damages for non-performance—note that in the latter case the same harm or loss may not be counted twice in the process of calculating the damages.

Since the enactment of the BGB it has been accepted that the remedies of *Rücktritt* and damages for non-performance may not be sought in cumulation. Thus it is probably incorrect to translate *Rücktritt* as simply "termination". It is closer to what happens in

---

[214] See §§ 542, 554 BGB—lease; §§ 620ff. BGB—contract of service; § 651e II BGB—travel contract.
[215] See further *infra* at 813.
[216] See also at 813.

English law when the innocent party both (a) terminates the contract and (b) seeks restitution of any benefits he has conferred on the other party instead of claiming damages. In this light, the impossibility of claiming both *Rücktritt* and damages for non-performance does not seem so striking, though it still differs from French law. The non-cumulation rule has been much criticized, and the Commission for the Reform of the Law of Obligations recommended its abolition.[217] However, it is unlikely to disadvantage the creditor in most cases. Some examples may make this clear:

(1) Where the creditor has not yet himself performed, the issue of restitution does not arise and damages for non-performance will be claimed in accordance with either the "difference theory" or the "surrogation method".

(2) Where the creditor's performance consisted of the payment of money—for example, the purchase price of goods—, he may recover this payment as minimum damages. In this case *Rücktritt* and damages for non-performance amount to the same thing.

(3) If the value of the performance already rendered by the creditor is in fact greater than the value of the debtor's counter-performance—for example, due to an initially bad bargain or a subsequent rise in the market—, it may be in the creditor's economic interest to obtain restitution of his performance—for example, the property delivered—and re-sell it in the market.

(4) As was pointed out earlier, damages other than those for non-performance may be claimed even when *Rücktritt* is sought.

In fact the creditor is disadvantaged only where he wishes the return of his performance and where, under other systems, he could have claimed damages in addition to this. This is in fact a fairly rare situation.[218]

It is interesting to compare Dutch law. Here termination is said not to be retrospective, BW Article 6:269, but termination results in each party being liable to make restitution of any benefits received under the contract: Article 6:271. This may be restitution of what was actually received or, if that is not possible—for example because the buyer has before termination resold the goods to a third party—restitution of the value of the benefit received.[219] However, after termination the creditor may claim damages for non-perfomance: Article 6:277.

In the international restatements termination is by notice and is prospective in effect:

Principles of European Contract Law   **6.PECL.71.**

Article 9:303: *Notice of Termination*
> (1) A party's right to terminate the contract is to be exercised by notice to the other party.

---

[217] *Abschlussbericht der Kommission zur Überarbeitung des Schuldrechts* (Bonn: Bundesministerium für Justiz, 1992) at 173 ff.

[218] See *J. von Staudingers Kommentar zum Bürgerlichen Gesetzbuch mit Einführungsgesetz und Nebengesetzen* (various editors), 13th edn. (Berlin: Sellier, de Gruyter, 1995), under 323 ff. BGB, para. 26; e.g. C sells piano for DM 1500,which was in fact worth DM 1000. C delivers the piano. D delays in paying. C may either recover the piano, *or* DM 1500, but not the piano *and* DM 500. In a commercial context C will of course opt to claim the DM 1500. But if the piano is of non-commercial value to C, then he is at a disadvantage because of the rule of non-cumulation of remedies

[219] See Hartkamp and Tillema, *Contract Law in the Netherlands* (The Hague/Boston: Kluwer, 1995), para. 189.

(2) The aggrieved party loses its right to terminate the contract unless it gives notice within a reasonable time after it has or ought to have become aware of the non-performance.

(3) (a) When performance has not been tendered by the time it was due, the aggrieved party need not give notice of termination before a tender has been made. If a tender is later made it loses its right to terminate if it does not give such notice within a reasonable time after it has or ought to have become aware of the tender.

(b) If, however, the aggrieved party knows or has reason to know that the other party still intends to tender within a reasonable time, and the aggrieved party unreasonably fails to notify the other party that it will not accept performance, it loses its right to terminate if the other party in fact tenders within a reasonable time.

(4) If a party is excused under Article 8:108 through an impediment which is total and permanent, the contract is terminated automatically and without notice at the time the impediment arises.

Article 9:305: *Effects of Termination in General*

(1) Termination of the contract releases both parties from their obligation to effect and to receive future performance, but, subject to Articles 9:306 to 9:308, does not affect the rights and liabilities that have accrued up to the time of termination.

(2) Termination does not affect any provision of the contract for the settlement of disputes or any other provision which is to operate even after termination.

6.4.2. BASIC RULES AND THE MEANS OF TERMINATION

Code civil **6.F.72.**

Article 1183: A resolutive condition is one which, when it operates, revokes the obligation and puts things back into the same position as if the obligation had never existed.

It does not suspend the performance of the obligation; it only obliges the creditor, if the event envisaged by the condition occurs, to restore what he has received.

Article 1184: In synallagmatic contracts, a resolutory condition is always implied for the case where one of the two parties does not fulfil his obligations.

In this case, the contract is not terminated automatically. The party to whom the obligation which has not been performed is owed has the choice of forcing the other party to perform, where this is possible, or of demanding termination and damages. Termination must be ordered by a court and may, according to the circumstances, be granted subject to a delay in favour of the debtor.

Note

The requirement that the aggrieved party seek resolution of the contract through court proceedings is subject to a number of exceptions. First, the parties may agree to a clause for *résolution en plein droit*.[220] Secondly, there are a number of cases in which it is permitted for a party to resolve the contract by a notice because of the urgency of the situation.

---

[220] This is dealt with *infra* at 787.

Cass. Civ. 1re, 28 April 1987[221]   **6.F.73.**

Unilateral termination

Faulty alarm system

A very serious non-performance may justify the creditor in terminating the contract without an action for résolution.

Facts: An alarm system installed by the plaintiffs never functioned satisfactorily and had caused many untimely alerts. The defendants purported to terminate the contract unilaterally.

Held: The Cour d'appel held that as, considering that, having regard to the price of the installation and the cost of maintenance, the installer "had proceeded with excessive negligence and casualness", the client was justified in unilaterally rescinding the contract; and also that various clauses which purported to exclude the alarm company's liability were ineffective.[222] The decision was affirmed by the Cour de cassation.

Judgment: THE COURT: . . . *On the two branches of the second appeal ground*:—Whereas it is also submitted that, since the equipment was not shown to be deficient, the court of appeal could not justify termination of the contract to the detriment of Abonnement Telephonique without reversing the burden of proof and infringing Articles 1134 and 1315 of the Civil Code; as secondly, it is submitted, having decided to declare the contract terminated on the ground of a latent defect, the court could not justify termination of the maintenance contract on a ground relating to the functioning of the installation;

—Whereas however, considering within the limits of its jurisdiction that, having regard to the price of the installation and the cost of maintenance, the installer "had proceeded with excessive negligence and casualness", the cour d'appel, without reversing the burden of proof, was entitled to infer therefrom that Pigranel SA was justified on those grounds in unilaterally rescinding the contract viewed in its totality;

—Whereas neither branch of the appeal ground is therefore well-founded;

. . .

On those grounds, the appeal is dismissed.

Note:

II.—The fate of the contract

A. Unilateral termination of the contract

10. *Unilateral Termination Of The Contract: An Original Solution.* In principle, contracts are binding. There can be no unilateral "declaration" of the termination or rescission of a contract. An application therefor may be made to the courts. However, that is not an absolute principle. It is perfectly open to the parties to agree that the contract shall be terminated on the occurrence of a stipulated event. It is simply a matter of including a clause providing for termination in a given case of non-performance. Moreover, legislative provisions allow the parties to terminate the contract before expiry of the period provided for. Thus, Article 1794 of the Civil Code confers on the owner the right to terminate a contract for a fixed sum. Article 1944 authorises the depositor to claim the item deposited, even though the contract provided for a fixed period before return of the item. And, under Article 2003 instructions may be unilaterally withdrawn by the principal. In contracts for an indefinite period, unilateral termination is also recognised. There again, this is governed by legislative provisions, but it should be remembered that those provisions have been extended to all

---

[221] D.1988.1, annotated by Ph. Delebecque.
[222] On this see *supra* at 529.

contracts providing for continuous performance. Finally and above all, the courts sometimes allow a creditor to break a contract without judicial intervention.

11. *Unilateral Termination: A Legitimate Solution*. At one time those cases were limited by the courts to very specific situations. Thus, premature termination was permitted in urgent cases where to continue the contract would be likely to cause irreparable harm, or on account of very close relations between the parties.[223] Subsequently, the courts became bolder, holding for example that a party could unilaterally break a contract where the other party had made such termination necessary by a serious failure to perform his side of the bargain. Thus, the Colmar court of appeal held that an unpaid vendor faced with a persistent refusal to pay by the buyer was entitled to bring about the termination of the sales agreement. In the same spirit, the Aix court of appeal held that an owner was entitled to terminate a contract in view of serious failures by his contracting partner to perform his obligations; the latter who had been entrusted with terracing work informed the owner that it was impossible for him to complete the works, although the contractual period for completion of the works had expired several weeks previously.

Note

In holding that the "negligence and casualness" of the installing company justified unilateral termination of the contract by the real estate agent, this judgment approves that analysis. The idea seems to accord with notions of justice. It is to give the parties the possibility of unilaterally bringing the contract to an end, even though it may be for the courts subsequently to determine whether such breach was well founded. It has the advantage both of overcoming the slowness of the administration of justice and of bringing the French system into line with solutions of foreign legal systems which favour unilateral termination subject to judicial review, and once again to highlight the part played by contractual good faith which focuses on the need for proper concertation in the performance of any contract or group of contracts.[224]

In German law, in contrast, it is not necessary for the creditor to start court proceedings to have the contract terminated. Instead in most cases he may have to set a notice period within which the debtor must perform and refuse performance thereafter. Exceptionally this notice period may be dispensed with.

BGB

6.G.74.

§ 323: (1) If the performance due from one party under a mutual contract becomes impossible because of a circumstance for which neither he nor the other party is responsible, he loses the claim for counter-performance; in cases of partial impossibility the counter-performance is diminished in accordance with §§ 472, 473 . . .

§ 325: (1) If the performance due from one party under a mutual contract becomes impossible because of a circumstance for which he is responsible, the other party may demand compensation for non-performance, or withdraw from the contract. In case of partial impossibility, if he does not desire the partial performance of the contract, he is entitled, subject to the conditions specified in § 280(2) to demand compensation for non-performance of the

---

[223] See Trib. Civ. Seine, 11 July 1939, S.1942.2.23.

[224] See also *Cahen* v. *Teyssonnier*, Cass. civ. 4.1.1910, S. 1911.1.195 (case of fraud; Pollard, *Sourcebook on French Law* 3rd edn. (London: Cavendish, 2000) at 475; *Estivant* v. *Dorigny*, Cass. civ 25.4.1936, Gaz.Pal. 1936.1.879 (employment; Pollard, op. cit., at 483).

entire obligation, or to withdraw from the entire contract. Instead of the claim for compensation and of the right of termination he may demand the rights specified in the situation provided for by § 323.

(2) The same applies in the situation provided for by § 283, if the performance is not made before the expiration of the period, or if at that time it is in part not made.

§ 326: (1) If, in the case of a mutual contract, one party is in delay in performing, the other party may give him a reasonable period within which to perform his part with a declaration that he will refuse to accept the performance after the expiration of the period. After the expiration of the period he is entitled to demand compensation for non-performance, or to withdraw from the contract, if the performance has not been made in due time; the claim for performance is barred. If the performance is only partly made before the expiration of the period, the provision of § 325(1), sentence 2, applies *mutatis mutandis*.

(2) If, in consequence of the delay, the performance of the contract is of no use to the other party, such other party has the rights specified in (1) without giving any period.

§ 327: The provisions of §§ 346 to 356 applicable to the contractual right of termination apply mutatis mutandis to the right of termination described in §§ 325, 326. If the termination occurs because of a circumstance for which the other party is not responsible, such other party is liable only under the provisions relating to the return of unjust enrichment.

Notes

(1) Where the creditor seeks to claim damages for delay under § 326, the notice period is required. In practice § 326 (1) is the most important provision allowing for *Rücktritt*. The purpose of the notice requirement is to allow the other party one last chance to fulfil his contractual obligations. Since the debtor must be in delay, he will already have been given notice (*Mahnung*) to perform under BGB § 284. It is possible, however, for the creditor to combine the notice putting the debtor into delay with a notice of refusal of performance, so that on expiry of the (single) notice period the creditor will be able to enforce one of his remedies under BGB § 326. However, the parties may stipulate a firm date for performance (*Fixgeschäft*) after which the contract may be terminated without notice.[225]

(2) Clauses which purport to fix agreed notice periods or to exclude the need for notice altogether may be subject to judicial control. For example, the AGBG provides:

AGBG   **6.G.75.**

Unenforceable in General Conditions of Business

10 no.2: . . . a clause permitting the proponent a disproportionately long or insufficiently determined period to accept or reject . . . the performance of an obligation

11 no. 4: . . . a clause freeing the proponent from a legal obligation .. to serve notice on the other party.

(3) Notice is not required in cases of subsequent impossibility for which the debtor is responsible (BGB § 325 (1) 1).

(4) In the case of a positive breach which is sufficiently serious to justify termination of the contract, the creditor must normally set a notice period.[226] Exceptionally a notice

---

[225] On the question of "collapse of the creditor's interest in performance" as per § 326 II BGB, see *infra* at 761 ff.
[226] See *Münchener Kommentar*, under § 275 BGB, para. 322.

may not be required, for example if the debtor indicates that he refuses to perform or where the basis of trust in the contract has been destroyed.[227]

BGH, 21st June 1985[228] **6.G.76.**

PERIOD SET IN *NACHFRIST* TO BE REASONABLE

Nachfrist

If a Nachfrist is set for too short a period, the creditor may terminate after a reasonable period. What is reasonable is to be judged objectively and it is immaterial that the creditor may wish to escape the contract for other reasons.

Facts: In a contract for the sale of land, an instalment of the price due on 27 January had not been paid by 29 January. On that day the vendor gave a *Nachfrist*, set to run until 4 February with refusal of performance thereafter. Payment was not forthcoming until after that date and the vendor declared *Rücktritt* on 11 February. The purchasers sought to enforce the contract.

Held: The lower courts upheld the plaintiff's claim on the ground that the period set in the *Nachfrist* was too short, but the BGH set aside their decision and referred the case back.

Judgment: By a notarial agreement of 22 December 1982 the plaintiffs bought from the defendant a housing plot which at that time was mortgaged to the Volksbank E. for DM 260.000. In regard to payment of the purchase price Article 4 of the agreement provided that the purchase price was DM 300.000. DM 100.000 was payable by 27 January 1983 and the remaining DM 200.000 by 15 February 1983. In case of non-payment interest was to be paid on the purchase price as from 28 January 1983 or as from 16 February 1983, as the case may be, at the rate of interest as calculated by the Volksbank E. for mortgages (III,1,2 and 3). The purchase price was to be paid to the vendor's account no. 203392 with the Volksbank E. The vendor was to assign by way of priority the first part of the purchase price amounting to DM 260.000 to the Volksbank E. The plaintiffs intended to finance the whole purchase price by way of life insurance. The payment of the loan was dependent on an application being made to the Land Registry for registration of a charge in favour of the insurance company. The application was lodged by the notary on 31 January 1983. After the first instalment of the purchase price of DM 100.000 had not been paid into the defendant's account on 27 January 1983, the defendant on Saturday 29 January 1983 gave the plaintiff a further period expiring at 10 o'clock Friday 4 February 1983 and stated that after that date he would refuse to accept performance. By a telegraphic transfer of 8 February 1983 the defendant's account was credited on 10 February 1983, backdated to 9 February 1983, with an amount of DM 288,996.08. By letter of 11 February 1983 the defendant gave notice of termination from the sales agreement since the sum due had not by that time been received. The plaintiffs who in the mean time had been registered in the Land Registry as the owners brought an action for vacant possession and delivery up of the land.

The *Landgericht* (Regional Court) upheld the claim. During the appeal procedure the defendant vacated the property in order to avert a writ of execution. He lodged a counter-claim for conveyance and delivery up of the property. The *Oberlandesgericht* (Higher Regional Court) dismissed the defendant's appeal and counter-claim. On appeal by the defendant on a point of law the judgment of the lower court was set aside and the case referred back.

---

[227] See *infra* at 777 ff.
[228] NJW 1985.2640.

Judgment: II.1. The judgment of the court *a quo* cannot be upheld on those grounds.

(a) The court *a quo* ought to have taken into consideration that generally a further period of too short a duration generally sets in motion a reasonable period . . .. It may exceptionally be otherwise where the creditor only sets a further period for the sake of appearance or has intimated that he will in no event accept performance even if effected within a reasonable period . . .. The court *a quo* did not establish any such exceptional circumstance. It merely considered that the suspicion had not been allayed that the defendant only withdrew because he regretted having entered into the transaction in the first place. Therefore, the court *a quo* ought to have established what further period would have been reasonable in the circumstances of this case and whether the plaintiffs in fact paid the first instalment of the purchase price within that period. The court *a quo* failed to make this assessment. This court cannot substitute its assessment for that of the lower court because the assessment of reasonableness is in principle a matter for the court trying the case on its merits. . . .

(b) The court hearing an appeal on a point of law can merely examine whether the court hearing the case on its merits applied lawful criteria. Nor judged against that yardstick can the judgment of the court below stand on the basis of the grounds given. The further period provided for by the law is intended to give the debtor a last chance properly to perform the contract. . . . It is intended to enable him to complete performance which has already begun to be effected. . . . What period of time is reasonable in that regard is determined in accordance with the circumstances of the case . . . In the case of periods within which payments are to be made it must be borne in mind that the debtor has to answer for his financial ability to pay. . . . Just as difficulties in obtaining credit cannot put off the occurrence of default by the debtor, neither can they affect the length of the further period to be set under § 326 BGB.

An additional factor in that connection is that the court *a quo* also did not find that the further period was objectively too short. It merely found that the period was "very tight in view of the specific nature of that real estate transaction", especially as the purchase price was not to be paid, as is usually the case, into the notary's client account but directly into the defendant's account with the Volksbank E. For that reason, the insurance company wished to make the loan available only after notification by the notary that he had applied for registration of the charge at the Land Registry and that there were no problems precluding registration. Evidently, the court *a quo* based its assessment that the further period had been too short on the suspicion that the defendant had only withdrawn because he regretted the whole transaction. That is wrong in law.

The reasonableness of a further period can only be assessed on objective criteria related to the stated purpose of the fixing of a further period in the event of default by the debtor . . .. Indeed in that connection the creditor's special interest in performance as punctual as possible by the debtor can be taken into consideration . . .. If, in spite of relevant factual submissions and evidence, the court *a quo* did not consider that the defendant had demonstrated any such special interest, it ought to have left that interest aside and appraised the reasonableness of the further period in the light of all the other circumstances. In that connection it should have formed a view on the plaintiffs' claim that, as borne out by the notarial confirmation of 3 February 1983, they could have managed to have the first instalment of the purchase price in the amount of DM 100.000 transferred by the insurance company, if the employee responsible for signing the payment order had not been away and only reachable again on 7 February 1983. If, however, the further period had been objectively adequate and also reasonable in the light of all other circumstances, the defendant's motives in setting that precise period and seeking to free himself from the contract would no longer be relevant . . .

Note

The wording of § 326 I BGB makes it clear that a creditor need only give notice that he intends invoking one of the remedies there enumerated without being required to specify which. However, he must subsequently choose between them. The BGB provides:

BGB **6.G.77.**

§ 349: Rescission is effected by declaration to the other party.

§ 355: If a period for the exercise of the right of termination has not been agreed upon, a reasonable period for its exercise may be given to the party entitled to it by the other party. The right of termination expires if termination is not declared before the expiration of the period.

Where *Kündigung* for breach of contract is the relevant form of termination, notice generally must be given to allow the other party to adjust their affairs before the ending of a legal relationship which has extended over time. This notice requirement may be dispensed with however, in cases of termination "for an important reason" (*Kündigung aus wichtigem Grund*) such as where it would be unreasonable to expect the terminating to continue with the contract: see §§ 553ff. § 626, § 651e II BGB.

In English law, a contract may be terminated if, within the time permitted under the contract, one party has failed to perform an obligation which is a condition of the contract. The distinction between a condition—breach of which gives rise to a right to terminate—and a warranty—breach of which does not give rise to a right to terminate but only to a claim for damages—was explained in section **6.3**.[229] We will see in section **6.4.4** that a party will also have a right to terminate if the other party fails to perform some other obligation in a way which deprives the first party of the substance of what it was contracting for.

Thus in English law the aggrieved party may not terminate the contract until the time for performance has expired.[230] A very important question is whether this happens as soon as the date for contractual performance has passed, or whether the other party, though in breach of contract and thus liable for damages for delay, is allowed additional time for performance. English law approaches this question in a similar way to breaches of other kinds: is the delay a breach of condition? If not, does it deprive the aggrieved party of the substance of what he was contracting for? However, the language used is often somewhat different. If prompt performance is a condition, then it is said that "time is of the essence" and the aggrieved party may terminate as soon as the date has passed. As was stated by McCardie J in *Hartley* v. *Hymans*:[231]

In ordinary commercial contracts for the sale of goods, the rule clearly is, that time is prima facie of the essence with respect to delivery.

---

[229] *Supra* at 736.

[230] This is subject to an exception which we will consider *infra* at 777. Sometimes there is in effect no question of time: for example, if a party promises not to do something and breaks the contract by doing the thing forbidden, the only question is whether the term broken was a condition.

[231] [1920] 3 KB 475, 484.

This means that if the seller is late in delivering the goods, the buyer may terminate the contract without further ado. This strict rule does not apply to all obligations even in a contract of sale:

Sale of Goods Act 1979   6.E.78.

Section 10(1): Unless a different intention appears from the terms of the contract, stipulations as to time of payment are not of the essence of a contract of sale.

If time is not of the essence, the aggrieved party may terminate if the delay is such that it frustrates the venture,[232] or if the other party repudiates the contract.[233]

However, in some situations where time is not of the essence, such as contracts for the sale of land and cases of the buyer failing to accept goods, English law has long recognized a procedure rather like the German *Nachfrist*. There are now dicta in the House of Lords suggesting that this procedure is generally applicable to *all* cases where time is not of the essence. On two occasions (*United Scientific Holdings Ltd.* v. *Burnley Borough Council*;[234] and in the next case) members of the House of Lords have approved the following passage from Halsbury's *Laws of England*:[235]

The modern law, in the case of contracts of all types, may be summarised as follows. Time will not be considered to be of the essence unless: (1) the parties expressly stipulate that conditions as to time must be strictly complied with; or (2) the nature of the subject matter of the contract or the surrounding circumstances show that time should be considered to be of the essence; or (3) a party who has been subjected to unreasonable delay gives notice to the party in default making time of the essence.

It is important to know whether the time for performance is or is not "of the essence". In some situations the answer, if not stated in the contract, is provided by established case law or by statute.[236] In other cases the court will have to decide as a matter of construction of the contract. We will return to this question in the next sub-section.

Principles of European Contract Law   6.PECL.79.

Article 8:103: *Fundamental Non-performance*
A non-performance of an obligation is fundamental to the contract if:
(a) strict compliance with the obligation is of the essence of the contract; or . . .

Article 8:106: *Notice Fixing Additional Period for Performance*
(3) If in a case of delay in performance which is not fundamental the aggrieved party has given a notice fixing an additional period of time of reasonable length, it may terminate the contract at the end of the period of notice. The aggrieved party may in its notice provide that if the other party does not perform within the period fixed by the notice the contract shall terminate automatically. If the period stated is

---

[232] See the judgment of Devlin LJ in *Universal Cargo Carriers* v. *Citati* [1957] 2 QB 401.
[233] On this see *infra* at 777.
[234] [1978] AC 904, 958.
[235] *Halsbury's Laws of England*, 4th edn., Vol. 9 (London: Butterworth, 1997) para. 481.
[236] As for delivery and payment in the sale of goods, see *supra*.

too short, the aggrieved party may terminate, or, as the case may be, the contract shall terminate automatically, only after a reasonable period from the time of the notice.

Article 9:303: *Notice of Termination*

(1) A party's right to terminate the contract is to be exercised by notice to the other party.

Article 9:305: *Effects of Termination in General*

(1) Termination of the contract releases both parties from their obligation to effect and to receive future performance, but, subject to Articles 9:306 to 9:308, does not affect the rights and liabilities that have accrued up to the time of termination.

(2) Termination does not affect any provision of the contract for the settlement of disputes or any other provision which is to operate even after termination.

Note

In the Principles of European Contract Law, the rules on termination appear to follow the model of the Common Law. First, termination is by notice. Secondly, whether the aggrieved party has the right to terminate depends on the nature of the term broken or the effect of the breach, rather than on the discretion of the court. Thirdly, the contract may not normally be terminated until the time for performance has elapsed; and this depends on whether time was originally fundamental or the aggrieved party has subsequently given reasonable notice fixing a period for performance. Fourthly, it is (as we saw in the last section) prospective in effect[237] and, fifthly, it does not preclude a claim for damages. The provisions of Unidroit are broadly similar (see Articles 7.3.1, 7.3.2 and 7.3.5).[238]

6.4.3. TERMINATION BECAUSE GOODS DELIVERED ARE DEFECTIVE

It is again necessary to consider the case where the seller has delivered defective goods. In the systems studied, there is a marked contrast between the Civil Law and the Common Law in this area. In English law, defective goods are subject to the same general rules as any other breach of contract, though, as we will see, there are a number of provisions applying those rules in a particular way. In France and Germany, on the other hand, a distinct body of rules applies to the issue of defective goods. It is helpful to give an account of those rules at this point.

Code civil   **6.F.80.**

Article 1641: The seller is bound by a guarantee against any hidden defect in a thing sold which renders it of no use for the intended purpose, or of less use for that purpose such that, had the buyer known of the defect, he would not have bought the thing or would only have bought it at a reduced price.

---

[237] Thus we will see that though after termination a party may return property it has received, there is only a right to restitution for benefits for which no counter-performance has been received, *infra* at 795.

[238] The rules on restitution after termination are different: cf. *infra* at 795.

Article 1642: The seller is not responsible for defects which were apparent and which the buyer could have seen for himself.

Article 1643: He is responsible for hidden defects, even if he could not have known of them, unless, in such a case, he has stipulated that that he will not be liable on any guarantee.

Article 1644: In the cases covered by Articles 1641 and 1643, the buyer has the choice of returning the thing and recovering the price or keeping the thing and recovering a proportion of the price, the proportion to be judged by experts.

Article 1645: If the seller knew of the defect in the thing, he is liable for damages to the buyer in addition to returning the price.

Article 1646: If the seller did not know of the defect in the thing, he is only liable to return the price and to reimburse the buyer for expenses occasioned by the sale.

Note

(1) In French law, delivery of defective goods may amount to non-performance of the contract, and may also render the seller liable under the *garantie des vices cachés*. If the buyer has not accepted the goods it can employ the usual remedies for non-performance, including an action for *résolution*—or unilateral *résolution* in the cases in which that is allowed. Alternatively it may rely on the *garantie*; and, if it has accepted the goods, it has only remedies under the *garantie*. Under the *garantie,* the buyer can claim either cancellation of the contract or a reduction in price. In principle, the seller is not liable for damages under Articles 1645 and 1646 unless the seller knew of the defect. This principle is now heavily qualified, as there is an irrebuttable presumption that a professional seller knew of the defects.[239]

(2) Subject to the point that damages are not the basic remedy, cancellation of the contract appears to be very much like termination for non-performance.[240] However, one difference is that the choice between the two remedies on the guarantee is the buyer's and does not depend on the seriousness of the defect or the court's discretion (though it must be remembered that the *garantie* applies only to defects which have "a certain seriousness . . . which make the thing sold unfit for the use that the buyer, if he had known of the defects, would not have bought the thing or would have done so only for a lower price".)

BGB   **6.G.81.**

§ 459: (1) The seller of a thing warrants the purchaser that, at the time when the risk passes to the purchaser, it is free from defects which diminish or destroy its value or fitness for its ordinary use, or the use provided for in the contract. An insignificant diminution in value or fitness is not taken into consideration.

(2) The seller also warrants that, at the time the risk passes, the thing has the promised qualities.

§ 460: A seller is not responsible for a defect in the thing sold if the purchaser knew of the defect at the time of entering into the contract. If a defect of the kind specified in §459(1) has remained

---

[239] See Ghestin and Desché, para. 851 ff.
[240] See *ibid.*, paras. 752–757.

unknown to the purchaser in consequence of gross negligence, the seller is responsible only if he has fraudulently concealed it, unless he has guaranteed that the thing is free from defect.

. . .

§ 462: On account of a defect for which the seller is responsible under the provisions of §§459, 460, the purchaser may demand annulment of the sale (cancellation; *Wandlung*), or reduction of the purchase price (reduction; *Minderung*).

§ 463: If a promised quality in the thing sold was absent at the time of the purchase, the purchaser may demand compensation for non-performance, instead of cancellation or reduction. The same applies if the seller has fraudulently concealed a defect.

. . .

§ 465: Cancellation is effected if the seller, on demand by the buyer, declares his consent thereto.

§ 466: If the buyer asserts against the seller a defect of quality, the seller may offer cancellation and require the buyer to declare within a reasonable fixed period whether he demands cancellation. In such a case cancellation may be demanded only before the expiration of the period.

. . .

§ 477: (1) The claim for cancellation or reduction and the claim for compensation on account of the absence of a promised quality are barred by prescription, unless the seller has fraudulently concealed the defect., in the case of moveables, in six months after delivery; in the case of land, in one year after the transfer. The prescriptive period may be extended by the contract.

Notes

(1) In a sale of specific goods, if the risk has not yet passed (i.e. before the time of delivery: § 446 BGB) the buyer may reject the goods and refuse to pay in accordance with § 320 BGB. After the passing of risk, as in French law, a seller is subject to guarantee liability (*Garantiehaftung*) under §§ 459 ff. Under § 477 BGB the limitation period for actions to enforce the obligations under §§ 459 ff is six months after delivery in the case of moveable property and one year after transfer in the case of real property. By contrast with the standard six-month limitation period for general sales in § 477 BGB, a commercial buyer is required to examine the goods and notify the seller of defects as soon as possible after delivery (§ 377 HGB).

(2) The defect in the goods must not be trivial, for example not one which will disappear of its own accord in a short period of time or one which the buyer himself could remove quickly and with minimal expense (§ 459 (1) 2 BGB).

(3) If the seller delivers goods of the wrong kind (*aliud*) this amounts to non-performance: the buyer may thus enforce the general remedies of §§ 320ff BGB is subject to the longer, thirty-year limitation period laid down in § 195 BGB. The boundary between this type of case and that of delivery of defective goods is not always easy to draw.[241]

(4) The seller's responsibility for defects in goods appears to be absolute: the seller cannot defeat a buyer's claim by showing that it was in no way his fault that the goods were "defective"—for example because no one could have discovered the defect. However, the

---

[241] *Münchener Kommentar*, under § 459 BGB, para. 15.

buyer does not necessarily have the full range of remedies. Under § 463, a buyer is able to claim compensation only for breach of a promise that the goods have a particular quality or for fraudulent concealment of a known defect. Otherwise, the buyer's only remedies will be cancellation (*Wandlung*) under § 459(1) or price reduction (*Minderung*) under § 462 BGB.

(5) The presence of particular qualities (§ 459(2) BGB) and thus also freedom from particular defects (§ 460 BGB) may be promised expressly or implicitly. Each case falls to be decided on an interpretation of the particular contract in accordance with §§ 133, 157 BGB.[242] Courts are more likely to find an implicit promise where there was particular reliance by the buyer on the seller's skill and knowledge, for example in sales of motor vehicles.[243] But the burden of proving that the seller made a promise, or fraudulently concealed the defect, is on the buyer—contrast this with French law, where a seller who knew of the defect is also liable in damages and there is a presumption that a professional seller knew of the defects in the goods.[244] The remedies of cancellation and price reduction are therefore of importance in the German law of sale.

(6) The buyer may choose damages only instead of—i.e. not as well as—reduction or cancellation (§ 463 BGB; again compare French law, under which the buyer may seek damages in addition to these remedies, CC Article 1645). Where damages are awarded this will be according to the expectation measure.

(7) § 465 BGB differs from the general provisions on termination (§§ 346ff BGB) in seeming to require not just a declaration by the buyer but the agreement of the seller to the cancellation. The dominant opinion is that a court judgment upholding the buyer's right to seek cancellation amounts to a consent by the seller.[245]

In English law, liability for defects in goods is subject to the same general rules as any other breach of contract, though there are a number of provisions applying those rules in a particular way. The Sale of Goods Act 1979 imposes implied terms that the goods must correspond to the description (section 13) or sample (section 15), and must be of satisfactory quality and fit for any particular purpose made known by the buyer to the seller (section 14), and provides that those terms are conditions of any contract of sale (sections 13–15). In accordance with the general law of contract, the buyer has the right to reject non-conforming or defective goods for a failure to comply with the implied conditions. Thus, once the time for delivery passes without tender of goods which do comply with the contract, the buyer has the right to terminate the contract and to claim damages for non-performance—on the seller's right to cure a non-conforming delivery, see *infra*.[246] We will see shortly that a non-consumer buyer's right to reject has recently been restricted.[247] English law is therefore in contrast to French and German law, where special regimes apply in relation to defects in goods sold.

In some ways, the right to terminate for defective goods under French and German law seems very similar to that under English law. In each system, if there is a defect which is

---

[242] See BGHZ 59.158.
[243] *Münchener Kommentar*, under §459 BGB, para. 56.
[244] See *supra*, at 757.
[245] Larenz, *SBT–I*, para. 41 II.
[246] At 790.
[247] See *infra* at 776–777.

more than trivial, the buyer has a right to recover the price paid—or to refuse to pay it if he has not yet done so. In French law this is under the *action rédhibitoire*; in German law it is through *Wandlung;* in English law it results from the fact that the implied term that the goods are of satisfactory quality is a condition. However, a significant difference between English and French law is that the French buyer may seek reduction of the price even though he or she has had considerable use for the goods, whereas in English law the right to reject the goods and terminate the contract is very quickly lost.[248] A further key difference is the role of damages as the basic remedy in English law.

6.4.4. THE SERIOUSNESS OF THE DEFAULT

Cass. civ., 27 November 1950[249]   **6.F.82.**

COURT'S DISCRETION TO PRONOUNCE *RÉSOLUTION*

Widow Doumenjou's rente viagère

It is within the appréciation souverain of the court to decide whether a non-performance is sufficiently serious to grant résolution.

Facts: The defendants had agreed to purchase the plaintiff's house in exchange for a *rente viagère* by which she would be provided with accommodation, food and care. The defendants failed to comply with their obligations and the plaintiff sought *résolution* of the agreement. She did not rely on a *clause de résolution de plein droit* (see below, p. 787).

Held: The lower court refused to grant *résolution* and awarded the plaintiff an annuity for maintenance in compensation. The appeal was dismissed.

Judgment: THE COURT: *On the second branch of the first appeal ground*:—Whereas it follows from the matters set out and assessed in the judgment appealed against that at no time of the procedure before the courts trying the case on its merits did Mrs Doumenjou rely on a fully applicable termination clause in support of her claim;
—Whereas accordingly, the allegation of an infringement of such a clause constitutes a fresh factual and legal plea, which cannot be raised for the first time before the Cour de cassation;
—Whereas that branch of the appeal ground is therefore inadmissible.

On the first branch of the first appeal ground:—Whereas in dismissing the claim by Mrs Doumenjou for termination, for non-execution of charges, of the sale agreed by her to Mr and Mrs Esquirol of a house in respect of which she was to retain during her lifetime partial enjoyment subject to a price converted into various obligations to feed and care for her, the confirmatory judgment appealed against, both in its own reasoning and in the reasoning adopted from the courts below, proceeded on the basis that the purchasers could not, in the absence of other unproven allegations, be criticised for what was in fact an involuntary delay in performing a part of their obligations, and had declared their readiness to perform them;
—Whereas where, as in the present case, no termination clause was relied on before them it is for the courts, in the event of non-performance of its obligations by one of the parties, to assess,

---

[248] On this question see *infra* at 806.
[249] Bull. civ. I.237.

760

depending on the circumstances of the case, whether non-performance was sufficiently serious for an immediate declaration of termination, or whether it is not sufficiently offset by an award of damages and interest; as that is an autonomous discretionary power;

—Whereas it follows that the cour d'appel, in so holding and ordering Mr and Mrs Esquirol to pay the sums for which they themselves acknowledge they are liable on account of their failures to fulfil their obligations, legally justified its decision; the first limb of that plea is therefore unfounded;

On the second appeal ground:—Whereas it is in fact acknowledged in the absolute discretion of the court below in the judgment appealed against which in that connection adopted the reasoning of the lower courts that the obligation on the purchasers to clothe, feed and care for the vendor had become impossible as a result of the misunderstanding between the parties;

—Whereas the courts trying the case on its merits were therefore entitled to substitute the payment to Mrs Doumenjou, widow, of a compensatory maintenance annuity in place of the positive obligation provided for in the agreement.

—Whereas in so deciding the court provided a legal basis for its decision.

On those grounds, the appeal on a point of law against the judgment given on 19 May 1947 by the Toulouse cour d'appel is dismissed.

Note

If *résolution* or *résiliation* requires the permission of a court, the judge will be able to prevent *résolution* in cases where that remedy would not be justified. Similarly, if a party claims to be entitled to resolve the contract without court proceedings on the basis of fraud or urgency, there is the in-built control that the court may later decide that the situation was not sufficiently serious. What if one party tries to use a clause permitting *résolution en plein droit* when the non-performance by the other side is not very grave?[250]

In German law the right of the creditor to choose either *Rücktritt* or the alternative of damages for non-performance[251] is generally available in cases of delay or impossibility in relation to main obligations (*Hauptpflichten*):[252] §§ 325, 326 BGB. It is also available in particularly serious cases of positive breach.

BGH, 13 November 1953[253] **6.G.83.**

NACHFRIST NOT REQUIRED

Ship not loaded

When a positive breach of contract is so serious that the aggrieved party cannot reasonably be expected to continue with the contract, he may terminate it without serving a notice requiring the other to perform.

Facts: Under a charter agreement a ship was to be ready to load in New York around 5 September. It arrived on 11 September. After repeated demands by the owners the charterers named as responsible for loading a stevedore firm who were not in fact involved at all. The plaintiffs set 12 September as the date on which loading was to begin or for a bank guarantee to be given. This was not done, the charterers making only a vague offer of

---

[250] We consider this in **6.4.6**, *infra* at 787.
[251] See *supra* at 000.
[252] See *supra* at 731
[253] BGHZ 11.80.

loading in New Orleans. On 13 September plaintiffs. declared they were withdrawing from contract and reserving all damages claims. It claimed damages.

Held: The Regional Court dismissed the action. The appeal court declared the claim well founded. The defendant's appeal on a point of law was dismissed.

Judgment: On 30 August 1950 the plaintiff entered into a charterparty with the defendant in the form of the Gencon charter. Under that charterparty the plaintiff undertook to make its steamer "Ouistreham" available around 5 September 1950 in New York.

On 11 September 1950 the "Ouistreham" arrived in New York and notified its readiness to load to C. Sh. Co whose name had finally been given to it by the defendant after repeated requests to that effect. That firm again informed the plaintiff that it had nothing to do with loading. In fact the defendant had no one for loading. On the same day the plaintiff informed the defendant that it would consider itself released from its obligations under the charterparty if loading of the vessel was not started by not later than mid-day on 12 September 1950, or if the defendant did not provide a bank guarantee for performance of the charterparty. The defendant did not proceed to load, nor did it present the promised guarantees by the Federal Government and the Bank but merely pointed to the possibility of a loading in New Orleans. Thereupon, the plaintiff informed the defendant on 13 September 1950 that as a result of the defendant's default it considered that the charterparty had not been performed, was withdrawing the "Ouistreham" and reserving all rights to damages arising out of the defendant's breach of contract.

According to the plaintiff, on the evening of 15 September 1950 the "Ouistreham" was brought into another dock in New York and on 28 September 1950 again made ready for regular service.

In its application the plaintiff claims recovery of its costs for unnecessarily sending the vessel to New York. It bases its claim to damages expressly on Clause 13 of the Charterparty ("indemnity for nonperformance of this charterparty, proved damages, not exceeding amount of freight").

The defendant contested the ground of action and the amount, contending that the plaintiff had not complied with § 577 HGB (Commercial Code).

The Regional Court dismissed the action. The appeal court declared the claim well founded. The defendant's appeal on a point of law was dismissed.

On those grounds:

In so far as the culpable breach does not involve impossibility of performance and delay specifically provided for in the Civil Code and occasions damage going beyond the interest in performance, such damage is to be made good in accordance with §§ 249ff. BGB. That does not apply to unilateral obligations not dependent on counter-performance but only to synallagmatic contracts . . .. In the case of synallagmatic contracts the injured party is not, however, limited to claiming such damage concerning the "negative" (breach of faith or compensatory) interest. The contracting party affected by the positive breach of contract can under certain circumstances claim further rights which as to content correspond to the rights arising out of §§ 325, 326 BGB but have their legal basis in § 242 BGB. Where, as a result of the breach, the object of the contract is jeopardised to the extent that the party faithfully adhering to the contract cannot, in light of all the circumstances of the case and in good faith, be expected to continue the contract or to perform its obligations under the contract, it can for its part refuse to perform the contract and opt either for damages for non-fulfilment, that is to say the "positive" interest in performance or indeed withdraw from the contract . . .

Whereas the claim for damages going beyond the interest in performance does not in principle affect performance of the contract, performance is precluded in the event of the "unreasonable jeopardising of the object of the contract". The party who may therefore withhold performance, is also entitled to withdraw from the contract or claim damages for non-performance. The subject-matter of the present dispute is not loss going beyond the interest in performamce. The claim for damages formulated in the action cannot, in the view of the *Reichsgericht* (Imperial Court), be founded merely on an application of § 276 BGB, as it may have seemed from the submissions of the plaintiff. The essential examination of whether, in light of the defendant's conduct, the plaintiff was entitled to withdraw prematurely from the contract depends upon whether the plaintiff in all the circumstances could in good faith still be expected to perform its obligations under the charterparty which were essentially to make the vessel available and to effect the carriage. According to general principles of law contained in the BGB—not the special provisions of the HGB—a party is released from those obligations where the charterer by his conduct culpably jeopardises the object of the contract to such an extent that the shipowner can no longer reasonably be expected to effect the performance stipulated by those obligations. The defendant is wrong in law to assert that the plaintiff, as the party required to effect performance first, was entitled to withhold performance only under the conditions set out in § 321 BGB. That provision only governs the special case of a significant deterioration occurring subsequently in the financial situation of the party receiving performance first, even in the absence of fault by that party. It does not, however, preclude further restrictions on the duty to effect performance from being justified in practice under the good faith requirement of § 242 BGB. Moreover, the prevailing opinion is that the party required to perform first is also entitled under § 242 BGB to withdraw from the contract if the party receiving performance first is not prepared to counteract the risk occurring to the object of the contract as a result of the deterioration in his financial situation by means of a step-by-step performance or by provision of security.

In the present case any default is sufficient in order to satisfy the definition of a positive breach of contract. Moreover, the decisive factor is merely whether the breach is so serious that not only the object of the contract is jeopardised but that, as a result of that risk, the injured party can no longer be expected to continue with the contract. . . . Where in light of all the circumstances, in particular the nature of the agreement and the specific situations and interests of the contracting parties, the breach of contract is so fundamental that the party complying with the terms of the contract can no longer be expected to continue to do so, the fixing of a period on expiry of which performance will not be accepted is no longer a requirement, at least as a general rule. . . . The party affected by the breach of contract may indicate the grounds which are decisive for him and withdraw from the contract straight away. In that connection the decisive grounds can only be those existing at the time of the party's declaration and stated as being significant in that connection. . . . A subsequent alteration in the conduct or the views of the parties to the contract cannot affect the justification of the declaration to withdraw from the contract. . . .

IV On the basis of these legal considerations the findings of the court *a quo* from the uncontested submissions of the parties entirely warrant the plaintiff's declared intention to withhold performance.

Although the defendant had no-one responsible for loading, on 7 September 1950 it gave the plaintiff the name of the non-existant Co. Sh. Co. and on 8 September 1950 C. Sh. Co. Inc. After the plaintiff had become suspicious of this repeatedly false information, the defendant sought to allay the plaintiff's suspicion on 9 September 1950 by stating that the A Bank had assumed responsibility for financing the transaction and had done so. This statement too turned out on immediate enquiry to be untrue. As a result of this conduct by the defendant the plaintiff must have had not only subjectively justifiable doubts as to the fulfillment of its interest in the proper performance of the charterparty but there was also the danger that the plaintiff's interests would be objectively frustrated in view of the defendant's culpable breach. Therefore, without erring in law, the court *a quo* found that even two days before arrival of the steamer in New York the situation had been such that the plaintiff must have had grave fears that the defendant would not fulfil the contract; the defendant repeatedly showed itself to be unreliable; even then its conduct would have justified the vessel's immediate withdrawal.

The duty incumbent on the shipowner to effect performance first generally entails a considerable financial risk which is only reasonable and tolerable if the charterer avoids anything which could undermine the basis of trust necessary for the carrying out of such a contract. On the undisputed facts of the case the defendant's unreliable conduct must have led the plaintiff seriously to doubt that the contract could properly be performed. Notwithstanding the undermining of the relationship of trust, the plaintiff did not straight away withdraw from the contract but gave the defendant a chance—in line with the provision contained in § 321 BGB—to remove the plaintiff's doubts and reservations as regards performance of the contract, by commencing loading or by providing a bank guarantee by 12 September 1950. By fixing this period the plaintiff did everything which could have been reasonably expected of it in accordance with the principle of good faith in order to preserve the interests of both contracting parties in the effecting of counter-performance. The defendant did not avail itself of the chance given to it. It did not fulfil conditions subject to which the plaintiff was prepared to continue with the contract. In that state of affairs the plaintiff, which is established abroad and could only have pursued its claims in Germany, could no longer be expected on account of the lack of certainty to expose itself to the continued risk of an ever-increasing loss occasioned by the vessel standing idle. The plaintiff's confidence in the defendant's adherence to the contract was thus finally so completely shaken that it could not be expected to continue to regard itself as bound by the contract. In such a case the initial jeopardising of interests is to be equated to frustration of interests. . . . By telex of 13 September 1950 the plaintiff expressly substantiated the allegation of breach of contract against the defendant and its decision to withdraw the vessel and seek damages on the ground of the defendant's unreliable conduct (". . . having been twice misled . . ."). By that statement the plaintiff was finally released from its duty of performance under the contract and entitled to claim damages under clause 13 of the charter party.

Notes

(1) We have seen[254] that the setting of a notice period (*Nachfrist*) in cases of delay may be dispensed with where further performance of the contract is of no interest to the creditor. The test applied to determine whether there has been such a collapse of interest is substantially similar to that applied in determining whether the aggrieved party can terminate for positive breach.

(2) If performance of the main obligations of the contract (*Hauptpflichten*) is only partly impossible, the remedy of termination—i.e. *Rücktritt* or damages for non-performance—is available where performance of the remaining part is of no interest to the creditor (§ 325 (1) 2 BGB).

(3) Termination is also permitted for breach of less important obligations of the contract (*Nebenpflichten*) through impossibility or delay for which the debtor is responsible (§§ 280 (2), 286 (2) BGB). In such cases the creditor has to prove that they no longer have any interest in performance of the rest of the contract.

As in English law termination is by act of the parties alone; the law must set criteria for when the non-performance is serious enough for the right to be exercised. We saw two such criteria in the last section on Withholding of Performance: in building contracts, the employer cannot terminate if there has been substantial performance; while more generally, a breach of condition entitles the aggrieved party to terminate while a breach of warranty does not.

---

[254] *Supra* at 750.

The second approach involves classifying the terms of the contract as conditions or warranties *a priori*, rather than looking at how serious the actual breach is on the facts of the case. This gives rise to difficulties when the term is one that may be broken in a number of different ways, some of which will be serious but others not. If the contract does not specify the status of the term, should the court classify it as a condition because it *might* be broken in a very serious way? If this is done, there is a danger that a party who has indeed suffered a breach of the term by the other party will terminate the contract even though on the facts the breach caused little or no loss—the "innocent" party's aim being to escape from a contract which has turned out unfavourably for other reasons, such as a fall in market prices since he entered the contract—remember that English law has no general doctrine of good faith or of abuse of rights. A more flexible approach seems to be needed.

Court of Appeal   **6.E.84.**
Hong Kong Fir Shipping Co. Ltd. v. *Kawasaki Kisen Kaisha*[255]

INTERMEDIATE TERMS

The *Hong Kong fir* case

The term that a chartered ship was to be fit in every way for cargo service was neither a condition nor a warranty. Whether breach of it gave rise to the right to terminate the contract depended on the consequences of the particular breach.

Facts: A twenty-four month time charter provided that the vessel was to be delivered to the charterers at Liverpool, she being in every way fitted for "ordinary cargo service". The "off-hire" clause provided that the charterers need not pay hire in respect of periods over twenty-four hours lost in carrying out repairs, and that such off-hire periods might, at the charterers' option, be added to the hire period. The vessel left for Newport News, to load a cargo of coal for carriage to Osaka. At the date of her delivery, the ship was unseaworthy because she had old engines which required careful supervision, whereas her engine ro6m staff was under-manned and inefficient. As a result, repairs had to be carried out on the way to Osaka and after her arrival there, and it took a total of eighteen weeks to make her seaworthy. This left a period of seventeen months during which she could be available to the charterers. There had been a steep fall in freight rates since the date of the charter, and the charterers purported to terminate.

Held: Salmon J held that the charterers had no right to terminate, and they appealed. The appeal was dismissed.

Judgment:

[SELLERS LJ held that there had been only a breach of warranty.]

UPJOHN LJ: . . . Why is this apparently basic and underlying condition of seaworthiness not, in fact, treated as a condition? It is for the simple reason that the seaworthiness clause is breached by the slightest failure to be fitted "in every way" for service. Thus, to take examples from the judgments in some of the cases I have mentioned above, if a nail is missing from one of the timbers of a wooden vessel, or if proper medical supplies or two anchors are not on board at the time of sailing, the owners are in breach of the seaworthiness stipulation. It is contrary to common sense to suppose that, in such circumstances, the parties contemplated that the charterer should at once be entitled to treat the contract as at an end for such trifling breaches. . . .

---

[255] [1962] 2 QB 26.

It is open to the parties to a contract to make it clear either expressly or by necessary implication that a particular stipulation is to be regarded as a condition which goes to the root of the contract, so that it is clear that the parties contemplate that any breach of it entitles the other party at once to treat the contract as at an end. That matter is to be determined as a question of the proper interpretation of the contract. Where . . . on the true construction of the contract, the parties have not made a particular stipulation a condition, it would be unsound and misleading to conclude that, being a warranty, damages is a sufficient remedy.

In my judgment, the remedies open to the innocent party for breach of a stipulation which is not a condition strictly so called, depend entirely on the nature of the breach and its foreseeable consequences. Breaches of stipulation fall, naturally, into two classes. First, there is the case where the owner by his conduct indicates that he considers himself no longer bound to perform his part of the contract: in that case, of course, the charterer may accept the repudiation and treat the contract as at an end. The second class of case is, of course, the more usual one, and that is where, due to misfortune such as the perils of the sea, engine failures, incompetence of the crew and so on, the owner is unable to perform a particular stipulation precisely in accordance with the terms of the contract try he never so hard to remedy it. In that case, the question to be answered is, does the breach of the stipulation go so much to the root of the contract that it makes further commercial performance of the contract impossible, or, in other words, is the whole contract frustrated? If yea, the innocent party may treat the contract as at an end. If nay, his claim sounds in damages only.

If I have correctly stated the principles, then, as the stipulation as to seaworthiness is not a condition in the strict sense, the question to be answered is, did the initial unseaworthiness as found by the learned judge, from which finding there has been no appeal, go so much to the root of the contract that the charterers were then and there entitled to treat the charterparty as at an end? The only unseaworthiness alleged, serious though it was, was the insufficiency and incompetence of the crew, but that surely cannot be treated as going to the root of the contract for the parties must have contemplated that, in such an event, the crew could be changed and augmented. In my judgment, on this part of his case counsel for the charterers necessarily fails.

I turn, therefore, to his second point: Where there have been serious and repeated delays due to the inability of the owner to perform his part of the contract, is the charterer entitled to treat the contract as repudiated after a reasonable time, or can he do so only if delays are such as to amount to a frustration of the contract? Some of my earlier observations on the remedy available for breach of contract are relevant here, but I do not repeat them. I agree with the conclusions reached by the learned judge and by Sellers LJ . . . Accordingly, I agree that this appeal must be dismissed.

DIPLOCK LJ: . . . Every synallagmatic contract contains in it the seeds of the problem: in what event will a party be relieved of his undertaking to do that which he has agreed to do but has not yet done? The contract may itself expressly define some of these events, as in the cancellation clause in a charterparty, but, human prescience being limited, it seldom does so exhaustively and often fails to do so at all. In some classes of contracts, such as sale of goods, marine insurance, contracts of affreightment evidenced by bills of lading and those between parties to bills of exchange. Parliament has defined by statute some of the events not provided for expressly in individual contracts of that class; but, where an event occurs the occurrence of which neither the parties nor Parliament have expressly stated will discharge one of the parties from further performance of his undertakings, it is for the court to determine whether the event has this effect or not. The test whether an event has this effect or not has been stated in a number of metaphors all of which I think amount to the same thing: does the occurrence of the event deprive the party who has further undertakings still to perform of substantially the whole benefit which it was the intention of the parties as expressed in the contract that he should obtain as the consideration for performing those undertakings? This test is applicable whether or not the event occurs as a result of the default of one of the parties to the contract, but the consequences of the event are different in the two cases. Where the event occurs as a result of the default of one party, the party in default cannot rely on it as relieving himself of the performance of any further undertakings on his part and the innocent party, although entitled to, need not treat the event as relieving him of the performance of his own undertakings. This is only a specific application of the fundamental legal and moral rule that a man should not be allowed to take advantage of his own wrong. Where the event occurs as a result of the default of neither party, each is relieved of the further performance of his own undertakings, and their rights in respect of undertakings previously performed are now regulated by the Law Reform (Frustrated Contracts) Act, 1943.

This branch of the common law has reached its present stage by the normal process of historical growth, and the fallacy in counsel for the charterers' contention that a different test is applicable when the event occurs as a result of the default of one party from that applicable in cases of frustration where the event occurs as a result of the default of neither party arises, in my view, from a failure to view the cases in their historical context. The problem: in what event will a party to a contract be relieved of his undertaking to do that which he has agreed to do but has not yet done? has exercised the English courts for centuries, probably ever since assumpsit emerged as a form of action distinct from covenant and debt, and long before even the earliest cases which we have been invited to examine: but, until the rigour of the rule in *Paradine* v. *Jane* was mitigated in the middle of the last century by the classic judgments of Blackburn J in *Taylor* v. *Caldwell* and Bramwell B in *Jackson* v. *Union Marine Insurance Co*, it was in general only events resulting from one party's failure to perform his contractual obligations which were regarded as capable of relieving the other party from continuing to perform that which he had undertaken to do. . . .

Once it is appreciated that it is the event and not the fact that the event is a result of a breach of contract which relieves the party not in default of further performance of his obligations, two consequences follow: (i) The test whether the event relied on has this consequence is the same whether the event is the result of the other party's breach of contract or not, as Devlin J pointed out in *Universal Cargo Carriers Corpn.* v. *Citati*. (ii) The question whether an event which is the result of the other party's breach of contract has this consequence cannot be answered by treating all contractual undertakings as falling into one of two separate categories: "conditions", the breach of which gives rise to an event which relieves the party not in default of further performance of his obligations, and "warranties", the breach of which does not give rise to such an event. Lawyers tend to speak of this classification as if it were comprehensive, partly for the historical reasons which I have already mentioned, and partly because Parliament itself adopted it in the Sale of Goods Act, 1893, as respects a number of implied terms in contracts for the sale of goods and has in that Act used the expressions "conditions" and "warranty" in that meaning. But it is no means true that of contractual undertakings in general at common law.

No doubt there are many simple contractual undertakings, sometimes express, but more often because of their very simplicity ("It goes without saying") to be implied, of which it can be predicated that every breach of such an undertaking must give rise to an event which will deprive the party not in default of substantially the whole benefit which it was intended that he should obtain from the contract. And such a stipulation, unless the parties have agreed that breach of it shall not entitle the non-defaulting party to treat the contract as repudiated, is a "condition". So, too, there may be other simple contractual undertakings of which it can be predicated that *no* breach can give rise to an event which will deprive the party not in default of substantially the whole benefit which it was intended that he should obtain from the contract; and such a stipulation, unless the parties have agreed that breach of it shall entitle the non-defaulting party to treat the contract as repudiated, is a "warranty". There are, however, many contractual undertakings of a more complex character which cannot be categorised as being "conditions" or "warranties" if the late nineteenth century meaning adopted in the Sale of Goods Act, 1893, and used by Bowen LJ in *Bentsen* v. *Taylor, Sons & Co*, be given to those terms. Of such undertakings, all that can be predicated is that some breaches will, and others will not, give rise to an event which will deprive the party not in default of substantially the whole benefit which it was intended that he should obtain from the contract; and the legal consequences of a breach of such an undertaking, unless provided for expressly in the contract, depend on the nature of the event to which the breach gives rise and do not follow automatically from a prior classification of the undertaking as a "condition" or a warranty". For instance, to take the example of Bramwell B in *Jackson* v. *Union Marine Insurance Co,* by itself breach of an undertaking by a shipowner to sail with all possible despatch to a named port does not necessarily relieve the charterer of further performance of his obligation under the charterparty, but, if the breach is so prolonged that the contemplated voyage is frustrated, it does have this effect.

As my brethren have already pointed out, the shipowner's undertaking to tender a seaworthy ship has, as a result of numerous decisions as to what can amount to "unseaworthiness", become one of the most complex of contractual undertakings. It embraces obligations with respect to every part of the hull and machinery, stores and equipment and the crew itself. It can be broken by the presence of trivial defects easily and rapidly remediable as well as by defects which must inevitably result in a total loss of the vessel. Consequently, the problem in this case is, in my view, neither solved nor soluble by debating whether the owners' express or implied undertaking to tender a seaworthy ship is a "condition" or a "warranty". It is, like so many other contractual terms, an undertaking one breach of which may give rise to an event which relieves the charterer of further performance of his undertakings if he so elects, and another breach of which may not give rise to such an event but entitle him only to monetary compensation in the form of damages. It is, with all deference to counsel for the charterers' skilful argument, by no means surprising that, among the many hundreds of previous cases about the shipowner's undertaking to deliver a seaworthy ship, there is none where it was found profitable to discuss in the judgments the question whether that undertaking is a "condition" or a "warranty": for the true answer, as I have already indicated, is that it is neither, but one of that large class of contractual undertakings, one breach of which may have the same effect as that ascribed to a breach of "condition" under the Sale of Goods Act, 1893, and a different breach of which may have only the same effect as that ascribed to a breach of "warranty" under that Act.
. . .

What the learned judge had to do in the present case as in any other case where one party to a contract relies on a breach by the other party as giving him a right to elect to rescind the contract, was to look at the events which had occurred as a result of the breach at the time at which the charterers purported to rescind the charterparty, and to decide whether the occurrence of those events deprived the charterers of substantially the whole benefit which it was the intention of the parties as expressed in the charterparty that the charterers should obtain from the further performance of their own contractual undertakings. One turns, therefore, to the contract, the Baltime 1939 Charter. Clause 13, the "due diligence" clause, which exempts the shipowners from responsibility for delay or loss or damage to goods on board due to unseaworthiness unless such delay or loss or damage has been caused by want of due diligence of the owners in making the vessel seaworthy and fitted for the voyage, is in itself sufficient to show that the mere occurrence of the events that the vessel was in some respect unseaworthy when tendered or that such unseaworthiness had caused some delay in performance of the charterparty would not deprive the charterer of the whole benefit which it was the intention of the parties he should obtain from the performance of his obligations under the contract-for he undertakes to continue to perform his obligations notwithstanding the occurrence of such events if they fall short of frustration of the contract and even deprives himself of any remedy in damages unless such events are the consequences of want of due diligence on the part of the shipowner.

The question which the learned judge had to ask himself was, as he rightly decided, whether or not, at the date when the charterers purported to rescind the contract, namely 6 June, 1957, or when the owners purported to accept such rescission, namely 8 Aug, 1957, the delay which had already occurred as a result of the incompetence of the engine-room staff, and the delay which was likely to occur in repairing the engines of the vessel and the conduct of the owners by that date in taking steps to remedy these two matters, were, when taken together, such as to deprive the charterers of substantially the whole benefit which it was the intention of the parties they should obtain from further use of the vessel under the charterparty. In my view, in his judgment—on which I would not seek to improve—-the learned judge took into account and gave due weight to all the relevant considerations and arrived at the right answer for the right reasons.

Notes

(1) It will be noted that Diplock LJ takes a slightly different approach to Upjohn LJ. According to Diplock LJ term will be a condition only if the agreement itself, or statute, so provides, or "if it can be predicated that every breach of [the term] must give rise to an event which will deprive the party not in default of substantially the whole benefit . . .". Upjohn LJ states that it is open to the parties to make it clear that a term is a condition either expressly or "*by necessary implication*". This seems to allow more terms to be classified as conditions even though not every breach of them would necessarily have serious consequences. The House of Lords has held that Upjohn LJ's approach is the correct one.[256]

(2) In *Cehave NV* v. *Bremer Handelsgesellschaft mbH, The Hansa Nord*,[257] the more flexible approach adopted in the *Hong Kong Fir* case was applied to a term in a cif sale contract that the goods be shipped "in good condition". A small quantity of the goods (citrus pulp pellets) had been damaged by overheating and the buyers rejected the whole cargo although the pellets were still perfectly good for the buyers' purpose—as was shown by the fact that the buyers then bought the goods again at a knock down price when they were auctioned on the orders of a court in Rotterdam after the sellers had refused to repay the price. The English trial judge considered that as the Sale of Goods Act refers only to conditions and warranties, and a breach of the term that the goods were to be shipped in good condition *might* have serious consequences, it must be a condition. Thus he held that the buyers were within their rights to reject. The Court of Appeal held that the Sale of Goods Act 1979 did not exclude the rules of the Common Law, under which the term would not be a condition. Thus the buyer would be entitled to reject the goods only if the breach had deprived them of the substance of what they were contracting for, which was not the case. The Court of Appeal also held that such a slight defect did not make the goods "unmerchantable" within the words of SGA section 14(2) as it then read—the section now refers to "satisfactory quality".[258] If the goods had been unmerchantable, the buyers *would* have had the right to reject, since section 14(2) also stated that it was a "condition" that the goods be of merchantable quality.

6.4.5. TIME STIPULATIONS—*FIXGESCHÄFTE*

BGB   **6.G.85.**

§ 361: If it is agreed in a mutual contract that the performance due from one of the parties is to be made exactly at a fixed time or within a fixed period, it is to be inferred, in case of doubt,

---

[256] See *infra* at 772.
[257] [1976] QB 44.
[258] See *supra* at 759.

that the other party shall be entitled to rescind if the performance is not made at the fixed time or within the fixed period.

HGB **6.G.86.**

§ 376: (1) If it is agreed that the performance of one of the parties should be rendered by a firmly set date or within a firmly set period, and if performance is not rendered by that date or within that period, the other party may terminate the contract or instead of performance, if the debtor is in delay, demand damages for non-performance. He may only demand performance if he notifies the other party of his insistence on performance immediately after the date has been passed or the period has expired.

BGH, 17 January 1990 [259] **6.G.87.**

WHETHER *FIXGESCHÄFT*

Aluminium bottle caps

A clause included in general conditions to the effect that the dates and notice periods were "fix"—is not enough of itself to make the contract into a Fixgeschäft if the circumstances showed differently.

Facts: The plaintiff was a wine producer; the defendant carried on business as a supplier to wine cellars and vintners. By a written order of 15 January 1986 the plaintiff ordered from the defendant 350 000 aluminium bottle caps for sealing wine bottles. On 21 September 1987 it once again ordered various quantities of aluminium caps that is to say, 400,000, 205,000 and 50,000 "for delivery by 1.10.1987". Both written orders contained a reference to the plaintiff's general terms and conditions of business printed on the back of the order form in which it is stated inter alia:

"(7) The delivery dates and periods agreed are mandatory and fixed (*fix*).
In the event of any delay in delivery the person placing the order shall be entitled without needing to fix a further period to pursue all the legal consequences of delay . . ."

The defendant delivered the caps covered by the first order on 29 January 1986, and the plaintiff paid the purchase price of DM 7,233.87. On 24 September 1987 when the plaintiff sought to use those caps the joins in the caps came apart immediately after the capping process as a result of uneven glueing. Of the second order on 1 October 1987 the defendant delivered 400,000 and 205,000 caps. For the 400,000 caps the defendant paid DM 8,664. After 5,000 of these caps had been used on 1 October 1987 the same defect as in the caps from the first order became apparent.

By letter dated 2 October 1987 the plaintiff complained to the defendant of the defectiveness of the caps, demanded repayment of the purchase price paid and gave notice that it would not accept delivery of the 50,000 caps undelivered as at 1 October 1987. The defendant confirmed that the uneven glueing of the joins constituted a latent defect, but refused to meet the plaintiff's claims and insisted on acceptance of the remaining 50,000 caps.

Held: The clause was not enough of itself to make the contract into a *Fixgeschäft* as the circumstances showed differently. (The clause was also invalid under §§ 3, 9 I AGBG.)

Judgment: On these grounds:

II.2.

(b) It cannot avail the appellant that the regional court granted the defendant's counter-claim to the purchase price of DM 1,083 for the 50,000 caps ordered on 21 September 1987 delivery of which has not yet been accepted. The plaintiff did not effectively withdraw from the sales agreement relating to these 50,000 caps. The regional court held that there was no right to withdraw under § 326 BGB, which is not contested on appeal and is not vitiated by an error of law. Nor can the plaintiff

---

[259] BGHZ 110.88.

derive any support for termination from the provision contained in § 376 (1) HGB for there was in fact no agreement that this should be a mandatory and fixed transaction (*Fixgeschäft*).

(aa) The regional court was unable to find any support from the individual contractual provisions and the surrounding circumstances for the proposition that the parties were at one on the fact that, in the event of the delivery period not being observed, the sales agreement entered into could straight away be terminated by the plaintiff. On appeal it is erroneously sought to find support for the contrary proposition from the delivery date precisely laid down. A *Fixgeschäft* requires not only the laying down of a precise delivery date or period but also consensus of the parties that the contract is to stand or fall on compliance or non-compliance with the delivery date whereby, in case of doubt, a contract is assumed not to be a time bargain. . . . It does not follow solely from the agreement of a specifically laid down (final) delivery date (in this case, "by 1.10.1987") that, in the event of non-compliance with that period, the plaintiff no longer has any interest in that transaction being effected. . . . That is borne out by the fact that the plaintiff used the caps delivered in January 1986 only twenty months later and gave no reason why observance of the delivery period in the case of the second order was of such great importance for it.

(bb) That appraisal is not altered by Clause 7(1) of the plaintiff's General Terms and Conditions of Business. It is true that the term *fix* used in that connection suggests that a time bargain was intended, in the absence of persuasive factors to the contrary. . . . Where, however, the conditions of a time bargain and of the basis of an individual agreement to that effect are not met, a standard provision which none the less makes the agreement appear to be in the nature of a time bargain is surprising in light of § 3 AGBG (Law on General terms and Conditions of Business) . . . and unreasonable in light of § 9 thereof. . . . For the contractual partner of the user, who did not agree with the latter that the transaction was to stand or fall with observance of the period, cannot reasonably be required in the circumstances to reckon on the General Terms and Conditions of Business making the transaction subject to strict adherence to the time limit. The unreasonable disadvantage within the meaning of § 9 (1) of that legislation follows from the fact that by means of clauses such as that now under consideration the user would in the result be relieved of the obligation to fix a further period under § 326 BGB which, in commercial transactions, may be agreed more effectively by means of standard clauses. . . . For if the clause were effective and it were sought—which may remain an open question—to attach to it the significance that the contract could essentially be determined as being a time bargain . . ., § 376 HGB, which would be applicable, would have the effect of allowing the purchaser to withdraw even without fixing a further period for performance of the other party's obligations and, in the event of delay by the seller, to claim damages.

Whether under §§ 3, 9 AGBG that appraisal would be different where, in sectors in which time bargains are common, the standard form additional wording *fix* is used directly in conjunction with the provision concerning the delivery period, does not need to be decided. . . . The clause is on the reverse side of the plaintiff's order form in the middle of a number of other standard terms. Furthermore, there is not the slightest indication that a time bargain is typically the contractual objective of agreements such as the one now under consideration.

Notes

(1) § 361 BGB and § 376 HGB—applying in contracts between business people only—are rules for interpreting the contract. Thus, the right to terminate in cases of such *Fixgeschäfte* is an agreed right coming directly within the standard case of § 346 BGB.[260]

[260] See *infra* at 789.

(2) Note that a non-commercial creditor may, instead of terminating, demand performance (as long as it remains possible) at any time after the stipulated date. A commercial creditor must insist on this immediately.[261]

(3) It is necessary to distinguish relative from absolute *Fixgeschäfte*. The former, as discussed, involve an agreed date for performance with an automatic right to terminate thereafter. The latter are contracts which, having regard to the their essential purpose, cannot meaningfully be performed after a certain date. Examples would be the case of a taxi reserved to take a passenger to a certain aeroplane flight or the delivery of flowers on the day of a wedding. Once the relevant date has been passed performance is viewed as being impossible and § 325 BGB applies. In the case of relative *Fixgeschäfte* performance delayed is still held to be possible, but subject to the agreed right to terminate (§ 361 BGB).

(4) A very slight delay in performance of obligations after a *Nachfrist* has expired or even under a *Fixgeschäft* may, for reasons of good faith (§ 242 BGB), be held insufficient to give rise to a right to terminate.

When a stipulation as to time is in question the English courts ask whether the time "was of the essence" of the contract, meaning, is it a condition of the contract that performance be completed by the time stated? The contract may state this expressly—see for an example *Lombard North Central* v. *Butterworth*.[262] If the contract simply states a date for performance without stating whether or not it is of the essence, the question again becomes one of construction of the contract. One question which lawyers discussed was whether the new "*Hong Kong Fir*" approach should apply to time stipulations.

Court of Appeal and House of Lords   **6.E.88.**
Bunge Corp. v. *Tradax S.A.*[263]

TIME OF THE ESSENCE

15 days' notice

A clause requiring the buyer under an FOB contract for bulk goods to give fifteen days' notice of the nominated vessel's readiness to load was a condition of the contract.

Facts: A contract for the purchase of 15,000 tons of soya FOB one US Gulf port (made on the GAFTA 119 form of contract) required the buyer to nominate a ship to collect the goods and to give the seller at least fifteen days' notice of the ship's probable readiness to load. The sellers would then select which Gulf port to direct the ship to in order to load the goods. The buyers gave less than fifteen days' notice and the sellers terminated the contract. They then claimed damages for non-performance by the buyers. The buyers argued that the sellers' purported termination was wrongful as the time for giving notice was not a condition but an intermediate term and the sellers had not shown that the delay caused them any difficulty.

Held: The arbitrator awarded damages to the sellers. On appeal to the Commercial Court the judge reversed that award, but the Court of Appeal allowed the sellers' appeal. An appeal by the buyers to the House of Lords was dismissed.

---

[261] See *Münchener Kommentar*, under § 361 BGB, para. 10.
[262] See *infra* at [0000].
[263] [1981] 2 All ER 513.

Judgment: MEGAW LJ: . . . I come to the second main issue: is the term of the contract which has been broken by the buyers a condition or an intermediate term? The sellers have, before us, made it clear that the term is not a condition, but is an intermediate term, they will not seek to contend that they can discharge the burden of showing that they were entitled to treat the contract as having been repudiated by the buyers.

The contract is, by its express terms, governed by English law. That is the effect of cl 25 of GAFTA 119.

It is an accepted principle of English law that in a mercantile contract for the sale of goods "prima facie a stipulated time of delivery is of the essence". This long-standing principle has recently been re-stated by Lord Diplock in *United Scientific Holdings Ltd.* v. *Burnley Borough Council* . . .

In the present case, then, there can be no doubt but that the obligation of the sellers to deliver the soya bean meal not later than 30 June 1975 was a condition of the contract. They had an obligation to tender the contractual quantity of the goods at the ship's rail so that they could be loaded in accordance with the contractual provision as to rate of loading, on or before that date. If they failed, in breach of contract, to carry out that obligation, and if the buyers thereupon were treat the contract as having been wrongfully repudiated by the sellers, it would be no answer for the sellers to say that the buyers had not proved that they, the buyers, had suffered any loss or would suffer any loss, if loading were to take place on 1 July. It would be unreal to suggest that one day's lateness in delivery would necessarily be a matter of serious consequence to the buyers. The lateness might or might not have such consequences. But the buyers' right to treat the contract as repudiated, and to treat themselves as freed from the performance of any further contractual obligations which they would otherwise have been required to perform under the contact, does not depend on the buyers being able to prove any such thing.

In para 5 of the award the board of appeal, having said that the term means "Buyers were to give at least 15 consecutive days' notice of probable readiness of vessel(s)", went on: "Such a provision is customarily treated in the trade as being for the purpose of giving to sellers sufficient time to make necessary arrangements to get the goods to the port for loading on board the nominated vessel." In other words, the parties have agreed, by acceptance of this term, that 15 days is "the time which is reasonably required by the sellers for the purpose of this particular contract, to enable them to make the arrangements necessary for the fulfilment by them of their contractual to deliver the goods by the due time. It would, in my view, be impossible for a court to hold that that was not the parties' intention in agreeing this term. There is no question here of the parties not being in an equal bargaining position. It would, in my opinion, be arrogant and unjustifiable for a court to substitute any view of its own for the view of the parties themselves as to what was a reasonable time for this purpose.

Unless there is some principle of law, or some authority binding on us, which leads necessarily to a contrary conclusion, it appears to me to follow that, just as the contractual time for delivery of the goods is a condition binding on the sellers, so that the contractual time by which the notice as to be given for the purpose of enabling the sellers to perform that condition should be regarded as a condition binding on the buyers. There is no more, and no less, reason to suppose that a breach of the time provision in the sellers' obligation will necessarily or probably lead to serious loss to the buyers than there is to suppose that a breach of the notice of readiness provision will necessarily or probably lead to serious loss to the sellers . . .

I come back to the purpose of the notice of probable readiness term in the present contract. The commercial reasons why advance notice is required are, I think, obvious. The sellers have to nominate the loading port. Is loading going to be possible, and if possible convenient, at port A, or port B, or port C? Until the probable date of readiness is known, it may be impossible to answer chose questions. Until they are answered, the sellers cannot perform their contractual duty of dominating the port. When the port is decided, arrangements have to be made to have the contract quantity (to be defined by the buyers by reference to "5% more or less") of the contract goods available when the vessel is ready. What is involved in making such arrangements? It may involve or include, buying goods, arranging for them to be moved by road, rail or water from wherever they may be; for warehousing them or moving them from one warehouse to another. Of course, in any given case, some or all of these tasks may be simply achieved, or their achievement may be possible in less than 15 days, in order to have the goods ready for loading where and when the vessel is ready for loading. It obviously cannot be predicated that 14 days' notice, instead of 15 days, would necessarily and in all circumstances cause sellers serious difficulties in respect of a contract containing these terms. What can and should be accepted is that the parties have agreed that, for the purpose of this contract, the reasonable time required to enable the sellers to perform their contractual obligations as to delivery of the goods is 15 days' notice of the probable readiness of the vessel to load. . . .

Apart from [a] particular reason, relating to the extension of shipment clause, Parker J was of the opinion that the term could not be a condition because of what he regarded as being "the principles established in the *Hong Kong Fir* case". . . and *Cehave NV* v. *Bremer Handelsgesellschaft mbH, The Hansa Nord*. In the latter case, Roskill LJ, while recognising that some terms of a contract of sale may be conditions, expressed the view that "a court" should not be over ready, unless required by statute or authority so to do, to construe a term in a contract as a "condition" . . .

The passage in the *Hong Kong Fir* case, to which Parker J referred, was that where Diplock LJ said this. . . .

> "No doubt there are many simple contractual undertakings, sometimes express, but more often because of their very simplicity ('It goes without saying') to be implied, of which it can be predicated that every breach of such an undertaking must give rise to an event which will deprive the party not in default of substantially the whole benefit which it was intended that he should obtain from the contract. And such a stipulation, unless the parties have agreed that breach of it shall not entitle the non-defaulting party to treat the contract as repudiated, is a condition."

If that statement is intended to be a definition of the requirements which must always be satisfied, in all types of contract and all types of clauses, in order that a term may qualify as, a condition, I would very respectfully express the view that it is not a correct statement of the law. I am confirmed in the view that it was not so intended because of what was recently said by Lord Diplock in a passage . . . from his speech in *United Scientific Holdings Ltd* v. *Burnley Borough Council* in relation to time being "of the essence" in certain commercial contracts. . . .

In the light of what was said by their Lordships in that case, I think it can fairly be said that in mercantile contracts stipulations as to time not only may be, but usually are, to be treated as being "of the essence of the contract", even though this is not expressly stated in the words of the contract. It would follow that in a mercantile contract it cannot be predicated that, for time to be of the essence, any and every breach of the term as to time must necessarily cause the innocent party to be deprived of substantially the whole of the benefit which it was intended that he should have . . .

In my opinion in the term with which we are concerned the provision as to time is of the essence of the contract. The term is a condition.

It is, I believe, a factor which is not without weight in that conclusion that, at least, it tends towards certainty in the law . . . The parties, where time is of the essence, will at least know where they stand when the contractually agreed time has passed and the contract has been broken. They will not be forced to make critical decisions by trying to anticipate how serious, in the view of arbitrators or courts, in later years, the consequences of the breach will retrospectively be seen to have been, in the light, it may be, of hindsight.

I must, however, return to the *Hong Kong Fir* case . . . No one now doubts the correctness of that decision: that there are "intermediate" terms, breach of which may or may not entitle the innocent party to treat himself as discharged from the further performance of his contractual obligation. No one now doubts that a term as to seaworthiness in a charterparty, in the absence of express provision to the opposite effect, is not a condition, but is an "intermediate" term. The question arising on that case which I think we are compelled to examine in the present case is the test by which it falls to be decided whether a term is a condition.

I have previously quoted a passage from the judgment of Diplock LJ. In its literal sense, the condition, then the term with which we are here concerned would not pass the test. The view which I have expressed that it is a condition would necessarily be wrong.

There are various reasons why I do not think that this was intended to be a literal, definitive and comprehensive statement of the requirements of a condition: and also, if it were, why, with great respect. I do not think that it represents the law as it stands today.

First, if it were intended to cover terms as to time in mercantile contracts, how could the requirements be said to be met in respect of stipulations in contracts of types in which, as Lord Diplock has recently said, time may be of the essence: for example, in respect of a stipulated time for delivery? It could never be said, as I see it, in any real sense, that *any* breach of such a stipulation *must necessarily cause the innocent* party to be deprived of *substantially all the benefit*.

Second, and following on what I have just said, I do not see how any contractual term, whether as to time or otherwise, could ever pass the test. Conditions would no longer exist in the English law of contract. For it is always possible to suggest hypothetically some minor breach or breaches of any contractual term which might, without undue use of the imagination, be wholly insufficient to produce serious effects for the innocent party, let alone the loss of substantially all the benefit.

Third, English law does recognise as conditions contractual terms which do not pass that test. For example, *Bowes* v. *Shand* and, I think a substantial number of other cases which are binding, at least on this court.

Fourth, it is clear law, reaffirmed by the House of Lords since *Hong Kong Fir* was decided, that where there has been a breach of a condition the innocent party is entitled to elect whether or not to treat the contracts as repudiated. . . .

How could this right of election be anything other than a legal fiction, a chimera, if the election can arise only in circumstances in which, as a result of the breach, an event has happened which will deprive the innocent party of substantially the whole benefit which it was intended that he should receive? This test, it is to be observed, is regarded (*Hong Kong Fir*) . . . as applying also where the term is an intermediate term, except that you then look to what has actually happened in order to see if the innocent party has lost substantially all the benefit. So, again, if the test be right, the former principle of English law that the innocent party has the right to elect is no longer anything but an empty shadow. For a right to elect to continue a contract, with the result that the innocent party will be bound to continue to perform his own contractual obligations, when he will, by definition, have lost substantially all, his benefit under the contract, does not appear to me to make sense.

Fifth, the same considerations as I have set out in the previous paragraph apply if the test be that a breach of contract gives a right to the innocent party to treat it as a repudiation only if the events which in fact have flowed from the breach would, if they had come about otherwise than by a breach of contract, amount to frustration of the contract. . . .

I would allow the appeal and, subject to any questions of detail which may arise as to the form of the order, I would restore the decision of the board of appeal.

BROWNE LJ: I agree that this appeal should be allowed, for the reasons given by Megaw LJ, with which I entirely agree.

[BRIGHTMAN LJ concurred.]
The House of Lords affirmed the judgment of the Court of Appeal:

Judgment: LORD WILBERFORCE: The fundamental fallacy of the appellants' argument lies in attempting to apply this analysis to a time clause such as the present in a mercantile contract, which is totally different in character. As to such a clause there is only one kind of breach possible, namely to be late, and the questions which have to be asked are: first, what importance have the parties expressly ascribed to this consequence? and, second, in the absence of expressed agreement, what consequences ought to be attached to it having regard to the contract as a whole?

The test suggested by the appellants was a different one. One must consider, they said, the breach actually committed and then decide whether that default would deprive the party not in default of substantially the whole benefit of the contract. They even invoked certain passages in the judgment of Diplock LJ in *Hong Kong Fir* to support it. One may observe in the first place that the introduction of a test of this kind would be commercially most undesirable. It would expose the parties, after a breach of one, two, three, seven and other numbers of the days, to an argument whether this delay would have left time for the seller to provide the goods. It would make it, at the time, at least difficult, and sometimes impossible, for the supplier to know whether he could do so. It would fatally remove the vital provision in the contract that certainty which is the most indispensable quality of mercantile contracts, and lead to a large increase in arbitrations. It would confine the seller, perhaps after arbitration and reference through the courts to remedy in damages which may be extremely difficult to quantify. These are all serious objections on practice. But I am clear that the submission is unacceptable in law. The judgment of Diplock LJ does not give any support and ought not to give any encouragement to any such proposition; for beyond doubt it recognises that it is open to the parties to agree that, as regards a particular obligation, any breach shall entitle the party not in default to treat the contract as repudiated. Indeed, if he were not doing so he would, in a passage which does not profess to be more than clarifactory, to be discrediting a long and uniform series of cases, at least from *Bowes* v. *Shand* onwards.

We have seen that the Sale of Goods Act 1979, as amended by the Sale and Supply of Goods Act 1994, provides a number of terms relating to the description and quality of goods which are implied into contracts for the sale of goods. Thus where the sale is by description, the goods must correspond to the description, section 13(1); and in sales in the course of a business, the goods must be of satisfactory quality, and may have to be fit for the buyer's particular purpose: section 14(2) and (3). The Act provides explicitly that the relevant implied terms "are conditions" (sections 13(1A) and 14(6)). However, the cases show that sometimes there may be a breach of one of these implied conditions which does not in fact have serious consequences for the buyer, yet the buyer takes advantage of the fact that there has been a breach of condition to escape from the contract for ulterior motives—typically because the market price for the goods has fallen since the date of the contract. On occasions the courts have seemed to strain the law to prevent this (for example the decision in *The Hansa Nord*,[264] that the goods were merchantable despite being damaged); on other occasions they have allowed the buyer to terminate even though the buyer's conduct smacked of abuse of rights—for example, *Arcos Ltd.* v. *E A Ronaasen & Son*.[265] In that case a buyer was permitted to reject a consignment of barrel staves (strips of wood for making barrels) that did not correspond to the contractual

---

[264] *Supra* at 769.
[265] [1933] AC 470.

description of half an inch thick, although they were only one-sixteenth of an inch too thick and were perfectly suitable for making barrels. (It will be recalled that English law does not have doctrines of good faith or abuse of rights.) To prevent these problems recurring, the Law Commission recommended that in commercial sales the law should be changed to prevent buyers from acting in this way:

Sale of Goods Act 1979 (as amended by Sale & Supply of Goods Act 1994) **6.E.89.**

Section 15A: (1) Where in the case of a contract of sale—
   (a) the buyer would, apart from this subsection, have the right to reject goods by reason of a breach on the part of the seller of a term implied by section 13, 14 or 15 above, but
   (b) the breach is so slight that it would be unreasonable for him to reject them,
   then, if the buyer does not deal as consumer, the breach is not to be treated as a breach of condition but may be treated as a breach of warranty.
   (2) This section applies unless a country intention appears in, or to be implied from, the contract.
   (3) It is for the seller to show that a breach fell within subsection (1)(b) above.

Note

It was thought that consumers should retain an absolute right of rejection, as a way of reducing the inequality between them and suppliers.[266]

6.4.6. TERMINATION BEFORE PERFORMANCE IS DUE

What if it is clear, before the date for performance, that the other party will not perform: he has announced this, or has put it out of his power to perform? Clearly, once the date for performance arrives, the innocent party will in all systems be able to terminate; but does he have to wait until that date to do so? If so, he may be left in some uncertainty, because he may want to make other arrangements, yet there may be the possibility that the other party will perform after all. Can the innocent party somehow prevent this? English and German law reach a fairly similar solution in this regard: he may terminate the contract, and bring an action for damages, either immediately (England) or after giving due notice (Germany). We shall see that French law takes quite a different approach.

Hochster v. de la Tour[267]   **6.E.90.**

PROCEEDINGS CAN BE COMMENCED ON REPUDIATION

The Courier

Where a contractual obligation is renounced before the date on which performance is due, the innocent party is entitled to treat the contract as terminated immediately and can bring proceedings for breach of contract before the date on which performance would have been due.

---

[266] See Law Commission Report no. 160, *Sale and Supply of Goods* (Cm 137, 1987), paras. 2.26, 4.1 4.24 and 6.18–6.20.
[267] (1853) [1843–60] All ER Rep. 12.

Facts: The defendant hired the plaintiff to travel with him as his courier for the purposes of a journey, his employment to commence on a set date. Before the date on which the journey was due to commence, the defendant informed the plaintiff that he no longer required the plaintiff's services and the plaintiff sought to bring an action against the defendant for breach of contract. The date for performance of the contract had not yet been reached.

Held: The plaintiff was entitled to treat the contract as terminated even though the date for performance had not yet occurred.

Judgment: LORD CAMPBELL CJ: On this motion in arrest of judgment, the question arises, whether, if there be an agreement between A and B, whereby B engages to employ A on and from a future day for a given period of time, to travel with him into a foreign country as a courier and to start with him in that capacity on that day, A being to receive a monthly salary during the continuance of such service, B may, before the day, refuse to perform the agreement and break and renounce it so as to entitle A, before the day, to commence an action against B to recover damages for breach of the agreement, A having been ready and willing to perform it till it was broken and renounced by B.

The defendant's counsel very powerfully contended that, if the plaintiff was not contented to dissolve the contract and to abandon all remedy upon it, he was bound to remain ready and willing to perform it till the day when the actual employment as courier in the service of the defendant was to begin, and that there could be no breach of the agreement, before that day, to give a right of action. But it cannot be laid down as a universal rule that, where by agreement an act is to be done on a future day, no action can be brought for a breach of the agreement till the day for doing the act has arrived. If a man promises to marry a woman on a future day and before that day marries another woman, he is instantly liable to an action for breach of promise of marriage: *Short* v. *Stone*. If a man contracts to execute a lease on and from a future day for a certain term, and, before that day, executes a lease to another for the same term, he may be immediately sued for breaking the contract: *Ford* v. *Tiley*. So, if a man contracts to sell and deliver specific goods on a future day, and before the day he sells and delivers them to another, he is immediately liable to an action at the suit of the person with whom he first contracted to sell and deliver them: *Bowdell* v. *Parsons*. One reason alleged in support of such an action is that the defendant has, before the day, rendered it impossible for the plaintiff to perform the contract at the day, but this does not necessarily follow, for, prior to the day fixed for doing the act, the first wife may have died, a surrender of the lease executed might be obtained, and the defendant might have re-purchased the goods so as to be in a situation to sell and deliver them to the plaintiff. Another reason may be that where there is a contract to do an act on a future day there is a relation constituted between the parties in the meantime by the contract, and that they impliedly promise that in the meantime neither will do any thing to the prejudice of the other inconsistent with that relation. As an example, a man and woman engaged to marry are affianced to one another during the period between the time of the engagement and the celebration of the marriage.

In the present case, of traveller and courier, from the day of the hiring till the day when the employment was to begin, the parties were engaged to each other, and it seems to be a breach of an implied contract if either of them renounces the engagement. This reasoning seems in accordance with the unanimous decision of the Exchequer Chamber in *Elderton* v. *Emmens* which we have followed in subsequent cases in this court. The declaration in the present case, in alleging a breach, states a great deal more than a passing intention on the part of the defendant which he may repent of, and could only be proved by evidence that he had utterly renounced the contract or done some act which rendered it impossible for him to perform it. If the plaintiff has no remedy for breach of the contract unless he treats the contract as in force, and acts upon it down to June 1, 1852, it follows that, till then, he must enter into no employment which will interfere with his promise "to start with the defendant on such travels on the day and year, and that he must then be properly equipped in all respects as a courier for a three months" tour on the continent of Europe.

But it is surely much more rational, and more for the benefit of both parties, that, after the renunciation of the agreement by the defendant, the plaintiff should be at liberty to consider himself absolved from any future performance of it, retaining his right to sue for any damage he has suffered from the breach of it. Thus, instead of remaining idle and laying out money in preparations which must be useless, he is at liberty to seek service under another employer, which would go in mitigation of the damages to which he would otherwise be entitled for a breach of the contract. It seems strange that the defendant, after renouncing the contract, and absolutely declaring that he will never act under it, should be permitted to object that faith is given to his assertion, and that an opportunity is not left to him of changing his mind. If the plaintiff is barred of any remedy by entering into an engagement inconsistent with starting as a courier with the defendant on June 1, he is prejudiced by putting faith in the defendant's assertion, and it would be more consonant with principle, if the defendant were precluded from saying that he had not broken the contract when he declared that he entirely renounced it.

Suppose that the defendant, at the time of his renunciation, had embarked on a voyage for Australia, so as to render it physically impossible for him to employ the plaintiff as a courier on the continent of Europe in the months of June, July and August, 1852. According to decided cases the action might have been brought before 1 June, but the renunciation may have been founded on other facts, to be given in evidence, which would equally have rendered the defendant's performance of the contract impossible. The man who wrongfully renounces a contract into which he has deliberately entered cannot justly complain if he is immediately sued for a compensation in damages by the man whom he has injured: and it seems reasonable to allow an option to the injured party, either to sue immediately or to wait till the time when the act was to be done, still holding it as prospectively binding for the exercise of this option, which may be advantageous to the innocent party, and cannot be prejudicial to the wrongdoer.

An argument against the action before 1 June is urged from the difficulty of calculating the damages, but this argument is equally strong against an action before 1 Sep, when the three months would expire. In either case, the jury in assessing the damages would be justified in looking to all that had happened, or was likely to happen, to increase or mitigate the loss of the plaintiff down to the day of trial.

We do not find any decision contrary to the view we are taking of this case. . . .

If it should be held that, upon a contract to do an act on a future day, a renunciation of the contract by one party dispenses with a condition to be performed in the meantime by the other, there seems no reason for requiring that other to wait till the day arrives before seeking his remedy by action, and the only ground on which the condition can be dispensed with seems to be that the renunciation may be treated as a breach of the contract. Upon the whole, we think that the declaration in this case is sufficient. It gives us great satisfaction to reflect that, the question being on the record, our opinion may be reviewed in a court of error. In the meantime we must give judgment for the plaintiff.

BGH, 21 March 1974[268] **6.G.91.**

REPUDIATION OF CONTRACT BEFORE DATE OF DUE PERFORMANCE

Geological survey demanded

If one party indicates, before he is due to perform, that he will not perform in accordance with the contract, the other may terminate the contract at that stage.

[268] BGH NJW 1974.1080.

Facts: Performance of building work was not yet due since planning permission had not yet been granted, but the contractor unjustifiably refused to continue excavation without a geological study.

Held: This was a sufficiently severe repudiation to amount to a positive breach and the employer could terminate the contract.

Judgment: By a contract dated 12/18 March 1969 the plaintiff entrusted the defendant with the earth-moving, concrete, reinforced concrete, masonry, canalisation and demolition work in connection with the partial demolition of an old production unit and the construction of a new one and the securing of a 2,000 square metre courtyard at the price of DM 104,851.49. Alongside special contractual conditions, the general trade conditions (VOB/B) were to apply.

The defendant started work on 25 March 1969. On excavating the foundations the water table was found to be higher than expected. On the orders of the directing building architect K. the defendant ceased work on 31 March 1969. In the ensuing days the architect repeatedly asked the defendant to resume work. The defendant declined to do so, taking the view that a geological investigation was first necessary. Sample drillings undertaken by another firm and the installation of a water-holding area were felt by the defendant to be insufficient. On 9 April 1969 the plaintiff informed the defendant in writing that he was in default by reason of delay, and that he had no alternative but to apply the provisions of the contract in that regard. On 16 April 1969 the plaintiff stated that he would decline to accept performance and was instructing another builder. The works were then carried out by the company, St. The plaintiff alleged that additional expenditure was thereby incurred amounting to DM 31,217.31. It finally brought an action for that amount, together with interest. The defendant counterclaimed for the amount of DM 2,180.55, together with interest, for work done up to 31 March 1969.

. . .

On these grounds: I. The court *a quo* disallowed the plaintiff's claim under the VOB/B on the ground that the defendant was not in default by reason of delay. The appeal on that point is also unsuccessful.

1. Delay could have occurred only if the claims arising out of the building contract were valid. That could not be the case so long as the building regulations authority had not issued the necessary authorisation. . . . Otherwise the continuance of the works would have contravened a legislative prohibition within the meaning of § 134 BGB, namely the Building Regulations for North-Rhine Westphalia.

II. Article 8(3)(2) VOB/B must however be applied by analogy where the contractor is guilty of such a serious positive breach of contract that the client is warranted in immediately withdrawing from the contract. . . . The court *a quo* has not hitherto adequately examined whether that condition is satisfied in the present case.

1. The court *a quo* also regards no claim as arising because the plaintiff prior to the issue of the building permit had no matured claim to have the works carried out and because it also adduced no factual evidence indicating any other than the interference with performance laid down in Article 5(4) VOB/B. In that connection the court stated that the defendant's refusal was not "absolute". Moreover it substantiated its refusal on objective grounds. Even if the geological investigation which it deemed essential may not have been necessary it was, however, convinced of the correctness of its view.

2. With the appellants on a point of law it must be agreed that the decision of the court *a quo* cannot be supported by this reasoning.

(a) Whether the plaintiff's claim was mature is not relevant in this connection. A positive breach of contract by the contractor may so undermine the client's confidence in proper performance of the contract that to wait until it was due would be an empty formality and could even give rise to an increase in the loss. Thus in its decision of 20 January 1969 this court allowed a claim for damages by a client by analagous application of Article 8(8)(2) **VOB/B** on the ground that the contractor seriously and definitively had withheld performance of the contract immediately after the conclusion thereof, that is to say prior to the date on which it was due.

(b) The situation may be the same in the present case. The court *a quo* considered that the defendant did not repudiate *every* duty to perform arising out of the building contract. The test as to whether performance has been seriously and definitively withheld must be a strict one. . . . The repeated statement by the defendant that he was unable to continue the works without a prior geological investigation, together with removal of machinery from the building site may however be equated to an absolute and a definitive withholding of performance where, as may be assumed from the findings of the court a quo, a geological investigation was not objectively necessary.

Notes

(1) This case highlights the distinction between a refusal before the date on which performance is due and a refusal after that date. The latter, is widely held to come within § 326 BGB as a type of delay.[269] However, cases of the former type cannot be said to involve delay since performance is not yet due. As indicated in the extract, the dominant opinion is that a refusal in such cases amounts to a positive breach.[270]

(2) Where a contract is to be performed over a period of time, failures to perform in the early stages may give the creditor reason to doubt that the debtor will perform adequately in future. This may constitute a sufficiently "important reason" to justify the creditor in serving a *Kündigung* without notice.[271]

French law has no doctrine of anticipatory breach as such. It appears that it is impossible to seek *résolution* of the contract before the date on which performance is due. However, the fact that a debtor has either refused performance or been responsible for making performance impossible may enhance the remedies available to the creditor, for example, damages greater than those merely foreseeable; greater likelihood of *résolution* being granted after the due date. Thus, by contrast with English and German law, Whittaker notes:[272]

in French law the fact that a breach of contract has occurred before the time for performance does not in general affect when any remedy based on breach becomes available, but its deliberate nature may have considerable effects on any subsequent remedy.

Principles of European Contract Law   **6.PECL.92.**

Article 9:304: *Anticipatory Non-Performance*

    Where prior to the time for performance by a party it is clear that there will be a fundamental non-performance by it, the other party may terminate the contract.

---

[269] See **6.4.2**, *supra* at 752. The notice requirement under that provision falls away where it is clear that the debtor is not going to perform.

[270] See *Münchener Kommentar*, under § 275 BGB, paras. 274–281.

[271] See **6.4.2**, *supra* at 754.

[272] Whittaker, "How Does French Law Deal with Anticipatory Breaches of Contract?" (1996) 45 ICLQ 662, at 666.

What if one party fears that the other may not perform, but the second party has not clearly repudiated his obligations or put it out of his power to perform? We saw earlier that this may give rise to a right to withhold performance; BW Article 6:263 states this in general terms, as does CISG Article 71. Other laws apply it to limited circumstances such as the other party's insolvency.[273] However the UCC § 2–609 and the PECL go further; they allow the party who is uncertain to demand and assurance and, if he does not get it, to terminate.

Principles of European Contract Law   **6.PECL.93.**

Article 8:105: *Assurance of Performance*
      (1) A party which reasonably believes that there will be a fundamental non-performance by the other party may demand adequate assurance of due performance and meanwhile may withhold performance of its own obligations so long as such reasonable belief continues.
      (2) Where this assurance is not provided within a reasonable time, the party demanding it may terminate the contract if it still reasonably believes that there will be a fundamental non-performance by the other party and gives notice of termination without delay.

There is some suggestion that termination in such circumstances may also be possible in German law. In cases where, before the due date, doubts arise about the likelihood of the debtor being able to perform, the creditor may set a notice period within which the debtor must declare—and in some cases prove—his willingness and ability to perform. If this declaration is not forthcoming on expiry of the notice period, the creditor may invoke his rights of *Rücktritt* or damages for non-performance.[274]

6.4.7. AGREED RIGHTS OF TERMINATION

As we have seen, in English law the aggrieved party may terminate either if the breach is one which deprives it of the substance of what it was contracting for or if the breach was a condition. In principle, a condition is a term which is so important that "it goes to the root of the contract". What if one party attempts to expand its right of termination to apply to cases in which the other has only committed what would normally be regarded as a minor breach?

Court of Appeal   **6.E.94.**
Financings Ltd. v. *Baldock*[275]

DAMAGES RECOVERABLE ONLY FOR INSTALMENTS DUE AT DATE OF TERMINATION

Power to terminate

Where a hire purchase contract is terminated and the goods have been repossessed by their owner, the owner cannot claim damages for its full loss under the agreement but only for instalments due at the date of termination.

---

[273] See *supra* at 740–741.
[274] BGH NJW 1983.989; see Emmerich, *Das Recht der Leistungsstörungen*, 3rd edn. (München: Beck, 1991), at 198, 239.
[275] [1963] 2 QB 104.

Facts: A hire-purchase agreement provided:

> "8. Should the hirer fail to pay the initial instalment . . . or any subsequent instalment . . . within ten days after the same shall have become due or if he shall die . . . the owner may . . . by written notice . . . forthwith and for all purposes terminate the hiring."

Clause 11 provided that if the agreement were terminated under clause 8, the hirer would pay to the owner "such further sum as with the total amount of any instalments previously paid hereunder will equal two-thirds of the total hiring cost . . .". The hirer failed to pay the second and third instalments, and the owners gave notice of termination under cl 8 and repossessed the vehicle. Clause 11 was invalid as a penalty clause.[276] Therefore the owners claimed damages from the hirer for their full loss.

Held: The Court of Appeal held that they were entitled to the overdue instalments up to the date of repossession, but no more. The failure to pay one or two instalments on time would not justify termination of the contract under the general law,[277] and Clause 8 merely conferred a right to terminate the agreement without making the failure to pay a breach of condition. If the hirer's failure to pay had amounted to a repudiation, as in *Overstone Ltd.* v. *Shipway*,[278] the hirer would have been liable in damages, but here the owners could only claim money due at the date of termination and any payments required under the termination clause itself (none in this case).

Judgment: DENNING LJ: (On the effect of clause 8) It seems to me that when an agreement of hiring is terminated by virtue of a power contained in it, and the owner retakes the vehicle, he can recover damages for any breach up to the date of termination but not for any breach thereafter, for the simple reason that there are no breaches thereafter. . . . That principle is implicit in what Salter J said as long ago as 1926 in *Elacy & Co Ltd* v. *Hyde*, an unreported case quoted by Jenkins LJ in *Cooden Engineering Co Ltd* v. *Stanford*. Salter J took the very case

> "where the hire is determined by the owner, because the hirer is in arrear with his payments. It is proved that this is a breach of this contract, and it is proved that that breach, apart from any termination of the hirer, would give the owner a right to damages against the hirer. But what would those damages be? They would be interest on the amount unpaid and nothing more. The fact that the hirer is in arrear with his payments will not entitle the owner to any damages for depreciation of these things. The reason that they have suffered is that they have second hand goods put on their hands before they have received very much money in respect of them. That is not the result of the hirer's breach of contract, in being late in his payments, it is the result of their own election to determine the hiring. That passage is in my view good law: and Jenkins LJ seems to have accepted the reasoning in it as correct."

DIPLOCK LJ: . . . [The hirer] was clearly in breach of his obligation to pay two instalments on the due dates but, in the absence of any express provision to the contrary in the contract, these breaches of a contract of hire expressed to be for a duration of 24 months would not of themselves go to the root of the contract or evince an intention on the part of the hirer no longer to be bound by the contract. The owners' only remedy would have been to sue for the two instalments overdue and their measure of damages would have been the amount of these instalments, together with interest at the agreed rate of 10 per cent per annum. They would also have continued to be liable to perform their own obligations under the contract, viz., to continue to hire the van to the hirer: for again, in the absence of express provision to the contrary, the non-payment of two instalments would not be an event which relieved the owners from their undertaking to do what they had agreed to do but had not yet done . . . Parties to a contract may incorporate in it provisions which expressly define the events, whether or not they amount to breaches of contract, which are to have this result. But such

---

[276] The rules on penalty clauses are explained in greater detail *infra* at 865 ff., but, in essence, if the parties agree on a sum which is to be paid as damages if one of them breaks the contract, the clause will be valid if it is a genuine pre-estimate of the loss which the breach is likely to cause ("liquidated damages"). If it exceeds this figure the clause will be invalid as a "penalty". Clause 11 in the *Financings* contract was penal because the same amount had to be paid by the hirer irrespective of the value of the car repossessed.

[277] See *supra* at 772.

[278] [1962] 1 All ER 52, CA.

a provision of itself may do no more than define an event which of itself, or at the option of one or other of the parties, brings the contract to an end and thus relieves both parties from their undertakings further to perform their obligations thereunder. Whether it does more than this and confers any other rights or remedies on either party on the termination of the contract, depends upon the true construction of the relevant provision. If it does not, then each party is left with such causes of action, if any, as had already accrued to him at the date that the contract came to an end, but acquires no fresh cause of action as a result of the termination.

Court of Appeal   **6.E.95.**
Lombard North Central plc v. *Butterworth*[279]

FUTURE INSTALMENTS RECOVERABLE WHERE TIME IS OF ESSENCE

Late payment for a computer

Where timely payment is a condition of a contract, and that condition is breached, the other party is entitled to claim all outstanding instalments by way of compensation for breach of the condition.

Facts: The plaintiff, a finance company, leased a computer to the defendant for a period of five years on payment of an initial sum of £584.05 and nineteen subsequent quarterly instalments of the same amount. Clause 2(a) of the hiring agreement made punctual payment of each instalment of the essence of the agreement and under cl 5 failure to make due and punctual payment entitled the plaintiffs to terminate the agreement. By clause 6 the plaintiffs were entitled on termination to all "arrears of instalments and all future instalments which would have fallen due had the agreement not been terminated less a discount for accelerated payment". Although the defendant paid the first two instalments promptly, the next three were paid very belatedly, and on four occasions payment made by direct debit was recalled by the bank. When the sixth instalment was six weeks overdue the plaintiffs wrote to the defendant terminating the agreement. Subsequently the plaintiffs recovered possession of the computer and sold it for only £172.88. The plaintiffs brought an action against the defendant claiming the amount of the unpaid sixth instalment and the thirteen future instalments or, alternatively, damages for breach of contract. They then applied for and obtained summary judgment under RSC Ord 14 for damages to be assessed.

Held: In assessing the damages the master held that the defendant had by his conduct repudiated the contract and accordingly the plaintiffs were entitled to recover damages in respect of all future instalments less certain credits. The defendant appealed, contending that he ought not to be held liable for more than the amount due and unpaid at the date of termination. The appeal was dismissed.

Judgment: MUSTILL LJ: . . . The hire agreement contained the following material provisions:

The LESSEE . . . AGREES . . .
2. (a) to pay to the lessor: (i) punctually and without previous demand the rentals set out in Part 3 of the Schedule together with Value Added Tax thereon punctual payment of each which shall be of the essence of this lease.
5. IN THE EVENT THAT (a) the Lessee shall (i) make default in the due and punctual payment of any of the rentals or of any sum of money payable to the Lessor hereunder or any part thereof . . . then upon the happening of such event . . . the Lessor's consent to the Lessee's possession of the Goods shall determine forthwith without any notice being given by the Lessor, and the Lessor may terminate this Lease either by notice in writing, or by taking possession of the Goods . . .
6. IN THE EVENT THAT the Lessor's consent to the Lessee's possession of the goods shall be determined under clause 5 hereof *(a)* the Lessee shall pay forthwith to the Lessor: (i) all arrears of rentals; and (ii) all further rentals which would but for the determination of the Lessor's consent to the Lessee's possession of the Goods have fallen due to the end of the fixed period of this Lease less a discount thereon for accelerated payment at the rate of 5 per cent per annum; and (iii) damages for any breach of this Lease and all expenses and costs incurred by the Lessor in retaking possession of the Goods and/or enforcing the Lessor's rights under this Lease together with such Value Added Tax as shall be legally payable thereon: *(b)* the Lessor shall be

[279] [1987] QB 527.

entitled to exercise any one or more of the rights and remedies provided for in clause 5 and sub clause *(a)* of this clause and the determination of the Lessor's consent to the Lessee's possession of the Goods shall not affect or prejudice such rights and remedies and the Lessee shall be and remain liable to perform all outstanding liabilities under this Lease notwithstanding that the Lessor may have taken possession of the Goods and/or exercised one or more of the rights and remedies of the Lessor; *(c)* any right or remedy to which the Lessor is or may become entitled under this Lease or in consequence of the Lessee's conduct may be enforced from time to time separately or concurrently with any other right or remedy given by this Lease or now or hereafter provided for or arising by operation of law so that such rights and remedies are not exclusive of the other or others of them but are cumulative.

Three issues were canvassed before us. (1) Is cl 6 of the agreement to be disregarded, on the ground that it creates a penalty? (Strictly speaking, this issue does not arise, since the judgment was for damages to be assessed, but cl 6 was relied on by the plaintiffs before the master and in this court, without objection.) (2) Apart from cl 2(a) of the agreement, was the master correct in holding that the conduct of the defendant amounted to a wrongful repudiation of the contract, and that the sum claimed was recoverable in damages? (3) Does the provision in cl 2(a) of the agreement that time for payment of the instalments was of the essence have the effect of making the defendant's late payment of the outstanding instalments a repudiatory breach?

As to the first two issues, I need say only that I have had the advantage of reading in draft the judgment to be delivered by Nicholls LJ, and that I am in such entire agreement with his conclusions and reasons that it is unnecessary to add any observations of my own.

The reason why I am impelled to hold that the plaintiffs' contentions are well-founded can most conveniently be set out in a series of propositions. (1) Where a breach goes to the root of the contract, the injured party may elect to put an end to the contract. Thereupon both sides are relieved from those obligations which remain unperformed. (2) If he does so elect, the injured party is entitled to compensation for (a) any breaches which occurred before the contract was terminated and (b) the loss of his opportunity to receive performance of the promisor's outstanding obligations. (3) Certain categories of obligation, often called conditions, have the property that any breach of them is treated as going to the root of the contract. On the occurrence of any breach of condition, the injured party can elect to terminate and claim damages, whatever the gravity of the breach. (4) It is possible by express provision in the contract to make a term a condition, even if it would nor be so in the absence of such a provision. (5) A stipulation that time is of the essence, in relation to a particular contractual term, denotes that timely performance is a condition of the contract. The consequence is that delay in performance is treated as going to the root of the contract, without regard to the magnitude of the breach. (6) It follows that where a promisor fails to give timely performance of an obligation in respect of which time is expressly stated to be of the essence, the injured party may elect to terminate and recover damages in respect of the promisor's outstanding obligations, without regard to the magnitude of the breach. (7) A term of the contract prescribing what damages are to be recoverable when a contract is terminated for a breach of condition is open to being struck down as a penalty, if it is not a genuine covenanted pre-estimate of the damage, in the same way as a clause which prescribes the measure for any other type of breach. No doubt the position is the same where the clause is ranked as a condition by virtue of an express provision in the contract. (8) A clause expressly assigning a particular obligation to the category of condition is not a clause which purports to fix the damages for breaches of the obligation, and is not subject to the law governing penalty clauses. (9) Thus, although in the present case cl 6 is to be struck down as a penalty, cl 2(a)(i) remains enforceable. The plaintiffs were entitled to terminate the contract independently of cl 5, and to recover damages for loss of the future instalments. This loss was correctly computed by the master.

These bare propositions call for comment. The first three are uncontroversial. The fourth was not, I believe, challenged before us, but I would in any event regard it as indisputable . . .

The fifth proposition is a matter of terminology, and has been more taken for granted than discussed. That making time of the essence is the same as making timely performance if condition was, however, expressly stated by Megaw and Browne LJJ in *Bunge Corp* v. *Tradax SA*[279a] and the same proposition is implicit in the leading speeches of Lord Wilberforce and Lord Roskill in the House of Lords.

The sixth proposition is a combination of the first five. There appears to be no direct authority for it, and it is right to say that most of the cases on the significance of time being of the essence have been concerned with the right to the injured party to be discharged, rather than the principles on which its damages are to be computed. Nevertheless, it is axiomatic that a person who establishes a breach of condition can terminate and claim damages for loss of the bargain, and I know of no authority which suggests that the position is any different where late performance is made into a breach of condition by a stipulation that time is of the essence.

I return to the propositions stated above. The seventh is uncontroversial, and I would add only the rider that when deciding on the penal nature of a clause which prescribes a measure of recovery for damages resulting from a termination founded on a breach of condition, the comparison should he with the common law measure, namely with the loss to the promisee resulting from the loss of his bargain. If the contract permits him to treat the contract as repudiated, the fact that the breach is comparatively minor should in my view play no part in the equation.

I believe that the real controversy in the present case centres on the eighth proposition. I will repeat it. A clause expressly assigning a particular obligation to the category of condition is not a clause which purports to fix the damages for breach of the obligation, and is not subject to the law governing penalty clauses. l acknowledge, of course, that by promoting a term into the category where all breaches are ranked as breaches of condition, the parties indirectly bring about a situation where, for breaches which are relatively small, the injured party is enabled to recover damages as on the loss of the bargain, whereas without the stipulation his measure of recovery would be different. But I am unable to accept that this permits the court to strike down as a penalty the clause which brings about this promotion. To do so would be to reverse the current of more than 100 years' doctrine, which permits the parties to treat as a condition something which would not otherwise be so. I am not prepared to take this step.

For these reasons I conclude that the plaintiffs are entitled to retain the damages which the master has awarded. This is not a result which I view with much satisfaction, partly because the plaintiffs have achieved by one means a result which the law of penalties might have prevented them from achieving by another and partly because if the line of argument under cl 2 had been developed from the outset, the defendant might have found an answer based on waiver which the court is now precluded from assessing, for want of the necessary facts. Nevertheless, it is the answer to which, in my view, the authorities clearly point. Accordingly, I would dismiss the appeal.

Notes

(1) Nicholls LJ (whose judgment is not extracted here but see BBF 535–537) held that cl. 6 was a penalty because it would allow the lessor to recover a greater amount than it would at common law. It seems odd that if the company's terms state that, in the event of the goods being repossessed, the company may recover its full loss, the clause is void as a penalty and the finance company can recover only the unpaid instalments; but that if time is stated to be of the essence the company can recover the full loss.

(2) Although the Court of Appeal held that the rules affecting penalty clauses did not apply to clause 2(a), such clauses in credit agreements are not completely uncontrolled in English Law. First, where the credit agreement is for hire-purchase or conditional sales it

---

[279a] *Supra* at 772.

may be regulated by the Consumer Credit Act 1974 (which applies to individuals who need not be buying for private purposes, but the transaction must be for less than £15,000). This may mean that repossession is subjected to a formal notice procedure. Secondly, this type of clause would now be subject to the Unfair Terms in Consumer Contracts Regulations 1994, if it were in a contract between a consumer and a seller or supplier and had not been individually negotiated.[280]

French law also recognizes the right of a party to insert a clause giving an express right to terminate the contract, the *clause de résolution en plein droit*. But the principal purpose of this clause is rather different: it is to allow termination without the need for court proceedings. Nevertheless, the following case shows us that the courts also monitor the use of such clauses through the concept of good faith.

Cass. civ. 3e, 8 April 1987[281]   **6.F.96.**

TERMINATION MUST BE IN GOOD FAITH

Widow Thomas' *rente viagère*

Where the terms of a contract have not been enforced over an extended period of time, and a party has been led to believe that the terms will not be enforced, it is not open to the other party to terminate the contract for a breach of those terms. In such a case, the termination clause is not relied upon in good faith.

Facts: Mr Thomas sold a house in 1970 to Mr and Mrs Andre-Renouvier. The sale contained an easement in favour of his wife and himself for a cash amount together with an annuity. After the death of Mr Thomas, his wife, invoking the termination clause in the contract for sale, gave formal notice to the debtors to pay the annuity which had never been claimed. Mr Andre and Mrs Renouvier refused to pay, and Mrs Thomas brought proceedings against them for repudiation of the sale.

Held: The creditors' claim for dissolution of the arrangement was dismissed on the basis that the termination clause was not relied on in good faith: by omitting for more than ten years to claim the annuity payment from the debtors, the creditor, and later his wife, had led the debtors to believe that the annuity would never be claimed. The Cour de cassation upheld the judgment on appeal.

Judgment: THE COURT: *On the first three appeal grounds taken together*: . . .—Whereas Mrs Thomas criticises the judgment for dismissing her claim whereas, in the terms of her first appeal ground, the termination clause in the deed of sale of 17 December 1970 was entirely lawful and binding on the parties and the courts; as furthermore, in her submission, once the courts found that effect had not been given to the claims in the summons, they had no power other then to hold that the contract had been terminated; as by excusing non-payment of arrears on alleged grounds of equity, the judgment appealed against infringed Articles 1134, 1184 and 1656 of the Civil Code;
—Whereas under the second appeal ground it is submitted that, although the court may examine points of law of its own motion, it must first invite the parties to submit their observations; as in holding there to have been an abuse of her rights by Mrs Thomas to the detriment of her adversaries the judgment appealed against infringed Articles 12 and 16 of the new Code of Civil Procedure;

---

[280] See *supra* at 526.
[281] Gaz.Pal. 1988.II.21037 annotated by Y. Picod.

—Whereas finally, under the third plea it is submitted that the exercise of a right cannot degenerate into an abuse unless it is exercised with the intention of harming another person or constitutes a serious fault equivalent to deception to be established by the court; as that is argued not to be the case here since Mrs Thomas merely availed herself of a right which accrued to her only on the death of her husband some months earlier, and whose exercise could have been foreseen by the debtors;
—Whereas the judgment appealed against is therefore said to be without legal basis under Articles 1382 et seq. of the Civil Code.
—Whereas the court of appeal found that, by omitting for more than 10 years to claim the annuity payment from the debtors the creditor then, after his death, his wife had led the debtors to believe that the annuity would never be claimed, the spouses having a particularly affectionate relationship with Mrs Renouvier, who was the foster sister of the creditor, and that the sudden change in the creditor's attitude which was solely due to dissension in Mrs Renouvier's daughter's family constituted a situation which was unforeseeable as far as the debtors were concerned, and prevented them from bringing themselves into conformity within the period allowed;
—Whereas the judgment is lawful on those grounds alone from which the court of appeal was entitled to infer, without infringing the principle of *audi alteram partem*, that the termination clause had not been relied on in good faith.

On the fourth appeal ground:—Whereas Mrs Thomas criticises the judgment for granting Mrs Renouvier a period of one year to pay the arrears accrued due. However, it is submitted on appeal that the court must confine itself to claims made before it, and Mrs Renouvier made no request for a period of grace;
—Whereas the judgment is therefore in breach of Article 5 of the new Code of Civil Procedure, since the grant of a period for payment of a debt is reserved to the debtor in difficulties and the courts trying the case on its merits must state the grounds relating to the debtor's situation on which it decides to grant the debtor a period of grace; as by stating no ground in that connection it is submitted that the judgment appealed against infringed Article 1244 of the Civil Code and Article 455 of the new Code of Civil Procedure;
—Whereas however, since a judgment which gives a decision on matters in respect of which no request was made may be rectified as provided for in Articles 462 and 463 of the new Code of Civil Procedure, that plea is inadmissible.

On those grounds: The appeal is dismissed.

Observations:
1. Where a contracting party seeks termination of the contract under Article 1184 of the Civil Code, the court may avail itself of wide-ranging powers. In order to uphold the contractual relationship, it may in particular appraise the importance of non-performance in relation to the benefit which the creditor was entitled to expect from the contract. It may also accede to an offer to perform by the debtor or grant him, in accordance with the legislation, a further period for compliance on account of difficulties encountered.
2. Judicial power also asserted itself when faced with an express termination clause in the contract. In fact, under the last paragraph of Article 1134 of the Civil Code, which provides that contracts must be performed in good faith, the courts have a moderating power which they do not hesitate to use in a proper case. In that way powers are returned to the courts which were thought by the parties to have been ousted by the insertion of clauses regarded as being of unlimited legal effect. Article 1134(3) of the Civil Code serves to mitigate the rigorous effects of a contractual provision which derives its validity from the first paragraph of that article. The judgment of the Cour de cassation of 8 April 1987 extends a line of authorities which began twenty years ago.

3. In this particular case the facts were as follows: On 17 December 1970 Mr Thomas sold to Mr and Mrs Andre-Renouvier a villa subject to an easement in favour of himself and his wife for a cash sum together with an annual payment. The vendor maintained a close affectionate relationship with the purchasers and for twelve years no annual payment was claimed. However, on 1 September 1982 the vendor's widow, relying on the termination clause in the deed of sale, formally put the debtors on notice to pay the arrears. No action having been taken in response to that notice she brought proceedings for termination of the sale and was successful before the lower court which merely noted that termination had occurred. That decision was overturned by a judgment of the court of appeal, Aix-en-Provence on the ground that the termination clause had not been relied on in good faith. According to that court, the creditor had by its attitude led the debtor to believe that payment would not be claimed and the sudden change in the plaintiff's attitude constituted for the debtor an unforeseeable situation. On 8 April 1987 the third Civil Chamber of the Cour de cassation affirmed that approach, thus dismissing the appeal brought by Mrs Thomas, widow, who had argued that the court had no power to control the exercise of the *clause résolutoire*, which was legal.

4. The Cour de cassation unambiguously acknowledges that the court's trying issues on their merits are empowered to review ex post facto whether termination clauses comply with the principle of good faith. Although the principle has been accepted for a number of years, the actual scope of the court's intervention depends on its definition of the concept of good faith. Often the courts perceive this concept negatively by penalising manifestly unfair attitudes and dishonest intentions. The courts will scrutinise the intentions of the parties and whenever bad faith appears to guide the actions of the creditor, they will set aside the termination clause. But it is not always easy to discern the intention of the contracting parties. However, good faith, construed as a duty to observe contracts, may also constitute a criterion for determining the substance of the contract. In that case it enables guide lines to be fixed in abstracto as regards the conduct of the parties. Which gives the courts greater latitude and certainty. The judgment of 8 April 1987 should be read in the light of this latter clarification.

BGB   **6.G.97.**

§ 346: If one party to a contract has reserved to himself the right of termination, and if termination takes place, the parties are obliged to return to each other whatever they received. For services rendered and for allowing the use of a thing the value shall be made good, or, if in the contract a counter-performance in money is stipulated for, this shall be paid.

AGBG   **6.G.98.**

§ 10 Nr 3: *Unenforceable in General Conditions of Business*:
     ... an agreement that the proponent has the right, for reasons unjustifiable on the facts and not enumerated in the contract, to free himself from his obligation to perform. This does not apply to contracts extending over a period of time.

Note

As mentioned above,[282] *Fixgeschäfte* within § 361 BGB are held to imply agreed rights to termination. As also noted earlier, to purport to terminate because of a very slight delay, even under a *Fixgeschäft*, would be contrary to good faith.

---

[282] **6.4.4**, *supra* at 769.

789

6.4.8. A LAST CHANCE TO PERFORM

If the debtor has committed a breach of contract which seems serious enough to warrant termination by the creditor, does the debtor still have a last chance to perform—if he can—and thereby avoid the contract being terminated?

Three issues require comment.

6.4.8.A. RIGHT TO PERFORM BEFORE DUE DATE

If the time for performance has not yet expired, the debtor will normally still have the right to perform. The creditor can of course withhold performance until the debtor has performed, but—subject to the rules on anticipatory breach which exist in some systems[283]—the creditor cannot terminate before that date. Thus in France the debtor may perform at any time before the court actually declares *résolution* of the contract and an action for *résolution* brought before the date on which performance is due will be dismissed as premature. In English law the situation is usually much the same because of the fact that the innocent party is normally not entitled to terminate until the date for performance has passed. In the case of *Borrowman, Phillips & Co.* v. *Free and Hollis*[284] the sellers tendered goods which were not in accordance with the contract and which the buyers rejected. However the contract period for delivery had not yet expired, and when within that period the sellers made a fresh tender of goods which did conform to the contract, the buyers had no right to reject the second tender. The result would be different in English law if there had been an anticipatory repudiation (see a case in which the first delivery was so defective that the court held that it amounted to a repudiation of the whole contract, which could be terminated right away: *Millar's Karri & Jarrah Co.* v. *Weddel, Turner & Co.*[285]).

In German law it is clear that a seller of goods is entitled to cure removable defects or supply a substitute item at any time before performance was actually due.[286]

Principles of European Contract Law   **6.PECL.99.**

Article 8:104: *Cure by Non-Performing Party*
> A party whose tender of performance is not accepted by the other party because it does not conform to the contract may make a new tender and conforming tender where the time for performance has not yet arrived or the delay would not be such as to amount to a fundamental non-performance.

6.4.8.B. REQUIREMENT OF NOTICE

As we have seen, in many systems a formal notice to the debtor is required before the debtor is treated as being in default. It operates to prevent sudden termination, as at least the debtor must first be put into default by serving the notice. For example, in French law

---

[283] See *supra* at 777.
[284] (1878) 4 QBD 500.
[285] (1909) 100 LT 128, KB.
[286] See *Münchener Kommentar*, § 459 BGB, para. 4.

the creditor must serve a *mise-en-demeure* (Article 1139), on the debtor before the debtor will be liable in damages: Article 1146. In principle this is required also for other remedies (except the *exception d'inexécution*), though if the creditor is merely seeking judicial *résolution*, the notice of action will probably suffice. A *mise en demeure* will be necessary before the creditor can rely on a *clause résolutoire* unless the clause dispenses with this. German law requires a *Mahnung*, putting the debtor into delay (§ 284 BGB), and frequently a *Nachfrist* (§ 326 BGB), before the contract may be terminated. All these requirements give the debtor a chance to perform.

Even English law, which does not generally require any advance warning to the debtor, requires a "default" notice before termination in certain cases, for example before termination of a consumer credit agreement (Consumer Credit Act 1974, sections 87–89; see also Law of Property Act 1925, section 146 (leases)).

6.4.8.C. COURT MAY GIVE ADDITIONAL PERIOD FOR PERFORMANCE

The court may have power to give the debtor an additional period to perform even if no notice is required, or if a notice has been given and has expired without the debtor performing. French Code civil Article 1184 allows the court to grant the debtor a *délai de grâce*, in other words, a last chance to perform. Traditionally this applied only to *résolution judiciare* but now it may also be granted where the creditor relies on a *clause de résolution en plein droit*: Article 1244–3, red.L., 9.7.1991). This delay is different from the "délai de grâce" of art. 1244–1, which may be given to every kind of debtor in distress. English law does not as a general rule allow the debtor extra time. However, there are a number of exceptions by statute and at common law. Most involve situations in which the debtor stands to forfeit property, or the right to possess property, if the contract is terminated. For example, under the Consumer Credit Act 1974, if a debtor under a hire-purchase or conditional sale agreement has paid more than one-third of the total price when he defaults, the creditor may not repossess the goods without a court order (section 90), and court may give the debtor extra time to pay (section 129). There are also provisions governing the forfeiture of leases of land for non-payment of rent (Common Law Procedure Act 1852, sections 210–212) and other breaches of covenant (Law of Property Act 1925, section 146). At common law, the House of Lords has held that equitable relief against forfeiture, in the form of extra time in which to pay before the other party will be allowed to terminate the contract, is confined to cases where a proprietary or possessory right is to be forfeited. Thus a time-charterer of a ship who has failed to pay the instalments of hire on time cannot invoke the jurisdiction to prevent the owner from withdrawing the ship under a clause which permits "withdrawal" for late payment: *Scandinavian Trading Tanker Co. AB* v. *Flota Petrolera Ecuatoriana, The Scaptrade*,[287] as a time-charter is a contract for services, not a contract giving the charterer any possessory rights. Relief has been given to hirers of machines who were late in paying: *Barton, Thompson & Co. Ltd.* v. *Stapling Machines Co.*[288] and *Transag Haulage Ltd.* v. *Leyland Daf Finance plc.*[289]

[287] [1983] 2 All ER 763.
[288] [1966] Ch. 499.
[289] [1994] 2 BCLC 88.

In German law an extension of the debtor's period for performance beyond the *Nachfrist* can only be justified on the basis of § 242 BGB; that is where not to do so would seriously infringe the interests of the debtor against the requirements of good faith. Such cases are likely to be most exceptional.[290]

6.4.9. EFFECTS OF TERMINATION

6.4.9.A. THE EFFECT OF TERMINATION ON CLAIMS FOR DAMAGES FOR NON-PERFORMANCE

It is quite clear that in French law the creditor may obtain both *résolution judiciare* and damages for non-performance. Equally in English law, termination of the contract may be combined with an action for damages for non-performance: *Johnson* v. *Agnew*.[291] In German law, as noted in section **6.4.2**, a claim for *Rücktritt* may not be combined with a claim for damages for non-performance. However, it has already been suggested that this difference is considerably less significant than at first appears. The creditor faced with a serious non-performance by the debtor must first put the debtor on notice that he will refuse performance after a certain time, whether he eventually seeks *Rücktritt* or claims damages for non-performance. Once this date is passed and the creditor resorts to either of the available remedies, the contract is effectively terminated in the sense in which we have been using that word here. That is: the creditor's claim for performance is expressly stated to be extinguished (in § 326 (1) 2 BGB) and the debtor's claim for performance must be similarly extinguished owing to the synallgamatic nature of the obligations. This is just the same effect as the process which in English law is referred to as termination.

To be precise, *Rücktritt* is not therefore the same as termination, but is a process of seeking restitution of the benefits conferred under the contract before the date of termination. This may also be possible—though, as we shall see, in much more limited circumstances—in English law, as the creditor who has terminated may be able to seek restitution. Though the English cases are not entirely clear, it seems that the creditor must elect between claiming in restitution and claiming damages.[292] The effect is thus similar to that in German law.[293]

6.4.9.B. THE EFFECT ON ANCILLARY OBLIGATIONS

Although the process of termination is often likened to that of avoidance for invalidity— for example, for fraud—, in all the systems there are at least two major differences. One is that just referred to, that the creditor may generally claim damages for non-performance. The other is that, though the main obligations to perform come to an end, the contract may continue to be binding in other respects; in particular, the ancillary clauses of the contract will continue to apply. Thus penalty clauses may continue to apply if that is what the agreement provides, see French Code civil Article 1142. Similarly, if there is a contract to manufacture patented goods under licence and the contract is terminated by the licensor

---

[290] See *Münchener Kommentar*, under § 326 BGB, para. 60.
[291] [1980] AC 367.
[292] See Beale, "Remedies: Termination" in *Towards a European Civil Code*, at 348.
[293] See further *infra* at 801 ff.

because of defaults by the licensee, clauses which forbid the licensee to divulge confidential information will still bind the licensee.

The same applies to other clauses of the contract such as arbitration clauses and clauses which limit one party's liability.

In English law this has long been accepted as far as arbitration clauses are concerned: for example *Heyman* v. *Darwins Ltd.*[294] At one time the English Court of Appeal took a different approach to exclusion and limitation clauses, arguing that these did not survive termination of the contract—the so-called doctrine of "fundamental breach". This was undoubtedly an attempt to control the use of such clauses, but it was rejected by the House of Lords both as a matter of principle and because it failed to distinguish between clauses which were unfair and those which represented a perfectly proper allocation of risks under the contract—see particularly the judgment of Lord Reid in *Suisse Atlantique*.[295] The doctrine of fundamental breach was finally laid to rest in *Photo Production Ltd* v. *Securicor Ltd.*[296] In that case Lord Diplock explained the general principle underlying the effect of termination in English law.

House of Lords   **6.E.100.**
Photo Production Ltd v. *Securicor Ltd*[297]

EFFECTS OF TERMINATION

[For the facts of this case and other extracts, see *supra* at 504].

LORD DIPLOCK: A basic principle of the common law of contract, to which there are no exceptions that are relevant in the instant case, is that parties to a contract are free to determine for themselves what primary obligations they will accept. They may state these in express words in the contract itself and, where they do, the statement is determinative; but in practice a commercial contract never states all the primary obligations of the parties in full; many are left to be incorporated by implication of law from the legal nature of the contract into which the parties are entering. But if the parties wish to reject or modify primary obligations which would otherwise be so incorporated, they are fully at liberty to do so by express words.

Leaving aside those comparatively rare cases in which the court is able to enforce a primary obligation by decreeing specific performance of it, breaches of primary obligations give rise to substituted or secondary obligations on the part of the party in default, and, in some cases, may entitle the other party to be relieved from further performance of his own primary obligations. These secondary obligations of the contract breaker and any concomitant relief of the other party from his own primary obligations also arise by implication of law—generally common law, but sometimes statute, as in the case of codifying statutes passed at the turn of the century, notably the Sale of Goods Act 1893. The contract, however, is just as much the source of secondary obligations as it is of primary obligations; and like primary obligations that are implied by law, secondary obligations too can be modified by agreement between the parties, although, for reasons to be mentioned later, they cannot, in my view, be totally excluded. In the instant case, the only secondary obligations and concomitant reliefs that are applicable arise by implication of the common law as modified by the express words of the contract.

[294] [1942] AC 356.
[295] [1967] 1 AC 361.
[296] *Supra*, at 504. Even now remnants may survive: see Treitel, *Contract* at 205 ff.
[297] [1980] AC 827.

Every failure to perform a primary obligation is a breach of contract. The secondary obligation on the part of the contract breaker to which it gives rise by implication of the common law is to pay monetary compensation to the other party for the loss sustained by him in consequence of the breach; but, with two exceptions, the primary obligations of both parties so far as they have not yet been fully performed remain unchanged. This secondary obligation to pay compensation (damages) for non-performance of primary obligations I will call the "general secondary obligation." It applies in the cases of the two exceptions as well.

The exceptions are: (1) Where the event resulting from the failure by one party to perform a primary obligation has the effect of depriving the other party of substantially the whole benefit which it was the intention of the parties that he should obtain from the contract, the party not in default may elect to put an end to all primary obligations of both parties remaining unperformed. (If the expression "fundamental breach" is to be retained, it should, in the interests of clarity, be confined to this exception.) (2) Where the contracting parties have agreed, whether by express words or by implication of law, that any failure by one party to perform a particular primary obligation ("condition" in the nomenclature of the Sale of Goods Act 1893), irrespective of the gravity of the event that has in fact resulted from the breach, shall entitle the other party to elect to put an end to all primary obligations of both parties remaining unperformed. (In the interests of clarity, the nomenclature of the Sale of Goods Act 1893, "breach of condition" should be reserved for this exception.)

Where such an election is made (a) there is substituted by implication of law for the primary obligations of the party in default which remain unperformed a secondary obligation to pay monetary compensation to the other party for the loss sustained by him in consequence of their non-performance in the future and (b) the unperformed primary obligations of that other party are discharged. This secondary obligation is additional to the general secondary obligation; I will call it "the anticipatory secondary obligation."

In cases falling within the first exception, fundamental breach, the anticipatory secondary obligation arises under contracts of all kinds by implication of the common law, except to the extent that it is excluded or modified by the express words of the contract. In cases falling within the second exception, breach of condition, the anticipatory secondary obligation generally arises under particular kinds of contracts by implication of statute law; though in the case of "deviation" from the contract voyage under a contract of carriage of goods by sea it arises by implication of the common law. The anticipatory secondary obligation in these cases too can be excluded or modified by express words.

When there has been a fundamental breach or breach of condition, the coming to an end of the primary obligations of both parties to the contract at the election of the party not in default, is often referred to as the "determination" or "rescission" of the contract or, as in the Sale of Goods Act 1893 "treating the contract as repudiated." The first two of these expressions, however, are misleading unless it is borne in mind that for the unperformed primary obligations of the party in default there are substituted by operation of law what I have called the secondary obligations.

The bringing to an end of all primary obligations under the contract may also leave the parties in a relationship, typically that of bailor and bailee, in which they owe to one another by operation of law fresh primary obligations of which the contract is the source; but no such relationship is involved in the instant case.

I have left out of account in this analysis as irrelevant to the instant case an arbitration or choice of forum clause. This does not come into operation until a party to the contract claims that a primary obligation of the other party has not been performed; and its relationship to other obligations of which the contract is the source was dealt with by this House in *Heyman* v. *Darwins Ltd.* [1942] A.C. 356.

In German law it is now agreed that termination of the contract, whether through making a declaration of *Rücktritt* or seeking damages for non-performance, merely transforms or recasts the main performance obligations (*Hauptpflichten*) of the contract into obligations either to make restitution or to pay damages.[298] Logically this recasting of performance obligations can have no effect on the continued validity of the other contractual obligations. We have, thus, already referred to the fact that notwithstanding his seeking *Rücktritt*, the creditor may also claim damages for delay in the performance of collateral obligations (*Nebenpflichten*), for breach of protective obligations etc.[299]

6.4.9.C. RESTITUTIONARY CLAIMS

Principles of European Contract Law   **6.PECL.101.**

Article 4.305: *Effects of Termination in General*
(1) Termination of the contract releases both parties from their obligation to effect and to receive future performance, but, subject to Articles 4.306, 4.307 and 4.308, does not affect the rights and liabilities accrued up to the time of termination.
(2) Termination does not affect any provision of the contract for the settlement of disputes or any other provision which is to operate even after termination.

Article 4.306: *Property Reduced in Value*
A party who terminates the contract may reject property previously received from the other party if its value to the first party has been fundamentally reduced as a result of the other party's non-performance.

Article 4.307: *Recovery of Money Paid*
On termination of the contract a party may recover money paid for a performance which he did not receive or which he properly rejected.

Article 4.308: *Recovery of Property*
On termination of the contract a party who has supplied property which can be returned and for which he has not received payment or other counter-performance may recover the property.

Article 4.309: *Recovery for Performance that Cannot be Returned*
On termination of the contract a party who has rendered a performance which cannot be returned and for which he has not received payment or other counter-performance may recover a reasonable amount for the value of the performance to the other party.

What if one or both parties has rendered some performance to the other before termination of the contract? Can the party who has performed claim restitution of what he transferred or, if there is nothing to be reclaimed *in specie*, its value?

From the point of view of the aggrieved party, it will not always matter much whether he can claim restitution: if he is left out of pocket, he can claim damages. However there is one case in which it will be critical. If the debtor is bankrupt, it will be very important to know whether any property transferred by the aggrieved party can be recovered, either from the debtor or from anyone else who now has possession of it.

---

[298] See *Münchener Kommentar* under § 346 BGB, paras. 45–46.
[299] See **6.4.2.**, *supra* at 751.

Obviously a party in breach who has transferred property to the aggrieved party, and who now finds the latter to be insolvent, may have a similar concern. However, the party in breach has a much greater interest in being able to claim in restitution even from a solvent aggrieved party, since the party in breach has no action for damages to fall back on.

Systems which regard termination as essentially retroactive seem to have little difficulty in allowing restitution as between the original contracting parties, in favour of either of them. As we shall see, the problem comes when creditors or other third parties are interested.

(1) France

Malaurie and Aynes[300]   **6.F.102.**

§ 743. *Retroactivity.* Termination produces the same retroactive effect as nullity: the situation is "as if" the contract had not existed: *resoluto jure dantis resolvitur jus accipienties* (where the right of the person giving is terminated, that of the person receiving is also terminated), which has consequences on the relations between the parties and in regard to third parties.

As between the parties: termination and its retroactive effect hardly give rise to any difficulties. If the contract has not been performed it is nullified save for the penalty clause whose raison d'être is precisely non-performance which constitutes a difference as opposed to nullity. If partial performance has taken place there must be restitution which must be settled in the same way as in the case of nullity where the property has suffered deterioration or undergone improvement. Moreover, damages may be awarded, which represents the application of contractual liability.

It is in regard to third parties that the disadvantages of retroactivity are encountered which puts third parties in serious jeopardy. In that connection termination produces the same effect as nullity: acts of disposition by the purchaser whose title is terminated are nullified but not acts of administration. Retroactive effect does not occur in contracts providing for continuous performance where there is only one act of repudiation.

§ 744. *Repudiation.* In synallagmatic contracts providing for continuous performance, such as leases, it is impossible to reopen completed acts. The terminated contract is repudiated as regards the future or more precisely as from the date from which the debtor ceased to fulfil his obligations, unless otherwise provided by law.

II—Restitution

The principle is that of a restoration to the *statu quo ante*: it is as if the contract had never existed. Under a contract declared null and void there must be restitution in respect of performance effected. The principle covers instalment contracts and there is an important exception in the case of unworthy conduct on the part of the claimant under the *nemo auditur* rule.

A. Principle

§ 586. *Reverse contract.* If the parties to a synallagmatic contract have already performed, in whole or in part, the obligations provided for under the contract, nullity imposes on them a reciprocal obligation of restitution in respect of consideration received. As Mr Carbonnier says, the situation is that of a "synallagmatic contract in reverse". That is only a metaphorical description: the

---

[300] Malaurie and Aynès, paras 743 ff. and 586 ff.

negation of the past (return to the *status quo ante*) always raises more difficulties than in the case of positions acquired (performance of the contract). Restitution is a species of repayment of amounts unduly paid (Art. 1376) where the condition of mistake is not required. When its subject-matter is property it obeys the same rules as those governing the claim.

(c) Successive contracts

A successive contract is performed by temporal instalments; examples are the lease or contract of employment. When it is declared null and void, it can obviously produce effects only after the declaration to that effect. In regard to effects produced prior to the declaration, the situation is more complex; a distinction must be made between non-pecuniary and other performance.

§ 589. *Non-pecuniary performance.* In regard to non-pecuniary performance, it is impossible to unravel the factual situation already established; the tenant whose rights under the lease are nullified has in fact been in occupation; the wage-earner under an invalid contract of employment has in fact carried out work, etc. The courts will equitably establish the pecuniary equivalent of performance which cannot be unravelled. Sometimes they will apply the provisions of the contract, though it has been declared null and void. Two examples may serve by way of illustration: one which has given rise to major controversy, the contract of employment, and the other, more recent, an agricultural contract.

Nullity of the contract of employment does not prevent the employee from obtaining remuneration for work done, certain allowances (paid holidays, period of notice) and certain ancillary rights (social security, pay slip). Academic writers have put forward a number of explanations for these solutions: unjust enrichment, equity, a kind of repudiation, a type of putative contract, that is to say one which has validity only in the minds of those who entered into it and whose nullity is effective only as regards the future. The Court of Cassation based those solutions on the notion of compensation, without further elucidation. Legislation has been enacted to deal with the most common question: the foreign worker under an invalid contract of employment is entitled to payment of his salary and ancillary benefits (Labour Code, Art. L. 341–6–1, Oct. 1981).

Similarly, where an agricultural contract is declared null and void after having been performed, return in kind to the *statu quo ante* is normally not possible: the feedstuffs have been eaten by the livestock and the animals will generally have been sold or slaughtered. There must therefore be equivalent restitution, that is to say in money, which raises greater difficulties than in regard to a lease or contract of employment, because of the greater degree of complexity involved in that kind of operation. Restitution must be made to the supplier in respect of the value of feedstuffs supplied, but not the price thereof so that he does not obtain a profit on his supplies. Conversely and above all restitution must be made to the farmer in respect of the value of the animals supplied. Moreover he must be paid compensation since the work he has done has conferred a benefit on the supplier of feedstuffs.

§ 590. *Monetary Performance.* In this regard the return to the *statu quo ante* raises no difficulties in principle: amounts paid under a nul and void contract must be repaid. However, under the policy in regard to the affect of nullity that rule may be set aside in two ways. . . .

Note
On the difficulty in French law noted by Malaurie and Aynès in respect of restitution when third parties have become interested in the property, see Cass. soc. 20 June 1952.[301]

[301] Bull. civ. IV.542.

The critical case is when the debtor has become bankrupt and is in possession of a specific piece of property transferred to him by the aggrieved party under the contract which has been resolved. In French law the retroactive effect of *résolution* means that, in principle, title to property which has been transferred under the contract re-vests in the transferor and it does not matter that third parties—who may include the transferee's creditors—have acquired rights to the property. However, third parties are protected in two ways. For immovables, the Code civil Article 2108 requires a seller who has not been paid to register his interest within two months of the date of the contract. For movables, Article 2279 lays down the principle, *la possession vaut titre*: a person who has acquired in good faith title from someone having lawful possession of the goods acquires title even if the possessor did not have a secure title. This does not protect the interests of other unsecured creditors of the debtor who might want to seize the goods: the original seller who has not been paid can take them back.[302]

There is another problematic issue in French law. Is the contract to annulled from the beginning (*résolution*) or merely terminated for the future (*résiliation*)? Frequently if it would be difficult to "unpick" what has already been done, in example a building contract, the court will simply grant *résiliation* for the future; for example Civ.1 1.January 1963, Bull. civ No.355, 119. But occasionally the decisions seem aimed at denying the party which has failed to perform any remedy so as to protect—or over-protect?—the other party.

Cass. civ. 1re, 13 January 1987[303]   **6.F.103.**

RÉSOLUTION OR *RÉSILIATION*?

Driving lessons

Where full payment has been made under an entire (inseparable) contract, and the payee later terminates the contract, there should be restitution of benefits paid to the payee.

Facts: A driving school had undertaken, in exchange for a single payment of FF7,100, to give Renard's sons sufficient lessons to enable them to pass their driving tests. It had later refused to go on. At first instance, Renard was refused restitution of moneys paid to the school.

Held: The judgment was set aside on appeal, and the case remitted to the cour d'appel at Amiens for adjudication.

Judgment: THE COURT: *On the second branch of the sole appeal ground*:—Under Articles 1183 and 1184 of the Civil Code, in contracts providing for performance by instalments, termination for partial non-performance affects the whole of the contract or certain of its instalments only depending on whether the parties intended to be bound by an inseparable contract or a series of contracts.
—Whereas on acquiring the business and taking over contracts entered into with existing customers, the Centre de Formation Routière Hubert (Hubert) refused to continue, unrestrictedly and until complete success in the obtaining of a driving licence, the theoretical and practical training of Daniel and Michel Renard on whose behalf their father had paid an agreed single payment of FF 7,100;
—Whereas the judgment appealed against declared the two contracts in question to be nullified and held the amount of loss suffered by Mr Renard on account of partial non-performance to be

[302] Ghestin, Jamin and Billiau, para. 509.
[303] Gaz.Pal. 1987.II.20860, annotated by Goubeaux.

FF 2,000; as the judgment appealed against which found that "the contracts at issue in the event of failure of the driving test provided for additional free training until it was successfully passed", nevertheless refused to award Mr Renard full restitution in respect of the amount of FF 7,100 actually paid;
—Whereas by so holding, even though it is clear from those very findings that the parties intended to be bound by an inseparable contract, the court of appeal infringed the abovementioned legislative provisions.

On those grounds and without there being any need to give a decision on the first limb of the plea the Cour de cassation quashes and sets aside the judgments given on 21 February 1985 between the parties by the Douai cour d'appel and refers the matter for adjudication to the Amiens Court of Appeal.

Observations (G. Goubeaux): Does this represent satisfactory resolution of a question which has long been discussed, namely the scope of termination of contracts providing for successive performance or, as the Cour de cassation prefers to put it, providing for performance by instalments? . . . It is often taught, with some simplification justified by pedagogical concerns, that although termination of synallagmatic contracts providing for immediate performance operates retroactively, the same sanction imposed on the defaulting parties affects contracts providing for successive performance only in regard to the future, nullification *ab initio* being converted into repudiation . . . But that doctrine has always been challenged by another tendency to apply more widely the device of retroactive nullification of the contract . . .

Yet in this case the Cour de cassation has established the criterion enabling room to be given to each of the two doctrines: "in contracts providing for performance by instalments, termination for partial non-performance affects the whole of the contract or certain of its instalments only depending on whether the parties intended to be bound by an inseparable contract or a series of contracts"
. . . .

There is every reason to be happy with a solution which promises to reduce divergencies and hesitations especially since it is an attractive solution, but will the firmness of the principle be sufficient? One cannot help feeling a certain scepticism when one envisages the application of the criterion. Above all, over and above the formulation of the solution, it is the practical consequences of the doctrine which are in fact questionable.

I. If the contract is performed by successive instalments, termination will not affect instalments already performed, that is to say past performance cannot be reopened: termination has effect only in regard to instalments not yet performed, in the manner of repudiation. Thus, in the case which is always cited as by way of illustration of a lease or a contract of employment properly performed for a time then terminated as a result of default by one of the parties, it is only from the date of such default that the contract will be nullified (in that connection *Cass. civ. 3e, 28 January 1975: Bull. civ. III.33*). To that extent traditional doctrine is thus confirmed, and also clarified.

It is to be noted that the Cour de cassation does not base that solution on the impossibility of going back in time and of unravelling completed acts . . .

. . . [T]ermination necessarily applies to the whole of the contract where the parties intended to be bound by an inseparable contract. The nullification of the contract in that case is total and operates retroactively. Whether it is a contract providing for successive performance and there has been part performance does not alter the situation; where the overall contract forms a single block it is maintained in force or wholly disappears with no possible half-measure.
. . .

III. From a practical point of view, if one contemplates the resulting restitution, the contradistinction between total termination of an inseparable contract and partial termination of a partially performed agreement becomes obvious. Thus, in the case here under discussion, the client of the driving instructor had paid the lump sum of 7,100 francs for the purpose of receiving driving lessons until the driver's licence had been obtained. If the view had been taken that termination should not call in question acts already giving effect to the agreement and should affect only future performance under it, the operator of the driving school would have retained a portion of the sum paid by the client corresponding to services already rendered, and would have been liable only to return the remaining amount. According to the courts trying the case on its merits, the sum to have been repaid would have been 2,000 francs. However, since it is an inseparable contract, a declaration of termination must be made in respect of the whole of the agreement and consequently the driving school must return the whole amount paid to it, namely 7,100 francs.

. . .

This solution is excessively severe. If the consequence of the inseparability of the contract were to be not only to nullify with retroactive effect the whole of the agreement but also that acts of performance under the contract were to be disregarded, the rigour of that judicial logic would give rise to cases of injustice.

In the case under discussion, it is perfectly true that the client of the driving school did not obtain the result bargained for on payment of the lump sum. None the less, driving lessons were given and, unless the pupil was exceptionally inept, they will have had some effect. When after termination of the contract the pupil applies to another driving school a smaller number of lessons will be sufficient to prepare him to pass the driving test. The result originally contemplated will be attained and it will cost the client a sum which is likely to be in the vicinity of 2,000 francs.

. . .

The appropriate solution is very simple and is neither new nor original. It is simply a case of applying Articles 1183 and 1184 of the Civil Code but of applying them to their fullest extent and not stopping half-way. Since under Article 1184 a judicial declaration of termination operates in the same way as a termination clause, its effect should be in the words of Article 1183 to "to restore matters to the situation which would have existed if there had been no contract." Accordingly, restitution must be afforded in respect of performance already effected—on a reciprocal basis. Reimbursement in full of the lump sum paid by the client of the driving school or the amount paid by the contracting partner of the defaulting publisher will not suffice. Regard must also be had to part performance by the other party. Certainly there cannot be restitution in kind but the value thereof may be assessed and an appropriate pecuniary award made.

Such assessment will be delicate but by no means impossible. . . . Since the purpose of restitution is to avoid unjust enrichment, the correct approach, it seems, is to apply by analogy the methodology of the *rem in verso* action and to take whichever of the two following amounts is less, the cost incurred by the party effecting part performance and the calculation of the benefit to the person receiving such consideration. . .

Notes

(1) English courts have also on occasion found that a contract was entire and the party who has partly performed thus entitled to no payment as a way of (over?) compensating the plaintiff.[304]

(2) In German law the driving lessons contract is either (1) one of service, in which case the remedy is *Kündigung*, with effect ex tunc (resiliation); or (2) one for services, in which case *Wandlung* (= *Rücktritt*) is available. In the latter case however the BGB expressly provides for the type of solution canvassed by M. Golbeaux—see below § 346 second sentence.

[304] See *Vigers* v. *Cook* [1919] 2 KB 475.

(2) Germany

German law in this area is not perhaps as clear it might be.[305] This is because a special restitution regime is established in §§ 346ff BGB for agreed rights of *Rücktritt*, although in the vast majority of cases the right will arise by operation of law. Furthermore, this special regime may yield in some instances to the general provisions on unjustified enrichment contained in §§ 812ff BGB.

BGB **6.G.104.**

§ 346: If in a contract one party has reserved to himself the right of *Rücktritt*, and if *Rücktritt* takes place, the parties are obliged to return to each other whatever they received. For services rendered and for allowing the use of a thing the value shall be made good, or if, in the contract a counter performance in money is stipulated for, this shall be paid.

§ 347: The claim to compensation for deterioration, destruction or impossibility of delivery arising from any other cause is determined, in the event of *Rücktritt*, and after receipt of whatever was handed over, according to the provisions which govern the relationship between an owner and a possessor after the date of commencement of an action on a claim for ownership. The same applies to the claim for delivery, compensation for emoluments and to the claim for compensation of disbursements. A sum of money bears interest from the time of its receipt.

§ 348: The obligations of the parties resulting from *Rücktritt* shall be fulfilled contemporaneously. The provisions of §§ 320, 322 apply *mutatis mutandis*.

§ 349: *Rücktritt* is effected by declaration to the other party.

Notes

(1) Under § 327 sentence 1 BGB the restitution regime governing agreed rights to *Rücktritt* that is laid down in §§ 346–356 BGB also applies to rights to *Rücktritt* provided by law (especially §§ 325, 326 BGB).

(2) The general rules on *Rücktritt* also apply to the remedy of *Wandlung* (cancellation) of a contract of sale (§ 467 BGB) or a contract of work (§ 634 IV BGB). By way of exception to this, § 349 BGB is displaced by § 465 BGB, whereby the consent of the seller/contractor to *Wandlung* is required.

(3) A declaration of *Rücktritt* imposes synallagmatic duties on the parties as creditor and debtor to a relationship governed by the law of obligations (§ 348 BGB). It has no direct effect on the property rights of the parties themselves or of third parties. Only when the obligations of both parties to make restoration are performed will property pass back.[306]

(4) The obligations of the possessor to compensate the owner for the destruction or diminution in value of the relevant item or generally where restoration is impossible, referred to in § 347 BGB, are enumerated in §§ 987ff. BGB. As well as a requirement to pay damages (§ 989 BGB) they also include obligations to account for profits made on the item (§ 987 I BGB) and to pay such amount as would have been made on the item but for

[305] See Emmerich, op. cit., at 127.
[306] See *Münchener Kommentar* under § 346 BGB, para. 36.

the fault of the party in possession (§ 987 II BGB). However, the party in possession may recover from the owner such expenditure as he was required to make to preserve the item (§ 994 BGB).

(5) Under §§ 347, 989 BGB a party who received performance before the contract was terminated will be obliged to make restitution even though he no longer retains the benefit of that performance.

However, there is an exception to the general rule set out above where restitution is sought from a person who is not at fault:

BGB   **6.G.105.**

§ 327: ... If the *Rücktritt* occurs because of circumstances for which the other party is not responsible, he is only liable in accordance with the provisions concerning restitution in cases of unjustified enrichment.

Notes

(1) The effect of the second sentence of § 327 BGB is to impose a less severe requirement upon a party who was not responsible for the circumstances giving rise to the *Rücktritt*. This is because such a party will be subjected to § 818 III BGB, under which the obligation to make restitution or to restore the value is excluded in sofar as the recipient is no longer benefited. Compare the position under § 346 BGB, note 4 above. The phrase "party not responsible" under § 327 is held to include the innocent party who declared *Rücktritt* after a default by the other party.[307]

(2) The party entitled to declare *Rücktritt* benefits from a lighter restitutionary burden (§ 812ff BGB) only up to the point where he becomes aware that he may make such a declaration. Thereafter he is subject to the stricter regime (§§ 347, 989 BGB).

(3) Although liability for defective goods is not dependent on fault, and therefore the seller is not responsible as such, it is generally held that, § 327 sentence 2 BGB also applies to *Wandlung* in such cases.[308]

(4) There is uncertainty about who the "other party" referred to in BGB § 327 sentence 2 is. The literal meaning of the words indicates that the "other party" is the party to whom the declaration of *Rücktritt* is addressed. This also seems to have been the intention of the drafters of the BGB.[309] But most cases of *Rücktritt* by operation of law arise under BGB §§ 325, 326, where by definition the "other party" is the one responsible for the circumstances (impossibility or delay) which gave rise to the right to terminate. Indeed, only one provision of the Code provides for a right of *Rücktritt* by operation of law without the other party being responsible for the relevant circumstances: BGB § 636 I. (This allows termination in cases of delay for which a provider of services is not responsible.) Many commentators and the preponderance of the case law, however, view this as too restrictive an application of BGB § 327 sentence 2, positioned as it is in the general part of the law of obligations. Instead the provision should apply to limit the obligation of either party to make restitution in accordance with BGB § 818 III, as long as they are not

---

[307] BGHZ 53.144 (148–149).
[308] OLG Köln, 13 January 1970 OLGZ 70.454.
[309] See *Palandt* under § 327, para. 2f; also Larenz, *SAT*, para. 26 I b.

responsible for the circumstances giving rise to a right of *Rücktritt*—so that the party who has declared *Rücktritt* is normally treated in a more favourable manner.

(3) England

English law is much less favourable to the party seeking restitution. Termination of the contract, being prospective only, does not re-vest property transferred in the transferor. An unpaid seller of goods can repossess them only if he has made specific provision in the agreement to that effect, typically by reserving title to the goods sold. If he has done this, it will give him the right to repossess goods from the buyer if the buyer is insolvent. Even then a sub-purchaser who has bought and paid for the goods without knowing of the seller's rights will get good title to them (Sale of Goods Act 1979, section 25). If the seller has not reserved title his only remedy is to sue for the price—and if the buyer is insolvent the seller will probably get little or nothing. Even as between the original parties, English law is much more restrictive on the use of restitution. It is necessary to distinguish between (a) the aggrieved party and the party in breach and (b) cases in which the benefit transferred was money and cases in which it was property or services which were performed.

(a) The position of the aggrieved party in English law

(i) Where money has been paid. English law allows recovery by the aggrieved party only where there has been "a total failure of consideration", in the sense that the innocent party has received no part of what he contracted for: see the *Fibrosa* case.[310] (The courts are somewhat flexible in their application of this: thus in *Ebrahim Dawood Ltd* v. *Heath (Est 1927) Ltd*[311] a buyer of steel sheets who had justifiably rejected part of a consignment of steel sheets was allowed to recover a proportionate part of the price, which was agreed at so much per ton.)

(ii) Where goods have been provided or services rendered. If the claiming party has completed its performance, or a severable part of it, the only remedy in English law is an action for the agreed price. In the situation of partial performance before the contract was terminated for breach, the aggrieved party may, as an alternative to claiming damages, claim a *quantum meruit*—i.e. recover a reasonable sum for the work done: see for example *Planché* v. *Colburn*.[312]

(b) The position of the party in breach

(i) Money paid. The party in breach may recover money paid for which he has received nothing in return, unless (a), the contract provides otherwise, for example by stating that the money was paid as a deposit;[313] or (b) broadly speaking, the money was a payment for work which has been done by the other party.[314]

---

[310] [1943] AC 32 HL.
[311] [1961] 2 Lloyd's Rep. 512.
[312] (1831) 8 Bing. 14.
[313] On which see further *infra* at 873 ff.
[314] See *Hyundai Heavy Industries Co Ltd.* v. *Papadopoulos* [1980] 2 All ER 29; Beatson (1981) 97 LQR 389.

(ii) Services rendered. If the party who rendered the service, but who failed to perform the contract properly in some way, has substantially performed the contract,[315] there will of course be no right to terminate: the contract has been performed. But what if the party has performed only part of an entire obligation? The contract price will not be payable; and it has been held that the other party need not pay anything for benefits he received, unless he could have returned them but decided not to.

Court of Appeal **6.E.106.**
Sumpter v. *Hedges*[316]

NO PAYMENT FOR PARTIAL PERFORMANCE OF ENTIRE OBLIGATION

Partially completed building

A builder employed to construct a house for a lump sum and who completes only part of the work is not entitled either to the contract price or to restitution of the value of the work done. The owner must pay for loose materials left behind by the builder and subsequently used by the owner.

Facts: The plaintiff had contracted to do building works for a lump sum of £565. After doing some of the work he ran out of money and abandoned the job, leaving behind some materials which the owner later used to finish the works. The plaintiff claimed the value of the materials and of the work done.

Held: The trial judge allowed the claim for the reasonable value of the materials but awarded nothing in respect of the work done. An appeal failed.

Judgment: COLLINS LJ. . . . I think the case is really concluded by the finding of the learned judge to the effect that the plaintiff had abandoned the contract. If the plaintiff had merely broken his contract in some way so as not give the defendant the right to treat him as having abandoned the contract, and the defendant had then proceeded to finish the work himself, the plaintiff might perhaps have been entitled to sue on a quantum meruit on the ground that the defendant had taken the benefit of the work done. But that is not the present case. There are cases in which, though the plaintiff has abandoned the performance of a contract, it is possible for him to raise the inference of a new contract to pay for the work done on a quantum meruit from the defendant's having taken the benefit of that work, but, in order that that may be done, the circumstances must be such as to give an option to the defendant to take or not to take the benefit of the work done. It is only where the circumstances are such as to give that option that there is any evidence on which to ground the inference of a new contract. Where, as in the case of work done on land, the circumstances are such as to give the defendant no option whether he will take the benefit of the work or not, then one must look to other facts than the mere taking the benefit of the work in order to ground the inference of a new contract. In this case I see no other facts on which such an inference can be founded. The mere fact that a defendant is in possession of what he cannot help keeping, or even has done work upon it, affords no ground for such an inference. He is not bound to keep unfinished a building which in an incomplete state would be a nuisance on his land. I am therefore of opinion that the plaintiff was not entitled to recover for the work which he had done.

[A L SMITH and CHITTY LJJ delivered concurring judgments.]

---

[315] See *supra* at 733.
[316] [1898] 1 QB 673.

Notes

(1) It may be argued that this case was wrongly decided, in that it seems to assume that the plaintiff can have restitution only if there was some agreement by the defendant to pay for what he had received. Whatever the strength of this argument, *Sumpter* v. *Hedges* remains good law and a proposal to change it to allow restitution has been rejected. In 1983 the Law Commission, in its Report No. 121, *Pecuniary Restitution for Breach of Contract*, recommended that the rule in *Sumpter* v. *Hedges* be reversed, so that if after taking into account any losses suffered by the owner the work done left the owner with a net benefit, the builder should be entitled to a sum by way restitution of that benefit. But one of the Commissioners dissented, pointing out that the present rule has a great advantage to the householder, who can say to the builder, "Unless you come back and finish the job, I shan't pay you a penny". The majority's recommendation was not accepted.

(2) In German law the remedy of *Wandlung* is rarely sought in the case of building contracts. This is primarily because the standard terms and conditions for building contracts (VOB/B) simply do not mention the remedy. Should it be invoked the returned price would be adjusted to reflect the value to the creditor of the work already done.[317] Under *Minderung* the price payable would be reduced by an amount proportionate with the diminution in value. However, § 13 Nr. 6 VOB/B seems to allow *Minderung* only in cases where a cure or replacement performance would be impossible or disproportionately expensive (by contrast in other work contracts the creditor can set a *Nachfrist* and thereafter go over from a right to cure to *Minderung/Wandlung*). Subject to what standard terms in England say, the German builder would thus seem to be in a much more favourable position, being able to cure as a matter of course, and even if not being entitled to something like a quantum meruit.

(3) Compare the result in the French "driving lessons" case.[318] What is the reason for denying relief to the party who has broken the contract?

6.4.9. LOSS OF RIGHT TO TERMINATE

This section will deal with the various ways in which the right to terminate may be lost: for example, waiver; delay in termination; and impossibility of restitution.

(1) Affirmation

Principles of European Contract Law **6.PECL.107.**

Article 9:303: *Notice of Termination*
(1) A party's right to terminate the contract is to be exercised by notice to the other party.
(2) The aggrieved party loses its right to terminate the contract unless it gives notice within a reasonable time after it has or ought to have become aware of the non-performance. . . .

---

[317] See *Münchener Kommentar*, under § 634 BGB, paras. 23–24.
[318] *Supra* at 798.

A party who knows that the other's non-performance gives him the right to terminate, but announces that he will not exercise that right, may lose the right to terminate.

In German law the innocent party may renounce his right to terminate, either explicitly or implicitly, for example by accepting late performance. It appears that the innocent party must have known that there had been non-performance.[319] In French law the right to *résolution* may be renounced, and it may be that the court would as a matter of discretion refuse *résolution* to a party who had appeared to waive his right.[320]

In English law, a party who knows he has a right to terminate and announces that he will not exercise it will be bound by the so-called doctrine of "election". In addition, a party who gives the appearance of affirming the contract may be bound by the doctrine of estoppel[321] if the other party acts on the apparent affirmation, even if the first party did not know he had a right to terminate: see *The Kanchenjunga*.[322]

(2) Lapse of Time

What if a party does not try to terminate the contract for a considerable time after the other party has purportedly performed it, simply because the first party did not yet know that there was anything wrong? In none of the systems does a simple lapse of time prevent termination. However, in all three systems there are special rules in sale of goods cases which require a buyer who has received defective goods to exercise any right to terminate the contract within a short period—or lose the right to terminate.

Sale of Goods Act 1979   **6.E.108.**

(as amended by Sale and Supply of Goods Act 1994, ss.2 and 3)

Section 34:   Unless otherwise agreed, when the seller tenders delivery of goods to the buyer, he is bound on request to afford the buyer a reasonable opportunity of examining the goods for the purpose of ascertaining whether they are in conformity with the contract and, in the case of a contract for sale by sample, of comparing the bulk with the sample.

Section 35:   . . .

(2) Where goods are delivered to the buyer, and he has not previously examined them, he is not deemed to have accepted them . . . until he has had a reasonable opportunity of examining them for the purpose—

(a) of ascertaining whether they are in conformity with the contract, and

(b) in the case of a contract for sale by sample, of comparing the bulk with the sample.

. . .

(4) The buyer is also deemed to have accepted the goods when after a lapse of a reasonable time he retains the goods without intimating to the seller that he has rejected them.

Notes

(1) In English law the buyer's right to reject is lost after the expiry of a reasonable time. It has been held that this does not mean a reasonable time in which to discover the specific

---

[319] Treitel, *Remedies* at 397–400, para. 290.
[320] *Ibid.*
[321] See *supra* at 17.
[322] [1990] 1 Lloyd's Rep 391, 399.

defect but simply a reasonable time to check the goods for apparent defects—and this may be quite short. In *Bernstein* v. *Pamson Motors (Golders Green) Ltd.*[323] the engine of a new car had seized up after only 140 miles. It was held that the car was not merchantable, but that as the buyer had had the car for nearly a month, a reasonable time had elapsed under section 35 and he could no longer reject it. It made no difference that the defect could not have been discovered earlier or that for much of the month the buyer had been ill and unable to drive the car. Rougier J said:[324]

[W]hat is a reasonable time in the circumstances? And here the 1979 Act ceases to be helpful. By s. 59 "a reasonable time" is defined as a question of fact, no more, as if it could be anything else.

The submission made on behalf of the defendants is that in the context of the sale of [a] new motor car a reasonable time must entail a reasonable time to inspect and try out the car *generally* rather than with an eye to any specific defect, and that to project the period further would be artificial and contrary to the general legal proposition that there should, whenever possible, be finality in commercial transactions. At first I regret to say this proposition got a hostile reception on the ground that a mere 140-odd miles, and some three weeks, part of which were occupied by illness, were not nearly enough to afford the plaintiff any opportunity of discovering this wholly latent defect.

However . . . [i]n my judgment, the nature of the particular defect, discovered ex post facto, and the speed with which it might have been discovered, are irrelevant to the concept of reasonable time in s. 35 as drafted. That section seems to me to be directed solely to what is a reasonable practical interval in commercial terms between a buyer receiving the goods and his ability to send them back, taking into consideration from his point of view the nature of the goods and their function, and from the point of view of the seller the commercial desirability of being able to close his ledger reasonably soon after the transaction is complete. The complexity of the intended function of the goods is clearly of prime consideration here. What is a reasonable time in relation to a bicycle would hardly suffice for a nuclear submarine.

But it is only the right to reject the goods (and thus to terminate the contract) which is lost. The buyer has the full normal limitation period (six years from the breach) in which to claim damages.

(2) In contrast a French buyer can claim cancellation on the basis of the *garantie des vices cachés* despite considerable use of the goods. The French buyer must bring any action within *un bref délai*—and failure to do this bars any remedy, not just redhibition; but the *délai* starts not from the date of sale or of delivery of the goods but from that date at which the buyer either discovered or (the jurisprudence in uncertain on this point) the date at which with reasonable diligence he could have discovered the defect.[325] The *garantie* period may be agreed; otherwise it will last for the normal lifetime of the goods.[326]

BGB 6.G.109.

§ 466: If the purchaser asserts against the seller a defect of quality, the seller may offer cancellation and require him to declare with a fixed reasonable period whether he demands cancellation

[323] [1987] 2 All ER 220.
[324] At 230.
[325] Ghestin and Desché, para. 737 ff.
[326] *Ibid.*, para. 741.

(*Wandlung*). In such a case cancellation may be demanded only before the expiration of the period.

§ 477: (1) The claim for cancellation or reduction on account of the absence of a promised quality is barred by prescription, unless the seller has fraudulently concealed the defect, in the case of moveables, after six months after delivery; in the case of land, after one year after the transfer. The prescription period may be extended by contract.

. . .

HGB

§ 377: (1) If the sale is a commercial transaction for both parties, the buyer should examine the goods immediately after their delivery by the seller, to the extent that this is possible in the ordinary course of business, and if a defect is found he should without delay notify the seller. (2) If the buyer fails to give notice, the goods are considered approved unless the defect was not one which was discernible upon examination.

Notes

(1) The rules contained in §§ 465 to 467 BGB and §§ 469 to 475 BGB also apply to cases where cancellation is sought for defects under a contract for work (*Werkvertrag*).

(2) If the seller sets an "unreasonable" period within § 466 BGB, it is effectively replaced by a reasonable period.

The differences between the Common Law and the Civil Law traditions came to a head with the Directive on Sale of Consumer Goods, 1999/44/EC. Articles 3 and 5(1) would extend the buyer's right to claim rescission or replacement to up to two years. This rule, taken literally, might have consequences which, to a common lawyer, seem remarkable. Can it really be intended that the buyer who finds non-conformity in the goods which existed at the time the goods were delivered may demand either the whole price back, or a—presumably new—replacement item, even though he has used the goods for over a year? In England it was argued that this seems unfair to the seller, likely to lead to unnecessary cost when the goods could satisfactorily be repaired, and possibly productive of opportunism by consumers who seize on some small defect as a ground for demanding a new item or their money back. This seems likely to be a particular problem with products in which prices are falling from year to year, such as computers.

In fact the common lawyers' alarm may be partly unfounded. First, if the English buyer still has the right to reject goods under SGA section 35, any use she has had from the goods before she rejects them is simply ignored. Under Civil Law systems it appears that the buyer who has had significant use from the goods before claiming *redhibition* may be liable to pay for the benefit received on a restitutionary basis—for example BGB §§ 467, 347. Recital 15 allows Member States to reduce the reimbursement due to the consumer to take account of the use the consumer has had from the goods. Secondly, Article 3(6) allows Member States to exclude the right to rescind where the defect is "minor".

(3) Impossibility of Restitution

What if a party seeking to terminate has received goods or other property and cannot restore it, or cannot restore it in the same condition, because the property has been destroyed or damaged: will termination be precluded? Broadly speaking, if the destruction or damage was due to the property having an inherent defect and thus not conforming to the contract, the party will still be entitled to terminate. If it was due to some other cause, the position in French law is that destruction or damage of the thing prevents termination.

Code civil **6.F.111.**

Article 1147: (1) If the thing has inherent defects and has perished because of its poor quality, the loss falls on the seller, who must repay the price to the buyer in addition to other damages as set out above.
(2) If the loss occurs by accident the loss falls on the buyer.

In German and English law, the position is more complex. If the destruction or damage was due to the fault of the buyer seeking to terminate, including a failure to look after the object properly, he will lose the right to terminate; but if the damage was due to an accident for which neither party was responsible, the buyer is still able to terminate in German law (§ 350 BGB) and probably in English law.[327]

In German law he will, however, be obliged to pay the value of the thing by way of damages to the seller (§§ 347, 989 BGB).[328]

As was mentioned above,[329] German law in this area is widely considered to be unclear and deficient. Specifically: the fault of one of the parties where the thing to be restored has been destroyed may be relevant to the issue of whether the right to *Rücktritt* has been lost; but fault may have different meanings in the context of the two different types of termination—i.e. agreed or by operation of law.

BGB **6.G.112.**

§ 350: *Rücktritt* is not precluded where the object received by the party entitled to terminate has been destroyed accidentally.

§ 351: The right of *Rücktritt* is barred if the party entitled is to blame for any significant deterioration, destruction, or impossibility of delivery for other reasons of the object received. The destruction of a considerable part is equivalent to the significant deterioration of the object; the fault of another person for whom, according to § 278, the party entitled is responsible, is equivalent to the party's own fault.

§ 352: The right of *Rücktritt* is barred if the party entitled has altered the form of the object received by processing or remodelling it into a thing of another kind.

§ 353: (1) If the party entitled has disposed of the object received or a considerable part of it, or has burdened it with a right in favour of a third party, the right of *Rücktritt* is barred if the conditions of § 351 or § 352 have arisen in the case of the party who has acquired the object because of the disposition.
(2) A disposition which is effected by means of compulsory execution or distraint, or by a trustee in bankruptcy, is equivalent to a disposition by the party entitled.

---

[327] See Guest (gen. ed.), *Benjamin's Sale of Goods*, 4th edn. (London: Sweet & Maxwell, 1997).
[328] See generally Treitel, *Remedies*, para. 285.
[329] *Supra* at 801–802.

Notes

(1) §§ 351ff BGB apply only to exclude the right of the aggrieved party to terminate where he has been at fault in some way in bringing about the mentioned circumstances. The aggrieved party will not lose his right to terminate where the fault of the other party has rendered impossible restitution of the item which he obtained under the contract. Instead the other party will have to pay damages in lieu of the destroyed item under §§ 347, 989 BGB.

(2) The exact meaning of fault in § 351 BGB has caused considerable debate. Where a right to terminate has been agreed the aggrieved party can be expected to treat the subject matter of the contract with a certain level of care. The concept of fault cannot however be that usually implied by § 276 BGB—negligence or deliberate wrongdoing—, since the aggrieved party, until discovering the grounds for a possible *Rücktritt*, will deal with it as his own. He is required, therefore, to exercise the care of a reasonable person in his own affairs.

(3) Where, however, the right to terminate arises by operation of law—for exmple, under §§ 325, 326 BGB—, the aggrieved party has no reason to exercise due care before this point. The requirement of fault seems wholly unsuitable in this context. Commentators have therefore confined it to mean only very unusual use of the item which significantly increases the risk of its destruction.[330]

(4) § 352 BGB excludes *Rücktritt* where the item has been transformed or used up, since this implicitly signals that the aggrieved party has foregone his right to terminate. The rules on *Rücktritt* are generally applicable to *Wandlung* (cancellation in the law of sale); but § 467(1) states that § 352 does not apply to preclude cancellation for defects in goods where the defects first become evident in the process of transformation of the goods.

(5) A party seeking *Rücktritt* is under a duty to obtain the item which was the subject of the contract if he has alienated it in favour of a third party. This applies, however, only where the item has not been culpably destroyed or significantly damaged through the fault of the other party (§ 353 BGB).

(6) Even where the right to *Rücktritt* is precluded by reason of § 350ff BGB, the creditor may still claim damages for non-performance. (He must not however have finally and conclusively declared in favour of *Rücktritt*.)

Further Reading on Termination

—V. Emmerich, *Das Recht der Leistungsstörungen*, 3rd edn. (München: Beck, 1991);

—K. Larenz, *Lehrbuch des Schuldrechts*, Vol. II, part I: *Besonderer Teil*, 13th edn. (München: Beck, 1986);

—K. Larenz, *Schuldrecht—Allgemeiner Teil*, 14th edn. (München: Beck, 1987);

—K. Rebmann and F. Säcker (eds.), *Münchener Kommentar zum Bürgerlichen Gesetzbuch*, 4th edn. (München: Beck, 2000);

—P. Schlechtriem, "Rechtsvereinheitlichung in Europa und Schuldrechtsreform in Deutschland" ZeuPR 1993.217;

[330] Cf. Larenz, *SAT* para. 26 b 1.

—*J. von Staudingers Kommentar zum Bürgerlichen Gesetzbuch mit Einführungsgesetz und Nebengesetzen* (various editors), 13th edn. (Berlin: Sellier, de Gruyter, 1995);
—G. Treitel, *Remedies for Breach of Contract* (Oxford: Clarendon, 1988), chapter XI;
—S. Whittaker, "How Does French Law Deal with Anticipatory Breaches of Contract?" (1996) 45 ICLQ 662.

6.5. DAMAGES

Principles of European Contract Law **6.PECL.113.**

Article 9:501: *Right to Damages*
(1) The aggrieved party is entitled to damages for loss caused by the other party's non-performance which is not excused under Article 8:108.
(2) The loss for which damages are recoverable includes:
(a) non-pecuniary loss; and
(b) future loss which is reasonably likely to occur.

Article 9:502: *General Measure of Damages*
The general measure of damages is such sum as will put the aggrieved party as nearly as possible into the position in which it would have been if the contract had been duly performed. Such damages cover the loss which the aggrieved party has suffered and the gain of which it has been deprived.

Article 9:503: *Foreseeability*
The non-performing party is liable only for loss which it foresaw or could reasonably have foreseen at the time of conclusion of the contract as a likely result of its non-performance, unless the non-performance was intentional or grossly negligent.

Article 9:504: *Loss Attributable to Aggrieved Party*
The non-performing party is not liable for loss suffered by the aggrieved party to the extent that the aggrieved party contributed to the non-performance or its effects.

Article 9:505: *Reduction of Loss*
(1) The non-performing party is not liable for loss suffered by the aggrieved party to the extent that the aggrieved party could have reduced the loss by taking reasonable steps.
(2) The aggrieved party is entitled to recover any expenses reasonably incurred in attempting to reduce the loss.

Article 9:506: *Substitute Transaction*
Where the aggrieved party has terminated the contract and has made a substitute transaction within a reasonable time and in a reasonable manner, it may recover the difference between the contract price and the price of the substitute transaction as well as damages for any further loss so far as these are recoverable under this Section.

Article 9:507: *Current Price*
Where the aggrieved party has terminated the contract and has not made a substitute transaction but there is a current price for the performance contracted for, it

may recover the difference between the contract price and the price current at the time the contract is terminated as well as damages for any further loss so far as these are recoverable under this Section.

Article 9:508: *Delay in Payment of Money*

(1) If payment of a sum of money is delayed, the aggrieved party is entitled to interest on that sum from the time when payment is due to the time of payment at the average commercial bank short-term lending rate to prime borrowers prevailing for the contractual currency of payment at the place where payment is due.

(2) The aggrieved party may in addition recover damages for any further loss so far as these are recoverable under this Section.

Article 9:509: *Agreed Payment for Non-performance*

(1) Where the contract provides that a party which fails to perform is to pay a specified sum to the aggrieved party for such non-performance, the aggrieved party shall be awarded that sum irrespective of its actual loss.

(2) However, despite any agreement to the contrary the specified sum may be reduced to a reasonable amount where it is grossly excessive in relation to the loss resulting from the non-performance and the other circumstances.

Article 9:510: *Currency by which Damages to be Measured*

Damages are to be measured by the currency which most appropriately reflects the aggrieved party's loss.

6.5.1. THE BASIC MEASURE OF DAMAGES FOR BREACH OF CONTRACT

Code civil   **6.F.114.**

Article 1149: The damages due to the creditor are, in general, the loss he has suffered and the gain of which he has been deprived, subject to the exceptions and modifications below.

Note

The distinction between *damnum emergens* and *lucrum cessans* dates from Roman law. If the creditor does not receive the goods promised and has to pay a higher price to buy substitute goods, this is *damnum emergens*, whereas if the creditor is prevented from making a profitable resale this is *lucrum cessans*. From this principle of full compensation (*réparation integrale*) the Code civil draws a number of rules on the assessment of damages, but it has been remarked that "what principally strikes the English lawyer is that the French analysis is relatively underdeveloped".[331] For example, the distinction between expectation (positive interest) and reliance (negative interest) damages known to both English and German law seems not to be recognized. One possible explanation for the lack of detailed rules is that the assessment of damages is within the full discretion of the court of first instance, though it has been pointed out that this is not a complete explanation as the Cour de cassation in principle controls the question of the kinds of loss for which compensation may be paid.[332]

[331] Nicholas, at 225.
[332] *Ibid.*

BGB **6.G.115.**

§ 249: A person who is obliged to make compensation shall restore the situation which would have existed if the circumstance rendering him liable to make compensation had not occurred. If the compensation is required to be made for injury to a person or damage to a thing, the creditor may demand, instead of restitution in kind, the sum of money necessary for such restitution.

§ 250: The creditor may fix a reasonable period for the restitution by the person liable to compensate with a declaration that he will refuse to accept restitution after the expiration of the period. After the expiration of the period the creditor may demand the compensation in money if the restitution is not effected in due time; the claim for restitution is barred.

§ 251: (1) insofar as restitution in kind is impossible or is insufficient to compensate the creditor, the person liable shall compensate him in money.
(2) The person liable may compensate the creditor in money if restitution in kind is only possible through disproportionate outlays.

§ 252: The compensation shall also include lost profits. Profit is deemed to have been lost which could probably have been expected in the ordinary course of events, or according to the special circumstances, especially in the light of the preparations and arrangements made.

Notes

(1) The German law on damages, as we saw earlier,[333] adopts the distinction between the positive interest and the negative interest. In cases of breach of contract the creditor may claim the positive interest. In contrast, under § 122 BGB (compensation where party avoids a contract) only negative interest damages are recoverable. It is provided that these may not exceed the value to the other party if the contract had been valid, i.e. may not exceed the positive interest.

(2) German law also recognizes the distinction between "abstract" assessments of damages, where the damages are measured by an abstract standard such as the market value of what the creditor would have received, and "concrete" assessment by reference to the actual loss, for example the actual cost of obtaining substitute goods.[334] In certain circumstances the German Commercial Code (HGB) expressly provides for the abstract measure of damages:

HGB **6.G.116.**

§ 430: If a carrier is obliged by a contract of carriage to make compensation for the total or partial loss of the item carried, he must pay the general market value or, in the absence of this, the general value which an item of the same type and character has in the place where delivery was to be made; the amount of customs and other costs spared as a result of the loss of the item is to be deducted from this.

(3) In German law it has sometimes been said that damages may be calculated according to the "exchange (or "surrogation") theory" and sometimes according to the "difference theory":

---

[333] In sections **2.2** on Pre-contractual liability, *supra* at 259 ff. and **3.2** on Validity, *supra* at 341 ff.
[334] See *infra* at 844 ff.

Schlechtriem[335] **6.G.117.**

There are two possible means of calculating the amount of compensation: the creditor can demand the whole value of the debtor's performance including all consequential loss and render his own performance in return. Damages are thus available for the full value of the debtor's performance, but in return for the whole of the (still possible) counter-performance of the creditor and are calculated accordingly ("surrogation" or "exchange" theory). The creditor can also, however, deduct the value of his performance from the amount of damages, but only if he has not yet rendered performance and wishes to retain it (the so-called-limited-"difference" theory). Where he owes a sum of money, for example the price of purchase, the same result is reached through setting off this amount against the (total) amount of damages, leaving only the difference between the loss due to non-performance and the purchase price.

The "difference" theory, which allows the creditor to retain his own performance and to take it into account in calculating his damages, is based essentially on a combination of withdrawal from the contract and damages for non-performance. It is nevertheless allowed and regularly used. The creditor may only demand the whole amount of damages under the "surrogation" theory if for his part he has already performed (and he does not and cannot take back his performance) or if he has a particular interest in rendering his own performance.

Court of Exchequer **6.E.118.**
Robinson v. *Harman*[336]

EXPECTATION MEASURE OF DAMAGES

[The facts and decision in this case need not be set out.]
PARKE B: (. . .) *The rule of the common law is, that where a party sustains a loss by reason of a breach of contract, he is, so far as money can do it, to be placed in the same situation, with respect to damages, as if the contract had been performed (. . .).*

Notes
(1) English law did not until recently distinguish openly between the positive and negative interests, but did in practice apply them. Thus in breach of contract cases, the plaintiff is to be put into the position he would have been in had the contract been performed, whereas in cases where liability is tortious, such as fraud, he is to be put back to the position he was in before the tort was committed.[337] However, the American author Fuller in his famous article with Perdue[338] adopted the parallel distinction between the expectation interest, the reliance interest, and the restitution interest and this terminology has now found its way, via the Canadian courts, into English case law: for example *C & P Haulage* v. *Middleton*.[339]

(2) Normally the plaintiff will be compensated for all three interests. The plaintiff will be given damages representing the value of what he would have received if the contract had been performed, less any sums already paid and any savings made as a result of the

---

[335] Schlechtriem, *SAT*, paras. 388–399.
[336] (1848) 1 Exch. 850, 855.
[337] E.g. *East* v. *Maurer* [1991] 2 All ER 733, noted *supra* at 342.
[338] 46 Yale LJ 52 (1936).
[339] [1983] 3 All ER 94.

breach. Thus suppose a manufacturer agrees to deliver a custom-built machine and accessories to a buyer for a price of £1,000. In accordance with the contract the manufacturer delivers some accessories worth £200 to the buyer and spends a further £500 in building the machine; meanwhile the buyer makes an advance payment of £250. Before the machine is finished the buyer repudiates the contract. The manufacturer would incur a further £100 in labour costs to finish the machine. The damages will be calculated as follows: from the total £1,000 the manufacturer would have received, one deducts the £250 already paid, the £100 needed to complete the machine (a saving) and also any scrap value of the machine (say £50); thus the seller will get £1,000 – £250 – £100 – £50 = £600. It will be seen that this sum, together with the money already paid and the scrap value of the machine (which is still in the seller's hands), in effect gives the seller not only the value of the accessories delivered (£200, the restitution interest) plus the wasted expenditure (£500, the reliance interest) but also the profit it should have made (£200, the expectation interest).[340]

(3) On occasion the plaintiff will claim only the reliance loss, because, for example, the loss of profit is hard to prove. For example in *Anglia TV* v. *Reed*,[341] the plaintiff had, even before the contract, incurred expenses in assembling a crew to make a film. The principal actor refused at the last moment to take part and the project was abandoned. The plaintiff was allowed to recover expenses including those incurred before the actor had agreed to take part. On other occasions the court will hold that the plaintiff has failed to prove that he would have made a profit but allows recovery of reliance loss (for example, *McRae* v. *Commonwealth Disposals Commission*[342]). However, the damages are in principle calculated by reference to the plaintiff's expectation; and if the profit he expected would not in fact have covered the reliance expenditure, so that he would have lost money anyway, the extra reliance loss is not recoverable: *C & P Haulage* v. *Middleton*.[343] The court will assume that the plaintiff would have recovered his costs unless the defendant shows otherwise: *CCC Films (London) Ltd* v. *Impact Quadrant Films Ltd*.[344]

Thus in all three systems, where there has been a non-performance for which a debtor is responsible, the creditor may—subject to various limitations to be noted—be able to recover damages; and these will aim to give the creditor what she would have received. There seems to be no practical difference between the "expectation" or "positive interest" formulae of English and German law and the traditional formulation of French Code civil Article 1149. The Principles of European Contract Law place both formulae in a single Article:

Principles of European Contract Law **6.PECL.119.**

Article 9:502: *General Measure of Damages*
    The general measure of damages is such sum as will put the aggrieved party as nearly as possible into the position in which it would have been if the contract had been

---

[340] Cf. *Hydraulic Engineering Co. Ltd.* v. *McHaffie* (1878) 4 QBD 670.
[341] [1971] 3 All ER 690, CA.
[342] (1950) 84 CLR 377, H.Ct.Aus. See *supra* at 388–9.
[343] (1950) 84 CLR 377 (High Ct. of Australia), noted *supra* at 388.
[344] [1984] 3 All ER 298.

duly performed. Such damages cover the loss which the aggrieved party has suffered and the gain of which it has been deprived.

In contrast, the equivalent Article of Unidroit speaks of "full compensation":

Unidroit Principles   **6.INT.120.**

Article 7.4.2: *Full compensation*

(1) The aggrieved party is entitled to full compensation for harm sustained as a result of the non-performance. Such harm includes both any loss which it suffered and any gain of which it was deprived, taking into account any gain to the aggrieved party resulting from its avoidance of cost or harm . . .

6.5.2. THE REQUIREMENT OF NOTICE

Normally the debtor will not become liable in damages until there has been a breach of contract—that is, until he has failed to perform by the date due, or has made it impossible for himself to perform, or he has committed some other breach of contract. (Note that in systems which recognize the doctrine of anticipatory breach or its functional equivalent[345] the debtor who announces in advance that he will not perform or who is clearly going to be unable to do so may become liable for non-performance even before the date set for performance.) However, in some systems, particularly in cases of delay, the debtor's liability for damages may not arise until he has also been given a warning or a demand for performance by the creditor.

Code civil   **6.F.121.**

Article 1146: Damages are only due when the debtor is in delay in fulfilling his obligation, except when the thing the debtor was bound to convey or to do could only be conveyed or done in a certain time which he has allowed to lapse. A clearly worded letter may constitute a *mise en demeure*.

Article 1139: The debtor is put *en demeure* by a *sommation* or by an equivalent act such as a letter in clear terms, or as the result of an agreement to the effect that the debtor will be *en demeure* after a certain time without any further act by the creditor.

Notes

(1) A *sommation* is a formal notice served by a *huissier* (bailiff).

(2) In principle a *mise en demeure* to inform the debtor that the creditor still requires performance is a prerequisite to any remedy except withholding of performance. If, however, the creditor seeks a judicial remedy (*exécution en nature* or *résolution*), commencement of the action will be sufficient. The same will be true of an action for damages but, if the creditor has not served a *mise en demeure* earlier, the damages will run only from the date of commencement of the action.

[345] See *supra* at 777 ff.

(3) The fact that the original contract fixed a time within which the debtor must perform does not amount to an agreement to dispense with a *mise en demeure* within Article 1139 (assuming that performance is still possible). But the parties may agree to dispense with the need for a *mise en demeure*, and the courts have held that this may be implicit.[346]

(4) Where performance is no longer possible—for example, an electricity company failed to supply power to a customer for a period of time now passed[347]—a *mise en demeure* is not required. In such a case the customer will be claiming compensation for the failure to perform (*dommages-intérêts compensatoires*) rather than for delay (*dommages-intérêts moratoires*).

BGB   6.G.122.

§ 284: (1) If after his obligation is due, the debtor does not perform after a warning (*Mahnung*) from the creditor, he is in delay. Bringing an action for performance and service of a judicial order for payment are equivalent to a warning.
(2) If a time is fixed by the calendar for the performance, the debtor is in delay without warning if he does not perform at the time fixed. The same rule applies if a notice is required to precede the performance, and the time is fixed in such a manner that it may be reckoned by the calendar from the time of notice.

§ 286: (1) The debtor shall compensate the creditor for any damage arising from his delay.
(2) If the creditor does not desire the performance because of the delay, he may, by refusing the performance, demand compensation for non-performance. The provisions of §§ 346–356 applicable to the contractual right of rescission (*Rücktritt*) apply *mutatis mutandis*.

§ 326: (1) If, in the case of a mutual contract, one party is in delay in performing, the other party may give him a reasonable period (*Nachfrist*) within which to perform his part with a declaration that he will refuse to accept the performance after the expiration of the period. After the expiration of the period he is entitled to demand compensation for non-performance, or to withdraw from the contract, if the performance has not been made in due time; the claim for performance is barred. If the performance is only partly made before the expiration of the period, the provision of § 325(1), sentence 2, applies *mutatis mutandis*.
(2) If, in consequence of the delay, the performance of the contract is of no use to the other party, such other party has the rights specified in (1) without giving any period.

Notes

(1) In German law also the debtor is put into delay by the creditor serving a warning (*Mahnung*). This need not be in any particular form provided that the debtor is warned that he is expected to perform. The warning is held to be subject to the same rules as an ordinary declaration of will. The most important of these is that it must be communicated to the debtor. No particular form is required, for example the warning could be expressed by the sending of a second demand for payment marked "urgent".

(2) In order to claim damages for non-performance arising out of delay in the performance of a main obligation, the creditor must provide a warning under § 284 BGB. If he wishes to terminate the contract and claim damages for non-performance he must

[346] Paris 28.3.1990, D. 1990.IR.98.
[347] Nicholas, at 239.

also set a period (*Nachfrist*) with a further warning that he will refuse performance after that period (§ 326 BGB). Both warnings may be combined in one declaration, however. Note that a *Nachfrist* is not necessary in cases of impossibility within § 325 BGB.[348]

(3) A warning is not required if the contract fixed a day for performance (*Fixgeschäft*). Nor is it required in cases of impossibility or positive breach, or where it would be pointless (§ 326 BGB), for example, where the debtor has conclusively refused to perform. In principle the parties can provide in the contract that no notice need be given, but this is not permissible as between a business and a consumer in a standard form contract: § 11 Nr.4 AGBG.

English law does not have any requirement of a notice to put the debtor into default—save in exceptional cases in which the debtor cannot know that he is in default until told by the creditor, for example a tenant must notify the landlord if a repair is needed. In the case of delay, damages will run from the date on which the debtor should have performed. This date may be agreed in the contract. If it is not, the debtor must perform within a reasonable time and damages will run from the expiry of that time; the creditor does not need to serve a notice to start the damages running. Notice is sometimes needed before termination is permitted.[349]

6.5.3. RESTRICTIONS ON DAMAGES RECOVERABLE

This sub-section deals with a number of rules which, in each system, limit the damages recoverable, so that the plaintiff may not in fact receive the measure of damages provided for under the general rules set out above.

6.5.3.A. UNFORESEEABLE OR INDIRECT LOSSES

Code civil **6.F.123.**

Article 1150: The debtor is liable in damages only for losses which were foreseen or could have been foreseen at the time the contract was made, provided that his non-performance was not fraudulent.

Article 1151: Even in the case in which non-performance of the agreement resulted from the fraud of the debtor, the damages for losses suffered by the creditor or gains by him prevented are only those which follow immediately and directly from the non-performance of the agreement.

Cass. civ., 22 November 1893[350] **6.F.124.**

LOSS NOT RECOVERABLE IF NOT FORESEEABLE

Machine for peeling artichokes

A party who has failed to perform cannot be ordered to pay compensation for losses which were not

---

[348] See *Münchener Kommentar*, under § 325 BGB, para. 18.
[349] See *supra* at 791.
[350] D.1894.1.358.

envisaged, and could not have been envisaged, at the time the contract was made.

Facts: The defendant railway company delayed in delivering a package containing a machine for peeling artichokes to the plaintiffs, who were consequently unable to use it in preparing vegetables for sale; the plaintiffs
therefore had to employ manual labour and some of the vegetables perished. They claimed damages for losses
of 1,200 FF.

Held: By the court of first instance, that the losses suffered were unforeseeable, and were also not proven in full,
so that only damages of 600FF would be awarded. The Cour de cassation set aside the judgment.

Judgment of the Tribunal de Commerce: whereas Benoit and Laurin commenced proceedings
against Compagnie Paris-Lyon-Méditerranée for an order requiring it to pay them FF 1,200 by way
of damages for the harm suffered by them following the said company's delay in delivering a
machine to be used in their factory; whereas the Company, without denying the delay of eight days
in delivery of the packages despatched on an urgent basis and without denying liability, offers as
compensation for the damage the sum of FF 50, together with transport costs amounting to FF 17;
but whereas the Company seeks to rely on Arts 1150 and 1151 of the Civil Code, contending that
carriers can be held liable only for loss envisaged or envisageable when the contract was concluded,
but never for damages. The harmful consequences suffered by the plaintiffs were not envisaged by
the parties when concluding the contract; since the parties could not have foreseen them, the contract of carriage was concluded outside the scope of those articles; it follows that the loss suffered
by Benoit and Laurin can be redressed only within the limits and scope of Article 1149 of the Civil
Code. Whereas it is not appropriate to assess the damage described by the Company as indirect
damage, but rather, in accordance with the abovementioned article, it is necessary to determine the
loss incurred by the plaintiffs and the profit of which they were deprived; whereas the delayed package, containing a machine for peeling artichokes, should have reached the addressees on 4 June; at
that time, they would have made arrangements to offer for sale a quantity of vegetables, using that
machine; since the machine did not arrive, they were obliged to employ workers; whereas part of
the goods deteriorated and the plaintiffs had to pay compensation of FF 300 to their suppliers; but
it has not been proved that their losses amount to the sum of FF 1,200 and the Court considers that
it must observe the requirements of Article 1149 of the Civil Code, by setting the total damages at
FF 600; accordingly, it orders the Company to pay the sum of FF 600 by way of damages.

APPEAL in cessation by Compagnie des chemins de fer de Paris-Lyon-Méditerranée, alleging
infringement of Articles 97 and 104 of the Commercial Code and 1150 of the Civil Code; misapplication of Article 1149 of the Civil Code, in that the contested judgment ordered the Company to
pay the respondents' damages, even though it was acknowledged that damages were not envisaged
and could not have been when the contract was concluded.

Judgment of the Cour de cassation: THE COURT: *On the first appeal ground*:—Under Article 1150 of
the Civil Code;
—Whereas, as a matter of law, a debtor is required by law, in the event of breach of an obligation,
to pay only the damages which were envisaged or were envisageable at the time when the contract
was concluded;
—Whereas, as a matter of fact, Benoit and Laurin sought from Compagnie des Chemins de Fer de
Paris-Lyon-Méditerranée redress for the loss caused them by the delay in delivery of a machine necessary for their business;
—Whereas, having found "that the harmful consequences suffered by the plaintiffs were not envisaged by the parties when concluding the contract and the parties could not have foreseen them",
the lower court nevertheless ordered the Company to pay the sum at which it set "the *total*" damage suffered;
—Whereas, by giving judgment to that effect, on the ground that "since the parties could not have
foreseen the loss, the contract of carriage was concluded outside the scope of Article 1150 of the

Civil Code", the judgment, formally, infringed that article;

On those grounds, and without its being necessary to adjudicate on the second ground of the appeal; the judgment is set aside . . .

Notes

(1) At one time the rule laid down in Article 1150 was seen as limiting the type of loss which would be recoverable, but not its extent. Now the rule is applied also to the extent.[351] Malaurie and Aynès point out that it acts as a financial limit on the defendant's liability.[352]

(2) The limitation of the debtor's liability to foreseeable losses under Article 1150 will not apply in cases of *dol* or *faute lourde,* nor will any limitation by way of a clause restricting the debtor's liability.[353] However, the debtor will still be liable only for losses which followed "immediately and directly" from the non-performance: Article 1151. The application of this directness test (also and more frequently applied in delict cases) is "elusive".[354] Malaurie and Aynès[355] still quote a passage from Pothier:[356]

If a trader sells me a cow which he knows to be infected with a contagious disease and conceals that defect from me, that concealment constitutes a deceit on his part rendering him liable for the damage suffered by me, not only in respect of the cow itself, which forms the subject-matter of his original obligation, but also with regard to any loss suffered by me in respect of any of my other livestock to which that cow has passed on the contagion—since it is as a result of that trader's deceit that I have suffered all of the damage in question. But is he liable for any other damage suffered by me which constitutes a more remote and less direct consequence of his deceit? For example, if the contagion passed to my cattle by the cow sold to me prevents me from cultivating my land, the damage which I suffer by reason of my land remaining uncultivated appears likewise to be a consequence of the deceit on the part of that trader, who has sold me an infected cow; but it is a more remote consequence than the loss which I have suffered in terms of my infected cattle. Is the trader liable for that damage? And what is the position if, by reason of the loss made by me on my cattle and the damage suffered by me as a result of my inability to cultivate my land, I am prevented from paying my debts, so that my creditors attach my assets and sell them at a totally inadequate price? Is the trader also liable for that damage? . . . The trader is not liable for the damage suffered by me in consequence of the attachment of my assets. That damage is nothing more than a very remote and indirect consequence of his deceit, and the requisite causal nexus does not exist, since, although the loss of my cattle which I have suffered as a result of his wrongful act may have had some influence on the upset in my financial position, that upset may have been caused by other factors . . . The loss which I have suffered as a result of the non-cultivation of my land appears to be a less remote consequence of the trader's deceit, but in my view he cannot be liable for it, or at least not for all of it. That non-cultivation is not a wholly necessary consequence of the loss of my cattle suffered by me as a result of the trader's deceit; despite that loss of cattle, I could avoid such non-cultivation by using other cattle to cultivate the land. . . . Nevertheless, since, by having recourse to that expedient, I would not have made as great a profit from my land as I would have done if I had used my own cattle, the loss of which was caused by the trader's deceit, that factor may be taken into account in the context of the damages for which he is liable.

[351] See Nicholas, at 230–1.
[352] Malaurie and Aynès, para. 839.
[353] E.g. Cass. req. 24 October 1932, D.P.1932.176 annotated by E. P.
[354] Nicholas, at 229.
[355] Malaurie and Aynès, para. 838.
[356] M. Dupin, *Œuvres de R.-J. Pothier* (Bruxelles: de Ode et Wadon, 1881), paras. 166–167.

Court of Exchequer 6.E.125.
Hadley v. *Baxendale*[357]

NATURAL AND PROBABLE CONSEQUENCES OF THE BREACH

The mill shaft

Where two parties have made a contract, which one of them has broken, the damages which the other party ought to receive in respect of such breach of contract should be such as may fairly and reasonably be considered either as arising naturally i.e. according to the usual course of things from such a breach of contract itself, or such as may reasonably be supposed to have been in the contemplation of both parties, at the time they had made the contract, as the probable result of the breach of it.

Facts: The plaintiffs, the owners of a flour mill, sent a broken iron shaft to an office of the defendants, who were common carriers, to be conveyed by them, and the defendant's clerk, who attended at the office, was told [that the mill was stopped—see note (1) below] that the shaft must be delivered immediately, and that a special entry if necessary, must be made to hasten delivery. The delivery of the broken shaft to the consignee, to whom it had been sent by the plaintiffs as a pattern by which to make a new shaft, was delayed by an unreasonable time; in consequence of which the plaintiff did not receive the new shaft for some days after the time it ought to have received it and it was consequently unable to work its mill for want of the new shaft, and thereby incurred a loss of profits.

Held: that, under the circumstances, such loss could not be recovered in an action against the defendants as common carriers.

Judgment: ALDERSON B: We think that there ought to be a new trial in this case; but in doing so we deem it to be expedient and necessary to state explicitly the rule which the Judge, at the next trial, ought, in our opinion to direct the jury to be governed by when they estimate the next damages ...

Now we think the proper rule in such a case as the present is this:—Where two parties have made a contract where one of them has broken, the damages that the other party ought to receive in the respect of such a breach of contract should be such as may fairly and reasonably be considered either arising naturally, i.e. according to the usual course of things, from such breach of contract itself or such as may reasonably be supposed to have been in contemplation of the both parties, at the time that they made the contract, as the probable result of the breach of it. Now, if the special circumstances under which the contract was actually made were communicated by the plaintiffs to the defendants, and thus known to both parties, the damages resulting from the breach of such a contract, which they would reasonably contemplate, would be the amount of injury which would ordinarily follow from a breach of contract under these special circumstances so known and communicated. But, on the other hand, if these special circumstances were wholly unknown to the party breaking the contract, he, at the most could only be supposed to have had in his contemplation the amount of injury which would arise generally, and in great multitude of cases not affected by any special circumstances, from such a breach of contract. For, had the special circumstances been known, the parties may have specially provided for the breach of contract by special terms as to the damage in that case; and of this advantage it would be very unjust to deprive them. Now the above principles are those by which we think the jury ought to be guided in estimating the damages arising out of any breach of contract.

Now, in the present case, if we are to apply the above principles laid down, we find that the only circumstances here communicated by the plaintiffs to the defendants at the time of the contract was made, were, that the article to be carried was the shaft of a mill, and that the plaintiffs were millers

[357] (1854) 9 Exch. 341.

of that mill. But how do these circumstances shew reasonably that the profits of the mill must be stopped by an unreasonable delay in the delivery of the broken shaft by the carrier to the third person? Suppose the plaintiffs had another shaft in their possession put up or putting up at the time, and that they only wished to send back the broken shaft to the engineer who made it; it is clear that this would be quite consistent with the above circumstances, and yet the unreasonable delay in the delivery would have no effect upon the intermediate profits of the mill. Or, again, suppose that, at the time of the delivery to the carrier, the machinery of the mill had been in other respects defective, then , also, the same results would follow. Here it is true that the shaft was actually sent back to serve as a model for a new one, and that the want, of a new one was the only cause of the stoppage of a mill, and that the loss of profits really arose from not sending down the new shaft in proper time, and that this arose from the delay in delivering the broken one to serve as a model. But it is obvious that, in a great multitude of cases of millers sending off broken shaft to the third persons by a carrier under ordinary circumstances, such consequences would not, in all probability, have occurred; and these special circumstances were here never communicated by the plaintiffs to the defendants. It follows, therefore, that the loss of profits here cannot reasonably be considered such a consequence of breach of contract as could have been fairly and reasonably contemplated by both the parties when they made this contract. For such loss would neither have flowed naturally from the breach of this contract in the greater multitude of such cases occurring under ordinary circumstances, nor were the special circumstances, which, perhaps, would have made it reasonable and natural consequence of breach of contract, communicated to or known by the defendants . . . there must therefore be a new trial . . .

Notes

(1) It has been said judicially that the headnote to the case, from which the statement of facts above is taken, actually gets the facts wrong: the words placed here in [. . .] should have been omitted. If the plaintiffs *had* told the defendant's clerk that the mill was stopped, they would have recovered: *Victoria Laundry (Windsor) Ltd* v. *Newman Industries Ltd*.[358]

(2) The words of Baron Alderson which are quoted in the summary are now known as "the rule in *Hadley* v. *Baxendale*". The rule seems to have been derived from French sources.[359]

(3) The rule in *Hadley* v. *Baxendale* works as a financial limit on the defendant's liability. In the *Victoria Laundry* case the buyers of a second-hand boiler wanted to use it immediately and suffered a loss of profits when the sellers delivered it late. The court held that this should have been obvious to the sellers. What the sellers could not have known was that the buyers wanted the boiler not for their normal laundering business but to fulfil some much more profitable Government dyeing contracts. The court held that the sellers were not liable for these higher losses but only for the normal loss of profits on laundering—though of course if the buyers had had the boiler on time they would not have used it for laundering but for dyeing!

(4) It is accepted that the extent of loss does not need to have been within the parties' contemplation provided the kind of loss was. Thus in *Balfour Beatty Construction (Scotland) Ltd* v. *Scottish Power plc* [360] the plaintiffs had contracted for a continuous supply of power

[358] [1949] 2 KB 528, 537–8.
[359] See Simpson (1975) 91 LQR 247. For a fascinating account of the background to the case see Danzig (1975) 4 JLS 249.
[360] 1993 SLT 1005.

to enable them to make a "continuous pour" of concrete to construct an aqueduct. As the "pour" was being made the power was interrupted; the plaintiffs had to demolish what had been done and start again. This could not have been contemplated by the defendants, but they were liable for the costs as they should have anticipated the necessity of some remedial work, such as cutting back the hardened concrete to form a joint with the new, and the difference was one of degree only.

(5) Similarly in English tort law, a defendant is only liable for loss caused by his breach of duty only if the loss is of a foreseeable type. In the leading case of *The Wagon Mound (No.1)*,[361] it was held to be foreseeable that crude oil spilled in a harbour would cause damage to a dock company by fouling its slipways, but not that the oil would cause damage by catching fire. However it seems that the defence will not apply if the kind of damage was foreseeable even as a remote possibility. In contract cases, however, the standard is different. It is not enough that the loss was foreseeable as a possibility. Alderson B. spoke of the "natural" or "probable" results of the breach. The House of Lords has held that, to be recoverable under *Hadley* v. *Baxendale*, the kind of loss must either have been known to the defendant or foreseeable by him as a substantial possibility: *The Heron II*.[362] The difference between the contract and tort rules has caused the courts some difficulty in those cases in which the defendant is liable in both contract and tort—there is no rule of *non-cumul* in English law.[363]

In German law two approaches to the remoteness of the harm sustained as a result of a breach of contract are taken. The chief means of deciding this question is by asking whether there was adequate causation of the harm; alternatively one may inquire about the scope of the protective purpose of the norm, here the contract.

Schlechtriem[364]   **6.G.126.**

The theory of adequate causation enables the exclusion from compensation of losses which were unforeseeable or highly improbable. The adequacy of causation is in particular judged from the perspective of an objective [or "optimal"] observer having regard to the events which he could have foreseen in the circumstances. The theory of adequate causation is also applied through giving legal form to a judgment as to probability: whether as a result of the initial harm the probability of the subsequent harm occurring was significantly increased. As against this the theory of the "purpose of the norm" or "normative connection" (*Rechtswidrigkeitszusammenhang*) requires a determination of whether the duty which was breached was supposed to protect the creditor from just the type of harm which in fact resulted.

The theory of the purpose of the norm is explored in the next sub-section.

The requirement that possible loss, beyond that which is foreseeable, be notified to the debtor is expressly included among the rules governing contribution and mitigation (§ 254(2) 1 BGB). Since this rule is part of the general law of obligations, it applies *inter*

---

[361] [1966] 1 AC 188, PC.
[362] [1969] 1 AC 350.
[363] See *supra* at 67 ff. and *H. Parsons (Livestock) Ltd* v. *Uttley Ingham & Co Ltd*; see also Bishop (1983) 12 JLS 241.
[364] Schlechtriem, *SAT*, at 225–6.

alia to both contract and tort. We shall see[365] that there are specific rules governing the extent of recoverable damages in the law governing sales and work contracts.

Thus in effect all three systems normally limit the liability of the party who has failed to perform to losses which, at the time the contract was made, were probable or foreseeable or which he was warned might be caused if the contract were not to be performed properly. The French rule that this limit does not apply in cases of *dol* or *faute lourde* does not appear in the other systems.[366] Nor does it appear in CISG[367] or the Unidroit Principles, but it is found in the Principles of European Contract Law.

Unidroit Principles   **6.INT.127.**

Article 7.4.4: *Foreseeability of harm*
> The non-performing party is liable only for harm which it foresaw or could reasonably have foreseen at the time of the conclusion of the contract as being likely to result from its non-performance.

Principles of European Contract Law   **6.PECL.128.**

Article 9:503: *Foreseeability*
> The non-performing party is liable only for loss which it foresaw or could reasonably have foreseen at the time of conclusion of the contract as a likely result of its non-performance, unless the non-performance was intentional or grossly negligent.

6.5.3.B. THE PROTECTIVE PURPOSE OF THE NORM

OLG Köln, 8 July 1982[368]   **6.G.129.**

THE PROTECTIVE PURPOSE OF THE CONTRACTUAL NORM

The bank which told the tax man

The loss for which compensation is sought must be within the protective purpose of the contract.

Facts: An official of the defendant bank gave information to the police concerning a number of bogus accounts held by the plaintiff customer. As a result the plaintiff was convicted of tax evasion. She sued for damages.

Held: The lower court held that there could be no recovery. The plaintiff's appeal against this decision was rejected on the basis that the purpose of the contract between the customer and the bank was not to protect the former against such harm.

Judgment: Until mid–1986 the plaintiff and her husband maintained various accounts in various names with the D. branch of the defendant bank. Towards the end of 1986, K., the manager of the branch, was summarily dismissed on account of his having committed serious criminal offences in the context of his employment. Upon being arrested on 10 December 1986, he was questioned by the police. He stated *inter alia*, in the light of documents comprised in a list of suspense accounts

---

[365] In **6.5.4.**, *infra* at 844.
[366] See Treitel, *Remedies* at 144–148, paras 123–126.
[367] See Art. 74.
[368] BB 1992, 2174.

824

dated November 1986, that he had played a significant role in the setting up of an index of creditors. He had drawn to the attention of the customers, and also of the directors of the bank, the existence of accounts in respect of which the identity of the account-holder was not the same as that of the creditor. Those accounts included the accounts maintained in several different names by the plaintiff. The accounts had been closed in mid–1986.

In June 1987 the plaintiff and her husband were the subject of a preliminary investigation by the public prosecutor concerning suspected tax evasion. Following an examination of the tax returns of the plaintiff and her husband, the department charged with investigating suspected tax offences, which had been instructed in the matter on 29 September 1987, summoned K. to give evidence. His evidence was taken on 20 November 1987. On that occasion, he provided further details regarding the accounts of the plaintiff and her husband. On 30 May 1988 the residence of Mr and Mrs D. was searched. Since 1973 they had declared only part of their unearned income in their income tax returns, and had failed to submit any capital tax returns. The plaintiff was convicted of tax evasion. Proceedings are now pending before the fiscal courts for payment of arrears of tax. The plaintiff has pleaded that the defendant is liable in damages to her and her husband, because K. was employed by the defendant in the performance of its obligations and breached, without justification, the bank's duty to maintain confidentiality. The plaintiff claims that, by reason of the statements made by K., she and her husband were prevented from availing themselves of the *Steueramnestiegesetz* (Law on tax amnesty) (Article 17 of the 1990 *Steuerreformgesetz* (Law on tax reform)), as they had firmly arranged to do at the end of 1987/beginning of 1988. Consequently, the loss and damage occasioned by the breach of contract included, according to the plaintiff, not only the fine and the legal costs but also the tax arrears payable up to and including 1985. She alleges that the defendant is additionally at fault since it was advised of K.'s breach of the duty of confidentiality but failed to inform the plaintiff and her husband of this. The *Landgericht* (Regional Court) dismissed the claim for damages in relation to the fine, the legal costs and the arrears of tax payable. The plaintiff's appeal against that judgment was likewise dismissed.

Grounds: The . . . plaintiff's appeal must be dismissed, without there being any need for further investigation of the factual matters at issue between the parties. . . . Even if K. unlawfully breached the duty of confidentiality owed by the defendant, the plaintiff has not in any event suffered any loss for which compensation is payable. The defendant was under no duty to furnish information.

1. On 10 December 1986 K. made a number of statements covered by the banking secrecy rules
. . .

2. The defendant remained under a duty to preserve banking secrecy following the closure of the accounts in 1986. Moreover, despite his dismissal, K. remained the agent of the bank for the purposes of the fulfilment of its obligations, and the defendant is in principle answerable for his actions.
. . .

4. There can be seen to exist a causal link between the statements made by K. and the pecuniary losses suffered by the plaintiff and her husband. There are grounds for supposing that, if it had not been for K.'s initial statement, there would have been no criminal proceedings and no liability to pay arrears of tax. That is a separate issue from the question whether the plaintiff would have availed herself of the tax amnesty legislation.

5. However, the claims for damages cannot be accepted as giving rise to liability to pay compensation. The prejudicial consequences of an offence which arise from a criminal conviction for that offence cannot, as a matter of principle, be shifted on to others. According to the relevant case law, the courts have hitherto been willing to accept the existence of a duty to pay compensation only

where there was some special reason in law for restraining the offender from committing the offence or for affording him legal protection against punishment. . . . That is not the position in the present case. Banking confidentiality is not intended to enable offences to be committed or kept secret, and its breach gives rise to liability, even in contractual relations, only in so far as may be necessary in order to safeguard a rule of law. . . . The commission by the plaintiff of criminal acts was not an issue to be taken into account by the defendant and K. The statements made by K. did not in themselves give rise to the suspicion of tax evasion; they had, moreover, already been superseded by the closure of the accounts.

The arrears of tax constitute an illegal pecuniary advantage which does not merit protection, and the plaintiff was not entitled to the continuance of that advantage.

No divergent conclusion can be drawn from the *Steueramnestiegesetz*, as regards either the criminal or the fiscal consequences of the matter. That statute, which entered into force in August 1988, lays down the way in which the plaintiff's loss could have been avoided, but does not affect the assessment of that loss.

Moreover, no special significance attaches to the fact that the point in time at which a criminal offence is discovered may produce effects as far as the person committing it is concerned, e.g. where it is no longer possible, subject to the detailed requirements laid down in that regard, to submit to the tax authorities a report of a false or incomplete tax declaration or to abandon the attempt to commit the offence, or where the running of the anticipated period of limitation for bringing a prosecution is interrupted. The fact that an offender is placed in the position in which he would have found himself if he had submitted a report of a false or incomplete tax declaration to the tax authorities or had abandoned his attempt to commit the offence, or if the limitation period had expired, in no way indicates whether a claim exists in contract.

Contrary to the view advanced by the plaintiff, the decisive factor which ultimately led to her exposure was the statement made by K. in December 1996, and not the evidence given by him in November 1987. The argument that the preliminary investigation by the public prosecutor would have been discontinued if K., invoking banking confidentiality, had refused to make a statement is not convincing. On the contrary, there are compelling grounds for supposing that he would then have been formally examined in a manner precluding a refusal to give evidence (§ 286 ZPO).

However, that in no way alters the fact that the course of events whereby the plaintiff and her husband found themselves no longer able to submit any rectifying tax declarations is irrelevant to the substance of any liability in damages which the defendant may have incurred.

6. Even if, contrary to the observations set out above, liability in damages for the loss suffered were to attach to the defendant, the plaintiff's claim would fall foul of § 254 BGB and would be bound to fail. The facts disclosed by K. were in themselves unimportant, and had already been overtaken by events, whereas the plaintiff and her husband were primarily instrumental in bringing about the prejudice which subsequently arose, in that they engaged in a course of wilful conduct over a period of many years.

7. Nor, finally, can the defendant be criticised for having failed to inform the plaintiff of the initial statement made by K., assuming that it was aware of the content of that statement. In that regard also, the position is such that the matter did not manifestly involve any interest of the plaintiff. The fact that the public prosecutor's suspicions may have been increased cannot constitute a criterion governing the defendant's obligations to give consideration to the matter and to exercise care.

Consequently, there is no need to consider the point in time at which the plaintiff and her husband would still have been able to escape a criminal prosecution by submitting to the tax authorities a confession in relation to their false or incomplete tax declarations, or to examine the question whether, had they known of the content of the statement made by K. on 10 December 1986, they would have decided to do so.

Notes

(1) The protective purpose of the norm approach is usually seen as limiting the recoverable harm to a greater extent than the theory of adequate causation. In other words, the debtor's breach of contract may have increased the probability that harm of the relevant type would occur, but such loss may still be held to be outside the purpose of the contractual norm. Thus, for example, in the case above it is very likely that a test of adequate causation would have applied in the plaintiff's favour.

(2) The precise scope of the protective purpose of the contract is a matter of fact to be determined in the light of all the circumstances, including especially the intentions of the parties. This gives judges considerable leeway. Tests applied in this connection take a more or less objective or subjective approach to intention.[369]

(3) It is doubtful whether any other legal systems would have permitted the plaintiffs to recover compensation for what was, in essence, the consequence of their own wrongdoing. There are alternative ways in which this could have been reached—for instance by holding that the loss was caused primarily by their own actions; contributory negligence; or a rule based on public policy denying compensation for the just desserts of criminal activity. But an approach which is rather similar to the purpose of the norm has been used in England to limit liability in cases which did not involve any criminal activity of any kind. Rather the court was concerned to relieve the debtor of liability for a loss which was foreseeable, and which would not have occurred but for its negligence, but which it did not seem fair to lay at the debtor's door. In *South Australia Asset Management Corp.* v. *York Montague Ltd,*[370] valuers had been employed by lenders to value properties which the lenders were promising to accept as security, but had negligently overvalued the properties. Had the valuation been done properly the lenders would not have accepted the security or made the loans. When the borrowers defaulted and the lenders tried to enforce the security it was found that they were worth much less than the amount owed, partly because of the overvaluation and partly because of a general fall in property values. The House of Lords held that the negligent valuers were not necessarily liable for a fall in market value. The purpose of the contract must be looked at, and it was not to protect the lenders against general falls in the market value. The valuers were liable for no more than the initial deficiency, i.e. the difference between the negligent over-valuation and what would have been a proper valuation at the time of the loan.

6.5.3.C. Losses which might have been avoided or reduced by the creditor

House of Lords   6.E.130.
British Westinghouse Electric and Manufacturing Co Ltd v. Underground Electric Railways Co of London Ltd[371]
Duty to mitigate

[The facts of this case are not relevant at this point as the case did not in fact involve mitigation.]
Viscount Haldane LC: . . . In order to come to a conclusion on the question as to damages thus raised, it is essential to bear in mind certain propositions which I think are well established. In some

[369] See Fuller and Lange, *Schadensersatz* (Tübingen: JCB Mohr (Paul Siebeck), 1979), at 79 ff.
[370] [1997] AC 191.
[371] [1912] AC 673, 688–9.

of the cases there are expressions as to the principles governing the measure of general damages which at first sight seem difficult to harmonise. The apparent discrepancies are, however, mainly due to the varying nature of the particular questions submitted for decision. The quantum of damage is a question of fact, and the only guidance which the law can give is to lay down general principles which afford at times but scanty assistance in dealing with particular cases. The judges who give guidance to juries in these cases have necessarily to look at their special character, and to mould for the purposes of different kinds of claim the expression of the general principles which apply to them, and this is apt to give rise to an appearance of ambiguity. Subject to these observations I think that there are certain broad principles, which are quite well settled. The first is that, as far as possible, he who has proved a breach of a bargain to supply what he contracted to get is to be placed, as far as money can do it, in as good a situation as if the contract had been performed. The fundamental basis is thus compensation for pecuniary loss naturally flowing from the breach; but this first principle is qualified by a second, which imposes on a plaintiff the duty of taking all reasonable steps to mitigate the loss consequent on the breach, and debars him from claiming in respect of any part of the damage which is due to his neglect to take such steps . . .

Notes

(1) This dictum is probably the clearest statement of the English law on the "duty to mitigate", as it is often called. In fact it is not a duty, since a duty must be owed to someone else; rather it is a rule that a party cannot recover a loss he could have avoided by taking reasonable steps. It is what in German is called an *Obliegenheit* (or requirement).

(2) The principle has two aspects. One is that the creditor should not act unreasonably in such a way as to risk making the loss worse—for example, by continuing to drive a car which he has bought if he knows it has defective brakes; the other, that he should take reasonable positive steps to reduce the loss, for example, by making a substitute contract.[372]

(3) The mitigation principle is so fundamental that it is often incorporated into statements of the damages recoverable. For example Sale of Goods Act 1979, sections 50(3) and 51(3):[373] each assumes that the creditor will normally mitigate by making, respectively, a substitute purchase or sale in the market.

(4) The creditor is expected only to take steps which are reasonable. A buyer who, when the seller fails to deliver, faces loss of profitable sub-sales is expected to buy replacement goods to meet its needs if these are readily available, but it need not "go hunting the globe" for goods which are not readily available: *Lesters Leather and Skin Co. Ltd.* v. *Home and Overseas Brokers Ltd.*[374] An employee who as the result of a partnership being dissolved has been dismissed without proper notice, but who is then offered immediate re-employment on the same terms by the new partners, is expected to accept the offer: *Brace* v. *Calder*;[375] whereas an employee who has had his trust in his old employer destroyed need not accept an offer of re-employment: *Yetton* v. *Eastwoods Froy Ltd.*[376]

(5) The creditor may recover the costs involved in mitigating, for example the costs of arranging a substitute sale or purchase. Sometimes what appeared to be a reasonable step

---

[372] See Treitel, *Contract*, at 881 ff.
[373] See *infra* at 844.
[374] (1948) 64 TLR 569.
[375] [1895] 2 KB 253.
[376] [1967] 1 WLR 104.

to mitigate loss does not reduce the loss as much as some other action might have done; the cost of the action taken is recoverable nonetheless: *Gebrüder Metelmann GmbH* v. *NBR (London) Ltd.*[377]

(6) Once the date for performance has passed, so that damages are payable, the creditor must take reasonable steps to mitigate her loss, and this may involve terminating the contract so as to make a substitute arrangement. It is not clear in what circumstances there may be a duty to mitigate before this date. If there has been an anticipatory breach of the contract and the creditor elects to terminate the contract right away, she comes under a duty to mitigate when she terminates; but if she does not so elect, it has been said that she is not under a duty to act: *Shindler* v. *Northern Raincoat Co Ltd.*[378] See however the cases following *White & Carter* v. *McGregor*,[379] which may qualify this statement to some extent.

(7) On the actual facts of the *British Westinghouse* case, the duty was not directly relevant. The plaintiffs had supplied turbines to the defendants which did not perform as efficiently as required by the contract. After several years the defendants had installed newer, much more efficient turbines made by another manufacturer. The House of Lords said that this was more than could reasonably have been required of them by the duty to mitigate. The question was whether the defendants could set the cost of installing these second turbines against the—still unpaid—contract price. It was held that they could not, because in fact the new turbines were so much more efficient than the old ones would have been, even if they had conformed to the contract, that the new machines paid for themselves. In other words, the plaintiff's actions had resulted in a saving to them which should be taken into account in reducing their damages.

BGB 6.G.131.

§ 254: (1) If any fault of the injured party has contributed to causing the damage, the omission to compensate the injured party and the extent of the compensation to be made depends upon the circumstances, especially upon how far the injury has been caused predominately by the one or the other party.

(2) This applies also if the fault of the injured party consisted only in an omission to call the attention of the debtor to the danger of unusually high damage which the debtor neither knew nor should have known, or in an omission to avert or mitigate the damage. The provision of § 278 applies mutatis mutandis.

§ 324: (1) If the performance due from one party under a mutual contract becomes impossible because of a circumstance for which the other party is responsible, the first party retains his claim for counter-performance. He must, however, deduct what he saves in consequence of release from the performance, or what he acquires or wilfully omits to acquire by different use of his labour.

(2) The same rule applies if the performance due from one party becomes impossible, because of a circumstance for which he is not responsible, at a time when the other party is in delay in acceptance.

---

[377] [1984] 1 Lloyd's Rep. 614, 634.
[378] [1960] 1 WLR 1038.
[379] Discussed *supra* at 721.

REASONABLE STEPS TO REDUCE LOSS

The architect and the defective building

The responsibility of the creditor to mitigate may include the enforcement of rights against third parties.

Facts: The creditor of a building contract sued the architect responsible for the work for loss caused by defective work on the roof. The architect claimed in response that the creditor was first obliged to proceed against the craftsman who actually carried out the work by way of mitigating his loss.

Held: The Landgericht and the Oberlandesgericht upheld the creditor's claim. The architect's appeal to the BGH was successful.

Judgment: On the grounds:
. . . II. The court below considers the head of claim to be substantiated under §§ 635 BGB. Accordingly, it correctly assesses the contract for architectural services covering building plans, direction and on-the-spot supervision entered into between the plaintiff and the defendant's husband as a contract for the provision of works.

. . .

2. However, the defendant's argument is relevant on another ground. The defendant claims that her husband and, after his death, she herself could have had the roof defects removed at a much lower cost. There was no need for a new roof. If that is true, the plaintiff's claim for damages may be reduced or nullified under § 254 II BGB . . ..

IV. It is contended in the context of this appeal that the plaintiff culpably omitted to avert or mitigate the damage (§ 254 II BGB), by not requiring the carpenter W., who assembled the roof structure, to carry out subsequent repairs (*Nachbesserung*, see § 633 BGB), thereby forfeiting his rights against the carpenter to the detriment of the defendant. This contention must be upheld and the case must be further examined under this aspect.

The court *a quo* did not decide the question whether the carpenter was jointly liable for the defects. Accordingly, for the purposes of the present proceedings there must be presumed to be joint liability with W.

It cannot be ruled out that the plaintiff was obliged first to require W. to carry out subsequent repairs, prior to seeking damages from the defendant's husband under the contract for architectural services. It is true that it is in principle open to the person giving instructions in respect of the building works to seek redress for building defects from the undertakings responsible or from the architect. But this right to choose is subject to the principle of good faith, as enshrined in § 254 BGB.

The architect and the craftsman are not jointly and severally liable. Irrespective of the fact that their obligations stem from different contracts, they do not contemplate the same contractual performance. It will not, therefore, be possible for the architect to demand compensation directly from the craftsman, for example, under § 426 BGB. The person directing the works as the creditor may not ignore that fact. He will therefore as a matter of principle be bound by the principle of good faith in relation to the architect also to seek redress from the craftsman. In particular he is obliged to avail himself of his right to call for subsequent repairs by the craftsman in order in that way to mitigate the loss for which the architect is liable (§ 254 II BGB), without, however, in this way being burdened by an unreasonable task.

[380] NJW 1962.149.

He cannot be expected to embark on a protracted dispute with the craftsman the outcome of which way be in doubt. Should appreciable difficulties in enforcing these rights against the craftsman already be foreseeable or even have already arisen, the architect cannot require that procedure to be followed but must accept liability for the full extent of the damage.

None the less, it does not appear to be free from doubt whether the particular circumstances under which the plaintiff had to seek redress from the building company are present in this case, if W. was required to adhere to the plans drawn up by the defendant's husband. However this requires further elucidation.

Notes

(1) Reasonable, rather than extraordinary, measures only need be taken in mitigation of harm. Thus, it has been held that a holidaymaker whose hotel becomes unavailable or unacceptable either before or during the trip, may be required—under § 254(2) BGB—to accept a substitute offer from the travel company. However, the substitute must be largely compatible with the original in terms of location and quality, and it must be offered without delay after the problem becomes known. In any event the requirement may not be imposed where the holidaymaker has lost all confidence in the company.[381]

(2) A disappointed buyer or seller is generally not required to enter into a cover transaction in mitigation of their loss unless the subject matter of the contract was perishable or its price is subject to frequent fluctuation.[382]

(3) However, the suggestion that the creditor should take action against one of two parties who are both liable before suing the other goes beyond anything found in English law. This is however a more general difference. For example, in German law a guarantor of a debt may not be sued by the creditor until the creditor has been unsuccessful in obtaining payment from the debtor; whereas in English law the creditor may recover from the guarantor as soon as the debtor is in default. The guarantor and the debtor are jointly and severally liable; if the guarantor pays he may recover from the debtor—if the latter is solvent!

(4) §§ 615, 649 BGB contain rules similar to § 324 BGB, allowing the reduction of damages in cases of default under contracts of service and work contracts respectively.

French law does not as such recognize the duty to mitigate. However a creditor who fails to warn the debtor that the contract is being broken and allows damages to mount up will not recover the additional loss, the loss being treated as his own fault: for example, *Gatelier* v. *Electricité de France*.[383]

Cour d'appel de Paris   6.F.133.
7 January 1924[384]

CREDITOR MUST NOT ALLOW DAMAGES TO ACCUMULATE WITHOUT PROTEST TO DEBTOR

Low gas pressure

A customer of the gas company is not entitled to a particular pressure, in the absence of any special agreement; but in any event it cannot recover damages for difficulties experienced over a period of time when it has not notified the gas company of the problem.

[381] See LG Frankfurt NJW 1986.1616.
[382] See Fuller and Lange, op. cit., at 369.
[383] Cass civ. 1re, 29 April 1981, JCP.1982.II.19730 annotated by Courbe
[384] DP 24.2.143.

Facts: The plaintiff hospice sued for losses caused allegedly by inadequate gas pressure over a two-year period. It had not notified the gas company of the difficulty.

Held: The first instance court allowed the claim but the decision was reversed on appeal.

Judgment:—Whereas Viollette, as Chairman of the administrative committee of the Dreux hospice, commenced proceedings against Société du gaz de Maubeuge for an order requiring it to pay FF 20,000 by way of damages, on the ground that from 1919 to 1921 the irregular and insufficient supply of gas disturbed the operation of the bath and sterilisation services; as since the hospice had no special arrangement guaranteeing minimum and constant pressure, it is necessary primarily to rely on the Company's terms and conditions; as those terms and conditions, it appears, do not require the concessionaire to observe any minimum pressure;

—Whereas it is therefore inappropriate to interpret a clause which does not exist and cannot be supplied; as the gas company, bound only by general contractual principles and the prevailing circumstance, was a fortiori entitled to moderate the pressure, varying it according to the times of day and corresponding needs;

—Whereas Article 1 of the Decree of 1 June 1917 required plants to interrupt supplies at times of low consumption, and Viollette does not even allege that that decree had been expressly repealed, except as regards Article 2 which limited the circulation of hot water in buildings; as it merely contends that it had fallen into desuetude and there had been no penalty; moreover, the expert's reports and other documents produced in the proceedings show that the alleged inadequacy was attributable above all to the malfunctioning of the installations, the maintenance of which is the responsibility of the hospice; as in any event, whatever the cause, that inadequacy should have been reported to the gas company as early as 1919, so that the latter could attend to repairing it;

—Whereas a person to whom a service is provided in a defective manner is not entitled to allow the loss to increase and possible damages to accumulate, without formally complaining or giving notice that the defective supply should be remedied promptly; as the gas company properly criticises Viollette for failing to serve any notice setting out his complaints before commencing proceedings;

—Whereas accordingly, this court sets aside the judgment of the Tribunal de Commerce, Dreux, of 6 January 1992, and directs that no interpretation, stay of proceedings or inquiry is appropriate.

Thus, although French law does not recognize the duty to mitigate, and though in German law the principle is not expressed in these terms, all three systems seem to reach the result that the creditor will not recover damages for loss which could have been avoided had the creditor taken reasonable steps. This is how it is formulated in the international restatements.

Principles of European Contract Law   **6.PECL.134.**

Article 9:505: *Reduction of Loss*

(1) The non-performing party is not liable for loss suffered by the aggrieved party to the extent that the aggrieved party could have reduced the loss by taking reasonable steps.

(2) The aggrieved party is entitled to recover any expenses reasonably incurred in attempting to reduce the loss.

Unidroit Article 7.4.8 (*Mitigation of harm*) is in similar terms.

6.5.3.D. CONTRIBUTORY NEGLIGENCE

Damages may also be reduced or refused altogether because the damage was partly due to the creditor's own conduct. Obviously, this principle might explain some cases of mitigation, but there is a wider rule. The duty to mitigate does not apply until the creditor knows that the debtor has broken the contract; it is only then that she is expected to take reasonable steps to reduce the loss. Here we are concerned with the case in which the creditor's carelessness contributed to the damage in some other way.

Cass. civ. 1re, 31 January 1973[385]   **6.F.135.**

DAMAGES REDUCED IF CREDITOR AT FAULT

The bad-tempered bear

A debtor whose non-performance has caused injury to the creditor should be liable in full for her injuries unless he is exonerated on the ground of force majeure or unless she contributed to her own injury through her own fault.

Facts: Mrs D. fell against a barrier designed to keep visitors a safe distance from a cage in which there was a bear. The barrier collapsed and the bear put its muzzle through the bars and bit her. She sued the zoo company.

Held: The court of appeal reduced her damages on the ground that her fall was an external event, but without finding that the fall was either unforeseeable or unavoidable, nor that it was the creditor's fault. On appeal the decision was quashed.

Judgment: THE COURT: *On the sole appeal ground*:—Under Article 1147 of the Civil Code;
—Whereas an act by the victim, which was neither unforeseeable nor inevitable, does not constitute grounds of partial exoneration for a person who entered into a specific obligation to ensure safety unless it involves fault;
—Whereas Mrs Dantony, who was visiting the zoo operated by Condour, fell against a barrier designed to keep visitors at a certain distance from the cage occupied by a bear; as the barrier collapsed under the weight of Mrs Dantony, and the bear stuck its muzzle through the bars of its cage and bit her arm;
—Whereas the cour d'appel (Lyon, 4 May 1971), having held that Condour was under an obligation to ensure safety vis-à-vis Mrs Dantony, exonerated it in part from its obligation on the ground that there was an external event, namely the victim's fall, when she lost her footing;
—Whereas by giving judgment to that effect, but not finding any fault on the part of Mrs Dantony, the court of second instance infringed the abovementioned provision;
   On those grounds, sets the judgment aside (. . .) and refers the matter back to the cour d'appel, Grenoble.

From the note:

Essentially, the court of second instance was criticised for exonerating C from some liability, without finding either that Mrs D's fall amounted to force majeure or that the event involved fault.
   Thus, the ground of appeal begged the question in two respects. It implied, first, that, in order even partially to escape his liability, a person subject to a particular obligation must prove that he could neither foresee nor prevent the harmful event. It implied, secondly, that, where the victim has

---

[385] D. 1973.149, annotated by Schmelck.

himself contributed to the occurrence of the damage, but without his involvement constituting *force majeure* for the defendant, the latter can be partially relieved of his obligation of redress only if he proved that such involvement amounted to fault. In other words, only fault, and not the mere act of the victim, is a reason for partially lifting contractual liability.

Of the two principles thus asserted, the first could not be accepted. Although eminent authors (Aubry and Rau, *Droit civil*, 5th edition, Vol. 4, No. 308, note 31) may have maintained in the past that the person who owes the obligation must always redress in its entirety the damage he causes to the person to whom he owes the obligation by failing to discharge the obligation which he entered into, even though the person to whom the obligation was owed for his part committed a fault without which the harm would not have been done, that view is now outdated. At the present time, legal authors are almost unanimous in recognising, in the areas both of contract and of delict, that whilst *force majeure* alone can totally exonerate the defendant, fault on the part of the victim remains a cause of partial exoneration (cf Mazeaud and Tunc, *Traité théor. et prat. de la responsabilité civile*, Vol. 2, 6th edition, p. 548, and the authors cited). Case law has gone the same way, since a judgment of 11 November 1942, which held that "the person owing the obligation, in the event of wrongfully failing to perform his contractual obligation, cannot be ordered to redress all the damage suffered by the person to whom the obligation is owed when it is proved that an independent fault, committed by that person and not attributable to the person owing the obligation, contributed to the occurrence of the harm". We may cite by way of example two judgments of the 1st Civil Chamber, one of 31 March 1965 (*Bull. civ. I, No. 236, p. 1 74*) and the other of 7 March 1966 (*Bull. civ. I. No. 165, p. 129*). The appeal was thus wrong to criticise the cour d'appel for exempting C from his liability without finding that the external cause which he invoked amounted to *force majeure*. There was no need for the judgment to make such a finding since the exoneration granted by it to the person owing the obligation was only partial.

In English law the position is complicated by the fact that in 1945 a statute was passed to allow the courts to reduce the damages awarded to a plaintiff who had been contributorily negligent. The statute, the Law Reform (Contributory Negligence) Act 1945, was aimed primarily at tort cases; before the Act, contributory negligence was a complete defence to a claim in tort. It has not been clear to what extent the Act applies also to cases of breach of contract. It is necessary to distinguish three cases: (i) where the defendant has broken a contractual duty of care and is concurrently liable in tort—remember that English law recognizes concurrent liability in contract and tort;[386] (ii) where the defendant has broken a contractual duty of care but would not be liable in tort—for example, his carelessness has caused only purely economic loss, which is seldom actionable in tort in English law;[387] and (iii) where the defendant's obligation was a "strict" obligation, even if in fact the defendant was negligent—but again he would not be liable in tort.

(1) *Concurrent Liability in Tort.* It is established that the Act applies where the defendant's breach of contract was also a tort. Thus in *Sayers* v. *Harlow UDC*[388] a lady used a public lavatory, for which she had to pay a penny. When she had finished she found there was no way of opening the door from the inside and, being in a hurry to catch a bus, she tried to climb out by standing on the toilet paper holder. This rotated under her foot and she fell, injuring herself. The Court of Appeal reduced her damages on

---

[386] See *supra* at 71.
[387] See *supra* at 54.
[388] [1958] 2 All ER 342.

the ground of contributory negligence. See also *Forsikringsaktielskapet Vesta* v. *Butcher*.[389]

(2) *No Liability in Tort.* It seems likely that the Act does not apply when the defendant's breach of contract was not also a tort, even if it was a breach of a contractual duty to use reasonable care and skill: dicta in *Forsikringsaktielskapet Vesta* v. *Butcher*.[390]

(3) *Strict Obligations.* Where the defendant's obligation was a strict one, neither the old doctrine of contributory negligence nor the 1945 Act applies—the Act refers to cases in which the damage was caused partly by the "fault" of the defendant, and fault is defined in a way that excludes a breach of a strict contractual obligation.

The Law Commission recommended that the power to reduce the plaintiff's damages should be extended to case (ii); but that it should not apply to case (iii) in which the defendant's contractual obligation was a strict one.[391] It said:

If the defendant commits himself to a strict obligation regardless of fault, the plaintiff should be able to rely on him fulfilling his obligation and should not have to take precautions against the possibility that a breach might occur.[392]

However, this recommendation was not accepted by the Government.

BGB   **6.G.136.**

§ 254: (1) If any fault of the injured party has contributed to causing the damage, the omission to compensate the injured party and the extent of the compensation to be made depends upon the circumstances, especially upon how far the injury has been caused predominantly by the one or the other party.

Kammergericht, 14 November 1984[393]   **6.G.137.**

CONTRIBUTORY NEGLIGENCE IN CONTRACT

The stolen double bass

A contract creditor who does not exercise reasonable care to avoid the occurrence of harm is liable to have an award of damages proportionately reduced.

Facts: The plaintiff was employed under a contract of service by the defendant, the arts department of a city district council, to give a recital with other musicians. After the recital he left his double bass unattended in another room while he changed. The instrument was stolen. He sued the department for breaching obligations of protection (positive breach of contract). The defendant claimed in turn that the plaintiff had been culpably careless in leaving the instrument unattended while there were still visitors in the building.

Held: The decision of the lower court (*Landgericht*) awarding damages but reducing them by 50% in accordance with § 254 BGB was upheld.

Judgment: 1. The *Landgericht* rightly approached the matter on the basis that a contract for services had been concluded between the parties (§ 611 BGB), whereby the plaintiff undertook to the

[389] [1988] 2 All ER 43, affirmed on other grounds [1989] 1 All ER 402.
[390] *Ibid.*
[391] *Contributory Negligence as a Defence in Contract*, Law Commission No. 219 (London: HMSO, 1993).
[392] Para. 4.2.
[393] NJW 1985.2137.

defendant (the T. arts directorate) to give a concert in the P. concert hall on the evening of 2 June 1983 in return for the payment of a specified fee. Contrary to the view taken by the *Landgericht*, however, the defendant owed the plaintiff a duty, on the basis of the contractual relationship existing between them, to protect the plaintiff's property against reasonably foreseeable loss and damage. It is generally recognised in case-law and academic legal literature that such a duty of protection forms a part of every contractual relationship (see RGZ 78, 240; Roth, in: *Münch. Komm*, § 242, note 182). Such duties of protection (or preservation) are intended to safeguard the party to whom they are owed not only against prejudice to his existing or future interest in the performance by the other party of the latter's obligations, but also against loss or damage to his other legally protected interests (as previously explained in detail by Stoll in *Die Lehre von den Leistungsstörungen*, 1936, p. 27). The duties involved are those existing under the contract, breach of which gives rise, in accordance with the principles of positive violation of contractual obligations, to liability in damages. If the other party to the contract uses another person to assist him in the fulfilment of the protection obligations imposed on him under the contract, he will be equally liable, pursuant to § 278 BGB, for fault on the part of that assistant as for his own fault.

In the present case, the defendant had taken it upon itself, through the T. arts directorate, to organise the performance of the concert featuring the plaintiff in the P. concert hall. That organisational duty (that is to say, the duty to ensure that the concert proceeded smoothly) also encompassed the collateral duty owed to plaintiff to take appropriate organisational steps to protect not only the plaintiff's person but also his property against loss and damage. In particular, the T. arts directorate was under an obligation to entrust one or more of its employees with the task of looking after the organisational aspects of the performance of the concert.

According to the facts, which were not contested in the proceedings before the appellate court below, the defendant only inadequately fulfilled that obligation, and this was the cause of the loss and damage suffered. It is common ground that two employees of the arts directorate were present during the concert, together with the caretaker employed by the horticultural department, who was entrusted with the task of unlocking and re-locking the doors. However, the event organised by the arts directorate did not finish at the end of the performance given by the artists; it continued until such time as the artists had left the auditorium and the neighbouring rooms. In view of this, it was possible and reasonable, and thus incumbent on the defendant, without incurring further expense, to ensure that one of its employees was continuously present in the *auditorium*, thereby performing the function of the organiser, until all the artists had departed. The defendant did not discharge that duty. It is common ground that the defendant's two employees left the building immediately after the end of the concert, that is to say, at a time when persons attending the concert had not yet left the auditorium. The task of the caretaker employed by the horticultural department was merely to be responsible for the unlocking and re-locking of the doors to the building. He had not been directed to take any measures connected with the actual organisation of the event. In those factual circumstances, either at least one of the defendant's employees should have remained present in the auditorium until the artists had left or the caretaker, who remained behind, should have been given the responsibility of seeing to the final completion of the event before himself leaving the building. The defendant has not asserted that any of its employees assigned the functions of the organiser to the caretaker in the manner described. Moreover, even if any such assignment of functions had taken place, the defendant would still have been liable, since the loss would in that event have been based on a failure by the caretaker to fulfil his duty of care as a person assisting in the performance of the contract (§ 278 BGB).

Since the defendant has failed, on account of negligence (§ 276 I BGB) on the part of its executive bodies or persons employed by it in the performance of its obligations, to fulfil its contractual duty to protect the plaintiff, it is liable in damages to the plaintiff in accordance with the principles of positive violation of contractual obligations.

2. As it is, the *Landgericht* rightly found that, in the context of the occurrence of the damage consisting of the loss of the instrument, the plaintiff had been contributorily negligent (§ 254 I BGB) and that, in consequence of that contributory negligence, the plaintiff was entitled to receive from the defendant damages representing only half of the loss sustained by him. According to § 254 BGB, a party suffering loss and/or damage will be [contributorily] negligent if he fails to fulfil the duty of care normally applied by an ordinary, reasonable person in order to avoid himself sustaining such loss and/or damage (RGZ 112, 284 [287]; BGHZ 9, 316 [318] = NJW 1953, 977). The plaintiff failed to fulfil that requirement obliging him to safeguard his own interests.

However, contrary to the view advanced by the defendant, the plaintiff cannot be said to have been contributorily negligent solely on account of the fact that, because of the circumstances relating to the space available, he did not take his musical instrument with him to the artists' dressing room immediately after the end of the concert, depositing it instead in a side room adjoining the auditorium. Nor does anything turn on the defendant's allegation, contested by the plaintiff, that the caretaker had indicated prior to the final rehearsal that it was risky to leave the instrument in the unsupervised, empty building. The plaintiff could not have inferred from that remark that the defendant would omit at the end of the concert to fulfil its contractual duty of protection. However, if (as the plaintiff himself stated in the proceedings before the Chamber) he deposited his valuable instrument in a side room adjoining the auditorium when he was aware that members of the public were still in the auditorium and the caretaker was just on the point of locking various doors to the auditorium, he should have made sure, by enquiring of the caretaker before going to the artists' dressing room, that his instrument would be watched over during his absence. Since, by that time, the employees of the arts directorate organising the event had already left the building, and the plaintiff did not in any event see that any employee of the defendant was still present when he deposited the double bass in the side room, there was no adequate basis on which he could be sure that a watch would be kept on his instrument, especially since the building was not designed for events of that kind. Accordingly, by failing to fulfil his own duty of care, the plaintiff was contributorily negligent and partially caused his own loss. Having regard to all the circumstances of the case, particularly the degree of causation and the extent of the fault attributable to each of the parties, the Chamber, applying § 287 ZPO (see BGH, NJW 1968, 985 et seq.), considers each of the parties to have contributed in equal measure to the cause of the loss. Consequently, responsibility for the damage suffered by the plaintiff must be divided equally between the parties.

Note

§ 254(1) BGB is an example of an *Obliegenheit*.[394] It applies not only to contract claims but also to tort and *culpa in contrahendo*.

Principles of European Contract Law   **6.PECL.138.**

Article 9:504: *Loss Attributable to Aggrieved Party*
The non-performing party is not liable for loss suffered by the aggrieved party to the extent that the aggrieved party contributed to the non-performance or its effects.

[394] Markesinis, Lorenz and Dannemann, *The German Law of Obligations*, Vol I: *The Law of Contracts and Restitution* (Oxford: Clarendon, 1997), at 662 with references.

6.5.3.E. NON-PECUNIARY LOSS (*PRÉJUDICE MORAL*)

Cass. civ. 1re, 16 January 1962[395]   **6.F.139.**

SENTIMENTAL DAMAGES

Lunus

Regardless of the material damage which it causes, the death of an animal may, for its owner, be the cause of subjective and affective harm, which may carry entitlement to compensation.

Facts: The first plaintiff's horse Lunus was hired to the second plaintiff, a trainer, and was placed by the latter in stables run by the defendant racecourse. Lunus bit through an electric cable and was electrocuted.

Held: The Cour d'appel of Poitiers held that not only should the owner be paid the market value of the horse but he should receive FF 500,000, and the trainer FF 75,000, for non-material damage. This decision was upheld, but its finding that various defendants were jointly liable was set aside.

Judgment: THE COURT: *On the first appeal taken in its two parts*:—Whereas in August 1952, Daille, the owner of the racehorse Lunus, hired it to the trainer Henri de Lotherie; the latter had the animal taken to Langon, where he was to take part on 26 and 27 July 1953 in races organised by Société hippique de Langon; as Fabre, the Chairman of that company, made available to the trainer a box in his stable to accommodate the horse; as on the morning of 27 July 1953, the animal grabbed between its teeth the wire of a mobile lamp known as a "baladeuse" ("walkabout lamp") and was electrocuted.—Whereas Daille commenced proceedings against Société hippique de Langon, Fabre personally, and de Lotherie, seeking damages; the contested judgment (Bordeaux, 5 July 1956) attributed responsibility for the death of the horse Lunus to Fabre as to 50 per cent, to Société hippique de Langon as to 25 per cent and to de Lotherie as to 25 per cent; whilst refusing to compensate Daille for the loss of such profits as the horse might have generated in the future, the cour d'appel held that in addition to the market value of the animal, which it put at Ff 350,000, Daille should receive an additional sum for the undoubted harm which he suffered as a result of the death of Lunus, and set the total amount of damages payable to Daille at FF 500,000, de Lotherie to receive the sum of FF 75,000;
—Whereas that decision is criticised for awarding damages intended to compensate for non-material damage suffered as a result of loss of the horse and for accepting that de Lotherie, under whose colours the horse was entered in the race, had himself suffered non-material damage, even though, first, such damage is conceivable only in respect of the loss of a cherished being, and there is nothing in common between the upset caused by the death of a person and that of an animal, and, secondly, it was allegedly for the court to prove, by reference to particular circumstances, the existence of damage which it merely affirmed but of which there was no evidence;
—Whereas regardless of the material damage which it entails, the death of an animal may, for its owner, be the cause of subjective and affective damage which may entail entitlement to redress; as in this case, the cour d'appel rightly considered that the harm suffered by Daille in respect of the death of his horse was not limited to the sum necessary to buy another animal having the same qualities, and that it was also necessary to bring into account, in calculating the damages, compensation intended to cover the harm suffered through loss of an animal to which he was attached; as regards de Lotherie, the court was also entitled to take note of the adverse effect on his interests as a trainer;

---

[395] D.1962.199, annotated by Rodière, S.1962.281, J.C.P.1962II.12447.

—Whereas it follows, that in giving judgment as it did, the court properly founded its decision;
But on the second appeal ground:—Under Having regard to Article 1202 of the Civil Code;
—Whereas, whilst each of the joint authors of a fault committed by more than one person may be ordered to redress in its entirety the damage to whose occurrence they contributed, the joint and several liability provided for in Article 1202 of the Civil Code can be declared against them only in the cases provided for by law.
—Whereas in finding Fabre, Société hippique de Langon, de Lotherle, and the insurance company, were jointly and severally liable vis-à-vis Daille and de Lotherie, the judgment merely notes that they shared the fault, but, having inferred from that finding alone that they were jointly and severally liable, the cour d'appel failed to indicate the legal basis of its decision;
On those grounds, the judgment is set aside . . . but only as regards this ground of appeal, and refers the matter back to the cour d'appel, Poitiers.

From the Note:

(1 and 2) The press has done this judgment the honour of devoting attention to it. The owner of a horse is awarded damages for his hurt against those responsible for killing the animal—that is indeed something unusual enough to be worth recounting and a great outcry may be expected!
1. First of all, there are the moralists, who will compare this compassion with the parents' of the animal with the indifference of public opinion to the violence which we witness daily and who will think that the immunity granted to some is not offset by the award of damages against those who, without wishing to do so, have run over "Mummy's little dog". A facile subject.
The pedants, imitating Rabelais who satirised the period in which he lived, will recall all the historic examples of disproportionate love for animals and will not fail to mention the horse Incitatus which Caligula wished to appoint as Consul, adding that Caligula did not exactly serve as a model of mental equilibrium.
Lovers of quotations, drawing a moral from the case, will recall two verses by Victor Hugo in "Les Contemplations":
"Les bêtes sont au Bon Dieu
Mais la bêtise est à l'homme",
without specifying to whom the second line refers.
Finally, lawyers will compare this decision with those which withhold any compensation from a fiancée overcome by the death of her loved one on the ground that she had no "blood relationship or relationship by marriage" with him, and will irreverently ask the Cour de cassation what exactly is the relationship by blood or marriage between the deceased horse and its master . . .
Anticipating all these ironical comments, the undersigned thought that this judgment needed at least a "Devil's advocate". He took the risk, with his lawyer's hat on, of course, and he will respond to the criticisms. In truth, the result is not very conducive to the continuing reliability of the case-law of the Civil Chamber.
2. Indeed, it is only possible to defend the judgment if the Civil Chamber abandons the solution which it has so far accepted in regard to proceedings by fiancé(e)s. It is necessary to refer specifically to the "Civil Chamber" since we know that the Criminal Chamber "requires no relationship by blood or marriage", which enables it to uphold actions by fiancé(e)s (Crim. 5 January 1956, D. 1956, 216) and those by foster parents (Crim. 30 January 1958, Gaz. Pal. 1958. 1.367).
The refusal to grant compensation to those who were not related by blood or marriage to the deceased is even less comprehensible in view of the fact that, in matters of contract, redress for non-material damage is quite usual, even though examples in the courts are not numerous.
Article 1382 requires any person who, by his fault, has caused damage to redress the same.
The courts must of course display circumspection and allow themselves to be convinced only on the basis of extensive evidence (R. Rodière, *Responsabilité civile*, No. 161 1) but *a priori* there is no

obstacle. Any profound and real pain deserves compassion and the assistance that judges can bring may consist in making the order for financial compensation requested of them by the plaintiff. Why, then, not take account of the pain caused by the death of a horse, a tom cat or a parrot if its "parents" were overcome by it . . .

The Devil's advocate rests his case. No need to say whether he himself is convinced.

Court of Appeal   **6.F.140.**
Jarvis v. Swans Tours[396]

DAMAGES FOR DISAPPOINTMENT

The solicitor's terrible holiday

Damages for mental distress can be recovered for a breach of contract where the purpose of the contract is to provide entertainment and enjoyment.

Facts: A solicitor booked a skiing holiday on the basis of a description in a brochure. The holiday failed to live up to the attractive terms in which it had been described.

Held: Overturning the first instance decision, the Court of Appeal awarded the plaintiff damages for mental distress and loss of enjoyment.

Judgment: LORD DENNING MR: . . . What is the legal position? I think that the statements in the brochure were representations or warranties. The breaches of them give Mr Jarvis a right to damages. It is not necessary to decide whether they were representations or warranties: because since the Misrepresentation Act 1967, there is a remedy in damages for misrepresentation as well as for breach of warranty.

The one question in the case is: What is the amount of damages? The judge seems to have taken the difference in value between what he paid for and what he got. He said that he intended to give "the difference between the two values and no other damages" under any other head. He thought that Mr Jarvis had got half of what he paid for. So the judge gave him half the amount which he had paid, namely, £31.72. Mr Jarvis appeals to this court. He says that the damages ought to have been much more.

What is the right way of assessing damages? It has often been said that on a breach of contract damages cannot be given for mental distress. Thus in *Hamlin* v. *Great Northern Railway Co.* (1856) 1 H. N. 408, 411 Pollock CB said that damages cannot be given "for the disappointment of mind occasioned by the breach of contract." And in *Hobbs* v. *London South Western Railway Co.* (1875) L.R. 10 Q.B. 111, 122, Mellor J said that "for the mere inconvenience, such as annoyance and loss of temper, or vexation, or for being disappointed in a particular thing which you have set your mind upon, without real physical inconvenience resulting, you cannot recover damages."

The courts in those days only allowed the plaintiff to recover damages if he suffered physical inconvenience, such as having to walk five miles home, as in *Hobbs'* case; or to live in an overcrowded house, *Bailey* v. *Bullock* [1950] 2 All E.R. 1167.

I think that those limitations are out of date. In a proper case damages for mental distress can be recovered in contract, just as damages for shock can be recovered in tort. One such case is a contract for a holiday, or any other contract to provide entertainment and enjoyment. If the contracting party breaks his contract, damages can be given for the disappointment, the distress, the upset and frustration caused by the breach. I know that it is difficult to assess in terms of money, but it is no more difficult than the assessment which the courts have to make every day in personal injury

---

[396] [1973] 1 All ER 71.

840

cases for loss of amenities. Take the present case. Mr Jarvis has only a fortnight's holiday in the year. He books it far ahead, and looks forward to it all that time. He ought to be compensated for the loss of it. A good illustration was given by Edmund Davies LJ in the course of the argument. He put the case of a man who has taken a ticket for Glyndbourne. It is the only night on which he can get there. He hires a car to take him. The car does not turn up. His damages are not limited to the mere cost of the ticket. He is entitled to general damages for the disappointment he has suffered and the loss of the entertainment which he should have had. Here, Mr Jarvis's fortnight's winter holiday has been a grave disappointment. It is true that he was conveyed to Switzerland and back and had meals and bed in the hotel. But that is not what he went for. He went to enjoy himself with all the facilities which the defendants said he would have. He is entitled to damages for the lack of those facilities, and for his loss of enjoyment.

. . . I think the damages in this case should be the sum of £125. I would allow the appeal, accordingly.

Notes

(1) This was the first English case in which damages for disappointment were awarded in contract. It was followed by others. For example, in *Heywood* v. *Wellers*[397] a woman employed solicitors to obtain an injunction to prevent a man molesting her. The solicitors failed to take proper steps and the molestation continued. She was awarded damages for mental distress.

(2) In *Heywood* James LJ suggested[398] that damages for distress could be awarded whenever distress was a foreseeable consequence of the breach. However, in *Watts* v. *Morrow*[399] this broad approach was rejected and it was said that, in contract, damages for disappointment or distress are recoverable only if the purpose of the contract was to provide enjoyment or peace of mind. In that case the plaintiffs bought a house in the country relying on a survey prepared by the defendant. The survey report had been prepared negligently and failed to reveal the need for major repairs. The trial judge included in the damages £8,000 for "distress and inconvenience." The Court of Appeal disallowed this, though it allowed £1,500 for "physical discomfort". Bingham LJ said:[400]

A contract-breaker is not in general liable for any distress, frustration, anxiety, displeasure, vexation, tension or aggravation which his breach of contract may cause to the innocent party. This rule is not, 1 think, founded on the assumption that such reactions are not foreseeable, which they surely are or may be, but on considerations of policy.

But the rule is not absolute. Where the very object of a contract is to provide pleasure, relaxation, peace of mind or freedom from molestation, damages will be awarded if the fruit of the contract is not provided or if the contrary result is procured instead. If the law did not cater for this exceptional category of case it would be defective. A contract to survey the condition of a house for a prospective purchaser does not, however, fall within this exceptional category.

In cases not falling within this exceptional category, damages are in my view recoverable for physical inconvenience and discomfort caused by the breach and mental suffering directly related to that inconvenience and discomfort. If those effects are foreseeably suffered during a period when defects are repaired I am prepared to accept that they sound in damages even though the cost of the repairs

---

[397] [1976] QB 446.
[398] *Ibid.* at 461.
[399] [1994] 4 All ER 937.
[400] *Ibid.* at 959–60.

is not recoverable as such. But I also agree that awards should be restrained, and that the awards in this case far exceeded a reasonable award for the injury shown to have been suffered.

Compare, however, the *Ruxley* swimming pool case.[401] This was a contract to build a swimming pool; the pool was less deep than the contract required though it was perfectly adequate for swimming and diving. The House of Lords seemed to accept that a similar award for "loss of amenity", which must mean loss of enjoyment, as there was no physical inconvenience to the owner, was proper, though strictly speaking this was obiter, as the trial judge's award of £2,500 for loss of amenity was not appealed: see the last words of Lord Jauncey's speech.[402] This suggests that the courts may now be ready to find that a contract was intended to provide enjoyment as well as its primary purpose of providing work or goods.

BGB **6.G.141.**

§ 253: For an injury which is not an injury to patrimony (*Vermögen*), compensation in money may be demanded only as provided by law.

Note

(1) § 253 BGB seems to imply that damages for non-patrimonial loss can only be awarded if there is specific statutory authorization. However, German courts in fact allowed compensation in "holiday" cases, similar to *Jarvis* v. *Swan's Tours*,[403] by treating the plaintiff as having a patrimonial right to his holiday entitlement, and by holding that this right had been destroyed by the bad holiday.[404] The matter is now covered by a specific legislative provision.[405]

(2) Commentators agree that the parties can set aside the rule in § 253 BGB by agreement,[406] for example through inserting an agreed damages clause into their contract. Thus under German law the plaintiff in a case like *Heywood* v. *Wellers* would be able to recover damages if she could show that the protection of her peace of mind was a purpose of her contract (*Schutzzweck des Vertrages*) with the lawyer.[407]

BGB **6.G.142.**

§ 651a: (1) Under the travel contract the tour operator is obliged to provide the traveller with a totality of travel services (travel). The traveller is obliged to pay to the tour operator the agreed travel price.

. . .

§ 651c: (1) The tour operator is obliged to provide the travel service in such a way that it has the characteristics warranted and is not vitiated by errors which negate or reduce its suitability for the normal or contractually agreed use

---

[401] *Supra* at 694.
[402] See *supra* at 695.
[403] See *supra* at 840.
[404] See BGHZ 63.98.
[405] See *infra*.
[406] BGH JZ 1955.581.
[407] See Fuller and Lange, op. cit., at 238.

(2) If the travel service is not of such a nature, the traveller may request assistance. The tour operator may refuse assistance if it demands a disproportionate amount of time or money.

(3) If the tour operator does not provide assistance within a reasonable period set by the traveller, the traveller may secure assistance himself and claim restitution in respect of the necessary expenditure of time and money. It shall not be necessary to set a period where assistance is refused by the tour operator or where immediate assistance is required owing to a particular need on the part of the traveller.

§ 651d: (1) If the travel service is defective within the meaning of § 651c(1) the travel price shall be reduced for the duration of the defect In accordance with § 472.

(2) Reduction shall not occur where the traveller culpably omits to give notice of the defect.

§ 651e: (1) If the travel service is appreciably affected by a defect of the kind mentioned in § 651c, the traveller may terminate the contract. The same shall apply where the traveller, as a result of such a defect, cannot be expected to make the journey for an important reason known to the tour operator.

(2) Termination shall be effective only if the tour operator has allowed a reasonable period set by the traveller to expire without providing assistance—it is not necessary to set a period where assistance is impossible, or is refused by the tour operator, or where immediate termination of the contract is justified by a particular need of the traveller.

(3) If the contract is terminated, the tour operator shall forfeit his right to the agreed price. He may nonetheless claim compensation, to be calculated in accordance with § 471, in respect of the services already provided or travel services to be provided in order to bring the journey to an end. This shall not apply where such services are of no interest to the traveller as a result of the cancellation of the contract.

(4) The tour operator shall be obliged to take the steps necessary as a result of cancellation of the contract; in particular, where the contract included recovery of the passenger, he shall bring the traveller home. Additional costs arising shall be borne by the tour operator.

§ 651f: (1) If the defect in the travel service is attributable to a factor for which the tour operator is responsible. the traveller may, notwithstanding a reduction or termination, claim damages for non-performance.

(2) If the travel service is rendered worthless or appreciably affected the traveller may also claim reasonable pecuniary compensation for holiday time spent to no avail.

Note

Council Directive 90/314/EEC on package travel, package holidays and package tours[408] imposes on Member States the obligation to regulate contracts for these services, and to provide for liability in cases of personal injury. Compensation for other losses, including disappointment over spoiled holidays, may however be subject to reasonable limitation in the holiday contract.

Though French law is the only one of the three to offer compensation for *préjudice moral* whenever it is a foreseeable consequence of the non-performance, English and German law seem each to be moving towards allowing recovery of this kind of loss. The principles of European Contract Law allow recovery for "non-pecuniary loss" (Article

[408] [1990] OJ L158/59.

9:501(2)(a)); the Unidroit Principles state that a party is entitled to full compensation for harm and that "such harm may be non-pecuniary and includes, for instance, physical suffering and emotional distress" (Article 7.4.2(2)). The Comments to Article 7.4.2 do not give disappointment as an example of such loss, but it should be remembered that the Unidroit Principles are for international commercial contracts in which personal disappointment or distress is less likely to occur.

6.5.4. SOME TYPICAL CASES

6.5.4.A. A SELLER OF GOODS FAILS TO DELIVER

Code civil **6.F.143.**

Article 1144: The creditor may also, in a case of non-performance, be authorised to perform the obligation himself at the expense of the debtor. The latter may be ordered to pay in advance the sums necessary for this performance.

Sale of Goods Act 1979 **6.E.144.**

Section 51: (1) Where the seller wrongfully neglects or refuses to deliver the goods to the buyer, the buyer may maintain an action against the seller for damages for non-delivery.
(2) The measure of damages is the estimated loss directly and naturally resulting, in the ordinary course of events, from the seller's breach of contract.
(3) Where there is an available market for the goods in question the measure of damages is prima facie to be ascertained by the difference between the contract price and the market or current price of the goods at the time or times when they ought to have been delivered or (if no time was fixed) at the time of refusal to deliver.

BGB **6.G.145.**

§ 252: The compensation shall also include lost profits. Profit is deemed to have been lost which could probably have been expected in the ordinary course of events, or according to the special circumstances, especially in the light of the preparations and arrangements made.

HGB **6.G.146.**

§ 376: (1) If it is stipulated that the performance of one party shall take place precisely at a fixed time or within a fixed period, the other party may, if the performance fails to take place at the fixed time or within the fixed period, rescind the contract or, in a case where it is the debtor who is delay, claim damages for non-performance instead of demanding performance. He may only demand performance, if immediately after the expiration of the time of the period he gives notice to the other party that he insists on performance.
(2) If the payment of damages for non-performance is demanded and the goods have a stock exchange or market price, the difference between the purchase price and the exchange or market price at the time and place of the performance owed may be demanded.

(3) The proceeds of a sale or purchase effected in a different way may, when the goods have a stock exchange or market price, be adopted as a basis of a claim for damages, only when the purchase or sale takes place immediately after the expiration of the stipulated time or period fixed for the performance. The sale or purchase, if not made by public auction, must be carried out at the current price by a commercial broker officially licensed for such sales or by a person who is an officially licensed auctioneer.

Notes

(1) Under the general law of sale in Germany, where the seller fails to deliver, the buyer may seek to enforce either the concrete or the abstract measure of damages. Under the *concrete measure*, the buyer will recover the difference between the cost of an actual cover purchase undertaken and the contract price. Where a cover purchase was not possible he may recover the difference between the contract price and the price he would have obtained from selling the goods on to another party. Under the *abstract measure,* the buyer may recover the difference between the market price of the goods—known as the price of a hypothetical cover purchase—and the contract price. Alternatively he may claim the difference between the contract price and the market price of the goods had he been able to resell them—known as a hypothetical further sale. In both cases it is obvious that where the cover purchase price, the market price or the further sale price was below the actual contract price no damages are recoverable—for non-performance at least.[409]

(2) An abstract calculation of damages amounts normally, in effect, to a lightening of the burden of proving loss which lies upon the creditor—here the seller. Thus, if the loss would have been caused in the normal course of events, it will be assumed that it was so caused in the particular case (see § 252, sent.2 BGB). However, it is always open to the debtor to prove that the case did not involve a "normal course of events". Indeed it is argued that where the buyer is not in business the abstract measure is not applicable at all since in these and related cases the seller will be able to prove that a further sale, for example, was improbable in the normal course of events.[410]

(3) The effect of § 376 HGB is to allow the seller or buyer, in the case of a commercial sale of goods, to claim damages where there is a delay in performance for which the other party is responsible. In such cases an abstract measure of damages is privileged over a concrete assessment by forcing the buyer to undertake a cover purchase immediately. It is in fact agreed that, whereas the abstract assessment in ordinary sales cases is merely a rebuttable presumption, easing the buyer's burden of proof, as to the measure of damages, the principle for calculation laid down in § 376(2) HGB is an irrebuttable rule of law.[411]

(4) When in French law the buyer/creditor is authorized to buy for himself the goods that the seller/debtor has failed to deliver, he will recover the actual cost of so doing—subject to it being shown that he did not act in good faith. English law refers only to an "abstract" method. The difference seems to depend on how the concrete measures are applied in practice. The English lawyer would defend the abstract principle by saying that if the buyer has paid more than the current market price for the replacement goods, he

---

[409] See generally *Münchener Kommentar*, under § 325 BGB, para. 87 ff.
[410] See BGH NJW 1980.172; Treitel, *Remedies* at 111–115, para. 102.
[411] See Fuller and Lange, op. cit., at 221.

has not acted reasonably. If he has managed to get them for less, this is a profitable deal he would have been able to make anyway, so that he should keep any profit. The international restatements provide both concrete and abstract methods.

Principles of European Contract Law   **6.PECL.147.**

Article 9:506: *Substitute Transaction*
> Where the aggrieved party has terminated the contract and has made a substitute transaction within a reasonable time and in a reasonable manner, it may recover the difference between the contract price and the price of the substitute transaction as well as damages for any further loss so far as these are recoverable under this Section.

Article 9:507: *Current Price*
> Where the aggrieved party has terminated the contract and has not made a substitute transaction but there is a current price for the performance contracted for, it may recover the difference between the contract price and the price current at the time the contract is terminated as well as damages for any further loss so far as these are recoverable under this Section.

See similarly Unidroit Articles 7.4.5 and 7.4.6.

6.5.4.B. A debtor fails to carry out work correctly

Under a contract for work such as a building contract, suppose that the contractor does some of the work defectively and refuses to put the defect right. What remedy will the employer have? In the continental systems, one possibility is that the contractor will be ordered to do the work; another, that the employer can have the work done at the contractor's expense.[412] English law will not normally grant specific performance of a building contract;[413] rather the normal remedy will be for the employer to engage another contractor to do the necessary work and to recover the cost from the defaulter in an action for damages. We have already pointed out that this is the functional equivalent of *exécution par un tiers*.[414]

However, what if the defect is not of great significance and repair would cost a disproportionate amount? We encountered this problem earlier, in section **6.2**.[415] We considered three cases. The first was a French case (Cass. civ. 17 January 1984[416]) in which the Cour d'appel had refused to give an order that a contractor should increase the number of the steps in a swimming pool from three to four, on the ground that it had not been shown that access with only three steps was more difficult. The Cour de cassation quashed the decision on the basis that, in deciding this without considering whether it was possible to make the pool conform to the contract, there was no legal basis for the decision. The second was a German case on replacement windows (BGH, 10 October 1985[417]) in which the BGH upheld new performance—at great expense—where a cure would be ineffective.

---

[412] For these possibilities, see *supra* at 684 ff.
[413] For this and an exception, see *supra* at 685.
[414] *Ibid.*
[415] *Supra* at 689 ff.
[416] Pourvoi no. 82–15.982 Lexis. See *supra* at 689.
[417] BGHZ 96.111. See *supra* at 691.

It was stated there that a proportionality requirement applied in relation to enforced performance in German law. The third was an English case (*Ruxley Electronics and Construction Ltd* v. *Forsyth*[418]) in which the House of Lords refused to award damages based on the cost of rebuilding a swimming pool to the correct depth on the ground that to rebuild it would be unreasonable when the pool was perfectly useable.

What if, as in *Ruxley*, the defect is so slight that it would be unreasonable to incur the cost of correcting it—or indeed, that the employer will not in fact spend any damages obtained on doing so? In English law the position is now fairly clear: first, if the employer will not in fact have the defect corrected, he may not recover the cost of doing so; nor can he if to do so would be unreasonable. In each case he may recover only any difference in value between the property with and without the defect and possibly damages for "loss of amenity".[419] What about the other systems?

Cass. civ., 11 April 1918[420]   **6.F.148.**

NO LOSS, NO DAMAGES

Wrong kind of wood

When a defect does not affect the usefulness or outward appearance of the finished work, the court may legitimately find that the employer has suffered no loss and award no damages, even if the material used is less expensive than that specified.

Facts: A shop-fitting contractor used a different kind of wood to that specified for furniture for a shop in Cairo. The usefulness and outward appearance of the finished furniture were not affected. The employer sought résolution of the contract and damages.

Held: The Tribunal Consulaire in Cairo refused to grant the employer *résolution* and, though it held that the contract had been broken, refused damages on the ground that there was no loss.

Judgment: . . . THE COURT: *On the first ground of appeal*:—Whereas from the introductory part and the grounds of the contested judgment, it appears that Francès brought an action against Collin and Courcier before the Tribunal Consulaire de France in Cairo for the cancellation of agreements concluded between them on 18 June and 12 July 1913 for the supply of furniture intended for the plaintiff's shops in Cairo, alleging in particular incomplete or incorrect compliance with the conditions laid down in the contract;
—Whereas the contested judgment, both adopting the grounds set out by the lower court and setting out its own grounds, examines the three complaints successively, and declares as follows:
1. The substitution of white Trieste pine for Swedish pine involves a significant price difference, but both woods can serve more or less the same purpose in the fitting out of a shop.
2. Although, according to the specification, the front of the furniture was to be of waxed oak and the interior of Swedish wood, the use of oak on only part of the external front side and Swedish wood inside was in conformity with cabinet-making usage, and a well-made veneer serves just as well as solid oak.
3. The bottom of the furniture was of the agreed thickness, and Collin and Courcier could not be criticised for reducing the thickness of the shelves by 0.02mm; hence, the judgment concludes that Francès's complaints, of a secondary nature, did not relate to the essential qualities of solidity and

---

[418] [1996] AC 344. See *supra* at 694.
[419] See *supra* at 842.
[420] S.1918.1.171.

847

elegance of the furniture sold, and could not therefore entail rescission, but only the award of damages;

—Whereas where a synallagmatic contract contains no express cancellation clause, it is for the courts to decide, in the event of partial non-performance and having regard to the factual circumstances, whether such non-performance is so significant that cancellation must be declared immediately or whether it might not be sufficiently remedied by an order awarding damages; that power of appraisal is absolute;

—Whereas consequently, the contested judgment, which did not, as wrongly alleged in the appeal, substitute new stipulations for those of the actual agreement, falls outside the scope of the Court of Cassation's review;

On the third appeal ground:—Whereas the appeal alleges finally that the contested judgment is vitiated by a contradiction in its grounds, because after recognising, as did the judgment which it upheld, the wrongful acts and negligence of which Collin and Courcier were guilty, it refused to grant Francès any right to damages, on the pretext that he did not suffer any loss;

—Whereas however, the only grounds taken over from the earlier decision are those which are not contrary to those of the judgment itself; the latter holds that, from all the facts, it is apparent that Francès had no grounds for complaining against the other parties, that he suffered no loss because of them, that the discount on the agreed prices willingly offered by Collin and Courcier constitutes adequate reparation, and that accordingly it is inappropriate to award higher damages;

—Whereas the finding as to the existence, extent or absence of loss falls within the absolutely unfettered powers of the trial court, and therefore the ground of appeal cannot be upheld;

—Whereas it thus follows that, by reaching the decision which it contains, the contested judgment did not infringe any of the articles referred to in the appeal;

The Court dismisses the appeal brought against the judgment delivered by the cour d'Aix, on 19 January 1916, etc.

BGB **6.G.149.**

§ 633: (1) The contractor is obliged to carry out the work in such a manner that it has the guaranteed attributes and that it is not subject to defects which negate or reduce its value or the usefulness for the purposes to which it would be put in the ordinary course of things or for those which were envisaged in the contract.

§ 635: If the defect in the work is due to a circumstance for which the contractor is responsible, the employer may seek damages instead of cancellation of the contract (*Wandelung*) or reduction of the purpose price (*Minderung*).

Notes

(1) The availability of damages for defects is greater in the case of a contract for services (*Werkvertrag*) than in the case of a contract of sale. In the case of sale, in order to recover damages the buyer must show that there was an express warranty or fraudulent concealment. By contrast, in the case of a contract for services the burden of disproving responsibility (including negligence) falls on the contractor.

(2) If a promised attribute is not present in the completed work, this still amounts to a defect within § 633(1) BGB, even where its absence does not reduce the value of the work or its usefulness for purposes to which it would ordinarily be put or which were envisaged in the contract. In such cases it has been said that the rights contained in §§ 634, 635

BGB—i.e. including the right to damages—will be limited by the principle of good faith only in "extremely exceptional cases".[421] Presumably this is the ground on which a German court would decide a case with the same facts as the *Ruxley* case.

(3) Apart from cases where a promised quality is absent, if a defect is significant, the employer can reject the work, refuse to pay the remuneration—or demand repayment if it has already been paid—and seek damages for the loss sustained—the "greater" damages claim. Alternatively the employer can retain the work and seek damages only for the reduction in the value of the work—the "lesser" damages claim. In this case the amount of damages can be set off against the contractor's claim for remuneration.

(4) A damages claim under § 635 BGB is not subject to the "disproportionality" restriction imposed upon both the right to a cure and the right to cancel the contract by § 633(2) sentence 3 BGB and § 634(3) BGB respectively.[422]

(5) Damages for non-performance recoverable under § 635 BGB may be calculated by reference to:
—the loss of profit of the employer;
—the reduction in the market value of the work (*Merkantiler Minderwert*);
—the cost to the creditor of removing the defect.

(6) In relation to the last mentioned means of calculating damages, in principle the "subjective" value, including the cost of securing conformity with the contract and not simply the difference in value, is to be paid. The decision of the English Court of Appeal in *Ruxley Electronics & Construction* v. *Forsyth*—which allowed the employer the cost of rebuilding the pool to the correct depth[423]—has been used to illustrate precisely this point of German law.[424]

(7) It is even the case that the employer will recover the cost of doing the work even though he has no intention of doing it.[425] In a number of tort cases it has been held that the owner of a car which has been damaged in an accident caused by the defendant's fault may recover the cost of hiring another car while his is being repaired even though he does not in fact hire a replacement.[426] The principle seems to be that what individuals do with their money/patrimony is their own business (*Privatautonomie*).

(8) By contrast, there is a personal injury case (BGH 14 January 1986[427]) in which the opposite result was reached. The plaintiff was left with scars after an accident. She was unable to recover the cost of an operation to remove the scars unless she had the operation. The BGH treated the personal injury as essentially and irreducibly injury to a different legal value (*Rechtsgut* or physical integrity or health). Damages compensate directly for this injury, for example, pain and suffering (*Schmerzensgeld*) (even for loss of earnings) and also money for an operation, but only if it is going to be used to restore the primary *Rechtsgut*, i.e. having a scarred face does not *per se* amount to being poorer, by contrast with having a scratched car.

[421] See *Münchener Kommentar*, under § 634 BGB, para. 27.
[422] *Münchener Kommentar*, under § 635 BGB, para. 4.
[423] See *supra* at 694.
[424] See Schlechtriem, *SAT*, para. 206.
[425] See BGHZ 61.28; 62.323.
[426] E.g. BGH 30 September 1963, BGHZ 40.345, BGH 15 April 1966, BGHZ 45.212 and other cases cit. in Markesinis, Lorenz and Dannemann, op. cit., at 626–8.
[427] BGHZ 97.14 cit. in Markesinis, Lorenz and Dannemann, op. cit., case 120.

Thus on the one hand English and French law seem to refuse the full cost of repair when this is greater than the loss of use or value of the property to the employer, at least if the employer does not in fact carry out the repair and probably if it would be unreasonable to do so because the cost would be disproportionate to the benefits to be obtained. German law seems prepared to award the full cost of repair in all cases. The international restatements do not address the question.

6.5.4.C. DEFECTS IN GOODS

As mentioned before, French and German law have special regimes governing the seller's liability for defects in goods.

In French law, if the goods have been accepted by the buyer, the seller's liability is normally limited to that under the *garantie des vices cachés*: see Code civil Articles 1641–1649.[428] The seller is responsible for returning the price, or a proportion of it, plus the expenses occasioned by the sale, but is not liable for damages unless it knew of the defect. This means that a seller who did not know of the defect is not liable for further losses to the buyer—however, a professional seller is presumed to know of any defects in goods it sells.[429]

Cancellation and reduction of the price were discussed earlier in connection with termination, which they closely resemble.[430] Under Article 1644, if the buyer claims a reduction in the price, this is to be adjudged by experts. More usually in civil law systems the price is reduced by the proportion that the value of the goods actually delivered bears to the value they should have had were they not defective, and this appears to be a restitutionary remedy rather than one measured by the buyer's loss.[431] It is not clear how it is regarded in French law.[432] Rather than a claim for damages, the *"action estimatoire"* is now considered as a kind of partial termination.[433]

The buyer is also entitled to expenses occasioned by the sale. At one time the courts applied this very broadly, so as to cover, for instance, expenses and inconvenience caused by a car breaking down,[434] and even the compensation the buyer had to pay to a third party injured by the defective car.[435] As Ghestin and Desché[436] say, this effectively made the good faith vendor liable for *damnun emergens*; it was only *lucrum cessans* which could not be recovered unless the vendor knew of the defect. But as the same authors argue,[437] in the light of developments which will be noted in the next paragraph, these broad decisions should no longer be followed, and they report various recent cases taking a narrower interpretation.

The development to which they refer is that a professional vendor is now presumed to know of defects in the goods it sold. A series of cases in the late 1950s and 1960s on the one hand rejected the broad interpretation of "expenses" referred to in the last paragraph,

---

[428] *Supra* at 664.
[429] See *infra* at 757.
[430] See *supra* at 756 ff.
[431] See Treitel, *Remedies* at 107–109, para. 100.
[432] See *ibid*.
[433] Ghestin and Desché, para 752.
[434] Cass.civ. 4 January 1965, D.1965.S.78.
[435] Cass., 21 October 1925, D.P.1926.1, Rapport Celice, annotated by Josserand.
[436] Ghestin and Desché, para. 853.
[437] Para. 743.

and on the other had held that a professional vendor ought to know of any defects in goods it sells and should therefore be liable in damages to the buyer.[438]

BGB **6.G.150.**

§ 472: (1) In the case of reduction, the purchase price shall be reduced in the proportion which at the time of the sale the value of the thing in a condition free from defect would have borne to the actual value.

(2) If, in the case of a sale of several things for an aggregate price, reduction is effected only in respect of some of them, then in reducing the price the aggregate value of all the things shall be taken as a basis.

§ 463: If a promised quality in the thing sold was absent at the time of the purchase, the purchaser may demand compensation for non-performance, instead of cancellation or reduction. The same applies if the seller has deceitfully concealed a defect.

BGH, 19 May 1993[439] **6.G.151.**

EXTENT OF SELLER'S GURARANTEE LIABILITY

Fake painting

A seller of goods who has guaranteed that they will have certain qualities is liable to pay damages in the amount of the expectation interest regardless of whether he could foresee the extent of such damages at the time of formation of the contract.

Facts: A painting was sold for DM 10,000. At the time of sale the seller made a written declaration that it was by the painter Edward Burra. It was later revealed to be a fake. If it had been an original it would have been worth DM 300,000. The plaintiff buyers sought damages of DM 290,000 on the basis that the seller had guaranteed an attribute of the painting under § 463 BGB and that they were therefore entitled to the expectation interest, i.e. the extra amount which they required to obtain an original. The lower courts rejected the buyer's claim for the following reasons. Even if the seller had guaranteed the authenticity of the painting he could not be taken by the buyer (having regard to the requirement of good faith § 157 BGB) to have assumed the huge financial risk which accrued in this case. The damages sought were furthermore beyond the protective purpose of the contract. Finally it would breach the "limits of normality", in the context of the law on defective goods, if the buyer were able to claim as damages a sum thirty times greater than the purchase price.

Held: The buyer's appeal was upheld. The buyer was required only to show that the seller had guaranteed a particular attribute, not that they had agreed to pay damages of a certain amount. As long as the first was proved the latter was irrelevant. The lower courts had confused loss arising directly from the defect with consequential loss. Only in the latter case would the protective purpose of the contract limit the amount recoverable. Ultimately provided that the original guarantee was proved, the buyer should not be deprived of the profit which he would have made on the contract, however large.

Judgment: I. The court immediately below did not determine the question whether the defendant's written declaration was already in existence when the contract was concluded, or whether the painting sold to the plaintiff was really a work by Burra. It held that the plaintiff's claim for damages was untenable on the basis of the plaintiff's own arguments, stating in that regard as follows:

---

[438] Cass. civ., 10 February 1959, JCP.1959.II.11063, annotated by Esmein, concl. Blanchet; D.1959.117; S.1959.45; RTD civ. 1959.338, annotated by Carbonnier and Mazeaud; Cass. civ. 4 February 1963, JCP.1963.II.13159, annotated by Savatier; S.1963.193, annotated by Meurisse; Cass. civ. 1re, 14 January 1965, D.1965.389; RTD civ. 1965.665. See Ghestin and Desché, para. 853.
[439] NJW 1993, 2103.

"It is true that, in his written declaration of 20.11.1990, the defendant gave an unequivocal assurance that the painting was genuine. Nevertheless, the lack of authenticity pleaded by the plaintiff cannot entitle him to the damages claimed by him under § 463 BGB. The quantum of damages payable under that provision depends on the significance to be attached to the assurance given. The decisive factor in that regard is the purpose which it was intended to achieve. The compensation payable is limited to that corresponding to the loss by the purchaser which the assurance given to him was intended to secure against. The purpose and scope of the assurance given by the defendant fall to be determined by means of the interpretation to be applied to it, and depend on the specific aspects of the particular case; they clearly show that the assurance as to the authenticity of the painting did not encompass an intention on the part of the defendant to guarantee that the picture sold for only DM 10,000 had a pecuniary and market value of DM 300,000. It would be completely contrary to common sense for the defendant, as a trader and a commercial art dealer, to have intended, on a sale at a price of DM 10,000, to warrant a capital appreciation of DM 290,000. Not even the plaintiff, having regard to the circumstances in which the contract was concluded, could, in good faith, have placed that interpretation on the conduct of the defendant. Moreover, the loss claimed does not fall within the scope of the protective purpose which § 459 et seq. of the BGB is designed to serve. The guarantee provisions applying to the sale of goods are intended to protect a purchaser who, in paying the price corresponding to goods which are supposed to be free from defects, has relied on the absence of such defects. However, looking at the matter from that standpoint, the plaintiff was not entitled to rely on the principle of the protection of persons acting in good faith, for the very reason that he did not pay the price payable for an item of property which was free from defects, that price being, according to his own submission, DM 300,000. Ultimately, liability under § 463 BGB in relation to the assurance given must be limited to a sum corresponding to those losses which that assurance would normally be intended to cover. No loss of the magnitude claimed has been suffered in the present case, since it would go beyond the 'bounds of normality' for an assurance regarding the subject-matter of a contract of sale to 'encompass a warranty that the value of the item of property in question was 30 times greater than the purchase price actually paid'".

It has not been conclusively shown that the defendant acted with deliberate intent to deceive, and no claim has been advanced for the amount of the purchase price actually paid by the plaintiff.

II. In various decisive respects, the foregoing statements do not stand up to scrutiny upon examination in the context of this appeal on a point of law.

1. The court below was correct in its view (which is not contested in this appeal) that the identity of the painter of the picture sold constituted an essential property of the subject-matter of the contract (see BGHZ 63, 369 [371] = NJW 1975, 970 = LM § 459 BGB, No 36; BGH, NJW 1988, 2597 = LM § 119 BGB, No 29 = WM 1988, 1415 (under II (1b)(aa)) and that the absence of that property, contrary to the assurance given, may found a claim for damages pursuant to § 463 BGB.

. . .

3. In the absence of any findings to the contrary by the appellate court below, it is necessary, for the purposes of determining this appeal, to assume that the painting sold was not by the painter Burra. On that assumption, the criteria for a claim in damages against the defendant under the first sentence of § 463 BGB are fulfilled. According to that provision, a purchaser may demand to be placed, by the payment to him of pecuniary compensation, in the position which he would have occupied if the object sold had possessed the property attributed to it by the vendor. If, like the plaintiff in the present case, he decides to claim what are known as "low damages", he is entitled to receive the difference in value between the hypothetical financial position which would have existed if, on the passing of risk, the object sold had been free from defects and the financial position which actually exists as a result of the material defect. . . . If the value of the painting sold to the plaintiff would have been around DM 300,000 had it been painted by the artist Burra, as must, in the absence of any findings to the contrary by the appellate court below, be assumed to be the case for the purposes of this appeal, that difference in value between the plaintiff's hypothetical and actual financial position, and thus the damages payable to him for non-performance amount to the sum claimed by him, namely DM 290,000.

4. Contrary to the view taken by the appellate court below, the question whether the defendant, in giving his assurance as to the authenticity of the picture, also intended to give a guarantee in respect of its market value exceeding the purchase price many times over, and to vouch for the

accrual to the plaintiff of a corresponding capital gain, is not material, in the particular circumstances of this case, for the purposes of determining the scope of the vendor's liability in damages under the first sentence of § 463 BGB. The views expressed in that connection by the appellate court below with regard to the purpose and scope of the assurance given are of relevance only in so far as concerns the liability of a vendor who has given an assurance for consequential losses flowing from the defect in question. Indeed, this depends decisively on the question whether the assurance given by the vendor was precisely intended, in addition, to secure the purchaser against consequential losses. . . . Moreover, the authors of the commentaries to which the appellate court sought to refer in support of its view are concerned solely with the vendor's liability for consequential losses. . . .

The issue in this case was, by contrast, the liability of the defendant vendor for the purchaser's immediate loss of bargain. A vendor who has given an assurance that the object sold possesses a property which it does not in fact possess is invariably liable for such loss under the first sentence of § 463 BGB, since the very essence of such an assurance lies in the fact that the vendor, in giving it, provides a contractually binding guarantee as to the presence of the property in question and thereby expresses his readiness to vouch for all and any consequences flowing from the absence of that property. . . . If an assurance is given regarding a property which the object sold does not in fact possess, the vendor will be liable, irrespective of what he thought at the time when the contract was concluded, for all consequences flowing directly from the absence of the property in question. The question wrongly raised in law by the appellate court below with regard to the quantum of damages, concerning the extent to which the defendant intended to stand surety for the consequences of the inauthenticity of the picture sold and as to the construction which the plaintiff was entitled, in good faith, to place on the defendant's declaration regarding the authenticity of the painting, is instead of decisive significance in relation to the more fundamental question needing to be answered for the purposes of interpreting the contract, namely whether a statement made in "unequivocal" terms as to the presence of a property in the object sold constitutes, in the legal sense, an assurance in respect of that property. . . .

5. Nor, contrary to the view taken by the appellate court below, can the defendant's liability for the plaintiff's immediate loss of bargain be denied on the ground that the loss and damage pleaded does not fall within the protective scope of the concept of liability under guarantees given on the sale of goods, pursuant to § 459 et seq. of the BGB. In so far as the appellate court below considers that the protective scope of the first sentence of § 463 BGB extends to cover only a purchaser who has paid the purchase price corresponding to the market value of the object sold, it is construing that provision too narrowly. That interpretation would afford no protection to a purchaser who succeeded (for whatever reason) in concluding the contract at a particularly favourable purchase price. There exist no grounds for such a restriction of liability under § 463 BGB. The judgment of the Eleventh Civil Chamber of the BGH of 30 January 1990 . . ., cited by the appellate court below in support of its contrary conclusion concerns a factual situation which is not comparable (limitation of liability on account of incorrect tax advice).

6. Nor, finally, are there any grounds for excluding the defendant's liability on the basis that the loss and damage pleaded in the present case go beyond the "bounds of normality". Once again (as is confirmed by the authority cited in that regard by the appellate court below), the principle that liability on an assurance under § 463 BGB encompasses only damage typically covered by such an assurance is solely concerned with the vendor's liability for consequential damage produced by a defect in the object sold. . . . No such restriction can be said to apply in the present case, relating as it does to liability for the direct loss of bargain suffered by the purchaser.

III. The appellant's complaint concerning the finding by the appellate court below that there was no conclusively proof of his having been fraudulently deceived over the inauthenticity of the painting cannot be upheld. The fact that, despite the doubts expressed by the plaintiff and supported by the information supplied by the English gallery, the defendant continues to insist that the painting is genuine, suggests that no fraudulent intent can be imputed to him. There is no need to determine the appellant's complaint that the defendant's account of the facts was ignored, since the plaintiff has not agreed and adopted that account.

. . .

Notes

(1) The reduction of the purchase price under § 472 BGB is calculated in the same way as in French law.

(2) Deceitful representation of the presence of a particular attribute is taken to be equivalent to deceitful concealment of a defect for purposes of § 463 BGB.

(3) Like a disappointed contractor under a contract for services, a buyer of defective goods may, where § 463 BGB applies, pursue either a lesser claim for damages or a greater claim for damages.[440] In both cases the buyer may also recover lost profit on any further sale of the goods, the costs of entering the contract and consequential loss.

(4) Whether the buyer demands cancellation or reduction, or seeks damages for non-performance, he may in addition recover damages for consequential loss (*Mangelfolge-schäden*). Consequential losses are those which are not directly related to the defects in the goods themselves, but which involve injury to another protected interest of the debtor. See, for example, RGZ 66, 289: a buyer of Indian maize, which was contaminated by poisonous castor seeds, had to pay damages to a further buyer whose horses died from eating the feed; it was accepted that he could recover this amount from the original seller. If the seller is taken to have assumed liability for consequential loss in the contract, the buyer will be able to recover damages under § 463 BGB, without proof of fault. In other cases of consequential loss the buyer must seek recovery on the basis of positive breach of contract which requires proof of fault, unless the harm originated within the area of risk specifically under the control of the seller, who bears the burden of disproving fault in such cases.[441] It is held that such claims for damages must be raised within the six-month limitation period laid down by § 477 BGB. Damages are also available for consequential loss caused by defects in work supplied under a work contract.[442] In the latter case however the general limitation period of thirty years applies (§ 195 BGB).

English law, in contrast, treats the delivery of defective goods as subject to the same rules as other breaches of contract. Thus if goods are not of satisfactory quality, the seller will be in breach of the term implied by Sale of Goods Act, section 14(2). This term is a condition, so the buyer will normally be entitled to reject the goods;[443] but whether the buyer rejects or not, she will be entitled to damages for any loss. These will be calculated under the normal rules.[444] The same approach is taken by PECL and Unidroit. CISG

---

[440] See *supra* at 813–814.

[441] See *Münchener Kommentar*, under § 275 BGB, para. 352.

[442] See BGH NJW 1982.2244.

[443] See *supra* at 736.

[444] Sale of Goods Act 1979 s. 53(1)(a) says that a buyer who has received defective goods may set up the defect "in diminution of the price", which may be a reflection of continental terminology but which is usually treated as referring to off-setting against the price the damages to which the buyer is entitled; see e.g P.S. Atiyah, *Sale of Goods,* 9th edn. with J. Adams (London: Pitman, 1995) at 489 ff.

provides for price reduction (Article 50) but also that the buyer may claim damages in addition (Article 45(1)(b)). (PECL also contains a provision on reduction of price, but its chief importance is in cases of excused non-performance.[445])

6.5.4.D. PLAINTIFF'S LOSS OR DEFENDANT'S GAIN?

The cases in which work has been done incorrectly raise the possibility that by breaking the contract, the defendant may make savings, or a profit, exceeding any loss to the plaintiff—this does not seem to have been the situation in the *Ruxley* case. We encountered the question in the French case about the contractor who used a cheaper kind of wood than had been specified to complete the contract,[446] but there the contractor seems to have offered to pay the employer the amount saved. In principle, damages are to compensate for loss, so recovery of any additional profit or any savings made by the debtor would have to be by way of restitution.[447] But occasionally cases seem to award damages where the loss is at best notional.

OLG Braunschweig, 26 January 1891[448]   **6.G.152.**

DEFENDANT MAY BE OBLIGED TO RESTORE GAINS ACQUIRED THROUGH BREACH OF CONTRACT

The bread rolls

Where a party receives goods that are worth less than they should have been he may recover damages even though he sells the goods for the same price for which he would have sold conforming goods.

Facts: A baker received quantities of dough from a bread dealer, to make into rolls for the customer. The baker kept some of the dough for himself but made the correct number of rolls, though they were smaller than they should have been. The bread dealer did not notice and re-sold the rolls for normal price to his customers. He later claimed damages.

Held: The baker was liable.

Judgment: The plaintiff, a bread dealer, had had a business relationship with the defendant, a baker, in the context of which he had dough delivered daily to the defendant in containers and baked by the defendant. It was established by the evidence of a number of witnesses that for the whole of this period, if not daily very frequently, the baker removed quantities of the dough delivered to him of up to five pounds and more to the value of 10 Marks to the pound and kept them for himself. Since the defendant was unsuccessful in his testimony that this procedure was based on an arrangement, he was ordered to pay damages and the plaintiff was requested to give sworn testimony of the estimate of his losses. At second instance the defendant went on to raise the plea that the action of damages should be struck out because the plaintiff had in reality not suffered any damage as a result of removal of the relevant quantities of bread dough on the ground that the bread rolls made for him by the defendant had always been sold at the full price, in spite of the reduction of the raw material delivered for that purpose. That objection was turned down.

Just as the defendant undoubtedly enriched himself by the unlawful taking of those quantities for his own use by the value thereof, to the same extent was the plaintiff harmed by the fact that

---

[445] See *supra* at 625.
[446] *Supra* at 847.
[447] See Treitel, *Remedies* at 76–77, para. 76.
[448] Seuff A 46 Nr. 173.

855

instead of the full number of bread rolls of full weight either a lesser quantity of bread rolls or rolls below full weight were delivered to him. It is irrelevant to the question of the occurrence of damage and the defendant's obligation to pay damages that the damage caused is imperceptible or subsequently balanced out on other grounds beyond the defendant's control—including the assertions made by him apparently at random and unsupported by evidence. Whilst the defendant's liability in damages is founded solely in the principles of the contract for the hire of services, which the court of first instance took sole cognisance of, there is no doubt concerning such liability under the principles of *condictio furtiva* the preconditions of which are all satisfied. For, according to these principles, the claim of the injured party is first to the return of the thing alienated together with all accessory rights or, if this is not possible, to its pecuniary value, even if a claim in respect of other damage may be made in addition (fr. 3. S. 13 de cond. furt. 18. 1; fr. 29 rer. amot. 25. 2), without the plaintiff being obliged to prove, understandably, particularly to the defendant, that, had the items in question not been removed he would have had use of them according to their value, or to prove that he suffered loss and, it so, the extent thereof, by removal of the items.

Notes

(1) This case predates the introduction of the BGB in 1901 and so was decided in accordance with the *gemeines Recht* (Common Law).

(2) In a similar case a brewer had wasted several vats of beer, but had made up the loss by weakening the strength of later quantities, thereby in fact making a profit for his employers beyond what could normally be expected. The Reichsgericht held him nonetheless liable—under the terms of his contract—to pay his employers for the wasted vats. The reasoning in these cases has been explained by Lange as follows:

In the brewery and bread roll cases a harm was undoubtedly suffered. The apparently purported elimination of the loss is not held to be sufficient because the defendant should not be able to derive any advantage from a further breach of the contract tending to damage the business interests of the plaintiff even more.[449]

(3) Although the case above (note 2) and that discussed previously involved a breach of contract, they also involved misappropriation of the plaintiff's property. The defendant is made to pay for the property even though the plaintiff does not show that he has lost by being deprived of it.

English cases with similar facts, in that in breach of contract the defendant has misused the plaintiff's property, have applied a similar rule. Thus in *Penarth Dock Engineering Co. Ltd.* v. *Pounds*[450] the defendant bought a pontoon which was on the plaintiffs' land and undertook to remove it. He failed to remove it until some months after the agreed date. The defendant was required to pay the plaintiffs damages based on what he would have had to pay to rent the land, although there was no evidence that the plaintiffs would either have rented or used the land themselves. Lord Denning MR applied a principle he had stated in the earlier case of *Strand Electric and Engineering Co. Ltd.* v. *Brisford Entertainments Ltd*:[451]

If a wrongdoer has made use of goods for his own purposes, then he must pay a reasonable hire for them, even though the owner has in fact suffered no loss. It may be that the owner would not have

---

[449] See Fuller and Lange, op. cit., at 163, footnote 7.
[450] [1963] 1 Lloyd's Rep. 588.
[451] [1952] 2 QB 246.

used the goods himself or that he had a substitute readily available which he used without extra cost to himself. Nevertheless the owner is entitled to a reasonable hire. . . . The claim for a hiring charge is therefore not based on loss to the plaintiff but on the fact that the defendant has used the goods for his own purposes. It is an action against him because he has had the benefit of the goods. It resembles therefore an action for restitution, rather than an action for tort.

Lord Denning seems to regard this as a form of restitution but the other members of the Court of Appeal in the *Strand Electric* case considered the damages to be compensatory.

There has been much discussion in England in recent years about whether the plaintiff can seek "restitution" of the savings or profit.

Court of Appeal   **6.E.153.**
Surrey County Council v. *Bredero Homes Ltd*[452]

PLAINTIFF CANNOT RECOVER PROFIT MADE BY DEFENDANT

Extra houses

The victim of a breach of contract may claim damages for its own loss, not to recoup a larger profit made by the defendant through breaking the contract.

Facts: The Council sold a site to Bredero, which was given permission to build seventy-two homes on the site but not more without the Council's permission. Without obtaining permission Bredero built seventy-seven homes. The Council did not object at the time. Later it claimed compensation. It was unable to show any loss suffered as the result of the breach but claimed a percentage of the additional profit made by Bredero.

Held: The trial judge held that the Council could recover only nominal damages and the Court of Appeal agreed.

Judgment: DILLON LJ: . . . The plaintiffs have merely sought damages which have been described as "damages at common law," as opposed to damages in equity under the Chancery Amendment Act 1858 (21 & 22 Vict. c. 27) (Lord Cairns's Act). The plaintiffs accept that they have not suffered any damage at all of the nature of damage to adjoining property owned or occupied by them.

What they claim as damages is essentially the profit made by the defendant by breaking the covenants and building 77 houses and not just 72—or, since the plaintiffs wish to be modest in their demands in putting forward a somewhat revolutionary development of the law of damages, such a part of the profit as would reflect the reasonable premium that the defendant should have paid them for contractual permission by way of relaxation of the covenants to build the 77 houses rather than 72.

. . .

The starting point, however, in my judgment is that the remedy at common law for a breach of contract is an award of damages, and damages at common law are intended to compensate the victim for his loss, not to transfer to the victim if he has suffered no loss the benefit which the wrongdoer has gained by his breach of contract . . . [The] innocent party is to be placed, so far as money can do so, in the same position as if the contract had been performed. That follows the statement of the rule of the common law by Parke B. *Harman* (1848) 1 Ex. 850, 855. That rule has been referred to in an argument in the present case as the "conventional" rule . . .

. . . Such damages may, in an appropriate case, cover profit which the injured plaintiff has lost, but they do not cover an award, to a plaintiff who has himself suffered loss, of the profit which the

---

[452] [1993] 1 WLR 1361.

857

defendant has gained for himself by breach of contract. In the field of tort there are areas where the law is different and the plaintiff can recover in respect of the defendant's gain. Thus in the tort of trespass it is well established that if one person has, without the leave of another, been using that other's land for his own purposes he ought to pay for such user. Thus even if he had done no actual harm to the land he was charged for the user of the land. This was applied originally in way leave cases where a person had without authority used his neighbour's land for passage: see, for instance, *Jegon* v. *Vivian* (1871) L.R. 6. Ch. App. 742 and *Phillips* v. *Homfray* (1871) L.R. 6 Ch.App. 770 . . . [In] a case of detinue the defendant was ordered to pay a hire for the chattels he had detained: *Strand Electric and Engineering Co. Ltd.* v. *Brisford Entertainments Ltd.* [1952] 2 Q.B. 246. Those cases do not apply in the present case as the defendant has made no use of any property of either plaintiff . . .

I come then to the *Wrotham Park* case [1974] 1 W.L.R. 798. In that case the predecessor in title of the plaintiffs had in 1935 sold some land to a predecessor in title of the defendants, subject to a restrictive covenant restricting building to a particular layout. That covenant was duly registered under the Land Charges Act 1925. In 1971 the land was sold to the defendants, who had no actual knowledge of the restrictive covenant and proceeded to build 14 houses on the land in breach of the covenant. In early 1972 the plaintiffs, as successors in title to the benefit of the covenant, issued their writ against the defendants claiming an injunction to restrain building in breach of the covenant, and demolition of anything built in breach. The plaintiffs made no application for an interim injunction. By the time the action came on for trial in July 1973, the 14 houses had all been completed and sold to purchasers with the benefit of indemnity insurance policies. At the trial Brightman J. held that the plaintiffs were indeed entitled to the benefit of the covenant and the defendants were bound by it. For obvious reasons however—he could not shut his eyes to the fact that the houses existed and it would be an unpardonable waste of much needed houses to direct that they be pulled down—he refused to grant a mandatory injunction. He commented that no damage of a financial nature had been done to the plaintiffs by the breach of the covenant and proceeded to consider what damages, if any, he should award under the jurisdiction which had originated under Lord Cairns's Act to award damages in substitution for an injunction.

It was submitted to him that the damages should be nil or purely nominal because the value of the Wrotham Park estate was not diminished by one farthing in consequence of the breach of covenant. But the judge concluded that such a result would be of questionable fairness. He said, at p. 812:

> "If, for social and economic reasons, the court does not see fit in the exercise of its discretion, to order demolition of the 14 houses, is it just that the plaintiffs should receive no compensation and that the defendants should be left in undisturbed possession of the fruits of their wrongdoing?"

He then referred to the wayleave cases . . . and the other cases which I have mentioned where the same principle has been applied. He concluded that the appropriate course was that the defendants should pay by way of damages the sum which the plaintiffs might hypothetically have been willing to accept—though actually they would never have been willing to relax the covenant—to permit the defendants to do what they wanted to do on the land. He fixed that at a small percentage of the defendants' anticipated profit from building the 14 houses on the land.

The difficulty about the decision in the *Wrotham Park* case is that in *Johnson* v. *Agnew* [1980] A.C. 367, 400G, Lord Wilberforce, after citing certain decisions on the scope and basis of Lord Cairns's Act which were not cited to Brightman J, stated in the clearest terms that on the balance of those authorities and on principle he found in the Act no warrant for the court awarding damages differently from common law damages. Sir William Goodhart submits that it follows from that analysis by Lord Wilberforce in *Johnson* v. *Agnew* . . . Given that the established basis of an award of damages in contract is compensation for the plaintiff's loss, as indicated above, I have difficulty in seeing how Sir William Goodhart's suggested common law principle of awarding the plaintiff who has suffered no loss the gain which the defendant has made by the breach of contract is intended to go. Is it to apply, for instance, to shipping contracts or contracts of employment or contracts for building works?

Sir William suggested, in his and Mr Weatherill's skeleton argument, that the conventional measure fails to do justice and a different measure should be applied where the following conditions are satisfied. (a) The breach is deliberate, in the sense that the defendant is deliberately doing an act which he knows or should know is plainly or arguably in breach of contract. (b) The defendant, as a result of the breach, has profited by making a gain or reducing a loss. (c) At the date of the breach it is clear or probable that damages under the conventional measure will either be nominal or much smaller than the profit to the defendant from the breach. (d) If the profit results from the avoidance of expenditure, the expenditure would not have been economically wasteful or grossly disproportionate to the benefit which would have resulted from it. He suggested in the skeleton argument that the underlying principle might be that the conventional measure of damages might be overridden in certain circumstances by the rule that no one should benefit from his deliberate wrongdoing.

In the course of his submissions Sir William limited his formulation and, while retaining conditions (a), (b) and (c), substituted for condition (d):

> "Damages for loss of bargaining power to perform the contract. Where no such possibility existed there was no bargaining power in reality and no right to damages for loss of it. Hence damages for loss of bargaining power cannot be awarded where there is, for example, a contract for the sale of goods or generally a contract of employment."

I find difficulty with that because in theory every time there is a breach of contract the injured party is deprived of his "bargaining power" to negotiate for a financial consideration a variation of the contract which would enable the party who wants to depart from its terms to do what he wants to do. In addition it has been held in *Walford* v. *Miles* [1992] 2 A.C. 128 that an agreement to negotiate is not an animal known to the law and a duty to negotiate in good faith is unworkable in practice, and so I find it difficult to see why loss of bargaining or negotiating power should become an established factor in the assessment of damages for breach of contract.

Beyond that, since we are looking for the measure of damages at common law for breach of contract apart from Lord Cairns's Act, I do not see why that should vary, depending on whether the party in breach could or could not have been restrained by injunction from committing the breach or compelled by specific performance to perform the contract. Injunction and specific performance were not remedies in the common law courts and were granted by the court of chancery, which, before Lord Cairns's Act, had no power to award damages, just because the common law remedy of damages was not an adequate remedy.

. . . I would dismiss this appeal.

STEYN LJ: I agree . . . Dillon LJ has reviewed the relevant case law. It would not be a useful exercise for me to try to navigate through those much travelled waters again. Instead, it seems to me that it may possibly be useful to consider the question from the point of view of the application of first principles.

An award of compensation for breach of contract serves to protect three separate interests. The starting principle is that the aggrieved party ought to be compensated for loss of his positive or expectation interests. In other words, the object is to put the aggrieved party in the same financial position as if the contract had been fully performed. But the law also protects the negative interest of the aggrieved party. If the aggrieved party is unable to establish the value of a loss of bargain he may seek compensation in respect of his reliance losses. The object of such an award is to compensate the aggrieved party for expenses incurred and losses suffered in reliance on the contract. These two complementary principles share one feature. Both are pure compensatory principles. If the aggrieved party has suffered no loss he is not entitled to be compensated by invoking these principles. The application of these principles to the present case would result in an award of nominal damages only.

There is, however, a third principle which protects the aggrieved party's restitutionary interest. The object of such an award is not to compensate the plaintiff for a loss, but to deprive the defendant of the benefit he gained by the breach of contract. The classic illustration is a claim for the return of goods sold and delivered where the buyer has repudiated his obligation to pay the price. It is not traditional to describe a claim for restitution following a breach of contract as damages . . .

In my view there are also other policy reasons which militate against adopting Sir William's primary or narrower submission. The introduction of restitutionary remedies to deprive cynical contract breakers of the fruits of their breaches of contract will lead to greater uncertainty in the assessment of damages in commercial and consumer disputes. It is of paramount importance that the way in which disputes are likely to be resolved by the courts must be readily predictable. Given the premise that the aggrieved party has suffered no loss, is such a dramatic extension of restitutionary remedies justified in order confer a windfall in each case on the aggrieved party? I think not. In any event such a widespread availability of restitutionary remedies will have a tendency to discourage economic activity in relevant situations. In a range of cases such liability would fall on underwriters who have insured relevant liability risks. Inevitably underwriters would have to be compensated for the new species of potential claims. Insurance premiums would have to go up. That, too, is a consequence which mitigates against the proposed extension. The recognition of the proposed extension will in my view not serve the public interest. It is sound policy to guard against extending the protection of the law of obligations too widely. For these substantive and policy reasons I regard it as undesirable that the range of restitutionary remedies should be extended in the way that we have been invited to do so . . .

[ROSE LJ agreed.]

Notes

(1) It is perhaps arguable that the County Council had in fact suffered a loss on the facts of this case.[453]

(2) On the assumption made by the court that there was no loss to the County Council, their claim is one for restitution of the profit made by the developers through breaking the contract. Note that this is quite different from the kind of restitution claim (common in contract cases) where a contract is avoided or terminated and a party then seeks restitution of property he had delivered or for other benefits transferred before the contract was brought to an end.

(3) There is a substantial body of academic opinion in favour of allowing a restitutionary claim at least in certain circumstances, and recently the Court of Appeal suggested that in some cases "restitutionary damages" may be appropriate. However, the House of Lords took a different approach, holding that on occasion the victim of a breach of contract may obtain an account of the profit made by the defendant through his breach of contract.

---

[453] See Beale, "Exceptional Measures of Damages: Contract" in Birks (ed.) *Wrongs and Remedies in the 21st Century* (Oxford: Clarendon, 1996), at 217.

House of Lords   **6.E.154.**
Attorney-General v. *Blake* [454]

RESTITUTIONARY DAMAGES?

The spy's book

Restitutionary damages may be awarded in two exceptional situations where profits are occasioned directly by a breach of contract and compensatory damages would be inadequate, namely where the defendant fails to provide the full extent of the services he has contracted to provide and for which he has charged the plaintiff, and where the defendant has obtained his profit by doing the very thing he contracted not to do.

Facts: The defendant was a former member of the Secret Intelligence Service ("S.I.S.") who in 1944 signed an undertaking not to divulge any official information gained as a result of his employment. Between 1951 and 1960 he disclosed valuable secret information to the Soviet Union. In 1961 he was convicted of spying and sentenced to 42 years' imprisonment, but in 1966 he escaped and went to live in Moscow, where he remained. In 1989 he wrote an autobiography substantial parts of which were based on information he had acquired in the course of his duties as an S.I.S. officer. By section 1(1) of the Official Secrets Act 19891 it was an offence for a person who had been a member of the intelligence services without lawful authority to disclose any information relating to intelligence which was in his possession by virtue of his position as a member of those services. The defendant entered into a publishing contract with the third party under which he was to receive an advance of £50,000, a further £50,000 on delivery of the final manuscript and £50,000 on publication. The defendant neither obtained permission from the Crown nor submitted the manuscript for prior approval, and the Crown had no knowledge of the book until its publication was announced in the press. After he had already received some £60,000 from the third party, the Attorney-General brought a private law action against the defendant claiming damages for breach of fiduciary duty and payment of all moneys received and to be received by him from the third party on the ground that the defendant owed the Crown a fiduciary duty not to use his position as a former member of the S.I.S. or make use of secret or confidential information acquired during his service so as to generate a profit for himself.

Held: The judge dismissed the action on the grounds that the lifelong duty owed by former members of the security services not to disclose secret or confidential information acquired during the course of their employment did not extend to information no longer secret or confidential and the disclosure of which would not damage the national interest, that the defendant had not expressly contracted not to publish any information relating to the intelligence service without the Crown's prior approval, nor could such an equitable obligation be implied, and that the breaches of section 1(1) of the Act of 1989 did not establish any breach of duty under the civil law for which the civil remedies sought could be claimed. The Attorney-General appealed, amending the statement of claim to raise issues of public law and claiming an injunction to restrain the defendant from receiving any payment or other benefit resulting from his criminal conduct.

On the appeal it was held, dismissing the appeal on the private law issues, that a fiduciary obligation did not continue after the determination of the particular relationship which gave rise to it; that a former employee did not owe a duty of undivided loyalty to his former employer nor was he under a duty to maintain the confidentiality of information which had ceased to be confidential; that, therefore, since the defendant's fiduciary relationship with the Crown had long since terminated and the information published in his autobiography was no longer confidential, the defendant was not in breach of any fiduciary duty to the Crown in publishing the information he obtained during his employment; but that by submitting the manuscript of his autobiography for publication without having first obtained clearance from the Crown the defendant was in breach of the express undertaking he signed when he joined the service of the Crown; that that obligation was not an unlawful restraint of trade since it did not exceed what was rendered unlawful by section 1(1) of the Official Secrets Act 1989; and that, accordingly, the defendant was in breach of contract, but, since the Crown had not sought an injunction to prevent publication, it could not establish loss and was therefore entitled to no more than nominal damages. The House of Lords held that, as a matter of private law, the Crown was entitled to an account of the profit made by Blake.

---

[454] [2000] 4 All ER 385.

861

Judgment: LORD NICHOLLS: . . .

Breach of contract

Leaving aside the anomalous exception of punitive damages, damages are compensatory. That is axiomatic. It is equally well-established that an award of damages, assessed by reference to financial loss, is not always "adequate" as a remedy for a breach of contract. The law recognises that a party to a contract may have an interest in performance which is not readily measurable in terms of money. On breach the innocent party suffers a loss. He fails to obtain the benefit promised by the other party to the contract. To him the loss may be as important as financially measurable loss, or more so. An award of damages, assessed by reference to financial loss, will not recompense him properly. For him a financially assessed measure of damages is inadequate.

The classic example of this type of case, as every law student knows, is a contract for the sale of land. The buyer of a house may be attracted by features which have little or no impact on the value of the house. An award of damages, based on strictly financial criteria, would fail to recompense a disappointed buyer for his head of loss. The primary response of the law to this type of case is to ensure, if possible, that the contract is performed in accordance with its terms. The court may make orders compelling the party who has committed a breach of contract, or is threatening to do so, to carry out his contractual obligations. . . .

All this is trite law. In practice, these specific remedies go a long way towards providing suitable protection for innocent parties who will suffer loss from breaches of contract which are not adequately remediable by an award of damages. But these remedies are not always available. For instance, confidential information may be published in breach of a non-disclosure agreement before the innocent party has time to apply to the court for urgent relief. Then the breach is irreversible. Further, these specific remedies are discretionary. Contractual obligations vary infinitely. So do the circumstances in which breaches occur, and the circumstances in which remedies are sought. The court may, for instance, decline to grant specific relief on the ground that this would be oppressive.

An instance of this nature occurred in *Wrotham Park Estate Co Ltd* v. *Parkside Homes Ltd* [1974] 2 All ER 321, [1974] 1 WLR 798. For social and economic reasons the court refused to make a mandatory order for the demolition of houses built on land burdened with a restrictive covenant. Instead, Brightman J made an award of damages under the jurisdiction which originated with Lord Cairns' Act. The existence of the new houses did not diminish the value of the benefited land by one farthing. The judge considered that if the plaintiffs were given a nominal sum, or no sum, justice would manifestly not have been done. He assessed the damages at 5 per cent of the developer's anticipated profit, this being the amount of money which could reasonably have been demanded for a relaxation of the covenant.

In reaching his conclusion the judge applied by analogy the cases mentioned above concerning the assessment of damages when a defendant has invaded another's property rights but without diminishing the value of the property. I consider he was right to do so. Property rights are superior to contractual rights in that, unlike contractual rights, property rights may survive against an indefinite class of persons. However, it is not easy to see why, as between the parties to a contract, a violation of a party's contractual rights should attract a lesser degree of remedy than a violation of his property rights. . . .

I turn to the decision of the Court of Appeal in *Surrey CC* v. *Bredero Homes Ltd* [1993] 3 All ER 705, [1993] 1 WLR 1361. . . .

This is a difficult decision. It has attracted criticism from academic commentators and also in judgments of Sir Thomas Bingham MR and Millett LJ in *Jaggard's* case. I need not pursue the detailed criticisms. In *Surrey CC* v. *Bredero Homes Ltd* ([1993] 3 All ER 705 at 709, [1993] 1 WLR 1361 at 1364) Dillon LJ himself noted that had the covenant been worded differently, there could have been provision for payment of an increased price if a further planning permission were forth-coming. That would have been enforceable. But, according to the *Bredero Homes Ltd* decision, a covenant not to erect any further houses without permission, intended to achieve the same result, may be breached with impunity. That would be a sorry reflection on the law. Suffice to say, in so far as the *Bredero Homes Ltd* decision is inconsistent with the approach adopted in the *Wrotham Park* case, the latter approach is to be preferred.

The *Wrotham Park* case, therefore, still shines, rather as a solitary beacon, showing that in con-tract as well as tort damages are not always narrowly confined to the recoupment of financial loss. In a suitable case damages for breach of contract may be measured by the benefit gained by the wrongdoer from the breach. The defendant must make a reasonable payment in respect of the ben-efit he has gained. In the present case the Crown seeks to go further. The claim is for all the profits of Blake's book which the publisher has not yet paid him. This raises the question whether an account of profits can ever be given as a remedy for breach of contract. The researches of counsel have been unable to discover any case where the court has made such an order on a claim for breach of contract. . . .

There is a light sprinkling of cases where courts have made orders having the same effect as an order for an account of profits, but the courts seem always to have attached a different label. . . .

These cases illustrate that circumstances do arise when the just response to a breach of contract is that the wrongdoer should not be permitted to retain any profit from the breach. . . .

My conclusion is that there seems to be no reason, *in principle*, why the court must in all circum-stances rule out an account of profits as a remedy for breach of contract. I prefer to avoid the unhappy expression "restitutionary damages". Remedies are the law's response to a wrong (or, more precisely, to a cause of action). When, exceptionally, a just response to a breach of contract so requires, the court should be able to grant the discretionary remedy of requiring a defendant to account to the plaintiff for the benefits he has received from his breach of contract. In the same way as a plaintiff's interest in performance of a contract may render it just and equitable for the court to make an order for specific performance or grant an injunction, so the plaintiff's interest in per-formance may make it just and equitable that the defendant should retain no benefit from his breach of contract.

The state of the authorities encourages me to reach this conclusion, rather than the reverse. The law recognises that damages are not always a sufficient remedy for breach of contract. This is the foundation of the court's jurisdiction to grant the remedies of specific performance and injunction. Even when awarding damages, the law does not adhere slavishly to the concept of compensation for financially measurable loss. When the circumstances require, damages are measured by reference to the benefit obtained by the wrongdoer. This applies to interference with property rights. Recently, the like approach has been adopted to breach of contract. . . . I consider it would be only a modest step for the law to recognise openly that, exceptionally, an account of profits may be the most appropriate remedy for breach of contract. It is not as though this step would contradict some recognised principle applied consistently throughout the law to grant or withholding of the remedy of an account of profits. No such principle is discernible.

The main argument against the availability of an account of profits as a remedy for breach of contract is that the circumstances where this remedy may be granted will be uncertain. This will have an unsettling effect on commercial contracts where certainty is important. I do not think these fears are well founded. I see no reason why, *in practice*, the availability of the remedy of an account of profits need disturb settled expectations in the commercial or consumer world. An account of profits will be appropriate only in exceptional circumstances. Normally the remedies of damages, specific performance and injunction, coupled with the characterisation of some contractual oblig-ations as fiduciary, will provide an adequate response to a breach of contract. It will be only in exceptional cases, where those remedies are inadequate, that any question of accounting for profits will arise. No fixed rules can be prescribed. The court will have regard to all the circumstances, including the subject matter of the contract, the purpose of the contractual provision which has been breached, the circumstances in which the breach occurred, the consequences of the breach and the circumstances in which relief is being sought. A useful general guide, although not exhaustive, is whether the plaintiff had a legitimate interest in preventing the defendant's profit-making activity and, hence, in depriving him of his profit.

It would be difficult, and unwise, to attempt to be more specific.

. . .

6.5.5. AGREED DAMAGES AND FORFEITURE CLAUSES

6.5.5.A. THE VALIDITY OF AGREED DAMAGES CLAUSES

Code civil **6.F.155.**

Article 1152: When the agreement provides that a party who fails to perform it shall pay a certain sum by way of damages, no larger or smaller sum may be awarded to the other party. Nonetheless, the judge may, of his own motion, moderate or increase the penalty which was agreed if it is manifestly excessive or derisory. Any provision to the contrary shall be of no effect.

Article 1228: The creditor may, instead of claiming the penalty fixed against the defaulting debtor, seek performance of the principal obligation.

Article 1229: (1) The penalty clause is compensation for the damages which the creditor suffers through non-performance of the principal obligation.
(2) He cannot at the same time claim both the penalty and the performance of the obligation, unless the penalty was only to apply to late performance.

Article 1230: Whether or not the original obligation was to be performed by a particular time, the penalty is not incurred until the party who is to deliver, to accept delivery or to do is *en demeure*.

Article 1231: When the obligation has been performed in part, the judge may of his own motion reduce the agreed penalty in proportion to the interest the creditor has in the part performance without prejudice to the application of Art.1152. Any provision to the contrary is of no effect.

Notes

(1) The traditional position of French law was that a penalty clause would be valid. The second and third sentences of Article 1152 were added in 1975.[455]

(2) If the debtor is guilty of *dol* or *faute lourde*, the creditor may claim full damages and is not limited to the amount agreed in the clause.[456]

---

[455] See Nicholas, at 235–6.

[456] E.g. Cass. civ 22 October 1975, D.S.1975.151. This presupposes that the amount of the penalty is less than the actual damage.

House of Lords **6.E.156.**
Dunlop Pneumatic Tyre Co. Ltd. v. *New Garage & Motor Co. Ltd.*[457]

PENALTY CLAUSE INVALID

Dunlop Tyres

A clause which requires a party who has broken the contract to pay a sum which is extravagant in rela-tion to the likely loss is invalid as a penalty; but a clause which represents a genuine pre-estimate of the likely loss is a valid liquidated damages clause. The clause may be valid even though the loss is hard to estimate.

Facts: The respondents had agreed, as part of a retail price maintenance scheme (not at the time considered to be anti-competitive) not to sell the appellants' tyres at less than the appellants' list prices; and, if they did, to pay the appellants £5 per tyre (including both "covers" and inner tubes).

Judgment: LORD DUNEDIN: . . .I shall content myself with stating succinctly the various propositions which I think are deducible from the decisions which rank as authoritative :–

1. Though the parties to a contract who use the words "penalty" or" liquidated damages" may prima facie be supposed to mean what they say, yet the expression used is.not conclusive. The Court must find out whether the payment stipulated is in truth a penalty or liquidated damages. This doctrine may be said to be found passim in nearly every case.
2. The essence of a penalty is a payment of money stipulated as in terrorem of the offending party; the essence of liquidated damages is a genuine covenanted pre-estimate of damage (*Clydebank Engineering aid Shipbuilding Co.* v. *Don Jose Ramos Yzquierdo y Castaneda* [1905] A.C. 6).
3. The question whether a sum stipulated is penalty or liquidated damages is a question of con-struction to be decided upon the terms and inherent circumstances of each particular contract, judged of as at the time of the making of the contract, not as at the time of the breach (*Public Works Commissioner* v. *Hills* [1906] A.C. 368 and *Webster* v. *Bosanquet* [1912] A.C. 394).
4. To assist this task of construction various tests have been suggested, which if applicable to the case under consideration may prove helpful, or even conclusive. Such are:
(a) It will be held to be penalty if the sum stipulated for is extravagant and unconscionable in amount in comparison with the greatest loss that could conceivably be proved to have followed from the breach. (Illustration given by Lord Halsbury in *Clydebank* case).
(b) It will be held to be a penalty if the breach consists only in not paying a sum of money, and the sum stipulated is a sum greater than the sum which ought to have been paid (*Kemble* v. *Farren* (1829) 6 Bing. 141). This though one of the most ancient instances is truly a corollary to the last test. Whether it had its historical origin in the doctrine of the common law that when A. promised to pay B. a sum of money on a certain day and did not do so, B. could only recover the sum with, in certain cases, interest, but could never recover further damages for non-timeous payment, or whether it was a survival of the time when equity reformed unconscionable bargains merely because they were unconscionable—a subject which much exercised Jessel MR in *Wallis* v. *Smith* (1882) 21 Ch.D. 243)—is probably more interesting than material.
(c) There is a presumption (but no more) that it is penalty when "a single lump sum is made payable by way of compensation, on the occurrence of one or more or all of several events, some of which may occasion serious and others but trifling damage" (Lord Watson in *Lord Elphinstone* v. *Monkland Iron and Coal Co.* (1886) 11 App. Cas. 332).

[457] [1915] AC 79.

On the other hand:

(d) It is no obstacle to the sum stipulated being a genuine pre-estimate of damage, that the consequences of the breach are such as to make precise pre-estimation almost an impossibility. On the contrary, that is just the situation when it is probable that pre-estimated damage was the true bargain between the parties (Clydebank *Case*, Lord Halsbury; *Webster* v. *Bosanquet*, Lord Mersey).

Turning now to the facts of the case, it is evident that the damage apprehended by the appellants owing to the breaking of the agreement was an indirect and not a direct damage. So long as they got their price from the respondents for each article sold, it could not matter to them directly what the respondents did with it. Indirectly it did. Accordingly, the agreement is headed "Price Maintenance Agreement," and the way in which the appellants would be damaged if prices were cut is clearly explained in evidence by Mr Baisley, and no successful attempt is made to controvert that evidence. But though damage as a whole from such a practice would be certain, yet damage from any one sale would be impossible to forecast. It is just, therefore, one of those cases where it seems quite reasonable for parties to contract that they should estimate that damage at a certain figure, and provided that figure is not extravagant there would seem no reason to suspect that it is not truly a bargain to assess damages, but rather a penalty to be held in terrorem.

The argument of the respondents was really based on two heads. They overpressed, in my judgment, the dictum of Lord Watson in *Lord Elphistone's Case*, reading it as if he had said that the matter was conclusive, instead of saying, as he did, that it raised a presumption, and they relied strongly on the case of *Willson* v. *Love* [1896] 1 Q.B. 626.

Now, in the first place, I have considerable doubt whether the stipulated payment here can fairly be said to deal with breaches, "some of which"—I am quoting Lord Watson's words—"may occasion serious and others but trifling damage." As a mere matter of construction, I doubt whether clause 5 applies to anything but sales below price. But I will assume that it does. None the less the mischief, as I have already pointed out, is an indirect mischief, and I see no data on which, as a matter of construction, I could settle in my own mind that the indirect H. damage from selling a cover would differ in magnitude from the indirect damage from selling a tube; or that the indirect damage from a cutting-price sale would differ from the indirect damage from supply at a full price to a hostile, because prohibited, agent. You cannot weigh such things in a chemical balance. The character of the agricultural land which was ruined by slag heaps in *Elphinstone's Case* (I) was not all the same, but no objection was raised by Lord Watson to applying an overhead rate per acre, the sum not being in itself unconscionable.

I think *Elphinstone's Case*, or rather the dicta in it, do go this length, that if there are various breaches to which one indiscriminate sum to be paid in breach is applied, then the strength of the chain must be taken at its weakest link. If you can clearly see that the loss on one particular breach could never amount to the stipulated sum, then you may come to the conclusion that the sum is penalty. But further than this it does not go; so, for the reasons already stated, I do not think the present case forms an instance of what I have just expressed.

[Lord Dunedin held that *Willson*'s case was also distinguishable.]

Notes

(1) In English law a clause which provides for a penalty—that is, a sum significantly greater than the loss which at the time the contract is made seems likely to follow for the breach penalized—is simply invalid. The creditor may then sue only for the actual loss.

(2) If the clause was a genuine attempt to pre-estimate the loss, it is a valid "liquidated damages" clause. In this case the creditor may recover the agreed amount even if the

actual loss is less or even nil—see *Clydebank Engineering & Shipbuilding Co* v. *Castenada*.[458] On the other hand if the actual loss is greater than the agreed sum the creditor cannot recover more than was agreed. There is some uncertainty whether, if the clause is invalid as a penalty and the actual loss is greater than the penalty, the sum fixed in the penalty clause acts as a "cap".[459]

(3) In English law a clause does not cease to be a valid liquidated damages clause because it sets the agreed damages too low: *Cellulose Acetate Silk Co Ltd* v. *Widnes Foundry (1925) Ltd*.[460] Thus the judge cannot simply increase the sum payable. However, it may be invalid under Unfair Contract Terms Act 1977 as an unreasonable limitation of liability clause; or under the Unfair Terms in Consumer Contracts Regulations 1999.

BGB **6.G.157.**

§ 339: If the debtor promises the creditor the payment of a sum of money as a penalty in case he does not perform his obligation or does not perform it in the proper manner, the penalty is forfeited if he is in default through delay. If performance due consists in a forbearance, the penalty is forfeited as soon as any act in contravention of the obligation is committed.

§ 340: (1) If the debtor has promised the penalty for the case of his not fulfilling his obligation, the creditor may demand the forfeited penalty in lieu of performance. If the creditor declares to the debtor that he demands the penalty, the claim for performance is barred.

(2) If the creditor has a claim for compensation for non-performance, he may demand the forfeited penalty as the minimum amount of the damage. Proof of further damage is not inadmissible.

§ 341: (1) If the debtor has promised the penalty for the case of his not performing the obligation in the proper manner, in particular not at the stipulated time, the creditor may demand the forfeited penalty in addition to the performance.

(2) If the creditor has a claim for compensation on account improper performance, the provisions of § 340(2) apply.

(3) If the creditor accepts the fulfilment, he may demand the penalty only if on acceptance he reserves the right to do so.

§ 342: If a performance other than the payment of a sum of money is promised as penalty, the provisions of §§ 339 to 341 apply; the claim for compensation is barred if the creditor demands the penalty.

§ 343: (1) If a forfeited penalty is disproportionately high, it may be reduced to a reasonable amount by judicial decree on the application the debtor. In the determination of reasonableness every legitimate interest of the creditor, not merely his property interest shall be taken into consideration. The claim for reduction is barred if the penalty has already been paid.

(2) The same rule applies also, apart from the cases provided for by §§ 339, 342, if a person promises a penalty for the case of his doing or forbearing some act.

---

[458] [1905] AC 6.

[459] See Hudson (1974) 90 LQR 31; Gordon (1974) 90 LQR 296; Hudson (1975) 91 LQR 25; Barton (1976) 92 LQR 20.

[460] [1933] AC 20.

§ 344: If the law declares the promised performance invalid, an agreement made for a penalty for non-fulfilment of the promise is also invalid even if the parties knew of the invalidity of the promise.

§ 345: If the debtor contests the forfeiture of the penalty on the ground of having performed his obligation, he is required to prove the performance unless the performance due from him consisted in a forbearance.

HGB **6.G.158.**

§ 348: A contract penalty, promised by a merchant operating a commercial concern, cannot be reduced on the basis of the provisions of § 343 BGB.

OLG Köln, 24 April 1974[461] **6.G.159.**

EXCESSIVE ESTIMATE OF DAMAGES A PENALTY

Plastic windows

Even though a clause may formally appear to contain a pre-estimate of damages, it is nonetheless open to be judged a penalty clause and to be subject to reduction under §343 BGB.

Facts: A clause provided that 50 per cent of the contract price be paid in the event of a customer cancelling a contract for the supply of windows. The customer, after various delays by the supplier, cancelled without giving proper notice, and the supplier claimed DM 3,000.

Held: The lower court granted the application, but on appeal the sum to be paid was reduced to DM 2,000, having regard to the fact that no work on the windows had yet been undertaken. Further, although the customer had unjustifiably cancelled the contract, the manufacturer had contributed to this by its delay and lack of clarity in specifying the time of delivery.

Judgment: The defendant instructed the firm G., whose claim is pursued by the plaintiff, to manufacture and fit plastic windows (contract value ca. DM 21,000). Forming part of the contract were General Conditions of Sale and Delivery, clause 10 of which requires the purchaser to pay 50 per cent of the contract value as compensation for loss of profit and costs arising, should he give notice to terminate the contract prior to the manufacture of the goods ordered. For various reasons supply of the windows was delayed. Without prior notice of termination and without warning of refusal to accept delivery, the defendant withdrew from the contract. The Regional Court granted an application for an order that the defendant should pay to the plaintiff DM 3,000. The defendant's appeal was successful in part.

On the following grounds: II. In accordance with clause 10 of the General Terms and conditions in conjunction with §§ 339ff BGB, §§ 398ff BGB, the plaintiff is entitled only to DM 2,000 as against the defendant.

1. It may remain open whether it is justified to make a distinction between the agreement of a contractual penalty within the meaning of §§ 339ff BGB and liquidated damages (*Schadenspauschale*)
. . .

For, even on the basis of the principles developed by the BGH, it cannot be said that this is an agreement for liquidated damages. It is true that the wording of Clause 10 of the Conditions mil-

[461] NJW 1974.1952.

itates in favour of such an agreement when it speaks of an amount of "50 per cent of the contract value for loss of profit and costs arising." The amount of the agreed damages, however, precludes such interpretation. For the significant factor is whether a serious attempt was made to estimate in advance the damage deemed possible. Only in such a case may it be assumed that the provision is intended to be for the purposes of the simplified enforcement of the anticipated claim for damages. Where the agreed liquidated damages are unreasonably high, all the indications are that the primary intention is that pressure should be exerted on the contractual partner in order to hold him to performance of the contract.

In this case the agreed liquidated damages are unreasonably high. The seller is to receive 50 per cent of the contract value, even if the contract is terminated prior to manufacture of the goods ordered. In the event that delivery is not taken of the goods already produced, the buyer was even obliged under Clause 10(1) of the General Conditions to pay the full price. 50 per cent as loss of profit is unreasonably high, even if one bears in mind that the firm G. has already incurred costs by instructing a fitter to re-measure [the windows]. A profit of this magnitude is not credible in light of the competitive situation in the building supplies market. Nor has it been demonstrated by the plaintiff that the firm G. works on such profit margins. It cannot therefore be assumed that the possible loss of profit was seriously calculated in advance. The plaintiff's submission that it works on a commission basis and therefore has an interest in performance of contracts also militates in favour of the construction of the clause as being in the nature of a contract penalty. Clause 10(2) of the General Conditions is therefore to be construed as a penalty clause. That is not altered by the fact that the plaintiff in its action is not claiming the full 50 per cent of the contract value, for the legal nature of an agreement cannot subsequently be altered by that fact.

2. The defendant is as a matter of principle obliged to pay the agreed penalty to the plaintiff. For it terminated the contract without notice prior to manufacture of the goods without good reason.

. . .

A contractual penalty in the amount of DM 2,000 is reasonable. The court has taken into account in determining that amount the fact that the plaintiff or the firm G. lost the profit on that contract and that it incurred expenditure in processing the contract and keeping the appointment for measurements. Expenditures incurred on partial or complete manufacture of the windows were not taken into account since, in the absence of submissions to the contrary, it may be assumed that G. had not yet started to manufacture the windows. Even if the loss of profit, together with the expenditure mentioned, reaches or even exceeds the amount claimed in the action, it does not appear to be justified to grant it in its full amount. For in assessing the contractual penalty account must also be taken of how it came about that the contract was terminated. It is true, as has already been stated, that the defendant unlawfully withdrew from the contract with G. Even though the conduct of G. did not justify termination without notice by the contractual partner, it did cause the defendant to hasten its decision. G's assurances as to dates were undesirably imprecise. It too could have taken steps, in the interests of avoiding ambiguities, in order to give the necessary clarity to the contractual arrangement.

Notes

(1) German law is like English law in distinguishing penalties from pre-estimates. It is like French law in allowing for the reduction of the amount of the penalty in cases of disproportionality. As in France, penalty clauses are viewed as having two functions: first, as an acceptable means of pressurizing the debtor into performing. This is seen as a particularly useful tool where the debtor's obligation is one of omission, particularly obligations to refrain from unfair competition;[462] and secondly to allow for a ready and

[462] See BGH NJW 1983.942.

expeditious calculation of damages. By contrast a genuine pre-estimate has only the second function. The distinction between the two types of clause is not so readily ascertained in practice.[463]

(2) The intention of the parties—was this clause meant to be a pre-estimate, or meant to be a penalty?—is important in the classification of the clause. The difficulty is that the intention of the parties may be hard to discern. Therefore, as the above case demonstrates, the amount payable, and whether it is excessive or proportionate to the loss likely to be suffered, may be the best guide to the purpose of the clause.

(3) Although German law accepts the need for penalty clauses, their use is (under § 343 BGB) effectively limited by reference to their purpose. Clauses are suspect if they are actually aimed at enriching the proponent, abusing a dominant market position or maliciously impoverishing the other party. Other factors to be considered in this regard are: the interest which the creditor had in performance; the previous behaviour—for example, reliability—of the debtor; the economic position of the debtor; and the comparative fault of the parties. The absence of harm in a particular case is not decisive.[464]

(5) In BGH NJW 54.998, although § 348 HGB applied, it was held that the enforcement of the penalty clause could still amount to an exercise of contractual rights against good faith. § 242 BGB may thus be applicable, to allow for review of the amount of a penalty. In that case the parties estimated the value of the object of sale at more than DM 1 million. It was in fact much less than this. The basis of the contract (*clausula rebus sic stantibus*) had changed radically and the court could reduce the penalty for non-performance from DM 20,000 to DM 5,000. The basis of the contract—i.e. the parties' estimation of value—was a question prior to that of the proportionality of the penalty.

(6) Should the clause not be challenged under § 343 BGB, or should such a challenge fail, the penalty will be payable in case of breach regardless of whether loss hs been suffered or not. Where there is a claim for damages this may not be claimed in addition to the penalty. Instead the penalty may be claimed as minimum damages and any excess of loss may be claimed in addition.

German law also provides for the invalidity of certain clauses containing pre-estimates of damages and penalty clauses where these are contained in standard conditions of business.

AGBG   **6.G.160.**

§ 11 Nr 5: *Unenforceable in general conditions of business . . .*
> the agreement of a lump sum claim in respect of damages or reduction in value in favour of the proponent if
> (a) the lump sum, in the type of case covered, exceeds the amount of damage or the usual diminution of value to be expected in the ordinary course of events, or
> (b) the other party is prevented from proving that damage or a reduction in value did not occur at all or that it was significantly less than the lump sum.

Nr 6:   . . . a provision according to which the proponent is promised a (contract) penalty payment if delivery is not taken or if there is delay in taking delivery, or in cases of delay in payment or where the other party seeks to escape from the contract.

---

[463] See *Münchener Kommentar*, under § 339 BGB, para. 3.
[464] See *ibid.*, under § 343 BGB, para. 14

Notes

(1) One purpose of pre-estimates in general conditions of business is to simplify the process of calculating damages. Hence the reference in § 11 Nr 5a AGBG to "damage . . . to be expected in the ordinary course of events" replicates the wording of § 252 BGB, the general rule on the calculation of damages for lost profits. It could be said that a pre-estimate is an *ex ante* calculation of damages on an abstract basis. Where a pre-estimate clause is challenged under § 11 Nr 5a AGBG, the proponent is thus obliged to show that the amount set is not more than the loss to be expected in the particular branch of business should such a breach occur.[465]

(2) Should a court hold a pre-estimate clause invalid under § 11 Nr 5a AGBG any damages will be calculated in the normal manner.[466]

(3) § 11 Nr 6 AGBG is not applicable in contracts between businesses. However, even if a clause is not caught by § 11 Nr 6 AGBG, for example due to the nature of the parties or the type of breach which gives rise to the penalty, it is still open to review under § 9 AGBG—general good faith clause.

(4) A penalty clause impermissible under either § 9 or § 11 Nr 6 cannot be adapted to become a pre-estimate.[467]

(5) Having regard to the foregoing, the following distinctions can be made as between clauses providing for payment of a liquidated sum in the event of a breach of contract:

(a) genuine pre-estimates;
(b) invalid pre-estimates in general conditions of business beyond what is to be expected in the ordinary course of events (§ 11 Nr 5 AGBG);
(c) acceptable penalties;
(d) invalid penalties for specific types of breach contained in general conditions of business (§ 11 Nr 6 AGBG);
(e) disproportionately high penalties (§ 343 BGB);
(f) penalties the enforcement of which would, in the circumstances, be contrary to good faith (§ 242 BGB).

Thus there are significant differences in the way in which penalty clauses are treated in the national laws. In England they are simply invalid. In France and Germany a penalty clause may be valid, but is subject to reduction by the court—and also to being struck down under legislation on unfair terms. In England, liquidated damages clauses are frequently used—for example, for delay in building contracts—but cases in which clauses are found to be contractual penalties are rare. In Germany it is said that penalty clauses are quite commonly used.

It may be suggested that by allowing penalty clauses German and French law are being consistent with their more generous approach to specific performance.[468] English law is being consistent with its hostile approach to specific performance by not allowing penalties. However, by controlling penalty clauses continental systems are also recognizing that

---

[465] See *ibid.*, under §11 Nr 5 AGBG, para. 64 ff.
[466] See *ibid.*, under §11 Nr 5 AGBG, para. 76.
[467] See OLG Frankfurt NJW 1982.2564.
[468] See **6.2**, *supra* at 674 ff.

there are limits to the coercion which maybe employed to ensure performance. English law, by banning all penalties, avoids the difficult question of what penalties are acceptable and which are not.

The international restatements both adopt the continental approach of accepting that a penalty clause may be valid but subjecting unreasonably high penalties to reduction by the court.

Principles of European Contract Law   **6.PECL.161.**

Article 9:509: *Agreed Payment for Non-performance*

(1) Where the contract provides that a party which fails to perform is to pay a specified sum to the aggrieved party for such non-performance, the aggrieved party shall be awarded that sum irrespective of its actual loss.

(2) However, despite any agreement to the contrary the specified sum may be reduced to a reasonable amount where it is grossly excessive in relation to the loss resulting from the non-performance and the other circumstances.

It appears that whether the sum agreed is excessive or not is to be judged in the light of the actual loss, as there is no reference to the circumstances envisaged at the time the contract is made: see Comment B. Unidroit Article 7.4.13 and its Comment are to the same effect.

6.5.5.B. DEPOSITS AND FORFEITURE CLAUSES

Contracts often call for one party to pay a sum of money when the contract is made. What will be the position if one of the parties then withdraws from the contract or refuses to perform? This is a complex topic and one in which English, French and German law have rather different rules.

The three systems agree on the position if the payment is merely part of the price paid on account (*accomptes*, *Anzahlung*). If before the contract has been performed either party refuses to go on with it and it is then terminated by the other party, the sum paid will normally have to be returned; but the usual remedies for non-performance will apply. Thus if a buyer pays part of the price in advance and then wrongly refuses to go with the contract, and the seller terminates the contract, the buyer may recover the sum paid but will be liable to the seller in damages for non-performance—and the seller will normally be entitled to set the damages off against the sum to be repaid.[469] If however the sum is paid as a deposit, or it is provided that it shall be forfeited, the position will depend on what the parties intended.

French law recognizes a distinction between part payment and earnest money (*arrhes*); and also that the parties may have intended that either party should be able to withdraw from the agreement (*faculté de dédit*).

---

[469] See Treitel, *Remedies* at 234–243, paras 182–186.

Code civil **6.F.162.**

Article 1590: If a promise of sale is made with earnest money either party is free to withdraw, in the case of the party who has paid the earnest money, on pain of losing it, and in the case of the other party, by paying twice the amount.

It has been held that the right to withdraw may be not exercised in bad faith, for example threatening to withdraw unless better terms are offered (Civ. 3, 11 May 1976[470]) but this decision is described as *"demeuré isolée"*.[471] In consumer contracts there is a presumption that sums paid in advance by the consumer give a *faculté de dédit* unless the contract provides otherwise: see Code de la consommation Article L. 114–1, al.4. Thus if the supplier were to withdraw it would have to reimburse double the sum paid.

However, it has been said by the Cour de cassation that Article 1590 merely "supplements the will of the parties",[472] and it is possible that *arrhes* may be paid without there being a *faculté de dédit*. Where the *arrhes* are substantial there is a presumption that they were merely *accomptes*, not to be forfeited in the case of default; but it seems possible that the contract could provide for forfeiture of a substantial sum which would operate as a penalty.

German law distinguishes between a sum which is paid as earnest (*Draufgabe*) and a sum of money which is to be forfeited (or paid) as the price of exercising a right to withdraw from the contract (*Reugeld*).

BGB **6.G.163.**

§ 336: (1) If, on entering into a contract, something is given as earnest, this is deemed to be proof of the conclusion of the contract.
(2) In case of doubt the earnest is not deemed to be a forfeit.

§ 338: The holder of the earnest is entitled to retain it if the performance due from the giver becomes impossible because of a circumstance for which he is responsible, or if the rescinding of the contract is due to his fault. If the holder of the earnest demands compensation for non-performance, the earnest shall, in case of doubt, be credited or, if this cannot be done, shall be returned on payment of the compensation.

§ 359: If the right to rescind is reserved on payment of a forfeit, the rescission is ineffective when the forfeit is not paid before or at the time rescission is declared, if the other party promptly rejects the declaration for this reason. The declaration is, however, effective if the forfeit is paid without delay after the rejection.

The BGB does not provide for double the earnest money to be paid if the payee defaults. However, if the earnest money were paid by a consumer under a clause which was not individually negotiated, the absence of "balance" might make it contrary to good faith. Compare the following provision, which includes on a "grey" list of terms those:

---

[470] D.1978.269, annotated by Taisne.
[471] Malaurie and Aynès, para. 748.
[472] Cass. civ. 1re, 16 July 1956, D. 1956. 609.

Directive on Unfair Terms in Consumer Contracts, 93/13/EEC[473] **6.EC.164.**

Annex 1: (d) permitting the seller or supplier to retain sums paid by the consumer where the latter decides not to conclude or perform the contract, without providing for the consumer to receive compensation of an equivalent amount from the seller or supplier where the latter is the party cancelling the contract.

§§ 336, 338 BGB seem to assume that the sum paid as *Draufgabe* is likely to be small. A very large *Draufgabe* is likely to be classed as a penalty clause and therefore to be subject to reduction under § 343 BGB where is it is held to be excessive as such.[474]

English law does not have any presumption that, when a party pays a sum of money in advance, he is entitled to withdraw from the contract on forfeiture of the sum paid, though such a right could be agreed expressly.[475] Deposits are paid frequently, for example for hotel bookings, and the sums are often substantial—in contracts for the sale of land, it is customary for the buyer to pay a 10 per cent deposit on exchange of contracts. If the buyer defaults, the seller may—subject to what is said below—retain the deposit; if the seller defaults, the deposit must be returned but there is no rule that that double the sum should be paid.

The position of deposits in English law is not wholly clear.

Privy Council (on appeal from Jamaica) **6.E.165.**
Workers Trust and Merchant Bank Ltd. v. *Dojap Investments Ltd.*[476]

LARGER DEPOSIT THAN CUSTOMARY INVALID

25 per cent deposit

Where for a particular kind of contract there is a custom to pay a certain percentage of the price in advance as a deposit, to be forfeited if the buyer defaults, the seller will not be able to retain a greater deposit unless there was a good reason for requiring the larger sum.

Facts: A contract for the sale of land in Jamaica provided for a deposit of 25 per cent of the purchase price. The purchaser paid the deposit but then defaulted. It claimed relief against forfeiture of the deposit by the vendor.

Held: The court of first instance (Zacca CJ) held that the deposit was reasonable. The Court of Appeal in Jamaica granted relief to the extent that the deposit exceeded 10 per cent. Both parties appealed. The Privy Council dismissed the vendor's appeal and allowed the purchaser's cross-appeal.

Judgment: LORD BROWNE WILKINSON: . . . In general, a contractual provision which requires one party in the event of his breach of the contract to pay or forfeit a sum of money to the other party is unlawful as being a penalty, unless such provision can be justified as being a payment of liquidated damages, being a genuine pre-estimate of the loss which the innocent party will incur by

---

[473] [1993] OJ L95/29.

[474] See *Münchener Kommentar*, under § 338 BGB, para. 1.

[475] See the right to withdraw from a hire-purchase agreement on making the payment up to a minimum sum, often 2/3 of the total credit price. It seems that such a provision, even if would give the finance company much more than it would lose through the hirer's termination, is not subject to the penalty rules as the latter apply only to sums payable upon breach of contract: see *Associated Distributors* v. *Hall* [1938] 2 KB 83; *Bridge* v. *Campbell Discount Co. Ltd* {1962] AC 600; Consumer Credit Act 1974, ss. 99, 100.

[476] [1993] AC 573.

reason of the breach. One exception to this general rule is the provision for the payment of a deposit by the purchaser on a contract for the sale of land. Ancient law has established that the forfeiture of such a deposit (customarily 10 per cent. of the contract price) does not fall within the general rule and can be validly forfeited even though the amount of the deposit bears no reference to the anticipated loss to the vendor flowing from the breach of contract. This exception is anomalous and at least one textbook writer has been surprised that the courts of equity ever countenanced it: see Farrand, *Contract and Conveyance*, 4th ed. (1983), p. 204. The special treatment afforded to such a deposit derives from the ancient custom of providing an earnest for the performance of a contract in the form of giving either some physical token of earnest (such as a ring) or earnest money. The history of the law of deposits can be traced to the Roman law of *arra* and possibly further back still: see *Howe* v. *Smith* (1884) 27 Ch.D. 89 101–102, per Fry LJ. Ever since the decision in *Howe* v. *Smith*, the nature of such a deposit has been settled in English law. Even in the absence of express contractual provision, it is an earnest for the performance of the contract: in the event of completion of the contract the deposit is applicable towards payment of the purchase price; in the event of the purchaser's failure to complete in accordance with the terms of the contract, the deposit is forfeit, equity having no power to relieve against such forfeiture.

However, the special treatment afforded to deposits is plainly capable of being abused if the parties to a contract, by attaching the label "deposit" to any penalty, could escape the general rule which renders penalties unenforceable. . . .

In the view of their Lordships . . . [it] is not possible for the parties to attach the incidents of a deposit to the payment of a sum of money unless such sum is reasonable as earnest money. The question therefore is whether or not the deposit of 25 per cent. in this case was reasonable as being in line with the traditional concept of earnest money or was in truth a penalty intended to act in terrorem. Zacca CJ tested the question of "reasonableness" by reference to the evidence before him that it was of common occurrence for banks in Jamaica selling property at auction to demand deposits of between 15 per cent. and 50 per cent. He held that, since this was a common practice it was reasonable. Like the Court of Appeal their Lordships are unable to accept this reasoning. In order to be reasonable a true deposit must be objectively operating as "earnest money" and not as a penalty. To allow the test of reasonableness to depend upon the practice of one class of vendor, which exercises considerable financial muscle, would be to allow them to evade the law against penalties by adopting practices of their own. However although their Lordships are satisfied that the practice of a limited class of vendors cannot determine the reasonableness of a deposit, it is more difficult to define what the test should be. Since a true deposit may take effect as a penalty, albeit one permitted by law, it as hard to draw a line between a reasonable, permissible amount of penalty and an unreasonable, impermissible penalty. In their Lordships' view the correct approach is to start from the position that, without logic but by long continued usage both in the United Kingdom and formerly in Jamaica, the customary deposit has been 10 per cent. A vendor who seeks to obtain a larger amount by way of forfeitable deposit must show special circumstances which justify such a deposit. . . .

Their Lordships agree with the Court of Appeal that this evidence falls far short of showing that it was reasonable to stipulate for a forfeitable deposit of 25 per cent. of the purchase price or indeed any deposit in excess of 10 per cent.

The question therefore arises whether the court has jurisdiction to relieve against the express provision of the contract that the deposit of 25 per cent. was to be forfeited. Although there is no doubt that the court will not order the payment of a sum contracted for (but not yet paid) if satisfied that such sum is in reality a penalty, it was submitted that the court could not order, by way of relief, the repayment of sums already paid to the defendant in accordance with the terms of the contract which, on breach, the contract provided should be forfeit. The basis of this submission was the view expressed in a considered obiter dictum of Romer LJ in *Stockloser* v. *Johnson* [1954] I Q.B. 476.

In that case there was a contract for the sale of quarry machinery to the plaintiff, the purchase price to be paid by instalments. The contract provided that in the event of a default in payment of the instalments, the vendor could retake the machinery and all instalments of the price previously paid should be forfeit. Pursuant to the contract, the plaintiff took possession and used the machinery but defaulted in payment of an instalment. The defendant forfeited the instalments already paid. In the action, the plaintiff sought to recover the instalments, alleging that their forfeiture was a penalty. The Court of Appeal unanimously held that the forfeiture did not constitute a penalty on the facts of that case but went on to express conflicting views, obiter, as to whether, if the forfeiture had been a penalty, the court had jurisdiction to order repayment. Somervell LJ and Denning LJ expressed the view that there was such jurisdiction. Romer LJ held that there was no general right in equity to mend the parties' bargain and that, even where there was jurisdiction to relieve from forfeiture, that could only be exercised by allowing a late completion to a party who was in default in performance but willing and able to carry out the terms of the contract belatedly.

Their Lordships do not find it necessary to decide which of those two views is correct in a case where a party is seeking relief from forfeiture for breach of contract to pay a price by instalments, the party in default having been let into possession in the meantime. This is not such a case. In the view of their Lordships, since the 25 per cent. deposit was not a true deposit by way of earnest, the provision for its forfeiture was a plain penalty. There is clear authority that in a case of a sum paid by one party to another under the contract as security for the performance of that contract, a provision for its forfeiture in the event of non—performance is a penalty from which the court will give relief by ordering repayment of the sum so paid, less any damage actually proved to have been suffered as a result of non-completion: *Commissioner of Public Works* v. *Hills* [1906] A.C. 368. Accordingly, there is jurisdiction in the court to order repayment of the 25 per cent. deposit. The Court of Appeal took a middle course by ordering the repayment of 15 per cent. out of the 25 per cent. deposit, leaving the bank with its normal 10 per cent. deposit which it was entitled to forfeit. Their lordships are unable to agree that this is the correct order. The bank has contracted for a deposit consisting of one globular sum, being 25 per cent. of the purchase price. If a deposit of 25 per cent. constitutes an unreasonable sum and is not therefore a true deposit, it must be repaid as a whole. The bank has never stipulated for a reasonable deposit of 10 per cent: therefore it has no right to such a limited payment. If it cannot establish that the whole sum was truly a deposit, it has not contracted for a true deposit at all.

Notes

(1) It seems curious that deposits, and clauses providing for the forfeiture of money paid by the party who has subsequently broken the contract, should not be subject to the penalty clauses rules—after all, they seem to have the same function. In the early twentieth century some cases did indeed apply the penalty rules to clauses requiring a deposit to be forfeited: for example, *Public Works Commisioner* v. *Hills*[477] and *Pye* v. *British Automobile Commercial Syndicate Ltd.*[478]. But other decisions suggest that this is not the case, at least where the deposit of not more than the customary 10 per cent. This figure does not have to represent a genuine pre-estimate of the seller's loss. It has been held that if the buyer defaults, the seller may keep the deposit whatever the actual loss (*Howe* v. *Smith*[479]); conversely, and surprisingly, if the actual loss is greater than the amount of the deposit, the seller can recover the difference (*Lock* v. *Bell*[480]).

[477] [1906] AC 368, PC.
[478] [1906] 1 KB 425.
[479] (1884) 27 Ch. D 89.
[480] [1931] 1 Ch. 35.

(2) This now seems to be subject to the restriction that where there is a customary fig-ure for the deposit, any greater deposit will be invalid unless it was reasonable to demand more.

(3) In a way, the *Worker's Trust* case was unusual. Had it been an English case, the court would have had power under the Law of Property Act 1925, section 49(2), to award the return of the deposit. That power applies only to sale of land cases.

(4) What is the position if the case is not one involving land and there is no customary amount for a deposit? Suppose a customer agrees to buy a new car from a dealer and pays a deposit of 10 per cent of the purchase price, the balance to be paid in cash on delivery of the new car. The customer repudiates the agreement—perhaps she loses her job, or is offered a new job with a company car provided—and the dealer resells the car for a sim-ilar price to another customer. Since the demand for this model exceeds the supply, the dealer resells the car without any difficulty and its loss is much smaller than the deposit—see *Charter* v. *Sullivan*[481] (car was re-sold with no loss to the dealer). Can the customer recover the deposit less the dealer's actual loss? The *Workers' Trust* case leaves the answer unclear.

(5) It is possible to infer from Lord Browne-Wilkinson's speech that he thought the use of deposits not related to the payee's loss is permitted *only* in the case of sales of land and that all other deposits must be genuine pre-estimates. This was one of the provisional solutions put forward by the Law Commission in its Working Paper No 61, *Penalty Clauses and Forfeiture of Monies Paid*, but it does not represent the present law as it is gen-erally understood to be.[482]

(6) In the Working Paper just cited, the Law Commission provisionally recommended that deposits and forfeiture clauses should be subjected to the penalty rules, and thus be valid only if they are genuine pre-estimates of the loss; but nothing further has been done.

The international restatements do not regulate deposits explicitly, either by giving a presumption that there is a right to withdraw on forfeiture of the deposit, or by stating that substantial deposits are subject to the rules on penalty clauses. However there is no doubt that those rules could be applied by analogy:

Principles of European Contract Law **6.PECL.166.**

Article 1:106: (2) Issues within the scope of these Principles but not expressly settled by them are so far as possible to be settled in accordance with the ideas underlying the Principles
. . .

Further Readings on Damages
—W. Bishop, "The Contract-Tort Boundary and the Economics of Insurance" (1983) 12 JLS 241;
—R. Danzig, "Hadley v. Baxendale: A Study in the Industrialization of the Law" (1975) 4 JLS 249;

---

[481] [1957] 2 QB 117, CA.
[482] E.g. Working Paper No.61, para.53.

—L. Fuller and H. Lange, *Schadensersatz* (Tübingen: JCB Mohr (Paul Siebeck), 1979);

—K. Larenz, *Schuldrecht—Allgemeiner Teil*, 14th edn. (München: Beck, 1987), paras. 28–30;

—K. Rebmann and F. Säcker (eds.), *Münchener Kommentar zum Bürgerlichen Gesetzbuch*, 4th edn. (München: Beck, 2000);

—P. Schlechtriem, *Schuldrecht—Allgemeiner Teil*, 4th edn. (Tübingen: Mohr, 2000)

—A.W.B. Simpson, "Innovation in Nineteenth Century Contract Law" (1975) 91 LQR 247;

—G. Treitel, *Remedies for Breach of Contract* (Oxford: Clarendon, 1988), chapters IV–VII.

CHAPTER SEVEN
THIRD PARTY CONSEQUENCES

7.1. THIRD PARTY BENEFICIARIES

7.1.1. INTRODUCTION

Principles of European Contract Law   **7.PECL.1.**

Article 6:110: *Stipulation in Favour of a Third Party*
> (1) A third party may require performance of a contractual obligation when its right to do so has been expressly agreed upon between the promisor and the promisee, or when such agreement is to be inferred from the purpose of the contract or the circumstances of the case. The third party need not be identified at the time the agreement is concluded.
>
> (2) If the third party renounces the right to performance the right is treated as never having accrued to it.
>
> (3) The promisee may by notice to the promisor deprive the third party of the right to performance unless:
>> (a) the third party has received notice from the promisee that the right has been made irrevocable, or
>>
>> (b) the promisor or the promisee has received notice from the third party that the latter accepts the right.

BGB   **7.G.2.**

§ 328: *Contract for benefit of a third party*
> (1) A contract may stipulate performance for the benefit of a third party, so that the third party acquires the right directly to demand performance.
>
> (2) In the absence of express stipulation it is to be deduced from the circumstances, especially from the object of the contract, whether the third party shall acquire the right, whether the right of the third party shall arise forthwith or only under certain conditions, and whether any right shall be reserved to the contracting parties to take away or modify the right of the third party without his consent.

Normally, the intention of persons who enter into a bilateral contract, such as a contract of sale, is that the contractual rights and obligations should attach to themselves alone. Contract is seen as a *vinculum iuris* binding two parties, and this is true even if they have provided that each of them may discharge his liability by rendering performance to someone else. If the buyer, at the seller's request, is to pay the price to the seller's creditor rather than to the seller himself, or if the seller is to deliver the goods to the buyer's order rather than to him personally, each party, in rendering performance to a third party, is performing an obligation which he owes only to his contractor and not to the third party. The situation is quite different where the parties' contract in such a manner that the third party, not himself involved in the formation of the original agreement, is to be entitled not only to receive the promised performance, but to demand that performance from the promisor.

It is not sufficient therefore if the parties have agreed that payment to a third party shall be a good discharge of the payor's debt. An agreement is a contract for the benefit of a third party, and the third party is a third party beneficiary if, and only if, the person for whose benefit the agreement is made can enforce it against the promisor.

Similarly, under Article 6:253 (1) BW there exists a contract for the benefit of a third party only if the contract "creates the right for a third person to claim a performance from one of the parties".

If a building contractor A enters into a contract with a landowner B whereby A undertakes to put a building on B's land and B undertakes to pay the agreed price directly to A's bank, the bank is *not* a third party beneficiary if payment to the bank is seen by the parties merely as a good discharge of B's debt. The bank is a third party beneficiary in the legal sense only if A and B understood that, by virtue of their agreement, the bank is to acquire an independent right to ask, and if necessary to sue, B for payment and thus to enforce an agreement to which it was not an original party.

The contract for the benefit of a third party must be distinguished from other legal institutions which may be functionally equivalent, but are legally distinguishable. One of these institutions is the *assignment*.[1] Take the case of the landowner who promised the building contractor to pay the price due under the contract directly to the contractor's bank. The parties may have intended the bank to acquire by virtue of the agreement a right against the landowner, but it is also possible—and indeed more likely—that the contractor will achieve the same result by assigning his rights under the building contract to the bank. In both cases the bank will acquire a right to enforce the claim against the landowner. However, in the case of an assignment, the right to demand payment forms part of the contractor's assets until, by virtue of a separate agreement, it is transferred by the contractor to the bank. On the other hand, when a third party beneficiary contract is used, the bank acquires the right to demand payment directly from the agreement made between the landowner and the contractor. Important consequences may follow from what appears to be merely a matter of legal construction. In particular, the position of the contractor's general creditors is likely to be more favourable if an assignment was made. In other cases, the practical difference may be negligible.

Contracts for the benefit of third parties must also be distinguished from the relationship arising where an agent, under the authority conferred on him by a principal, enters into a contract with another party on the principal's behalf (*agency*).[2] In that case, the principal may have an enforceable claim against the other party, not because he is a third party beneficiary, but because he himself is a party to a contract made on his behalf by his agent under authority conferred on him either expressly or impliedly.

---

[1] See *infra*, **7.2**.
[2] See *infra*, **7.3**.

7.1.2. PARTY BENEFICIARIES: THE POSITION IN GENERAL

All modern Continental legal systems agree that a contract may be concluded by the parties so as to create an enforceable right in a third person who is a stranger to the contract. To the modern lawyer this may seem rather obvious, but one should not forget that Roman law was opposed to this idea (*"alteri nemo stipulari potest"*) and that it was only in the nineteenth century that the numerous restrictions on the use of the third party beneficiary contract were whittled down and a general theory of the institution emerged. The economic force which fuelled this development was the enormous growth in the nineteenth century of insurance, particularly life insurance. Thus, life insurance policies are frequently based on a contract between the insured and the insurance company whereby the latter promises upon certain conditions to pay money to a third party beneficiary. It is clear that in this case the contracting party wishes the beneficiary to be able to maintain a suit on the policy and that the proceeds should belong to him rather than to the insured's estate.

The development of French law provides a good example. The Code civil starts off with the proposition in Article 1165 that agreements have effect only between the parties to them and can neither benefit nor bind a third party. Likewise, Article 1119 asserts that a person making an agreement can thereby bind or benefit only himself. However, Article 1121 is by way of exception:

Code civil **7.F.3.**

Article 1121: One may stipulate for the benefit of a third party when such is the condition of a stipulation which one makes for oneself or of a gift which one makes to another.

If these requirements were taken seriously a beneficiary of a life insurance policy would acquire an enforceable right against the insurer (promisor) only if either the insured (promisee) were himself the beneficiary of a stipulation made for his benefit by the insurer, or if the insurer had received something from the insured as a gift. Under the pressure of the recognition and enforcement of third party rights under insurance contracts the courts have dismantled these restrictions. They have held that the performance which the promisee must make to the promisor under Article 1121 need not be a "gift" in the technical sense; *any* performance, such as the payment of a premium, will suffice. The alternative requirement of Article 1121, that the promisee must at the time of the contract always stipulate something for himself, has been understood by the courts as being satisfied if any *profit moral* accrues to him as a result of the transaction. In the case of insurance such a *profit moral* exists in the insured's certainty that the insured sum will be paid to the third party on the occurrence of the insured event. Thus, the limiting requirements of Article 1121 have been effectively struck out by the courts, since it is hardly conceivable that a promisee who intends to benefit a third party, by way of an insurance contract or any other agreement, does not derive at least a *profit moral* from the assurance that his intention will eventually be implemented.

In contrast to all jurisdictions of the European continent, English law has not yet been able to bring itself to adopt the contract for the benefit of third parties as a legal institution of general application though we will see that recent statutory reform has moved significantly in that direction.[3] There are two common law doctrines which make it very difficult for a stranger to sue on a contract to which he is not a party. Under the doctrine of privity rights and duties can be created by way of contract only for and against those who are parties to it. And the doctrine of consideration[4] states that promises are legally enforceable only if they are given in return for a "consideration" from the promisee, i.e. some counterpromise or counterperformance. It follows that only the promisee can enforce a promise and even then must show that he, not someone else, has provided consideration for it.

House of Lords   **7.E.4.**
Dunlop Pneumatic Tyre Co. Ltd. v. *Selfridge & Co. Ltd.*[5]

THE DOCTRINE OF PRIVITY OF CONTRACT

The tyre retailer

A person who is a not party to a contract cannot enforce it or any of its terms. Even if the person can show that one of the parties to the contract was acting as his agent, he will still be unable to enforce it if he has not provided consideration.

Facts: Dunlop had sold some of their tyres to Dew & Co. on terms that Dews would not resell at less than Dunlop's list prices and that, if they resold them to trade buyers, they would extract from them a similar undertaking. Dews resold the tyres to Selfridge who agreed to observe the restrictions and "to pay to the Dunlop Pneumatic Tyre Co. Ltd. the sum of £5 for each and every tyre . . . sold or offered in breach of this agreement, as and by way of liquidated damages". Selfridge supplied tyres to two of their customers at below the list price, and Dunlop sought to recover two sums of £5 each.

Held: Upholding the decision of the Court of Appeal, the House of Lords held that Dunlop (the defendants) could not enforce the term as they were not parties to the contract; and even if Dews were acting as agents for Dunlop, Dunlop had not provided any consideration to Selfridge (the respondents).

Judgment: VISCOUNT HALDANE LC: My Lords, in the law of England certain principles are fundamental. One is that only a person who is a party to a contract can sue on it. Our law knows nothing of a *jus quaesitum tertio* arising by way of contract. Such a right may be conferred by way of property, as, for example, under a trust, but it cannot be conferred on a stranger to a contract as a right to enforce the contract *in personam*. A second principle is that if a person with whom a contract not under seal has been made is to be able to enforce it consideration must have been given by him to the promisor or to some other person at the promisor's request. These two principles are not recognised in the same fashion by the jurisprudence of certain Continental countries or of Scotland, but here they are well established. A third proposition is that a principal not named in the contract may sue upon it if the promisee really contracted as his agent. But again, in order to entitle him so to sue, he must have given consideration either personally or through the promisee, acting as his agent in giving it.

My Lords, in the case before us, I am of opinion that the consideration, the allowance of what was in reality part of the discount to which Messrs. Dew, the promisees, were entitled as between

---

[3] See s. 1 of the Contracts (Rights of Third Parties) Act 1999, *infra* at 893.
[4] See *supra* at 140 ff.
[5] [1915] AC 847.

882

themselves and the appellants, was to be given by Messrs. Dew on their own account, and was not in substance, any more than in form, an allowance made by the appellants. The case for the appellants is that they permitted and enabled Messrs. Dew, with the knowledge and the desire of the respondents, to sell to the latter on the terms of the contract of 2 January 1912. But it appears to me that even if this is so the answer is conclusive. Messrs. Dew sold to the respondents goods which they had a title to obtain from the appellants independently of this contract. The consideration by way of discount under the contract of 2 January was to come wholly out of Messrs. Dew's pocket and neither directly nor indirectly out of that of the appellants. If the appellants enabled them to sell to the respondents on the terms they did this was not done as any part of the terms of the contract sued on.

No doubt it was provided as part of these terms that the appellants should acquire certain rights, but these rights appear on the face of the contract as *jura quaesita tertio*, which the appellants could not enforce. Moreover, even if this difficulty can be got over by regarding the appellants as the principals of Messrs. Dew in stipulating for the rights in question, the only consideration disclosed by the contract is one given by Messrs. Dew, not as their agents, but as principals acting on their own account.

The conclusion to which I have come on the point as to consideration renders it unnecessary to decide the further question as to whether the appellants can claim that a bargain was made in this contract by Messrs. Dew as their agents; a bargain which, apart from the point as to consideration, they could therefore enforce. If it were necessary to express an opinion on this further question, a difficulty as to the position of Messrs. Dew would have to be considered. Two contracts—one by a man on his own account as principal, and another by the same man as agent—may be validly comprised in the same piece of paper. But they must be two contracts, and not one as here. I do not think that a man can treat one and the same contract as made by him in two capacities. He cannot be regarded as contracting for himself and for another *uno flatu*.

My Lords, the form of the contract which we have to interpret leaves the appellants in this dilemma, that, if they say that Messrs. Dew contracted on their behalf, they gave no consideration, and if they say they gave consideration in the shape of a permission to the respondents to buy, they must set up further stipulations, which are neither to be found in the contract sued upon nor are germane to it, but are really inconsistent with its structure. That contract has been reduced to writing, and it is in the writing that we must look for the whole of the terms made between the parties. These terms cannot in my opinion consistently with the settled principles of English law, be construed as giving to the appellants any enforceable rights as against the respondents.

I think that the judgment of the Court of Appeal was right, and I move that the appeal be dismissed with costs.

LORD DUNEDIN: My Lords, I confess that this case is to my mind apt to nip any budding affection which one might have had for the doctrine of consideration. For the effect of that doctrine in the present case is to make it possible for a person to snap his fingers at a bargain deliberately made, a bargain not in itself unfair, and which the person seeking to enforce it has a legitimate interest to enforce. Notwithstanding these considerations I cannot say that I have ever had any doubt that the judgment of the Court of Appeal was right.

My Lords, I am content to adopt from a work of *Sir Frederick Pollock*, to which I have often been under obligation, the following words as to consideration: "An act or forbearance of one party, or the promise thereof, is the price for which the promise of the other is bought, and the promise thus given for value is enforceable." (*Pollock* on Contracts, 8th ed., p. 175).

Now the agreement sued on is an agreement which on the face of it is an agreement between Dew and Selfridge. But speaking for myself, I should have no difficulty in the circumstances of this case in holding it proved that the agreement was truly made by Dew as agent for Dunlop, or in other words that Dunlop was the undisclosed principal, and as such can sue on the agreement. None the less, in order to enforce it he must show consideration, as above defined, moving from Dunlop to Selfridge.

In the circumstances, how can he do so? The agreement in question is not an agreement for sale. It is only collateral to an agreement for sale; but that agreement for sale is an agreement entirely between Dew and Selfridge. The tyres, the property in which upon the bargain is transferred to Selfridge, were the property of Dew, not of Dunlop, for Dew under this agreement with Dunlop held these tyres as proprietor, and not as agent. What then did Dunlop do, or forbear to do, in a question with Selfridge? The answer must be, nothing. He did not do anything, for Dew, having the right of property in the tyres, could give a good title to any one he liked, subject, it might be, to an action of damages at the instance of Dunlop for breach of contract, which action, however, could never create a *vitium reale* in the property of the tyres. He did not forbear in anything, for he had no action against Dew which he gave up, because Dew had fulfilled his contract with Dunlop in obtaining, on the occasion of the sale, a contract from Selfridge in the terms prescribed.

To my mind, this ends the case. That there are methods of framing a contract which will cause persons in the position of Selfridge to become bound, I do not doubt. But that has not been done in this instance; and as Dunlop's advisers must have known of the law of consideration, it is their affair that they have not so drawn the contract.

I think the appeal should be dismissed.

Notes

(1) There are two main objections against giving the third party an enforceable right as against the promisor. One is that no promise was made by the promisor to the third party, and the other is that the third party did not provide consideration. The first objection can be overcome if one accepts Lord Dunedin's view that Dews made the agreement with Selfridge as agent for Dunlop. Since this would make Dunlop a party to the agreement, Selfridge's promise could be viewed as having been made to Dunlop. To overcome the second objection the agreement between Dews and Selfridge would have to be framed so as to show that Dunlop provided some sort of consideration in return for Selfridge's promise to pay £5 to Dunlop in the event of a breach of the restrictions imposed by them.

(2) In *Beswick* v. *Beswick*[6] a coal merchant more than seventy years old made a written contract with his nephew: the merchant was to transfer his whole coal business to the nephew, and in return the nephew was to pay £6 per week to the coal merchant while he lived and, after his death, £5 per week to his widow. After the old man died, the nephew refused to make the agreed payments to his widow, and the widow sued him both in her own right and as administratrix, i.e. as a person appointed by law to manage the estate of her deceased husband who had died intestate. The House of Lords held that the widow had no claim in her own right, English law knowing nothing of a *ius quasitum tertio* by way of contract. It was only in her capacity as administratrix that the House of Lords was able to award her a decree ordering the nephew to perform the agreement specifically. Suppose the nephew had been the administrator, rather than the widow. Do you think it would have been fair to let the widow go away empty-handed? How could the agreement between the coal merchant and the nephew have been arranged so as to give the widow an indisputable right to the £5 per week?

(3) The unquestionable need to recognize the rights of strangers to a contract was, until recently, satisfied in English law by a number of isolated, albeit important,

[6] [1968] AC 58.

exceptions. Section 11 of the Married Women's Property Act 1882 provides that a husband or wife and/or their children may sue the insurance company on a life insurance policy made for their benefit by a spouse or parent. This Act does not apply if the insured intended a niece or a charitable organization to benefit from the policy. But it would probably mean commercial ruin for an insurance company to set up the privity rule as a defence against the beneficiary's claim. Other statutes provide that third parties may enforce marine and fire insurance policies, and this applies also to some other types of liability insurance, such as motor insurance.

Court of Appeal   **7.E.5.**
Darlington Borough Council v. *Wiltshier Northern Ltd.*[7]

CALLS FOR REFORM

Darlington Recreational Centre

Under the privity rule, a contract cannot be treated as having been made for the benefit of a third party so as to enable the latter to sue on it. Although there is a powerful case for reform of the rule, it might only be reformed by statute or by resolution of the House of Lords in an appropriate case.

Facts: A borough council wanted to create a new recreational centre on land which the council already owned. The straightforward way of going about that would have been for the council to enter into a building contract with a construction company and to raise the money to pay for the work by borrowing. However, as there were restrictions on local authority borrowing, a finance company (Grenfell) entered into the contract with Wiltshier Northern Ltd, a construction company, to build the recreational centre. Pursuant to an agreement with the council Grenfell then assigned to it all rights and causes of action against Wiltshier to which Grenfell was entitled under the contract.

Held: The Court of Appeal held that, since the building contract, to the knowledge of both parties, was entered into for the benefit of the council, damages for loss caused by Wiltshier's breaches could be claimed by the council as assignee. Among the hurdles which the Court of Appeal had to surmount to reach this result was the principle that a third party cannot sue for damages on a contract to which he was not a party. On the Continent no such hurdle would exist since Grenfell's contract with Wiltshier would be regarded as having been made for the benefit of the council so as to entitle the latter to sue on it. To the regret of Steyn LJ this approach was not open under English law.

Judgment: STEYN LJ: In order lawfully to avoid the financial constraints of the Local Government Act 1972 Morgan Grenfell acted as financier to the council in connection with the construction of the Dolphin Centre in Darlington. Morgan Grenfell entered into building contracts with Wiltshier for the benefit of the council. That is how the transaction was structured and that is how all three parties saw it. And it is, of course, manifest that the council, as the third party, accepted the benefit of the building contract. But for the rule of privity of contract the council could simply have sued on the contract made for its benefit.

The case for recognising a contract for the benefit of a third party is simple and straightforward. The autonomy of the will of the parties should be respected. The law of contract should give effect to the reasonable expectations of contracting parties. This principle certainly requires that a burden should not be imposed on a third party without his consent. But there is no doctrinal, logical or policy reason why the law should deny effectiveness to a contract for the benefit of a third party where that is the expressed intention of the parties. Moreover, often the parties, and particularly

---

[7] [1995] 1 WLR 68

third parties, organise their affairs on the faith of the contract. They rely on the contract. It is therefore unjust to deny effectiveness to such a contract . . .

While the privity rule was barely tolerable in Victorian England, it has been recognised for half a century that it has no place in our more complex commercial world. Indeed, as early as 1915, in *Dunlop Pneumatic Tyre Co. Ltd.* v. *Selfridge & Co. Ltd.* [1915] A.C. 847, 855, when the House of Lords restated the privity rule, Lord Dunedin observed in a dissenting speech that the rule made

> "it possible for a person to snap his fingers at a bargain deliberately made, a bargain not in itself unfair, and which the person seeking to enforce it has a legitimate interest to enforce."

Among the majority, Viscount Haldane LC asserted as a self-evident truth, at p. 853, that "only a person who is a party to a contract can sue on it". Today the doctrinal objection to the recognition of a *stipulatio alteri* continues to hold sway. While the rigidity of the doctrine of consideration has been greatly reduced in modern times, the doctrine of privity of contract persists in all its artificial technicality.

In 1937 the Law Revision Committee in its Sixth Report (Cmd. 5449, para. 41–48) proposed the recognition of a right of a third party to enforce the contract which by its express terms purports to confer a benefit directly on him. In 1967, in *Beswick* v. *Beswick* [1968] A.C. 58, 72, Lord Reid observed that if there was a long period of delay in passing legislation on the point the House of Lords might have to deal with the matter. Twelve years later Lord Scarman, who as a former chairman of the Law Commission usually favoured legislative rather than judicial reform where radical change was involved, reminded the House that it might be necessary to review all the cases which "stand guard over this unjust rule": *Woodar Investment Development Ltd.* v. *Wimpey Construction U.K. Ltd.* [1980] 1 W.L.R. 277, 300 G. . . . In 1983 Lord Diplock described the rule as "an anachronistic shortcoming that has for many years been regarded as a reproach to English private law": *Swain* v. *The Law Society* [1983] 1 A.C. 598, 611 D.

But as important as judicial condemnations of the privity rule is the fact that distinguished academic lawyers have found no redeeming virtues in it: see, for example, Markesinis (1987) 103 L.Q.R. 354; Reynolds (1989) 105 L.Q.R. 1; Beatson (1992) 45 C.L.P. 1 and Adams and Brownsnword (1993) 56 M.L.R. 722. And we do well to remember that the civil law legal systems of other members of the European Union recognise such contracts. That our legal system lacks such flexibility is a disadvantage in the single market. Indeed it is a historical curiosity that the legal system of a mercantile country such as England, which in other areas of the law of contract (such as, for example, the objective theory of the interpretation of contracts) takes great account of the interests of third parties, has not been able to rid itself of this unjust rule deriving from a technical conception of a contract as a purely bilateral *vinculum iuris*.

In 1991 the Law Commission revisited this corner of the law. In cautious language appropriate to a consultation paper the Law Commission has expressed the provisional recommendation that "there should be a (statutory) reform of the law to allow third parties to enforce contractual provisions made in their favour": Privity of Contract: Conflicts for the Benefit of Third Parties, Consultation Paper No. 121, p. 132. The principal value of the consultation paper lies in its clear analysis of the practical need for the recognition of a contract for the benefit of third parties, and the explanation of the unedifying spectacle of judges trying to invent exceptions to the rule to prevent demonstrable unfairness. No doubt there will be a report by the Law Commission in the not too distant future recommending the abolition of the privity of contract rule by statute. What will then happen in regard to the proposal for legislation? The answer is really quite simple: probably nothing will happen.

But on this occasion I can understand the inaction of Parliament. There is a respectable argument that it is the type of reform which is best achieved by the courts working out sensible solutions on a case by case basis, e.g. in regard to the exact point of time when the third party is vested with enforceable contractual rights: see Consultation Paper, No. 121, para. 5.8. But that requires the door to be opened by the House of Lords reviewing the major cases which are thought to have entrenched the rule of privity of contract. Unfortunately, there will be few opportunities for the House of Lords to do so. After all, by and large, courts of law in our system are the hostages of the arguments deployed by counsel. And Mr Furst for the council, the third party, made it clear to us that he will not directly challenge the privity rule if this matter should go to the House of Lords. He said that he is content to try to bring his case within exceptions to the privity rule or what Lord Diplock in *Swain* v. *The Law Society* [1983] 1 A.C. 598, 611 D, described as "juristic subterfuges. . . to mitigate the effect of the *lacuna* resulting from the non-recognition of a *jus quaesitum tertio* . . .".

Note
The report by the Law Commission mentioned by Steyn LJ (now Lord Steyn) was published in 1996.[8] It did indeed recommend the recognition of third party rights in limited circumstances: and it was implemented by Contracts (Rights of Third Parties) Act 1999.[9]

7.1.3. THE BASIS OF THIRD PARTY CLAIMS

Once a legal system has recognized a third person's right to enforce a contract to which he is not a party, the further question arises under what conditions the third party will be accorded a right of action. There are many contracts whose performance will be of some benefit to some third person or persons; since not every such contract should be enforceable by the third person, the legislatures or the courts must establish standards and guidelines so as to bring some order and predictability into the question whether in a given case a beneficially interested third person can enforce a contract as a third party beneficiary.

In many cases this decision is not difficult. Where A contracts with B to erect an apartment building on B's land, the owner of the adjoining land C will not be permitted to enforce the contract against A or B even though he may run on the adjoining land a department store which will benefit from the construction of the building. On the other hand, where an insurance company promises the insured to pay an agreed sum to the insured's wife after his death there will be little doubt that the wife can enforce the policy by bringing a suit against the insurer in her own name.

Between these two cases there is a large area in which the decision is more difficult. The test used in virtually all continental jurisdictions to distinguish between genuine third party beneficiaries and merely "incidental" beneficiaries is the test of "intention to benefit". In other words, it must be asked whether the parties have intended to confer on the third party an enforceable claim. If this intention is not clearly spelled out in the text of the agreement the court will ascertain the parties' "implied" intention by looking at the purpose of the agreement, the interests of the parties, and the circumstances of the individual case. In reading the following cases one should always ask whether the decision was based on an actual or implied "intention" of the parties or rather on "objective" considerations of what was fair and equitable in the circumstances—however, we will also see

---

[8] *Privity of Contract: Contracts for the Benefit of Third Parties*, Law Com. No. 242 (London: TSO, 1996).
[9] This will be considered in more detail *infra* at 893, 908–912.

from other cases that third parties may occasionally be able to bring a claim on a basis other than "intention to benefit".

BGH, 28 June 1979[10]   **7.G.6.**

CONSUMER A BENEFICIARY

Isolar glass

Where a manufacturer issues a guarantee in relation to goods sold to an intermediary, intending that guarantee to be enforceable by the ultimate consumer of the goods, the guarantee is treated as a contract made for the benefit of the consumer which can be enforced by the consumer directly against the manufacturer.

Facts: The plaintiff had asked the firm F to install panes of glass in his house. F bought panes described as "ISOLAR-Glas" from the defendant. A letter in which the plaintiff's architect complained of the opaqueness of the panes was passed on by F to the defendant, and the defendant's answer of 8 November 1974 denying liability was passed on by F to the plaintiff. It was only from this letter that the plaintiff learned that the following statement was printed under the heading "Guarantee" on prospectuses disseminated by the defendant for marketing purposes:

> "The manufacturers of ISOLAR glass guarantee, for a period of 5 years calculated from the date of initial delivery, that under normal conditions the transparency of ISOLAR glass will not be impaired either by the formation of a film or by deposits of dust between the panes."

F denied all liability under its contract with the plaintiff. In an action for damages the defendant argued that he had no contract with the plaintiff. (A separate point was also raised that the five year-period had already run; this argument was dismissed by the court in parts of the judgment not extracted here.)

Held: The plaintiff was the beneficiary of the warranty given by the defendant manufacturer.

Judgment: The appellate court took the view that no direct contractual relationship had come into existence between the defendant, as the manufacturer of the glass panes, and the plaintiff, as the ultimate purchaser thereof. There is no need to determine whether that view is correct. As it is, the contested judgment cannot be valid, since a guarantee agreement for the benefit of the plaintiff as the final consumer (i.e. a contract in favour of a third party) came into existence between the defendant and Messrs F.

(a) The appellate court also held that no such [guarantee] contract existed; it stated that, as a general rule, there could not be said to have been any intention on the part of either the manufacturer or the intermediate supplier, who did not enter into direct contractual relations with the final consumer, to create any rights benefiting the latter or to burden themselves with any obligations . . .

(b) The appellant rightly contests those arguments.

The defendant's guarantee . . . took effect from the date of initial delivery, i.e. from the date when the glass was delivered to F. Clearly, therefore, the defendant intended to be contractually bound as from that date. This accorded with the interests of the intermediate supplier, which likewise benefited from the creation of the guarantee contract in favour of the final consumer, since, in the event of a defect arising which was covered by the guarantee, it would itself be absolved from liability *vis-à-vis* its customer, inasmuch as the manufacturer would for its part be obliged to make good the defect pursuant to the contractual guarantee. It follows that F must necessarily have wished

---

[10] BGHZ 75, 75.

888

the guarantee contract to be constituted as rapidly as possible, in order thereby to secure for itself the indirect exemption afforded by that guarantee and to extricate itself from involvement in any subsequent contingencies which might arise (concerning, e.g., the question whether the final consumer, as a third party, acquired knowledge of the guarantee) . . .

(c) Thus, inasmuch as it was in the interests of all the parties concerned that the guarantee relating to a contract benefiting a third party should be constituted as quickly as possible (§ 328 BGB), it must also be assumed that the defendant and F intended such contractual relations to be established. This is also borne out by the fact that, according to the defendant's letter of 8 November 1974, it regarded F as its customer as far as the guarantee contract was concerned. Otherwise, the defendant would have referred not to a complaint about the glass made by Messrs F but to notification of a defect by the plaintiff, and would have argued the matter out primarily with the plaintiff, as the final consumer, and not with Messrs F.

That result is not affected by the fact that, in the contractual circumstances prevailing in the present case, the identity of the "third party" had not yet been established at the time when the contract between the defendant and Messrs F was concluded. As far as the contracting parties were concerned, the identity of the future end consumer was at the outset immaterial. It was enough that they agreed that the third party beneficiary should be *whoever was the final consumer*. That agreement rendered the third party beneficiary sufficiently ascertainable.

Note

There are many other cases in which German courts have made use of the third party beneficiary contract. If for example the lessor of a private clinic provides in the lease that a named specialist should have the right to reserve beds in it, the contract may be construed under § 328 so as to give the specialist an independent contractual right against the lessee.[11] The circumstances under which a person opens an account in a bank or savings bank, especially the name chosen for the account, may show that a third party should also have an immediate right to draw on the funds in the account.[12] The dowry promised by the bride's father to his future son-in-law can be construed as a contract in favour of the daughter.[13] If a collective agreement between a trade union and an employers' federation contains a promise not to strike and the promise is broken, an individual employer may be able to claim damages in respect of the harm suffered by him, since the contract made by the employers' federation is to this extent a contract in favour of the individual employers who are its members.[14] If a holiday tour operator charters from an airline seats on certain flights a customer, after having booked one of those seats with the operator, is a third party beneficiary of the charter agreement and has therefore an independent right to sue the airline for damages if he was wrongfully denied his seat as booked.[15]

[11] BGH 16 November 1951, BGHZ 3, 385.
[12] BGH 25 June 1956, BGHZ 21, 148.
[13] RG 12 December 1907, RGZ 67, 204.
[14] BAG 10 February 1956, NJW 1957, 647.
[15] BGH 17 January 1985, BGHZ 95, 271.

RESTRICTIONS ON BUSINESS OF TENANTS MAY BE ENFORCED BY OTHER TENANTS

Selling bread

Where a landlord leases two neighbouring properties and inserts a clause into one lease restraining the lessee from using the property for the same purposes as the second property, that clause is made for the benefit of the lessee of the second property and cannot be deleted from the lease without his consent.

Facts: These were stated by the lower court (Bordeaux, 22 February 1984) as follows: ". . . Mr and Mrs Gomez are the owners of commercial premises situated in the same building which were let (a) to Mr Esteban for use as a cake shop/confectioner's shop, subject to a restriction prohibiting their use for the sale of bread, and (b) to Mr Frappier for use as a baker's shop; by a rider to the lease granted to Mr Esteban, the restriction prohibiting the use of his premises for the sale of bread was removed with effect from 1 September 1978; Mr Frappier brought proceedings against Mr and Mrs Gomez and Mr Esteban, by which he sought an order restraining the use of the latter's premises for the sale of bread and, in addition, compensation for the loss suffered."

Held: The cour d'appel held that Frappier could enforce the covenant given by Esteban to Gomez. The Cour de cassation agreed.

Judgment: As regards the first two pleas, considered together: . . .—Whereas Mr and Mrs Gomez and Mr Esteban contest the judgment of the cour d'appel allowing those claims; as according to their appeal ground, they argue, first, that it was not open to the cour d'appel, having itself ruled that a stipulation for the benefit of a third party must be express and that the absence of such an express stipulation in Mr Frappier's favour proved that the parties had not intended to confer a benefit on him, to go on to decide that, in the present case, despite the absence of any such form of wording, the parties had stipulated in favour of Mr Frappier; as, in so ruling, it is submitted that the cour d'appel infringed Article 1121 of the Civil Code and that the clause permitting the lessee to "carry on the business of selling pastries, cakes and confectionery, dairy products and dietary products but excluding the sale of bread" does not constitute a provision for the benefit of a third party, being instead a clear, precise clause relating to the intended purpose of the premises which is binding solely on the lessee and the lessor; as they contend that the cour d'appel has thus infringed Article 1121 of the Civil Code and that in addition, matters agreed in a contract take effect only as between the contracting parties; as in deciding that Mr Frappier, who was not a party to the contract and was not mentioned in it, should have been a party to the rider of 1 September 1978 deleting the clause at issue, the cour d'appel infringed Article 1165 of the Civil Code; as moreover, and in any event, even if the clause at issue were capable of being construed as a stipulation for the benefit of a third party, it could only vest in the baker an acquired right such that he could only be deprived of it without his consent if he had declared that he wished to avail himself of it; as in the absence of such a declaration, the cour d'appel has consequently infringed Article 1121 of the Civil Code by ruling that the rider of 1 September 1978 deleting the clause in issue could not be relied on as against Mr Frappier. Second, . . .

—Whereas in seeking to determine the common intention of the parties to the lease of the premises to be used as a cake shop/confectioner's shop, the cour d'appel found however, in its power of appreciation, that the clause prohibiting Mr Esteban from using the premises let to him for the sale of bread could only have been intended to benefit the lessee of the neighbouring baker's shop and that it constituted a stipulation, binding on the parties thereto, for the benefit of a third party: as the cour d'appel correctly held that, in order to be valid, the rider deleting that prohibition required the consent of Mr Frappier; on those grounds alone, it lawfully justified its decision in that regard . . .;

On those grounds, the Court dismisses the appeal . . .

[16] Gaz. Pal. 1986.370.

Cass. civ. 2e, 17 December 1954[17]

7.F.8.

RECIPIENT OF BLOOD TRANSFUSION MAY BE BENEFICIARY

Contaminated blood

A patient who receives a blood transfusion in a public hospital is a third party beneficiary of a contract under which the National Blood Transfusion Service supplies blood to hospitals and can thus recover if the blood is contaminated, unless the National Blood Transfusion Service shows force majeure.

Facts: In the course of treatment at a hospital, the claimant was given a transfusion of blood which the hospital had obtained under a contract between the public services and the national blood transfusion centre. The blood was contaminated and the claimant was infected by it.

Held: The Court of Appeal held that she could recover even though no fault had been shown. The Cour de Cassation upheld the decision.

Judgment: THE COURT: *As regards the first two pleas, considered together*:—Whereas it appears from the contested judgment that a blood transfusion was ordered in the course of treatment which Mrs L was undergoing at the Boucicaut Hospital; the staff of that establishment requested assistance from the Centre National de Transfusion Sanguine [National Blood Transfusion Centre], which nominated Miss V as the blood donor.
—Whereas it is complained in the appeal that the cour d'appel wrongly held, in an essentially contractual matter, that the Centre National de Transfusion Sanguine was liable in tort for the commission of a fault in relation to Mrs L, and that it based its assessment of the damage caused to her on matters of pure conjecture, notwithstanding that no fault of any kind whatever was proved to have been committed by the member of the medical staff concerned and that, according to the medical practices accepted and recognised at the time of the accident, no fault attached to anyone;
—Whereas whilst simultaneously applying to the Administrative Court for a declaration that the public services were liable for the acts of its own servants, Mrs L obtained from the civil courts, on the basis of Article 1382, an order requiring the Centre National de Transfusion Sanguine to pay damages
—Whereas it is however for the Cour de cassation to determine the true nature of the legal relationships inferred by the lower courts from the findings of fact made by it in its absolute discretion;
—Whereas it is not disputed that the agreement concluded between the public services and the appellant Centre National de Transfusion Sanguine was intended to procure for the hospitalised patient the assistance of a blood donor with a view to providing medical treatment which had been prescribed and that that agreement was thus accompanied by a stipulation intended to benefit a third party; the stipulation in question was imposed on behalf of Mrs L, who, although she was not a party to the original contract and was not in any way referred to in it, was none the less intended to benefit from the contractual obligation entered into for her sake; as the non-performance of that obligation by the party by whom it was owed was consequently such as to make the latter directly liable for the resulting damage to the party to whom it was owed, by virtue of the combined effect of Articles 1121 and 1135 of the Civil Code.
—Whereas the background of the contractual relationship which it has itself pleaded, the appellant has moreover neither proved nor even alleged that the breach of the obligation at issue arose, in accordance with Article 1147 of the Civil Code, as a result of some extraneous cause, such as

---

[17] D. 1955.269 annotated by Rodière; J.C.P. 1955.II.8490 annotated by Savatier.

force majeure, which cannot be attributed to it; as in finding that, in circumstances not involving any negligence of a medical nature, "Mrs L was infected with contaminated blood", the court adjudicating on the substance of the case established that the Centre National de Transfusion Sanguine had failed to provide the proper service which Mrs L was entitled to expect, and based on the fault this gives a right to receive compensation; on that legal ground, which automatically supplants all others, it follows that the contested judgment is justified in law.

On those grounds, the Court dismisses the appeal.

Notes

(1) The Court's adoption of a third party beneficiary theory was clearly motivated in this case by its desire to make up for what it felt to be a deficiency of tort law. The plaintiff had originally based her claim on tort but had not been able to prove defendant's negligence under Article 1382 of the French Civil Code. The device of putting into the plaintiff's hands one end of the contractual *vinculum iuris* made it possible for the Court to improve significantly her position. On a contractual approach, Article 1147 of the French Civil Code requires the defendant to prove that no negligence on his part was involved in passing on contaminated blood and that this was due to *force majeure*.

(2) A similar motivation underlies the series of famous cases in which the Court decided in 1933 and 1934 that contracts concluded between passengers and carriers must always be understood to confer a direct contractual right against the carrier on those dependants of a fatally injured passenger who have a legally recognized right to be supported by the latter.[18] It cannot seriously be argued that every time a passenger boards a bus or train and pays for a ticket he has the actual or implied intention of making a kind of testamentary disposition by stipulating, for the benefit of a statutorily defined class of relatives, a right to sue the carrier in contract in case of a fatal accident. This theory is based on what Josserand has called in his annotation a "purely fictitious mental operation invented to satisfy the needs of the case". Clearly, the Court's basic motive was the desire to further a strong social policy of granting maximum protection to the innocent dependants of fatally injured accident victims. It may be noted in passing that there is today no longer any need for the dependants of accident victims to sue as contract beneficiaries. Since the 1930s French courts have improved the protection of tort law significantly. Under Article 1384(1) of the French Civil Code the dependants must prove only that their relative was killed through the operation of a bus, train or other "thing" under the control of the defendant at the time of the accident. It is then up to the defendant to show that the accident was caused by *force majeure* or by the act of a third person for which he was not responsible.

The civil law is prepared, by looking at the purpose of the agreement and the circumstances of the case, to imply an intention to benefit the third party. In contrast the English Contracts (Rights of Third Parties) Act 1999, which follows the bill drafted by the Law Commission,[19] takes a more cautious line:

---

[18] See Cass. civ. 6 December 1932 and 24 May 1933, D.P. 1933.1.137 annotated by Josserand (**1.F.36**, *supra* at 42); S. 1934.1.81 annotated by Esmein (**1.F.37**, *supra* at 43).
[19] See *supra* at 887.

Contracts (Rights of Third Parties) Act 1999   **7.E.9.**

Section 1:   (1) Subject to the provisions of this Act, a person who is not a party to a contract
(a "third party") may in his own right enforce a term of the contract if—
(a) the contract expressly provides that he may, or
(b) subject to subsection (2), the contract purports to confer a benefit on him.
(2) Subsection (1)(b) above does not apply if on a proper construction of the contract it appears that the parties did not intend the term to be enforceable by the third
party.
(3) The third party must be expressly identified in the contract by name, as a member of a class or as answering a particular description but need not be in existence
when the contract is entered into.

Compare the following:

Principles of European Contract Law   **7.PECL.10.**

Article 6:110 (1): (1) A third party may require performance of a contractual obligation when its
right to do so has been expressly agreed upon between the promisor and the
promisee, or when such agreement is to be inferred from the purpose of the contract or the circumstances of the case. The third party need not be identified at
the time the agreement is concluded.

The following three cases from France, Germany and England have a common theme: an
expert enters into a contract with his client under which he is to render an expert's opinion for a fee. Due to the expert's carelessness his opinion is erroneous and misleading. If
it is not the client but a third party who relies on the accuracy of the opinion, can that
party bring a claim for damages against the expert? Does the third party's action lie in
contract or tort? As we shall see, the systems studied sometimes permit a third party to
make a claim by virtue of a test other than that of "intention to benefit". For example, in
these cases, French law adopts the "intention to benefit" approach, whereas German law
adopts a different contract–based approach. In English law, on the other hand, the expert
is liable in the tort of negligence.[20]

Paris, 18 June 1957[21]   **7.F.11.**

AN APPRAISER EMPLOYED BY A SELLER MAY BE LIABLE TO THE BUYER OF THE
PROPERTY APPRAISED

The "Double de Genève"

*A valuer who is employed by the seller of a rare stamp to give an expert opinion on it for the purpose
of sale and who fails to report that the stamp has been repaired is liable to a purchaser of the stamp
who pays the value of an unrepaired stamp.*

---

[20] Negligence is a liability in tort depending on whether the defendant owed a duty of care to the plaintiff
and caused him damage by a breach of that duty.
[21] J.C.P. 1957.II.10134 (2d case) annotated by Lindon

Facts: Cosnelle employed Busser to appraise a Swiss "Double de Genève" stamp which he was hoping to sell to Fabre. Busser gave a certificate that the stamp had "a fine appearance, authentic and not repaired". Relying on this certificate, Fabre bought the stamp for 300,000 francs. When he came to sell it in 1953, Fabre discovered that the stamp had been repaired and re-coated and was worth only some 100,000 francs. Fabre claimed from Busser the difference between this and the value the stamp would have had if it had been in the condition stated by Busser.

Held: The first instance court dismissed Fabre's claim on the ground that there was no connection between Fabre and Busser. The court of appeal reversed this decision but remitted the case for further findings of fact.

Judgment:—Ruling on the appeal lodged by Fabre against a judgment delivered by the tribunal de commerce de la Seine on 13 December 1954, declaring his claim inadmissible, alternatively unfounded, and dismissing the same;

—Whereas it is common ground that Busser, to whom Mr Cosnelle had submitted for examination a Swiss postage stamp dating from 1843 known as a "Double de Genève", issued on 1 March 1947 an expert's certificate containing a description of the stamp and stating "stamp having a fine appearance, authentic and not repaired", and further that, in early 1953, Fabre offered for sale, at a price of 600,000 francs, a "Double de Genève" stamp accompanied by the aforementioned certificate;

—Whereas Fabre states that on 1 March 1947 he acquired the stamp in relation to which Busser had provided his expert's opinion, paying therefor the sum of 300,000 francs, and that in January 1953, just when he was putting it up for sale, that stamp was found to have been "repaired and re-coated", its value in that condition being approximately 100,000 francs; as he maintains that Busser committed a fault or was negligent in his expert appraisal, and claims that he should be ordered to pay him the sum of 800,000 francs, representing the difference between the current value which the stamp in question would have had if it were in good condition and the value which it is actually recognised as having;

—Whereas in dismissing Fabre's claim, the court hearing the case at first instance considered that there was no legal connection between Fabre and Busser and, moreover, that it had not been established that the same stamp was involved or that the condition of the stamp in 1947 was the same as that which it was found to possess in 1953;

—Whereas it appears from the attestation made by Cosnelle on 11 May 1953 that on 1 March 1947 Fabre acquired a Swiss "Double de Genève" (No 1) postage stamp dating from 1843 through the intermediary of Cosnelle, who had previously submitted the stamp in question to Busser for examination and expert appraisal by the latter. The expert appraisal was requested by Cosnelle and carried out by Busser on behalf of the purchaser, namely Fabre; as Fabre was thus the beneficiary of a stipulation which was made for his benefit by Cosnelle and accepted by Busser and which created a direct contractual link between Busser and himself;

—Whereas the wording of the said attestation shows furthermore that Cosnelle acted in the circumstances as Fabre's agent and that both the expert appraisal of the stamp and its acquisition were organised by him in pursuance of that agency, so that Fabre, as the principal, was in a contractual relationship with Busser;

—Whereas in the event that any fault attributable to Busser became apparent, it would consequently render the latter liable to Fabre

—Whereas however, the Court does not have before it, as matters stand, sufficient evidence enabling it to assess the matter and to determine whether any fault was even committed or, if it was, to adjudicate on the quantum of damage; Whereas it is consequently necessary to order an expert appraisal on the terms hereinafter set out . . .

Note

It is a pity that the judgment tells us so little about the facts of the case. It seems that the court gave two alternative grounds for the decision. One was that Cosnelle made the agreement with Busser (in his own name but) *"pour le compte"* of Fabre and that Fabre could therefore be considered as a third party beneficiary. The other ground was that Cosnelle made the agreement with Busser *"comme mandataire"* (as an agent) of Fabre (presumably acting in Fabre's name).

BGH, 26 November 1986[22]   **7.G.12.**

SELLER'S APPRAISER LIABLE TO BUYER'S BANK

Tax consultant's "rosy view"

A tax consultant employed by the owner of a company to prepare a balance sheet for use in selling the company may, if the balance sheet is inaccurate, be liable not only to the purchaser but also to the bank financing the purchase.

Facts: A was the sole shareholder of a company which he wanted to sell. He requested the defendants, his tax consultants, to draw up a balance sheet. They were negligent in painting the company's financial position in too rosy a light. A copy of the balance sheet was passed on by A to B as a potential purchaser of the company, and B in turn passed it on to his bank, the plaintiff, in support of an application for credit to finance the purchase price. The bank was duly impressed and lent B DM 500,000, taking a pledge on the company's shares as security. The bank lost all its money when shortly thereafter both B and his newly acquired company became insolvent and went into liquidation. The bank brought proceedings against the tax consultants.

Held: The Court awarded the plaintiff damages for a breach by the tax consultants of their contractual duty to use proper care in drawing up the balance sheet. This duty was primarily owed by them to A with whom they had a contract. The Court held, however, that they owed this duty also to third parties who they knew or ought to have known might rely on the accuracy of the balance sheet. This included not only B (and other potential purchasers of the company who might be shown the balance sheet), but also the bank to whom the balance sheet had been submitted by the purchaser in support of an application for a loan to finance the acquisition.

Judgment: . . . The present case affords grounds for supposing that the contracting parties intended to include third parties within the scope of protection provided by the contract. As stated above, it cannot be assumed that [the balance sheet] was intended solely for the edification of the defendant's client; on the contrary, it was meant to serve as the basis on which a third party—either the purchaser or a lender—might reach a decision. In such a case, it is clear that the third party is to be included within the scope of protection afforded by the contract. It cannot be argued, in opposition to the claim in the present case, that the interests of the purchaser or lender, on the one hand, and of the tax adviser's client, on the other, ran counter to each other. Where a person instructs another person recognised by the State as possessing expert knowledge in a particular field (e.g. a publicly appointed expert, chartered or certified accountant, publicly appointed surveying engineer or tax adviser) to produce an expert's report or to give an expert opinion (e.g. an accountant's or tax adviser's attestation) to be used in dealings with a third party, the client generally has an interest in ensuring that the results of the work carried out have the requisite probative value. This can only be guaranteed, however, if the author of the report or opinion produces it on an objective basis and does so to the best of his knowledge and belief, and if he is also able to vouch for it *vis-à-vis* the third party.

The inclusion of the plaintiff within the scope of protection afforded by the contract does not depend on whether the defendant was aware of the fact that [the balance sheet] was to be submitted to the plaintiff; it will suffice in that regard if the defendant realised, or ought to have realised, that the results of his work were intended either for a purchaser or for a lender (bank). The

---

[22] NJW 1987,1758.

Bundesgerichtshof has previously held on numerous occasions that a duty of protection exists, in cases in which the person owing that duty was aware neither of the number nor of the names of the persons entitled to such protection [citations omitted]. This does not mean, however, that the group of persons to whom the duty of protection is owed may be extended *ad infinitum*; on the contrary, that duty must be restricted to a discernible, clearly circumscribed group of persons. Accordingly, it does not appear unacceptable to include within the scope of protection afforded by the contract the person for whom [the balance sheet] was clearly intended to serve as the basis for a decision, since in this case the scope of such protection would extend to cover only the purchaser and whoever might lend money to the purchaser.

Notes

(1) Note that the plaintiff in this case is not a beneficiary of a "genuine" contract made for his benefit as spelled out by §§ 328 *et seq.* BGB, since the bank acquired no right to ask the tax consultants to perform the contract specifically. They were allowed to claim only damages for breach of a contractual duty which the Court held was owed to them by the tax consultants. For this type of third party beneficiary contract German doctrine has coined the term "contracts having protective effect for third parties", discussed further in the *Carelessly Drafted Divorce Settlement* case.[23]

(2) Assume (a) that B had bought the company with his own money and had submitted the balance sheet to his bank in order to obtain a loan for other purposes; (b) that B, by submitting the balance sheet to his suppliers, had persuaded them to make deliveries to the company on credit. Would the bank or the sellers be able to sue the tax consultants for breach of contract? Where does the ball stop rolling?

English law has sometimes produced a rather similar effect; but, before the enactment of Contracts (Rights of Third Parties) Act 1999—and possibly even afterwards, because of the narrow terms of that Act[24]—this could not be done by imposing liability in contract. Instead, the plaintiff had to bring an action in tort for negligence.

House of Lords **7.E.13.**
Smith v. *Bush*[25]

VALUER EMPLOYED BY LENDER LIABLE IN NEGLIGENCE TO PURCHASER/BORROWER

Negligent building society survey

A valuer who is employed by a building society to value a property on which a loan for the purchase price is to be secured will be liable to the purchaser/ borrower if the property is negligently overvalued.

Facts: The plaintiff applied to a building society for a mortgage to assist her in purchasing a house. The building society instructed the defendants, a firm of surveyors and valuers, to carry out a visual inspection of the house and to report on its value and any matter likely to affect its value. The defendants' valuer who carried out the inspection was careless in failing to check whether the chimneys were adequately supported. He stated that the house needed no essential repairs. The building society supplied a copy of the report to the plaintiff who purchased the house. The chimneys were not adequately supported and one of them subsequently collapsed. The plaintiff claimed damages from the defendants in negligence.

[23] See *infra* at 898. For a full comparative discussion of this type of agreement and of their relationship with tort law see Markesinis, *The German Law of Torts*, 3rd edn (Oxford: Clarendon, 1995) at 285 ff.

[24] See *supra* at 893.

[25] [1990] 1 AC 831.

Held: The court of first instance upheld the claim. The Court of Appeal reversed this decision on the ground that the survey contained a disclaimer of responsibility which prevented the surveyor being liable, as in *Hedley Byrne & Co Ltd.* v. *Heller & Partners Ltd.* [1964] AC 465. The House of Lords allowed the purchaser's appeal. [Parts of the judgment dealing with the effect of the disclaimer are extracted above, p. 548.]

Judgment: LORD GRIFFITHS: I therefore return to the question in what circumstances should the law deem those who give advice to have assumed responsibility to the person who acts upon the advice or, in other words, in what circumstances should a duty of care be owed by the adviser to those who act upon his advice ? I would answer—only if it is foreseeable that if the advice is negligent the recipient is likely to suffer damage, that there is a sufficiently proximate relationship between the parties and that it is just and reasonable to impose the liability. In the case of a surveyor valuing a small house for a building society or local authority, the application of these three criteria leads to the conclusion that he owes a duty of care to the purchaser. If the valuation is negligent and is relied upon damage in the form of economic loss to the purchaser is obviously foreseeable. The necessary proximity arises from the surveyor's knowledge that the overwhelming probability is that the purchaser will rely upon his valuation, the evidence was that surveyors knew that approximately 90 per cent. of purchasers did so, and the fact that the surveyor only obtains the work because the purchaser is willing to pay his fee. It is just and reasonable that the duty should be imposed for the advice is given in a professional as opposed to a social context and liability for breach of the duty will be limited both as to its extent and amount. The extent of the liability is limited to the purchaser of the house—I would not extend it to subsequent purchasers. The amount of the liability cannot be very great because it relates to a modest house. There is no question here of creating a liability of indeterminate amount to an indeterminate class. I would certainly wish to stress that in cases where the advice has not been given for the specific purpose of the recipient acting upon it, it should only be in cases when the adviser knows that there is a high degree of probability that some other identifiable person will act upon the advice that a duty of care should be imposed. It would impose an intolerable burden upon those who give advice in a professional or commercial context if they were to owe a duty not only to those to whom they give the advice but to any other person who might choose to act upon it.

Notes

(1) Would it have made a difference if the building society had not shown the report to the plaintiff, but had simply offered him a mortgage? Would the House of Lords have awarded damages in tort to the plaintiff bank in the German case[26] if the test proposed by Lord Griffiths had been used?

(2) If a person possessed of a special skill, such as an expert, a surveyor, a chartered accountant or a banker, negligently makes an erroneous or misleading statement he will be liable in damages to another who, as he knows or should know, has relied on the statement and suffered loss. Note, however, that in this case the liability of the professional person is based not on a breach of contract, but on the tort of negligence: see the leading case of *Hedley Byrne & Co.* v. *Heller & Partners*[27] and the re-statement of the present law in *Caparo Industries Plc* v. *Dickman*.[28]

What if a professional person carelessly fails to take the steps necessary to comply with his client's intention to benefit a third party? Will the professional person be liable to the third party—even though a statement was neither made nor relied on? This problem is discussed in the next two judgments.

[26] See *supra* at 895.
[27] [1964] AC 465
[28] [1990] 2 AC 605.

ATTORNEY LIABLE TO THIRD PARTY WHO LOSES THROUGH ATTORNEY'S NEGLIGENCE

Carelessly drafted divorce settlement

An attorney employed to draw up a divorce settlement which will benefit the children of the marriage but who fails to ensure that the settlement is adequate to protect those children may be liable to them.

Facts: The defendant was an attorney who had represented M in divorce proceedings. In January 1972 Mr and Mrs M met in the defendant's office, where they signed a divorce agreement drawn up by the defendant. It contained the following clause:

"§ 6. As to the house, the parties agreed that the half belonging to Mrs. M is to be transferred to the three children in equal parts. Mr. M hereby agrees not to sell his half but to transfer it to his present legitimate children. An appropriate notarial contract to this effect is to be concluded immediately after the divorce is final. Mr. M further promises that once the divorce is final he will indemnify Mrs. M against any liabilities arising from the house or its construction . . ."

A divorce decree was granted in February 1972, and the defendant, in the name of his client, waived any rights of appeal, as did Mrs M's attorney. Mrs M then refused to transfer her interest in the property to M's son and his siblings. The minor son, represented by his father as his statutory representative, thereupon claimed damages from the defendant on the ground that he had failed, before waiving his client's rights of appeal, to take the steps necessary to create, by way of a notarial contract, a legally binding obligation of Mrs M to transfer her interest in the house to the plaintiff and his siblings.

Held: The defendant had indeed acted carelessly and was liable to the plaintiff even though there was no contract with him.

Judgment: . . . Nor is there anything wrong in law with the Court of Appeal's holding that although there was no contract between the plaintiff and the defendant, the plaintiff could sue the defendant for damages for his faulty breach of contract.

(a) The Court of Appeal found that there was here a contract with protective effect for third parties and that the plaintiff's claim arose therefrom. We do not have to decide whether this is so.

(aa) Certainly an important factor pointing in that direction is that the plaintiff was the son of the attorney's client and was entitled to care and protection from him (compare BGHZ 61, 227, 233). The usual problem in cases of contracts with protective effects for third parties is whether the victim was someone the debtor could expect to be harmed by a breach of the contract. That is not the problem here. The very words of § 6 of the divorce agreement drawn up by the defendant show that the children were its sole beneficiaries, the only people apt to suffer if the agreement proved invalid.

The only question here is how far the protective effect of this contract works in favour of the children, in particular whether they have any claim for damages for breach of contract in their own right. Now the contract between client and attorney is such, given its nature and structure, that it can only be very seldom, whether one interprets the contract extensively or invokes § 242 BGB (see BGHZ 56, 269, 273; NJW 1975, 977), that the duties it generates can be sued on by third parties, for the fiduciary relationship between client and attorney makes it strongly bilateral and self-contained [references omitted]. Thus the fact that third parties have an interest in what an attorney does will not normally lead to any extension of his liability, even if those persons are named or known to him. However, an exception must be made where a contract drafted by the attorney is designed to vest rights in third parties specified therein, especially third parties who, as in the present case, are represented by the client. It is true that most of the cases where the courts have granted third parties a

---

[29] NJW 1977.2073. Translation by Tony Weir in Markesinis and Unberath, *The German Law of Torts: A Comparative Treatise*, 4th edn. (Hart Publishing, Oxford, 2002).

claim for damages arising out of a contract to which they were not parties have involved personal injury or property damage and its consequences (BGHZ 49, 350, 355; NJW 1955, 257; [other references omitted]), but it is not impossible for a third party to have a personal claim for economic loss caused by breach of subsidiary contractual duties (NJW 1968, 1929; BGH NJW 1975, 344). In drawing the line here one must certainly apply an especially stringent test: the circle of persons to whom the protective effect of a contract extends is to be narrowly drawn, so as to avoid blurring the line between contractual and tortious liability in an unacceptable manner (BGHZ 66, 51, 57; NJW 1974, 1189). It must always be borne in mind, in claims for purely economic loss, that the debtor is not to be made liable for the mere ricochet effect of his conduct on third parties.

(bb) Despite this, we cannot, on the special facts of the present case, fault the Court of Appeal's holding that the plaintiff was drawn into the protective ambit of the attorney's contract. The respondent invokes a decision of this court of 6 July 1965 (NJW 1965, 1955), but this is not quite in point. The court there did allow the daughter of a client to sue the attorney although she was not herself a party to the contract, but the court was reluctant to categorise the contract as one with protective effect for third parties [references omitted]. Contracts with protective effect for third parties are concerned with breach of subsidiary duties by the contractor (see BGH NJW 1975, 344) whereas in that case the question was really whether the attorney could be made liable towards the client's daughter, the third party, for a breach of specific duties of performance [reference omitted]. Our case is clearly distinguishable.

(b) The plaintiff might also base his claim here on the concept of *Drittschadensliquidation*, a doctrine which borders on, if it does not actually overlap, the area of application of the doctrine of contracts with protective effect for third parties (see BGHZ 49, 350, 355). It would have been quite proper for the defendant's client to indemnify his son, the plaintiff, for the harm he had suffered, and one could then infer from the fact that he brought suit as his son's statutory representative that he was making an assignment of his own claim which the plaintiff, on the threshold of majority, could implicitly accept. But we need not pursue the matter here.

(c) In whatever legal or doctrinal category one puts the present litigated facts, the result must be that the plaintiff has a direct claim against the defendant attorney for compensation for the harm which he suffered as a result of the defendant's failure to tell his father of the need to implement the agreement in § 6 of the divorce document. Any other conclusion would be inconsistent with the meaning and purpose of the attorney's contract here and of the father-son relationship between the client and the plaintiff of which the defendant was well aware.

Note

For similar cases see BGH 6 July 1965, NJW 1965, 1955 and 13 July 1994, NJW 1995, 51.

House of Lords   **7.E.15.**
White v. *Jones*[30]

Dɪsᴀᴘᴘᴏɪɴᴛᴇᴅ ʙᴇɴᴇғɪᴄɪᴀʀʏ ᴍᴀʏ ʀᴇᴄᴏᴠᴇʀ ғʀᴏᴍ ɴᴇɢʟɪɢᴇɴᴛ ʟᴀᴡʏᴇʀ

Will not drawn up in time

A solicitor who is employed by a testator to draw up a new will leaving property to the plaintiff but who negligently fails to prepare the will before the testator dies will be liable to the disappointed beneficiary.

---

[30] [1995] 2 WLR 187.

Facts: The testator had been reconciled with his daughters and instructed a solicitor to draw up a new will, leaving £9,000 to each daughter, to replace an earlier will which left them nothing. The solicitor failed to prepare the will before the testator died.

Held: The first instance court dismissed the plaintiffs' action on the ground that the solicitor owed them no duty of care. This decision was reversed by the Court of Appeal. By a majority the House of Lords dismissed the solicitor's appeal.

Judgment: LORD GOFF OF CHIEVELEY: My Lords, in this appeal, your Lordships' House has to consider for the first time the much discussed question whether an intended beneficiary under a will is entitled to recover damages from the testator's solicitors by reason of whose negligence the testator's intention to benefit him under the will has failed to be carried into effect. In *Ross* v. *Caunters* [1980] Ch. 297, a case in which the will failed because, through the negligence of the testator's solicitors, the will was not duly attested, Sir Robert Megarry V.-C. held that the disappointed beneficiary under the ineffective will was entitled to recover damages from the solicitors in negligence. In the present case, the testator's solicitors negligently delayed the preparation of a fresh will in place of a previous will which the testator had decided to revoke, and the testator died before the new will was prepared. The plaintiffs were the two daughters of the testator who would have benefited under the fresh will but received nothing under the previous will which, by reason of the solicitor's delay, remained unrevoked. It was held by the Court of Appeal, reversing the decision of Turner J, that the plaintiffs were entitled to recover damages from the solicitors in negligence. The question which your Lordships have to decide is whether, in cases such as these, the solicitors are liable to the intended beneficiaries who, as a result of their negligence, have failed to receive the benefit which the testator intended they should receive . . .

The fact that the problems which arise in cases such as the present have troubled the courts in many jurisdictions, both common law and civil law, and have prompted a variety of reactions, indicates that they are of their very nature difficult to accommodate within the ordinary principles of the law of obligations. It is true that our law of contract is widely seen as deficient in the sense that it is perceived to be hampered by the presence of an unnecessary doctrine of consideration and (through a strict doctrine of privity of contract) stunted through a failure to recognise a *jus quaesitum tertio*. But even if we lacked the former and possessed the latter, the ordinary law could not provide a simple answer to the problems which arise in the present case, which appear at first sight to require the imposition of something like a contractual liability which is beyond the scope of the ordinary *jus quaesitum tertio*. In these circumstances, the effect of the special characteristics of any particular system of law is likely to be, as indeed appears from the authorities I have cited, not so much that no remedy is recognised, but rather that the system in question will choose its own special means for granting a remedy notwithstanding the doctrinal difficulties involved.

We can, I believe, see this most clearly if we compare the English and German reactions to problems of this kind. Strongly though I support the study of comparative law, I hesitate to embark in an opinion such as this upon a comparison, however brief, with a civil law system; because experience has taught me how very difficult, and indeed potentially misleading, such an exercise can be. Exceptionally however, in the present case, thanks to material published in our language by distinguished comparatists, German as well as English, we have direct access to publications which should sufficiently dispel our ignorance of German law and so by comparison illuminate our understanding of our own.

I have already referred to problems created in the English law of contract by the doctrines of consideration and of privity of contract. These, of course, encourage us to seek a solution to problems of this kind within our own law of tortious negligence. In German law, on the other hand, in which the law of delict does not allow for the recovery of damages for pure economic loss in negligence, it is natural that the judges should extend the law of contract to meet the justice of the case. In a case such as the present, which is concerned with a breach of duty owed by a professional man, A, to his client, B, in circumstances in which practical justice requires that a third party, C, should have a remedy against the professional man, A, in respect of damage which he has suffered by reason of the breach, German law may have recourse to a doctrine called *Vertrag mit Schutzwirkung für Dritte* (contract with protective effect for third parties), the scope of which extends beyond that of an ordinary contract for the benefit of a third party: see Professor Werner Lorenz in *The Gradual Convergence*, edited by Markesinis (1994), pp. 65, 68–72). This doctrine was invoked by the German Supreme Court in the *Testamentfall* case (BGH 6 July 1965, NJW 1965, 1955) which is similar to the present case in that the plaintiff, C, through the dilatoriness of a lawyer, A, (instructed by her father, B) in making the necessary arrangements for the father's will, was deprived of a testamentary benefit which she would have received under the will if it had been duly made. The plaintiff, C, was held to be entitled to recover damages from the lawyer, A. Professor Lorenz has expressed the opinion (p. 70) that the ratio of that case would apply to the situation *Ross* v. *Caunters* itself. In these cases, it appears that the court will examine "whether the contracting parties intended to create a duty of care in favour of" the third person (BGH NJW 1984, 355, 356), or whether there is to be inferred "a protective obligation . . . based on good faith . . ." (BGHZ 69, 82, 85 *et seq.*). (Quotations taken in each case from Professor Markesinis's article on "An Expanding Tort Law—the Price of a Rigid Contract Law" (1987) 103 L.Q.R. 354, 363, 366, 368.) But any such inference of intention would, in English law, be beyond the scope of our doctrine of implied terms; and it is legitimate to infer that the German judges, in creating this special doctrine, were extending the law of contract beyond orthodox contractual principles.

I wish next to refer to another German doctrine known as Drittschadensliquidation, which is available in cases of transferred loss (*Schadensverlagerung*). In these cases, as a leading English comparatist has explained:

> "the person who has suffered the loss has no remedy while the person who has the remedy has suffered no loss. If such a situation is left unchallenged, the defaulting party may never face the consequences of his negligent conduct; his insurer may receive an unexpected (and undeserved) windfall; and the person on whom the loss has fallen may be left without any redress." See Markesinis, *The German Law of Torts*, 3rd ed. (1994), p. 56.

Under this doctrine, to take one example, the defendant, A, typically a carrier, may be held liable to the seller of goods, B, for the loss suffered by the buyer, C, to whom the risk but not the property in the goods has passed. In such circumstances the seller is held to have a contractual claim against the carrier in respect of the damage suffered by the buyer. This claim can be pursued by the seller against the carrier; but it can also be assigned by him to the buyer. If, exceptionally, the seller refuses either to exercise his right for the benefit of the buyer or to assign his claim to him, the seller can be compelled to make the assignment: see Professor Werner Lorenz in *Essays in Memory of Professor F.H. Lawson* (1986), pp. 86, 89–90, and in *The Gradual Convergence*, pp. 65, 88–89, 92–93; and Professor Hein Kötz in 10 Tel Aviv University Studies in Law (1990), pp. 195, 209. Professor Lorenz (*Essays*, at p. 89) has stated that it is at least arguable that the idea of *Drittschadensliquidation* might be "extended so as to cover" such cases as the *Testamentfall* case, an observation which is consistent with the view expressed by the German Supreme Court that the two doctrines may overlap (BGH 19 January 1977, NJW 1977, 2073 = VersR 1977, 638: translated in Markesinis, *The German Law of Torts*, p. 293). At all events both doctrines have the effect of extending to the plaintiff the benefit of what is, in substance, a contractual cause of action; though, at least as seen through English eyes, this result is achieved not by orthodox contractual reasoning, but by the contractual remedy being made available by law in order to achieve practical justice . . .

I therefore return to the law of tort for a solution to the problem. For the reasons I have already given, an ordinary action in tortious negligence on the lines proposed by Sir Robert Megarry V.-C. in *Ross* v. *Caunters* [1980] Ch. 297 must, with the greatest respect, be regarded as inappropriate, because it does not meet any of the conceptual problems which have been raised . . . Even so it seems to me that it is open to your Lordships' House . . . to fashion a remedy to fill a lacuna in the law and so prevent the injustice which would otherwise occur on the facts of cases such as the present. In the *Lenesta Sludge* case [1994] 1 A.C. 85, as I have said, the House made available a remedy as a matter of law to solve the problem of transferred loss in the case before them. The present case is, if anything, *a fortiori*, since the nature of the transaction was such that, if the solicitors were negligent and their negligence did not come to light until after the death of the testator, there would be no remedy for the ensuing loss unless the intended beneficiary could claim. In my opinion, therefore, your Lordship's House should in cases such as these extend to the intended beneficiary a remedy under the *Hedley Byrne* principle by holding that the assumption of responsibility by the solicitor towards his client should be held in law to extend to the intended beneficiary who (as the solicitor can reasonably foresee) may, as a result of the solicitor's negligence, be deprived of his intended legacy in circumstances in which neither the testator nor his estate will have a remedy against the solicitor. Such liability will not of course arise in cases in which the defect in the will comes to light before the death of the testator, and the testator either leaves the will as it is or otherwise continues to exclude the previously intended beneficiary from the relevant benefit. I only wish to add that, with the benefit of experience during the 15 years in which *Ross* v. *Caunters* has been regularly applied, we can say with some confidence that a direct remedy by the intended beneficiary against the solicitor appears to create no problems in practice. That is therefore the solution which I would recommend to your Lordships . . .

Cass. civ. 1re, 21 November 1978[31]   **7.F.16.**

SECURITY COMPANY UNDER CONTRACT TO BANK LIABLE TO CUSTOMER

The Carrefour takings

A security company employed by a bank to collect takings from one of its customer's stores and which carried the takings in an ordinary car instead of the armoured vehicle stipulated is liable to the customer if the takings are stolen as a result.

Facts: On 8 March 1972 employees of the Société Parisienne de Surveillance ("S.P.S.") were engaged in loading into the boot of a Mercedes motor-car a trunk containing the takings of a Carrefour store operated by the Société des Grands Magasins Garonne-Adour ("Sogara"), with a view to transporting it to the head office of the Crédit Commercial de France ("C.C.F.") in Bordeaux, when armed raiders appeared, wounded one of the employees of S.P.S., seized the trunk and fled. Sogara brought legal proceedings for damages against S.P.S., which regularly transported funds to and from the store and C.C.F. pursuant to an agreement dated 28 June 1971 which had been concluded between C.C.F. and S.P.S. Sogara claimed that S.P.S. had failed to take all necessary precautions, and in particular that it had used a private motor-car instead of an armoured vehicle.

Held: The cour d'appel found that C.C.F. had imposed a stipulation for the benefit of a third party, namely Sogara and, declaring that S.P.S. had failed to fulfil its contractual obligations, ordered the latter to pay damages to Sogara. The Cour de cassation upheld this decision.

Judgment: THE COURT: *On the sole ground taken in its two branches*:—Whereas the appellant contests the decision of that appellate court, arguing, first, that a stipulation for the benefit of a third party cannot be said to exist merely by reason of the fact that the third party has an interest in the contract to which it was not a party; as a stipulation for the benefit of a third party can only exist where the contract creates a right in favour of the third party and does not impose any obligation on that third party and whereas second, it asserts that the cour d'appel omitted to deal with S.P.S.'s

[31] J.C.P. 1980.I.19315, annotated by Rodière.

submission that Sogara had not objected to the transportation of the money in a Mercedes motor-car and had thus exonerated the carrier from liability;

—Whereas however, the cour d'appel, adopting one of the grounds on which the decision of the first-instance court was based, held that S.P.S. had undertaken in the agreement of 28 June 1971 to make armoured vehicles available to C.C.F. and to provide teams of drivers and accompanying personnel with a view to ensuring the safe carriage of cash in consideration of the payment of a fixed-rate fee, and that it had further covenanted to take out insurance to cover the period from the time when the valuables were handed over to its personnel until the time when they were placed in the C.C.F.'s safe; as the cour d'appel could so consider that the contract created a right in favour of Sogara and held that that contract, which was concluded in the interests of both C.C.F. and Sogara, contained a stipulation for the benefit of a third party, namely Sogara; as the appellate court found that the fact that the contract required Sogara to settle the invoices—a requirement which that company accepted—did not preclude the existence of a stipulation for the benefit of a third party;

—Whereas second, the cour d'appel—adopting, again, one of the grounds on which the decision at first instance had been based—found that it was not open to S.P.S. to maintain that Sogara had authorised the use of the Mercedes, since Rolland, an employee of S.P.S., had admitted that the decision to use it had been taken by him alone and in so concluding, the cour d'appel dealt with the submissions relied on; as none of the appeal grounds is consequently well-founded.

On those grounds, the Court dismisses the appeal lodged against the judgment delivered on 29 June 1977 by the cour d'appel, Bordeaux.

Note

German courts have developed a special technique (referred to as *Drittschadens-liquidation*) to deal with cases in which A enters into a contract with B under which B is to store, guard, repair, manage or—as in this case—carry a chattel owned by C. If a breach of B's contractual duties results in damage to C's chattel, A has a contractual claim against B for the damages *sustained by C*, and C, as assignee, may then enforce that claim himself against B.[32] The same technique is used where a seller contracts with a carrier for the carriage of goods sold to a buyer and the goods are damaged or lost *in transitu* owing to the carrier's negligence. In these cases, as a result of the agreement between the seller and the buyer, the loss falls on, or is "transferred' to, the buyer as he must pay the full price despite the fact that the goods were lost or destroyed. The buyer has no remedy against the carrier, either in contract as he is not a party to the contract of carriage, or in tort as title to the goods was in the seller at the time when the loss or damage occurred. In this situation German courts have held, first, that the seller has a contractual claim against the carrier for the loss suffered by the buyer, and, secondly, that there is an express or implied assignment under which the seller has assigned his claim for damages to the buyer so that the latter, as the real party in interest, has a right to sue of his own.[33] See also Lord Goff's discussion of *Drittschadensliquidation* in *White* v. *Jones*.[34] In French law, Drittschadensliquidation is considered as a form of "stipulation pour autrui" and treated as such.

---

[32] BGH 10 July 1963, BGHZ 40, 91, at 100 ff.; BGH 10 May 1984, NJW 1985, 2411.
[33] BGH 29 January 1968, BGHZ 49, 356, at 360 ff.
[34] See *supra* at 901.

7.1.4. EXEMPTION CLAUSES FOR THE BENEFIT OF THIRD PARTIES

So far we have discussed cases in which a person acquires an enforceable right by virtue of a contract to which he is not a direct party. A similar problem arises in cases where a third party wishes to avail himself of an immunity, a limitation or exclusion of liability, or another defence which is based on a contract made by others but intended by them, either expressly or impliedly, to benefit the third party. In other words, can the benefit conferred on one not a direct party to a contract consist not only of a sword, but also of a shield?

BGH, 7 December 1961[35]   **7.G.17.**

VICARIOUS IMMUNITY

The patrolman and the stove

A clause which protects an employer from liability to its customer may be interpreted as also protecting the employees who carry out the contract on behalf of the employer.

Facts: A firm had entered into a contract with a security organization under which the firm's plant was to be guarded by patrolmen during the night. A clause in the "Special Conditions" of the contract provided that liability for damages resulting from negligence in guarding machines, stoves and heaters was excluded. When a fire occurred because of a patrolman's negligent failure to look after a stove, suit was brought by the firm's insurer, as subrogee of the firm's claims, against the patrolman in his personal capacity. His defence was that he was entitled to the protection of the exemption clause in his employers' contract with the plaintiffs.

Held: The Oberlandesgericht held that the patrolman was protected by the clause, even though the clause did not refer to the liability of employees. The BGH agreed.

Judgment: . . . Thus the decision [to be made in this case] depends on whether the defendant was included within the scope of protection afforded by the exemption clause agreed between the security firm and the company. The Chamber concurred with the OLG in answering that question in the affirmative.

However, the "Special Conditions" contain no express provisions in that regard. Furthermore, it is correct to say that, where such stipulations are contained in general terms and conditions of business, they are to be interpreted narrowly and must, where doubt arises, be construed against the party who drafted them and whom they are intended to benefit (*contra preferentem*).

That is not, however, the sole deciding factor. It is not the wording of the exemption clause but its purpose, discernible to the other contracting party, which is decisive. Thus, where any doubt exists in that regard, it is not merely permissible but mandatory to take the appropriate steps to supplement the deficiency in accordance with § 157 BGB (citation omitted).

1. The security firm obviously intended that the protection afforded by the stipulation should extend to its employees, if only because it was arguably bound to secure such protection for them by virtue of its duty to have regard for their interests and welfare.

It had undertaken to perform the task of protecting the things which it was guarding against damage. It regarded the potential risk involved as so significant that it felt it had to limit its liability; indeed, as regards the task of guarding and attending to the stoves, it considered that it had to exclude even gross negligence on the part of its employees. As the Oberlandesgericht correctly

---

[35] NJW 1962, 388.

states, it would have been inconceivable for it to have sought to shift the risk which it recognised in that connection off its own shoulders but to have intended that that risk should be borne by its employees. The employees were in an economically weaker position and even less able than their employer to bear the consequences of the negligent acts and omissions which, as human beings, they might perpetrate—*a fortiori* since, according to the findings made by the Oberlandesgericht, the employees in question were in many cases elderly persons whose mental faculties were beginning to wane.

In those circumstances, the duty incumbent on the security firm to have regard for the welfare and interests of its employees was in itself such as to require it to include those employees within the scope of the protection which it regarded as necessary. In the absence of any evidence indicating otherwise, it clearly intended to fulfil that duty by means of the exemption clause in issue.

. . .

3. However, the intention on the part of the security firm to include its employees within the scope of protection afforded by the exemption clause will only be of any consequence if it was sufficiently apparent to the other party to the contract. The Chamber has no hesitation in concurring, in this respect also, with the conclusion reached by the Oberlandesgericht and in finding that it was so apparent.

The company is itself an employer. Thus, like all other clients of the security firm finding themselves in a similar position, it was clearly aware of those considerations. It is inconceivable that a contracting party willing to accept limitations of liability as far-reaching as those agreed in the present case should intend to exonerate the well-to-do other party to the contract yet to insist that the economically weaker employees of that other party should assume the more onerous liability.

Notes

(1) This was a fairly clear case as there seemed to be little merit in a claim brought against an impecunious patrolman in order to circumvent an exemption clause to which the firm had agreed knowing no doubt that its property was fully protected by insurance. Compare the following:

BW   **7.NL.18.**

Article 6:257: Where a contracting party can derive a defence from the contract against his co-contracting party to shield him from liability for conduct by his servant, the servant may also invoke this defence, as if he were a party to the contract, if he is sued by the co-contracting party on the basis of that conduct.

(2) Most cases in which the problem of "vicarious immunity" arises deal with situations involving the carriage of goods where stevedores, warehousemen and other third parties seek to shield behind exemption clauses contained in contracts of carriage to which they are not direct parties. It has been held in many German cases that they were allowed to do so, at least where the shipper knew or ought to have known that the goods were to be handled not only by the carrier himself but also by stevedores and other independent contractors.[36] The Dutch Civil Code has express provisions to this effect: See for example BW Article 7:608, 8:71.

---

[36] BGH 28 April 1977, VersR 1977, 717.

The issue of the stevedore's liability has also raised the enforceability of exemption clauses by third parties to the contract in English law. In *Adler* v. *Dickson*[37] the plaintiff, as a passenger on board the *Himalaya*, suffered injuries caused by the negligence of the shipping company's servants. Since the contract of carriage exempted the company from all liability, suit was brought by the passenger against the ship's master and boatswain. The Court of Appeal held that the defendants were not entitled to the protection of the exemption clause since its wording could not be construed so as to express an intention by the passenger to give up any claims against the shipping company's servants. According to the majority, even if the clause had expressly mentioned the employees, they would not have been protected by it because they were not parties to it. Clauses in contracts of carriage designed to extend its protections and immunities to the carrier's servants, agents and subcontractors have ever since been called "*Himalaya* clauses" in the shipping industry.

House of Lords   **7.E.19.**
Scruttons Ltd. v. *Midland Silicones Ltd*[38]

LACK OF PRIVITY MEANS SUB-CONTRACTOR NOT PROTECTED

Stevedores and the drum of chemicals

Stevedores to whom the task of unloading goods is sub-contracted are not protected by a clause in the contract of carriage between the carrier and the goods owner which limits the carrier's liability; and because of the doctrine of privity the stevedores would still not be protected even if the clause purported to apply to them.

Facts: The respondents were consignees, and at the material time owners, of a drum of chemicals consigned to them from America by ship under a bill of lading signed on behalf of the shipowners as carriers which exempted them from all liability for loss to the goods exceeding $500. The shipowners had asked the respondents, a firm of stevedores, to unload the ship's cargo in the port of London. In the course of their duties the respondents negligently dropped the drum causing damage in excess of $500. They admitted negligence but contended that they were entitled to limit their liability to $500 by virtue of the main contract. The defence failed.

Held: The stevedores were not protected by the clause, nor would they have been protected even if the clause had expressly purported to limit their liability rather than just that of the shipowner.

Judgment: LORD REID: . . . We were informed that questions of this kind frequently arise and that this action has been brought as a test case.

In considering the various arguments for the appellants, I think it is necessary to have in mind certain established principles of the English law of contract. Although I may regret it I find it impossible to deny the existence of the general rule that a stranger to a contract cannot in a question with either of the contracting parties take advantage of provisions of the contract, even where it is clear from the contract that some provision in it was intended to benefit him. That rule appears to have been crystallised a century ago in *Tweddle* v. *Atkinson* and finally established in this House in *Dunlop Pneumatic Co. Ltd.* v. *Selfridge & Co Ltd*. There are, it is true, certain well established exceptions to that rule—though 1 am not sure that they are really exceptions and do not arise from other principles. But none of these in any way touches the present case.

---

[37] [1955] 1 QB 158.
[38] [1962] AC 446.

The actual words used by Lord Haldane in the *Dunlop* case were made the basis of an argument that, although a stranger to a contract may not be able to sue for any benefit under it, he can rely on the contract as a defence if one of the parties to it sues him in breach of his contractual obligation—that he can use the contract as a shield though not as a sword. I can find no justification for that. If the other contracting party can prevent the breach of contract well and good, but if he cannot I do not see how the stranger can. As was said in *Tweddle* v. *Atkinson*, the stranger cannot "take advantage" from the contract.

It may be that in a roundabout way the stranger could be protected. If A, wishing to protect X, gives to X an enforceable indemnity, and contracts with B that B will not sue X, informing B of the indemnity, and then B does sue X in breach of his contract with A, it may be that A can recover from B as damages the sum which he has to pay X under the indemnity, X having had to pay it to B. But there is nothing remotely resembling that in the present case.

The appellants say that through the agency of the carrier they were brought into contractual relation with the shipper and that they can now found on that against the consignees, the respondents. And they say that there should be inferred from the facts an implied contract, independent of the bill of lading, between them and the respondents. It was not argued that they had not committed a tort in damaging the respondents' goods.

I can see a possibility of success of the agency argument if (first) the bill of lading makes it clear that the stevedore is intended to be protected by the provisions in it which limit liability, (secondly) the bill of lading makes it clear that the carrier, in addition to contracting for these provisions on his own behalf, is also contracting as agent for the stevedore that these provisions should apply to the stevedore, (thirdly) the carrier has authority from the stevedore to do that, or perhaps later ratification by the stevedore would suffice, and (fourthly) that any difficulties about consideration moving from the stevedore were overcome. And then to affect the consignee it would be necessary to show that the provisions of the Bills of Lading Act, 1855, apply.

But again there is nothing of that kind in the present case. I agree with your lordships that the "carrier" in the bill of lading does not include stevedore, and if that is so I can find nothing in the bill of lading which states or even implies that the parties to it intended the limitation of liability to extend to stevedores. Even if it could be said that reasonable men in the shoes of these parties would have agreed that the stevedores should have this benefit, that would not be enough to make this an implied term of the contract. And even if one could spell out of the bill of lading an intention to benefit the stevedore, there is certainly nothing to indicate that the carrier was contracting as agent for the stevedore in addition to contracting on his own behalf. So it appears to me that the agency argument must fail.

And the implied contract argument seems to me to be equally unsound. From the stevedores' angle, they are employed by the carrier to deal with the goods in the ship. They can assume that the carrier is acting properly in employing them and they need not know who the goods belong to. There was in their contract with the carrier a provision that they should be protected, but that could not by itself bind the consignee. They might assume that the carrier would obtain protection for them against the consignee and feel aggrieved when they found that the carrier did not or could not do that. But a provision in the contract between them and the carrier is irrelevant in a question between them and the consignee. Then from the consignees' angle they would know that stevedores would be employed to handle their goods, but if they read the bill of lading they would find nothing to show that the shippers had agreed to limit the liability of the stevedores. There is nothing to show that they ever thought about this or that if they had they would have agreed or ought as reasonable men to have agreed to this benefit to the stevedores. I can find no basis in this for implying a contract between them and the stevedores. It cannot be said that such a contract was in any way necessary for business efficiency.

In the light of this decision contract planners have returned to the attack and have produced *Himalaya* clauses by which the carrier is dressed up as the stevedore's agent. A clause of this type to be included in a bill of lading may be worded as follows:

> It is hereby expressly agreed that no servant or agent of the Carrier (including every independent contractor from time to time employed by the Carrier) shall in any circumstances whatsoever be under any liability whatsoever to the Shipper, Consignee or Owner of the goods or to any holder of this Bill of Lading for any loss or damage or delay of whatsoever kind arising or resulting directly or indirectly from any act neglect or default on his part while acting in the course of or in connection with his employment and, without prejudice to the generality of the foregoing provisions in this Clause, every exemption, limitation, condition and liberty herein contained and every right, exemption from liability, defence and immunity of whatsoever nature applicable to the Carrier or to which the Carrier is entitled hereunder shall also be available and shall extend to protect every such servant or agent of the Carrier acting as aforesaid and for the purpose of all the foregoing provisions of this Clause the Carrier is or shall be deemed to be acting as agent or trustee on behalf of and for the benefit of all persons who are or might be his servants or agents from time to time (including independent contractors as aforesaid) and all such persons shall to this extent be or be deemed to be parties to the contract in or evidenced by this Bill of Lading.

This clause was tested in *New Zealand Shipping Co. Ltd.* v. *A. M. Satterthwaite & Co. Ltd. (The Eurymedon)*.[39] The Privy Council held that the terms of the bill of lading amounted to an offer by the shipper to the stevedore, made through the carrier as the stevedore's agent, that if the stevedore unloaded the goods, it should have the benefit of the exemption clause. This offer had been accepted, and consideration provided, by the stevedore through performing, or promising to perform, the agreement made with the carrier for the unloading of the cargo. Note, however, that *Himalaya* clauses do not always work, for example, if the damage occurred before the unilateral offer had been accepted by starting unloading[40] or if the promisee was not authorised to act on the third party's behalf and the latter cannot ratify.[41]

Fortunately, these complications can now be avoided under the following statute:

Contracts (Rights of Third Parties) Act 1999   **7.E.20.**

Section 1(6): Where a term of the contract excludes or limits liability in relation to any matter references in this Act to the third party enforcing the term shall be construed as references to his availing himself of the exclusion or limitation.

In other words, if the term excluding or restricting liability purports to protect the third party by mentioning him or describing him, the third party will be protected by it.

---

[39] [1974] 1 All ER 1015.
[40] *Raymond Burke Motors* v. *Mersey Docks and Harbour Co.* [1986] 1 Lloyd's Rep. 155.
[41] *Southern Water* v. *Carey* [1985] 2 All ER 1077.

7.1.5. MODIFICATION AND RESCISSION

A question to be answered by all legal systems recognizing the third party beneficiary contract is whether and up to what time the promisor and the promisee, or one of them, has the freedom to modify or rescind the contract without the beneficiary's consent. In one group of legal systems the actual or implied intention of the parties is the controlling factor. § 328(2) BGB provides that, in the absence of specific contractual provisions, it is to be inferred from the circumstances, and especially from the purpose of the contract, not only whether a third person is to acquire a right to enforce the contract at all, but also "whether his right arises at once or only under certain conditions, and whether the contracting parties retain the power to annul or modify the right of the third party without his consent". In ascertaining the parties' implied intention the judge gets no help from the Code except that § 331 paragraph 1 lays down a presumption if the performance to the third party is to take place after the promisee's death. In that situation, the third party shall in case of doubt acquire the right to performance only at the time of the promisee's death. It follows that, in the absence of stipulations to the contrary, the third party's position before the promisee's death amounts to a mere *nuda spes*.

The majority of Continental legal systems have followed the French solution laid down in Article 1121 sentence 2 of the French Civil Code. According to this provision the promisee's right of revocation shall cease once the beneficiary has made it clear that he wishes to avail himself of the benefit to be conferred on him by virtue of the contract. Similar provisions are Article 112(3) of the Swiss Code of Obligations, Article 1257(2) of the Spanish Civil Code, Article 412 of the Greek Civil Code, Article 6:253(2) BW. Article 1411(2) of the Italian Civil Code follows the French rule, but provides that in cases in which the performance may be demanded by the third person only after the promisee's death, the promisee can revoke the benefit "notwithstanding that such third person has declared that he intends to avail himself of it, unless, in this latter case, the promisee has waived in writing his power of revocation". Consider also:

Principles of European Contract Law   **7.PECL.21.**

Article 2.115 (3): The promisee may by notice to the promisor deprive the third party of the right to performance unless:
(a) the third party has received notice from the promisee that the right has been made irrevocable; or
(b) the promisor or the promisee has received notice from the third party that the latter accepts the right.

A very detailed and elaborate solution is to be found in section 2 of the Contracts (Rights of Third Parties) Act 1999.

Contracts (Rights of Third Parties) Act 1999   **7.E.22.**

Section 2: (1) Subject to the provisions of this section, where a third party has a right under section 1 to enforce a term of the contract, the parties to the contract may not by agreement

909

rescind the contract, or vary it in such a way as to extinguish or alter his entitlement under that right without his consent if—
   (a) the third party has communicated his assent to the term to the promisor;
   (b) the promisor is aware that the third party has relied on the term; or
   (c) the promisor can reasonably be expected to have foreseen that the third party would rely on the term and the third party has in fact relied on it.
(2) The assent referred to in subsection (1)(a) above—
   (a) may be by words or conduct; and
   (b) if sent to the promisor by post or other means, shall not be regarded as communicated to the promisor until received by him.
(3) Subsection (1) is subject to any express term of the contract under which
   (a) the parties to the contract may by agreement rescind or vary the contract without the consent of the third party, or
   (b) the consent of the third party is required in circumstances specified in the contract instead of those set out in subsection (1)(a) to (c).

7.1.6. DEFENCES AVAILABLE TO THE PROMISOR

There is general agreement that if suit is brought by the third party the promisor may rely on all defences, set-offs and counterclaims which would have been available to him in an action by the promisee. See § 334 BGB, Article 1413 of the Italian Civil Code, Article 449 of the Portuguese Civil Code. The Contracts (Rights of Third Parties) Act 1999 provides in section 3 that, subject to any express terms to the contrary in the contract:

Contracts (Rights of Third Parties) Act 1999 **7.E.23.**

Section 3: (2) The promisor shall have available to him by way of defence or set-off any matter that—
   (a) arises from or in connection with the contract and is relevant to the term and
   (b) would have been available to him by way of defence or set-off if the proceedings had been brought by the promisee.
   . . .
(4) The promisor shall also have available to him—
   (a) by way of defence or set-off any matter, and
   (b) by way of counterclaim any matter not arising from the contract,
   that would have been available to him by way of defence or set-off or, as the case may be, by way of counterclaim against the third party if the third party had been a party to the contract.

In Cass. com. 25 March 1960,[42] the buyer in a contract for the sale of a going business had promised the seller to purchase a certain quantity of grain from C at a stated price. When C, tendering the grain, sued the buyer for the price, the buyer asked the court to stay the proceedings until an action, brought by him against the seller of the business for rescission of the contract because of a breach by the seller, had been decided. The Cour de

---

[42] Bull. IV 118.

cassation held that the lower court was right in staying the proceedings since the agreement for the benefit of C "constituted an agreement for the benefit of a third party whose validity was subordinated to that of the sales agreement on which it was based".

On the other hand, there may be cases in which the promisor's right to raise certain defences *vis-à-vis* the third party has been excluded. In BGH 17 January 1985,[43] it was held that an airline was not allowed to deny a passenger a seat as booked on the ground that the tour operator (an intermediary) had not paid for the seats as provided in the charter agreement:

The defendant concluded the charter agreement with Messrs T, a tour operator . . . Consequently, it necessarily had to expect that those seats were to be available, and would be taken, pursuant to travel agreements concluded by the tour operator with passengers, and that those passengers would pay the air fare included in the price of the tour prior to commencing their journey, regardless of whether or not they were obliged to do so. The defendant also agreed that air tickets were to be issued by Messrs T in respect of the seats chartered from it. Thus it must also have been aware—as the appellate court correctly found—that the passengers booking a package tour inclusive of flights, who would have had no knowledge of the specific legal terms and conditions of the contract of carriage, would assume, and would be entitled to assume, that they had the right to be carried on the flight without demur and without any plea or objection being raised to their detriment. Consequently, it was not open to the defendant, as the party chartering out the aircraft, to plead, as against Mrs H, non-fulfilment of the charter agreement. On the contrary, the need to ensure that it received by the due date the payments made by the passengers for the flight was a matter falling within the scope of the risks which it assumed.

7.1.7. REMEDIES AVAILABLE TO THE PROMISEE

Normally the person mainly interested in enforcing the promise made for the benefit of a third party is the third party himself. There may be cases, however, in which the promisee has a strong interest in the promise's performance or where enforcement by the third party is impractical. For example, in a case involving a service company's promise to a municipality to provide services to its residents, an action by one of the individual contract beneficiaries against the company may be unlikely or unreasonable because the cost of litigation is much higher than what the plaintiff may hope to recover. In such cases the municipality is clearly the more efficient plaintiff. Accordingly, all Continental jurisdictions recognizing the third party beneficiary contract allow the promisee not only to enforce the contract specifically for the benefit of the third party, but also to claim damages from the promisee for breach of the promise. See § 335 of the German Civil Code, Article 112 of the Swiss Code of Obligations, Article 6:256 of the Dutch Civil Code, Civ. 1e 12 July 1956, D. 1956, 749; Com. 14 May 1979, D.S. 1980, 157. See also:

Contracts (Rights of Third Parties) Act 1999   **7.E.24.**

Section 4: Section 1 does not affect any right of the promisee to enforce any term of the contract.

In contrast, English law has traditionally taken the position that the promisee may recover only his own losses, not those of the third party. Moreover, at the suggestion of

---

[43] BGHZ 93, 271.

the Law Commission[44] this matter is not dealt with in the new Contracts (Rights of Third Parties) Act but is left to the Common Law to develop. There have been a number of recent cases on the point, including *Linden Gardens Trust Ltd* v. *Lenesta Sludge Disposals Ltd.*,[45] in which the majority held that the promisee can recover the loss suffered by the third party only where the contract was in connection with property which the parties contemplated would be sold to a third party; *Darlington Borough Council* v. *Wiltshier Northern Ltd.*,[46] and *Alfred McAlpine* v. *Panatown*.[47] In the last case the House of Lords confirmed the basic rule that a party to a contract can recover damages only for the losses he has himself suffered. There are exceptions, such as that referred to in the *Linden Gardens* case, but they apply only where the third party would otherwise be left without a remedy. On the facts of *Panatown*, the contractors had been employed by Panatown to construct a building for the third party who owned the land. The contractors had executed a deed giving the land-owners a direct remedy against the contractor for any failure on its part to exercise reasonable care and skill in the construction process.[48] The work was defective. It was held, by a majority, that because the third party land-owners had a direct remedy against the contractors, the employers could not recover substantial damages on the land-owners' behalf.

7.2. AGENCY

7.2.1. INTRODUCTION

Principles of European Contract Law   **7.PECL.25.**

Article 3:201: *Express, Implied and Apparent Authority*
(1) The principal's grant of authority to an agent to act in its name may be express or may be implied from the circumstances.
(2) The agent has authority to perform all acts necessary in the circumstances to achieve the purposes for which the authority was granted.
(3) A person is to be treated as having granted authority to an apparent agent if the person's statements or conduct induce the third party reasonably and in good faith to believe that the apparent agent has been granted authority for the act performed by it.

Article 3:202: *Agent acting in Exercise of its Authority*
Where an agent is acting within its authority as defined by Article 3:201, its acts bind the principal and the third party directly to each other. The agent itself is not bound to the third party.

---

[44] *Privity of Contract: Contracts for the Benefit of third Parties* (Law Com. No. 242, 1996 para. 5.11).
[45] [1994] AC 85, HL.
[46] [1995] 1 WLR 68, CA; see *supra* at 885.
[47] (1998) 88 Building LR 67, CA; *Alfred Mcalpine* v. *Panatown*, [2000] 4 All ER 97, HL.
[48] Presumbaly the direct warranty was made by deed in part to avoid problems of consideration: see above, **1.0.0**. The reasons for this complex arrangement were said to be to reduce the incidence of VAT.

The device of agency is an unavoidable necessity in any developed economic system which depends on the division of labour for the production and distribution of goods and services. The most obvious example is the employee of a firm who has a power to enter into contracts binding on the firm. The firm may also confer such power on self-employed traders. Thus a manufacturing company may delegate the sale of its products in a certain market on a "commercial agent". An export firm may ask a "forwarding agent" to arrange for goods to be transported to a foreign destination, and a houseowner may instruct an "estate agent" to find a buyer for his house. The entrepreneur who delegates the procurement of materials to a member of his staff, the heirs who commission an auctioneer to sell the inherited property, the landowner who has a "factor" run the estate, the manufacturer whose distributive chain includes independent salesmen as well as staff of his own, all these people who for one reason or another cannot or will not act personally, expand their sphere of activity by engaging others to effect contracts with third parties "for them", "on their account", "on their behalf", "as their agents", "in their interest" or "in their name".

In the common law agency is defined as a relationship which arises when one person, called the principal, authorizes another, called the agent, to act on his behalf, and the other agrees to do so. Its most important effect is that it enables the agent to affect the principal's legal position in respect of third parties, in particular by the making of contracts between the principal and third parties. A civil lawyer would regard this definition as too wide. What is needed in the Civil Law is not only that the principal has conferred authority on the agent to act on his behalf. A contract made by the agent with a third party will bind the principal only if the agent acted "in the name" of the principal and the third party therefore knows or has reason to know, either from the agent or from the circumstances, that the contract was intended to become binding on the principal. If the agent acts "in his own name" he alone acquires rights and liabilities under the contract with the third party even though he may have acted solely on the principal's business and account. Common lawyers, on the other hand, are perfectly willing to accept that if a duly authorized agent and a third party enter into a contract the third party acquires rights against both the agent and the principal even though the agency was "undisclosed" at the time the contract was made.

For these reasons the term "agency" is wider than the civil law term "*représentation*", "*rappresentanza*" or "*Stellvertretung*".

Obligationenrecht (Switzerland)   **7.CH.26.**

Article 32: If somebody who is authorised to represent another enters into a contract in the other's name, it is the other, and not the representative, who acquires rights and duties under the contract.

BGB   **7.G.27.**

§ 164: (1) A declaration of intention by which a person makes in the name of a principal within the scope of his agency operates directly both in favour of and against the principal. It makes no difference whether the declaration is made expressly in the name of the principal, or if the circumstances indicate that it was to be made in his name.

(2) If the intention to act in the name of another is not apparent, the agent's absence of intention to act in his own name is not taken into consideration.

(3) The provisions of (1) apply mutatis mutandis if a declaration of intention required to be made to another is made to his agent.

Article 1388 of the Italian Civil Code is to similar effect. Article 1984 of the French Civil Code states that a contract of mandate exists where one person confers on another "the power to do something for the mandator and in his name". But it is recognized that even where the mandatary acts in his own name there may still be a contract of mandate. Such a mandate, however, according to the writers, is a *"mandat sans représentation"* and the principal is not directly affected. For this to happen *"représentation"* is required, and this needs the transaction to have been conducted "in the name" of the principal.

The Geneva Convention on Agency in the International Sale of Goods (1983) has adopted the wider approach of the common law:

Geneva Convention on Agency in the International Sale of Goods **7.INT.28.**

Article 1: (1) This Convention applies where one person, the agent, has authority or purports to have authority on behalf of another person, the principal, to conclude a contract of sale of goods with a third party.
. . .
(4) It applies irrespective of whether the agent acts in his own name or in that of the principal.

Another difference of a more doctrinal nature exists even among the continental systems themselves. Some of them regard the authority of the agent as merely an aspect of the agreement between the parties. Thus, Article 1984 of the French Civil Code discusses the authority of one person to bind another as a mere side-effect of the contract of mandate. Other legal systems draw a sharp line between the authority of an agent and the contract linking him to the principal. They therefore distinguish between the *authorisation*, which they consider a purely unilateral act of the principal intended to confer on the agent the power to bind him directly, and the underlying *contractual relationship* between principal and agent which produces rights and duties in their internal relationship. Once this approach is accepted it becomes possible for the codes to draw a distinction between the general rules dealing, on a fairly high level of abstraction, with the authorization of another and its legal consequences, and the rules on the various types of agency agreements. This system was first adopted by the German Civil Code and has been followed by the Swiss Law of Obligations (1911), the Swedish Contract Act (1915), the Greek Civil Code (1940), the Italian Civil Code (1942), the Portuguese Civil Code (1966) and the new Dutch Civil Code (1992).

7.2.2. DISCLOSED AGENCY

Principles of European Contract Law **7.PECL.29.**

Article 3:102: *Categories of Representation*
(1) Where an agent acts in the name of a principal, the rules on direct representation apply (Section 2). It is irrelevant whether the principal's identity is revealed at the time the agent acts or is to be revealed later.

(2) Where an intermediary acts on instructions and on behalf of, but not in the name of, a principal, or where the third party neither knows nor has reason to know that the intermediary acts as an agent, the rules on indirect representation apply (Section 3).

A disclosed principal is one of whose existence the third party is aware at the time of contracting. This will generally be the case where the agent entered into the contract "as agent for X", "for X", "in the name of X" or where other circumstances existed from which the third party concluded, or had reason to conclude, that it was the agent's intention not to bind himself, but to bind another person as principal. The principal is a "named" principal if the third party knows his identity. If the third party knows that the agent is contracting as an agent but is unaware of the principal's identity, there may still be a case of disclosed agency if the agent and the third party are in agreement that the principal shall be identified at some later stage.

On the other hand, there may be cases in which the third party knows that the agent is acting on behalf of another, but where it follows from the circumstances that the agent undertakes to bind himself only. In civil law systems this will be assumed in cases in which the agent has acted as a "commission agent" (*commissionnaire, Kommissionär*). According to trade usage, custom or statute a contract made by a commission agent will normally be held to be binding only on the agent, even though the third party may know not only that the agent, as commission agent, acts on behalf of a principal, but may even know about the principal's identity. See, for example, Article 94 of the French Commercial Code, Article 1731 of the Italian Civil Code, Article 425 of the Swiss Obligations Law and the following provision:

HGB   **7.G.30.**

§ 383: A commission agent is a person who engages, for business purposes, in the sale or purchase in his own name of goods or securities for the account of another (the principal).

Suppose A, a shoe wholesaler, is buying shoes in large quantities from M, a manufacturer, and is reselling them to retail firms. In this case A bears the risk that the shoes become unsaleable or can be sold only at very low prices. If A wishes to shift this risk to M and M is willing to bear this risk, they may agree that A should operate on the basis of a "commission contract". Under a commission contract, A sells the shoes to retailers "in his own name", and as a result the retailers will acquire contractual rights only against A (and will be insulated from contractual liabilities *vis-à-vis* M) even though they may be fully aware of M's identity and of A's role as M's agent.[49] However, since A is dealing only *pour le compte* (*für Rechnung, per conto*) of M, the economic risk of his dealing in M's shoes will be borne by M, and A's reward will typically be only a percentage of what he is paid by the retailers.

Where a duly authorized agent has made a contract with a third party on behalf of a disclosed principal a direct contractual relationship arises between principal and third party so that the principal can sue and be sued by the third party on such contract. The Geneva Agency Convention provides:

[49] For some exceptions to this principle see *infra* at 922 *et seq.*

Geneva Convention on Agency in the International Sale of Goods   **7.INT.31.**

Article 12: Where an agent acts on behalf of a principal within the scope of his authority and the third party knew or ought to have known that the agent was acting as an agent, the acts of the agent shall directly bind the principal and the agent to each other, unless it follows from the circumstances of the case, for example by a reference to a contract of commission, that the agent undertakes to bind himself only.

These rules are fairly clear in the abstract. However, the words used by contracting parties will not always facilitate the easy application of the rules. It may not be clear whether a person was contracting "as agent" of another or whether it was intended by the parties that the contract should become binding only on the "agent". In other cases it may be clear that the person has been acting as agent for a principal, but there is doubt about who the principal is. Sometimes a person may contract both on his own behalf and on behalf of a principal. The following cases illustrate some of these difficulties, and the different approaches taken in the different systems studied.

Swiss Federal Court, 19 December 1934[50]   **7.CH.32.**

PERSON ACTING "IN NAME OF" OTHER UNIDENTIFIED PERSON IS PRINCIPAL

In the name of a group of banks

Where a party arranges finance for a borrower "in the name of a group of banks" but those banks are not identified, that party should be treated as principal, so that the banks have no direct claim against the borrower.

Facts: Elektra Corp. needed a substantial amount of money for an investment project. They approached the bankers Brupbacher & Co. and obtained from them a loan of sfrs 5 million under a contract dated 30 January 1928 which provided in its introductory passage that it was made between Elektra Corp., on the one hand, and "Messrs. C.J. Brupbacher & Cie in Zurich, in the name of a group of banks, hereinafter called the "bank", on the other hand". The same formula was used in a contract dated 4 June 1931 by which the loan was extended until 15 March 1933. In September 1930 Brupbacher became insolvent. An action was brought against Elektra Corp. by 14 banks which, as members of a consortium formed by Brupbacher, had contributed shares ranging between sfrs 50.000 and sfrs 1.5 million to be made available to Elektra Corp. through Brupbacher. The defendant Elektra pleaded that, despite the wording of the contracts, its only creditor was Brupbacher, and that the plaintiffs had no cause of action.

Held: Brupbacher had been acting as principal so the banks had no action against Elektra.

Judgment:

1. It is undisputed that Messrs Brupbacher & Cie concluded the two loan agreements of 30 January 1929 and 4 June 1931. The opening wording of those contracts merely stated that Brupbacher was acting "in the name of a group of banks". The defendant was not informed of the identity of the members of that group of banks, nor of the sums contributed by them. Indeed, it was not even certain, upon the conclusion of the first contract and, in part, on that of the second, who would be participating; on the contrary, it was only subsequently that the undertakings now claiming as the plaintiffs in this action, alternatively, their predecessors in title, committed themselves to the grant of the credit. Accordingly, they did not in any event, by virtue of the two contracts, become

---

[50] BGE 60 II 492.

creditors of the defendant in accordance with the ordinary rules of agency, since it is normally a condition of direct agency (Article 32 *et seq.* OR), which alone is capable of having that effect, that the identity of the principal must, at the time when the contract is concluded, be objectively established and must, in addition, not be left unspecified in subjective terms, that is to say, *vis-à-vis* the other contracting party, or at least not intentionally.

However, the plaintiffs rely, in advancing their claims as alleged creditors, on the principle of "acting on behalf of those whom it may concern".

2. According to that principle, "acting on behalf of those whom it may concern" takes place when, upon conclusion of the contract, an intermediary is involved on behalf of one of the parties and either the person for whom he is acting has not yet been specified in objective terms or, at least, his identity has not yet been revealed to the other contracting party. The most obvious example of this is where the intermediary buys something and "reserves" to himself the right to identify the buyer. Since the intermediary makes it clear to the other contracting party that he is not contracting on his own behalf, such cases represent a particular type of direct agency. They differ from the form usually taken, in that the identity of the principal on whose behalf the transaction is entered into is for the time being left unspecified. Where the legal order permits this, the situation is such that the principal acquires direct rights and assumes direct obligations under the contract.

The plaintiffs rely on the opening wording of the contracts, which stated that Messrs Brupbacher & Cie were acting "in the name of a group of banks". According to normal legal parlance, that wording does indeed permit the conclusion to be drawn that direct agency was involved. However, that conclusion is not irrebuttable; it is open to the other party to adduce evidence to show that, in the particular case at issue, the formula in question bore a different meaning, and that the intention was that the rights and obligations arising under the contract should vest in the person of the alleged agent himself.

In that connection, the defendant . . . correctly points out that the identity of the plaintiffs as contracting parties is not apparent from the ensuing wording of the contracts. In that further wording, the lender is specified as "the Bank", without there being any clear indication from the explanation given in the opening wording whether that term was intended to constitute an abbreviated reference to Messrs Brupbacher & Cie or a reference to the group of banks. Moreover, no reference is made, in the context of the signature by Messrs Brupbacher & Cie, to its acting in any agency capacity. True, it may be argued that there was no need to repeat the reference to its involvement in the capacity of an agent, given that it had been definitively stated in the opening wording that the firm of Brupbacher & Cie was acting on behalf of the group of banks. However, had the contracting parties really considered that the group of banks was to stand directly, in legal terms, in the position of lender *vis-à-vis* the defendant, then it is clear, given the broad implications attaching to the question, that the position should have been expressed unambiguously, instead of merely being alluded to in a formula consisting of a few words in the opening wording . . .

The very nature of the transaction suggests that it was Messrs Brupbacher & Cie that was to be regarded as the creditor. In credit transactions, especially those involving millions, it is, from the outset, in the interests not only of the creditor but also, to a limited extent, of the debtor to know the identity of the other contracting party. The grant of the loan makes the debtor financially dependent on the creditor, with the result that the latter's identity cannot be a matter of indifference to him. One has only to consider in that regard that the debtor may subsequently run into problems over the making of payments and may have to ask for time to pay or for some other form of alleviation of his difficulties. For those reasons, it is hardly likely that an undertaking seeking such large amounts of credit would needlessly engage in a contract with unspecified third parties.

In addition, the plaintiffs claim that, even after the conclusion of the contracts, the defendant did not have the right to be informed of the composition of the consortium; and, in point of fact, the identity of its individual members did not come to light until the collapse of Messrs Brupbacher &

Cie prompted them to emerge from their anonymity. As explained above, that in itself operates to deprive of all legal effect the plea that the case involved an agent "acting on behalf of those whom it may concern". Quite apart from this, however, it is apparent from the facts of this case that the parties cannot have had the intention alleged. It runs counter to the natural interpretation of the case, and to all normal business practice, to claim that, in the transaction of such a substantial deal, one party should remain, unidentified and unidentifiable, in the background and that the other party should renounce the right at any time to discover with whom it was dealing as the other party to the contract.

Contrast the approach of the Swiss courts in this case with that of the English courts in *The Ariadne Irene:*

House of Lords 7.E.33.
Universal Steam Navigation Co. Ltd. v. *James McKelvie & Co.*[51]

SIGNATURE "AS AGENT" PRECLUDES LIABILITY

The Ariadne Irene

A party who signs "as agent" is not personally liable even if elsewhere in the contract he is referred as if he were the principal.

Facts: A charterparty was expressed to be made between T.H. Seed & Co. Ltd., as agents for the owners of a steamer, and "James McKelvie & Co., Newcastle-on-Tyne, Charterers". The charterparty contained numerous provisions imposing obligations on the "Charterers", including an obligation to pay demurrage in the event of the steamer being detained beyond the stipulated time either at the port of loading or at the port of discharge. The charterparty was signed "For and on behalf of James McKelvie & Co. (as agents). J.A. McKelvie." Liability for demurrage at the port of discharge having been incurred the owner brought an action against the defendants. They pleaded that they had signed the charterparty merely "as agents" for a third party and were therefore not personally liable.

Held: The defendant having signed "as agents" were not liable notwithstanding that they were described as "Charterers" in the body of the charterparty.

Judgment: VISCOUNT CAVE LC: If the respondents had signed the charterparty without qualification, they would of course have been personally liable to the shipowners; but by adding to their signature the words "as agents" they indicated clearly that they were signing only as agents for others and had no intention of being personally bound as principals. I can imagine no other purpose for which these words could have been added; and unless they had that meaning, they appear to me to have no sense or meaning at all.

[After a discussion of various cases his Lordship continued] To this current of authority the only exception is the case of *Lennard* v. *Robinson* (1855) 5 E. & B. 125. There the defendants were named in the charterparty itself as parties, but signed "by authority of and as agents for" a person named; and it was held that they contracted personally. There may be minute distinctions between that case and the present; but I think it best to say that in my opinion that case cannot now be treated as law. It is, as Bankes LJ said, to the interest of the commercial community that a signature "as agent" should have a generally accepted meaning, and I agree with him that such a qualification of the signature should be taken as a deliberate expression of intention to exclude any personal liability on the part of the signatory.

---

[51] [1923] AC 492.

LORD SHAW OF DUNFERMLINE: . . . The first question is in what character Messrs. McKelvie signed this document? I see no ground whatsoever for denying effect to the express word "agents": it was undoubtedly in that character that the contract was signed: there is as little ground for cutting out the express character in which it was signed as for cutting out the signature itself.

The second question is, whether, although thus denominating themselves as "agents," Messrs. McKelvie were yet signing a contract which by its terms made them principals therein. But its terms do not refer to either "principals" or "agents"; the body of the document can be applied to either category. As for the names of the parties, I hold that the names of McKelvie followed by "Charterers" with nothing said of agency, is definitely stamped with agency by the express affirmation of the signature.

LORD PARMOOR: . . . My Lords, the question in this appeal is whether the respondents are personally liable, under the terms of a charter-party, for demurrage, in discharging the steamship *Ariadne Irene*. The defence of the respondents is that they signed the charterparty "as agents", and did not incur thereunder any personal liability. The charterparty was signed as follows: "For and on behalf of James McKelvie & Co. (as agents).—J.A. McKelvie." The words "as agents" are, in my opinion, clearly words of qualification and not of description. They denote, in unambiguous language, that the respondents did not sign as principals, and did not intend to incur personal liability. The signature applies to the whole contract, and to every term in the contract. I think it would not be admissible to infer an implied term, or implied terms, in the contract inconsistent with the limitation of liability directly expressed in the qualification of the signature, since the effect of such an implication would be to contradict an express term of the contract. It is not impossible that by plain words in the body of the document, persons signing "as agents", may expressly undertake some form of personal liability as principals, but I can find no trace of any intention of the respondents to incur any such liability in the charterparty, which is in question in the present appeal.

[LORD SUMNER delivered a speech to the same effect. LORD BIRKENHEAD concurred.

Cour d'appel, Lyon, 6 December 1985[52]   **7.F.34.**

COMMISSION AGENT

Supplies of paper

A purchasing co-operative which orders goods on behalf of another firm but specifies that orders are to be sent to it is a commission agent even if the supplier looks first to the other firm for payment.

Facts: Le Progrès, a purchasing co-operative, ordered paper to be supplied to IMA but used its own headed paper and required confirmations of orders and all invoices to be sent to it. The suppliers looked first to IMA for payment but when IMA went into liquidation, brought an action against Le Progrès.

Held: Le Progrès was not a true agent but a commission agent and was thus responsible to the supplier.

Judgment:—Whereas the Swiss company Holzstoff commenced proceedings against SA Le Progrès Centrale d'Achat, Chassieu, before the Tribunal de Commerce, Lyon, for an order requiring it to pay the equivalent in French francs of DM 388 136.54 in respect of orders for paper placed by Le Progrès; as Le Progrès refused to pay for those goods on the ground that the orders had been placed on behalf of the printing firm Maurice André which was alone responsible for payment of that sum; as by judgment of the Tribunal de Commerce, Lyon, of 30 March 1983, Le Progrès was

---

[52] Cahiers de droit de l'entreprise 1986.27.12.

ordered to pay the sum claimed by Holzstoff . . .; as Le Progrès has appealed against that decision. It contends that it acted only as agent for Maurice André and not as commission agent (*commissionnaire*) and that it is not therefore liable for the debts of that printing firm; as it therefore contends that Holzstoff's claim should be dismissed;

—Whereas the respondent calls for the judgment to be affirmed on the ground . . . that Le Progrès in this case acted as *commissionnaire* and should therefore be held liable for the debts of the printing firm Maurice André;

—Whereas on dates between 7 December 1981 and 14 January 1982 Le Progrès placed several orders for paper with Mr Daclin, the Lyon representative of Holzstoff; the orders were contained in letters on paper with the letterhead of "Le Progrès Centrale d'Achats de Chassieu"; the letters referred to orders which in some cases were to be invoiced to the company "Hebdo" and in others to the company "Imprimerie Maurice André";

—Whereas in that correspondence, Le Progrès specified that all the invoices, regardless of the place of delivery, were to be made out to Le Progrès itself, at its own address, namely 93 Chemin de St-Priest, 69680 Chassieu; Holzstoff was also asked to send confirmation of acceptance of the orders to Le Progrès at the same time as to the addressees;

—Whereas Imprimerie Maurice André was unable, having become insolvent, to pay for a number of orders placed with Holzstoff in a total sum of DM 388,136.54, equivalent to FF 995,221.83 as at the date of the insolvency;

—Whereas the abovementioned creditor seeks from Le Progrès itself payment of that sum which it has been unable to obtain from its debtor;

—Whereas it is apparent from the documents before the Court that Le Progrès acted, when placing those orders, as a "Centrale d'Achats" (purchasing cooperative); as the indication of that standing on the order letters, the indication that its address was to appear on the invoices and its requests for confirmations of orders show that Le Progrès placed those orders not as an agent but as a *commissionnaire* for two companies in which it had, moreover, acquired holdings and of which it could legitimately reveal the names;

—Whereas although, when the orders were placed, Le Progrès indicated the names of the addressee companies, the fact of delivery being made direct to the latter does not relieve the Centrale d'Achats from the obligations of a *commissionnaire* incurring liability vis-à-vis the supplier even if the latter initially took action against the principal to secure payment;

—Whereas furthermore, as emphasised by the judges at first instance, Le Progrès never indicated in its correspondence with Holzstoff that it was acting as the agent of Maurice André; by stating that the invoices should be sent to Le Progrès' address at Chassieu and not to that of Imprimerie Maurice André at St-Etienne, Le Progrès clearly demonstrated its intention to ask the other party to the contract to deliver the goods direct to the addressees but without thereby releasing itself from its obligations as a *commissionnaire* which had taken the order from its principal and placed the order in its own name, stating that delivery should be made to the principal, but remaining liable to third parties as primary obligor even if the latter took the view that they should institute proceedings in the first instance against the principal.

—Whereas in short, the judgment under appeal was correct in upholding the claim by Holzstoff and should be confirmed . . .

On those grounds, the Court upholds the contested judgment in every respect.

Note

The court held that the defendant, as *commissionnaire*, was fully liable to the plaintiffs on the contracts he had made with them *en son propre nom* and *pour le compte* of Maurice André, the printers. It appears that the plaintiffs not only knew of Maurice André as the ultimate recipient of the goods, but had demanded and received from him payment for part of the goods. In the court's analysis, however, Maurice André would have been entitled to refuse such payments. He may have paid because he misunderstood the legal position or simply for the sake of convenience.

BGH, 16 April 1957[53]   **7.G.35.**

"OWNER" IS PERSON WHO HAS INSTRUCTED AGENT TO SELL

Timber sold by non-owner

A person who makes a contract to sell timber "as agent for the owner" is merely stating that he is acting on behalf of the person who instructed him and not on behalf of the true owner if that turns out to be someone else; therefore he is not liable for breach of warranty of authority on the basis that the true owner had not authorized the sale.

Facts: After R. had brought from I a quantity of timber stored in a forest, he had authorized the defendant to sell the timber on his behalf. Thereupon the defendant had entered into a written contract with the plaintiff which was expressed to be made by the defendant "as agent for the owners" of the timber. After paying the defendant the plaintiff tried to take possession of the timber but was prevented from doing so by K., its real owner. The plaintiff brought an action (not against R. who had apparently become insolvent, but) against the defendant arguing that the defendant had acted as agent (not for R., but) for the real owners and was therefore personally liable for breach of an implied warranty of authority.

Held: The Court of Appeal dismissed the action; the BGH dismissed a further appeal.

Judgment: The appellate court has stated that when the defendant held himself out, on the conclusion of the contract, as acting "as agent for the owner", without identifying the latter by name, he intended to act only on behalf of the person by whom he had in fact been given authority to act. According to that court, it is inconsistent with the realities of life to interpret his statement as meaning that he intended to act on behalf of the actual owner, regardless of who that person might be. On the contrary, the use of the word "owner" in his contractual statement merely indicated he believed that the person whom he represented was the owner. On an objective assessment, the plaintiff must likewise have interpreted the defendant's statement as having that meaning. According to the appellate court, the plaintiff intended to conclude the contract not with someone who was completely unknown to him but with a person who, although not named, was nevertheless comprehensively specified, namely the person behind the defendant who had given the latter that authority to conclude the contract.

The criticisms levelled against those findings in the notice of appeal are without merit. The court below found that the defendant had acted on behalf of the person who had given him authority to sell the timber. It did not make any assumptions as to the identity of the person on whose behalf the defendant would have been acting had he known that K. was in fact the owner of the timber; nor did it regard the defendant's intention, which was not revealed and which was never expressed in any way, as decisive. The reasons given by the court below for its finding that, on an objective assessment, the plaintiff would necessarily have likewise interpreted the defendant's declaration as meaning that the latter was acting on behalf of the person who actually gave him authority to act clearly show that that court chose the correct basis for its decision as to the nature of the intention declared to, and discernible by, the plaintiff, and as to the way in which the latter must, according to the principles of good faith, have construed that declaration. There exist no grounds in law for criticising the appellate court's conclusion, based on experience of life as it is lived, that an agent

---

[53] Lindenmaier-Möhring, *Nachschlagewerk des Bundesgerichtshofes* § 164 BGB Nr. 10.

921

who declares that he is acting "as agent for the owner" is not stating that he is contracting on behalf of a person unknown to him who may subsequently turn out to be the true owner of the goods sold, but is instead acting on behalf of the person by whom he has been instructed to act and whose identity he has declined, for whatever reason, to specify, since he is assuming, like the other party to the contract, that the person who instructed him to act intended to sell something actually belonging to that person and not something which the latter had yet to acquire. In the light of the statements made, both parties should have regarded the defendant's principal as being the person who instructed the defendant to act on his behalf, and whom they assumed at the same time to be the owner of the goods. The question whether the plaintiff did in fact interpret the defendant's declaration in that way, or whether he may have regarded the defendant as being the agent of the true owner of the goods and intended to contract on that basis, is irrelevant, since it is only discernible conduct that counts. Nor can it be said on that basis that the present case concerns a hidden absence of consensus. According to the statements made by both parties, it was the person who had instructed the defendant to act that was the seller of the timber.

7.2.3. UNDISCLOSED AGENCY

We now turn to cases in which the agent, by entering into a contract with a third party, has acted on behalf of a principal, but without disclosing the existence of the agency relationship so that the third party neither knew nor had reason to know that the agent was acting as an agent. The general rule in the Civil Law is that in this case only the agent can sue and be sued on the contract and that the contract is for the principal a mere *res inter alios acta*.

The common law adopts a different approach. Not only does it allow the undisclosed principal to sue the third party, but it also allows the third party, once the identity of the principal has been revealed to him, to bypass the agent and sue the principal directly. This is difficult to reconcile with the doctrine of privity which says that a contract cannot confer rights or impose obligations arising under it on any person except the parties to it. A good deal of academic discussion has been devoted to reconcile the doctrine of privity and the rules on undisclosed agency. But, in the words of Fridman:[54]

all these varied, and imaginative theories do not completely explain this strange, peculiarly English doctrine. Perhaps the most satisfying attitude to adopt is that the idea of the undisclosed principal is an anomaly, introduced into and accepted by the common law for reasons of mercantile convenience.[55]

We shall first discuss cases in which the undisclosed principal is suing the third party. The paramount consideration is to avoid prejudice to the third party who honestly thought at the time of contracting that he was only dealing with the agent.

Given that there is no general "doctrine of undisclosed agency" in the civil law, the principal cannot generally proceed against the third party. However, if the principal cannot obtain what he is owed by the agent he is sometimes allowed to intervene in a contract concluded on his behalf by an agent with a third party. If, for example, the agent is owed money by the third party under the contract and then becomes insolvent the principal is

---

[54] Fridman, *Law of Agency*, 6th edn (London: Butterworths, 1990) at 230.
[55] On what these "reasons of mercantile convenience" may be, see *infra* at 924–5.

given priority over the agent's general creditors in respect of his claim against the third party. This applies where goods have been sold on behalf of the principal by a "commission agent"; see § 392 paragraph 2 of the German Commercial Code, § 61 of the Swedish Law on Commission Agents (1914). Other legal systems grant the same right to all undisclosed principals: see Article 401 of the Swiss Obligations Law, Article 1705 paragraph 2, 1721 of the Italian Civil Code, Article 412 paragraph 1 of the New Dutch Civil Code. See Article 13(2) of the Geneva Convention:

Geneva Convention on Agency in the International Sale of Goods **7.INT.36.**

Article 13: (1) Where the agent acts on behalf of a principal within the scope of his authority, his acts shall bind only the agent and the third party if

    (a) the third party neither knew nor ought to have known that the agent was acting as an agent, or

    (b) it follows from the circumstances of the case, for example by a reference to a contract of commission, that the agent undertakes to bind himself only.

  (2) Nevertheless

    (a) Where the agent, whether by reason of the third party's failure of performance or for any other reason, fails to fulfil or is not in a position to fulfil his obligations to the principal, the principal may exercise against the third party the rights acquired on the principal's behalf by the agent, subject to any defences which the third party may set up against the agent.

    . . .

The following English case illustrates that, even though English law recognizes undisclosed agency, there are constraints on the principal's ability to proceed against the third party:

King's Bench Division   **7.E.37.**
Said v. *Butt*[56]

UNDISCLOSED PRINCIPAL WITH WHOM THIRD PARTY WOULD NOT HAVE CONTRACTED

The unwelcome theatre critic

An undisclosed principal who knows that the third party would not have contracted with him directly cannot claim against the third party.

Facts: The plaintiff was minded to attend the first night of a play but the management of the theatre was ill-disposed towards him and would have refused to sell him a ticket, so he had the ticket purchased by a friend, Mr Pollock. This did him no good, since the defendant, the manager of the theatre, refused to allow the plaintiff to his seat. The plaintiff sued on the ground that he was entitled as undisclosed principal to demand admission on the basis of the contract concluded by Mr Pollock as his agent. The action was dismissed.

Held: Action dismissed

Judgment: MCCARDIE J: . . . A first night at the Palace Theatre is, as with other theatres, an event of great importance. The result of a first night may make or mar a play. If the play be good, then word of its success may be spread, not only by the critics, but by the members of the audience. The nature

---

[56] [1920] 3 KB 497.

and social position and influence of the audience are of obvious importance. First nights have become to a large extent a species of private entertainment given by the theatrical proprietors and management to their friends and acquaintances, and to influential persons, whether critics or otherwise. The boxes, stalls and dress circle are regarded as parts of the theatre which are subject to special allocation by the management. Many tickets for those parts may be given away. The remaining tickets are usually sold by favour only. A first night, therefore, is a special event, with special characteristics. As the plaintiff himself stated in evidence, the management only disposes of first night tickets for the stalls and dress circle to those whom it selects. I may add that it is scarcely likely to choose those who are antagonistic to the management; or who have attacked the character of the theatre officials.

In my opinion the defendant can rightly say, upon the special circumstances of this case, that no contract existed on 23 December 1919, upon which the plaintiff could have sued the Palace Theatre. The personal element was here strikingly present. The plaintiff knew that the Palace Theatre would not contract with him for the sale of a seat for 23 December. They had expressly refused to do so. He was well aware of their reasons. I hold that by the mere device of utilising the name and services of Mr Pollock, the plaintiff could not constitute himself a contractor with the Palace Theatre against their knowledge, and contrary to their express refusal. He is disabled from asserting that he was the undisclosed principal of Mr Pollock.

Geneva Convention on Agency in the International Sale of Goods   **7.INT.38.**

Article 13: (6) The principal may not exercise against the third party the rights acquired on his behalf by the agent if it appears from the circumstances of the case that the third party, had he known the principal's identity, would not have entered into the contract.

In *Greer* v. *Downs Supply Co.*[57] the defendant made a purchase from an agent only because he had a time-barred claim against the agent which he hoped to be able to set off against the price; the undisclosed principal, on whose account the agent had contracted, was not allowed to sue. The third party can also defend on the ground that he has already performed to the agent, believing him to be the other party to the contract, and he can set off against the principal's claim any claim he had against the agent at the time the contract was formed (*Montagu* v. *Forwood*[58]). It follows that the third party, if sued by an undisclosed principal, is protected much in the same way as a debtor who has a new creditor thrust on him without his consent by way of an assignment.[59]

While the Common Law and the Civil Law are not far apart in regard to the undisclosed principal's rights against the third party, the two systems diverge in relation to the third party's rights against the principal. Whilst the Common Law recognizes the third party's right to sue the undisclosed principal, it is much harder for the Civil Law to accept the view that the third party should be able to sue a principal of whom he was unaware when the contract was concluded. Take the case of an agent who bought goods on credit from a third party on behalf of an undisclosed principal: if the third party was unaware of the existence of a principal at the time of contracting, it is arguable that the third party, having failed to take the usual precaution of reserving title, should bear the risk of the

---

[57] [1927] 2 KB 28.
[58] [1893] 2 QB 350.
[59] See *infra* at 942 *et seq.*

agent's insolvency. Why should he be able to bypass the (insolvent) agent and sue the principal if his existence is revealed to him, perhaps by accident, at some later stage? The common lawyer would defend this result on the ground that the principal, by giving the agent authority to buy on his behalf, created the risk of his becoming insolvent and cannot complain if he is held liable to the third party for the consequences of his agent's activities:

Court of Appeal   **7.E.39.**
Irvine v. *Watson*[60]

UNDISCLOSED PRINCIPAL LIABLE DESPITE HAVING PAID AGENT

Agent paid by principal

An undisclosed principal is liable to the third party even though the principal has paid the agent, unless the third party has led the principal to believe that he had already settled with the agent.

Facts: The plaintiffs sold certain casks of oil, and on the face of the contract Conning appeared as the purchaser. Conning was acting for the defendants as principals. When the casks had been delivered to Conning the defendants paid the price to him. In the action brought against the defendants for payment of the price it was regarded by the court as self-evident that the plaintiffs had a right to sue them directly.

Held: The main issue was whether the defendants were discharged of their liability to the plaintiffs by having paid the agent. Bowen J had found in favour of the plaintiffs. The Court of Appeal affirmed his judgment.

BRAMWELL LJ: The question is whether such payment discharged [the defendants] from their liability to the plaintiffs. I think it is impossible to say that it discharged them, unless they were misled by some conduct of the plaintiffs into the belief that [Conning] had already settled with the plaintiffs, and made such payment in consequence of such belief. But it is contended that the plaintiffs here did mislead the defendants into such belief, by parting with the possession of the oil to Conning without getting the money. The terms of the contract were "cash on or before delivery", and it is said that the defendants had a right to suppose that the sellers would not deliver unless they received payment of the price at the time of delivery. I do not think, however, that that is a correct view of the case. The plaintiffs had a perfect right to part with the oil to the broker without insisting strictly upon their right to prepayment, and there is, in my opinion, nothing in the facts of the case to justify the defendants in believing that they would so insist. No doubt if there was an invariable custom in the trade to insist on prepayment where the terms of the contract entitled the seller to it, that might alter the matter; and in such cases non-insistence on prepayment might discharge the buyer if he paid the broker on the faith of the seller already having been paid. But that is not the case here; the evidence before Bowen J, shows that there is no invariable custom to that effect.

Apart from all authorities, then, I am of opinion that the defendants' contention is wrong, and upon looking at the authorities, I do not think that any of them are in direct conflict with that opinion. It is true that in *Thomson* v. *Davenport* (1829) 9 B. & C. 78 both Lord Tenterden and Bayley J suggest in the widest terms that a seller is not entitled to sue the undisclosed principal on discovering him, if in the meantime the state of account between the principal and the agent has been altered to the prejudice of the principal. But it is impossible to construe the dicta of those learned judges in that case literally; it would operate most unjustly to the vendor if we did. I think the judges who uttered them did not intend a strictly literal interpretation to be put on their words. But whether they did or not, the opinion of Parke, B in *Heald* v. *Kenworthy* (1855) 10 Exch. 739 seems

---

[60] (1880) 5 QBD 414.

to me preferable; it is this, that "If the conduct of the seller would make it unjust for him to call upon the buyer for the money, as for example, where the principal is induced by the conduct of the seller to pay his agent the money on the faith that the agent and seller have come to a settlement on the matter, or if any representation to that effect is made by the seller, either by words or conduct, the seller cannot afterwards throw off the mask and sue the principal" That is in my judgment a much more accurate statement of the law.

[BRETT LJ and BAGGALLAY LJ delivered judgments to the same effect.]

The Geneva Agency Convention follows the common law approach. As seen above, Article 13(1) provides that, as a rule, the acts of an agent shall be binding on him only if the third party neither knew nor ought to have known that he was acting as an agent. However, according to Article 13(2)(b):

Geneva Convention on Agency in the International Sale of Goods   **7.INT.40.**

Article 13(2)(b): Where the agent fails to fulfil or is not in a position to fulfil his obligations to the third party, the third party may exercise against the principal the rights which the third party has against the agent, subject to any defences which the agent may set up against the third party and which the principal may set up against the agent.

BW   **7.NL.41.**

Article 7:412: If a mandatary who has entered into a contract with a third person in his own name does not perform his obligations with respect to the mandator or goes bankrupt, the mandator can have those rights of the mandatary with respect to the third person, which are susceptible of transfer, transferred to him by a written declaration to both of them, except to the extent that these rights belong to the mandatary in his mutual relationship with the mandator.

Principles of European Contract Law   **7.PECL.42.**

Article 3:301: *Intermediaries not acting in the name of a Principal*
(1) Where an intermediary acts:
(a) on instructions and on behalf, but not in the name, of a principal, or
(b) on instructions from a principal but the third party does not know and has no reason to know this,
the intermediary and the third party are bound to each other.
(2) The principal and the third party are bound to each other only under the conditions set out in Articles 3:302 to 3:304.

Article 3:302: *Intermediary's Insolvency or Fundamental Non-performance to Principal*
If the intermediary becomes insolvent, or if it commits a fundamental non-performance towards the principal, or if prior to the time for performance it is clear that there will be a fundamental non-performance:
(a) on the principal's demand, the intermediary shall communicate the name and address of the third party to the principal; and

(b) the principal may exercise against the third party the rights acquired on the principal's behalf by the intermediary, subject to any defences which the third party may set up against the intermediary.

Article 3:303: *Intermediary's Insolvency or Fundamental Non-performance to Third Party*
If the intermediary becomes insolvent, or if it commits a fundamental non-performance towards the third party, or if prior to the time for performance it is clear that there will be a fundamental non-performance:
(a) on the third party's demand, the intermediary shall communicate the name and address of the principal to the third party; and
(b) the third party may exercise against the principal the rights which the third party has against the intermediary, subject to any defences which the intermediary may set up against the third party and those which the principal may set up against the intermediary.

Article 3:304: *Requirement of Notice*
The rights under Articles 3:302 and 3:303 may be exercised only if notice of intention to exercise them is given to the intermediary and to the third party or principal, respectively. Upon receipt of the notice, the third party or the principal is no longer entitled to render performance to the intermediary.

7.2.4. AGENT ACTING *ULTRA VIRES*

7.2.4.A. APPARENT AUTHORITY

A principal will be bound to the third party only by acts which are within the agent's authority. Most obviously this applies to what the principal has expressly authorized the agent to do. However a grant of authority may also be implied, either because (though it was not mentioned) it was a normal part of what the agent was expressly authorized to do (thus a lawyer retained to litigate a case has implied authority to accept an offer by the other side to settle the case out of court: *Waugh* v. *HB Clifford*[61]) or if it is a normal duty of someone who is given the job that the agent has been appointed to do (thus a shop assistant may have authority to give information about the goods to customers as well as to sell them). But the principal may exclude authority which would normally be implied by indicating to the agent that he or she is not authorized to do the act in question.

A contract made by the agent in excess of that authority will not affect the principal unless he adopts what the agent has done in accordance with the doctrine of ratification.[62] Nevertheless, a principal will be bound, despite the absence of a ratification, if by words or conduct, he has allowed another person, to appear to the outside world to be his agent, and a third party acting on the reasonable inference that the person is an agent, has entered into a contract with him. In this situation the principal cannot afterwards repudiate this "apparent" or "ostensible agency" if to do so would cause injury to the third party. See Principles of European Contract Law, Article 3:201(3)[63] and:

---

[61] [1982] Ch 374.
[62] See *infra* at 930–2.
[63] See *supra* at 912.

Article 3:61(2):   Where a juridical act has been performed in the name of another person, the other party who, on the basis of a declaration or conduct of that other person, has presumed and in the given circumstances could reasonably presume the existence of a sufficient authority, may not have invoked against him the inaccuracy of this presumption.

Geneva Convention on Agency in the International Sale of Goods   **7.INT.44.**

Article 14:   (1) Where an agent acts without authority or acts outside the scope of his authority, his acts do not bind the principal and the third party to each other.
(2) Nevertheless, where the conduct of the principal causes the third party reasonably and in good faith to believe that the agent has authority to act on behalf of the principal and that the agent is acting within the scope of that authority, the principal may not invoke against the third party the lack of authority of the agent.

Court of Appeal   **7.E.45.**

Freeman & Lockyer v. *Buckhurst Park Properties (Mangal) Ltd.*[64]

Apparent authority

Acting as managing director

A director who has not been appointed as managing director of a company but who has been allowed by the board of directors to act as such, has apparent authority to bind the company.

Facts: The defendant company had bought a plot of land intending to develop and resell it. Mr Kapoor was a director of the company but, not having been appointed managing director, had no actual authority to enter into contracts with third parties regarding the development of the land. Nevertheless, he instructed the plaintiffs to prepare an application for planning permission. The plaintiffs executed the work and filed an action against the defendant company claiming their fee. The defendant argued that Mr Kapoor had no authority to enter into the contract.

Held: it was held at first instance and by the Court of Appeal that Kapoor had authority to act.

Judgment: Diplock LJ: It is necessary at the outset to distinguish between an "actual" authority of an agent on the one hand, and an "apparent" or "ostensible" authority on the other. Actual authority and apparent authority are quite independent of one another. Generally they co-exist and coincide, but either may exist without the other and their respective scopes may be different. As I shall endeavour to show, it is upon the apparent authority of the agent that the contractor normally relies in the ordinary course of business when entering into contracts.

An "actual" authority is a legal relationship between principal and agent created by a consensual agreement to which they alone are parties. Its scope is to be ascertained by applying ordinary principles of construction of contracts, including any proper implications from the express words used, the usages of the trade, or the course of business between the parties. To this agreement the contractor is a stranger; he may be totally ignorant of the existence of any authority on the part of the agent. Nevertheless, if the agent does enter into a contract pursuant to the "actual" authority, it does create contractual rights and liabilities between the principal and the contractor.

---

[64] [1964] 2 QB 480.

An "apparent" or "ostensible" authority, on the other hand, is a legal relationship between the principal and the contractor created by a representation, made by the principal to the contractor, intended to be and in fact acted upon by the contractor, that the agent has authority to enter on behalf of the principal into a contract of a kind within the scope of the "apparent" authority, so as to render the principal liable to perform any obligations imposed upon him by such contract. To the relationship so created the agent is a stranger. He need not be (although he generally is) aware of the existence of the representation but he must not purport to make the agreement as principal himself. The representation, when acted upon by the contractor by entering into a contract with the agent, operates as an estoppel, preventing the principal from asserting that he is not bound by the contract. It is irrelevant whether the agent had actual authority to enter into the contract . . .

The representation which creates "apparent" authority may take a variety of forms of which the commonest is representation by conduct, that is, by permitting the agent to act in some way in the conduct of the principal's business with other persons. By so doing the principal represents to anyone who becomes aware that the agent is so acting that the agent has authority to enter on behalf of the principal into contracts with other persons of the kind which an agent so acting in the conduct of his principal's business has usually "actual" authority to enter into.

[His Lordship then applied these rules to the case where the principal is not a natural person, but a corporation. In this case there are] four conditions which must be fulfilled to entitle a contractor to enforce against a company a contract entered into on behalf of the company by an agent who had no actual authority to do so. It must be shown:

(1) that a representation that the agent had authority to enter on behalf of the company into a contract of the kind sought to be enforced was made to the contractor;
(2) that such representation was made by a person or persons who had "actual" authority to manage the business of the company either generally or in respect of those matters to which the contract relates;
(3) that he (the contractor) was induced by such representation to enter into the contract, that is, that he in fact relied upon it; and
(4) that under its memorandum or articles of association the company was not deprived of the capacity either to enter into a contract of the kind sought to be enforced or to delegate authority to enter into a contract of that kind to the agent.

In the present case the findings of fact by the county court judge were sufficient to satisfy the four conditions. In particular the Court of Appeal could see no good ground for interfering with the judge's finding that Kapoor, although never appointed as managing director, had throughout been acting as such, and that this was well known to the board of the company. For these reasons it was held that Kapoor had "apparent" authority to enter into contracts on behalf of the company for services in connection with the sale of the company's property, including the obtaining of development permission with respect to its use.

[PEARSON LJ and WILLMER LJ delivered judgments to the same effect

Note
The effect of a company entering a contract which is outside its powers has, since this case, been altered substantially by the Company Law First Directive (68/151/EEC), Article 9.

Cass. Assemblée plénière, 13 December 1962[65] **7.F.46.**

APPARENT AUTHORITY

Two signatures required

An organization which has represented to a third party that a person has authority to act on its behalf may be bound by the rule of apparent authority even without proof of fault on its part.

Facts: The President of the Banque canadienne gave a guarantee to the Administration des domaines signed in his name alone. The Bank refused to honour the guarantee, arguing that its statues required the signature of two authorized personnel.

Held: The Administration des domaines was entitled to believe that the President was authorized to act in this way. The Assemblée plénière upheld this decision.

Judgment: THE COURT, *On the sole ground taken in its two branches*:—Whereas it is apparent from the content and grounds of the contested judgment (Poitiers, 6 May 1957) that C . . ., the chief executive of Banque Canadienne, Société Anonyme, issued under his sole signature on behalf of that bank, in favour of the *Administration des Domaines*, a joint and several guarantee for a scrap company in the sum of FF 700,000 in May 1973; as the administration called for that guarantee to be enforced, whereupon the bank contended that it could not be enforced against it since its *statuts* required in such cases the signatures of two duly authorised agents of the company;
—Whereas in finding against the bank, the contested judgment states that in this case the administration was legitimately entitled to think that it was dealing with an agent acting within the limits of his normal authority, and holds that accordingly the bank is bound by reason of ostensible agency;
—Whereas according to the plea put forward, ostensible agency presupposes a fault which was imputable to the alleged principal and gave rise to the error made by the third party; it is contended not only that the contested judgment does not identify any such fault but also that, since the very nature of the commitment calls for a special authority which the administration ought to have demanded, it was the administration which displayed a lack of care in the circumstances of this case;
—Whereas on the one hand, however, a principal can be bound on the basis of ostensible authority even in the absence of any fault of which it might be accused if the third party's belief as to the extent of the agent's powers is legitimate, and it is legitimate if the circumstances are such that the third party is entitled to refrain from verifying the precise limits of his powers;
—Whereas on the other hand, to examine the allegation of imprudence made against the administration in this case would necessitate undertaking an investigation of points of fact which the Cour de Cassation is not able to carry out; neither branch of the appeal ground can be upheld.
On these grounds, the appeal is dismissed.

7.2.4.B. RATIFICATION

There is general agreement that a contract made by an unauthorized agent with a third party becomes binding on the principal if he ratifies it, i.e. affirms it either expressly or impliedly by conduct showing clearly that he approves and adopts what has been done on his behalf. Rules to this effect are laid down in most civil codes although they differ in details. See for example §§ 177, 178 of the German Civil Code, Article 38 of the Swiss Obligations Law, Article 1399 of the Italian Civil Code, Article 3:69 of the New Dutch Civil Code.

[65] D. 1963.277 annotated by Calais-Auloy; J.C.P. 1963.II.13105 annotated by Esmein.

Article 15: (1) An act by an agent who acts without authority or who acts outside the scope of his authority may be ratified by the principal. On ratification the act produces the same effects as if it had initially been carried out with authority.

(2) Where, at the time of the agent's act, the third party neither knew nor ought to have known of the lack of authority, he shall not be liable to the principal if, at any time before ratification, he gives notice of his refusal to become bound by a ratification. Where the principal ratifies but does not do so within a reasonable time, the third party may refuse to be bound by the ratification if he promptly notifies the principal.

(3) Where, however, the third party knew or ought to have known the lack of authority of the agent, the third party may not refuse to become bound by a ratification before the expiration of any time agreed for ratification or, failing agreement, such reasonable time as the third party may specify.

(4) The third party may refuse to accept a partial ratification.

(5) Ratification shall take effect when notice of it reaches the third party or the ratification otherwise comes to his attention. Once effective, it may not be revoked.

(6) Ratification is effective notwithstanding that the act itself could not have been effectively carried out at the time of ratification.

(7) [Omitted]

(8) Ratification is subject to no requirement as to form. It may be express or may be inferred from the conduct of the principal.

Note

Article 15(1) gives ratification retrospective effect: the situation is as if the agent had been authorized all along. See also *Bolton Partners* v. *Lambert*[66] (the other party purported to repudiate the contract before the principal had ratified; it was held that if the principal ratified the repudiation was ineffective and the other party was bound).

Principles of European Contract Law   **7.PECL.48.**

Article 3:207: *Ratification by Principal*

(1) Where a person acting as an agent acts without authority or outside its authority, the principal may ratify the agent's acts.

(2) Upon ratification, the agent's acts are considered as having been authorised, without prejudice to the rights of other persons.

In the Civil Law it follows from the wording of the code provisions that ratification by a principal is possible only where the agent's (unauthorized) statements were reasonably understood by the third party as being made in the name of a principal. What, under the common law, if the third party had no reason to assume that he was dealing with an agent? Can a principal, by way of a ratification, acquire rights and liabilities as a result of a contract made by an undisclosed agent acting outside his authority?

---

[66] (1888) 41 Ch.D 295.

House of Lords   **7.F.49.**
Keighley, Maxstead & Co. v. *Durant*[67]

Ratification by undisclosed principal

A person cannot ratify an act done by another who was not authorized to act as he did in advance and who did not disclose to the third party that he was acting as agent.

Facts: Roberts bought corn from the sellers at a price above that at which he had been instructed to buy by the appellants. He intended to buy for them, but did not disclose this fact to the sellers. The appellants later purported to ratify the contract, but then refused to accept delivery. The sellers sued them for damages.

Held: The Court of Appeal held for the sellers on the ground that the appellants' ratification was valid. The House of Lords allowed the appeal.

Judgment: LORD MACNAGHTEN: . . . By a wholesome and convenient fiction, a person ratifying the act of another, who, without authority, has made a contract openly and avowedly on his behalf, is deemed to be, though in fact he was not, a party to the contract. Does the fiction cover the case of a person who makes no avowal at all, but assumes to act for himself and for no one else? . . . Ought the doctrine of ratification to be extended to such a case? On principle I should say certainly not. It is, I think, a well-established principle in English law that civil obligations are not to be created by, or founded upon, undisclosed intentions. That is a very old principle . . . and in my opinion it is not to be put aside or disregarded merely because it may be that, in a case like the present, no injustice might be done to the actual parties to the contract by giving effect to the undisclosed intentions of a would-be agent.

I think the appeal must be allowed.

LORD LINDLEY: . . . It is not necessary to write a treatise on the doctrine of ratification in order to dispose of this case. Historically that doctrine is no doubt derived from the Roman law; but it has been extended and developed in this country conformably to our own legal principles and to meet our own commercial necessities; and it is to our own decisions rather than to the Digest and commentaries upon it that English Courts must look for guidance. It is well known that in matters of contract we pay far less attention judicially to unexpressed intentions than is paid to them in other countries which have followed the Roman law more closely than we have: see *Byrne* v. *Van Tienhoven* (1880) 5 C.P.D. 344 . . .

It was strongly contended that there was no reason why the doctrine of ratification should not apply to undisclosed principals in general, and that no one could be injured by it if it were so applied. I am not convinced of this. But in this case there is no evidence in existence that, at the time when Roberts made his contract, he was in fact acting, as distinguished from intending to act, for the defendants as possible principals, and the decision appealed from, if affirmed, would introduce a very dangerous doctrine. It would enable one person to make a contract between two others by creating a principal and saying what his own undisclosed intentions were, and these could not be tested.

[Judgments to the same effect were delivered by the other Law Lords.]

---

[67] [1901] AC 240.

7.2.4.C. TERMINATION OF AUTHORITY

Principles of European Contract Law   **7.PECL.50.**

Article 3:209: *Duration of Authority*

(1) An agent's authority continues until the third party knows or ought to know that:

(a) the agent's authority has been brought to an end by the principal, the agent, or both; or

(b) the acts for which the authority had been granted have been completed, or the time for which it had been granted has expired; or

(c) the agent has become insolvent or, where a natural person, has died or become incapacitated; or

(d) the principal has become insolvent.

(2) The third party is considered to know that the agent's authority has been brought to an end under paragraph (1)(a) above if this has been communicated or publicised in the same manner in which the authority was originally communicated or publicised.

(3) However, the agent remains authorised for a reasonable time to perform those acts which are necessary to protect the interests of the principal or its successors.

BGB   **7.G.51.**

§ 170: If a power of attorney is conferred by declaration to a third party, it remains in force with respect to him until he is notified of the termination by the principal.

Note

These sections represent a general principle to which there are exceptions; for example, if the third party knows that an agent had been given authority for an indefinite period, and does not know that the authority has in fact been terminated, the agent's acts on behalf of the principal will still bind the principal.[68] Thus in *Waugh* v. *HB Clifford*[69] a lawyer retained to litigate a case had implied authority to accept an offer by the other side to settle the case out of court. The lawyer had received an offer and had in fact contacted his client (the principal) to ask if he should accept. The client sent an instruction not to accept (thus revoking the implied authority) but the instruction never reached the lawyer, who accepted the offer. The other party knew nothing about the client's instruction not to accept. It was held that the lawyer had apparent authority to act and the client was bound by the settlement agreement.

7.2.4.D. LIABILITY OF AGENT

The general principle of the Common Law is that everyone who professes to act as an agent on behalf of somebody else impliedly warrants that he has authority to make the contract which has been made, unless the third party knows that he is lacking such

---

[68] See Kötz, *European Contract Law* at 231, note 68.
[69] [1982] Ch. 374.

authority. It follows that the self-styled agent will be fully liable to the third party even though he may have honestly believed in his authority.

Court of Appeal   **7.E.52.**
Yonge v. *Toynbee*[70]

WARRANTY OF AUTHORITY

Principal insane

An agent whose principal has become incapable by reason of insanity is liable on an implied warranty of authority, even though he had no reason to know of his lack of authority.

Facts: The defendant solicitor had been conducting litigation against the plaintiff on behalf of a client who became insane. After this had happened but before the solicitor had heard of it he took further steps in the action. The question was whether the plaintiff could recover from the solicitor the costs incurred by him in consequence of his having continued the litigation after his authority to do so had come to an end because of his client's incapacity.

Held: The plaintiff succeeded in recovering his costs from the solicictor.

Judgment: BUCKLEY LJ: . . . I can see no distinction in principle between the case where the agent never had authority and the case where the agent originally had authority, but that authority has ceased without his knowledge or means of knowledge. In the latter case as much as in the former the proposition, I think, is true that without any mala fides he has at the moment of acting represented that he had an authority which in fact he had not. In my opinion he is then liable on an implied contract that he had authority, whether there was fraud or not. In *Collen* v. *Wright* (1857) 8 E. & B. 647 Willes J. in giving judgment of the Court uses the following language: "I am of opinion that a person who induces another to contract with him, as the agent of a third party, by an unqualified assertion of his being authorised to act as such agent, is answerable to the person who so contracts for any damages which he may sustain by reason of the assertion of authority being untrue . . . The fact that the professed agent honestly thinks that he has authority affects the moral character of his act; but his moral innocence, so far as the person whom he has induced to contract is concerned, in no way aids such person or alleviates the inconvenience and damage which he sustains. The obligation arising in such a case is well expressed by saying that a person professing to contract as agent for another, impliedly, if not expressly, undertakes to or promises the person who enters into such a contract, upon the faith of the professed agent being duly authorised, that the authority which he professes to have does in point of fact exist." This language is equally applicable to each of the two classes of cases to which I have referred . . . The question is not as to his honesty or *bona fides*. His liability arises from an implied undertaking or promise made by him that the authority which he professes to have does in point of fact exist. I can see no difference of principle between the case in which the authority never existed at all and the case in which the authority once existed and has ceased to exist . . .

The same strict rule has been adopted by Article 3:70 of the New Dutch Civil Code and Article 16 of the Geneva Agency Convention. Under this rule the damages will be fixed so as to put the plaintiff into the position he would have been in had the agent had authority.

---

[70] [1910] KB 215.

Principles of European Contract Law   **7.PECL.53.**

Article 3:204: *Agent acting without or outside its Authority*
(1) Where a person acting as an agent acts without authority or outside the scope of its authority, its acts are not binding upon the principal and the third party.
(2) Failing ratification by the principal according to Article 3:207, the agent is liable to pay the third party such damages as will place the third party in the same position as if the agent had acted with authority. This does not apply if the third party knew or could not have been unaware of the agent's lack of authority.

According to § 179 paragraph 2 of the German Civil Code the agent is treated more leniently if he honestly believed in his authority: he will then be liable only for the third party's reliance interest, i.e. for the loss incurred by the third party as a result of his reliance on the agent's authority. The same solution is adopted by Article 39 of the Swiss Obligations Law; however, if the agent's belief in his authority was careless the judge may award higher damages if he thinks that it would be just and equitable to do so.

7.3. ASSIGNMENT

7.3.1. INTRODUCTION

An assignment is a transaction whereby a right is transferred by its owner, called the assignor, to another person, called the assignee, as a result of which the assignee becomes entitled to sue the person liable, called the debtor. In most cases, an assignment will refer to the transfer of a money claim arising by way of contract, such as a seller's right to the purchase money, or a contractor's right under a building contract to demand payment from his employer, or an insured's right to be paid the agreed sum by the insurer. The rules on assignment are equally applicable to the transfer of other intangibles, such as patent rights or copyrights.

Special rules apply to the assignment of contractual rights arising out of negotiable instruments, such as bills of exchange, promissory notes, cheques or other documents which have been held, either by statute or trade usage, to be negotiable. The essential feature of a negotiable instrument is that it represents the debt owed in physical form. If the holder of such an instrument endorses it, by writing his name on the back, and delivers it to another party, this party, upon taking the instrument in good faith and for value, obtains a good title despite any defect in the title of the transferor and any defences available to the debtor against his original creditor. Nor does it matter whether the debtor knew, or could have known, of the transfer of the instrument. In this respect the position of the "holder in due course" of a negotiable instrument is much stronger than if he had acquired the right by way of an ordinary assignment, since an assignee takes the right "subject to equities", i.e. subject to any defects in the assignor's title and subject to certain defences which the debtor may have against the assignor.[71]

---

[71] See *infra* at 952 *et seq*.

There is no assignment if the creditor simply requests his debtor to make payment to a third party. If the debtor pays the third party he will be discharged not because the third party had become his creditor by virtue of an assignment, but because the third party received payment as the creditor's agent and on his behalf (even though he may keep the money if that is what he and the creditor have agreed). Nor is there an assignment if the creditor and debtor have reached an agreement that a third party shall be entitled to demand performance from the debtor. In this case the third party is a "third party beneficiary", since his right arises directly from the agreement made between the creditor and the debtor, and not as a result of the transfer of the right by the creditor without the debtor's consent. It is to be noted, however, that some legal systems do not fully recognize third party beneficiaries.[72]

An assignment may take place pursuant to different underlying agreements. An assignment may occur because the assignor and the assignee are parties to a contract under which the assignor has assumed a duty, in consideration of the assignee's promise to pay a price, to transfer a right to the assignee as the buyer of that right. This seems to be the main situation the authors of the French Civil Code had in mind when they drafted the Code's provisions on assignment, since these provisions (Article 1689 ff.) form part of the section on sales contracts. However, it is clear that a right may also be assigned pursuant to a gift promise, or in lieu of money owed, or as security for a loan made by the assignee. One can also assign something by way of an outright gift with no prior promise. Even then there will be an agreement that the donee is to receive the assigned right without paying or owing anything in return.

Most assignments are made for the purpose of securing debts, for example, when a bank lending money to a customer accepts as security an assignment of his claims which the customer has against third parties. Nowadays whole packages of claims are sold or transferred as security by a single transaction; credit institutions often take a bulk assignment of hundreds of claims at a time as security from those who borrow from them. This is what happens in "factoring contracts", made when manufacturers or dealers whose customers have yet to settle their accounts need cash in hand now. They do not use their "accounts receivable" as security but sell them outright to a factor for rather less than their nominal value, the difference representing the interest the factor forgoes on the cash advanced, the trouble of collecting on the debts and sometimes the risk of non-payment.

7.3.2. VALIDITY OF ASSIGNMENT

7.3.2.A. FORMAL REQUIREMENTS

The minimum requirement of a valid assignment is that there must be an agreement between the assignor and the assignee on the transfer of the right. In the Continental legal systems many civil codes expressly provide that it is by virtue of a "contract" between a creditor and another party that the creditor's claim may be transferred to that party. English law does not see assignment as a "contract"; accordingly there need not be any

---

[72] See *supra* at 882 *et seq.*

consideration[73] given or promised by the assignee. However, in the words of Treitel, an assignment has no effect unless it is communicated to the assignee by the assignor . . . or unless it is made in pursuance of a prior agreement between assignor and assignee.[74] If the assignee has become aware of the assignment English law seems to allow him to repudiate the transfer.[75] If he does not do so the assignment is valid. The same result would be reached on the Continent since it would normally be inferred from the circumstances that the assignee's silence constitutes an acceptance of the assignor's offer.

While an agreement between assignor and assignee is needed in each of the systems studied, it is highly controversial whether this agreement is sufficient to transfer the right to the assignee so as to make him, as against the whole world, the new owner of the assigned claim. This is the position taken under German, Austrian and Swiss law. Thus:

BGB 7.G.54.

§ 398: A claim or debt may, by agreement between the creditor and another, be transferred by the former to the latter (assignment). Upon the conclusion of such an agreement, the new creditor takes the place of the former creditor.

It follows that the assignment is fully effective without the debtor's consent and indeed even where the debtor knows nothing about it. Once the agreement referred to in § 398 BGB has been made the right no longer forms part of the assignor's assets. It can no longer be attached by the assignor's creditors nor does it fall in the estate of a bankrupt assignor provided that the agreement referred to in § 398 of the German Civil Code was made before the attachment order or the opening of the bankruptcy proceedings. If the assignor makes successive assignments of the same debt to two different assignees the debt is acquired by the party to whom it was first assigned (*prior tempore potior iure*) while the second assignee takes nothing (*nemo dat quod non habet*). However, if the debtor pays the assignor the payment will form part of the assignor's estate; the assignee will have merely a personal claim against the assignor. The claim may be of either a contractual or a restitutionary nature. This is for the protection of the debtor who has not been notified of the assignment and who pays the assignor.[76]

A different position is taken by the French Civil Code and by most legal systems based on the French tradition. Under Article 1689 of the French Civil Code the agreement between assignor and assignee results in a transfer of the right only as between the parties. As against third parties the assignment is to be treated as complete only when the assignor or assignee has notified the debtor of the assignment by making the appropriate communication through an official process-server (*signification*) or, alternatively, when the debtor has accepted the assignment by a notarial document (*acceptation faite par le débiteur dans un acte authentique*; cf. Article 1690):

---

[73] See *supra* at 140 ff.
[74] Treitel, *Contract* at 626.
[75] *Ibid.*
[76] See *infra* at 952 *et seq.*

Code civil 7.F.55.

Article 1690: (1) The assignee is not treated as acquiring the debt as against third parties until the debtor has been notified.
(2) However, acceptance of the assignment by the debtor in a notarial act also vests the debt in the assignee.

This rule has been received, in one form or another, by most civil codes which have to some extent used the French Civil Code as a model. In some cases, the codes provide that the assignment is valid as against third parties only if a "secure date" of the assignment has been laid down in a public document evidencing the debtor's acknowledgement (Article 1264, 1264, 2704 of the Italian Civil Code). Similarly strict formal requirements are applicable if a contract right is to be pledged. According to Article 2075 of the French Civil Code the debtor must in that case be notified of, or must accept, the pledge agreement in the same formal manner as prescribed by Article 1690 for an outright transfer of the right.

To some extent, the formalities prescribed by Article 1690 of the French Civil Code have been mitigated by the courts. Thus it has been held that the assignee's statement of claim against the debtor, if filed with the court, may amount to a *signification* in the sense of Article 1690.

Cass. com., 18 February 1969[77] 7.F.56.

STATEMENT OF CLAIM IS SIGNIFICATION

Service of statement of claim

A statement of claim served on the debtor in an action by the assignor, if it gives sufficient detail to show that there has been an assignment, is sufficient to amount to a signification to the debtor perfecting the assignment.

Facts: H assigned to EL a debt owed it by R. EL did not give a formal notice to R but simply commenced a process to recover the debt from R.

Held: The service of a statement of claim was sufficient signification. Appeal dismissed.

Judgment: *On the sole appeal ground:*—Whereas the appellant contests the judgment of the lower court (Paris, 25 May 1966) on the ground that it accepted that the company Epirotiki Lines could bring an action against Rouquie pursuant to the assignment to Epirotiki of the debt owed by Rouquie to the company Hercules, the process served on the appellant having replaced notification of the assignment as provided for by Article 1690 of the Civil Code, and according to the appellant, that was possible only if the process stated the date on which the assignment was effected and the price paid in consideration, which Rouquie formally contested without being in way contradicted on that point by the judgment in issue.

—Whereas however, in order for the process to count as notification of the assignment of the debt, it is sufficient for it to provide, as notification, a copy of the assignment making the transfer unconditional; as in its notice and grounds of appeal, without pleading failure to mention the price

---

[77] Bull. civ. IV. 65.

paid for the assignment of the debt, Rouquie had maintained that the process contained no details of the essential provisions of that assignment; as the contested judgment rejects that plea, pointing out that the process stated that Hercules had assigned the debt owed to it to Epirotiki by private instrument of 31 March 1965 and that Rouquie challenged the *locus standi* of neither the assignor nor the assignee; as the cour d'appel therefore showed good reason for its decision.
—As the appeal ground is unfounded.

On those grounds: the Court dismisses the appeal against the judgment delivered by the cour d'appel, Paris, on 25 May 1966.

Similarly, the courts have been fairly generous in dispensing with the requirement of a formal notification or acceptance if enforcement of the assigned claim by the assignee can do no harm to any rights that may have accrued in the meantime to a third party.

Cass. civ. 1re, 8 January 1955[78]   **7.F.57.**

PROCESS SUFFICIENT NOTICE IF THIRD PARTY NOT AFFECTED

Assignment of option to purchase

When an option to purchase land is assigned, the validity of the assignment is not affected by lack of a formal notification to the original grantor of the option if no third party rights would be affected by the enforcement of the option.

Facts: Landowners granted an option to purchase to R, who assigned it to AFI who assigned it to the plaintiff. The grantors were not formally notified before the plaintiffs commenced proceedings.

Held: The last assignee could enforce the option.

Judgment: *As to the first appeal ground*:—Whereas it is apparent from the contested judgment that Jacques Richepin, the original promisee of a unilateral promise to sell made by Henri Bernard relating to property of approximately 4 hectares situated at Mougins, assigned the benefit thereof to the Association Foncière et Immobilière, which in turn assigned it to the Société de Golf de la Croix des Gardes;
—Whereas the appellant challenges the contested judgment on the grounds that while it declares that that assignment was duly made and may be relied on against Mr and Mrs Bernard, as the heirs of Henri Bernard, it does not find that the assignment was made in accordance with Article 1690 of the Civil Code.
—Whereas however, while the right arising from a unilateral promise to sell is a personal right the assignment of which is governed by Article 1690 of the Civil Code, and while service of notice of the assignment on the promisor or his acceptance of the assignment in a notarially recorded instrument is necessary, in principle, if the assignee is to be able to enforce against third parties the right which he has acquired, the fact nevertheless remains that failure to comply with those formalities does not mean that the assignee is estopped from requiring the promisor to perform his obligation, provided that that performance is not liable adversely to affect any right which has accrued since the debt was created, either to the person liable to pay the debt or perform the obligation assigned or to another person a third party to the assignment.
—Whereas the contested judgment finds that the promise of sale signed by Henri Bernard in favour of Jacques Richepin had not lapsed at the time when Société de Golf de la Croix des Gardes claimed the rights under it; as furthermore, at no time did Mr and Mrs Bernard prove,

[78] Bull.civ. I.13.

939

offer to prove or even allege that they had received notification from any other persons, transferees in particular, or creditors of intermediate promisees, of some right conflicting with that of the latest assignee.

—Whereas in the absence of any circumstance altering in favour of Henri Bernard, his heirs or third parties the legal situation arising from the original undertaking, no plea of inadmissibility based on failure to comply with the formalities of Article 1690 of the Civil Code may be raised against Société de Golf de la Croix des Gardes in its action brought as the assignee of the right, this being outside the particular case contemplated by Article 2214 of the Civil Code

—As it follows that the first appeal ground is unfounded.

The same view has been taken in many other cases (see for example Cass. civ. 3e, 26 February 1985[79]). It applies only, however, if there is no third party who may have a better claim to the assigned right than the assignee. If, for example, the assignor makes successive assignments of the same claim to two different assignees, it is acquired not by the one to whom it was first assigned, but by the one who first complied with the formalities of Article 1690. The same rule applies if the assigned claim has been attached by the assignor's creditors or is claimed by the assignor's trustee in bankruptcy.

It goes without saying that the heavy formalism of Article 1690 of the French Civil Code and similar provisions in other legal systems have prevented the use in these countries of general assignment law as a basis for a workable system of selling, or using as security, contract claims on a large scale. In order to facilitate the transfer of such claims in commercial transactions special legislation has been enacted in France, Italy and Belgium. Most important is the French Law of 2 January 1981 (*Loi Dailly*) which provides for the transfer on an *en masse* basis to banks and other credit institutions of contract rights, either as outright sales (*cession*) or as collateral security (*nantissement*), by the simple delivery of a memorandum (*bordereau*) which identifies the rights in prescribed form and is signed by the transferor.

Loi Dailly (Law of 2 January 1981) as amended

7.F.58.

Article 1: Where any credit is granted by a credit establishment to a legal person constituted under private law or public law, or to a natural person engaged in the performance of his professional activities, the recipient of the credit may transfer or charge to that establishment, by the simple delivery of a memorandum, any debt which may be due to him from a third party who is a legal person constituted under public law or private law or a natural person engaged in the performance of his professional activities.

Debts which are of a fixed amount and payable, even if not until a future date, may be transferred or charged. Debts arising from an event which has already occurred or which has yet to occur, but the amount and maturity of which have not yet been determined, may also be transferred or charged.

Article 4: The transfer or charge shall take effect between the parties and become enforceable against third parties on the date inscribed on the memorandum.

Article 5: The credit establishment may at any time serve on the debtor from whom the debt transferred or charged is due a notice prohibiting him from paying the signatory of the memorandum. Upon the giving of notice to that effect, the form of which shall be prescribed

---

[79] J.C.P. 1986.II.20607 annotated by Petit.

by the decree of the Conseil d'État provided for in Article 13, the debtor shall be released from his obligation only if he makes payment to the credit establishment.

In Belgium, mounting criticism of the formalism of Article 1690 has led to the replacement of this provision by a new text (enacted by Article 4 of the Law of 6 July 1994):

Code civil (Belgium)   **7.B.59.**

Article 1690: By virtue of the conclusion of an agreement for the transfer or assignment of a debt, that transfer or assignment shall be effective against third parties other than the debtor whose debt has been transferred or assigned.

The transfer or assignment shall not be effective against the debtor whose debt has been transferred or assigned until such time as notice thereof is given to the debtor or the transfer or assignment is acknowledged by him.
Where the assignor has assigned the same rights to more than one assignee, preference shall be given to the assignee who is able in good faith to rely on the fact of having been the first to give the debtor notice of the transfer or assignment of the debt or of having been the first to receive acknowledgement thereof from the debtor.
The transfer or assignment shall not be effective against a *bona fide* creditor of the assignor to whom the debtor has validly made payment in good faith and before he received notice of the transfer or assignment.

Article 1691: A debtor who pays his debt in good faith before receiving notice of the transfer or assignment thereof or before acknowledging the same shall be discharged from liability.

A *bona fide* debtor may rely, as against the assignee, on the consequences of any legal act executed in relation to the assignor before he received notice of the assignment or transfer or prior to his acknowledgement thereof.[80]

Law of Property Act 1925   **7.E.61.**

Section 136: *Legal assignment of things in action*
(1) Any absolute assignment by writing under the hand of the assignor (not purporting to be by way of charge only) of any debt or other legal thing in action, of which express notice in writing has been given to the debtor, trustee or other person from whom the assignor would have been entitled to claim such debt or thing in action, is effectual in law (subject to equities having priority over the right of the assignee) to pass and transfer from the date of such notice—
(a) the legal right to such debt or thing in action;
(b) all legal and other remedies for the same; and
(c) the power to give a good discharge for the same without the concurrence of the assignor:
Provided that, if the debtor, trustee or other person liable in respect of such debt or thing in action has notice—
(a) that the assignment is disputed by the assignor or any person claiming under him; or

---

[80] For a detailed discussion of the new provisions of the Belgian Civil Code see van Ommeslaghe, "Le nouveau régime de la cession et de la dation en gage des créances", JT 1995, 529.

(b) of any other opposing or conflicting claims to such debt or thing in action, he may, if he thinks fit, either call upon the persons making the claim thereto to interplead concerning the same, or pay the debt or other thing in action into court under the provisions of the Trustee Act 1925.

. . .

Note

(1) In English law a distinction is made between "statutory assignments" and "equitable assignments". Before statute intervened, assignments were recognized only by the courts of equity, and the assigneee could not sue without joining the assignor as a party to the action. Under the Law of Property Act 1925 a "legal" assignment is possible which enables the assignee to sue without joining the assignor. Section 136(1) provides that, for a statutory assignment to be effective, the assigned right must be a debt (such as a claim for the repayment of a loan, or for the price of goods, or for damages for breach of contract), notice must have been given in writing to the debtor, the assignment must be in writing signed by the assignor, and the assignment must be "absolute". An assignment is not absolute if it is for only a part of the debt, if it is conditional (for instance a debt is assigned as security for a loan until such time as the loan is repaid to the assignee), or if for some other reason the assignor retains an interest in the assigned right. These cases in which the assignment is not absolute are ones in which it will normally be desirable to ensure that both the assignor and assignee are before the court, so the assignee cannot sue alone. Otherwise, as stated above, provided the formalities of the Law of Property Act 1925 section 136(1) have been met the assigned right will be acquired by the assignee so as to enable him to sue the debtor in his own name, and to sue alone, i.e. without joining the assignor as a party to the action.

(2) If the requirements of an effective statutory assignment are not satisfied, whether because the debtor was not informed or because the assignment was oral or partial or not absolute, the transaction may still be a valid equitable assignment, with the result that the assignee may have to join the assignor in the action. Finally, an equitable chose of action (such as the claim of a beneficiary under a trust or of a legatee under a will) may be assigned by way of a statutory or equitable assignment. According to the Law of Property Act 1925 section 53(1)(c) an assignment of an "equitable chose of action" must be in writing.

7.3.2.B. SUBSTANTIVE REQUIREMENTS

Agreements providing for the transfer of a right are void, unenforceable or subject to being set aside where they have been entered into by a person lacking capacity, have been procured by undue influence, seek to defraud creditors, or are against public policy. There are a few vitiating factors which are peculiar to assignments.

(a) Unassignability of Rights Tied to Personal Relationships. A right cannot be assigned when it is "of a strictly personal character" (Article 1260 paragraph 1 of the Italian Civil Code) or when performance to an assignee would involve "an alteration of its substance" (§ 399 of the German Civil Code).

Chancery Division   **7.E.62.**
Griffith v. Tower Publishing Co. Ltd. and Moncrieff [81]

COMPANY CANNOT ASSIGN RIGHT TO PUBLISH AUTHOR'S BOOKS

Assignment by publishing company

A publishing contract may not be assigned by the publisher, even where the publisher is a company, because of the nature of the relationship between publisher and author.

Facts: The plaintiff was an author who had entered into three agreements with the defendant company for the publication of certain novels. The company became insolvent and Mr Moncrieff was appointed receiver. He informed the plaintiff of his intention to sell his books, together with all the company's rights under the above agreements to another publishing firm. The plaintiff did not approve of this firm. He moved for an injunction to restrain the defendants from selling or assigning without his consent the company's rights under the above agreements.

Held: An injunction would be granted to prevent the intended assignment.

Judgment: STIRLING J. [after stating the facts and referring to the first agreement]: If the agreement in question had been entered into with an individual or a partnership firm, it is clear, upon the cases, that the contract would be of a personal nature, and that the benefit of it would not be assignable . . . It is suggested that there is a difference between a company contractor and an individual contractor, and that though a contract entered into between an author and an individual publisher or a publishing firm consisting of individuals may not be assignable, yet a similar contract entered into between an author and a limited company is capable of assignment. I should hesitate long before accepting that view . . . An author may have confidence in a limited company as well as in an individual publisher. A limited company may have a reputation for producing books in good style and attractive form, and an author selecting such a company as his publisher may do so in the reasonable expectation that the company, although its members and its officers may fluctuate, may nevertheless consider itself under an obligation to maintain its reputation. In the present case what attracted the plaintiff was that the company had published certain books in a form and style of which he approved. No doubt part of the inducement was also that the company had a very efficient manager. It was said that the company might have discharged him the next day without giving the plaintiff cause to complain. That observation is well founded. The company might have discharged its manager the next day, and appointed new officers at any time; but still the plaintiff might well act on the assumption that the Tower Company and those who directed its affairs would select a manager who would maintain the reputation of the company.

It seems to me that it would be wrong to draw any such distinction as is suggested between an agreement entered into by an author with an individual publisher and a similar agreement between an author and a limited company; and agreements of the former kind being non-assignable, I hold that agreements of the latter description are also incapable of being assigned.

I think, therefore, that an injunction ought to be granted.

Note
Lord Watson refers to the Bills of Sale Acts (Bills of Sale Acts 1878, 1890, 1891 and Bills of Sale (Amendment) Act 1882). This is legislation which requires any written agreement to sell goods which remain in the buyer's possession, or any written mortgage of goods, to be in a particular form and to be registered. As Lord Watson says, debts are not covered by this legislation.

[81] [1897] 1 Ch. 21.

King's Bench   **7.E.63.**
Peters v. *General Accident & Life Assurance Corp. Ltd.*[82]

INSURANCE POLICY NOT ASSIGNABLE

Motor policy assigned to car buyer

An insurance policy, as opposed to sums payable under a policy, cannot be assigned as the identity of the assured is material to the insurer.

Facts: The plaintiff had been injured in a road accident caused by Mr Pope's negligence while driving his car. Shortly before the accident Mr Pope had bought the car from Mr Coomber who had taken out liability insurance with the defendant insurance company under a policy which extended the cover to any person driving with the consent or permission of the insured. The car had been delivered to Mr Pope together with the policy. The plaintiff argued that there was an assignment of the policy and that he was therefore entitled to recover damages from the defendant company.

Held: The buyer was not entitled to the benefit of the policy.

Judgment: GODDARD J: . . .The last point that was taken . . . was that there was an assignment of the policy. I have already said why I do not think that there was an assignment in fact. I do not think that you can assign a policy of this nature at all. You can assign your right to receive money under it. If an accident has occurred, and you have a right to be indemnified by your insurers, or if your car has been destroyed, so that you have a right to be paid by your insurers, you can assign your right to anybody you choose, subject to the Road Traffic Act . . . You cannot thrust a new assured upon a company against its will. If you do that, you must have a novation. You must have the release of the assured and the acceptance of a new assured. It is not a question of assigning a chose in action, such as a debt, a right to recover money. A little reflection, I think, will show what a serious state of affairs might otherwise exist. The proposal form in this case, as in every case of motor insurance, asks questions with regard to the previous driving history of the proposer. The company want to know whether he is a man whose record is such that they can take him, and, if so, at what premium. His driving history or his driving experience must, I think, be a material fact. The moral factor, as it has been called, enters into these matters very considerably, not only in motor insurance, but also in most classes of insurance of this description. For instance, take the case of a person who wishes to insure jewellery. There may be people whose character is such that no insurance company would insure their jewellery for a single moment. There may be people who have had such an unhappy record of fires or such an unhappy record of losses of jewellery that only the most charitable could believe that those were fortuitous happenings. An insurance company, in those circumstances, would probably be very shy—I mean, respectable insurance companies; there are some insurance companies which, I have no doubt, as long as they can get a premium, will take it, though whether they will pay out at the end is another matter. However, I am considering respectable and proper insurance companies, and the moral factor is a factor which is more common in an action, where the policy is disputed on the ground of non-disclosure, than to say: "You have not disclosed a material fact here, namely, the accidents that you have had, or the fires that you have had, or the losses of jewellery that you have had." I have no doubt therefore, that you cannot assign a motor policy in the way that it is suggested it was done here . . .

(b) Assignment of Future Rights. There is general agreement that a right under an existing contract may be assigned even though the right is not yet due or is conditional on

---

[82] [1937] 4 All ER 628.

some event that has not yet occurred. If, for example, a building contractor secures a bank loan by assigning to the bank his claim under an existing, but still executory, construction contract, the assignment is valid even though the contractor's right to payment is conditioned on his own future performance of the contract.

A different problem arises where someone attempts to assign a right to payment under a contract he hopes to make with a third person in the future. Courts have always had conceptual and practical difficulties in accepting such assignments as valid. The conceptual difficulty lies in the old rule that nobody is able to transfer property he does not yet own (*nemo dat quod non habet*). There is also the fear that by admitting the assignment of "mere expectancies" the door to fraud might be opened or improvident assignors might be encouraged to sell or pledge all contract rights they might acquire at any time in the future. It is arguable that if there are clear policy reasons for disallowing the assignment of future claims such invalidity should be openly based on these reasons rather than on the view that the rights to be transferred are "not yet in existence". Moreover, there is a growing need of the business community to make use of future contract rights for the purpose of securing a present loan.

House of Lords   **7.E.64.**
Tailby v. *Official Receiver*[83]

ASSIGNMENT OF FUTURE PROPERTY

Assignment of book debts

An assignment of book debts (broadly speaking, these are trade debts) is effective to transfer to the assignee even book debts which were not in existence at the time of the assignment, provided that when they come into existence they are sufficiently identifiable.

Facts: Izon assigned all his book debts to Tyrell; Tyrell's interest was later obtained by the appellant. Later Izon supplied goods to Wilson, who were notified by the appellant that they should pay him, which they did. Izon went bankrupt and his trustee in bankruptcy, the respondent, claimed that the appellant should repay this money.

Held: The Court of Appeal held that the assignment was ineffective because it was too vague. The House of Lords reversed this decision.

Judgment: LORD WATSON: . . . My Lords, the circumstances which have given rise to this litigation may be very shortly stated.

Henry George Izon, who at that time carried on the business of a packing-case manufacturer in Birmingham, by mortgage dated the 13th of May 1879 assigned, for valuable consideration received, to the late John Tyrell, his stock-in-trade, and "all the book debts due and owing or which may during the continuance of this security become due and owing to the said mortgagor." In the months of October and November 1884 Izon supplied a firm of Wilson Brothers & Co., upon credit, with goods to the value of £10 7s. 11d. The appellant, who had acquired Tyrell's interest in the debt, gave notice of the assignment to that firm, and required them to make payment of it to himself, which they accordingly did. Some time after the date of the notice Izon was adjudged bankrupt, and the respondent, who is trustee of his estate, now sues the appellant for repayment of the amount received by him from Wilson Brothers & Co.

---

[83] (1888) 13 App.Cas. 523, 532–530.

It does not clearly appear whether the debt in question was incurred to the mortgagor in the business in which he was engaged in May 1879, or in some other trade. In the argument addressed to your Lordships it was rightly assumed that the assignment comprehends every future book debt becoming due to Izon, in any profession or trade which may be followed by him in any place and at any time during the continuance of the security constituted by the mortgage. The respondent admitted that the liability of Wilson Brothers & Co., whenever it emerged, was, and until satisfied by payment continued to be, a proper book debt, due and owing to the mortgagor. He maintained his right to it, in competition with the appellant, upon the single ground that the assignment of future book debts, in the mortgage of 1879, is ineffectual to carry any equitable interest to the assignee . . .

The rule of equity which applies to the assignment of future choses in action is, as I understand it, a very simple one. Choses in action do not come within the scope of the Bills of Sale Acts, and though not yet existing, may nevertheless be the subject of present assignment. As soon as they come into existence, assignees who have given valuable consideration will, if the new chose in action is in the disposal of their assignor, take precisely the same right and interest as if it had actually belonged to him, or had been within his disposition and control at the time when the assignment was made. There is but one condition which must be fulfilled in order to make the assignee's right attach to a future chose in action, which is, that, on its coming into existence, it shall answer the description in the assignment, or, in other words, that it shall be capable of being identified as the thing, or as one of the very things assigned. When there is no uncertainty as to its identification, the beneficial interest will immediately vest in the assignee. Mere difficulty in ascertaining all the things which are included in a general assignment, whether in esse or in posse, will not affect the assignee's right to those things which are capable of ascertainment or are identified.

In the case of book debts, as in the case of choses in action generally, intimation of the assignee's right must be made to the debtor or obligee in order to make it complete. That is the only possession which he can attain, so long as the debt is unpaid, and is sufficient to take it out of the order and disposition of the assignor. In this case the appellant's right, if otherwise valid, was, in any question with the respondent, duly perfected by his notice to Wilson Brothers & Co. before Izon became a bankrupt.

The learned judges of the Appeal Court were unanimously of opinion that the description of book debts in the assignment of Tyrell is "too vague," and it is upon that ground only that they have held the assignment to be invalid. The term which they have selected, in order to express what they conceived to be the radical defect of the assignment, is susceptible of at least two different meanings. It may either signify that the description is too wide and comprehensive, without implying that there will be any uncertainty as to the debts which it will include, if and when these come into existence, or it may signify that the language of the description is so obscure that it will be impossible, in the time to come, to determine with any degree of certainty to what particular debts it was intended to apply. In the latter sense the description of future book debts in the mortgage of 1879 does not incur the imputation of vagueness. No one has suggested that the expression "book debt" is indefinite; and it is, in my opinion, very clear that every debt becoming due and owing to the mortgagor, which belongs to the class of book debts (a fact quite capable of ascertainment), is at once identified with the subject-matter of the assignment . . .

When the consideration has been given, and the debt has been clearly identified as one of those in respect of which it was given, a Court of Equity will enforce the covenant of the parties, and will not permit the assignor, or those in his right, to defeat the assignment upon the plea that it is too comprehensive.

The problem is of enormous practical significance in Germany since it is quite common for a buyer, having acquired on credit goods to be resold to third parties, to assign to the vendor his future claims against the buyers of those goods. So long as the goods are in the possession of the buyer the vendor is protected by a reservation of title clause. Once the goods have been resold the vendor's title is "prolonged" into the contract rights to be acquired by the buyer against third parties upon the resale of the goods. The validity of such assignments used to be doubtful, partly because they were believed to be against public policy, partly because they might be incompatible with the rule that there can be no effective transfer of property unless the asset to be transferred is "determined" or at least "determinable" at the time the transfer is made. All doubts were laid to rest when the Bundesgerichtshof decided that the assigned right need not be "determinable" at the time of the assignment but only at the time it comes into existence.

BGH, 25 October 1952[84]   **7.G.65.**

The master plumber's debts

Where goods have been sold subject to a retention of title clause, with a provision that if the goods are sold or otherwise disposed of, sums due from the persons to whom they were disposed of shall be assigned to the original supplier, with a provision for re-assignment if the amount so received exceeds the sum due, the assignment is valid.

Facts: Between the end of May 1949 and January 1950, the defendant supplied goods having a total value of approximately 17,000 DM to S, a master plumber. Of the total purchase price, it received only approximately 1,700 DM. The supplies were subject to the defendant's general terms and conditions of sale and delivery, Clause 14 of which read as follows:

"Supplies shall be made by us solely on the basis of the reservation by us of title to and ownership of the goods supplied pending payment in full. Title to the goods shall not pass to the purchaser until such time as he has discharged all his liabilities and obligations arising from the supply of goods by us . . . The purchaser shall be entitled to alienate the goods supplied in the ordinary course of business . . . The alienation by the purchaser of the goods supplied by us—regardless of the state or condition thereof—shall operate with immediate effect as an assignment by him to us, pending the discharge in full of all debts due from him to us in respect of goods supplied by us, of claims vesting in him by virtue of [such] alienation against the person acquiring the goods in question, together with all ancillary rights relating thereto . . .

In the event that the value of the security provided to us exceeds, in the aggregate, the amount of our claims for goods supplied by more than 20 per cent, we shall be required, upon request by the purchaser, to re-assign to him our rights to that extent."

Under a contract with K, S had installed the materials bought from the defendant in K's house. Subsequently, S had assigned part of his outstanding claim against K to the plaintiff. Since K did not know which party had the better claim he paid the money into court and left it to the parties to fight the matter out between themselves.

The plaintiff claims an order requiring the defendant to consent to the payment, out of the sum paid into court, of the debts due to the plaintiff in priority to those due to the defendant. The plaintiff relies in support of his claim on the assignment of 8 December 1949, and asserts that the assignment of future claims provided for by Clause 14 of the defendant's general terms and conditions of sale and delivery is ineffective and inoperative.

Held: The lower courts had found for the plaintiff on the ground that the assignment pursuant to Clause 14 of the defendant's general terms of business was invalid. The BGH allowed an appeal and dismissed the action.

Judgment: . . . The second sentence of § 398 BGB provides that, upon the conclusion of an assignment agreement, the new creditor takes the place of the former creditor. According to § 401 BGB,

---

[84] BGHZ 7, 365.

the ancillary and preferential rights specified in that provision are to pass, along with the claim assigned, to the new creditor. That provision is to be understood as meaning that the amount of an assigned claim must be adequately determined or determinable, since, if it is not, uncertainty will subsist as to the extent to which the claim remains vested in the old creditor and the extent to which it is vested in the new creditor. In the interests of legal certainty, however, it is necessary that the position should be clear in that regard. Thus, it is acknowledged in the relevant case-law [citations omitted] and jurisprudence [citations omitted] that an assignment of future claims shall be valid in law only if the amount of the claim assigned is adequately determined or determinable.

The defendant bases its claim to entitlement to the moneys paid into court on the fact that the contracts concluded with S were subject to the its general terms and conditions of sale and delivery, and that these contained, in Clause 14, a general assignment of future claims . . .

The recent case-law of the *Reichsgericht* has indeed attached excessively stringent requirements to the determinability of the scope of pre-assigned claims as provided for in standard-form legal documents. As stated above, it must be borne in mind that standard-form terms and conditions are to be construed without regard to the distinctive characteristics of individual cases. That follows from their very nature. Consequently, in the case of assignments of future claims pursuant to standard-form terms and conditions, it is necessary, first of all, to undertake an objective examination of the significance attaching to an assignment of future claims based on a standard-form document, leaving out of consideration the incidental aspects of the individual case in question. By means of the results thus obtained from the ascertainment of the meaning of the assignment clause, it is necessary then to proceed to examine whether the general assignment of future claims contained in the standard-form assignment clause, as construed from the interpretation of its standard characteristics, covers the claim at issue in the individual case. If it does, the next question will be whether that claim is adequately determined or determinable having regard to the results of the above-mentioned investigations. In the present case, the following results emerge from the test to be applied from those various standpoints: the nature of the defendant's business is such that it supplies goods to, in particular, plumbers and fitters who do not simply resell, pursuant to sales contracts, the goods supplied to them by the defendant but conclude contracts for work and materials and use those goods in order to complete the works which they have contracted to carry out. The standard-form stipulations contained in Clause 14 of the defendant's general terms and conditions of sale and delivery take those commercial circumstances into account. They provide for the possibility that the customer may process or adapt the goods subject to the retention of title clause, and that the customer may "alienate them, in whatever state or condition they may be". Thus, the possibility of alienation of the goods subject to the retention of title clause, even in a processed or adapted state, is covered by the clause at issue. It further follows from a logical interpretation of the contractual provision in question, having regard to the statement, set out above, of the principles of construction applying to standard-form legal documents, that the clause in issue also covers cases in which the customer has used the goods subject to the retention of title in carrying out contracts for work and materials (§ 651 BGB), has thereafter handed over the completed work to the person commissioning it, and has acquired, as against that person, a claim for remuneration under the contract. It further follows from this, however, that the phrase "claims vesting in him by virtue of [such] alienation" contained in the clause must be understood as covering entitlement to the whole of the remuneration—in other words, the sum which, in the case of contracts for work and materials, is made up of the value of the goods, the business profit made and the reward for the labour itself. The fact that, contrary to the view taken by the appellate court, the defendant's standard-form terms and conditions of sale and delivery must be interpreted in that way is apparent, above all, from the final paragraph of Clause 14. That paragraph provides that, in the event that the value of the security provided to the defendant exceeds, in the aggregate, the amount of its claims for goods supplied by more than 20 per cent, it is to be required, upon request by the purchaser, to re-assign to him its rights to that extent. That stipulation assumes that the assignment may cover not only the amount of the value of the goods subject to the retention of title but the entire remuneration which the purchaser of those goods is entitled to receive from the person who has commissioned the works pursuant to the contract for work and materials concluded with the latter. The appellate court, referring to the decision of the *Reichsgericht* reported at RGZ 155, 32, considered that such total assignment could not be regarded as feasible, especially having regard to the economic aspects involved. The doubts expressed by the appellate court might be justified, were it not for the existence of the final paragraph of Clause 14. However, they are removed by the very fact of the stipulations contained in that final paragraph, which take into account the legitimate interests of both parties. If the provisions of the final paragraph of Clause 14 are taken sufficiently into consideration, it becomes clear that the assignment of future claims does not excessively restrict the freedom of economic activity of the purchaser of the goods subject to the retention of title, and that the standard-form stipulations do not in themselves infringe § 138 BGB. This further has the result of removing the objection expressed by the *Reichsgericht* (RGZ 155, 32) that there could be an assignment the value of which was disproportionately high in relation to the value of the goods supplied. The following conclusions may be drawn from this objective interpretation of a standard-form document: the contract concluded between the defendant and S is legally valid, since the appellate court made no findings of fact concerning special circumstances which might have rendered it void under § 138 BGB. Furthermore, S assigned to the defendant in advance his claim against K for the whole of the fixed price agreed with the latter. That being so, the amount of the assigned claim is adequately determined, and there can thus be no doubt in that regard concerning the validity of the assignment in law.

The assignability of "future" contract rights does not seem to be of major practical importance in France. Unpaid sellers frequently protect themselves by a reservation of title clause (*clause de réserve de propriété*) and it is clear that, if the buyer becomes insolvent and bankruptcy proceedings are opened, the seller takes priority over the buyer's other creditors not only with respect to the goods delivered but also, if the goods have been sold in their original condition, with respect to the outstanding claims against the sub-purchasers (see Article 121 and 122 of the Insolvency Law of 25 January 1985). However, this follows not, as under German law, from an assignment of these claims agreed in advance between the seller and the buyer in their contractual agreement, but from an application of the doctrine of *subrogation réelle*.[85] A similar result is reached in England when goods are supplied under reservation of title and the seller authorises the buyer to resell them on condition that he accounts for the proceeds of sale ("Romalpa clause"). Here the seller will be given an equitable right to "trace" those proceeds and to recover them by a proprietary action. However, subsequent cases have made it very difficult for the supplier to "trace" the proceeds. The courts are very concerned that an agreement that the proceeds from the resale of the goods should be held by the buyer for the supplier will amount to a form of charge, and a charge will not be valid unless the charge is registered (Companies Act 1989, section 395). Although in principle it is possible for the proceeds to belong to the supplier outright, the courts are very reluctant to interpret the contract as giving the supplier entitlement to any more than the amount which it is owed by the buyer—and that would be a charge.[86]

---

[85] See Cass com. 8 March 1988, Bull.civ. IV 99; Com. 20 June 1989, D. 1989, 431 annotated by Pérochon.
[86] See e.g. *Pfeiffer Weinkellerei-Weineinkauf GmbH & Co* v. *Arbuthnot Factors Ltd* [1988] 1 WLR 150.

(c) *Assignments Contrary to No-assignment Clauses.* Frequently, parties include in their contract a term prohibiting the creditor, without the written consent of the debtor, to assign to third parties rights arising under the contract. In the building industry, it is quite common for employers, particularly for the government, to include in their standard terms a "non-assignment clause" and thereby to prevent the contractor from assigning his right to money under the building contract without the employer's consent.

Helstan Securities Ltd. v. *Hertfordshire County Council*[87]   **7.E.66.**

ASSIGNMENT PROHIBITED; ASSIGNMENT INEFFECTIVE

Prohibition on Assignment

A purported assignment of a claim under a contract which the contract states may not be assigned is ineffective.

Facts: The Hertfordshire County Council ("the county council") contracted with Renhold Road Surfacing Ltd. ("Renholds") for road-works to be carried out. There were a number of these agreements. They were all in the form of the Institution of Civil Engineers Conditions of Contract (known as the ICE Conditions of Contract 4th Ed.). Renholds got into very severe financial difficulties. They said that they were owed, in one way or another, £46,437 by the county council under the contracts and sold these debts to the plaintiffs. The plaintiffs gave notice of these assignments to the county council, who did not consent to the assignments. The plaintiffs as assignees of the debts have sued the county council claiming that sum of £46,437.

Held: The purported assignment was without effect.

Judgment: CROOM-JOHNSON J: . . . This case asks what is the effect, where there is a purported assignment of a chose in action, of a condition in the contract which forbids assignment without consent? [He stated the facts as above and continued:]

The county council say that they are under no obligation to pay, for two reasons. The first is that each contract contained a condition prohibiting the assignment of the debts. It read as follows: "(3) The contractor [that is to say Renholds] shall not assign the contract or any part thereof or any benefit or interest therein or thereunder without the written consent of the employer [that is to say the county council]." Condition 4 of the contract forbids subletting the whole of the works and deals with subcontracting parts of the works . . .

If the reported cases are not a sure guide, one is thrown back in this case on the agreement. There are certain kinds of choses in action which, for one reason or another, are not assignable and there is no reason why the parties to an agreement may not contract to give its subject-matter the quality of unassignability. In these circumstances, one has to look at the clause itself. The words "benefit or interest therein or thereunder" do cover the debts which result from the performance of the contract. I cannot draw the distinction which the plaintiff's counsel asked me to draw, namely that there is a difference between a right to payment on an engineer's certificate and the resulting debt. If there is such a difference, both are caught by this clause. It is the contract which creates the entitlement to be paid, and that is a benefit or interest under the contract.

I find no ambiguity such as would lead me to consider the background against which the contract was made as an aid to interpretation. If I did, the background would not help the plaintiffs. The clause is obviously there to let the employer retain control of who does the work. Condition 4, which deals with subletting, has the same object. But closely associated with the right to control who does the work, is the right at the end of the day to balance claims for money due on the one

---

[87] [1978] 3 All ER 262.

had against counterclaims, for example, for bad workmanship on the other. The plaintiffs say that such a counterclaim may be made against the assignees instead of against the assignors. But the debtors may only use it as a shield by way of set-off and cannot enforce it against the assignees if it is greater than the amount of the debt: *Young* v. *Kitchin* (1878) 3 Ex D 127. And why should they have to make it against people whom they may not want to make it against, in circumstances not of their choosing, when they have contracted that they shall not?

Although arguments showing potential hardship cannot prevail over the construction of the clause, I should mention two which have been advanced. It is said by the plaintiffs that if the assignment is void, the debtor can take the benefit of the work done by the assignor and avoid paying the assignee. The defendants reply that the assignee must make proper enquiries before he buys a debt, and these enquiries may go to the likelihood of the debtor having the money with which to pay, or the prospect of a counterclaim which would extinguish the debt, or the existence of a prohibitory condition such as the present. On all of these things depends the price he is prepared to pay. There is no injustice in expecting the purchasers of debts to make these enquiries.

My decision . . . is that condition 3 does in this case make the assignment invalid, and in those circumstances the defendants are entitled to judgment against the plaintiffs and this action fails.

This holding was confirmed by the House of Lords in *Linden Gardens Trust Ltd.* v. *Lenesta Sludge Disposals Ltd.*[88] Under § 399 BGB and Article 164 paragraph 1 of the Swiss Law of Obligations a claim is unassignable if an agreement between debtor and creditor so provides. The courts have treated no-assignment clauses as fully effective on the ground that the debtor has a legitimate interest to avoid the administrative expense of keeping track of one or more (partial) assignments and to protect himself against the risk of having to pay twice if he overlooks the receipt of a notice of assignment. A further reason is that, while the debtor can set up against the assignee all defences that have arisen before the receipt by him of a notice of assignment (see below at 952 *et seq.*), he may wish to set up "new" defences as well and to avoid a fight with the assignee over the thorny question whether a defence is "new" or "old".

On the other hand, it is clear that no-assignment clauses, if upheld as valid, can severely limit the creditor's ability to use his contract rights as security. An unassignable claim is not good security for a loan; indeed it is arguable that the general recognition of no-assignment clauses has serious commercial implications, especially for small and medium-sized companies which can, as a practical matter, finance their undertakings only by assigning book debts to financial institutions. In Germany, after a lively debate of the pros and cons of no-assignment clauses, Parliament has finally reacted by invalidating such clauses if the right which the parties have purported to treat as unassignable arises from a commercial operation (as defined in §§ 343–345 German Commercial Code) or if the debtor is a government entity. § 354a German Commercial Code (as enacted by a Law of 25 July 1994) now provides:

HGB **7.G.67.**

§ 354a: Where the assignment of a money claim is excluded by agreement with the debtor in accordance with § 399 BGB, and the transaction giving rise to that claim constitutes, for both parties, a commercial transaction, or the debtor is a legal person under public law . . ., the

---

[88] [1993] 3 All ER 417, at 427–43, *per* Lord Browne-Wilkinson.

assignment shall nevertheless be valid. However, the debtor may, with the effect of discharging the debt, pay the sum due to the former creditor. Any agreement to the contrary shall be ineffective.

The French Civil Code says nothing on the validity of no-assignment clauses nor are there modern authorities dealing with the problem. It seems safe to say, however, that French law would take a dim view of such clauses if only because of a strong policy against restraints on alienation of property which dates back to the French Revolution. An old case in point is Cass. civ. 1 June 1853,[89] in which such a clause was invalidated on the ground that it "tends to go further than provided by law in restricting the free use of property and thus to place assets outside the free flow of commerce that must in the present state of the law remain freely transferable". See also Article 1260 paragraph 2 of the Italian Civil Code which provides that a no-assignment clause does not prevent the assignee from acquiring a good title to the assigned right unless he had knowledge of the clause at the date of the assignment.

The trend towards the invalidity of no-assignment clauses has also manifested itself in the law of the United States (see § 9–318 paragraph 4 of the Uniform Commercial Code) and in the Unidroit Convention on International Factoring. Article 6 of the Convention provides that the assignment of a contract right by a supplier (assignor) to a factor (assignee) shall be effective "notwithstanding any agreement between the supplier and the debtor prohibiting such assignment".[90]

7.3.3. PROTECTION OF THE DEBTOR

The law of assignment is dominated by the conflict between two interests. One of these is the interest of commerce in increasing the circulation of credit: money claims, like other items of wealth, should be capable of being transferred by mere agreement between assignor and assignee so that the transfer is effective against all third parties without any further requirement, especially without any need for any form of co-operation or agreement on the part of the debtor. Opposed to this is the interest of the debtor in not having his legal position adversely affected by the transfer of the claim against him.

The general principle recognized in all legal systems is that while the assignee of a contract right succeeds to all the rights of the assignor, a debtor is not affected by the assignment unless he has notice thereof. If he pays his indebtedness to the assignor in ignorance of the assignment he is relieved from all liability to the assignee. (In such a case the assignee will have to try to recover the money from the assignor, see above, p. 937. He may also set up against the claim of the assignee any defences, such as a release, a stay or a modification of the claim, acquired by way of an agreement made with the assignor prior to notice of the assignment.)

---

[89] D.P. 1853.1.191.
[90] For details see *e.g.* Goode [1988] J.Bus.L. 347; Rebmann, RabelsZ 1989.599.

(1) Notice to the Debtor
The formulas used in the civil codes vary somewhat. The debtor is not discharged by paying the assignor if he does so after "knowing" of the assignment (§ 407 of the German Civil Code) or after "the assignee has been made known to him" (§ 1396 of the Austrian Civil Code) or although he was not "in good faith" in paying "the previous creditor" (Article 167 of the Swiss Law of Obligations). Similarly, Article 5 of the *Loi Dailly*[91] provides that when the debtor has been notified of the assignment by the assignee bank he will not be discharged unless payment is made by him to the bank.

In applying the notice requirement the courts have required the notification to record clearly and definitely the fact of assignment and to indicate that payment must be made to the assignee.

Court of Appeal   **7.E.68.**
James Talcott Ltd. v. *John Lewis & Co. Ltd. and North American Dress Co. Ltd*[92]

NOTICE TO DEBTOR MUST MAKE CLEAR THAT RIGHT TRANSFERRED

Ambiguous notice

A debtor who receives what was intended as a notice of assignment but which does not make it clear that the right to the debt has been transferred to the intended assignor, rather than that he may pay that party, cannot be made to pay a second time if he pays the assignor.

Facts: The second defendants, the North American Dress Co., Ltd., agreed to sell certain goods to John Lewis & Co., Ltd., the first defendants. They sent those four instalments of goods to John Lewis & Co., Ltd., and four invoices for payment. On each of the invoices sent by the suppliers of the goods, the North American Dress Co., Ltd., to John Lewis & Co., Ltd., there was a rubber stamp imposed in the following terms:

> "To facilitate our accountancy and banking arrangements, it has been agreed that this invoice be transferred to and payment in London funds should be made to James Talcott, Ltd., 6–8 Sackville Street, London, W.1. Errors in this invoice must be notified to James Talcott, Ltd., immediately . . ."

Subsequently, John Lewis & Co., Ltd., paid the amount of the invoices to the North American Dress Co., Ltd., by their cheque and the North American Dress Co., Ltd., received the money. Then the plaintiffs intervened, and made a claim on John Lewis & Co., Ltd., that the debt represented by those invoices had been assigned to them, and that, therefore, they had a right to claim that John Lewis & Co., Ltd., should pay the money to them a second time, basing their claim upon the ground that there had been an assignment of the debt to them, and that they had given notice thereof to John Lewis & Co., Ltd.

Held: The plaintiff's claim was dismissed at first instance. The Court of Appeal upheld this decision.

Judgment: MACKINNON LJ: This is a very short point, but, I think, not by any means an easy one. [He stated the facts as above and continued:] By correspondence between the solicitors for the plaintiffs and those for the first defendants, it was agreed that that question depended upon the construction of this clause which was stamped by the rubber stamp on the invoices. It was admitted by the solicitors for John Lewis & Co., Ltd., and it appears from a document with which I have been furnished—indeed, there is no doubt whatever—that the North American Dress Co., Ltd., had assigned those debts to the plaintiffs by a completely formal document. The whole question in this case is whether there was such sufficient notice to John Lewis & Co., Ltd., of that assignment, as

---

[91] See *supra* at 940.
[92] [1940] 3 All ER 592.

created a legal obligation on John Lewis & Co., Ltd., to pay the plaintiffs, and to pay them only, so that, though they had paid the original debt, they must none the less pay the plaintiffs over again . . .

One may have a notice to a debtor from his creditor asking him to pay the money to a third party. The terms of it may be such as to indicate that it is to be paid to that third party because that third party has, by virtue of an assignment, become the person entitled to receive it. On the other hand, it may be a request to pay the debt to a third party, not because that third party has a right to it, but because, as a matter of convenience, the creditor desires that it shall be paid to that third party as his agent to receive it in respect of the right of the creditor still surviving to receive the debt himself. Plainness of meaning is necessary in order that the debtor who has received a notice to pay a third party shall be rendered liable to pay the money over again if he disregards the notice. The language is immaterial if the meaning is plain, but that plain meaning must be that the debt and the right to receive it have been transferred to the third party. It is not merely that I have made some arrangements by which I request another to pay this money to the third party as my agent. The question is whether this stamped clause put upon the invoices did amount to a plain intimation to the first defendants that the right to receive this money had been transferred to the plaintiffs.

First of all, it is not a notice sent by the plaintiffs at all. If it were sent direct by the plaintiffs to the first defendants, the mere fact that it emanated from them would go some little way to indicate that they were doing so pursuant to a right of theirs. I do not say that there is very much in that, but the fact that it is stamped on their own invoice by the North American Dress Co., Ltd., makes it a communication from them, and not a communication from John Lewis & Co., Ltd., to the plaintiffs . . . It would have been so simple for James Talcott Ltd., to give a correct notice, "This debt has been assigned to us", or to insist that the North American Dress Co., Ltd. should in clear terms give that intimation, that it is a matter of extreme wonder and speculation why this stamp should have been couched in this extremely vague and obscure language.

We have been told (I think that it appears from one of the letters) that the wording of this extraordinary sentence was actually settled by counsel. I can only conceive that it was couched in this obscure language to conceal the fact that the North American Dress Co., Ltd., were carrying on their business with borrowed money, and had assigned to the plaintiffs the money to which they themselves were entitled.

The words begin—and they are the first words to be read by anybody who did read them—"To facilitate our accountancy and banking arrangements . . ." The word "our" suggests that it is still a debt due to the North American Dress Co., Ltd., and that it is only a matter of their internal business arrangements. It is true that the words go on "it has been agreed", and it is suggested that that must mean an agreement between the North American Dress Co., Ltd., and the plaintiffs, though I do not know why it should. There is nothing to show that it has been agreed between those parties. There are the vague, uncertain words "it has been agreed". Then it goes on to say "that this invoice be transferred to". It is suggested that those words in themselves ought to be taken to mean that the debt due upon this invoice shall be assigned, but they do not say so. The invoice is transferred "and payment in London funds should be made to James Talcott Ltd. . . . Errors in this invoice must be notified to James Talcott Ltd., immediately."

As I have said, it is not enough to make the debtor liable to pay over again if he has creditors, if he has merely received a notice that he is to pay to some other party merely as agent for his creditor. He is not bound to pay over again unless he has received a sufficiently plain notice that the right to receive the money has been transferred to the third party, so that he will at his peril neglect that notice and neglect the right of the third party. I think that this notice stamped on the invoice was ambiguous. I think that it is equally consistent with being merely a request to pay to the plaintiffs, as agents of the creditor to receive the money, and it does not indicate sufficiently clearly that there has been an assignment of the debt to the plaintiffs so that they should become the real creditors of the first defendants, be the only persons entitled to be paid the money. That was the view taken by MacNaghten J, with the result that he dismissed the claim. I think that his decision was right, and that this appeal fails.

[Du PARCQ LJ made a speech to the same effect. GODDARD LJ dissented.]

(2) Defences Available to the Debtor
One type of defence is based on the debtor's contention that the assignment itself was invalid so that the assignee never became his true creditor. Assignment law requires the debtor to determine, at his own risk, the validity of assignment of claims against him. He will not get a good discharge if he pays the assignee and it later turns out that the assignment was a forgery, was procured by an assignee who lacked capacity to contract, or, having been extorted by duress or fraud, was set aside by the assignor.

The problem of protecting the debtor can also arise when there is no doubt about the assignee's entitlement, but the question is what defences the debtor can raise against his claim for payment. Since the assignment can take place without the consent of the debtor, the invariable principle is that the assignment does not curtail the defences he can raise against the assignee. The Common Law's metaphor is that the assignee "stands in the assignor's shoes" or that the assignee "takes subject to equities"; in the Civil Law the rule is sometimes explained as being based on the principle that *nemo plus iuris transferre potest quam ipse habet*. Unlike the holder in due course of a negotiable instrument, the assignee of a non-negotiable claim has no greater rights against the debtor than the assignor.

It follows that the assignee is vulnerable to defences raised by the debtor on the ground that the assignor failed to perform the contract or that a condition limiting the debtor's duty to render the counter-performance occurred. This applies whether the events giving rise to the defence have occurred before or after the assignment or before or after the debtor has acquired notice thereof. Some code provisions seem to take a narrower view since defences available against the assignor are available against the assignee only "if they were justified at the time of the assignment" (§ 404 of the German Civil Code) or "if they existed at the time when the debtor was notified of the assignment" (Article 169 paragraph 1 of the Swiss Law of Obligations). However, it has been held in numerous cases that the debtor can invoke a breach committed by the assignor even though the facts giving rise to the breach did not occur until after the assignment and notice to the debtor. These cases assert that the defence need not have fully materialized at the time of the assignment or of its notification; only a general basis for the defence must have existed at that time in the contractual relationship between the debtor and the assignor.

Reichsgericht, 11 November 1913[93] **7.G.69.**

ASSIGNEE SUBJECT TO DEFENCES UNDER CONTRACT, INCLUDING LATER BREACHES

Termination of building contract after date of assignment: Germany

If after the assignment of money which should become payable under a contract, compensation becomes due to the debtor because of the assignor's failure to perform, the debtor may raise this as a defence against the assignee.

[93] RGZ 83, 279.

Facts: By a contract dated 23 October 1908, G, a building contractor, agreed to construct a new dwelling-house for the defendant. He accomplished part of the building works, but their completion was delayed. The defendant granted him a period of grace, until 5 April 1909, in which to resume the works, warning him that, in the event of failure by G to comply, the defendant would refuse to accept the services supplied and would claim damages for non-performance. Upon the failure by G to comply with the time-limit, the defendant ceased to employ him for the construction and had the building works carried out by another builder. Out of the amount due to him by way of remuneration for the partial work carried out to him, G had on 7 February 1909 assigned to the plaintiff, to whom he owed 4,441.10 marks for stones supplied for use in the construction, a claim in an equivalent sum, which the plaintiff proceeded to demand. The defendant was obliged to expend considerably more in order to have the construction completed than he would have had to pay to G under the contract with the latter. In opposition to the claim made against him, he sought compensation for that loss, which exceeded the remuneration due to G for the partial services performed by the latter.

Held: The *Landgericht* and the *Oberlandesgericht* dismissed the plaintiff's claim. The plaintiff's appeal on a point of law was likewise dismissed.

Judgment: According to the contract for work and services, the contractor was responsible for the performance of the building works in their entirety, and the customer was required, in consideration thereof, to pay the agreed remuneration. Even on the basis of a stipulation that instalments of the remuneration were to become payable to the contractor as the works proceeded, nevertheless, on a proper construction of the agreement, and having regard to the principle of good faith, it is clear from the particular nature of the synallagmatic contract concerned that the entitlement to partial remuneration was not definitively fixed, as to the existence and amount thereof, on an autonomous, independent basis; instead, it was dependent on the continuing existence of the legal relationship. For a contractor to demand, without any reduction, the remuneration corresponding to the completed part of the undivided whole of the work to be carried out by him, whilst at the same time being liable to pay his customer damages under the same contract on account of fault on his part, and particularly on account of delay, is contrary to the nature of things, and is incompatible with the meaning of damages for non-performance of synallagmatic contracts pursuant to the second sentence of § 326(1) BGB, as established by the case-law of the *Reichsgericht* . . . It is not permissible to determine the amount of the loss and then offset it against the remuneration for the work or against that part thereof which has become due. On the contrary, the contractor liable to pay damages has no further claim whatever arising out of the contract, not even for the partial remuneration which is due. He retains only the significance attaching to an invoiced sum which affects the amount of the claim for damages (citations omitted). If partial remuneration for work done is set against a claim for damages for non-performance arising out of the same contract for work and services, that amounts not to a set-off in accordance with § 379 et seq. of the BGB, but to a settlement of accounts, that is to say, the determination of the arithmetical result . . .

The customer commissioning the works may argue, in opposition to the claim for part of the remuneration, that the change in the debt relationship, as described in the present case, occurred as a result of the delay on the part of the contractor. For the contractor to be able, by assigning his claim to partial remuneration for the work, to preclude the customer from raising any objection to that claim and to prevent the latter from thus recouping his losses by means of recourse to the partial remuneration due is not only contrary to the principle of good faith but also incompatible with § 404 BGB, according to which a debtor may raise, as against the new creditor, any objections and defences which were established against the former creditor at the time of the assignment. As at the date of the assignment in the present case (7 February 1909), the defendant's claim for damages was already established within the meaning of § 404 BGB, alternatively he had a legitimate objection or defence under § 326 BGB, since it was based on the reciprocal debt relationship which existed at the time of the assignment, notwithstanding that the facts and matters as a result of which the legal basis of the objection or defence (inherent in the debt relationship) became effective did not occur until after the assignment (citations omitted). In the case of a synallagmatic contract in particular, the new creditor must accept that there may be raised against him all and any objections and defences which, like those asserted in the present case, do not emerge until a later stage in the legal relationship (citations omitted). The claim assigned passes, together with the preferential and ancillary rights attaching to it, but also with its weaknesses and defects, to the new creditor. Consequently, in this case too, the defendant is entitled to raise his claim for damages as against the plaintiff, with the effect described, since, in accordance with its legal basis, his defence lies in the debt relationship which already existed at the time of the assignment.

Cass. com., 9 February 1993[94]   **7.F.70.**

ASSIGNEE SUBJECT TO DEFENCES UNDER CONTRACT, INCLUDING LATER BREACHES

Termination of building contract after date of assignment: France

If after the assignment of money which should become payable under a contract, compensation becomes due to the debtor because of the assignor's failure to perform, the debtor may raise this as a defence against the assignee.

Facts: According to the contested judgment (Versailles, 4 January 1991), the Banque Populaire des Pyrénées-Orientales, de l'Aude et de l'Arriège ("the Bank") became, in the form provided for by the Law of 2 January 1981 [the Loi Dailly], the assignee of a debt due from SCI (Société Immobilière pour le Commerce et l'Industrie, a company formed to let commercial and industrial premises), and notified that company of the assignment. When the debt fell due, the SCI claimed termination of the works contracts concluded with the assignor undertaking, since the latter had not completed the performance thereof.

Held: SCI need not pay the sum claimed by the bank. An appeal by the bank was dismissed.

Judgment: . . .—Whereas the Bank challenges the contested judgment in that it allowed the objection pleaded against it to be relied upon, whereas, according to the appeal, Articles 1 and 4 of the Law of 2 January 1981 make it clear that a debtor may raise against an assignee only such objection as he could have raised against the assignor before the assignment; as having found that the termination of the works contract which gave rise to the assignment of debts of 2 May 1988 in favour of the Bank took place on 19 May 1988, that is to say, later than the assignment, from which it followed that the debtor's objection regarding the assignor's failure to perform its contractual obligations could not be pleaded against the assignee, the cour d'appel infringed those provisions by none the less relying on that fact in order to dismiss the Bank's application for payment.

—Whereas however, since the debtor company had not consented to the assignment of the debt, the cour d'appel was fully entitled to hold that the objection relating to that non-performance could be relied upon against the assignee Bank, without there being any need to inquire whether the non-performance of the contract on which the debt in issue was founded took place after notification of the assignment; as the appeal ground is accordingly unfounded.

On those grounds, the appeal is dismissed.

The rule under which a debtor may avail himself, as against the assignee, of all defences he could have raised against his original creditor renders the assignee's position somewhat precarious, and it comes as no surprise that assignees, dissatisfied with their vulnerability under this rule, have sought protection against the debtor's defences. One possibility is for the assignee to ask the debtor for an "acknowledgement" of the debt, i.e. for a declaration by which the debtor confirms the existence of the assigned claim and states that he will

---

[94] Bull. civ. IV.51.

raise no defences or counterclaims when payment is demanded. Since such waivers are as a rule made on forms provided by the assignee, ambiguities are interpreted *contra preferentem*. The courts are also inclined to consider defences as waived only to the extent to which the debtor at the time of the waiver knew, or ought to have known, of the facts giving rise to the defence.

BGH, 18 October 1972[95]

7.G.71.

AMBIGUITY IN WAIVER OF DEFENCE CONSTRUED AGAINST ASSIGNEE

Of tools assigned

Where a debtor has completed a form drafted by an assignee and confirmed that it has no claim against the assignor, but in fact the debtor does have a claim against the assignor, that ambiguity should be construed against the party that drafted the form i.e. the assignee.

Facts: On 20 January 1966 the defendant firm purchased tools from S GmbH. The purchase price was DM 97,850, and the tools were to be delivered over a period of time. S GmbH assigned its claim for payment to the plaintiff bank, which granted it credit.

The defendant received a notice of assignment dated 29 June 1966; this was signed by S GmbH and was on a form used by the plaintiff. Attached to that form was a further form filled out by the plaintiff, which contained a clause stating that there existed no rights vested in any third party to the DM 80,000 residual debt or any counterclaims to that sum which the defendant itself might raise by way of set-off. The defendant signed the latter form, dated it 11 July 1966 and sent it, in accordance with an imprint on the form, to the plaintiff.

In July 1967 S GmbH became bankrupt. By that time, it had provided the defendant with possession and ownership of only some of the tools sold. The plaintiff demanded from the defendant payment of a residual debt of DM 39,526.20 together with interest. The defendant refused to pay, on the ground that some of the tools had not yet been delivered and that it had already paid in excess of the sums due for those which had been delivered. The plaintiff argued that the defendant, by its "confirmation" of 11 July 1966, had in any event lost any right to raise such a defence.

Held: The courts below found in favour of the plaintiff and ordered the defendant to pay the DM 39,526.20 claimed plus interest. This decision was reversed by the BGH.

Judgment: . . . 2(a) The court below regarded the defendant's statement of 20 January 1966 as a confirmatory acknowledgement of indebtedness, against which no objection can be raised. According to that court, that acknowledgement must be interpreted as meaning that the defendant waived its right to assert, as against the plaintiff, the objection which it now raises, namely that the contract was not performed (§ 320 BGB). This Chamber, adjudicating in the dispute, is unable to concur with that interpretation.

(b) Where—as in the present case—a bank accepts from its customer, for the purposes of securing indebtedness, an assignment of a claim vested in the bank's customer against that customer's own customer, and obtains from the latter confirmation of the claim assigned, there arises a typical situation involving a juxtaposition of interests. On the one hand, the bank, in the interests of securing the credit given or to be given by it, attaches importance—in such a way that the debtor may be aware of it—to ensuring as far as possible that it is protected against any subsequent objections which the debtor may raise in relation to the claim assigned, by thus seeking to exclude such objections on the basis of the confirmation of the debt. On the other hand, as must *ipso facto* be manifestly apparent to the bank, it cannot as a general rule be in the interests of the debtor to waive his right to contest the claim assigned, since he has no reason to waive that right. Nor is he under any obligation *vis-à-vis* the creditor or the bank to declare, in response to the request made to him, that

---

[95] NJW 1973, 39.

he confirms the debt claim. If he gives that confirmation, in accordance with normal commercial practice, the interpretation to be applied to it will depend on the way in which it should have been understood by the recipient of the declaration, that is to say, the bank. However, since the bank knows that it cannot necessarily reckon on a waiver by the debtor of his right to raise objections, it can only infer such a waiver from the debtor's declaration if and in so far as this is clearly and unambiguously expressed in that declaration, in such a way that it cannot be misunderstood by the debtor either. It is *a fortiori* necessary to apply that requirement where the debtor does not himself formulate the wording in which his declaration is couched but merely signs a declaration the wording of which has been prepared for him in advance by the bank. The consequences of any lack of clarity in the wording must be borne by the bank, which chose and filled out the form used. Where, however, the declaration contains an express waiver by the debtor of his right to raise any objection, such that, on a careful examination of its terms, it cannot be misconstrued by the debtor, then he must accept—subject to the possibility of contesting it on the ground of mistake, which does not arise in the present case—that his declaration is to be interpreted as a waiver of his right to raise objections, even where he was not conscious, when signing the declaration, that it would have that scope.

(c) In the form used in this case, the defendant confirmed on 11 July 1966 that it owed S GmbH a balance of DM 80,000 in respect of the supply of tools, and that there existed "no rights vested in any third party to the DM 80,000 residual debt or any counterclaims to that sum which [the defendant itself] might raise by way of set-off". Contrary to the view taken by the court below, the defendant had no reason necessarily to infer from the description of the sum in question as a "residual debt"—which was the description applied to it by the plaintiff—that the plaintiff believed that S GmbH had already entirely performed its part of the contract or that the bank was relying on that belief. Where a bank agrees to take an assignment of debts owed to one of its customers and is unclear as to those debts, it must either obtain clarification from its customer, the assignor, or ask the debtor by whom the debts assigned are owed to explain the position in such a way as to clarify the point and remove any ambiguity . . . If it fails to do so, and instead contents itself with confirmation that the debt exists and that the debtor has no counterclaims which may be set off against that debt, then such a confirmation cannot be construed as a waiver by the debtor of his right under any circumstances to raise any such objections as he may be entitled to assert by reason of subsequent failure by the party with whom he has contracted properly to perform the contract (whether consisting of a total failure to provide consideration or of defective performance). In those circumstances, the confirmation of the debt dated 11 July 1966 cannot outweigh the objection by the defendant that the contract had (in part) not been performed. That objection was already "established", within the meaning of § 404 BGB, at the time when the assignment took place (June 1966). It is sufficient for that purpose that, by that time, the sale and purchase contract from which the defendant derives its objections had already been concluded between it and S GmbH. Consequently, the defendant is entitled also to assert that objection against the plaintiff, as assignee.

Loi Dailly (Law of 2 January 1981) **7.F.72.**

Article 6: Upon demand by the person in whose favour the memorandum is provided, the debtor may undertake to make payment direct to that person; such undertaking shall be valid only if it is in writing and headed: "Act of acceptance of the transfer, assignment or charge of a trade debt". In such circumstances, the debtor may not raise against the credit establishment any objections founded on his personal relations with the signatory of the memorandum unless the credit establishment, in acquiring or taking over the benefit of the debt, knowingly acted to the detriment of the debtor.

Cass. com., 3 December 1991[96] **7.F.73.**

ACCEPTANCE OF DEBT BY DEBTOR

Acceptance under Loi Dailly

If the debtor notifies the assignee that it accepts the debt, under Article 6 of the Loi Dailly it cannot then raise against the assignee any defence based on its relationship with the assignor.

Facts: According to the contested judgment (Douai, 23 November 1989), the company Cogny, a subcontractor of the company Santerne, executed successively assignments to three banks, in the form provided for by the Law of 2 January 1981, of the debt due to it from the latter company. The first of those assignees, Banque Hervet, obtained an acceptance of the arrangement from Santerne, but its right to receive payment of the amount of the debt was challenged both by that company and by the Banque du Bâtiment et des Travaux Publics, another assignee bank.

Held: The appeal court held that Santerne could not rely on the debtor's non-performance as against the Banque Hervet. The appeal was dismissed.

Judgment: *On the sole appeal ground in the main appeal, taken in its two branches*:—Whereas Santerne contests the judgment of the lower court on the ground that it ordered it to pay to Banque Hervet the total sum stated on the memorandum of transfer of the debt whereas by its appeal, it argues, first, that the assignment of a trade debt can only operate to transfer to the assignee a right to payment of the debt definitively found to be due and owing upon completion of the works, when they are accepted by the party commissioning them, and in accordance with their quantity and quality, and that such assignment can only operate to require the debtor, even if he has accepted the assignment, to pay the debt thus determined upon the outcome of the works; as the appellant submits that, in deciding to the contrary, the contested judgment misapplied, and thus infringed, the second paragraph of Article 6 of the Law of 2 January 1981; as on the other hand, it maintains that a debtor who has accepted an assignment may none the less raise against the assignee objections and defences which are based on his personal relations with the signatory of the memorandum but which had not yet come into existence as at the date of acceptance; as consequently, according to Santerne, it was entitled to raise, in opposition to Banque Hervet, the existence of bad workmanship affecting the works carried out by the assignor which did not become apparent until after the date of acceptance of the assignment, on which date those works had not yet even been carried out; as it asserts that the contested judgment thus infringed, the second paragraph of Article 6 of the Law of 2 January 1981.

—Whereas however, having found that Santerne had acknowledged its acceptance of an assignment of a debt in a fixed sum, which was not subject to the carrying out of the works, the cour d'appel correctly inferred from that finding, in accordance with the provisions of Article 6 of the Law of 2 January 1981, that that company was liable to pay the sum provided for on the due date, and that it could not raise against the assignee credit establishment any objections based on its personal relationship with the signatory of the memorandum; as it follows that none of the branches of the appeal ground is well founded . . .

On those grounds, and without there being any need to rule on the second branch of the sole appeal ground advanced in the interlocutory appeal, the Court quashes and annuls the judgment delivered on 23 November 1989 by the Douai cour d'appel, restores the action and the parties to the position in which they found themselves prior to delivery of that judgment, and refers the case to the cour d'appel of Reims.

---

[96] Bull. civ. IV.370.

A seller planning to assign to his bank money claims arising under contracts of sale may include in his standard terms of business a waiver-of-defence clause under which the buyer agrees, in the event of an assignment, not to set up any defences against the assignee. Such clauses have been invalidated if the buyer is a consumer, i.e. a natural person who is acting for purposes which can be regarded as outside his trade or profession.

Council Directive of 22 December 1986 for the approximation of **7.EC.74.**
the laws . . . concerning consumer credit[97]

Article 9: Where the creditor's rights under a credit agreement are assigned to a third person, the consumer shall be entitled to plead against that third person any defence which was available to him against the original creditor, including set-off where the later is permitted in the Member State concerned.

According to Article 14 paragraph 1 of the Directive Member States "shall ensure that credit agreements shall not derogate, to the detriment of the consumer; from the provisions of national law implementing or corresponding to this Directive".

---

[97] [1987] OJ L42/48.

Index

Numbers refer to pages

Page references in italics indicate a short note or explanation on the meaning of the word or expression.

Page references in bold indicate a discussion of the subject-matter in the excerpted materials and the note thereto.

Index

Index

Index

Index

Index

Index

Index

Index

Index

Index

Index

Index

Index

Index

Index

Index

Index

Index

Index

Index

Index

Index

Index

Index

Index

Index

989

Index

Index

Index

Index